HUMAN RESOURCE MANAGEMENT

HUMAN RESOURCE MANAGEMENT

A Contemporary Approach

Seventh edition

Edited by

Julie Beardwell
and
Amanda Thompson

De Montfort University, Leicester

PEARSON

Harlow, England • London • New York • Boston • San Francisco • Toronto • Sydney • Auckland • Singapore • Hong Kong
Tokyo • Seoul • Taipei • New Delhi • Cape Town • São Paulo • Mexico City • Madrid • Amsterdam • Munich • Paris • Milan

Pearson Education Limited

Edinburgh Gate
Harlow CM20 2JE
United Kingdom
Tel: +44 (0)1279 623623

Web: www.pearson.com/uk

First published 1994 (print)
Second edition published 1997 (print)
Third edition published 2001 (print)
Fourth edition published 2004 (print)
Fifth edition published 2007 (print)
Sixth edition published 2010 (print), 2011 (electronic)
Seventh edition published 2014 (print and electronic)

© Longman Group Limited 1994 (print)
© Financial Times Professional Limited 1997 (print)
© Pearson Education Limited 2001, 2010 (print), 2011 (electronic)
© Pearson Education Limited 2014 (print and electronic)

The Financial Times. With a worldwide network of highly respected journalists, *The Financial Times* provides global business news, insightful opinion and expert analysis of business, finance and politics. With over 500 journalists reporting from 50 countries worldwide, our in-depth coverage of international news is objectively reported and analysed from an independent, global perspective. To find out more, visit **www.ft.com/pearsonoffer.**

ISBN: 978-1-292-00272-9 (print)
       978-1-292-00275-0 (PDF)
       978-1-292-00274-3 (eText)

British Library Cataloguing-in-Publication Data
A catalogue record for the print edition is available from the British Library

Library of Congress Cataloging-in-Publication Data
A catalog record for the print edition is available from the Library of Congress

10 9 8 7 6 5 4
18 17

Cover image: © Mlenny Photography

Print edition typeset in 10/12 pt Minion Pro by 75
Print edition printed and bound by Neografia, Slovakia

NOTE THAT ANY PAGE CROSS REFERENCES REFER TO THE PRINT EDITION

Brief contents

Contents

Contents

9   Organisational development
Mairi Watson   301

Part 4
THE EMPLOYMENT RELATIONSHIP

10   The employment relationship and employee rights at work
Alan J. Ryan   347

11   Employee engagement
Julia Pointon   389

Contents

Lecturer Resources

For password-protected online resources tailored to support the use of this textbook in teaching, please visit **www.pearsoned.co.uk/beardwell**

ON THE WEBSITE

Guided tour

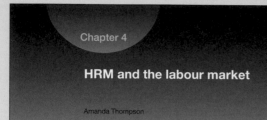

Chapter 4

HRM and the labour market

Amanda Thompson

Objectives

- To explain the nature and composition of the UK labour market.
- To identify the major social forces responsible for shaping the nature and extent of people's engagement with paid employment.
- To highlight developments in the nature of work and employment in the late twentieth and early twenty-first centuries and to show how these trends have influenced organisational requirements for labour.
- To present a critical assessment of workers' experiences of employment in contemporary Britain.

Introductory case study

Underemployment can be as corrosive as unemployment – and it's on the rise

Lots of people are wondering why the employment figures aren't worse, since we're in such a slump. Well, if you measure them properly, they are.

In August 2012, Stephanie Flanders, the BBC's Economics Editor, described it as puzzling, the fact that unemployment hadn't shot up amidst the slump. Her interrogation of the figures prompted Iain Duncan Smith, the Coalition's Work and Pensions Secretary, to accuse Flanders of simultaneously 'dumping on the government' and 'peeing all over British industry'. Ministers, of course, are naturally protective of jobless stats: they're about the only bit of good economic news around to cling on to. At a time when the economy remains wedged in the U-bend, the public-finance targets look either broken or thoroughly bent and the export boom, the surge in business investment and other unicorns promised by the Office for

Budget Responsibility are still stubbornly elusive, at least the labour market affords a less gloomy vista. Even though more than 2.5 million people are out of work, 2012 was the best year for employment growth since the bursting of the dotcom bubble.

The question on the tip of Flanders' tongue is just how this can be, when almost 7,000 public-sector jobs are shed each month and the economy hovers on the edge of a triple-dip recession? One explanation for the rise in employment must be the rise in Britain's population. Another might be that the lull in the growth of dole queues is temporary, and that unemployment will soon pick up. Perhaps the most important explanation though is that the headline figures miss important groups, such as the part-time workers who want to go full-time but can't, or the freelancers and self-employed who are barely attracting enough work or

107

> **Objectives**
> Provide an overview of the topics to be covered in each chapter, giving a clear indication of what you should expect to learn.

> **Introductory case study**
> Designed to stimulate interest and provoke thought as you begin your exploration of the chapter and consider how it might relate to the real World.

> **Figures**
> Are used to illustrate key points, models, theories and processes.

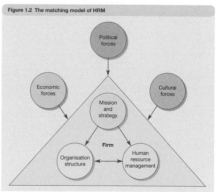

Models of HRM

Figure 1.2 The matching model of HRM

Source: Devanna et al. (1984) in Fombrun et al. (1984: 35). Reproduced with permission.

- Appraisal, monitoring performance and providing feedback to the organisation and its employees.
- Rewards for appropriate performance.
- Development of the skills and knowledge required to meet business objectives.

The matching model is closely allied with the 'hard' interpretation of HRM, i.e. the deployment of human resources to meet business objectives. Two assumptions underpin this model. The first is that the most effective means of managing people will vary from organisation to organisation and is dependent on organisational context. The second assumption is that of unitarism, i.e. the assumption that conflict, or at least differing views, cannot exist in the workplace because everyone (managers and employees) is working to achieve the same goal, the success of the organisation. This model has formed the basis of the 'best fit' school of HRM, discussed further in Chapter 2.

Universalism – more is better

A second influential model, illustrated in Figure 1.3, was developed by Beer *et al.* (1984) at Harvard University. 'The map of HRM territory', as the authors titled their model, recognises that there are a variety of 'stakeholders' in the organisation, which include shareholders, various groups of employees, the government and the community. The model recognises the legitimate interests of various groups, and assumes that the creation of HRM strategies will have to reflect these interests and fuse them as much as possible into the human resource strategy and ultimately the business strategy.

9

Chapter 7 Learning and development

and active role, withdrawing when participants' confidence and capability has risen. The learners, by contrast, can be expected to interact with an increasing number of participants and at a higher frequency as time passes.

Explore

Look first at the right-hand side of Figure 7.6.

• During the processes and interactions involved in e-learning, what activities will the e-moderator be engaged in at each stage of the process?
• Think again about the description of e-learning as one of 'guided-discovery' (Colvin-Clark and Mayer, 2011). How does Salmon's model help to understand this process?

The skills of e-learners

Learning theories (considered earlier in the chapter) still have relevance in the e-learning world, although they may be challenged by the new context in which learning is taking place. Cognitive theories, for example, involve selection, organisation and integration. Using this model, we can consider the skills required for e-learning (Mayer, 2005):

• *Selection.* Learners are much more active participants in shaping their own learning in the e-learning context (Sharpe, 2010). One of the challenges of e-learning for the learner is navigating the vast landscape of material that is potentially useful – there is 'too much of a good thing' (Colvin-Clark and Mayer, 2011: 19). Thus, establishing skills associated with selection (which resource is valid?) and choice of material for learning – such as establishing criteria for value and worth in the context of learning – should be included at the outset of any process.

• *Organising.* The mental and practical organisation of material discovered during the process of e-learning requires the learner not only to select appropriately, but to link in a way that provides a coherent representation of what they have discovered. In addition to the activities that the e-facilitator undertakes to guide learning, the learner needs skills in navigating the landscape and organising what they have discovered. This may involve simply good IT skills, or encouragement in logging and recording activity through blogging.

• *Remembering and integrating.* Reusing learning in the context of work may be more challenging in the absence of physical manuals or instructions, if learning has taken place entirely in a virtual environment. Integrating the learning environment with the workplace can enhance learning – for the learner, this will involve understanding how devices in the workplace can enable access to previous learning and materials.

Key Controversy

Revisit the earlier sections of this chapter that consider individual processes of learning. Which, for you, helps to explain the process of learning from the perspective of the e-learner? Can the theories adequately explain experience in this new context?

Explore

Look now at the left-hand side of Figure 7.6.

• What activities might the e-learner be engaged in at each stage of the process?

Summarising e-learning

At its best, e-learning provides learning which is more accessible, more flexible and adaptable to individual circumstances, and provides a broader and cheaper range of alternatives. It is attractive because of its flexibility and accessibility whereby learning is available when learners

244

Explore
Features appear throughout the text to reinforce learning through the use of self-reflection, problems and practical exercises, helping you to better understand the links between theory and practice.

Key controversy
Features invite you to reflect critically, challenge assumptions and relate scenarios to your own experience, helping to develop skills for use in future employment.

Employment relations in emerging economies: China and India

Box 16.1   Confucian values and HRM: the case of the retail sector in China

China's social context and institutions play a major role in the way firms operate and manage their employees. Confucian values such as respect for authority, interpersonal harmony and role and importance of *guanxi* guide individual action and attitudes in modern Chinese society. This has led to some scholars claiming the emergence of 'Confucian HRM in China', a hybrid management model of Western HRM underpinned by the Chinese traditional value of harmony. A study of retail firms in China, SOEs and foreign MNCs, explored how these traditional norms might impact upon HRM. As the societal values interact with foreign ventures in the retail sector, some fundamental and far-reaching changes are noticeable in the HR practices of retail firms.

The respect for authority that stems from strong hierarchical and authoritarian traditions in China implies that a participative style of management is likely to be constrained. Chinese managers are likely to feel threatened and employees might not involve themselves in decision-making. This is often the case in SOEs where employee involvement and interpersonal communications are weak because of the traditional as well as Maoist legacy of hierarchical structures. By contrast, MNCs that have more developed HRM had significantly higher levels of employee participation practices. In a similar vein, the role and importance of *guanxi* prevail in aspects such as recruitment and career progression at the workplace, both in SOEs and in MNCs in China. However, many employees in MNCs prefer the management in MNCs to the complicated relationships and particularistic connections in Chinese firms. According to one employee, 'In state enterprises, relationships are more complicated. In foreign firms *guanxi* is much less relevant; instead there's good management. It's a real nuisance to be concerned with who is who's cousin.' Likewise, some MNCs have been able to transfer their flatter organisational structures to their Chinese workplace, which is in stark contrast to the rigid hierarchical structures in SOEs.

Thus, the MNCs in China are influenced by Chinese societal norms but can also successfully bypass such norms. One of the significant reasons is that they are not embedded in the traditional environment as are the SOEs. Their financial strength and prestige allow them to be more innovative. Also, being 'outsiders' MNCs can introduce novel practices without alienating traditional norms. Lastly, the retail sector employs a largely young Chinese workforce that is not influenced by norms or Maoist legacy to the same extent as the older SOE employees and is more open to new and innovative practices.

Source: based on Gamble (2006b, 2012).

Questions

1 How do traditional values impact on HRM? Assess with respect to either respect for authority or the role of *guanxi*.
2 Why do SOEs display many of the traditional norms in their employee management practices?
3 Why are MNCs able to bypass traditional norms in implementing HR practices?
4 To what extent are Confucian values likely to continue to exert an influence on HRM in a globalising China?

Early research on MNCs operating in China showed that the host country influence was stronger due to high cultural and institutional distance, and MNCs faced difficulty in implementing Western HR practices in China, e.g. performance appraisal systems (Child, 1994; Lu and Bjorkman, 1997; Gamble, 2003). *Guanxi* continued to operate in recruitment processes. Values such as respect for authority and seniority would make it difficult to encourage employee participation and avoidance of conflict, and saving 'face' implied difficulties in

584

Boxes
Contain a variety of business and organisational examples to demonstrate theory in practice, providing you with the knowledge to succeed in future employment.

various national schemes to develop skills. It is therefore crucial that managers and policy-makers understand the processes of learning and development.

Of course, learning and development are significant for individuals, too, both to prosper in employment and society and, more importantly, to fulfil their potential. Their learning and development take place through life, not just during their employment, so that employers both benefit from and contribute to it. It has to be recognised, therefore, that human resource development has a moral dimension, and juggles with empowering and controlling employees.

Summary

This chapter has covered broad ground, from the individual experience of learning, through learning and development as an organisational process and then as a national process. For example, the chapter has discussed:

- Learning and development are of strategic importance to organisations, and of high importance to the broader economy, reflected in organisational plans and government policies.
- There are many definitions of 'learning' and 'development' and many ways in which learning and development can play out in organisations.
- The significance of learning and development for individuals.
- Adult learners have particular expectations of, and requirements from, learning and development opportunities.
- Theories of learning provide explanations of how learning takes place and assistance in optimising the effectiveness of organisational learning interventions.
- In organisations, the planned process of learning and development includes: identifying learning needs, aims and objectives; determining learning strategies; planning and implementation; and evaluation.
- E-learning, or online learning, has grown exponentially in the last few years, with new supportive technologies to enhance the experience, but also to pose skills challenges for learners and facilitators alike.
- The national context of learning and development – or government skills policy – has a significant impact on the quality and impact of learning and development in organisations.

Questions

1. What are the main definitions of learning and development? How do these differ? Why do you consider that to be the case?
2. What are the main components of employability?
3. What impact can the learning theories discussed in the first section of this chapter have on the design and delivery of learning interventions in your organisation?
4. To what extent can learning and development support the business strategy?
5. Who are the stakeholders in learning and development?
6. How idealistic or cynical are calls for activities such as mentoring and coaching in today's flexible organisations?
7. What are the differences between mentoring and coaching?
8. Is mentoring elitist or empowering? Are there other possible interpretations?
9. Consider an off-the-job learning experience you have had recently. Did you enjoy it? Did you learn something that you were able to apply to your job on return to the workplace? If it was successful, what contributed to this? If it was unsuccessful, why do you think this was the case?
10. What would be the advantages and disadvantages of each method of training delivery for the people in your organisation? Which methods would be best for which skills?

257

Summary
Sections at the end of the chapters recap the key topics within each chapter and enable you to review and check your understanding of them.

Questions
Can be used for self-testing, class exercises or debates.understanding of them.

Chapter 15 Comparative HRM and responses to global crises

Case study 1

'Toyota committed to Japan'

In summer 2012, Akio Toyoda, president of the Toyota Motor Corporation, committed the firm to maintaining itself as a Japanese car producer whereby the multinational will continue to produce three million cars, or 40 per cent of its global output, in Japan. This is only about one million cars fewer than before the onset of the global financial crisis. This commitment came in the face of the impact of a strong yen on Japanese exports and despite the fact that Toyota's domestic rivals, Honda and Nissan, produce about 75 per cent of their cars abroad to enable them to compete with local rivals such as South Korean firm Hyundai. Toyota has not closed any car plants in Japan or curtailed its pattern of lifetime employment for core workers – rather it has consolidated some of its subsidiary operations into the core of the firm and bought out minority shareholders who are more focused on global strategies and investor and shareholder value. Toyota's global operations secured its profitability worldwide, whereas its domestic operations lost nearly 400 billion yen.

Questions

1. What does Toyota's commitment tell us about the embeddedness of the Japanese business and HR model in some Japanese firms?
2. What is it that enables Toyota and other firms such as Honda and Nissan to retain a significant level of domestic production and more localised production in Europe and the USA?

Case study 2

Mercedes-Benz in Alabama

In Alabama, USA, Mercedes, in partnership with the state of Alabama, has formalised a $1.6 million contract to open a graduate training school to train and develop apprentices in mechtronics – the integration of mechanics, electronics and computer science in the manufacturing process, metallurgy, welding and electrical skills. Mechtronics students must complete seven terms of instruction, and after completing this and associated coursework will receive an associate degree. The top 75 per cent of students will secure jobs in full-time production. In addition, a percentage of these apprentices may go on to do further study that will qualify an apprentice for higher-grade maintenance positions in the plant. The Mercedes programme aims to secure, grow and develop the local workforce, and the local plant will be one of four global plants producing the Benz C-Class and its successor generation. Mercedes training programmes are identical across the world, in large measure because the firm does not produce different versions of cars for different territories. Mercedes has developed the programme recently diffused in Alabama throughout Asia, Europe and Canada.

Questions

1. Why is it necessary for Mercedes to do this in its global operations?
2. Does the global rollout of a German approach to VET represent a strong country-of-origin effect or Mercedes's aspiration to become a global firm?

References and further reading

Almond, P. and Ferner, A. (eds) (2006) *American Multinationals in Europe.* Oxford: Oxford University Press.
Appelbaum, E., Batt, R. and Clark, I. (2013) 'Implications for employment relations research: evidence from breach of trust and implicit contracts in private equity buy-outs' *British Journal of Industrial Relations.* Published online 1 March.
Araki, T. (2005) 'Corporate governance, labour and employment relations in Japan: the future of the shareholder model?' in H. Gospel and A. Pendleton (eds) *Corporate Governance and Labour Management: An International Comparison.* Oxford: Oxford University Press, pp. 254–83.
Araki, T. (2009) 'Changes in Japan's practice-dependent stakeholder model and employee centred corporate governance' in Whittaker, D.H. and Deakin, S. (eds) *Corporate Governance and Managerial Reform in Japan.* Oxford: Oxford University Press, pp. 227–54.

566

Case studies
Appear at the end of each chapter and provide an opportunity to consider what you have learnt from the chapter in the context of a real World scenario. Discover how you might apply both theory and practice and prepare yourself for life beyond academic study.

References and further reading
Are provided at the end of each chapter. Comprehensive details of the leading literature and sources in the subject area are provided and those that are asterisked are especially recommended for further reading, helping you to take the subject further and begin to understand the links across the subject area.

Preface

Human resource management (HRM) is a continually evolving field of theory and practice. In its successive editions, this book has provided critical reflection upon new developments as the issues and policies associated with HRM have multiplied considerably. Previous editions have traced the debates over the role of the HRM specialist in organisations, the role and nature of HRM in relation to organisational change initiatives such as total quality management (TQM), and the strategic role of HRM and its effects on organisational performance. They have also reflected on how, in academic circles, the search for a universal HRM paradigm has given way to an emphasis on understanding how HRM operates in diverse situations and what contribution it can make to organisational effectiveness and profitability, focusing on high-performance work systems, the resource-based view of HRM and 'bundles' of HR policies.

More recent editions have explored issues raised by globalisation and the growing importance of multinational enterprises. The discussion has considered whether distinctive national patterns of HRM can survive in the face of globalisation, how HRM is developing in the emerging economies of China and India, and the ways in which multinational companies are influencing not only HRM ideas and practice across the globe, but also the national and international policy environments in which HRM operates.

This edition continues to explore these themes and also reflects significant contemporary events, such as the financial crisis and the economic downturn affecting many Western economies. Our concern to address contemporary developments has led to new chapters on employee voice, employee engagement and organisational development, as well as substantial changes to chapters on the labour market, employee development and HRM in the emerging economies of China and India. We recognise that the huge and expanding area in and around HRM cannot be contained within a single book and we apologise for any omissions. Nevertheless, we are confident that we have covered the broad sweep of the HRM field and some aspects of it in considerable detail.

As with HRM, the team of contributors is a continually evolving one. When the first edition of this book was published in 1994, all the contributors were members of the HRM department at De Montfort University (DMU). Since that time, some long-standing contributors have moved to other institutions (Universities of Leicester, London, East Anglia and Northampton) while others have retired. Over the same time period, new members of the department at DMU have joined the team of contributors. As ever, we thank all our contributors for their hard work and willing cooperation in getting this edition to press. We would also like to thank partners, family members and colleagues for their help and support in the arduous process of academic writing. Thanks, too, to Pearson for their commitment to successive editions of this book and for the enthusiastic help and encouragement we have received from the editorial team.

Some previous contributors have chosen not to be involved this time round and we would like to thank Bob Carter, Trevor Colling, Linda Glover and Sue Marlow for their input into earlier editions. Finally, we would like to thank Tim Claydon for his judicious work as co-editor on the fourth, fifth and sixth editions. You're a hard act to follow, Tim.

Julie Beardwell
Amanda Thompson

Plan of the book

Part 1		
HUMAN RESOURCE MANAGEMENT AND ITS ORGANISATIONAL CONTEXT		
Chapter 1 An introduction to human resource management	Chapter 2 Strategic human resource management	Chapter 3 Contextualising HRM

Part 2		
RESOURCING THE ORGANISATION		
Chapter 4 HRM and the labour market	Chapter 5 Talent management	Chapter 6 Managing equality and diversity

Part 3		
DEVELOPING THE HUMAN RESOURCE		
Chapter 7 Learning and development	Chapter 8 Leadership and management development	Chapter 9 Organisational development

Part 4				
THE EMPLOYMENT RELATIONSHIP				
Chapter 10 The employment relationship and employee rights at work	Chapter 11 Employee engagement	Chapter 12 Performance management	Chapter 13 Employee reward	Chapter 14 Employee voice

Part 5		
INTERNATIONAL HUMAN RESOURCE MANAGEMENT		
Chapter 15 Comparative HRM and responses to global crises	Chapter 16 Employment relations in emerging economies: China and India	Chapter 17 International HRM

How to use this book

This text is designed to meet the needs of a range of students who are studying HRM as a core or option subject on undergraduate degrees in Business and Social Science, MBAs, specialised Master's programmes or the CIPD's Advanced Level Qualification.

All the chapters are designed to take a critically evaluative approach to their subject material. This means that the book is not written in a prescriptive or descriptive style as are some other HRM textbooks, although there will be sections that must necessarily incorporate aspects of that approach. Given this stance, some chapters will be more easily absorbable by the novice student than others. For example, Chapters 1 (Introduction to HRM) and 2 (Strategic HRM) are good introductions to the subject, while Chapter 3 takes a more unconventional perspective on contextualising HRM and developing critical thinking that will prove rewarding to the more able student.

The critically evaluative approach is reflected in the 'Explore' and 'Key controversy' features in every chapter. We use 'Explore' points to encourage readers to examine issues in more depth and to consider how the theories and concepts they have read about in the text apply to organisational settings with which they are familiar. 'Key controversy' boxes are designed to highlight the most contentious debates and urge readers to formulate their own considered conclusions. Each chapter begins and ends with a case study to illustrate the practice of HRM in a diverse range of contexts. As in earlier editions, there are also questions at the end of each chapter. These features can be used by lecturers as coursework exercises, and the Lecturer's Guide that accompanies this edition gives detailed suggested answers. Additional material is also available on the companion website.

The outlines that follow are intended to indicate how the material in this book can be used to cover the requirements for a selection of postgraduate programmes. There is no corresponding outline for undergraduates because we recognise the multiplicity of courses at this level. Nevertheless, it is hoped that these suggested 'routes' through the book will be helpful guidelines for tutors who have responsibility for some or all of these programmes.

MBA Route

Introduction: Chapters 1, 2, 3
Core: Chapters 4, 5, 7, 10, 12, 13, 14, 15
Options: Chapters 6, 8, 9, 11, 16, 17

MA/MSc Route

Introduction: Chapters 1, 2, 3, 4
Core: Chapters 5, 6, 8, 11, 12, 13, 14, 15
Options: Chapters 7, 9, 10, 16, 17

'At a glance' - quick reference guide for CIPD students

This text is designed to be beneficial to a range of student audiences. Several chapters in particular complement the CIPD Advanced level modules. The following table is designed to provide a simple guide to direct CIPD students to those chapters which contain *primary* and/or *secondary* sources of information for each of the CIPD Advanced level modules (see p.xviii).

CIPD Advanced level modules	Primary sources	Secondary sources
Human Resource Management in Context (7HRC)	Ch 1 – An introduction to HRM Ch 2 – Strategic HRM	Ch4 – HRM and the labour market Ch 10 – The employment relationship and employee rights at work
Leading, Managing and Developing People (7LMP)	Ch1 – An introduction to HRM Ch 7 – Learning and development Ch 8 – Leadership and management development	Ch 11 – Employee engagement Ch 9 – Organisational development
Leadership and Management Development (7LMD)	Ch 8 – Leadership and management development	Ch 3 – Contextualising HRM
Organisational Design and Development (7ODD)	Ch 9 – Organisational development	Ch 1 – An introduction to HRM Ch 2 – Strategic HRM
Performance Management (7PFM)	Ch12 – Performance management	Ch 13 – Employee reward
Reward Management (7RWM)	Ch13 – Employee reward	Ch 6 – Managing equality and diversity Ch 12 – Performance management
Resourcing and Talent Management (7RTM)	Ch 5 – Talent management	Ch 6 – Managing equality and diversity
Managing Employment Relations (7MER)	Ch 14 – Employee voice	Ch 4 – HRM and the labour market Ch 10 – The employment relationship and employee rights at work Ch 16 – Employment relations in emerging economies
Employment Law (7ELW)	Ch 10 – The employment relationship and employee rights at work	Ch 6 – Managing equality and diversity
Employee Engagement (7EEG)	Ch 11 – Employee engagement	Ch 5 – Talent/Management
Learning and Talent Development (7LTD)	Ch 7 – Learning and development	Ch 5 – Talent management Ch 8 – Leadership and management development
Designing, Delivering and Evaluating Learning and Development Provision (7DDE)	Ch 7 – Learning and development	Ch 9 – Organisational development
Knowledge Management and Organisational Learning (7KML)	Ch 9 – Organisational development	
Understanding and Implementing Coaching and Mentoring (7ICM)	Ch 8 – Leadership and management development	Ch 7 – Learning and development

Contributors

Phil Almond, BSc, MA, PhD, is Professor of Comparative Employment Relations at De Montfort University. His main research interests are international and comparative HRM and the relationships between multinational corporations and their host economies. His publications include *American Multinationals in Europe: Managing Employment Relations across National Borders*. He recently led an ESRC-funded comparative study of relationships between multinational corporations and regional governance agencies in different countries.

Julie Beardwell, BA, MA, PhD, FCIPD, is Honorary Professor of HRM at Glasgow Caledonian University, Chief Moderator Standards for the CIPD and Chair of the Police Promotions Examinations Board for the College of Policing. She was awarded her PhD for her study into people management in engineering companies and continues to be interested in HRM in small and medium-sized workplaces. She is also co-editor of *Human Resource Development: Theory and Practice,* now in its second edition. Julie left De Montfort University in 2011 and is now co-owner and director of an online retail business, Knit 'n' Caboodle.

Peter Butler, BA, MA, PhD, is Senior Lecturer in Employment Relations in the Department of Human Resource Management, De Montfort University. He teaches Employment Relations at undergraduate and postgraduate level. He has written on the topic of non-union employee representation and the management of managerial careers in US-owned multinational companies. More recently, along with Dr Linda Glover and Prof. Olga Tregaskis, he has published on the theme of partnership working in British industry.

Ian Clark, BA, MA, PGCE, PhD, is Professor of Employment Relations at the University of Leicester where he is Deputy Director of the MRC + ESRC-funded Centre for Sustainable Work and Employment Futures. Ian has written extensively on industrial relations and economic performance, and the influence of the US business system on HRM and industrial relations in the UK. Ian is currently working on an EU-funded transatlantic project examining the diffusion of new business models associated with financial capitalism and the rise of private equity and the recent financial crisis. In addition to these areas, Ian recently managed a research team which examined NHS strategies for skill mix in hospitals and the effect of this strategy on health care assistants. In terms of impact and public policy, Ian provided oral and written evidence to the UK Government Treasury Select Committee during its investigation into private equity between 2007 and 2009.

Tim Claydon, BSc, MSc (econ), PhD, retired as Head of the Department of Human Resource Management at De Montfort University at the end of August 2011. He has written on trade union history, union derecognition, union–management partnership and ethical issues in HRM. His current interests include perceptions of organisational justice and injustice, and the development of employment relations under New Labour. Since retiring he has been a visiting lecturer at the Universities of Warwick and Birmingham.

Audrey Collin, BA, DipAn, PhD, is Professor Emeritus of Career Studies, De Montfort University and Fellow of the National Institute for Career Education and Counselling. Her early career was in personnel management, and she is a Chartered Member of the Chartered Institute of Personnel and Development. She has researched and published on career and life-span studies, mentoring and the employment of older people. She has co-edited (with Richard A. Young) two books on career which reflect her questioning of traditional understandings of career and her commitment to interpretive research approaches, and another with Wendy Patton: *Vocational Psychological and Organisational Perspectives on Career: Towards a Multidisciplinary Dialogue.* Now formally retired, she continues her writing on career for the international academic readership, while also addressing the relationship between theory and practice.

Nicky Golding, BA, MSc, CIPD, is a former Senior Lecturer in Human Resource Management at De Montfort University. She lectured on a range of postgraduate and post-experience courses in the area of Strategic Human Resource Management and Learning and Development. She led and was involved in a range of consultancy projects in the public and private sector, advising senior management teams on SHRM and the management of change.

Anita Hammer, BA (Hons.), MA, MSc, PhD, is a Senior Lecturer in Comparative and International HRM in the Department of HRM, De Montfort University. Anita's research interests lie in the political economy of India as well as its sub-national variations, explored from a comparative capitalist framework. Her research focuses on employment relations in multinational firms with a special focus on New Industrial Zones/Special Economic Zones in India. Anita has industry experience as Head of HR of a public sector organisation. She currently lectures on International HRM at both undergraduate and postgraduate levels.

Mike Noon, BA, MSc, PhD, is Professor of Human Resource Management at Queen Mary University of London. He has previously researched and taught at Imperial College London, Cardiff Business School, Lancaster University and De Montfort University. Mike's research explores the effects of contemporary management practices on the work of employees, and his main focus is equality, diversity and discrimination. In addition to publishing in academic journals, he has co-authored or co-edited the following books: *The Realities of Work,* co-authored with Paul Blyton and Kevin Morrell, the fourth edition of which was published by Palgrave in 2013; *Equality, Inequalities and Diversity: Contemporary Challenges and Strategies,* co-edited with Geraldine Healy and Gill Kirton (Palgrave, 2011); *Equality, Diversity and Disadvantage in Employment,* co-edited with Emmanuel Ogbonna (Palgrave, 2001); and *A Dictionary of Human Resource Management,* co-authored with Ed Heery, the second edition of which was published by Oxford University Press in 2008.

Julia Pointon, BA, MA, PGCE, D.Ed., CIPD, is Principal Lecturer in Organisational Behaviour and HRM in the Department of Human Resource Management at De Montfort University and a National Teacher Fellow. She teaches principally on postgraduate courses and is Course Director of the Management of Human Resources MA. She has served on the CIPD membership and Education Committee and has also been Chair of the CIPD branch in Leicester.

Deborah Price, DMS, DipM, MBA, PhD, is a Senior Lecturer in Human Resource Management at De Montfort University. Following a career in nursing, she has worked as an independent consultant and a senior manager in both Higher Education and the NHS. Her research interests focus on the psycho-social role of identity and identification in the creation of organisational relationships, on leadership in safety critical contexts and on qualitative research methods. She has co-authored a CIPD research methods textbook, *Business Research Methods: A Practical Approach,* with Sheila Cameron and has produced an edited textbook, *The Principles and Practice of Change.*

Alan J. Ryan, BA, LLM, AcadMCIPD is Principal Lecturer in the Department of HRM at De Montfort University. His teaching is focused on the implications of legal change for the management of people at work and the development of managerial responses to legislative activity. He teaches courses at undergraduate and postgraduate level as well as delivering courses and programmes to corporate clients. His research interest lies in the development of soft systems analysis as a way of understanding changes in managerial behaviour following the introduction of legislation. He has undertaken some consultancy work in both the private and the voluntary sector. He has written on reward management, participation regimes in SMEs and the legal implications of flexibility.

Amanda Thompson, BA, MA, CertEd, FCIPD, is Head of the Department of Human Resource Management and Head of the Department of Corporate Development at Leicester Business School, De Montfort University. Alongside her managerial roles, she contributes to the teaching of equality and diversity at final year undergraduate level and employee resourcing at postgraduate level. She has previously published work on the nature of the employment relationship in small and medium-sized enterprises, focusing upon how firm growth influences the dynamic of informality. Amanda is a CIPD National Examiner, Regional External Moderator for the Southern Region and a CIPD Quality Panel Member.

Olga Tregaskis, BSc, MSc, PhD, is Professor of International Human Resource Management at the University of East Anglia, Norwich Business School. Her research examines employment practices in multinational firms, with a particular focus on networks, learning and multi-level global actors. Her work has been supported through Research Council, EU and private firm funding. She is a founding member of the INTREPID network, which is a collaborative network of over 40 researchers from Argentina, Australia, Canada, Denmark, Ireland, Mexico, Norway, Singapore, Spain and the UK. She is also a member of CRIMT which is an inter-university research centre on Globalisation and Work co-ordinated by the University of Montreal.

Mairi Watson, LLB, LLM, PGCE, MBA, PhD, MCIM, AcadMCIPD, is Deputy Dean (Development) at Northampton Business School (NBS), the University of Northampton. Prior to that, she was Head of Corporate and Postgraduate Programmes there, and previously, Academic Director of Corporate Programmes and Principal Lecturer in Organisational Behaviour and Human Resource Management at De Montfort University. She is a Member of the Chartered Institute of Management and an Academic Member of the Chartered Institute of Personnel and Development. At NBS she has strategic responsibility for the leadership of research, and the design and development of the portfolio, including corporate and online programmes, postgraduate and undergraduate provision, enterprise activity and international and other partnerships. She also leads on marketing and recruitment in the School. Her research interests include managerial identity and policy implementation in constrained circumstances. Mairi's research has been conducted in prisons, as her previous career was as a prison governor.

Acknowledgements

We are grateful to the following for permission to reproduce copyright material:

Figures

Figure 1.1 adapted from *Managing Today and Tomorrow,* Palgrave Macmillan (Stewart, R. 1991) Copyright © Rosemary Stewart 1991, reproduced with permission of Palgrave Macmillan, cited in Rollinson and Dundon (2007); Figure 1.2 from M.A. Devanna, C.J. Fombrun and M.A. Devanna, A framework for strategic human resource management, in, *Strategic Human Resource Management,* p. 35 (Fombrun, C.J., Tichy, M.M. and Devanna, M.A. (eds.) 1984), Copyright © 1984 by John Wiley & Sons, Inc., with permission from John Wiley & Sons, Inc.; Figure 1.3 from *Managing Human Assets,* Free Press (Beer, M., Spector, B., Lawrence, P.R., Quinn Mills, D. and Walton, R.E. 1984) p. 16, Copyright © 1984 by The Free Press, reprinted with permission of The Free Press, a division of Simon & Schuster; Figure 1.4 from *Strategy and Human Resource Management,* 3rd ed., Palgrave Macmillan (Boxall, P. and Purcell, J. 2011) p. 95, Copyright © Peter Boxall and John Purcell 2003, 2008, 2011, reproduced with permission of Palgrave Macmillan; Figure 1.5 adapted from Strategic human resource management and performance: an introduction, *International Journal of Human Resource Management,* Vol. 8 (3), pp. 257-62 (Paauwe, J. and Richardson, R. 1997), cited and adapted in Boselie et al (2005); Figure 1.6 from *Strategy and Human Resource Management,* 3rd ed., Palgrave Macmillan (Boxall, P. and Purcell, J. 2011) p. 5, Copyright © Peter Boxall and John Purcell 2003, 2008, 2011, reproduced with permission of Palgrave Macmillan; Figure 2.1 from *Contemporary Strategy Analysis: Concepts, Techniques, Applications,* 6th ed., Blackwell (Grant, R.M. 2008) p. 7, Copyright © 1991, 1995, 1998, 2002, 2005, 2008 by Robert M. Grant, reproduced with permission of Blackwell Publishing Ltd.; Figure 2.2 from The Strategy Concept I: Five Ps For Strategy, *California Management Review,* Vol. 30 (1), pp. 11-24 (Mintzberg, H. 1987), p. 14, Figure 1, Copyright © 1987 by The Regents of the University of California, used with permission of the publisher, University of California Press; Figure 2.3 from *What is Strategy and Does It Matter?,* 2nd ed., Thomson Learning (Whittington, R. 2001) p. 3; Figure 2.4 from *Human Resource Management,* 4th ed., Prentice Hall (Torrington, D. and Hall, L. 1998) p. 27, Copyright © Prentice Hall Europe 1987, 1991, 1995, 1997; Figure 2.5 from Towards a unifying framework for exploring fit and flexibility in strategic human resource management, *Academy of Management Review,* Vol. 23 (4), p. 758 (Wright, P. and Snell, S. 1998), Copyright 1998 by Academy of Management (NY); Figure 2.6 from *Understanding the People and Performance Link: Unlocking the Black Box,* London: CIPD (Purcell, J., Kinnie, N., Hutchinson, S., Rayton, B. and Swart, J. 2003), with the permission of the publisher, the Chartered Institute of Personnel and Development, London (www.cipd.co.uk). The People and Performance Model was developed by Bath University for the CIPD; Figure 4.2 from *The Realities of Work,* 3rd ed., Palgrave Macmillan (Noon, M. and Blyton, P. 2007) p. 368, Copyright © Mike Noon and Paul Blyton 1997, 2002, 2007, reproduced with permission of Palgrave Macmillan; Figure 5.1 adapted from *Successful Selection Interviewing,* Blackwell (Anderson, N. and Shackleton V. 1993) p. 30, with permission from Professor Neil Anderson; Figure 5.2 from Quit stalling, *People Management,* p. 34 (Bevan, S. 1997), with permission from Stephen Bevan; Figure 6.2 adapted from *The Realities of Work* 3rd ed., Palgrave Macmillan (Noon, M. and Blyton, P. 2007) p. 297, Copyright © Mike Noon and Paul Blyton 1997, 2002, 2007, reproduced with permission of Palgrave Macmillan; Figure 7.1 after Design for learning in management training and development: a view, *Journal of European Industrial Training,* Vol. 4 (8), p. 22 (Binsted, D.S. 1980), with permission from MCB University Press; Figure 7.4 from *Learning and Talent Development Survey,* London: CIPD (2012) p. 8, with the permission of the publisher, the Chartered Institute of Personnel and Development, London (www.cipd.co.uk); Figure 7.5 from *Effective Coaching: Lessons from the Coach's Coach,* 3rd ed. (Downey, M. 2003) p. 23, © 2003 South Western, a part of Cengage Learning, Inc., used with permission of the author; Figure 7.6 from *E-moderating: The Key to Online Teaching and Learning,* London: Routledge (Salmon, G. 2011) used with permission of Taylor and Francis Group, LLC; Figure 7.7 Qualification levels diagram, http://ofqual.gov.uk/help-and-advice/comparing-qualifications/, © Crown Copyright 2013, Ofqual 2013, contains public sector information licensed under the Open Government Licence v2.0, www.nationalarchives.gov.uk/doc/open-government-licence; Figure 8.1 from *UK Highlights: Global Leadership Forecast 2011,* London: CIPD (2011) p. 6, Figure 6, with the permission of the publisher, the Chartered Institute of Personnel and Development, London (www.cipd.co.uk); Figure 8.2 from Leadership development in organisations: multiple discourses and diverse practice, *International Journal of Management Reviews,* 15 (4), pp. 359-80 (Mabey, C. 2012), © 2012 The Author, International Journal of Management Reviews © 2012 British Academy of Management and John Wiley and Sons Ltd., with permission of John Wiley and Sons; Figure 8.3 from W. Tate, Linking development with business, in, *Leadership in Organizations: Current Issues and Key Trends,*

2nd ed., p. 196, Figure 11.2 (Storey, J. (ed.) 2010), London: Routledge, reproduced with permission of Routledge, permission conveyed through Copyright Clearance Center, Inc.; Figure 8.4 adapted from M. Clarke, D. Butcher and C. Bailey, Strategically aligned leadership development, in, *Leadership in Organizations: Current Issues and Key Trends*, p. 287 (Storey, J. (ed.) 2004), Routledge; Figure 8.5 from *UK Highlights: Global Leadership Forecast 2011*, London: CIPD (2011) pp. 8-9, Figures 8 and 9, with the permission of the publisher, the Chartered Institute of Personnel and Development, London (www.cipd.co.uk); Figure 8.6 adapted from J. Burgoyne and B. Jackson, The arena thesis: management development as a pluralistic meeting point, in, *Management Learning: Integrating Perspectives in Theory and Practice*, p. 63, Table 3.2 (Burgoyne, J. and Reynolds, M. (eds) 1997), Copyright © John Burgoyne and Brad Jackson 1997, reproduced by permission of Sage Publications, London, Los Angeles, New Delhi and Singapore; Figure 9.1 from Wanted: OD more alive than dead!, *Journal of Applied Behavioural Science* Vol. 40 (4), pp. 374-391 (Greiner, L. and Cummings, T. 2004), Copyright © 2004, NTL Institute, reprinted by permission of SAGE Publications; Figure 9.4 from *Organization Development in Schools*, National Press Books (Schmuck, R.A. and Miles, M.B. 1971) p. 5, used with permission of the authors; Figure 9.6 from Peter de Jager, http://www. technobility.com, © 2013 Peter de Jager, reprinted with express permission of the owner, pdejager@technobility.com; Figure 9.7 from Models of change agency: a fourfold classification, *British Journal of Management*, Vol. 14, pp. 131-142 (Caldwell, R. 2003), Copyright © 2003, John Wiley and Sons, with permission of John Wiley and Sons; Figure 9.8 from *Organisation Development: A Practitioners Guide* London: Kogan Page (Cheung-Judge, M.-Y. and Holbeche, L. 2011) p. 146, Figure 7.3, Copyright © Mee-Yan Cheung-Judge and Linda Holbeche 2011, used with permission of Kogan Page; Figure on page 335 adapted from *Strategic Change and the Management Process*, Basil Blackwell Ltd. (Johnson, G. 1987) p. 224, Figure 7.2, reproduced with permission of Blackwell Publishing Ltd.; Figure 9.10 from *Organisational Culture and Leadership*, Jossey Bass (Schein, E.H. 2004) p. 26, Copyright © John Wiley & Sons, Inc., all rights reserved, reproduced with permission of John Wiley & Sons, Inc.; Figure 10.1 from *Law Express: Employment Law*, Pearson Longman (Cabrelli, D. 2008) p. 11, Copyright © Pearson Education Ltd. 2008; Figure 11.1 from *The Drivers of Employee Engagement Report 408* Institute for Employment Studies UK (Robinson, D., Perryman, S. and Hayday, S. 2004), with permission of Institute for Employment Studies (IES); Figure 12.3 from Managing cross-national and intra-national diversity, *Human Resource Management*, Vol. 32 (4), pp. 461-77 (Tung, R. L. 1993), p. 465, Figure 1, Copyright © 1993 Wiley Periodicals, Inc., a Wiley Company, with permission of John Wiley and Sons, adapted from Rieger, F. and Wong-Rieger, D. (1991); Figure 13.2 from *Paying for Contribution: Real Performance-Related Pay Strategies*, Kogan Page (Brown, D. and Armstrong, M. 1999) p. 81; Figure 13.3 from J. Adams, Inequity in social exchange, in, *Advances in Experimental Social Psychology*, 2nd ed., pp. 267–96 (Berkowitz, L. (ed.) 1965), with permission from Elsevier, http://www.elsevier. com; Figure 13.7 adapted from *Paying for Contribution: Real Performance-Related Pay Strategies,* Kogan Page (Brown, D. and Armstrong, M. 1999) p. 137; Figure 17.2 from An integrative framework of strategic international human resources management, *Journal of Management,* Vol. 19 (2), pp. 419-59 (Schuler, R., Dowling, P. and De Ceri, H. 1993), Copyright © 1993 Southern Management Association, reprinted by permission of SAGE Publications.

Tables

Table 1.1 from *Improving Health Through Human Resource Management: A Starting Point for Change,* London: CIPD (Hyde, P., Boaden, R., Cortvriend, P., Harris, P., Marchington, M., Pass, S., Sparrow, P. and Sibald, B. 2006), with the permission of the publisher, the Chartered Institute of Personnel and Development, London (www.cipd.co.uk); Table 1.2 from Role call, *People Management,* Vol. 11 (12), pp. 24-28 (Ulrich, D. and Brockbank, W. 2005), with permission from D. Ulrich and W. Brockbank; Table 2.1 adapted from *What is Strategy and Does It Matter?,* 2nd ed., Thomson Learning (Whittington, R. 2001) p. 39; Table 2.2 from Linking competitive strategies with human resource management, *Academy of Marketing Executive* Vol. 1 (3), pp. 207-219 (Schuler, R.S. and Jackson, S.E. 1987), Copyright 1987 by Academy of Management (NY); Table 2.3 from Modes of theorizing in strategic human resource management, *Academy of Management Journal,* Vol. 39 (4), pp. 802-35 (Delery, J.E. and Doty, H. 1996), Copyright 1996 by Academy of Management (NY); Table 2.4 from *The Human Equation: Building Profits by Putting People First,* Harvard Business School Press (Pfeffer, J. 1998) Copyright © 1998 by the Harvard Business School Publishing Corporation, reprinted by permission of Harvard Business School Press, all rights reserved; Table 2.6 from The romance of human resource management and business performance, and the case for big science, *Human Relations,* Vol. 58 (4), pp. 429-63 (Wall, T.D. and Wood, S.J. 2005), Copyright © 2005 The Tavistock Institute, reprinted by permission of SAGE Publications and the authors; Table 2.7 'Non-financial metrics most valued by investors' adapted from *Measures That Matter,* Ernst and Young (1997) © Ernst & Young LLP, all rights reserved, Cited and adapted in *Strategic Human Resource Management: The Key to Improved Business Performance*, London: CIPD (Armstrong, M. and Baron, A. 2002) p. 63, used with the permission of the publisher, the Chartered Institute of Personnel and Development, London (www.cipd.co.uk); Table 4.1 from Office for National Statistics, contains public sector information licensed under the Open Government Licence v.2.0, www.nationalarchives.gov.uk/doc/open-government-licence, cited in Rutherford 2012; Table 4.2 from Labour Force Survey Household Datasets, UK Data Service, Office for National Statistics, contains public sector information licensed under the Open Government Licence v.2.0, www.nationalarchives.gov.uk/doc/open-government-licence; Tables 4.3 and 4.4 from Labour Force Survey, Office for National Statistics, contains public sector information licensed under the Open Government Licence v.2.0, www.nationalarchives.gov.uk/doc/open-government-licence; Table 4.6 from *Working Futures 2010-2020: Main Report,* UK Commission for Employment and Skills, UKCES Evidence Report No. 41 (Wilson, R. and Homenidou, K. 2012) p. 41, used with permission of UK Commission for Employment and Skills; Table 4.7 from *Working Futures 2010-2020: Main Report,* UK Commission for Employment and Skills, UKCES Evidence Report No. 41 (Wilson, R. and Homenidou, K. 2012) p. 83, used with permission of UK Commission for Employment and Skills; Table 4.8 from *The 2011 Workplace Employee Relations Study - First Findings,* London: BIS (Van Wanrooy, B., Bewley, H., Bryson, A., Forth, J., Freeth, S., Stokes, L. and Wood, S. 2013) p. 9, contains public sector information licensed under the Open Government License v2.0, www.nationalarchives.gov.uk/doc/open-government-licence, and used with permission of the Steering Committee; Table 5.1 from Talent management for the twenty-first century, *Harvard Business Review,* March, p. 78 (Capelli, P. 2008), Copyright © 2008 by the Harvard Business School Publishing Corporation, all rights reserved, reprinted by permission of Harvard Business School Press; Table 5.2 from *Recruitment and Selection,* Advisory booklet No. 6, Advisory, Conciliation and Arbitration Service (ACAS) (1983) © ACAS, Euston Tower, 286 Euston Road, London NW1 3JJ, Crown Copyright material is produced with the permission of the Controller, Office of Public Sector Information (OPSI); Table 5.3 from *Resourcing and Talent Planning Survey Report,* London: CIPD (2011) p. 18, with the permission of the publisher, the Chartered Institute of Personnel and Development, London (www.cipd.co.uk); Table 8.1 from Management development for the individual and the organisation, *Personnel Management,* June, pp. 40-44 (Burgoyne, J. 1988), with permission from Dr. J. G. Burgoyne; Table 8.2 from *Talent Management and Succession Planning,* London: CIPD (Cannon, J. and McGee, R. 2007), with the permission of the publisher, the Chartered Institute of Personnel and Development, London (www.cipd.co.uk); Table 9.1 from Organizational discourse and new organization development practices, *British Journal of Management,* Vol. 19, pp. 7-19 (Marshak, R. and Grant, D. 2008), Copyright © John Wiley and Sons, used with permission of John Wiley and Sons; Table 9.2 from *Planning and Managing Change. Change Management Volume 2: Understanding and Managing Change Through Organisational Development.,* Milton Keynes, Open University Business School (Pugh, D. and Mayle, D. 2009) Copyright © Open University; Table 10.2 from The Employment Tribunals and Employment Appeals Tribunals Fees Order 2013, http://www.legislation.gov.uk/ukdsi/2013/9780111538654, contains public sector information licensed under the Open Government Licence v2.0 www.nationalarchives.gov.uk/doc/open-government-licence; Table on page 378 from *Employment Tribunal Service Annual Report 2012,* contains public sector information licensed under the Open Government Licence v2.0 www.nationalarchives.gov.uk/doc/open-government-licence; Table 11.1 from *18 Critical Factors to Improve Employee Satisfaction and Engagement: Keys for Improving Employee Satisfaction and Engagement,* Society for Human Resource Management (Heathfield, S.M. 2013), reprinted with permission of Society for Human Resource Management (SHRM); Table 11.2 from *Global Employee Engagement Index™,* Effectory (2011); Table 13.1 from *Reward Management Annual Survey Report 2012,* London: CIPD pp. 38-39, with the permission of the publisher, the Chartered Institute of Personnel and Development, London (www.cipd.co.uk); Table 13.4 from *Job Evaluation: Consideration and Risks,* London: ACAS (2010) © ACAS, Euston Tower, 286 Euston Road, London NW1 3JJ, Crown Copyright material is produced with the permission of the Controller, Office of Public Sector Information (OPSI); Table 13.5 from *Employee Reward,* 3rd ed., London: CIPD (Armstrong, M. 2002) p. 306, with the permission of the publisher, the Chartered Institute of Personnel and Development, London (www.cipd.co.uk); Table 14.1 adapted from *Managing Employee Involvement and Participation,* London: Sage (Hyman, J. and Mason, B. 1995) p. 25, Table 2.1, © Jeff Hyman and Bob Mason 1995, reproduced by permission of Sage Publications, London, Los Angeles, New Delhi and Singapore; Table 14.2 after *The 2011 Workplace Employee Relations Study - First Findings,* London: BIS (Van Wanrooy, B., Bewley, H., Bryson, A., Forth, J., Freeth, S., Stokes, L. and Wood, S. 2013) p. 18, Figure 1, contains public sector information licensed under the Open Government License v2.0, www.nationalarchives.gov.uk/doc/open-government-licence, and used with permission of the Steering Committee; Table 14.3 from *The 2011 Workplace Employee Relations Study - First Findings,* London: BIS (Van Wanrooy, B., Bewley, H., Bryson, A., Forth, J., Freeth, S., Stokes, L. and Wood, S. 2013) p. 22, Table 1, contains public sector information licensed under the Open Government License v2.0, www.nationalarchives.gov.uk/doc/open-government-licence, and used with permission of the Steering Committee; Table 14.4 from *The 2011 Workplace Employee Relations Study - First Findings,* London: BIS (Van Wanrooy, B., Bewley, H., Bryson, A., Forth, J., Freeth, S., Stokes, L. and Wood, S. 2013) p. 22, Table 1, contains public sector information licensed under the Open Government License v2.0, www.nationalarchives.gov.uk/doc/open-government-licence, and used with permission of the Steering Committee; Table 16.1 from Asian business systems: institutional comparison, clusters and implications for varieties of capitalism and business systems theory, *Socio-Economic Review,* Vol. 11 (2), pp. 265-300 (Witt, M.A. and Redding, G. 2013), p. 268, Table 1, Copyright © 2013 Oxford University Press, by permission of Oxford University Press; Table 17.2 from N. Adler and F. Ghadar, Strategic human resource management: a global perspective, in *Human Resource Management: An International Comparison,* p. 240, Table 1 (Pieper, R. (ed.) 1990), used with permission of the authors.

Text

Case Study on page 31 from RBS was 'disaster waiting to happen', *Daily Telegraph,* 21 March 2009 (Winnett, R. and Corrigan, T.), Copyright © Telegraph Media Group Limited

2009; and on page 33 adapted from Stephen Hester lays out RBS departure plan, *The Telegraph,* 15 June 2013 (Ahmed, K.), Copyright © Telegraph Media Group Limited; Case Study on page 72 from What are the goals of a football club?, *Financial Times,* 26 April 2013 (Palin, A.), © The Financial Times Limited 2013, all rights reserved; Quote on page 73 from John Webster from 1985 advertisement for The Guardian, reproduced in memory of John Webster (1934–2006); Case Study on page 100 from Fear and loathing after the credit crisis, *Financial Times,* 3 October 2008 (Willman, J.), Copyright © The Financial Times Limited 2008, all rights reserved; Box 5.4 from Employee retention of McDonald's, http://www.managementparadise.com/forums/human-resources-management-h-r/219372-emplyee-retention-mcdonald-s.html; Box 5.5 from Caught by the fizz, *People Management,* 7 August 2008, p. 24 (Chynoweth, C.), with permission of the author; Box 6.4 from Equality policies, http://www.equalityhumanrights.com/advice-and-guidance/guidance-for-employers/equality-policies-equality-training-and-monitoring/equality-policies/, The copyright and all other intellectual property rights in the material to be reproduced are owned by, or licensed to, the Commission for Equality and Human Rights, known as the Equality and Human Rights Commission ("the EHRC"); Extract on page 221 from *Effective Teaching and Mentoring,* 1st ed., Jossey-Bass (Daloz, L.A. 1986) pp. 24-26, Copyright © 1986 Jossey-Bass Inc., Publishers, reproduced with permission of John Wiley & Sons, Inc.; Box 8.1 from Continuing growth in the recruitment scheme for HR graduates aims to build a pipeline of candidates for top government jobs, *People Management,* 29 August 2012 (Churchard, C.), with the permission of the publisher, the Chartered Institute of Personnel and Development, London (www.cipd.co.uk); Case Study on page 263 from Leadership research reveals managers 'struggle with basic skills', *People Management,* 11 February 2013, with the permission of the publisher, the Chartered Institute of Personnel and Development, London (www.cipd.co.uk); Case Study on page 295 adapted from Jersey Telecom's leadership development initiative, *People Management* 24 September 2012 (Reeves, N.), with the permission of the publisher, the Chartered Institute of Personnel and Development, London (www.cipd.co.uk), and the author; Case Study on page 301 from Taking first steps in making health clubs fit for purpose, *The Times,* 29 April 2013 (Walsh, D.) © News Syndication 2013; Box 9.1 from HR and organisation development: separate past, joint future? Podcast 44, http://www.cipd.co.uk/podcasts/_articles/_organisationdevelopment.htm?link=title, with the permission of the publisher, the Chartered Institute of Personnel and Development, London (www.cipd.co.uk); Box 9.6 adapted from training materials provided by Frank Jordan, University of Northampton 2013; Case Study on page 338 from *NHS staff 'should face prosecution over mistake cover-ups',* 7 February 2013, London: CIPD (Stevens, M.) http://www.cipd.co.uk/pm/peoplemanagement/b/weblog/archive/2013/02/07/nhs-staff-should-face-prosecution-over-mistake-cover-ups.aspx, with the permission of the publisher, the Chartered Institute of Personnel and Development, London (www.cipd.co.uk); Case Study on page 385 from Ageism more widespread than sexism, *Financial Times,* 31 March 2013 (Groom, B.), © The Financial Times Limited 2013, all rights reserved Case Study on page 389 from A journey to award-winning employee engagement, *Human Resource Management International Digest,* Vol. 20 (5), pp. 31-34 (Powis, A. 2012), Copyright © 2012, Emerald Group Publishing Limited, all rights reserved; Case Study on page 417 adapted from *A study of the link between Performance Management and Employee Engagement in Western multinational corporations operating across India and China,* Society for Human Resource Management (Farndale, E., Hope-Hailey, V., Kelliher, C. and van Veldhoven, M. 2011); Case Study on page 449 from Creating a company-wide, on-line, performance management system: A case study at TRW Inc., *Human Resource Management,* Vol. 41 (4), pp. 491-98 (Neary, D.B. 2002), Copyright © 2002 Wiley Periodicals, Inc., with permission of John Wiley and Sons; Case Study on page 454 from How do I get my pay up?, *Financial Times,* 29 January 2013 (Kellaway, L.), Copyright © The Financial Times Limited 2013, all rights reserved; Case Study on page 524 based on a case study by Dr. Enda Hannon, Kingston University; Case Study on page 497 from Trade union warns of further strikes, *Financial Times,* 6 September 2012 (Groom, B.), © The Financial Times Limited 2012, all rights reserved; Box 15.1 from Keidenran's Okuda lauds Japanese management for revival, *The Nikkei Weekly,* 16 January 2006; Case Study on page 602 from Trade unions in a constrained environment: workers' voices from a New Industrial Zone in India, *Industrial Relations Journal,* Vol. 41 (2), pp. 168-184 (Hammer, A. 2010), © 2010 The Author, Journal compilation © 2010 Blackwell Publishing Ltd., with permission of John Wiley and Sons.

Articles sourced from the Financial Times have been referenced with the FT logo. These articles remain the Copyright of the Financial Times Limited and were originally published between 2008 and 2013. All Rights Reserved. FT and 'Financial Times' are trademarks of The Financial Times Ltd. Pearson Education is responsible for providing any translation or adaptation of the original articles.

In some instances we have been unable to trace the owners of copyright material, and we would appreciate any information that would enable us to do so.

Part 1

HUMAN RESOURCE MANAGEMENT AND ITS ORGANISATIONAL CONTEXT

Introduction to Part 1

Human resource management (HRM) has become a pervasive and influential approach to the management of employment in a wide range of market economies. The original US prescriptions of the early 1980s have become popularised and absorbed in a wide variety of economic settings: there are very few major economies where the nature of HRM, to include its sources, operation and philosophy, is not actively discussed. As a result, the analysis and evaluation of HRM are major themes in academic, policy and practitioner literatures.

These first three chapters are strongly related, in that they consider the nature of HRM from a number of perspectives. The first chapter outlines the different ways in which HRM has been interpreted and introduces two of the early influential models. It then explores the current preoccupation in the relationship between HRM and organisational performance and the extent to which research studies are able to demonstrate a link between the two. The chapter then goes on to explore the impact that the global financial crisis and recession have had on the adoption of HRM practices. The chapter concludes by considering the impact of HRM on human resources professionals.

Chapter 2 examines the strategic nature of HRM in more depth: how it is aligned to and configured with organisational strategy and how the debate incorporates multiple perspectives, including the 'best fit', the 'configurational approach', the 'resource-based view' and 'best practice'. In considering claims for the importance of the strategic nature of HRM, it raises questions as to its efficacy in helping to meet organisational objectives, creating competitive advantage and 'adding value' through 'high-performance' or 'high-commitment work practices'. Whether or not the claims for these approaches are supportable, it is becoming clear that no one system or approach can be applied to all organisations, owing to the increasing complexity of organisational forms and organisational contexts.

Chapter 3 continues this contextual theme by exploring the various strands that are woven together to form the pattern of meanings that constitute HRM. This helps to enrich our understanding of HRM and unravel some of the assumptions and philosophical stances that lie behind it. The purpose of the discussion is to create a critical awareness of the broader context in which HRM operates, not simply as a set of operational matters that describe the functional role of people management, but as part of a complex and sophisticated process that helps us to understand the nature of organisational life. The chapter concludes with a consideration of ethical issues.

The type of questions raised by HRM indicates the extent to which it has disturbed many formerly accepted concepts in the employment relationship. For some, it has become a model for action and application; for others it is no more than a map that indicates how the management of employees might be worked out in more specific ways than can adequately be dealt with by HRM as a set of general principles.

Chapter 1

An introduction to human resource management

Julie Beardwell

Objectives

- To define human resource management (HRM).
- To explore the origins of HRM.
- To review and evaluate the main models of HRM.
- To explore the association between HRM and business performance.
- To explore HRM in practice and the impact of the recession on HRM practice.
- To review the impact of HRM on the roles of human resources professionals.

Introductory case study

Winning HRM practices

For the third year in a row, the commercial radio operator UKRD has been voted the best company to work for in the *Sunday Times* '100 Best Companies' poll. UKRD is the fourth largest commercial radio operator in the UK, employing 275 staff. As well as owning and running 17 radio stations, the company also develops software and has a number of websites.

The company's culture is described as open, fair, honest and unconventional. The chief executive, William Rogers, works without a PA, spends most of his time on the road visiting staff and knows everyone by name. Employees thrive on maximum autonomy, lots of training and development, constant motivation and regular recognition. Thank-yous range from a bottle of wine or champagne to concert tickets or a trip to the races, as well as cakes and presents on employees' birthdays. Training includes coaching, developing leadership skills and a course on how to have 'courageous conversations' to tackle difficult issues with colleagues. The group's drive to improve its remuneration package and working conditions has meant an end to the traditional 6-day week for presenters and journalists, with no reduction in pay, and an increase in holidays from 20 to 25 days for new staff.

Source: http://features.thesundaytimes.co.uk/public/best100companies/live/list.

Introduction

The first edition of this book was published in 1994 and the then editors described HRM as a newly emerging phenomenon that added 'a powerful and influential perspective' to debates about the nature of the contemporary employment relationship. They noted (Beardwell and Holden, 1994: 5):

> Any assessment of the emergence of Human Resource Management has, at least, to take account of this changing context of employment and provide some explanations as to the relationships that exist between the contribution HRM has made to some of these changes on the one hand and, on the other hand, the impact that such changes have had on the theory and practice of HRM itself.

Human resource management continues to both influence and be influenced by the changing context of employment, but, while still relatively new, it can no longer be described as an emerging phenomenon. Boxall and Purcell (2011: 2) suggest that HRM is the most widely recognised term in the English-speaking world to refer to management activities in organising work and employing people. However, there is still little universal agreement on what precisely constitutes HRM, and debates around the meaning of the term and the impact of the concept continue. To enable us to identify how 'understanding HRM' has changed over time and to consider the impact this change has had on the management of people, this chapter aims to explore the key themes within the debates that surround HRM under the six headings in the list of objectives.

Definitions of HRM

Human resource management refers to a collection of policies used to organise work in the employment relationship and centres on the management of work and the management of people who undertake this work. Therefore, HRM is concerned with recruitment, selection, learning and development, reward, communication, teamwork and performance management. While it is relatively easy to list activities that make up HRM, it is a subject that has stimulated much debate and disagreement. Thus, despite the popularity of the term HRM, there is still no universally agreed definition of its meaning. Watson (2002: 369) suggests that a 'rather messy situation currently exists whereby the term HRM is used in a confusing variety of ways'. In its broadest sense HRM can be used as a generic term to describe any approach to managing people; for example, Boxall and Purcell (2011: 3) use the term to encompass 'the management of work and the management of people to do the work'.

For others, though, HRM encompasses a new approach to managing people that is significantly different from more traditional practices. They claim that HRM offers two advantages over traditional approaches to managing people. First, it is more strategic, in that HRM policies are designed to reinforce each other and support the organisation's business strategy. This strategic dimension incorporates vertical integration, i.e. the alignment of human resources (HR) strategy with business strategies, whereas the operational dimension emphasises horizontal integration, i.e. that HR policies and practices must be compatible with each other. Secondly, appropriately designed and integrated HRM policies create an organisational climate in which workers are more highly motivated and committed to cooperating with management to achieve organisational goals. This approach has been summed up by Storey (2007: 7) as follows:

> a distinctive approach to employment management which seeks to achieve competitive advantage through the strategic deployment of a highly committed and capable workforce, using an array of cultural, structural and personnel techniques.

However, it begs the question as to whether HRM policies designed to achieve strategic goals, such as competitive costs or the ability to respond rapidly to changes in markets, can also provide a climate of trust and cooperation between workers and managers. Some commentators have argued that HRM is essentially about creating a climate of employee commitment (e.g. Pfeffer, 1998) and cooperation, while others have maintained that the term HRM can relate to policies for managing people that are designed to further the strategic goals of the organisation (e.g. Legge, 2005; Huczynski and Buchanan, 2007). Consequently, there is some ambiguity in the meaning of HRM, which has led to it becoming a contested concept.

Explore

- What does the term HRM mean to you?
- To what extent is it possible to have policies and practices that meet the needs and objectives of organisations and individuals?

This ambiguity has led to various attempts to clarify the meaning or, indeed, the meanings of HRM. Some of the earliest contributions drew a distinction between 'soft' and 'hard' variants of HRM (Guest, 1987; Storey, 1992), with 'soft HRM' used to describe approaches aimed at enhancing the commitment, quality and flexibility of employees, while 'hard HRM' is used to describe the emphasis on strategy where human resources are deployed to achieve business goals in the same way as any other resource. 'Hard HRM' can also have a harsher interpretation associated with strategies of cost reduction (e.g. subcontracting, outsourcing, lower wages, minimal training and tighter monitoring and performance management) and lean production (downsizing, work intensification) associated with these strategies. However, this attempt at clarification is also problematic. For example, if hard HRM is used to describe a strategic approach to people management, then soft and hard HRM are 'not necessarily incompatible' (Legge, 2005). Hard variants can contain elements of soft practice, while soft variants can deliver hard outcomes in terms of tightness of fit with business strategy. However, if hard HRM is used to describe a cost minimisation approach, then soft and hard HRM may be 'diametrically opposed' (Truss *et al.*, 1997: 54).

As the debate on HRM continues, further terms have been introduced, e.g. 'high-commitment management' (HCM) and 'high-involvement management' have eclipsed soft HRM, whereas 'strategic HRM' appears to have replaced hard HRM. Nonetheless, the underlying tensions within HRM that were captured in the 'hard' vs 'soft' dichotomy remain. In addition, the preoccupation with the relationship between HR practices and improved business performance has been reflected in the use of 'high-performance work practices' (HPWPs) as a term to describe 'a set of complementary work practices covering three broad categories: high employee involvement practices, human resource practices, and reward and commitment practices' (Sung and Ashton, 2005:5). There are subtle variations in the meanings of these labels, but there is also considerable overlap and some authors (e.g. Pfeffer, 1998) use the terms interchangeably. Both the high-commitment and high-involvement models reflect 'a system of human resources practices thought to enhance employees' levels of skill, motivation, information and empowerment' (Guthrie, 2001: 180) and performance expectations are high in the commitment model (Walton, 1985). An element that all the models have in common is that they are seen as a contrast with a Taylorist, control type of management (Wood, 1999).

High commitment vs control

Walton (1985: 78) compared the high-commitment model with 'the traditional, control-oriented approach to workforce management'. This contrast can be misleading, as high-commitment and control-based approaches to people management are both means of achieving organisational control, i.e. 'the regulation of organisational activities so that some targeted element of performance remains within acceptable limits' (Barney and Griffin, 1992: 329). What varies between them is the type of control exercised and the desired employee behaviours.

Stewart (1991) identifies three distinct control strategies: manager-directed control, bureaucratic control and employee-centred control. Rollinson and Dundon (2011) depict these strategies on a continuum (see Figure 1.1).

At the predictability end of the continuum, manager-directed control reflects Taylorist assumptions about worker competence and management authority. Control is exercised through supervisors giving direct instruction and closely monitoring work. The middle ground, bureaucratic control, relies less on close monitoring and seeks to limit employee discretion through fixed job definitions, reliance on rules and procedures, differentiated status, equitable pay and a restricted flow of information. Guest (1991) labels this the 'compliance' model. Employee-centred control, at the other end of the continuum, equates with the high-commitment model. This form of control emphasises employee discretion and aims to get employees to exercise self-control and behave in ways that are congruent with organisational objectives (Rollinson and Dundon, 2011).

The high-commitment/high-performance paradigm has come to be promoted as 'best practice' for both employers and employees, and many of the HR practices associated with this type of approach are included in the measures used to compile the *Sunday Times* 'Best Companies to Work For' list, as illustrated in the introductory case study. Employers are seen to benefit on the grounds that the practices associated with it yield performance levels above those associated with more traditional workplace practices (Godard, 2004: 349). Employees are seen to benefit from the ability to exercise discretion and experience high levels of trust. Guest and Conway (1999) found that employees in workplaces with a high number of HRM practices reported higher levels of job satisfaction and a more positive management–worker relationship than employees who did not. However, there is a danger that the terms used to

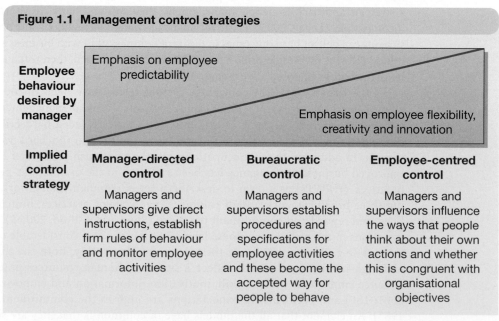

Figure 1.1 Management control strategies

Employee behaviour desired by manager	Emphasis on employee predictability		Emphasis on employee flexibility, creativity and innovation
Implied control strategy	**Manager-directed control**	**Bureaucratic control**	**Employee-centred control**
	Managers and supervisors give direct instructions, establish firm rules of behaviour and monitor employee activities	Managers and supervisors establish procedures and specifications for employee activities and these become the accepted way for people to behave	Managers and supervisors influence the ways that people think about their own actions and whether this is congruent with organisational objectives

Source: adapted from Stewart 1991 in Rollinson and Dundon (2011: 344).

define HRM imply positive outcomes that may not necessarily be warranted. For example, greater demands on employee commitment and tighter systems for performance management are likely to further the interests of the organisation, its owners and investors at the expense of employees. Enhancements in employee discretion, associated with 'high-commitment/involvement' practices, may be achieved at the 'expense of stress, work intensification and job strain' (Ramsay *et al.*, 2000: 505). Similarly, Wall and Wood (2005: 432) challenged the assumption of an established link between HRM practices and organisational performance, implied in the 'high performance' label – this is discussed more fully later in the chapter.

The origins of HRM

There is rather more consensus that the origins of HRM lie within employment practices associated with welfare capitalist employers in the USA during the 1930s. Both Jacoby (2005) and Foulkes (1980) argue that this type of employer exhibited an ideological opposition to unionisation and collective employment relations. As an alternative, welfare capitalists believed the organisation, rather than third-party institutions such as the state or trade unions, should provide for the security and welfare of workers. To deter any propensity to unionise, especially once President Roosevelt's New Deal programme began after 1933, welfare capitalists often paid efficiency wages, introduced healthcare coverage, pension plans and provided lay-off pay. Equally, they conducted regular surveys of employee opinion and sought to secure employee commitment via the promotion of strong, centralised corporate cultures and long-term permanent employment. Welfare capitalists pioneered individual performance-related pay, profit-sharing schemes and what is now termed teamworking. This model of employment regulation had a pioneering role in the development of what is now termed HRM, but rested on structural features such as stable product markets and the absence of marked business cycles. While the presence of HRM was well established in the US business system before the 1980s, it was only after that period that HRM gained external recognition by academics and practitioners.

There are a number of reasons for its emergence since then, among the most important of which are the major pressures experienced in product markets during the recession of 1980–82, combined with a growing recognition in the USA that trade union influence was waning. By the 1980s the US economy was also being challenged by overseas competitors, most notably Japan. This led to discussions that focused on two issues: 'the productivity of the American worker', particularly compared with the Japanese worker, 'and the declining rate of innovation in American industries' (Devanna *et al.*, 1984: 33). From this sprang a desire to create a work situation free from conflict, in which both employers and employees worked in unity towards the same goal – the success of the organisation (Fombrun, 1984: 17). Beyond these prescriptive arguments and in a wide-ranging critique of institutional approaches to industrial relations analysis, Kaufman (1993) suggested that a preoccupation with pluralist industrial relations within and beyond the period of the New Deal excluded the non-union sector of the US economy for many years. He argued that this was a misreading of US employment relations because welfare capitalist employers (soft HRM) and anti-union employers (hard HRM or no HRM) are embedded features within the US business system, whereas the New Deal Model was a contingent response to economic crisis in the 1930s.

In the UK, the business climate also began to favour changes in the employment relationship in the 1980s. As in the USA, this was partly driven by economic pressure in the form of increased product market competition, the recession in the early part of the decade and the introduction of new technology. However, a very significant factor in the UK, generally absent from the USA, was the desire of the government to reform and re-shape the conventional model of industrial relations. This provided support for the development of more employer-oriented employment policies on the part of management (Beardwell, 1992, 1996). The restructuring of the economy saw a rapid decline in the old industries and a relative rise in the service sector and in new industries based on 'high-tech' products and services, many of which were comparatively free from the established patterns of what was sometimes termed the 'old' industrial relations. These changes were overseen by a muscular entrepreneurialism promoted by the Conservative government led by Margaret Thatcher in the form of privatisation and anti-union legislation, 'which encouraged firms to introduce new labour practices and to re-order their collective bargaining arrangements' (Hendry and Pettigrew, 1990: 19).

At the same time, the influence of the US 'excellence' literature (e.g. Peters and Waterman, 1982; Kanter, 1984) associated the success of 'leading edge' companies with the motivation of employees by involved management styles that also responded to market changes. Consequently, the concepts of employee commitment and 'empowerment' became another strand in the ongoing debate about management practice and HRM.

A review of these issues suggests that any discussion of HRM has to come to terms with at least three fundamental problems:

- that HRM is derived from a range of antecedents, the ultimate mix of which is wholly dependent upon the stance of the analyst, and which may be drawn from an eclectic range of sources;

- that HRM is itself a contributory factor in the analysis of the employment relationship, and sets part of the context in which that debate takes place;

- that it is difficult to distinguish where the significance of HRM lies – whether it is in its supposed transformation of styles of employee management in a specific sense, or whether in a broader sense it is in its capacity to sponsor a wholly redefined relationship between management and employees that overcomes the traditional issues of control and consent at work.

Models of HRM

Following on from our earlier discussion of the different definitions and meanings of HRM, two broad models have proved particularly influential, at least in academic circles, in the interpretation of HRM. On the one hand, contingency-based approaches have developed into strategic HRM to suggest that HRM must match with business strategy. On the other hand, what might be termed an absolute position – more is better – has developed around ideas of mutuality and stakeholding at the organisation level.

Contingency – the matching model

The 'matching' model, developed by academics at the Michigan Business School, introduced the concept of strategic HRM, in which HRM policies are inextricably linked to the 'formulation and implementation of strategic corporate and/or business objectives' (Devanna *et al.*, 1984: 34). The model is illustrated in Figure 1.2.

The authors emphasise the necessity of a 'tight fit' between HR strategy and business strategy and the use of a set of HR policies and practices that are integrated with each other and with the goals of the organisation. Price (2004: 45–46) outlines the following key areas for the development of appropriate HR policies and systems:

- Selection of the most suitable people to meet business needs.
- Performance in the pursuit of business objectives.

Figure 1.2 The matching model of HRM

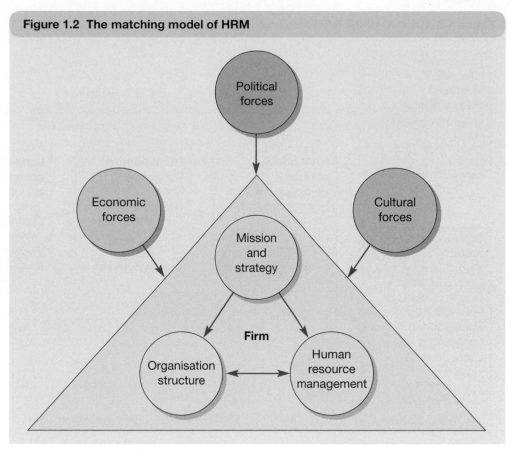

Source: Devanna *et al.* (1984) in Fombrun *et al.* (1984: 35). Reproduced with permission.

- Appraisal, monitoring performance and providing feedback to the organisation and its employees.
- Rewards for appropriate performance.
- Development of the skills and knowledge required to meet business objectives.

The matching model is closely allied with the 'hard' interpretation of HRM, i.e. the deployment of human resources to meet business objectives. Two assumptions underpin this model. The first is that the most effective means of managing people will vary from organisation to organisation and is dependent on organisational context. The second assumption is that of unitarism, i.e. the assumption that conflict, or at least differing views, cannot exist in the workplace because everyone (managers and employees) is working to achieve the same goal, the success of the organisation. This model has formed the basis of the 'best fit' school of HRM, discussed further in Chapter 2.

Universalism – more is better

A second influential model, illustrated in Figure 1.3, was developed by Beer *et al.* (1984) at Harvard University. 'The map of HRM territory', as the authors titled their model, recognises that there are a variety of 'stakeholders' in the organisation, which include shareholders, various groups of employees, the government and the community. The model recognises the legitimate interests of various groups, and assumes that the creation of HRM strategies will have to reflect these interests and fuse them as much as possible into the human resource strategy and ultimately the business strategy.

Figure 1.3 The map of the HRM territory

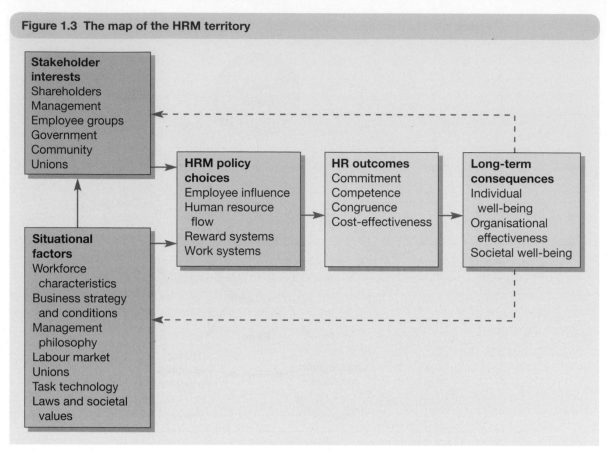

Source: Beer *et al.* (1984: 16). Reprinted with permission of The Free Press, a division of Simon & Schuster. Copyright © 1984 by The Free Press.

This recognition of stakeholders' interests raises a number of important questions for policymakers in the organisation (Beer *et al.*, 1984: 8):

> How much responsibility, authority and power should the organisation voluntarily delegate and to whom? If required by government legislation to bargain with the unions or consult with workers' councils, how should management enter into these institutional arrangements? Will they seek to minimize the power and influence of these legislated mechanisms? Or will they share influence and work to create greater congruence of interests between management and the employee groups represented through these mechanisms?

The recognition that employees and their representatives are important stakeholders who at least need to be included in the equation initially led to greater acceptance of this model by academics and commentators in the UK, although some still criticised it as being too unitarist (Hendry and Pettigrew, 1990). However, the main influence of this model is based less on considerations of stakeholder interests and situational factors and more on the benefits to employers of adopting a 'soft' approach to HRM that seeks to enhance the quality and commitment of the workforce. Building on this model, Guest (1989: 42) developed a set of propositions that combine to create more effective organisations:

- *Strategic integration* is defined as 'the ability of organisations to integrate HRM issues into their strategic plans to ensure that the various aspects of HRM cohere and for line managers to incorporate an HRM perspective into their decision making'.

- *High commitment* is defined as being 'concerned with both behavioural commitment to pursue agreed goals and attitudinal commitment reflected in a strong identification with the enterprise'.
- *High quality* 'refers to all aspects of managerial behaviour, including management of employees and investment in high-quality employees, which in turn will bear directly on the quality of the goods and services provided'.
- *Flexibility* is seen as being 'primarily concerned with what is sometimes called functional flexibility, but also with an adaptable organisational structure with the capacity to manage innovation'.

This reflects an assumption that it is possible to balance the strategic integration associated with the matching model and the high-commitment elements of the universal model.

The assumption of universalism that underlies the 'best practice' school of HRM is that a set of practices aimed at high commitment or high performance will benefit any organisation regardless of context (public sector, private sector or voluntary sector).

The elements of best practices identified by Pfeffer (1998) are now widely recognised, if not universally accepted:

- Employment security
- Sophisticated selection
- Teamworking and decentralisation
- High wages linked to organisational performance
- Extensive training
- Narrow status differentials
- Communication and involvement.

There is still no widely accepted theoretical rationale for favouring any particular set of practices as being essential to HRM (Boselie *et al.*, 2005) and reviews of the field (e.g. Boselie *et al.*, 2005; Wall and Wood, 2005; Hyde *et al.*, 2006) continue to show considerable variety in the number and types of practices included in lists within different studies. However, these studies have also identified some areas of common ground. For example, Wall and Wood's (2005: 435) review of 25 studies found that 'they typically cover a substantial range of the following: sophisticated selection, appraisal, training, teamwork, communication, job design, empowerment, participation, performance-related pay, harmonisation and employment security'. More specifically, Boselie *et al.*'s (2005: 73) review of 104 articles identified the top four practices, in order, as 'training and development, contingent pay and reward schemes, performance management (including appraisal) and careful recruitment and selection'. Guest (2001) notes a broad consensus around the territory to be covered:

> There is a plausible list of practices that includes selection, training, communication, job design and reward systems. There are also practices on the margin such as family-friendly and equal opportunity practices as well as some that cannot apply across all sectors, such as profit-related pay and employee-share ownership schemes (Guest, 2001: 1096).

Best-practice HRM is discussed more fully in Chapter 2 and will be revisited later in this chapter in relation to HRM and organisational performance. However, it is worth noting here that there are some challenges to the universal applicability of best-practice HRM. For example, Marchington and Zagelmeyer (2005: 4) suggest that a high-commitment approach to HRM is dependent on the ability of employers to take a long-term perspective and on the prospect of future market growth. They also suggest that it is easier to engage in high-commitment HRM when labour costs form a low proportion of total costs. Boxall and Purcell (2011) agree that any list of best practices is unlikely to have universal application because of the influence of organisational context. However, they differentiate between the surface layer of policy and practice that is likely to be contingent on a range of internal and external factors and the underpinning layer that reflects 'certain desirable

Figure 1.4 The 'best fit' vs 'best practice' debate: two levels of analysis

Surface layer: HR policies and practices – heavily influenced by context (societal, sectoral, organisational)

Underpinning layer: generic HR processes and general principles of labour management

Source: Boxall and Purcell (2011: 95).

principles which, if applied, will bring about more effective management of people' (Boxall and Purcell, 2011: 95–96; see Figure 1.4).

HRM and organisational performance

Over the last 20 years, there have been many studies investigating the links between HRM and organisational performance. These have mainly focused on the extent to which high-commitment practices lead to improvements in employee outcomes and organisational performance (Marchington and Wilkinson, 2012: 401). The view that HRM improves the performance of organisations is widespread, yet which aspects of performance are important and how they might be measured are not clearly defined. HRM may contribute to sustaining competitive advantage, but this does not necessarily have to rely on high-commitment HRM. A key issue relates to the type of sector and product market in which a firm competes. Broadly these fall into two categories: cost advantage, which is crucial to competitiveness in contexts where the imperative is cost control if not cost reduction, e.g., mass service or mass production sectors; labour differentiation, where quality and services are at a premium and the focus of HR strategies is to attract and retain good-quality recruits and the design of superior organisational processes to promote both vertical and horizontal fit.

Guest (2011: 4) identified six overlapping phases in research into the links between HRM and performance. These are briefly outlined here and then discussed in more detail as the chapter progresses:

- Phase 1: Development of HRM frameworks
- Phase 2: Survey-based studies
- Phase 3: Backlash against claims linking HRM to improved organisational performance
- Phase 4: Conceptual refinement about HRM practices, outcomes and the link between them
- Phase 5: Focus on HR processes and the importance of workers' perceptions
- Phase 6: Growing sophistication and complexity of data collection methods and statistical analysis.

The first phase, which occurred in the 1980s, 'presented the promise of HRM in the form of semi-prescriptive analytical frameworks alongside somewhat anecdotal cases that appeared to confirm the promise of an association between HRM and performance' (Guest, 2011: 4); two such frameworks have been introduced in the chapter.

The second phase emerged in the 1990s when survey-based studies emerged (primarily from the USA) which showed that the adoption of more HR practices was associated with higher organisational performance. The starting point for this empirical approach came from the USA, in particular the work of Arthur (1992, 1994), McDuffie (1995) and Huselid (1995). The unifying theme of these studies is that particular combinations of HRM practices, especially where they are refined and modified to fit with particular organisational contexts, can give quantifiable improvements in organisational performance. Arthur's work studied 54 mini-mills (new technology steel mills using smaller workforces and new working practices) and demonstrated that firms using a 'commitment' model of HRM saw higher productivity, lower labour turnover and lower rates of rejected production. McDuffie's work examined 70 plants in the world car industry and the use of HR techniques that were regarded as innovative. His analysis argued that superior performance is achieved when practices are used together, rather than in isolation. An important part of this analysis is the extent to which employees gave 'extra' in the form of discretionary effort that would otherwise not have been forthcoming without the cumulative effect of the chosen practices. Three factors were noted in particular: buffers (the extent to which plants adopted flexibility); work system (the work arrangements that complemented flexibility); and HRM policies (the HRM practices that complemented flexibility). The marked effect on performance was in the combined impact of all three factors working together. Huselid's study examined the relationships between the HR system (the groups of practices rather than individual practices), outcome measures (such as financial performance as well as HR data on turnover and absence), and the fit between HR and competitive strategy in 986 US-owned firms employing more than 100 employees. Huselid's results indicated a lowering of labour turnover, higher sales performance, improved profitability and higher share valuations for those firms that performed well on his indices.

The benefits of adopting HRM were also evident in the study undertaken by Ichniowski et al. (1997). The authors identified four different types of HR system on the basis of innovative practices in relation to selection, reward, communication, work organisation, training and employment security. The HR systems were numbered from one to four, ranging from system 1 (innovative HR practices in all areas) to system 4 (no innovative HR practices). Systems 2 and 3 lay between the two extremes and included innovative practices in some areas but not others. The findings showed a positive association between innovative HRM practices and both productivity and product quality. Furthermore, the authors claimed that a move from system 4 to system 2, if maintained for 10 years, would increase operating profits by over $10 million simply as a result of the HRM changes (Ichniowski et al., 1997). A US study conducted by Chadwick and Cappelli (1998) identified two approaches to managing people: an 'investment HR system' (including extensive training, employee involvement, teamworking) and a 'contractual HR system' (average pay, use of atypical workers, importance of industry credentials for selection). The findings suggested that not only were investment systems more likely to improve performance than contractual systems, but also that contractual systems could have a detrimental effect on performance.

Similar findings emerged from the UK at the same time. Thompson's (1998) study of the aerospace industry found that innovative HRM practices were positively associated with higher added value per employee. A longitudinal study of single-site, single-product manufacturing firms (Patterson et al., 1997) concluded that HRM practices accounted for 19 per cent of variation in profitability and 18 per cent of variation in productivity. More recently, a cross-sector study (Tamkin et al., 2008) reported that increased investment in people, using measures associated with HRM, resulted in increased profits and sales growth. Positive results were not limited to manufacturing. In 2002, a study of HR practices in NHS acute hospital trusts found that certain HR practices (the sophistication and extensiveness of appraisal and training for hospital employees and the percentage of staff working in teams) were significantly associated with measures of patient mortality (West et al., 2002).

The results of these studies seemed to provide convincing evidence that HRM has a positive impact on organisational performance. The third phase, identified by Guest (2011: 4) is the backlash that emerged once it became recognised that 'the rush to empiricism had occurred at the expense of sufficient consideration of some key conceptual issues'. The first criticism related to a lack of consensus about which HR practices should be included. For example, a

Table 1.1 Numbers of empirical papers showing types of association between elements of HRM and performance

Element of HRM	Type of association			Main association between this element and performance	Total number of papers exploring this association
	Positive	Negative	Non-significant		
Training/development	24	1	19	Positive	44
Pay/incentives[a]	21	6	20	Positive	47
Involvement/voice[b]	16	5	17	Non-significant	38
Selection/recruitment	7	4	12	Non-significant	23
Teamworking	7	0	7	Positive or non-significant	14
Performance appraisal	6	0	12	Non-significant	18
HR index/bundle	37	3	20	Positive	60
Security	0	0	2	Non-significant	2
Job design (including work–life balance)	8	1	12	Non-significant	21
Equal opportunities	1	0	2	Non-significant	3
Career development (including mentoring)	2	0	6	Non-significant	8

[a]Including 'pay for performance'. [b]Including 'information sharing/communication'

Source: from *Improving Health Through Human Resource Management: A Starting Point for Change,* Chartered Institute of Personnel and Development (Hyde, P., Boaden, R., Cortvriend, P., Harris, P., Marchington, M., Pass, S., Sparrow, P. and Sibald, B. 2006), with the permission of the publisher, the Chartered Institute of Personnel and Development, London (**www.cipd.co.uk**).

literature review of empirical studies that examined the link between HRM and performance (Hyde *et al.*, 2006) found little consistency in results. Training, pay, employee involvement and 'bundles' of HR practices were more likely to be positively associated with performance, but these same elements also had the highest number of non-significant associations with performance. Pay and employee involvement also had the highest number of negative associations with performance. Table 1.1 provides an overview of the results.

Explore • What factors might account for the diversity of these results?

The second criticism was related to the variation in how these practices were measured (Becker and Gerhart, 1996; for a fuller discussion see Chapter 2) and to how organisational performance could be measured. The review of 97 academic papers undertaken by Hyde *et al.* (2006) found over 30 different performance measures used in the papers, with no single measure used in all the papers. A further criticism was that a concentration on the association between HRM and organisational performance could ignore other measures of managerial effectiveness and thus overstate the impact of HRM (Richardson and Thompson, 1999). There is also the issue of causality: does the introduction of HRM practices lead to enhanced organisational performance, or is it that better-performing organisations can afford to invest in the more sophisticated practices associated with HRM? Figure 1.5 illustrates the association between HRM activities and HRM outcomes and business performance, and 'indicates the possibility of two-way causation, i.e. that firm performance itself will give rise to a change (very often perceived as an improvement) in HRM practices' (Paauwe and Richardson, 1997).

Issues about the direction of causality were revealed in a study exploring the relationship between HRM and performance in 366 UK companies in the manufacturing and service sectors (Guest *et al.*, 2003). The study covered nine main areas of HRM: recruitment and

Figure 1.5 HRM activities in relation to HRM outcomes and performance

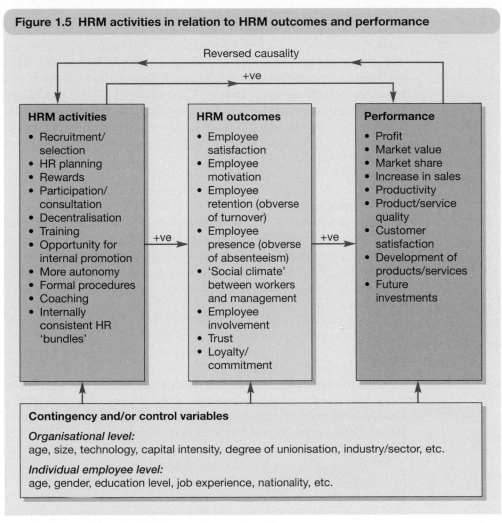

Source: Paauwe and Richardson (1997) adapted in Boselie *et al.* (2005: 68). http://www.tandf.co.uk/journals.

selection; training and development; appraisal; financial flexibility; job design; two-way communication; employment security and the internal labour market; single status and harmonisation; and quality. Measures of performance included employment relations items (e.g. labour turnover, absence and industrial conflict); labour productivity and financial performance compared with the average for the industry; and performance data such as value of sales and profit per employee. The findings show a positive association between HRM and profitability, but appear to 'lend stronger support to the view that profitability creates scope for more HRM rather than vice versa' (p. 309). Overall, the results are described as 'very mixed and on balance predominantly negative' (Guest *et al.,* 2003: 307):

> The tests of association show a positive relationship between the use of more HR practices and lower labour turnover and higher profitability, but show no association between HR and productivity. The test of whether the presence of more HR practices results in a change in performance shows no significant results.

As Guest and his colleagues argue, the focus of research on HRM and performance over the past decade has been slightly schizophrenic; on the one hand, it appeared to establish that

HRM has a positive effect on organisational performance, but, on the other, a number of commentators argue that such claims are premature. Wall and Wood (2005) demonstrate that the methodological limitations of most studies on HRM and performance undermine claims of any positive performance effect. In particular, Wall and Wood (2005: 450) claim that not all measures of improved performance, especially financial measures, are concurrent, i.e. they do not cover the same period of analysis. Thus, it is often the case that the data collected necessarily reflect prior performance and it follows from this that studies of HRM and performance may need to build a lag into their analysis. Alternatively, studies could be under-estimating the strength of the relationship between HRM and performance because of inadequate measurement of HR practices.

The fourth phase, identified by Guest (2011: 5), centres on conceptual refinement about HRM practices, outcomes and the link between them. At least part of the explanation for the continuing ambiguity about HRM and its impact on organisational performance can be attributed to an absence of 'a coherent theoretical basis for classifying HRM policy and practice' (Guest, 1997: 266). Three theoretical frameworks have had a major impact on the study of HRM: AMO theory (Appelbaum *et al.*, 2000), contingent theory and resource-based theory (Barney, 1991). AMO theory, which states that individual performance is a function of employee ability, motivation and opportunity, underpins many of the assumptions regarding which practices to include in a high-commitment/high-performance model (see Figure 1.6; Boxall and Purcell, 2011: 5). These aspects of performance are seen to contribute to organisational commitment, motivation and job satisfaction (e.g. Purcell *et al.*, 2003) and to enhance discretionary behaviour, a key factor in the link between individual and organisational performance (Appelbaum *et al.*, 2000).

AMO theory underpins both 'best practice' and 'best fit' schools of thought, although they differ with respect to the precise nature of the HR practices required to enhance organisational performance. According to proponents of the best-practice, or universal, approach (e.g. Pfeffer, 1998), the adoption of a 'synergistic set of practices' (Wood, 1999) that fosters employee involvement and commitment will enhance performance regardless of organisational context.

By contrast, proponents of the best-fit approach combine AMO with contingency theory and argue that there is no single best way; rather, people management practices need to be tailored to an organisation's specific circumstances. Thus different combinations of HRM practices may be effective and practices may change in response to specific external or internal influences. Well-known 'best fit' models are based on a variety of contextual factors, including life cycle (e.g. Kochan and Barocci, 1985), competitive advantage (e.g. Schuler, 1989; Sisson

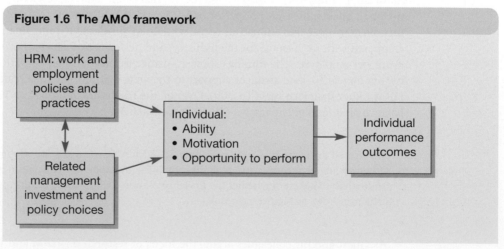

Figure 1.6 The AMO framework

Source: Boxall and Purcell (2011: 5).

and Storey, 2000), and strategic configurations (e.g. Delery and Doty, 1996), and are discussed more fully in Chapter 2.

Resource-based theory, also discussed more fully in Chapter 2, states that a firm's human resources can be a source of sustained competitive advantage, particularly if they are 'inimitable' and 'non-substitutable' (Barney, 1991). The resource-based view also reflects elements of AMO and contingent theories, but here the set of HRM practices, which could be easily imitated (Wright *et al.*, 1994), is less important than the human and social capital held by the workforce. HR practices contribute to this through 'building the human capital pool and stimulating the kinds of human behaviour that actually constitute an advantage' (Boxall and Steeneveld, 1999: 445).

Much of the research into HRM and performance has focused on HR practices, but the fifth and overlapping phase identified by Guest (2011: 5) turns its attention to HR processes and, in particular, to 'the key role of workers and the importance of workers' perceptions and behaviour in understanding the relationship between HRM and performance'. An example of research in this phase is work undertaken by Purcell *et al.* (2003), which explored the links between people management and performance. They concluded that a critical link is the extent to which HR practices influence employee attitudes and improve worker performance in ways that are beneficial to the organisation, and identified that front-line managers play a key role in this (see Chapter 2 for more detail).

Phase 6 of research into HRM and performance, identified by Guest (2011: 5–6), can be defined in terms of growing sophistication and complexity, which include the use of multiple sources of information and the application of more sophisticated statistical techniques.

This is partly in response to the criticisms identified in phase 3. A further criticism concerns the accuracy of data gathered from a single source. The vast majority of studies to date have relied on a single respondent for all the information, but one person is unlikely to have sufficient knowledge to answer questions across the board. Sixty per cent of the studies reviewed by Wall and Wood (2005) used estimates of organisational performance provided by the same person who had given information about HR practices and it can be argued that 'these two pieces of data should come from different sources to minimize bias' (Marchington and Wilkinson, 2012: 414). Multiple sources of information can also shed light on the presence of HRM practices, as research evidence suggests that managers generally report a higher incidence of HR practices than are reported by workers in the same organisation (Guest, 2011). Asking for views of workers can also provide insights into the effectiveness of HR practices: a study undertaken by Nishii *et al.* (2008) found that the way in which workers interpret the intention of HR practices can influence how they respond to them.

This section has outlined the key phases in research into the links between HRM and organisational performance. There is still some debate about the degree of association and the direction of causality, but the extensive body of research has increased our knowledge and understanding of the field. In addition, as Guest (2011) identifies, the significant number of studies has helped to refine the core research question, which started out as 'What impact does HRM have on performance?' and has now been extended in two directions. The first is the contingency question: 'Under what circumstances does HRM have an impact on performance?' The second concerns process and asks: 'What is the process whereby HRM can have an impact on performance?' (Guest, 2011: 7).

HRM in practice

The studies discussed in the previous section provide some support for the argument that the systematic deployment of HRM will enhance organisational performance and productivity. Findings of studies undertaken by the Chartered Institute of Personnel and Development

(CIPD, 2006) and the Economic and Social Research Council (ESRC, 2004), and other research such as the Conference Board (2005), make an important contribution to the wider debate about HRM and performance. These studies indicate that effective people management in conjunction with contemporary systems of work organisation can make a demonstrative difference to organisational performance and productivity. However, if, as the cited studies demonstrate, effective people management does make a difference in terms of performance and productivity, a key question for both academics and practitioners is why so few firms deploy these practices. The UK and the USA are frequently cited as liberal market economies where short-termism and shareholder capitalism predominate over longer-term stakeholder approaches to management. The established research on HRM in the USA does suggest that high-performance, high-commitment approaches to HRM do not have a widespread presence, but their presence is greater than in the UK. So, while there is a strong case to be made that HRM has a positive effect on performance, we are left with the question of why, in the UK, short-termism appears to have generated strong barriers to the wider diffusion of HRM practices.

Fifteen years ago, the Sheffield study (Patterson *et al.*, 1997) concluded that the finding of a positive association between HRM and organisational performance was 'ironic, given that our research has also demonstrated that emphasis on HRM practices is one of the most neglected areas of managerial practice within organisations' (p. 21). Since then, empirical data (e.g. Guest *et al.*, 2000; Kersley *et al.*, 2006) continue to show that, although the use of individual practices is extensive, workplaces that adopt full-blown HRM, i.e. a high number of HRM practices, remain in the minority. UK studies such as the Workplace Employee Relations Surveys (WERS; Cully *et al.*, 1999; Kersley *et al.*, 2006; Van Wanrooy *et al.*, 2013) and the Future of Work Study (Guest *et al.*, 2000) consistently report that only a minority of organisations are making extensive use of HRM practices (Guest *et al.*, 2000: ix):

> Concentrating on a list of 18 typical practices, only 1 per cent of companies have more than three-quarters in place and applying to most workers, and only 26 per cent apply more than half of them. At the other extreme, 20 per cent of organisations make extensive use of less than a quarter of these practices.

Sung and Ashton (2005) investigated the adoption of 35 'high-performance work practices'. The findings show that the more of these practices an organisation uses, the more effective it is in delivering adequate training provision, motivating staff, managing change and providing career opportunities. However, the findings also show that about 60 per cent of the sample uses less than 20 practices.

Key Controversy

If there is a link between HRM and organisational performance, why is there not a more extensive use of HRM practices?

Sisson (2001: 80–81) first proposed two explanations for the limited adoption of an integrated set of HRM practices some time ago, but they continue to be relevant today. The first is that the time resources and costs associated with change may tempt managers to adopt an incremental approach, i.e. to 'try one or two elements and assess their impact before going further, even though this means forgoing the benefits of the integration associated with "bundles" of complementary practices'. The low take-up of HRM is also attributed to system inertia, particularly in established organisations. There are three possible causes of this inertia (CIPD/ EEF, 2005): firms get locked into their initial choice of people management practices and face resistance to change; they experiment with change but abandon it when it does not appear to work; and change in people management practices may also require new production or distribution technologies and therefore will incur additional costs.

Another, and in Sisson's words, 'less comfortable' explanation is that 'competitive success based on the quality and upskilling that HRM implies is only one of a number of strategies available to organisations' and other strategies such as cost-cutting, new forms of Taylorism, mergers and joint ventures may be applied instead. Legge (1989: 30) suggests the potential incompatibility between business strategies and best-practice HRM: 'if the business strategy should dictate the choice of HRM policies, will some strategies dictate policies that. . . fail to emphasise commitment, flexibility and quality?'

Explore

- What factors might influence the take-up of practices associated with high-commitment HRM?

While many of the supporters of HRM (e.g. Huselid, 1995; Pfeffer, 1998) argue for its universal applicability, others suggest that the attractiveness of HRM to employers can depend on HR requirements. For example, McDuffie (1995: 199) suggests three conditions that enable HRM to contribute to improved economic performance:

- Employees possess knowledge and skills that managers lack.
- Employees are motivated to apply this skill and knowledge through discretionary effort.
- The organisation's business strategy can only be achieved if employees contribute such discretionary effort.

In a similar vein, Marchington and Wilkinson (2012: 75) suggest that best-practice HRM is more likely when:

- employers are able to take a long-term perspective;
- the cost of labour is low compared with other costs;
- knowledge workers are expected to use their discretion;
- organisations and workers are in a strong market position.

In the absence of these conditions, the business case for investing in high-commitment/best-practice HRM may be weak. Indeed, organisations may perceive more benefits, at least in the short term, from adopting an 'intensification' or cost reduction approach. Cost considerations are clearly important. Godard (2004: 367) suggests that many of the claims about the positive association between HRM and business performance underestimate the costs involved in adopting HRM practices: 'These costs can reflect higher wages, more training, possible inefficiencies arising from participatory decision-making processes and various resource requirements needed to maintain high involvement levels.' As a result, Godard suggests that, for most employers, the use of an integrated set of HRM practices often has little or no overall advantage over traditional personnel practices with a few high-performance practices grafted on, and may even have negative effects for some employers. Organisation size can also be a key factor. Small and medium-sized enterprises (SMEs), which account for 94 per cent of all employers in the UK economy, are less likely than larger organisations to use a number of HRM practices, such as sophisticated selection, extensive training, teamworking, problem-solving and functional flexibility (Forth *et al.*, 2007).

The impact of the recession on HRM practice

The high-commitment HRM model assumes that employers are able to take a long-term perspective and 'ride out' difficult economic circumstances. Marchington and Wilkinson (2012: 75) suggest that this might include: hiring during lean times when labour is plentiful, investing in workers' development when finances are tight and retaining workers during downturns. The global financial crisis and subsequent recession have certainly resulted in difficult conditions for many organisations, so has this context acted as an enabler or inhibitor of the adoption of HRM practices? Brewster and King (2013) suggest that the impact of the recession on HRM is paradoxical because it increases the importance of managing people in the most cost-effective and efficient way at the same time as making it more difficult to do so. They suggest that many HRM practices 'are under threat as short-term survivalist thinking begins to dominate longer term success orientations' (Brewster and King, 2013: 1) and describe a scenario of job cuts, reduced hiring and a greater focus on cost-cutting.

An exploration of HRM in recession-hit Ireland (Roche *et al.*, 2011) found evidence of both 'hard' and 'soft' approaches. The study found two broad patterns of 'hard' HRM. About half the firms had implemented 'general HR retrenchment programmes' which included pay freezes, curbs on overtime, short-time working, redundancies and more rigorous work regimes. The others had implemented fewer of these measures, focusing mainly on pay freezes, curbs in overtime and greater rigour in the management of work regimes. The study also found that firms often combined these cost-driven measures with 'softer' aspects of HRM in an attempt to maintain staff motivation and commitment. These practices included a great emphasis on communications and employee engagement, as well as involving employees in the development of measures of responding to the recession (Roche *et al.*, 2011: 11) There was also evidence of a greater emphasis on implementing existing HR policies concerned with employee performance, particularly relating to discipline, attendance and time-keeping. Emphasis on performance management and employee communication was revealed in a study undertaken by Ipsos Mori and Talent 2 (2009: 3), which asked organisations to identify their biggest current priorities during these turbulent economic conditions. The top three priorities were performance management, leadership/management development and employee communication and engagement.

A survey undertaken by King's College, London, and employment law specialists, Speechly Bircham (Clinton and Woollard, 2010) confirmed the significant effect of the recession, with 83 per cent of respondents reporting a negative impact on their business. Cost-cutting measures were apparent with many organisations reporting reductions in pay rises, the size of bonus pools and development budgets. The study also found that there was a shift away from the use of compulsory redundancies towards an increase in the use of flexible and part-time working and the use of other methods to downsize. The recession also appears to be taking its toll on the employment experience, with a higher proportion of respondents reporting an increase in levels of stress among employees, an increase in employment relations problems and an increase in employee grievances, mainly concerning bullying and harassment and relations with senior or line managers. The respondents to this survey identified their top three major HR challenges as maintaining employee engagement, succession planning, and managing growth and expansion, implying that an upturn is anticipated. This survey focused on the views of senior HR professionals. A survey of 2,000 UK employees conducted by YouGov (CIPD, 2013) revealed that redundancies, training cuts, pay freezes and recruitment freezes were more common in the public sector than in the private sector, while the private sector was more likely to have cut back on the hours people work. Eighteen per cent of employees working in the private sector reported that their organisation had not been affected by the economic downturn, compared with only 4% in the public sector.

Explore

- To what extent can HR practices designed to maintain employee motivation and commitment offset the effects of cost-cutting practices such as pay freezes and redundancies?

The impact of HRM on the roles of HR professionals

'There have been notable attempts to capture the changing nature of personnel roles in response to major transformations in the workplace and the associated rise of HRM' (Caldwell, 2003: 983). In many organisations, the personnel department was essentially an administrative support function, which focused on expert knowledge, procedural efficiency and compliance, and was perceived as being remote from business performance issues (Storey, 2007). The emergence of HRM and the emphasis on its contribution to the achievement of business goals have been perceived by many practitioners as presenting an opportunity to 'raise their game'. In order to overcome the traditional marginalisation and poor reputation of the personnel function, Ulrich (1998) proposed that HR professionals should become more proactive and strategic 'business partners' through the adoption of four key roles:

1 *Strategic partner* – working with senior and line managers in strategy execution. HR should identify the underlying model of the company's way of doing business, i.e. the organisational architecture, and undertake regular audits in order to identify aspects in need of change.

2 *Administrative expert* – improving administrative processes, often through the application of technology, in order to improve the efficiency of the HR function and the entire organisation.

3 *Employee champion* – ensuring that employees are 'engaged', i.e. that they feel committed to the organisation and contribute fully. This is achieved through acting as the voice for employees in management discussion as well as offering them opportunities for personal and professional growth, and providing the resources that help them to meet the demands placed on them.

4 *Change agent* – building the organisation's capacity to embrace and capitalise on change by shaping processes and by helping an organisation to identify key success factors and assess its strengths and weaknesses in relation to each factor.

The 'Ulrich model of business partnering' has been widely espoused in the USA and the UK, partly because of its rhetorical simplicity and its forceful message to change the HR function (Caldwell, 2008). In addition, steeply climbing salaries and an increased perception of status and prestige mean that the business partner term seems to have become the title of choice for ambitious HR practitioners (Francis and Keegan, 2006). However, not all aspects of the role have been embraced with equal enthusiasm. Although Ulrich (1998) suggested that the HR function needs to fulfil all four roles, empirical evidence suggests that HR practitioners are more likely to aspire to the strategic roles of strategic partner and change agent rather than the more operationally focused roles of administrative expert and employee champion. Survey findings in the UK (e.g. CIPD, 2003) show that a higher proportion of HR practitioners regard themselves as strategic partners and change agents than regard themselves as administrative experts and employee champions. Similarly, HR practitioners are also more likely to aspire to the strategic partners and change agent roles than they are to become administrative experts or employee champions.

Explore

- Why do you think so few HR professionals want to be employee champions?

There is a danger that the emphasis in the HR literature on the achievement of business-oriented performance outcomes has minimised the contribution of the employee champion role and obscured the importance of employee well-being in its own right (Peccei, 2004; cited in Francis and Keegan, 2006). However, a number of studies (e.g. Guest and King, 2004;

Table 1.2 Evolution of HR roles

Mid-1990s	Mid-2000s	Evolution of thinking
Employee champion	Employee advocate	Focuses on the needs of today's employee
	Human capital developer	Focuses on preparing employees to be successful in the future
Administrative expert	Functional expert	HR practices are central to HR value. Some HR practices are delivered though administrative efficiency and others through policies and interventions
Change agent	Strategic partner	Being a strategic partner has multiple dimensions: business expert, change agent, strategic HR planner, knowledge manager and consultant
Strategic partner	Strategic partner	As above
	Leader	Being an HR leader requires functioning in each of these four roles. However, being an HR leader also has implications for leading the HR function, collaborating with other functions, setting and enhancing the standards for strategic thinking and ensuring corporate governance

Source: from 'Role call', *People Management* 11(12), pp. 24–28 (Ulrich, D. and Brockbank, W. 2005), with permission from D. Ulrich and W. Brockbank.

Hope-Hailey *et al.*, 2005) have shown that the neglect of people-centred roles can have a negative effect on the sustainability of organisational performance.

A subsequent variant of this model (Ulrich and Brockbank, 2005a) redefines the employee champion and administrative expert roles, integrates the change agent role into the strategic partner role and introduces the new role of HR leader (see Table 1.2). These 'subtle but important changes' are described as reflecting the 'changing roles we are observing in the leading organisations with which we work' (p. 24), but also serve to correct the imbalances of business partnering roles (Caldwell, 2008). Ulrich and Brockbank (2005b: 201) argue that 'caring for, listening to, and responding to employees remains the centerpiece of HR work'. So, the employee champion role is enlarged and focuses on building the workforce of the future, as well as addressing employees' current needs. Functional experts are not only concerned with administrative efficiency, but also apply their expert knowledge to the design and implementation of HR practices that 'improve decisions and deliver results' (Ulrich and Brockbank, 2005a: 26). HR leaders are responsible for leading the HR function in order to enhance its credibility.

Explore

- To what extent do you believe that these changes increase the attractiveness of operational HR roles?

While many HR practitioners aspire to a more strategic role, survey data suggest that operational and administrative work is still dominant. The CIPD (2007) survey into the roles and responsibilities of HR practitioners asked respondents to identify the most time-consuming activities and the most important activities in terms of their contribution to the organisation. The most important activities in terms of adding value to the organisation were identified as developing HR strategy, business strategy, change management and providing specialist HR expertise. By contrast, the most time-consuming activities were identified as providing support to line managers, HR administration, implementing HR policies and change management. The fact that these lists only overlap on one element (change management) helps to illustrate the ongoing tensions between competing role demands on the HR function and the difficulties in creating an entirely new role and agenda for the function that 'focuses not on traditional HR activities such as staffing and compensation, but on outcomes' (Ulrich, 1998: 124).

A recent survey, undertaken on behalf of CIPD, suggests that, in reality, many HR professionals see their main role as transactional rather than strategic. The results, which draw on responses from 1,500 HR practitioners across the UK, show that only a fifth (22%) consider that the purpose of the HR function they work in is to drive sustainable organisation performance and only 43 per cent see this as the purpose of a best practice HR function. By contrast, 43 per cent consider that their main purpose is 'ensuring the organisation has the best people in the right jobs, doing the right work' and 29 per cent see their main purpose as providing payroll, pensions, learning and administration (CIPD, 2011: 2). The same study also reports that the majority of respondents (60 per cent) think that 'HR needs to build its ability to understand business issues', and only half consider that 'HR is viewed as adding significant value' to their organisation (CIPD, 2011: 3). Similar results are evident in a study commissioned by KPMG International (KPMG, 2012: 14), which found that only 17 per cent of respondents felt that HR was able to demonstrate measurably its value to the business.

Key Controversy

There 'remains a vast gulf between the perceived importance and the perceived effectiveness of HR today'(KPMG, 2012: 14). Why do you think this gap exists and how can HR professionals best address it?

The authors of the KPMG International study (KPMG, 2012: 15–17) argue that, in order to improve HR's contribution and image, executives need to:

- *Make the value of HR more prominent and understood.* HR work is frequently undertaken behind the scenes, so others in the organisation may be unaware of HR's contribution. HR professionals need to understand the business, ensure that they are included in strategic discussions and demonstrate strong leadership.

- *Think, understand and communicate in the language of business.* HR professionals need to consider the impact of HR on business outcomes and make a strong business case for any proposals. They also need to take a full perspective on the whole business and create HR strategies to fit; this 'requires a far deeper grasp of the organisation's core business model and strategy and the implications this holds for the rest of the business – to date, something that far too few HR practitioners have mastered' (p.15).

- *Transfer appropriate responsibilities to line managers.* 'Constrained budgets and improved technology are also leading to a shift in direct responsibility for employees away from HR and back to line managers as the latter become empowered to handle their own transactions' (p.16).

- *Move from administration to higher-value activities.* Advances in technology can enable HR to focus more on strategic activities rather than transactional administration. However, in order to have the credibility to focus on higher-value activities, the authors argue that HR first needs to prove that it is capable of delivering value to the business.

One response to raising the credibility of the HR function is to ensure that the competence and capability of HR professionals reflect the needs of contemporary organisations. Behavioural competence becomes more critical as people develop into senior roles, and research suggests that HR professionals need to develop a broader skill-set if they are to meet the challenges facing business today (CIPD, 2009). The emphasis on critical behaviours, coupled with the rise of the 'HR business partner', has led to an enormous growth in HR competency models (see Caldwell, 2008).

Ulrich *et al.* (2012) identified new roles that HR professionals need to adopt to tackle the challenges currently facing organisations, including the economic crisis, globalisation and technological advances. These six roles are as follows:

- Strategic positioner
  - Knows the business context and understands how political, economic, social, technological, legal and environmental trends impact on the organisation.
  - Contributes to the development of relevant business strategies and helps translate strategies into business plans and goals.

- Credible activist
  - Gets things done and delivers results.
  - Has strong interpersonal skills and makes sound business decisions based on good-quality data and thoughtful opinions.

- Capability builder
  - Helps to define and build organisational capabilities, i.e. what the organisation is good at and known for.
  - Helps ensure that capabilities reflect organisational values.

- Change champion
  - Develops organisational capacity for change and translates this into effective change processes and structures.
  - Overcomes resistance to change by engaging key stakeholders in decisions and building their commitment.
  - Ensures that the necessary resources, including time, people, capital and information, are available.
  - Captures the lessons of success and failure.

- Human resource innovator
  - Able to innovate and integrate HR practices around critical business issues.
  - Aligns HR practices, processes, structures and procedures with identified organisational capabilities and desired business results.

- Technology proponent
  - Applies social networking technology to help people stay connected with each other and with the organisation
  - Contributes to the effective management of information.

In the UK, the CIPD has developed a Profession Map, which, it is claimed, 'captures what successful and effective HR people do and deliver across every aspect and specialism of the profession' (**www.cipd.co.uk**). The map covers 10 professional areas, eight behaviours and four bands of competence.

Explore

Examine the Profession Map at http://www.cipd.co.uk/cipd-hr-profession/hr-profession-map/.

- To what extent do you agree that these behaviours are important for effective HR professionals?
- What do you see as the key differences between the competencies identified by Ulrich and those identified by the CIPD?

Concluding comments

Human resource management has now become the most widely used term in the English-speaking world to refer to the activities of management in the employment relationship (Boxall and Purcell, 2011), but debates around the meaning of the term and the impact of the concept continue. In order to differentiate the generic use of the term, i.e. to cover all activities relating to people management and its more specific meaning as an approach focusing on enhancing the discretionary behaviour of individuals, a number of other terms have been introduced, such as high-commitment management, high-involvement management and high-performance work systems. From its early origins, a key theme in the HRM debate has concerned the relationship between HRM practice and organisational performance. The results are somewhat ambiguous in that, while there appear to be associations between HRM and organisational performance, a question remains about which comes first: does HRM lead to better organisational performance, or are better-performing organisations more able to invest in HRM practices? Either way, it still seems that the majority of organisations have embraced HRM in a partial rather than a complete way. The impact of the global financial crisis and recession on HRM has been paradoxical, as they have increased the importance of managing people in the most cost-effective and efficient way while making it more difficult to do so. Survey data suggest that many organisations have attempted to temper 'hard' HR practices, such as redundancies and pay freezes, with 'softer' practices, designed to maintain commitment and motivation. The association between HRM and organisational performance appears to have had some impact on the role and status of HR professionals, particularly apparent in the growing recognition of the business partner role. However, while HR models have emphasised the potential for HR professionals to adopt a strategic focus, the operational focus continues to be a reality for many, and questions still exist about the extent to which HR can demonstrate its value to the business.

The different interpretations of HRM can be confusing, but they are also part of the attraction of HRM for academics and practitioners and help to ensure that 'the domain remains lively, vibrant and contested' (Storey, 2007: 17). Whatever the perspective taken, it seems that the advent of HRM has raised questions about the nature of people management that have stimulated one of the most intense and active debates on the subject in the last 40 years and there is every likelihood that this will continue for some considerable time yet.

Summary

- **Defining HRM**. There is no universally agreed definition of HRM and definitions can refer to people management activities in the broadest sense or in the specific meanings of high-commitment management or a strategic approach to people management.

- **Models of HRM**. By the early 1980s, a number of US analysts were writing about HRM and devising models and explanations for its emergence, which can be traced back to the 1930s. Among the most significant of these are Devanna (fit and the matching model) and Beer (the Harvard model).

- **HRM and business performance**. Guest (2011) has identified six phases in the growing body of research into the association between HRM and organisational performance. Results from empirical studies suggest that there is a link, but the direction of causality is inconclusive, as is the assumption that a set of practices can have universal applicability.

- **HRM in practice**. Empirical evidence continues to show that, although there is a high use of individual HRM practices, few organisations appear to adopt a full-blown version of high-commitment HRM. The general low level of take-up can be attributed to organisational inertia and cost considerations, but may also suggest that some organisations seek to achieve competitive advantage through a 'low road' approach of cost-cutting or new forms of Taylorism rather than the 'high road' approach of HRM. The financial crisis and recession have increased the use of cost-cutting HR practices such as pay freezes, overtime bans and redundancies in order to survive, but many organisations have tried to balance these with softer practices to maintain employee motivation and commitment.

- **HRM and the HR function?** The emergence of HRM and the emphasis on its contribution to the achievement of business goals have been perceived by many practitioners as presenting an opportunity to improve the power and status of the HR function. One of the most influential models over years has been developed by Ulrich (1998). However, survey findings continue to show that, while many practitioners aspire to adopt a more strategic role, the administrative role is still dominant and HR often struggles to demonstrate that it adds significant value to the business. A number of models have been developed identifying the key competencies that HR professionals need in order to meet the challenges of organisations now and in the future.

Questions

1 The 'matching model' (Devanna *et al.*, 1984) and the 'map of the HR territory' (Beer *et al.*, 1984) were conceived 30 years ago. To what extent are they still relevant to the study of HRM in organisations today?
2 Studies of HRM and performance differ on a number of grounds, including the HR practices considered, methods of data collection and the respondents asked to provide information. How does this lack of consensus affect our understanding of the association between HRM and organisational performance?
3 To what extent can demonstration of the competencies identified by Ulrich *et al.* (2012) and CIPD's Profession Map help to raise the perceived added value of HR? What other factors should also be considered?

Case study

Amazon unpacked

By Sarah O'Connor

When Amazon opened a warehouse in the struggling former coal-mining town of Rugeley, locals were thrilled. But for many, this soon turned to bitter disappointment as they began to experience the working conditions – and job insecurity – at the company.

Between a sooty power station and a brown canal on the edge of a small English town, there is a building that looks as if it should be somewhere else. An enormous long blue box, it looks like a smear of summer sky on a damp industrial landscape. Inside, hundreds of people in orange vests are pushing trolleys around a space the size of nine football pitches, glancing down at the screens of their handheld satnav computers for directions on where to walk next and what to pick up when they get there. They do not dawdle – the devices in their hands are also measuring their productivity in real time. They might each walk between seven and 15 miles today. It is almost Christmas and the people

working in this building, together with seven others like it across the country, are despatching a truck filled with parcels every three minutes or so. Before they can go home at the end of their three-hour shift, or go to the canteen for their 30-minute break, they must walk through a set of airport-style security scanners to prove they are not stealing anything. They also walk past a life-sized cardboard image of a cheery blonde woman in an orange vest. 'This is the best job I have ever had' says a speech bubble near her head.

As online shopping explodes in Britain, more and more jobs are moving from high-street shops into warehouses like this one. Amazon has invested more than £1 billion in its UK operations and announced last year that it would open another three warehouses over the next two years and create 2,000 more permanent jobs.

Workers in Amazon's warehouses, known by the company as 'fulfilment centre associates', are divided into

Case study continued

four groups. There are people on the 'receive lines' and the 'pack lines', They either unpack, check and scan every product arriving from all around the world, or they pack up customers' orders at the other end of the process. Another group stows away suppliers' products wherever there is a free space. Only Amazon's vast computer brain knows where everything is because workers use their handheld computers to scan both the item they are stowing away and a barcode on the spot on the shelf where they put it. The last group, the 'pickers', push trolleys around and pick up customers' orders from the aisles. Amazon's software calculates the most efficient walking route to collect all the items to fill a trolley, and then simply directs the worker from one shelf space to the next via instructions on the screen of the handheld satnav device. 'You're sort of like a robot, but in human form,' said the Amazon manager, 'It's human automation, if you like.'

The unassuming efficiency of these warehouses is what enables Amazon to put parcels on customers' doorsteps so quickly, even when it is receiving 35 orders a second. Every warehouse has its own 'continuous improvement manager', who uses 'kaizen' techniques pioneered by Japanese car company Toyota to improve productivity. Every day, managers take a 'genba walk', which roughly means 'go to the place' in Japanese, to discover how to help staff perform better. Some people also patrol the warehouse pushing tall little desks with laptops on them – they are 'mobile problem-solvers' looking for any hitches that might be slowing down the operation.

What did the people of Rugeley make of all this? For many it was a culture shock. Some have found the pressure intense. Several former workers said the hand-held computers, which look like clunky scientific calculators with handles and big screens, gave them a real-time indication of whether they were running behind or ahead of their latest target and by how much. Managers could also send text messages to these devices to tell workers to speed up, they said. 'People were constantly warned about talking to one another by the management, who were keen to eliminate any form of time-wasting,' one former worker added.

Other employees complained that they were getting blisters from the safety boots some were given to wear, which workers said were either cheap or the wrong size. In a statement, Amazon said, 'Some of the positions in our fulfilment centres are indeed physically demanding and some associates may log between seven and 15 miles walking per shift. We are clear about this in our job postings and during the screening process and, in fact, many associates seek these positions as they enjoy the active nature of the work. Like most companies, we have performance expectations for every Amazon employee – managers, software developers, site merchandisers and fulfilment centre associates – and we measure actual performance against those expectations.'

Not all of the workers in the warehouse are employed directly by Amazon. Many are initially employed by the employment agency. After three months, a worker who has performed well is able to apply to be an Amazon employee, although there is no guarantee that they will succeed. Amazon employees wear blue badges and workers supplied by agencies wear green badges. In the most basic roles, they perform the same tasks for the same pay (just above the minimum wage), but Amazon employees also receive a pension and shares. Discipline is strict with a 'three strikes and release' policy.

Amazon said it employed 'hundreds of permanent and temporary associates' at Rugeley and had recently given a further 200 permanent jobs to temporary workers there. It said it was proud of giving associates 'a great working environment', including on-the-job training, opportunities for career progression, competitive wages, performance-related pay, stock grants, healthcare, a pension plan, life assurance, income protection and an employee discount. It added: 'In order to ensure that we are providing our customers with the highest level of service, we do take on temporary associates during periods of high demand. When we have permanent positions available, we look to the top performing temporary associates to fill them.'

 Source: O'Connor, S. (2013) Amazon unpacked, *Financial Times*, 8 February. www.ft.com/cms/s/2/ed6a985c-70bd-11e2-85d0-00144feab49a.html

Questions

1. Identify the balance between 'hard' and 'soft' HRM practices at Amazon. To what extent do they complement or contradict each other?

2. How do HRM practices contribute to organisational efficiency?

3. What are the advantages and disadvantages of the approach adopted by Amazon for the organisation and individual workers?

References and further reading

Those texts marked with an asterisk are recommended for further reading.

Applebaum, E., Bailey, T., Berg, P. and Kalleberg, A. (2000) *Manufacturing Advantage: Why High-performance Systems Pay Off.* Ithaca, NY: ILR Press.

Arthur, J.B. (1992) 'The link between business strategy and industrial relations systems in American steel mini-mills', *Industrial and Labour Relations Review,* 45, 3: 488–506.

Arthur, J.B. (1994) 'Effects of human resource systems on manufacturing performance and turnover', *Academy of Management Journal,* 37, 3: 670–87.

Barney, J. (1991) 'Firm resources and sustained competitive advantage', *Journal of Management,* 17, 1: 99–120.

Barney, J. and Griffin, R. (1992) *The Management of Organisations: Strategy, Structure, Behavior.* Boston, MA: Houghton Mifflin.

Beardwell, I.J. (1992) 'The new industrial relations: a review of the debate', *Human Resource Management Journal,* 2, 2: 1–8.

Beardwell, I.J. (1996) 'How do we know how it really is?' in I.J. Beardwell (ed.) *Contemporary Industrial Relations.* Oxford: Oxford University Press, pp. 1–10.

Beardwell, I. and Holden, L. (1994) *Human Resource Management: A Contemporary Perspective.* London: Pitman.

Becker, B. and Gerhart, B. (1996) 'The impact of human resource management on organisational performance: progress and prospects', *Academy of Management Journal,* 39, 4: 779–801.

*Beer, M., Spector, B., Lawrence P.R., Quinn Mills, D. and Walton, R.E. (1984) *Managing Human Assets.* New York: Free Press.

Boselie, P., Dietz, G. and Boon, C. (2005) 'Commonalities and contradictions in HRM and performance research', *Human Resource Management Journal,* 15, 3: 67–94.

Boxall, P. and Purcell, J. (2011) *Strategy and Human Resource Management,* 3rd edn. Houndmills: Palgrave Macmillan.

Boxall, P. and Steeneveld, M. (1999) 'Human resource strategy and competitive advantage: a longitudinal study of engineering and competitive advantage: a longitudinal study of engineering consultancies', *Journal of Management Studies,* 36, 4: 443–63.

Brewster, C. and King, Z. (2013) *HRM and the Recession: Insights from Henley Business School.* Online: **http://www.henley.ac.uk/testing2/test-henley/hbs-insightsfromhbs-brewster.aspx** (accessed 15 May 2013).

Caldwell, R. (2003) 'The changing role of personnel managers: old ambiguities, new uncertainties', *Journal of Management Studies,* 40, 4: 983–1004.

Caldwell, R. (2008) 'HR business partner competency models: re-contextualising effectiveness', *Human Resource Management Journal,* 18, 3: 275–94.

Chadwick, C. and Cappelli, P. (1998) 'Alternatives to generic strategy typologies in strategic human resource management' in P. Wright, L. Dyer, J. Boudreau and G. Milkovich (eds) *Research in Personnel and Human Resource Management.* Greenwich, CT: JAI Press.

CIPD (2003) *Where we are: where we're heading?,* Survey Report. London: CIPD.

CIPD (2006) *People, Productivity and Performance – Work Smart.* London: CIPD.

CIPD (2007) *The Changing HR Function,* Survey Report, September. London: CIPD.

CIPD (2009) *Taking the Temperature on 'HR Skills for Survival',* Survey Report, April. London: CIPD.

CIPD (2011) *HR Outlook,* autumn. London: CIPD.

CIPD (2013) *Employee Outlook,* spring. London: CIPD.

CIPD/EEF (2005) *Maximising Employee Potential and Business Performance: The Role of High Performance Working,* CIPD Report, December.

Clinton, M. and Woollard, S. (2010) *From recession to recovery? The stage of HR in this challenging economic environment,* Survey Report. London: Kings College and Speechly Bircham.

Conference Board: McGuckin, R. and van Ark, B. (2005) *Performance 2005: Productivity, Employment and Income in the World's Economies,* August. New York: Conference Board.

Cully, M., Woodland, S., O'Reilly, A. and Dix, G. (1999) *Britain at Work: As Depicted by the 1998 Workplace Employee Relations Survey.* London: Routledge.

Delery, J.E. and Doty, H. (1996) 'Modes of theorizing in strategic human resource management: tests of universalistic, contingency and configurational performance predictions', *Academy of Management Journal,* 39, 4: 802–35.

*Devanna, M.A., Fombrun, C.J. and Tichy, N.M. (1984) 'A framework for strategic human resource management' in C.J. Fombrun, M.M. Tichy and M.A. Devanna (eds) *Strategic Human Resource Management.* New York: John Wiley, pp. 33–56.

ESRC (2004) *The UK's Productivity Gap: What Research Tells Us and What We Need to Know.* Swindon: ESRC.

Fombrun, C.J. (1984) 'The external context of human resource management' in C.J. Fombrun, N.M. Tichy and M.A. Devanna (eds) *Strategic Human Resource Management.* New York: John Wiley, pp. 1–18.

Forth, J., Bewley, H. and Bryson, A. (2007) *Small and Medium-sized Enterprises: Findings from the 2004 Workplace Employment Relations Survey.* London: Department for Business, Enterprise and Regulatory Reforms.

Foulkes, F. (1980) *Personnel Policies in Large Non-union Companies.* Englewood Cliffs, NJ: Prentice Hall.

Francis, H. and Keegan, A. (2006) 'The changing face of HRM: in search of balance', *Human Resource Management Journal,* 16, 3: 231–49.

Godard, J. (2004) 'A critical assessment of the high-performance paradigm', *British Journal of Industrial Relations,* 42, 2: 349–78.

Guest, D. (1987) 'Human resource management and industrial relations', *Journal of Management Studies,* 24, 5: 503–21.

Guest, D. (1989) 'Human resource management: its implications for industrial relations and trade unions' in J. Storey (ed.) *New Perspectives on Human Resource Management.* London: Routledge, pp. 41–55.

Guest, D. (1991) 'Personnel management: the end of orthodoxy?' *British Journal of Industrial Relations,* 29, 2: 149–75.

Guest, D. (2001) 'Industrial relations and human resource management', in J. Storey (ed.) *HRM: A Critical Text.* London: Thomson Learning.

Guest, D. (2011) 'Human resource management and performance: still searching for some answers', *Human Resource Management Journal,* 21, 1: 3–13.

Guest, D. and Conway, N. (1999) 'Peering into the black hole: the downside of the new employment relations in the UK', *British Journal of Industrial Relations*, 37, 3: 367–89.

Guest, D. and King, Z. (2004) 'Power, innovation and problem solving: the personnel managers' three steps to heaven?' *Journal of Management Studies*, 41, 3: 401–23.

Guest, D., Michie, J., Sheehan, M., Conway, N. and Metochi, M. (2000) *Effective people management: initial findings of the future of work study*, CIPD Research Report. London: CIPD.

Guest, D., Michie, J., Conway, N. and Sheehan, M. (2003) 'Human resource management and corporate performance in the UK', *British Journal of Industrial Relations*, 41, 2: 291–314.

Guthrie, J. (2001) 'High-involvement work practices, turnover and productivity: evidence from New Zealand', *Academy of Management Journal*, 44, 1: 180–90.

Hendry, C. and Pettigrew, A. (1990) 'Human resource management: an agenda for the 1990s', *International Journal of Human Resource Management*, 1, 1: 17–43.

Hope-Hailey, V., Farndale, E. and Truss, C. (2005) 'The HR department's role in organizational performance', *Human Resource Management Journal*, 15, 3: 49–66.

Huczynski, A. and Buchanan, D. (2007) *Organizational Behaviour*, 6th edn. Harlow: FT/Prentice Hall.

*Huselid, M. (1995) 'The impact of HRM practices on turnover, productivity and corporate financial performance', *Academy of Management Journal*, 38, 3: 635–72.

Hyde, P., Boaden, R., Cortvriend, P., Harris, C., Marchington, M., Pass, S., Sparrow, P. and Sibbald, B. (2006) *Improving health through human resource management: a starting point for change*, Change Agenda. London: CIPD.

Ichniowski, C., Shaw, K. and Prennushi, G. (1997) 'The effects of human resource management practices on productivity: a study of steel finishing lines', *American Economic Review*, 87, 291–313.

Ipsos Mori and Talent 2 (2009) *The Impact of the Economic Recession on HR*. Survey Report.

Jacoby, S. (2005) *The Embedded Corporation: Corporate Governance and Employment Relations in Japan and the United States*. Princeton, NJ: Princeton University Press.

Kanter, R. (1984) *The Change Masters*. London: Allen & Unwin.

Kaufman, B. (1993) *The Origins and Evolution of the Field of Industrial Relations*. New York: ILR Press.

Kersley, B., Alpin, C., Forth, J., Bryson, A., Bewley, H., Dix, G. and Oxenbridge, S. (2006) *Inside the Workplace: Findings from the 2004 Workplace Employment Relations Survey*. London: Routledge.

Kochan, T. and Barocci, T. (1985) *Human Resource Management and Industrial Relations*. Boston, MA: Little Brown.

KPMG International (2012) *Rethinking Human Resources in a Changing World*. Online: **http://www.kpmg.com/Global/en/IssuesAndInsights/ArticlesPublications/hr-transformations-survey/Documents/hr-transformations-survey-full-report.pdf** (accessed 29 August 2013).

*Legge, K. (1989) 'Human resource management: a critical analysis' in J. Storey (ed.) *New Perspectives on Human Resource Management*. London: Routledge, pp. 19–40.

*Legge, K. (2005) *HRM: Rhetorics and Realities*. Basingstoke: Macmillan Business.

McDuffie, J.P. (1995) 'Human resource bundles and manufacturing performance', *Industrial and Labour Relations Review*, 48, 2: 197–221.

Marchington, M. and Wilkinson, A. (2012) *Human Resource Management at Work*, 5th edn. London: CIPD.

Marchington, M. and Zagelmeyer, S. (2005) 'Foreword: linking HRM and performance – a never-ending search?' *Human Resource Management Journal*, 15, 4: 3–8.

Nishii, L., Lepak, D. and Schneider, B. (2008) 'Employee attributions of the "why" of HR practices: their effects on employee attitudes and behaviours and customer satisfaction', *Personnel Psychology*, 61, 3: 503–45.

Paauwe, J. and Richardson, R. (1997) 'Introduction', *International Journal of Human Resource Management*, 8, 3: 257–62.

Patterson, M., West, M., Lawthorm, R. and Nickell, S. (1997) 'The impact of people management practices on business performance', *Issues in People Management*, 22. London: IPD.

Peters, T.J. and Waterman, R.H. (1982) *In Search of Excellence: Lessons from America's Best Run Companies*. New York: Harper & Row.

Pfeffer, J. (1998) *The Human Equation*. Boston, MA: Harvard Business School Press.

Price, A. (2004) *Human Resource Management in a Business Context*, 2nd edn. London: Thomson Learning.

Purcell, J., Kinnie, N., Hutchinson, S., Rayton, B. and Swart, J. (2003) *Understanding the People and Performance Link: Unlocking the Black Box*. London: CIPD.

Ramsay, H., Scholarios, D. and Harley, B. (2000) 'Employees and high-performance work systems: testing inside the black box', *British Journal of Industrial Relations*, 38, 4: 501–31.

Richardson, R. and Thompson, P. (1999) 'The impact of people management practices on business performance: a literature review', *Issues in People Management*. London: IPD.

Roche, W., Teague, P., Coughton, A. and Fahy, H. (2011) *Human Resource Management in the Recession: Results of Survey of Employers*, Final Report Presented to the Labour Relations Commission, January.

Rollinson, D. and Dundon, T. (2011) *Understanding Employment Relations*. London: McGraw-Hill.

Schuler, R. (1989) 'Strategic human resource management and industrial relations', *Human Relations*, 42, 2: 157–84.

Sisson, K. (2001) 'Human resource management and the personnel function: a case of partial impact?' in J. Storey (ed.) *Human Resource Management: A Critical Text*, 2nd edn. London: Thomson Learning.

Sisson, K. and Storey, J. (2000) *The Realities of Human Resource Management*. Buckingham: Open University Press.

Stewart, R. (1991) *Managing Today and Tomorrow*. London: Macmillan.

Storey, J. (1992) *Developments in the Management of Human Resources: An Analytical Review*. London: Blackwell.

Storey, J. (2007) 'Human resource management today: an assessment' in J. Storey (ed.) *Human Resource Management: A Critical Text*, 3rd edn. London: Thomson Learning, pp. 3–20.

Sung, J. and Ashton, D. (2005) *High Performance Work Practices: Linking Strategy, Skills and Performance Outcomes*. London: DTI/CIPD.

Tamkin, P., Cowling, H. and Hunt, W. (2008) *People and the Bottom Line, Report 448*. Brighton: IES.

Thompson, M. (1998) 'Jet setters', *People Management*, 4, 8: 38–41.

Truss, C., Gratton, L., Hope-Hailey, V., McGovern, P. and Stiles, P. (1997) 'Soft and hard models of human resource management: a reappraisal', *Journal of Management Studies*, 34, 1: 53–73.

Ulrich, D. (1998) *Human Resource Champions*. Boston, MA: Harvard Business School Press.

Ulrich, D. and Brockbank, W. (2005a) 'Role call', *People Management*, 11, 12: 24–28.

Ulrich, D and Brockbank, W. (2005b) *The HR Value Proposition*. Boston, MA: Harvard University Press.

Ulrich, D., Younger, J., Brockbank, W. and Ulrich, M. (2012) *HR from the Outside In*. New York: McGraw Hill.

Van Wanrooy, B., Bewley, H., Bryson, A., Forth, J., Freeth, S., Stokes, L. and Wood, S. (2013) *The 2011 Workplace Employment Relations Study, First Findings,* Department for Business, Innovation and Skills, ACAS, ESRC, UKCES and NIERS.

Wall, T. and Wood, S. (2005) 'The romance of human resource management and business performance and the case for big science', *Human Relations,* 58, 4: 429–62.

Walton, R.E. (1985) 'From control to commitment in the workplace', *Harvard Business Review,* 63, 2: March–April, 76–84.

Watson, T. (2002) *Organising and Managing Work*. Harlow: FT/Prentice Hall.

West, M., Borrill, C., Dawson, J., Scully, J., Carter, M., Anelay, S., Patterson, M. and Waring, J. (2002) 'The link between the management of employees and patient mortality in acute hospitals', *International Journal of Human Resource Management,* 13, 8: 1299–310.

Wood, S. (1999) 'Human resource management and performance', *International Journal of Management Reviews,* 1, 4: 367–413.

Wright, P., McMahan, G. and McWilliams, A. (1994) 'Human resources and sustained competitive advantage: a resource-based perspective', *International Journal of Human Resource Management,* 5, 2: 301–26.

Chapter 2

Strategic human resource management

Nicky Golding and Julie Beardwell

Objectives

- To explore the meaning and application of strategic human resource management (SHRM).
- To evaluate the relationship between strategic management and SHRM.
- To examine the different approaches to SHRM, including:
  - the best-fit approach to SHRM;
  - the configurational approach to SHRM;
  - the resource-based view of SHRM;
  - the best-practice approach to SHRM.
- To evaluate the relationship between SHRM and organisational performance.

Introductory case study

Changes at RBS

The crisis

In 1998, when Sir Fred Goodwin joined Royal Bank of Scotland (RBS) as the deputy chief executive, it was a modest high-street bank with a celebrated history at the heart of Edinburgh and Scottish life. However, the youthful executive had ambitious plans to transform RBS into a global banking powerhouse.

Within three years of Sir Fred joining, RBS stunned the City of London by buying NatWest – in a deal that he masterminded. Sir Fred was charged with integrating the two institutions and soon earned his 'Fred the Shred' nickname, thanks to the ruthless zeal he showed for the task. By 2001, he was chief executive, flying around the world in the bank's private jet.

RBS prided itself as a cautious lender on the British high street, an image far removed from the scenes in the trading rooms of the investment banking division. Traders were under instructions to buy up assets – office buildings, aircraft, ships and whatever else they could find. Huge private equity deals were financed and the mantra was 'accumulate assets'. At RBS Greenwich Capital in Stamford, Connecticut, the bank established what is reputed to be the 'largest trading floor in the world'. Those in charge were earning up to $25 million a year in cash bonuses. Another unit of RBS was also embarking on an equally risky strategy to move into sub-prime mortgages.

Citizens Bank was a well-established New England institution which had not engaged in the more risky mortgage businesses. It had been owned by RBS since the 1980s, but during the past decade it took over several US regional banks. In 2007, it is understood to have begun buying up sub-prime mortgages from other banks. Although Citizens, headed by Larry Fish, was not offering sub-prime loans itself, it quickly amassed billions of pounds in sub-prime exposure. It is not known why it adopted this strategy, which was not authorised by the RBS board. It went disastrously wrong and Citizens is understood to have about £14 billion in 'toxic' loans. Several senior executives at the bank were 'severely reprimanded' over the move into sub-prime. Mr Fish retired last year with a pension worth $27 million (£18.6 million), which pays him more than $2.2 million (£1.5 million) annually.

It is alleged that the way in which bonuses were paid – based on the interest earned on assets – encouraged traders to take on riskier prospects that offered higher rates of return. One former senior executive at the bank said: 'The place was totally dysfunctional. Everywhere you looked they were taking on assets – billions of dollars worth of planes, billions of dollars of ships, commercial real estate across America and Britain. They were buying everything to meet Goodwin's targets and his targets were assets.'

It was against this background that – despite Sir Fred's public statements – traders started buying into the American sub-prime mortgage market. In 2007, mortgage portfolios were bought from other banks and huge lines of credit were offered to lenders with questionable records. Crucially, RBS was piling into the market

as others were fleeing. The plan was to package up the sub-prime debts and sell them on, but RBS was unable to offload the 'toxic' mortgages. By the end of 2007, RBS was forced to begin announcing that the value of many of its assets was less than previously thought.

By February 2009, the bank admitted the scale of its disastrous mistakes, unveiling a £28 billion loss. The taxpayer now effectively owns the toxic debts. One former executive estimates that losses could total more than £100 billion before the end of the recession. Despite the huge public liabilities, political attention has focused on the £17 million pension awarded to Sir Fred after he was forced to step down from RBS last October. However, directors say that the pension row underlines the dysfunctional nature in which the bank was run. The board only learnt of the settlement at the January 2009 meeting.

Sir Fred's subordinates were terrified of bringing problems to his attention. 'The bank was all about what Sir Fred wanted,' said one insider. 'It was still being run like a small Scottish bank rather than a major multinational company.' Gordon Pell, the bank's deputy chief executive, said that the bank would scrap many of the business divisions blamed for its downfall. Meanwhile politicians from all parties started pushing for an investigation into the downfall of RBS and other British banks.

Source: Winnett and Corrigan (2009).

The bailout

Stephen Hester is Britain's highest-profile financier and chief executive of the bank the nation loves to hate – the one that cost taxpayers £45 billion of bailout money in 2008 and 2009, the one that won't lend to Britain's struggling small businesses but pays out bonuses hand over fist, the one that is still, humiliatingly, 82 per cent owned by the government. Hester was parachuted in as chief executive four-and-a-half years ago to replace the disgraced Fred Goodwin. He came from British Land, a property group where he had overseen another dramatic restructuring. Now, as he likes to say, 'RBS is something approaching a normal bank'.

As a menu is brought to us, I pose the question Hester has been asked virtually throughout his stint at RBS. How long will he stay in a job that, notwithstanding the £1.2m salary plus bonuses of up to six times that, is often described as the most challenging, and thankless in British business? Usually, it is an issue Hester deflects with a few set responses. He has often talked,

colourfully but formulaically, of his focus on the five-year task of 'defusing the timebomb' on RBS's balance sheet – a reference to the bad loans he has sought to restructure or sell before they blow up and burn through the group's financial resources. Another standard default statement is that he wants to 'see the job through', which is generally taken to mean that he would like to lead the bank's reprivatisation over the next couple of years. But over lunch he is somewhat franker. Apologising if he sounds 'pompous', Hester says the RBS job was something he took on as a 'mission. I could have stayed out of the limelight at British Land but I wanted the challenge. Now that I've taken it on, it commands all my focus'. Returning RBS to sustainable profitability and to private sector ownership will be the key measures of success. 'I hate not winning, I hate it,' he says with a glimmer of passion.

At RBS he has spent the bulk of his time in charge resisting the reformist pressures of politicians and regulators, whether over his own bonuses or the size and scope of the group's investment bank and foreign operations. In the past year, however, he has been reinventing himself as more of a compliant public servant. First, he waived a bonus after an embarrassing IT glitch that saw customers unable to access their money, then he agreed to sell RBS's US subsidiary and scale back its investment banking arm.

We are meeting the day after RBS has received a rare piece of good news from regulators – that the bank will not be forced to raise swathes of fresh capital to absorb loan losses as some had predicted. Things may be looking up for RBS – assuming a report due next week from an influential parliamentary commission does not recommend breaking up the bank.

 Source: adapted from Jenkins, P. (2013) Lunch with the FT: Stephen Hester – 'I hate not winning', *Financial Times*, 8 June. http://www.ft.com/cms/s/2/6f05854c-ce98-11e2-8e16-00144feab7de.html axzz2tc7VV4B7 © The Financial Times Limited 2013. All Rights Reserved.

The future

Just after the interview in the preceding section was published, it was announced to a shocked City that Hester would be departing as the chief executive of RBS at the end of the year. The morning after this announcement, the share price dipped by 8 per cent and by the close it was down 3.7 per cent. It soon became obvious that Hester had not decided to quit of his own volition. It was the board, led by Sir Philip Hampton, that initiated the departure discussions three weeks previously, telling Hester that he had successfully negotiated the rescue phase of the bank and it was now time for a 'fresh face' to oversee its return to the private sector. Since then, it has become clear that in fact the not-quite-hidden hand of the Treasury had been in play. Those close to RBS revealed that tensions existed between Hester and the Government. As the 81 per cent majority shareholder, the Chancellor of the Exchequer, George Osborne, ultimately calls the shots.

According to Hester, 'RBS is in much better shape than we had any right to think it could be. RBS has gone from bust bank to pretty close to normal bank, we're ready now for the journey from normal to good, which will have privatisation as its next big milestone.'

Source: excerpts taken from Ahmed, K (2013) 'Stephen Hester lays out RBS departure plan', *The Telegraph*, 15 June © Telegraph Media Group Limited 2013.

Introduction

This chapter charts the development of strategic human resource management (SHRM). It assumes a certain familiarity with the evolution of HRM, early HRM models and frameworks and their theoretical underpinning as discussed in other chapters (in particular, see Chapter 1). The aim of this chapter is to trace the development of SHRM, so that you will be able to understand the synthesis both within and between SHRM and strategic management in its various forms.

Since the early 1980s, when HRM arrived on the managerial agenda, there has been considerable debate concerning its nature and its value to organisations. From the seminal works emerging from the Chicago School and the matching model of HRM (Fombrun *et al.*, 1984), the emphasis has very much concerned its *strategic* role in the organisation. Indeed, the literature rarely differentiates between HRM and SHRM. When attention was first focused on SHRM, some writers associated HRM with the strategic aspects and concerns of 'best fit' in vertically aligning an organisation's human resources to the organisational strategy (Fombrun, *et al.* 1984) or by creating 'congruence' or 'horizontal alignment' between various managerial and HRM policies (Beer *et al.*, 1984; Walton, 1985). Others focused on HRM as a means of gaining commitment and linked this to outcomes of enhanced organisational performance and business effectiveness (Beer *et al.*, 1984; Guest, 1987; Wood and De Menezes, 1998; Guest *et al.*, 2000a) through best-practice models (Pfeffer, 1994, 1998; MacDuffie; 1995; Arthur, 1994) or high-performance work practices (Guest, 1987; Huselid, 1995). Others recognised the 'harder' nature of SHRM (Storey, 1992), emphasising its contribution to business efficiency. Interlaced with this debate has been the wider controversy concerning the nature of business strategy itself, from which SHRM takes its theoretical constructs.

In addition to this are the transformations in organisational forms, which have had a simultaneous impact on both structures and relationships in organisations. The need for increased flexibility (Atkinson, 1984) or 'agility' (Rahrami, 1992: 35) in organisational structures and relationships has led to 'delayering, team-based networks alliances and partnerships and a new employer–employee covenant' or psychological contract. These changes in organisational structuring and employer–employee relationships have led to difficulties in finding new organisational forms that both foster creativity and avoid chaos. Thus tensions can arise between 'innovation and maintaining focus, between rapid response and avoiding duplication, between a focus on future products and meeting time to market criteria, between long-term vision and ensuring performance today'. These tensions have become more apparent with the global financial crisis and subsequent recession, as organisations grapple with remaining lean and focused through 'right-sizing', yet needing to maintain a motivated core base of skill and knowledge capable of creativity and rapid response in the future. These dilemmas are not new to the SHRM literature. Kanter (1989) noted contradictions between remaining 'lean, mean and fit', on the one hand, and being seen as a great company to work for on the other.

Developments in SHRM thinking, explored in this chapter through the development of the best-fit approach, the configurational approach, the resource-based approach and the best-practice approach, have a profound impact on our understanding of the contribution SHRM can make to organisational performance, through increased competitive advantage and added value. Indeed, it becomes clear that whether the focus of SHRM practices is on alignment with the external context or on the internal context of the firm, the meaning of SHRM can only really be understood in the context of something else, namely organisational performance, whether that be in terms of economic value added and increased shareholder value, customer value added and increased market share, or people value added through increased employee commitment and reservoirs of employee skills, knowledge and talent.

The debate therefore becomes extremely complex in its ramifications for analysing processes, evaluating performance and assessing outcomes. The observer must come to the view, in the best postmodern tradition, that the profusion and confusion of policy make straightforward analysis of SHRM in empirical and analytical terms extremely difficult and contingent on positional stances of the actors and observers involved in the research process. However, some kind of analytical context is useful in beginning our evaluations.

In order to understand the development of SHRM, and to recognise that it is more than traditional HRM prefixed with the word 'strategic', it is necessary to consider the nature of strategic management. This will provide an understanding of the 'strategic' context within which SHRM has developed, and enable us to understand the increasingly complex relationship between strategic management and SHRM.

Understanding the business context

The nature of business strategy

Boxall (1996: 60) has commented that 'any credible attempt at model-building in strategic HRM involves taking a position on the difficult questions: what is strategy? (content) and how is strategy formed? (process)'. It is the intention of this section to explore these questions and identify the difficulties and complexities involved in the 'strategy-making' process. This section provides an overview of some of the issues and debates, and sets the context for the SHRM debate discussed later in the chapter.

The roots of business strategy stretch far back into history (Alexander the Great, 356–323 BC; Julius Caesar, 100–44 BC), and early writers linked the term 'strategy' to the ancient Greek word *strategos*, which means 'general' and has connotations of 'to lead' and 'army'. Thus it is not surprising that many dictionary definitions convey a military perspective, such as the following from the *Oxford Pocket Dictionary*:

> *Strategy*. The art of war, especially the planning of movements of troops and ships etc. into favourable positions; plan of action or policy in business or politics etc.

Early writings on business strategy adopted a military model combined with economics, particularly the notion of rational–economic man (Chandler, 1962; Sloan, 1963; Ansoff, 1965). This is known as the classical or rational-planning approach, and has influenced business thinking for many decades. The meaning of strategy has changed, however, and become more complex, as the literature has moved from emphasising a long-term planning perspective (Chandler, 1962) to a more organic evolutionary process occupying a shorter time-frame (Ansoff and McDonnell, 1990; Aktouf 1996). Thus strategic management in the twenty-first century is seen to be as much about vision and direction as about planning, mechanisms and structure:

> Throughout the first half of our century and even into the early eighties, planning – with its inevitable companion, strategy – has always been a key word, the core, the near ultimate weapon of 'good' and 'true' management. Yet many firms including Sony, Xerox, Texas Instruments . . . have been remarkably successful . . . with minimal official, rational and systematic planning.
>
> Aktouf (1996: 91)

Explore

- How would you define the word 'strategy'? Note down five words you associate with strategy.

Strategy is a difficult concept to define, and sometimes it is easier to think about it in terms of metaphors. We have already been introduced to the military metaphor of 'strategy as the art of war'.

- What other metaphors might you use to define strategy?
- What metaphor would best describe the 'strategy-making' process in your organisation or one with which you are familiar?

Approaches to the strategy-making process

This chapter uses the four distinctive approaches to strategy-making identified by Whittington (1993, 2001) as a model of analysis:

- the classical or rational-planning approach
- the evolutionary approach
- the processual approach
- the systemic approach.

As you will see, an organisation's approach to its 'strategy making' process has implications for our understanding and application of SHRM.

Classical or rational-planning approach

This view suggests that strategy is formed through a formal and rational decision-making process. The key stages of the strategy-making process emphasise a comprehensive analysis of the external and internal environments, which then enables an organisation to evaluate and choose from a range of strategic choices that, in turn, allows for plans to be made to implement the strategy. With this approach, profitability is assumed to be the only goal of business and the rational-planning approach is the means to achieve it. Alfred Chandler (1962), a business historian, Igor Ansoff (1965), a theorist and Alfred Sloan (1963), president of General Motors, identified these key characteristics of the classical approach in their work and writings. Chandler (1962: 13) defined strategy as:

> the determination of the basic, long-term goals and objectives of an enterprise, and the adoption of courses of action and the allocation of resources necessary for those goals.

Grant (2010) highlights the classical approach in his model of common elements in successful strategies (Figure 2.1), where clear goals, understanding the competitive environment, resource appraisal and effective implementation form the basis of his analysis.

Within the classical perspective, strategy can be, and often is, viewed at three levels: first, at the corporate level, which relates to the overall scope of the organisation, its structures, financing and distribution of key resources; secondly, at a business level, which relates to its competitive positioning in markets/products/services; and thirdly, at an operational level, which relates to the methods used by the various functions of marketing, finance, production and, of course, human resources to meet the objectives of the higher-level strategies. This approach tends to separate out operational practices from higher-level strategic planning. This is not always helpful in reality, as it is often operational practices and effective systems that are 'strategic' to success in organisations (Boxall and Purcell, 2011), thus prompting Whittington (2001: 107) to comment that 'the rigid separation of strategy from operations is no longer

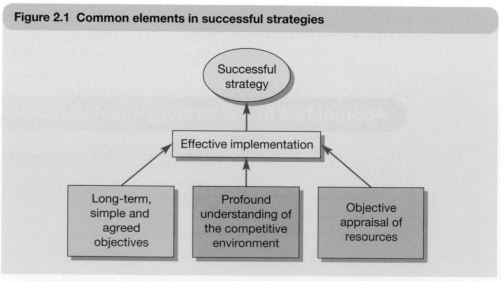

Figure 2.1 Common elements in successful strategies

Source: Grant (2010: 7).

valid in a knowledge-based age'. This is not to suggest that external analysis and planning should be ignored, but proposes a recognition that operational practices or 'tactical excellence' may provide sustainable competitive advantage by ensuring an organisation is adaptable and can flex with the environment. This becomes significant in contributing to our understanding of SHRM later in the chapter.

Key Controversy

The classical approach can be seen to underpin SHRM approaches, yet it 'relies upon an image of detached senior managers who determine the best plans for deploying workers to achieve victory over the competition in chosen market situations' (Marchington and Wilkinson, 2012: 13). How likely is this in reality?

Mintzberg (1990) clearly identified the 'basic premises' of the classical approach as being the disciplined 'readiness and capacity of managers to adopt profit-maximising strategies through rational long-term planning'. He questioned the feasibility of adopting this approach as either a model for prescription of best practice or a model of analysis, as he considered it to be an inflexible and oversimplified view of the 'strategy-making' process, relying too heavily on military models and their assumed culture of discipline. This can often lead to a disproportionate emphasis on analysis and decision-making about strategic choices at the expense of the key stage of implementation which, after all, delivers the results. Mintzberg (1987) therefore argued that making strategy in practice tends to be complex and messy and that he preferred to think about strategy as 'crafting' rather than 'planning'.

The classical approach is, however, the basis for much strategy discussion and analysis, and, as we will see later, underpins much strategic HRM thinking, particularly the 'best fit' school of thought and the notion of vertical integration. If, however, we accept that devising and implementing strategies in organisations is a complex and organic process, then it highlights the complexity of both defining and applying SHRM.

Evolutionary approach

An alternative view of the strategy-making process is the evolutionary approach. This suggests that strategy is made through an informal evolutionary process which relies less upon top managers to plan and act rationally and more upon the markets to secure profit maximisation. Whittington (2001) highlighted the links between the evolutionary approach and the 'natural law of the jungle'. Henderson (1989: 143) argued that 'Darwin is probably a better guide to business competition than economists are', as he recognised that markets are rarely static and indeed likened competition to a process of natural selection, where only the fittest survive. Darwin noted that more individuals of each species are born than can survive, and thus there is a frequently recurring struggle for existence. Evolutionists, therefore, argue that markets not managers choose the prevailing strategies. Thus, in this approach, the rational-planning models that analyse the external and internal environments in order to select the most appropriate strategic choices and then to identify and plan structural, product and service changes to meet market need become irrelevant. The evolutionary approach suggests that markets are too competitive for 'expensive strategizing and too unpredictable to outguess' (Whittington, 2001: 19). From this perspective, sophisticated strategies can only deliver a temporary advantage, and some suggest focusing instead on efficiency and managing the 'transaction costs'.

Processual approach

Quinn (1978) recognised that, in practice, strategy formation tends to be fragmented, evolutionary and largely intuitive. His 'logical incrementalist' view, therefore, while acknowledging the value of the rational–analytical approach, identified the need to take account of the psychological, political and behavioural relationships that influence and contribute to strategy. Quinn's view fits well within Whittington's (2001) processual approach, which recognises 'organisations and markets' as 'sticky, messy phenomena, from which strategies emerge with much confusion and in small steps' (p. 21).

The foundations of the processual school can be traced back to the work of the American Carnegie School according to Whittington (2001) and the work of Cyert and March (1956) and Simon (1947). They uncovered two key themes, first the cognitive limits of human action, and secondly, that human beings are influenced by 'bounded rationality' (Simon, 1947). Thus no single human being, whether he be the chief executive or a production worker, is likely to have all the answers to complex and difficult problems, and we all often have to act without knowing everything we would like to. Thus complexity, uncertainty and the need to take on board a range of interests become facts of life in strategic management and consequently in SHRM (Boxall and Purcell, 2011). It is important for organisations to recognise this, to avoid falling into a fog of complacency or the 'success trap' (Barr *et al.*, 1992), and it also highlights the limitations of some of the prescriptions for success advocated both in the strategic management and SHRM literature. In practice, an organisation's approach to SHRM has considerable influence here on the strategic management process, as to effectively manage the environment better than their competitors, some writers would suggest that the organisation needs to adopt a learning and open systems perspective. Mintzberg (1987) recognised this in his ideas on 'crafting strategy', and the fluid and organic nature of the strategy-making process. He compared the skills required of those involved in the process to those of a traditional craftsperson – traditional skill, dedication, perfection, mastery of detail, sense of involvement and intimacy through experience and commitment. Thus he recognised that planned strategies are not always realised strategies, and that strategies can often emerge and evolve (Figure 2.2). Thus the classic sequence of plan first, implementation second can become blurred, as 'strategy is discovered in action (March, 1976). Secondly, the processualists noted the significance of the micro-politics within organisations, a theme since developed by Pettigrew (1973, 1985) and Wilson (1992). This approach recognises the inherent rivalries and conflicting goals present within organisations and the impact this can have on strategy implementation. As we will see later in the chapter, it is these pluralist tensions that are sometimes ignored in certain branches of the SHRM literature, most notably the 'best practice' approach.

Explore

- Why might an intended strategy not be realised in practice?
- Why do strategies sometimes emerge?

Systemic approach

This leads us on to the final perspective identified by Whittington (1993, 2001), the systemic approach. This approach suggests that strategy is shaped by the social system within which it operates. Strategic choices, therefore, are shaped by the cultural and institutional interests of a broader society. So, for example, state intervention in France and Germany has shaped HRM in a way that is different from the USA and the UK. A key theme of the systemic approach is that 'decision makers are not detached, calculating individuals interacting in purely economic transactions' (Whittington, 2001: 26), but are members of a community 'rooted in a densely

Figure 2.2 Emergent strategy

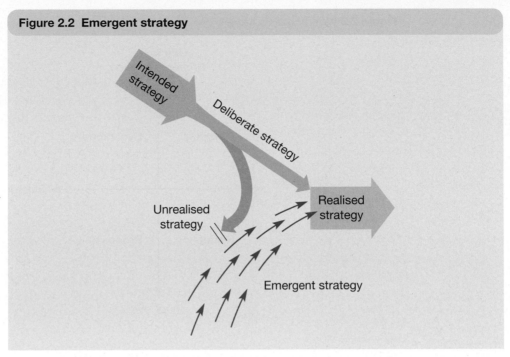

Unrealised strategy

Realised strategy

Emergent strategy

Source: from The Strategy Concept 1: Five Ps for Strategy, *California Management Review*, 30(1), pp. 11–24 (Mintzberg, H.). Copyright © 1987 by The Regents of the University of California, by permission of the publisher, University of California Press.

interwoven social system'. Therefore in reality, organisations and their members' choices are embedded in a network of social relations (Whittington, 1993). Thus, according to this approach, organisations differ according to the social and economic systems in which they are embedded.

Explore

- What are the implications for multinational organisations if we assume a systemic view of strategy?
- What are the implications for the HR professional involved in mergers and acquisitions?

The four approaches to strategy identified differ considerably in their implications for advice to management. Understanding that strategy formulation does not always occur in a rational, planned manner, due to complexities in both the external and internal environments, is significant for our understanding of SHRM. Whittington (1993) summarised his four generic approaches of classical, evolutionary, systemic and processual approaches in the model in Figure 2.3.

By plotting his model on two continua of outcomes (profit maximisation – pluralistic) and processes (deliberate – emergent), Whittington (1993, 2001) recognises that the strategy process changes depending upon the context and outcomes. In terms of SHRM, therefore, the term 'strategic' has broader and more complex connotations than those advocated in the prescriptive 'classical' strategy literature. As turbulence in the environment increases, organisations are recognising the importance of HR to their competitive performance, and therefore its role at a strategic level rather than an operational one.

Figure 2.3 Whittington's model

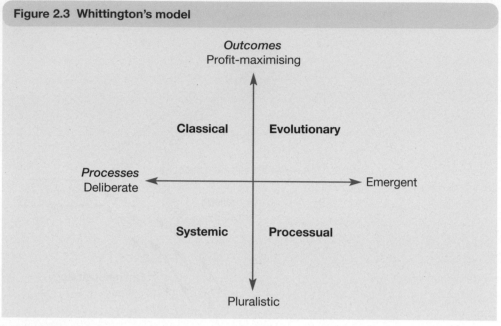

Source: Whittington (2001: 3).

Explore

Revisit the case study at the beginning of this chapter.

• Using Whittington's typology, can you explain how and why RBS's strategy developed and failed under Sir Fred Goodwin?

• How did the strategy change under the leadership of Stephen Hester?

By now you should be familiar with different approaches to understanding the nature of strategy and should have gained an appreciation of the complexities involved in the strategic management process. You may have realised that our understanding and interpretation of SHRM will, to a certain extent, be influenced by our interpretation of the context of strategic management. It is to the definition and the various interpretations of SHRM that we turn next.

The rise of SHRM

The contribution that HR may make to an organisation's performance and effectiveness has been the subject of scrutiny for some time. This interest has been linked to changes in the business environment, with the impact of globalisation leading to the need for increased competitiveness, flexibility, responsiveness, quality and the need for all functions of the business to demonstrate their contribution to the bottom line. As we have already recognised, it is against this backdrop that the traditional separation between strategy and operational activities, such as HRM, has become blurred, particularly within a knowledge-based age.

There is confusion over the differentiation between HRM and SHRM. Part of the reason for this confusion will be familiar to you, as it arises from the varying stances of the literature, those of prescription, description or critical evaluation. Some writers see the two terms as synonymous (Mabey *et al.*, 1998), while others consider there are differences. A wealth of literature has appeared to prescribe, describe and critically evaluate the way organisations manage their human resources. It has evolved from being highly critical of the personnel function's contribution to the organisation, as being weak, non-strategic and lacking a theoretical base (e.g. Drucker, 1968; Watson, 1977; Legge, 1978; Purcell, 1985), through the development of HRM models and frameworks (e.g. Beer *et al.* 1984; Fombrun *et al.* 1984; Guest, 1987; Schuler and Jackson, 1987), criticism of the HRM concept, questioning the empirical, ethical, theoretical and practical base of the subject (Blyton and Turnbull, 1992; Keenoy, 1990; Keenoy and Anthony, 1992; Clarke and Newman, 1997; Legge, 2005), and on to a wave of SHRM literature focusing on the link (or vertical integration) between HR practices and an organisation's business strategy, in order to enhance performance (Schuler and Jackson, 1987; Kochan and Barocci, 1985; Miles and Snow, 1984), and also on the relationship between best-practice or high-commitment HR practices and organisational performance (Pfeffer, 1994, 1998; Huselid, 1995; MacDuffie, 1995; Guest, 2001).

Confusion arises because embedded in much of the HRM literature is the notion of strategic integration (Beer *et al.*, 1984; Fombrun *et al.*, 1984; Guest, 1987), but critics have been quick to note the difference between the rhetoric of policy statements and the reality of action (Legge, 2005); the somewhat piecemeal adoption of HRM practices (Storey, 1992, 1995); and the ingrained ambiguity of a number of these models (Keenoy, 1990; Blyton and Turnbull, 1992). Thus, while the early HRM literature appeared to emphasise a strategic theme, there was much critical evaluation that demonstrated its lack of strategic integration. Thus terms such as 'old wine in new bottles' became a familiar explanation for the development from personnel to HRM to SHRM.

Explore

Consider the reading you have done previously in this book (see Chapter 1) and draw your own model of HRM, demonstrating its theoretical and applied origins.

- In what ways do you believe SHRM to be different from your model of HRM?
- Would you make any alterations to your model to ensure its strategic nature?

Exploring the relationship between strategic management and SHRM: the best-fit school of SHRM

The best-fit (or contingency) school of SHRM explores the close link between strategic management and HRM by assessing the extent to which there is *vertical integration* between an organisation's business strategy and its HRM policies and practices. This is where an understanding of the strategic management process and context can enhance our understanding of the development of SHRM, both as an academic field of study and in its application in organisations.

The notion of a link between business strategy and the performance of every individual in the organisation is central to 'fit' or vertical integration. Vertical integration can be explicitly demonstrated through the linking of a business goal to individual objective setting, to the measurement and rewarding of attainment of that business goal. Vertical integration between business strategy or the objectives of the business and individual behaviour and ultimately individual, team and organisational performance is at the core of many models of SHRM. Inherent in most treatments of fit is the premise that organisations are more efficient and/or effective when they achieve fit relative to when there is a lack of fit (Wright and Snell, 1998: 757). This vertical integration or 'fit' where 'leverage' is gained through procedures, policies and processes is widely acknowledged to be a crucial part of any strategic approach to the management of people (Dyer, 1984; Mahoney and Deckop, 1986; Schuler and Jackson, 1987;

Fombrun *et al.*, 1984; Gratton *et al.*, 1999). Vertical integration therefore ensures an explicit link or relationship between internal people processes and policies and the external market or business strategy, and thereby ensures that competencies are created that have a potential to be a key source of competitive advantage (Wright *et al.*, 1994).

Tyson (1997) saw the move towards greater vertical integration (between HRM and business strategy) and horizontal integration (between HR policies themselves and with line managers) as a sign of 'HRM's coming of age'. In recognising certain shifts in the HRM paradigm, Tyson identified 'vertical integration' as the essential ingredient that enables the HR paradigm to become strategic. In practice, this requires not only a statement of strategic intent, but also planning to ensure an integrated HR system can support the policies and processes in line with the business strategy. It is worthwhile considering the earlier discussions on the nature of strategic management here, as a number of critics, notably Legge (2005), have questioned the applicability of the classical–rational models on the grounds that there is a dearth of empirical evidence to support their credibility. Legge (2005: 135) tends to prefer the processual framework (Whittington, 1993), which is grounded in empirical work and recognises that 'integrating HRM and business strategy is a highly complex and iterative process, much dependent on the interplay and resources of different stakeholders'.

Explore

- In what way does Whittington's (1993, 2001) typology of strategy impact on your understanding of 'vertical integration'? You may find it useful to use Table 2.1 to guide your thinking.

There have been a number of SHRM models that have attempted to explore the link between business strategy and HR policies and practices, and to develop categories of integration or 'fit'. These include the lifecycle models (Kochan and Barocci, 1985; Lengnick Hall and Lengnick Hall, 1988; Sisson and Storey, 2000) and the competitive advantage models of Miles and Snow (1978) and Schuler and Jackson (1987), based on the influential work of Porter (1985).

Lifecycle models

A number of researchers have attempted to apply business and product life cycle thinking or 'models' to the selection and management of appropriate HR policies and practices that fit the relevant stage of an organisation's development or life cycle (Kochan and Barocci, 1985; Baird and Meshoulam, 1988). So, for example, according to this approach, during the start-up phase of the business there is an emphasis on 'flexibility' in HR to enable the business to grow and foster entrepreneurialism, whereas in the growth stage, once a business

Table 2.1

	Classic	Processual	Evolutionary	Systemic
Strategy	Formal and planned	Crafted and emergent	Efficient	Embedded
Rationale	Profit maximisation	Vague	Survival of the fittest	Local
Focus	Fitting internal plans to external contexts	Internal (politics)	External (markets)	External (societies)
Processes	Analytical	Bargaining/learning	Darwinian	Social/cultural
Key influences	Economics/military	Psychology	Economics/biology	Sociology
Emergence	1960s	1970s	1980s	1990s

Source: adapted from Whittington (2001: 39).

grows beyond a certain size, the emphasis would move to the development of more formal HR policies and procedures. In the maturity stage, as markets mature and margins decrease, and the performance of certain products or the organisation plateaus, the focus of the HR strategy may move to cost control. Finally, in the decline stage of a product or business, the emphasis shifts to rationalisation, with downsizing and redundancy implications for the HR function (Kochan and Barocci, 1985). The question for HR strategists here is, first, how can HR strategy secure and retain the type of human resources that are necessary for the organisation's continued viability, as industries and sectors develop; and secondly, which HR policies and practices are more likely to contribute to sustainable competitive advantage as organisations go through their life cycle (Boxall and Purcell, 2011)? Retaining viability and sustaining competitive advantage in the 'mature' stage of an organisation's development are at the heart of much SHRM literature. Baden-Fuller (1995) noted that there are two kinds of mature organisation that manage to survive industry development, 'one is the firm that succeeds in dominating the direction of industry change and the other is the firm that manages to adapt to the direction of change' (Boxall and Purcell, 2011: 198). Abell (1993), Boxall (1996) and Dyer and Shafer (1999) argue that the route to achieving human resource advantage as organisations develop and renew lies in the preparation for retaining viability and competitive advantage in the mature phase. The need for organisations to pursue 'dual' HR strategies, which enable them to master the present while preparing for and pre-empting the future, and to avoid becoming trapped in a single strategy is identified by Abell (1993), while Dyer and Shafer (1999) developed an approach that demonstrates how an organisation's HR strategy could contribute to what they termed 'organisational agility'. This implies an in-built capacity to flex and adapt to changes in the external context, which enables the business to change as a matter of course. Interestingly, this work appears to draw on the resource-based view and best-practice view of SHRM discussed later in the chapter, as well as the best-fit approach, reflecting the difficulty of viewing the various approaches to SHRM as distinct entities.

Competitive advantage models

Competitive advantage models tend to apply Porter's (1985) ideas on strategic choice. Porter identified three key bases of competitive advantage: cost leadership, differentiation through quality and service and focus on 'niche' markets. Schuler and Jackson (1987) used these as a basis for their model of SHRM, where they defined the appropriate HR policies and practices to 'fit' the generic strategies of cost reduction, quality enhancement and innovation. They argued that business performance will improve when HR practices mutually reinforce the organisation's choice of competitive strategy. Thus, in Schuler and Jackson's model (see Table 2.2), the organisation's mission and values are expressed through their desired competitive strategy. This, in turn, leads to a set of required employee behaviours, which would be reinforced by an appropriate set of HR practices. The outcome of this would be desired employee behaviours that are aligned with the corporate goals, thus demonstrating the achievement of vertical integration.

As you can see, the 'cost reduction'-led HR strategy is likely to focus on the delivery of *efficiency* through mainly 'hard' HR techniques, whereas the 'quality enhancement' and 'innovation'-led HR strategies focus on the delivery of *added value* through 'softer' HR techniques and policies. Thus, all three of these strategies can be deemed 'strategic' in linking HR policies and practices to the goals of the business and the external context of the firm, and in therefore contributing in different ways to 'bottom-line' performance. Another commonly cited competitive advantage framework is that of Miles and Snow (1978), who defined generic types of business strategy as *defenders, prospectors* and *analysers* and matched the generic strategies to appropriate HR strategies, policies and practices – the rationale being that if appropriate alignment is achieved between the organisation's business strategy and its HR policies and practices, a higher level of organisational performance will result.

Table 2.2 Business strategies and associated HR policies

Strategy	Employee role behaviour	HRM policies
Innovation	A high degree of creative behaviour	Jobs that require close interaction and coordination among groups of individuals
	Longer-term focus	Performance appraisals that are more likely to reflect long-term and group-based achievement
	A relatively high level of cooperative interdependent behaviour	Jobs that allow employees to develop skills that can be used in other positions in the firm
	A moderate degree of concern for quality	Pay rates that tend to be low, but allow employees to be stockholders and have more freedom to choose the mix of components that make up their pay package
	A moderate concern for quantity; an equal degree of concern for process and results	Broad career paths to reinforce the development of a broad range of skills
	A greater degree of risk-taking; a higher tolerance of ambiguity and unpredictability	
Quality enhancement	Relatively repetitive/predictable behaviours	Relatively fixed and explicit job descriptions
	A more long-term or immediate focus	High levels of employee participation in decisions relevant to immediate work conditions and job itself
	A moderate amount of cooperative interdependent behaviour	A mix of individual and group criteria for performance appraisal that is mostly short-term and results-oriented
	A high concern for quality	Relatively egalitarian treatment of employees and some guarantees of job security
	A modest concern for quantity of output	Extensive and continuous training and development of employees
	High concern for process; low risk-taking activity; commitment to the goals of the organisation	
Cost reduction	Relatively repetitive and predictable behaviour	Relatively fixed and explicit job descriptions that allow little room for ambiguity
	A rather short-term focus	Narrowly designed jobs and narrowly defined career paths that encourage specialisation expertise and efficiency
	Primarily autonomous or individual activity	Short-term results-oriented performance appraisals
	Moderate concern for quality	Close monitoring of market pay levels for use in making compensation decisions
	High concern for quantity of output	Minimal levels of employee training and development
	Primary concern for results; low risk-taking activity; relatively high degree of comfort with stability	

Source: Schuler and Jackson (1987: NY). Copyright 1987 by ACADEMY OF MANAGEMENT (NY).

Explore

- What are the advantages and disadvantages inherent in the competitive advantage models?
- What factors might present difficulties in applying them to organisations?

Configurational models

One criticism often levelled at the contingency or best-fit school is that its proponents tend to oversimplify organisational reality. In attempting to relate one dominant variable external to the organisation (e.g. compete on innovation, quality or cost) to another internal variable (e.g. HRM), they tend to assume a linear, non-problematic relationship. It is unlikely, however, that an organisation will only pursue a single focus strategy, as organisations have to compete in an ever-changing external environment where new strategies are constantly evolving and emerging. Thus organisations tend to develop hybrid strategies where a quality-focused strategy, for example, will often be combined with elements of cost reduction and even innovation. How often in organisational change programmes have organisations issued new mission and value statements, proclaiming new organisational values of employee commitment, etc., on the one hand, with announcements of compulsory redundancies on the other? Thus cost-reduction reality and high-commitment rhetoric often go hand in hand, particularly in a short-termist economy. Delery and Doty (1996) noted the limitation of the contingency school, and proposed the notion of the configurational perspective. This approach focuses on how unique patterns or configurations of multiple independent variables are related to the dependent variable, by aiming to identify 'ideal type' categories not only of the organisation strategy but also of the HR strategy. The significant difference here between the contingency approach and the configurational approach is that these configurations represent 'non-linear synergistic effects and higher-order interactions' that can result in maximum performance (Delery and Doty, 1996: 808). As Marchington and Wilkinson (2012: 91) note, the key point about the configurational perspective is that it 'identifies an internally consistent set of HR practices that maximise horizontal integration and then links these to alternative strategic configurations in order to maximise vertical integration'. Thus, put simply, SHRM according to configurational theorists, requires an organisation to develop an HR system that achieves both horizontal and vertical integration, or a form of 'idealised fit'. Delery and Doty use Miles and Snow's (1978) categories of 'defender' and 'prospector' to theoretically derive 'internal systems' or configurations of HR practices that maximise horizontal fit, and then link these to strategic configurations of, for example, 'defender' or 'prospector' to maximise vertical fit (Table 2.3).

The configurational approach provides an interesting variation on the contingency approach, and contributes to the SHRM debate in recognising the need for organisations to achieve both vertical and horizontal fit through their HR practices, so as to contribute to an organisation's competitive advantage and therefore be deemed strategic. While Table 2.3 only provides for the two polar opposites of 'defender' and 'prospector' type strategies, the approach does allow for deviation from these ideal-type strategies and recognises the need for proportionate deviation from the ideal-type HR systems.

Explore

- Chart the differences between the two theoretical perspectives identified in the discussion so far (contingency and configurational approaches).
- In what ways have these approaches contributed to your understanding of *strategic* HRM?

In analysing the level of vertical integration evident in organisational practice, it soon becomes clear that organisations pursue and interpret vertical integration in different ways. Some organisations adopt a top-down approach to HR 'strategy making', with senior management cascading defined strategic objectives to functional departments, who in turn cascade and roll out policies to employees, while others might recognise HRM as a key business partner and involve HR in the strategic process. Torrington et al. (2008) have explored the varying interpretations of 'fit' or 'integration' by attempting to qualify the degree or levels of integration between an organisation's business strategy and its HR strategy. They identified five different relationships or levels of 'vertical integration' (see Figure 2.4).

Table 2.3 Gaining maximum vertical and horizontal fit through strategic configurations

HR practices	Internal career opportunities	Training and development	Performance management	Employment security	Participation	Role of HR
Defenders						
Low-risk strategies Secure markets Concentration on narrow segments Focus on efficiency of systems	Sophisticated recruitment and selection systems Build talent and skills Career development opportunities Retention of key skills valued	Focus is on longer-term development for the future and emphasis on learning	Appraisals are development-oriented Clear grading structure and transparency valued Employee share schemes	Job security highly valued	Employee voice valued, through established systems of employee involvement, grievance and trade unions where recognised Commitment to the organisation emphasised	Potential for strategic role Well established department, with established HR systems
Prospectors						
Innovative, high-risk strategies Change and uncertainty Focus on entering new markets	Buy in talent and skills Limited internal career paths	Focus is on short-term skill needs Onus is on individual to take responsibility for personal learning and development	Appraisals are results-oriented Reward is short-term incentive based Performance-related pay based on bottom-line measures	Employability valued	Participation and employee voice limited	Administrative role Support role

Source: Delery and Doty (1996: 802–35). Copyright 1996 by ACADEMY OF MANAGEMENT (NY).

In the separation model, there is clearly no vertical integration or relationship between those responsible for business strategy and those responsible for HR, and thus there is unlikely to be any formal responsibility for human resources in the organisation. The 'fit' model according to Torrington *et al*. recognises that employees are key to achieving the business strategy, and therefore the HR strategy is designed to fit the requirements of the organisation's business strategy. This 'top-down' version of fit can be seen in the matching model (Fombrun *et al*., 1984) and in the best-fit models of Schuler and Jackson (1987) and Kochan and Barocci (1985). As you have probably already identified, these models assume a classical approach to strategy. Thus they assume that business objectives are cascaded down from senior management through departments to individuals.

The 'dialogue' model recognises the need for a two-way relationship between those responsible for making business strategy decisions and those responsible for making HR decisions. In reality, however, in this model the HR role may be limited to passing on essential information to the board to enable them to make strategic decisions. The 'holistic' model, on the other hand, recognises employees as a key source of competitive advantage rather than just a mechanism for implementing an organisation's strategy. HRresource strategy in this model becomes critical, as people competencies become key business competencies. This is the underpinning assumption behind the resource-based view of the firm (Barney, 1991; Barney and Wright, 1998),

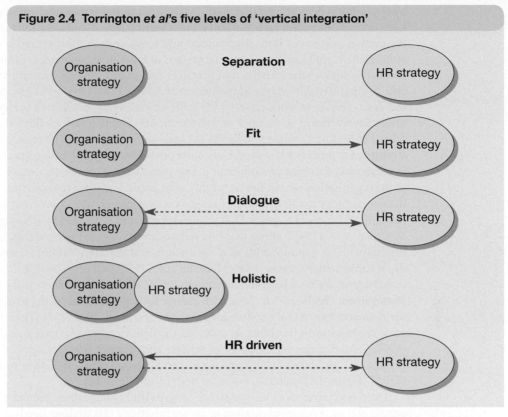

Figure 2.4 Torrington *et al*'s five levels of 'vertical integration'

Source: Human Resource Management, 4th ed., Prentice Hall (Torrington, D. and Hall, L. 1998) p. 27, Copyright © Prentice Hall Europe 1987, 1991, 1995, 1997.

discussed later in this chapter. The final degree of integration identified by Torrington *et al.* is the HR-driven model, which places HR as a key strategic partner.

Key Controversy

The assumption that it is possible to have a close relationship between organisational strategy and HRM that underpins 'best fit' models of SHRM fails to take account of the messy reality of a dynamic business environment, obstacles to change and how decisions are made. To what extent do you agree with this statement and why?

Limitations of the best-fit models of SHRM

Criticisms of the best-fit approach have identified a number of problems, both in its underlying theoretical assumptions and in its application to organisations. One of these key themes is the reliance on the classical rational-planning approach to strategy-making, its reliance on determinism and the resulting lack of sophistication in its description of generic competitive strategies (Miller, 1992; Ritson, 1999; Boxall and Purcell, 2011), together with its rejection of societal and national cultural influences on HR strategy. As Boxall and Purcell (2011: 61) noted, the firm can never be the complete author of its own HRM. This criticism is partly answered by the configurational school, which recognises the prevalence of hybrid strategies and the need for HR to respond accordingly (Delery and Doty, 1996). A further criticism is that best-fit models tend to ignore employee interests in the pursuit of enhanced economic performance. Thus, in reality, alignment tends to focus on 'fit' as defined by Torrington *et al.* (2008), and relies on assumptions of unitarism rather than the alignment of mutual

47

interests. It has been argued that 'multiple fits' are needed to take account of pluralist interests and conventions within an organisation, by ensuring that an organisation's HR strategy meets the mutual interests of both shareholders and employees. A third criticism could be levelled at the lack of emphasis on the internal context of individual businesses within the same sector and the unique characteristics and practices that might provide its main source of sustainable competitive advantage. Marchington and Wilkinson (2012: 95) ask, for example, why did Tesco choose to work closely with trade unions while Sainsbury's preferred to minimise union involvement? A number of these criticisms imply a lack of flexibility in the best-fit school of SHRM as, while a 'tight' fit between an organisation's HR strategy and its business strategy may provide a key source of competitive advantage in a stable business environment, in a dynamic changing environment it may prove to be a source of competitive disadvantage as the organisation cannot flex as quickly as its rivals. For some time, writers have argued that fit is sometimes not desirable and can be counter-productive in an environment of change (Lengnick Hall and Lengnick Hall, 1988). Wright and Snell (1998), drawing on the work of Milliman *et al.* (1991), argue that this reflects an 'orthogonal perspective', suggesting fit and flexibility are at opposite ends of a continuum, and therefore cannot co-exist. They support the 'complementary perspective' (Milliman *et al.*, 1991) and propose that fit and flexibility can co-exist, and are both essential for organisational effectiveness. They argue that the strategic management challenge is to cope with change by continually adapting to achieve fit between the firm and its external environment (Wright and Snell, 1998: 757). Thus SHRM must promote organisational flexibility in order for the firm to achieve dynamic fit. Wright and Snell (1998: 759), drawing on the work of Schuler and Jackson (1987), Capelli and Singh (1992), Wright and McMahan (1992) and Truss and Gratton (1994), therefore propose a model of SHRM (Figure 2.5) which accounts for both fit and flexibility.

The model assumes a classical stance towards the strategic management process, as it demonstrates how the implementation of an organisation's HR strategy needs to 'fit' the strategic choice made by the business in providing a process where the firm's strategy identifies the required or anticipated skills and behaviours, which then drive the intended HR practices, which in turn are operationalised in 'actual' HR practices, which influence the 'actual' skills and behaviours developed. When aligned, these then contribute to organisational performance. This alignment may endure and be effective in a stable and predictable environment because it supports the competitive needs of the organisation. Thus, fit may exist without any need for flexibility being built into the system. However, when the environment becomes unpredictable, it may become more difficult for managers to obtain the information they need and align the HR systems with the strategic process. Wright and Snell (2005) suggest that in such environments, achieving fit over time may be dependent upon the extent to which flexibility exists in the system, thus requiring a flexible HR system. Flexibility is demonstrated in their model by developing HR systems that can be adapted quickly, by developing a human capital pool with a broad range of skills and by promoting behavioural flexibility among employees. Thus employees develop a repertoire of skills and behaviour that reflects their capability to react to and flex with strategic changes.

Explore

- Reflect on Wright and Snell's fit/flexibility model (see Figure 2.5). How might an HR professional facilitate flexibility?

We have explored the best-fit school of SHRM and its relationship to strategic management through the contingency and configurational approaches. The contingency approach recommends a strong relationship to strategic management, whether it be to an organisation's life cycle or to competitive forces. This obviously assumes a classical, rational-planning

Figure 2.5 A fit/flexible model

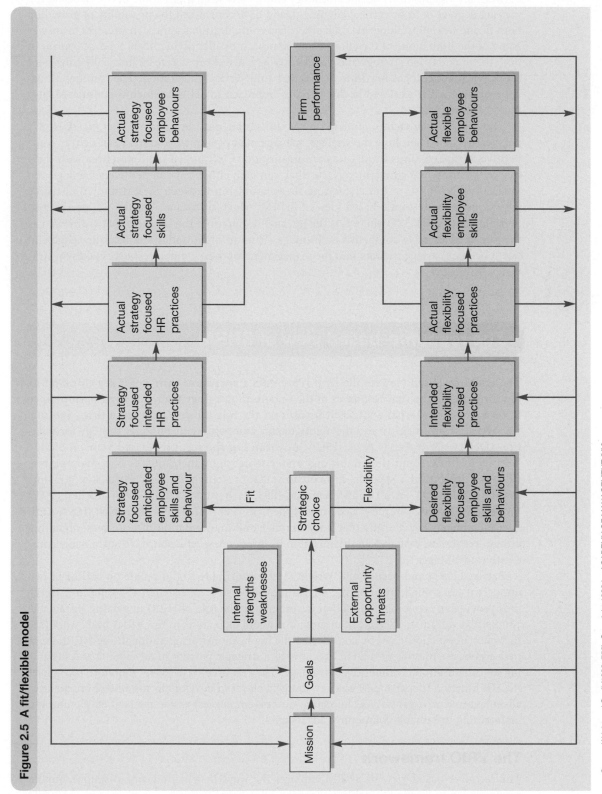

Source: Wright and Snell (1998: 758). Copyright 1998 by ACADEMY OF MANAGEMENT (NY).

model of strategic management. We have considered this relationship, or vertical integration between an organisation's business strategy and its HR strategy, in some detail, defining the varying degrees of fit or vertical alignment, and have considered the possibility of providing both fit and flexibility alongside each other. The configurational approach attempts to answer some of the limitations of the contingency approach by identifying 'ideal type' categories of both the organisation strategy and the HR strategy. It seeks to derive an internally consistent set of HR practices that maximise horizontal amd vertical integration. The configurational approach is further explored in the 'bundles' approach to SHRM, which is considered later in this chapter.

The best-fit approach to strategic HRM utilises an 'outside-in' (Wright *et al.*, 2004: 37) perspective to explain how the strategic management of human resources can deliver competitive advantage; thus by aligning an organisation's HR policies and practices with their market position and competitive focus they can gain enhanced competitive advantage. An alternative approach to understanding the relationship between SHRM and competitive advantage is the resource-based view of SHRM, which utilises an 'inside-out' perspective (Wright *et al.*, 2004: 37), where it is the internal resources of the business that are viewed as the key to sustainable competitive advantage. Thus an organisation's skills, knowledge and talent become 'strategic assets' and the management of these human resources takes on strategic significance.

The resource-based view of SHRM

The resource-based view of the firm represents a paradigm shift in SHRM thinking by focusing on the internal resources of the organisation rather than analysing performance in terms of the external context. It focuses on the relationship between a firm's internal resources, its profitability and the ability to stay competitive through its strategy formulation (Delery, 1998; Ferris *et al.*, 1999). Advocates of the resource-based view on SHRM help us to understand the conditions under which human resources become a scarce, valuable, organisation-specific, difficult-to-imitate resource, in other words key 'strategic assets' (Winter, 1987; Amit and Shoemaker, 1993; Barney and Wright, 1998; Mueller, 1998). Proponents of the resource-based view of the firm (Penrose, 1959; Wernerfelt, 1984; Amit and Shoemaker, 1993) argue that it is the range and manipulation of resources, including human resources, that give an organisation its 'uniqueness' and source of sustainable competitive advantage.

Barney (1991) and Barney and Wright (1998) contribute to the debate on SHRM in two important ways. First, by adopting a resource-based view (Wernefelt, 1984; Barney, 1991), they provide an economic foundation for examining the role of HRM in gaining sustainable competitive advantage. Secondly, in providing a tool of analysis in the VRIO framework (see the following section), and by considering the implications for operationalising HR strategy, they emphasise the role of the HR executive as a strategic partner in developing and sustaining an organisation's competitive advantage. The resource-based view therefore recognises the HR function (department) as a key strategic player in developing sustainable competitive advantage and an organisation's human resources (employees) as key assets in developing and maintaining sustainable competitive advantage.

The VRIO framework

The resource-based view of SHRM explores the ways in which an organisation's human resources can provide sustainable competitive advantage. This is best explained by the VRIO framework:

- Value
- Rarity
- Inimitability
- Organisation.

Value

Organisations need to consider how the HR function can create value. It is quite common in organisations to reduce costs through HR, such as the reduction in headcount and the introduction of flexible working practices, but it is also important to consider how they might increase revenue. Reicheld (1996) has identified human resources' contribution to the business as *efficiency,* but also as customer selection, customer retention and customer referral, thus highlighting the impact of HR's contribution through enhanced customer service and customer added value. This view is reflected by Thompson (2001) in recognising the paradigm shift from traditional added value through economy and efficiency to ensuring the potential value of outputs is maximised by making sure they fully meet the needs of the customers that the product or service is intended for. The suggestion of the resource-based view is that if the HR function wishes to be a 'strategic partner', it needs to be understood which human resources contribute the most to *sustainable competitive advantage* in the business, as some human resources may provide greater leverage for competitive advantage than others. Hamel and Prahalad (1993) therefore identify that productivity and performance can be improved by gaining the same output from fewer resources (*right-sizing*) and by achieving more output from given resources (*leveraging*). In order to achieve this, the HR function must ask themselves the following questions:

- On what basis is the firm seeking to distinguish itself from its competitors? Production efficiency? Innovation? Customer service?
- Where in the value chain is the greatest leverage for achieving differentiation?
- Which employees provide the greatest potential to differentiate a firm from its competitors?

Explore

- Try to answer the above questions with regard to your organisation or one you are familiar with.

The value of an organisation's resources is not sufficient on its own, however, for sustainable competitive advantage, because if other organisations possess the same value, then it will only provide *competitive parity*. Therefore an organisation needs to consider the next stage of the framework: rarity.

Rarity

The HR manager needs to consider how to develop and exploit rare characteristics of a firm's human resources to gain competitive advantage. For example, US fashion store Nordstrom operates in the highly competitive retail industry where you would usually expect a lower level of skill and subsequently high labour turnover. Nordstrom, however, focused on individual salespeople as a key source of its competitive advantage, investing in attracting and retaining young, college-educated people who were looking for a career in retailing. To ensure horizontal integration, it also provided a highly incentive-based compensation system (up to twice the industry average) and it encouraged employees to make a 'heroic effort' to attend customers' needs. Thus, by investing in its human resources and ensuring an integrated approach to development and reward, Nordstrom has taken a 'relatively homogeneous labour pool and exploited the rare characteristics to gain a competitive advantage' (Barney and Wright, 1998: 34).

Explore

Consider current advertising campaigns, either on television, radio or in the media.

- Can you identify any organisations that are attempting to exploit the rare characteristics of their employees, as a key source of their competitive advantage?
- Once you have identified an organisation, try to find more out about that organisation, their business strategy and their organisational performance in relation to their competitors.

Inimitability

If an organisation's human resources add value and are rare, they can provide competitive advantage in the short term, but if other firms can imitate these characteristics, then over time competitive advantage may be lost and replaced with competitive parity.

The third element of the VRIO framework requires the HR function to develop and nurture characteristics that cannot be easily imitated by the organisation's competitors. Barney and Wright (1998) recognise the significance of 'socially complex phenomena' here, such as an organisation's unique history and culture, which can be used to identify unique practices and behaviours that enable organisations to 'leapfrog' their competitors. Alchian and Demsetz (1972) also identified the contribution of *social complexity* in providing competitive advantage in their work on the potential *synergy* that results from effective teamwork. They found that this ensured a rare and difficult-to-copy commodity for two reasons; first, it provided competitive advantage through its *causal ambiguity,* as the specific source of the competitive advantage was difficult to identify; secondly, a synergy resulted from its *social complexity* as team members were involved in socially complex relationships that are not transferable across organisations. So characteristics such as trust and good relationships become firm-specific assets that provide value, are rare and are difficult for competitors to copy.

Southwest Airlines is an example of an organisation that demonstrates the strength of inimitability in that it exemplifies the role that socially complex phenomena such as culture can play in gaining competitive advantage. Top management attribute the company's financial success to its 'personality', a culture of 'fun' and 'trust', that empowers employees to do what it takes to meet the customers' needs and which the CEO, Herb Kelleher, believes cannot be imitated by competitors. This personality is reinforced through an extensive selection process, and a culture of trust and empowerment reinforced by the CEO. In addition to the extensive selection process, employees are empowered to create an entertaining travelling environment by a strong organisational culture that values customer satisfaction (Barney and Wright, 1998: 35). So the human resources of Southwest Airlines serve as a source of sustained competitive advantage because they create value, are rare and are virtually impossible to imitate.

Organisation

Finally, to ensure that the HR function can provide *sustainable* competitive advantage, the VRIO framework suggests that organisations need to ensure that they are organised, so that they can capitalise on adding value, rarity and imitability. This implies a focus on horizontal integration, or *integrated, coherent systems of HR practices* rather than individual practices, that enables employees to reach their potential (Guest, 1987; Wright and Snell, 1991; Wright *et al.* 1996; Gratton *et al.*, 1999). This requires organisations to ensure that their policies and practices in the HR functional areas are coordinated and coherent, and not contradictory.

To conclude our remarks on the VRIO framework, if there are aspects of human resources that do not provide value, they can only be a source of competitive disadvantage and should be discarded. Aspects of the organisation's human resources that provide value and are rare provide competitive parity only, while aspects that provide value and are rare but are also easily copied provide temporary competitive advantage, but in time are likely to be imitated and then only provide parity. So to achieve competitive advantage that is sustainable over time, the HR function needs to ensure the organisation's human resources provide value, are rare, are difficult to copy and that there are appropriate HR systems and practices in place to capitalise on this.

Mueller (1998), in advocating the resource-based view of SHRM, argues that 'the existing theorising in strategic HRM needs to be complemented by an evolutionary perspective on the creation of human resource competencies'. He echoes Mintzberg's (1987) concerns that an overly rationalistic approach to strategy-making tends to focus too much attention on past successes and failures, when what is really needed is a level of strategic thinking that is radically different from the past. He identifies a lack of theoretical and empirical evidence to justify the emphasis on rational, codified policies of HRM, and reflects Bamberger and Phillips (1991) in describing HR strategy as an 'emergent pattern in a stream of human-resource related decisions occurring over time'. Thus the strategic planning approach may be viewed by some as a 'metaphor employed by senior management to legitimise emergent decisions and actions' (Giojia and Chittipeddi, 1991: 440). Unlike contingency and universalist theorists (Miles and Snow, 1978; Kochan and Barocci, 1985; Schuler and Jackson, 1987; Pfeffer, 1994, 1998; Huselid, 1995), Mueller (1998) is more wary of the claimed relationship between SHRM and the overall financial performance of an organisation. He recognises that enlightened best-practice HR activities do not automatically translate into competitive superiority, but rather require more complex and subtle conditions for human resources to become 'strategic assets'. He defines these as 'the social architecture' or 'social patterns' within an organisation that build up incrementally over time and are therefore difficult to copy. The focus on 'social architecture' rather than culture is deliberate, as it provides an emphasis on developing and changing behaviours rather than values, which are notoriously difficult to change (Ogbonna, 1992). Mueller identifies an organisation's 'social architecture' as a key element in the resource-based view of SHRM, together with an embedded 'persistent strategic intent' on the part of senior management and embedded learning in daily work routines, which enable the development of 'hidden reservoirs' of skills and knowledge, which in turn can be exploited by the organisation as 'strategic assets'. The role of HR is then to channel these behaviours and skills so that the organisation can tap into these hidden reservoirs. This thinking is reflected in the work of Hamel and Prahalad (1993, 1994), discussed in the following section.

Applying the resource-based view of SHRM

In adopting a focus on the internal context of the business, HR issues and practices are core to providing sustainable competitive advantage, as they focus on how organisations can define and build core competencies or capabilities that are superior to those of their competitors. One key framework here is the work of Hamel and Prahalad (1993, 1994) and their notion of 'core competencies' in their 'new strategy paradigm'. Hamel and Prahalad (1994) argue that in most companies, the emphasis is on competing in the present which means that too much management energy is devoted to preserving the past and not enough to creating the future. Thus it is organisations that focus on identifying and developing their core competencies that are more likely to be able to stay ahead of their competitors. The key point here is not to anticipate the future but to create it, by not only focusing on organisational transformation and competing for market share, but also regenerating strategies and competing for opportunity share. In creating the future, strategy is not only seen as learning, positioning and planning but also forgetting, foresight and strategic architecture, where strategy goes beyond achieving 'fit' and resource allocation to achieving 'stretch' and resource 'leverage'. The level of both tacit and explicit knowledge within the firm, coupled with the ability of employees to learn, becomes crucial. Indeed, Boxall and Purcell (2011) argue that there is little point in making a distinction between the resource-based view and the knowledge-based view of the firm, as both approaches advocate that it is a firm's ability to learn faster than its competitors that leads to sustainable competitive advantage.

When organisations grow through mergers or acquisitions, it has been argued that the resource-based view takes on further significance. When mergers and acquisitions fail, it is often not at the planning stage but at the implementation stage (Hunt *et al.*, 1987), and people and employee issues have been noted as the cause of one-third of such failures in one survey (Marks and Mirvis, 1982). Thus 'human factors' have been identified as crucial to successful mergers and acquisitions. The role of human resources shifts to a 'strategic' focus on 'managing capability' and 'know-how', and ensuring that organisations retain both tacit and explicit knowledge (Nonaka and Takeuchi, 1995) in order to become more innovative, as organisations move to knowledge-based strategies as opposed to product-based ones.

The resource-based view of SHRM has recognised that both human capital and organisational processes can add value to an organisation, but they are likely to be more powerful when they mutually reinforce and support one another. The role of the HR function in ensuring that exceptional value is achieved and in assisting organisations to build competitive advantage lies in its ability to implement an integrated and mutually reinforcing HR system that ensures appropriate talent is identified, developed, rewarded and managed in order to reach its full potential. This theme of *horizontal integration* or achieving congruence between HR policies and practices is developed further in the next section on the best-practice approach to SHRM.

Key Controversy

The resource-based view focuses on the internal resources (including people) that can provide competitive advantage to organisations, but has been criticised for paying insufficient attention to the external environment. To what extent do you agree with this view?

Limitations of the resource-based view

The resource-based view is not without its critics, particularly in relation to the strong focus on the internal context of the business. Some writers have suggested that the effectiveness of the resource-based view approach is inextricably linked to the external context of the firm (Porter, 1991; Miller and Shamsie, 1996). They have recognised that the resource-based view approach provides more added value when the external environment is less predictable. Other writers have noted the tendency for advocates of the resource-based view to focus on differences between firms in the same sector as sources of sustainable competitive advantage. This sometimes ignores the value and significance of common 'baseline' or 'table stake' (Hamel and Prahalad, 1994) characteristics across industries, which account for their legitimacy in that particular industry. Thus in the retail sector, there are strong similarities in how the industry employs a mix of core and peripheral labour, with the periphery tending to be made up of relatively low-skilled employees who traditionally demonstrate higher rates of employee turnover. Thus, in reality, economic performance and efficiency tend to be delivered through right-sizing, by gaining the same output from fewer and cheaper resources, rather than through leverage by achieving more output from given resources. The example of B&Q in the UK, employing more mature people as both their core and particularly their peripheral workforce, shows how an organisation can partially differentiate themselves from their competitors by focusing on adding value through the knowledge and skills of their human resources. Thus leverage is gained as the knowledge of B&Q's human resources adds value to the level of customer service provided, which theoretically in turn will enhance customer retention and therefore shareholder value. An exploration of the empirical evidence to support this relationship between SHRM and organisational performance is discussed in more detail in the next section: the best-practice approach to SHRM.

Best-practice SHRM: high-commitment models

The notion of best-practice or 'high-commitment' HRM was introduced in the previous chapter (see Chapter 1) and can be identified as a key theme in the development of the SHRM debate. These models argue that all organisations will benefit and see improvements in organisational performance if they identify, gain commitment to and implement a set of best HRM practices. Since the early work of Beer *et al.* (1984) and Guest (1987), there has been much work done on defining sets of HR practices that enhance organisational performance. These models of best practice can take many forms; while some have advocated a *universal* set of HR practices that would enhance the performance of all organisations they were applied to (Pfeffer, 1994, 1998), others have focused on high-commitment models (Walton, 1985; Wood and de Menezes, 1998; Guest, 2001) or 'human capital-enhancing' practices (Youndt *et al.*, 1996) and high-involvement practices (Wood, 1999; Guthrie, 2001) which reflect an underlying assumption that a strong commitment to the organisational goals and values will provide competitive advantage. Others have focused on 'high-performance work systems/practices' (Berg, 1999; Applebaum *et al.*, 2000). There is now an extensive body of research exploring the relationship between these 'sets of HR practices' and organisational performance, but it is still difficult to reach generalised conclusions from these studies (Guest, 2011). This is mainly as a result of conflicting views about what constitutes an ideal set of HR best practices, whether they should be horizontally integrated into 'bundles' that fit the organisational context or not and the contribution these sets of HR practices can make to organisational performance.

Universalism and high-commitment bundles

One of the best-practice models most commonly cited is Pfeffer's (1998) list of seven practices (see Table 2.4). The relevance of this list in a European context has been questioned due to Pfeffer's lack of commitment to independent worker representation and joint regulation

Table 2.4 Pfeffer's (1998) list of seven practices of successful organisations

Practices	Rationale
Employment security	Employees are more willing to share knowledge and seek productivity improvements Will result in more careful and leaner hiring
Selective hiring	Rigorous selection methods and selection based on the skills and attributes identified as most critical for the organisation result in a better organisation–employee 'fit'
Self-managed teams and teamworking	Workers exercise greater autonomy and discretion, resulting in intrinsic rewards and job satisfaction
High pay contingent on organisational performance	Salary levels send a message to the workforce. Contingent pay helps to motivate effort because people can share in the results of their work
Training	High-performance working requires a skilled and motivated workforce that has the knowledge and capacity to perform the required tasks
Reduction of status differentials	Helps make all organisational members feel important and valued
Sharing information	Employees need information in order to contribute to organisational performance Sends message that employees are trusted

Source: from *The Human Equation: Building Profits by Putting People First*, Harvard Business School Press, Boston, MA (Pfeffer, J. 1998). Copyright © 1998 by the Harvard Business School Publishing Corporation, all rights reserved, reprinted by permission of Harvard Business School Press.

(Boxall and Purcell, 2011). Marchington and Wilkinson (2012: 56) have adapted Pfeffer's list and drawn on additional sources to add 'employee involvement and participation, worker voice', 'performance review, appraisal and career development' and 'work–life balance' to the key components of high-commitment HRM.

With the universalist approach or 'ideal set of practices' (Guest, 1997), the concern is how close organisations can get to the ideal set of practices, the hypothesis being that the closer an organisation gets, the better it will perform in terms of higher productivity, service levels and profitability. The role of HR therefore becomes one of identifying and gaining senior management commitment to a set of HR best practices and ensuring they are implemented and that reward is distributed accordingly. The key to Pfeffer's universal approach is the provision of employment security, as this underpins the effectiveness of the other practices. Pfeffer recognises that employees are unlikely to commit to the organisation and share their knowledge and ideas without some mutual recognition of employment security. Critics of Pfeffer have questioned the feasibility of providing employment security, particularly in a weak economic climate, as 'downsizing' or 'right-sizing' is often viewed as the favoured HR option when faced with an economic downturn. However, there have been examples of organisations, such as Toyota, in which management and worker representatives negotiated a reduction in pay and hours rather than cutting jobs in order to maintain employment security and employee commitment (Millward, 2009).

As discussed previously (see Chapter 1), one of the difficulties with the best-practice approach is the variation in what constitutes best practice. Lists of best practices vary in their constitution and in their relationship to organisational performance. A sample of these variations is provided in Table 2.5. Such discrepancies in lists of best practices result in confusion about which particular HR practices constitute high commitment and in a lack of empirical evidence and 'theoretical rigour' (Guest, 1987: 508) to support claims of universal application. Capelli and Crocker-Hefter (1996: 7) argue that 'a single set of best practices may, indeed, be overstated . . . We argue that [it is] distinctive human resource practices that help to create unique competencies that differentiate products and, in turn, drive competitiveness'.

A key theme that emerges in relation to best-practice HRM is that individual practices cannot be implemented effectively in isolation (Storey, 1992); combining them into integrated and complementary bundles is therefore crucial (MacDuffie, 1995). MacDuffie believes that a 'bundle' creates the multiple, reinforcing conditions that support employee motivation, given that employees have the necessary knowledge and skills to perform their jobs effectively (Stavrou and Brewster, 2005). Thus the notion of achieving horizontal integration within and between HR practices gains significance in the best-practice debate. Horizontal alignment with other functional areas has also been highlighted by some writers as a key element in enhancing the effectiveness of other organisational practices and therefore organisational performance. Lawler *et al.* (1995) identified the link between HRM and total quality management (TQM), and similarly MacDuffie (1995) identified HR practices as integral to the effectiveness of lean production.

The need for *horizontal integration* in the application of SHRM principles is one element that is found in the configurational school of thought, the resource-based view approach and in certain best-practice models. It emphasises the coordination and congruence between HR practices through 'a pattern of planned action' (Wright and McMahan, 1999). In the configurational school, cohesion is thought likely to create synergistic benefits, which in turn enable the organisation's strategic goals to be met. Roche (1999: 669), in his study on Irish organisations, noted that 'organisations with a relatively high degree of integration of human resource strategy into business strategy are much more likely to adopt commitment-oriented bundles of HRM practices'. Where some of the best-practice models differ is in those that advocate the 'universal' application of SHRM, notably Pfeffer (1994, 1998). Pfeffer's argument is that best practice may be used in any organisation, irrespective of product life cycle, market situation or workforce characteristics, and improved performance will ensue. This approach ignores potentially significant differences in organisations, industries, sectors and countries. The work of Delery and Doty (1996) has highlighted the complex relationship between the

Table 2.5 Variations among lists of best practice

Pfeffer (1998)	MacDuffie (1995)	Huselid (1995)	Arthur (1994)	Delery and Doty (1996)	Luthans and Sommer (2005)	Stavrou and Brewster (2005)
Employment security	Self-directed work teams	Contingent pay	Self-directed work teams	Internal career opportunities	Information-sharing	Training
Selective hiring	Job rotation	Hours per year of training	Problem-solving groups	Training	Job design programmes	Share options
Extensive training	Problem-solving groups	Information-sharing	Contingent pay	Results-oriented appraisals	Job analysis methods	Evaluation of HR
Sharing information	TQM	Job analysis	Hours per year of training	Profit-sharing	Participation programmes	Profit-sharing
Self-managed teams	Suggestions forum	Selective hiring	Conflict resolution	Employment security	Incentive-based compensation bundle	Group bonus
High pay contingent on company performance	Contingent pay	Attitude surveys	Job design	Participation	Benefits	Merit pay
Reduction of status differentials	Hiring criteria, current job vs learning	Employment tests	Percentage of skilled workers	Job descriptions	Training	Joint HR–management bundle
	Induction and initial training provision	Grievance procedure	Supervisor span of control		Grievance	Communication on strategy
	Hours per year of training	Formal performance appraisal	Social events		Selection and staffing	Communication on finance
		Promotion criteria	Average total labour costs		Performance appraisal	Communication on change
		Selection ratio				Communication on organisation of work
		Benefits/total labour costs				Career
						Wider jobs
						Communication to management

TQM, total quality management.

Source: adapted from Becker and Gerhart (1996: 785) and Stavrou and Brewster (2005).

management of human resources and organisational performance, and their research supports the contingency approach (Schuler and Jackson, 1987) in indicating that there are some key HR practices, specifically internal career opportunities, results-oriented appraisals and participation/voice, that must be aligned with the business strategy (in other words, that are context-specific). The best-practice 'bundles' approach, however, is additive, and accepts that as long as there is a core of integrated high-commitment practices, other practices can be added or ignored and still produce enhanced performance. Within many high-commitment-based models, there is an underlying assumption of unitarism, which ignores the inherent pluralist values and tensions present in many organisations. Coupled with further criticisms of context avoidance and assumed rationality between implementation and performance, the best-practice advocates, particularly the universalists, are not without their critics.

Key Controversy

To what extent is Pfeffer's list of practices truly relevant to all organisations, regardless of size and context? What key factors might impact on the effectiveness of these practices in enhancing organisational performance?

HRM and performance

In recognising HRM systems as 'strategic assets' and in identifying the strategic value of a skilled, motivated and adaptable workforce, the relationship between SHRM and organisational performance moves to centre stage. The traditional HR function, when viewed as a cost centre, focuses on transactions, practices and compliance. When this is replaced by an SHRM system, it is viewed as an investment and focuses on developing and maintaining a firm's strategic infrastructure (Becker *et al.*, 1997). The strategic role of HRM then might be characterised as 'organisational systems designed to achieve *competitive advantage* through people' (Snell *et al.*, 1996: 62). In turn, competitive advantage may be defined as a set of capabilities or resources giving an organisation an advantage that leads to superior performance relative to that of its competitors (Wiggins and Ruefli, 2002: 84). Thus the relationship between HRM and organisational performance becomes significant, both in terms of defining appropriate HR systems and in terms of identifying methods to evaluate and measure the contribution of HR systems.

It is not surprising, therefore, that there is an extensive body of work that focuses on the contribution of such HR systems to organisational performance (MacDuffie, 1995; Stroh and Caligiuri, 1998; Perry-Smith and Blum, 2000; Stavrou and Brewster, 2005). This systems approach and concentration on 'bundles' of integrated HR practices is at the centre of thinking on high-performance work practices. The seminal work of Huselid (1995) and Huselid and Becker (1996) identified integrated systems of high-performance work practices – those activities that improve employees' knowledge, skills and abilities and enhance employee motivation – as significant economic assets for organisations, concluding that 'the magnitude of the return on investment in high performance work practices is substantial' (Huselid, 1995: 667) and that plausible changes in the quality of a firm's high-performance work practices are associated with changes in market value of between $15,000 and $60,000 per employee. Zigarelli (1996: 63) identified that Huselid's study went beyond merely justifying the existence of the HR manager. In an increasingly competitive business environment where sources of competitive advantage are scarce, Huselid's work identified that SHRM can provide such an edge, as a high-quality, highly motivated workforce is a difficult advantage for competitors to replicate.

This differs from the universal approach, and is indicative of a configurational approach (Delery and Doty, 1996) in that high-performance work practices are recognised as being highly idiosyncratic and in need of being tailored to meet an individual organisation's specific context in order to provide maximum performance. These high-performance work practices will only have a strategic impact, therefore, if they are aligned and integrated with each other and if the total HRM system supports key business priorities. Instead of focusing on the effects of individual HR policies and practices on individual outcomes, then, it becomes necessary to explore the impact-specific configurations, or systems of HRM on organisational-level outcomes (Luthans and Sommer, 2005: 328). This requires a 'systems' thinking approach on the part of HR managers, which enables them to avoid 'deadly combinations' (Delery, 1998) of HR practices that work against each other (e.g. team-based culture and individual performance-related pay) and seek out 'powerful connections' or synergies between practices (e.g. building up new employees' expectations through sophisticated selection and meeting them through appropriate induction, personal development plans and reward strategies).

The impact of HRM practices on organisational performance has been recognised as a key element of differentiation between HRM and SHRM. Much research interest has been generated in exploring the influence of high-performance work practices on shareholder value (Huselid, 1995) and on human capital management (Ulrich *et al.*, 1995; Ulrich, 1997). For example, Youndt *et al.* (1996) demonstrated that productivity rates were higher in manufacturing plants where the HR strategy focused on enhancing human capital, and Huselid *et al.*

(1997) found that increased HRM effectiveness corresponded to a 5.2 per cent estimated increase in sales per employee, a 16.3 per cent increase in cash flow and an estimated 6 per cent increase in market value. Studies in the UK have demonstrated similar findings. A survey by Patterson *et al.* (1997), published for the CIPD, cited evidence for HRM as a key contributor to improved performance. Patterson *et al.* argued that 17 per cent of the variation in company profitability could be explained by HRM practices and job design, as opposed to just 8 per cent from research and development, 2 per cent from strategy and 1 per cent from both quality and technology. Other studies have reviewed the links between high-commitment HRM and performance, and two studies by Guest *et al.* (2000a,b) have argued the economic and business case for recognising people as a key source of competitive advantage in organisations and therefore as key contributors to enhanced organisational performance. Further, Gelade and Ivery (2003) noted significant correlations among work climate, HR practices and business performance in the UK banking industry. Stavrou and Brewster (2005) have noted, however, that while the connection between HRM and performance has been extensively researched in the USA, there is a need for further studies to explore HRM approaches that are indigenous to the European Union.

Becker and Gerhart (1996: 793) argued that future work on the strategic perspective of HRM 'must elaborate on the black box between a firm's HR systems and the firm's bottom line'. They recognised that there was a need to understand how and why HR policies influence performance which goes beyond a basic input–output model. It could be argued that the AMO theory of Applebaum *et al.* (2000) (see Chapter 1) sets out to do this, where organisational performance is viewed as the sum of employees' abilities, motivations and opportunities to participate, which when managed appropriately will encourage employees to demonstrate discretionary behaviour. An employee's willingness to demonstrate discretionary behaviour was found to have clear links to organisational performance. Purcell *et al.* (2003) developed the AMO concept in their Bath People and Performance model, which identified 11 HR practices that contributed to organisational performance, through supporting the development of employee ability, motivation and providing opportunities to demonstrate discretionary behaviour (Figure 2.6). They reflected that the critical link in the HRM black box is how HR practices influence employee attitudes and improve worker performance in ways that are beneficial to the employing organisation (Purcell and Hutchinson, 2007). This led to recognition of the key role of the front-line manager in the SHRM/organisational performance equation. Front-line managers were seen as key to enacting HR policy and practice and engaging in leadership behaviour that translates strategic HR choices to effective implementation, thereby influencing employee attitude and behaviour. Thus, whilst much HR literature has focused on exploring the relationship with organisational performance in terms of HR strategic choices in relation to identifying appropriate HR roles (Ulrich and Brockbank, 2005), or in selecting appropriate HR practices that either fit the business strategy (Schuler and Jackson, 1987) or generate high commitment (Huselid, 1995; MacDuffie, 1995; Pfeffer, 1998), there has not been much attention paid to the key influencers in the effective implementation of HR strategy, the role of the front-line manager (Purcell and Hutchinson, 2007).

SHRM and performance: the critique

While research studies devoted to demonstrating the link between SHRM and performance have increased (Wright and Haggerty, 2005), they are still the subject of much criticism. Criticisms aimed at advocates of the high-commitment/performance link are mainly centred on the validity of the research methods employed (Wall and Wood, 2005), the lack of theoretical underpinning (Dyer and Reeves, 1995; Becker and Gerhart, 1996; Wright *et al.*, 2003), problems associated with inconsistencies in the best-practice models used (Becker and Gerhart, 1996; Wright and Gardner, 2003; Marchington and Wilkinson, 2012) and the lack

Figure 2.6 The Bath People and Performance model

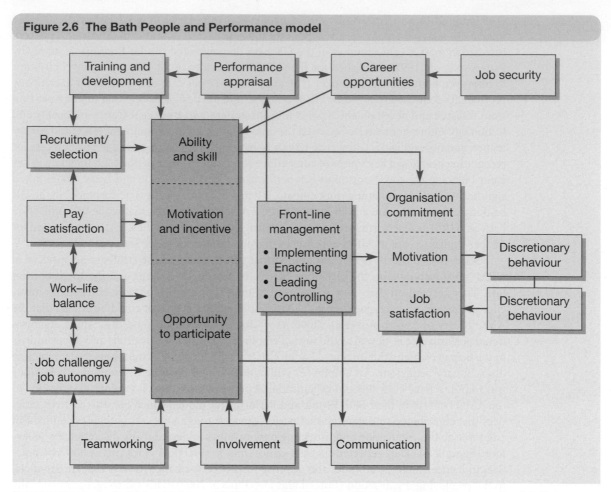

Source: from *Understanding the People and Performance Link: Unlocking the Black Box*, Chartered Institute of Personnel and Development (Purcell, J., Kinnie, N., Hutchinson, S., Rayton, B. and Swart, J. 2003), with the permission of the publisher, the Chartered Institute of Personnel and Development, London (**www.cipd.co.uk**). The People and Performance Model was developed by Bath University for the CIPD.

of emphasis on the examination of the level of either vertical or horizontal alignment (Wall and Wood, 2005). This has led some researchers to be more circumspect in their analysis of the relationship between SHRM and performance (Marchington and Grugulis, 2000). In their 2003 study, Wright and Gardner (2003: 312) suggest that HR practices are only 'weakly' related to firm performance and Godard (2004: 355) suggests that in liberal market economies the generalisability is likely to be low.

In terms of research methodology, Wall and Wood (2005) identified that the least satisfactory survey method is to use single source respondents. In their review of 25 research studies, including many of the key studies on SHRM and performance, they identified that 21 of the studies had used single respondents as the sole source of data. Some of the studies reviewed are presented in Table 2.6. Wall and Wood (2005) therefore argue that future progress in justifying the relationship between SHRM and organisational performance depends on using large-scale, long-term research or 'big science' in partnership among research, practitioner and government communities (Wall and Wood, 2005: 429).

In terms of evidence, it is difficult to pinpoint whether it is the HR practices that in turn lead to enhanced organisational performance or whether financial success has enabled the implementation of appropriate HR practices. It is difficult to see how organisations operating in highly competitive markets, with tight financial control and margins, would be able to invest in some of the HR practices advocated in the best-practice models. This is not to say that HR could not make a contribution in this type of business environment, but rather that

Table 2.6 A review of research studies evaluating the SHRM/performance link

Research study and response rates (%)	HRM dimensions	HRM measure and source	Dependent variable measures
Arthur (1994): 30 US mini steel mills (56%)	Control and commitment focus	Questionnaire: single source HR managers	Self-report: scrap rates and productivity
Guest and Hoque (1994): 119 UK manufacturing sites mainly (39%)	Four a priori types 2 × 2: whether or not claim HRM strategy and use more or less than half of 22 HRM practices	Questionnaire: single source principal HR manager or line manager	Self-report: productivity and quality
Huselid (1995): 968 companies with 100+ staff (28%)	Two scales: skills and structures (communication, QWL, training, grievance procedures) and motivation (performance appraisals, promotion on merit)	Questionnaire: single source mailed to senior HRM professional	Objective: productivity, Tobin's Q and GRATE
MacDuffie (1995): 62 car assembly plants worldwide (69%)	Two scales: work systems (participation, teams, quality role) and HRM policies (selection, performance-related pay, training)	Questionnaire: a contact person, often the plant manager, sections completed by different people	Objective: productivity (labour hours per vehicle)
Delaney and Huselid (1996): 50 for-profit and non-profit US firms (51%)	Five scales: staffing, selectivity, training, incentive pay, decentralisation, internal promotion	Telephone survey: single source, multiple respondents in a few cases	Self-report, organisational and market performance
Delery and Doty (1996): 216 US banks, 101 in some analyses (18%)	Seven scales: internal promotion, training, appraisal, profit-sharing, security, participation, job specification and two strategy measures	Questionnaire: single source, senior HR manager (+ strategy from president)	Objective: return on assets (ROA), return on equity (ROE)
Youndt et al. (1996): 897 manufacturing plants in US (19%)	Two scales: administrative HR (appraisal, incentives) and human capital enhancing HR (selection and training for problem-solving, salaried pay)	Questionnaire: multiple source (at least two respondents per plant, mean score) general and functional managers	Self-report: customer alignment (quality), productivity and machine efficiency
Huselid et al. (1997): 9,293 US firms (manufacturing, finance, miscellaneous) (response rate unclear)	Two scales: SHRM (teamwork, empowerment) and technical HRM (recruitment, training). Ratings of perceived effectiveness	Questionnaire: single source, executives in HR (92%) and line (8%) positions (effectiveness of HR practices)	Objectivity: productivity, GRATE and Tobins Q
Wood and de Menezes (1998): Representative sample of 1,693 UK workplaces	Four types of workplace, ranging from high- to low-commitment management	Interviews: single source, HR manager or senior manager responsible for HR	Self-report: productivity, productivity change over last 3 years and financial performance
Hoque (1999): 209 UK hotels (35%)	Overall HRM (21 practices used, including harmonisation, job design, training, merit pay)	Questionnaire: single source, respondents unclear	Self-report: productivity, service quality and financial performance
Capelli and Neumark (2001): 433–666 US manufacturing plants (response rates unclear)	Extent of job rotation, self-managed teams, teamwork training, cross-training pay for skill/knowledge, profit/gain	Telephone survey: single source: plant/site manager	Self-report: sales per employee, total labour cost per employee and sales/value/labour costs sharing, meetings and TQM

(continued)

Table 2.6 Continued

Research study and response rates (%)	HRM dimensions	HRM measure and source	Dependent variable measures
Guthrie (2001): 164 New Zealand firms, heterogeneous sample (23%)	Single high-involvement work practices (HIWP) scale based on 12 practices (e.g. performance-based promotion, skill-based pay, training participation)	Questionnaire: single source, various staff from CEO to junior manager	Self-report: productivity (annual sales per employee)
Batt (2002): 260 call centres (54%)	Skill level (education and training); job design (discretion and teamwork); HR incentives (supportive HR training, feedback, high pay, security)	Telephone survey: single source, general managers	Self-report:% change in sales in prior 2-year period
Wright et al. (2003): 50 business units, US food service companies (response rate unclear)	Single overall HR practices scale: nine items covering selection, pay for performance, training, participation	Employee attitude survey: multiple source: rank and file employees	Objective (from company records), productivity and profit-subsequent for period 3–9 months after measurement of HR practices

Source: Wall and Wood (2005: 429–63).

the contribution would not be that espoused by the best-practice models. Here, the enhanced performance could be delivered through the efficiency and tight cost control more associated with 'hard' HR practices (Storey, 1995) and the contingency school. A further difficulty is the underlying theme of 'unitarism' pervading many of the best-practice approaches. As Boxall and Purcell (2011) note, many advocates of best-practice, high-commitment models tend to 'fudge' the question of pluralist goals and interests. If the introduction of best-practice HR could meet the goals of all stakeholders within the business equally, the implementation of such practices would not be problematic. However, it is unlikely that this would be the case, particularly within an economy driven by short-term thinking, where the majority of organisations are looking primarily to increase return on shareholder value. Thus, if this return can best be met through cost-reduction strategies or increasing leverage in a way that does not fit employees' goals or interests, how can these practices engender high commitment and therefore be labelled 'best practice'? It is not surprising, therefore, that ethical differences between the *rhetoric* of human resource best practice and the *reality* of human resource real practices are highlighted (Legge, 1998). High-commitment models, therefore, which at first appear to satisfy ethical principles in treating employees with respect and as ends in their own right, rather than as means to other ends (Legge, 1998), in reality can assume a utilitarian perspective, where it is deemed ethical to use employees as a means to an end, if it is for the greater good of the organisation. This might justify downsizing and right-sizing strategies.

Key Controversy

If 'best practice' HRM is applied to meet the strategic goals of the organisation, to what extent are these practices also in the best interests of key stakeholders, particularly employees, in the organisation?

One of the key components of Pfeffer's list of HRM practices (Table 2.4) is pay contingent on organisational performance, i.e. when an organisation is performing well, employees will be rewarded accordingly. However, there have been many recent cases where senior managers of poorly performing organisations have been rewarded with large payoffs. To what extent do such practices undermine the principles of 'best practice' HRM?

Measuring the impact of SHRM on performance

We have so far considered the complexity of the SHRM debate and recognised that our understanding and application of SHRM principles are contingent upon the particular body of literature in which we cite our analysis. It is now appropriate to consider in more detail how strategic management processes in firms can be improved to deal more effectively with key HR issues and take advantage of HR opportunities. A study by Ernst & Young in 1997 (cited in Armstrong and Baron, 2002) found that more than a third of the data used to justify business analysts' decisions were non-financial, and that when non-financial factors, notably 'human resources', were taken into account, better investment decisions were made. The non-financial metrics most valued by investors are given in Table 2.7.

This presents an opportunity for HR professionals to develop business capability and demonstrate the contribution of SHRM to organisational performance. One method that is worthy of further consideration is the balanced scorecard (Kaplan and Norton, 1996, 2001). This is also concerned with relating critical non-financial factors to financial outcomes by assisting firms to map the key cause–effect linkages in their desired strategies. Interestingly, Kaplan and Norton challenge the short-termism found in many Western traditional budgeting processes and, as with the Ernst & Young study, they imply a central role for HRM in the strategic management of the firm and importantly suggest practical ways for bringing it about (Boxall and Purcell, 2011).

Kaplan and Norton identify the significance of executed strategy and the implementation stage of the strategic management process as key drivers in enhancing organisational performance. They recognise, along with Mintzberg (1987), that 'business failure is seen to stem mostly from failing to implement and not from failing to have wonderful visions' (Kaplan and Norton, 2001: 1). Therefore, as with the resource-based view, implementation is identified as a key process which is often poorly executed.

Table 2.7 Non-financial metrics most valued by investors

Metric	Question to which measurable answers are required
1 Strategy	How well does management leverage its skills and experience? Gain employee commitment? Stay aligned with shareholder interests?
2 Management credibility	What is management's behaviour? And forthrightness in dealing with issues?
3 Quality of strategy	Does management have a vision for the future? Can it make tough decisions and quickly seize opportunities? How well does it allocate resources?
4 Innovativeness	Is the company a trendsetter or a follower? What's in the R&D pipeline? How readily does the company adapt to changing technology and markets?
5 Ability to attract talented people?	Is the company able to hire and retain the very best people? Does it reward them? Is it training the talent it will need for tomorrow?
6 Management experience	What is the management's history and background? How well have they performed?
7 Quality of executive compensation	Is executive pay tied to strategic goals? How well is it linked to the creation of shareholder value?
8 Research leadership	How well does management understand the link between creating knowledge and using it?

Source: Adapted from *Measures That Matter*, Ernst and Young LLP, all rights reserved, cited and adapted in *Strategic Human Resource Management: The Key to Improved Business Performance*, London: CIPD (Armstrong, M. and Baron, A. 2002) p. 63, with the permission of the publisher, the Chartered Institute of Personal and Development, London (www.cipd.co.uk).

Kaplan and Norton adopt a stakeholder perspective, based on the premise that for an organisation to be considered successful it must satisfy the requirements of key stakeholders, namely investors, customers and employees. They suggest identifying objectives, measures, targets and initiatives on four key perspectives of business performance:

1 *Financial*: 'To succeed financially, how should we appear to our shareholders'?

2 *Customer*: 'To achieve our vision, how should we appear to our customers'?

3 *Internal business processes*: 'To satisfy our shareholders and customers, what business processes must we excel at'?

4 *Learning and growth*: 'To achieve our vision, how will we sustain our ability to change and improve'?

They recognise that investors require financial performance, measured through profitability, market value and cash flow or economic value added (EVA). Customers require quality products and services, which can be measured by market share, customer service, customer retention and loyalty or customer value added (CVA). Employees require a healthy place to work, which recognises opportunities for personal development and growth. These can be measured by attitude surveys, skill audits, performance appraisal criteria, which recognise not only what they do, but what they know and how they feel, or people value added (PVA). They can be delivered through appropriate and integrated systems, including HR systems. The balanced scorecard approach therefore provides an integrated framework for balancing shareholder and strategic goals, and extending those balanced performance measures down through the organisation, from corporate to divisional to functional departments and then on to individuals (Grant, 2010).

By balancing a set of strategic and financial goals, the scorecard can be used to reward current practice and also offer incentives to invest in long-term effectiveness, by integrating financial measures of current performance with measures of 'future performance'. Thus it provides a template that can be adapted to provide the information that organisations require now and in the future for the creation of shareholder value. The balanced scorecard at Sears, for example (Yeung and Berman, 1997: 324; Rucci *et al.*, 1998), focused on the creation of a vision that the company was 'a compelling place to invest', 'a compelling place to shop' and 'a compelling place to work', whereas the balanced scorecard at Mobil North American Marketing and Refining (Kaplan and Norton, 2001) focused on cascading down financial performance goals into specific operating goals, through which performance-related pay bonuses were determined.

Kaplan and Norton (2001) recognise the impact key HR activities can have on business performance in the learning and growth element of the balanced scorecard. Employee skills, knowledge and satisfaction are identified as improving internal processes, and therefore contributing to CVA and EVA. Thus the scorecard provides a mechanism for integrating key HR performance drivers into the strategic management process. Boxall and Purcell (2011) highlight the similarities between Kaplan and Norton's (2001: 93) learning and growth categories of *strategic competencies* (skills and knowledge required by employees to support the strategy), *strategic technologies* (information support systems required to support the strategy) and *climate for action* (the cultural shifts needed to motivate, empower and align the workforce behind the strategy) and the *AMO theory of performance*, where performance is seen as a function of employee ability, motivation and opportunity. Thus the balanced scorecard contributes to the development of SHRM, not only in establishing goals and measures to demonstrate cause–effect linkages, but also in encouraging a process that stimulates debate and shared understanding between the different areas of the business. However, the balanced scorecard approach does not escape criticism, particularly in relation to the measurement of some HR activities that are not directly linked to productivity, thus requiring an acknowledgement of the multidimensional nature of organisational performance and a recognition of multiple 'bottom lines' in SHRM. Boxall and Purcell (2011) suggest the use of two others besides labour productivity: *organisational flexibility* and *social legitimacy*. So although the balanced scorecard has taken account of the impact and influence of an organisation's human resources in achieving competitive advantage, there is still room for the process to become more HR-driven.

Concluding comments

Given the increasing profile of SHRM in creating organisational competitive advantage and the subsequent complexity in interpreting and applying SHRM principles, there appears to be agreement on the need for more theoretical development in the field, particularly regarding the relationship between strategic management and HRM and the relationship between SHRM and performance (Wright and McMahan, 1992; Guest, 1997; Wright and McMahan, 1999; Boxall and Purcell, 2011). This chapter has reviewed key developments and alternative frameworks in the field of SHRM in an attempt to clarify its meaning so that the reader is able to make an informed judgement as to the meaning and intended outcomes of SHRM. Thus SHRM is differentiated from HRM in a number of ways, particularly in its movement away from a micro perspective on individual HR functional areas to the adoption of a macro perspective (Butler *et al.* 1991; Wright and McMahan, 1992), with its emphasis on vertical integration (Schuler and Jackson, 1987; Guest, 1989; Tyson, 1997) and horizontal integration (Baird and Meshoulam, 1988; MacDuffie, 1995). It therefore becomes apparent that the meaning of SHRM tends to lie in the context of organisational performance, although organisational performance can be interpreted and measured in a variety of ways. These may range from delivering efficiency and flexibility through cost-reduction-driven strategies through the implementation of what may be termed 'hard HR techniques' (Schuler and Jackson, 1987), to delivering employee commitment to organisational goals through 'universal sets' of HR practices (Pfeffer, 1994, 1998) or 'bundles' of integrated HR practices (Huselid, 1995; Delery and Doty, 1996), to viewing human resources as a source of human capital and sustainable competitive advantage (Barney, 1991; Barney and Wright, 1998) as well as a core business competence and a key strategic asset (Hamel and Prahalad, 1993, 1994). As you can see, there are conflicting views as to the meaning of SHRM and the contribution SHRM can make to an organisation.

Summary

- This chapter has charted the development of SHRM, exploring the links between the strategic management literature and SHRM. It has examined the different approaches to SHRM identified in the literature, including the best-fit approach, the best-practice approach, the configurational approach and the resource-based view, in order to understand what makes HRM strategic.

- A key claim of much SHRM literature is a significant contribution to a firm's *competitive advantage,* whether it is through cost-reduction methods or more often *added value* through best-practice HR policies and practices. An understanding of the business context and particularly of the 'strategy-making' process is therefore considered central to developing an understanding of SHRM.

- Whittington's (1993, 2001) typology was used to analyse the different approaches to 'strategy-making' experienced by organisations and to consider the impact this would have on our understanding of the development of SHRM. The influence of the classical, rational-planning approach on the strategic management literature and therefore SHRM literature was noted, with its inherent assumption that strategy-making is a rational, planned activity. This ignores some of the complexities and 'messiness' of the strategy-making process identified by Mintzberg and others. Other approaches that recognised the constituents of this 'messiness', namely the processual approach, the evolutionary approach and the systemic approach, were identified. These took account of changes and competing interests in both the external and internal business environments. Significantly for HRM, there is a recognition that it is not always appropriate to separate operational policies from higher-level strategic planning, as it is often operational policies and systems that provide the source of 'tactical excellence', and thus the traditional distinction between strategy and operations can become blurred.

- The best-fit approach to SHRM explored the close relationship between strategic management and HRM by considering the influence and nature of vertical integration. Vertical integration, where leverage is gained through the close link of HR policies and practices to the business objectives and therefore the external context of the firm, is considered to be a key theme of SHRM. Best fit was therefore explored in relation to lifecycle models and competitive advantage models, and the associated difficulties of matching generic business-type strategies to generic HRM strategies were considered, particularly in their inherent assumptions of a classical approach to the strategy-making process. The inflexibility of 'tight' fit models in a dynamic, changing environment was evaluated, and consideration was given to achieving both fit and flexibity through complementary SHRM systems.

- The configurational approach identifies the value of having a set of HR practices that are both vertically integrated to the business strategy and horizontally integrated with each other, in order to gain maximum performance or synergistic benefits. This approach recognises the complexities of hybrid business strategies and the need for HRM to respond accordingly. In advocating unique patterns or configurations of multiple independent variables, they provide an answer to the linear, deterministic relationship advocated by the best-fit approach.

- The resource-based view represents a paradigm shift in SHRM thinking by focusing on the internal resources of the firm as a key source of sustainable competitive advantage, rather than focusing on the relationship between the firm and the external business context. Human resources, as scarce, valuable, organisation-specific and difficult-to-imitate resources, therefore become key strategic assets.

- The best-practice approach highlights the relationship between 'sets' of good HR practices and organisational performance, mostly defined in terms of employee commitment and satisfaction. These sets of best practice can take many forms; some have advocated a universal set of practices that would enhance the performance of all organisations to which they were applied (Pfeffer, 1994, 1998), others have focused on integrating the practices to the specific business context (high-performance work practices). A key element of best practice is horizontal integration and congruence between policies. Difficulties arise here, as best-practice models vary significantly in their constitution and in their relationship to organisational performance, which makes generalisations from research and empirical data difficult.

- In endeavouring to gain an understanding of the meaning of SHRM, it soon becomes apparent that a common theme of all approaches is enhanced organisational performance and viability, whether this be in a 'hard' sense, through cost-reduction and efficiency-driven practices or through high-commitment and involvement-driven value added. This relationship is considered significant to understanding the context and meaning of SHRM. The need to conduct further empirical research, particularly in Europe, is identified (Stavrou and Brewster, 2005) and the lack of methodological rigour and the extensive use of single source respondents in current research studies evaluating the SHRM/performance link are noted (Wall and Wood, 2005).

Questions

1 In what ways do models of the four distinct approaches to strategy-making contribute to our understanding of SHRM?
2 Compare and contrast life cycle, competitive advantage and configurational models of SHRM.
3 To what extent can organisations apply both 'outside-in' and 'inside-out' approaches to SHRM?
4 Evaluate the relationship between SHRM and organisational performance. What challenges exist in attempting to monitor and measure the existence of the relationship?'
5 To what extent is best-practice SHRM universally applicable?

Case study

Jaguar Land Rover

In August 2012, Jaguar Land Rover's (JLR) Halewood plant, on Merseyside in the UK, moved to 24-hour production in order to meet demand for a new SUV, the Evoque, as well as JLR's older model, the Freelander. Halewood begins its working week at 5a.m. on Mondays and carries on until 12.30a.m. on Saturdays. Over the past two years, the factory has trebled its staff to 4,500 to keep up with the insatiable global demand.

Halewood has not worked night shifts since the 1990s, the heyday of Ford's Escort, and even then it did not work round the clock. According to Richard Else, the plant's operations director, 'Based on what we have on at the moment, we are above capacity.' In automotive terms, this is a small miracle. Most of Europe's car plants right now are cutting shifts or working days because of a slowdown in demand. Three-shift, 24-hour production is a rarity in this part of the world, apart from a few successful companies such as Germany's premium car giant BMW or South Korea's fast-growing Hyundai and Kia brands.

Jaguar Land Rover is in the midst of a five-year, £7.5 billion investment programme approved by its owner, Indian carmaker Tata Motors, in 2010. Tata bought Jaguar and Land Rover just as the car industry was heading into a deep crisis in 2008, paying Ford $2.3 billion when no other top-drawer carmaker wanted them. Almost as soon as the ink was dry on the contract, demand for SUVs evaporated because of higher petrol prices and the fallout from the US sub-prime crisis. On the weekend Lehman Brothers collapsed, JLR had US customers cancelling orders; within weeks, some of its overseas markets were down by half. By early 2009, JLR had let 3,500 workers go on a voluntary basis, and the company's production was at a crawl. At Halewood, workers were engaging in

'busy work', such as maintaining robots and repainting stripes on the factory floor.

The low point came that October, when JLR said it would have to close one of its two West Midlands plants. Solihull and Castle Bromwich are just eight miles apart, but then operated separate overheads, and workers did not move between them. Tata was hinting it might move more of its production to low-cost India.

Jaguar Land Rover – and Halewood particularly – has a tradition of union militancy that stretched back to the many wildcat strikes that plagued Ford. The unions were initially defiant, vetoing the conditions management was seeking to keep the plants open: a closing of the final pension scheme and a cut in starting pay. The impasse lasted for several months before a compromise emerged, when JLR dangled an ambitious project plan before unions. This would allow the carmaker to grow into its outsize UK manufacturing footprint: £7.5 billion invested in new cars, engines and variants over five years.

In exchange, unions agreed to let workers move between the two West Midlands plants. They also signed off a novel pay structure under which new hires join as temporary workers for a year at 80 per cent of normal pay, then as staff at 90 per cent after a year. The compromise allowed JLR to factor lower manufacturing costs into its business plan and also rejuvenated the company's workforce.

Jaguar Land Rover is having a good year, with record sales and good reviews for the new Range Rover and Jaguar F-type. However, it has formidable competitors. In a business where the biggest producers have the greatest competitive advantage, JLR sells about 400,000 vehicles a year – a fraction of the 1.7 million sold by BMW, the industry's

Case study continued

largest premium producer, or the 1.3 million sold by Volkswagen's Audi.

Jaguar Land Rover has also been a latecomer to overseas manufacturing in the emerging countries that now provide most of the car industry's biggest growth. China is one of Land Rover's biggest markets,

but it pays steep tariffs to get its cars in. The company is remedying this: it is close to finalising a plan to build its first factory there. JLR is also considering assembling Freelanders from kits in Brazil, as it does in India. This, in turn, is making unions anxious, potentially causing threats to JLR's competitiveness.

 Source: Adapted from: Reed, J. (2012) The car that saved JLR, *Financial Times*. 28 September. Http://www.ft.com/cms/ s/2/93481c40-0831-11e2-a2d8-00144feabdc0.html
© The Financial Times Limited 2013. All Rights Reserved.

Questions

1 Using Whittington's model, identify the dominant strategic approach at JLR.

2 Which approach to SHRM discussed in this chapter best explains JLR's approach to SHRM and change?

3 How has JLR enhanced organisational performance through the implementation of HR practices?

4 What advice would you give JLR to reduce the risk of industrial action in the face of overseas expansion?

References and further reading

Those texts marked with an asterisk are recommended for further reading.

Abell, D.F. (1993) *Managing with Dual Strategies: Mastering the Present, Pre-empting the Future*. New York: Free Press.

Ahmed, K. (2013) 'Stephen Hester lays out RBS departure plan', *The Telegraph*, 15 June.

Aktouf, O. (1996) *Traditional Management and Beyond: A Matter of Renewal*. Montreal: Gaetan Morin.

Alchian, A. and Demsetz, H. (1972) 'Production information costs and economic organisation', *American Economic Review*, 62: 777–95.

Amit, R. and Shoemaker, P. (1993) 'Strategic assets and organisational rent', *Strategic Management Journal*, 14: 33–46.

Ansoff, H.I. (1965) *Corporate Strategy*. Harmondsworth: Penguin.

Ansoff, H.I. and McDonnell, E. (1990) *Implanting Strategic Management*, 2nd edn. Hemel Hempstead: Prentice Hall.

Applebaum, E., Bailey, T., Berg, P. and Kalleberg, A. (2000) *Manufacturing Competitive Advantage: Why high-performance Systems Pay Off*. Ithaca, NY: ILR Press.

Armstrong, M. and Baron, A. (2002) *Strategic Human Resource Management: The key to improved business performance*. London: CIPD.

Arthur, J. (1994) 'Effects of human resource systems on manufacturing performance and turnover', *Academy of Management Journal*, 37, 3: 670–87.

Atkinson, J. (1984) 'Manpower strategies for the flexible organisation', *Personnel Management*, August, 28–31.

Baden-Fuller, C. (1995) 'Strategic innovation, corporate entrepreneurship and matching outside-in to inside-out approaches to strategy research', *British Journal of Management*, 6 (special issue): 3–16.

Baird, L. and Meshoulam, I. (1988) 'Managing two fits of strategic human resource management', *Academy of Management Review*, 13, 1: 116–28.

Bamberger, P. and Phillips, B. (1991) 'Organisational environment and business strategy: parallel versus conflicting influences on human resource strategy in the pharmaceutical industry', *Human Resource Management*, 30, 2: 153–82.

Barney, J.B. (1991) 'Firm resources and sustained competitive advantage', *Journal of Management*, 17, 1: 99–120.

Barney, J.B. and Wright, P.M. (1998) 'On becoming a strategic partner: the role of human resources in gaining competitive advantage', *Human Resource Management*, 37, 1: 31–46.

Barr, P., Stimpert, J. and Huff, A. (1992) 'Cognitive change, strategic action, and organisational renewal', *Strategic Management Journal*, 13: 15–36.

Batt, R. (2002) 'Managing customer services: human resource practices, quit rates and sales growth', *Academy of Management Journal*, 45: 587–97.

Becker, B. and Gerhart, B. (1996) 'The impact of human resource management on organisational performance: progress and prospects', *Academy of Management Journal*, 39, 4: 779–801.

Becker, B.E., Huselid, M.A., Pickus, P.S. and Spratt, M.F. (1997) 'HR as a source of shareholder value: research and recommendations', *Human Resource Management*, 36, 1: 39–47.

Beer, M., Spector, B., Lawrence, P.R., Quinn Mills, D. and Walton, R.E. (1984) *Managing Human Assets*. New York: Free Press.

Berg, P. (1999) 'The effects of high performance work practices on job satisfaction in the US steel industry', *Industrial Relations*, 54: 111–35.

Blyton, P. and Turnbull, P. (1992) (eds) *Reassessing HRM*. London: Sage.

Boxall, P. (1996) 'The strategic HRM debate and the resource-based view of the firm', *Human Resource Management Journal*, 6, 3: 59–75.

Boxall, P. and Purcell, J. (2011) *Strategy and Human Resource Management*, 2nd edn. Basingstoke, Palgrave MacMillan.

Butler, J. E., Ferris, G. R. and Napier, N.K. (1991) *Strategy and Human Resource Management*. Cincinnati, OH: Sothwestern Publishing.

Capelli, P. and Crocker-Hefter, A. (1996) 'Distinctive human resources are firms' core competencies', *Organisational Dynamics*, 24, 3: 7–22.

Capelli, P. and Neumark, D. (2001). 'Do "High performance work practices" improve establishment-level outcomes?' *Industrial and Labor Relations Review*, 54, 737–75.

Capelli, P. and Singh, H. (1992) 'Integrating strategic human resources and strategic management' in D. Lewin, O.S. Mitchell and P. Sherer (eds) *Research Frontiers in Industrial Relations and Human Resources*. Madison, WI: Madison Industrial Relations Research Association, pp. 165–92.

Chandler, A.D. (1962) *Strategy and Structure: Chapters in the History of the American Industrial Enterprise*. Cambridge, MA: MIT Press.

Clarke, J. and Newman, J. (1997) *The Managerial State*. London: Sage.

Cyert, R.M. and March, J.G. (1956) 'Organisational factors in the theory of monopoly', *Quarterly Journal of Economics*, 70, 1: 44–64.

Delaney, J.T. and Huselid, M.A. (1996) 'The impact of human resource management practices on perceptions of organisational performance', *Academy of Management Journal*, 39, 919–69.

Delery, J.E. (1998) 'Issues of fit in strategic human resource management: implications of research', *HRM Review*, 8, 3: 289–309.

Delery, J. and Doty, H. (1996) 'Modes of theorizing in strategic human resource management', *Academy of Management Journal*, 39, 4: 802–35.

Drucker, P. (1968) *The Practice of Management*. London: Pan.

Dyer, L. (1984) 'Studying human resource strategy', *Industrial Relations*, 23, 2: 156–69.

Dyer, L. and Reeves, T. (1995) 'Human resource strategies and firm performance: what do we know and where do we need to go?' *International Journal of HRM*, 6, 3: 656–70.

Dyer, L. and Shafer, R. (1999) 'Creating organisational agility: implications for strategic human resource management' in P. Wright, L. Dyer, J. Boudreau and G. Milkovich (eds) *Research in Personnel and HRM*. Stamford, CT and London: JAI Press. (Supplement 4: *Strategic Human Resource Management in the Twenty-first Century*.)

Ferris, G.R., Hochwater, W.A., Buckley, M.N., Harrell-Cook, G. and Frink, D. (1999) 'Human resource management, some new direction', *Journal of Management*, 25, 385–418.

Fombrun, C., Tichy, N. and Devanna, M. (eds) (1984) *Strategic Human Resource Management*. New York: John Wiley.

Gelade, G. and Ivery, M. (2003) 'The impact of human resource management and work climate on organisational performance', *Personnel Psychology*, 56, 383–401.

Giojia, D.A. and Chittipeddi, K. (1991) 'Sensemaking and sensegiving in strategic change initiation', *Strategic Management Journal*, 12, 6: 433–48.

Godard, J.A. (2004) 'A critical assessment of the high performance paradigm', *British Journal of Industrial Relations*, 42, 349–78.

*Grant, R.M. (2010) *Contemporary Strategy Analysis: Concepts, Techniques, Applications*, 7th edn. Oxford: Blackwell.

Gratton, L., Hope-Hailey, V., Stiles, P. and Truss, C. (1999) 'Linking individual performance to business strategy: the people process model' in R.S. Schuler and S.E. Jackson (eds) *Strategic Human Resource Management*. Oxford: Blackwell, pp. 142–58.

Guest, D. (1987) 'Human resource management and industrial relations', *Journal of Management Studies*, 24, 5: 503–21.

Guest, D. (1989) 'Personnel and HRM: can you tell the difference?' *Personnel Management*, 21, 48–51.

Guest, D. (1997) 'Human resource management and performance: a review and research agenda', *International Journal of Human Resource Management*, 8, 3: 263–76.

Guest, D. (2001) 'Human resource management: when research confronts theory', *International Journal of Human Resource Management*, 12, 7: 1092–106.

Guest, D. (2011) 'Human resource management and performance: still searching for some answers', *Human Resource Management Journal*, 21, 1: 3–13.

Guest, D. and Hoque (1994) 'The good, the bad and the ugly: employee relations in new non-union marketplaces', *Human Resource Management Journal*, 5: 1–14.

Guest, D., Michie, J., Sheehan, M. and Conway, N. (2000a) *Employment Relations, HRM and Business Performance: An Analysis of the 1998 Workplace Employee Relations Survey*. London: CIPD.

Guest, D., Michie, J., Sheehan, M., Conway, N. and Metochi, M. (2000b) *Effective People Management: Initial Findings of the Future of Work Study*. London: CIPD.

Guthrie, J.P. (2001) 'High involvement work practices, turnover and productivity: evidence from New Zealand', *Academy of Management Journal*, 44: 180–90.

Hamel, G. and Prahalad, C. (1993) 'Strategy as stretch and leverage', *Harvard Business Review*, 71, 2: 75–84.

Hamel, G. and Prahalad, C. (1994) *Competing for the Future*. Boston, MA: Harvard Business School Press.

Henderson, B.D. (1989) 'The origin of strategy', *Harvard Business Review*, 67, 6, 139–43.

Hoque, K. (1999). 'Human resource management and performance in the UK hotel industry', *British Journal of Industrial Relations*, 37, 419–43.

Hunt, J., Lees, S., Grumber, J. and Vivian, P. (1987) *Acquisitions: The Human Factor*. London Business School and Egon Zehender International.

Huselid, M.A. (1995) 'The impact of human resource management on turnover, productivity, and corporate financial performance', *Academy of Management Journal*, 38: 635–72.

Huselid, M. and Becker, B. (1996) 'Methodological issues in cross-sectional and panel estimates of the HR-firm performance link', *Industrial Relations*, 35: 400–22.

Huselid, M.A., Jackson, S.E. and Schuler, R.S. (1997) 'Technical and strategic human resource management effectiveness as a determinant of firm performance', *Academy of Management Journal*, 40: 171–88.

Jenkins, P. (2013) 'Lunch with the FT: Stephen Hester – I hate not winning', *Financial Times*, 8 June.

Kanter, R. (1989) 'The new managerial work', *Harvard Business Review*, November–December: 85–92.

Kaplan, R. and Norton, D. (1996) *The Balanced Scorecard: Translating Strategy into Action*. Boston, MA: Harvard Business School Press.

Kaplan, R. and Norton, D. (2001) *The Strategy-Focussed Organisation*. Boston, MA: Harvard Business School Press.

Keenoy, T. (1990) 'HRM: A case of the wolf in sheep's clothing', *Personnel Review*, 19, 2: 3–9.

Keenoy, T. and Anthony, P. (1992) 'HRM: metaphor, meaning and morality' in P. Blyton and P. Turnbull (eds) *Reassessing Human Resource Management*. London: Sage, pp. 233–55.

Kochan T. and Barocci, T. (1985) *Human Resource Management and Industrial Relations*. Boston, MA: LittleBrown.

Lawler, E.E., Mohrman, S.A. and Ledford, G.E. (1995) *Creating High Performance Organisations*. San Francisco, CA: Jossey-Bass.

Legge, K. (1978) *Power, Innovation and Problem-Solving in Personnel Management*. London: McGraw-Hill.

Legge, K. (1998) 'The morality of HRM' in C. Mabey, G. Salaman and J. Storey (eds) *Strategic Human Resource Management, A Reader*. London: Open University/Sage, pp. 18–29.

Legge, K. (2005) *Human Resource Management: Rhetoric and Realities*. London: Macmillan.

Lengnick Hall, C.A. and Lengnick Hall, M.L. (1988) 'Strategic human resource management: a review of the literature and a proposed typology', *Academy of Management Review,* 13: 454–70.

Luthans, K.W. and Sommer, S.M. (2005) 'The impact of high peformance work on industry-level outcomes', *Journal of Managerial Issues,* 17, 3: 327–46.

Mabey, C., Salaman, G. and Storey, J. (eds) (1998) *Strategic Human Resource Management, A Reader*. London: Open University/Sage.

MacDuffie, J.P. (1995) 'Human resource bundles and manufacturing performance', *Industrial Relations Review,* 48, 2: 199–221.

Mahoney, T. and Deckop, J. (1986) 'Evolution of concept and practice in personnel administration/human resource management', *Journal of Management,* 12: 223–41.

March, J.G. (1976) 'The technology of foolishness' in J. Marsh and J. Olsen (eds) *Ambiguity and Choice in Organisations*. Bergen: Universitetsforlaget.

Marchington, M. and Grugulis, I. (2000) 'Best practice human resource management: perfect opportunity or dangerous illusion?', *International Journal of Human Resource Management,* 11: 905–25.

Marchington, M. and Wilkinson, A. (2012) *Human Resource Management at Work: People Management and Development,* 5th edn. London: CIPD.

Marks, M. and Mirvis, P. (1982) 'Merging human resources: a review of current research', *Merger and Acquisitions,* 17, 2: 38–44.

Miles, R. and Snow, C. (1978) *Organisational Strategy, Structure and Process*. New York: McGraw Hill.

Miles, R.E and Snow, C.C. (1984) 'Designing strategic human resource systems', *Organisational Dynamics,* Summer: 36–52.

Miller, D. (1992) 'Generic strategies; classification, combination and context', *Advances in Strategic Management,* 8, 391–408.

Miller, D. and Shamsie, J. (1996) 'The resource based view of the firm in two environments: the Hollywood film studios from 1936–1965', *Academy of Management Journal,* 39, 3: 519–43.

Milliman, J., Von Glinow, M.A. and Nathan, M. (1991) 'Organisational life cycles and international strategic human resource management in multinational companies: Implications for congruence theory', *Academy of Management Review,* 16, 318–39.

Millward, D. (2009) *Daily Telegraph*. 11 March.

Mintzberg, H. (1987) 'Crafting strategy', *Harvard Business Review,* 65, 4: 65–75.

Mintzberg, H. (1990) 'The design school: reconsidering the basic premises of strategic management', *Strategic Management Journal,* 11: 171–95.

Mueller, F. (1998) 'Human resources as strategic assets: An evolutionary resource-based theory' in C. Mabey, G. Salaman and J. Storey (eds) *Strategic Human Resource Management*: A Reader. London: Open University/Sage, pp. 152–69.

Nonaka, I. and Takeuchi, H. (1995) *The Knowledge-Creating Company*. New York: Oxford University Press.

Ogbonna, E. (1992) 'Organisational culture and human resource management, dilemmas and contradictions' in P. Blyton and P. Turnbull (eds) *Reassessing Human Resource Management*. London: Sage, pp. 74–96.

Patterson, M.G., West, M.A., Lawthom, R. and Nickell, S. (1997) *The Impact of People Management Practices on Business Performance*. London: IPD.

Penrose, E. (1959) *The Theory of the Growth of the Firm*. Oxford: Blackwell.

Perry-Smith, J. and Blum, T. (2000) 'Work-family human resource bundles and perceived organisational performance', *Academy of Management Journal,* 43: 1107–17.

Pettigrew, A.M. (1973) *The Politics of Organisational Decision-Making*. London: Tavistock.

Pettigrew, A.M. (1985) *The Awakening Giant: Continuity and Change in ICI*. Oxford: Blackwell.

Pfeffer, J. (1994) *Competitive Advantage through People*. Boston, MA: Harvard Business School Press.

Pfeffer, J. (1998) *The Human Equation: Building Profits by putting People First*. Boston, MA: Harvard Business School Press.

Porter, M. (1985) *Competitive Advantage: Creating and Sustaining Superior Performance*. New York: Free Press.

Porter, M. (1991) 'Towards a dynamic theory of strategy', *Strategic Management Journal,* 12 (Winter): 95–117.

Purcell, J. (1985) 'Is anybody listening to the corporate personnel department?' *Personnel Management,* September: 28–31.

Purcell, J. and Hutchinson, S. (2007) 'Front-line managers as agents in the HRM-performance causal chain: theory, analysis and evidence', *Human Resource Management Journal,* 17, 1: 3–20.

Purcell, J., Kinnie, N., Hutchinson, S., Rayton, B. and Swart, J. (2003) *Understanding the People and Performance Link: Unlocking the Black Box*. London: CIPD.

Quinn J.B. (1978) 'Strategic change: Logical incrementalism', *Sloan Management Review,* 1, 20: 7–21.

Rahrami, H. (1992) 'The emerging flexible organisation: perspectives from Silicon Valley', *California Management Review,* 34, 4: 33–48.

Reed, J. (2012) 'The car that saved JLR', *FT Weekend Magazine,* 28 September. Online: http://www.ft.com/cms/s/2/93481c40-0831-11e2-a2d8-00144feadc0.html#slide0 (accessed January 2014).

Reicheld, F. (1996) *The Loyalty Effect: The Hidden Force Behind Growth, Profits and Lasting Value*. Boston, MA: Harvard Business School Press.

Ritson, N. (1999) 'Corporate strategy and the role of HRM: critical cases in oil and chemicals', *Employee Relations,* 21, 2: 159–75.

Roche, W. (1999) 'In search of commitment-oriented HRM practices and the conditions that sustain them', *Journal of Management Studies,* 36, 5: 653–78.

Rucci, A. Kirn, S. and Quinn, R. (1998) 'The employee–customer–profit chain at Sears', *Harvard Business Review,* 76, 1: 82–97.

Schuler, R. and Jackson, S. (1987) 'Linking competitive strategies with human resource management', *Academy of Management Executive,* 1, 3: 207–19.

Simon, H.A. (1947) *Administrative Behaviour*. New York: Free Press.

Sisson, K. and Storey, J. (2000) *The Realities of Human Resource Management*. Buckingham: Open University Press.

Sloan, A.P. (1963) *My Years with General Motors*. London: Sidgwick & Jackson.

Snell, S.A., Youndt, M. and Wright, P.M. (1996) 'Establishing a framework for research in strategic human resource management: merging resource theory and organisation learning', *Research in Personnel and Human Resources Management,* 14: 61–90.

Stavrou, E.T. and Brewster, C. (2005) 'The configurational approach to linking strategic human resource management bundles with business performance: myth or reality?', *Management Revue,* 16, 2: 186–202.

Storey, J. (1992) *Developments in the Management of Human Resources.* Blackwell: Oxford.

Storey, J. (1995) *Human Resource Management: A Critical Text.* London: Routledge.

Stroh, L. and Caligiuri, P.M. (1998) 'Strategic human resources: a new source for competitive advantage in the global arena', *International Journal of Human Resource Management,* 9: 1–17.

Thompson, J. (2001) *Understanding Corporate Strategy.* London: Thomson Learning.

Torrington, D. and Hall, L. (1998) *Human Resource Management,* 4th edn. Europe: Prentice Hall.

Torrington, D., Taylor, S. and Hall, L. (2008) *Human Resource Management* (7th edn). Harlow: Pearson Education.

Truss, C. and Gratton, L. (1994) 'Strategic human resource management: a conceptual approach', *International Journal of Human Resource Management,* 5: 663–86.

Tyson, S. (1997) 'Human resource strategy: a process for managing the contribution of HRM to organisational performance', *International Journal of Human Resource Management,* 8, 3: 277–90.

Ulrich, D. (1997) 'Measuring human resources: an overview of practice and a prescription for results', *Human Resource Management,* 36, 3 (Fall): 303–20.

Ulrich, D. and Brockbank, W. (2005) *The HR Value Proposition.* Boston, MA: Harvard Business Review School Press.

Ulrich, D., Brockbank, W., Yeung, A. and Lake, D. (1995) 'Human resource competencies: An empirical assessment', *Human Resource Management,* 34: 473–95.

Wall, T.D. and Wood, S.J. (2005) 'The romance of human resource management and business performance, and the case for big science', *Human Relations,* 58, 4: 429–62.

Walton, R. (1985) 'From control to commitment in the workplace', *Harvard Business Review,* 63, 2: 76–84.

Watson, J. (1977) *The Personnel Managers: A Study in the Sociology of Work and Employment.* London: Routledge & Kegan Paul.

Wernefelt, B. (1984) 'A resource based view of the firm', *Strategic Management Journal,* 5, 2: 171–80.

Whittington, R. (1993) *What is Strategy and Does it Matter?* London: Routledge.

*Whittington, R. (2001) *What is Strategy and Does it Matter?,* 2nd edn. London: Thomson Learning.

Wiggins, R.R. and Ruefli, T.W. (2002) 'Sustained competitive advantage: temporal dynamics and the incidence and persistence of superior economic performance', *Organisation Science,* 13: 82–108.

Wilson, D. (1992) *A Strategy of Change.* London: Routledge.

Winnett, R. and Corrigan, T. (2009) *Daily Telegraph,* 21 March.

Winter, S. (1987) 'Knowledge and competence as strategic assets' in D.J. Teece (ed.) *The Competitive Challenge: Strategies for Industrial Innovation and Renewal.* Cambridge, MA: Ballinger, pp. 159–84.

Wood, S. (1999) 'Human resource management and performance', *International Journal of Management Reviews,* 1, 4: 367–413.

Wood, S.J. and de Menezes, L. (1998) 'High commitment management in the UK: evidence from the workplace industrial relations survey and employers' manpower and skills practices survey', *Human Relations,* 51: 485–515.

Wright, P.M. and Gardner, T.M. (2003) 'The human resource-firm performance relationship: methodological and theoretical challenges' in D. Holman, T.D. Wall, C.W. Clegg, P. Sparrow and A. Howard (eds) *The New Workplace: A Guide to the Human Impact of Modern Working Practices.* Chichester: John Wiley.

Wright, M.W. and Haggerty, J.J. (2005) 'Missing variables in theories of strategic human resource management: time, cause and individuals', *Management Revue,* 16, 2: 164–74.

Wright, P.M. and McMahan, G.C. (1992) 'Alternative theoretical perspectives for strategic human resource management', *Journal of Management,* 18: 295–320.

Wright, P.M. and McMahan, G.C. (1999) 'Theoretical perspectives for strategic human resource management' in R.S. Schuler and S.E. Jackson (eds) *Strategic Human Resource Management.* Oxford, Blackwell Business, pp. 49–72.

Wright, P. and Snell, S. (1991) 'Towards an integrative view of strategic human resource management', *Human Resource Management Review,* 1: 203–25.

Wright, P.M. and Snell, S.A. (1998) 'Towards a unifying framework for exploring fit and flexibility in strategic human resource management', *Academy of Management Review,* 23, 4: 756–72.

Wright, P.M. and Snell, S.A. (2005) 'Partner or guardian? HR's challenge in balancing value and values', *Human Resource Management Journal,* 44, 2: 177–82.

Wright, P. McMahan, G. and McWilliams, A. (1994) 'Human resources and sustained competitive advantage: a resource-based perspective', *International Journal of Human Resource Management,* 5, 2: 301–26.

Wright, P., McCormick, B., Sherman, S. and McMahan, G. (1996) 'The role of human resource practices in petrochemical refinery performance', Paper presented at the 1996 Academy of Management, Cincinnati, OH.

Wright, P.M., Gardner, T.M. and Moynihan, L.M. (2003) 'The impact of HR practices on the performance of business units', *Human Resource Management Journal,* 13: 21–36.

Wright, P., Snell, S. and Jacobsen, P. (2004) 'Current approaches to HR strategies: inside-out vs. outside-in', *Human Resource Planning,* 27: 36–46.

Yeung, A. and Berman, B. (1997) 'Adding value through human resources: reorienting human resource management to drive business performance', *Human Resource Management,* 36, 3: 321–35.

Youndt, M., Snell, S., Dean, J. and Lepak, D. (1996) 'Human resource management, manufacturing strategy and firm performance', *Academy of Management Journal,* 39: 836–66.

Zigarelli, M. (1996) 'Human resources and the bottom line', *Academy of Management Executive,* 10: 63–64.

Chapter 3

Contextualising HRM

Audrey Collin

Objectives

- To identify the challenge of conceptualising and representing context.
- To contextualise human resource management (HRM) and enrich understanding of it by examining its background, uncovering some of the strands in its thinking and their underpinning assumptions, and highlighting some of the tensions it addresses.
- And thereby to develop readers' capacity for critical thinking and recognition of ethical issues in relation to HRM.

Introductory case study

What are the goals of a football club?

By Adam Palin

What is the purpose of a publicly listed football club: to win trophies or turn a profit? The teaching faculty from the European School of Management and Technology in Berlin have examined this question in their recently published research.

Urs Müller and Ulrich Linnhoff, with Bernhard Pellens of Ruhr-Universität Bochum, take the example of Borussia Dortmund, Germany's only football club to be listed on the stock exchange.

The club was taken public in 2000 – at the height of its on-pitch success – having won European club football's most prestigious tournament, the Uefa Champions League, in 1997. Its transformation to a for-profit company coincided with the sport's rapid commercialisation fuelled by rising broadcasting revenues.

Increased revenues were, however, offset by 'rocketing expenses, in particular players' salaries', the authors observe. Pursuing success in lucrative tournaments, the Ruhr club assembled a star-studded squad of players with an accompanying wage bill that reached €60m a season at its peak, they write. Although topping the Bundesliga, the German league, in 2002, Borussia struggled to sustain its success and by the end of 2004 was on the brink of financial collapse.

A rescue package – launched in 2005 – dramatically cut labour costs and allowed the club to repurchase its stadium, which had been sold in 2002. On a more sustainable financial footing, Borussia has since returned to success, winning the Bundesliga in both 2011 and 2012. However, from its flotation on the stock market in 2000, to 2009, the club amassed a cumulative loss of more than €145m, Mr Müller notes.

In their research – available online at ECCH – the writers ask what goals should Borussia set itself? Does the club have a higher obligation to its fans and traditions through the pursuit of sporting success, or to its shareholders, who suffered the collapse in its share price from €11 at flotation to less than €1 in 2009?

For Mr Müller, these 'very essential' questions relating to Borussia's identity are relevant to every organisation.

'What is the higher purpose?' he asks. 'The definition of the main purpose of an organisation – whether business, association or any other institution – is a permanent management challenge.' **https://www.esmt.org/**

Source: Palin, R. (2013) What are the goals of a football club? *Financial Times.* 26 April. Http://www.ft.com/cms/s/2/2a3bbcac-ae49-11e2-bdfd-00144feabdc0.html#axzz2tcGBag9f

Introduction

The significance and nature of context

An event seen from one point-of-view gives one impression. Seen from another point-of-view it gives quite a different impression. But it's only when you get the whole picture you fully understand what's going on.

(Reproduced in memory of John Webster, 1934–2006)

The need to be aware of the context of human affairs was demonstrated dramatically in this prize-winning advertisement for *The Guardian* newspaper that is still remembered today. We can easily misinterpret facts, events and people when we examine them out of context, for it is their context that provides us with the clues necessary to understand them. Context locates them in space and time and gives them a past and a future, as well as the present that we see. It gives us the language to understand them, the codes to decode them, and the keys to their meaning.

From the various models of human resource management (HRM) discussed earlier in the book (see Chapter 1), you will recognise that it is shaped by its context, and that its context is complex, diverse and dynamic. This chapter will therefore carry forward your thinking about the issues raised in that chapter, by exploring the various strands within the context of HRM that are woven together to form the pattern of meanings that constitute it. As explained previously, and as will be amplified by the rest of the book, HRM is far more than a portfolio of policies, practices, procedures and prescriptions concerned with the management of the employment relationship. It is this, but more. And because it is more, it is loosely defined and difficult to pin down precisely, being a basket of overlapping and shifting meanings, which users of the term do not always specify. Its 'brilliant ambiguity' (Keenoy, 1990) derives from the context in which it is embedded, a context within which there are multiple and often competing perspectives upon the employment relationship, some ideological, others theoretical, and yet others conceptual. HRM is inevitably a contested terrain, and the various definitions of it reflect this.

The context of HRM is multi-layered. The organisation constitutes the immediate context of the employment relationship, and it is here that the debate about how that relationship can be managed begins. The nature of organisation and the tensions between the stakeholders in it give rise to issues that have to be addressed by managers, e.g. choices about how to orchestrate the activities of organisational members and whose interests to serve. Beyond the organisation itself lie the economic, social, political and cultural layers, and beyond them again the historical, national and global layers of context. Considerable change is taking place within those layers, making the whole field dynamic. It is not the purpose of this chapter to register all these changes. You will become aware of some of them as you read the remainder of this book; others you will experience in your own lives. However, we need to note here that the events and changes in the wider context have repercussions for organisations and HRM, and present further issues to be managed and choices to be made. Indeed, Mayo and Nohria (2005) argue that successful managers have what they have coined 'contextual intelligence', which enables them to be deeply sensitive to their organisation's context.

The several layers of HRM's context, however, are not like the skins of an onion. They exist in more than one conceptual plane: some have a concrete nature, like a local pool of labour, and others are abstract, like the values and stereotypes that influence an employer's views of a particular class of person in the labour market. The abstract world of ideas and values overlies and intersects with the other layers of the context of HRM: theories of organisation and management; the ways of organising society, acquiring and using power, and distributing resources; the ways of relating to, understanding and valuing human beings and their activities; the ways of studying and understanding reality and of acquiring knowledge; and the stocks of accumulated knowledge in theories and concepts.

To understand the context of HRM, then, we need to recognise it as more than the environment or the surrounding circumstances that exert 'external influences' on a given topic: context gives it a third dimension. By contextualising HRM, you will come to recognise the breadth of its field, uncover its foundations and give it a backstory, and this will enrich your understanding of it.

The challenge of conceptualising and representing context

How can we begin to understand anything that is embedded in a complex context? We seem to have awareness at an intuitive level, perceiving and acting upon the clues that context gives to arrive at 'tacit knowledge' (see Chapter 7). However, context challenges our formal thinking. First, we cannot stand back to take in the complete picture, which has traditionally been one way to gain objective knowledge of a situation. Because we are ourselves a part of our context, it is not possible for us to obtain a detached perspective upon it. In that respect, we are like the fish in water that 'can have no understanding of the concept of "wetness" since it has no idea of what it means to be dry' (Southgate and Randall, 1981: 54). However, humans are very different from the 'fish in water'. We can be *reflexive,* recognising what our perspective is and what its implications are; *open,* seeking out and recognising other people's perspectives; and *critical,* entering into a dialogue with others' views and interrogating our own in the light of theirs, and vice versa. We shall see later that this is also the approach needed to recognise and make an appropriate response to ethical issues in organisations.

Secondly, we need the conceptual means to grasp the wholeness (and dynamic nature) of the picture. To understand a social phenomenon such as HRM, we cannot just wrench it from its context and examine it microscopically in isolation. To do this is to be like the child who digs up a newly planted and now germinating seed to see 'whether it is growing'. In the same way, if we analyse context into its various elements and layers, then we are already distorting our understanding of it, because it is an indivisible whole. Rather, we have to find ways to examine HRM's interconnectedness and interdependence with other phenomena in its context. Here the very representation of our thinking in written language is not helpful, for it is linear, which undermines our ability to communicate a dynamic, interrelated complexity clearly and succinctly. Nevertheless, as we shall discuss later, there are ways that enable us to conceptualise and express the many loops and circularities of these complex interrelationships in an often dynamic context. We could also perhaps think in terms of 'rich pictures' or 'mind maps' (Senge, 1990; Cameron, 1997), but meanwhile we shall use metaphor to conceptualise context, i.e. to envisage it in terms of something concrete that we already understand.

We have already mentioned that the metaphor of the many-skinned onion, although depicting multiple layers, is insufficient to convey the interconnectedness and texture of context. We could, instead, think of it as a tapestry. This is a 'thick hand-woven textile fabric in which design is formed by weft stitches across parts of warp' (*Concise OED*, 1982). The warp threads run the length of the tapestry and the weft are the lateral threads that weave through them to give colour, pattern and texture. In this chapter, we propose that the warp is constituted from the basic structures of society, such as the social and economic systems, demography, etc., that are the foundation upon which employing organisations are built. The weft threads are the ways of thinking about those structures – the various ways of defining reality. Events, people and ephemeral issues are the stitches sewn into the surface of the tapestry to elaborate its pattern. This metaphor helps us to visualise how interwoven and interrelated are the various elements of the context of HRM; and how the pattern of HRM itself is woven into them, as in Figure 3.1. It reminds us again that an analytical approach to the study of context, which would take it apart to examine it closely, would be like taking a tapestry to bits: we would be left with threads. The tapestry itself inheres in the whole, not its parts.

This tapestry that is the context of HRM is being woven continuously from threads of different colours and textures. At times one colour predominates, but then peters out. In parts of the tapestry, patterns may be intentionally fashioned, while observers (such as the authors of this book) believe they can discern a recognisable pattern in other parts. Of course, it will not be feasible here, or indeed necessary, to attempt to portray the whole tapestry that is HRM's context. This chapter can only examine part of it, so we will pick out a number of the threads for you to identify and follow through the remainder of the book. You should observe the interconnections and interrelationships between them, and how their interweaving gives us changes in the pattern and colour of the tapestry, some distinct and others subtle.

Figure 3.1 The metaphor of tapestry to convey HRM in context

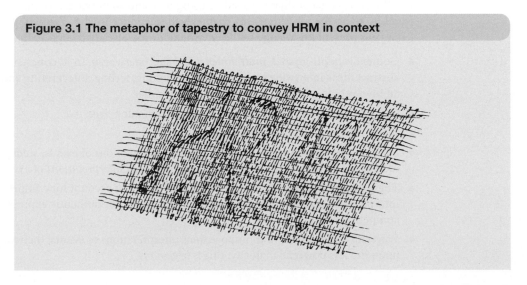

It will be a challenge to find new ways of thinking in order to seek the whole picture rather than take the customary formal, detached and analytical approach. However, as well as giving you a greater understanding of the context of HRM and its effects, this will develop and exercise your capacity for critical thinking, as it will allow you to recognise some significant perspectives that often remain unnoticed or ignored. It will also highlight some of the ethical issues in HRM that can otherwise be obscured. This will be of value both to those studying HRM and to reflective practitioners. It has been predicted that HR will see a major transformation, with its core becoming more analytical and critical (Czerny, 2005) and turned 'from a department and a transaction into a philosophy leading the organisation' (Pickard, 2005: 15). And from 2005 the concept of the 'thinking performer', 'who applies a critically thoughtful approach to their job' (Whittaker and Johns, 2004: 32), has underpinned the professional standards of the Chartered Institute of Personnel and Development (CIPD).

Before beginning to read about the context of HRM, you will find it helpful to make the following exploration.

Explore

Reflect upon this way of understanding context.

- How different is it from the way in which you would have defined the context of HRM based, for example, on the various models presented in Chapter 1?
- Does this challenge the way you generally think and, if so, in what way?

The concepts and language needed to understand issues raised by the context of HRM

By examining context, this chapter suggests, you can develop your critical thinking, in the sense of questioning and uncovering the basic issues, not of arguing against something. The concepts and language needed for this may be largely unfamiliar to you, but you will probably find that you already understand much of their meaning. You are already likely to have experience of thinking about and responding to issues in the natural, physical environment, which is another aspect of context that incorporates both the concrete world and abstract ideas. Such issues as climate change, genetically modified food and threats to the survival of many species will also have promoted critical thinking and raised ethical issues, and it will have given you the basic concepts that we shall be using here and so provide a useful set of 'hooks' upon which to hang the ideas that this chapter will introduce to you. You will probably find that from your present knowledge of the environment you already recognise that:

- Context is *multi-layered, multidimensional* and *interwoven*. In it, concrete events and abstract ideas intertwine to create issues; thinking, feeling, interpreting and behaving are all involved. It is like the tapestry described earlier.
- Our interpretation of our context depends upon our *perspective*.
- It also depends upon our *ideology*.
- Different groups in society have their own interpretations of events, stemming from their ideology. There are therefore *competing* or *contested interpretations* of events.
- These groups use *rhetoric* to express their own, and to account for competing, interpretations, thus distorting, or even suppressing, the authentic expression of competing views.
- Powerful others often try to impose their interpretations of events, their version of reality, upon the less powerful majority: this is *hegemony*.

The immediate context of HRM

Human resource management concerns the management of the employment relationship. The nature of the organisation and the way it is managed therefore form the immediate context within which HRM is embedded, and this is overlaid by the interpretations made by theorists, which will be examined shortly.

The nature of organisations and the role of management

At its simplest, an organisation comes into existence when the efforts of two or more people are pooled to achieve an objective that one would be unable to complete alone. The achievement of this objective calls for the completion of a number of tasks. Depending upon their complexity and degree of interdependence, the availability of appropriate technology and the skills of the people involved, these tasks may be subdivided into a number of sub-tasks and more people employed to help carry them out. This division of labour constitutes the lateral dimension of the structure of the organisation. Its vertical dimension is constructed from the generally hierarchical relationships of power and authority between the owner or owners, the staff employed to complete these tasks, and the managers employed to coordinate and control the staff and their work. Working on behalf of the organisation's owners or shareholders, and with the authority derived from them, managers draw upon a number of resources to enable them to carry out their task: raw materials, finance, technology, people, information, and legitimacy, support and goodwill from the organisation's environment. They manage the organisation by ensuring that there are sufficient people with appropriate skills; that they work to the same ends and timetable; that they have the resources and authority needed to complete their tasks; and that their tasks dovetail and are performed to the required standard and at the required pace.

The very nature of work organisations in a capitalist society therefore generates a number of significant tensions: between people with different stakes in the organisation, and therefore different perspectives upon and interests in it; between what owners and other members of the organisation might desire and what they can feasibly achieve; and between the needs, capabilities and potentials of organisational members and what the operation of the organisation demands of and permits them. Management (see Watson, 2000) is the process that keeps the organisation from flying apart because of these tensions, that makes it work, secures its survival and, according to the type of organisation, its profitability or effectiveness. Inevitably, however, managerial control is a significant and often contentious issue. (Until recently, that had been seen in terms of managers controlling employees. What has recently been learnt about the banking industry and other large corporations, however, now raises the issue of how senior managers are themselves controlled.)

Moreover, the nature of people and their relationships and the way they constitute an organisation make management complex. Although the organisation of tasks packages people into organisational roles, individuals are larger and more organic than those roles have traditionally been. The organisation, writes Barnard (1938, in Schein, 1978: 17) 'pays people only for certain of their activities . . . but it is whole persons who come to work'. Unlike other resources, people interact with those who manage them and among themselves; they have needs for autonomy and agency; they think and are creative; they have feelings; and they need consideration for their emotional and their physical needs, security and protection. This greatly complicates the tasks of managers, who can work only with and through people to ensure that the organisation survives and thrives in the face of increasing pressures from its environment. The management of people is therefore not only a more diffuse and complex activity than the management of other resources, but also an essentially moral one (again, see Watson, 2000).

As organisations become larger and more complex, the division of managerial labour often leads to a specialist 'people' function to advise and support line managers in the complex and demanding tasks of managing their staff. This was originally personnel management (which has since changed in name and nature to become HRM). It developed a professional expertise in aspects of managing people, such as selection, training and industrial relations, which it offered in an advisory capacity to line managers, who nevertheless remain the prime managers of people. However, this division of managerial labour has fragmented the management of people: the development of HRM to subsume personnel management can be seen as a strategy to reintegrate the management of people into the management of the organisation as a whole.

Explore

- In your own experience of being employed, however limited that might be so far, have you been aware of some of these tensions?
- What were their effects upon you and your colleagues at work?
- How did the management of the organisation respond to these tensions?
- Has this coloured how you look at management and HRM?

Managers' strategies to resolve the tensions in organisations

Those tensions have to be resolved through the process of managing, or rather continuously resolved, for they are inherent in organisations. Hence Weick (1979: 44) writes that organising is a continuous process of meaning-making: 'organisations keep falling apart . . . require chronic rebuilding'. A continuing issue, therefore, is that of managerial control: how to orchestrate organisational activities in a way that meets the needs of the various stakeholders. The owners of organisations, or those who manage them on their behalf, have explored many ways to resolve these tensions. The strategies they have adopted are embodied in their employment policies and practices and the organisational systems they put in place. They are also manifested in the psychological contract between organisation and employees that embroiders the legal employment contract (CIPD, 2012). The notion of the psychological contract now in current use goes back to a much earlier literature (e.g. Schein, 1970) and it is some of the earlier terminology that is used below.

Managers have adopted various strategies to deal with these tensions, but we can note only a few here. In practice they might be less easy to distinguish, and some managers adopt a hybrid version appropriate to their particular organisation. They will always be seeking new approaches to deal more effectively with those tensions, or to deal with variations in them as circumstances change. You can elaborate upon the material here by reading further in an organisational behaviour or management theory textbook, such as Huczynski and Buchanan (2010) or Clark *et al.* (1994).

An early twentieth-century strategy was *scientific management* (or the classical school of management theory). This addressed the tensions in the organisation by striving to control how people worked and to keep down their costs. It emphasised the need for rationality, clear objectives, the managerial prerogative – the right of managers to manage – and adopted work study and similar methods. It led to the reduction of tasks to their basic elements and the grouping of similar elements together to produce low-skilled, low-paid jobs, epitomised by assembly-line working. Workers were treated relatively impersonally and collectively ('management and labour'), and rather like machine components themselves. The nature of the psychological contract with them was calculative (Schein, 1970), with a focus on extrinsic rewards and incentives. Such a strategy encouraged a collective response from workers, and hence the development of trade unions.

This approach to management evolved in North America, and provided a firm foundation for modern bureaucracies (Clegg, 1990). In Britain they overlaid the norms of a complex, though changing, social class system that framed the relationships between managers and other employees (Child, 1969; Mant, 1979). The legacy of this early strategy continued well on into the century in many management practices, such as organisation and method study, job analysis and description, selection methods, an overriding concern for efficiency and the 'bottom line', appraisal and performance management. This has not been completely abandoned (see Clegg, 1990; Ritzer, 1996 on 'McDonaldization'; and debates about employment in call centres, e.g. Hatchett, 2000; Callaghan and Thompson, 2002; Holman and Wood, 2002; Taylor et al., 2002).

A second approach to the tensions in organisations, the *human relations* strategy, emerged during the middle years of the twentieth century, and developed in parallel with an increasingly prosperous society in which there were strong trade unions and (later) a growing acceptance of the right of individuals to self-fulfilment. Child (1969) identifies its emergence in British management thinking as a response to growing labour tensions. It tempered scientific management by its recognition that people differed from other resources, that if they were treated as clock numbers rather than as human beings they would not be fully effective at work and could even fight back to the point of subverting management intentions. It also recognised the significance of social relationships at work – the informal organisation (Argyris, 1960). Managers therefore had to pay attention to the nature of supervision and the working of groups and teams, and to find ways of involving employees through job design, motivation, and a democratic, consultative or participative style of management. The nature of the psychological contract was cooperative (Schein, 1970).

Human resource management is another strategy adopted by managers to address the tensions within the organisation. It developed much later in the century as major changes and threats were experienced in the context of organisations (recession, international competition and globalisation). It was a response to the need to achieve flexibility in the organisation and workforce, and improved performance, by devolved decision-making and empowerment. As noted later in the book (see Chapter 7), employees have had to become multi-skilled and to work across traditional boundaries. Unlike the two strategies above, HRM approaches the organisation holistically and often with greater attention to its culture, leadership and 'vision', the 'soft' Ss of McKinsey's 'Seven S' framework (Pascale and Athos, 1982: 202–6). It attempts to integrate the needs of employees with those of the organisation in an explicit manner: the psychological contract embodies mutuality (Schein, 1970). It recognises that people should be invested in as assets so that they achieve their potential for the benefit of the organisation. It also pays greater attention to the individual rather than the collective, so that these notions of developing the individual's potential have been accompanied by individual contracts of employment, performance appraisal and performance-related pay. However, the very title of human resource management suggests that this is also an instrumental strategy. Although it differs greatly from the approaches that see labour as a 'cost', to be reduced or kept in check, it nevertheless construes the human being as a resource for the organisation to use.

Another, more *humanistic* approach aimed to construct the organisation as an appropriate environment for autonomous individuals to work together collaboratively for their common good. This is the approach of many cooperatives (and, to some extent, of mutuals such as the John Lewis Partnership). It informed the early philosophy of organisation development (see Huse, 1980), although the practice of that is now largely instrumental. It also underpins the notion of the learning organisation (see Senge, 1990 and Chapter 8).

Explore

Some of you will have worked in a call centre. Working on your own or in a group, examine your experiences of working there.

- Could you identify one or more of these managerial strategies in your workplace?
- What might have been your experiences had the management adopted a different strategy?

Since the global financial crisis hit in 2007, managers have had to grapple with many new tensions. To ensure organisational survival, they are having to balance, *inter alia,* the need to reduce the size of the workforce with ways of maintaining motivation and retaining essential skills for the future.

Key Controversy

Working on your own or in a group, identify some of the new tensions that are arising.
● What new strategies are you aware of?
● How would you describe the basis of their psychological contract with employees?
● Do they raise new ethical issues?

Ideas and theories in the immediate context of HRM

Here we shall note some of the abstract ideas that we suggested overlie and intersect with what happens in the immediate context of HRM, and find not only that have they varied over time, but also that several strongly competing interpretations co-exist. Managers themselves are to some extent influenced by such concepts and language, if not their arguments. Again, this chapter can only skim over this material, but you can pursue the issues by reading, for example, Child (1969), who traces the development of management thought in Britain, or Morgan (2006), who sets out eight different metaphors for organisations through which he examines in a very accessible way the various ways in which theorists and others have construed organisations. Reed and Hughes (1992: 10–11) identified the changing focus of organisation theory over the previous 30 or so years, from a concern with organisational stability, order and disorder, and then with organisational power and politics, to a concern with the construction of organisational reality.

The reification of the organisation by managers and others, and the general acceptance of the need for it to have rational goals to drive it forward in an effective manner, have long been challenged (see the Introductory case study). Simon (see Pugh *et al.*, 1983) recognised that rationality is 'bounded' – that managers make decisions on the basis of limited and imperfect knowledge. Cyert and March adopted a similar viewpoint: the many stakeholders in an organisation make it a 'shifting multigoal coalition' (see Pugh *et al.*, 1983: 108) that has to be managed in a pragmatic manner. Others (see Pfeffer, 1981; Morgan, 1997) recognised the essentially conflictual and political nature of organisations: goals, structures and processes are defined, manipulated and managed in the interests of those holding the power in the organisation. A range of different understandings of organisations has developed over time: the systems approach (Checkland, 1981), the learning organisation (Senge, 1990), transformational leadership and 'excellence' (Peters and Waterman, 1982; Kanter, 1983), knowledge management (see Chapter 7) and the significance of rhetoric (see later, and Eccles and Nohria, 1992). This range is widening to include even more holistic approaches, with recent interest in the roles in the workplace of emotional intelligence (Pickard, 1999; Cherniss and Goleman, 2001; Higgs and Dulewicz, 2002), spirituality and love (Welch, 1998; Zohar and Marshall, 2001). The influence of many of these new ideas can be seen in the concern for work–life balance (e.g. CIPD, 2013a).

The established views of managers are subject to further interpretations. Weick (1979) argued the need to focus upon the process of organising rather than upon the organisation, which is its reified outcome. As we noted earlier, he regards organising as a continuous process of meaning-making: '[p]rocesses continually need to be re-accomplished' (p. 44). Cooper and Fox (1990) and Hosking and Fineman (1990) adopted a similar interpretation in their discussion of the 'texture of organising'.

Like the Introductory case study, Brunsson (1989) shone a different light on the nature and goals of organising, based on his research in Scandinavian municipal administrations.

He suggested that the outputs of these kinds of organisations are 'talk, decisions and physical products'. He proposed two 'ideal types' of organisation: the *action* organisation, which depends on action for its legitimacy (and hence essential resources) in the eyes of its environment; and the *political* organisation, which depends on its reflection of environmental inconsistencies for its legitimacy. Talk and decisions in the action organisation (or an organisation in its action phase) lead to actions, whereas the outputs of the political organisation (or the organisation in its political phase) are talk and decisions that may or may not lead to action:

> . . . hypocrisy is a fundamental type of behaviour in the political organisation: to talk in a way that satisfies one demand, to decide in a way that satisfies another, and to supply products in a way that satisfies a third.
>
> Brunsson (1989: 27)

There are similarly competing views upon organisational culture, as we see in Aldrich (1992) and Frost *et al.* (1991). The established view interprets it as a subsystem of the organisation that managers need to create and maintain through the promulgation and manipulation of values, norms, rites and symbols. The alternative view argues that culture is not something that an organisation *has*, but that it *is*.

These competing ideas challenge us to recognise that, underlying the management of people in organisations, are some fundamental assumptions about the nature of organisations and of reality itself and how we can understand it. Those assumptions inform the practices and policies of management, and hence define the organisational and conceptual space that HRM fills, and generate the multiple meanings of which HRM is constructed. In terms of the tapestry metaphor we used earlier, they constitute some of the weft threads in the tapestry/context of HRM. They also highlight ethical issues in its practice. We shall return to these issues later in the chapter.

The wider context of HRM

The definition of the wider context of HRM could embrace innumerable topics (from, for example, demography to globalisation) and a long-time perspective (from the organisation of labour in prehistory, as at Stonehenge, to today). Such a vast range, however, could only be covered in such a perfunctory manner here that it rendered the exercise valueless. It is more appropriate to give examples of some of the influential elements and how they have affected HRM, and to encourage you to identify others for yourself.

Explore

Go back to the models of HRM presented earlier (see Chapter 1) and, working either individually or in a group, start to elaborate upon the various wider contextual elements that they include. Look, for example, at the external forces of the 'matching model' illustrated in Figure 1.2.

- What in detail constituted the elements of the economic, political and cultural forces at the time Devanna *et al.* (1984) were writing? What would they be now?
- What other elements would you add to those, both then and now?
- What are the relationships between them, both then and now?
- And what, in your view, has been their influence upon HRM, both then and now?

Echoes from the wider context

Here the focus will be on distant events from the socio-political sphere that have neverthe-less influenced the management of the employment relationship and still do so indirectly. Although what follows is not a complete analysis of these influences, it illustrates how the field of HRM resonates with events and ideas from its wider context.

The world wars

The two world wars, though distant in time and removed from the area of activity of HRM, have nevertheless influenced it in clearly identifiable and very important ways, some direct and some indirect. These effects can be classified in terms of changed attitudes of manag-ers to labour, changed labour management practices, the development of personnel tech-niques, and the development of the personnel profession. We shall now examine these, and then note how some outcomes of the Second World War continue, indirectly, to influence HRM.

Changed attitudes of managers to labour

According to Child (1969: 44), the impact of the First World War upon industry hastened changes in attitudes to the control of the workplace that had begun before 1914. The develop-ment of the shop stewards' movement during the war increased demand for workers' control; there was growing 'censure of older and harsher methods of managing labour'. The recognition of the need for improved working conditions in munitions factories was continued in the post-war reconstruction debates: Child (1969: 49) quotes a Ministry of Reconstruction pamphlet that advised that 'the good employer profits by his "goodness"'. The outcome of these various changes was a greater democratisation of the workplace (seen, for example, in works councils) and, for 'a number of prominent employers', a willingness 'to renounce autocratic methods of managing employees' and 'to treat labour on the basis of human rather than commodity market criteria' (pp. 45–46). These new values became incorporated in what was emerging as a distinctive body of management thought, practice and ideology, upon which later theory and practice are founded.

Changed labour management practices

The need to employ and deploy labour effectively led to increased attention to working con-ditions and practices during both wars. The changes that were introduced then continued and interacted with other social changes that ensued after the wars (Child, 1969). For exam-ple, the Health of Munitions Workers Committee, which encouraged the systematic study of human factors in stress and fatigue in the munitions factories during the First World War, was succeeded in 1918 by the Industrial Fatigue Research Board [Department of Scientific and Industrial Research (DSIR), 1961; Child, 1969; Rose, 1978]. During the postwar reconstruc-tion period, progressive employers advocated minimum wage levels, shorter working hours and improved security of tenure (Child, 1969).

'The proper use of manpower whether in mobilising the nation or sustaining the war econ-omy once reserves of strength were fully deployed' was national policy during the Second World War (Moxon, 1951). As examples of this policy, Moxon cites the part-time employment of married women, the growth of factory medical services, canteens, day nurseries and special leave of absence.

The development of personnel techniques

Both wars encouraged the application of psychological techniques to selection and training, and stimulated the development of new approaches. Rose (1978: 92) suggests that, in 1917, the American army tested two million men to identify 'subnormals and officer material'. Seymour (1959: 7–8) writes of the Second World War:

the need to train millions of men and women for the fighting services led to a more detailed study of the skills required for handling modern weapons, and our understanding of human skill benefited greatly . . . Likewise, the shortage of labour in industry led . . . to experiments aimed at training munition workers to higher levels of output more quickly.

The wars further influenced the development of the ergonomic design of equipment, and encouraged the collaboration of engineers, psychologists and other social scientists (DSIR, 1961). Moreover, the exigencies of war ensured that attention and resources were focused upon activities that are of great significance to the field of employment, while the scale of operations made available for testing large numbers of candidates, ensuring robust statistics.

The development of the personnel profession

Very significantly, the Second World War had a major influence on the development of the personnel profession. According to Moxon (1951: 7), the aims of national wartime policy were:

(i) to see that the maximum use was made of each citizen, (ii) to see that working and living conditions were as satisfactory as possible, (iii) to see that individual rights were reasonably safeguarded and the democratic spirit preserved. The growth of personnel management was the direct result of the translation of this national policy by each industry and by each factory within an industry.

Child (1969: 11) reports on how government concern in 1940 about appropriate working practices and conditions 'led to direct governmental action enforcing the appointment of personnel officers in all but small factories and the compulsory provision of minimum welfare amenities'. Moxon (1951) comments on the 'four-fold increase in the number of practising personnel managers' at this time (p. 7). Child (1969) records the membership of what was to become the Institute of Personnel Management as 760 in 1939, and 2,993 in 1960 (p. 113). He also notes a similar increase in other management bodies. (The Institute has now become the Chartered Institute of Personnel and Development, with an individual membership of 135,000 in 2013.)

The postwar reconstruction of Japan

The chapter has so far noted some of the direct influences that the two world wars had upon the field of HRM. It now points to an indirect and long-continuing influence. The foundation of the philosophy and practice of total quality management (TQM), which has been of considerable recent significance in HRM, was laid during the Second World War. Edward Deming and Joseph Juran were consultants to the US Defence Department and during the Second World War ran courses on their new approaches to quality control for firms supplying army ordnance (Pickard, 1992). Hodgson (1987: 40) reports that 'vast quantities of innovative and effective armaments were produced by a labour force starved of skill or manufacturing experience in the depression'.

However, after the war, America 'could sell everything it could produce' and, because it was believed that 'improving quality adds to costs', the work of Deming and Juran was then ignored in the West. However, Deming became an adviser to the Allied Powers Supreme Command and a member of the team advising the Japanese on postwar reconstruction (Hodgson, 1987: 40–41). He told them that 'their war-ravaged country would become a major force in international trade' if they followed his approach to quality. They did. Western organisations have since come to emulate the philosophy and practices of quality that proved so successful in Japan and that have led on to, for example, the 'high-performance working of today' (Armitage and Keeble-Allen, 2007).

Wider contextual influences on HRM today

Once again, there are innumerable topics that could be mentioned. The two world wars are, for us, history: interpretations of them have by now become established and, to a large degree, generally accepted, though always open to question. However, those of our own time are not yet fully formed or understood, and may have the potential to unsettle and possibly disrupt established thinking, and hence practice.

The failure of the US sub-prime mortgage market

The case study at the end of the chapter **(p. 100)** indicates responses at the time to the effects of the collapse of financial markets following disastrous investments in the American sub-prime mortgage market. Major firms were shrinking in size or disappearing altogether, small businesses were being lost, unemployment was rising alarmingly, and some taken-for-granted capitalist values were being challenged. The impact on HRM, its practices, policies and strategies, was potentially enormous. It could not be gauged at the time because the story was still unfolding. However, you – who will have had experience of the fallout from those distant beginnings – will be able to identify the subsequent influence on HRM when you answer the questions on that case study.

The impact of social media in organisations

The development of social media has had a major impact on communication and the spread of ideas and attitudes generally, e.g. in politics. In organisations, these media make connections between employees, respond to people's interests and needs, and create and share information outside the formal relationships and communication channels. They have considerable potential to influence HRM (see CIPD, 2013b).

Explore

- What other distant socio-political events or developments have influenced or are influencing HRM?

Ideas and theories in the wider context of HRM

Just as we noted some of the ideas and theories that overlie and intersect with what happens in the immediate context of HRM, so here we note a few of the very many that are influential in the wider context of HRM. We shall pay them and others greater attention later when we examine their underlying assumptions and alternatives to them.

Belief in science

This is the generally accepted view inculcated in the majority of members of our society through the processes of socialisation and education, and sustained through sanctions against deviation. For example, most people have traditionally trusted in rationality and 'orthodox medicine' and have had doubts about the paranormal and 'alternative medicine'. We do not generally question our orthodox beliefs: they 'stand to reason', they work, everyone else seems to think in the same way. By definition, therefore, we do not pay much attention to them; we do not consider how they frame the interpretations we make of our world, or what other alternatives there could be.

The concept of the individual

A key building block in Western thinking is the concept of the individual (Collin, 1996: 9). Its emphasis on individuality, the need for autonomy and fulfilment has underpinned the philosophy and practices of HRM, and is the moral basis for employment conditions and contracts.

Gender differences

Sexual equality and feminist ideas have long been accepted in our society, yet gender differences have continued to be issues. Equal pay, the glass ceiling, the appropriateness of positive discrimination remain live issues in many organisations.

Modernism and postmodernism

These are included as examples of ideas that have been both imported from other disciplines and adopted in the attempt to understand HRM better. They achieved some degree of currency for a while but now appear to have lost it.

These ideas from art and architecture spread through the fields of culture (Harvey, 1990) and the social sciences, and were adopted by some to express a critical perspective in organisation studies (e.g. Gergen, 1992; Hassard and Parker, 1993; Hatch, 1997; Morgan, 1997) and in the HRM field (Townley, 1993; Legge, 1995). Connock (1992) included postmodern thinking among the contemporary 'big ideas' of significance to HR managers, while Fox (1990) interpreted strategic HRM as a self-reflective cultural intervention responding to postmodern conditions. Attempts were made to classify issues of post-industrialism, post-Fordism and the present stage of capitalism in modernist and postmodernist terms (see Reed and Hughes, 1992; Legge, 1995).

Some saw the differences between them in terms of historical period ('post-modern'), others of epistemological position ('postmodern'). For example, Clegg (1990: 180–81) suggested that the modernist organisations with which we had been familiar until the last decade or so of the twentieth century were rigid, addressed mass markets and were premised on technological determinism; their jobs were 'highly differentiated, demarcated and de-skilled'. 'Postmodern' organisations, however, were flexible, addressed niche markets, and were premised on technological choices; their jobs were 'highly de-differentiated, de-demarcated and multiskilled'. Since Clegg's analysis, hierarchical modern organisations have often been contrasted with 'post-modern' networking. As for their epistemological position (discussed later in this chapter), while 'modernism' was based on the belief that there existed a universal objective truth, which we could come to know by means of rational, scientific approaches (though often only with the help of experts), 'postmodernism' denied that. It assumed that truth was local and socially constructed (discussed later in this chapter) from a particular perspective. Instead it recognised the claims of diverse and competing interpretations, and accepted that everything is open to question, that there are always alternative interpretations.

Nevertheless, Legge (1995: 324–25) considered HRM to be both 'post-modern' and 'postmodern'. 'From a managerialist view' it was 'post-modern' in terms of epoch and its basic assumptions (p. 324), whereas 'from a critical perspective' it was a 'postmodernist discourse' (p. 312). HRM, with its ambiguous, or contested, nature, emerged alongside the spread of 'post-modern' organisations and 'postmodern epistemology'. The recognition of multiple, coexisting yet competing realities and interpretations, the constant reinterpretation, the eclecticism, the concern for presentation and re-presentation, the significance of theory lying not in its 'truth' but in its usefulness for practice, could be interpreted as a 'postmodern' rendering of the debate about the nature of the employment relationship. However, its relativity proved to be challenging and unsettling for those socialised into a 'modern' understanding of the world. By the second edition of her book, Legge (2004: 3) considered that there was 'a retreat from postmodern approaches to HRM' and that discussion of HRM as a post-modern/postmodern phenomenon had 'a slightly passé feel'.

It could also be suggested that 'postmodernism' in the social sciences was a forerunner of social constructionism (see later), which has very similar views but which did not become established as a possible alternative to traditional views until somewhat later.

Underlying assumptions

When we examine these examples of the influence of ideas upon the immediate and wider contexts of HRM, we can recognise that they are underpinned by assumptions that differ significantly.

Defining reality

However, we need first to recognise that submerged even more deeply beneath those are the fundamental ways we define reality, which shape the very way we think. Some are so deeply ingrained that they are difficult to identify and express, but they are nevertheless embodied in the way we approach life.

Perception

Human beings cannot approach reality directly, or in a completely detached and clinical manner. The barriers between ourselves and the world outside us operate at very basic levels: 'Despite the impression that we are in direct and immediate contact with the world, our perception is, in fact, separated from reality by a long chain of processing' (Medcof and Roth, 1979: 4).

This processing includes the selection of stimuli to which to respond and the organisation and interpretation of them according to patterns we already recognise. (You can read more about this in Huczynski and Buchanan, 2010.) In other words, we develop a set of filters through which we make sense of our world. Kelly (1955) calls them our 'personal constructs', and they channel the ways we conceptualise and anticipate events (see Bannister and Fransella, 1971).

Defence mechanisms

Our approach to reality, however, is not just through cognitive processes. There is too much at stake for us, for our definition of reality has implications for our definitions of ourselves and for how we would wish others to see us. We therefore defend our sense of self – from what we interpret as threats from our environment or from our own inner urges – by means of what Freud called our 'ego defence mechanisms'. In his study of how such behaviour changes over time, Vaillant (1977: 7) wrote: 'Often such mechanisms are analogous to the means by which an oyster, confronted with a grain of sand, creates a pearl. Humans, too, when confronted with conflict, engage in unconscious but often creative behaviour.'

Freudians and non-Freudians (see Peck and Whitlow, 1975: 39–40) have identified many forms of such unconscious adaptive behaviour, some regarded as healthy, while others are considered unhealthy and distorting. We may not go to the lengths of the 'neurotic' defences that Vaillant (1977: 384–85) describes, but a very common approach to the threats of the complexity of intimacy or the responsibility for others is to separate our feelings from our thinking, to treat people and indeed parts of ourselves as objects rather than subjects. The scene is set for a detached, objective and scientific approach to reality in general, to organisations in particular, and to the possibility of treating human beings as 'resources' to be managed.

Assumptions about organisations

Managers make assumptions about the nature of the organisation, many interpreting it as having an objective reality that exists separately from themselves and other organisational members – they reify it (see Glossary). They make assumptions about the nature of their own and the organisation's goals, which many interpret as rational and objective. However, as the Introductory case study illustrates, these may not be straightforward. Managers make assumptions about the appropriate distribution of limited power throughout the organisation, and how people in the organisation should be regarded and treated.

However, many managers do not identify or question their own assumptions. They leave them unstated, unaddressed and so rarely challenged; thus their actions appear, both to themselves and to others, to be based upon reason and organisational necessity. In the same way, many theorists leave unstated the fact that the organisations about which they write exist within a particular economic system that has to meet the needs of capital. They ignore the material and status needs of owners and managers, and their emotional (Fineman, 1993) and moral selves (Watson, 2000). Many might assert the need for equal opportunities to jobs, training and promotion, but do not necessarily challenge the process of managing itself despite its often gender-blind nature (Hearn *et al.*, 1989; Hopfl and Hornby Atkinson, 2000). Moreover, many other members of the organisation appear to accept those premises on which they are managed, even though those might conflict with their own experiences, or virtually disempower or disenfranchise them. This is also the case with many of the ideas current in the wider context of HRM. They are clearly not espoused by all, but alternatives to them are frequently not made explicit. They tend to be identified and discussed only by those writers who wish to persuade their readers to accept a different interpretation (e.g. Braverman, 1974; Hearn *et al.*, 1989; Calas and Smircich, 1992).

Alternative ways of thinking

The examination we have made of the context of HRM has alerted us to questions about the assumptions that managers and theorists are making. These prompt the recognition that different assumptions might generate different ways of thinking (see Pirsig, 1976). These might include the way we conceptualise, theorise about and manage the employment relationship, and so have important implications for our interpretation of HRM. We shall now examine some of these.

Differing epistemological positions

Positivism

The commonly accepted epistemological position (theory of the grounds of knowledge) in Western thinking is based on *positivism*. This forms the basis of scientific method, and applies the rational and ordered principles of the natural sciences to human affairs generally. It manifests itself (see Heather, 1976; Rose, 1978: 26) in a concern for objectivity, in the construction of testable hypotheses, in the collection of empirical data, in the search for causal relationships and in quantification. It is therefore uneasy with subjective experience, and in research attempts to maintain distance between the researcher and those studied (called 'subjects', though regarded more as objects). Scientific method has informed much social science research, which in turn has reproduced traditional Western interpretations through the kind of new knowledge generated, and hence it 'reigns' in much HRM research (Legge, 1995: 308). It will be clear from the discussion of the immediate context of HRM that many managers and theorists of management espouse it, and it underpins many HRM activities such as psychometric testing for selection and human resource planning models.

We shall pay greater attention here to some of the alternatives to commonly accepted ways of thinking, not only because we are more familiar with it than with them but also because the contrast they make with it emphasises its nature. You could read more about them in Denzin and Lincoln (2005). The approaches here have different origins and, to some extent, values and constituencies. They differ from positivism, being concerned not with objective reality, but with our lived, subjective, experience and interpretations of it. They pose a challenge to conventional thinking which could be perceived as threatening:

> A scientist . . . depends upon his [sic] facts to furnish the ultimate proof of his propositions . . . these shining nuggets of truth . . . To suggest [as Kelly (1955) does] . . . that further human

> reconstruction can completely alter the appearance of the precious fragments he has accumulated, as well as the direction of their arguments, is to threaten his scientific conclusions, his philosophical position, and even his moral security . . . our assumption that all facts are subject . . . to alternative constructions looms up as culpably subjective and dangerously subversive to the scientific establishment.
>
> Bannister and Fransella (1971: 17–18)

Phenomenology

This is concerned with understanding the individual's conscious experience. Rather than analysing this into fragments, it deals with it as a whole, i.e. holistically. It acknowledges the significance of subjectivity, which positivism subordinates to objectivity. Phenomenological researchers try to make explicit the conscious phenomena of experience of those they study, seeking access to them empathically, through shared meanings and inter-subjectivity. This is not a commonplace approach in the field of HRM and management (Sanders, 1982), although it is sometimes discussed in qualitative research studies.

Constructivism and social constructionism

Constructivism and social constructionism are also concerned with individual experience. The differences between them are often not clearly stated but, for our purpose, constructivism emphasises the individual's cognitive processes. It does not deny the existence of an external reality, but holds that we cannot know it, only the models of it that we construct ourselves: 'each individual mentally constructs the world of experience . . . the mind is not a mirror of the world as it is, but functions to create the world as we know it' (Gergen, 1999: 236). (Note that some constructivists appear to retain something of the positivist approach.)

We deal with social constructionism in more detail because it is a greater challenge to conventional thinking. It does not assume that a reality independent of the observer exists. Reality is only what we construct ourselves, and that not through our own cognitive processes, as with constructivism, but through the social processes of language, discourse and social interaction (see Raskin and Bridges, 2002). As Checkland (1981: 277) stated: 'Human beings in the social process are constantly creating the social world in interaction with others. They are negotiating their interpretations of reality, those multiple interpretations at the same time constituting the reality itself.'

To make sense of our experiences, we have to interpret and negotiate meaning with others. There can be no single objective meaning but, Hoffman (1990: 3) suggests:

> an evolving set of meanings that emerge unendingly from the interactions between people. These meanings are not skull-bound and may not exist inside what we think of as an individual 'mind'. They are part of a general flow of constantly changing narratives.

Hence social contructionism has considerable significance for HRM. It recognises that multiple and competing views of organisations and HRM are legitimate; that the significance of theory lies not in its 'truth' but in its usefulness for practice.

Social constructionism throws into question (Kvale, 1992; Hassard and Parker, 1993) the traditional (Western) understanding of the individual as a 'natural entity', independent of society, with 'attributes' that can be studied empirically, a natural object, bounded, reified, highly individualised and autonomous, having rather than being a self (Collin, 1996: 9). That orthodox interpretation has provided the foundation for HRM thinking and practices, such as psychometric testing, competencies and assessment, but social constructionism challenges that (Brittain and Ryder, 1999).

This epistemological position also recognises that *knowledge is constructed* and a social phenomenon (Hoffman, 1990). Far from being objective and universal as in scientific thinking, it is constructed through the interplay of relationships, the workings of power, and often the dominance of the most powerful. Hence social constructionism uncovers how traditional ways of thinking are reproduced through ideologies and hegemony (see the section on 'hegemony' later in this chapter). It asks 'What truth?', 'Whose truth?' and 'Who says so?'. Hence it challenges the authority of the established view, for example, of the 'meta-narratives' of 'progress', 'the value of science' or 'Marxism vs capitalism', which had become the accepted framework of twentieth-century understanding. It makes a critical interpretation of established bodies of thought such as psychology (Kvale, 1992), which could be seen as a Western cultural product (Stead and Watson, 1999). It also encourages self-reflexivity and, therefore, a critical suspicion towards one's own interpretations, and an ironic and playful treatment of one's subject.

Traditional thinking assumes that language is neutral, 'the vehicle for communicating independent "facts"' (Legge, 1995: 306). The constructionist argument, however, is that this is not the case (see Reed and Hughes, 1992; Hassard and Parker, 1993). Rather than depicting objective reality, *language constructs meaning*. Weick (1979: 1) quotes a baseball story that illustrates this nicely:

> Three umpires disagreed about the task of calling balls and strikes. The first one said, 'I calls them as they is.' The second one said, 'I calls them as I sees them.' The third and cleverest umpire said, 'They ain't nothin' till I calls them.'

Language 'itself constitutes or produces the "real"' (Legge, 1995: 306). Moreover, it is 'ideological' (Gowler and Legge, 1989: 438), both the means through which ideologies are expressed and the embodiment of ideology, and can work through rhetoric (discussed later in this chapter). This can be seen in sexist and racist language, and in 'management-speak'.

Social constructionism highlights the significance of *discourse*. 'Why do we find it so congenial to speak of organisations as structures but not as clouds, systems but not songs, weak or strong but not tender or passionate?' (Gergen, 1992: 207). The reason, Gergen goes on to say, is that we achieve understanding within a 'discursive context', and the organisational context understands structure. A discourse is a 'set of meanings, metaphors, representations, images, stories, statements and so on that in some way together produce a particular version of events' (Burr, 1995: 48), a version belonging to a particular group of people. It provides the language and meanings whereby members of that group can interpret and construct reality, and gives them an identifiable position to adopt upon a given subject, thereby constituting their own identity, behaviour and reality (Gavey, 1989). By interpreting competing positions in its own terms, the group's discourse shuts down all other possible interpretations but its own. For example, in order to engage in academic discourse, academics have to learn (Parker and Shotter, 1990: 9):

> a vocabulary and a set of analytic procedures for 'seeing' what is going on . . . in the appropriate professional terms. For we must see only the partially ordered affairs of everyday life, which are open to many interpretations . . . as if they are events of a certain well-defined kind.

Using the contrast between 'everyday talk' and academic writing, Parker and Shotter (1990: 2–3) explain how academic text standardises its interpretations:

> The strange and special thing about an academic text . . . is that by the use of certain strategies and devices, as well as already predetermined meanings, one is able to construct a text which can be understood (by those who are a party to such 'moves') in a way divorced from any reference to any local or immediate contexts. Textual communication can be (relatively)

> decontextualised. Everyday talk, on the other hand, is marked by its vagueness and openness, by the fact that only those taking part in it can understand its drift; the meanings concerned are not wholly predetermined, they are negotiated by those involved, on the spot, in relation to the circumstances in which they are involved. . . . Everyday talk is situated or contextualised, and relies upon its situation (its circumstances) for its sense.

There are many discourses identifiable in the field of organisation and management studies – managerial, humanist, critical, industrial relations – that offer their own explanations and rhetoric. You can explore them further in, for example, the chapters that follow, and in Clark *et al.* (1994), but you should remain aware that academic discourse itself enables writers to exercise power over the production of knowledge and to influence their readers. Awareness of discourse is also important for the understanding of organisations (Baxter, 1999: 49):

> organisational life is made up of many 'discourses' – that is, flows of beliefs, experiences, meanings and actions. Each of these discourses shapes the behaviour of the organisation and of teams and individuals within it. These discourses are in turn created and reworked by individuals' actions and their expressed beliefs. This may not sound much, but it shifts the management of change, for example, from a simplistic view of changing culture, processes and structures to one of altering these aspects of organisational life by building on and reshaping the various discourses flowing around a company.

As also suggested by Pepper's (1942) contextualism, discussed later in this chapter, this view of the social construction of meaning implies that we cannot separate ourselves from our created reality: 'man [*sic*] is an animal suspended in webs of significance he himself has spun' (Geertz, 1973: 5). This approach emphasises the significance of perspective, the position from which an interpretation is made (remember *The Guardian* advertisement at the start of this chapter?).

While the social construction of meaning appears a very abstract notion, it is apparent in everyday life in the stories we tell: narrative is how we make meaning (Polkinghorne, 1988). 'We dream in narrative, daydream in narrative, remember, anticipate, hope, despair, believe, doubt, plan, revise, criticise, construct, gossip, learn, hate, and love by narrative' (Hardy, 1968: 5). Listening to narratives is an approach increasingly favoured by those trying to understand organisations (Gabriel, 2000).

The reproduction of traditional thinking

In the face of so many possible alternatives, how has traditional thinking come about? Social constructionism uncovers some of the mechanisms whereby it is reproduced.

Ideology

Gowler and Legge (1989) define ideology as 'sets of ideas involved in the framing of our experience, of making sense of the world, expressed through language' (p. 438). It has a narrower focus than the traditional ways of thinking we have been discussing in previous sections, and can be seen as a localised orthodoxy, a reasonably coherent set of ideas and beliefs that often goes unchallenged. According to Sloan (1992: 174): 'Ideology operates as a reifying, congealing mechanism that imposes pseudoresolutions and compromises in the space where fluid, contradictory, and multivalent subjectivity could gain ground.'

Ideology purports to explain reality objectively, but within a pluralist society it actually represents and legitimates the interests of members of a subgroup. It is a 'subtle combination of facts and values' (Child, 1969: 224), and achieves its ends through language and rhetoric. What we hear and what we read are conveying someone else's interpretations. The way those are expressed may obscure the ideology and vested interest in those interpretations. For example, in contrast to the generally accepted view of culture, Jermier argues that culture is 'the objectified product of the labour of human subjects . . . there is a profound forgetting of the fact that the world is socially constructed and can be remade . . . . Exploitative practices are mystified and concealed' (Frost *et al.*, 1991: 231).

As you will recognise from this chapter, the organisation is an arena in which ideologies of many kinds are in contest: capitalism and Marxism, humanism and scientific approaches to the individual, feminism and a gender-biased view.

Child (1969) discusses the ideology embodied in the development of management thinking, identifying how the human relations approach chose to ignore the difference of interests between managers and employees and how this dismissal of potential conflict influenced theory and practice. Commentators such as Braverman (1974), Frost *et al.* (1991) and Rose (1978), and many of the readings in Clark *et al.* (1994), will help you to recognise some of the ideologies at work in this field.

Hegemony

Hegemony is the exertion of a group's authority over subordinate groups by imposing its definition of reality over other possible definitions, with the result that less powerful people are disempowered, overlooked, remain silent and left without a 'voice' (Mishler, 1986; Bhavnani, 1990).

This does not have to be achieved through direct coercion, but by 'winning the consent of the dominated majority so that the power of the dominant classes appears both legitimate and natural'. In this way, subordinate groups are 'contained within an ideological space which does not seem at all "ideological": which appears instead to be permanent and "natural", to lie outside history, to be beyond particular interests' (Hebdige, 1979: 15–16).

It is argued that gender issues are generally completely submerged in organisations and theories of them (Hearn *et al.*, 1989; Calas and Smirich, 1992; Hopfl and Hornby Atkinson, 2000) so that male-defined realities of organisations appear natural, and feminist views unnatural and shrill. You could use the readings in Clark *et al.* (1994) to identify instances of hegemony and the outcomes of power relations, such as the 'management prerogative'. Watson (2000) throws light on the manager's experience of these.

Rhetoric

Rhetoric is 'the art of using language to persuade, influence or manipulate' (Gowler and Legge, 1989: 438). '*[I]ts high symbolic content allows it to reveal and conceal but above all develop and transform meaning*' (Gowler and Legge, 1989: 439, their italics). It '*heightens and transforms meaning by processes of association, involving both evocation and juxtaposition*'. In other words, its artfulness lies in playing with meanings, and it can be used for various effects. It is something with which we are familiar, whether as political 'spin' or as the terminology used in effecting organisational change (Atkinson and Butcher, 1999). In the 'eco-climate' of an organisation, where meanings are shared and negotiated, power and knowledge relations are expressed rhetorically. For example, changes to structure and jobs might be described as 'flexibility' rather than as the casualisation of work, and increased pressures upon employees as 'empowerment'. Legge (1995: xiv) proposes that one way of interpreting HRM is to recognise it as 'a rhetoric about how employees should be managed to achieve competitive advantage' that both 'celebrates' the values of its stakeholders while 'at the same time mediating the contradictions of capitalism'. In other words, it allows those stakeholders to 'have their cake and eat it'. Nevertheless, Eccles and Nohria (1992: 10) regard rhetoric as

something that can be used and abused, but it *cannot* be avoided [original italics]. Rather, it constantly serves to frame the way we see the world. In our view, rhetoric is used well when it mobilises actions of people in a way that contributes both to the individuals as people and to the performance of organisations as a whole.

It is effective when it is flexible enough 'to incorporate the different meanings, emphases, and interpretations that different people will inevitably give it' (p. 35).

Differing 'world hypotheses'

Writing about Kelly's (1955) personal construct theory, Bannister and Fransella (1971: 18) argue: 'we cannot contact an interpretation-free reality directly. We can only make assumptions about what reality is and then proceed to find out how useful or useless those assumptions are.' However, we have developed our assumptions from birth, and they have been refined and reinforced by socialisation and experience so that, generally, we are not even aware of them. We do not, therefore, generally concern ourselves with the theory of knowledge, or epistemology, and often find the discussion of philosophical issues difficult to follow. Nevertheless, we are undoubtedly making significant assumptions about 'what it is possible to know, how may we be certain that we know something' (Heather, 1976: 12–13). These assumptions underpin thinking and contribute to the filters of perception: they therefore frame any understanding of the world, including the ways in which researchers, theorists and practitioners construe HRM. To understand something of HRM, we need at least to recognise some of the implications of these epistemological and philosophical issues.

Pepper's (1942) 'world hypotheses' help us distinguish some of the fundamentally different assumptions that can be made about the world. He classifies them as two pairs of polarised assumptions. The first pair is about the universe. At one pole is the assumption that there is an ordered and systematic universe, 'where facts occur in a determinate order, and where, if enough were known, they could be predicted, or at least described' (Pepper, 1942: 143). At the other pole, the universe is understood as a 'flowing and unbroken wholeness' (Morgan, 1997: 251), with 'real indeterminateness in the world' (Harré, 1981: 3), in which there are 'multitudes of facts rather loosely scattered and not necessarily determining one another to any considerable degree' (Pepper, 1942: 142–43). Pepper's second polarity is about how we approach the universe: through analysis, fragmenting a whole into its parts in order to examine it more closely, or through synthesis, examining it as a whole within its context.

Western thinking stands at the first pole in both pairs of assumptions: it takes an analytical approach to what is assumed to be an ordered universe. Hence 'we are taught to break apart problems, to fragment the world' (Senge, 1990: 3); we examine the parts separately from their context and from one another, 'wrenching units of behaviour, action or experience from one another' (Parker, 1990: 100). These approaches, which underpin the scientific approach and positivism outlined earlier, lead us in our research to examine a world that we interpret as 'abstract, fragmented, precategorized, standardised, divorced from personal and local contexts or relevance, and with its meanings defined and controlled by researchers' (Mishler, 1986: 120).

By contrast, and of particular relevance to this chapter, there is 'contextualism'. This is Pepper's world hypothesis that espouses the assumptions at the second pole of both pairs above. This regards events and actions as processes that are woven into their wider context, and so have to be understood in terms of the multiplicity of interconnections and interrelationships within that context. This is what our tapestry metaphor has attempted to convey. We can use further metaphors to glimpse just how different this view is from our orthodox understanding of the world: from the user's perspective, the latter is like using a library, while the former is more like using the internet (Collin, 1997). The information in a library is structured and classified by experts in a hierarchical system according to agreed conventions; users have to follow that system, translating their needs for information into a form recognised by that system. The internet, however, is an open-ended network of providers of information, nonlinear, constantly changing and expanding. It presents users with a multitude of potential connections to be followed at will and, moreover, the opportunity to participate through dialogue with existing websites or through establishing their own web page or blog.

Differences as basic as those between Pepper's world hypotheses inevitably lead to very different ways of seeing and thinking about reality and, indeed, of understanding our own role in the universe. However, we are rarely aware of or have reason to question our deepest assumptions. Not only does our generally accepted approach itself impede our recognition of these epistemological issues, but the processes of socialisation and education in any given society nudge its members in a particular direction [although some may wander off the highway into the byways or, like the author of *Zen and the Art of Motorcycle Maintenance* (Pirsig, 1976), into what are assumed to be badlands]. It can be easier to discern these issues in the contrast offered by the epistemological positions adopted in other societies. We can, for example, recognise more of our own deeply embedded assumptions when we encounter a very different world view such as revealed in an anthropologist's account of his apprenticeship to a Yaqui sorcerer (Castaneda, 1970). Of this, Goldschmidt (1970: 9–10) writes:

> Anthropology has taught us that the world is differently defined in different places. It is not only that people have different customs; it is not only that people believe in different gods and expect different post-mortem fates. It is, rather, that the worlds of different peoples have different shapes. The very metaphysical presuppositions differ: space does not conform to Euclidean geometry, time does not form a continuous unidirectional flow, causation does not conform to Aristotelian logic, man [*sic*] is not differentiated from non-man or life from death, as in our world . . . The central importance of entering worlds other than our own – and hence of anthropology itself – lies in the fact that the experience leads us to understand that our own world is also a cultural construct. By experiencing other worlds, then, we see our own for what it is . . .

Most of the epistemological threads in the tapestry examined in this chapter reflect Western orthodoxy [note how this has exerted hegemony (discussed earlier; **also see Glossary**) over non-Western thinking (Stead and Watson, 1999)]. However, this orthodoxy itself might be gradually changing; some commentators have argued that it has reached a 'turning point' (Capra, 1983), that they can detect signs of a 'paradigm shift' **(see Glossary)**. Indeed, over the last decade or so there have emerged new developments in the natural sciences (see below), and elsewhere (e.g. feminist thinking; see the following section) that challenge accepted thinking.

Explore

- How could you use Pepper's ideas to explain the challenges to conventional thinking made by social constructionism?

Feminist thinking

Recognition of the differences between the world-views of women and men challenges what is increasingly regarded as the male world-view of the positivist approach (Gilligan, 1982; Spender, 1985). Gilligan's (1982) landmark study concluded that women value relationship and connection, whereas men value independence, autonomy and control. Bakan (1966) made a distinction between 'agency' and 'communion', associating the former with maleness and the latter with femaleness. Agency is 'an expression of independence through self-protection, self-assertion and control of the environment' (Marshall, 1989: 279), whereas the basis of communion is integration with others: 'The agentic strategy reduces tension by changing the world about it; communion seeks union and cooperation as its way of coming to terms with uncertainty. While agency manifests itself in focus, closedness and separation, communion is characterised by contact, openness and fusion' (Marshall, 1989: 289).

Therefore, Marshall (1989) argues, feminist thinking 'represents a fundamental critique of knowledge as it is traditionally constructed . . . largely . . . by and about men' and either ignores or devalues the experience of women:

its preoccupation with seeking universal, immutable truth, failing to accept diversity and change; its categorisation of the world into opposites, valuing one pole and devaluing the other; its claims of detachment and objectivity; and the predominance of linear cause-and-effect thinking. These forms reflect male, agentic experiences and strategies for coping with uncertainty. By shaping academic theorising and research activities, they build male power and domination into the structures of knowledge . . . (p. 281)

Calas and Smircich (1992: 227) discuss how gender has been 'mis- or under-represented' in organisation theory, and explore the effects of rewriting it in. Those would include the correction or completion of the organisational record from which women have been absent or excluded, the assessment of gender bias in current knowledge, and the making of a new, more diverse organisation theory that covers topics of concern to women. Hopfl and Hornby Atkinson (2000) point to the gendered assumptions made in organisations, while Hearn *et al.* (1989) identify similar shortcomings in organisation theory in their discussion of the sexuality of organisations.

However, it is important to note that it is only the non-positivist forms of feminist thinking that are cited here: in other words, there are also positivist versions.

Systems and ecological thinking

Systems thinking takes a different perspective from that of traditional Western thinking, and has much in common with ecological thinking. It allows us to see the whole rather than just its parts and to recognise that we are a part of that whole: we argued at the start of the chapter that this was needed for the understanding of context. It registers patterns of change, relationships rather than just individual elements, a web of interrelationships and reciprocal flows of influence rather than linear chains of cause and effect. As with feminist thinking, there are both positivist and alternative views of systems, but here we are concerned with the latter. For example, in his 'soft systems methodology', Checkland (1981) employs systems not as 'descriptions of actual real-world activity' (p. 314), but as 'tools of an epistemological kind which can be used in a process of exploration within social reality' (p. 249).

The concept of system denotes a whole, complex entity, comprising a hierarchy of subsystems, where the whole is greater than the sum of its parts. Much of what has been written about systems draws upon General Systems Theory, a meta-theory that offered a way to conceptualise phenomena in any disciplinary area. Very importantly, the systems approach does not argue that social phenomena are systems, but rather that they can be modelled (conceptualised, thought about) as though they had systemic properties. The concept of system used in the social sciences is therefore a very abstract kind of metaphor. However, we can give only a brief outline of systems concepts here: you will find further detail in Checkland (1981), Checkland and Scholes (1990), Senge (1990) and Morgan (1997). [Note that, while Checkland and Scholes (1990) updates the methodology of Checkland (1981), it does not repeat the discussion of its philosophical underpinnings.]

Systems may be 'open' (like biological or social systems) or 'closed' to their environment (like many physical and mechanical systems). As shown in Figure 3.2, the open system imports from, and exchanges with, its environment what it needs to meet its goals and to survive. It converts or transforms these inputs into a form that sustains its existence and generates outputs that are returned to the environment either in exchange for further inputs or as waste products. The environment itself comprises other systems that are also drawing in inputs and discharging outputs. Changes in remote parts of any given system's environment can therefore ripple through that environment to affect it eventually. There are feedback loops that enable the system to make appropriate modifications to its subsystems in the light of its changing environment. Thus the system constantly adjusts to achieve equilibrium internally and with its environment.

Reflecting upon the management approaches identified earlier, we can now recognise that the scientific management, human relations and perhaps also the humanistic approaches

Figure 3.2 Model of an open system

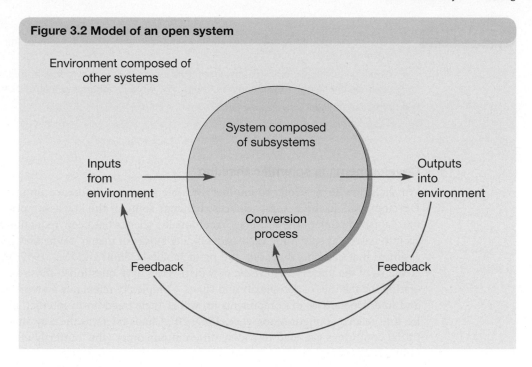

treated the organisation as a closed system, whereas the human resource approach recognises it as open to its environment. Brunsson's (1989) identification of the 'action' and 'political' organisations could also be seen as an open systems approach.

The significance of systems thinking, then, lies in its ability to conceptualise complex, dynamic realities – the system and its internal and external relationships – and model them in a simple, coherent way that is capable of further elaboration when necessary. This means that we can use it to hold in our minds such complex ideas as those discussed in this book, without diminishing our awareness of their complexity and interrelationships.

According to Senge (1990: 12–13), systems thinking is essential for the development of the effective organisation – the learning organisation:

> At the heart of a learning organisation is a shift of mind – from seeing ourselves as separate from the world to connected to the world, from seeing problems as caused by someone or something 'out there' to seeing how our own actions create the problems we experience. A learning organisation is a place where people are continually discovering how they create their reality. And how they can change it.

Systems thinking therefore enables us to contextualise organisations and HRM. It conceptualises an organisation in an increasingly complex and dynamic relationship with its complex and dynamic global environment. Changes in one part of the environment – climate change, collapse of the banks, failed harvests, wars – can change the nature of the inputs – raw materials, money and other resources – into an organisation. This can lead to the need for adjustments in and between the subsystems – new marketing strategies, technologies, working practices – either to ensure the same output or to modify the output. The environment consists of other organisations, the outputs of which – whether intentionally or as by-products – constitute the inputs of others. A change in output, such as a new or improved product or service, however, will constitute a change in another organisation's input, leading to a further ripple of adjustments. Consider, for example, how flexible working practices and call centres have been developed. Sherwood (2002) illustrates how to apply systems thinking to practical HRM issues.

- How would you represent an organisation in a changing world in terms of the open systems model?
- Working individually or in groups, identify its inputs (where they come from, and how they could be changing), how it converts these, and what its (changing?) outputs might be.
- What are its feedback mechanisms?

Developments in scientific thinking

We shall now turn briefly to another possible source of influence upon the HRM field. Developments in the natural sciences challenge some of the key assumptions of Newton's mechanistic notion of the universe. Traditionally, science has been 'reductionist' in its analysis into parts and search for 'the basic building blocks of matter' (Wheatley, 1992: 32). It had assumed that 'certainty, linearity, and predictability' (Elliott and Kiel, 1997: 1) were essential elements of the universe. However, new discoveries have questioned those assumptions, generating the theories of complexity and chaos. Complexity refers to a system's 'interrelatedness and interdependence of components as well as their freedom to interact, align, and organise into related configurations' (Lee, 1997: 20). Chaos refers to the way small differences in initial conditions can lead to widely different outcomes (the 'butterfly effect'). As Morgan (1997: 262) wrote:

> Because of this internal complexity, random disturbances can produce unpredictable events and relationships that reverberate throughout a system, creating novel patterns of change . . . however, . . . despite all the unpredictability, coherent order *always* [emphasis in original] emerges out of the randomness and surface chaos.

To understand complexity, new approaches that recognise the whole rather than just its parts – a holistic approach – and attention to relationships between the parts are needed, and these are being developed.

Although theories of complexity and chaos are sometimes referred to as a 'postmodern science', this is a 'common misconception', for 'while recognising the need for a modification of the reductionist classical model of science, [these theories] remain grounded within the "scientific" tradition' (Price, 1997: 3). They are, nevertheless, recognised as relevant to the understanding of complex social systems. For example, 'chaos theory appears to provide a means for understanding and examining many of the uncertainties, nonlinearities, and unpredictable aspects of social systems behaviour' (Elliott and Kiel, 1997: 1). The literature on the application of these theories to social phenomena tends to be very demanding (e.g. Eve *et al.*, 1997; Kiel and Elliott, 1997). However, Morgan's (1997) and Wheatley's (1992) applications to organisations are more accessible. There has been some application in the HRM field. For example, Cooksey and Gates (1995) use non-linear dynamics and chaos theory as a way of conceptualising how common HRM practices translate into observable outcomes. Brittain and Ryder (1999: 51) draw on complexity theory in their attempt to improve the assessment of competencies, and conclude that 'HR professionals and psychologists need to challenge widely held beliefs about assessment processes, move away from simplistic assumptions about cause and effect and take a more complex view of the world.'

- What similarities do you see between systems thinking and these developments in science?

Ethical issues in HRM

Ethics is the branch of philosophy that concerns the values of right and wrong in human conduct, and such considerations are inherent in managing people in organisations. Indeed, the professional practice of HRM has ethical standards on a wide range of topics, such as health and safety and the need for equity and fairness in employment, compensation and appraisal. You can read about some of the debates on these issues in Greenwood (2002) and Winstanley and Woodall (1996, 2000).

Ethics are also an issue at the corporate and strategic level, their significance highlighted by the growing reputation of stakeholder theory (Freeman, 1984). The CIPD (2013c) is concerned that the needs and interests of stakeholders be recognised, that relationships be based on confidence, trust and respect, and that practices provide opportunity, diversity, inclusion and dignity. And there is now considerable interest in the development of the 'third generation' of quality management (Foster and Jonker, 2007) in which emphasis is placed on the social network of stakeholders and on relational and not just instrumental values.

Our examination of the context of HRM has drawn attention to issues that raise ethical questions. We have noted that managers have to respond to the tensions in their organisations generated by:

* the existence of several stakeholders in the employment relationship;
* their differing aims, interests and needs;
* their differing perspectives upon and interpretations of events, experiences and relationships;
* the interplay between formal organisation and individual potential and needs.

The strategy they choose to adopt will affect employees differently and so it has an ethical dimension. Similarly, there are ethical issues raised in the Introductory case study. These are clearly visible, but are they openly discussed? What we have noted of the workings of ideology and hegemony suggests that the basis of many management decisions will not only be obscured but will benefit a powerful minority, not the majority of employees.

The chapter has also emphasised that there are alternative, and very different, ways of thinking that are based on interpretations of reality and underlying assumptions. However, many of those assumptions are obscured or submerged and so are not open to interrogation or debate. Indeed, the managers themselves might not be fully aware of them, and so might be unable to take them into account when making their decisions. Equally, they might be unaware of the interpretations and underlying assumptions of their colleagues, superiors or subordinates, and hence would not be fully aware of all factors they needed to know in order to act ethically (and effectively).

So attention to context promotes recognition of the need for managers to be aware of epistemological and other underlying assumptions on which their decisions are made. In order to act ethically and responsibly, they need to be willing to question themselves and to reflect on the implications of their views; to be transparent and discuss their assumptions; to listen and give due weight and representation to others' thinking; and to have policies to deal with issues of conscience.

Concluding comments

This chapter has responded to the challenge of representing context by using the metaphor of a tapestry. We have pulled out for examination various strands of meaning that managers and academics are drawing upon to construct – i.e. both to create and to make sense of – HRM. The basic foundations of society are the warp threads that run the length of the tapestry, while alternative ways of thinking are the weft. Woven together, they produce the context that has HRM interwoven into it. The nature of the threads is generally not visible on the surface, but they are more apparent when the tapestry is turned over. Issues and events such as multiculturalism, NEETs (young people who are not in education, employment, or training), workfare, European directives and the Eurozone constitute the surface stitching that is drawn through the warp and weft and elaborate the pattern that is HRM.

Multiple meanings are continuously being woven into the organisational and conceptual pattern that is HRM, and awareness of this allows us to recognise that yet further meanings, and hence potentials for the management of the employment relationship, remain to be constructed.

By pointing to the need to recognise the significance of the context of HRM, this chapter is also acknowledging that you will find herein more interpretations than this book of 'academic text' (Parker and Shotter, 1990), shaped by its writers' own agendas and values and the practicalities of commercial publication, can offer you. The process both of writing and of publication is that of decontextualisation, fragmentation, standardisation and presentation of knowledge as 'entertaining education', in bite-sized chunks of knowledge or sound bites. But by urging you to become aware of the context of HRM, this chapter is at the same time inviting you to look beyond what this book has to say, to recognise the nature of its discourse or, rather, discourses, to challenge its assumptions (and, indeed, your own) and to use your own critical judgments informed by your wider reading and personal experience. This chapter had a further aim (and this betrays this writer's agenda and values), which is to orientate your thinking generally towards an awareness of context, to think contextually, for ultimately awareness of context is empowering. One of the outcomes could well be greater knowledge but less certainty, the recognition that there could be competing interpretations of the topic you are considering, that the several perspectives on the area could all yield different conclusions. Attention to context, therefore, encourages us not to be taken in by our initial interpretations, or to accept unquestioningly the definitions of reality that others would have us adopt (hegemony). There are, however, no easy answers, and we have to make the choice between alternatives. Reality is much messier and more tentative than theory and, like 'everyday talk', it is 'marked by its vagueness and openness', its meaning open to interpretation through negotiation with others. The acceptance of this, however, is one of the marks of the mature learner: the ability to recognise alternative viewpoints but, nevertheless, to take responsibility for committing oneself to one of them.

By definition, one chapter cannot begin to portray the details of the context of HRM. Those, after all, are constantly changing with time. It will have achieved its purpose if it causes you to recognise the significance of context and the need to adopt ways of thinking that enable you to conceptualise it. It can point you in some directions, and you will find many others in the chapters that follow, but there are no logical starting points, because context is indivisible – and you will never reach the end of the story because, from the perspective of context, the story is never-ending.

Summary

- The chapter argues that the keys to the understanding of human affairs, such as HRM, lie within their context. Although context is difficult to conceptualise and represent, readers can draw on their existing understanding of environmental issues to help them comprehend it. Awareness and comprehension of context are ultimately empowering because they sharpen critical thinking by identifying and challenging our own and others' assumptions.

- Multiple interests, conflict and stressful and moral issues are inherent in the immediate context of HRM, which comprises the organisation (the nature of which generates a number of tensions) and management (defined as the continuous process of resolving those tensions). Over time, managers have adopted a range of approaches to their task, including scientific management, the human relations school, humanistic organisation development and HRM. Examination of this immediate context uncovers the existence of some significant assumptions that inform managers' differing practices and the competing interpretations that theorists make of them. It also highlights ethical issues.

- The wider social, economic, political and cultural context of HRM is diverse, complex and dynamic, but some very different and unconnected strands of it are pulled out for examination, such as the legacies of the two world wars in relation to the management of the employment relationship. Other threads are the alternative ways of thinking that locate HRM within a contemporary framework of ideas that challenge assumptions about the management of the employment relationships.

- The chapter, however, finds it insufficient to conceptualise context as layered, like an onion. Rather, HRM is embedded in its context. The metaphor of a tapestry is therefore used to express the way in which its meaning is constructed from the interweaving and mutual influences of the basic structures of society, with alternative ways of thinking derived from perceptual, epistemological, philosophical and ideological positions. These include positivism, phenomenology, constructivism, social constructionism, feminist thinking, systems thinking and new developments in science, which make their impact though ideology, hegemony and rhetoric. People, events and issues are the surface stitching.

- The nature of this tapestry, with its multiple and often competing perspectives, ensures that HRM, as a concept, theory and practice, is a contested terrain. However, the chapter leaves readers to identify the implications of this through their critical reading of the book.

- This examination of context challenges readers to develop their critical thinking and highlights ethical issues.

Questions

1 In what ways does the conceptualisation of context adopted by this chapter differ from more commonly used approaches (e.g. in the models of HRM in Chapter 1)? Does it add to the understanding they give of HRM and, if so, in what way?

2 What assumptions and 'world hypotheses' underpin those models in Chapter 1, and what are the implications for your use of them?

3 What assumptions and 'world hypotheses' appear to underpin the tapestry metaphor of this chapter, and what are the implications for your use of it?

4 Identify some recent events that are likely to play a significant part in the context of HRM.

5 This chapter has been written from a British perspective. If you were working from a different perspective – South African, perhaps, or Scandinavian – what elements of the context of HRM would you include?

6 The chapter has been written for students of HRM. Is it also relevant to practitioners of HRM and, if so, in what way?

Case study

Fear and loathing after the credit crisis

By John Willman

Historical events change behaviour and attitudes. The two world wars, the Great Depression of the 1930s and the 9/11 terrorist attacks on the US each shaped the way a generation thought and acted. The financial crisis will be no different.

Exactly how attitudes will change is not easy to forecast, however. As Niels Bohr, the Danish physicist, once observed, prediction is never easy – particularly about the future. But already some elements of the changed social landscape are emerging.

One is a deep scepticism – loathing, even – of the financial wizards who got the world's markets into this mess. When the House of Representatives voted down Hank Paulson's $700bn bank rescue package on Monday, they did so because they feared the wrath of the voters.

Main Street faced economic ruin with the credit markets closed for business, but those who inhabit it were determined to block any measure that appeared to shore up Wall Street. New York had the feeling of a war zone, said one executive, as angry demonstrators jeered at shell-shocked bankers in the financial district.

The two archbishops at the head of the Church of England also caught the British public mood with their attacks on the City of London last week. Rowan Williams, archbishop of Canterbury and head of the Anglican church, said it was right to ban short selling, while John Sentamu, Archbishop of York, called traders who cashed in on falling prices 'bank robbers and asset strippers'.

'We have all gone to this temple called money,' Dr Sentamu said in an interview. 'We have all worshipped at it. No one is guiltless.'

Full marks for honesty: the Church Commissioners who administer the church's assets had lent stock to short sellers, sold a mortgage portfolio last year and bought shares in the biggest listed hedge fund. But there is little doubt that the archbishops' sentiments were closer to the views of the parishioners who no longer attend their services than those who spoke up for short selling.

Bankers, in any case, have never been popular. In London and New York, they bid up the price of homes, forcing ordinary mortals to commute from ever more distant suburbs. And the arrogance and hubris of a group who felt themselves to be masters of the universe means they are winning no more sympathy in these straitened times than Sherman McCoy did when he fell from grace in Tom Wolfe's *Bonfire of the Vanities*.

A second consequence of the financial crisis, therefore, is likely to be a surge of recruits from the best universities into professions such as teaching, social work and public administration. Investment banking and its support industries have sucked up the talent for two decades, offering an appalling work–life balance in return for sufficient money to permit retirement at 30. Henceforth it will be the teachers and the engineers who will command the envy of the upwardly mobile, with their more secure careers and a positive contribution to society.

A third change is that no one will be able to borrow for many years to come the prodigious amounts of credit offered recently to people with no incomes, no jobs or assets – the so-called Ninjas. But few are likely to want to take out such massively leveraged loans either, given the misery already unfolding for the overborrowed, and the happy fact that homes will be much more affordable as prices continue to plummet.

Lending institutions will return to prehistoric practices, such as requiring homebuyers to save some money before they take on such an expensive commitment. Potential borrowers are unlikely to demur, having become more risk-averse as a result of the credit crunch.

Savers are also becoming more risk-averse – understandably, given the runs on banks around the world. Soaring gold purchases are one symptom, but so are transfers of funds between savings institutions in search of a safe home for savings.

Northern Rock, the UK mortgage bank whose collapse was one of the first of the credit crunch, this week closed several savings accounts to new savers who saw a government-owned institution as a safe haven. Thousands queued to open post office savings accounts run by Bank of Ireland whose deposits are guaranteed by the Irish government.

Before Northern Rock, most savers had no idea about the interest rate on their nest-eggs and 42 per cent always used the same bank. A survey published yesterday by Mintel, the market research group, found most saying they now think carefully about where to save and invest.

Case study continued

Attitudes will also change to society's casualties, who have enjoyed less public sympathy when markets boomed and jobs were plentiful. If the slowdown turns into a recession, expect voters to be more amenable to increased welfare payments.

At the same time, they will become less supportive of public services, as household budgets come under strain and tax cuts look more compelling. Ipsos Mori's regular poll of British attitudes to social issues has already shown concern about the National Health Service, education and defence falling as concern about the economy rises to levels not seen in decades.

None of this will mean there will be no new global crisis in the future. The first world war was not 'the war to end all wars', and the dotcom bust only temporarily blighted the attractions of technology investments. But it will take many years for finance and its high priests to return to their position of unchallenged power – which will be no bad thing.

The writer is UK business editor.

Questions

You can tackle these questions on your own or in a small group. Note the date of this article. It identifies some of the knock-on effects of the 2008–09 global financial crisis that were being experienced in its early stages.

1 The situation has changed considerably in the intervening years since then. To update it, what other events would you need to note?

2 Which of the predictions here have come to pass, and which have failed? Why might this be the case?

3 Make a systems map to help you explain why the situation has developed as it has.

4 What have been the most significant effects of this crisis on organisations?

5 In the light of those, make a systems map and use it to identify what have been the most significant effects on HRM strategies, policies and practice. (If you are working in a group, split into two, one half looking at this from the perspective of an HR director of a large private-sector organisation, and the other from that of an HR director of a public-sector organisation. Compare the two models. Are there differences between them? Why?)

6 Can you identify some of the rhetoric used by bankers and by their critics? What does it tell you about what they believe? What other rhetoric has since developed?

References and further reading

Aldrich, H.E. (1992) 'Incommensurable paradigms? vital signs from three perspectives' in M. Reed and M. Hughes (eds) *Rethinking Organization: New Directions in Organization Theory and Analysis*. London: Sage, pp. 17–45.

Argyris, C. (1960) *Understanding Organisational Behaviour*. London: Tavistock Dorsey.

Armitage, A. and Keeble-Allen, D. (2007) *Using the Past to Improve our Future: Can High Performance Working Learn from TQM?* CIPD: Professional Standards Conference, Keele University.

Atkinson, S. and Butcher, D. (1999) 'The power of Babel: lingua franker', *People Management*, 5, 20: 50–52.

Bakan, D. (1966) *The Duality of Human Existence*. Boston, MA: Beacon.

Bannister, D. and Fransella, F. (1971) *Inquiring Man: The Theory of Personal Constructs*. Harmondsworth: Penguin.

Baxter, B. (1999) 'What do postmodernism and complexity science mean?', *People Management*, 5, 23, 25 November: 49.

Bhavnani, K.-K. (1990) 'What's power got to do with it? empowerment and social research' in I. Parker and J. Shotter (eds) *Deconstructing Social Psychology*. London: Routledge, pp. 141–52.

Braverman, H. (1974) *Labor and Monopoly Capital: The Degradation of Work in the Twentieth Century*. New York: Monthly Review Press.

Brittain, S. and Ryder, P. (1999) 'Get complex', *People Management*, 5, 23, 25 November: 48–51.

Brunsson, N. (1989) *The Organization of Hypocrisy: Talk, Decisions and Actions in Organizations*. Chichester: Wiley.

Burr, V. (1995) *An Introduction to Social Constructionism*. London: Routledge.

Calas, M.B. and Smircich, L. (1992) 'Re-writing gender into organizational theorising: directions from feminist perspectives' in M. Reed and M. Hughes (eds) *Rethinking Organization: New Directions in Organization Theory and Analysis*. London: Sage, pp. 227–53.

Callaghan, G. and Thompson, P. (2002) 'We recruit attitude: the selection and shaping of routine call centre labour', *Journal of Management Studies*, 39, 2: 233–54.

Cameron, S. (1997) *The MBA Handbook: Study Skills for Managers*, 3rd edn. London: Pitman.

Capra, F. (1983) *The Turning Point: Science, Society and the Rising Cultures*. London: Fontana.

Castaneda, C. (1970) *The Teachings of Don Juan: A Yaqui Way of Knowledge*. Harmondsworth: Penguin.

Checkland, P. (1981) *Systems Thinking, Systems Practice*. Chichester: John Wiley.

Checkland, P. and Scholes, J. (1990) *Soft Systems Methodology in Action*. Chichester: John Wiley.

Cherniss, C. and Goleman, D. (eds) (2001) *The Emotionally Intelligent Workplace: How to Select for, Measure, and Improve Emotional Intelligence in Individuals, Groups, and Organizations*. San Francisco, CA: Jossey-Bass.

Child, J. (1969) *British Management Thought: A Critical Analysis*. London: George Allen & Unwin.

CIPD (2012) *The Psychological Contract*, Factsheet. London: CIPD (**www.cipd.co.uk/hr-resources/factsheets**).

CIPD (2013a) *Health and Well-being at Work*, Factsheet. London: CIPD (**www.cipd.co.uk/hr-resources/factsheets**).

CIPD (2013b) *Social Media and Employee Voice: The Current Landscape*, Research Report, March. London: CIPD.

CIPD (2013c) *Corporate Responsibility*, Factsheet. London: CIPD.

Clark, H., Chandler, J. and Barry, J. (1994) *Organization and Identities: Text and Readings in Organisational Behaviour*. London: Chapman & Hall.

Clegg, S.R. (1990) *Modern Organizations: Organization Studies in the Postmodern World*. London: Sage.

Collin, A. (1996) 'Organizations and the end of the individual?', *Journal of Managerial Psychology*, 11, 7: 9–17.

Collin, A. (1997) 'Career in context', *British Journal of Guidance and Counselling*, 25, 4: 435–46.

Concise Oxford English Dictionary (1982) 7th edn. Oxford: Clarendon Press.

Connock, S. (1992) 'The importance of "big ideas" to HR managers', *Personnel Management*, June, pp. 24–7.

Cooksey, R.W. and Gates, G.R. (1995) 'HRM: a management science in need of discipline', *Asia Pacific Journal of Human Resources*, 33, 3: 15–38.

Cooper, R. and Fox, S. (1990) 'The "texture" of organizing', *Journal of Management Studies*, 27, 6: 575–82.

Czerny, A. (2005) 'Lean future looms for HR functions', *People Management*, 11, 11, 2 June: 9.

Denzin, N.K. and Lincoln, Y.S. (eds) (2005) *The SAGE Handbook of Qualitative Research*, 3rd edn. Thousand Oaks, CA: Sage,

Department of Scientific and Industrial Research (DSIR) (1961) *Human Sciences: Aid to Industry*. London: HMSO.

Devanna, M.A., Fombrun, C.J. and Tichy, N.M. (1984) 'A framework for strategic human resource management' in C.J. Fombrun, M.M. Tichy and M.A. Devanna (eds) *Strategic Human Resource Management*. New York: John Wiley, pp. 33–56.

Eccles, R.G. and Nohria, N. (1992) *Beyond the Hype: Rediscovering the Essence of Management*. Boston, MA: Harvard Business School Press.

Elliott, E. and Kiel, L.D. (1997) 'Introduction' in L.D. Kiel and E. Elliott (eds) *Chaos Theory in the Social Sciences: Foundations and Applications*. Ann Arbour, MI: University of Michigan Press, pp. 1–15.

Eve, R.A., Horsfall, S. and Lee, M.E. (eds) (1997) *Chaos, Complexity, and Sociology: Myths, Models, and Theories*. Thousand Oaks, CA: Sage.

Fineman, S. (ed.) (1993) *Emotion in Organizations*. London: Sage.

Foster, D. and Jonker, J. (2007) 'Towards a third generation of quality management: searching for a theoretical re-conceptualisation of contemporary organisations based on the notions of stakeholders and transactivity', *International Journal of Quality & Reliability Management*, 24, 7: 683–703.

Fox, S. (1990) 'Strategic HRM: postmodern conditioning for the corporate culture', in S. Fox and G. Moult (eds) *Postmodern Culture and Management Development*. special edition: Management Education and Development, 21, 3: 192–206.

Freeman, R.E. (1984) *Strategic Management: A Stakeholder Approach*. Boston, MA: Pitman.

Frost, P.J., Moore, L.F., Louis, M.R., Lundberg, C.C. and Martin, J. (1991) *Reframing Organizational Culture*. Newbury Park, CA: Sage.

Gabriel, Y. (2000) *Storytelling in Organizations: Facts, Fictions, and Fantasies*. Oxford: Oxford University Press.

Gavey, N. (1989) 'Feminist poststructuralism and discourse analysis: contributions to feminist psychology', *Psychology of Women Quarterly*, 13: 459–75.

Geertz, C. (1973) *The Interpretation of Cultures*. New York: Basic Books.

Gergen, K.J. (1992) 'Organization theory in the postmodern era', in M. Reed and M. Hughes (eds) *Rethinking Organization: New Directions in Organization Theory and Analysis*. London: Sage, pp. 207–26.

Gergen, K.J. (1999) *An Invitation to Social Construction*. London: Sage.

Gilligan, C. (1982) *In a Different Voice: Psychological Theory and Women's Development*. Cambridge, MA: Harvard University Press.

Goldschmidt, W. (1970) 'Foreword' in C. Castaneda, *The Teachings of Don Juan: A Yaqui Way of Knowledge*. Harmondsworth: Penguin, pp. 9–10.

Gowler, D. and Legge, K. (1989) 'Rhetoric in bureaucratic careers: managing the meaning of management success' in M.B. Arthur, D.T. Hall and B.S. Lawrence (eds) *Handbook of Career Theory*. Cambridge: Cambridge University Press, pp. 437–53.

Greenwood, M. (2002) 'Can HRM be ethical?' *Journal of Business Ethics*, 36: 261–78.

Hardy, B. (1968) 'Towards a poetics of fiction: An approach through narrative', *Novel*, 2: 5–14.

Harré, R. (1981) 'The positivist-empiricist approach and its alternative' in P. Reason and J. Rowan (eds) *Human Inquiry: A Sourcebook of New Paradigm Research*. Chichester: John Wiley, pp. 3–17.

Harvey, D. (1990) *The Condition of Postmodernity*. Oxford: Blackwell.

Hassard, J. and Parker, M. (eds) (1993) *Postmodernism and Organizations*. London: Sage.

Hatch, M.J. (1997) *Organization Theory: Modern, Symbolic and Postmodern Perspectives*. Oxford: Oxford University Press.

Hatchett, A. (2000) 'Call collective: ringing true', *People Management*, 6, 2, January: 40–42.

Hearn, J., Sheppard, D.L., Tancred-Sheriff, P. and Burrell, G. (1989) *The Sexuality of Organization*. London: Sage.

Heather, N. (1976) *Radical Perspectives in Psychology*. London: Methuen.

Hebdige, D. (1979) *Subculture: The Meaning of Style*. London: Methuen.

Higgs, M. and Dulewicz, V. (2002) *Making Sense of Emotional Intelligence*, 2nd edn. London: Previson.

Hodgson, A. (1987) 'Deming's never-ending road to quality', *Personnel Management*, July, pp. 40–44.

Hoffman, L. (1990) 'Constructing realities: an art of lenses', *Family Process*, 29, 1: 1–12.

Holman, D. and Wood, S. (2002) *Human Resource Management in Call Centres*. Sheffield: Institute of Work Psychology.

Hopfl, H. and Hornby Atkinson, P. (2000) 'The future of women's career' in A. Collin and R.A. Young (eds) *The Future of Career*. Cambridge: Cambridge University Press, pp. 130–43.

Hosking, D. and Fineman, S. (1990) 'Organizing processes', *Journal of Management Studies*, 27, 6: 583–604.

Huczynski, A. and Buchanan, D. (2010) *Organizational Behaviour: An Introductory Text*, 7th edn. Harlow: FT/Prentice Hall.

Huse, E.F. (1980) *Organization Development and Change*, 2nd edn. St Paul, MN: West Publishing.

Kanter, R.M. (1983) *The Change Masters*. New York: Simon & Schuster.

Keenoy, T. (1990) 'Human resource management: rhetoric, reality and contradiction', *International Journal of Human Resource Management*, 1, 3: 363–84.

Kelly, G.A. (1955) *The Psychology of Personal Constructs*, vols 1 and 2. New York: W.W. Norton.

Kiel, L.D. and Elliott, E. (eds) (1997) *Chaos Theory in the Social Sciences: Foundations and Applications*. Ann Arbour, MI: University of Michigan Press.

Kvale, S. (ed.) (1992) *Psychology and Postmodernism*. London: Sage.

Lee, M.E. (1997) 'From enlightenment to chaos: towards non-modern social theory', in R.A. Eve, S. Horsfall and M.E. Lee (eds) *Chaos, Complexity, and Sociology: Myths, Models, and Theories*. Thousand Oaks, CA: Sage, pp. 15–29.

Legge, K. (1995) *Human Resource Management: Rhetorics and Realities*. Basingstoke: Macmillan Business.

Legge, K. (2004) *Human Resource Management: Rhetorics and Realities*, 2nd edn. Basingstoke: Palgrave Macmillan.

Mant, A. (1979) *The Rise and Fall of the British Manager*. London: Pan.

Marshall, J. (1989) 'Re-visioning career concepts: a feminist invitation', in M.B. Arthur, D.T. Hall and B.S. Lawrence (eds) *Handbook of Career Theory*. Cambridge: Cambridge University Press, pp. 275–91.

Mayo, A.J. and Nohria, N. (2005) *In Their Time: The Greatest Business Leaders of the 20th Century*. Boston, MA: Harvard Business School Press.

Medcof, J. and Roth, J. (eds) (1979) *Approaches to Psychology*. Milton Keynes: Open University Press.

Mishler, E.G. (1986) *Research Interviewing: Context and Narrative*. Cambridge, MA: Harvard University Press.

Morgan, G. (2006) *Images of Organization*. Thousand Oaks, CA: Sage.

Moxon, G.R. (1951) *Functions of a Personnel Department*. London: Institute of Personnel Management.

Parker, I. (1990) 'The abstraction and representation of social psychology', in I. Parker and J. Shotter (eds) *Deconstructing Social Psychology*. London: Routledge, pp. 91–102.

Parker, I. and Shotter, J. (eds) (1990) 'Introduction' in *Deconstructing Social Psychology*. London: Routledge, pp. 1–14.

Pascale, R.T. and Athos, A.G. (1982) *The Art of Japanese Management*. Harmondsworth: Penguin.

Peck, D. and Whitlow, D. (1975) *Approaches to Personality Theory*. London: Methuen.

Pepper, S.C. (1942) *World Hypotheses*. Berkeley, CA: University of California Press.

Peters, T.J. and Waterman, R.H., Jr (1982) *In Search of Excellence: Lessons from America's Best Run Companies*. New York: Harper & Row.

Pfeffer, J. (1981) *Power in Organizations*. London: Pitman.

Pickard, J. (1992) 'Profile: W. Edward Deming', *Personnel Management*, June, p. 23.

Pickard, J. (1999) 'Emote possibilities: sense and sensitivity', *People Management*, 5, 21, 28 October: 48–56.

Pickard, J. (2005) 'HR will be a philosophy rather than a department', *People Management*, 11, 22, 10 November: 15.

Pirsig, R.M. (1976) *Zen and the Art of Motorcycle Maintenance*. London: Corgi.

Polkinghorne, D.E. (1988) *Narrative Knowing and the Human Sciences*. Albany, NY: State University of New York Press.

Price, B. (1997) 'The myth of postmodern science', in R.A. Eve, S. Horsfall and M.E. Lee (eds) *Chaos, Complexity, and Sociology: Myths, Models, and Theories*. Thousand Oaks, CA: Sage, pp. 3–14.

Pugh, D.S., Hickson, D.J. and Hinings, C.R. (1983) *Writers on Organizations*, 3rd edn. Harmondsworth: Penguin.

Raskin, J.D. and Bridges, S. K. (eds) (2002) *Studies in Meaning: Exploring Constructivist Psychology*. New York: Pace University Press.

Reed, M. and Hughes, M. (eds) (1992) *Rethinking Organization: New Directions in Organization Theory and Analysis*. London: Sage.

Ritzer, G. (1996) *The McDonaldization of Society: An Investigation into the Changing Character of Contemporary Social Life*. Thousand Oaks, CA: Pine Forge Press.

Rose, M. (1978) *Industrial Behaviour: Theoretical Development since Taylor*. Harmondsworth: Penguin.

Sanders, P. (1982) 'Phenomenology: a new way of viewing organizational research', *Academy of Management Review*, 7, 3: 353–60.

Schein, E.H. (1970) *Organizational Psychology*, 2nd edn. Englewood Cliffs, NJ: Prentice Hall.

Schein, E.H. (1978) *Career Dynamics: Matching Individual and Organizational Needs*. Reading, MA: Addison-Wesley.

Senge, P. (1990) *The Fifth Discipline: The Art and Practice of the Learning Organization*. London: Century.

Seymour, W.D. (1959) *Operator Training in Industry*. London: Institute of Personnel Management.

Sherwood, D. (2002) *Seeing the Forest for the Trees: A Manager's Guide to Applying Systems Thinking*. London: Nicholas Brealey.

Sloan, T. (1992) 'Career decisions: a critical psychology', in R.A. Young and A. Collin (eds) *Interpreting Career: Hermeneutical Studies of Lives in Context*. Westport, CT: Praeger, pp. 168–76.

Southgate, J. and Randall, R. (1981) 'The troubled fish: barriers to dialogue' in P. Reason and J. Rowan (eds) *Human Inquiry: A Sourcebook of New Paradigm Research*. Chichester: John Wiley, pp. 53–61.

Spender, D. (1985) *For the Record: The Making and Meaning of Feminist Knowledge*. London: Women's Press.

Stead, G.B., and Watson, M.B. (1999) 'Indigenisation of psychology in South Africa' in G.B. Stead and M.B. Watson (eds)

Career Psychology in the South African Context. Pretoria, South Africa: Van Schaik, pp. 214–25.

Taylor, P., Mulvey, G., Hyman, J. and Bain, P. (2002) 'Work organisation, control and the experience of work in call centres', *Work, Employment and Society,* 16, 1: 133–50.

Townley, B. (1993) 'Foucault power/knowledge, and its relevance for human resource management', *Academy of Management Review,* 18, 3: 518–45.

Vaillant, G.E. (1977) *Adaptation to Life: How the Brightest and Best Came of Age*. Boston, MA: Little Brown.

Watson, T.J. (2000) *In Search of Management: Culture, Chaos and Control in Managerial Work*. London: Thomson Learning.

Weick, K.E. (1979) *The Social Psychology of Organizing*. New York: Random House.

Welch, J. (1998) 'The new seekers: creed is good', *People Management,* 4, 25, 24 December: 28–33.

Wheatley, M.J. (1992) *Leadership and the New Science: Learning about Organization from an Orderly Universe*. San Francisco, CA: Berrett-Koehler.

Whittaker, J. and Johns, T. (2004) 'Standards deliver', *People Management,* 10, 13, 30 June: 32–34.

Winstanley, D. and Woodall, J. (1996) 'Business ethics and HRM' *Personnel Review,* 25, 6, 5–12.

Winstanley, D. and Woodall, J. (eds) (2000). *Ethical issues in contemporary HRM*. Basingstoke: Macmillan.

Zohar, D. and Marshall, I. (2001) *Spiritual Intelligence: The Ultimate Intelligence*. London: Bloomsbury.

Part 2

RESOURCING THE ORGANISATION

Introduction to Part 2

This part deals with how organisations define and meet their needs for labour and how they are influenced by factors both internal and external to the organisation.

For students and practitioners of management, the main theme in recent times has been one of global economic crisis and resulting deep uncertainty in product and labour markets. Intense competition for goods and services remains a key feature of the landscape and something that almost all organisations need to learn to accommodate and respond to. In employment terms, the key reaction has been to reduce the size of workforces and/or look for ways to achieve cost-effective approaches to resourcing, greater labour flexibility and improved levels of employee engagement and retention. In other sectors, more resilient to the effects of economic depression, sophisticated forms of recruitment and selection, designed to seek out the most talented hires, have become paramount in the quest for a sustainable source of competitive advantage.

Chapter 4 explains the labour market context within which the aforementioned employee resourcing decisions are taken. It starts by explaining the concept of the labour market and considering the nature and composition of the labour force in the UK as shaped by a number of demographic factors. Next it examines patterns of labour market participation set against a discussion of the changing nature of demand for labour in the UK. Here we examine how developments in the nature of work and employment have influenced organisational requirements for labour and affected the type and quality of employment opportunities available to different labour market groups. It concludes with a critical assessment of workers' fractured experiences of employment in contemporary Britain.

Chapter 5 takes up the theme of changing organisational requirements for labour by focusing on the growing interest in talent management. The need to attract, retain, motivate and develop individuals is of increasing importance as organisations seek to do more with less and this chapter explores the initiatives used to create and sustain a suitable talent pool to meet future requirements. The chapter also considers the relative merits of 'growing' or 'buying' talent and discusses whether talent management opportunities should apply to the total workforce or only a chosen few.

Chapter 6 picks up the themes of advantage and disadvantage in employment scoped more broadly in Chapter 4, by examining the nature and effects of unfair discrimination in employment, why managers should act to promote fairness at work and the different, sometime conflicting ideas about how they should do so. It highlights the complex nature of the issues raised by attempts to tackle disadvantage due to unfair discrimination. For example, should managers treat all employees the same regardless of ethnicity or gender, or should they take these differences into account when framing their employment policies? Should policies for combating disadvantage aim at equality of opportunity or equality of outcome? It also discusses the significance of the recent tendency to shift the focus of discussion away from the traditional idea of 'equal opportunities' to the concept of 'managing diversity'.

Chapter 4

HRM and the labour market

Amanda Thompson

Objectives

- To explain the nature and composition of the UK labour market.
- To identify the major social forces responsible for shaping the nature and extent of people's engagement with paid employment.
- To highlight developments in the nature of work and employment in the late twentieth and early twenty-first centuries and to show how these trends have influenced organisational requirements for labour.
- To present a critical assessment of workers' experiences of employment in contemporary Britain.

Introductory case study

Underemployment can be as corrosive as unemployment – and it's on the rise

Lots of people are wondering why the employment figures aren't worse, since we're in such a slump. Well, if you measure them properly, they are.

In August 2012, Stephanie Flanders, the BBC's Economics Editor, described it as puzzling, the fact that unemployment hadn't shot up amidst the slump. Her interrogation of the figures prompted Iain Duncan Smith, the Coalition's Work and Pensions Secretary, to accuse Flanders of simultaneously 'dumping on the government' and 'peeing all over British industry'. Ministers, of course, are naturally protective of jobless stats: they're about the only bit of good economic news around to cling on to. At a time when the economy remains wedged in the U-bend, the public-finance targets look either broken or thoroughly bent and the export boom, the surge in business investment and other unicorns promised by the Office for

Budget Responsibility are still stubbornly elusive, at least the labour market affords a less gloomy vista. Even though more than 2.5 million people are out of work, 2012 was the best year for employment growth since the bursting of the dotcom bubble.

The question on the tip of Flanders' tongue is just how this can be, when almost 7,000 public-sector jobs are shed each month and the economy hovers on the edge of a triple-dip recession? One explanation for the rise in employment must be the rise in Britain's population. Another might be that the lull in the growth of dole queues is temporary, and that unemployment will soon pick up. Perhaps the most important explanation though is that the headline figures miss important groups, such as the part-time workers who want to go full-time but can't, or the freelancers and self-employed who are barely attracting enough work or customers to get by. Neither of these groups are out of work; but nor are they fully employed. And while they are included in some totting up by the Office for National Statistics, it is at a pretty basic level.

The underemployment index compiled by David Bell and David Blanchflower, published in the National Institute Economic Review, is probably the best study yet of Britain's hidden unemployment problem. The index totals the net sum of all the extra hours at current wages that Britons want to work, but can't. Until 2007, Bell and Blanchflower find, as many people felt over-worked as felt under-worked. Then came the crash. Today, Britons would work an extra 20 million hours if they could only get them. Had this hidden unemployment been taken into account in the headline figures, according to Bell and Blanchflower, the jobless rate at the end of 2012 would have been not 8 per cent, but 10 per cent.

We're conditioned by previous slumps to think of the victims as those who just can't find work: a Jarrow Marcher, say, or Yosser Hughes. But the face of this depression is the shop worker on a zero-hours contract, the part-timer who can't go full-time, the self-employed consultant whose phone hasn't rung for days. Nominally, these people are in work; in reality, they don't consider that they have a working income. And, Bell and Blanchflower find, full-time employees increasingly want more hours – so they too increasingly count as *underemployed*. This is likely a direct product of how British wages since the banking crisis have failed to keep up with inflation, so that real incomes are now 10 per cent down from 2008 – and show no sign of picking up any time soon. Chronic joblessness leads to mental illness, broken marriages and even suicides; but what's striking in Bell and Blanchflower's study is that the impact of forced *underemployment* is almost as corrosive to one's sense of well-being.

Source: adapted from an article by Aditya Chakrabortty, *The Guardian,* 15 April 2013; http://www.guardian.co.uk/commentisfree/2013/apr/15/underemployment-corrosive-unemployment-on-rise

Introduction

This chapter is concerned principally with the size, composition and condition of the UK labour market and, more specifically, with how the labour market shapes employers' choices concerning people management and utilisation. An appreciation of labour markets and how they operate is especially relevant for students of human resource management (HRM) as human resources (HR) policies and practices are initiated, modified and in some cases abandoned in response to prevailing labour market characteristics and key labour market predictions. Sophisticated forms of selection, for example, become more paramount when labour is in short supply (described as a shortage labour market or 'tight' labour market); organisations must deploy all of their skills to assuredly secure the necessary quantity and quality of resources. Conversely, loose labour markets (a 'surplus' labour market), where unemployment is running high and labour supply exceeds demand, call for a more targeted approach to recruitment and selection in order to identify appropriate resources quickly and efficiently. Understanding the nature and composition of labour markets alongside an appreciation of other external and internal factors having an impact on the organisation facilitates a strategic approach to HRM (for a full assessment of the processes and activities of strategic HRM, see Chapter 2). A strategic stance is considered attractive because it offers organisations scope to select an appropriate employment system and a set of complementary HR practices to 'fit' the external operating environment, placing the firm in a better position to exploit competitive advantage.

The chapter is divided into four main sections to draw upon a range of contemporary labour market issues and consider the significance of each for the practice of HRM. In the first, we discuss the nature of labour markets and the considerations that influence the employment strategies of firms. In the second, we explore recent political and social developments and the implications of these for the supply of labour. The third section explores the changing nature of work and employment and is designed to focus on emergent themes in employers' demand for labour. The final section of the chapter considers key dimensions of job quality and discusses these in relation to workers' experiences of employment in contemporary Britain. Necessarily, the chapter deals with a number of controversial issues some of which are touched on briefly in the opening case; here we see challenges to official employment statistics, doubt cast over the 'true' quantity and quality of work available in the current labour market and an insight into the way in which labour market experiences impact on individuals' health and well-being.

The nature of labour markets

The most general definition of the labour market is that it consists of workers who are looking for paid employment and employers who are seeking to fill vacancies. The amount of labour that is available to firms – *labour supply* – is determined by the number of people of working age who are in employment or seeking employment and the number of hours that they are willing to work. This number will be determined by the size and age structure of the population and by the decisions made by individuals and households about the relative costs and benefits of taking paid employment. These decisions are influenced by various factors, one of which is the level of wages on offer. Generally speaking, a higher wage will attract more people into the labour market, whereas a lower wage will attract fewer people, as long as other factors, such as the level of welfare benefits and people's attitudes towards work, remain constant.

The number of jobs on offer to workers *labour demand* – is the sum of people in employment plus the number of vacancies waiting to be filled. The demand for labour is determined by the level of demand for the goods and services produced by firms in the market. When sales and production are rising, firms' demand for labour rises. When sales stagnate or fall and production is cut back, firms' demand for labour declines. This is aptly illustrated by the job losses incurred as music, film and games retailer HMV closed stores, and sold the Waterstones book chain, the entertainment venue Hammersmith Apollo and HMV Live, which owned 13 live music venues and operated five music festivals in the UK. The retailer HMV's like-for-like sales were down 12.1 per cent in the financial year 2011–12 as it tried unsuccessfully to stave off increased competition, particularly from music downloads (BBC, 2012).

The simplest view of the labour market is that it is an arena of competition. Workers enter the arena in search of jobs and employers enter it in search of workers. Competition between employers for workers and between workers for jobs results in a 'market wage' that adjusts to relative changes in labour demand and supply. Thus, when labour demand rises relative to labour supply, the market wage rises as firms try to outbid each other for scarce labour. When labour demand falls relative to labour supply, the market wage falls as workers compete with each other for the smaller number of available jobs.

Competition means that no individual firm can set a wage that is out of line with the competitive market wage. Neither can workers demand such a wage. Should a firm try to offer a wage that is below the market rate, it will be unable to hire workers. Should a firm set a wage above the market rate, it will go out of business because its costs of production will be above those of its competitors. For the same reason, workers who demand a wage higher than the market rate will price themselves out of jobs. No firm will hire them because to do so would increase their costs of production relative to those of their competitors.

While it is undeniable that competitive forces operate in the labour market to a degree, few would seriously pretend that this is a wholly accurate description of the real world. There are limits to competition between firms and among workers. Wages do not respond instantly to changes in labour demand. Nor is there a uniform wage in the labour market. Empirical research has shown that rates of pay vary between firms, even in the same industry and operating in the same local labour market (Nolan and Brown, 1983). Other employment policies also vary among firms. For example, some firms employ labour on a hire-and-fire basis and make heavy use of casualised forms of employment such as temporary work and zero-hours contracts, while others offer long-term employment security and career development. The policies that employers adopt are influenced to a great extent by the characteristics they seek in their workforce, including:

- *The need for a stable workforce.* A stable workforce is advantageous to employers because it reduces: the costs of labour turnover, i.e. disruption of production due to the unplanned reductions in the workforce that result from workers leaving; the costs of recruitment and selection, such as the financial costs of advertising for recruits and the cost in terms of management time spent in recruiting and selecting replacements; and the cost of training new recruits. These costs may be particularly high where skilled labour is scarce and replacements are hard to find, or where employers have invested considerable amounts in training workers. In these situations, employers have a strong interest in limiting the extent of labour turnover.

- *The need for worker cooperation in production.* A central issue in managing people at work is how to manage their performance. One way of trying to ensure that workers supply the required level of effort is by subjecting them to direct controls (Friedman, 1977). Traditionally, this took the form of direct personal supervision by a superior and externally imposed discipline. Today, direct supervision is supplemented with electronic surveillance, 'mystery customers' and customer questionnaire surveys in a managerial effort to make workers' effort levels increasingly visible. However, there are limits to the extent that employers can rely on direct controls. This is because the nature of the product or the production process often makes it difficult to define what the appropriate effort levels are for each worker and to measure how hard they are actually working. Therefore, employers have to rely on sufficiently motivated workers using their initiative to ensure efficiency and quality in the production of goods and the delivery of services. This makes it difficult for managers to impose effort levels without the workers' agreement. Heavy reliance on supervision and surveillance may also be counterproductive because of the resistance that it can generate among workers. The alternative is to encourage workers to exercise responsible autonomy at work (Friedman, 1977). In other words, it may be more cost-effective for managers to offer positive incentives to ensure that workers cooperate voluntarily with management and use their job knowledge and their initiative to maintain and improve efficiency and quality.

Explore

Think about a range of industries and sectors.
- What types of workforce will have low turnover costs and why?
- What types of workforce will have high turnover costs?

The greater the employer's need for a stable, highly cooperative workforce, the more likely the firm is to introduce policies to retain workers and create a basis for mutual trust and cooperation. These policies, which are associated with the 'best-practice HRM' principle of treating employees as valued assets rather than disposable commodities (see Chapter 2), *internalise* employment by fostering long-term employment relationships and giving workers a degree of protection from external labour market pressures. They include guarantees of long-term

Box 4.1   Contingent labour

An academic study has explored how construction companies use contingent labour, i.e. subcontractors and workers supplied by agencies. It found widespread use of contingent labour, but many firms would have made less use of contingent labour had it not been for the difficulties they had in recruiting directly employed workers. The researchers also found that the vast majority of employers valued long-term relationships with workers even when using contingent contracts and tried to develop long-term relationships with suppliers, especially in the case of subcontract labour and to a lesser extent with temporary agencies.

Source: Forde and Mackenzie (2007).

Questions

1 What advantages are there for construction industry employers in using contingent labour?

2 Why, in view of these advantages, do the great majority of construction employers value long-term employment relationships and seek to foster long-term links with suppliers of contingent labour?

employment security, opportunities for training and internal promotion, fringe benefits and pay that is higher than the market rate. However, these policies are themselves costly. Therefore the extent to which employers seek to internalise employment depends on the cost of labour turnover and the extent of the limits to direct control. Where these are low, employers are more likely to treat labour as a disposable commodity, in other words *externalising* the employment relationship.

It is evident that employers make strategic choices concerning the extent to which they internalise or externalise employment, but these choices are influenced by the specific labour market contexts in which individual firms operate (see Box 4.1). Two key elements of this context are the overall state of the labour market and the way in which the labour market is segmented, giving rise to advantaged and disadvantaged labour market groups. To be able to understand how these influences operate, we first need to examine the two sides of the labour market: labour supply and demand.

The supply of labour

As Marx suggested (Marx, 1932), the worker is a commodity, his existence is bought under the same condition as the existence of every other commodity and he is lucky if he can find a buyer. Given that the labour market is a competitive arena, it follows that firms in competition with one another for workers will be interested in the current and future 'stock' of this good and seek to plan accordingly to be sure to secure the amount they require at any given time. Conventionally, the process of human resource planning involves forecasting the supply and demand for labour so that suitable plans can be put in place to address situations of labour shortage or surplus (see Chapter 5).

The number of people seeking work in the labour market is influenced by factors relating to the size and composition of the population; as such, practitioners of HRM and others involved in human resource planning are advised to keep abreast of shifting populace trends. Within this section of the chapter, we consider the main demographic factors affecting total labour supply, namely population and population change, the age structure of the population, gender and ethnicity.

Population

National population trends

The supply side of the labour market derives from the country's population, specifically, for statistical counting purposes, people aged between 16 and 64 years of age. Clearly, therefore, information on the total size of the current population and predictions of future patterns of population growth and decline are important for estimating the current and future supply of labour.

Population is affected by birth and death rates. When live births exceed the number of deaths, a net natural population increase arises, and when mortality rates exceed birth rates, a net natural decline in population occurs. Population change is also influenced by net migration, i.e. the effect caused by people moving into and out of the country. In the 1950s and 1960s, population growth was largely attributable to net natural change. Within this period, a relatively stable death rate coupled with the baby boom that followed the Second World War caused net natural growth. In the 1980s, the net inflow of migrants began to increase, tilting the key trigger for population growth from net natural change to net migration. Certainly in the years following the early 1990s, migration became a big contributory factor to population growth, continuing through to the mid-2000s when the A8 accession countries joined the European Union (Vargas-Silva, 2013a). Latest census data [Office for National Statistics (ONS), 2012a] show that from the period of the last census in March 2001 to the date of the recent census in March 2011, there were 6.6 million births and 5.0 million deaths in England and Wales, leading to a net natural increase in the population of 1.6 million. At this level, natural change accounts for around 44 per cent of the total increase (3.7 million) in the population size in England and Wales across the period March 2001 to March 2011, with the remainder being due to the effects of migration. Considering the UK as a whole, census 2011 data (ONS, 2013a) show that on the day of the census in March 2011, the population of the UK stood at 63.2 million, the largest it has ever been. Indeed over the last 100 years the population of the UK (as currently constituted) has increased by 21.1 million, representing an increase of 50 per cent (ONS, 2012b). Looking forward, projections indicate that the UK population is set to increase by a further 4.9 million to 67.2 million in the 10-year period 2010–2020, equivalent to an average annual rate of growth of 0.8 per cent (ONS, 2011), and the population will rise further still, exceeding 70 million in 2028 and reaching 73.2 million by 2035 (Rutherford, 2012; see also Table 4.1). Population increases remain, of course, jointly attributable to net natural increase and migration, although in more recent years, net natural increase, driven by the changes in the numbers of births rather than the numbers of deaths, has been propelling population growth as opposed to net migration (Barnes, 2012).

Correspondingly, the net inflow of migrants to the UK is slowing. According to ONS (2013b), 515,000 people immigrated to the UK in the year ending June 2012, significantly lower than the 589,000 people who migrated to the UK in the previous year. The numbers of people leaving the UK, however, were similar for the years ending June 2011 and June 2012. The consequence of declining inflow, set against relatively stable emigration, is a fall in net migration, allowing the situation described above where once again net natural change has become the most important driver of population increase. The data show that the number of migrants coming

Table 4.1 Estimated and projected population of the UK and constituent countries 2010–2035 (figures in 000s)

	2010	2015	2020	2025	2030	2035
United Kingdom	62,261	64,775	67,173	69,404	71,393	73,207
England	52,234	54,468	56,607	58,607	60,410	62,078
Wales	3,006	3,083	3,170	3,250	3,315	3,369
Scotland	5,222	5,365	5,486	5,596	5,686	5,755
Northern Ireland	1,799	1,859	1,910	1,951	1,982	2,005

Source: Rutherford (2012), ONS 2010-based population projections.

to the UK from both New Commonwealth countries and the EU accession countries, such as Poland, Estonia, and the Czech Republic, decreased, as did the number of people entering the UK with study visas and visitor and transit visas. It remains to be seen whether the inflow of migrants will continue to fall; much depends on prevailing political persuasion. Immigration is undoubtedly a critical issue at the ballot box, however, as demonstrated by the success of the UK Independence Party (UKIP) in the May 2013 local elections in England and Wales. Whether or not net migration continues to fall, the effects of migration will continue to influence population growth in the UK as the birth rate in migrant families is taken into account.

The way in which the country's population expands, whether as a result of natural change or migration patterns, affects the gender composition, age profile and ethnic diversity of the labour market. At a local level, patterns of regional population density resulting from a combination of natural causes, international migration and internal migration (the movement of people between regions within the UK) lead to variations in the *amount of labour* available in different parts of the country. While labour tends to move to parts of the country where work is more plentiful, those organisations relying on local labour in areas of the country with low population density and/or net population loss are confronted with a different set of labour market circumstances from those operating in areas of higher population density. ONS (2013a) illustrates that the population density of the UK ranges from 13,871 people per square kilometre in the London Borough of Islington to just nine people per square kilometre in Highland and Eilean Siar, two Scottish local authorities. Outside of London, the most densely populated local authority is Portsmouth with 5,074 people per square kilometre. The age profile, ethnicity and skills mix of workers in local labour markets can also vary considerably, affecting the *type of labour* available. These factors combine to pose different employment challenges and opportunities for firms operating in different regions of the country.

Explore

- Consider how HRM practices aimed at attracting and retaining suitable labour would need to vary according to population density and population composition in different regions of the UK.

Regional population trends

Regional populations form an interesting focal point for study, with important implications for the supply of labour. ONS (2012b) shows that in the period between the two most recent censuses (March 2001 to March 2011), the largest population increases were witnessed in London, the South East, the East Midlands and East England and Northern Ireland. The three local authorities with the largest percentage population increases over the period were Tower Hamlets and Newham in London, with rises of 26.4 per cent and 23.5 per cent, respectively. Outside of London, Dungannon in Northern Ireland saw a 20.9 per cent increase. Meanwhile, local authorities experiencing population decline are concentrated in the West of Scotland and in the North East and North West areas of England. Regional populations reflect births and deaths and the effects of international and internal (within the UK) migration. Some interesting patterns are evident in terms of internal migration. Consistently, those most likely to move regions are young adults; ONS data (2012c) depicts peaks in internal migration at ages 19 and 22, which can be largely attributed to moves to and from universities and other higher education establishments. The capital experiences the greatest net loss through internal migration; for example, in the year ending June 2011, some 40,000 more people moved out of London to other regions than made internal moves to London. London also experiences the highest level of population churn of any region in England and Wales. In terms of regional population gains due to internal migration, the South East region had the largest positive net difference, with approximately 20,700 more migrants arriving than leaving. Indeed, the South East was the recipient region for around 40 per cent of London leavers. As far as local authorities are concerned, Cornwall Unitary Authority was the only authority in the top 10 absolute net flows table to record more migrants arriving than leaving (ONS, 2012c). The effects of international migration can, of course, counter the net losses of within-UK (internal) migration, so while the number of people moving out of London to other parts of England and Wales regularly exceeds those moving to London from other regions in England and Wales, London's population continues to rise as a consequence of the inflow of international migrants.

Age structure of the population

The age structure of the population is a key determinant of labour supply as firms draw employees from the portion of the total population that is of working age. The age structure is closely associated with past trends in migration; such trends, referred to in the previous section, can also be used to explain regional differences in the population's age profile as migrants establish communities in certain areas of the country. White ethnic groups, particularly the white Irish population, have an older age structure than other ethnic groups as a consequence of past fertility and immigration patterns. Among non-white ethnic groups, younger age profiles are exhibited within groups migrating to the UK relatively recently whilst, as might be expected, those groups with an earlier history of large-scale migration to the UK have now begun to contain larger proportions of people within older age brackets.

As well as past trends in migration, the age structures of the total population and of regional populations are affected by trends in births and deaths. Records show a fairly erratic pattern in the number of live births occurring in the UK at different phases throughout the twentieth century. Notable decreases in the number of births occurred during the two world wars (1914–1918 and 1939–1945) and after a sharp increase immediately after the First World War; births fell again and remained relatively low for most of the inter-war period. A further baby boom occurred after the Second World War, causing another, more modest, upsurge in the late 1980s and early 1990s as members of the baby boomer generation produced their own children. The smaller cohorts of women born in the 1970s (reaching their reproductive peak in the 1990s), coupled with lower fertility rates (fewer children born per woman), led to a decline in births by 2000. ONS (2008) data show that births reached their lowest point since 1977 in 2001 (at around 670,000) but have risen again every year since. Recent data (ONS, 2012d) show a small rise in live births in 2011, confirming a continuation in the upward trajectory witnessed since 2001. Indeed, the number of live births increased by 22 per cent in the period 2001–2011 and fertility rates rose from an average of 1.63 children per woman in England and Wales to 1.93.

There are a number of explanations for the rise in the total fertility rate, notably women born in the 1960s and 1970s who postponed childbearing in their 20s now catching up in their 30s and 40s plus the effects of increases in the number of foreign-born women in the population who present above-average fertility rates and are in the younger age strata of the population (ONS, 2012d). To illustrate, 25.5 per cent of live births in England and Wales in 2011 were to mothers born outside of the UK, compared with 16.5 per cent in 2001 and 11.6 per cent in 1990. Poland is now the top nationality for creating second-generation immigrants to the UK; in 2001 fewer than 2,000 babies were born in Britain to Polish mothers, but by 2011 this figure had risen at least 11 times to 23,000 (Mason, 2012). Women from Pakistan, India, Bangladesh, Nigeria, Somalia, Germany, South Africa, Lithuania and China have the next highest number of babies.

Together with birth rates, the age structure of the population is influenced by the death rate (number of deaths as a percentage of the population). ONS (2008) reports that every year since 1901, with the exception of 1976, there have been fewer deaths than births in the UK. ONS (2012d) reports that there were 6,236 deaths per million population for males and 4,458 deaths per million population for females in England and Wales in 2011, giving rise to a situation where the age-standardised mortality rate (ASMR) for both males and females in 2011 was the lowest ever recorded. Essentially, death rates in the UK have fallen due to the combined factors of stable absolute death figures and a growing population. General improvements in living standards, changing occupational structure from hard physical labour to office/white collar work and advancements in health and medicine have contributed to increased life expectancy for both men and women. ONS (2013c) records that life expectancy at birth in England and Wales for babies born in the period 2009–2011 is 82.6 years for girls and 78.7 years for boys, assuming mortality rates remain at 2009–2011 levels. Whereas life expectancy used to be much higher for women than men, figures show growing convergence; for example, for babies born in 1980–1982 a girl's life expectancy was predicted to be six years longer than that of a boy, whereas by 2009–2011 the gap had narrowed to four years. Life expectancy at older ages also continues to climb steadily; for example, ONS (2013c) depicts rises in life expectancy at age 65 and at 85 since 1980–1982. The number of centenarians is also at unprecedented levels, having risen five-fold in the period 1980–2010. Whilst more women live to a hundred and beyond, the proportion of men doing so is rising more rapidly, once more showing convergence of life expectancy between the sexes.

We have seen in this section that the age structure of the population is affected by migration, births and deaths. While some non-white ethnic groups display relatively young age profiles, the overall picture in the UK is of an ageing population. The number of children under the age of 16 is predicted to increase to 13.0 million by 2020 (a 6.2 per cent increase on 2010), stabilise and then start a modest decline post-2025 (Rutherford, 2012). The number of people aged 65 and over, however, is set to rise to 12.7 million in 2018 (from 10.3 million in 2010), a percentage increase of 22 per cent over the period. Growth in this age group is expected to persist for the foreseeable future, with the over-65 population reaching 16.9 million by 2035. At this point, there are projected to be four million more people aged over 65 than under 16 (Rutherford, 2012).

In terms of HRM, the implications of changes in the age structure of the population are numerous. The following points indicate some of the challenges presented by an ageing population:

- The prospect of a shrinking pool of people of working age as the 'baby boomers' born in the 1950s and 1960s move into retirement.
- Intensified competition for school leavers/young workers as there become fewer younger people of working age.
- Identifying employment strategies to attract and retain older workers.
- Meeting the needs and aspirations of older workers in work.
- Career management and development.
- Managing sickness absence.
- Growing elder care responsibilities for those in employment as the number of elderly dependants rises.
- Concerns over the adequacy of pension arrangements.

In addition, employers are obliged to comply with the anti-age discrimination provisions of the Equality Act 2010 which make it unlawful for employers to discriminate on the grounds of age in recruitment and selection, promotion, provision of training, dismissal, etc. This imperative, coupled with the removal of the default retirement age in October 2011, compels organisations to embrace older workers and erase stubbornly held stereotypical views where these prevail.

Explore

- How might employees' care responsibilities for elderly relations impact upon their presence and attention to paid work?
- Thinking about the organisation you work for, or one with which you are familiar, do you think elder care will soon begin to pose a greater challenge to managers and employees than childcare? Why?
- What measures, if any, do you think employers should consider introducing to assist employees with elder care responsibilities?

The gender composition of the population

ONS (2008) reports that more boys than girls have been born every year in the UK since 1922; however, there are more females than males in the population. At the time of the last census in 2011, there were 31 million men and 32.2 million women residing in the UK (ONS, 2012b). Analysis of the country's population by gender and age shows that although there are more male than female newborns, the number of women in the population closes in on the number of men with the passage of time. The numbers are closest at the age of 23 where there is a difference of just 100 in favour of young women. This pattern reversal is commonly attributed to a higher mortality rate among young adult males in the 16–24 age group, although a recent report by Townsend and Westcott (2012) for the BBC suggests that part of the 'disappearance of men' could be that they are not good form fillers and so their details do not register in the census. They argue that men are also more likely than women to spend time working abroad or travelling and so potentially did not feature in the census for this reason. In the older age groups (over 65) the gap between the number of men and women in the population broadens; however, as noted in the previous section, male life expectancy is catching up with women's and so is contributing to a gradual expansion of the male population at older ages.

The female population is also supplemented by more women migrating to, than emigrating from, the UK, whereas for men the reverse is in evidence (more male emigrants than immigrants). The net in-migration figure for females is thus higher, despite the fact that the proportion of male migrants coming to the UK has been greater than the proportion of women in almost every year since 1993 (Vargas-Silva, 2013b).

Later in the chapter we consider the ways in which gender shapes people's experiences of work. In particular, we explore the interplay of gender and age and look at gendered roles within the family to understand differences in the patterns of male and female participation in the labour market.

Ethnicity and the population

In previous sections, we have referred to migration and demonstrated that in the postwar period the UK has granted residency to people from a variety of different countries, including Pakistan, India, Bangladesh, China, parts of Africa and the Caribbean, and more recently from countries within Eastern Europe. As a consequence, a number of distinct minority ethnic groups have joined the nation's historically white British heritage to form a more multicultural and diverse (ethnically and religiously) Britain. The census collects ethnicity data by asking people which group they see themselves belonging to. When the census was last conducted in March 2011, it showed that the majority of the usual resident population of England and Wales reported their ethnic group as white (86 per cent); of these, white British formed the largest group (80.5 per cent) whilst the category 'any other white' attracted 4.4 per cent of the response (ONS, 2012e). Indian was the second largest ethnic group (2.5 per cent) followed by Pakistani (2.0 per cent). The remaining ethnic groups each accounted for up to 2 per cent of the population in 2011. In terms of religious denomination, the 2011 census records 59.3 per cent of the residents of England and Wales as Christians and 4.8 per cent as Muslims, around a quarter of people reported no religion in 2011 (ONS, 2012f).

The data depict a changing landscape, with a decline in the broad white ethnic group over the last two decades and a rise in minority ethnic groups since the 1991 census (ONS, 2012e). While in general terms it is accurate to say the total population of England and Wales is becoming more ethnically diverse, certain regions and certain local authority districts contain high concentrations of (non-white) ethnic minority groups and others remain strongly white/ white British. Across the regions London was the most ethnically diverse area, with the highest proportion of minority ethnic groups and the lowest proportion of the white ethnic group; the second most diverse area was the West Midlands, incorporating Birmingham. Conversely Wales, the South West and the North East are the least diverse areas, all showing populations that are in excess of 95 per cent white. In terms of local authorities the lowest proportions of white British are to be found in the London boroughs of Newham, Brent, Ealing and Tower Hamlets, for example, and outside London in Slough (Berkshire) where 34.5 per cent of the population described themselves as white British. Other local authorities are notable; for example, Leicester has the highest proportion of those reporting to be Indian in England and Wales (28.3 per cent), whilst Boston in Lincolnshire had the highest increase of 'any other white' between 2001 and 2011 (an 11.4 per cent increase) as a consequence of EU citizens from the A8 accession countries locating to the authority for work purposes.

Key Controversy

The uneven geographical spread of ethnic minority groups means that some local labour markets remain practically monocultural, while others are considerably diverse. How might high levels of ethnic diversity impact upon labour markets and the firms operating within them?

The workforce

The workforce has conventionally been drawn from the segment of the population between the ages of 16 and state retirement age. Since October 2011, however, the notion of a state retirement age (formerly set at 65) has been removed and individuals are at liberty to continue working for as long as they wish, unless the organisation they work for is able to demonstrate an employer-justified retirement age (EJRA). However, for the purpose of compiling labour market statistics, the ONS starts from the premise that the working population will be drawn from those aged 16–64; of course, not everyone of working age will be in employment at any one time. Figure 4.1 is a useful framework for analysing the activities of people of working age.

A proportion of those over the age of 16 will not be in work or seeking work; this portion of the workforce is classified as *economically inactive*. There are a number of reasons why people might be economically inactive. This group typically includes those with caring responsibilities for children or other dependants, those who have retired from work, students, people who are incapacitated through ill-health or disability and those choosing not to work or seek

Figure 4.1 Plan of the workforce

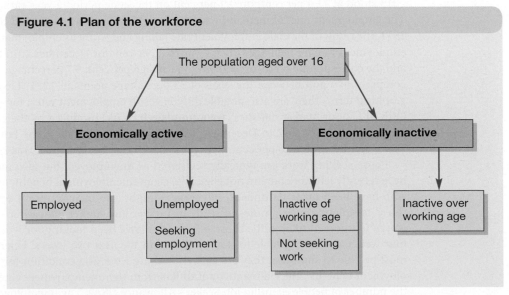

Source: adapted from *SCER* (2001: 10).

work. People within this group may voluntarily decide to enter (or re-enter) the labour market once their circumstances alter. Others may need to be enticed back to work through incentives and/or government-orchestrated benefit reforms. The UK government is, at the time of writing (2013), in the midst of reforming the welfare framework designed to help people into work, whilst supporting the most vulnerable. The Conservative–Liberal Democrat Coalition Government believes that the current system of social welfare is too complex and there are insufficient incentives to encourage people on benefits to start paid work or increase their hours (supply greater amounts of labour to the labour market). A system of universal credits has been introduced in some areas from spring 2013, as a pilot, bringing together a range of working-age benefits into a single payment. The idea behind the system is that it will smooth transitions into and out of work and it will encourage people into work by making sure that work pays. In a departure from the pre-existing system, universal credits will be applicable to those in work and on a low income as well as those out of work. To accompany this system, the government will also introduce a cap on the total amount of benefits working age people can receive so that households on working age benefits can no longer receive more in benefits than the average working wage for working families.

The amount of labour available to firms at any one time is determined by the number of people of working age who are in employment or seeking employment; in other words those classified as *economically active*. ONS (2013d) shows that there were 29.70 million people in employment age 16 and over, up nearly half a million from a year earlier, and 8.95 million people of working age were economically inactive.

The employed segment of the workforce contains those in paid work; this incorporates those working full-time or part-time, temporarily or permanently as employees (under a contract *of service*), workers (under a contract *for services*) or on a self-employed basis. A number of factors affect individuals' propensity to take work, including the availability and proximity of suitable employment opportunities, travel links, the levels of pay and benefits offered, the type of contract offered and so forth. These factors also influence people's decisions to move between jobs within the labour market.

The employment rate (the proportion of the UK's working-age population in employment) is subject to fluctuations associated with the economic cycle and shows variations both within and between different regions of the country. There are also different trends for men and women, some differences according to educational attainment and differences at different age brackets. The employment rate for those aged 16–64 in the period December 2012 to February 2013 stood at 71.4 per cent, up 0.9 per cent on the same period a year earlier (ONS, 2012d). The employment rates of men and women of working age have converged considerably since 1971, the result of the male employment rate falling and women's employment rate rising. The employment rate for men aged 16–64 was 76.3 per cent for December 2012 to February 2013 and the corresponding rate for women stood at 66.6 per cent, 9.7 percentage points lower; this compares to a gulf between the sexes of 33 percentage points in 1971 (ONS, 2008). In geographical terms there are also notable differences in employment rates; for example, NOMIS Official Labour market statistics (**www.nomisweb.co.uk**) produced by the ONS show that in the period January 2012 to December 2012 the employment rate in the London Borough of Tower Hamlets was 61.6 per cent, whereas in South Cambridgeshire it was 79.3 per cent.

Those seeking work are typically registered as unemployed, but also include those who have recently left work but are not eligible to claim unemployment benefit, for example, those who have been made redundant. Job seekers might also include recent school leavers and those completing programmes of study in further and higher education. The term *unemployed* is reserved to describe those people who have been looking for work within the last four weeks and are available to start work within the next two weeks. Unemployed workers must be able to show that they are actively seeking work as a condition for receiving unemployment benefits. The claimant count differs from the unemployment figure and is simply the number of people claiming Job Seeker's Allowance (JSA). The unemployed group consists of people affected by different types of unemployment:

- *Long-term unemployment or structural unemployment* – those unemployed as a result of the demise of whole industries or distinct occupations, e.g. mine workers, shipbuilders, textile workers.
- *Frictional unemployment* – those temporarily out of work because they are between jobs.
- *Seasonal unemployment* – those made jobless as a result of seasonal fluctuations in the availability of work. Seasonal unemployment is characteristic of land workers and those whose work is connected with holiday seasons.

It is also likely that some of those registered unemployed will never work again, as they lack the skills and competencies sought by employers. This group of unemployed workers is sometimes referred to as the *residual* unemployed.

Unemployment rates, as might be expected, are also subject to variation across regions of the UK. Nationally, however, the unemployment rate in the UK stood at 7.79 per cent (2.56 million people) in the period December 2012 to February 2013, an increase of 0.2 percentage points from September to November 2012 and up for the third successive quarter, but down 71,000 from a year earlier. Although unemployment is currently climbing and the economy is teetering on the edge of a triple-dip recession, unemployment has yet to reach levels commensurate with those experienced in 1984 when 3.3 million were unemployed.

Focus on youth unemployment

In the current climate, the unemployment rate for 20- to 24-year-olds remains a key concern as it does in several other parts of the European Union, notably in Spain where Eurostat report that youth unemployment is at a staggering 55.7 per cent (Baccardax, 2013). In the UK in the three months to February 2013, the number of young people out of work reached close to one million, at 979,000, pushing the youth unemployment rate to 21.1 per cent, up 0.6 percentage points on the previous quarter. This figure includes people in full-time education if they have been looking for work in the last four weeks and are available to start week within the next two weeks. Excluding people in full time education, there were 670,000 unemployed 16 to 24-year-olds for December 2012 to February 2013 (19.1 per cent of the economically active population for 16 to 24-year-olds not in full-time employment). Young people are in a particularly difficult position in a depressed labour market as they often lack the employ-ability skills and experience organisations are seeking and so find themselves losing out in the competitive stakes to workers with greater proven capacity to work.

Patterns of labour market participation

This section of the chapter explores patterns of participation in paid employment by gender, parental/family status, age and ethnicity.

The operation of the labour market is influenced by broader societal developments, government ideology and policy, and the behaviour of employees and employers. In social terms, attitudes to marriage and partnership and men and women's respective responsibilities for childcare and domestic duties shape the labour market decisions made by individuals, couples and families. In so far as government policies are concerned, issues such as the school curriculum and funding for post-compulsory education affect the skills set and level of educational attainment with which young people join the labour market and also influence the age at which young people enter employment. As we saw earlier, the government also acts to stimulate labour supply by implementing policies designed to get the unemployed into work and schemes to encourage the economically inactive to enter into employment.

Some people's ability to find employment is constrained by their inability to understand the labour market and acquire and exploit 'social capital' (SCER, 2001: 17). In other words, some people will lack the necessary information and contacts to search for and take advantage of employment opportunities. The Scottish Centre for Employment Research (SCER) notes that this is particularly likely to be the case for the unemployed and for new entrants to the labour market. However, the SCER (2001: 18) also states that 'even with the right information, skills and qualifications, there still exist barriers to full or appropriate labour market participation for some people . . . one such barrier is discrimination, typically race and sex discrimination'. Whilst anti-discrimination legislation exists to help eradicate unfair discrimination in employment, employers' policies and practices may still harbour prejudice and unfairness, resulting in patterns of disadvantage in the labour market for certain groups and individuals.

Patterns of male and female participation

Over the last 30 years or so, the employment rates of men and women have converged considerably. A major doorway to the world of work has clearly opened up for women, but, as we shall see here and later in the chapter, the career paths and fortunes of men and women in the labour market are often distinctly gendered.

One of the deeper influences attributable to gender that serves to structure women's participation in paid employment is domestic work. Women continue to perform the bulk of housework and to shoulder the primary responsibility for childcare in the majority of households, and this shapes the amount of paid work they do. Recent research points to the division of domestic labour becoming more equally divided between men and women, in part through women doing less housework (Cooke and Baxter, 2010) and also because both men and women now spend more time with their children (Craig, 2006). Other research (Crompton and Lyonette, 2009), however, suggests egalitarian attitudes are perhaps more prevalent than egalitarian behaviours; 69 per cent of British couples said that household duties should be shared, whilst only 34 per cent reported that they are shared as opposed to mostly male or female. Further, Laurie and Gershuny (2000) find that women continue to do more than 60 per cent of the domestic work even in couples where both partners work full-time.

The evidence about the participation of women and men in the labour market and the reality of childcare arrangements shows that progress towards a more equal division of caring responsibilities between women and men is still very slow. As Table 4.2 depicts, the

Table 4.2 Number and percentage of women by economic activity and age of youngest dependent[a] child, April–June 2012, UK (numbers are in 000s)

	All women	Women with dependent children (by age of youngest dependent child, years)				Women without dependent children[b]
	16–64	All 0–18	0–3	4–10	11–18	
In employment[c] of whom:	13,414	5,146	1,535	1,781	1,830	8,268
Full-time	7,392	2,245	646	659	940	5,147
Part-time	5,291	2,766	851	1,078	836	2,524
Unemployed	1,046	399	123	180	96	647
Economically Active[d]	14,459	5,545	1,658	1,961	1,926	8,915
Economically Inactive	5,710	2,015	994	587	434	3,694
Total[e]	20,169	7,560	2,652	2,548	2,360	12,609
Employment rate (%)[f]	66.5	68.1	57.9	69.9	77.5	65.6
Unemployment rate (%)[g]	7.2	7.2	7.4	9.2	5.0	7.3

[a]Dependent children are children aged under 16 and those aged 16–18 who have never married and are in full-time education.
[b]Includes women with non-dependent children or no children.
[c]Sum of the subgroups may not equal total in employment due to unknown responses.
[d]Economically active are those in employment plus the unemployed i.e. in work or actively seeking work.
[e]The total is the number in employment plus the number unemployed and the number inactive.
[f]The employment rate is the number in employment divided by the total.
[g]The unemployment rate is the number unemployed divided by the economically active group.

Source: Labour Force Survey Household datasets.

employment rate of women is affected by the age of their youngest dependent child. Moreover, women with very young children (aged 0–3) present a significantly lower employment rate than women with older dependent children and women with no dependent children or no children at all. Women with dependent children are also more likely than women with no dependent children/no children to work part-time as opposed to full-time; this is pronounced for women whose youngest child is under the age of 10.

The differences between men and women's participation patterns in paid employment are illustrated in ONS labour market statistics reproduced by the EHRC (2013a). The statistics show that between March 2011 and October 2012 the vast majority of men in employment worked full-time (86–87 per cent) compared with just over half of all women in employment (56–57 per cent). Significantly more women than men in employment were working part-time (43 per cent vs 13 per cent).

The findings from the fourth Department for Business Innovation and Skills work–life balance survey (Tipping *et al.,* 2012) also show a gendered divide in employment patterns between women and men with dependent children. The survey found that there are significant associations between women with dependent children and the take-up of part-time working, with 59 per cent of women with dependent children taking up part-time working, compared with 16 per cent of men with dependent children. Take-up of part-time working was also very common among lone parent mothers (56 per cent) and mothers who were part of a couple (59 per cent), as compared with coupled fathers (15 per cent). Fifty-four per cent of lone parents of both sexes had taken up part-time working, compared with 39 per cent of coupled parents, presumably in an attempt to combine work with care in the absence of a partner with whom to share care responsibilities and/or in response to the often prohibitive costs of childcare. At the other end of the spectrum, Tipping *et al.* (2012) found that men are more likely to work long hours, with one in ten (10 per cent) of male employees working more than 48 hours per week, compared with just two per cent of female employees.

While parenthood continues to affect women's employment rates disproportionately to men's, the proportion of working-age mothers with dependent children who are in employment has risen exponentially, from 47 per cent in 1973 to the rate of 68.1 per cent shown in Table 4.2, narrowing the participation gap between men and women considerably. Most employees do return to work following maternity leave; evidence collated by the Women's Business Council (2013) shows that in 2010–2011, 77 per cent of mothers were back at work after 12 months, and 84 per cent of these were back with the same employer, compared with 59 per cent of mothers returning to the same employer in 2002. The decision to return to work is undoubtedly complex and influenced by a variety of factors; however, women were less likely to return to work if they had been in their pre-birth job less than a year and/or had not received any maternity pay.

We can see from this short insight into the working patterns and economic activity rates of women that they have indeed come a long way in terms of labour market participation. However, as we shall see later in the chapter there are still gender-based inequalities that segment the labour market experiences of and opportunities for different sorts of women.

Ethnicity and patterns of labour market participation

Employment participation rates for ethnic minorities are significantly lower than those for the population as a whole. As Table 4.3 shows, the employment rate of white people in the UK in the three months ending September 2012 was higher than the employment rate of those in each of the each of the minority ethnic groups at age 16–34 and 35–59. The disparity is most acute among the younger age group, particularly Bangladeshi, Pakistani, Chinese and other Asian 16- to 34-year-olds. Unemployment rates amongst minority ethnic groups are also higher than for white people of working age of all ages as Table 4.4 demonstrates.

There are noticeable variations in activity and employment rates between different ethnic minority groups. For example, the employment rate among people of Indian origin is 64 per cent, compared with just 47 per cent among Bangladeshis and among Pakistanis (see Table 4.3). Activity and employment rates also vary within each ethnic group, being generally higher among

Table 4.3 Employment rate (%) by ethnicity, age and sex, in the three months ending September 2012, UK (not seasonally adjusted)

	White	Mixed	Indian	Pakistani	Bangladeshi	Chinese	Other Asian	Black/ African/ Caribbean	Other
People aged 16-34									
Total	13	17	15	19	25	19	13	23	15
Male	13	14	13	13	20	20	9	26	13
Female	12	19	18	29	34	18	17	20	19
People aged 35-59									
Total	5	8	6	10	8	5	10	11	12
Male	5	5	6	9	–[a]	–[a]	7	12	11
Female	4	11	6	12	18	–[a]	13	11	13

People aged 60 and over	White	Non-white[b]
Total	4	6
Male	4	7
Female	2	5

[a]Estimates are considered too unreliable for practical purposes.
[b]Includes: mixed, Indian, Pakistani, Bangladeshi, Chinese, Other Asian, Black/African/Caribbean and other ethnicities.
Source: Labour Force Survey.

Table 4.4 Unemployment rate (%) by ethnicity, age and sex, in the three months ending September 2012, UK (not seasonally adjusted)

	White	Mixed	Indian	Pakistani	Bangladeshi	Chinese	Other Asian	Black/ African/ Caribbean	Other
People aged 16-34									
Total	69	57	64	47	47	34	50	52	53
Male	73	62	71	61	65	40	64	54	65
Female	66	52	56	33	30	27	38	49	40
People aged 35-59									
Total	81	74	80	58	56	79	74	72	67
Male	86	81	87	81	81	87	85	77	75
Female	76	68	71	36	25	73	64	68	58
People aged 60 and over									
Total	18	22	22	11	–[a]	24	19	13	27
Male	24	–[a]	32	18	–[a]	18	42	17	35
Female	14	25	14	6	–[a]	29	–[a]	12	18

[a]Estimates are considered too unreliable for practical purposes.
Source: Labour Force Survey.

British-born members of ethnic minorities than among immigrants (Wadsworth, 2003). Also, as Table 4.3 shows, ethnic minority women are less likely to participate in employment than men.

A report by the National Audit Office (2008) attributes the under-achievement of the ethnic minority population in the labour force to three key factors:

- *Human capital* – some ethnic minority groups have lower levels of education and skills than the white population.

- *Geography* – many ethnic minorities live in deprived areas with high unemployment.
- *Discrimination* – unequal treatment by employers on grounds of race or colour represents a further barrier to employment.

There may also be a range of cultural and familial factors that dissuade ethnic minorities from engaging in the labour market or with certain types of work or certain employers.

But how robust are these explanations in accounting for the differences in employment outcomes for ethnic minority individuals and the majority white population? Certainly with reference to the human capital assertion, Dustmann *et al.* (2011) argue that second-generation ethnic minority immigrants tend to be better educated than their parents' generation, and better educated than their white native peers. Indeed, they assess that the relative enhancement in education between the parent and descendant generation is far greater for ethnic minorities than it is for white natives. British-born ethnic minorities, despite their initial disadvantage in the British educational system, as measured at the time of entry to primary school, step up the pace continually throughout the compulsory school system, performing astonishingly well in terms of educational attainments and achieving a higher proportion of college education than their British-born white contemporaries. Note, however, that there is considerable heterogeneity between different minority ethnic groups, with some faring much better than others. Despite their educational accomplishments, the employment probabilities for ethnic minorities are lower than those of whites, and for some ethnic minority groups markedly so.

Similarly, research by Wadsworth (2003) found that educational attainment plus age and region explained hardly any of the difference in employment rates between ethnic minorities and British-born whites, calling into question the efficacy of the human capital explanation and the geographical explanation cited earlier.

In other related work, Heath and Cheung (2006), found ongoing evidence of 'ethnic penalties' in the labour market. In particular, they found that a number of ethnic minority groups, notably Pakistani, Bangladeshi, Black Caribbean and Black African men, continue to experience higher unemployment rates, greater concentration in routine and semi-routine work, and lower hourly earnings than members of the comparison group of British and other whites. Women from these ethnic minority groups also experience higher rates of unemployment than the comparison group, but for those in work, average hourly earnings tend to match or exceed those of white women as corroborated by Dustmann *et al* (2011). Heath and Cheung (2006) draw particular attention to the levels of disadvantage experienced by Pakistani and Bangladeshi groups, where male unemployment and levels of male economic inactivity are high. In addition, where individuals from these groups are in employment, they are disproportionately represented in semi-routine and routine work. The differentials Heath and Cheung found are not confined to those born and educated outside the UK; indeed, the ethnic penalties they refer to also appear to be experienced by second-generation ethnic minority groups who were born and schooled in the UK.

Later in the chapter we extend this discussion of labour market participation according to gender and ethnicity, to look more closely at labour market inequalities experienced by these groups.

Labour demand

Aggregate demand for labour

The aggregate demand for labour consists of total employment plus unfilled vacancies. As the demand for labour is derived from the demand for goods and services, it follows the economic cycle, rising in upswings and falling in recessions. Changes in labour demand are reflected in changes in the unemployment rate.

Low levels of unemployment are usually taken as a sign that the economy is growing and is in good shape. For employers, however, the combination of record employment, low unemployment and high numbers of economically inactive people creates a labour market that is referred to as a 'tight labour market'. Tight labour markets mean that employers have to compete more actively for workers and workers have a wider choice of employment opportunities. This will lead to higher rates of labour turnover as workers leave organisations for better jobs elsewhere. In response, firms may be forced to increase pay. They may also adopt other policies aimed at retaining employees, as vacancies arising from labour turnover will be hard to fill. Therefore, there will be more internal promotion and redeployment and this may necessitate increased investment in training. While these responses might be seen as moves towards internalising employment, they are not driven by the technical and skill requirements of production or a long-term employment strategy, but by immediate pressures from the labour market. These pressures may be reinforced by stronger trade union bargaining power as a result of low unemployment and unfilled vacancies. Once established, these employment practices may become embedded, although employers may seek to reverse them should labour demand slacken and unemployment rise.

Tight labour markets characterised the period from 2001 until 2008. There was low unemployment, a record number of people in employment and a large number of economically inactive people. All this meant that many employers experienced recruitment difficulties and skill shortages, although these problems were eased by an inflow of immigrant workers, including those from countries such as Latvia, Poland and Slovenia, which joined the EU on 1 May 2004. However, during 2008 the economy moved into recession as a result of the 'credit crunch' and the ensuing financial crisis and global recession, and has been struggling to recover its position ever since. As economic activity has been in the doldrums, high levels of unemployment have become a feature of the economy. The latest labour market statistics (ONS, 2013d) show unemployment at 7.9 per cent of the economically active population – 2.56 million people are officially unemployed. The fall in labour demand has meant that tight labour market conditions have given way to a 'slack' labour market in which there are more people seeking work than there are jobs available. Employers tend not to replace workers who leave because they need a smaller workforce, as demand for their product falls. Where they do need to fill vacancies, many prefer to hire on a temporary basis in view of uncertainties about future demand.

Whereas tight labour markets improve the bargaining position of workers relative to employers, the reverse is true when labour demand falls. Workers' and unions' anxiety about job losses may lead them to accept lower wage increases or even lower absolute wages in order to save jobs. They are also more likely to support changes to production methods in order to improve the chances of company survival, even if this leads to some job losses.

As well as examining changes in aggregate demand for labour, we need to look at how the employment experience of different labour market groups varies as the result of structured patterns of inequality of employment opportunity. As we shall see, slack labour markets are likely to have disproportionate effects on those who are already disadvantaged in the labour market, such as those with little education and low skill levels and those who are subject to various forms of discrimination. We also need to examine the changing pattern of demand for labour in the long run and how it affects different labour market groups.

Labour market inequality

The quality of jobs on offer in the labour market varies. Some workers are in 'good jobs' with high earnings, good working conditions, employment security and opportunities for training and career development. Others are in 'bad jobs' with low status and pay, poor working conditions, little access to training and few, if any, opportunities for promotion. How good and bad jobs get created has been a matter of ongoing debate surrounding the theory of labour market segmentation. One classical line of explanation, advanced by two economists, Doeringer and Piore (1971), is based on the analysis of employers' labour requirements outlined earlier. Some firms face strong pressures to internalise the employment relationship in order to train, develop and retain suitably skilled workers and gain their voluntary cooperation in production. Others do not and are able to meet their labour requirements by following the commodity labour approach and externalising the employment relationship.

Another explanation (Gordon *et al.*, 1982) is that some firms enjoy monopoly power in their product markets and are able to use this power to increase the selling price of the product, thereby increasing profits. Some of these companies are faced by workers who have developed strong trade unions that can use their bargaining power to gain a share of these profits in the form of high wages and other benefits, including job security provisions. At the same time, management seeks to limit union solidarity and bargaining power by dividing the workforce into horizontal segments and offering the prospect of promotion to those who are cooperative and trustworthy. Firms that are unable to use monopoly power to raise their prices do not have surplus profits to share with trade unions, so terms and conditions of employment are less favourable. As it is more likely that large rather than small firms are able to exercise monopoly power, primary sector employment is concentrated in large, rather than small firms.

One of the central predictions of the labour segmentation thesis is that there will be little movement of workers between the primary and secondary sectors of the labour market. Workers in the primary sector are unwilling to move to the secondary sector and the high level of employment security they enjoy means they are unlikely to be forced to through job loss. Workers who make up the disadvantaged segments of the labour market are unable to move up into the primary sector because employers see them as undesirable candidates for jobs. Primary sector employers want disciplined, cooperative workers with good work habits, so when selecting from among applicants for jobs, primary sector employers will tend to reject those with unstable employment histories that involve frequent unemployment and job changes, because they will assume that this indicates a poor-quality worker. This will automatically rule out secondary sector workers, regardless of their personal qualities, since by definition secondary workers are in unstable, insecure jobs. It is also the case, however, that because of their experience of poor work, some secondary sector workers will tend to develop negative attitudes and poor patterns of work behaviour that reinforce employers' prejudices against secondary sector workers as a whole.

These explanations for labour market segmentation emphasise the way in which firms' employment decisions influence the wider labour market by dividing it into advantaged and disadvantaged groups. But despite this analysis, the quality of the jobs that people do is not determined simply by their abilities, educational attainment and skills acquired through training. The chances of someone being in a good or a bad job are also influenced by their membership of particular socioeconomic groups. There is clear evidence that the labour market is segmented along lines that reflect 'broader social forces leading to discrimination within the labour market' (Rubery, 1994: 53).

Discrimination in the labour market means that workers' chances of gaining access to 'good' or 'bad' jobs are unfairly influenced by non-work characteristics such as gender, race, class, work-unrelated disability and age. Thus two equally skilled workers will likely find themselves in different sectors of the labour market because one is a white male from a middle-class social background and the other is a working-class black woman. This reflects deep-seated patterns of discrimination within society in general as well as in the labour market. Here we build on the earlier segment of the chapter that focused on patterns of male, female and ethnic minority participation in employment to examine more closely how gender and ethnicity influence people's *experiences* in the labour market.

As we have touched upon already, women and ethnic minority groups occupy a disadvantaged place in the labour market. Women's employment disadvantage reflects deep-seated societal norms concerning the family and the respective roles of women and men in domestic roles and paid work. The domestic roles played by many women mean that their employment opportunities are restricted geographically and contractually. This is particularly true of women with children as we have seen. In the absence of highly developed systems of state support for childcare, childcare responsibilities mean that many women cannot travel long distances to work or work 'standard' hours. Therefore they are invariably restricted to part-time work in the immediate locality. This means that they have limited choice of employment and therefore little bargaining power and may have to accept secondary sector terms and conditions of employment. Ethnic minority workers, as well as facing racial prejudice and discrimination, may be faced with additional limits to their choice of employment because they live in areas where business activity is low and public transport facilities are poorer. For these reasons it is also likely that women and ethnic minority workers will be disproportionately affected by unemployment generated by recession. This is because they are less able to compete for the jobs that are available should they lose their current employment and it is easier for employers to discriminate against women and ethnic minorities when there are many people competing for a limited number of jobs.

Philpott (2011) advises that the 2008–2009 recession is sometimes referred to as a 'mancession' as men were more acutely affected than women, as a result of blue collar job losses in the private sector, notably in construction and manufacturing. Women were more shielded from recessionary effects as a consequence of their representation in the public sector (which actually saw a small rise in employment during the recession), and their presence in part-time work which held up better than full-time employment. The recession ended in the third quarter of 2009 and the economy benefited from a moderate fillip in activity in 2010 before economic growth stagnated once again in 2011. The country plunged into another recession in early 2012, referred to widely as a 'double dip' recession due to the proximity to the 2008–2009 recession. The period of sustained austerity and public sector cuts leading up to and subsequent to the 2012 recession has been uncomfortable for women, as mass job losses have imploded on the public sector and a slowdown in consumer spending has impacted sectors such as retail which employ a good proportion of female workers.

Gender-based inequalities in employment opportunity

The social forces identified in the previous section mean that there are major differences in the types of work that men and women tend to do, and the way in which male and female employment is segregated by time. Patterns of occupational segregation are strongly in evidence in the labour market, creating a division between male and female work. For example, women occupy 77 per cent of administration and secretarial posts but only 6 per cent of engineering and 14 per cent of architects, planners and surveyors roles; 83 per cent of people employed in personal services are women (EHRC, 2013b).

As shown in Table 4.5, patterns of vertical segregation also loom large, with men continuing to dominate highly rewarded, senior roles in politics, business, media and culture and the public and voluntary sectors (Centre for Women and Democracy, 2013).

Table 4.5 Women's share of a selection of senior ranked roles since 2005

Role	2005	2006	2007–2008	2010–2011	2012
Members of parliament	19.7	19.5	19.3	22.2	22.3
Local authority council leaders	16.2	13.8	14.3	13.2	12.3
Directors in FTSE 100 companies	10.5	10.4	11.0	12.5	16.7
Editors of national newspapers	13.0	17.4	13.6	9.5	5.0
Directors of major museums and art galleries	21.7	17.4	17.4	26.1	28.0
Chief executives of national sports bodies	6.7	6.7	13.3	25.0	23.8
Local authority chief executives	17.5	20.6	19.5	22.8	22.9
Senior ranks in the armed forces	0.8	0.4	0.4	1.0	1.8
Senior police officers	9.8	12.2	11.9	16.8	17.6
University vice-chancellors	11.1	13.2	14.4	14.3	14.2
Health service chief executives	28.1	37.9	36.9	31.4	34.8

Source: an extract from Centre for Women and Democracy (2013), *Sex and Power; Who Runs Britain?* p. 7.

Explore

• To what extent are broader patterns of occupational segregation useful for explaining the varying levels of representation of women in senior roles as shown in Table 4.5?

Men's and women's jobs are also segregated by hours of work, sometimes referred to as gendered time segregation. As we have seen, generally women are more likely than men to work part-time, but particularly so if they have dependent children. Part-time working is invariably low-paid and this is reflected in the stubbornly persistent gender pay gap that exists between women working part-time and men working full-time (Longhi and Platt, 2009). The preponderance of women in part-time work may also help to explain that in 2011 around 28,000 men aged over 21 were earning at or just below the national minimum wage (NMW) compared with around 50,000 women, suggesting that nearly two-thirds of those earning at or just below the NMW are women (The Fawcett Society, 2013). At the complete opposite end of the spectrum the 25th anniversary issues of the Sunday Times Rich List (*Sunday Times*, 2013) is dominated with tales of (overwhelmingly male) wealthy business tycoons; indeed, the highest position in the list held by a woman in her own right (i.e. not part of a couple or part of a wealthy family) is 116th. Ironically this place belongs to Slavica Ecclestone, an ex-model, whose wealth has been amassed, not as a result of her success in business, but as a result of her divorce from Formula One magnate Bernie Ecclestone!

Female heterogeneity

The population, and hence the labour market, comprises different sorts of women, fractured by age, class, ethnicity, qualification level, background and experience. So, while generalisations about the relative positions of men and women in employment serve some purpose, an understanding of the different employment experiences of different sorts of women is useful.

While we have seen that women are typically casualties of segregation in employment, some women will be in a more advantageous labour market position than others (and some men). The level of educational qualifications women attain is a key determinant of the extent to which they subsequently participate in paid employment. As Plunkett (2011) demonstrates, the UK has very low employment rates among women with low educational achievements and there is considerable disparity between the employment rates of women with and without post-secondary education. Indeed, the UK employment rate amongst women who left school prior to completing A-level education is 43 per cent, compared with 86 per cent for women who completed degrees and other higher education awards. Some of the more highly educated women in the labour market will be mothers who have been able to return to well-paid jobs following maternity leave, something women without qualifications are less likely to be able to do. The resultant impact on lifetime earnings is demonstrable; women with degrees are estimated to face only a 4 per cent loss in lifetime earnings as a result of motherhood, while mothers with mid-level qualifications face a 25 per cent loss and those with no qualifications a 58 per cent loss (EHRC, 2013b).

The employment rates of women also vary according to ethnicity, reflecting in part different cultural norms and family circumstances. The EHRC (2013b) reports that despite some growth in their employment rates, only one in four Bangladeshi and Pakistani women work, and many face practical barriers preventing them from doing so. Black Caribbean women are more likely to be in full-time work than any other group of women, including white women. Almost half of Bangladeshi (49 per cent) and Pakistani (44 per cent) women are looking after the family or home full time, compared to 20 per cent or fewer of other groups.

Progress?

It is the case that some, but not all, women are making significant strides in training and in occupations traditionally dominated by men. For example, in the nine years between 2001 and 2010 the proportion of female solicitors, lawyers, judges and coroners increased from

36.9 to 44.9 per cent, the number of female scientists increased by 11.7 percentage points from 34.7 to 46.4 per cent, and the proportion of female certified and chartered accountants increased 7.1 percentage points to 38.6 per cent (Cracknell, 2012). The latest General Medical Council statistics released in April 2013 show that 47.9 per cent of doctors on the General Practitioner register are female.

Management is another key area where women have made progress. Headline figures show that the proportion of women in managerial and senior positions, aggregated across the UK labour force, rose by 4.5 percentage points between 2001 and 2010 to reach 35.5 per cent (Cracknell, 2012). However, as with so many occupations (e.g. teaching, policing, healthcare) a closer examination of the gender composition at different levels of management and at management in different sectors reveals distinct patterns of horizontal and vertical segregation *within* management careers. Cracknell (2012), for example, shows that women are far more likely to be personnel, training and industrial relations managers, customer care managers or managers in restaurants and catering than they are production managers or information technology and communication managers. Turning to patterns of vertical segregation within management careers, the dominance of men in the most senior management positions is aptly illustrated by the findings of the Cranfield *Female FTSE Board Report 2013* (Sealy and Vinnicombe, 2013), an annual report examining the representation of women on the boards of the FTSE 100 companies:

- Burberry, the luxury clothing and accessories firm, tops the 2013 female FTSE index with three women directors out of eight (37.5 per cent of the board). Both the chief executive and the chief financial officer roles at Burberry are held by women. Further it is the only FTSE 100 company to have two female executive directors. In second place is drinks firm Diageo, with four women directors out of 11 (36.4 per cent of the board).

- Women hold 21.8 per cent of non-executive directorships in the FTSE 100 (up from 18.3 per cent in 2012) but only 5.8 per cent of executive directorships, down from 6.6 per cent in 2012.

- Only 17 companies in the FTSE 100 have female executive directors, the same as in 2012.

- Just a quarter of the FTSE 100 companies have 25 per cent or more women on their boards (the target to be attained by 2015, set by Lord Davies in 2011).

- Six of the FTSE 100 companies have exclusively all-male boards.

- Of the 31 new executive director appointments made across FTSE 100 boards in the 12 months to January 2013, women took just two, which equates to just 6.5 per cent.

- There is only one FTSE 100 company with a woman holding the position of chairman (Alison Carnwath at Land Securities).

The ability for women to get so far and then find the very senior positions difficult or impossible to access is metaphorically referred to as the 'glass ceiling' phenomenon. Women can see the jobs at the very top but cannot penetrate the invisible barrier that prevents them securing the positions. The findings gathered by Sealy and Vinnicombe (2013) suggest that women find it harder to be promoted internally than men and often find it necessary to move between companies to show their mettle before succeeding in executive roles. They call for more vigorous talent management strategies to be implemented to identify talented women who can be 'pulled through'.

Explore

- Why does the glass ceiling persist in the twenty-first century and what prospect is there for smashing it?
- Do you think Lord Davies' target is achievable by 2015? How can change be effected?

It is clear from the extract of the 2013 *Sex and Power Report* shown in Table 4.5 and other research referred to in this section that some women are making considerable progress in employment. We have also seen that the level of earnings penalty is strongly mediated by levels of education, as women with higher-level qualifications are able to secure better-quality roles within the labour market. Better qualifications therefore afford women greater opportunities within the labour market, but do not entirely safeguard against disadvantage. Patterns of occupational segregation and vertical segregation persist, causing even relatively advantaged women, such as those in the esteemed professions, to find that their roles and opportunities for advancement are limited because of their gender. As Marlow and Carter (2004: 16) wrote: 'Women can stretch the ties that bind but cannot sever them.'

Ethnically based labour market inequality

People from ethnic minorities experience disadvantage compared with whites in terms of their access to employment, their level of occupational attainment, and pay. The EHRC (2013b) reports that between 1995 and 1997, and again in the period 2006–2008, prior to the recession, a steady growth in the number of jobs raised the percentage of women and of black people of working age in employment by twice the average, and the percentage of Bangladeshi and Pakistani people of working age in employment by three times the average. However, over the longer term, some groups with low employment rates have not fared well, particularly those pushed to the margins of the labour market. We focus here on ethnicity, but equally other social factors such as disability or age can marginalise individuals in the labour market and interplay with ethnicity, resulting in inferior outcomes (lower employment rates, greater likelihood of unemployment, lower pay, poor-quality jobs and so forth). For example, black people and disabled people in their early 20s are twice as likely to be not in employment, education or training (NEET) as white people and non-disabled people (EHRC, 2013b).

Ethnic minorities in general are less likely than whites to be employed in professional and managerial occupations and more likely to be in semi-routine and routine occupations (Heath and Cheung, 2006). These disadvantages could theoretically reflect differences in education and skills. We know that unemployment is higher and wages are lower among lower educated, unskilled workers. However, these disadvantages remain even when educational qualifications are taken into account. In other words, 'ethnic penalties' can be demonstrated that impede the occupational success of ethnic minorities during the job search, hiring and promotion process. As a result, ethnic minorities suffer from a general inability to convert their high educational attainments into comparable occupational outcomes. A related scenario is 'over-education' whereby people hold qualifications over and above those required for their job. Rafferty (2012: 2) advances our understanding of the concept of ethnic penalties to suggest that a disproportionate number of ethnic minority women and men are employed in roles that do not require their levels of educational attainment. Focusing on graduates, he seeks to explore whether the accessibility of a university education has facilitated an equalising of labour market outcomes for ethnic minority individuals with comparably qualified white men and women. Whilst the expansion of higher education has enabled wider segments of the population to improve their employment prospects relative to older generations and to the less well qualified, Rafferty (2012: 15) concludes that for minority ethnic men and women 'higher level qualifications still do not appear to provide a panacea or facilitate an equalisation of labour market outcomes to those of comparably educated white UK born men and women'. Li *et al.* (2008) concur, noting that while the acquisition of educational credentials facilitates entry into the labour market and enhances income levels for all groups, education only protects against lower employment rates and earning levels to an extent, and many people from ethnic minority groups experience poorer employment rates and lower incomes than white people. Full-time degree graduates from all minority ethnic groups have higher initial unemployment rates than white graduates, with the highest rates among African, Chinese, Pakistani and Bangladeshi groups (AGCAS Race Equality Task Group, 2008). Evidently, ethnic or racial stereotyping and inhospitable workplace cultures related to both gender and ethnicity can place significant barriers to those seeking to access certain professions and/or advance their careers.

Ethnic heterogeneity

Although people from ethnic minorities as a whole are disadvantaged in the labour market, there is noticeable variation in the experience of different ethnic groups and between men and women within ethnic groups. As we saw earlier (see Tables 4.3 and 4.4) the employment rates and unemployment rates of different minority ethnic groups vary. Levels of occupational attainment also vary between different ethnic minority groups. Chinese and Indians of both sexes are more likely to be in professional and managerial occupations than whites, as are black African and black Caribbean women; however, they remain significantly under-represented when qualifications are taken into account. With the exception of Indians and Chinese, ethnic minority workers are more likely to be in semi-routine or routine occupations than whites (Heath and Cheung, 2006: 15).

There are also variations in average earnings across ethnic minorities. Dustmann (n.d.), suggests that the disadvantage experienced by Pakistani and Bangladeshi minorities in employment is reflected in the pay they receive. In 2009, Pakistani men earned on average 26 per cent less than white people in employment, while Bangladeshi men received wages 35 per cent below the average earnings of white people in employment. However, while for the Bangladeshi minority, wage differentials can be shown to be slowly converging with the average earnings of white people over time (from –53 per cent in 1993 to –50 per cent in 2000 and –35 per cent in 2009), for the Pakistani ethnic group wage differentials are relatively stable. Among the other minority ethnic groups black Caribbean men displayed a 27 per cent wage disadvantage in 2009. Black Caribbean women did not display significant wage differentials to white women in 2009, but exhibited average wage rates 15 per cent higher than indigenous white women in earlier years. Indian men and women earned 14 and 18 per cent, respectively, more than white indigenous workers in 2009. These complex outcomes indicate considerable heterogeneity, with wage disadvantages for some ethnic minority groups and wage advantages for others. Overall Dustmann (n.d) demonstrates a wage advantage for British-born ethnic minorities of 4.8 per cent. Breaking this down by gender shows that British-born ethnic minority males face a wage disadvantage of 2.7 per cent, while British-born ethnic minority females face a wage advantage of 13.3 per cent. These figures may be driven by the educational advantage of ethnic minorities compared with the white British population as well as by different regional distributions, notably the concentration of ethnic minorities in London where wages are higher on average. The substantial wage advantage experienced by ethnic minority women can be explained by the fact that ethnic minority women are less likely to take part-time jobs than white women. Full-time jobs are noticeably better paid than part-time jobs, and it is this that accounts largely for the apparent lack of pay disadvantage among ethnic minority women.

Rubery (1994) argues that the presence of disadvantaged groups in the labour market increases the range of options open to some employers by allowing them to fulfil their requirements for a stable, cooperative workforce without having to offer the positive incentives associated with internalised employment relationships (see Box 4.2). This is because, as indicated earlier, disadvantaged groups face barriers to employment, curtailing choice in terms of jobs and careers; in short, they often have to accept what they can get. The absence of better alternatives makes these jobs more attractive than they would otherwise be and therefore more highly valued by workers. This is reflected in the willingness of many disadvantaged workers to remain with their employer and cooperate with management in order to keep their jobs (see Box 4.2).

Box 4.2 **Advantages to employers of using immigrant labour from eastern Europe**

Research carried out for the Joseph Rowntree Foundation into the position of central and eastern European immigrant workers in the UK found that immigrant workers from there often had skills and qualifications that were significantly higher than those needed in their jobs. Many of these workers were willing to take low-paid work in the UK because there were even fewer employment opportunities in their home countries. The research also found that employers regarded them as 'high quality workers for low-skilled work' and that employers 'were often trying to balance the requirement for workers who were easy to hire and fire on the one hand but were also reliable and easy to retain'.

Source: Anderson *et al*. (2006: 115).

Key Controversy

Is it rational for an employer to refuse to hire workers on the basis of their ethnicity or nationality? Do employers who hire ethnic minority workers nevertheless benefit from the presence of racism in society as a whole?

Changing patterns of demand

The period since the 1980s has seen significant changes in the pattern of demand for labour and therefore in the types of jobs available to workers. These shifts reflect inter-linked changes in the structure of the economy, government policy for the labour market, and employers' labour requirements.

A shift of employment from manufacturing to services

The proportion of workers employed in manufacturing has declined in the UK, the USA and all the major European Union economies since the 1960s. This reflects the effects of economic growth and rising incomes on people's consumption patterns. As people get richer, the proportion of their income that they spend on manufactured goods declines (although people may still spend more money on them in absolute terms) and the proportion spent on services increases. This means that output, and hence employment, grow faster in the service sector than in the manufacturing sector.

The decline of manufacturing has been particularly rapid in the UK since 1980. This has reflected additional forces, such as the effects of government monetary and exchange rate policy during the 1980s, which raised the price of British exports in foreign markets and cheapened foreign imports; the long-term inability of UK manufacturing to respond adequately to foreign competition; and organisational restructuring whereby manufacturing firms have tried to cut costs by hiving off certain 'non-core' and specialist activities, such as security, cleaning and catering, to outside suppliers of these services. This has meant that the workers who used to deliver these services are now counted as being in the service sector rather than manufacturing.

The growth of service sector employment has been a major factor in the increase in part-time employment in the UK and has therefore expanded employment opportunities for women with dependent children and also, more recently, young people in full-time education who value the income from part-time employment to assist with the costs of tuition fees and general living expenses.

Table 4.6 Changes in the distribution of employment by broad sector, 1990–2020 (percentage share of total employment)

	1990	2000	2010	2015[a]	2020[a]
Primary sector and utilities	3.9	2.5	2.5	2.5	2.3
Manufacturing	17.2	13.6	8.3	7.9	7.3
Construction	8.3	6.6	6.9	7.1	7.3
Trade, accommodation and transport	26.9	27.3	26.2	26.4	26.2
Business and other services	22.3	26.9	29.2	30.8	31.6
Non-market services	21.3	23.0	26.9	25.2	25.3

[a]Projected figures.

Source: Wilson and Homenidou (2012: 41).

Wilson and Homenidou's study 'Working Futures' (2012) projects a continuation of the trend away from manufacturing towards service-sector employment. They anticipate that private services will form the main source of jobs growth during the period 2010–2020. Business and other services will also be a particularly vital component, with employment expansion equivalent to in excess of one million additional jobs. The period is expected to see a shift in the balance of the economy away from public-sector employment as cuts to public-sector services are rolled out. The share of total employment accounted for by non-market services is projected to fall from 27 per cent in 2010 to 25 per cent in 2020 (see Table 4.6).

Explore

- How specifically has the growth of the service sector boosted part-time and female employment?
- What sorts of jobs have been created?

Changes in the occupational structure of employment

The occupational structure refers to how employment is apportioned among different jobs in the economy. Changes in the occupational structure of employment reflect changes in the types of skill demanded by employers. The declining relative importance of manufacturing means that, over time, the share of occupations associated with manufacturing has also declined, while the share of occupations associated with the delivery of business services, retail services, etc. has increased. Changes in the occupational structure also reflect changes in the demand for skills *within* industries. These changes are generated by new technologies and by organisational changes that alter the way in which goods are produced and services delivered.

Past changes and projected changes in the occupational structure of employment are aptly illustrated by the data in Table 4.7. Sisson (2011) claims that over the longer term the economy has shifted in emphasis away from routine production towards a knowledge base, causing new jobs to be created in large numbers in high-skill, high-wage managerial and professional occupations. However, the last decade or so has also seen growth in lower-wage service occupations, combined with a reduction in middle-wage occupations as advances in technology 'hollow out' demand for routine workers in administrative and secretarial, and process, plant and machine operative occupations. Some commentators use the term 'hourglass economy' to reflect this changing occupational structure. In short, the routine tasks that can be replaced by technology are neither the managerial roles at the top nor the low-skilled ones at the bottom, such as cleaning, bar work or shelf-stacking. The roles that are vulnerable are in fact those in the middle of the occupational structure, including manual work, and it is these jobs that will thin out over time (CBI, 2011). Concern is expressed that an hourglass-shaped economy will lead to stark polarisation between high-wage 'lovely' occupations and low-wage 'lousy' occupations (Holmes and Mayhew, 2012).

Table 4.7 Changes in the occupational structure (percentage share of total employment), using standard occupational classifications (SOCs), 2010 – major groups

	1990	2000	2010	2015[a]	2020[a]
Managers, directors and senior officials	7.9	8.7	9.9	10.6	11.1
Professional occupations	14.5	16.5	19.2	20.1	21.0
Associate professional and technical	10.6	12.2	12.9	13.4	14.0
Administrative, clerical and secretarial	15.4	14.0	12.1	11.2	10.3
Skilled trades occupations	16.5	12.9	11.6	11.0	10.3
Caring, leisure and other services	5.0	7.3	8.9	9.1	9.5
Sales and customer service	8.0	8.5	8.6	8.3	8.2
Process, plant and machine operatives	9.8	8.0	6.4	5.9	5.4
Elementary occupations	12.2	11.8	10.4	10.4	10.2

[a]Projected figures.

Source: Wilson and Homenidou (2012: 83).

Despite misgivings about a growing chasm between good and bad jobs and regardless of recession, which has impacted considerably on employment levels for all occupations, Wilson and Homenidou (2012) suggest that broad trends in employment share have not derailed. We continue to see rising employment levels and shares for higher-level, white collar groups such as managers, directors and senior officials, professionals and associate professional and technical occupations; rapid increases for leisure-related and other personal service occupations; a decline in employment for administrative and secretarial occupations; and declining employment levels and employment share for most blue collar/manual occupations. Accompanying these trends, the demand for skills as measured by formal qualifications is projected to rise, as is the supply of people holding higher-level qualifications; for example, the number of jobs in occupations typically requiring a degree is expected to continue to grow, but perhaps more slowly than previously forecast, as a result of overall slow growth in the economy as it emerges from recession. One of the negative consequences of these patterns, coupled with stilted economic growth characterised by high unemployment, is the risk of basic-level jobs being increasingly filled by those with intermediate-level skills, reducing the opportunities for those with only basic skills (CBI, 2011).

We need to be careful in drawing conclusions about what these trends mean in real terms for employment opportunities in the labour market. To assume that there will be an absence of job vacancies in declining occupations ignores the fact that in addition to net growth or decline in demand for workers within particular occupations, there will be a demand for workers to replace those leaving occupations, mainly for reasons of retirement. 'Replacement demand' means that, although total employment in an occupation may be declining, there could still be a large number of jobs on offer within it at any one time. Wilson and Homenidou (2012) project that around 12 million job vacancies will be created by those who leave the labour market between 2010 and 2020, around eight times the estimated 1.5 million openings from the creation of new jobs (so-called expansion demand). Replacement demand creates opportunities in all sectors and across all occupations, including those predicted to slump significantly. Individuals planning careers and embarking on training ought therefore to consider that declining occupations and industries may nevertheless provide decent career prospects.

One of the dangers for employers is that skill shortages may arise, not because there is a dearth of applicants to vacancies but because employers cannot locate the necessary skills to fulfil replacement demand in declining occupations. The CBI brief (2011) suggests that the key to securing increased levels of employment in the economy is the ability to match skills supply with demand in different parts of the economy.

Holmes and Mayhew (2012) express some concern that the pace at which workers are becoming increasingly well-qualified may lead to their skills being under-utilised. Similarly, Sisson (2011: 19) worries that when competition for jobs is intense and relatively high-skilled workers have lost their jobs or are struggling to find work they 'bump down' and compete with unskilled workers for lower-wage/lower-skilled jobs. This scenario has two consequences: first, for those with few skills and qualifications, competition for work becomes extreme and the penalties for unemployment get higher (in other words, losing a job is more catastrophic as the chances of getting another are reduced); and secondly, for those who are 'bumping down', concerns centre around wage degradation, under-utilisation of skills and potentially lower levels of job satisfaction.

Wilson and Homenidou (2012) are a little more optimistic. Whilst they acknowledge that the qualification profile of the workforce will improve significantly over the next decade (running the distinct risk that the supply of highly qualified workers will exceed demand for such workers), they are confident there is evidence to suggest that labour market rates of return to higher qualifications, although faltering a little, are generally holding up pretty well. In other words, there are still significant positive benefits to be accrued from investing in education and training.

Changing forms of employment

During the 1980s and 1990s, senior managers initiated programmes of organisational change aimed at reducing costs and increasing the speed with which their organisations could respond to changes in market conditions. A central feature of organisational change programmes was workforce 'restructuring' or 'business process re-engineering', which involved large-scale reductions in headcount, achieved partly through redundancies, early retirement and non-replacement of departing workers and partly by contracting out non-core and specialist services. This was accompanied by the reorganisation of work and, in many cases, the wider use of part-time, fixed-term contract and temporary labour and, in a minority of cases, highly casualised forms of employment such as zero-hours contracts (Cully *et al.*, 1999; Millward *et al.*, 2000). These changes were aimed at increasing managers' ability to achieve greater *numerical labour flexibility,* in other words to be able to adjust the size of the workforce more easily in response to changes in demand.

The result was that, although the total number of jobs grew, there was a net reduction in the number of *full-time* jobs in Britain during the 1990s. All of the growth in employment was accounted for by a growth of part-time jobs, which increased from 22.9 per cent of total employment in 1992 to 24.6 per cent in 1999. The early and mid-1990s also saw an increase in the share of fixed-term and temporary employment from 5.9 per cent in 1992 to 7.6 per cent in 1997. These developments led some to argue that the full-time, permanent job was likely to become the exception rather than the rule (Bayliss, 1998). However, while part-time employment continued to increase its share of total employment after 1997, reaching 25.8 per cent in 2004 before levelling off and dropping slightly to 25.5 per cent at the end of 2008, the trend of temporary and fixed-term employment has been downward, the share falling to 5.5 per cent in 2008 (ONS 2005, 2009). Full-time, permanent jobs continue to be the most common form of employment.

The latest Workplace Employment Relations Study (WERS) data (van Wanrooy *et al.,* 2013: 10) provides an updated assessment of the prevalence of non-standard forms of working arrangements. The first findings of the survey report an increase (over the period 2004–2011) in the proportion of workplaces making some use of non-standard working provisions, such as shifts, annualised hours and zero-hours contracts. In fact, the percentage of workplaces that had some employees on zero-hours contracts doubled between 2004 and 2011, but only from a low base of 4 per cent. van Wanrooy *et al.* (2013) find little change in the use of fixed-term or temporary contracts, the use of agencies or employers contracting services in or out. In response to the recession, some employers reported cutting rather than increasing the number of agency workers. The CBI (2011), on the other hand, suggest that, as the recession eased, firms took on temporary workers to meet growing staffing needs while remaining watchful of continued economic uncertainty. They claim that the number of temporary workers and their share of the labour force are both now higher than pre-recession levels. According to the CBI (2011), the number of part-time workers was 5 per cent higher after the recession.

There is some evidence that people are occupying part-time roles because they are unable to secure the full-time work they desire. Kollowe (2012), for example, reports that in the second quarter (Q2) of 2012, part-time employment reached a record high of 8.07 million; however, the number of people working part-time only because they cannot find a full-time job also reached a new high, of 1.42 million. This problem of *underemployment* is referred to in the introductory case study at the beginning of this chapter.

Labour market outcomes: the quality of employment

In this section of the chapter, we examine how changes in the labour market have affected the quality of the employment experience. How should we assess the quality of jobs? What indices should we use? Traditionally, economists have used pay as the measure of job quality. Other social scientists have stressed the level of skill as a key measure on the grounds that skilled work not only provides workers with better pay but also more variety, personal autonomy and involvement, and ultimately more control over their effort. We have seen that there has been an overall trend towards increased skill requirements in jobs, so on the face of things at least it seems plausible that the quality of jobs available in the labour market has, on balance, improved. However, recent research has uncovered unexpected disjunctures between skill and other measures of job quality, such as employment security, the ability to control one's level of effort and to exercise control over how the job is done. In this section, we review evidence relating to these dimensions of job quality to assess whether recent changes in the demand for labour have improved the quality of employment experience in the UK.

Job security

Job security is generally regarded as an important factor determining job quality. Employment security has also been linked positively to skill level, with skilled workers enjoying greater job security than unskilled workers. Management-led organisational change during the 1980s and 1990s led to a growing concern at what appeared to be an increase in employment insecurity. It was argued widely in the press and by some academics that organisational restructuring and associated changes in patterns of labour demand were creating a new era of insecurity for workers, who were faced with higher risks of job loss and increased costs of job loss, leading to a subjective sense of employment insecurity.

The risk of job loss is affected by movements in the labour market, particularly changes in the rate of unemployment. The risk of job loss is greater when unemployment is rising than when it is constant or falling. However, during the 1990s, some observers argued that the risk of job loss was increasing independently of the level of unemployment; in other words for any given level of unemployment, the risk of job loss was higher than it used to be. Proponents of this argument pointed to redundancy dismissals and the replacement of permanent, full-time jobs with part-time and temporary jobs among previously secure groups such as managerial and professional workers and public-sector workers, and some argued these developments marked the end of internalised employment relationships that offered 'jobs for life' and clear career paths linked to length of service. Supporters of the insecurity thesis also argued that the costs of job loss had risen, because the level of social security payments had fallen relative to average wages and workers who had lost permanent full-time jobs were less able than previously to find equivalent replacements because of the trend away from full-time, permanent jobs to part-time and temporary jobs. They also argued that these developments generated heightened feelings of insecurity among workers.

Table 4.8 Perceptions of job security (%)

	Strongly agree or agree	Neither agree nor disagree	Strongly disagree or disagree
'I feel my job is secure in this workplace'			
2004	67	18	15
2011	60	21	18
Number of changes as a result of recession			
None	72	18	10
1	60	23	17
2	50	24	26
3	45	24	32
4 or more	32	25	43

Source: van Wanrooy *et al.* (2013: 9).

The empirical evidence showed that there was not a step increase in employment insecurity during the 1990s. While there was a slight increase in the proportion of workers in jobs lasting less than one year between 1991 and 1998, there was also an increase in the proportion of people employed in long-term jobs, i.e. those lasting 10 years or more (Sparrow and Cooper, 2003: 77). Neither was there a long-term increase in people's feelings of employment insecurity. The 'employment insecurity debate' subsided as quickly as it had arisen, figuring less and less in public discussion as we moved into the new millennium.

With the dawn of the credit crunch and the ensuing recession in the late 2000s, the state of job security in the labour market is once again under the microscope. It is inevitable perhaps that as unemployment bites, workers in employment will feel more insecure as the chance of losing their job increases and the likelihood of finding another lessens. WERS 2011 (van Wanrooy *et al.*, 2013: 9) does indeed show that workers are feeling more insecure than they did at the time of the last survey in 2004 (see Table 4.8).

As Table 4.8 shows, employees who had experienced change as a result of the recession were less likely to agree that their job was secure. Overell *et al.* (2010: 5), however, find that, although feelings of job insecurity will be heightened as a result of the recession, there is a paucity of evidence to support the notion that disposable, casual and hence insecure forms of employment are displacing the 'proper job' in the long run. They confirm that more than 80 per cent of jobs have permanent contracts and whilst full-time employment might have fallen and part-time employment increased, two-thirds of UK employees continue to be employed on a full-time basis. Additionally there has been no *significant* trend towards greater self-employment or temporary work in the UK, with levels of temporary work low in comparison to some other EU countries.

Explore

- Discuss with fellow students your perceptions of your own job security or insecurity generally in the current economic climate.
- What factors influence your assessment?

Worker discretion and autonomy

Worker discretion and autonomy are usually associated with skill. In fact, the skill content of a job is partly defined in terms of the extent to which workers are required to exercise their own judgment in deciding how the job should be done, the other elements being task complexity and variety. The fewer the prescribed instructions to workers and the greater the number of decisions that workers have to make in the course of the job, the more skilled it is considered to be. We have already seen that changes in the demand for labour have led to an increase in the average skill requirements of jobs. But does this mean that workers are enjoying increasing influence and control over how they work?

On the contrary, various studies have cast doubt on how far the up-skilling of jobs has been accompanied by increased discretion and control for workers – see Ramsay *et al*. (1991) for a discussion of the increased supervision of white collar workers in local government, Dent's (1991) study of bureaucratic controls affecting teachers and academics and Gallie *et al*. (1998) for an assessment of skilled workers subject to increased supervision when working with new technology. National survey data also show that the overall increase in skill levels has not been accompanied by increased worker discretion; if anything, the reverse has occurred (Green, 2006: 105). Overell *et al*. (2010: 6) persist, arguing that there has been insufficient recognition of the 'collapse of autonomy'. Using skills survey data, they find that workers' level of influence over the order, pace and nature of job tasks is much lower than it was 20 years ago. The proportion of respondents reporting a great deal of influence over how they did a task declined from 56.9 per cent in 1992 to 42.7 per cent in 2006, while those with a great deal of personal control over work effort has reduced from 70.7 to 52.5 per cent. This fall in autonomy is reported to affect *all* occupational groups.

So, rather than the shift in favour of more skilled jobs providing workers with greater control over their work, there has been a marked overall decline in discretion for all workers but particularly among professionals, who are among the most highly skilled workers. The reasons for this probably include the effects of new technology, financial pressures in the public sector, the spread of subcontracting and the increased public accountability to which professions have been subjected in the interests of improving public services such as health and education (e.g the NHS Patient's Charter). New technologies allow the implementation of routine processes and the closer monitoring of individual workers. Professional workers are also concentrated in the public sector, where government-imposed financial constraints have encouraged closer managerial control of professional workers. At the same time, political pressure to reform and improve public services has involved criticisms of established standards and practices among professional groups that have led to managerial interventions to limit professional autonomy.

Explore

- Identify as many examples as you can of politically inspired managerial interventions that have affected public service sector professional workers. The Patient's Charter cited in the segment above should help you on your way with your list.

Effort and work pressure

Since the 1980s, many have argued that work pressure has been increasing on two fronts in the UK. First, managers have been putting workers (and each other) under increasing pressure to work long hours. The prevalence of the 'long hours culture' in the UK is indicated by the fact that average working hours are higher in the UK than elsewhere in the European Union (EU). The British government has been accused of supporting a long-hours culture by seeking to limit the effect of the EU Working Time Directive in the UK. Secondly, since the mid-1980s, analysts have argued that work is being intensified; in other words, workers are being made to work harder during their working hours.

Green (2006) notes that there is a widespread belief that work is encroaching on other aspects of workers' lives, restricting the time available for non-work activities and consequently subjecting people to increased time pressures. This has fuelled recent discussion of 'work–life balance' (see the following section). Statistical evidence, however, shows that there has not been a *long-term* increase in average hours worked in the UK. Average hours worked per employed person fell from the 1950s to the 1980s but has remained relatively unchanged since. WERS 2011 (van Wanrooy *et al.*, 2013) found that in 2011 the distribution of usual hours worked among employees in workplaces with five or more employees was similar to that observed in 2004; the majority were working full-time hours of 30 or more per week, just under half (46 per cent) were working 40 or more hours per week, and 11 per cent of employees were working more than 48 hours per week. ONS (2012g) cites 39.1 hours per week as the mean weekly paid number of hours per week for full-time employees in both 2011 and 2012. What have increased, however, are the working hours per household as the proportion of households where all the adults are working has grown. The growing proportion of women with dependent children who are in work has been a major influence here. According to Green (2006), it is the increase in the total hours worked per household rather than an increase in hours worked per worker that has made it more difficult to balance work and non-work activities and put people under pressure of time.

The other contributory factor to pressures at work is the intensity of the work itself and the amount of work conducted within the hours worked. Whilst we have established that people are not, on the whole, working longer than they were in previous decades, there is evidence that work is harder, requiring people to apply higher levels of 'intensive effort', in other words more mental or physical effort. It is argued that work intensification has been driven mainly by macro-level influences such as increased competitive pressures and technological change. The 'effort-biased' nature of technical change (Green, 2006) enables management to exercise closer control over workers' effort. A clear example of this is the automated call distribution technology that is used in call centres. This ensures that call centre operators receive a continuous stream of incoming and outgoing calls, setting the pace of work in a similar way to the assembly line of an automated manufacturing plant. Another factor contributing to work intensification may be change in the labour market environment, particularly the decline of collective bargaining. This has given employers greater freedom to introduce certain HRM practices aimed at stimulating effort either directly, through, for example, performance-related pay and other new pay systems, or indirectly as a side-effect of other HR outcomes such as organisational commitment and employee engagement (Green, 2006).

Increased workloads were reported by 32 per cent of full-time employees and 19 per of part-time employees responding to the 2011 WERS (van Wanrooy *et al.*, 2013). Incidences of reported workload increases were felt by more managerial employees (39 per cent) than non-managerial staff (27 per cent). Further, there was a 6 per cent increase between 2004 and 2011 in the percentage of employees who strongly agreed with the statement 'my job requires I work very hard'.

Interestingly, there is also a growing body of evidence that part-time workers and those engaging in other forms of flexible working are experiencing work intensification. Walsh (2007) found that whilst employees in her study liked part-time work, there was evidence that fragmented work schedules, mandated overtime and difficulties in taking time off work at times to suit the employee created tensions in both the work and family sphere. Kelliher and Anderson (2010) also present findings to show that employees who worked from home for part of the week and employees working reduced hours experienced work intensification. Kelliher and Anderson (2010) report that flexible workers can be exposed to three different forms of intensification:

- *Imposed intensification* – e.g. when a full-time member of staff elects to reduce his/her hours, but their workload is not reduced accordingly. Such circumstances could result in increased 'extensive' effort, working at times when they are not scheduled to work and/or increased 'intensive' effort while working (working harder during hours of work).
- *Enabled intensification* – where the form of work organisation makes it easier for people to work harder, e.g. working from home incurs fewer distractions and negates travel time and so permits more time to work.
- *Reciprocal or exchange induced intensification* – where the ability to take advantage of flexible working options may engender a reaction in employees, which results in them expending greater discretionary effort.

Despite WERS evidence of employees working harder (van Wanrooy *et al.*, 2013: 40), the proportion of employees who were very satisfied or satisfied with all aspects of their job, except job security, rose between 2004 and 2011. Similarly, few of the respondents in Kelliher and Anderson's study of work intensification in flexible forms of work objected or cited negative outcomes of intensification.

Explore

Think about your own workplace.

● What systems and technologies are in place to regulate your effort?

● Have you noticed an increase or decrease in the intensity of your work over time?

● Why do you think employees report job satisfaction despite recognising intensification?

Responses to work pressure: the quest for 'work–life balance'

Work–life balance is a broad issue concerning how to mediate the conflicting demands of corporate profitability on the one hand and the concerns of workers who are under work pressure and life strain on the other.

Work–life balance is not an easily defined term. The word 'balance' suggests the search for equilibrium between work and life; a settled point perhaps at which work and the rest of life's activities can comfortably reside side by side. Noon and Blyton (2007) suggest work–life balance is about individuals being able to run their working lives and non-work lives without pressure from one detracting from the other. Part of the problem associated with the notion of striking a balance or equilibrium, however, is that for many, work and non-work aspects of life are increasingly inextricably entwined and overlapped; propelled by the accessibility of tablets and smart phones, we can work in a number of locations and be available instantly, at least in a virtual sense! Employee efforts to make individual and household adjustments to help bring about a better work–life balance are valuable in combating work–life conflict, but these endeavours are shaped by action at community, organisational and societal levels (see Figure 4.2).

Figure 4.2 Levels of response to work–life balance pressures

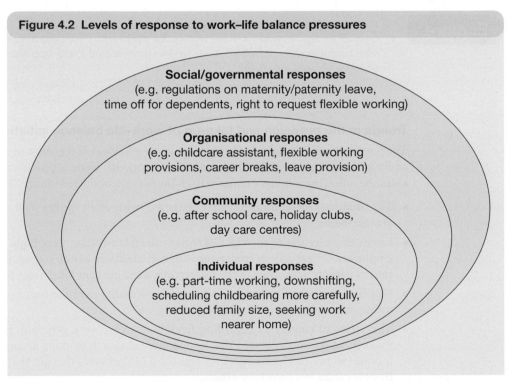

Social/governmental responses
(e.g. regulations on maternity/paternity leave,
time off for dependents, right to request flexible working)

Organisational responses
(e.g. childcare assistant, flexible working
provisions, career breaks, leave provision)

Community responses
(e.g. after school care, holiday clubs,
day care centres)

Individual responses
(e.g. part-time working, downshifting,
scheduling childbearing more carefully,
reduced family size, seeking work
nearer home)

Source: Noon and Blyton (2007: 368).

- Are you content with your work–life balance?
- What could you conceivably do to improve your work–life balance?
- How do governmental/social, organisational and community responses to work–life balance pressures (as detailed in Figure 4.2) help or hinder you in your ability to improve your work–life balance?

Organisational responses to work–life balance

There are arguably strong business reasons why employers should offer arrangements to employees to help achieve a better integration of work and non-work aspects of their lives. Clutterbuck (2004) suggests that creating an enabling culture in which employees can amend and re-apportion the time and attention they pay to work to meet their particular needs and circumstances can be a source of sustainable competitive advantage. More specifically, Edwards and Wajcman (2005) refer to international survey evidence to show that graduates care more about work–life balance than pay when they are selecting an employer, the implication being that employers who attend to the work–life balance needs of their employees are more likely to be employers of choice in the competitive graduate market. However, finding the right blend of organisational interventions to help individuals is complex; work–life balance is a movable target in the sense that different people have different ideas of what constitutes a satisfactory work–life balance. In practice, employers' responses to work–life balance have been mixed. According to WERS 2011 (van Wanrooy *et al.,* 2013), most managers (76 per cent) strongly agree or agree that it is up to individual employees to balance their work and family responsibilities. Managers in private-sector organisations were more likely than those in the public sector to take this view. In line with these findings, there was no reported general increase in employers' provision of flexible working practices to help employees achieve a better work–life balance.

- Think of an organisation you have worked for where some work–life balance practices were available. Why do you think this organisation elected to develop and introduce work–life balance initiatives?

Trends in the provision and take-up of work–life balance initiatives

The Fourth Work–Life Balance Survey (Tipping *et al.,* 2012) is the latest in a series of surveys embarked upon first in 2000, to track trends in work–life balance provision. The survey provides the following summary remarks from the survey conducted in early 2011:

- The majority of employees were satisfied with their hours and current working arrangements.
- Levels of awareness of the right to request flexible working were high; 75 per cent of all employees, 73 per cent of employees with non-childcare caring responsibilities and 79 per cent of parents were aware of the right, rising to 82 per cent for parents of young children.
- Flexitime, working from home and part-time working were the forms of flexible working most commonly taken up by employees.
- The views of employees regarding flexible working were generally positive. The vast majority of employees agreed that having more choice in working arrangements improves morale (90 per cent), although over one-third (35 per cent) thought that people who work flexibly create more work for others.

- The availability of flexible working was important for just over two in five employees (41 per cent) when they made their decision to work for their current employer. Those with flexible working arrangements were more likely to work long hours, suggesting that such practices facilitate greater labour market involvement.

The survey is extremely rich in detail and reveals perceptions of the availability of a host of different forms of flexible working by employee and employer characteristics. It is beyond the scope of this chapter to extract and discuss these findings. Suffice to say that gender, age, occupation/occupational status and qualifications are among the factors influencing the availability of forms of flexible working to employees. Employers' propensity to offer flexible working arrangements is driven by a number of factors, including but not limited to sector, mode of production/nature of operations, the gendered composition of the workforce, workplace size and unionisation.

It is conjectured that progress in addressing work–life balance issues will continue to be uneven given the trend to smaller workplaces combined with limited trade union presence. Moreover, even in those organisations where opportunities for flexible working are offered, barriers to their take-up by employees can prevail; 'organisations need not only to have policies for work–life balance in place, but also an underlying culture that supports employees who use flexible working options' (Noon and Blyton, 2007: 373). Potential obstacles to take-up include the irreducible nature of work tasks in many cases, possible damage to career prospects resulting from taking flexible work options and, for low earners, loss of earnings resulting from some options.

Concluding comments

The evidence discussed in this chapter suggests that, despite the widespread rhetoric of high commitment and high involvement and the tendency among advocates and practitioners of HRM to present the employment relationship in terms of mutual consent, it continues to be characterised by conflicts of interest. Currently these centre on hours of work, work intensity, lack of discretion and control over how work is performed, and structured inequalities in the labour market.

The main labour market developments from 1997 to just before the recession in 2008 were sustained growth of employment accompanied by increasing inequality in the distribution of pay as a result of the polarised nature of employment growth. While employment and pay have risen for all groups of workers since 1993, the *relative* position of less skilled workers in terms of unemployment, access to jobs and pay is worse than it was at the start of the 1980s and is now further compounded by economic instability and austerity measures. The rise in unemployment, resulting from the economy dipping in and out of recession since 2008, will continue to have disproportionate effects on the most disadvantaged sections of the population.

In addition, long-standing patterns of inequality and disadvantage remain. The difference in employment rates between women and men has not really changed over the last 10 years, nor has there been much change in the quality of jobs occupied by women. They are still concentrated in occupations and industries where rates of pay are low and working conditions are poor. While the overall pay gap between women and men has narrowed, it is the minority of women who are working full-time in higher-paid occupations who have benefited. This group have also benefited from statutory maternity leave provisions, which have given them the right to return to their jobs after childbirth. The pay gap for the majority of working women, who are in part-time jobs, has not narrowed. Established patterns of labour market inequality between ethnic minorities and whites have also persisted.

These features of the contemporary labour market suggest that there are serious long-term issues to face. First, it is clear that there has been a mismatch between, on the one hand, the way managers are organising work and designing jobs and, on the other, how workers' job aspirations are developing. Widespread job dissatisfaction is a risk that stands to weaken employees' commitment to their employers and erode the goodwill that is necessary for cooperative behaviour in the workplace. Recent attention to work–life balance issues may go some way to addressing these issues, but as long as, in the words of the UK Commission for Employment and Skills (2009: 10), there are 'too few high performance workplaces, too few employers producing high quality goods and services, too few businesses in high value-added sectors', there will continue to be too many people struggling to get by in jobs for which they are more than likely over-qualified and in which they consequently find insufficient fulfilment.

Secondly, discrimination against ethnic minorities, women and older workers represents a waste of human resources, as it leads to under-utilisation of skills possessed by these groups. However, employers individually may benefit from the presence of disadvantaged groups, who can be exploited because they lack alternative job opportunities. Therefore there is a case for stronger 'active' state intervention to combat unfair discrimination in the labour market.

Summary

- Labour markets are often seen as arenas of competition in which forces of supply and demand determine wage and employment levels. In reality, however, there are limits to competition in labour markets.

- Employers have some freedom to make a strategic choice between internalising or externalising the employment relationship. Their choices are influenced, although not completely determined, by the nature of their labour requirements and by features of the labour market context in which they operate.

- The aggregate supply of labour – the size of the workforce – is determined by demographic factors such as the size and age structure of the population and by social and political factors that influence the participation rate of different socioeconomic groups within the population. In the UK, differential participation rates can be observed between men and women of different age groups and different ethnic groups.

- Aggregate labour demand consists of total employment plus unfilled vacancies. The demand for labour is derived from the demand for goods and services. In conditions of low unemployment – tight labour markets – employers have to compete more actively to attract and retain workers.

- The demand for labour is segmented into job offers of varying quality. Unfair discrimination along lines of gender and ethnicity means that women and ethnic minorities are disadvantaged in terms of access to good jobs.

- There has been a long-term change in labour demand away from manufacturing to services. This has been an important force driving the long-term growth of part-time employment and women's employment.

- Since the 1980s, there has been a shift in the occupational structure of labour demand mainly towards highly skilled occupations but also leading to the growth of some low-skilled occupations. There has been a relative decline in intermediate occupations. Some refer to this as the hollowing out of the occupational structure to create an hourglass economy.

- Since the 1980s, managers have restructured their organisations and their workforces. This has involved a retreat from internalised employment relationships.

- Contrary to what might have been predicted from the overall trend towards more highly skilled work, the quality of jobs has deteriorated in terms of work pressure and worker autonomy, although not (up until recently) in terms of job stability. These factors have contributed to falling levels of job satisfaction compared with the early 1990s. The demand for better work–life balance is a recent response to growing work pressure.

Questions

1 Explain the factors that influence the differential labour market participation rates of women and men, and black and minority ethnic (BME) individuals and whites.
2 How has the structure of demand for labour changed over the last three decades or so?
3 Why have levels of job satisfaction declined since the early 1990s?
4 Who have been the main beneficiaries of changes in the labour market since the 1980s and who have been the main losers?

Case study

Is a Bulgarian and Romanian influx on the cards?

Romania and Bulgaria are among the poorest countries in Europe and when they joined the European Union in 2007, 'transitional' work restrictions were imposed amidst fears about mass migration. These measures will be lifted from 1 January 2014, giving Bulgarians and Romanians the same rights to work across the union as other EU citizens.

Some in the UK have voiced fears that ending restrictions will trigger a huge influx of Romanian and Bulgarian immigrants seeking work, as happened in 2004 when the UK allowed people from EU accession states, including Poland, Hungary and the Czech Republic, to work freely. Many of the people who came to the UK from Poland and other eastern European countries did so without a job awaiting them. However, the results of polls conducted in each country in February 2013 by BBC's *Newsnight* programme (both comprising 1000+ citizens) suggest that, for now at least, most Romanians and Bulgarians would only come to the UK with a firm offer of work.

The polls are relatively small; however, looking at Romania, of the 90 people who said they were planning to work in the UK, 65 per cent would do so only with an offer from a recruitment agency, or directly from a company. For the 138 Bulgarians answering this question, 60 per cent said they would do so only with an offer from a recruitment agency, or directly from a company. When looking at what kind of people are interested in moving to the UK, the Bulgarian survey suggested they tend to be younger and they are more likely to be unemployed than the average in the survey. The Romanian survey suggested that people interested in moving to the UK are more likely to have a university degree, more likely to be employed, and are likely to be more affluent than those looking to move elsewhere in the EU.

In truth, the ministers do not know how many Romanians and Bulgarians will come to the UK in 2014 and beyond. The Home Office has said it has not produced forecasts, and Downing Street has insisted it would not publish predictions on the number of people who could move to the UK following the relaxation of rules on the movement of people from the EU member states. The formula on the website, however, suggests 4,613 Bulgarians and 8,155 Romanians will head to the UK. The communities secretary, Eric Pickles, has said that he has no confidence in such estimates – the government could only monitor 'pull factors' attracting migrants, he said.

'All the government can do is to just be careful about the pull factors that might range from the health service, through housing, through benefits within the law to try and ensure there isn't an extra attraction to come here. Already there are people working in Lincolnshire and our crops being brought in (by people) that come from Romania and Bulgaria and the truth is very few carrots would be picked without that help that is there.'

Migration Watch UK, which campaigns for tougher controls on immigration, estimates that 250,000 Romanians and Bulgarians will move to the UK in the first five years after access restrictions are lifted (2014–2019).

Source: adapted from 'Romania and Bulgaria immigration: "No idea" on numbers', *BBC Politics*, 19 March 2013, http://www.bbc.co.uk/news/uk-politics-21850751 and 'Polls: No indication of huge Romanian-Bulgarian influx', *BBC Politics*, 22 April 2013 (http://www.bbc.co.uk/news/uk-22221841).

Case study continued

Questions

1 What challenges and opportunities does the prospect of the arrival of migrants from Bulgaria and Romania present for the UK, both economically and socially?

2 If, as the *Newsnight* poll predicts, Romanians and Bulgarians will likely only move to the UK if they have a firm job offer, how robust are anti-immigration claims that an influx of migrants will place undue pressure on jobs and employment and be catastrophic for the UK?

3 Eric Pickles implies that migrant workers do the jobs indigenous workers prefer not to do. How critical is migrant labour to the UK economy?

References and further reading

AGCAS Race Equality Task Group (2008), *What Happens Next? A Report on Ethnicity and the First Destinations of Graduates 2006*. Sheffield: AGCAS.

Anderson, B., Ruths, M., Rogaly, B. and Spencer, C. (2006) *Fair Enouth? Central and Eastern European Migrants in Low-wage Employment*. York: Joseph Rowntree Foundation.

Baccardax, M. (2013) 'Spain: quarterly unemployment surges to record high 27.2%', *International Business Times,* 25 April 2013.

Barnes, L. (2012) *Measuring national well-being, social trends 42 – population*, ONS.

Bayliss, V. (1998) *Redefining Work: An RSA Initiative*. London: Royal Society for the Encouragement of Arts, Manufactures and Commerce.

BBC (2012) *Business News,* 'HMV posts annual loss as sales decline'. Online: **http://www.bbc.co.uk/news/business-19190829** (accessed 9 August 2012).

CBI (2011) *Mapping the route to growth: rebalancing employment*, Brief, June 2011.

Centre for Women and Democracy (2013) *Sex and Power; Who Runs Britain?* Counting Women in Coalition, funded by the Joseph Rowntree Charitable Trust.

Clutterbuck, D. (2004) *Managing Work–Life Balance in the 21st Century*. London: CIPD.

Cooke, L. and Baxter, J. (2010) 'Families in international context; comparing institutional effects across western societies', *Journal of Marriage and Family,* 72(3): 516–36.

Cracknell, R. (2012) *Women in public life, the professions and the boardroom*, House of Commons Library, Standard Note SN05170.

Craig, L. (2006) 'Children and the revolution; a time diary analysis of the impact of motherhood on daily workload', *Journal of Sociology,* 42: 125–43.

Crompton, R. and Lyonette, C. (2009) 'Partners' Relative Earnings and the Domestic Division of Labour', Conference presentation at Gender Equality Network Conference; Gender Inequalities in the 21st Century, University of Cambridge, 26 March.

Cully, M., Woodland, S., O'Reilly, A. and Dix, G. (1999) *Britain at Work. As Depicted by the 1998 Workplace Employee Relations Survey*. London: Routledge.

Dent, M. (1991) 'Autonomy and the medical profession: medical audit and management control' in C. Smith, D. Knights and H. Willmott (eds) *White-Collar Work: The Non-Manual Labour Process*. Basingstoke: Macmillan, pp. 65–88.

Doeringer, P.B. and Piore, M.J. (1971) *Internal Labour Markets and Manpower Analysis*. Lexington, MA: Heath.

Dustmann, C., Frattini, T. and Theodoropoulos, N. (2011) 'Ethnicity and second generation immigrants' in P. Gregg and J. Wadsworth (eds) *The Labour Market in Winter. The State of Working Britain*. Oxford: Oxford University Press.

Edwards, P. and Wajcman, J. (2005) *The Politics of Working Life*. Oxford: Oxford University Press, pp. 220–39.

EHRC (2013a) *Women, men and part-time work*, January. Online: **http://www.equalityhumanrights.com/scotland/legal-news-in-scotland/articles/women-men-and-part-time-work/** (accessed 16 January 2014).

EHRC (2013b) *How Fair is Britain? Equality, Human Rights and Good Employment Relations in 2010. The First Triennial Review*. Online summary: **http://www.equalityhumanrights.com/key-projects/how-fair-is-britain/online-summary/employment/** (accessed 16 January 2014).

Forde, C. and MacKenzie, R., (2007) 'Getting the mix right? The use of labour contract alternatives in UK construction', *Personnel Review*, 36, 4: 549–63.

Friedman, A. (1977) *Industry and Labour*. London: Macmillan.

Gallie, D., White, M. and Cheng, Y. (1998) *Restructuring the Employment Relationship*. Oxford: Clarendon Press.

Gordon, D.M., Edwards, R. and Reich, M. (1982) *Segmented Work, Divided Workers: The Historical Transformation of Labour in the United States*. Cambridge: Cambridge University Press.

Green, F. (2006) *Demanding Work: The Paradox of Job Quality in the Affluent Economy*. Oxford: Princeton University Press.

Heath, A. and Cheung, S.Y. (2006) *Ethnic Penalties in the Labour Market: Employers and Discrimination*. Research Report 341. London: DWP.

Holmes, C. and Mayhew, K. (2012) *The Changing Shape of the UK Job Market and its implications for the Bottom Half of Earners*. London: Resolution Foundation.

Kelliher, C. and Anderson, D. (2010) 'Doing more with less? flexible working practices and the intensification of work', *Human Relations*, 63(1): 83–196.

Kollowe, M. (2012) 'UK unemployment falls due to temporary Olympics jobs boost', *The Guardian,* 15 August 2012.

Laurie, H. and Gershuny, J. (2000) 'Couples, work and money' in R. Berthoud and J. Gershuny (eds) *Seven Years in the Lives of British Families*. Bristol: Polity Press, pp. 45–72.

Li, Y., Devine, F. and Heath, A. (2008), *Equality Group Inequalities in Education, Employment and Earnings: A Research Review and Analysis of Trends over Time*. Manchester: EHRC.

Longhi, S. and Platt, L. (2009) *Pay Gaps and Pay Penalties by Gender and Ethnicity, Religion, Disability, Sexual Orientation and Age*. London: EHRC.

Marlow, S. and Carter, S. (2004) 'Accounting for change: professional status, gender disadvantage and self-employment', *Women in Management Review*, 19, 1: 5–17.

Marx, K. (1932) *Economical and Philosophic Manuscripts of 1844*. Moscow: Progress Publishers.

Mason, R. (2012) 'One in four British babies born to foreign mothers', *The Telegraph*, 25 October 2012.

Millward, N., Bryson, A. and Forth, J. (2000) *All Change at Work? British Employment Relations as Portrayed by the Workplace Industrial Relations Survey Series*. London: Routledge.

National Audit Office (2008) *Department for Work and Pensions. Increasing Employment Rates for Ethnic Minorities. Report by the Comptroller and Auditor General*. London: The Stationery Office.

Nolan, P. and Brown, W. (1983) 'Competition and workplace wage determination', *Oxford Bulletin of Economics and Statistics*, 45: 269–87.

Noon, M. and Blyton, P. (2007) *The Realities of Work: Experiencing Work and Employment in Contemporary Society*, 3rd edn. Basingstoke: Macmillan.

ONS (2005) *Labour Market Trends*, 113, 12.

ONS (2008) *Social Trends*, No. 38, 2008 edn. Office for National Statistics. Basingstoke: Palgrave MacMillan.

ONS (2009) *Economic and Labour Market Review*, April, Table 2.03. Online: **http://www.ons.gov.uk/ons/rel/elmr/economic-and-labour-market-review/no--4--april-2009/index.html** (accessed 19 January 2014).

ONS (2011) *Summary: UK Population Projected to Reach 70 Million by Mid-2027*, 26 October 2011.

ONS (2012a) *2011 Census – Population and Household Estimates for England and Wales, March 2011*. Statistical Bulletin, 16 July 2012.

ONS (2012b) *2011 Census – Population Estimates for the United Kingdom, March 2011*. Statistical Bulletin, 17 December 2012.

ONS (2012c) *Internal Migration by Local Authorities in England and Wales, year ending June 2011*, September 2012.

ONS (2012d) *Births and Deaths in England and Wales, 2011* (Final), 17 October 2012.

ONS (2012e) *Ethnicity and National Identity in England and Wales 2011*, 11 December 2012.

ONS (2012f) *Religion in England and Wales 2011*, 11 December 2012.

ONS (2012g) *Annual Survey of Hours and Earnings, 2012 Provisional Results*, 22 November 2012.

ONS (2013a) *2011 Census – Population and Household Estimates for the United Kingdom, March 2011*. Statistical Bulletin, 21 March 2013.

ONS (2013b) *Migration Statistics Quarterly Report*, February 2013.

ONS (2013c) *Interim Life Tables, England and Wales 2009–2011*, 21 March 2013.

ONS (2013d) *Labour Market Statistics*. Statistical Bulletin, April 2013.

Overell, S., Mills, T., Roberts, S., Lekhi, R. and Blaug, R. (2010), *The Employment Relationship and the Quality of Work*, Provocation Paper 7, The Good Work Commission, The Work Foundation.

Philpott, J. (2011) *How Men and Women have Fared in the Post-Recession UK Jobs Market*, Work Audit. London: CIPD.

Plunkett, J. (2011) *The Missing Million; The Potential for Female Employment to Raise Living Standards in Low to Middle Income Britain*, a Resolution Foundation Briefing.

Rafferty, A. (2012) 'Ethnic penalties in graduate level over-education, unemployment and wages: evidence from Britain', *Work, Employment and Society*, 26, 6: 987–1006.

Ramsay, H., Baldry, C., Connolly, A. and Lockyer, C. (1991) 'Multiple microchips: the computerised labour process in the public service sector', in C. Smith, D. Knights and H. Willmott (eds) *White-Collar Work: The Non-Manual Labour Process*. Basingstoke: Macmillan, pp. 35–64.

Rubery, J. (1994) 'Internal and external labour markets: towards an integrated analysis', in J. Rubery and F. Wilkinson (eds) *Employer Strategy and the Labour Market*. Oxford: Oxford University Press, pp. 37–68.

Rutherford, T. (2012) *Population Ageing; Statistics*. House of Commons Library Standard Note SN/SG/3228.

SCER (2001) *SCER Report 1 – Understanding the Labour Market*. Glasgow: University of Strathclyde, Department of Human Resource Management.

Sealy, R. and Vinnicombe, S. (2013) *The Female FTSE Board Report 2013: False Dawn or Progress for Women on Boards?* Cranfield: Cranfield University.

Sissons, P. (2011) *The Hour Glass and the Escalator; Labour Market Change and Mobility*. London: The Work Foundation.

Sparrow, P.R. and Cooper, C.L. (2003) *The Employment Relationship: Key Challenges for HR*. London: Butterworth Heinemann.

The Fawcett Society (2013) *The Changing Labour Market; Delivering for Women, Delivering for Growth*. London: The Fawcett Society.

Tipping, S., Chanfreau, J., Perry, J. and Tait, C. (2012) *The fourth work life balance employee survey*, Employment Relations Research Series 122. London: The Department for Business Innovation and Skills.

Townsend, L. and Westcott, K. (2012) 'Census 2011: five lesser-spotted things in the data', *BBC News Magazine*, 17 July.

The Women's Business Council (2013) *Getting On and Branching Out, Evidence Paper: Transitions in Work, Flexible Working and Maternity*.

UK Commission for Employment and Skills (2009) *Ambition 2020: World Class Skills and Jobs for the UK*. London: UKCES (**www.ukces.org.uk**).

van Wanrooy, B., Bewley, H., Bryson, A., Forth, J., Freeth, S., Stokes, L. and Wood, S. (2013) *The 2011 Workplace Employment Relations Study, First Findings*. Department for Business, Innovation and Skills, ACAS, ESRC, UKCES and NIERS.

Vargas-Silva, C. (2013a) *Long-term International Migration Flows to and from the UK*. Oxford: The Migration Observatory at the University of Oxford.

Vargas-Silva, C. (2013b) *Geographical Distribution and Characteristics of Long-term International Migration Flows to the UK*. University of Oxford: The Migration Observatory.

Wadsworth, J. (2003) 'The labour market performance of ethnic minorities in the recovery' in R. Dickens, P. Gregg and J. Wadsworth *The Labour Market under New Labour: The State of Working Britain*. Basingstoke: Palgrave, pp. 116–33.

Walsh, J. (2007), 'Experiencing part time work; temporal tensions, social relations and the work family interface', *British Journal of Industrial Relations*, 45, 1: 155–77.

Wilson, R. and Homenidou, K. (2012), '*Working Futures 2010–2020: Main Report*'. UK Commission for Employment and Skills, UKCES Evidence Report No. 41.

Chapter 5

Talent management

Julie Beardwell and Audrey Collin

Objectives

- To define talent and talent management.
- To consider ways of identifying talent to meet organisational requirements.
- To identify the contribution of recruitment and selection to talent management.
- To investigate initiatives designed to enhance employee retention.
- To identify the contribution of employee development activities, succession planning and career management to talent management.

Introductory case study

The contribution of talent management

What exactly is talent? According to the director of talent at PwC, Sonja Stockton, PwC looks for intellectual agility, drive and resilience, but the definition of talent really depends on the person: 'Some people have deep subject specialisms but others have a range of skills and can move from one role to another and transfer those skills. Talent can be inspired in different ways and at different times of people's lives'.

In 'The Human Age', a report published last month, Manpower's Mr Joerres claims that how companies and their employees relate is changing. He says the recession has driven companies to excel at 'doing more with less', which has led them to focus on seeking a relatively rare but valuable skill set – which is what he defines as talent: 'Talent isn't just people, it's people with specific skills, behaviours and a way of operating in a chaotic, global environment, that fits the needs of the organization.' However, he continues by saying that pinning all of a company's hopes on acquiring talent is already passé: 'Companies know that their current way of operating can't continue.' He believes the power in the employment relationship is shifting from the company to the individual – or at least those individuals with skills that are in demand. To deal with this, he says, companies will need to spend more time addressing the needs of individual employees rather than taking a one-size-fits-all approach.

 Source: Griggs, T (2011) 'The self-imposed talent shortage', *Financial Times*, 10 February. http://www.ft.com/cms/s/0/32b7ba98-3461-11e0-993f-00144feabdc0.html#axzz2tcGBag9f
© The Financial Times Limited 2011. All Rights Reserved.

Introduction

The preoccupation with talent has grown considerably in recent years. There continues to be an abundance of TV shows that are based on a competitive elimination process to identify the most 'talented' individual in a variety of fields, from modelling to singing to baking. This interest in searching for and identifying talented individuals is not restricted to the media. Talent has become an important issue in the workplace and talent management is fast gaining top priority for organisations across many countries (Bhatnagar, 2008). A global study of human resources (HR) leaders shows that talent management is *the* most critical issue facing HR departments worldwide. The study, conducted by the Boston Consulting Group and the World Federation of Personnel Management Associations (WFPMA), involved an online survey of nearly 5,000 executives and over 200 in-depth interviews, and the results reveal that talent management was at the top, or near the top, of executive agendas in almost all of the 83 countries surveyed (Phillips, 2008). These findings pre-date the 2008 financial crisis, but a recent survey undertaken by the Chartered Institute of Personnel and Development (CIPD, 2012a) found that the current economic situation has led almost half of all organisations to increase their focus on talent management. This highlights the importance of an effective workforce when times are difficult and recognition that organisations cannot afford to tolerate inadequate performance (CIPD, 2012a: 20).

But what do we mean by talent management? The term was first coined by the McKinsey Group in the late 1990s when they warned that a 'war for talent' was imminent due to a predicted shortage of people with leadership potential. Since then, the use of the term has become increasingly common, but its meaning still remains somewhat elusive and open to a number of different interpretations. This chapter will therefore begin by defining the terms 'talent' and 'talent management' and will then explore the activities associated with talent management and their effectiveness.

Defining talent management

The *Compact Oxford English Dictionary* defines talent as 'natural aptitude or skill' and 'people possessing such aptitude and skill', so that talent can apply equally to specific skills and to the people who possess these skills. In the workplace context, talent can be defined as 'those individuals who can make a difference to organisational performance, either through their immediate contribution or in the longer term by demonstrating the highest level of potential' (CIPD, 2006: 3). Thus, talent can be used to refer to everyone, on the assumption that people all possess individual skills and abilities, or talent can be used in a more exclusive sense only to refer to those who can demonstrate high performance or potential. The initial McKinsey report focused on the recruitment and retention of 'A players', the top-performing 20 per cent of managers (Guthridge and Lawson, 2008), arguing that 'managerial talent is not the only type of talent that companies need to be successful, but it is a critical one' (Michaels *et al.,* 2001). More recently, consideration of talent has broadened to reflect recognition of the valuable contribution of 'B players', i.e. the capable, steady performers that make up the majority of the workforce (Guthridge and Lawson, 2008). A third interpretation suggests that the focus of any talent management activity should be on the key positions that are important to fill in any organisation (CIPD, 2006). Thus talent can be used in an exclusive sense, to refer to a select group of high-flyers; in an inclusive sense, to refer to all employees; or in a hybrid sense to refer to key workers or roles that are critical to organisational success but which may be at different levels of the organisation.

A critical review of the literature (Lewis and Heckman, 2006: 140–41) identifies three distinct perspectives on talent management:

- *Talent management as HR management.* Talent management is seen to encompass typical HR practices, functions, activities or specialist areas, such as recruitment, selection, development, and career and succession management. From this perspective, the emphasis is on HR doing what it has always done but 'doing it faster (via the internet or outsourcing) or across the enterprise rather than within a department or function' (Lewis and Heckman, 2006: 140).

- *Talent management as HR planning.* Talent management is viewed primarily as a set of processes designed to ensure an adequate flow of employees into jobs throughout the organisation. Here the focus is on projecting staffing needs and ensuring an adequate and appropriate talent pipeline.

- *Talent management as a general good.* This third perspective focuses on talent generically, without considering organisational boundaries or specific positions. Two different approaches emerge in this perspective: organisations that focus their attention on attracting, developing and retaining high-performing individuals (the exclusive approach identified earlier) and organisations that aim to manage everyone to better performance (the inclusive approach).

Explore

- Are these perspectives mutually exclusive?
- What are the implications of these different perspectives for the understanding and application of talent management?

Research undertaken on behalf of the Corporate Research Forum (Hirsh, 2012: 23) found that at least half of the respondents use talent management as a general set of human resource management (HRM) practices, while three-quarters operate around the second perspective with a focus on succession planning. Responses to the survey show two main aims for talent management:

- Echoes of long-established definitions of workforce planning – phrases like 'the right people, in the right place at the right time'.

- Developing the workforce, either in its entirety or those with high or leadership potential – i.e. building the talent pipeline.

Strategic talent management

Whichever perspective is applied, there is nothing particularly new about the individual activities that comprise talent management. In fact, Lewis and Heckman (2006: 141) suggest that the first two perspectives are little more than a rebranding of HR practices and workforce planning practices which do little to advance our understanding of 'the strategic and effective management of talent'. Others, however, do suggest that talent management is a strategic process closely aligned with business strategy; for example, Armstrong (2009: 560) sees talent management as an integrated bundle of activities, 'the aim of which is to secure the flow of talent in an organization, bearing in mind that talent is a major corporate resource' (Armstrong, 2009: 580). CIPD (2012b: 1) defines talent management as 'the systematic attraction, identification, development, engagement, retention and deployment of those individuals who are of particular value to an organisation, either in view of their "high potential" for the future or because they are fulfilling business/operation-critical roles'. In addition, CIPD (2012c: 11) suggests that 'in today's challenging economic climate, the effective and strategic management of talent is critical to differentiate organisations from their competitors and drive business success'.

The existence of a strategy can support the development of plans that are concerned with attracting sufficient high-quality external applicants and making effective use of the internal labour market through the retention, deployment and engagement of the existing workforce. These plans are based on predictions of demand, i.e. the numbers of people and skills that the organisation will need in the future, and supply, i.e. the availability of those people and skills already in the organisation and in the external labour market. Reconciliation of these plans can help organisations to determine the optimum balance between external and internal recruitment. Some organisations prefer to fill as many vacancies as possible with existing employees in order to motivate and develop people and retain critical skills. This approach requires considerable investment in training and development and the support of a performance management system with an emphasis on identifying potential and on securing commitment from employees. However, the internal recruitment pool is likely to be relatively small so the potential downside of internal recruitment is that the organisation does not necessarily get the best person for the job.

An emphasis on external recruitment might help to bring new ideas and new styles of working into the organisation, but this approach may also reflect a short-term focus and an unwillingness or inability to invest in the existing workforce. Within the UK the unwillingness may arise from a fear of engaging in costly development activities with staff, which could make them attractive to competitors. Alternatively, management may believe that future changes can pose problems in offering long-term employability or promotion and do not want to raise unrealistic expectations amongst the workforce. At the same time, rapidly changing organisational requirements may mean there is no time to develop the required competencies in-house. In practice, many organisations adopt a combination of both external and internal recruitment, depending on the positions to be filled and the skills available in-house. Cappelli (2008) argues that adopting a supply chain perspective and applying operations principles to talent management can help to address the risks associated with estimating demand and the uncertainty of supply (see Table 5.1).

A KPMG white paper 'Tune into Talent' (2013: 3) suggests that, too often, organisations 'make plans for tomorrow based on people they have and the situation they are in today' rather

Table 5.1 Operations principles applied to talent management

Principle 1 – Make and buy to manage talent	A deep bench of talent is expensive, so companies should undershoot their estimates of what will be needed and plan to hire from outside to make up for any shortfall. Some positions may be easier to fill from outside than others, so firms should be thoughtful about where they put their resources in development. Talent management is an investment, not an entitlement.
Principle 2 – Adapt to the uncertainty in talent demand	Uncertainty in demand is a given, and smart companies find ways to adapt to it. One approach is to break up development programmes into shorter units. Rather than put management trainees through 3-year functional programmes, for instance, bring employees from all the functions together for an 18-month course that teaches general management skills, and then send them back to their functions to specialise. Another option is to create an organisation-wide talent pool that can be allocated among business units as the need arises.
Principle 3 – Improve the return on investment in developing employees	One way to improve the payoff is to get employees to share in the costs of development. That might mean asking them to take on additional stretch assignments on a volunteer basis. Another approach is to maintain relationships with former employees in the hope that they may return some day, bringing back your investment in their skills.
Principle 4 – Preserve the investment by balancing employee–employer interests	Arguably, the main reason good employees leave an organisation is that they find better opportunities elsewhere. This makes talent management a perishable commodity. The key to preserving your investment in development efforts for as long as possible is to balance the interests of employees and employer by having them share in advancement decisions.

than taking 'a cold, hard look at current processes and technologies – and being prepared to radically evolve them to meet the needs of the next generation of employees'. Empirical evidence appears to support the criticism that few organisations are adopting a strategic approach to talent management. Survey data (CIPD, 2006) found that 60 per cent of organisations had no formal talent management strategy and 80 per cent had no formal definition of talent management. A more recent survey (CIPD, 2012c) found that, although just over half (54 per cent) of organisations undertake talent management activities, the main objectives are to develop high-potential employees (62 per cent) or grow senior managers (59 per cent) rather than meeting future skill requirements (28 per cent). However, whether talent management is a strategic or reactive process, its key components are concerned with attracting, identifying, developing and retaining talented individuals. The chapter will explore each of these activities in turn, considering the different methods that organisations may use and the effectiveness of different approaches.

Attracting talent

Attracting talent is primarily aimed at the external labour market and involves the use of recruitment and selection techniques to identify the skills required and then to attract and choose the most suitable people to meet an organisation's HR requirements. Recruitment and selection are integrated activities, and where recruitment stops and selection begins is a moot point (Anderson, 1994). Nevertheless, it is useful to try to differentiate between the two areas. Whitehill (1991) describes the recruitment process as a positive one, 'building a roster of potentially qualified applicants', as opposed to the 'negative' process of selection. So a useful definition of recruitment is 'searching for and obtaining potential job candidates in sufficient numbers and quality so that the organisation can select the most appropriate people to fill its job needs' (Dowling and Schuler, 1990: 51). Selection is concerned more with 'predicting which candidates will make the most appropriate contribution to the organisation – now and in the future' (Hackett, 1991: 49), but also affects the ability to attract suitable candidates, as applicants may be put off if the selection practices appear unfair or unprofessional.

External recruitment

The recruitment process involves identifying the skills and abilities required and then choosing the most effective recruitment methods to attract a pool of suitable candidates. When organisations choose to recruit externally rather than internally, the search takes place in local, regional, national and/or international labour markets, depending on numbers, skills, competencies and experiences required, the potential financial costs involved and the perceived benefits involved to the organisation concerned. External recruitment often poses problems for organisations, particularly in the public sector: 82 per cent of respondents to the CIPD (2012a) *Resourcing and Talent Planning Survey* report recruitment difficulties. The main causes cited are:

- lack of necessary specialist or technical skills (59 per cent);
- lack of relevant sector/industry experience (39 per cent);
- looking for more pay than could be offered (38 per cent).

The survey no longer identifies how organisations are responding to these recruitment difficulties, but earlier surveys (e.g. CIPD, 2008) have found that common approaches include appointing people with potential, taking account of a broader range of qualities, redefining the job and increasing starting salaries. Other initiatives that were applied include:

- providing a realistic job preview;
- using employer brand as a recruitment tool;
- offering flexible working.

Box 5.1	Realistic job previews at easyJet

The easyJet careers website provides an interactive quiz to help prospective applicants understand more about what it is like to work as a member of cabin crew. The company encourages prospective applicants to take the quiz as many times as they like so that they can make the right decision about whether or not to apply. The quiz includes a range of scenarios commonly encountered by cabin crew and asks the applicant to select how they may react to the situation. For example:

> You have been working on a flight to Hamburg and are just about to start preparations for the return flight home when your cabin manager tells you that there is a technical issue with the aircraft that means you'll be delayed in Hamburg for at least five hours. This will disrupt the plans you'd made to spend the evening out for a friend's birthday. How do you feel?
>
> A I understand the reasons, but I feel a little frustrated.
> B I'm resolved to do my best to help make the situation better.
> C I accept that sometimes things like this happen.

After each scenario, the applicant receives some feedback on their response. Based on the feedback received, candidates can then make more informed decisions about whether to apply for the post or continue searching for roles that may be more suited to their skills and working preferences.

Source: http://careers.easyjet.com/try-before-you-fly/

Questions

1 What are the advantages and disadvantages of online realistic job previews for organisations and prospective employees?

2 What other methods could be used to give candidates an accurate picture of job requirements?

Realistic job previews

The purpose of a realistic job preview is to help prospective candidates to better understand the demands of the job and the culture and values of the organisation. Realistic job previews can be presented in a variety of ways, including online questionnaires, videos and workplace visits (see Box 5.1). The information included in a realistic job preview should be important to most recruits, not widely known outside the organisation and related to the reasons why newcomers leave (Wanous, 2009). A realistic job preview can improve the 'fit' between employee and organisational expectations and reduce the numbers of employees who leave the organisation after a short time. A study of the effectiveness of a realistic job preview for expatriate assignments in a multinational company (Caliguiri and Phillips, 2003) found that candidates who received a realistic job preview reported higher perceived ability to make an informed decision about whether to accept a global assignment than those who did not. On the other hand, some excellent candidates may be deterred from applying if the preview draws too much attention to the potential drawbacks of the role. Taylor (2010) suggests that it may be wise to keep back some of the more negative aspects of the job for discussion at the selection interview.

Employer branding

Over recent years, skills shortages and a tough economic environment have meant that employers are obliged to compete more fiercely with one another to attract and keep effective staff, whilst often being constrained in the extent to which they can do this by paying higher salaries (CIPD, 2007). One response to these difficulties has been to promote a strong employer brand that markets what the organisation has to offer potential and existing employees. Employer branding adopts similar techniques to those developed by marketeers to attract customers and maintain their loyalty, but in this case applies them to employees. Employer branding can therefore be defined as (CIPD, 2007: 3):

> A set of attributes and qualities – often intangible – that makes an organisation distinctive, promises a particular kind of employment experience, and appeals to those people who will thrive and perform best in its culture.

All organisations have an employer brand, regardless of whether they have consciously sought to develop one. This brand will be based on the way they are perceived as a 'place to work' by potential recruits, existing employees and leavers (CIPD, 2012d). Developing an employer brand involves creating a compelling employer image and convincing employees and prospective employees of its worth (Suff, 2006). A strong employer brand should therefore connect an organisation's values and its people management strategy and be intrinsically linked to a company brand (CIPD, 2012d). Employer branding also reflects recruitment and selection as a social process, i.e. recognising that it is not only the organisation that selects the applicant but also the applicant who selects the organisation (Nickson *et al.*, 2008).

Explore

Think about an organisation where you have worked or would like to work.
- How would you describe its brand?
- How is this brand communicated to potential and existing employees?

Taylor (2010: 199) suggests that a positive employer brand can not only make the organisation more attractive to potential recruits but also reduce recruitment costs. Raising the organisation's profile and increasing its reputation in the labour market mean that fewer advertisements need to be placed to attract the candidates the organisation needs. In addition to being able to attract high-quality applicants, organisations also have to be able to keep them. A strong employer brand is frequently associated with being an 'employer of choice' and is seen as a key element of winning the 'war for talent' (Williams, 2000: 31):

> In essence, creating a winning environment consists of developing a high-achieving company with values and brand images of which employees can be proud. At the same time, their jobs should permit a high degree of freedom, give them a chance to leave a personal mark and inject a constant flow of adrenalin. Leadership, of course, should be used to enhance, enable and empower, rather than to inhibit, constrain or diminish.

However, not all commentators view employer branding in a positive light. Taylor (2010: 213) identifies two criticisms contributing to significant debate about the concept. The first is based on the principle that this kind of marketing activity is essentially manipulative and serves the interests of employers at the expense of employees. To put it another way, employer branding is used to recruit and retain without increasing wages. In response, Taylor points out that publications on employer branding repeatedly state that 'branding exercises that are dishonest in nature invariably fail' (p. 214). Furthermore, the growth of social media means that risks associated with the employee experience not matching that promised by the employer brand are greater than in the past. Employees can and do use social media to comment on their organisations and what it is like to work there. Frank Durrell, TMP Worldwide Head of Digital, commented in a recent CIPD paper (CIPD, 2012e) that 'social media can make or break the employer brand and encourage talent to come knocking or redirect it to the competition'.

The second criticism views employer branding as merely another management fad which will soon run its course. However, there is little to indicate that the interest in employer branding is waning: on the contrary, a number of commentators (see, for example, CIPD, 2009) have suggested that the emphasis on branding has increased in response to the current economic conditions. Managing the perceptions of employees and potential candidates is particularly important in difficult times; for example: 'the handling of job cut announcements can have a significant impact on the reputation of the organisation as an employer (CIPD, 2009: 2).

Key Controversy

Is employer branding beneficial for individuals and organisations? What steps could be taken to ensure that employer branding is handled ethically?

Whether or not an organisation actively engages in employer branding, the process of recruitment involves identifying the types of applicants that the organisation wants in terms of skills, experience and attributes. Traditionally, this approach has been very job-focused, i.e. identifying the specific vacancy to be filled and then identifying the person who can best meet the job requirements. More recently there has been a move towards being more people-focused, i.e. identifying the key attitudes and behaviours that will make a valuable employee and then training to match specific job needs. This chapter now considers the advantages and disadvantages associated with both approaches.

Defining the talent required

The traditional approach to defining the type of people an organisation wants to attract involves writing a comprehensive job description of the job to be filled. This enables the recruiter to know exactly what the purpose, duties and responsibilities of the vacant position will be and its location within the organisation structure. The next step involves drawing up a person specification that is based on the job description, and which identifies the personal characteristics required to perform the job adequately. Characteristics are usually described within a framework consisting of a number of broad headings. Two frequently cited frameworks are the seven-point plan (Rodger, 1952) and the five-fold grading system (Munro Fraser, 1954), illustrated in Table 5.2. Both frameworks are dated now, and some headings can appear to be potentially discriminatory (e.g. physical make-up and circumstances), but nevertheless they continue to form the basis of many person specifications in current use. It is common to differentiate between requirements that are essential to the job and those that are merely desirable.

Whatever exact format is used, the person specification can form the basis of the recruitment advertisement, it can help to determine the most effective selection methods and, if applied correctly, can ensure that selection decisions are based on sound, justifiable criteria. However, the compilation of a person specification needs to be handled with care. Predetermined criteria can contribute to effective recruitment and selection only if full consideration has been given to the necessity and fairness of all the requirements. Preconceived or entrenched attitudes, prejudices and assumptions can lead, consciously or unconsciously, to requirements that are less job-related than aimed at meeting the assumed needs of customers, colleagues or the established culture of the organisation. Examples of this might include insistence on qualifications or experience that are not specifically required to undertake the role or sex role stereotyping.

The job-based approach to recruitment and selection can be inflexible in a number of ways. For example, the job description may fail to reflect potential changes in the key tasks, or

Table 5.2 Person specification frameworks

Rodger (1952)	Munro Fraser (1954)
Physical make-up – health, appearance, bearing and speech	Impact on others – physical make-up, appearance, speech and manner
Attainments – education, qualifications, experience	Acquired qualifications – education, vocational training, work experience
General intelligence – intellectual capacity	
Special aptitudes – mechanical, manual dexterity, facility in use of words and figures	Innate abilities – quickness of comprehension and aptitude for learning
Interests – intellectual, practical, constructional, physically active, social, artistic	Motivation – individual goals, consistency and determination in following them up, success rate
Disposition – acceptability, influence over others, steadiness, dependability, self-reliance	Adjustment – emotional stability, ability to stand up to stress and ability to get on with people
Circumstances – any special demands of the job, such as ability to work unsocial hours, travel abroad	

Source: ACAS (1983).

the list of duties and responsibilities may be too constraining, especially where teamworking is introduced. This concentration on a specific job and its place in a bureaucratic structure may be detrimental to the development of the skills and aptitudes needed for the long-term benefit of the organisation. In order to accommodate the need for greater flexibility and the desire to encourage working 'beyond contract', many organisations have replaced traditional job descriptions with more generic and concise job profiles, consisting of a list of 'bullet points' or accountability statements.

The recognition that jobs can be subject to frequent change can also reduce the importance of the job description and increase the relative importance of getting the 'right' person. This approach has the potential for greater flexibility, as it enables organisations to focus less on the job itself and more on an individual's attitude to work and their adaptability. For example, research into call centre recruitment and selection found that a positive attitude was more important in candidates than their ability to use a keyboard (Callaghan and Thompson, 2002).

In a talent management approach, a combination of the job-oriented and person-oriented approaches may be adopted in order to recruit people who can not only fill a specific vacancy but can also contribute to the wider business goals of the organisation. One way to achieve this is via the use of competencies. The term 'competency' can be interpreted in different ways but is generally used to refer to personal attributes of individuals' i.e. 'the behaviours that individuals must have, or must acquire, to perform effectively at work' (CIPD, 2012f: 1). Competency-based recruitment and selection involve the identification of a set of competencies that are seen as important across the organisation, such as planning and organising, managing relationships, gathering and analysing information and decision-making. Each competency can then be divided into a number of different levels, and these can be matched to the requirements of a particular job.

Feltham (in Boam and Sparrow, 1992) argues that a competency-based approach can contribute to the effectiveness of recruitment and selection in three main ways:

- The process of competency analysis helps an organisation to identify what it needs from its human resources and to specify the part that selection and recruitment can play.

- The implementation of competency-based recruitment and selection systems results in a number of direct practical benefits.

- Where systems are linked to competencies, aspects of fairness, effectiveness and validity become amenable to evaluation. These competence frameworks can be used for more than just recruitment and selection.

However, competency frameworks can be difficult to apply in practice and therefore may not achieve the goals of the organisation. The main reasons for this are that managers do not see the benefit of the competency framework and are not trained adequately in its use; there are not clear links to what the business is aiming to achieve; and many frameworks are a mix of different concepts, which makes them unwieldy (Whiddett and Hollyforde, 2007).

What a competency-based approach may discover is that recruitment is not always the answer. There are usually a variety of strategies for achieving a particular competency mix and no 'right' solutions. For example, if specialist skills are scarce, an organisation may choose to replace the skills with new technology, train existing staff, or hire specialist consultants when needed in preference to employment of permanent staff (Feltham, 1992). Where recruitment and selection is deemed appropriate, a competency-based approach achieves a visible set of agreed standards that can form the basis of systematic, fair and consistent decision-making. A recent variation is in the use of a 'strengths-based' approach to recruitment, which involves 'identifying individuals' strengths, such as roles they particularly enjoy or at which they excel, and then matching them to appropriate types of work, hence enhancing individual performance' (CIPD, 2012f: 1).

Recruitment methods

The choice of methods and media used to attract candidates can determine the numbers and quality of candidates and whether or not they decide to apply for the role. Organisations have a wide variety of methods to choose from, including the use of:

- the internet, including corporate websites and social media;
- advertising, including local and national press, specialist publications, radio and TV;
- informal personal contacts, such as word of mouth and speculative applications;
- formal personal contacts, such as employee referral schemes, careers fairs and open days;
- notice boards, accessible by current staff and/or the general public;
- external assistance, including job centres, careers service, employment agencies and 'head-hunters'.

Decisions about the most appropriate method (or methods, as many organisations will use more than one) are likely to be influenced by the level of the vacancy and its importance within the organisation. Other factors to be taken into account when choosing the most appropriate method include the resources available within the organisation (in terms of people and finance), the perceived target groups, and the organisation's stance on internal versus external recruitment. HRM literature emphasises the need to have well-developed internal labour market arrangements for promotion, training and career development, which would suggest that many openings can and should be filled internally (Beaumont, 1993). However, a number of organisations, particularly those in the public sector, have policies that require the majority of posts to be advertised externally. Survey findings suggest that, although the majority of workplaces treat external and internal applicants equally, one-fifth give preference to internal candidates and one in 10 prefer to recruit externally (Kersley *et al.*, 2006).

E-recruitment

Over recent years, there has been a significant increase in use of technology to recruit candidates and the majority of respondents to the latest CIPD survey on recruitment (CIPD, 2012a: 9) considered their own corporate website to be the most effective recruitment method. Online recruitment enables organisations to reduce the time and cost of recruitment and reach more potential applicants. Online recruitment can be used in a number of ways:

- to advertise vacancies on a corporate website, job sites or social networking sites;
- to deal with applications, e.g. email enquiries, emailed applications forms or CVs, online application forms;

- to enhance employer brand;
- to create a personal relationship with the talent pool, e.g. through the use of recruitment blogs.

The impact of technology on the recruitment process can vary depending on whether online methods are used to supplement or replace more traditional approaches. For example, corporate and external websites can be used to advertise vacancies in addition to press adverts, while the handling of enquiries and applications via email can lead to a duplication of activity (electronic as well as paper-based systems) rather than a replacement of one system with another. Online recruitment can help to speed up the recruitment process and simplify administration, thus reducing costs. It can reinforce employer branding and provide more tailored information on the post and the organisation. The global coverage also helps to reach a wide pool of applicants and can provide a cost-effective means of building a talent pool for future vacancies. However, the downside is that online recruitment can lead to application overload or, conversely, restrict the applicant audience to those who search for jobs online and can make the process impersonal, which may be off-putting for some candidates. In response to this, an increasing number of organisations are using social networking sites to target potential employees.

Social networking

Frank Durrel, TMP Worldwide Head of Digital (CIPD, 2012e: 8), suggests a number of ways that social media can be used in the recruitment process, from simply providing information to candidates to arguably more effective interaction and engagement with the target audience. For example, Jaguar Land Rover created a video and enabled graduates to personalise this with an image of themselves and then share it on social media. Interaction can also be used to identify the most suitable candidates: GCHQ launched a code-cracking campaign on social media and only those candidates who could crack the code were directed to the organisation's website to apply for the job in cyber-security. A survey undertaken by Eurocom Worldwide (2012) found that the most popular social media sites for technology companies are LinkedIn (74 per cent), Twitter (67 per cent), Facebook (64 per cent) and YouTube (56 per cent) (see Box 5.2).

Recruitment documentation

The response to applicants should indicate the overall image that the organisation wishes to project. Some organisations prepare a package of documents, which may include the job description, the person specification, information about the organisation, the equal

---

Box 5.2 | **Recruitment at the Hard Rock Café**

When the Hard Rock Café opened a restaurant in Florence in Spring 2011, the company needed to hire 120 people in four weeks. Using the services of a company called Work4Labs, Hard Rock first created a unique Facebook page for the restaurant. After running ads to target locals who 'liked' Rock and Roll, the company allowed potential hires to submit their applications directly through the social network.

The result was a fully staffed restaurant for a fraction of the normal spend and 25,000 new Facebook fans.

Source: Colao, J.J (2012) 'With Facebook your recruitment pool is one billion people', forbes.com 12/9/12 (accessed: 28 March 2013).

Questions

1 What are the advantages and disadvantages of the approach adopted by the Hard Rock Café?

2 What factors should an organisation take into account before deciding to use social media as the primary source of potential candidates?

opportunities policy, the rewards package available and possible future prospects. Some give candidates the opportunity to discuss the position with an organisational representative on an informal basis. This allows the candidate to withdraw from the process with the minimum activity and cost to the organisation. Much relevant information can now be supplied online, thus improving access and reducing costs.

The design of application forms can vary considerably, but the traditional approach tends to concentrate on finding out about qualifications and work history, and usually includes a section in which candidates are encouraged to 'sell' their potential contribution to the organisation. A more recent development is the adoption of a competency-based focus, requiring candidates to answer a series of questions in which they describe how they have dealt with specific incidents such as solving a difficult problem or demonstrating leadership skills. Some organisations, particularly in the retail sector, include a short questionnaire in which applicants are asked to indicate their preferred way of working.

A variant on the traditional application form, 'biodata' (short for biographical data), may also be used. Forms usually consist of a series of multiple-choice questions that are partly factual (e.g. number of brothers and sisters, position in the family) and partly about attitudes, values and preferences (Sadler and Milmer, 1993). The results are then compared against an 'ideal' profile, which has been compiled by identifying the competencies that differentiate between effective and non-effective job performance in existing employees. Biodata questionnaires are costly to develop and need to be designed separately for each job (Taylor, 2010). There are also problems with potential discrimination and intrusion into privacy, depending on the information that is sought. Taylor (2010: 250) suggests that the apparently arbitrary nature of making selection decisions on the basis of questions such as university attended or preferred holiday destination 'is disturbing, however effective the approach might be at determining job performance'. Few employers report the full-blown use of biodata, but the principles appear to influence the design of longer and more sophisticated application forms, often completed online (Reynolds and Weiner, 2009).

Explore

- How much time and effort does it take you to obtain details about a post and complete an application that shows how your skills and experiences match the requirements of the job?
- Why is it important for organisations to be aware of the answers to the above question?

Selecting talent

The stages described in the previous sections constitute recruitment, and are primarily concerned with generating a sufficient pool of quality applicants. The focus now shifts to selection and the next stages concentrate on assessing the suitability of candidates.

Shortlisting

It is extremely unlikely that all job applicants will meet the necessary criteria, and so the initial step in selection is categorising candidates as probable, possible or unsuitable. This should be done by comparing the information provided on the application form or CV with the predetermined selection criteria. The criteria may either be explicit (detailed on the person specification) or implicit (only in the mind of the person doing the shortlisting). However, this latter approach is potentially discriminatory, and would provide no defence if an organisation was challenged on the grounds of unlawful discrimination. Potentially suitable candidates will continue to the next stage of the selection process.

Other developments chiefly reflect a desire to reduce the time and effort involved in short-listing from large numbers of applicants. One option is to encourage unsuitable candidates to self-select themselves out of the process. The chapter has already discussed the use of realistic job previews that allow candidates to answer online questionnaires and receive feedback on their answers and potential suitability for the post prior to completing a job application. A variant on this is to use 'killer' questions; these are asked at certain stages of an online application process and an incorrect answer will terminate the application at that point (IRS, 2003). Another option is to use software packages that compare CVs with the selection criteria and separate the applications that match the criteria from those that do not. This has the advantage of removing some of the subjectivity inherent in human shortlisting, but does rely on the selection criteria being correctly identified in the first instance. It can also reject good candidates who have not used the right keywords and so needs to be handled with caution. A third option is to reduce large numbers of applicants via random selection. Although there is concern that this may operate against equal opportunities, it is also claimed that 'randomised selection may produce a better shortlist than one based on human intervention where the wrong selection criteria are used consistently or where the correct selection criteria are applied inconsistently' (IRS, 1994: 6).

Selection techniques

Various selection techniques are available, and a selection procedure will frequently involve the use of more than one. The most popular techniques are outlined here (see Table 5.3), and their validity and effectiveness are discussed later in the chapter.

Interviews

Interviewing continues to be the most popular selection method but can be applied in a wide variety of ways. Differences can include both the number of interviewers and the number of interview stages. The format can be biographical, i.e. following the contents of the application form, or it can be based on the key competencies required for the job. Over the years, interviews have received a relatively bad press as being overly subjective, prone to interviewer bias, and therefore unreliable predictors of future performance. Such criticisms are levelled particularly at unstructured interviews, and in response to this, developments have focused on structuring the interview more formally or supplementing it with less subjective selection tools, such as psychometric tests and work sampling.

Table 5.3 Popularity of selection methods

	%
Competency-based interviews	70
Interviews following contents of CV/application form (i.e. biographical)	63
Structured interview (panel)	56
Tests for specific skills	49
Telephone interviews	43
Literacy and/or numeracy tests	38
Personality/aptitude questionnaires	35
Assessment centres	35
Pre-application elimination/progression questions	25
General ability tests	23
Group exercises (e.g. role-playing)	21
Pre-interview references	9

N – 605

Source: from the *Resourcing and Talent Planning Survey* report, CIPD (2011) p. 18, with the permission of the publisher, the Chartered Institute of Personnel and Development, London (**www.cipd.co.uk**).

There are different types of structured interview, but they have a number of common features (Anderson and Shackleton, 1993: 72):

- The interaction is standardised as much as possible.
- All candidates are asked the same series of questions.
- Replies are rated by the interviewer on pre-formatted rating scales.
- Dimensions for rating are derived from critical aspects of on-the-job behaviour.

The two most popular structured interview techniques are behavioural and situational interviews. Both use critical incident job analysis to determine aspects of job behaviour that distinguish between effective and ineffective performance (Anderson and Shackleton, 1993). The difference between them is that in behavioural interviews, the questions focus on past behaviour (e.g. 'Can you give an example of when you have had to deal with a difficult person? What did you do?'), whereas situational interviews use hypothetical questions (e.g. 'What would you do if you had to deal with a team member who was uncooperative?').

Explore

Imagine you are responsible for selecting operators to work in a call centre.

- Prepare a set of behavioural questions suitable for the interview. You are looking for evidence of strong social skills (e.g. good verbal communication, positive attitude, good sense of humour, energy and enthusiasm) and good technical skills (e.g. numeracy and keyboard skills).
- Test out these questions on friends and colleagues to assess their effectiveness. What do you see as the key strengths and weaknesses of this approach?

Behavioural and hypothetical questions generally form the basis of competency interviews with the supplementary use of probing questions focused on exploring in detail the extent to which candidates can demonstrate the key behaviours and attributes deemed necessary for the role in question. The focus on specific incidents makes it harder for candidates to make up answers and, from an interviewer's perspective, provides a good basis for justifying selection decisions (Taylor, 2010).

A recent development is the adoption of a strengths-based approach to recruitment, used by 40 per cent of organisations (CIPD, 2011). Whilst competencies relate to capability, strengths focus on what people enjoy doing. Professor Alex Linley defines strength as 'a pre-existing capacity for a particular way of behaving, thinking or feeling that is authentic and energizing to the user and enables optimal functioning, development and performance' (**www.cappeu.org**). When people are using their strengths they demonstrate a real sense of energy and engagement; they become engrossed in what they are doing; they will rapidly learn new information and will reach high levels of performance (Isherwood, 2008). Strengths-based recruitment is based on the principles of positive psychology, defined as 'a psychology of positive human functioning . . . that achieves a scientific understanding and effective interventions to build thriving in individuals, families and communities' (Seligman and Csikszentmihalyi, 2000: 13). Advocates of strengths-based recruitment (e.g. Isherwood, 2008) argue the benefits for both organisations and individuals, as it enables organisations to match the strongest candidates to roles that will help them achieve their potential and allows candidates to make informed and authentic choices. According to the CIPD survey (CIPD, 2011: 18), 78 per cent of organisations using a strengths-based approach to recruitment believe it brings benefits in terms of increased individual performance; 67 per cent believe it improves retention; 63 per cent believe it improves levels of engagement; and 39 per cent report that it results in greater diversity of skills in the workplace.

Tests

The types of test used for selection are ability and aptitude tests, intelligence tests and personality questionnaires. Ability tests (such as typing tests) are concerned with skills and abilities already acquired by an individual, whereas aptitude tests (such as verbal reasoning tests or numerical aptitude) focus on an individual's potential to undertake specific tasks. Intelligence tests can give an indication of overall mental capacity and have been used for selection purposes for some considerable time. Personality questionnaires allow quantification of characteristics that are important to job performance and difficult to measure by other methods (Lewis, 1985). The debate about the value of personality tests is ongoing, and centres around lack of agreement on four key issues (Taylor, 2010: 257):

- the extent to which personality is measurable;
- the extent to which personality remains stable over time and across different situations;
- the extent to which certain personality characteristics can be identified as being necessary or desirable for a particular job;
- the extent to which completion of a questionnaire can provide sufficient information about an individual's personality to make meaningful inferences about their suitability for a job.

Tests have the benefit of providing objective measurement of individual characteristics, but they must be chosen with care. Armstrong (2009) lists four characteristics of a good test:

- It is a *sensitive* measuring instrument which discriminates well between subjects.
- It has been *standardised* on a representative and sizeable sample of the population for which it is intended, so that any individual's score can be interpreted in relation to others.
- It is *reliable* in the sense that it always measures the same thing. A test aimed at measuring a particular characteristic should measure the same characteristic when applied to different people at the same time, or to the same person at different times.
- It is *valid* in the sense that it measures the characteristic which the test is intended to measure. Thus, an intelligence test should measure intelligence and not simply verbal facility (Armstrong, 2009: 572).

One relatively recent development has been the increased popularity of online testing, particularly in the recruitment of graduates and where employers are faced with high volumes of applicants. Online testing has the potential to reduce delivery costs, thus making testing more affordable for lower-paid jobs. However, there are also some potential disadvantages, including lack of control of the environment in which the test takes place and problems verifying that the individual taking the test is the actual candidate.

Assessment centres

An assessment centre is not a place but rather a process that 'consists of a small group of participants who undertake a series of tests and exercises under observation, with a view to the assessment of their skills and competencies, their suitability for particular roles and their potential for development' (Fowler, 1992). There are a number of defining characteristics of an assessment centre:

- A variety of individual and group exercises are used, at least one of which is a work simulation.
- Multiple assessors are used (frequently the ratio is one assessor per two candidates). These assessors should have received training prior to participating in the centre.
- Selection decisions are based on pooled information from assessors and techniques.
- Job analysis is used to identify the behaviours and characteristics to be measured by the assessment centre.

Assessment centres are used by a third of organisations (CIPD, 2011), usually in the appointment of graduates or management positions. The assessment centre process allows organisations

| Box 5.3 | **Graduate recruitment at KPMG** |

KPMG is one of the world's leading professional services organisations with a global network of member firms operating in 144 countries. The organisation keeps in touch with new and prospective graduate applicants via Twitter and Facebook. It also provides details of the selection process on its website:

Stage 1: Online Application Form covering academic background and work experience.

Stage 2: Situational Judgment Test is a multiple choice test featuring a series of hypothetical, challenging situations that could be encountered as a trainee with KPMG.

Stage 3: Online Numerical and Verbal Reasoning Tests. Applicants who are successful with their initial application and SJT are asked to take numerical and verbal tests designed specifically for KPMG.

Stage 4: First Round Interview. Applicants who are successful in the online tests are invited to participate in a 45-minute telephone interview focusing on behavioural capabilities.

Stage 5: Immersive Assessment Centre. All activities during the day are centred on a fictional organisation (based on KPMG), thus enabling candidates to experience a 'day in the life' of a KPMG trainee. Activities include:

Virtual office exercise – a laptop-based in-tray exercise

Analysis exercise – review complex information and prepare written recommendations

Lunch with current trainees

Two simulated meetings – client and internal meeting

Source: www.kpmgcareers.co.uk/graduates/how-to-apply/application-process/ (accessed 29/03/12).

Questions

1 What further action might KPMG take to ensure that the selection process fully reflects the nature of the business?

2 What criteria should KPMG use to measure the effectiveness of the immersive assessment centre?

to observe candidate behaviour in a work-related setting. Typical exercises can include presentations, role-plays, group discussions as well as interviews and psychometric testing. Combining group and individual exercises can improve the consistency and objectivity of the selection process. In addition, the use of such a sophisticated technique, if handled well, can help the organisation to display a positive image to potential candidates. The drawbacks primarily relate to the costs and resources required. For this reason, assessment centres are most likely to be used in public-sector organisations and by larger private-sector employers (see Box 5.3).

Social media

The chapter has already discussed the use of social media to attract candidates, but networking sites are also often used to screen applicants. The annual Eurocom Worldwide study has found that 40 per cent of respondent companies check out potential employees' profiles on social media and, according to the most recent survey, almost one in five technology firms has rejected a job applicant because of their social media profile (Eurocom, 2012). An article in the *Wall Street Journal* (Kwoh, 2012) reports on a study undertaken by the Corporate Executive Board, which found that, when screening using social media, 44 per cent of organisations have rejected applicants for badmouthing their current employer, 30 per cent for inappropriate language and 17 per cent for excessive personal information. The same report suggests that some companies are reluctant to add social media checks to their hiring process because employers can become aware of information that cannot be legally considered in the selection process, such as religion, race, gender and health status. In addition to potential claims for unlawful discrimination, risks to employers can also include ensuring compliance with data protection legislation and breaching trust and confidence (Cronly-Dillon, 2007).

Key Controversy

To what extent should organisations include information available on social media in their screening process?
How far should you consider future job prospects when posting information on social media sites?

Factors influencing choice of selection techniques

What determines the choice of different techniques? One could reasonably assume that a key factor in determining the type of method would be its ability to predict who is suitable and who is unsuitable for the position. In other words, whatever technique is used, people who do well should be capable of doing the job and people who do badly should not.

Accuracy

Accuracy should be a key determinant but no single technique can predict with certainty which individuals will perform well in a particular role (Marchington and Wilkinson, 2012). Figure 5.1 shows the accuracy of selection methods measured on the correlation coefficient between predicted and actual job performance, with zero for chance prediction and 1.0 for perfect prediction.

Figure 5.1 The predictive accuracy of selection methods

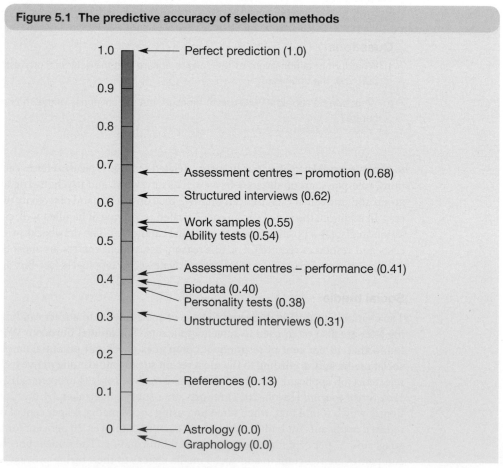

1.0 ← Perfect prediction (1.0)

0.7 ← Assessment centres – promotion (0.68)

← Structured interviews (0.62)

← Work samples (0.55)
← Ability tests (0.54)

← Assessment centres – performance (0.41)
← Biodata (0.40)
← Personality tests (0.38)

0.3 ← Unstructured interviews (0.31)

← References (0.13)

0 ← Astrology (0.0)
← Graphology (0.0)

Source: adapted from Anderson and Shackleton (1993: 30).

The increased use of more accurate methods, such as assessment centres and selection testing, can help to improve the effectiveness of the selection process, although findings from a survey (CIPD, 2011) show that interviews are still the most widely used selection methods. Concerns about accuracy appear to have encouraged employers to adopt more structured interview formats or supplement the interview with other selection methods such as tests or work simulation. However, the extent to which the drive for accuracy is the key influence is open to question. A study into the use of selection tests (Wolf and Jenkins, 2006) suggests that their increased use has been driven more by organisations' desire to protect themselves from legal challenges to selection decisions and by the growing professionalism of HR departments than by considerations of the technical qualities and predictive validity of tests. As a result, the article concludes that 'further increases in test use are very likely, but . . . there is no reason . . . to expect that these will necessarily increase the effectiveness of the selection process' (p. 208).

Level of vacancy

The level of vacancy can have a significant influence on the choice of selection methods used. Assessment centres, in particular, are more likely to be used for managerial and graduate posts. This may indicate an organisation's willingness to invest more heavily in future managers than in other parts of the workforce, but may also be due to candidate expectations and the organisation's need to attract the highest-quality applicants for key positions.

Cost of selection techniques

There is no doubt that recruitment and selection can be costly activities, and the costs incurred by some selection techniques can make them prohibitive for all but a few 'key' vacancies in an organisation. For example, assessment centres require considerable investment of resources and substantial time commitment from assessors. A CIPD survey (CIPD, 2102a: 14) reported median recruitment costs to be £8,000 for senior management/director positions and £2,500 for other employees. However, in deciding on the most cost-effective methods, the 'up-front' costs need to be balanced against the costs of wrong decisions. Jaffee and Cohen (cited in Appelbaum *et al.*, 1989: 60) suggest that consideration of costs should include some or all of the following:

- the start-up time required by a replacement for the jobholder;
- the down-time associated with the jobholder changing jobs internally or externally;
- training and/or retraining for the replacement and the jobholder;
- relocation expenses;
- the shortfall in productivity between an effective and ineffective jobholder;
- the psychological impact on the 'failed' jobholder and the morale of others in the department.

Making the selection decision

The aim of the overall recruitment and selection process is to provide enough information to enable recruiters to differentiate between those who can do the job and those who cannot. The prescriptive approach stresses that the final decision should involve measuring each candidate against the selection criteria defined in the person specification and not against each other (Torrington *et al.*, 2008). Searle (2003: 114–16) suggests a number of sources of error and bias in interviewers' decision-making process, including:

- 'similar to me effect', where interviewers enhance the ratings of those who look like themselves, respond in a similar way, or appear to have equivalent experiences;
- 'halo effect', where one aspect of the candidate's qualities (most commonly physical attractiveness) influences all other aspects and so boosts their overall rating;
- 'horns effect', where over-attention to some negative aspect reduces a candidate's overall rating.

The combination of a number of different selection methods and the increased use of more objective methods can enhance the quantity and quality of information about each candidate, although Anderson and Shackleton (1993) warn of the dangers of information overload in selection.

Retaining talent

Up until now, this chapter has focused on attracting new talent to the organisation, i.e. the external element of talent management. However, that is only part of the equation and talent management is also concerned with the ability to keep high-quality employees and continue to maximise their contribution to the organisation, i.e. the internal element. The chapter therefore now focuses on the internal element of talent management by exploring talent retention, talent development, succession planning and career management.

The retention of key staff is a major component of talent management as labour turnover can lead to a loss of skills and knowledge and a consequent reduction in productivity (CIPD, 2012a: 30). Any retention strategy needs to have information on why employees leave the organisation. Investigating labour turnover can include the use of quantitative and qualitative techniques.

Investigating labour turnover – quantitative methods

The most common method of measuring labour turnover is to express leavers as a percentage of the average number of employees. The labour turnover index is usually calculated using the following formula:

$$\frac{\text{Number of leavers in a specified period}}{\text{Average number employed in the same period}} \times 100\%$$

This measure is used most effectively on a comparative basis and frequently provides the basis for external and internal benchmarking. Labour turnover can vary significantly between different sectors and industries; for example, a recent survey into labour turnover (CIPD, 2012a) reports that the median labour turnover rate in the UK is 12.7 per cent, but this varies between different sectors (e.g. 9.5 per cent in manufacturing and production and 16.1 per cent in private services). There is no single best level of labour turnover, but external comparisons can be useful to benchmark labour turnover against other organisations in the same industry, sector or location. However, even organisations with lower than average turnover rates can experience problems if people have left from critical jobs or from posts that are difficult to fill. Conversely, high turnover is not necessarily problematic and may be used by cost-focused firms to minimise labour costs (Batt and Colvin, 2011). The labour turnover index is thus a relatively crude measure that provides no data on the characteristics of leavers, their reasons for leaving, their length of service or the jobs they have left. So, while it may indicate that an organisation has a problem, it gives no indication about what the specific problem might be, or what might be done to address it.

Knowledge about the location of leavers within an organisation can be gained by analysing labour turnover at the department or business unit level or by job category. For example, managers generally have lower levels of resignation than other groups of employees. Any areas with turnover levels significantly above or below organisational or job category averages can then be subject to further investigation. Most attention is levelled at the cost and potential disruption associated with high labour turnover, but low levels of labour turnover should not be ignored as they may be equally problematic.

Low labour turnover can cause difficulties as a lack of people with new ideas, fresh ways of looking at things and different skills and experiences can cause organisations to become stale and rather complacent. It can also be difficult to create promotion and development opportunities for existing employees. Nevertheless, many organisations are keen for some levels of stability. While the labour turnover index focuses on leavers, the stability index focuses on the percentage of employees who have stayed throughout a particular period, often one year. This therefore allows organisations to assess the extent to which they are able to retain workers. The formula used to calculate stability is:

$$\frac{\text{Number of employees with one year's service at a given date}}{\text{Number employed one year ago}} \times 100\%$$

Quantitative methods of turnover analysis can be useful for benchmarking the organisation against competitors and for analysing the relative performance of different parts of the organisation. Year-on-year comparisons can also be used to monitor the effectiveness of any retention initiatives. The major drawback of quantitative methods is that they provide no information as to the reasons why people are leaving. So, quantitative analyses can help to highlight problems but they give those responsible for talent management no indication about how these problems might be addressed.

Investigating labour turnover – qualitative methods

Investigations into reasons for turnover are usually undertaken via qualitative means. A variety of approaches are used in UK organisations. Exit interviews are the most commonly used methods of finding out why people leave. The benefits of exit interviews are that they are flexible enough to investigate reasons for leaving, identify factors that could improve the situation in the future and gather information on the terms and conditions offered by other organisations. Generally, exit interviews collect information on the following (IRS, 2002):

- reasons for leaving;
- conditions under which the exiting employee would have stayed;
- improvements the organisation can make for the future;
- the pay and benefits package in the new organisation.

There can also be a number of problems. The interview may not discover the real reason for leaving, either because the interviewer fails to ask the right questions or probe sufficiently or because some employees may be reluctant to state the real reason in case this affects any future references or causes problems for colleagues who remain with the organisation, e.g. in instances of bullying or harassment. Conversely, some employees may choose this meeting to air any general grievances and exaggerate their complaints. Some organisations collect exit information via questionnaires. These can be completed during the exit interview or sent to people once they have left the organisation. They are often a series of tick boxes with some room for qualitative answers. The questionnaire format has the advantage of gathering data in a more systematic way, which can make subsequent analysis easier. However, the standardisation of questions may reduce the amount of probing and self-completed questionnaires can suffer from a low response rate.

Reasons for leaving can generally be divided into four main categories:

- *voluntary, controllable* – people leaving the organisation due to factors within the organisation's control, e.g. dissatisfaction with pay, prospects, colleagues;
- *voluntary, uncontrollable* – people leaving the organisation due to factors beyond the organisation's control, e.g. relocation, ill-health;
- *involuntary* – determined by the organisation, e.g. dismissal, redundancy, retirement;
- *other/unknown*.

Attention is usually concentrated on leavers in the voluntary, controllable category as organisations can potentially take action to address the factors causing concern. However, distinctions between controllable and uncontrollable factors can become blurred. For example, in some instances, advances in technology and greater flexibility can facilitate the adoption of working methods and patterns to accommodate employees' domestic or personal circumstances. The involuntary category is also worthy of attention as high numbers of controlled leavers can be indicative of organisational problems, e.g. a high dismissal rate might be due to poor recruitment or lack of effective performance management.

Whilst exit interviews or exit surveys can provide some information about why people are leaving, they do not necessarily identify the triggers that made someone decide to leave. For example, someone might say that they are leaving to go to a job with better pay, but this does not show what led the person to start looking for another job in the first place. In order to address labour turnover problems and improve retention, organisations need to differentiate between 'push' and 'pull' factors. Once an individual has decided to look for another job, they are likely to base their decision on 'pull' factors, i.e. the attractions of the new job or organisation in relation to their existing circumstances. However, the decision to look for another job can be triggered by 'push' factors, i.e. aspects of the current role or organisation that are deemed unsatisfactory. A study into turnover of health care professionals in the UK (Loan-Clarke *et al.*, 2010: 402) found that reasons for leaving NHS employment were more often stated in terms of what was wrong with the NHS (push factors) rather than what was right with the alternative (pull factors). Mitchell *et al.* (2001) also suggest that decisions to leave or stay are influenced by the degree of job-embeddedness. This relates to how well an individual fits their job (i.e. alignment of skills with job demands), their community (interpersonal relationships) and what they would have to give up if they left.

One way to identify potential 'push' factors is to conduct *attitude surveys* within the organisation. Attitude surveys have an advantage over exit interviews and leaver questionnaires in that they can identify potential problems experienced by existing employees rather than those that have already decided to leave. This means that any response can be proactive rather than reactive. However, it also means that organisations can make problems worse if they do not act on the findings: 'Telling employees that an organisation cares enough to get their opinion and then doing nothing can exacerbate the negative feelings that already existed, or generate feelings that were not present beforehand' (IRS, 2002: 40).

The final method to investigate labour turnover to be discussed here is risk analysis. This involves identifying two factors: the likelihood that an individual will leave and the consequences of the resignation (Bevan *et al.*, 1997). Statistically, people who are younger, better qualified and who have shorter service, few domestic responsibilities, marketable skills and relatively low morale are most likely to leave (IRS, 2001). The consequences of any resignations are likely to be determined by their position in the organisation, performance levels and the ease with which they can be replaced. The risk analysis grid (Bevan, 1997) shows how the two factors can be combined (Figure 5.2). This then enables the organisation to target resources or action at the people it would be most costly to lose. However, the results should be treated with caution as the process does assume an element of predictability, whereas research suggests that decisions to leave are often complex and dynamic, and may be unpredictable or precipitated by sudden events (Morrell and Arnold, 2007).

Information from current employees and leavers can help organisations determine the most effective steps to avoid high levels of turnover and improve employee retention. However, De Vos and Meganck (2009) suggest that some retention initiatives are often based on HR managers' understanding of employees' reasons for leaving rather than their reasons for staying, which can reduce their impact. Findings from the CIPD (2012a: 31) survey show the most common steps taken by organisations to improve retention:

- increased learning and development opportunities (47 per cent);
- improved line management people skills (46 per cent);
- improved induction process (43 per cent);

Figure 5.2 Risk analysis grid

		Likelihood of leaving	
		High	*Low*
Impact on organisation	*High*	Danger zone	Watching brief
	Low	'Thanks for all you've done'	No immediate danger

Source: from Quit stalling, *People Management*, p. 34 (Bevan, S. 1997), with permission from Stephen Bevan.

- improved employee involvement (39 per cent);
- improved selection techniques (37 per cent);
- improved pay (28 per cent).

Explore

Think about an organisation you have left or are considering leaving.

- What impact would the factors listed above have on your decision?
- Why?

Attention to the skills and abilities of managers is perceived by some as a key element of retention: 'put simply, employees leave managers not companies' (Buckingham, 2000: 45). Buckingham (2000) argues that employees are more likely to remain with an organisation if they believe that their manager shows interest and concern for them; if they know what is expected of them; if they are given a role that fits their capabilities; and if they receive regular positive feedback and recognition. However, he also suggests that 'most organisations currently devote far fewer resources to this level of management than they do to high-fliers' (p. 46). Box 5.4 outlines a staff retention initiative from McDonald's.

Box 5.4 Improving retention at McDonald's

McDonald's Corporation is the world's largest chain of hamburger fast food restaurants, serving more than 58 million customers daily. One of the most common reasons that employees leave is that they want a different environment and don't think they can have that without changing jobs.

McDonald's Europe decided to do something about this perception. In September 2006, it launched its McPassport programme, an official certification programme designed to support the movement of restaurant employees throughout the European Union. 'The McPassport is a physical document, resembling a real passport, that certifies crew competencies and thus enables a McPassport holder to be eligible for a McDonald's job in the 25 countries of the European Union', says Carmen Vroonen, spokesperson for McDonald's Europe.

To earn McPassport certification, employees must be trained and earn a 'good' rating or above in the following stations: service, dining area, hospitality, production, fried products,

Box 5.4 continued

grills, buns and dressing. No minimum seniority is required. If an employee decides to leave one McDonald's restaurant, that particular operator has to look for another employee but at least the chain itself isn't losing a reliable employee and the time and money spent training the employee are not lost, as the new employer can take advantage of it.

Since launching McPassport, Vroonen says that both employees and operators have been excited about the programme. The first McPassport holders are currently working in the UK, Spain and Italy.

Source: http://www.managementparadise.com/forums/human-resources-management-h-r/219372-emplyee-retention-mcdonald-s.html (accessed 6 April 2013).

Questions

1 What steps would you recommend to improve retention even further?

2 How might your recommendations be best implemented?

3 How would you monitor the effectiveness of action taken?

Developing talent

Learning and performance improvement have always been an integral part of talent management (Frank and Taylor, 2004). Learning and development are discussed in detail in Chapter 7, so this section is merely intended to highlight the key developmental practices associated with talent management. Research undertaken by CIPD (CIPD, 2012c: 13) found that the talent management activities deemed to be most effective by respondents are:

● coaching (51 per cent);

● in-house development programmes (33 per cent);

● high-potential development schemes (26 per cent);

● mentoring and buddying schemes (25 per cent);

● 360-degree feedback (22 per cent).

The most appropriate methods are likely to be influenced by the size and nature of the talent pool, the organisation's focus on talent management, i.e. whether it is exclusive, inclusive or hybrid, and by organisational context. For example, the survey findings show that small and medium-sized companies were most likely to rate courses at external institutions and action learning sets as most effective, whereas larger organisations were more likely to rank high-potential development schemes and graduate development programmes among their most effective initiatives (CIPD, 2012c: 13). The survey also shows that, in the majority of UK organisations, talent management activities are aimed at developing high-potential employees (62 per cent) and growing future senior managers/leaders (59 per cent) and so are frequently associated with succession planning and career management.

Research undertaken by CIPD (CIPD, 2010) explored the perceptions of senior employees who were part of a talent pool or talent programme in their organisation. The results showed that 'the power and energy created from the formation of peer groups amongst the highest-performing individuals across the business . . . provides a significant opportunity for organisations to harness talent' (CIPD, 2010: 3). Respondents to the study valued coaching, mentoring and networking above the more formal development activities of a talent management programme. The results also demonstrate the importance of having a selection process for the talent programme, as this enhances the value of the programme to successful applicants. There is a danger of lower levels of organisational commitment from those who are not successful, so organisations need to give full consideration to how this group will be handled.

Two inter-linked key processes that underpin the creation and development of a talent pipeline are succession planning and career management. Succession planning is primarily driven by organisational requirements and is a process by which successors are identified for key posts and development activities and career moves are planned in the short and long term (Hirsh, 2012). Career management can be seen as a process that allows individuals to identify future career moves (either within or beyond the existing organisation) and the skills and knowledge required to prepare themselves to gain these roles. The key elements of each approach are considered below.

Succession planning

Succession planning can be seen as a means of ensuring that an organisation is creating a 'talent pipeline', i.e. developing a pool of individuals who are capable of filling key positions in the future in order to ensure that the future needs of the business are met (see Box 5.5). There

---

Box 5.5 | **Creating a talent pipeline at Coca-Cola**

When soft drinks giant Coca-Cola was forced to look outside the organisation to recruit senior marketing professionals, it decided it was time to establish a programme to identify the talent it had internally. In 2005, the Group HR Director, Steven J. Sainte-Rose, attended the global marketing people development forum, a quarterly meeting of marketing leaders from each of Coca-Cola's eight geographical divisions. At this meeting they identified a particular senior role – division marketing manager – as central to the company's succession planning in each region.

The next step was to create a joint job description so that each region had the same understanding of what the role required. Underlying these discussions was the information that had sparked concern in the first place: a worldwide engagement survey, which showed that marketing staff felt that the company was spending more time buying talent to fill roles than developing existing talent.

A global senior marketing leadership development centre was created, which reflected Coca-Cola's marketing and core leadership competencies. Sainte-Rose and marketing leaders from around the business decided that testing for this critical combination of competencies needed to be based on reality rather than on a series of hypothetical situations, so the development centre includes actual events with the names and some information changed to protect confidentiality. The two-day development centre, which is shaped around a 'day in the life of' exercise, also includes dealing with an unexpected issue, coaching, developmental sessions, presenting and feedback based on personality preferences and a 360-degree review. When participants leave the centre, they are given feedback that links in to their existing development programmes.

The development centre is now held twice a year and each geographical region nominates participants from their list of potential divisional marketing managers. This means that each event brings eight top people from across the globe into one place and so marketing leaders get to see the high calibre of talent internationally. As a result, there has been an increase in poaching talent from one region to another, but this is seen as a good thing as this movement creates a flow of fresh ideas for the company, benefits individual development and helps recruitment by showing the international opportunities available within the company.

Of the 31 participants who have taken part in the marketing development centre to date, 22 have been promoted or taken on significantly expanded job responsibilities.

Source: Caught by the fizz, *People Management*, p. 24 (Chynoweth, C.), 7 August 2008, with permission of the author.

Questions

1 What are the main benefits of this type of succession planning for the organisation and individuals?

2 What potential drawbacks also need to be considered?

is nothing new about organisations identifying and grooming people to fill key posts. The traditional approach to succession planning relied on identifying a few key individuals who would be ready to take on senior roles at certain points in time. However, to be effective, this requires a stable environment and long-term career plans. In response to a rapidly changing environment where the future is uncertain, the focus has moved away from identifying an individual to fill a specific job towards developing talent for groups of jobs as well as planning for jobs that do not yet exist. Succession planning can help to retain talent by providing career development opportunities for individuals and make sure that the organisation has the skills it needs to respond to the rapidly shifting sands that make up today's business environment (Hills, 2009).

A study undertaken for the Corporate Research Forum, *Planning for Succession in Changing Times* (Hirsh, 2012: 20), identifies two broad reasons why organisations undertake succession planning: first, mitigating the short-term business risk of not being able to fill a key job role, especially at senior level; and secondly, the longer-term development of pipelines of people with the skills, knowledge and career experiences to meet future business needs. The study (Hirsh, 2012: 21) further suggests that these drivers are being sharpened by contemporary business pressures including:

- governance pressures from regulators, governments and investors – increasing the need for robust succession planning for senior roles;
- rapid and large-scale strategic refocusing of some businesses into new markets – leading to the need for global pipelines of internal successors with different skills and experiences;
- global deployment – leading to a need for more consistent processes for identifying and developing potential across the organsiation.

A key issue in contemporary succession planning is the balance between internal and external labour markets. Succession planning can be used as a means to retain and motivate key members of the existing workforce, but there is a danger that the organisation can become stale in the absence of 'new blood'. Some senior external appointments are therefore necessary to improve diversity and to bring on board people with different skills and experience, but too many can result in frustration and the loss of some key talent if existing employees feel that they have been overlooked.

A study of over 1,000 employers in the UK (Parry, 2008) found that the majority of employers believe that internal development brings greater benefits to the organisation than external recruitment. The main benefits are perceived as cost-effectiveness, better staff retention and increased employee motivation. However, the same study found that more than half fill their vacancies by external recruitment. A high proportion of organisa-tions also appear to rely on external recruitment rather than succession planning to fill the most senior positions. For example, a study of chief executives in 20 large organisations in the USA (Cohn *et al.*, 2005: 65) found that only a quarter have talent pipelines that extend three levels below them. More recently, research undertaken by the Institute of Leadership and Management (ILM, 2012) focused on the state of the UK's management talent pipe-line and where it could be improved. The study of 750 organisations across the public and private sectors found that most lack a functional talent management pipeline, with many having no talent plan at all. As a result, many UK organisations are 'heavily reliant on external recruitment for management vacancies, especially at senior levels [and this] is driven in large part by shortcomings in internal leadership and management development' (ILM, 2012: 2).

A number of studies suggest that, even where succession planning does occur, the results are less than satisfactory. The CRF study (Hirsh, 2012), mentioned earlier, found that 76 per cent of organisations use some formal succession planning (although this falls to only 28 per cent in small and medium-sized companies) but only 56 per cent of survey respondents were satisfied with their organisation's ability to fill senior positions and 42 per cent were actively dissatisfied.

Similarly, research undertaken by CIPD (CIPD, 2012c: 12) found that only 6 per cent of organisations rate their talent management activities as 'very effective' and only half rate them as 'fairly effective'. The public sector, in particular, appear to view their talent management activities unfavourably, with nearly a quarter (23 per cent) rating their talent management activities as 'fairly' or 'very' ineffective.

Key Controversy

Consider these two questions posed by Clutterbuck (2012: 26):

- If succession planning and talent management work, how come the wrong people so often get to the top?
- If succession planning and talent management work, why – in spite of so much effort to bring about change – is the diversity at the bottom of organisations not reflected in senior positions?

Succession planning is often linked to competency frameworks and part of the problem may be that these frameworks focus on competencies demonstrated by successful leaders in the past, rather than the skills, behaviours and abilities that are required now and in the future. As a result, Clutterbuck (2012: 27) argues that:

The system [talent planning] does work, in the sense that, if you identify a particular group and give them lots of opportunities to experience and to learn, they are likely to advance faster than less privileged colleagues. But that doesn't prove that these were the most talented employees. In reality, those people might have taken the hint and gone off to work elsewhere, often for themselves, where their talent is appreciated.

Careers and talent management

The second core element for internal talent development is career management. Career can be a complex concept so this section begins by defining career and its multi-faceted meanings and perspectives before exploring the contribution of career management and development to talent management practice. The section then considers changes in career and, in particular, the impact of the global financial crisis.

Defining career

Career is a familiar term in everyday speech and formal discourse, where it has been defined as:

- 'a succession of related jobs, arranged in a hierarchy of prestige, through which persons move in an ordered, predictable sequence' (Wilensky, 1960: 554)
- 'the evolving sequence of a person's work experiences over time' (Arthur et al., 1989: 8).

It has other related meanings, too, for it is used in different contexts, from different perspectives and for different purposes, but all are grounded in settled arrangements in society, the economy and the organisation of work.

Elements in the meaning of career

The various meanings of 'career' have the following elements, explicitly or implicitly:

- Movement of an individual, group or groups of individuals through social space:
  - connecting roles and establishing regular sequences and continuities;
  - so often regarded as more than 'just a job'.
- Movement often seen as advancement: forward (metaphor of pathway) or upwards (metaphor of ladder):
  - roles often arranged hierarchically.

- Some sequences recognised as contributing to the individual's social capital by giving social status, financial, reputational rewards and 'success':
  - career sometimes regarded as elitist.
- Movement through time:
  - connecting past, present and future;
  - having a strong future orientation;
  - weaving a continuing thread; forming a trajectory.
- Implicating the individual's sense of self and need for self-fulfilment:
  - linking an individual's dreams, goals, actions and achievements;
  - interacting with individual development;
  - giving the basis of a narrative;
  - creating relationships.
- Interaction of individual biography and social or organisational structure:
  - individual thereby contributing to that wider structure;
  - and from it deriving overarching framework of norms, values, meanings which provides goals, directions, limits and guidelines for life.
- Interaction of factors internal and external to individual in career and contribution to the process of socialisation.
- Dual aspects of career – the individual's outer and inner worlds:
  - objective career – observable movement through social space and time;
  - subjective career – the personal experience people have of that movement and its private meaning and significance for them.

Career in different contexts

Career is used in many contexts where different aspects of it may be emphasised, from 'a criminal career' to the 'career of an illness'. It is commonly used in occupational, organisational and professional contexts, where its elements of movement, sequence, progression and advancement are particularly significant. In the field of education, it links self-fulfilment and self-development, aspiration and social status with the means of gaining a role in society through earning a living and contributing to the economy. Government policies in the UK and more widely (OECD, 2003) recognise the significance of career guidance for the efficiency of labour markets and the education system, the promotion of equity and as a contribution to lifelong learning, although they do not define career itself.

Career seen from different perspectives

Further understandings of career arise from the differing perspectives from which it can be viewed. These vary from those of an individual, an organisation, the economy or society and from the various academic disciplines concerned with them. These include vocational, organisational and occupational psychology, various branches of economics, sociology, education, counselling, HRM (see, for example, Arthur *et al.*, 1989; Adamson *et al.*, 1998;). These disciplines have generated a rich fund of theories addressing different aspects of career, or the same aspects but from different disciplinary perspectives, e.g. vocational psychology and organisational psychology, on career development and career management (Collin and Patton, 2009).

Some theories explain career in terms of external influences upon the individual, e.g. the economic system and labour markets; social class, social structure and social mobility; education; organisational and occupational structure; and mobility. Other theories examine factors internal to the individual, e.g. age, gender, psychoanalytical explanations; personality traits; life span development; and implementation of self-concept. There are also theories about the interaction of internal and external factors, e.g. decision-making and social learning. Further theories address careers in organisations, e.g. career development, career planning and career management. There are also theories concerned with subjective experiences, and how to interpret and study them (see Chapter 3), e.g. narrative approaches, relational approaches and social constructionist approaches.

'Career' used for different purposes

A particular meaning of 'career' may be specified by a speaker or writer, whether informally or formally, while others may be left vague. Intentionally or otherwise, the user may elide them or use them interchangeably or inconsistently. Nevertheless, this does not seem to confuse listeners/readers. Rather, they accept the multi-layered richness of the term, and this lends it a rhetorical power to convey more than is actually stated, or to obscure what the user prefers to remain hidden. For example, the manager may use 'career' to motivate employees to learning and application in work, to encourage aspiration, or to endorse particular pathways as desirable or rewarding. At the same time, however, such wording could be glossing over or obscuring the actual prospects of mundane jobs or the ways in which organisational incentives and structures are in effect regulating and controlling employees. And the employees themselves may be constructing the career they want by piecing together parts of their work, social and personal lives.

Career development and career management

From the individual perspective, career development is a unique lifelong process of learning, work and leisure that takes place through a series of planned and unplanned stages, transitions, influences and decisions (McIlveen, 2009). The individual's career management, or self-management, is an active process that aims to achieve a fulfilling career. It includes strategies such as learning a new skill or gaining a mentor (see Chapter 7), and other behaviours, such as becoming more self-aware, choosing realistic goals, making decisions effectively and negotiating transitions (McIlveen, 2009).

From the organisational perspective, the organisation manages the career development of its employees primarily to meet its own needs and only secondarily for its employees' benefit (Creed and Hood, 2009). It requires sufficient and appropriately skilled employees to be available for its present and expected future effective functioning and to enhance its competitive advantage. It uses a range of activities to achieve this, such as succession planning, assessment centres, performance appraisal, mentoring, career counselling and secondments (Baruch, 2009).

Career development and career management in talent management

Career development and management play a part in talent management through attracting new talent, and retaining and developing it by:

- offering a long-term career perspective;
- suggesting stability and security;
- suggesting enlightened employment policies;
- indicating the possibility of future progress and rewards;
- having recognisable career patterns, pathways and ladders;
- shaping employees' expectations and needs;
- providing future goals for employees;
- providing incentives for individual effort;
- encouraging employees to invest in their own career development;
- investing in and rewarding employees;
- motivating and persuading them;
- encouraging and supporting their development;

- investing in their individual learning and development;
- influencing employees' behaviour in desirable directions;
- shaping their organisational identity.

At the same time, employees may have their own career development and management plans. Some of these may work synergistically with those of their employers, while for others there may be a discrepancy between their goals which would undermine effective talent management.

Changes in the nature of career

According to Kanter (1989) there are three principal forms of career:

- *The professional form* – weakly connected to employing organisations, and defined by craft or skill; occupational status achieved through monopolising socially valued knowledge and reputation.
- *The entrepreneurial form* – developed by creating valued new outputs or organisational capacity; it offers freedom, independence and control over tasks and surroundings, but entrepreneurs have only what they grow themselves.
- *The bureaucratic form* – defined by advancement in a formally defined hierarchy. This form had come to dominate the view of organisational careers generally.

In the final quarter of the twentieth century, globalisation, major technological and other developments resulted in, *inter alia,* flatter and more flexible forms of organisation and changes in the organisation of work, and these threatened the 'onward and upward' bureaucratic career. New forms of career began to be identified, such as:

- *The subjective career.* According to Weick and Berlinger (1989: 321), in 'self-designing organisations' in which the advancement and stable pathways of the typical career would be absent, the objective career 'dissolves' and the subjective career 'becomes externalized and treated as a framework for career growth' and a resource for the further organisational self-design.
- Weick and Berlinger (1989: 323–26) liken this to the '*Protean career*' (Hall, 1976) in which people engage in 'interminable series of experiments and explorations'. This calls for frequent substantial career moves in order to incorporate a changing, complex and multi-layered sense of self; the 'decoupling' of identity from jobs; the preservation of the ability to make choices within the organisation; the identification of distinctive competence; and the synthesis of complex information.
- *The portfolio career* in which workers, perhaps self-employed, manage several concurrent streams of work, jobs or contracts (Handy, 1990).
- *The boundaryless career.* Whereas traditionally careers took place 'through orderly employment arrangements' within organisations, many are now crossing traditional boundaries between organisations, and home and work (Arthur and Rousseau, 1996: 3).

Nevertheless, Guest and McKenzie Davey (1996: 22) cautioned against writing off the traditional career: in their own research they had found little evidence of major organisational transformations. Moynagh and Worsley (2005), drawing on the Economic and Social Research Council (ESRC) Future of Work research programme (**www.leeds.ac.uk/esrcfutureofwork/**), also considered that long-term jobs and careers would continue to exist. Meanwhile, it was thought that attributes of the 'professional' and 'entrepreneurial' forms were likely to be found more extensively in the twenty-first century (CIPD, 2002).

After the global financial crisis of 2007–08

The global financial crisis (see Chapter 15) has brought about considerable change, which is disrupting the UK labour market and employment contracts (see Chapter 4). At the time of publication, this seems likely to continue. Some of its directions and dimensions are not yet agreed upon or fully understood, although aspects such as the development of some forms of apprenticeship (Richard, 2012), and increases in temporary work for those who want it, are welcomed.

The changes include severe and rising unemployment, and especially youth unemployment, reduced permanent and full-time work, increased temporary and part-time work, zero-hours contracts, agency work, self-employment (including the 'odd job' culture of part-time work undertaken to avoid unemployment), outsourcing, underemployment (desire for permanent work by those with temporary contracts), various forms of unpaid work such as workfare and internships. Those having such experiences are labelled the 'precariat' by Standing (2011); they are without long-term jobs, stable occupational identities, careers, stable social protection or protective regulations.

Such changes affect many of the elements of career noted earlier, and working life is fragmenting for young and adult workers. Traditional continuities, sequences and trajectories are being disrupted or destroyed, the future time perspective eroded, advancement is becoming irregular, rewards less certain and aspirations dampened. With increasing competition for first jobs, the start of the career is delayed, and with demographic changes dictating delayed pension age, the overall familiar shape of working life is no longer predictable. It is now essential to manage one's own career, to invest in learning and development and to remain employable (see Chapter 7). Questions still need to be asked about the future, not only of careers but of the concept of the career itself (Collin and Young, 2000). It could be that the subjective career may become more significant than before.

Key Controversy

Study the labour market changes regularly reported in the CIPD's quarterly reports (**www. cipd.co.uk**) and the Institute for Employment Studies' reports (**www.employment-studies. co.uk**) and consider their implications for careers.

Are labour market myths confusing the understanding of contemporary careers?

Explore

- What contribution could the subjective career make to talent management?

Explore

- Do you consider that you will have a career in the future?
- How do you envisage it?
- How will it be likely to differ from the careers of your parents' and grandparents' generations?

Concluding comments

Organisations appear to be sending out some mixed messages regarding talent management. On the one hand, survey respondents suggest that talent management is a top priority for the majority of organisations and most HR professionals consider that it can have a positive impact on an organisation's financial performance. On the other hand, many organisations do not have a talent management strategy and there appears to be a tendency to buy in talent through external recruitment rather than 'growing your own' through employee development activities. Even where talent management activities are in place, evidence of their effectiveness is 'woefully thin' (Clutterbuck, 2012: 26). Survey data (CIPD, 2008) suggest that relatively high numbers of employees leave their organisation for 'pull' factors such as promotion or 'push' factors such as lack of development and career opportunities. These results suggest that many organisations could benefit from paying the same attention to the talent within the existing workforce as they do to attracting talent externally. The majority of employers claim that internal recruitment brings greater benefits to the organisation than external recruitment (Parry, 2008), so why does there seem to be this gap between the rhetoric and the reality?

One explanation is that, whilst there have been a number of significant developments in the activities encompassed within the talent management umbrella, e.g. the growing interest in employer branding, employee engagement and the benefits of being an employer of choice, in many cases talent management activities lack the integration necessary to secure the flow of talent that organisations will require in the future (Armstrong, 2009). However, it may be that the difficult current economic circumstances are actually helping organisations to focus more attention on the talent that exists within the current workforce. In a recent survey conducted by the CIPD (CIPD, 2012a), 70 per cent of respondents reported that they are looking to develop more talent in-house and 55 per cent are focusing more on retaining rather than recruiting talent (these figures add up to more than 100 per cent because some organisations are adopting multiple strategies). This does not mean the end of the external labour market: 60 per cent of respondents are still continuing to recruit key talent and only a quarter (28 per cent) are planning on reducing the number of new recruits. However, it does suggest that a number of organisations appear to be following the principles outlined by Cappelli at the beginning of the chapter. Time will tell whether the practice lives up to expectations.

Summary

- Talent can be used in an exclusive sense to refer to a select group of high-flyers; in an inclusive sense to refer to all employees; or in a hybrid sense to refer to key workers or roles that are critical to success, wherever they are in the organisation. The focus of talent management activities can therefore vary, but definitions include the need to attract, retain, motivate and develop individuals.

- Methods used to identify the skills required can be job-based or person-based. The emphasis on identifying people with the 'right' attitudes has led to a growth in competency frameworks, but these can be difficult to apply in practice.

- Recruitment activities can contribute to talent management by attracting a pool of suitable candidates. In recent years there has been significant growth in the use of e-recruitment, which can help organisations to reach more candidates and to develop a 'personal' relationship with the talent pool. The purpose of selection methods is to differentiate between suitable and unsuitable candidates and, if handled effectively and professionally, these can also convey a strong image of the organisation.

- Employee retention is a key element of talent management, as selecting and developing high-quality employees are of limited value if the organisation then loses their skills and expertise. A number of initiatives have been introduced to aid retention, and the most popular are increased learning and development opportunities and improved line management people skills.

- Learning and performance improvement have always been an integral part of talent management. A combination of development activities, succession planning and career management can be used to retain and motivate the workforce and ensure that the organisation has a talent pipeline to meet future requirements. However, evidence suggests that these activities are not yet as effective as they might be at ensuring organisations have the talent they need for the future.

Questions

1 Compare and contrast an exclusive and inclusive approach to talent management. What factors might influence the approach adopted by an organisation?
2 What steps can organisations take to ensure that they identify and nurture the skills, abilities and knowledge to drive organisational success in the future?
3 Skills shortages remain in many sectors. Should organisations be more proactive in managing the careers of their employees?

Case study

Recruitment and retention of workers in childcare

The UK childcare sector has grown rapidly in recent years. The expansion reflects increased demand from working parents as well as a series of government-led initiatives. Issues of recruitment and retention are important with high turnover levels leading to potential skills shortages. Marilyn Carroll and colleagues investigated issues of recruitment and retention in 33 nurseries across the north-west of England (Carroll *et al.*, 2008).

The study found that three-fifths of managers had experienced difficulties attracting staff and just less than one-half saw staff recruitment as a major problem impacting on the running of the business. This suggests that a focus on retention could be beneficial.

The study also investigated employee perspectives on retention. Responses were analysed using the four categories of labour turnover identified by Torrington *et al.* (2005):

- *Functional turnover* – when resignations are welcomed by both parties. The study found that staff turnover was highest among trainees and younger workers who found that working in a nursery was not what they had imagined it would be. Managers also reported that some of these recruits lacked the right characteristics and the ability to fit in.
- *Outside factors* – factors unrelated to the job itself. Reasons for leaving included relocation, leaving to have a baby, leaving because childcare arrangements had broken down, or leaving for another job with shorter hours in order to combine work and family responsibilities. Some employers had responded to this by offering reduced fees at the nursery or some flexibility in working hours.
- *'Push' factors* – aspects of the job or organisation that cause dissatisfaction. The study found that one of the key 'push' factors was a perceived lack of

appreciation, reflected in low pay and limited training and development opportunities. The limited career opportunities in the sector are compounded by operational constraints: 'When an employee receives training in work time, managers must ensure that Ofsted ratios are adhered to. In some small businesses, finances meant that employees were not paid for training days . . . . for employees on low wages it does little to encourage career investment or a sense of value' (p. 67).

- *'Pull' factors* – relative attractions of other employers. The study found that employees often made comparisons with the retail sector, arguing that they could earn more as a checkout operator, although few wanted to move into shop work. Career progression was often cited as a reason for leaving, either to go to a different nursery or to move out of the sector into other professions such as midwifery or teaching assistants.

Source: from Carroll *et al.* (2008) Recruitment and retention in front-line services: the case of childcare, *Human Resource Management Journal*, 19, 1: 57–74.

Questions

1 What recruitment and selection processes might employers consider to ensure that nursery workers understand the realities of the job and have the necessary qualities for the role?

2 Given operational constraints, what might employers do to improve perceptions of appreciation amongst their employees?

3 What impact might government plans to increase acceptable staff:children ratios and improve the qualification levels of nursery workers have on recruitment and retention in the sector?

References and further reading

The text marked with an asterisk is recommended for further reading.

ACAS (1983) *Recruitment Selection,* Advisory Booklet No. 6. London: ACAS.

Adamson, S. J., Doherty, N. and Viney, C. (1998) 'The meanings of career revisited: implications for theory and practice', *British Journal of Management,* 9: 251–9.

Anderson, A.H. (1994) *Effective Personnel Management: A Skills and Activity-Based Approach.* Oxford: Blackwell Business.

Anderson, N. and Shackleton, V. (1993) *Successful Selection Interviewing.* Oxford: Blackwell.

Appelbaum, S., Kay, F. and Shapiro, B. (1989) 'The assessment centre is not dead! How to keep it alive and well', *Journal of Management Development,* 8, 5: 51–65.

Armstrong, M. (2009) *Armstrong's Handbook of Human Resource Management Practice,* 11th edn. London: Kogan Page.

Arthur, M.B. and Rousseau, D.M. (1996) (eds) *The Boundaryless Career: A New Employment, Principle for a New Organizational Era.* Oxford: Oxford University Press.

Arthur, M.B., Hall, D.T. and Lawrence, B.S. (eds) (1989) *Handbook of Career Theory.* Cambridge: Cambridge University Press.

Baruch, Y. (2009) 'Career planning and management interventions from the organizational perspective', in A. Collin and W. Patton (2009) (eds) *Vocational Psychological and Organisational Perspectives on Career: Towards a Multidisciplinary Dialogue.* Rotterdam: Sense Publishers, pp. 131–145.

Batt, R. and Colvin, A. (2011) 'An employment systems approach to turnover: human resources practices, quits, dismissals and performance', *Academy of Management Journal,* 54, 4: 695–717.

Beaumont, P. (1993) *Human Resource Management: Key Concepts and Skills.* London: Sage.

Bevan, S. (1997) 'Quit stalling', *People Management,* 20 November.

Bevan, S., Barber, I. and Robinson, D. (1997) *Keeping the Best: A Practical Guide to Retaining Key Employees.* London: IES.

Bhatnagar, J. (2008) 'Managing capabilities for talent engagement and pipeline development', *Industrial and Commercial Training,* 40, 1: 19–28.

Boam, R. and Sparrow, P. (eds) (1992) *Designing and Achieving Competency: A Competency-based Approach to Developing People and Organisations.* Maidenhead: McGraw-Hill.

Buckingham, G. (2000) 'Same indifference', *People Management,* 17 February: 4–46.

Callaghan, G. and Thompson, P. (2002) 'We recruit attitude: the selection and shaping of routine call centre labour', *Journal of Management Studies,* 39, 2: 233–54.

Caliguiri, P. and Phillips, J. (2003) 'An application of self-assessment realistic job previews to expatriate assignments', *International Journal of Human Resource Management,* 14, 7: 1102–16.

Cappelli, P. (2008) 'Talent management for the twenty-first century', *Harvard Business Review,* March: 74–81.

Carroll, M., Smith, M., Oliver, G. and Sung, S. (2008) 'Recruitment and retention in front-line services: the case of childcare', *Human Resource Management Journal,* 19, 1: 59–74.

CIPD (2002) *The Future of Careers.* London: CIPD.

CIPD (2006) *Talent management: understanding the dimensions,* Report, October. London: CIPD.

CIPD (2007) *Employer branding: A no-nonsense approach,* CIPD Guide, October. London: CIPD.

CIPD (2008) *Recruitment, retention and labour turnover,* Annual Survey Report. London: CIPD.

CIPD (2009) *Employer branding: maintaining momentum in a recession,* CIPD Guide, June. London: CIPD.

CIPD (2010) *The talent perspective: what does it look like to be talent managed?* Survey Report, Summer. London: CIPD.

CIPD (2011) *Resourcing and talent planning 2011,* Survey Report, June. London: CIPD.

CIPD (2012a) *Resourcing and talent planning 2012,* Survey Report, June. London: CIPD.

CIPD (2012b) *Talent Management: an overview,* Factsheet, August. London: CIPD.

CIPD (2012c) *Learning and talent development survey 2012,* Survey Report, April. London: CIPD.

CIPD (2012d) *Employer Brand,* Factsheet. London: CIPD.

CIPD (2012e) *Harnessing social media for organizational effectiveness,* Research Report, June. London: CIPD.

CIPD (2012f) *Competence and competency frameworks,* Factsheet, July. London: CIPD.

Clutterbuck, D. (2012) 'The talent wave', *People Management,* October: 26–29.

Cohn, J., Rakesh, K. and Reeves, L. (2005) 'Growing talent as if your business depended on it', *Harvard Business Review,* October: 63–70.

Colao, J.J. (2012) 'With Facebook your recruitment pool is one billion people', 12 September. Online: **http://www.forbes.com/sites/jjcolao/2012/09/12/with-facebook-your-recruitment-pool-is-one-billion-people/** (accessed 16 January 2014).

Collin, A. and Patton, W. (2009) (eds) *Vocational Psychological and Organisational Perspectives on Career: Towards a Multidisciplinary Dialogue.* Rotterdam: Sense Publishers.

Collin, A. and Young, R. A. (eds) (2000) *The Future of Career.* Cambridge: Cambridge University Press.

Creed, P. and Hood, M. (2009) 'Career development, planning, and management from the organisational perspective' in A. Collin and W. Patton (eds) *Vocational Psychological and Organisational Perspectives on Career: Towards a Multidisciplinary Dialogue.* Rotterdam: Sense Publishers, pp. 41–6.

Cronly-Dillon, M. (2007) 'Face up to rules on researching recruits on line', *People Management,* 13, 21: 20.

De Vos, A. and Meganck, A. (2009) 'What HR managers do versus what employees value: exploring both parties' views on retention management from a psychological contrat perspective', *Personnel Review,* 38, 1: 45–60.

Dowling, P.J. and Schuler, R.S. (1990) *International Dimensions of HRM.* Boston, MA: PWS-Kent.

Eurocom (2012) 'One in five technology firms has rejected a job applicant because of social media profile – Eurocom Worldwide Annual Survey', Press release. Online: **http://www.eurocompr.com/prfitem.asp?id=14921** (accessed 23 March 2013).

Feltham, R. (1992) 'Using competencies in selection and recruitment' in R. Boam and P. Sparrow (eds) *Designing and Achieving*

Competency: A Competency-based Approach to Developing People and Organisations. Maidenhead: McGraw-Hill.

Fowler, A. (1992) 'How to plan an assessment centre', *PM Plus,* December: 21–23.

Frank, F. and Taylor, C. (2004) 'Talent management: trends that will shape the future HR', *Human Resource Planning,* 27, 1: 33–41.

Griggs, T. (2011) 'The self-imposed talent shortage', *Financial Times,* 10 February.

Guest, D. and McKenzie Davey, K.M. (1996) 'Don't write off the traditional career', *People Management,* 22 February: 22–5.

Guthridge, M. and Lawson, E. (2008) 'Divide and survive', *People Management,* 18 September: 40–44.

Hackett, P. (1991) *Personnel: The Department at Work.* London: IPM.

Hall, D.T. (1976) *Careers in Organizations.* Pacific Palisades, CA: Goodyear.

Handy, C. (1990) *The Age of Unreason.* New York: McGraw-Hill.

Hills, A. (2009) 'Succession planning – or smart talent management', *Industrial and Commercial Training,* 41, 1: 3–8.

Hirsh, W. (2012) *Planning for succession planning in changing times,* Research Report, London: CRF.

ILM (2012) *The leadership and management talent pipeline,* Research Report. London: ILM.

IRS (1994) 'Ensuring effective recruitment' and 'Random selection', *Employee Development Bulletin 51,* March: pp. 2–8.

IRS (2001) 'Risk analysis and job retention', *Employee Development Bulletin,* 141, September: 3–4

IRS (2002) 'The changing face of succession planning', *IRS Employment Review 756,* 22 July: 37–42.

IRS (2003) 'Spinning the recruitment web', *IRS Employment Review 767,* 10 January: 34–40.

Isherwood, S. (2008) 'Flaws exposed in talent spotting models', Guest column, *Financial Times,* 13 October.

Kanter, R.M. (1989b) 'Careers and the wealth of nations: a macro-perspective on the structure and implications of career forms' in M.B. Arthur, D.T. Hall and B.S. Lawrence (eds) *Handbook of Career Theory.* Cambridge: Cambridge University Press, pp. 506–21.

Kersley, B., Alpin, C., Forth, J., Bryson, A., Bewley, H., Dix, G. and Oxenbridge, S. (2006) *Inside the Workplace: Findings from the 2004 Workplace Employment Relations Survey.* Abingdon: Routledge.

Kwoh, L. (2012) 'Beware: potential employers are watching you', *Wall Street Journal,* 29 October. Online: **http://online.wsj.com/article/SB10000872396390443759504576314100938 79278.html** (accessed 23 March 2013).

KPMG (2012) *Tune into Talent.* White Paper.

Lewis, C. (1985) *Employee Selection.* London: Hutchinson.

Lewis, R. and Heckman, R. (2006) 'Talent management: a critical review', *Human Resource Management Review,* 16: 139–54.

Loan-Clarke, J., Arnold, J., Coombs, C., Hartley, R. and Bosley, S. (2010) 'Retention, turnover and return – a longitudinal study of allied health professionals in Britain', *Human Resource Management Journal,* 20, 4: 391–406.

Marchington, M. and Wilkinson, A. (2012) *Human Resource Management at Work,* 5th edn. London: CIPD.

McIlveen, P. (2009) 'Career development, planning, and management from the vocational psychology perspective' in A. Collin and W. Patton (eds) *Vocational Psychological and Organisational Perspectives on Career: Towards a Multidisciplinary Dialogue.* Rotterdam: Sense Publishers, pp. 63–90.

Michaels, E., Handfield-Jones, H. and Axelrod, E. (2001) *The War for Talent.* Boston, MA: Harvard Business School Press.

Mitchell, T., Holtom, B., Lee, T. Sablynski, C. and Erez, M. (2001) 'Why people stay: using job embeddedness to predict voluntary turnover', *Academy of Management Journal,* 44, 6: 1102–1122.

Morrell, K. and Arnold, J. (2007) 'Research article: look after they leap: illustrating the value of retrospective reports in employee turnover', *International Journal of Human Resource Management,* 18, 9: 1683–99.

Moynagh, M. and Worsley, R. (2005) *Working in the Twenty-First Century.* Leeds/Norfolk: ESRC/The Tomorrow Project.

Munro Fraser, J. (1954) *A Handbook of Employment Interviewing.* London: Macdonald & Evans.

Nickson, D., Warhurst, C., Dutton, E. and Hurrell, S. (2008) 'A job to believe in: recruitment in the Scottish voluntary sector', *Human Resource Management Journal,* 18, 1: 20–35.

OECD (2003) *Education Policy Analysis 2003.* Paris: OECD.

Parry, E. (2008) *Nurturing talent: A Research Report,* October. Cranfield University.

Phillips, L. (2008) 'Talent management is a global preoccupation', *PM Online,* 14 April.

Reynolds, D. and Weiner, J. (2009) *Online Recruiting and Selection.* Chichester: Wiley-Blackwell.

Richard, D. (2012) *The Richard Review of Apprenticeships Summary* (**www.bis.gov.uk**).

Rodger, A. (1952) *The Seven Point Plan.* London: National Institute of Industrial Psychology.

Sadler, P. and Milmer, K. (1993) *The Talent-intensive Organisation: Optimising your Company's Human Resource Strategies.* Special Report P659. London: The Economist Intelligence Unit.

Searle, R. (2003) *Selection and Recruitment: A Critical Text.* Milton Keynes: Open University Press.

Seligman, M. and Csikszentmihalyi, M (2000) 'Positive psychology: an introduction', *American Psychologist,* 55, 1: 5–14.

Standing, G. (2011) *The Precariat: The New Dangerous Class.* London: Bloomsbury.

Suff, R. (2006) 'More than just a pretty face: building an employer brand', *IRS Employment Review,* 857, October: 42–5.

*Taylor, S. (2010) *People Resourcing,* 5th edn. London: CIPD.

Torrington, D., Taylor, S. and Hall, L. (2005) *Human Resource Management* (6th edn). Harlow: Pearson Education.

Torrington, D., Hall, L. and Taylor, S. (2008) *Human Resource Management,* 7th edn. Harlow: Prentice Hall.

Wanous, J. (2009) 'Realistic job previews' in C. Cooper (ed.) *Blackwell Encyclopedia of Management.* Blackwell Reference (**http://www.blackwellreference.com**).

Weick, K.E. and Berlinger, L.R. (1989) 'Career improvisation in self-designing organizations' in M.B. Arthur, D.T. Hall and B.S. Lawrence (eds) *Handbook of Career Theory.* Cambridge: Cambridge University Press, pp. 313–28.

Whiddett, S. and Hollyforde, S. (2007) *Competencies,* Toolkit. London: CIPD.

Whitehill, A.M. (1991) *Japanese Management: Tradition and Transition.* London: Routledge.

Wilensky, H. L. (1960) Work, careers and social integration. *International Social Science Journal,* 12: 543–74.

Williams, M. (2000) 'Transfixed assets', *People Management,* 3 August: 28–33.

Wolf, A. and Jenkins, A. (2006) 'Explaining greater test use for selection: the role of HR professionals in a world of expanding regulation', *Human Resource Management Journal,* 16, 2: 193–213.

Chapter 6

Managing equality and diversity

Mike Noon

Objectives

- To define discrimination and explain the forms of legal protection in the workplace.
- To describe, evaluate and compare the social justice and business case arguments for pursuing policies of equality and diversity.
- To explain the deep-rooted causes of the problems of equality and diversity using the concept of institutional discrimination.
- To explain the purpose of equality and diversity policies and assess their limitations.
- To define and explain the meanings of positive action and positive discrimination.
- To explain the concepts of 'sameness' and 'difference', and evaluate their importance in guiding policy within organisations.
- To assess the process of discrimination in an organisation and outline its possible consequences.

Introductory case study

Inequality at the top

'The progress of women to positions of authority in Britain has been tortuously slow. . . . While women make progress in some sectors, that progress regularly stalls or even reverses in other sectors. . . .

British women are better educated than ever before. They are attending university in ever increasing numbers and achieve better degree results than men. Intelligent, competent women are flooding the junior ranks of law firms, accountancies and medical practices.

These women step on the career ladder and work hard, with a position at the top firmly in sight. In their 20s they level peg with men and we would expect them to enter the management ranks at the same rate as men. However, several years down the track a different picture emerges – one where many

have disappeared from the paid workforce or remain trapped in the 'marzipan layer' below senior management, leaving the higher ranks to be dominated by men.'

Source: Equality and Human Rights Commission (2011: 1)

'We have often been told that we live in a meritocracy in which women could achieve high office if they wanted to, and that the failure of women to do so when they have equality of opportunity is more about them than it is about power, structures or prejudice. We agree that women more often want training, mentoring and support to take on senior roles, and indeed we regard this as a strength rather than a weakness, since it suggests that women want to prepare properly for responsibility. But we see no evidence to suggest that there actually is a meritocracy so far as women (or other under-represented groups) are concerned.'

Source: Centre for Women and Democracy (2013: 15)

These comments are from two reports evaluating the presence of women in Britain's 26,000 top positions of power. Of particular concern is the under-representation of women in boardrooms. The Equality and Human Rights Commission (EHRC) report estimates that, based on the current rate of change, it will take 70 years to achieve an equal number of female and male directors of FTSE 100 companies.

The problem of qualified women failing to reach senior roles in organisations in the same proportions as men is echoed across Europe and in other developed economies around the world, with reports showing that the proportion of women on boards of companies is typically below 20 per cent, and often as low as single digits in countries like Italy (Deloitte, 2011).

As a result, some people have called for the introduction of gender quotas to force organisations to appoint more women in the top roles, and some countries have already put legislation in place. The prime example is Norway, which requires a gender balance of at least 40 per cent of men and 40 per cent of women on all listed company boards. Belgium, Denmark, Finland, France, Iceland, Italy and Spain also have some form of quota law in place or in process.

But the issue of quotas is highly controversial. Opponents argue that businesses should be free to appoint the best person for the job, and that quotas distort this. They say that quotas lead to the suspicion that someone has been appointed not on the basis of merit but because of their gender. They argue that quotas are bad for business and demeaning for women, and that the problem of under-representation stems from there being insufficient women with relevant experience who can be promoted.

By contrast, supporters of quotas argue that research reveals how managers tend to appoint those who are similar to themselves, so without quotas there will simply be the perpetuation of the status quo: the domination of senior roles by men. They argue that quotas not only encourage board members to think more broadly about the types of qualities needed for the role, but also force senior managers in organisations to think about the 'talent pipeline' and look more seriously at the development opportunities they provide for women managers.

Not surprisingly, many of the voices of opposition come from men, but among women the split between opponents and supporters is fairly evenly balanced. For instance, a survey of 2,960 business leaders by the Institute of Leadership and Management (ILM, 2011) in the UK found that 47 per cent of female respondents were in favour of quotas. Similarly, in an international survey of 1,067 board directors from 58 countries (Groysberg and Bell, 2012), 51 per cent of women directors believed quotas were an effective tool (although only 39 per cent would personally support them). In both of these surveys, only 25 per cent of men supported quotas and, according to the Groysberg and Bell survey, the explanations for the worse position of women differ between the sexes.

'Women place the responsibility squarely on board leadership, while men see it as both a pipeline and a leadership issue. Women view the board chairs, lead directors and nominating committee chairs as the real change agents in building a diverse boardroom'.

Henrietta Fore, co-chair of the global survey sponsors, Women Corporate Directors (p. 3).

Between the opponents and supporters of quotas are those who take a middle road: they are against the idea of enforced quotas, but agree that something needs to be done. They argue that, left alone, nothing will change – or the rate of change will be incredibly slow – so they suggest there needs to be encouragement through methods such as voluntary codes of best practice, targets and 'comply or explain' initiatives, which require disclosure about diversity policies and progress in company annual reports and websites.

These 'middle roaders' also call for evidence to show how a diverse senior management team can help to improve the performance of the organisation. They often argue that diversity is good for business and that proving this is the best way of getting male senior managers to appoint more women (see, for example, the McKinsey & Co 'Women Matter' programme of research, **http://www.mckinsey.com/features/women_matter**).

However, some of the evidence is mixed. For example, in Norway quotas have undoubtedly been effective in gender-balancing the membership of boards, but an analysis of company performance by Kenneth Ahern, a professor of finance from the University of Michigan, led him to conclude (quoted in Alexander, 2012):

'The quota led to younger and less experienced boards, and deterioration in operating performance, consistent with less capable boards. . . . In Norway they knew that the value of their companies would drop, but society there cared more about equality than finance. It was a conscious decision'.

Introduction

The opening case study illustrates the type of inequality problem that managers can be faced with. Problems like this cannot, and should not, be ignored. In fact, the case raises five common core issues and associated dilemmas that need to be addressed – five issues that this chapter will focus upon in detail, but which are outlined here:

- First, the opening case raises issues about the forms of discrimination and the legal protection in place. Are women being refused access to board directorship because of their sex, or are they being excluded because they had previously not been given (or not taken) sufficient managerial experience to make them strong candidates? In other words, was there direct discrimination against women or is it that women lack the requisite experience – so no unfair discrimination is occurring? And if it is the latter, might this in some circumstances also be a form of discrimination (indirect discrimination) if unjustifiable criteria of selection are applied that disadvantage women as a group because they are not given the same promotion opportunities as men in order to build experience? Moreover, in either circumstance what legal issues might managers need to consider?

- Secondly, the opening case raises the issue of why inequality is a problem. Discussion of equality problems tends to revolve around fairness and inefficiency. So in the case study there is the concern with the unfairness of women not getting access to the senior roles, but also the problem of the inefficiency of this because organisations are potentially missing out on the talents of 50 per cent of the population. These two sets of arguments can be described as the social justice and business case arguments for equality and diversity, and are applicable to many contemporary equality problems.

- Thirdly, there is the issue of identifying the underlying causes of the problem of inequality within organisations. Can it simply be explained away as blatant discrimination by individuals? Or is it more deep-rooted and caused in more subtle ways by the dominant organisational processes, procedures, structures and cultures? So in the opening case, is it that men do not want women in senior roles because, for instance, they do not think women have the capability? Or is it that the men have tended to perpetuate ways of operating that make it more difficult for women to progress through the ranks and compete on equal terms with the men?

- Fourthly, there is the issue of how to deal with the problem. In the opening case there are some people calling for regulation through the introduction of quotas (an interventionist approach) while others are suggesting that it should be left to the organisations themselves (a voluntarist approach). There are also those taking a middle position who think something should be done, but do not want high levels of regulation – this type of approach is often associated with calls for taking 'positive action', and it forms the backbone of most equality and diversity policies and practices in organisations.

- Finally, there is the challenge of devising effective policies and initiatives. This task should not be under-estimated because there will be conflicting opinions about whether the policy should be aimed at treating everyone the same, or whether it should take people's differences into account. And if the latter, should policies be mindful of differences between groups, or should they focus on individuals. So, in the opening case, ought an organisation wishing to gain a better gender balance seek to implement policies that encourage a simple gender-blind approach, or should they have policies that take into account the relative disadvantage of women in the hierarchy? Should certain women be fast-tracked? Or is there a need for a complete overhaul of the processes of selection and promotion throughout the management structure?

So these five issues – discrimination and legal protection, the problem of inequality, the underlying causes of the problem, the ways of dealing with the problem and the devising of effective equality and diversity policies and initiatives – form the core structure of this chapter.

Discrimination and legal protection in the workplace

'Discrimination' is the process of judging people according to particular criteria. For example, in the selection process for a teaching post, the appointment panel might discriminate in favour of a candidate who answers their questions clearly and concisely, and discriminate against a candidate who mutters and digresses from the point. However, when most people use the term 'discrimination', they tend to mean *unfair* discrimination. The word is mainly used to denote that the criteria on which the discrimination has occurred are unjust. It is likely that most people would not describe the teaching post example above as 'discrimination', because they would not consider the criteria the panel used (clarity and conciseness) as unfair. However, if the criterion the appointment panel used to choose between candidates was gender or race, then most people would call it 'discrimination'. So this chapter will adopt the commonly understood meaning of the term 'discrimination' to describe situations where there is less favourable treatment that cannot be justified.

Where can discrimination occur?

In all of the chapters in this book you will have encountered issues where people (usually managers) are making choices that affect the lives of others in the workplace. It is at these decision points where judgments might be made that are unfairly discriminatory. In other words, there are numerous sites of potential discrimination that you have already encountered. To illustrate, the following list shows some human resource management (HRM) issues where equal opportunities must be considered unless an organisation wants to run the risk of legal action being taken against it by disgruntled employees (or prospective employees) who have been unfairly treated:

- Advertising of posts
- Recruitment procedures
- Selection techniques
- Contractual terms and conditions of employment
- Pay
- Dress codes
- Working hours
- Workplace disciplinary procedures
- Appraisal interviews
- Allowances and bonus payments
- Dismissal procedures
- Occupational pensions
- Employee involvement arrangements
- Training opportunities
- Workplace culture and norms
- Custom and practice arrangements
- Promotion procedures
- Selection for redundancy

Explore

Fairness at decision points

Consider the list of HRM issues above.

- Select five of these and in each case give an example of how equal opportunity considerations need to be taken into account. (For instance, in considering the advertising of posts, managers might want to bear in mind the demographics of the readership of the newspaper, magazine or website where the advert is placed.)

Legal protection against unfair discrimination

In Europe there has been a move towards a common platform of human rights in relation to equality and fairness. One of the key developments has been the attempt to harmonise the protection against discrimination at work. Within each country there have been changes in national legislation – either amendments to existing laws or the introduction of new laws – in compliance with European Union (EU) directives. The basic principle behind the directives is a right to equal treatment irrespective of sex/gender, racial or ethnic origin, religion or belief, disability, age or sexual orientation. In other words, if someone considers they have been unfairly treated because of their sex, age, religion and so forth, they have a legal right to challenge their employer and seek compensation. Within the UK, the Equality Act 2010 uses the term 'protected characteristics' to denote those aspects where there is legal protection:

- age;
- disability;
- gender reassignment;
- marriage and civil partnership;
- pregnancy and maternity;
- race (includes, colour, nationality, ethnic or national origins);
- religion or belief (covers philosophical belief, and includes a lack of religion or belief);
- sex;
- sexual orientation.

Of course, there are other characteristics that could be added to this list, such as size (both height and weight), appearance (haircut, tattoos, piercings, norms of attractiveness), health, class (socioeconomic group), accent, schooling or university. None of these other characteristics is covered directly by European law or UK legislation, so it is often lawful for an employer to discriminate against someone on any of these grounds, although in some instances there might be some protection for the individual through laws that cover indirect discrimination (see below), or the violation of human rights.

Explore

Experiences of discrimination

- On the basis of the preceding discussion reflect on your own experiences by identifying the ways you might have been disadvantaged personally in your past or current employment (or in any other aspect of your life). You do not need to think of dramatic examples of discrimination (although you might have experienced these) but think of instances where characteristics that are part of your identity have influenced a person's decision, behaviour or attitude towards you. Remember you can consider the unprotected characteristics as well as the protected ones.

The forms of legal protection

In many countries, legislation sets limits to lawful managerial action and places obligations on managers to act in accordance with principles of fairness. In other words, some equality and diversity practices are the result of a legal obligation, rather than management choice. Bearing this general point in mind, you should also note the following:

- The type and extent of this legislation vary from country to country, so it is important to read about the specific legislation in your own national context.
- Opinion varies as to whether state regulation is necessary or the extent to which it is legitimate or practical to legislate to prevent discrimination and promote equality of opportunity.

- Even when legislation is in place there is no guarantee that this will ensure equality of opportunity. This might be because the legislation is ignored (unlawfully) or because it is ineffective (too weak, too many loopholes, difficult to enforce and so on).

Within European workplaces EU directives have provided a shared platform of protection and established common legal definitions of four forms of discrimination (although, of course, interpretation of the meaning and the application might still vary in different national contexts). The descriptions and examples below are taken from the UK's application of the directives through the Equality Act 2010.

1 *Direct discrimination* occurs when a person is treated less favourably than another is, has been or would be treated in a comparable situation on one of the protected grounds (sex/gender, racial or ethnic origin, etc.) (see Box 6.1). **Example** (HMSO, 2010: 18): 'If an employer recruits a man rather than a woman because she assumes that women do not have the strength to do the job, this would be direct sex discrimination.'

   In addition to protection against less favourable treatment due to the possession of one of the characteristics, the UK's Equality Act 2010 also covers cases where a person is treated less favourably because (a) they are wrongly assumed to have a protected characteristic, or (b) they are associated with someone who has one of the protected characteristics (except marriage and civil partnership). **Example of (a)** (HMSO, 2010: 19): 'If an employer rejects a job application form from a white man whom he wrongly thinks is black, because the applicant has an African-sounding name, this would constitute direct race discrimination based on the employer's mistaken perception.' **Example of (b)** (HMSO, 2010: 18): 'If a Muslim shopkeeper refuses to serve a Muslim woman because she is married to a Christian, this would be direct religious or belief-related discrimination on the basis of her association with her husband.'

2 *Indirect discrimination* occurs where a policy, provision, criterion or practice that applies in the same way for everyone has an effect that disadvantages a group of people because of their age, disability, gender reassignment, marital/civil partnership status, race, sex or sexual orientation. Someone from that group can then claim they have been indirectly discriminated against. It will be deemed indirect discrimination unless the employer can justify the policy or action as a proportionate means of achieving a legitimate aim (see Box 6.1).

   Example (HMSO, 2010: 24): 'An observant Jewish engineer who is seeking an advanced diploma decides (even though he is sufficiently qualified to do so) not to apply to a specialist training company because it invariably undertakes the selection exercises for the relevant course on Saturdays. The company will have indirectly discriminated against the engineer unless the practice can be justified.'

3 *An instruction to discriminate* is where one person obliges another to act in a discriminatory manner against a third party covered by one of the protected grounds. In such situations, it is the employee being told to act in a discriminatory manner who can make a claim for direct discrimination against his or her employer.

Box 6.1 Direct and indirect discrimination

A Muslim woman applied for a job as a stylist in a hair salon in London, but she was rejected because she wore a headscarf and the salon owner argued that all the stylists should display their own hair.

In this case there is no *direct discrimination* on the ground of her religion, because the owner of the salon would have rejected a non-Muslim who wore a headscarf.

Potentially, there is *indirect discrimination* because the salon owner's rule of no headscarves would affect Muslim women more than non-Muslims, as it is a dress code observed in the main by Muslim women.

Explore

Direct and indirect discrimination

The key issue in Box 6.1 is whether the requirement that stylists display their hair is a 'proportionate means of achieving a legitimate aim'. If it is, then a claim of indirect discrimination would fail. If it is not, then the salon owner is indirectly discriminating.

- What do you think?
- Using the same reasoning as above, consider the following situation and explain the grounds on which a claim of discrimination might be made: The managers of a tourist attraction in Glasgow advertised for a worker no taller than 1.7 metres (5ft 6in) to fit into a costume for an exhibition.

Example (HMSO, 2010: 19): 'If the manager of a nightclub is disciplined for refusing to carry out an instruction to exclude older customers from the club, this would be direct age discrimination against the manager unless the instruction could be justified.'

4 *Harassment* is where unwanted conduct related to the protected grounds of discrimination takes place with the *purpose or effect* of violating someone's dignity and of creating an intimidating, hostile, degrading, humiliating or offensive environment.

Examples (HMSO, 2010: 29): 'An employer who displayed any material of a sexual nature, such as a topless calendar, may be harassing her employees where this makes the workplace an offensive place to work for any employee, female or male. A shopkeeper propositions one of his shop assistants. She rejects his advances and then is turned down for promotion which she believes she would have got if she had accepted her boss's advances. The shop assistant would have a claim of harassment.'

Differences between and within social groups

One of the assumptions sometimes made is that all discrimination is the same, irrespective of whether it is based on sex, race/ethnicity, disability and so forth. While it is certainly the case that the consequences of discrimination (the disadvantage suffered) are the same (or very similar) for the victims, the reactions and attitudes of the members of the social groups affected can differ. The term 'social group' refers to people who share similar characteristics; for example, it is possible to refer to women as a social group, or people with a disability as a social group. Of course, it would be also possible to break these social groups down even further – for instance, white women; or Muslim men with a disability; or even white, partially sighted, lesbian atheists under 25. For our purposes at this stage, the social group is defined by one of the key characteristics (sex, age, ethnicity, etc.), although shortly we shall explore why this is an over-simplification.

It is important to acknowledge differences *between* social groups. Although they may all be victims of discrimination, it would be inaccurate to assume the experience of being discriminated against because you are a woman is the same as that of being discriminated against on the grounds of sexual orientation; or that the discrimination experienced by disabled employees is the same as that endured by ethnic minority employees. For example, someone's social group might be identifiable because of visible characteristics, such as sex, race/ethnicity, some forms of disability, and religions that require certain codes of dress. Other characteristics, such as sexual orientation and some religions or beliefs, can be hidden, enabling potential victims to avoid disadvantage and discrimination through behaviour that disguises their true identities.

A further issue to consider is that some people experience discrimination because of more than one characteristic they possess. This has been discussed by researchers in two ways:

- *Multiple discrimination.* This refers to situations where a person suffers unfair treatment due two or more characteristics – e.g. their sex and their age. The conclusion drawn by some researchers (e.g. Berthoud, 2003) is that there is some sort of additive effect. In other words, for example, in terms of getting a job, there is a disadvantage associated with being a woman to which is added the disadvantage of being an older worker. It is sometimes referred to as 'double jeopardy'.

- *Intersectionality*. This term is also used to describe situations of multiple discrimination, but there is an important distinction. Researchers conclude that the disadvantages caused by two or more characteristics are not simply additive, but they produce a totally different experience for the person (see, for example, Acker, 2006; Bradley and Healy, 2008). For instance, the experience of being from an ethnic minority background and also a woman is not simply the sum of the two disadvantages (ethnicity and sex) but rather the product of the interaction between these two characteristics. It can be described as producing a new and potentially greater disadvantage that is distinct to the specific category (the intersection). For example, an employee might be discriminated against because she is both a woman and Asian, and might therefore not share the same concerns about, or experiences of, discrimination as her white women colleagues or black male colleagues. Researchers argue that for this reason it is important to study the intersections between the various strands, because these are distinct categories in their own right.

Finally, it is important to recognise differences *within* social groups, rather than consider each group to be homogeneous. For instance, Reynolds *et al.* (2001) point out how disability can be a diverse and wide-ranging categorisation. People may move into a state of disability from ill-health, work accidents or ageing, and so while some people are 'born disabled', there is an increasing proportion of employees who 'become disabled'. Moreover, the needs of those with different 'disabilities' are so wide-ranging that it might be suggested there is very little meaning in such a broad category as 'disability'. The same conclusion might be reached for race/ethnicity. Commentators (e.g. Modood *et al.*, 1997; Pilkington, 2001; Nazroo and Karlsen, 2003) argue that research evidence suggests there is so much ethnic diversity that to describe discrimination as being the same across different ethnic groups fails to take into account its differential impact. This means it is essential to recognise the differences between ethnic groups not only in terms of their experiences of discrimination, but also in their varied requirements for redressing the discrimination.

Key Controversy

The extent to which it is meaningful or helpful to consider equality and disadvantage in relation to social groups is subject to debate because, as discussed above, people may fall into more than one group and the differences within groups may be as large as the differences between them.

What are the implications for managers?

The overall situation is that managers must operate within a legal context that has established rights for individuals that protect employees and job applicants. Of course, this does not stop some managers from ignoring or flouting these laws, but this carries both a pecuniary and a reputational risk for the organisation. Within this legal framework, managers must also be aware of the differences in the needs of the various groups and individuals that experience discrimination. These are important issues because it means:

- Managers should not assume that discrimination means the same thing irrespective of the social group concerned.
- Managers should not assume that a solution to rectify disadvantage for one social group (e.g. women) will be appropriate or welcomed by a different social group (e.g. disabled people).

- Managers should expect that attitudes will differ within social groups (e.g. Asian employees and black employees).

The recognition of this diversity has led some commentators to argue that rather than defining people by their similarities to others, managers should see all employees as individuals with unique skills and needs. This is an issue that we return to later in the chapter.

Why is inequality a problem and why should managers be concerned with it?

A key question that needs to be addressed is why managers should care whether some people are disadvantaged and suffer unfair treatment. In answering this question, it is useful to distinguish between two different sets of arguments, which can be labeled 'the social justice case' and 'the business case'.

The social justice case

The social justice case is that managers have a moral obligation to treat employees with fairness and dignity. Part of this involves ensuring that decisions are made without resorting to prejudice and stereotypes (for definitions of these terms, see Box 6.2). If decisions are made free from prejudice and stereotyping then there is a lower risk of any particular group being disadvantaged and therefore less chance of an individual feeling that he or she has been discriminated against.

Social justice arguments typically centre around one or more of the following points.

Equality of opportunity

The 'level playing field' argument is that managers have a responsibility to ensure that everyone is given the same opportunity to access jobs and promotion opportunities, and what separates the winners from the losers are the skills and abilities they possess. Managers might therefore need to intervene to ensure that such equality of opportunity is provided, otherwise factors other than skills and abilities will determine success. The particular objective is ensuring procedural justice so that the processes at key decision points are free from bias and distortion.

Equality of outcome

The focus is on the outcome of any process. Are the rewards (jobs, pay, bonuses, training opportunities, etc.) distributed in a manner that truly takes into account skill and abilities or, put more prosaically, does everyone get 'a fair share of the cake'? While procedures are essential, it is vital not to overlook the outcomes, so there also needs to be a concern with distributive justice. Importantly, this approach can help draw attention to how individuals from some groups can enter a 'level playing field', yet they do so from a position of prior disadvantage, which is rarely taken into account. As we saw in the Introductory case study about women on company boards, some people argue there is a need for quotas to address the disadvantage women face in climbing the management hierarchy in order to compete for the board positions.

Fairness and human rights

Treating people fairly is an end in itself and it should not be seen merely as the means to an end. From an ethics perspective, this means taking a *deontological* stance where an action is not evaluated in terms of its consequences but is judged in relation to the act itself. In other

| Box 6.2 | **Prejudice and stereotyping** |

The following definitions come from a dictionary of HRM;

Prejudice – this means holding negative attitudes towards a particular group, and viewing all members of that group in a negative light, irrespective of their individual qualities and attributes. Typically we think of prejudice as being against a particular group based on gender, race/ethnicity, religion, disability, age and sexual orientation. However, prejudice extends much further and is frequently directed at other groups based on features such as accent, height, weight, hair colour, beards, body piercings, tattoos and clothes. It is extremely rare to find a person who is not prejudiced against any group – although most of us are reluctant to admit to our prejudices.

Source: Heery and Noon, 2008: 359

Stereotyping – this is the act of judging people according to our assumptions about the group to which they belong. It is based on the belief that people from a specific group share similar traits and behave in a similar manner. Rather than looking at a person's individual qualities, stereotyping leads us to jump to conclusions about what someone is like. This might act against the person concerned (negative stereotype) or in their favour (positive stereotype). For example, the negative stereotype of an accountant is someone who is dull, uninteresting and shy – which, of course, is a slur on all the exciting, adventurous accountants in the world. A positive stereotype is that accountants are intelligent, conscientious and trustworthy – which is an equally inaccurate description of some of the accountants you are likely to encounter. The problem with stereotypes is that they are generalisations (so there are always exceptions) and can be based on ignorance and prejudice (so are often inaccurate). It is vital for managers to resist resorting to stereotyping when managing people; otherwise, they run the risk of treating employees unfairly and making poor-quality decisions that are detrimental to the organisation.

Source: Heery and Noon (2008: 443–44)

words, the everyday processes of managing needs to take into account fair treatment because this is the right (ethical) thing to do, not because of the benefits it brings or the absence of harm caused. This line of thinking is counter-intuitive to business, whereby success is typically measured in terms of outcome rather than process (a teleological ethical stance). However, the recognition by some large organisations of the importance of corporate social responsibility in relation to their public image, consumer taste and pressure from social movements means that adopting ethical, rights-based stances might be an obligation and a necessity, or might even offer commercial advantages. There is, of course, a sleight of hand here, because arguing that fairness is a worthy ethical value due to the business advantages it brings is wholly different from arguing that it is the right approach irrespective of those benefits.

| Explore | **Prejudice and stereotyping** |

Read the definitions in Box 6.2, be honest with yourself and think about the prejudices you have and the stereotypes you use to categorise people.

- Try to think of at least two examples for each. (Even the most politically correct among us have deep-seated prejudices and stereotypes. By recognising and confronting our prejudices and stereotypes, we have a better chance of not letting them influence the decisions we make.)

Limitations of the social justice argument

The social justice approach is not unified. It can be seen from the three sets of arguments in the previous section that there is a different emphasis in each, which can lead to different policy suggestions as to how organisations should address the problems of disadvantage and inequality. Most notably, those who favour procedural intervention tend to advocate a 'light touch' in terms of legal regulation and best-practice guidelines, while those who focus on outcomes advocate stronger legislation and/or more radical changes to organisational processes and practices. These types of differences in approach are returned to later in this chapter when examining policy choices for managers.

Critics of the social justice case tend to argue that while the pursuit of fairness is laudable, it is not the prime concern of organisations. The goals of managers in organisations are profit and efficiency, rather than morality. If social justice was to guide their decision-making, it might have a detrimental effect on the operation of the business and ultimately the bottom line. This line of argument has led to an additional rationale for equality and diversity: the business case.

The business case

The second set of arguments that can be used to justify why managers should be concerned with eliminating disadvantage is based on making a business case. The point is that, aside from any concerns with social justice, fair treatment simply makes good business sense for five key reasons:

1 *It is a better use of human resources.* If managers discriminate on the basis of sex, race/ethnicity, disability and so on, they run the risk of neglecting or overlooking talented employees. The consequence is that the organisation fails to maximise its full human resource potential and valuable resources are wasted through either under-utilising the competences of existing employees, or losing disgruntled, talented staff to other organisations. These considerations are vital for effective talent management (see Chapter 5).

2 *It provides more opportunity for innovation.* The greater the range of employees from different backgrounds and with different perspectives, the greater the opportunity for the development of new ideas about products, services, ways of working and problem-solving. This might help place an organisation at the cutting edge within its industry and help generate a creative and vibrant working environment/culture.

3 *It leads to a wider customer base.* An organisation with a diverse workforce might be in a better position to identify and exploit new market opportunities and attract new customers. This might be particularly important where face-to-face service delivery is a central part of the business and requires an empathy with the customers.

4 *It creates a wider pool of labour for recruitment.* When managers are open-minded about the people they could employ for various jobs at different levels in the organisation, they will have a wider pool of talent from which to recruit. This is particularly important when an organisation is attempting to secure scarce resources, such as employees with specific skills or experience.

5 *It leads to a positive company image.* If there is a clear statement of the organisation's commitment to fair treatment, backed by meaningful practices that result in a diverse workforce, managers will be able to project a positive image of the organisation to customers, suppliers and potential employees. In terms of employees, the organisation will be perceived as good to work for because it values ability and talent, and so will be more likely to attract and retain high-calibre people.

Key Controversy

Although the business case arguments are quite persuasive, there might be some circumstances when 'good business sense' provides the justification for not acting in the interest of particular groups.

Limitations of the business case arguments

Cunningham and James (2001) found that line managers often justified their decision not to employ disabled people on the grounds that the necessary workplace adjustments would eat into their operating budgets. Indeed, equality and diversity initiatives often have a cost associated with them, the recovery of which cannot always be easily measured and might only be realised in the long term. The danger (highlighted by commentators such as Dickens, 1994, 2000; and Webb, 1997) is that such initiatives can only be justified as long as they contribute to profit. For example in Webb's (1997) case study of an international computing systems manufacturer, the corporate philosophy was to encourage employee diversity to bring in new ideas, meet customer needs and achieve success in the global marketplace. However, at divisional level in the UK, the requests from women for childcare provision and flexible hours were rejected on the basis that these would adversely affect profitability. Furthermore, although managerial opportunities were open to women, this was clearly on men's terms, as Webb (1997: 165) explains:

> Women graduate engineers are aware that they have to fit in as 'one of the boys' and however supportive the line manager, these are all men: 'I think the difficulty is still being able to sit down, map out your career and possibly say that at a certain time you many well wish to have a family...' (graduate sales rep.) ... Even for those willing to adopt male work norms, the corporate orientation to innovation and change means that the uncertainties experienced by managers are likely to result in the continuing exclusion of women, who continue to be regarded as a riskier bet than men.

This type of problem is common and is expressed vividly by Liff and Wajcman (1996: 89) in the following quote:

> Managers' perceptions of job requirements and procedures for assessing merit have been shown to be saturated with gendered assumptions ... Feminists can argue (as they have for years) that not all women get pregnant, but it seems unlikely that this will stop managers thinking, 'Yes, but no men will.'

Explore

The building supplies firm

The managing director of a small business supplying building and gardening materials says: 'This diversity stuff is political correctness gone mad. I like to employ people I understand and that means people who are from backgrounds similar to mine. I'm not prejudiced and I'm not against employing women. In fact I have a couple of girls answering the phone in the office, but my customers prefer to deal with men. You see, most of my customers are local tradesmen and they want to deal with men who know all about the materials we supply. I've got a good set of employees but the biggest problem is labour turnover. It doesn't take long to train them up, but the good ones don't stay long.'

● Assuming he would listen to you, what points could you make to persuade him that there might be a business case for changing his approach?

A further problem is the issue of measuring the effects of extending opportunities. The underlying assumption is that all initiatives will have a positive effect on business (hence they

191

make good business sense). But this logic requires that they are subsequently measured and evaluated to assess their effects. This poses two difficulties:

1 *Finding a meaningful measure.* In some instances, this is feasible. For example, it would be possible to recruit more Asian salespeople in order to increase sales to Asian customers, and in this case appropriate measures would be the number and value of sales and the number of Asian customers (identified by their family name). However, in other instances, measurement is very difficult. For example, how would you measure the impact of diversity-awareness training? Or the effects of flexible working arrangements? In both cases, it might be possible to measure the effects in terms of attitudes or changes in performance, but it would be more difficult to attribute these solely to the specific initiatives.

2 *Measuring in the short term.* In many instances, the full effects of an equality or diversity initiative would only be realised in the long term. For many managers within organisations, this would be a disincentive to invest in such initiatives, particularly if the performance of their department was measured in the short term. Moreover, it would be an even greater disincentive to invest if the manager's salary or bonus was affected by the short-term performance of their department.

Overall, the business case argument can make an impact – e.g. in circumstances of skills shortages, needs for particular types of employees, or local labour market conditions – but this is likely to be variable and patchy. As Dickens (1999: 10) states:

> The contingent and variable nature of the business case can be seen in the fact that business case arguments have greater salience for some organisations than others. . . . The appeal of a particular business case argument can also vary over time as labour or product markets change, giving rise to 'fair weather' equality action.

In summary, there are three sets of problems associated with the business case.

- There will not always be a business case for equality and diversity initiatives because it depends on the particular circumstances of the organisation.
- The business case might be difficult to prove (in quantitative terms), even if it seems persuasive.
- Even if there is a business case that can be proven at a given time, circumstances change (not least economic ones) so the particular business case might cease to have relevance.

By contrast, the social justice case applies to all organisations, does not require proof (as it is based on a universal principle) and is far more resilient because it is not affected by the vagaries of the market (see Noon, 2007).

Justice and business sense

As you might have realised, the two sets of arguments are not necessarily mutually exclusive. Indeed, it is feasible and practical for managers to use both sets to justify equality or diversity initiatives in their organisations. By stressing both arguments, there is more chance of gaining commitment to equality and diversity from a wider group of people. It does not really matter whether a manager is committed to equality for reasons of justice or because of a compelling business case – it is the fact they are committed that counts. Of course, this is not quite as simple in practice, because once commitment has been gained, there is then the question of how to deal with the problems of discrimination. A starting point is to identify the underlying causes of the discrimination, inequality or lack of diversity.

What are the embedded and deep-rooted causes of the problems of equality and diversity within an organisation?

Institutional discrimination

One of the key issues that managers must face is whether their organisations operate in ways that are fundamentally discriminatory. This is sometimes referred to as institutional racism, institutional sexism, institutional homophobia and so on. The term means that discrimination is deep-rooted in the processes and culture of an organisation, and cannot simply be explained as the actions of individuals who are blatantly prejudiced against particular groups. The discrimination might be intentional – e.g. a promotion process might be known by managers to favour men over women, but no one challenges it or wishes to improve it. Equally, the discrimination might be unintentional – e.g. the managers simply do not realise that holding team-building meetings in the pub after work might be disadvantageous for employees with young families and may conflict with some religious beliefs.

Examples of processes that are sometimes described as evidence of institutional discrimination are:

- word-of-mouth methods for recruitment;
- dress codes that prevent people from practising their religious beliefs;
- promotions based on informal recommendations, rather than open competition;
- informal assessments rather than formal appraisals;
- assumptions about training capabilities;
- assumptions about language difficulties and attitudes.

Often these types of processes are not recognised as being discriminatory and have been in operation for many years. It is only when a company is faced with a legal challenge that such practices are seen to be having a discriminatory impact. HR managers should regularly scrutinise organisational procedures, and collect and analyse data on the demographic profile of the organisation across different levels and jobs, and particularly in the different formal processes, such as appraisal, promotion, training and discipline.

Institutional discrimination can be perpetuated through some workplace cultures when they have the effect of excluding people from particular social groups by making them feel unwelcome or uncomfortable. This is a key issue for managers because organisations might have cultures that are long established and deeply embedded. An interesting review of the way organisational cultures can marginalise social groups is provided by Kirton and Greene (2005: 83–109). Most notable among their conclusions are the following points:

- Organisational cultures are infused with gendered meanings, which are often unarticulated and thus rendered invisible. The gendered hierarchy is an example, as are various unwritten codes, rules, customs and habits which guide gendered behaviour and underpin expectations of organisational members.
- Sexual harassment and the use of sexual humour are pervasive and the outcome of workplace gendered social relations, which are powerful mechanisms for the control and subordination of women.
- Stereotypes (based on gender, race, disability, sexual orientation and age) are reinforced through jokes and humour, leading to negative organisational experiences for some people.
- Non-disabled people's lack of contact with disability reinforces their fear and ignorance surrounding the issue.
- Employer ageism is often mediated by other factors, particular gender.

193

Box 6.3 | **Fair selection?**

Hotels.com (part of the Expedia group) is an online consumer platform that prides itself on being agile to keep up with the pace of technological change and so is always on the hunt for technical experts to develop and maintain products, such as smartphone apps. As well as using job adverts, its website, Twitter and LinkedIn, **Hotels.com** makes extensive use of its existing staff members by relying on their referrals. In the London office, the method has proved highly successful in bringing in technical staff who have the skills yet also fit with the culture of the organisation.

Source: 'Driving culture through recruitment', AskGrapevine HR, November 2012, pp, 28–30.)

Pret à Manger, the sandwich chain, hit the headlines in 2012 when the London mayor, Boris Johnson, raised concerns about why there were virtually no young Londoners employed in their outlets. Pret denied it was biased but it has an unusual final stage in its selection process. Those applicants who make it through the first stages (an online application, and a telephone interview or meeting at Pret's recruitment centre) are invited to an 'experience day'. The company describes this as follows on their website:

> There's no better way of finding out if you would enjoy working at Pret than trying it for yourself. Our Experience Day will see you working as part of the team in a shop for a whole day. You get to check us out and we get to check you out. At the end of the day, each member of the team tells the manager whether they think you'd be a good fit at Pret and the manager tells you there and then whether you've been successful. If unfortunately you haven't, we'll explain why and pay you for the day's work that you've done. If you are successful (hurrah!) you'll be welcomed into the team and the hours you've worked will be included in your first week's pay.

The members of the team who have had contact with the applicant during the morning rate him or her on the company's key behaviours: passion, clear-talking and team-working. The manager totals the scores and adds their own before making a decision.

Sources: 'Why can't a Brit get a job at Pret?', Evening Standard, 23 January 2012, pp. 20–21; Pret à Manger, **http://www.pret.co.uk/jobs/Recruitment_centre.htm** (accessed 20 January 2013).

Explore | **Fair selection**

- The recruitment and selection practices used by **Hotels.com** and **Pret à Manger** outlined in Box 6.3 are effective, but do they raise any concerns in relation to equality and diversity?
- Review the recruitment and selection practices in your own organisation with respect to equality and diversity.

Two problems with institutional discrimination

The first problem is inertia. Even when institutional discrimination has been identified there is no incentive to make changes because those people in positions of influence have benefited (and continue to benefit) from the system. Furthermore, those people most likely to change policies within the organisation (the 'victims' of discrimination) are denied access to decision-making processes.

The second problem is with the concept of institutional discrimination itself. Some critics argue that it can lead to a tendency to blame 'the system', rather than focusing on the people who shape and sustain the system. In some circumstances, this can be helpful, because by removing blame from individuals it might be easier to encourage action to address the problem. In other circumstances, it can result in nothing being done, because no one is deemed responsible or held accountable.

In defence of the concept of institutional discrimination, it can be argued that it alerts people to the way that the fundamental structures and processes can be detrimental to equality and diversity, and that unless action is taken to address these fundamentals, nothing will improve. This is an important point, because it suggests that in many instances the drive to equality and diversity requires some radical changes, rather than just equality/diversity statements and positive action initiatives.

Using equality and diversity policies to deal with the problems

If the issue of disadvantage is to be addressed in a systemic and consistent way within an organisation, then it is essential to have an overall policy that guides decision-making and action. Increasingly, such policies are being created, although the terminology differs from organisation to organisation: some call them equal opportunity policies, others diversity policies and more recently the term 'inclusion' is being used (see Oswick and Noon, 2014). To confuse matters further, some organisations blend all three terms. The rationale for the adoption of policies can be based on a mix of justice and business sense arguments, as was noted earlier. The EHRC in the UK recommends that all organisations have an equality policy, as well as putting in place effective methods of ensuring the policy is actually put into practice. For advice on the possible content of the policy and the means of enforcing it, see Box 6.4.

Box 6.4   Equality policy advice from the UK's Equality and Human Rights Commission

An equality policy should apply to every aspect of employment, from recruitment through pay, access to facilities and employment benefits, discipline and grievance procedures and so on up to the end of the contractual relationship and beyond, e.g. when you provide references.

A policy might include:

- statements outlining your organisation's commitment to equality;
- identification of the types of discrimination that an employer (and, if this applies to you, a service provider) is required to combat across the protected characteristics of age, disability, gender reassignment, marriage and civil partnership, pregnancy and maternity, race, religion or belief, sex and sexual orientation;
- statements outlining the type of work environment your organisation aims to create, including what is and is not acceptable behaviour at work (also referring to conduct near the workplace and at work-related social functions where relevant);
- information about how policy will be put into action, including how you will deal with any breaches of the policy by your workers, and how concerns and complaints will be dealt with, whether these come from your workers or (if you have them) from your customers, clients or service users;
- who is responsible for the policy;
- how you will monitor the policy and when you will review it;
- details covering how the policy is linked in with your other policies.

Your equality policy could also describe the type of working environment you want to create. For example: 'We aim to create a working environment in which all people are able to give of their best, there is no bullying and harassment or discrimination and all decisions are based on merit.'

Box 6.4 continued

Alongside your equality policy, you can have a separate harassment and bullying policy, or you could put both policies together as a 'dignity at work' policy.

To make sure an equality policy is put into practice in an organisation, there should be:

- a demonstrable commitment to the policy from the very top of your organisation;
- the agreement, understanding and support of all your staff and stakeholders (such as trade unions) regarding the policy's implementation;
- involvement of your staff and stakeholders in the drafting of the policy;
- extensive promotion of the policy both within your organisation and to potential workers, contractors and suppliers;
- training provided to all your staff to explain what the equality policy says and what it means to them;
- incorporation of the policy into your organisation's business strategy;
- an explicit willingness to challenge and, if necessary, discipline anyone not following the policy;
- reference made to the equality policy in other policies within your organisation;
- an action plan in place which includes a commitment to a regular policy review – your review should examine your progress in delivering the action plan and ensure that this information is shared.

Source: Equality policies, **http://www.equalityhumanrights.com/advice-and-guidance/guidance-for-employers/ equality-policies-equality-training-and-monitoring/equality-policies/**, The copyright and all other intellectual property rights in the material to be reproduced are owned by, or licensed to, the commission for Equality and Human Rights, known as the Equality and Human Rights Commission ("the EHRC") (accessed 20 January 2013).

The form of equality policies varies between organisations, and Table 6.1 shows how organisations might be categorised according to the extent to which they are actively engaging with equality issues. At one extreme are those organisations that do the absolute minimum – barely meeting the legal requirements – and at the other extreme are those fully committed to an equality/diversity agenda.

One particular technique recommended by advocates of equality and diversity as a way of embedding policy is 'discrimination proofing' the organisation. This entails auditing the HR processes to assess the potential areas where unfair practice might occur. The identification

Table 6.1 Types of equal opportunity organisation

The negative organisation	Has no equal opportunity policy
	Makes no claims of being an equal opportunity employer
	Might not be complying with the law
The minimalist organisation	Claims to be an equal opportunity employer
	Has no written equal opportunity policy
	Has no procedure or initiatives, but will react to claims of discrimination as they arise
The compliant organisation	Has a written equal opportunity policy
	Has procedures and initiatives in place to comply with some aspects of good practice recommendations
The proactive organisation	Has a written policy backed up with procedures and initiatives
	Monitors the outcomes of initiatives to assess their impact
	Promotes equality using a full set of good practice guidelines, and might even go beyond these

Source: based on Healy (1993) and Kirton and Greene (2005).

of unfairness might signal the absence of clear policy or procedures, or the failure of existing procedures, often through a managerial lack of knowledge or training. The purpose of such an exercise is to identify the areas of vulnerability and to take action to make improvements where they carry an unacceptable level of risk.

Explore

Categorising equality approaches

Look at Table 6.1.

- In which category would you place the organisation where you study and where you work (or have previously worked)?
- Explain your reasoning.

Two key components: positive action and equality monitoring

To ensure the effectiveness of equal and diversity policies, there needs to be positive action initiatives and effective equality monitoring in place. These two components are a feature of those organisations with a 'proactive' approach to equality and diversity.

Positive action

Positive action means one or more specific initiatives designed to compensate for present or past disadvantages that have been caused by unfair discrimination. Typically, positive action initiatives encourage under-represented groups to apply for jobs or promotion within the organisation. Positive action might also be concerned with making changes to working arrangements to encourage the retention of employees by making the environment more suited to the needs they have that differ from the majority of employees. Here are a few examples of the type of initiatives that could be described as 'positive action':

- Launching a recruitment campaign in specific locations known to have a high density of ethnic minorities.
- Ensuring company social events, where partners are invited, include same-sex partners.
- Introducing a vocational training scheme open only to employees aged 55 or over.
- Adapting the uniform or dress code requirements to take into account religious requirements.
- Introducing flexible working hours to accommodate family needs.
- Providing a sign language interpreter for a training course.

You will encounter other examples of positive action throughout the chapter, and there will be some subtle distinctions made between different types of positive action. There is one important distinction that must be made: positive action is not the same as 'positive discrimination'. The latter means the preferential treatment of a person because of their sex, ethnicity, age and so forth, and this is unlawful under most discrimination law within Europe. For example, imagine that a school had no black or Asian teachers, so the governing body decided to shortlist only ethnic minority candidates for the next teaching post that became available. This would be *positive discrimination* and is unlawful because the candidates have been shortlisted due to their ethnicity, not due to their skills, experience, qualifications, etc. (see Box 6.5 for a discussion on positive discrimination). On the other hand, an entirely lawful *positive action* initiative would be for the school to state on the advert that 'applications from ethnic minorities would be particularly welcome'; and this could result in a preponderance of applications from black and Asian candidates with stronger CVs than white applicants and consequently perhaps a shortlist composed exclusively of candidates from ethnic minority backgrounds.

Box 6.5   **Time to rethink positive discrimination?**

I have made arguments in favour of adopting some forms of positive discrimination in two journal articles (Noon, 2010, 2012). My view is that positive discrimination is often misunderstood because it is often assumed to be simply about quotas, when in fact it can take different forms. There are typically four main objections made by people who criticise the idea of positive discrimination: it fails to select the 'best' candidate; it undermines meritocracy; it has a negative impact on the beneficiaries; and it leads to the injustice of reverse discrimination. In the articles, I argue that it is possible to logically challenge each of these criticisms. The extract below is the challenge I make to the second of these criticisms, namely that positive discrimination undermines meritocracy. My argument is that meritocracy is not as prevalent, objective or fair as we are sometimes led to believe.

The issue of meritocracy raised by the critics is frequently an appeal to principles of economic individualism. Typically it finds an expression among those who argue for non-interventionary approaches to securing equality. For example, the head of diversity at PricewaterhouseCoopers stated, 'It makes commercial sense to create an environment where meritocracy prevails. Anything other than this is de-motivating for everyone and productivity will inevitably drop' (Hilpern, 2007: 13).

There are at least four challenges that can be made to the veracity of statements such as this:

1 It might not be in the interests of managers to ensure meritocracy due to internal politics, and might not be possible due to well-known processes that influence the selection of candidates (e.g. stereotyping, halo/horns effects, cronyism, 'old boys' network' etc.).
2 If it is a superior business model that produces greater advantages of productivity and commitment, then why are not all companies following it?
3 It is difficult to prove quantitatively the commercial advantages.
4 There is a contingent nature to these advantages: in some instances there will be a business case for meritocracy, while in other instances it might be to a business's advantage to discriminate unfairly (Dickens, 1994; Noon, 2007).

An additional problem is that the concept of merit is not as value neutral as it might first appear. How is merit to be measured? Should it be focused on talent and ability, or should it also reflect effort and achievement? If elements of the latter category were included then merit would recognise personal achievements against the odds; for example, someone from an underprivileged background, state schooling and a low ranking university might be more meritorious than a middle-class person from a private school and a top university, even if the latter had better qualifications.

Objections based on the principle of merit can of course be used to disguise prejudicial views about certain groups being unable or unsuitable to perform certain work. The view promulgated is that some social groups fail due to inability (typically a biological essentialist perspective) or personal choice (typically a preference theory perspective), but such arguments surface even in the absence of positive discrimination initiatives; in other words, positive discrimination does not cause those views to be held, rather it provides the excuse for them to be expressed. [. . .]

An observation made by Reyna et al. (2005) is that both opponents and supporters of US initiatives designed to redress disadvantages in access to college, jobs or promotions (sometimes called affirmative action programmes) claim the principle of merit to be their main concern in taking their stance. Opponents argue that it infringes merit by giving preferential treatment based on social group characteristics (sex, race, etc.) while supporters argue that only by taking these characteristics into consideration can a truly meritocratic process be ensured. Overturning the notion of meritocracy produces an uncomfortable alternative proposition for the advantaged group: that meritocracy is not the prevalent norm and so, logically, some people in the advantaged group do not deserve to be in their jobs. Intuitively people may know this proposition to be plausible – most people are able to point to instances of favouritism, cronyism, nepotism and the like – but the issue is how widespread this is believed to be. People are unlikely to argue that their own position was gained through a

Box 6.5 continued

non-meritocratic process, even though they might claim this is the case for their superordinates or their co-workers.

Source: abridged from pp. 733–34 of M. Noon (2010) 'The shackled runner: time to rethink positive discrimination?' *Work, Employment and Society,* 24 (4): 728–39.

Key Controversy

In some instances, positive action is not going to be radical enough to tackle deep-seated, historical patterns of disadvantage, yet positive discrimination is unlawful in the UK and provokes considerable controversy whenever it is raised.

There is sometimes a fine line that distinguishes positive action from positive discrimination, but it should be drawn where the initiative goes beyond encouragement and persuasion. In other words, if an initiative means that a person is selected primarily because of their ethnicity, sex, age, religion, sexual orientation, etc., then this is likely to be unlawful positive discrimination. But the boundary is far from clear. In France the positive action on disability is more like positive discrimination because there is a requirement for 6 per cent of the workforce to be disabled – and similar quota-based systems (or quota-levy systems where employers can opt out through paying a tax to a special fund) operate in countries as diverse as Japan, Venezuela, Poland and Austria. In the UK, the disability discrimination legislation allows employers to discriminate in favour of individuals because of their disability; indeed, there is no legal protection for someone to claim that they have been treated unfairly because they are *not* disabled. There are also some other exceptions (see Box 6.6) and in the UK employers are allowed to take into account protected characteristics in the selection and promotion when making a decision between candidates that are equally qualified for the job. This 'tie break' clause was introduced (to the indignation of much of the UK media) by the Equality Act 2010 and although it is clearly stated to be a form of positive action, it reveals just how blurred the boundary between positive action and positive discrimination can become.

Box 6.6 | Lawful 'positive discrimination' in the UK

There are some exceptional circumstances where an organisation can claim there is an 'occupational requirement' explicitly to take into account one of the characteristics; for example, an organisation offering support services for women who are victims of sexual assault can employ only female counsellors, or an advertising agency can interview only people with disabilities for a photo-shoot for a disability charity's publicity campaign. The organisation must show that the requirement is really genuine for commercial or operating purposes, so, for example, it would be difficult for a games software company to require all its game developers to be under the age of 25 or even a Catholic school to require all staff to be practising Catholics.

Questions

1 Decide in each of the three cases below whether the action is likely to be lawful and explain your reasoning:

   (a) A theatre company wants to put on a production of Shakespeare's *Macbeth*. It only auditions female actors for the role of Lady Macbeth.
   (b) A Chinese restaurant in the West End of London only recruits waiters of Chinese origin.
   (c) A meat supplier advertises for workers in its factory in East Anglia. The advert states that 'Applicants must speak Polish.' The managers explain that this is because all the workforce are Polish migrants and all the health and safety training is in Polish.

Understandably, the distinction between positive action and positive discrimination is often misunderstood. This means that completely lawful positive action is sometimes misconstrued in the media and in blogosphere, and is frequently disparaged as being positive discrimination – usually followed with the words, 'It's political correctness gone mad!' But setting this confusion aside, it is generally true to say that lawful positive action initiatives almost always meet with disapproval from those who will not benefit from them. So a recruitment campaign targeted at attracting women into a male-dominated workplace will often be questioned by the men who see no need for change. However, if those who are openly hostile or resistant to the action are told what the social and organisational benefits are, they might moderate their position. Important in this respect is the production of the argument and evidence of the need for a change. As was noted earlier, business case arguments can sometimes be used to convince sceptics that equality of opportunity needs to be addressed. In addition, the collection of data (particularly statistical information) is not only important for demonstrating current inequalities, but also vital as a tool for evaluating the effects of any positive action initiatives – and hence assessing their worth. The process of systematic data collection is called equality monitoring.

Equality monitoring

One of the key ways of helping to ensure the effectiveness of policies is through the use of equality monitoring. This is a process of systematically collecting and analysing data on the composition of the workforce, particularly with regard to recruitment and promotion. The rationale behind monitoring is that it is impossible for managers to make an assessment of what action to take (if any) unless they are aware of the current situation. Of course, the supposition behind this is that managers might want to take action – but if this is not the case, then logically managers might not see the value in collecting the data in the first place. Therefore, equality monitoring has both advocates and detractors who marshal different arguments to justify their position; these are summarised in Table 6.2. Once again there is also variation in practice, depending on the national context. For example, in France it is unlawful for data to be collected on the ethnic composition of the workforce, because this contravenes

Table 6.2 The arguments for and against monitoring

The case in favour of equal opportunities monitoring	The case against equal opportunities monitoring
It allows managers to demonstrate what is being done and identify particular problem areas so they can take action	It stirs up trouble and discontent, and can create problems that would otherwise not arise
It encourages managers to think creatively about positive action initiatives	It puts undue pressure on managers, and might encourage them to lower standards or appoint for the wrong reasons
It removes the need for stronger legislation, such as quotas (positive discrimination)	It is positive discrimination 'by the back door'
The data can be kept confidential, just like any other information	It is an invasion of privacy and open to abuse
It provides useful information to help management decision-making	It creates the requirement to collect information that is unnecessary
Organisations conducting their activities in line with the legal requirements have nothing to fear	Organisations with no problems regarding equal opportunities do not need this burdensome bureaucratic mechanism
The costs are modest	It is an unnecessary expenditure
It is good business practice	The business should focus on its commercial activities

French policy on ethnic integration. By contrast, in the UK, public authorities now have a legal requirement to collect ethnic monitoring data on staff in post, applications for employment, promotion and training, and then to analyse these data and act upon any evidence of unfairness or disadvantage.

Criticism of equality and diversity policies

Naturally, there are some criticisms of equality and diversity policies. The first is that the policies are sometimes not worth the paper they are written on. Just because an organisation has a policy does not mean that the policy is effective. Indeed, research has found that in the majority of cases equality and diversity policies are not backed up with equality practices, so therefore lack substance and have little impact in ensuring that equality of opportunity prevails (Hoque and Noon, 2004). It might further be argued that in some organisations managers want to present the positive image of being aware of equality concerns, but do not wish to introduce procedures or initiatives that might (in their opinion) constrain or limit their decisions about whom to appoint, train, promote and so on. However, when policies are backed up with strong equality practices, they can be very effective in ensuring equal treatment (Noon and Hoque, 2001).

A second criticism is that formal policies do not prevent managers from finding ways of evading or distorting the procedures. For example, in their case study of a local government authority in the UK, Liff and Dale (1994) interviewed a black woman on a clerical grade who had been told that she needed to get a professional qualification if she wanted promotion: 'After obtaining the qualification she was turned down again, this time in favour of a white woman without qualification: a decision justified [by the managers] on the grounds of "positive action"' (p. 187). In another study (Collinson *et al.*, 1990) even the personnel/HR managers, who are supposedly the guardians and promoters of good practice, were colluding with line managers to avoid equal opportunity guidelines.

A third criticism is that even where managers are working within the procedures, there is a huge amount of informal practice and discretion that means unfair treatment can persist. In the following quote, Liff (2003: 434) gives examples from two studies that show how this might occur during selection interviewing:

Collinson *et al.* (1990), during detailed observation of interviews, found that managers used different (gender-based) criteria to assess whether applicants were able to meet the job requirements. For example, a form of behaviour described as 'showing initiative' and assessed as desirable when demonstrated by a male applicant, in a woman applicant was seen as 'pushy' and undesirable. Similarly Curran (1988: 344) showed that managers often found it hard to separate the assessment of a characteristic such as leadership from the concept of masculinity, or a 'requirement for a pleasant personality and one for a pretty girl with a smile'. What is important about these findings is that they show that for some managers at least, gender becomes part of their assessment of suitability criteria... Such findings also reduce the force of the prescriptive advice to excluded groups that they can succeed simply by gaining the necessary skills and demonstrating their ability at job-related tasks.

Explore

Criticisms of equality and diversity policy

- To what extent do the criticisms outlined above apply to the equality and diversity policy in your own organisation?

It will be noted that these three types of criticism are concerned with the ineffectiveness of equality and diversity policies; however, there are other critics who simply reject the whole idea of the needs for such policies. They tend to suggest that policies and positive action initiatives are providing special privileges for particular groups. It is a viewpoint that is common among those of an extreme, right-wing political persuasion and sometimes stems from a belief in the inferiority of some groups. Within organisations it can manifest itself in the form of verbal abuse and harassment, as the following cutting from the press illustrates (*Metro,* 28 February 2012, p. 27):

> One of Britain's biggest breweries has been branded racist after sacking a black worker who was nicknamed 'Sooty'.
>
> Greene King fired Joel Perry, whose boss also called him 'the black man' and asked him to stand by the lights so he could be seen.
>
> But when the 31-year-old made a formal complaint, he was suspended and later sacked for 'stealing drinks'.
>
> After disciplining his manager, Janet Wolszczak, Greene King dismissed the abuse as 'banter' and promptly handed her another pub to run.
>
> [. . .] The employment tribunal criticised Greene King's response to the 'casual racism' and deplored the 'lack of steps taken to ensure such conduct did not happen again'.

Devising equality and diversity policies

It has been noted above that equality and diversity policies are seen as desirable and that recommendations are often made to organisations about how to frame such policies. Ultimately, however, it is up to the decision-makers within organisations to choose the form and content of their policies – although there will be certain legal requirements within which they are expected to operate.

When formulating policy, managers are faced with addressing the key question of how to treat people at work in order to ensure fairness. Or, to express this more specifically: to ensure fairness, should managers ignore the differences between people and treat them the same, or should managers acknowledge differences and treat people differently? The way the question is answered will determine the types of policies and initiatives that can be implemented. To help explain this, Figure 6.1 categorises the perspectives and the sections below analyse each category.

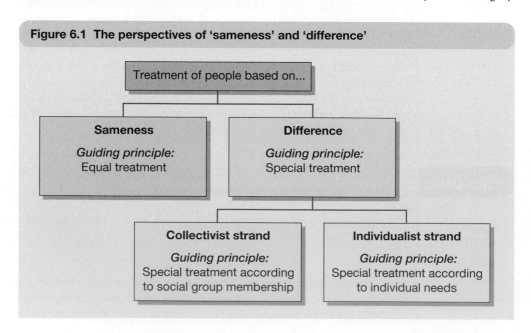

Figure 6.1 The perspectives of 'sameness' and 'difference'

The sameness perspective

A word of warning is needed here. This concept of 'sameness' acknowledges genuine differences between people, but suggests that attributes such as intelligence, potential to develop skills, values, emotions and so forth are distributed evenly across different social groups. Consequently, it is argued that any differences between people on these attributes are not determined by their gender, ethnicity, age, sexual orientation and so forth, but arise from their upbringing, experiences, socialisation and other contextual factors. Therefore, the important guiding principle for managers is that people should be treated equally regardless of their sex, ethnic group, age and so forth.

Below are a few examples of the kinds of practices that this perspective might lead organisations to adopt:

- Ensure that age is not used as a criterion to decide whether an employee is suitable for training.
- Ensure the same questions are asked of men and women during selection interviews.
- Ensure that gender-specific language does not appear in job adverts, job descriptions and other organisation documents.
- Ensure part-time working opportunities are available to men and women.
- Ensure any company benefits (e.g. pensions, insurance rights, health scheme subsidies) are available to partners of non-married couples and same-sex partners.
- Ensure the same pay for the same job.
- Ensure the rules regarding the display of religious symbols apply to all employees regardless of their religion or beliefs.

The guiding policy behind these types of initiative is *equal treatment*. Obviously, any such organisational initiatives are influenced by the legal context in which the organisation is based. There is likely to be legislation that requires organisations to undertake some actions. For instance, in the UK, the legislation sets some of the parameters in the recruitment process (see Chapter 4), in terms and conditions of employment (Chapter 10) and in reward systems (Chapter 13).

Explore

Equality and diversity initiatives

- Draw up a list of the initiatives designed to address equality and diversity in your organisation (if you work full-time or part-time) or an organisation with which you are familiar (if you are a full-time student). Your list does not need to be exhaustive, but try to include initiatives additional to the examples already given.
- Which of the initiatives have arisen because of legal requirements and which have been introduced out of choice (i.e. voluntarily)?
- Select one or two of those initiatives that have been introduced voluntarily and assess the influences that led to the initiatives being adopted. These could be internal or external pressures.

Limitation of the sameness approach

There is a substantial problem with this sameness approach. It assumes that disadvantage arises because people are not treated the same. While this is sometimes the case, disadvantage can also arise due to treating people the same when their differences ought to be considered. This is eloquently summed up by Liff and Wajcman (1996: 81) in relation to gender:

All policies based on same/equal treatment require women to deny, or attempt to minimize, differences between themselves and men as the price of equality. This, it is suggested, is neither feasible nor desirable. Such an approach can never adequately take account of problems arising from, say, women's domestic responsibilities or their educational disadvantage. Nor does it take account of those who want to spend time with their children without this costing them advancement at work. Sameness is being judged against a norm of male characteristics and behaviour . . . [The sameness approach to equal opportunities takes] an over-simplistic view both of the problem of inequality (seeing it as a managerial failure to treat like as like) and its solution ('equality' can be achieved by treating women the same as men).

Explore

'Treat them the same'

If you were to ask someone who has not studied HRM how they would ensure equality of opportunity at work, they would very likely reply: 'Treat everyone the same.' This tends to be the 'common sense' view. If you were then to say to the person you have asked, 'So does this mean that if someone in a wheelchair applied for an office job you would expect them to walk up a flight of stairs to the interview room if there was no lift', you are most likely to get the answer 'no'. This means they are willing to make exceptions – hence they are accepting the principle that to ensure fair treatment sometimes people have to be treated differently.

- Now try it out on a real person!

The difference perspective

The 'difference' perspective assumes that key differences exist between people and that these should be taken into account when managers are making decisions. Ignoring such differences can lead to people being disadvantaged.

Again there is a word of warning. There are two branches of this perspective: the collectivist branch and the individualist branch. This conceptual distinction must be made because each branch leads to different conclusions about the appropriate policy to put into place.

The collectivist branch

This approach argues that the differences between people are associated with the social groups to which a person belongs (based on gender, ethnicity, disability, etc.). For example, as the earlier quote from Liff and Wajcman (1996) underlines, women's domestic responsibilities are different in general from those of men – most notably in the time spent on childcare – so, to ignore this difference will disadvantage women. In practical terms, it means that two candidates (one male, the other female) might be of the same age and both have children, but the female candidate is likely to have less direct work experience because she has had to take time out to have children and might have chosen to take extended maternity leave. By ignoring the differences associated with childbirth and childcare, the woman might appear a weaker candidate; by recognising the differences, the woman's achievements within her more restricted periods of employment can be assessed.

The collectivist branch therefore argues that differences between social groups exist and should be considered in relation to ensuring fairness at work. This means that it might be relevant to introduce practices that are based on recognising differences between social groups, rather than ignoring differences. The following are some examples of the types of initiative that might arise from taking this collectivist difference perspective:

- Single-sex training schemes (developing skills to allow access to a wide range of jobs).
- Payment for jobs based on principles of equal value (see also Chapter 13).
- Job advertisements aimed at encouraging applications from under-represented groups.
- Reassessment of job requirements to open opportunities up to a wider range of people.
- Choice of food in the workplace cafeteria that reflects different cultural needs.

The guiding policy behind these types of positive action initiative is *special treatment according to social group membership*. There is a wide range of such initiatives, and the legal context must be taken into account because some principles, such as 'equal value', might be a legal requirement for all organisations, while others are left entirely to the discretion of managers.

The general policy of special treatment offers a persuasive approach because it recognises that disadvantage is often an intrinsic part of existing organisational structures, practices and culture – see the section above on institutional discrimination. Simply adopting a policy of same treatment would not remove this existing disadvantage; instead something has to be done to get to the root of the problem and redress the existing imbalance. A good example of this is the UK legislation covering disability discrimination which requires managers to undertake reasonable adjustments to accommodate the needs of employees (and prospective employees) with disabilities. This 'special treatment' is not designed to give an advantage to such employees, but rather to recognise that the existing conditions mean that they are disadvantaged, so changes must be made in order to redress this unfairness.

Explore

A reasonable request?

A disabled worker has been awarded £6,000 damages after the world's most famous stairlift maker refused to install one of its own devices at its headquarters.

The Stannah employee was told a stairlift could not be fitted because 'everyone would want to ride on it and no work would get done', an employment tribunal was told.

The IT designer, who suffers back problems and uses crutches, told the hearing he had problems walking to and from his second floor office.

His boss laughed when he asked if the company could put in a stairlift, he alleged.

The company, based in Andover Hampshire, promptly terminated the employee's contract saying it had concerns about his conduct and training.

Source: 'Stair case costs Stannah £6,000', *Metro*, 10 January 2007.

- Evaluate this incident from the point of view of:
  - the employer
  - the employee.

The individualist branch

The second branch of the difference perspective focuses on the individual rather than the social group. This approach emphasises the individuality of all employees, pointing out that people have unique strengths and weaknesses, abilities and needs. It suggests that it is not important to focus on characteristics that associate people with a particular group – for instance, their sex or whether they have a disability – but rather to concentrate on their individuality.

A label that is often associated with this approach is 'managing diversity'. It is increasingly being used by organisations as a term to describe their approach to ensure fairness and opportunities for all. However, a particular problem is that the term 'managing diversity' can have various meanings. It has become one of those widely used management phrases, so can mean different things in different organisations. At one extreme it is simply a synonym for 'equal opportunities' – used because the latter is seen as old-fashioned or backward-looking – and therefore has no distinct or special meaning of its own. At the other extreme, managing diversity represents a new approach to dealing with disadvantage at work.

A notable example of the new approach based on recognising individual differences is Kandola and Fullerton (1994). They argue that managing diversity is superior to previous approaches to equality at work for five reasons:

- It ensures all employees maximise their potential and their contribution to the organisation.
- It covers a broad range of people; no one is excluded.
- It focuses on issues of movement within an organisation, the culture of the organisation, and the meeting of business objectives.
- It becomes the concern of all employees and especially all managers.
- It does not rely on positive action/affirmative action.

Below are some examples of the types of initiatives that might arise from taking this individualist difference perspective:

- Offer employees a choice of benefits from a 'menu' so they can tailor a package to suit their individual needs.
- Devise training and development plans for each employee.
- Provide training to ensure managers are aware of and can combat their prejudices based on stereotypes.
- Explore and publicise ways that diversity within the organisation improves the organisation – e.g. public perceptions, sensitivity to customer needs, wider range of views and ideas.
- Re-evaluate the criteria for promotion and development and widen them by recognising a greater range of competences, experiences and career paths.

The guiding policy behind these types of initiative is *special treatment according to individual needs*. Of course, this approach has its critics, and in particular three objections can be raised:

1 The approach tends to understate the extent to which people share common experiences. It has a tendency to reject the idea of social groups, which is somewhat counter to people's everyday experiences. For example, while several disabled people might differ considerably across a whole range of attributes and attitudes, their common experience of disability (even different forms of disability) might be sufficient to create a feeling of cohesion and solidarity. In particular, some people might actively look for social group identity if they feel isolated or vulnerable.

2 The approach ignores material similarities between social groups. For example, Kirton and Greene (2005: 131) note that 'women of all ethnic groups typically take on the responsibility for childcare and elder care, and are less able to compete for jobs with men, notwithstanding qualitative ethnic differences in how women...may "juggle" their multiple roles.'

3 The approach has a tendency to emphasise the value of diversity in terms of the business sense arguments outlined earlier in the chapter. As was noted, such arguments have their limitations because they focus only on those initiatives that can be shown to contribute to the profitability or other performance indicators of the organisation. In practice, this extends opportunities only to a selective number of individuals whose competencies are in short supply or have been identified as being of particular value.

Sameness and difference

As has been shown in the preceding discussion, disadvantage can arise by treating people the same or by treating people differently, so any policy that emphasises one perspective more than the other runs the risk of leaving some disadvantages unchecked. What is called for is a mixed policy because this recognises that to eliminate disadvantage it is necessary in some circumstances to treat people the same, and in other circumstances to treat people differently. Of course, this is a challenge in itself, because in what circumstances do you apply one criterion and not the other? For example, imagine the following situation.

A woman applies for a job as an adviser selling financial products in a company that is dominated by men.

- *Scenario 1.* She has the same qualifications and experience as male applicants, but the all-male selection panel might reject her because they consider that she would not 'fit in' with the competitive, aggressive culture of the organisation.

- *Scenario 2.* She has the same qualifications as male applicants but has taken a career break for childcare purposes. The selection panel reject her because compared with men of the same age she has less work experience.

The panel reject her in the first scenario by using the criterion of difference (recognising gender); in the second by using the criterion of sameness (ignoring gender). But if the panel were to reverse their logic of difference and sameness, it might lead them to different conclusions. In the first scenario, if the panel ignored gender, they would arrive at the conclusion that she was appointable. In the second scenario, if they recognised that, because of her gender, she has had extra domestic commitments so cannot be compared with men of the same age then again they might conclude she is appointable. This illustrates that managers have a key role in dealing with disadvantage, because they determine the criteria and define the circumstances in which sameness and difference are either recognised or ignored.

Long and short agendas

Some commentators argue that fundamental change is needed if the elimination of disadvantage is to be achieved. Foremost among these commentators is Cockburn (1989, 1991), who points out that many of the positive action policies and initiatives adopted by managers in organisations are concerned only with the short term. Typically they are concerned with fixing current problems, responding to outside pressures, or perhaps attempting to impress customers and clients. The proposition advanced by Cockburn is that, as well as this short agenda (with its laudable aim of eliminating bias), there is the need to consider the long agenda. This would be a challenging project of organisational transformation, requiring fundamental changes to the processes, roles, norms, attitudes and relationships within organisations. Cockburn (1989: 218) explains:

> As such it brings into view the nature and purpose of institutions and the processes by which the power of some groups over others in institutions is built and renewed. It acknowledges the needs of disadvantaged groups for access to power. [...] But it also looks for change in the nature of power, in the control ordinary people of diverse kinds have over institutions, a melting away of the white male monoculture.

The obvious problem for enacting the long agenda is that those in positions of influence within organisations have little incentive to make changes that might challenge their own power and dominance. The long agenda therefore has to be led by activists and advocates. This might be through committed individuals within organisations, but it would also require collective voice and action. It might need a political context that encourages a more active approach by organisations to ensuring equality of opportunity – through, for example, compulsory monitoring or employment quotas for disadvantaged groups.

Key Controversy

Whilst it is recognised that the long agenda is necessary and would be beneficial for society, organisational responses tend to focus on the short agenda only.

The process of discrimination in an organisation

The discussion so far in this section has explored the complexity of taking into account concerns about 'sameness' and 'difference'. It is also important to consider other pressures and influences that are likely to have an impact. Figure 6.2 is a flowchart that maps the relationship between the key components and thereby shows how the process of discrimination occurs in organisations (Noon and Blyton, 2007). Each of the components of this flowchart is discussed in this section, and is linked with many of the issues raised in the earlier part of the chapter.

At the centre of the process lie two vital questions: what should be the basis of any specific policy, and is the policy fair? Try to envisage this in terms of specific policies, such as promotion, awarding of merit pay, entitlement to career development opportunities and so on. The first question is of vital concern to managers, as their decisions are going to shape a particular policy. However, as the diagram shows, such decisions are not made in isolation but are subject to a range of influences: personal influences (belief, values and political agenda), external pressures and organisational pressures:

- *Personal influences.* A manager will have their individual beliefs and values that fundamentally guide behaviour and influence decisions. So, for instance, a strong belief in social justice is going to affect the choices that a manager makes, as is a particular prejudice or stereotype about a social group. Combined with this is the individual political agenda of the manager, which might moderate the values and beliefs in some way. For example, a male manager might believe that women do not make good leaders but knows that in order to get promotion he must suppress this view in order not to alienate his boss – who is a

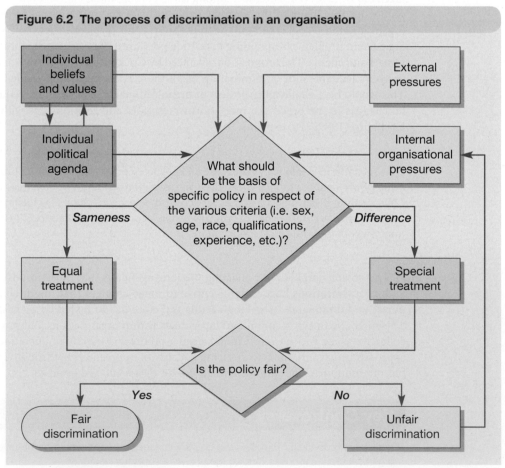

Figure 6.2 The process of discrimination in an organisation

Source: adapted from Noon and Blyton (2007).

woman. This reflects the micro-politics of organisational life and will operate at all levels. The intermixing of beliefs, values and political manoeuvring is going to have an influence on the manager's decisions.

- *External pressures.* In addition to these personal pressures, the manager is faced with external pressure. This could be legislation requiring (or prohibiting) certain action, public opinion, customer or client pressure, supplier influence, labour supply issues and so forth. For instance, it was noted in the discussion about the business case that managers might adopt equal and diversity initiatives in order to improve the public image of their organisations, or to access a wider customer base.

- *Internal organisational pressures.* The final set of pressures arise from within the organisation. These pressures might come from other managers, employees (especially through engagement surveys and grievances), trade unions, works councils and so forth. There might also be pressure as a result of data collected within the organisation. For example, high levels of employee turnover might encourage positive action initiatives that help to retain employees, develop and make better use of skills, and provide a more supportive and encouraging environment. In addition, there are likely to be pressures because of the workplace culture and traditions of the organisation – the sorts of issues that were discussed in the section on institutional discrimination.

These combined pressures establish the context in which decisions are made about specific policies within the organisation. As was noted earlier in the chapter, managers must make choices between people and therefore criteria have to be used to differentiate people. For example, imagine you are running a recruitment process and have received a pile of application forms. In deciding your shortlisting policy (i.e. who to call for an interview) you might use the criterion of 'previous experience' as a way of choosing between applicants. Those who meet the minimum requirements are interviewed; those who do not are rejected. At the same time, you might think that formal qualifications are irrelevant for the particular job and so you do not take these into account when shortlisting the applicants. Hence your shortlisting policy is based on 'difference' with regard to experience, and 'sameness' with regard to formal qualifications. There is nothing wrong with this mixture – it reflects the possibility of combining principles of sameness and difference. The consequence of this combination is that someone with a university degree will be treated the same as someone without a degree (equal treatment), but if they have previous work experience they will get treated more favourably (in this instance, shortlisted) compared with someone without appropriate previous experience.

Logically, this raises the question of whether this is fair (note the next stage in the flow-chart). If you think such a shortlisting policy is fair then you are likely to be in agreement with the decisions about the criteria for equal and special treatment. However, if you think this is unfair, this might be because you feel either or both of the following:

- equal treatment was applied inappropriately (e.g. formal qualifications should have been taken into account);
- special treatment was given inappropriately (e.g. previous experience should not have been taken into account).

If you were an employee in the organisation then this feeling of unfairness might simply produce a feeling of discontent. On the other hand, it might drive you to take action, such as voicing your opinion to managers, going to the trade union, discussing the issue with other employees or even looking for a job elsewhere. Such actions might then produce internal organisational pressures on future decisions (shown by the feedback loop in Figure 6.2).

Mapping out the process in this way reveals that every managerial decision about appointments, promotions, allocation of work, bonuses, training opportunities and so forth is likely to be met with a variety of responses: some individuals and groups will interpret the decision as fair and others as unfair, depending on whether they consider the equal or special treatment to be justifiable. The extent to which employees concern themselves with issues of fairness will vary according to the circumstances and is likely to reflect whether they are directly involved with, or affected by, the outcome.

Reflecting on fairness

- Have you directly experienced or observed treatment you considered unfair?
- If so, what did you do about it?
- What other options did you have?

Concluding comments

The chapter is focused on equality and diversity, but recently a new concept has surfaced: inclusion. Strictly speaking, the idea of inclusion has always been present in the equality and diversity debate, but some commentators are now making a clear distinction between diversity and inclusion. For instance, the UK's Chartered Institute of Personnel and Development (CIPD) has a specialist adviser on diversity who is quoted as follows in an article by Evans (2006: 26):

> We talk much more about inclusion now, which is a dynamic… It is not about visible or non-visible traits of characteristics such as race or gender, sexuality or disability, which can all be stereotyped. It is about celebrating difference as an asset, since everyone is unique, and recognising that everyone can make a contribution."

In an attempt to bring some clarity, Roberson (2006) assesses the views of a range of practitioners about what they mean by diversity and inclusion. She finds that their definitions of 'diversity' tend to focus on differences and the demographic composition of groups or the organisation, while their definitions of 'inclusion' focus on organisational objectives to increase participation of all employees and to leverage diversity effects in the organisation. While Roberson's findings generally suggest conceptual distinctiveness, she also adds a caveat noting how, in operational terms, there is likely to be overlap between diversity and inclusion, and that for some organisations a change of emphasis from diversity to inclusion might simply be a change in language and might not make any difference to policies and initiatives.

Generally, it seems that academic commentators, consultants and practitioners are beginning to suggest that while diversity is concerned with recognising the value of differences within the workforce and managing them for commercial advantage, inclusion is concerned with the processes that incorporate differences into business practices and thereby help to realise the value. It could mean that we are at the start of a new trend towards managing inclusion (see Oswick and Noon, 2014), adding even more complexity to the topic area, and creating an even wider range of issues for managers to consider when developing policies and initiatives to address discrimination and disadvantage in organisations. But since we are only at the start of this possible change, it has to be a matter left for the next edition of this book.

Summary

- Discrimination can occur at any decision point within an organisation. Employees are legally protected in terms of certain characteristics. The type and extent of protection necessarily vary from country to country, although within the EU there is a common platform of protection. A key feature is the protection against direct and indirect discrimination.

- It is vital to recognise the diversity between social groups and also within social groups. It is also important to acknowledge that some people are discriminated against due to more than one characteristic – an effect that is described by academic commentators as multiple discrimination or intersectionality, depending on the assumed impact on the individual. This diversity means policies need to be sensitive to different experiences of discrimination and different needs of disadvantaged groups and individuals.

- The reason for managers to intervene in order to prevent discrimination can be based on arguments of social justice or business needs – or both. The social justice case stresses the moral argument with reference to equality of opportunity, equality of outcome, fairness and human rights. Critics argue that managers should be concerned with profit and efficiency, not morality. The business case stresses various ways that equality and diversity are good for business needs (effective use of human resources, innovation, attracting customers, wider recruitment and company image), but critics point to limitations of the business case, including instances where it can make good business sense *not* to act in the interests of equality and diversity.

- Deep-rooted problems are often caused by institutional discrimination. This term is used to describe organisations that have processes and practices that are fundamentally discriminatory – sometimes without managers realising it – and are reinforced through existing organisational structures and workplace cultures. Tackling such fundamental problems might require a more radical agenda than that being proposed by many advocates of equality and diversity.

- Equality and diversity policies vary between organisations; they range from those that are simply empty statements to others that are backed up by effective action programmes. For policies to be effective, they need to have positive action initiatives to ensure policy is implemented, and monitoring to assess the effectiveness of the initiatives over time. It is important to recognise that positive action and positive discrimination are not the same – although they are often confused – and offer very different solutions to the problems of discrimination and disadvantage.

- Managers devise equality and diversity policies based on assumptions of sameness or assumptions of difference. These two perspectives help to explain why there is often a lack of agreement about how to ensure fairness. The sameness perspective emphasises similarities between people and advocates equal treatment. The difference perspective emphasises diversity either between social groups or between individuals. These two branches of the difference perspective are similar in that they both advocate special treatment that takes the differences between people into account, but they differ in their suggestions about the types of initiatives that organisations should adopt.

- The term 'managing diversity' is often used to describe the approach to fairness that emphasises the individual differences between people. In some instances, it is an alternative approach advocated by commentators who think traditional equal opportunities policies have failed and are fundamentally flawed.

- It is important for managers to recognise that unfair treatment sometimes results from treating people differently when they ought to be treated the same, and sometimes from treating people the same when key differences ought to be recognised. Policies, procedures and attitudes within an organisation should therefore be based on recognising both the similarities and differences between people.

- The process of discrimination can be seen as the combination of personal, external and internal pressures on managers to make choices according to principles of sameness or difference, in their decisions about appointments, promotions, allocation of work, training opportunities and so forth. Perceptions of unfairness are the result of a mismatch between the expectations of employees and the manager's decisions. Viewed in this way, all decisions are susceptible to claims of unfairness, depending on the perspective of the individuals concerned, the perceived appropriateness of the criterion for the decision and the individual and social acceptability of the type of treatment (special or equal).

- A recent development within the field has been the emergence of the concept of managing inclusion, which seems to be an acknowledgement of the need for managers not only to recognise the value of diversity but also to develop policies, processes and initiatives that harness the differences to better and more productive effect.

Questions

1 'We don't employ people over 50 years old because they find it difficult to learn new skills.' This statement was made by a training manager in a call centre.

   Comment on the statement using the concepts of stereotyping, prejudice, social justice and the business case.

2 What is the purpose of equality and diversity policies? Why do they sometimes fail to live up to expectations?

3 Without looking back through the chapter, give at least one example of a workplace initiative from each of the following approaches:
   (a) the sameness perspective;
   (b) the collectivist strand of the difference perspective;
   (c) the individualist strand of the difference perspective.

4 'I treat everyone the same – so that's how I ensure fairness.' This quote is from a section manager in a supermarket. Explain why such an approach can sometimes lead to unfairness.

5 'Everyone is unique. Everyone is an individual. As a manager you should treat them as such.' If you were being critical of this opinion, what points would you make?

6 If an organisation is accused of being institutionally racist, sexist and homophobic, what does it mean? How would you evaluate whether such a description was legitimate?

Case study

Employees of conscience?

Read through the scenarios below which all concern discrimination on the basis of religion.

Scenario 1 – the airline check-in desk worker

An airline has a strict uniform policy that prohibits the display of any jewellery. Ms E is a devout Christian and started to wear a small plain silver cross on a necklace that could be seen above her uniform. She worked on the check-in desks and managers asked her to remove it, because it was in breach of the uniform policy. She refused because she felt that she had the right to express her faith while at work. The company offered her the opportunity to move to another non-customer-facing role where the uniform policy did not apply, but she was not prepared to accept this. She was sent home on unpaid leave.

Scenario 2 – the nurse

A hospital introduced a uniform policy that prevented nurses from wearing necklaces because of health and safety concerns. Mrs C was an experienced nurse who had been wearing a cross necklace on wards for 30 years without incident. She refused to remove the cross but offered to have a magnetic clasp fitted (so the necklace would come apart easily if it was grabbed by a patient). The hospital insisted that she removed the necklace, but she refused to do so and was moved to a desk job.

Scenario 3 – the relationship guidance counsellor

Mr M was a counsellor employed by a charity providing relationship guidance. He made it clear during a training session that he would have difficulty counselling same-sex couples because this conflicted with his strongly held Christian principles. He argued that managers should make allowances to take into account his beliefs. He was suspended pending an investigation and then dismissed.

Case study continued

Scenario 4 – the registrar

Ms L was a registrar, licensed by the local authority to conduct civil marriage services. She took up employment many years prior to the introduction of same-sex civil partnerships, but as soon as these became legal she made it clear that she was not prepared to conduct them as a matter of conscience, because it was against her Christian beliefs. At first she was able to swap duties with other registrars, but then a change in working conditions introduced by the local authority meant this was no longer possible. She argued she was being forced to choose between her religious beliefs and her job. She claimed she was shunned and accused of being homophobic by managers and work colleagues. She was eventually dismissed.

Questions

1 Compare scenario 1 and scenario 2.
   (a) Evaluate the key issues in each and decide whether the employees have suffered discrimination.
   (b) What issues must managers bear in mind when deciding how to proceed?

2 Compare scenario 3 and scenario 4.
   (a) Who is being discriminated against, and why?
   (b) Who has the stronger case, Mr M or Ms L? Explain your reasoning.

3 Based on all four scenarios, did you think employees should be allowed to exercise their conscience in this way in the workplace? Explain your reasoning.

References and further reading

Acker, J. (2006) 'Inequality regimes: gender, class and race in organisations', *Gender, Work and Society*, 20, 4: 441–64.

Alexander, H. (2012) 'Norway's businesswomen and the boardroom bias debate' *The Telegraph*, 18 March. Online: **http://www.telegraph.co.uk/news/worldnews/europe/norway/9150165/Norways-businesswomen-and-the-boardroom-bias-debate.html** (accessed November 2012).

Berthoud, R. (2003) *Multiple Disadvantage in Employment: A Quantitative Analysis*. York: Joseph Rowntree Foundation.

Bradley, H. and Healy, G. (2008) *Ethnicity and Gender at Work*. London: Palgrave.

Centre for Women and Democracy (2013) *Sex and Power 2013*. Leeds: Centre for Women and Democracy.

Cockburn, C. (1989) 'Equal opportunities: the short and long agenda', *Industrial Relations Journal*, 20, 3: 213–25.

Cockburn, C. (1991) *In the Way of Women*. Basingstoke: Macmillan.

Collinson, D.L., Knights, D. and Collinson, M. (1990) *Managing to Discriminate*. London: Routledge.

Cunningham, I. and James, P. (2001) 'Managing diversity and disability legislation', in M. Noon and E. Ogbonna (eds) *Equality, Diversity and Disadvantage in Employment*. Basingstoke: Palgrave, pp. 103–17.

Curran, M. (1988) 'Gender and recruitment: people and places in the labour market', *Work, Employment and Society*, 2, 3: 335–51.

Deloitte (2011) *Women in the Boardroom. A Global Perspective*. Deloitte Global Services Ltd.

Dickens, L. (1994) 'The business case for equal opportunities: is the carrot better than the stick?' *Employee Relations*, 16, 8: 5–18.

Dickens, L. (1999) 'Beyond the business case: a three-pronged approach to equality action', *Human Resource Management Journal*, 9, 1: 9–19.

Dickens, L. (2000) 'Still wasting resources? equality in employment', in S. Bach and K. Sissons (eds) *Personnel Management*, 3rd edn. Oxford: Blackwell, pp. 137–69.

Equality and Human Rights Commission (2011) *Sex and Power 2011*. London: Equality and Human Rights Commission.

Evans, R. (2006) 'Variety performance', *People Management*, 23 November: 26.

Groysberg, B. and Bell, D. (2012) *2012 Board of Directors Survey*. Heidrick & Struggles International and Women Corporate Directors (WCD).

Healy, G. (1993) 'Business and discrimination' in Stacey, R. (ed.) *Strategic Thinking and the Management of Change*. London: Kogan Page, pp. 169–89.

Heery, E. and Noon, M. (2008) *A Dictionary of Human Resource Management*. Oxford: Oxford University Press.

Hilpern, K. (2007) 'A question of positive motives', *Employers' Law*, October: 12–13.

HMSO (2010) *Equality Act 2010 – Explanatory Notes*. London: HMSO.

Hoque, K. and Noon, M. (2004) 'Equal opportunities policy and practice in Britain: evaluating the "empty shell" hypothesis', *Work, Employment and Society*, 18, 3: 481–506.

ILM (2011) *Ambition and Gender at Work*. London: ILM.

Kandola, R. and Fullerton, J. (1994) *Managing the Mosaic*. London: IPD.

Kirton, G. and Greene, A-M. (2005) *The Dynamics of Managing Diversity*, 2nd edn. Oxford: Butterworth-Heinemann.

Liff, S. (2003) 'The industrial relations of a diverse workforce', in P. Edwards (ed.) *Industrial Relations*, 2nd edn. Oxford: Blackwell, pp. 420–46.

Liff, S. and Dale, K. (1994) 'Formal opportunity, informal barriers: Black women managers within a local authority', *Work, Employment and Society*, 8, 2: 177–98.

Liff, S. and Wajcman, J. (1996) '"Sameness" and "difference" revisited: which way forward for equal opportunity initiatives?', *Journal of Management Studies*, 33, 1: 79–94.

Modood, T., Berthoud, R., Lakey, J., Nazroo, J., Smith, P., Virdee, S. and Beishon, S. (1997) *Ethnic Minorities in*

Britain: Diversity and Disadvantage. London: Policy Studies Institute.

Nazroo, J.Y. and Karlsen, S. (2003) 'Patterns of identity among ethnic minority people: Diversity and commonality', *Ethnic and Racial Studies:* 26, 5: 902–30.

Noon, M. (2007) 'The fatal flaws of diversity and the business case for ethnic minorities', *Work, Employment and Society,* 21, 4: 373–84.

Noon, M. (2010) 'The shackled runner: time to rethink positive discrimination?' *Work, Employment and Society,* 24, 4: 728–39.

Noon, M. (2012) 'Simply the best? the case for using threshold selection in hiring decisions', *Human Resource Management Journal,* 22, 1: 76–88.

Noon, M. and Blyton, P. (2007) *The Realities of Work,* 3rd edn. Basingstoke: Palgrave.

Noon, M. and Hoque, K. (2001) 'Ethnic minorities and equal treatment: the impact of gender, equal opportunities policies and trade unions', *National Institute Economic Review,* 176: 105–16.

Oswick, C. and Noon, M. (2014) 'Discourses of diversity, equality and inclusion: Trenchant formulations or transient fashions?', *British Journal of Management,* 25, 1: 23–39.

Pilkington, A. (2001) 'Beyond racial dualism: Racial disadvantage and ethnic diversity in the labour market' in M. Noon and E. Ogbonna (eds) *Equality, Diversity and Disadvantage in Employment.* Basingstoke: Palgrave, pp. 172–89.

Reyna, C., Tucker, A., Korfmacher, W. and Henry, P.J. (2005) 'Searching for common ground between supporters and opponents of Affirmative Action', *Political Psychology,* 26, 5: 667–82.

Reynolds, G., Nicholls, P. and Alferoff, C. (2001) 'Disabled people, (re)training and employment: A qualitative exploration of exclusion' in M. Noon and E. Ogbonna (eds) *Equality, Diversity and Disadvantage in Employment.* Basingstoke: Palgrave, pp. 190–207.

Roberson, Q. M. (2006) 'Disentangling the meanings of diversity and inclusion in organizations', *Group & Organization Management,* 31, 2: 213–36.

Webb, J. (1997) 'The politics of equal opportunity', *Gender, Work and Organisation,* 4, 3: 159–69.

Part 3

DEVELOPING THE HUMAN RESOURCE

Introduction to Part 3

Changes in the context of the organisation increase the need to train and develop its members to ensure effectiveness, quality and responsiveness. Because these changes are not being made once and for all, the need for attention to human resource development (HRD) is more important than ever before.

Part 3 examines the various forms that HRD takes: the development of the employee both as an individual and as an employee; the development of the employee by the employer or by him or herself; training; education; career development; group development; staff development; professional development; management development; and, even more widely, organisation development.

Chapter 7 identifies the strategic importance of HRD in organisations, and considers the significance of learning and development for the individual. It examines the processes and activities intentionally undertaken within organisations to enable employees to acquire, improve or update their skills, including e-learning. The chapter then explores the influence of the national context on the quality and impact of learning and development in organisations.

Chapter 8 discusses the development of leaders and managers and explores the significance of leadership and management development to organisational success. It examines the methods, techniques and processes used to develop leaders and managers and how these may be varied to suit different needs and contexts. The chapter also speculates on the likely direction of leadership and management development in the future.

The inclusion of Chapter 9 in this edition of the textbook reflects the renewed interest in organisational development (OD) and its contribution to sustainable organisational performance. The chapter traces the historical development of OD and examines contemporary views on the concept. It then investigates the key techniques and practices associated with OD and the skills required by OD practitioners. It concludes with an examination of the relationship between OD and organisational strategy, structure and culture.

Chapter 7

Learning and development

Audrey Collin and Mairi Watson

Objectives

- To define learning and development.
- To identify the strategic importance of learning and development in the light of the significant changes taking place in organisations.
- To examine the significance of learning and development for individuals.
- To examine theories of learning and development and their impact on practices.
- To identify the key components of the planned process of learning and development in organisations.
- To explore the benefits and challenges of e-learning.
- To consider the influence of the national context on the quality and impact of learning and development in organisations.

Introductory case study

Talent management – the politics of skill

All organisations need skilled employees. HR professionals devote much of their time and energy to providing skilled resources: recruiting, developing, paying for and retaining them. It would be easy, therefore, to assume that everyone sees skill as a good thing, something to be developed and exploited as much as possible. But real people aren't like that. Skill has a value and so some people will seek to restrict it, or restrict access to it. In order to prevent injustice, most organisations create systems designed to ensure fairness, such as competency and performance management models. But these may create false objectivity and mask 'political behaviours' (think office politics) –

behaviours that can lead to unspoken practices that subvert organisational values and undermine performance and pleasure in the workplace. Some examples of these behaviours include: skills monopolies; managers who ensure their favourites get promoted; employees who do nothing to help others up the career ladder; and inadequate job handovers. While no means an exhaustive list, these examples may help HR professionals to spot the signs of skill restriction and take action to reduce the resulting harm.

Source: extracted from Barton, R. 'Talent management: The politics of skill', *People Management* 24 April 2012.

Introduction

According to Honey (1998: 28–29), learning would be 'the central issue for the twenty-first century':

> Changes are bigger and are happening faster, and learning is the way to keep ahead…to maintain employability in an era when jobs for life have gone. It enables organisations to sustain their edge as global competition increases. Learning to learn . . . [is] the ultimate life skill.

That was true at the start of the century and is even more so today as transformations in work, organisations, the economy and society identified throughout the textbook are continuing. This chapter addresses this 'central issue'. It starts by explaining that learning and development are of crucial importance to individuals and that their outcomes are of strategic importance to organisations (and beyond them to the wider economy). It then examines the processes of individual learning and development, which human resource (HR) managers need to understand, and the ways in which human resource development (HRD) mobilises that understanding in order to meet both organisational goals and the learning needs of employees. The chapter closes by explaining the national significance of learning and development, and noting the policies and frameworks that aim to achieve them.

The strategic importance of learning and development for organisations

The labels given to today's world – the global economy, the network society (Castells, 1996), the knowledge society (Drucker, 1969;UNESCO, 2005) – give a clue to the challenges that many individuals are now facing. New technologies and ways of working are not only creating new tasks but demanding new ways of thinking about work, doing work and relating with one another (Bayliss, 1998). People need conceptual, 'helicopter' and analytical thinking (Wisher, 1994: 37). Whether employed or not, they need to be able to challenge traditional ways of thinking and working; to think and work 'outside the box' of traditional job descriptions; to work without prior experience, clear guidelines or close supervision; to be flexible and prepared to change, to undertake new tasks, move to another organisation; or to recognise the opportunities for self-employment. This all means that people have to learn and develop continuously and effectively in order to adapt to their changing world, construct a meaningful and fulfilling role in it, and acquire the knowledge, skills, competencies, capabilities and employability that will give them satisfaction and the ability to make their way.

Organisations also need those outcomes from their employees' learning and development, for they, too, are being challenged by this changing world. To adapt and survive and be competitive, they have had to become more flexible, innovative, quality-conscious, customer-orientated, constantly improving their performance to remain competitive. They have to 'think global and act local' and need people who have a 'matrix of the mind', who will share learning and create new knowledge (Ulrich and Stewart Black, 1999). They need what Castells (1998: 341) calls the 'self-programmable' labour in the global economy, which has 'the capability constantly to redefine the necessary skills for a given task, and to access the sources for learning these skills'. It is his view that work that does not require such abilities will be undertaken by 'generic' labour, which, lacking self-programmable skills, would be '"human terminals" [which could] be replaced by machines, or by any other body around the city, the country, or the world, depending on business decisions. While they are collectively indispensable to the production process, they are individually expendable' (Castells, 1998: 341).

Employers have to promote the kind of learning that, through critical thinking and reflection, can recognise, appraise, transmit and apply contextually embedded learning. Human capital approaches and the learning organisation (see Chapter 8), and the establishment of the Investors in People award indicate that many employers are now aware of this need. So also is the increasing adoption of knowledge management, which has come about with the recognition that the wealth of information produced by advances in information and communications technologies becomes meaningful and of competitive advantage to the organisation only when people share, interpret and elaborate it. Knowledge management embraces the creation, validation, presentation, distribution and application of knowledge (see Nonaka, 1991; Malhotra, 1998; Hwang, 2003). It recognises that not all knowledge is explicit: 'the knowledge needed to develop a new product is largely in people's heads . . . [it] cannot be written down, because an individual may not even know it is there until the situation demands a creative response' (Dixon, 2000: 37). It has also been suggested (Snowden, 2002) that knowledge is not an 'abstract, objective truth' but a cultural construction within 'communities of practice', and hence 'essentially pragmatic, partial, tentative and always open to revision' (Blackler, 2000: 61). Hence to address the complexities of knowledge, high levels of technical, cognitive and 'soft' interpersonal skills are called for and this places a great premium on the individual's learning and development. Organisations need to understand those processes in order to invest in their human capital and facilitate, mobilise and support the learning and development of their employees because '[p]eople are our only source of differentiation and sustainable competitive advantage. Essential to that is learning' (Beattie, 2002). As Guest *et al.* (1997: 3) wrote:

> Creating, disseminating and embodying knowledge – tacit and explicit – becomes a key strategic resource to be leveraged. It holds the key to unlocking the organisation's ability to learn faster than its environment is changing. In summary, learning and development lie at the heart of innovation in organisations.

Learning and development are thus now of strategic importance for organisations. Those responsible for HRD in organisations, according to their professional body, the Chartered Institute of Personnel and Development (CIPD, 2002), have an increasingly strategic role and need to become 'thinking performers' (CIPD, 2007) who apply 'a critically thoughtful approach to their job' (Whittaker and Johns, 2004: 32).

Learning and development are also crucial for the wider economy. Skills are 'the most important lever within our control to create wealth and to reduce social deprivation' (Leitch, 2006; see also **www.ukces.org/uk**). The government also recognises their strategic significance nationally and has established the UK Commission for Employment and Skills (**www.ukces.org.uk**; see also **www.delni.gov.uk**). It is also now widely recognised that we need to become a learning society, in which there is a culture of, and opportunities for, lifelong learning in order to provide the skills required for competitiveness in a global economy.

Explore

Before proceeding further, on your own or in a small group identify some of the changes taking place in organisations you know in response to changes in their context.

● What are the implications for HRD and for the learning and development of individuals?

Individual learning and development

From birth, humans, like all animals, engage actively in the processes of learning and development: they do not have learning and development done to them. Senge (1990: 4) said: 'Deep down, we are all learners. No one has to teach an infant to learn. . . . They are intrinsically inquisitive, masterful learners . . . not only is it our nature to learn but we love to learn.'

They continue learning throughout life, whether encouraged or not, whether formally taught or not, whether the outcomes are valued by society or not. This personal learning knows no boundaries: learning in one domain – job, hobbies or maintenance of home and car – cross-fertilises that in another and thereby achieves a wider understanding and more finely honed skills. According to Daloz (1986: 1), 'Most of us have learnt a good deal more out of school than in it . . . from our families, our work, our friends . . . from problems resolved and tasks achieved but also from mistakes confronted and illusions unmasked.'

Society facilitates and fosters, channels and controls the learning and development of its members through socialisation and education so that they yield outcomes that contribute to and are acceptable to it. However, although individuals gain a lifetime's experience of being learners, some of their experiences (especially those in formal educational settings) might not have been happy ones (Honey, 1999). They might be experienced learners, but not necessarily competent or confident learners, and might not learn what society and its institutions want them to learn.

Defining learning and development

The words 'learning' and 'development' are sometimes used loosely and even interchangeably, but to understand them they need to be distinguished and clearly defined.

Learning is 'a process within the organism which results in the capacity for changed performance which can be related to experience rather than maturation' (Ribeaux and Poppleton, 1978: 38). It is not just a cognitive process that involves the assimilation of information in symbolic form (as in book learning), but it is also an affective and physical process (Binsted, 1980). Emotions, nerves and muscles are involved, too. Moreover, intelligence is not a unitary concept [see Gardner (1985, 1999) on multiple intelligences; Mayo and Nohria (2005) on 'contextual intelligence'], or just a cognitive capacity [see Pickard (1999) on emotional intelligence].

Learning leads to skilful and effective adaptation to and manipulation of the environment, which is one element in a much-quoted definition of intelligence (Wechsler, 1958). Through learning, a person 'qualitatively [changes] the way he or she conceived something' (Burgoyne and Hodgson, 1983: 393) or experiences 'personal transformation' (Mezirow, 1977). Learning leads to change, whether positive or negative for the learner. It can be more or less effectively undertaken, and it could be more effective when it is paid conscious attention.

Development, whether of an organism, individual or organisation, is the process of becoming increasingly complex, more elaborate and differentiated as a result of learning and maturation. It is a process of both continuity and discontinuity. (It is sometimes interpreted as progression and advancement; it is irreversible, although regression to earlier phases can occur.) Quantitative changes lead to qualitative changes or transformations. The disintegration of the existing phase creates the conditions for a new one that is 'not entirely new – it is a transformation. Each succeeding phase is more complex, integrating what has gone before' (Pedler, 1988: 7–8). This opens up the potential for new ways of acting and responding to the environment, which in turn leads to the need and opportunity for even further learning, and so on.

Overall, then, development is not synonymous with learning, but it cannot take place without learning. Lifelong learning and development mean continuous adaptation. Increased knowledge and improved skills enlarge the individual's capacities to adapt to the environment and to change that environment, so allowing new possibilities to emerge. As the systems model shows (see Chapter 3), external changes will lead individuals on to further internal changes: in their ability to respond to and make their way in their particular environment (their perceptual-motor, intellectual, social and interpersonal skills); in the way they think, feel and interpret their world (their cognition, affect, attitudes, overall philosophy of life); in their social status and the way they see themselves, their self-concept, confidence, and self-esteem. Hence learning sets in train potentially far-reaching changes in the individual. Daloz (1986: 24–26) draws on elements of folk tales to convey the significant effect of this in adult learning:

> The journey tale begins with an old world, generally simple and uncomplicated, more often than not, home. . . . The middle portion, beginning with departure from home, is characterised by confusion, adventure, great highs and lows, struggle, uncertainty. The ways of the old world no longer hold, and the hero's task is to find a way through this strange middle land, generally in search of something lying at its heart. At the deepest point, the nadir of the descent, a transformation occurs, and the traveller moves out of the darkness towards a new world that often bears an ironic resemblance to the old.
>
> Nothing is different, yet all is transformed. It is seen differently. . . . Our old life is still there, but its meaning has profoundly changed because we have left home, seen it from afar, and been transformed by that vision. You can't go home again.
>
> *Source*: reprinted with permission of John Wiley & Sons, Inc.

Key Controversy

As learning and development have the potential to promote a profound effect on a person's life, what responsibility does the HRD manager have to employees, and how could it be discharged?

Explore

- Has your learning caused you to develop?
- What has the experience of that been for you?
- Will you be able to 'go home again'?

Many types of learner in the workplace

Learners in the workplace are adults and so, to understand how they learn, a model of adult learning (androgogical) rather than of children's learning (pedagogical) has to be used. According to Knowles and Associates (1984), this takes into account the fact that adult learners are self-directing, and motivated by their need to be recognised, to prove something to themselves and others, to better themselves and to achieve their potential. Their learning does not take place in a vacuum. Not only are they ready to learn when they recognise their need to know or do something, but they have experience on which to draw and to hang their new learning and assess its utility.

However, the earlier learning experiences of many adults might have been far from effective or comfortable, and contribute to significant barriers to effective learning. Some of these can be internal: poor learning skills or habitual learning styles that constrain them; poor communications skills; unwillingness to take risks; lack of confidence, low expectations and aspirations; and anxiety, fear or insecurity. Other barriers can be thrown up by their situation: lack of learning opportunities or support, inappropriate time or place (see Mumford, 1988), or negative stereotyping from society. These will often be the experience of disabled people whose numbers in employment are likely to increase because of government policies.

It has also to be recognised that, as well as personal circumstances, traits and inclinations, the particular context, culture, socialisation and education influence what and how people learn. Earlier in the book (Chapter 3) several areas were identified on which there could be significant differences between dominant and alternative assumptions about reality, perhaps embodied in the construction of knowledge and of language, which might affect the experience of, and outcomes from, learning. This could be the case for women and members of cultural and ethnic minorities. Their learning experiences might have generated different knowledge and attitudes that may not be recognised or valued by the mainstream society and so have to be fought for, or subsumed or negotiated to fit in. Of course, this does not always result in negative experiences, and could even offer an advantage in developing some of the skills that organisations now need.

Until recently, older workers were widely discriminated against when seeking employment and, when employed, they were often not given training (Naylor, 1987; Dennis, 1988; Laslett, 1989; Waskel, 1991). They have been commonly stereotyped as having failing cognitive and physical abilities, as being inflexible, and unwilling and unable to learn new ways. However, traditional attitudes towards older workers have started to change because of today's concern for knowledge management and investment in human capital (*People Management*, 2005b) and demographic changes [see also Smethurst (2006), via the Centre for Research into the Older Workforce at Surrey University, and via a CIPD Factsheet *Age and Employment*]. With the raising of the state pension age, working lives will be extended and many older people will have to continue learning in order to keep up with the new technologies and practices that will come along. Despite the past negative stereotyping of older people, this will not necessarily be a problem for them. Although there is deterioration in performance with age, it is less than popularly believed: 'Except where such abilities as muscular strength are of predominant importance, age is not a good discriminator of ability to work; nor of the ability to learn' (The Carnegie Inquiry into the Third Age, Trinder *et al.*, 1992: 20). Trinder *et al.* (1992) also note that performance is influenced as much by experience and skill as by age: skill development in earlier years will encourage adaptability in later life. Moreover, although older people are 'at a disadvantage with speedy and novel (unexpected) forms of presentation', Coleman (1990: 70–71) reports little or no decline with age in memory and learning, particularly 'if the material is fully learnt initially'. The continuing ability of older people to learn was demonstrated in an apprenticeship programme for older workers organised by BMW. It was completed in 60 per cent of the time taken by the youth apprenticeship scheme: 'They already had life skills and were used to factory work, making it easier to acquire new skills. But they were also motivated and knew what they wanted to do' (*People Management*, 2005a: 17).

Significant outcomes of learning and development for people at work

The outcomes discussed in the following are of considerable significance not only to individuals themselves but also to the organisations that employ them. (You can read more about them in Bloom *et al.*, 1956.)

Psychomotor skills

These 'doing' skills are needed at every level of an organisation, from the senior manager's ability to operate a desktop computer to the cleaner's operation of a floor-scrubbing machine, while more sophisticated skills are needed to operate complex and expensive technology. Skill can be defined as:

> ...the performance of any task which, for its successful and rapid completion, requires an improved organisation of responses making use of only those aspects of the stimulus which are essential to satisfactory performance. Ribeaux and Poppleton (1978: 53–54)
>
> ...an appearance of ease, of smoothness of movement, of confidence and the comparative absence of hesitation; it frequently gives the impression of being unhurried, while the actual pace of activity may of course be quite high ... increasing skill involves a widening of the range of possible disturbances that can be coped with without disrupting the performance. Borger and Seaborne (1966: 128–129)

The acquisition of such skills starts with the ability to make a general response to a signal, after which a learner develops a chain of two or more stimulus–response links, including verbal chains and associations; then the ability to make different responses to similar though different stimuli; to achieve concept learning and identify a class of objects or events; to learn rules through the acquisition of a chain of two or more concepts; and, finally, to combine rules and so achieve problem-solving (Gagné, 1970, in Stammers and Patrick, 1975). Recognising and understanding this process suggests how to facilitate learning and prevent failure to learn at the various levels.

'Soft' skills

These are the 'feeling' skills: self-management, interpersonal, language and social skills. They include, for example, asking, listening and focusing; responding, interpreting and questioning; arguing, persuading and criticising; developing, modifying and comparing; acting, influencing and solving. These are needed for communication, teamworking and leadership in organisations (see CIPD, 2010).

Cognitive skills

These 'thinking' skills can be defined in terms of sequences of increasing levels or hierarchies, with the lower levels being prerequisites for, and subsumed by, the higher. This is seen in Bloom *et al.*'s widely used taxonomy of cognitive skills (as revised by Anderson and Krathwohl, 2001: 67–68):

- remembering (retrieving, recognising, and recalling relevant knowledge from long-term memory);
- understanding (constructing meaning from oral, written and graphic messages through interpreting, exemplifying, classifying, summarising, inferring, comparing and explaining);
- applying (carrying out or using a procedure through executing, or implementing);
- analysing (breaking material into constituent parts, determining how the parts relate to one another and to an overall structure or purpose through differentiating, organising and attributing);
- evaluating (making judgments based on criteria and standards through checking and critiquing);
- creating (putting elements together to form a coherent or functional whole; reorganising elements into a new pattern or structure through generating, planning or producing)

The higher-order skills need to be deployed in order to be effective in complex and challenging situations.

Knowledge

There are several kinds of knowledge, and these are learned in different ways. Sometimes a simple distinction is drawn between propositional knowledge, or '*know-that*', which is derived from formal thinking and learned through education, and '*know-how*', which is in part learned from performance. Gardner (1985:68) noted:

> ...many of us know how to ride a bicycle but lack the propositional knowledge of how that behaviour is carried out. In contrast, many of us have propositional knowledge about how to make a soufflé without knowing how to carry this task through to successful completion.

Bloom et al. (Anderson and Krathwohl, 2001) elaborated that distinction and identified four increasingly challenging levels of knowledge: factual knowledge is of basic elements and terminology; conceptual knowledge is of classifications, principles, theories and models; procedural knowledge concerns techniques, methods and when to use them; and meta-cognitive knowledge is strategic and self-knowledge.

Practical knowledge is sometimes ranked lower than other cognitive skills in the social hierarchy of skills, and associated with lower-level occupations. That, however, misrepresents it. According to Jarvis (2004), practical knowledge combines 'know-that', 'know-how', everyday knowledge acquired through the senses, attitudes/beliefs/values, skills and tacit knowledge (see discussion of situated learning in the section on 'Overarching theories of learning'). It is needed at all levels of occupation, from sweeper to surgeon, though occupations differ in the balance they need between its components. Collins (1993: 17), for example, writes about:

> the all too invisible laboratory technician. . . . Look into a laboratory and you will see it filled with fallible machines and the manifest recalcitrance of nature. . . . Technicians make things work in the face of this. . . . Notoriously, techniques that can be made to work by one technician in one place will not work elsewhere. The technician has a practical understanding of aspects of the craft of science beyond that of many scientists. But does the technician 'understand science'?

There are further aspects of knowledge to be noted. The first is explicit, which can easily be documented, while the second is implicit, which could be, but has not yet been, documented. Then there is *tacit knowledge,* which is what 'we know but cannot tell' (Polanyi, 1966). Sternberg (1985: 169) recognises this in his definition of practical intelligence: 'Underlying successful performance in many real-world tasks is tacit knowledge of a kind that is never explicitly taught and in many instances never even verbalised.'

Tacit knowledge is drawn upon for the fluent performance of psychomotor skills (see the definition earlier); it is recognised as crucial in knowledge management. It would seem to be acquired through performance and experience rather than through instruction, and is embedded in the context in which this experience is taking place. This can be seen in stage 2 of the model of Dreyfus *et al.* (1986; see the section on 'Sequential models'), in which the learner becomes independent of instruction through the recognition of the contextual elements of the task, and thereafter develops the ability to register and 'read' contextual cues. However, unlike the formal knowledge that it accompanies, this tacit knowledge never becomes explicit. It has to be apprehended in context, and can perhaps be glimpsed by paying attention to the stories that are told in organisations (e.g. Gabriel, 2000). Myers and Davids (1992: 47) question whether 'tacit skills' can be taught, and identify that they are often transmitted in 'an environment of intensive practical experience' and in task performance: 'We may yet be able to learn much from "sitting next to Nellie"!'

Competency/competence

Both terms are used, but the difference in meaning between them has not been agreed [see the CIPD Factsheet *Competence and Competency Frameworks,* revised July 2012; for the history, purpose and nature of these developments, see Harrison (1992: 17–77, 2005)]. In their comparison of English and some European understandings of competence, Brockmann *et al.* (2008) point out that in England it refers to skills-based performance of narrowly defined tasks, whereas in France, for example, it refers to knowledge-based performance that integrates practical and theoretical knowledge with personal and social qualities.

However, common definitions refer to the ability to apply knowledge and skills with understanding to a work activity which is assessed via performance, as in:

- an underlying characteristic of a person which results in effective and/or superior performance in a job (Boyatzis, 1982);
- the ability to perform the activities within an occupational area to the levels of performance expected in employment (Training Commission, 1988).

Competencies/competences can be seen as instances of practical knowledge that have been specifically constructed to meet the purposes of employing organisations. They represent the behavioural and technical abilities an employee must have in order to meet the organisation's goals. They are a means of 'aligning what people can offer – their competencies – against the demands of customers rather than against the ill-fitting and ill-designed demands of jobs' (Martin, 1995: 20).

Considerable effort has been paid to identifying and defining competencies/competences and, crucially, to expressing them in measurable terms. They are now used to form a comprehensive and continually updated national framework agreed across all sectors and occupations in which elements in an individual's learning and development, whether achieved through formal education, training or experiential learning across the life span, are identified and assessed against nationally agreed standards. This framework is now often used by organisations in recruitment, assessment, the articulation of learning needs, and the design of training and development. Its language, philosophy and procedures are thus likely to shape individuals' perceptions of their own learning and learning needs. However, it should be noted that this institutionalised, trans-organisational framework has wrenched competencies/competences from their context and hence from the tacit knowledge that characterises practical knowledge.

Employability

Since the 1990s, as employment insecurity has grown, attention has focused on employability, an indirect outcome of learning and development. It has become the 'new security': individuals who lose their jobs would be capable of finding another elsewhere. Hence it is now a matter of concern not only for individuals but also for government employment policies and provisions and for educational institutions, which aim to help their students develop it.

Employability is the capability to gain initial employment, maintain it and obtain new employment if required (Hillage and Pollard, 1998). It focuses on the individual's assets (knowledge, skills, attributes and behaviours), how the individual deploys them and presents them to an employer, and the context of the work that is sought. UKCES (2009) sees the foundation of employability as a positive approach, upon which the functional skills of effectively using numbers, language and IT can be built. To these are added the personal skills of self-management, thinking and solving problems, working together and communicating, understanding the business. Increasingly, employers are emphasising the need for those 'soft skills' (e.g., CBI/NUS, 2011).

These employability skills are defined by criteria set by employers. However, there is also concern for 'sustainable employability' which takes a longer-term view of it and relates it to individual learning and development. Yorke and Knight (2006) suggest that it should cover understanding, beliefs about self-efficacy, the deployment of skills and metacognition, and Watts (2006) adds career development skills. These echo Bloom *et al.*'s (1956) levels of learning, and can be achieved via experiential and action learning, work experience and the opportunity for reflection and integration.

People achieve employability by investing in their human capital of skills and reputation, and this means that they must engage in continuous learning and development, update their skills and acquire others that might be needed in the future by their current or future employer.

- How is employability defined in your college or university?
- How would you assess your own employability?

Theories of learning

Both individuals and HRD managers need to understand how such learning outcomes may be achieved, so the chapter will now examine some of the more influential theories of learning and development. (You can read about others in Nolen-Hoeksema *et al.,* 2009.) However, it is worth noting that, in their recent review, McGurk and Sadler-Smith (2012) find that HR developers tend to make use of only a few of them (e.g., Honey and Mumford, Kolb, learning styles: see below), and suggest that they should look to neuroscience and the study of the brain for new understandings of learning.

Overarching theories of learning

Three of these will now be presented, one concerning behaviour, another cognition, and the third context and social relationships. Some of the differences between them are due in part to their underpinning assumptions, whether positivist, constructivist and social constructionist, as outlined earlier in the book (see Chapter 3).

Behaviourist approach

The behaviourist (positivist) approach is frequently used to encourage desired behaviours in children and animals, and in basic forms of training. It regards learning as the process by which a particular stimulus (S), repeatedly associated with, or conditioned by, desirable or undesirable experiences, comes to evoke a particular response (R). This conditioning can be of two kinds. With classical conditioning, a stimulus leads automatically to a response, as in Pavlov's experiment in which dogs were conditioned to salivate at the sound of a bell rung before food was presented. Operant conditioning reinforces or rewards a desired response, which increases the probability of the repetition of the same response when the stimulus recurs. Experimental research (including many animal studies) has shown that negative reinforcement, or punishment, is not as effective for learning as positive reward, and that reinforcement at variable intervals is more effective than continuous reinforcement. Behaviour can be shaped by reinforcing responses that approximate to what is desired until that behaviour is finally achieved.

Cognitivist approach

That behaviourist S–R approach pays no attention to the cognitive processes that come to associate a stimulus with a particular response: it does not investigate what is in the 'black box'. However, cognitivist learning theories, influenced by constructivism, again originally based on animal studies, do so. They see learning as an association of stimulus with stimulus (S–S). The learner develops expectations that stimuli are linked and so develops a cognitive 'map' or latent learning. Hence insightful behaviour appropriate to a situation takes place without the strengthening association of S–R bonds. Social learning theory also addresses what is in the 'black box'. It recognises the role in learning of the observation and imitation of the behaviour of others, but as seen in, say, the debates around the influence of the media upon children's behaviour, there are clearly many moderating variables.

Social constructivist approach

Learning, according to the behavioural and cognitivist theories, is largely decontextualised. The social constructivist approach to the understanding of learning, however, recognises the significance of context, culture and social interaction. Rather than being a solely individual experience, learning is a social process that takes place through interaction and collaboration with others (Vygotsky, 1978). This view places emphasis upon language, which it considers to be socially constructed, and on the role of other people in an individual's learning. Lave and Wenger (1991) develop this further in their notion of situated learning. Individuals learn through socialisation and imitation as they try to address problems in a specific context and in interaction with others. This takes place in a 'community of practice', which is a group of people who create a shared identity by participating in a communal activity. Through the relationships between practitioners, their practice and the social organisation of their communities, they develop their practical knowledge.

The process of learning

There are several models of the process through which learning occurs, which HR developers could use to point to ways in which learning might be facilitated, made more effective or impeded.

Sequential models

One approach is to see learning as an information-processing system in which a signal, containing information, is transmitted along a communication channel of limited capacity and subject to interference and 'noise' (Stammers and Patrick, 1975). The signal has to be decoded before it can be received, and then encoded to pass it on. Data received through the senses are filtered, recognised and decoded through the interpretative process of perception; this information is then translated into action through the selection of appropriate responses. The effectiveness of learning depends on attention being paid only to the relevant parts of the stimuli, the rapid selection of appropriate responses, the efficient performance of them, and the feeding back of information about their effects into the system. Overload or breakdown of the system can occur at any of these stages.

Gagné (1974, in Fontana, 1981: 73) analysed the *sequence* of learning, a chain of events, some internal and others external to the learner. It begins with the learner's readiness to receive information (motivation or expectancy), and continues as the learner perceives it, distinguishes it from other stimuli, makes sense of it and relates it to what is already known. The information is then stored in the short- or long-term memory. Thereafter, it can be retrieved from memory, generalised to, and put into practice in, new situations. Its final phase is feedback from knowledge of the results obtained from this practice.

Fitts (1962) uses *a three-stage* approach, to the acquisition of psychomotor skills in particular. First, the learner has to understand what is required, its rules and concepts, and how to achieve it: *the cognitive stage*. Then the learner has to practise and establish the stimulus–response links, the correct patterns of behaviour, gradually eliminating errors: *the associative stage*. Finally, the learner refines the motor patterns of behaviour until external sources of information become redundant and the capacity simultaneously to perform secondary tasks increases: *the autonomous stage*.

Burgoyne and Hodgson (1983) use a variation of this in their analysis of how managers learn. Managers gradually build up experience created out of specific learning incidents, internalise this experience and use it, both consciously and unconsciously, to guide their future action and decision-making. The three levels in this process are:

- *Level 1 learning,* which occurs when managers simply take in some factual information or data that is immediately relevant but does not change their views of the world.

- *Level 2 learning,* which occurs at an unconscious or tacit level. Managers gradually build up a body of personal 'case law' that enables them to deal with future events.
- *Level 3 learning,* when managers consciously reflect on their conception of the world, how it is formed, and how they might change it.

Dreyfus *et al.* (1986, in Cooley, 1987: 13–15 and Quinn et al., 1990: 314–15) set out a more elaborate model of the acquisition of skills that is relevant to understanding the development of cognitive skills. Their five-stage model moves from the effective performance of lower- to higher-order skills.

- *Stage 1: the novice.* Novices follow context-free rules, with relevant components of the situation defined for them; hence they lack any coherent sense of the overall task.
- *Stage 2: the advanced beginner.* Through their practical experience in concrete situations, learners begin to recognise the contextual elements of their task. They begin to perceive similarities between new and previous experiences.
- *Stage 3: competent.* They begin to recognise a wider range of cues, and become able to select and focus upon the most important of them. Their reliance upon rules lessens; they experiment and go beyond the rules, using trial and error.
- *Stage 4: proficient.* Those who arrive at this stage achieve the unconscious, fluid, effortless performance referred to in the definitions of skill given earlier. They still think analytically, but can now 'read' the evolving situation, picking up new cues and becoming aware of emerging patterns; they have an involved, intuitive and holistic grasp of the situation.
- *Stage 5: expert.* At this stage, according to Cooley (1987: 15), 'Highly experienced people seem to be able to recognise whole scenarios without decomposing them into elements or separate features.' They have 'multidimensional maps of the territory'; they 'frame and reframe strategies as they read changing cues' (Quinn *et al.*, 1990: 315). With this intuitive understanding of the implications of a situation, they can cope with uncertainty and unforeseen situations.

Cyclical models and learning styles

The Lancaster model is an example of learning as a *cyclical process,* and is based on analysis of managers' learning. It represents all types of learning 'including cognitive, skill development and affective, by any process' (Binsted, 1980: 22). It identifies three different forms of learning: receipt of input/generation of output, discovery and reflection. As Figure 7.1 shows, they take place in both the inner and outer worlds of the individual. Learners receive input as they are taught or given information, or read it in books. They proceed round the discovery loop (action and feedback) through action and experimentation, opening themselves to the new experiences generated, and becoming aware of the consequences of their actions. They follow the reflection loop (conceptualising and hypothesising) when making sense of the information they receive and the actions they undertake, and then, on the basis of this, theorising about past or future situations. Each form of learning is cyclical, and the cycles can be linked in various ways (e.g. learning in formal classroom settings links the receipt of input with reflection), but in effective learning the learner will complete the overall cycle.

The best-known model of the learning cycle in the management field is that of Kolb. Learning has two dimensions (Kolb *et al.*, 1984): concrete/abstract (involvement/detachment) and active/reflective (actor/observer). Effective learning is an integrated cognitive and affective cyclical process. The learner moves in a cyclical manner from becoming fully involved in concrete, new experiences (CE); through observation and reflection on these experiences from many perspectives (RO); using concepts and theories to integrate their observations (AC); to active experimentation in decision-making and problem-solving (AE), and so on (Kolb, 1983).

Figure 7.1 The Lancaster model of the learning cycle

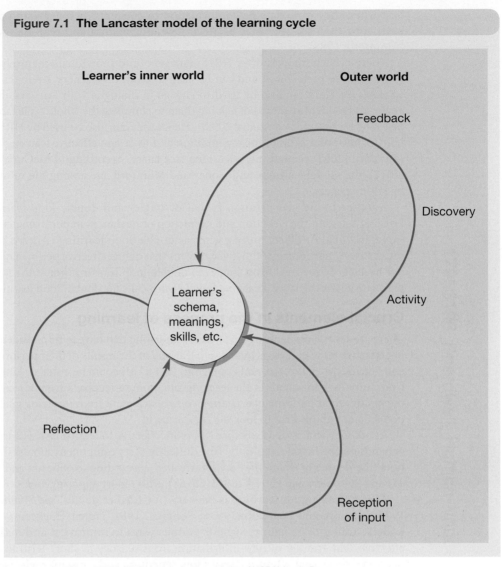

Source: based on Binsted (1980: 22). Reproduced with permission of MCB University Press.

Importantly, these cyclical models draw attention to the significance of learning through action and reflection, as well as through the traditional channels of teaching/learning. They also emphasise that effective learning is achieved by completing the whole cycle and by using methods appropriate to its various phases. They also recognise that individuals might have a preference for a particular phase and so do not complete the cycle and hence do not learn as effectively or as comprehensively as they could. Thus they have different *learning styles*. Kolb's Learning Styles Inventory identifies these preferences (Mumford, 1988: 27). The 'converger' (AC and AE) prefers the practical and specific; the 'diverger' (CE and RO) looks from different points of view and observes rather than acts; the 'assimilator' (AC and RO) is comfortable with concepts and abstract ideas; and the 'accommodator' (CE and AE) prefers to learn primarily from doing.

Honey and Mumford (1992) also identify four learning styles, based on the individual's preference for one element in the learning cycle, and have developed norms based on the results of those who have completed their Learning Styles Questionnaire. Their activists learn best when they are actively involved in concrete tasks; reflectors learn best through reviewing and reflecting upon what has happened and what they have done; theorists learn best when they can relate new information to concepts or theory; and pragmatists learn best when they see relevance between new information and real-life issues or problems (Mumford, 1988).

These cyclical models offer HRD managers (and individuals themselves) the means to identify those preferences, and can be used to build on learners' strengths and reduce their weaknesses They can also be used to engage in dialogue with learners about their preferences; and to identify means of helping them to complete the whole cycle [see CIPD Factsheet *Learning Styles* (updated August 2008)]. Hence they can also be used by HR managers to facilitate higher-order skills in the organisation and to design effective learning events, including, Mumford (2002) reminds us, e-learning (see later). According to McGurk and Sadler-Smith (2012), the models of Kolb, and Honey and Mumford, are among the most commonly used by HR managers.

Another useful classification is that of single- and double-loop learning. Single-loop learning refers to the detection and correction of deviances in performance from established (organisational or other) norms, whereas double-loop learning (Argyris and Schön, 1978) refers to the questioning of those very norms that define effective performance. Individuals do not necessarily progress from single- to double-loop learning, nor is the former an essential prerequisite for the latter. Learning how to learn calls for double-loop learning.

Crucial elements in the process of learning

There are several elements of the process of learning that have to be considered to make learning effective. One of these is *feedback* to learners of the results of their performance (Stammers and Patrick, 1975; Ribeaux and Poppleton, 1978). This could be visual or kinaesthetic feedback from responses to stimuli in the learning situation; or feedback from an external source during or after their performance. Learners may also benefit from receiving guidance before their performance about what to look out for during it.

Another crucial issue is whether it is more effective to learn a task as a *whole* or *in parts*. It depends on the task's 'complexity' (the difficulty of its component subtasks) and its 'organisation' (the degree to which they are interrelated), according to Ribeaux and Poppleton (1978: 61) and Stammers and Patrick (1975: 85–88), who report opposing views.

Also significant for learning is *memory* (for further details, see Stammers and Patrick, 1975; Ribeaux and Poppleton, 1978; Fontana, 1981; Nolen-Hoeksema et al., 2009). An understanding of its nature suggests various ways to improve it and make learning more effective. The transfer of new information from sensory to short-term to long-term memory is clearly crucial: attention, recitation, repetition and constant revision (or *overlearning*) are needed. The coding and organisation of material to be stored are also important; this is helped by associating the new information with what is already familiar, especially using visual imagery, by attending to the context giving rise to the information to be learned, and by making the effort to understand the information so that it can be stored in the appropriate 'files'. The learning context or event should not provoke anxiety. It should also be recognised that memory is an active and a constructive process, and not like a camera that has recorded what happened. The process of memory draws inferences from its data inputs and so elaborates upon them, filtering them through the individual's stereotypes, mindset and worldview. What is then stored is this enhanced and repackaged material.

Explore

- On your own or in a group, go through this section on theories of learning and list what you consider to be the key components of learning that will be needed in designing and implementing the training of (i) technical apprentices; (ii) retail staff; (iii) supervisory staff.

Theories of the process of development

Development, defined earlier, is the process whereby people achieve greater degrees of complexity, even transformation, as they live their lives. There are several approaches to understanding how this process takes place, and they differ in the assumptions they make about reality (see Chapter 3). Some appear to be based on the assumption that the social and economic environment provided an objective, orderly, stable framework for individual lives. These would then follow a largely common pattern of sequential phases or stages, sometimes seen in terms of progression or advancement, and the individual had to complete a 'developmental task' in order to move on to the next stage. It was assumed that this pattern provided universal norms against which an individual's development could be calibrated. The development of women and minorities were generally seen in terms of those norms even those that had been based on the experiences of majority white males. [Hence Gallos (1989) questioned the relevance of many of the accepted views of development to women's lives and careers, while Thomas and Alderfer (1989) noted that the influence of race on the developmental process was commonly ignored in the literature.] Individuals were socialised to conform to the patterns of behaviour or norms of their social group. These could be expressed as legal constraints – the age of consent, marriage, attaining one's majority (becoming an adult) – as quasi-legal constraints, such as the age at which the state pension is paid and hence at which most people retire from the labour force, or as social and peer group expectations. For example, Neugarten (1968) recognised how family, work and social statuses provided the 'major punctuation marks in the adult life' and the 'way of structuring the passage of time in the life span of the individual, providing a time clock that can be superimposed over the biological clock' (p. 146).

The workplace was another arena in which development took place, and it could facilitate or hinder it. Stable organisations in the past had their own 'clocks'. Sofer (1970: 239) notes how his respondents were 'constantly . . . asking themselves whether they were on schedule, in front of schedule or behind schedule . . . they had a set of norms in mind as to where one should be by a given age'.

One influential theory which seems to assume this stable framework for individual lives is Erikson's (1950) psychosocial model of development. It identifies stages of ego development and the effects of maturation, experience and socialisation (see Levinson et al., 1978; Wrightsman, 1988). Each stage builds on the ones before, and presents the expanding ego with a choice or 'crisis'. The successful resolution of that 'crisis' achieves a higher level of elaboration in individuality and adaptation to the demands of both inner and outer worlds, and hence the capacity to deal with the next stage. An unsuccessful or inadequate resolution hinders or distorts this process of effective adaptation in the subsequent stages. For example, according to Erikson, the adolescent strives for a coherent sense of self, or identity, perhaps experimenting with several different identities and as yet uncommitted to one; entry to work and choice of work role play a part here. The adolescent, however, has to make a choice and assume responsibility for its consequences: unless this occurs, there is identity confusion. Young adults have to resolve another choice. This is between achieving closeness and intimate relationships and being ready to isolate themselves from others. The choice for those aged 25–65 years is between the stagnation that would result from concern only for self, indulging themselves as though they were 'their own only child' (Wrightsman, 1988: 66), and 'generativity'; that is, the reaching out beyond the need to satisfy self in order to take responsibility in the adult world, and show care for others, the next generation, or the planet itself. The choice of the final stage of life is between construing life as having been well spent and construing it as ill spent.

Another influential theory that does not question the assumption of a stable framework of life is Levinson et al.'s (1978) model of the male life span, which they based on their study of the experiences of men in mid-life. They saw this life span in terms of alternating, age-related, periods of stability and instability. In the stable period, lasting six to eight years, a man built and enriched the structure of his life: work, personal relationships and community involvement. That structure, however, could not last, and so there followed a transitional period, of four to five years, when the individual reappraised that structure and explored new possibilities. These could be uncomfortable or painful experiences, but they were the essential prelude to adapting or changing the life structure, and so achieving a further stable period. By defining the periods within the life span in terms of chronological age – e.g. between ages 22 and 28 a man embarked on a stable period and entry into the adult world, and between ages 33 and 40 entered another stable period in which he settled down – this model was making assumptions about the universal, normative patterning of experiences.

Now, and certainly since globalisation and the economic upheavals of the early twenty-first century, it is no longer possible to assume the existence of a normative and stable framework for individuals' lives. This gives support to an alternative theoretical perspective on development, which emphasises that the environment offers particular opportunities and threats for different people's lives. The biological, social, economic and psychological strands of their life interweave and they have to negotiate a balance between changing self and changing environment. This can be conceptualised using the systems model introduced earlier in the book (Chapter 3). The process of development or elaboration takes place as the individual's innate capacity to grow and mature unfolds within a particular context, which in turn facilitates or stunts growth, or prompts variations upon it. The interaction and accommodation between individuals and their environment cannot, therefore, be meaningfully expressed in a cross-cultural or universal model.

A further theoretical perspective on individual development acknowledges the significance of a person's subjective experiences, which some interpret as socially constructed. This emphasises the significance of context, and the dynamic, intersubjective processes through which individuals interpret and make decisions about their lives and careers.

The individual's own learning and development within an organisation

Before turning to how learning and development become embodied in organisational practices to achieve organisational ends, it should be noted that employees' own learning and development will continue informally and unplanned. They often learn for themselves how to carry out their jobs and improve their performance: through doing and observing and 'sitting next to Nellie', and through trial and error. Other people in the work context, their peers, supervisors and subordinates, may well provide models to follow, instruction and feedback, support and encouragement, confidence-building, informal mentoring and coaching, and perhaps even inspiration.

Employees may outgrow their jobs as they learn, and seek promotion or to move into new jobs that will allow them to continue their development. They may also take the initiative to acquire additional skills, knowledge or understanding by attending educational and other courses. However, they might not necessarily be exposed to best practice, and learn poor lessons; or learn ineffectively and in an unnecessarily uncomfortable, effortful or wasteful manner. Thus they might not necessarily themselves benefit from the learning and development they contribute to their organisation, although they would not be able to withhold some of its benefits from their employers. Because of this, employee learning is problematical.

With the increasing flexibility of organisations and their contracts of employment, individuals need to engage in lifelong learning; their need for *self-development,* both 'of self' and 'by self' (Pedler, 1988), associated with their need for employability, is likely to be greater than ever in the future. They will need to take responsibility for their own learning, identify their own learning needs and how to meet them, often through the performance of everyday work, monitor their own progress, assess the outcomes, and reassess their goals. Others might have a role in an individual's self-development, not as teacher, trainer or coach, but perhaps as a mentor, counsellor or learning resource.

Although self-development is regarded positively as proactive and entrepreneurial, it can be difficult for the individual to provide evidence of it without some form of accreditation. This can be achieved through the Credit Accumulation and Transfer Scheme, and the Accreditation of Prior Learning and of Experiential Learning. These allow individuals to claim accreditation for a range of learning experiences, while Scottish Vocational Qualifications (SVQs) and National Vocational Qualifications (NVQs) (see Chapter 8) allow them to gain recognition for aspects of their work performance. Employee development schemes should also help individuals in their self-development, whether systematic or sporadic.

While these informal methods of learning might have their weaknesses, they also have strengths. They variously embody characteristics of learning identified earlier. They encourage employees to make use of several types of knowledge – propositional, practical, implicit and tacit. They incorporate the use of feedback. They can offer whole rather than part learning, and the opportunity to reflect. They may stimulate individuals to engage in double-loop learning as they start to examine their underlying assumptions, and to follow the learning cycle of input, action and reflection. They may draw on the experiences of an employee group. Not only would they benefit from their combined various learning styles, but the identification of problems and implementation of their solutions would be embedded in the learning context, which would be likely to increase the effectiveness of their learning.

Learning and development: the organisational context

'Learning and development' as an organisational phenomenon exists on several levels:

- *Practical*: delivering or facilitating training, learning and development interventions, e.g. training, on-the job learning, e-learning, coaching, mentoring, secondments, etc.

- *Professional*: hosting a set of plans, policies and strategies to achieve a pre-determined set of strategic goals, to coordinate the production of information and evaluation, providing expertise and advice on learning and development as experts in the practice of ethical learning and development, who understand the nature of effective design and delivery.

- *Partnership*: building relationships intra-organisationally between HRD and HRM, HRD and the wider organisation.

- *Strategic*: ensuring that learning and development activity contributes to plugging performance gaps identified in strategic planning.

- *Cultural*: developing a culture that values learning and principles associated with it.

- *Extra-organisational*: building strategically beneficial relationships outside the organisation to ensure that learning and development in the organisation are up-to-date, relevant and appropriately develop the organisation's skills base.

In order to design, implement and evaluate effective learning events or HRD interventions (including training, but sometimes covering learning and development more broadly), a cyclical process or system of formal planning ought to be followed (Walton, 1999; Reid, et al., 2004; Harrison, 2009; Mankin, 2009; Beevers and Rea, 2010). However, the popularity of planning cycles is more evident in the rhetoric of the literature than in organisational reality, with only 48 per cent of employers having a training plan specifying in advance the level and types of training that employees will need in the coming year and only 36 per cent with a budget for training expenditure. Organisations with more than 25 people are much more likely to see these activities as 'standard' and to have them in place. Where businesses have a formal plan of business objectives, they are more likely to have a training plan, and where there is a training plan, it is more likely that there will be a training budget (Shury *et al.*, 2008, 2012).

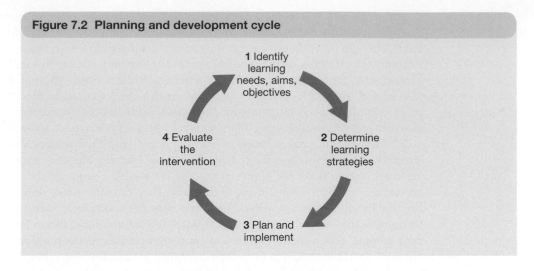

Figure 7.2 Planning and development cycle

The learning and development planning cycle (see Figure 7.2) comprises logical stages to ensure the consideration of the needs of the individual and the organisation at the early stages; to establish appropriate aims and objectives; to ensure optimum methods of design and delivery; and to carry out effective evaluation of the learning intervention.

This approach stems from strategic planning approaches, popular for several decades (Rothwell and Kazanas, 1989; Walton, 1999). It matches most organisations' tendency to treat strategic issues formally, using written documents with aims, objectives, targets, priorities and performance indicators and recognition frameworks, such as Investors in People (**www.investorsinpeople. co.uk**), relying heavily on analysis, planning and foresight, logical thinking and clarity of organisational objectives. Yet, the approach underestimates iterations of, or interuptions in or to, the process; overlooks changes in material aspects of the process; and ignores influences external or internal to the process. It does not take account of the need for evaluation to happen at all stages of the process, or the way that needs change and develop as the process moves on. It matches well the classical or rational planning approach to strategy, which suggests that organisational strategy is formed through a formal, rational decision-making process (see Chapter 2 on strategic HRM), but not with alternative approaches (e.g. evolutionary, processual or systemic (Whittington, 1993), outlined in Chapter 2) that conceptualise strategy as something more informal, fragmented and embedded in the social systems (cultural and institutional aspects) of the business.

Stages in the process

The next sections cover in sequence:

- identifying learning needs, aims and objectives;
- determining learning strategies;
- planning and implementation;
- evaluating learning and development interventions.

Identifying learning needs, aims and objectives

Identifying learning needs establishes how learning and development strategies, policies, practices and activities can bridge the gap between where the organisation is now and where it needs to be in order to achieve its strategic objectives (CIPD, 2013). A learning need exists when there is a gap between the future requirements of the job and the current capabilities of the incumbent, whether this is measured in terms of skills, attitudes or knowledge, and it is anticipated that a planned learning intervention will overcome the deficiency or barrier (see Figure 7.3).

Figure 7.3 The nature of learning needs

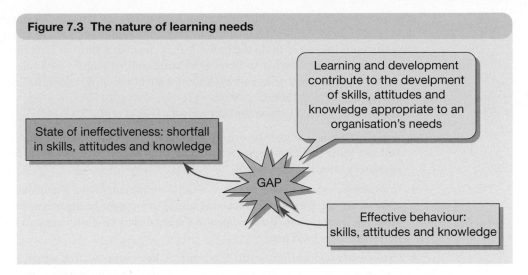

Given the multi-level nature of the learning and development process discussed earlier, one would expect multi-level analysis of learning and development needs. So, while this section considers the analysis of learning needs at just three levels: organisational, job and individual (CIPD, 2013), others consider more. McGoldrick *et al.* (2002), for example, offer a comprehensive structure that suggests seven levels of analysis:

- *Extra-organisational*: beyond organisational boundaries, attempting to understand, anticipate and create change in the environment and translate it into the advantage of the organisation. This involves practical and analytical research and learning and changing in response to this.

- *Inter-organisational*: between organisations, transferring learning and information, sharing best practices through collaboration and exchange.

- *Intra-organisational*: between departments, cross-fertilisation of ideas, encouraging diversity.

- *Organisational*: recognising the uniqueness of the organisation and responding to its needs for learning and change.

- *Departmental*: encouraging self-development and creativity through learning by experimentation.

- *Group*: through good communication, identifying and solving problems to lead to learning and improvement.

- *Individual*: personal responsibility for identifying learning and improvement needs in knowledge, skills, aptitude and performance.

Despite the aspirations of authors, articles and textbooks, very few organisations have developed or used appropriate measures (Anderson, 2007). Only half of employers (52 per cent) formally assess the extent to which employees currently have gaps in their skills against formal written job descriptions, and 30 per cent do not have formal written job descriptions (Shury *et al.,* 2008).Whichever level of activity is engaged, the process – if treated appropriately as one that is ongoing, iterative and reviewable – is resource- and time-intensive (Mankin, 2009).

For the organisation

The first level of analysis of learning needs is at the level of the whole organisation. This step provides the link between the broader strategy of the organisation and the HRD strategy; ensures that the learning processes, systems and interventions support the direction in which the business is heading; considers the 'fit' with the values and priorities of the organisation;

examines feedback provided by evaluation of previous learning and development interventions; and aims to identify the quantity and type of learning required to ensure all employees have the skills they need to do their jobs. It may consider a short or long time-frame and will aid decisions about whether to develop existing staff or employ new talent (Taylor, 2008). However, it is not one that has always received attention, or if it does, it is considered a 'one-off' or 'special' review (Mankin, 2009).

In practice, this level of analysis can consist of (Reid et al., 2004: 243):

- *A global review* – where the organisation examines its short- and longer-term objectives and the skills and knowledge required to meet them. This takes the form of a detailed whole-organisation job analysis.

- *Competence-based global review* – where competence and performance management approaches are used to align training and development to organisational objectives. It is attractive because it is firmly related to the organisation's objectives and can be the basis of performance-related pay.

- *Critical incident analysis* – this is a positive, key event focused strategy which considers the main processes in the organisation and considers the learning needs associated with them.

- *Priority problem analysis* – where the aim is not to consider comprehensively learning needs, but to identify and prioritise the main problems of the organisation and respond using HRD interventions.

At this level, information can be found in strategic and HR plans, succession planning data, performance management data, management information systems and financial plans.

For the job

Job level analysis has as its purpose the identification of the skills, knowledge and attributes of the job. The most commonly used approaches include interviews with job holders, managers and supervisors, job logs, questionnaires and group discussions. The outcomes of this level of analysis are usually a job description, job specification and job training specification. Job level analysis can be categorised on four levels (Harrison, 2009; Mankin, 2009):

- *Comprehensive analysis* – consists of a full and exhaustive analysis of the job, producing a detailed job specification of all the tasks, roles and performance levels associated with the job and the level of knowledge, skills and attitudes required to perform the job effectively.

- *Key task analysis* – consists of an analysis of the tasks central to effective performance of the job.

- *Problem-centred analysis* –focuses on problems or performance deficiencies and seeks to identify HRD solutions.

- *Critical incident analysis* – identifies critical or significant tasks in job performance.

The outcome of the intervention is a job training specification which forms the basis of planning for HRD interventions for each post-holder.

For the individual

Analysis of training needs at the job level, while common, is not the whole picture, and it is not without its critics, among them Ashworth (2006:1):

> It is tempting to address training needs at [job] level: deciding the training needed for particular roles then rolling out this training to all employees with that job. This approach has the benefit of ensuring all employees have the skills to perform their role effectively. Yet it also has drawbacks, with its 'sheep dip' tactics resulting in people attending training they do not need. The consequences are wasted training spend, poor perception of the training department and wasted working time. Addressing training needs analysis at the most individual level possible is

time-consuming and can be more costly. But it yields greater benefits . . . financially . . . organisationally . . . and individually. What can make us more a part of the strategic direction of the organisation than delivering the employee resource with the exact skills profile required to realise it?

The individual level of analysis, or person analysis, examines whether those in the job have the necessary capabilities to perform at the correct level. It is often considered to be a response to gaps or failures in performance, identifying where there are areas where individuals are not performing effectively or where they have insufficient knowledge, skills or abilities. However, Ashworth (2006) argues that this is potentially the best way for organisations to address strategic learning needs. Information can come from person specifications, personal profiles, self-, peer or manager assessments, the appraisal system and assessment centres.

Determining learning strategies

Organisations have a choice about which learning strategy or intervention they identify to meet the needs established in the previous stage and the decision is highly circumstantial or contextual. Criteria can be employed to help to make the appropriate decision, which can include the extent to which the learning (Reid *et al.*, 2004):

- *Fits with objectives*: for example, if the objective is practical knowledge, then practical/hands-on experience should be sought, rather than classroom-based education.
- *Is likely to be transferred to the work place*: for example, whether the learning intervention is sufficiently related to the objectives that have to be met, and whether there are systems in place (such as coaching) to support transfer of learning on return to the workplace.
- *Matches available resources*: for example, practical concerns such as time, money and the availability of internal or external expertise.
- *Takes into account learner-related factors*: for example, the learner's preferences in terms of time, location and learning, taking account of the nature of their contract and reasonable expectations on how they use their time.

What do organisations do?

Given the extent of expenditure on training and learning activity in organisations (CIPD, 2012c; Shury *et al.*, 2012), the cost-effective use of training methods ought to be an investment that companies and organisations consider carefully. Most employers engage in some form of workplace development activity – in the 12 months prior to The UK Commission's Employer Perspectives Survey (Shury *et al.*, 2012), 73 per cent of establishments had provided some form of training to staff, with internal training being more common than external training. The annual National Employers' Skills Survey (published by UKCES) reports employer investment in skills. In the year to the end of 2011 (the most recent report at time of publication), a total of £49 billion (£3,275 per person trained) had been spent on training over 117.3m days (4.3 days per annum per employee).

However, many commentators report that organisations choose inappropriate methods that are costly, time-consuming, have a deleterious effect on employees' perceptions of the value of training and development and ultimately do little to increase skills levels in organisations.

The CIPD and the UKCES produce annual reports which include information on training and development activity in organisations. These are available online:

- National Employers Skills Survey 2011 (published May 2012) – **www.UKCES.org.uk**
- Annual Survey Report 2012: Learning and Development (published April 2012) – **www.cipd.co.uk**.

The National Employer Skills Survey 2011 notes the division of training into (Davies *et al.*, 2011):

- *On-the-job training* – defined as activities that would be recognised as training by staff, and that take place at the individual's immediate work position, *but not* the sort of learning by experience that takes place on an ongoing basis. This type of training significantly increased between 2005 and 2011 (Davies *et al.,* 2011). The report recognises that 'broader activity can take place which leads to skills development but which may not be classified as training' (Davies *et al.,* 2011: 100), e.g. supervision, learning through observation, job enhancement, review and feedback.

- *Off-the-job training* – which takes place away from the individual's immediate work position, whether on the premises or elsewhere.

The type of provision of training by employers varies, with 46 per cent providing off-the-job training and 42 per cent providing on-the-job training (Davies *et al.,* 2011).

A summary of some of the main learning interventions is given in the following section. In order to broaden the definitions and provide recognition of the many ways that staff are developed, here the reference is to on- and off-the-job *learning* rather than *training*.

On-the-job learning

On-the-job learning is learning that takes place at the individual's immediate work situation and includes activities that may not always be recognised by staff as development, e.g. staff meetings, discussion, reflection, observation, teamworking, undertaking a project, assignment or consultancy, taking on a new area of responsibility, changing work practices or systems and much more. It is popular because it is job-specific and relevant, immediate and flexible. However, identifying the learning that has occurred as a result is more challenging – particularly where it occurs informally, even if planned.

In 2012, the CIPD survey identified that it was also one of the most *effective* methods of training, topped only by in-house development programmes and coaching by line managers, which have grown considerably in popularity in the last three years. However, both positive and negative behaviours and skills can be passed on, underlining the need for suitable role models and opportunities to be identified and developed as part of the organisation's HRD strategy. On-the-job training ought not to be haphazard and accidental. The most commonly used planned methods are now discussed (see Figure 7.4).

Observation

Obtaining job knowledge from colleagues is the most obvious and cheapest method of on-the-job development and is how the vast majority of employees learn their job and how best to perform it. Social learning theory provides the conceptual basis for this approach (see earlier). Both the strengths and the limitations of this approach are based on its central premise – that people learn well by watching others. It is popular because it is immediate and accessible to most employees. While much of this type of learning happens in an *ad hoc,* unplanned way, it can be a valid, planned way of transferring learning and knowledge in the workplace. In order to be effective, it relies on good structuring, planning and monitoring. The limitations of this approach are well documented. The underlying assumption is that the role model is an experienced, well-practised and skilled performer who has a good understanding of what needs to be passed on. However, they may not be good at their job, may exhibit inefficient job practices or inappropriate behaviour. There might be someone else who is better, or the role model may not have been trained in the practices they are modelling. Often this is a result of poor structure, design and planning, but it can result in the passing on of bad or even dangerous working practices.

Reflective practice

Reflective practice is commonly encouraged by professional organisations such as the CIPD and is central to their professional standards (CIPD, 2005). This is discussed in detail in the next chapter.

Mentoring

The terms mentoring and coaching are sometimes used interchangeably, but there is a difference in the relationship between the participants in the process. Mentoring has a much longer

Figure 7.4 The most commonly used planned methods of on-the-job training

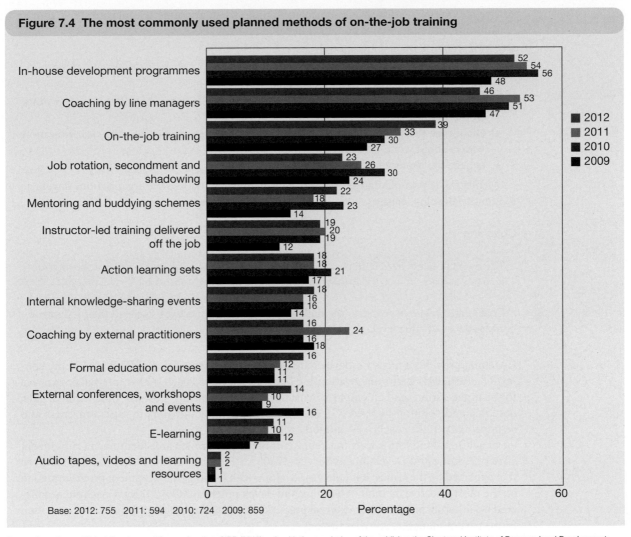

Base: 2012: 755   2011: 594   2010: 724   2009: 859

Source: *Learning and Talent Development Survey*, London: CIPD (2012) p. 8, with the permission of the publisher, the Chartered Institute of Personnel and Development, London (www.cipd.co.uk)

history than coaching, as Mentor was, in ancient Greek literature, the friend to whom Ulysses entrusted the care of his young son before embarking on his epic voyages.

The mentoring relationship is most often orientated towards an 'exchange of wisdom, support, learning or guidance for the purpose of … career growth; sometimes [it is] used to achieve strategic business goals … content can be wide ranging' (Parsloe and Wray, 2000: 12).

Mentoring is based on a 'role model' relationship where a more senior or experienced employee takes a supporting role in the development of a new or younger employee. It can be formal or informal and relies on the development of a positive advisory relationship. As such, it includes the skills of coaching, facilitating, counselling and networking. The relationship is often mutually beneficial as mentors gain from being challenged to understand their own jobs and their organisation, and so find ways of helping their protégé share this understanding effectively.

Effective mentoring relies on the following characteristics:

- *Status and character of the mentor* – mentors will generally be senior managers, outside line management, who should have the skills and qualities that protégés respect: good empathic and people development skills. Not all managers will make appropriate mentors.

- *The protégé* – should have potential and be capable and willing to develop it.

- *The relationship* – this should be one of mutual trust, and unless limits are set, it should continue until the protégé no longer needs support.
- *The activities* – the mentor should:
  - encourage the protégé to analyse their performance and to identify strengths and weaknesses – feedback should be offered and accepted;
  - act as a sounding boards for protégés' ideas and give commentary in the context of the work environment;
  - encourage the protégé to observe and analyse the organisation at work, learning more widely about work;
  - engage the protégé in their networks.

Mentoring is part of a range of 'talent management' activities that organisations engage in to identify, develop, engage, retain and deploy the most talented individuals (CIPD, 2012c).

Coaching

> The coach does not need to impart knowledge, advice or even wisdom. What he or she must do is speak, and act, in such a way that others learn and perform at their best.   Downey (2003: 17)

> Coaching...requires people to see things from others' perspectives, suspend their judgment and listen at a higher level.   Hall (2005)

Coaching provides a focus for developing individual performance (CIPD, 2012a) in the context of a (usually) one-to-one relationship between a trained coach (either internal or external to the organisation) and an employee/coachee. The relationship is usually time-limited; goal, outcome and solution-focused (Greene and Grant, 2006); and aims to raise awareness and responsibility in the coachee (Whitmore, 2009).

Coaching, along with e-learning, represents the largest growth area identified in subsequent CIPD Learning and Development Surveys (2005–2012) with staying power that has outlived that expected by the critics. It is considered, along with in-house development programmes, to be the most effective method of learning and development (CIPD, 2012c). Coaching is delivered by either in-house staff or external practitioners (Knights and Poppleton, 2008) and often forms part of managers' job descriptions.

At the centre of coaching are models of *structure* and *skills*. The structure of coaching, or the coaching process, is firmly focused on the outcome or longer-term objective that the participants want to achieve. The most popular model is the 'GROW' model (Gallway, 1986; Downey, 2003; Cox *et al.*, 2009; Whitmore, 2009) (see Box 7.1). The model takes the participants through four overlapping stages in an iterative process of interaction between the coach and the coachee. This usually takes the form of the coach asking questions in order to raise the awareness and responsibility of the coachee, and allows them to develop practicable solutions or actions in order to achieve the goal. It enables the coach to structure the conversation and deliver a result that emphasises the accountability and responsibility of the coachee and the will to achieve the outcome.

Box 7.1   Typical GROW model

Goal: What is the longer term objective? What is the objective for *this* discussion?

Reality: What is the situation now? Who is involved? What is it costing? What is happening?

Options: What are the possible (not necessarily practicable) solutions? What could be done?

Will: What will be done? When? With whose support?

Within this conversational process, the coach is using a range of *skills*: Downey (2003) suggests that the coach can use all of the skills on the spectrum shown in Figure 7.5. He indicates that the most effective skills of the coach lie at the non-directive end of the spectrum. For Downey, the skills of the coach are more valuable than experience of the problem the coachee is attempting to resolve. He indicates that while there will be times when the coachee is stuck and the coach knows the solution, there are limitations to the directive approach – namely, the coach has to know the answer already or be able to work it out, the answer is unlikely to be the one that fits the problem best, and the experience of the coachee is excluded. Aside from the generic skills of coaching, expertise from the behavioural sciences is commonly included or expected, e.g. psychology and psychoanalysis (Stober and Grant, 2006; Palmer and Whybrow, 2007), and different theoretical approaches are employed, e.g. cognitive behavioural, adult learning, psychodynamic, person-centred or transpersonal (Cox *et al.*, 2009).

Coaching is beset by a number of debates, not least the one concerning the appropriate way to regulate the profession and develop the skills of those who practise it (Hall, 2005). Professional bodies have been established in the UK (**www.associationforcoaching.com**), Europe (**www.emccouncil.org**) and the USA (**www.coachfederation.org**), providing verified levels of membership and ethical and behavioural codes of practice. Moreover, many universities and professional bodies have introduced development programmes for would-be coaches, and most organisations have a system to measure the abilities or performance of the coaches they use.

The emphasis has shifted in the last few years from developing effective coaches and processes to developing a coaching culture (Knights and Poppleton, 2008), with the aim of improving individual and organisational performance.

Job rotation, secondment and shadowing

In an economic climate where opportunities for progression and advancement may be reduced, job rotation can reduce boredom, vary activities and develop or increase skill levels by encouraging employees to change jobs periodically. If properly structured it can be a positive learning experience for employees and have spin-off benefits for business performance. It is usually part of a larger agenda of *job enrichment* which aims to motivate staff and increase productivity. However, it has been criticised for being insufficiently planned and structured, with less focus on employee development and more on achieving organisational outcomes of flexibility and efficiency.

Figure 7.5 Spectrum of coaching skills

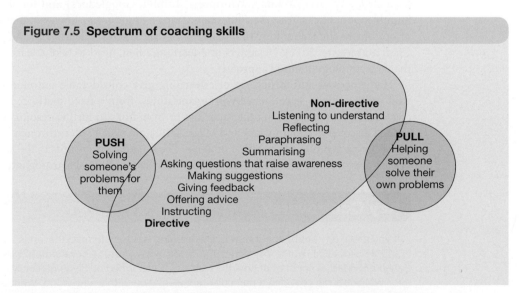

Source: from *Effective Coaching: Lessons from the Coach's Coach*, 3rd edn. (Downey, M.) p. 23. © 2003 South Western, a part of Cengage Learning, Inc., reproduced by permission of Cengage Learning, Inc., **www.cengage.com/permissions** and the author.

Secondment encourages the cross-fertilisation of ideas and usually involves an employee leaving, temporarily, their workplace to work for another organisation. Usually it will be a similar job in a different sector, or a similar area of work with a different focus, e.g. practical versus theoretical. It is usually for a fixed period of time with a structured procedure for feedback and learning.

Shadowing is another popular technique where employees gain an understanding of a job or role in a different department. Usually, the participant is not expected to carry out the job role they are shadowing, but learn about a job by walking through the work day as a shadow to a competent worker. Normally it is temporary, and allows the participant to view at first hand the work environment and skills in practice, with the intention of gaining skills and experience in that area in order to inform job choices, or to develop cross-departmental understanding.

E-learning

'E-learning (or 'electronic' learning) may be defined as learning that is delivered, enabled or mediated using electronic technology for the explicit purpose of training, learning or development in organisations' (CIPD, 2012b: 1).

E-learning, online learning, or technology-enhanced learning has revolutionised the learning landscape generally, and at work has improved access and availability enormously. While many large organisations invest in an online learning platform to provide formal course-based learning (technical or managerial, professional development or legal compliance), a broader range of more informal activities and techniques fall under the umbrella of e-learning, e.g.:

- group based activities such as discussion boards, webinars and podcasts (to replace face-to-face interactions in a classroom);
- individual activities such blogging and micro-blogging (for developing reflective practice).

Moreover, easy access to free high-quality university-led learning opportunities on the web (e.g. through the arrival of MOOCs – massive, open, online courses – see Corbyn, 2012; Parr, 2013) has transformed the landscape of learning more broadly. Social media platforms, open (Twitter, Pinterest) and closed (Blackboard, Moodle, Facebook), have also expanded the opportunities for co-creation and collaboration in learning, enabling links between learners with common interests and of learners to resources. A proliferation of 'apps' or programmes to support the process have emerged: for online reading (Kindle, Ibooks, Coursesmart), for connectedness (Facebook, LinkedIn, Twitter, Instagram), for working together (Wikispace, Mediawiki, Vocaroo, Wimba, Wordpress, Tumblr, Googledocs) and for sharing (Pinterest, Stumbleupon, Flickr, Youtube, Slideshare, Trapit). Some argue, however, that the proliferation of options in the technology of e-learning has sidelined the learner in the process (Colvin-Clark and Mayer, 2011). Designers of e-learning, then, need to take a learner-focused rather than a technology-focused approach.

The processes and structures of e-learning give considerable autonomy to the learner, who will be able to select, usually in organisations, from a fixed platform such as a webinar or e-course, from a range of other activities or from links to further resources. This process of 'guided discovery' (Colvin-Clark and Mayer, 2011) can take learners through activities synchronously or asynchronously, together or alone. The boundaries or limits to the activities and focus of the e-learner are therefore far less well defined than traditional learning interventions.

Key Controversy

If you are in any doubt about how online learning has transformed the landscape of learning and development, watch Wensch (2007: **http://www.youtube.com/watch?v=NLlGopyXT_g**), who provides an account of how the web has transformed our lives generally.

Wensch's clip provides a particular representation of this new world. What is the impact of Wensch's account for e-learning? What is missing from Wensch's account?

The degree and pace of change have set challenges in terms of:

- understanding and regulation, as companies grapple with how to manage access to social media;
- quality, as easy access is no guarantee of veracity or value;
- security, as the easy sharing of material threatens traditional frameworks of ownership and privacy;
- capability, as a distinct set of skills are required to effectively facilitate e-learning and to effectively engage in it.

The next sections consider the last point in detail.

The skills of e-facilitators

Online learning has changed the nature of the activities in which facilitators are expected to engage. The 24/7, 365-day nature of online learning has an impact on expectations not only of technical skills of e-facilitators, but also in communication skills, time and resource management and learning design.

Salmon's work on matching the stages of learning online with the skills of e-facilitators (Sharpe, 2010; Salmon, 2011) has been highly influential in developing practice in the field. Each stage of engagement in e-learning requires the e-moderator to display different sets of skills (see Figure 7.6). At the beginning of the process, e-moderators have a more hands-on

Figure 7.6 Skills required by the e-moderator at different stages of e-learning

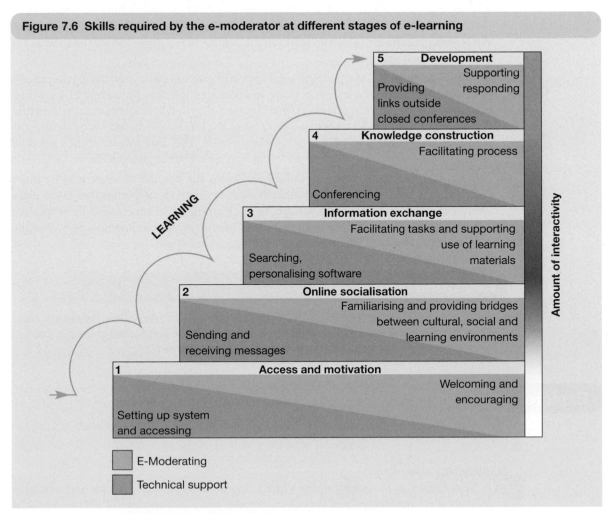

Source: From Salmon (2011) *E-moderating: The Key to Online Teaching and Learning*, 3rd edn, p. 32.

and active role, withdrawing when participants' confidence and capability has risen. The learners, by contrast, can be expected to interact with an increasing number of participants and at a higher frequency as time passes.

Look first at the right-hand side of Figure 7.6.

- During the processes and interactions involved in e-learning, what activities will the e-moderator be engaged in at each stage of the process?
- Think again about the description of e-learning as one of 'guided-discovery' (Colvin-Clark and Mayer, 2011). How does Salmon's model help to understand this process?

The skills of e-learners

Learning theories (considered earlier in the chapter) still have relevance in the e-learning world, although they may be challenged by the new context in which learning is taking place. Cognitive theories, for example, involve selection, organisation and integration. Using this model, we can consider the skills required for e-learning (Mayer, 2005):

- *Selection.* Learners are much more active participants in shaping their own learning in the e-learning context (Sharpe, 2010). One of the challenges of e-learning for the learner is navigating the vast landscape of material that is potentially useful – there is 'too much of a good thing' (Colvin-Clark and Mayer, 2011: 19). Thus, establishing skills associated with selection (which resource is valid?) and choice of material for learning – such as establishing criteria for value and worth in the context of learning – should be included at the outset of any process.

- *Organising.* The mental and practical organisation of material discovered during the process of e-learning requires the learner not only to select appropriately, but to link in a way that provides a coherent representation of what they have discovered. In addition to the activities that the e-facilitator undertakes to guide learning, the learner needs skills in navigating the landscape and organising what they have discovered. This may involve simply good IT skills, or encouragement in logging and recording activity through blogging.

- *Remembering and integrating.* Reusing learning in the context of work may be more challenging in the absence of physical manuals or instructions, if learning has taken place entirely in a virtual environment. Integrating the learning environment with the workplace can enhance learning – for the learner, this will involve understanding how devices in the workplace can enable access to previous learning and materials.

Key Controversy

Revisit the earlier sections of this chapter that consider individual processes of learning. Which, for you, helps to explain the process of learning from the perspective of the e-learner? Can the theories adequately explain experience in this new context?

Look now at the left-hand side of Figure 7.6.

- What activities might the e-learner be engaged in at each stage of the process?

Summarising e-learning

At its best, e-learning provides learning which is more accessible, more flexible and adaptable to individual circumstances, and provides a broader and cheaper range of alternatives. It is attractive because of its flexibility and accessibility whereby learning is available when learners are available to learn. It allows for learning to be completed in 'granules' in the workplace during working hours, rather than through a fixed, inflexible traditional training course.

However, its limitations lie in its use simply as a high-tech alternative to textbook learning where it plays down the social or interactive aspects of learning. The most successful and effective reports of e-learning come from businesses which use a 'blended learning' approach (CIPD, 2008) – e-learning combined with multiple additional routes that support and facilitate learning (Sloman and Rolph, 2003). This can be through e-learning supported by periodic face-to-face learning, or with the knowledge component delivered through e-learning and skills component delivered face-to-face, perhaps supported by online discussions and resource links. The possibilities and combinations are endless and changing and it has been used by organisations as diverse as the National Health Service (Scott, 2008) and Councils (Phillips, 2008) and has demonstrable advantages for a diverse range of employees (Jarvis and Hooley, 2004).

Key Controversy

Some argue generational differences in engagement in e-learning. For example, Prensky (2001) sparked extensive debate with his metaphor of 'digital natives and digital immigrants'. Prensky argues that 'native' young people who have grown up in a world of technology pose a challenge for 'digital immigrants' in adapting their methods of teaching and learning for a 'new' generation.

Find out more about Prensky's metaphor and why it has been so enduring. To what extent do you agree with his assertion? What are the consequences of your views for the development of your skills and those of others?

Off-the-job learning

Off-the-job learning is simply learning that takes place away from the place of work of the employee. However, it is frequently pigeonholed as the 'old' way of doing things – and typified as teacher-centred, classroom-based, process-focused and providing learning that is difficult to transfer to the workplace. It is often criticised as wasteful of time and money, taking the employee away from the practical context in which he or she will have to apply the theoretical knowledge. Yet, learning that takes place away from the place of work gives the employee time and space to consider the new learning, and, if the event includes learners from other departments, workplaces or sectors, allows the cross-fertilisation of ideas and innovations, the chance to consider notions free from distractions, and the opportunity to network with like-minded individuals. Off-the-job learning is epitomised by formal education courses or instructor-led training delivered off the job. Formal education courses normally take place in further or higher education colleges or universities. Instructor-led training is usually delivered by training professionals either directly employed by the organisations or contracted to deliver the event as a training consultant.

Planning and implementation

The planning and implementation stages of learning and development comprise a broad range of practical and specialist activities which include careful consideration of the learning theories explained in the early sections of this chapter.

Planning

Beavers and Rea (2010) suggest that the design stage of the learning and development process in organisations might include:

- Clarifying factors that affect design, both:
  - individual – learning needs and how best to meet them, learning styles, previous experiences;
  - organisational – business priorities, resources, funding, culture, preferences, importance of external accreditation, regulations or rules, legal requirements.

- Identifying aims and objectives – taking into account best practice as well as stakeholder input and influence.
- Determining and sequencing learning content – taking into account the learning needs analysis and the depth of information, this provides information about what is essential, desirable and achievable in the time available.
- Selecting methods and designing learning materials – considering in detail learning theory, which will enable the appropriate selection of different methods and approaches and encourage variety in delivery. (The initial sections of this chapter considered the individual experience of learning and development – pivotal in the design of activities.)
- Selecting assessment and evaluation activities – considering formative and summative assessment for individuals and groups, and the requirements of stakeholders in the design of evaluation (see later).
- Agreeing the plan with stakeholders and relating outcomes to strategy.

Implementation

Given the extensive variation between learning interventions, similarly there are variations in style of delivery. While 'most people will conjure up the image of a trainer delivering a traditional classroom-based intervention' (Mankin, 2009: 232), delivery can take many forms and require many different skill sets.

Explore

Consider the different sets of skills required in order to successfully deliver or effect training or development interventions in the following forms:
  Coach – for support in achieving goals and improving effectiveness
  Mentor – for advice on and support in career and development
  Facilitator – for outcome-based learning
  Trainer – for practice-based learning
  Online tutor – for e-learning
  Teacher – for theory-based learning
  Manager – for facilitating on the job learning, providing feedback, for career development
  Colleague – for learning by observation
  Individual – for self-directed learning
There are some excellent online (e.g. **www.cipd.co.uk**) and paper resources (via popular online and high-street book retailers) for skills development in each of these areas.

- Identify an area where you would like to develop your skills and ask colleagues, tutors or the author (via Twitter, @MairiWatson) for suggestions on suitable resources in each case.

Evaluating learning and development interventions

Despite its strategic importance, the evaluation of HRD is rarely carried out in any organisationally useful way (Anderson, 2007). Two-thirds of workplaces that train their employees also formally assess the impact of training on their performance (Davies *et al.,* 2011), leaving a significant number of organisations where evaluation is not undertaken. Often it is simply because organisations are not sure how to undertake evaluation beyond tried-and-tested approaches and techniques; or, if they are sure how to do it, they are not sure what to do with the results. There is also a fear that it will be expensive and time-consuming, and offer little in the way of results. Finally, because evaluation is often tagged on at the end of training, learning or development, the event or intervention will not have been designed with the end in mind (evaluation and feedback into the next intervention). However, there may be a more fundamental challenge in measuring the impact of learning and development, which compounds the challenges associated with evaluation. The assumption that HRD can add something to 'the bottom line' of a business, and that it can be measured, springs from the literature on high-performance work practices and the best-practice literature (see Chapter 2 on strategic HRM). However, there are issues around the capability of current HR data to provide the type of information stakeholders require (King, 2010): HR data quantify a range of activities from which there may also be qualitative outputs. Green (1999) argues that businesses rarely give sufficient emphasis to researching the impact that specific interventions or tools can have on improved performance. He says that a business's success will be achieved by asking challenging questions such as: Why is the organisation doing this activity? What difference does it make? Does the difference (return) justify the investment? Could we get the same results in a more cost-effective way? Does the difference anticipated align with our business strategy and objectives? These can be simplified to: Why should we do this? What difference do we want? How are we going to measure it? Is it cost-effective?

The benefits of engaging in the process of measuring the value of HRD include improving its position as an employer of choice through a positive effect on motivation and morale; enhancing employee contribution; and supporting the delivery of company objectives by developing the skills in line with organisational needs. HRD is an aspect of the psychological contract in organisations, and potentially skills the workforce to be better than the competition. At the very least, HRD sometimes means a business can operate within legal requirements. Measurements should go beyond post-course evaluation to measuring wastage, error rates, cost benefit, customer satisfaction, staff opinions and motivation, and can attempt to link specific outcomes to the training delivered, analyse cost-effectiveness, demonstrate contribution to strategic objectives, and link HRD to performance via a performance management system.

That said, evaluation is less of a calculation than it is a judgment (Kearns, 2005). A rigorous scientific approach to evaluation, though desirable in theory, is not practical. Therefore, it involves a number of subjective considerations – the measurement itself is subjective, the interpretation of the results is subjective, and the values and goals of the stakeholders in the process are different and potentially conflicting. Attaching a financial value to HRD, which means estimating the financial impact of employee behaviour, is at least challenging. However, one might argue, it is no less challenging than assessing the impact on the organisation of marketing efforts, such as advertising or networking. Isolating the impact of HRD is therefore not insurmountable: for example, alongside the many tools suggested in this section, one might establish a control group, consider the impact of other influences (e.g. market or financial changes in the environment) or use professional judgment.

One remaining conundrum concerns what evaluation purports to measure: most models we consider here are concerned with *intermediate* outcomes, which may or may not lead to business success, e.g. cost of training, reduction of turnover or absence, improved morale or motivation, all of which, it is hoped, will have some broader business impact. These *performance* indicators may not give the best information, as they measure only the specific outcome they purport to measure and nothing more. Writers still struggle to elevate the measures associated with HRD to a higher, strategic level.

Such questions are at the heart of evaluation, and this section outlines some of the key models and approaches to judging the contribution HRD behaviour can make to organisational performance. Evaluation at its best flows throughout learning in the organisational context, and happens as events unfold using multiple methods of feedback and communication, rather than on a piece of paper at the end of a training course.

Categorising evaluation

Three themes are apparent in the development of measurement and evaluation in HRD (Wang and Spitzer, 2005):

- *Evaluating practice* – typified by the seminal work of Kirkpatrick (1960 – see the next section) and considering the impact of (usually) training interventions.
- *Evaluating process* – typified by the return on investment (ROI) work seeking to justify training and HRD expenditure based on the measurements of benefits versus costs of training.

- *Evaluating experience* – based on an awareness of business reality and, by extension, of the strategic contribution that HRD can make, which is still an emerging field of analysis.

Evaluating practice

This stage in the development of evaluation literature relies heavily on Kirkpatrick's (1960) enduring work, which, while it has been criticised (Swanson, 2001), has had enviable staying power in the world of learning evaluation. Kirkpatrick proposed four levels of evaluation of learning and training. A close examination reveals that Kirkpatrick was more concerned with the transfer of learning to the workplace and organisational results than is often represented:

1 *Reactions* for Kirkpatrick are defined as 'how well the trainees liked a particular training program'. Reactions are typically measured formally, and immediately, at the end of training, but can be measured informally by the trainer/facilitator during the event.

   Measures include: reaction questionnaires, observation of reactions, relationships, body language, participant interactions, questioning by trainer and questions asked by participants.

2 *Learning* is defined by Kirkpatrick as the 'principles, facts, and techniques [that] were understood and absorbed by the conferees'. This has the purpose of measuring the change in the knowledge of the learner post-event, compared with the knowledge pre-event.

   Measures include: written, verbal and practical tests, interviews with participants and managers at pre-determined times after the event, self-assessment, performance review procedures, questionnaires, interviews, peer group discussion.

3 *Behaviour* is about changes in on-the-job behaviour, which must be evaluated in the workplace itself.

   Measures include: self, peer and manager appraisals, observation, measurement of outputs/results, interviews, product/service sampling.

4 *Results*. Kirkpatrick relied on a range of examples to make clear his meaning here: 'Reduction of costs; reduction of turnover and absenteeism; reduction of grievances; increase in quality and quantity of production; or improved morale which, it is hoped, will lead to some of the previously stated results.'

   Measures include: measurement of performance indicators, e.g. absenteeism, grievances, production, customer satisfaction, turnover, targets, stakeholder feedback, return on investment (ROI) measures (see the following section).

It is difficult to over-estimate the popularity of Kirkpatrick's model. Some 91 per cent of those surveyed in the CIPD's Learning and Development Survey 2006 evaluated training, learning and development activities and 98 per cent of those used exercises to measure Kirkpatrick's level 1 outcomes. Some 75 per cent used level 2 evaluation exercises, 62 per cent level 3 and 36 per cent go as far as level 4.

Missing from Kirkpatrick's model is any consideration of the pre-event state of affairs or an assessment of how level 4 results affect the business. Hamblin (1974, 2007) added this 'ultimate level' to consider the extent to which the event has affected the ultimate profitability and survival of the organisation.

Kirkpatrick's model has operational and practitioner appeal, and a role in demonstrating the value that learning and development activities can add to organisations. Even at this level, organisations identify that their efforts to measure the impact of learning and development activities do not go far enough, and while there is an increasing emphasis on evaluation, cost, time, lack of effective measures, organisational priorities and lack of knowledge and understanding act against the best attempts of those who seek to establish the contribution that learning and development make to business performance (CIPD, 2012c).

Evaluating process

As noted by Scott (2010:14):

> In difficult times, HR gets a mindless fixation on return on investment.... Everybody thinks they should measure the return on investment on training. But most people in learning and development don't know what it means, or understand that it has specific technical requirements.

An increasing awareness of the business reality of global competition, pressure from adverse economic conditions and increased demands for managerial accountability (Wang and Spitzer, 2005) and availability of advanced HR metrics (Scott, 2010) have contributed to the popularity of ROI approaches. These measures have stimulated much critical debate in the world of HRD (Phillips, 2005). At its simplest, ROI calculates of the costs and benefits of training events, and it is usually represented as an (apparently) straightforward formula:

$$\frac{\text{Benefits from training} - \text{Costs of training}}{\text{Costs of training} \times 100\%} = \%\text{ROI}$$

There the simplicity ends, as measuring the costs and benefits of the training is often far from straightforward. Thompson (2005) argues that to measure ROI effectively, training has to be divided into two categories: knowledge and technical skills (content or 'hard' training); and attitude and interpersonal skills (process or 'soft' training). The former is fairly easy to assess for ROI purposes, but the latter (often the larger proportion of companies' training effort in terms of time, money or profile) is a 'problem area of evaluation'. The usefulness or otherwise of the measure is dependent on the quality of the information that feeds it. Sophisticated models (Swanson, 2001; Phillips, 2002; Kearns, 2005) emphasise the importance of:

- the collection of information post-event or programme, including evaluation instruments that are purposeful, timely, and multilevel;
- isolating the effects of the training or programme;
- converting the data to monetary value;
- calculating ROI;
- identifying other, intangible benefits.

Potentially, the sophisticated emphasis on financial and strategic measurement of outputs is at odds with the values-based practice of training and development, and Dee and Hatton (2006:40) argue for an incremental approach:

> Learning and development should demonstrate a business benefit, but it is often impossible to go from training straight to ROI. A possible alternative is a staged process which focuses on improving the quality of programmes, increasing the transfer of learning to the workplace and measuring against specific metrics established from the outset.

Phillips (2012) suggests that the key to effectiveness in ROI measurements is in planning for them at the outset of learning and development activities. Moreover, ROI measures (or metrics) should be attempted at each level of Kirkpatrick's model, which may include:

- *Measures of training activity* – how much training and development take place? Percentage of payroll, training amount spent per employee per annum, average number of training days per employee/manager per annum, HRD staff per 100 employees.

- Measures of training results:
  - at reaction level: average percentage of positive course ratings;
  - at learning level: average percentage gain in learning per-course based on difference between pre- and post-course results;
  - at behaviour level: average percentage of improvement in on-the-job performance after training;
  - bottom line: profits per employee per year;
  - cost savings as a ratio of training expenses.
- *Measures of training efficiency* – training cost per delegate hour.

Despite the limitations, discussion of ROI has increased the awareness among HRD practitioners that, in order to justify the existence of HRD interventions, there has to be some attempt to measure the financial contribution it makes to the organisations, however challenging this is in practice (Thompson, 2005; Phillips, 2012).

Thompson (2005) suggests five methods of gathering information to inform an ROI judgement:

- Refining end-of-course 'happy sheets' to ask 'What will you do/do differently as a result of this training?' and 'How exactly will each element of this course help you to do a better job?'
- Following up with line managers and participants at a later date, asking for feedback on the things they have used from the training.
- E-mailing a sample of people, asking them about past 'critical incidents' (e.g. in management of communication), what skills they used to deal with them, and where they acquired those skills without hinting that training could be the primary source.
- Interviewing participants, their managers and other significant stakeholders before and after training.
- Asking participants to complete pre- and post-event evaluations.

Benchmarking can also provide information on the evaluation of process in HRD (see Box 7.2). Benchmarking is a set of related activities that support and enhance strategies of imitation or collaboration leading to a competitive advantage. Walton (1999: 303) notes that 'some organisations have relied excessively on comparative performance data as a key plank in their competitive strategy . . . this may help a company meet competitors' performance, but it is unlikely to reveal practices to beat them'. Harrison (2009: 250) also argues that benchmarking measures best value or best practice and not the value added to the organisation by the training or learning intervention. To measure added value, Harrison argues, means asking and answering a different question: 'What critical difference has the service made to the organisation's capability to differentiate itself from other similar organisations, thereby giving it a leading edge?'.

Box 7.2   **Benchmarking**

For HRD, Walton (1999: 313) suggests three levels at which benchmarking can operate:

- The level of organisational learning:
  - How have other organisations generated a learning climate?
- The level of organisation-wide HRD processes:
  - How have other organisations identified and developed competencies for staff?
  - How have other organisations balanced on- and off-the-job learning?
- The level of training and development activity and resource allocation:
  - What percentage of payroll is devoted to training and development in other organisations?

There are three types of benchmarking: competitive benchmarking, which assesses key parts of the organisation's processes, systems and procedures against those of chosen competitors in the field; best-practice/functional benchmarking, which compares particular aspects of an organisation's product or service with organisations considered to be 'the best' in this area, and may involve collaboration; and internal benchmarking, which considers and compares similar processes within an organisation to achieve internal best practice, e.g. induction, appraisal.

Evaluating experience

The evaluation of experience draws on a desire to demonstrate overall contribution to business performance (Anderson, 2007) in a way that goes beyond the previous section. For example, Brinkerhoff (2005) supports this view that traditional evaluation models and methods do little to improve organisational performance. His 'success case method' argues that the main challenge for organisations is how to leverage learning – consistently, quickly and effectively – into improved performance. Responsibility for this does not lie solely with HRD professionals, and while the diffusion of responsibility poses challenges, especially for evaluation, it opens the way for a consideration of a 'whole organisation approach' to evaluation, which will ultimately be more effective in turning learning into organisational advantage. He uses the metaphor of marriage to explain that most evaluation considers the wedding (the training), whereas what we really need to know about is the whole marriage (the training, plus what comes afterwards), the entire training to organisational performance process.

Making evaluation work: closing the loop

The initial diagrams for planning learning and development represented the process as a loop, where evaluation ultimately fed into the development of future plans. Closing the loop gives purpose to the evaluation activities, and without that there is little point in engaging in what is potentially difficult, complex and judgmental.

Learning and development: the national perspective

Considering the broader national and international context of skills development has clear relevance for organisational HRD strategies, as the frameworks relate to how new recruits have acquired and continue to acquire knowledge and skills relevant to work. Thus, making the right choices about training and development is central to a country's national competitiveness (Finegold and Soskice, 1999; Van den Berg et al., 2006; Descy and Tchibozo, 2009; Garrett et al., 2010; Sheehan, 2012). To ensure that a country achieves the level of skills it needs to compete internationally, they ought also to be the concern of governments and European bodies (Leitch, 2006). Set against a backdrop of an ageing population and high youth unemployment, there is scope for a fresh look at the nature and purposes of the skills policy in the UK. Thus, at the level of government policy, a consideration of how weaknesses in the national approach to skills development translate into skills deficiencies and shortages in organisations, and correspondingly how strengths translate into innovation and organisational strength, helps to underline the increasing importance of workplace learning as a source of competitiveness. At the level of the business, there is strong evidence that investment in training and development generate substantial gains for firms (Ballot, 2003; Descy and Tchibozo, 2009). Furthermore, the research under-emphasises macro-social outcomes (crime, social cohesion, citizenship, civic and political participation). In addition, for the individual, there are likely to be substantial personal benefits – including improved health, better parenting, crime reduction and social inclusion (Descy and Tchibozo, 2009).

However, researching the link between education and training and economic growth is limited by the poor quality of data, particularly in inter-country comparisons, and by the fact that human capital is mostly measured by formal education, training and qualifications (Descy and Tessaring, 2005: 16). National vocational education and training systems (NVETs), which provide country-wide training within a framework of standards, exist internationally but with differences in key features, aims and objectives and underlying principles. The consideration of NVET systems is complex and context-bound; however, it is essential to ensure an understanding of the extent to which, on an increasingly competitive international stage, individual countries can meaningfully compete.

Moreover, rapidly changing economic conditions make learning and replication difficult, if not impossible. Furthermore, drawing conclusions about the link between education and macro-social outcomes is difficult, as these 'effects are mostly indirect and conditional on other – often more powerful – contextual determinants' (Descy and Tessaring, 2005: 37) and embedded in the broader socioeconomic system (Descy and Tchibozo, 2009).

Explore

- Read Descy and Tshibozo's (2009) full report at **http://www.cedefop.europa.eu/EN/ Files/4068_en.pdf**

The European dimension

Skills policy and skills development in the UK are located in the broader context of European frameworks and regulations. The difficulty with this area is not that there is a dearth of information available, but that there is so much, in so many places. The European Commission (EC), the Organisation for Economic Co-operation and Development (OECD), the European Centre for the Development of Vocational Training (CEDEFOP) and the Chartered Institute of Personnel and Development (CIPD) all provide information across a range of national systems of vocational education and training. However, because of the variety of information available and given the different political, social, economic, technological and legal development paths as well as different styles of management and cultural understanding, realistic comparison is not easy.

Explore

CEDEFOP has published reports on vocational education and training research since 1998, including its 'VET in Europe' series, presenting a comprehensive review of current research, its results and the implications for policy, practice and future research (see **http://libserver. cedefop.europa.eu**). They also attend to the theoretical and methodological foundations with reference given to economic, sociological, pedagogical and other fields of research.

- Using this resource, explore the approaches of at least two other European countries, e.g.:
  - Germany: VET in Europe: Country Report 2012: **http://libserver.cedefop.europa.eu/ vetelib/2012/2012_CR_DE.pdf**
  - France: VET in Europe: Country Report 2011: **http://libserver.cedefop.europa.eu/ vetelib/2011/2011_CR_FR.pdf**

Explore box continued

● As you read through the information, consider the following:
  – What are the strengths and weaknesses of the approach about which you are reading?
  – What aspects of the VET system would be transferable to the UK context?
  – What challenges could be faced in doing so?
  – What are the limitations of seeking to transfer ideas from other national contexts?

Each European country has a number of routes through education and training. While the sequential nature of the French system contrasts with the dual system of the German approach, you will see from the next section that the UK's approach is the most diffuse, complex and lacking in clarity. Keep and Mayhew (2001) describe the UK approach as a 'blizzard of initiatives' with a system of qualifications that is a 'sprawling, complex mess, incomprehensible to employers and trainees alike' which involves 'near-ceaseless organisational change' that does not produce results, and fails to deliver lasting and significant change on a number of fronts. Arguably, the link between learning and work is less well cemented in the UK than in the other countries we have considered. Attempts at imposing order and reform (Leitch, 2006) have been threatened by more recent changes which reflect the current economic conditions.

Skills policy in the UK

The government's skills policies in the UK have typically been concerned with the development of vocational education from around the age of 14 to adulthood. Sometimes the soubriquet, National Vocational Education and Training (NVET), is used as an umbrella description for activity in this area, which allows comparison (as we have seen) with other national approaches. In England, all NVET sits within the National Qualifications Framework (**www.ofqual.gov.uk**), which in turn sits within the European Qualifications Framework (**http://ec.europa.eu/education/lifelong-learning-policy/eqf_en.htm**). Qualifications are classified according to levels – entry to 8. Ofqual (**www.ofqual.gov.uk**; see Figure 7.7) and the Quality Assurance Agency (**www.qaa.org.uk**) are government agencies that have a regulatory role in ensuring the appropriate application of the framework, the former in GCSEs, A-levels and vocational qualifications to level 3 and the latter in higher education (bachelor degrees, masters and doctorates) from levels 4 to 8.

Figure 7.7 The UK qualifications framework (www.ofqual.gov.uk)

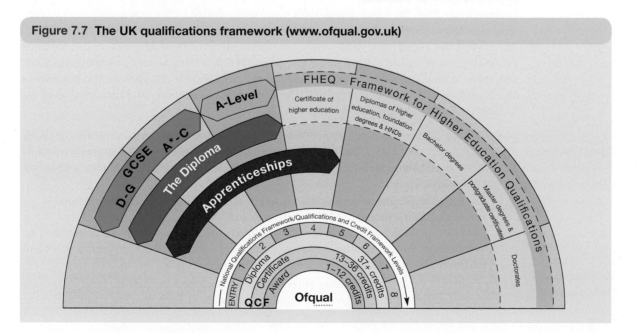

In terms of the government policy that supports this area, significant changes have taken place in UK skills policy since the last edition. The dramatic fall in the financial fortunes of the UK since the start of 2008, the growth in unemployment (particularly long-term) and issues in the UK banking system have highlighted the importance of developing workplace skills in the success or failure of the UK in a globally competitive marketplace. However, the declining fortunes of the economy and a change of government have required a refocusing on the structures and funding of the systems and processes that support it. For example, Train to Gain, The Learning and Skills Councils and a number of government departments that underpinned the previous government's skills policy have been disbanded.

The journey of policy development in the UK has taken the country from an era where there was no clear national skills policy (1970s) to one, in the last decade, that emphasised voluntarism and joint investment (employer, employee and government). Despite activity to raise levels of qualification in the population, to increase employability and improve competitiveness and productivity in the UK (Leitch, 2006), major decisions about workplace training and HRD are primarily in the hands of employers and the VET system is still one based on voluntarism (CIPD, 2012d). For a review of the skills policy in the UK up to 2010, please see the previous edition of this book (Chapter 8). This edition picks up the story at the change of government in 2010.

2011–2013: from the Wolf Report to 'Rigour and Responsiveness in Skills': the Coalition Government's activities

With the change of government came a change of direction and emphasis in skills policy, and a number of government-sponsored reports and reviews were conducted to allow policy to be refreshed in line with the Coalition Government's priorities and policies.

Two government departments share responsibility for the development and funding of the post-16 learning and skills policy in the UK:

- For 16–18 education – the Department for Education (**www.education.gov.uk**)
- For 19 years old and over – the Department for Business, Innovation and Skills (BIS) (**https://www.gov.uk/government/organisations/department-for-business-innovation-skills**). BIS is supported by the UK Commission for Employment and Skills (**www.UKCES.org.uk**)

Pre-19 vocational education

In September 2010, Professor Alison Wolf was commissioned by the new government to conduct a review of vocational education for 14–19 year-olds. The report was published in March 2011 (Wolf, 2011) and made wide-ranging recommendations about the area's reform, focusing on linking vocational education to the labour market, providing accurate information about the value of qualifications and simplifying the system dramatically. Following consultation, the government's response in May 2011 (Department for Education, 2011) accepted all of the recommendations and promised:

- All young people will study and achieve in English and Mathematics, ideally to GCSE A*-C by the age of 19. The 'academic core' of education would be supplemented by vocational development. Lower attaining pupils would be supported to achieve appropriate qualifications.
  - See **http://www.education.gov.uk/schools/teachingandlearning/qualifications/otherqualifications/a00222542/vocational-qualifications-16-19-year-olds** for information on the current review of vocational qualifications for 16–19 year-olds. The outcomes of the consultation will affect vocational education from September 2014 and will be reported in performance tables from September 2016.
- Performance tables and funding rules would be reviewed to provide information on content, assessment and progression. Funding would move from funding qualifications to funding learners.

- The Education Funding Agency (EFA) provides revenue and capital funding for education for learners between the ages of 3 and 19, or the ages of 3 and 25 for those with learning difficulties and disabilities. Their website – **http://www.education.gov.uk/aboutdfe/executiveagencies/efa** – provides up-to-date information on how pre-19 education is funded.

- The Skills Funding Agency, however, has a role in providing funding for Apprenticeships for 16–18 year-olds, as well as a broader remit post-19. Along with the National Apprenticeship Service they distribute government funding for workforce training to colleges and providers. Their updated funding rules – **http://readingroom.lsc.gov.uk/SFA/Funding_Rules_2013_14_Jan_2013.pdf** – outline their broader responsibilities across vocational education for all ages.

- The simplification of apprenticeships (16 and over) so as to make it easier for employers to offer them, and young people to access them.

  - The National Apprenticeship Service (NAS) supports, funds and co-ordinates the delivery of Apprenticeships throughout England. Their website – **http://www.apprenticeships.org.uk/** – provides up-to-date information on the development of apprenticeships' structure and funding

Explore

- Read the full Wolf report at: https://www.education.gov.uk/publications/eOrderingDownload/The%20Wolf%20Report.pdf

- Consider in detail the 27 recommendations from page 12 onwards. To what extent have the recommendations been implemented and how? (For more information on the report's history and development, visit http://www.education.gov.uk/search/results?q=vocational+education)

Post-19 vocational education and skills

In post-19 vocational education and skills, the degree of change has been equally great. In November 2010, the government published two sets of documents to set out their new strategy for further education and skills:

- *Skills for Sustainable Growth* (**https://www.gov.uk/government/publications/skills-for-sustainable-growth-strategy-document**), which set out the government strategy for improving and using skills for sustainable growth and extending social mobility and inclusion.

- A series of documents on the theme 'New Challenges, New Chances' covered further education funding (**https://www.gov.uk/government/consultations/new-challenges-new-chances-next-steps-in-implementing-the-further-education-reform-programme**).

  - In addition, the government is currently piloting major changes to the skills funding regime for vocational qualifications in England. The 'Employer Ownership of Skills' pilot, overseen by the UK Commission for Employment and Skills (UKCES), routes skills funding directly to employers in England providing the opportunity through bids for direct access to up to £250 million of public investment over the next two years to design and deliver their own training solutions (**www.ukces.org.uk/ourwork/employer-ownership**).

More recently, *Rigour and Responsiveness in Skills* (April 2013) – **https://www.gov.uk/government/publications/rigour-and-responsiveness-in-skills** – provides an updated skills strategy outlining priorities in making the system more rigorous and responsive to need.

The UKCES is a key body in this area: its establishment was a key strand of the previous government's policy in this area (Leitch Review, 2006). As a non-departmental public body, it provides leadership on skills and employment issues for the four nations of the UK. Under the new government its role is to:

- provide world-class labour market intelligence;
- work with sectors and business leaders to develop and deliver solutions to generate greater employer investment in skills;
- maximise the impact of changed employment and skills policies and employer behaviour to help drive jobs, growth and an internationally competitive skills base.

In 2012–13, their 'priority outcomes' were:

- more employers investing in the skills of their people;
- more career opportunities for young people;
- more collective action by employers through stronger sectors and local networks;
- more employers stepping up and taking ownership of skills.

In April 2010, the Commission became the guardian of Investors in People (**www.investorsinpeople.co.uk**). The Investors in People (IiP) Standard was developed in 1990 and revised in 2004 (placing emphasis on employee involvement and on maximising their potential) and is a national quality standard setting a level of good practice for improving an organisation's performance and competitiveness through a planned approach to setting and communicating business objectives and developing people to meet these objectives.

New entities to replace the former 'Regional Development Agencies' – Local Enterprise Partnerships (LEPs) – have also been established as part of the government reforms. LEPs sit between the Department for Business, Innovation and Skills and The Department for Communities and Local Government to provide leadership on economic priorities, including skills strategies for local areas.

Explore

The government's skills policy represents a simplification of the previous arrangement for skills development in the UK. However, it also firmly re-establishes employer responsibility in this area.

- Read the upbeat assessment of the UKCES pilot at **http://www.peoplemanagement.co.uk/pm/articles/2012/11/government-announces-extra-150m-in-skills-funding.htm**
- What are the challenges for employers in taking ownership of skills development?
- How can LEPs support businesses in the development of skills?

Scotland, Wales and Northern Ireland

Throughout this section, the predominant view has been that of the UK, but in many sections this applies only to England as the devolution of governance in the UK means that the government and institutional frameworks in England, Wales, Northern Ireland and Scotland are different. For example, in Scotland, the government has launched its own skills strategy – 'Skills for Scotland: Accelerating the Recovery and Increasing Sustainable Ecomonic Growth' – available at **http://www.scotland.gov.uk/Publications/2010/10/04125111/0**.

Concluding comments

Learning and development are not just of significance for individuals, but also of strategic importance to employers. This is recognised by many of the organisations which have invested in their human resource development, as *People Management* reports in its regular company profiles and annual features on the National Training Awards. It is also acknowledged in the various national schemes to develop skills. It is therefore crucial that managers and policy-makers understand the processes of learning and development.

Of course, learning and development are significant for individuals, too, both to prosper in employment and society and, more importantly, to fulfil their potential. Their learning and development take place through life, not just during their employment, so that employers both benefit from and contribute to it. It has to be recognised, therefore, that human resource development has a moral dimension, and juggles with empowering and controlling employees.

Summary

This chapter has covered broad ground, from the individual experience of learning, through learning and development as an organisational process and then as a national process. For example, the chapter has discussed:

- Learning and development are of strategic importance to organisations, and of high importance to the broader economy, reflected in organisational plans and government policies.

- There are many definitions of 'learning' and 'development' and many ways in which learning and development can play out in organisations.

- The significance of learning and development for individuals.

- Adult learners have particular expectations of, and requirements from, learning and development opportunities.

- Theories of learning provide explanations of how learning takes place and assistance in optimising the effectiveness of organisational learning interventions.

- In organisations, the planned process of learning and development includes: identifying learning needs, aims and objectives; determining learning strategies; planning and implementation; and evaluation.

- E-learning, or online learning, has grown exponentially in the last few years, with new supportive technologies to enhance the experience, but also to pose skills challenges for learners and facilitators alike.

- The national context of learning and development – or government skills policy – has a significant impact on the quality and impact of learning and development in organisations.

Questions

1 What are the main definitions of learning and development? How do these differ? Why do you consider that to be the case?

2 What are the main components of employability?

3 What impact can the learning theories discussed in the first section of this chapter have on the design and delivery of learning interventions in your organisation?

4 To what extent can learning and development support the business strategy?

5 Who are the stakeholders in learning and development?

6 How idealistic or cynical are calls for activities such as mentoring and coaching in today's flexible organisations?

7 What are the differences between mentoring and coaching?

8 Is mentoring elitist or empowering? Are there other possible interpretations?

9 Consider an off-the-job learning experience you have had recently. Did you enjoy it? Did you learn something that you were able to apply to your job on return to the workplace? If it was successful, what contributed to this? If it was unsuccessful, why do you think this was the case?

10 What would be the advantages and disadvantages of each method of training delivery for the people in your organisation? Which methods would be best for which skills?

11 What are the benefits of investing in measuring the impact of training and learning on organisational outcomes?

12 Why are most organisations reluctant to carry out any meaningful analysis? What evaluation techniques have you used or been subject to?

13 How would you summarise the UK's skills policy?

Case study

Learning and development at First Group

By using interactive drama, First Group has got the message across to staff that safety is not just about implementing rules and regulations, it's about people's lives.

The challenge

Getting the health and safety message across is a constant and daunting challenge in any company. But when the organisation concerned is leading transport operator First Group, which employs 130,000 people in the UK and US and is responsible for carrying billions of passengers every year, it is a challenge that has to be met. Traditional training methods that use teaching formats, with staff expected to listen and absorb, don't have the necessary impact to shift staff perspectives, says Naveed Qamar, the group's safety director. 'Talking at people just makes them resistant; they sit there with folded arms. We needed something different.'

The programme

That 'something' was interactive drama with a health and safety message. The idea was to trigger an emotional response and encourage staff to see health and safety as a personal concern. 'We wanted to challenge perspectives on safety – that it isn't just a bunch of rules and regulations that have to be implemented; it's about people's lives,' says Qamar.

L&D consultancy Forum Interactive came up with a series of scenarios highlighting relevant issues, from which they developed 20-minute plays. They started with the aftermath of a fatal accident where a young child is hit by a bus, and focused on the emotional impact on the bus driver, his family and colleagues, as well as on the little girl's family. The play encouraged the audience to ask themselves how they would cope and to think about the impact their actions could have on others.

The play was first unveiled at a safety conference for senior directors in September 2006 and since then has been seen by more than 1,500 operators. 'The reaction when it was first performed was beyond our expectations,' says Qamar. 'There was a real buzz.'

Subsequent plays have dealt with issues such as the little girl's mother suing the bus company on discovering that safety procedures have not been implemented. This highlighted liability issues and encouraged managers to think about leadership and implementing procedures. The message that comes across is that every staff member is personally responsible for health and safety and that, ultimately, it's the individual's actions that count.

The results

Drama-based learning has had a significant effect on First Group's safety record. Since January 2007 there has been a 47 per cent reduction in time lost through injury, with passenger injuries down by 24 per cent, according to Qamar. He puts the drop in collision and red signal mistakes (when a driver fails to stop at a warning signal) at 30 per cent. Meanwhile the number of US schoolchildren who get left on the bus – usually because they fall asleep and the driver doesn't check – has more than halved. 'In fact,' adds Qamar, 'last month, out of several million journeys, the figure was zero.'

The HR view

Naveed Qamar is group safety director at First Group. Drama-based training was the 'something completely different' that the company needed to switch people onto safety issues, says Qamar, and Forum Interactive came up with storylines that covered the issues they experience. 'They were very powerful,' he recalls, 'and I actually got emotional just reading them. The first session was totally secret – people knew something was happening but had no idea what – and some of the toughest people in the company were brought to tears. The actors are right in their faces and screaming and they have to pay attention.' The safety conference is the right setting, he believes, because all the directors are in one place and the message cascades down. 'However,' he adds, 'we have taken the interactive training to various subdivisions and to the US.

Case study continued

Scenarios from last year's conference have also been put on DVD. The aim is to teach staff about ways to have better conversations on safety and to engage them, prompting them to report hazards and report injuries.'

The employee view

John Evans is group HR director at First Group. 'I am HR director but this drama-based training was introduced before I joined the company so I have experienced it rather than implemented it,' explains Evans. He believes any interactive training builds understanding and the scenarios help reinforce the fact that safety is the core value of the organisation. 'It also challenges our thinking and own behaviour,' he says.

'You come out thinking, "I could do that differently" – it's a bit like holding up a mirror to your own behaviour. The scenes encourage us to talk about the issues and bring home that every passenger is an individual with a specific reason for travelling.' They help everyone appreciate what passengers' issues are, he says, whether it is carrying a pram or physical infirmity, for example. 'The power of this is such that we never manage to complete the session,' he admits.

'We always run out of time. It would be fantastic to get everybody involved but it's a challenge – money, time, logistics – so the primary focus is on senior managers.'

Source: http://www.hrmagazine.co.uk/hr/case-studies/1015070/learning-development-study-first-group

Questions

1 How can the learning theories described in the first part of the chapter explain why learning in this way can be effective?

2 What are the benefits – and the challenges – of using techniques like those described in the case study?

References and further reading

Those texts marked with an asterisk are recommended for further reading.

Anderson, V. (2007) *The Value of Learning: From Return on Investment to Return on Expectation*. London: CIPD.

Anderson, L. W. and Krathwohl, D. R. (eds) (2001) *A Taxonomy for Learning, Teaching and Assessing: A Revision of Bloom's Taxonomy of Educational Objectives: Complete Edition*. New York: Longman.

Argyris, C. and Schön, D.A. (1978) *Organisational Learning: A Theory of Action Perspective*. Reading, MA: Addison-Wesley.

Ashworth, L. (2006) 'Training Needs Analysis is better carried out at an individual level than as a 'sheep-dip', *People Management*, 23 March: 1.

*Atkinson, R.L., Atkinson, R.C., Smith, E.E., Bem, D.J. and Nolen-Hoeksema, S. (1999) *Hilgard's Introduction to Psychology*, 13th edn. New York: Harcourt Brace College Publishing.

Ballot, G. (2003) *Firms investment in human capital: Sponsoring and Effect on Performance*. European Conference on The Future of Work: challenges for the European Employment Strategy, Athens.

Bayliss, V. (1998) *Redefining Work: An RSA Initiative*. London: The Royal Society for the Encouragement of the Arts, Manufactures and Commerce.

Beattie, D. (2002) *President's Message, Annual Report 2002*. London: CIPD.

Beevers, K. and Rea, A. (2010). *Learning and Development Practice*. London: CIPD.

Binsted, D.S. (1980) 'Design for learning in management training and development: a view', *Journal of European Industrial Training*, 4, 8 (whole issue).

Blackler, F. (2000) 'Collective wisdom', *People Management*, 22 June: 61.

Bloom, B.S., Englehart, M., Furst, E., Hill, W. and Krathwohl, D. (1956) *Taxonomy of Educational Objectives, Handbook 1: The Cognitive Domain*. London: Longmans Green.

Borger, R. and Seaborne, A.E.M. (1966) *The Psychology of Learning*. Harmondsworth: Penguin.

Boyatzis, R.E. (1982) *The Competent Manager: A Model for Effective Performance*. New York: Wiley.

Brinkerhoff, R. O. (2005). 'The success case method: a strategic evaluation approach to increasing the value and effect of training', *Advances in Developing Human Resources*, 7(1): 86–102.

Brockmann, M., Clarke, L. and Winch, C. (2008) 'Knowledge, skills and competence: European divergences in vocational education and training (VET) – the English, German, and Dutch cases', *Oxford Review of Education*, 34, 5: 547–67.

Burgoyne, J.G. and Hodgson, V.E. (1983) 'Natural learning and managerial action: a phenomenological study in the field setting', *Journal of Management Studies*, 20, 3: 387–99.

Castells, M. (1996) *The Information Age: Economy, Society and Culture. I: The Rise of the Network Society*. Oxford: Blackwell.

Castells, M. (1998) *The Information Age: Economy, Society and Culture. III: End of Millennium*. Oxford: Blackwell.

CBI/NUS (2011) *Working Towards Your Future: Making the Most of your Time in HE*. London: CBI.

CIPD (2002) *Training in the Knowledge Economy*. London: CIPD.

CIPD (2005) *A Barometer of HR Trends and Prospects 2005: An Overview of CIPD Surveys*. London: CIPD.

CIPD (2006) *Learning and Development*, Annual Survey Report. London: CIPD.

CIPD (2007) *The Changing HR Function: Transforming HR*. London: CIPD.

CIPD (2008) *Learning and Development*, Annual Survey Report. London: CIPD.

CIPD (2010) *Using the head and heart at work: a business case for soft skills*, Research Report. London: CIPD.

CIPD (2012a) *Coaching*, Factsheet. London: CIPD. Online: **http://www.cipd.co.uk/hr-resources/factsheets/coaching-mentoring.aspx** (accessed August 2013).

CIPD (2012b) *E Learning*, Factsheet. London: CIPD. Online: **http://www.cipd.co.uk/hr-resources/factsheets/e-learning. aspx** (accessed August 2013).

CIPD (2012c) *Learning and Talent Development Survey*. London: CIPD.

CIPD (2012d) *Skills Policy in the UK*. London, CIPD. Online: **http://www.cipd.co.uk/hr-resources/factsheets/skills-policy-uk.aspx** (accessed August 2013).

CIPD (2013) *Identifying learning and talent development needs*. London: CIPD. Online: **http://www.cipd.co.uk/hr-resources/factsheets/identifying-learning-talent-development-needs. aspx** (accessed August 2013).

*Chartered Institute of Personnel and Development (ongoing) Factsheets.

Coleman, P. (1990) 'Psychological ageing' in J. Bond and P. Coleman (eds) *Ageing and Society: An Introduction to Social Gerontology*. London: Sage, pp. 62–88.

Collins, H. (1993) 'Untidy minds in action', *Times Higher Education Supplement*, 1066, 9 April: 15, 17.

Colvin-Clark, R. and Mayer, R. (2011). *E-Learning and the Science of Discovery*. San Francisco CA: John Wiley.

*Cooley, M. (1987) *Architect or Bee? The Human Price of Technology*. London: Hogarth Press.

Corbyn, Z. (2012) 'This could be huge', *Times Higher Education*, 6 December. Online: **http://www.timeshighereducation. co.uk/422034.article** (accessed January 2014).

Cox, E., Bachkirova, T. and Clutterbuck, D. (2009) *The Complete Handbook of Coaching*. London: Sage.

*Daloz, L.A. (1986) *Effective Mentoring and Teaching*. San Francisco, CA: Jossey-Bass.

Davies, B., Gore, K., Shury, J., Vivian, D. and Winterbotham, M. (2011) *UK Commission's Employer Skills Survey 2011: UK Results*. London, UKCES.

Dee, K. and Hatton, A. (2006). 'How to face training evaluation head-on', *People Management*, 23 March: 40–41.

Dennis, H. (1988) *Fourteen Steps in Managing an Ageing Work Force*. Lexington, MA: D.C. Heath.

Department for Education (2011) *Wolf Review of Vocational Education: Government Response*. London: Department for Education.

Department of Innovation, Universities and Skills (2008) *Shaping the Future – A New Adult Advancement and Careers Service for England*. London: HMSO.

Descy, P. and Tchibozo, G. (2009) *Modernising Vocational Education and Training: Fourth Report on Vocational Education and Training Research in Europe*. Luxembourg: CEDEFOP.

Descy, P. and Tessaring, M. (2005) *The Value of Learning: Evaluation and Impact of Education and Training': Third Report on Vocational Training Research in Europe*. Luxembourg: CEDEFOP.

Dixon, N. (2000) 'Common knowledge: the insight track', *People Management*, 17 February: 34–9.

Downey, M. (2003) *Effective Coaching*. New York: Thompson Texere.

Dreyfus, H.L., Dreyfus, S.E. and Athanasion, T. (1986) *Mind Over Machine: The Power of Human Intuition and Expertise in the Era of the Computer*. New York: Free Press.

Drucker, P. (1969) *Age of Discontinuity: Guidelines to our Changing Society*. New York: Harper & Row.

Erikson, E. (1950) *Childhood and Society*. New York: W.W. Norton.

Finegold, D. and Soskice, D. (1999) 'Creating self-sustaining high-skill ecosystems', *Oxford Review of Economic Policy*, 15(1): 60–79.

Fitts, P.M. (1962) 'Factors in complex skills training' in R. Glaser (ed.) *Training Research and Education*. New York: Wiley, pp. 177–98.

Fontana, D. (1981) 'Learning and teaching' in C.L. Cooper (ed.) *Psychology for Managers: A Text for Managers and Trade Unionists*. London: British Psychological Society and Macmillan, pp. 64–78.

Gabriel, Y. (2000) *Storytelling in Organisations: Facts, Fictions, and Fantasies*. Oxford: Oxford University Press.

Gagné, R.M. (1970) *The Conditions of Learning*, 2nd edn. New York: Holt, Rinehart & Winston.

Gagné, R.M. (1974) *Essentials of Learning for Instruction*. Hinsdale, IL: Dryden Press.

Gallos, J.V. (1989) 'Exploring women's development: implications for career theory, practice, and research', in M.B. Arthur, D.T. Hall and B.S. Lawrence (eds) *Handbook of Career Theory*. Cambridge: Cambridge University Press, pp. 110–32.

Gallway, T. (1986). *The Inner Game of Golf*. London: Pan.

Gardner, H. (1985) *Frames of Mind: The Theory of Multiple Intelligences*. London: Paladin.

Gardner, H. (1999) *Intelligence Reframed: Multiple Intelligences for the 21st Century*. New York: Basic Books.

Garrett, R., Campbell, M. and Mason, G. (2010). *The Value of Skills: An Evidence Review*. London: UKCES.

Green, K. (1999). 'Offensive Thinking', *People Management*, 5, 8: 27.

Greene, J. and Grant, A. (2006). *Solution-focussed Coaching: Managing People in a Complex World*. Harlow: Pearson Education.

Guest, D., Storey, Y. and Tate, W. (1997) *Opportunity Through People*. IPD Consultative Document, June. London: IPD.

Hall, L. (2005) 'Coach class', *People Management*, September: 46.

Hamblin, A. C. (1974) *Evaluation and Control of Training*. Maidenhead, McGraw-Hill.

Hamblin, B. (ed.) (2007) *Towards Evidence-based Management Development. Management Development: Perspectives from Research and Practice*. Abingdon: Routledge.

Harrison, R. (1992) *Employee Development*. London: IPD.

Harrison, R. (2009) *Learning and Development*, 5th edn. London: CIPD.

Hillage, J. and Pollard, E. (1998) *Employability: Developing a Framework for Policy Analysis*. Research Report RR 85. London: Department for Education and Employment.

Honey, P. (1998) 'The debate starts here', *People Management*, 1 October: 28–9.

Honey, P. (1999) 'Not for the faint-hearted', *People Management*, 28 October: 39.

Honey, P. and Mumford, A. (1992) *Manual of Learning Styles*, 3rd edn. London: Peter Honey.

Hwang, A.-S. (2003) 'Training strategies in the management of knowledge', *Journal of Knowledge Management*, 7, 3: 92–104.

Jarvis, P. (2004) *Adult Education and Lifelong Learning: Theory and Practice*, 3rd edn. Abingdon: Routledge-Falmer.

Jarvis, J. and Hooley, A. (2004) 'Access all areas', *People Management*, 9 December: 40–42.

Kearns, P. (2005) 'From return on investment to added value evaluation: the foundation for organisational learning', *Advances in Developing Human Resources*, 7, 1: 135–46.

Keep, E. and Mayhew, K. (2001) *The Skills System in 2015. The future of learning for work,* Executive Briefing. London: CIPD.

King, Z. (2010) *Human Capital Reporting: What Information Counts in the City?,* Research Report. London: CIPD.

Kirkpatrick, J. (1960) 'Techniques for evaluating training programmes', *Journal of American Society for Training and Development*, 14, 13–18: 25–32.

Knights, A. and Poppleton, A. (2008) *Developing Coaching Capability in Organisations: Research into Practice.* London: CIPD.

Knowles, MSC and Associates (1984) *Androgogy in Action.* San Francisco, CA: Jossey-Bass.

Kolb, D.A. (1983) *Experiential Learning.* New York: Prentice Hall.

Kolb, D. (1984) *Experiential Learning: Experience as the Source of Learning and Development.* Englewood Cliffs, NJ: Prentice Hall.

Kolb, D.A., Rubin, I.M. and MacIntyre, J.M. (1984) *Organizational Psychology: An Experiential Approach,* 4th edn. New York: Prentice Hall.

Laslett, P. (1989) *A Fresh Map of Life: The Emergence of the Third Age.* London: Weidenfeld & Nicolson.

Lave, J. and Wenger, E. (1991) *Situated Learning: Peripheral Participation.* Cambridge: Cambridge University Press.

Leitch, S. (2006) *Leitch Review of Skills: Prosperity for All in the Global Economy – World Class Skills.* London: HMSO. Online: **http://www.delni.gov.uk/leitch_finalreport051206[1]-2.pdf** (accessed January 2014).

Levinson, D.J., Darrow, C.M., Klein, E.B., Levinson, M.H. and McKee, B. (1978) *The Seasons of a Man's Life.* New York: Alfred A. Knopf.

Malhotra, Y. (1998) *Knowledge Management for the New World of Business,* WWW Virtual Library on Knowledge Management (**http://www.brint.com/km/**).

Mankin, D. (2009) *Human Resource Development.* London: Oxford University Press.

Martin, S. (1995) 'A futures market for competencies', *People Management*, 23 March: 20–24.

Mayer, R. (2005) 'Cognitive theory of multimedia learning', *The Cambridge Handbook of Multimedia Learning.* Cambridge: Cambridge University Press.

Mayo, A.J. and Nohria, N. (2005) *In Their Time: The Greatest Business Leaders of the 20th Century.* Boston, MA: Harvard Business School Press.

McGoldrick, J., Stewart, J. and Watson, S. (2002) *Understanding Human Resource Development: A Research Based Approach.* London: Routledge.

McGurk, J. and Sadler-Smith, E. (2012) 'Practising HRD in transition: From 'steady state' to 'ready state'', *University Forum for Human Resource Development,* 3 November 2012.

Mezirow, J. (1977) 'Personal transformation', *Studies in Adult Education* (Leicester: National Institute of Adult Education), 9, 2: 153–64.

Mumford, A. (1988) 'Learning to learn and management self-development' in M. Pedler, J. Burgoyne and T. Boydell (eds) *Applying Self-Development in Organisations.* New York: Prentice Hall, pp. 22–7.

Mumford, A. (2002) 'Horses for courses', *People Management,* 27 June: 51.

Myers, C. and Davids, K. (1992) 'Knowing and doing: tacit skills at work', *Personnel Management,* February: 45–7.

Naylor, P. (1987) 'In praise of older workers', *Personnel Management,* November: 44–8.

Neugarten, B.L. (1968) 'Adult personality: towards a psychology of the life cycle' in B.L. Neugarten (ed.) *Middle Age and Ageing: A Reader in Social Psychology.* Chicago, IL: University of Chicago Press, pp. 137–47.

Nolen-Hoeksema, S., Fredrickson, B., Loftus, G. and Wagenaar, W. (2009) *Atkinson and Hilgard's Introduction to Psychology,* 15 edn. Andover: Cengage Learning.

Nonaka, I. (1991) 'The knowledge creating company' in *Harvard Business Review on Knowledge Management.* Cambridge, MA: Harvard Business School Press, pp. 21–45.

Palmer, S. and Whybrow, A. (2007) *Handbook of Coaching Psychology.* London: Routledge.

Parr, C. (2013) 'MOOC providers expand', *Times Higher Education*, 17 October.

Parsloe, E. and Wray, M. (2000) *Coaching and Mentoring: Practical Methods to Improve Learning.* London: Kogan Page.

Pedler, M. (1988) 'Self-development and work organisations' in M. Pedler, J. Burgoyne and T. Boydell (eds) *Applying Self-Development in Organisations.* New York: Prentice Hall, pp. 1–19.

People Management (2005a) 'Older staff train faster at BMW', 27 October: 17.

People Management (2005b) 'Troubleshooter', 27 October: 64–5.

Phillips, J. (2002) *How to Measure Training Success: A Practical Guide to Evaluating Training.* New York: McGraw Hill.

Phillips, J. (2005) 'Measuring Up.' *People Management.* Online: **http://www.cipd.co.uk/pm/peoplemanagement/b/weblog/archive/2013/01/29/measuringup-2005-04.aspx** (accessed September 2013).

Phillips, L. (2008) 'Council rolls out diversity e-learning course', *People Management,* 27 February.

Phillips, J. (2012) *Training Evaluation: Measurement and Methods.* London: Routledge.

Pickard, J. (1999) 'Emote possibilities: sense and sensitivity', *People Management,* 28 October: 48–56.

Polanyi, M. (1966) *The Tacit Dimension.* London: Routledge and Kegan Paul.

Prensky, M. (2001) 'Digital natives, digital immigrants', *On the Horizon,* 9, 5. Online: **http://www.marcprensky.com/writing/Prensky%20-%20Digital%20Natives,%20Digital%20Immigrants%20-%20Part1.pdf** (accessed September 2013).

Quinn, R.E., Faerman, S.R., Thompson, M.P. and McGrath, M.R. (1990) *Becoming a Master Manager.* New York: Wiley.

Reid, M. A., Barrington, H. and Brown, M. (2004) *Human Resource Development: Beyond Training Interventions.* London: CIPD.

Ribeaux, P. and Poppleton, S.E. (1978) *Psychology and Work: An Introduction.* London: Macmillan.

Rothwell, W. J. and Kazanas, H. (1989) *Strategic Human Resource Development.* Englewood Cliffs, NJ: Prentice Hall.

Salmon, G. (2011) *E-moderating: The Key to Online Teaching and Learning.* London: Routledge.

Scott, A. (2008) 'Seven-way collaboration produces modular, customised package, *People Management,* 20 June: 13.

Scott, A. (2010). 'Learning: development opportunity', *People Management,* 16 September 2010.

*Senge, P. (1990) *The Fifth Discipline: The Art and Practice of the Learning Organisation.* London: Century.

Sharpe, R. (2010) *Rethinking Learning for a Digital Age: How Learners are Shaping their Own Experiences.* London: Routledge.

Sheehan, M. (2012) 'Investing in managment development in turbulent times and perceived organisational performance:

A study of UK MNCs and their subsidiaries', *International Journal of Human Resource Management,* 23, 12: 2491–513.

Shury, J., Davies, B., Riley, T. and Stanfield, C. (2008) *Skills for the Workplace: Employer Perspectives.* London: UKCES.

Shury, J., Vivian, D., Gore, K. and Huckle, C. (2012) *UK Commission's Employer Perspectives Survey.* London, UKCES.

Sloman, M. and Rolph, J. (2003) *E-learning: the Learning Curve.* Change Agendas Series. London: CIPD. Online: **http://www. cipd.co.uk/hr-topics/e-learning.aspx**.

Smethurst, S. (2006) 'State of mind', *People Management,* 12 January: 24–9.

Snowden, D. (2002) 'Complex acts of knowing: paradox and descriptive self-awareness', *Journal of Knowledge Management,* 6, 2, May: 100–11.

Sofer, C. (1970) *Men in Mid-Career.* Cambridge: CUP.

Stammers, R. and Patrick, J. (1975) *The Psychology of Training.* London: Methuen.

Sternberg, R.J. (1985) *Beyond IQ: A Triarchic Theory of Human Intelligence.* Cambridge: CUP.

Stober, D. and Grant, A. (2006) *Evidence Based Coaching: Putting Best Practices to Work for your Clients.* London: John Wiley.

Swanson, R. A. (2001) *Assessing the Financial Benefits of Human Resource Development.* Cambridge, MA: Perseus.

Taylor, J. (2008) *Identifying Learning and Training Needs.* London: CIPD.

Thompson, I. (2005) *Training Evaluation: Making it Happen.* Online: **http://www.cipd.co.uk/subjects/training/trneval/treva. htm** (accessed August 2013)

Thomas, D.A. and Alderfer, C.P. (1989) 'The influence of race on career dynamics: theory and research on minority career experiences' in M.B. Arthur, D.T. Hall and B.S. Lawrence (eds) *Handbook of Career Theory.* Cambridge: Cambridge University Press, pp. 133–58.

Training Commission (1988) *Classifying the Components of Management Competences.* Sheffield: Training Commission.

Trinder, C., Hulme, G. and McCarthy, U. (1992) *Employment: the Role of Work in the Third Age,* The Carnegie Inquiry into the Third Age, Research Paper Number 1. Dunfermline: The Carnegie United Kingdom Trust.

UKCES (2009) *The Employability Challenge.* London: UK Commission for Employment and Skills.

Ulrich, D. and Stewart Black, J. (1999) 'All around the world: worldly wise', *People Management,* 25 October: 42–6.

UNESCO (2005) *Towards Knowledge Societies,* UNESCO World Report. Paris: UNESCO.

Van den Berg, N., Meijers, F. and Sprengers, M. (2006) 'More vocational education and supplementary training through equalisation of costs?', *Human Resource Development International,* 9(1): 5–24.

Vygotsky, L. (1978) *Mind in society: The Development of Higher Psychological Processes.* Cambridge, MA: Harvard University Press.

Walton, J. (1999) *Strategic Human Resource Development.* Harlow: Pearson Education Limited.

Wang, G. G. and Spitzer, D.R. (2005) 'Human resource development measurement and evaluation: looking back and moving forward', *Advances in Developing Human Resources* 7, 1: 5–16.

Waskel, S. A. (1991) *Mid-life Issues and the Workplace of the 90s: A Guide for Human Resource Specialists.* New York: Quorum.

Watts, A.G. (2006) *Career Development Learning and Employability.* York: Higher Education Academy.

Wechsler, D. (1958) *The Measurement and Appraisal of Adult Intelligence,* 4th edn. London: Baillière, Tindall & Cox.

Wensch, M. (2007) *The Maching is Us/ing Us.* Online: **http://www. youtube.com/watch?gl=GB&hl=en-GB&v=NLlGopyXT_g** (accessed August 2013).

Whitmore, J. (2009) *Coaching for Performance.* London: Nicholas Brearley Publishing Ltd.

Whittaker, J. and Johns, T. (2004) 'Standards deliver', *People Management,* 30 June: 32–4.

Whittington, R. (1993) *What is Strategy and why does it Matter?* London, Routledge.

Wisher, V. (1994) 'Competencies: the precious seeds of growth', *Personnel Management,* July: 36–9.

Wolf, A. (2011) *Review of Vocational Education.* London: Department for Education.

Wrightsman, L.S. (1988) *Personality Development in Adulthood.* Newbury Park, CA: Sage.

Yorke, M. and Knight, P.T. (2006) *Embedding Employability into the Curriculum.* York: Higher Education Academy.

Chapter 8

Leadership and management development

Mairi Watson

Objectives

- To explain the meanings and nature of management and leadership development in organisations.
- To acknowledge the significance of management and leadership development to organisational success.
- To contrast key conceptual approaches to management and leadership development.
- To examine the methods, techniques and processes used to develop managers and leaders.
- To draw attention to the way management and leadership development can be varied to meet different needs and in different contexts.
- To speculate about the future direction of management and leadership development in the UK and beyond.

Introductory case study

Leadership research reveals managers 'struggle with basic skills'

Business leaders are 'struggling with basic management skills' as budget cuts and efficiencies increase the pressure on organisations, research from Roffey Park has revealed. The institute's annual Management Agenda report, which surveyed 1,460 managers, found that the issue was so serious 55 per cent of employers had made 'leadership development' a top priority for the year ahead. Businesses put this training ahead of other strategies for growth such as developing new products and services, bringing in new technology or improving employee engagement.

[...]

Worryingly, almost half of respondents (45 per cent) said they received 'low levels of support' from their organisation, yet they faced an increased use of 'stretch assignments' and enhanced responsibilities. Nearly two-thirds of managers (61 per cent) said their employer had given them 'increased responsibility' as a developmental incentive, while 41 per cent said they had been given 'stretch assignments' and 35 per cent had received coaching.

But in contrast, pay rises and bonuses were bottom of the list of incentives received by managers, at just 5 per cent and 9 per cent, respectively.

Roffey Park warned that without proper support, the 'developmental deal' for employees who step up risks being a 'dumping' rather than 'stretching' exercise for the individual.[...]

Michael Jenkins, chief executive of Roffey Park, said: 'With the financial crisis and recent corporate scandals around bonuses and tax, it's leaders at the very top who've been in the firing line. Now, as focus must shift from responding to the crisis to steering a more stable course through austerity, we're seeing managers further down the line struggling to cope with basic issues such as implementing change and dealing with underperforming staff.'

Source: extracted from *People Management,* 11 February 2013, 'Leadership research reveals managers struggle with basic skills' with the permission of the publisher, the Chartered Institute of Personnel and Development, London (www.cipd.co.uk).

Introduction

The effective management of both private- and public-sector organisations is widely perceived to be of critical importance to organisational success and, more broadly, to national economic well-being. Some critics, moreover, argue that the UK has certain deficiencies in respect of the qualities and skills of its management base when compared with managers at the global level. This means that the development of managers to help sustain their performance at the highest levels possible is a particularly crucial element of wider organisational learning strategies.

CIPD (2012b)

Since the last edition of this textbook was published, the UK – and the worldwide economy – has experienced an unprecedented period of turbulence which has changed the landscape of HR and threatened in-company expenditure on HR activities, particularly learning and development, the umbrella under which leadership and management development (LMD) would normally sit. Greater scrutiny of budgets has led to a reduction in investment which could, in the long term, threaten organisational (and national) performance and competitiveness (Sheehan, 2012; Stevens, 2013). For example, in the CIPD Learning and Talent Development Survey (2012), three-quarters of organisations reported a deficit in highly valued management and leadership skills; however, budget issues were most frequently quoted as a reason for not investing in LMD (CIPD, 2012a). Optimistically, however, 80 per cent of organisations expressed an intention to conduct leadership development activities in the subsequent 12 months. All is not, it seems, lost.

Within this new context of operation, the chapter will assist in developing an understanding of LMD within increasingly complex and diverse organisational contexts and challenging economic circumstances. To this end, the chapter identifies issues that must be explored in order to develop a critical analysis of LMD, poses questions and encourages you to engage in activities and exercises that take you beyond the confines of the book.

Defining leadership and management development (LMD)

The changing nature of management and leadership

In practice, managers and leaders have to deal with the ambiguities and complexities that arise from tensions in their position in the organisation, dealing with the different aims, expectations and interests of those they manage and those who set their goals. Furthermore, theoretical conceptions of 'management' or 'leadership' have changed significantly. In the 1990s – and in some organisations still – it was common to see typologies that dichotomised the nature of management and leadership roles, emphasising the visionary and inspirational nature of leadership functions against the practical and controlling nature of management. While it is appealing, this type of work caricatures rather than describes the roles and functions of managers and leaders. Furthermore, this leadership and management split is based on dubious assumptions about the structure of organisations as long hierarchical chains (Mabey and Finch-Lees, 2008). Arguably the dominance of a Western view of leadership that reinforces the split between leadership and management does so without considering the potential range of leadership behaviours that can be observed across the globe (House *et al.,* 2002; Mabey and Finch-Lees, 2008) and the value that accrues from different types of leaders, and different ways of leading.

Recent work has suggested that the required competencies of managers and leaders are converging (Salaman, 2004) and that it is leadership – not management – that has become the pervasive feature in organisations (Storey, 2010a,c) and a 'highly sought-after and highly valued commodity' (Northhouse, 2013: 1). Increasingly, the blurring of management and leadership roles has led to a redefinition of the roles and competencies of those who organise, control and inspire across organisations (Storey, 2010a,c).

For example, Boddy (2010) identifies several different positions in a hierarchy for managers in organisations with the amount of management, leadership and non-management work varying within these positions:

- *Performing direct operations* – this is likely to contain some element of managerial work, but in lower level jobs this will be limited. Managerial work may be greater where this applies to professions such as lawyers and accountants or to small business owners who may perform significant levels of direct operations alongside managerial work.

- *Managing staff on direct operations* – this includes supervisors or first-line managers who have responsibility for staff performing the daily operations of the business.

- *Managing managers* – usually this means 'middle managers' who are expected to ensure supervisors achieve organisational goals through monitoring and supporting. They also provide a link to the board/those who manage the business and ensure information flows up and down appropriately.

- *Managing the business* – this is the work of a small group of people at the top of the organisation who are most responsible for the overall performance and direction of the organisation.

While it is difficult to draw a clear line between management and leadership, using Boddy's typology would suggest that there are leadership *and* management responsibilities at all levels of the organisation. Thus leadership is no longer the preserve of senior figures in the organisation (Storey, 2010c). Leadership acts can be observed at all levels, and leadership is dispersed or distributed rather than concentrated in the hands of managers. Current thinking, therefore, favours a line of argument that sees 'leadership is a necessary quality of managers at all levels' (Salaman, 2004: 77; Lee, 2003; Passmore, 2010) and more controversially as 'the answer to a whole array of intractable problems' (Storey, 2010c: 7). Arguably, in practice the word manager has been replaced by the word leader (Salaman, 2010), but not without consequence:

Key Controversy

Salaman (2010: 56) argues that there have been repeated crises in the practice of leadership 'of a very serious nature and with catastrophic impacts' because 'leadership . . . is seen as the best and only solution to the problems caused by leadership'. He discusses examples from the last decade, particularly in the financial sector, that have had long-running effects on how we live and work.

What examples can you identify of 'irresponsibility and incompetence' in leadership that have had an impact on the way we live and work today?

As you read through the rest of the chapter, consider how leadership and management development could have contributed to a more positive picture of leadership in contemporary organisations.

Leadership and management development therefore has to address the complexities of varied managerial and leadership roles and the diverse needs of the individuals who occupy them (Storey, 2010a). In other words, any investment in development has to be congruent with the 'reality' of what managers do, and not (however well intentioned) be rooted in abstract or increasingly redundant models or stereotypes of what others might think they should do or used to do (Mole, 2010; Sturges, 2010). In short, LMD has to 'measure up' (Tyler, 2004: 152) and develop the skills that are critical to managers' and organisational performance. CIPD (2011) identified the need for both a current and future perspective of the identification and development of managerial skills: what do we need now, and what do we need for the future? (Figure 8.1).

In addressing issues in LMD, this chapter therefore conflates the titles of management and leadership on purpose. This signifies that the roles, responsibilities and development of managers and leaders are best considered as one single topic, which may, over history, have been popular as one term (management development, 1985–1990s) and then another (leadership development, 1990s–2000s), but now there is a clear recognition in the literature of the overlapping and intertwining nature of the roles, which makes distinguishing between the two less important. This is appropriate, as management and the work of managers and leaders are not simple processes but complex matters that are specific to individuals and organisations (Mumford and Gold, 2006; Storey, 2010b).

Definition of LMD

Management development is the structured process by which managers enhance their skills, competencies and/or knowledge, via formal or informal learning methods, to the benefit of both individual and organisational performance.

CIPD (2012b: 1)

Figure 8.1 Critical skills needed in the next three years (UK/global)

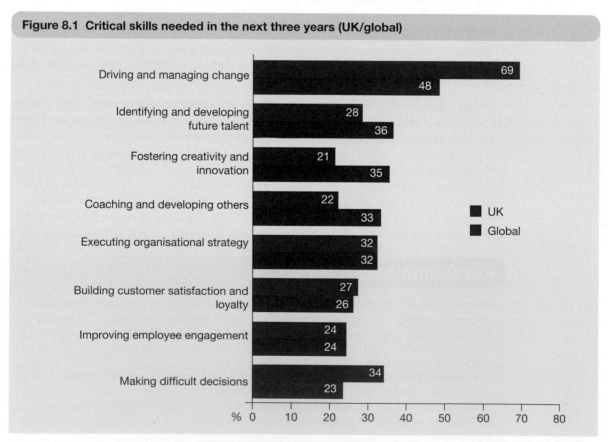

Source: from UK Highlights: Global Leadership Forecast 2011, London: CIPD (2011) p. 6, Figure 6, with the permission of the publisher, the Chartered Institute of Personnel and Development, London (www.cipd.co.uk).

Leadership and management development is a multifaceted activity that involves not just formal training but also broader, informal processes of learning, including learning from experience, which enhances the quality and outputs of leadership and management in an organisation. A range of different approaches to LMD can be identified in different organisational contexts (public, private, not-for-profit, large, small, national, multinational and multi-cultural); for different levels of management (from junior to senior or board level leaders); and for different degrees of experience (from novice to expert). This section considers the multiple purposes and priorities of LMD and the broad range of activities that can be considered as contributing to those purposes.

Key Controversy

Mabey and Finch-Lees (2008) and Mabey (2013) present a challenging and critical view of the multiple discourses of leadership and its development, which argues that the contrasting conceptions of what leadership represents 'will have profound implications for the way leadership development in organizations is articulated, practiced, experienced and researched' (Mabey, 2013). The four discourses are represented in Figure 8.2.

One aspect of the importance of their work is to draw attention to the language of leadership as something that is not neutral. Nor is it normally scrutinised. Accepting that there are multiple discourses allows a more nuanced interpretation of events and brings a number of lenses through which to examine the artefacts of leadership and its development.

Read Mabey (2013) and reflect on what this means for your understanding of leadership and its development and how you measure the impact of LMD in your organisation.

Figure 8.2 The four discourses of leadership development (LD)

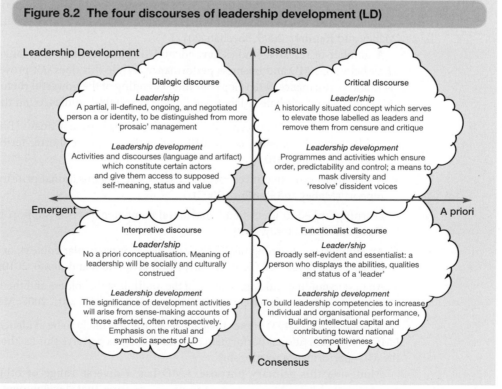

Source: from Mabey (2013).

The purposes of LMD

Explicit in definitions of the activities of LMD is the requirement of improvement in individual or organisational performance through developing the knowledge, skills and abilities of managers and leaders so that they can appropriately provide direction, use resources, work with internal and external stakeholders and facilitate the achievement of organisational priorities (including change). As a primary aim of LMD (Sheehan, 2012), its contribution to organisational performance (and the achievement of the organisational strategy) is of paramount importance (CIPD, 2012a). Nowadays, no investment in development is likely to be made without strong evidence of potential – or actual – results, raising the value and importance of evaluating LMD programmes.

However, while the rhetoric of the strategic significance of LMD is appealing, unravelling this in practice is challenging (Sheehan, 2012). There are those who argue strongly in favour of LMD's contribution to the achievement of strategic goals, and there is evidence to suggest that some employers identify strategically driven LMD, implemented over time, as making a significant difference to business performance (CIPD, 2012a; Sheehan, 2012). LMD is usually credited with a role in organisational success and strategic achievement, as it can develop successful business leaders. On the other hand, many organisations do not understand the relationship between management capability and business performance (CIPD, 2005) or the value of the processes of LMD (Bailey *et al.,* 2010). Thus, while crediting LMD with positive business effects is appealing, it is by no means settled (Tyler, 2004; Tate, 2010) and a belief in its effectiveness is not always supported by evidence of tangible successes (Bailey *et al.,* 2010). Thus, while investment in LMD in some larger organisations often amounts to a sizeable proportion of the HR budget, it can be argued that companies continue to support such training and development largely as an act of faith. To be fair, in part this reliance on faith can be explained by the challenges in evaluating LMD (Edwards and Turnbull, 2013). However, recent work suggests that if an organisation carefully cultivates the development of its managerial cadre, this will, in time, lead to improvements in morale, motivation and corporate capability, which will in turn, other things being equal, lead to a more productive organisation (Mabey and Ramirez, 2005; Sheehan, 2012).

A number of research studies have identified characteristics of organisations that report a link between LMD and business performance. While this does not prove the link between LMD and performance, it develops our understanding of the powerful rhetoric that surrounds LMD and its strategic halo (Mabey and Finch-Lees, 2008). Studies found the following:

- A careful alignment between LMD and a longer-term strategic focus (Brown, 2005; Mabey and Ramirez, 2005; Bailey *et al.,* 2010), rather than with the shorter-term learning needs of individuals (Tate, 2010).

- A sustained, proactive investment in LMD as an organisational priority with board level support (Mabey and Ramirez, 2005).

- Learning linked to identified behavioural competencies that support business purposes (Salaman, 2004; Storey, 2010a).

- An emphasis on learning tied to the workplace, or particular context, or the managers and leader being developed (Brown, 2007; Antonacopoulou and Bento, 2010; Mole, 2010).

- An understanding and appreciation of the multiple stakeholders and their multiple interests in human resource development (HRD; Stansfield and Stewart, 2007; Mabey, 2013).

Sheehan (2012: 2,493) argues that, above all, there is likely to be evidence of a link between LMD and organisational performance where managers *perceive* this as 'the glue that cements the MD–performance relationship'.

Alongside this primary purpose, LMD has a diverse range of other purposes (Hill and Stewart, 2007). As well as organisations ensuring that development is linked to their philosophies and strategic objectives, decision-makers must also take account of individual needs, expectations and aspirations. This can often be a difficult balance to achieve and frequently becomes a source of tension (Sturges, 2010). Narrowly defined, its central purpose is to provide the structures and systems necessary for individual development (more broadly known as a 'humanistic perspective' – Mankin, 2009). From this individual perspective, engaging in LMD is linked to personal career, self-esteem, prestige and job security. From an organisational perspective, LMD serves a much broader agenda. For example, it is viewed as a 'tool' or device for attaining competitive advantage by enhancing knowledge and skills, which in turn lead to improvements in efficiency, productivity and innovation. It can also be used as a device to 'engineer' organisational change, especially culture change, which requires a longer-term perspective on the outcomes of LMD (Carter *et al.,* 2005; Amagoh, 2009). However, reconciling and managing the contradictions and incongruities that sometimes emerge when organisations seek to balance organisational goals and personal aspirations is a major challenge. It is therefore vital that organisations view LMD as a long-term investment and select an approach that is suited to their specific needs and requirements.

Key Controversy

If we accept the argument that LMD contributes significantly to organisational performance, then organisations should structure their investment in such a way that they achieve strategic LMD. Mumford and Gold (2004) describe six levels of strategic maturity in organisational activity related to LMD.

Study Mumford and Gold's model. Identify where you believe your organisation is positioned in relation to the different 'types' and 'levels of maturity'. What action would they have to take to develop a strategic approach to LMD?

Developing an LMD strategy

As stated earlier, if we accept the argument that LMD contributes significantly to organisational performance, then organisations should structure their investment in such a way that they achieve strategic LMD. Mumford and Gold (2006) review Burgoyne's (1988) model of strategic maturity in organisations' investment in LMD, from the unsystematic to the highly strategically integrated (see Table 8.1). Sadly, unsystematic approaches to LMD are all too common (Bailey *et al.,* 2010; Mole, 2010). Such approaches contribute to the failure of LMD to fulfil personal and organisational expectations (Mole, 2010). Not only do they waste investment, time and effort, but there is also a risk of damage to existing levels of morale and commitment among managers as efforts to develop them founder on organisational barriers to change.

The need for a broader and more contextualised perspective of LMD is central to a strategic approach (Hill and Stewart, 2007). Many approaches to development have characteristics similar to Burgoyne's levels 1 and 2 and accordingly may be labelled as piecemeal. Implementing piecemeal approaches will almost certainly lead to inefficient and ineffective development.

Unsystematic or piecemeal approaches to development are characterised by the following:

● There is no LMD infrastructure. Development is not linked to business strategy. Activities are unrelated, and lack overall direction or philosophy. They fail to reinforce each other, and reduce the potential for organisational effectiveness.

● Development often focuses on the needs of the organisation, and fails to meet the learning needs and aspirations of individuals and groups.

Table 8.1 Levels of maturity of organisational management development

1	2	3	4	5	6
No systematic management development	Isolated management development	Integrated and coordinated structural and development tactics	A management development strategy to implement corporate policy	Management development strategy input to corporate policy formation	Strategic development of the management of corporate policy
No systematic or deliberate management development in a structural or developmental sense; total reliance on laissez-faire, uncontrived processes of management development	There are isolated and *ad hoc* tactical management development activities, of either structural or developmental kinds, or both, in response to local problems, crises, or sporadically identified general problems	The specific management development tactics that impinge directly on the individual manager, of career structure management, and of assisting learning, are integrated and coordinated	A management strategy plays its part in implementing corporate policies through managerial human resource planning, and providing a development strategic framework and direction for the tactics of career structure management and of learning, education and training	Management development processes feed information into corporate policy decision-making processes on the organisation's managerial assets, strengths, weaknesses and potential, and contribute to the forecasting and analysis of the manageability of proposed projects, ventures, changes	Management development processes enhance the nature and quality of corporate policy-forming processes, which they also inform and help implement

Source: from 'Management development for the individual and the organisation', *Personnel Management,* June, pp. 40–44 (Burgoyne, J, 1988), with permission from Dr J. G. Burgoyne.

- Development is largely defined in terms of a range of universal, off-the-shelf internal or external courses.
- There is tacit support for management education and training because it is seen as a 'good thing to be doing' irrespective of organisational needs.
- There is a lack of common vision among those responsible for LMD. For instance, some managers see development as a central part of their job, while others see it as peripheral and a nuisance.
- LMD effort can be wasted because it is used as a solution to the wrong problem. Rather than developing managers, the correct solution may be to change aspects of organisation structure or systems.
- It is difficult to evaluate the effectiveness of a piecemeal approach that lacks clear direction and established objectives.

Explore

Study Burgoyne's model.

- Identify where you believe your organisation is positioned in relation to the different 'levels of maturity'.
- Why?
- What action would they have to take to develop a strategic approach to LMD?

Whatever action you have identified in the previous activity, an LMD policy can be useful to express an organisation's commitment to development, and set out clearly a framework within which it can take place (Mabey, 2002). Policies make explicit who is responsible for development, the support that is available, the methods used and key stakeholders. Research over time has consistently suggested that those organisations having a formal policy for developing their managers undertake significantly more management training than companies without (Thompson *et al.*, 2001; CIPD, 2012b).

The first stage of developing a policy is to link LMD explicitly to an organisation's strategy (Tate, 2010). We identified earlier the importance of a strategic approach and the link between HR practices and strategy is considered in detail in Chapter 2. While this is not without significant challenges (Bailey *et al.*, 2010), there are steps that can be taken to design a workable set of *intentions,* encapsulated in an LMD policy.

The remainder of the chapter is structured around the other key components of an LMD policy. LMD policies will normally include the following (Mumford and Gold, 2006; Bailey *et al.*, 2010):

- *Choosing who to develop.* Who will be targeted? Will our provision be tailored or standardised?

- *Choosing what to do.* What are the development needs of the managers and leaders? What will be done? When will it be done? Are there frameworks to support us?

- *Identifying who to involve and how.* Who are the stakeholders? Who will be responsible for managing LMD activities?

- *Deciding how to evaluate.* What are our metrics? What do we want to achieve? How will we measure it?

Each of these issues will be considered as this chapter progresses, so that by the end of the chapter you will be equipped to begin the process of design and development of an LMD policy for your organisation.

Key Controversy

The use of the word 'intentions' (highlighted in the previous section) hints at the potential mismatch between the promises of policy and the reality of practice in some organisations, which means that policies may be viewed with some scepticism – especially during times of radical downsizing involving the loss of managerial jobs. Moreover, organisations face challenges in aligning their needs with individual career requirements as careers become more individualised (Sturges, 2010). There are also difficulties in evaluating the effectiveness of policies in achieving desired outcomes (Tyler, 2004; Hamblin, 2007).

Does your organisation have an LMD policy? If so, locate it and identify the extent to which it is delivered in practice. How closely is it related to the organisation's strategy? If it does not have a policy, consider what the impact may have been on the business.

It is worth bearing in mind as you reflect on the next sections that the policy should also take account of the different stages of the manager or leader's relationship with the company (see Figure 8.3) (Tate, 2010). The development process requires careful managing by line managers and HRD specialists such that development activities vary along the employment spectrum appropriate to the stage of the manager's relationship with the company (Sheehan, 2012). Investment in, for example, high-value development should be limited in the final stages of the employee's tenure.

Figure 8.3 Managing leadership along the employment spectrum

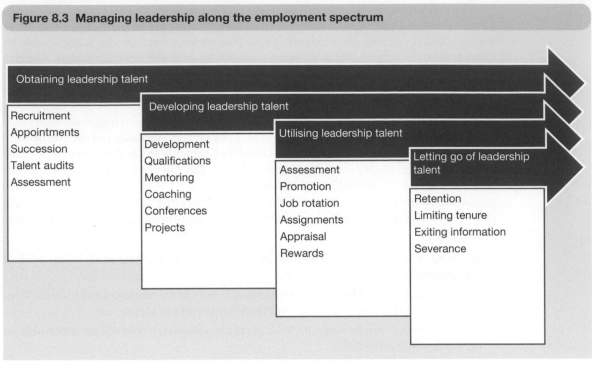

Source: from Tate (2010).

Choosing who to develop

There are many ways that organisations can cut their cloth when deciding who to develop. For example, they may choose graduate entrants to the organisation (common in larger organisations and captured in an annual 'milk round' – e.g. see **www.milkround.com**), senior managers on an executive development programme or choose people via 'talent spotting' programmes to recognise those in the organisation who may be operating at a level below their potential.

A deciding factor in the process is whether to develop those with 'high potential' or those who are currently exhibiting levels of 'high performance' (the differences between them are presented in Table 8.2; Cannon and McGee, 2007). A growing interest in 'talent management'

Table 8.2 High-potential versus high-performance employees (Cannon and McGee, 2007)

A high-potential employee	A high-performance employee
• Has the respect and trust of peers, supervisors and subordinates	• Consistently produces measurable results above expectations
• Maintains a high level of competence in their role/job	• Self-manages in a manner that fosters learning and high performance
• Has a bias for action, is a proactive catalyst for change	• Ensures that team goals are achieved within ethical and cultural guidelines
• Thinks and solves problems creatively and from a position of enquiry (vs advocacy)	• Manages and leads teams that demonstrate a sense of loyalty and community
• Is open to constructive criticism and feedback	• Strives to deliver and exceed customers' needs
• Uses critical judgment	• Arranges and leverages resources within the organisation
• Has a broad understanding of the organisation's business and their role in achieving its goals	• Has high resilience
• Has a high capacity to learn	

Source: Talent Management and Succession Planning, London: CIPD (Cannon, J, and McGee, R. 2007), with the permission of the publisher, the Chartered Institute of Personnel and Development, London (www.cipd.co.uk).

(Tansey *et al.,* 2007; see also Chapter 5) has fostered an exclusive/targeted approach in many organisations where high-potential individuals are the focus of considerable development investment (Bailey *et al.,* 2010). As businesses become contextually more complex, those with talent and leadership potential are more difficult to find (Strack and Krinks, 2008) and so identifying and developing internal staff with high potential becomes vital to business success.

One organisation that takes development of high potential very seriously is eBay (Crush, 2013), where:

> Managers continually discuss career aspirations with staff, in addition to twice-yearly formal conversations. . . . Every top position now has successors earmarked, with 50 per cent of positions having a "ready-now" successor. More than 70 per cent of directors have been promoted internally.

However, Bailey *et al.* (2010) argue that high-potential development schemes ought to run alongside more inclusive approaches to ensure a balanced approach to LMD. They identify four separate approaches (Figure 8.4) that support strategic objectives in businesses. These approaches are not mutually exclusive; rather they identify that each is appropriate for different purposes and different levels of managers and leaders.

However, many organisations are not sufficiently focused when identifying their target population for LMD (Mabey, 2002; Bailey *et al.,* 2010). Given the sensitivity that surrounds role identification and the prestige that is often attached to inclusion in LMD programmes (Mabey and Finch-Lees, 2008), issues of power and identity influence decision-makers. However, having devised and communicated a clear policy for LMD, those responsible for implementing development need to think through and be able to justify why they are developing an individual manager (or a group of managers).

Figure 8.4 Leadership and management development strategy framework

		Who?	
		Targeted	*Inclusive*
What?	*Individualised content*	**High potential tailored:** structured, targeted, individual, tailored activities to aid succession planning	**Self-motivated:** no prescribed methods or content, development open to all, individual motivation central
	Corporate consistency	**High potential programme:** planned and consistent activities driven by business needs and corporate message	**Generic programmes:** develops organisational capabilities, available to all

Source: adapted from Clarke *et al.* (2004: 287).

Choosing what to do

Once the target population has been identified, a number of questions can be asked so as to tailor provision for the groups or individuals:

- What are the LMD needs?
  - What are the specific needs of the individuals?
  - How are these linked to the strategy of the organisation through competency, development or performance frameworks?
  - Does the programme seek to develop new attitudes and values, e.g. after a takeover or merger?
  - Does the programme aim to develop technical, financial, business or interpersonal skills? What are the priorities?
  - Does the programme seek to change existing managerial behaviours and styles to reflect an internal organisational restructuring, such as the introduction of new technology?

- What LMD interventions are appropriate?
  - Where will the development take place? Should development be on-the-job in the office, factory or sales territory, or off-the-job in a residential hall, academic institution or individual's home, or a combination of all of these?
  - What are the most cost-effective/appropriate techniques available?
  - How much scope is there to accommodate individual learning needs and preferences?
  - How much choice is delegated to the individual over the choice of development techniques?
  - How is conflict resolved between individual and organisational needs?

Answering these questions will help the business decide the most appropriate range of activities to undertake, because when people refer to LMD, they usually refer to the activities that are planned and deliberate (Mumford and Gold, 2006). However, there is more to LMD than that.

Identifying LMD needs

In those organisations that take a structured and strategic approach to LMD, there are a number of frameworks that can be used to support LMD policies and their implementation. Three will be considered here: competency frameworks, career development and appraisals.

Competency frameworks

It has been argued for some time that the UK has deficiencies in management competencies that have an impact on the country's international competitiveness (CIPD, 2012b). Competency-based development (CBD) in LMD provides a formalised and structured method for informing the development of managers and leaders. Competency frameworks describe the knowledge, skills and behaviours that are required for individuals to perform their role effectively (IDS, 2012). Their strengths lie in accepting the argument that, while it may not be possible to teach leadership, it is possible to develop the skills and competencies of leadership (Mole, 2010). Despite their long pedigree, competency frameworks as a way of structuring leadership development are alive and well (see Case study 1 at the end of the chapter).

National standards for competency management were originally devised in the early 1990s by the then lead body for management standards – the Management Charter Initiative (MCI). The national standards have undergone several periods of redevelopment and renegotiation and now, as standards for management and leadership, are part of the National Occupational Standards Framework (**www.ukces.org.uk**) and form the basis for national vocational qualifications (NVQs), Scottish vocational qualifications (SVQs) and vocationally related qualifications (VRQs). There has been considerable effort in the development of the standards to introduce some contextualisation – e.g. the Management and Leadership Standards available in 2013 are divided into nine further categories to take account of different trade, sector and professional specialisms in management.

Explore

Locate the National Occupational Standards for Management and Leadership at **www.ukces.org.uk**.

● Which category is most relevant for your occupational specialism?
● Could you find one that fits?

Since their inception, competence-based national standards have attracted considerable criticism. Some have questioned how far competencies can be generalised beyond a particular organisational context (Mole, 2010). Thus CBD can generate frustration and resentment when the competence-based approach is seen not to be appropriate or relevant to the needs of managers in their organisational situation (Antonacopoulou and Bento, 2010) or where managers who may be viewed as competent in one contextual setting are deemed 'incompetent' when reviewed in another context.

Others have also argued that there has been too much emphasis on assessment and not enough on learning (Antonacopoulou and Bento, 2010) or have expressed concerns about the way competence-based approaches are seen to operate (cost, time, bureaucracy, inflexibility, etc.). Further, the view that competencies are either scientifically neutral or objectively measurable has been challenged (Mabey and Finch-Lees, 2008), especially where they reinforce gender stereotypes of management behaviour (Kyriakidou, 2012).

Alongside the national standards, many organisations prefer to link competencies to strategic expectations of leaders' performance. Rather than engage with a somewhat costly, bureaucratic, prescriptive and rigid framework of national standards, they develop competence frameworks for managers that are more fragmented and differentiated as they seek to adapt to changing individual circumstances.

Explore

One example of how leadership competences can inform LMD is the NHS's leadership framework. Explore the framework from the following link: **http://www.leadershipacademy. nhs.uk/discover/leadership-framework/**. In particular, notice the competence-based language that is used in the examples offered at **http://www.leadershipacademy.nhs.uk/ discover/leadership-framework-in-practice/**.

If one considers organisational competency frameworks as simply 'high-level job analysis' (Mole, 2010), competencies can be used as predictors of successful management and leadership behaviour and form the basis for formal learning interventions, particularly if they are not considered to be the only source of information for decision-making. Thus competency-based development can inform policy-making and implementation in LMD.

Key Controversy

Competency-based development is not without its critics. The extent to which competencies reflect capability in the role is questioned and organisations may be accused of paying 'lip service' to the frameworks that act as its foundation.

If your organisation already operates CBD, how effective has it been? If not, to what extent would CBD make a difference to the way managers in your organisation are currently being developed?

Career development

In the past, an individual's career was tied to progression in a single organisation. Hierarchical progression upwards through clearly defined junior, middle and senior management roles was based on tenure, the possession of specialist skills and the display of patterns of expected behaviours. However, the nature of the career has changed radically (see Chapter 5 for more detail); traditional pathways have been replaced by uncertain and less clearly defined routes where 'automatic' promotion is no longer available to the majority. Individuals may experience a punctuated or 'boundaryless' career in which there will be less job security and career progression opportunities will be limited (Tams and Arthur, 2010). Career progression is likely to involve a greater emphasis on horizontal or diagonal rather than vertical movement, e.g. projects, overseas secondments and postings, departmental and job shifts, internal consultancy roles, acting as mentors and coaches. In the new career, success accrues to those who display greater flexibility and adaptability.

In terms of LMD, the emergence of the new career is characterised by three points of difference from the 'traditional' career (Sturges, 2010):

- an increase in individual (rather than organisational) management, making self-development more important in LMD;
- an emphasis on career mobility where security with one employer is no longer guaranteed, meaning an increased desire for the individual to develop generic, portable skills;
- an increasing recognition that work is just one part of life, meaning individuals are not prepared to devote long periods away from work to development and training that could take place in work time.

Thus, as the challenges have changed the landscape for individuals, so has it changed for organisations: as management structures have delayered, so opportunities for progression have reduced and organisations no longer treat individuals as indispensable or irreplaceable, nor are they inclined to invest highly in their development. The impact of this change in expectations about career has meant that the responsibility for LMD may have shifted for many from the organisation to the individual, or at best be shared between the two parties (Tams and Arthur, 2010). LMD, in short, is now an individual rather than a corporate experience (Sturges, 2010).

Moreover, as careers become more individualised, the challenges in balancing individual and organisational needs become more acute (Sturges, 2010). For example, the key way to increase the effectiveness of LMD is to place an emphasis on developing *managers within the context in which they manage* rather than just in the classroom, the training suite or the hotel conference room. However, this is likely to make managers' skills less portable if their organisation is no longer able to employ them. While the UK system has traditionally relied on developing generic, rather than specific, management skills (Ramirez, 2004), this may suit individuals' career plans, but it will not do so much for organisations.

Performance management

The principles and structures of performance management are covered in detail later in the book (see Chapter 13), but performance management systems can also provide the basis of LMD and allow a more individualised approach. They have the potential to motivate and reward managers who contribute to strategic goals and objectives and, by implication, to exert sanctions on or 'punish' those who fail to deliver anticipated performance levels. The achievement of objectives is closely linked to management training and education, which act to provide the skills and knowledge required to meet objectives. Performance appraisal provides the forum for identifying development needs. It also serves as the mechanism for feeding back information to managers about their current levels of performance, enabling them to identify and negotiate adjustments or further development needs.

Explore

Do you have a personal development plan?

- If you have not, make a mental note to discuss this with your boss at your next appraisal interview.
- If you have got a plan, when was it last reviewed?
- Is it still valid and up to date?

In addition to performance appraisal, another method of establishing a personal development plan is through a development centre. Development centres are used to determine career development needs and talent potential (Harrison, 2009). Practically, development centres are workshops that measure the abilities of participants against the agreed success criteria for a job or role. The main aim of a development centre is to obtain the best possible indication of a person's actual or potential competence to perform at the target job or job level. In that sense they are useful – albeit expensive in time and other resources – for the organisation and the individual in clarifying values, motivation and potential. The result is the crafting of a development plan, which may include endorsement of suitability for a more senior role. Such schemes are common in large organisations across all sectors, e.g. HM Prison Service or Nationwide.

Most development centres operate in the following way:

1 There is careful selection of job-related criteria. These may be in the form of competences, dimensions, attributes or critical success factors.

2 A group of managers is identified and brought together in the form of a workshop normally lasting one or two days. In the workshops, a series of diagnostic instruments and/or multiple assessment techniques are administered that aim to measure an individual's ability to perform against the job-related criteria. These can take the form of psychometric tests, planning exercises, in-tray exercises, interviews, games or simulations.

3 A team of trained assessors observe and measure performance, evaluate and provide structured feedback and guidance to individuals.

4 After the workshop, line managers and/or trainers utilise the feedback to help the individual construct a personal development plan.

A number of criticisms have been levelled at poor practice in this area: for example, assessment techniques that do not relate to the task or job, poor organisation, poorly trained assessors, ineffective feedback and the lack of follow-up action.

LMD interventions: which ones are appropriate?

Like other learning and development interventions (see Chapter 7), LMD methods are often divided into formal and informal (Mankin, 2009; Hanson, 2013), in-house or external (Storey, 2010a), or taught and experiential (Antonacopoulou and Bento, 2010), and LMD delivery can be as individual as the organisation in which it is based. However, LMD usually includes the following (Mabey and Finch-Lees, 2008; CIPD, 2011, 2012a):

- *Formal learning (e.g. workshops, training courses and seminars)* – specific interactions designed to address and achieve specific competencies, e.g. workshops, training courses (face to face, blended or virtual), seminars (internal skills programmes, external courses), conferences or formal qualifications (from NVQs to MBAs).

- *Informal learning* – work-based methods designed to structure the informal learning that takes place in the workplace, e.g. mentoring or coaching, in company job rotation, special projects (internal or external assignments, placements or secondments).

Formal interventions are used more frequently and are perceived to be the most effective (see Figure 8.5). Most of the interventions that are available, be they formal or informal, contain one or more of the following aspects (Storey, 2004, 2010c):

- learning about leadership theory and its application;
- self and/or team analysis through questionnaires and instruments;
- experiential learning and simulation through one-to-one coaching or team-based activities.

The transitional process from learning through analysis to application forms the core of best-practice LMD. It is widely recognised that central to the success of LMD is contextualisation to the role and organisation of the individual (Duerden, 2006).

Formal methods of delivering LMD

> By simply asking the question, 'Can leadership be taught?', one is immediately in danger of ringing alarm bells and raising hackles on a truly grand scale. That is because an enormous amount of business activity, on a global basis, is based on creating the belief among buyers that not only can leadership be taught, but that there are many who are qualified to teach it, through a variety of methods.
>
> Mole (2010: 113)

Formal methods of LMD rely heavily on input from trainers, teachers and other 'experts', and the LMD industry is big business (Mole, 2010). LMD is often seen as synonymous with formal education. The emphasis on formal education makes it easier to demonstrate LMD's link to the strategic intentions of the organisation, as participation can be clearly identified and tracked through performance management systems. Such formal LMD can take place 'on the job' (within the workplace environment, e.g. at a training centre) or 'off the job' (away from the workplace in a college, university or conference/seminar; Mumford and Gold, 2006). The differences between on- and off-the-job approaches to learning generally have been explained (see Chapter 7), but here we consider LMD specifically.

However, despite the popularity of formal methods of development (CIPD, 2011, 2012a), there is considerable debate about whether 'teaching' leadership is an effective way of developing managers (Antonacopoulou and Bento, 2010; Mole, 2010). Programmes or courses may be the least appropriate way to develop individuals or groups of managers and may even generate resistance and frustration (Mole, 2010). Furthermore, it is debatable whether leadership *can* be taught, or must be developed experientially (Ng *et al.*, 2009; Antonacopoulou and Bento, 2010). While formal programmes may be effective in giving knowledge about leadership, they are less effective at developing leadership skills *per se*. Typically, formalised methods are less contextualised or applied, yet the most effective are 'connected and aligned to' (Hanson, 2013: 106) both the specific organisational contexts in which the managers and leaders operate, and the outcomes for which those leaders and managers are responsible (Mole, 2010; Hanson, 2013). One way in which to build this comprehensive picture to effectively inform LMD is through competency frameworks, which are described and discussed in the previous section.

Corporate universities

Corporate universities have, for some larger organisations, been the vehicle for delivering in-house formal LMD (Paton *et al.*, 2010). These vary in structure and arrangements: they have as their purpose the meeting of corporate learning requirements through a highly structured and visible in-house provision, usually based in corporate headquarters. They often rely on competency frameworks to structure the delivery of LMD and in that sense there is a clear link between the activity of the corporate university and organisational performance (Paton *et al.*, 2010). In the UK there are now an estimated 200 organisations professing to have established a corporate university. Organisations include Veolia Environnment, Anglian Water,

Figure 8.5 Leadership and management development methods: frequency of use versus effectiveness

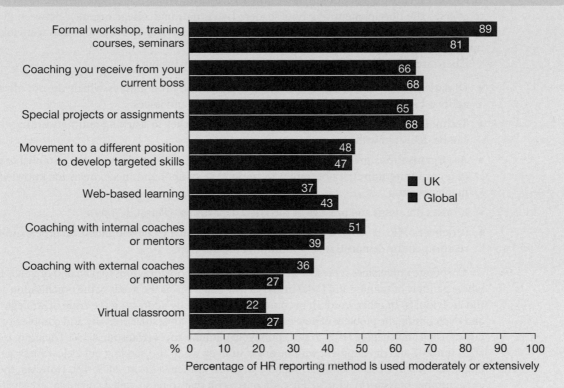

Percentage of HR reporting method is used moderately or extensively

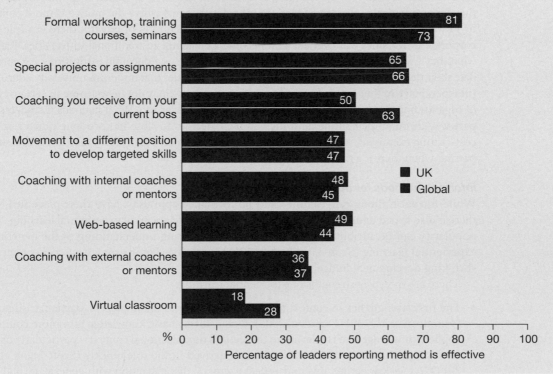

Percentage of leaders reporting method is effective

Source: UK Highlights: Global Leadership Forecast 2011, London: CIPD (2011) pp. 8–9, Figures 8 and 9, with the permission of the publisher, the Chartered Institute of Personnel and Development, London (www.cipd.co.uk).

Unipart, Lloyds TSB and British Aerospace. Similar models exist in the public sector in the National College for School Leadership (discussed by Alimo-Metcalfe and Alban-Metcalfe, 2010), an executive agency of the Government's Department for Education, which was formed to oversee the development of school leaders (**www.nationalcollege.org.uk**). Between 2000 and its merger with the Teaching Agency on 13 March 2013, over 160,000 places were taken up on the leadership development courses it offered.

There are a number of factors that have led to this expansion:

- Dissatisfaction with the generic nature of academic programmes which do not always address localised and unique management problems and issues.
- Technological development, facilitating new approaches to learning and networking that can be delivered with ease and cost-effectively.
- As organisations grow increasingly more complex and ambiguous, the establishment of a corporate university becomes an important symbol and mechanism for knowledge management.
- It raises the status and prestige of the HRD department (Persaud, 2004).
- It delivers HR benefits, e.g. access to a high standard of development facilities, aiding recruitment by demonstrating commitment to develop.

Corporate universities represent a coherent attempt by organisations to plan and organise the whole panoply of training and LMD in such a way that it meets the needs of the organisation and the individuals. In other words, it becomes a way of directly addressing the issue of strategic fit and overcoming the problem of how to meet the needs of contextual diversity and complexity by customising and shaping HRD to suit contingent circumstances (Hanson, 2013). Their aim is 'to align training and development with business strategy while also sending out a clear message to employees that the organisation is prepared to invest in them' (Arkin, 2003: 42). However, there are a number of issues to address. First, there is a risk that some so-called corporate universities may be nothing more than re-badged training departments where the motive is more political or PR than learning or development. Second, at forecasted rates of growth, there is a fear that corporate universities will overtake and become a challenge to traditional universities. Rather, what they say they are seeking is a collaboration with Higher Education institutions, e.g. to validate their degree offerings. But there are fears that the values that underpin university education (independence of thought and critical analysis and debate) may not be welcome in certain types of organisational culture. Third, there are practical concerns too. What happens if students are part-way through their studies and the company decides to close its corporate university as a cost-cutting exercise? Universities too may be chary of linking themselves too closely to a single partner when there is a risk of commercial failure (Arkin, 2003).

Informal methods for developing managers

While formal training programmes and performance appraisals have their place in LMD, there is also broad understanding of the benefits and efficiencies of experiential learning. This popularity can be attributed, at least in part, to a growing understanding of the benefits of experiential learning (Scott-Ligon *et al.*, 2011), as well as being a practical consequence of shrinking development budgets (CIPD, 2012a).

There are three key strengths of experiential learning:

- The first strength lies in contextualising the learning to the managers' particular situation (Thomson *et al.*, 2001; Duerden, 2006). It transforms basic knowledge into more complex, applied knowledge that is relevant to the leader's organisational context – particularly useful for high-potential managers who may have arrived in the role quickly (Scott-Ligon *et al.*, 2011). As we saw earlier, this may reflect a general dissatisfaction with generic, formal off-the-shelf courses or education programmes when they do not meet unique organisational, contextual or individual needs (Thomson *et al.*, 2001; Mole, 2010).

- The second strength is that experiences develop both skill and identity in the role (Mumford *et al.,* 2007; Scott-Ligon *et al.,* 2011). The exercise of problem-solving and decision-making skills is a feature of addressing the challenges that experiences offer, thereby developing cognitive capabilities for future situations.

- Finally, and pragmatically, it is inexpensive. The growth in popularity of experiential learning may also reflect the desire by individuals and organisations to take advantage of more flexible and cost-effective methods, often using innovative technologies (Scott, 2004) that fit with changing lifestyles and rapidly changing or unique organisational situations (Scott-Ligon *et al.,* 2011) and increasingly individualised careers (Sturges, 2010).

The experiences themselves can be *planned* experiences (McCall, 2010), e.g. projects or placements, or *unplanned* experiences during normal workplace activity. They can be false (e.g. outdoor pursuits and games) or real: Tate (2010) distinguished between 'ostensibly realistic' (resembling typical work activity such as case studies or practice tasks, but not in the learner's own company), 'potentially real' (using company materials but agreed as a learning opportunity) and 'live reality' (where work problems are considered in a context from which to learn and take action). Whatever the experience, the process of learning occurs through the more formal activity of reflective practice (Marsick and Watkins, 1997; Moon, 2004). On the whole, then, 'experiences are compelling as developmental tools' (Scott-Ligon *et al.,* 2011: 301).

The remainder of this section covers some examples of experiential learning along Tate's (2010) continuum, from false, to live reality:

- active learning;
- projects and secondments;
- coaching and mentoring;
- action learning sets;
- reflective practice.

Active learning

> Active learning...[includes] business simulations, games, improvisation, outdoor learning and a whole host of increasingly esoteric learning metaphors ranging from African drumming through to horse-whispering and community engagement. Gold et al. (2010: 31)

Active learning in LMD encompasses a range of methods of development that rely on physical activity or practical tasks analogous to challenges in the workplace, but which take place in contexts that are unlike their everyday working environment. The goal is usually a 'time-compressed simulation of getting something done collectively' (Gold *et al.,* 2010: 31). They require careful management to ensure that:

- external providers understand organisational priorities;
- individual and organisational development intentions are achieved;
- issues of hierarchy, gender and ability are sensitively considered;
- they are not perceived as an expensive diversion from the 'real' challenges of leadership.

Active learning also encompasses outdoor LMD (OMD), which can include 'anything from an afternoon of activities on a hotel lawn to a month of outdoor adventure training in the Scottish wilderness' (Jones and Oswick, 2007: 327). Managers are exposed to emotional, physical and mental risks and challenges in which skills such as leadership and teamwork become *real* to the individuals and groups concerned. While the consequences may be real during the experience of OMD, it is not always clear what the longer-term benefits are or how likely learning is to be transferred to the workplace, as noted by Tarrant (2005: 25):

> Depending on your bent or glee at seeing a difficult colleague disappear down a river without a paddle, the experience [of OMD] invariably delivered 'war stories' of hilarity and terror with widely questioned benefits to the team at the real coalface back at the office.

With this issue in mind, Jones and Oswick (2007) identify that the most effective OMD aims to improve participants' management of themselves and others, is embedded in a broader process of LMD, addresses the *specific* learning needs of the individuals and teams involved, and requires both individual discretion and cooperative effort. Furthermore, tasks have to increase in difficulty as the OMD progresses, and review and feedback are regular and focused on process issues, rather than on technical ones.

While physical challenges are still popular, there has been a noticeable shift to more sophisticated forms of active learning that focus on problem-solving, innovation and changing behaviour in the classroom and beyond. For example, Arkin (2003) describes how Sony (Europe) took its senior managers on a 'leadership journey' across Europe linked to team and individual exercises designed for them to experience the anxiety and uncertainty their employees felt during radical change. Allen (2003: 36) also describes how managers are engaging with community-based projects linked to corporate social responsibility, arguing that active learning is moving towards 'experiences that are carefully designed to provide a true metaphor for the workplace'.

Projects and secondments

Secondments and projects are popular and organisationally beneficial ways of developing the knowledge and skills of managers within their working context. For example, multinational companies have highly sophisticated management exchange programmes that are used not only to develop important language and cultural skills in managers (Ng *et al.*, 2009), but also to reinforce the organisation's central belief and value systems. Exchange programmes also exist between public and private sector organisations to transfer knowledge and broaden understanding (Alimo-Metcalfe and Alban-Metcalfe, 2010). Some larger organisations are seconding their managers to various initiatives designed to assist small business ventures and community programmes. Tate (2010) identifies the dual use of projects, assignments and secondments in both *developing* leadership talent and *utilising* leadership talent as a component of a strategic approach to LMD and one which ensures best value for money.

Coaching and mentoring

Coaching and mentoring were described in detail earlier (see Chapter 7), where the dual concerns of raising awareness and developing responsibility (Whitmore, 2009) were identified and explained. Distinguishing between coaching and mentoring is important in order to identify the different sets of roles and responsibilities in the relationships (see Chapter 7).

As an LMD tool, coaching, in particular, has received significant recent attention (Lee, 2003; Passmore, 2010) for its role in raising self-awareness and focus on achieving specific outcomes. Furthermore, significant value rests on the process of capturing learning from the day-to-day activities of managers. There has been considerable investment by some organisations in providing external, or developing internal, coaches to support managers and leaders at all levels and it is part of management development activities in 46 per cent of organisations (CIPD, 2012a); 51 per cent of organisations consider coaching to be the most effective method of development (CIPD, 2012a), while, conversely, 40 per cent of organisations identified that there was a lack of skills in coaching and mentoring in leaders (CIPD, 2012a).

Action learning sets

> There is no learning without action and no (sober and delicate) action without learning.
>
> Revans (1983)

Action learning, as distinct from active learning, is attributed to Reg Revans. Revans argued that learning by doing, reflecting on personal actions and experience, was a powerful tool in improving performance. Action learning is common in leadership development models (Skipton-Leonard, 2009).

Revans saw learning (L) as a combination of what he terms 'programmed knowledge' (P) and 'questioning insight' (Q): thus $L = P + Q$. When facing unprecedented changes, managers cannot know what programmed knowledge they will need. Instead, they need to 'understand the subjective aspects of searching the unfamiliar, or learning to pose useful and discriminating questions'. Therefore action learning becomes a 'simple device of setting them to tackle real problems that have so far defied solution' (Revans, 1983: 11).

Revans (2011) identified 20 key principles of action learning that explain the importance of action and lived experience to effectiveness as a leader or manager. Revans argues that managerial learning has to embrace both 'know-how' and 'know-that', and be rooted in real problem-solving, where 'lasting behavioural change is more likely to follow the reinterpretation of past experiences than the acquisition of fresh knowledge' (p. 14). Managers will be more able to make their interpretations, which are 'necessarily subjective, complex and ill-structured' (p. 14), and reorder their perceptions by working with colleagues who are engaged in the same process, as well as with non-managers, such as management teachers, who are 'not exposed to real risk in responsible action'. Therefore, the principles include the fact that formal instruction is not sufficient, that asking challenging questions is important and that voluntarism is essential.

A central aspect of action learning is the contribution of peers – that is, that managers learn from managers and non-managers by checking their perceptions and actions against those of others. This process is formalised through the 'action learning set' (groups of four to six people) who, with the aid of a facilitator, work together and learn to give and accept criticism, advice and support.

Therefore, in LMD, action learning sets have become a popular intervention for general development purposes (Pedler, 2008; Alimo-Metcalfe and Alban-Metcalfe, 2010) and specifically in facilitating change (Butler and Leach, 2011).

However, there are some doubts about the efficacy of action learning, e.g. in the extent to which managers will truly engage in action learning if this challenges current management cultures and political structures with concomitant risks for the individual (Pedler, 2008). That said, interest is still alive in the benefits of action learning to the manager's experience (Kesby, 2008).

Reflective practice

> It is not sufficient simply to have an experience in order to learn. Without reflecting upon this experience it may quickly be forgotten, or its learning potential lost. It is from the feelings and thoughts emerging from this reflection that generalisations or concepts can be generated. And it is generalisations that allow new situations to be tackled effectively.   Gibbs (1988: 16)

A greater focus on experiential learning in the workplace, coupled with a reaction against the 'remoteness', complication and institutionalisation of LMD, has encouraged organisations to adopt new methods of learning, which include reflective practice. While the process is not without its critics (well articulated by Hunt, 2005), the value of reflecting on practice is well established in many professions (e.g. HRM, nursing, teaching) and underlines the notion of the manager as practitioner, rather than scientist (Moon, 2004; Gold et al., 2007; Thompson and Thompson, 2008).

Introduced by *The Reflective Practitioner* (Schön, 1984) and closely associated with action learning, the ideas associated with reflective practice have gained ground in the last 30 years. Schön's work argued that the gap between theory and practice was widening and in order to address that, managers ought to be encouraged to be reflective practitioners. This area is closely related to social learning theory, (see Chapter 7).

Reflective practice is a set of abilities and skills to indicate the taking of a critical stance on your practice or experience as an individual. The process relies on participants engaging in *active observation* and *critical reflection,* both of which require particular sets of skills.

Active observation can be described as a 'lean forward' activity which requires engagement and absorption by the observer in the process. Learning by observation involves four separate processes (Bandura, 1997):

- *Attention.* Observers learn when they pay attention to events around them. This may be influenced by expectations about the event or person that is being observed and personal liking or respect.

- *Retention.* Observers learn when they remember the event or behaviour observed. This is reliant on the observer's ability to remember the information in a way that allows them to reuse it.

- *Production.* Observers must be capable of producing the act. Observing a complex action or event is quite different from being able to repeat it. *Masterchef* fans will know this from the 'taste test' challenge that participants must successfully pass in order to proceed in the competition!

- *Motivation.* Observers will only repeat what they have observed if they are motivated to do so. Reinforcement or reward can assist in the process.

Attention and retention account for acquisition or learning of a model's behaviour; production and motivation control the quality of subsequent performance. On the whole, however, observation itself is of limited value unless the object and purpose of observation is clearly defined to the observer.

Critical reflection provides time and space for the individual to direct their attention to new interpretations of events and a means through which personal competences and capabilities can be examined and interpreted so as to develop deeper understanding and self-awareness. Critical reflection is often captured in writing through reflective diaries or accounts (Bolton, 2010). This process gives order to the disparate events and captures the reflective process in a way that allows the writer to reflect on future action (Moon, 2004). The most effective critical reflection is the deepest. Hatton and Smith (1995) suggest four levels of reflective writing:

- *Descriptive writing* – not reflective, no discussion beyond description.

- *Descriptive reflection* – description of events, alternative viewpoints accepted, but not embraced.

- *Dialogic reflection* – demonstrates a stepping back from events, a 'conversation with yourself', mulling about the events and actions. Recognises different qualities of judgment and alternative explanations. Analytical.

- *Critical reflection* – demonstrates an awareness that actions and events are not only located within and explicable by multiple perspectives, but are located in and influenced by multiple contexts.

In essence, it is a readiness to constantly evaluate and review your practice in the light of new learning (which may arise from within the context of your professional practice) and at its broadest is an orientation to problem-solving or state of mind (Moon, 2004) that adds sophistication to the process of learning from experience. However, learners can create any number of meanings, intended or otherwise, out of the same learning experience: accuracy and relevance can be improved through practice.

In reflective writing, the learner will normally ask a series of questions of themselves in relation to the event or experience and recount these in a written statement: what happened; so what; now what? Much of the theory relating to reflective practice is drawn from the work of Kolb (1984) and Honey and Mumford (1989), who introduced the concept of a learning cycle in which managers learn through a process of:

- implementation
- reflection
- making changes
- initiating further action.

In summary, this section has outlined some of the formal and informal methods that are currently being used to develop managers. However, it must be borne in mind that a great deal of development takes place in ways that are not only less formal, but are also incidental and opportunistic. There may be times when the individual manager is unaware that development has even taken place, e.g. trial and error, learning from mistakes, playing political games. This suggests that development may have as much to do with the provision of organisational support and facilitation for the creation of a learning culture and managing the influence of organisational context (social, political, cultural) in which managers operate as it does with the selection and implementation of specific development methods. An entirely upbeat view of reflective practice may be misguided, however, and we should consider the hazards, as well as the hopes, of critical reflection (Trehan and Rigg, 2008).

Identifying who to involve and how

Leadership and management development is, in many organisations, both high-profile and politically contentious, largely because of the vested interests of a wide range of stakeholders both intentionally identified as having a responsibility in its management and peripherally involved because of their broader contribution or interest (Mabey, 2013), e.g. government or professional agencies, in-house trainers or development units, consultancy firms, HR managers, line managers and the managers or leaders involved in the development intervention.

Therefore, to be constructive, development demands the involvement of a range of stakeholders, each of whom will have an impact on the development process and its outcomes (Mabey and Finch-Lees, 2008;). Figure 8.6 identifies a number of key stakeholders, each of whom shares a measure of responsibility. Clarifying these at the outset is central to ensuring continued support for the process and for minimising resistance. Having determined its policy guidelines, the next step for the organisation is to consider how it should approach the development of its managers (Mumford and Gold, 2006). Traditionally, responsibility for development has rested with the HR function, with some input from the manager's boss through the performance management system (Duerden, 2006) (see below and Chapter 12). The individual manager was often passive in the process: they were only required to 'turn up and be developed'. If a development programme is to be successfully planned and implemented, there has to be clear and unambiguous allocation of responsibility and a willingness to accept that responsibility by the parties involved.

Explore

Prepare a list of those who are responsible for your development.

- How clearly are their roles delineated and communicated?
- How effective is the support you receive?
- How can you clarify and improve the roles of stakeholders in LMD in your organisation?

An active process of discussion and negotiation should ensure that each set of stakeholders accepts and owns a share of the responsibility for supporting the process, e.g. through supporting the manager, setting development objectives, planning and implementing the process. However, as Mabey and Salaman (1995: 176) identify, the linkages between each stakeholder

Figure 8.6 Stakeholders in leadership and management development

Reasons for supporting	Stakeholder	Reasons for resisting
Personal development, status/prestige, improved career, break from the norm	**Manager/leader**	Waste of time, unwillingness to accept new responsibilities
Improved management and direction, expresses commitment to development	**Team**	Resistance to changes, absence of manager when training, waste of time
Solves performance problems, commitment to development, reward/incentive	**Line managers**	Creates line problems (manager's absence)
Strengthens skills, opportunity to demonstrate professional knowledge, improves political ties in organisation	**HR professionals**	Might be able to see better alternative
Demonstrates action to other stakeholders, improves financial performance	**Senior managers**	Might not be sufficiently tied to the bottom line
Concrete message about commitment to employees, improved financial performance	**Boards**	May be disruptive, cause divisions
Financial opportunity demonstrates commitment to improving national skills	**External funding agencies**	Limited involvement in design doesn't generate sufficient new knowledge or skills, not tied to national standards

Source: adapted from Burgoyne and Jackson (1997: 63).

are complex and each will 'help shape the ethos and practice of training and development within organisations'.

Deciding how to evaluate

Organisations undertake LMD with the assumption that there will be some beneficial outputs (Tyler, 2004; Tate, 2010) and so measuring LMD is vital to demonstrate the value of the programme in terms of monetary value or achievement of organisational goals (Mabey and Finch-Lees, 2008). Traditionally, the literature on evaluation has focused heavily on the training and education 'components' of development (Warr *et al.*, 1970; Rae, 2002; also see Chapter 7). However, evaluation of leadership development programmes has been criticised for a reliance on structured or quantitative evaluation models that do not account for:

- broad or qualitative outcomes (Edwards and Turnbull, 2013) such as improvements in leader relationships (Cunliffe and Eriksen, 2011);
- the longer-term impact or sustainability of development (Jarvis *et al.*, 2013);

- the context in which the development takes place (Tyler, 2004; Hanson, 2013): 'it makes little sense to send newly trained people back into unchanged organisations' (Peters and Baum, 2007:64);

- the input and impact of stakeholders (Grandy and Holton, 2013; McCauley-Smith *et al.*, 2013).

For example, Jarvis *et al.* (2013) identify the 'tensions' in seeking evidence for the effectiveness of leadership development through traditional quantitative/return on investment (ROI) calculations. They argue that such measurements are flawed in their attempts to link inputs from leadership development to outputs in leadership behaviour. By way of an alternative, they propose a qualitative/ethnographic approach which recognises the messy complexity of management learning. The methods identified included guided conversations on critical incidents and key learning points, placing greater emphasis on the everyday experience of participants in applying their learning and establishing 'What is really going on here?' Therefore, with increased pressure on resources, being able to demonstrate the contribution is vital. Aside from financial measures, other success criteria are possible and identifying these in advance is vital if there is to be effective evaluation (Hamblin, 2007; Tate, 2010).

Explore

Identify a recent LMD initiative that you were involved in.

- What were the desired outcomes of this initiative?
- How could these be measured taking into account the criticisms made of most evaluations in the previous paragraph?
- How would you account for these measurements to the stakeholders?

LMD in different contexts or for different needs

Throughout the chapter, the importance of considering the context in which LMD takes place has been explained as a core component of its strategic success. Tailoring interventions to contexts requires careful consideration of local factors; however, there are a number of generic contexts that have received attention in the literature, outlined here: different national contexts, senior manager development, developing professionals as managers, graduate LMD, LMD in the small firm, LMD in the public sector, international LMD and the development groups under-represented in management.

LMD in different national contexts

Leadership and management development is located in the cultural, social and economic context in which it is set (Geppert *et al.*, 2002), such that the impact of industrial relations, social protection, professional associations, legislation, regulation and economic conditions will play a part in determining LMD practices at a national level (Mabey and Finch-Lees, 2008). In short, the context will frame the choices that businesses make about investments in LMD and the appropriateness of various interventions.

Explore

The differences between approaches to LMD across the world are well reported elsewhere – for example, for a full review of practices across Europe, read Ramirez (2004).

However, there has been limited debate on the differences required in development interventions so as to take account of culture-specific views of management and leadership; for example, the global growth of the (Western) MBA as a leadership development tool is evidence of the relative insensitivity to cultural norms about leadership (Saks *et al.,* 2011).

Senior manager development

The separate treatment of the most senior managers – or those with potential to fall into that category – in an organisation is a well-established approach (Lee, 2003; Trehan and Shelton, 2007; McCall, 2010). Arguably, their position high in the organisational hierarchy, their strategic responsibilities, a requirement for cross- or extra-organisational working and special benefits linked to their status mean that they require special consideration (CIPD, 2008).

That they are likely to be far fewer in number will mean that their development will need to be more tailored and specific, requiring additional planning and investment (CIPD, 2008). Their isolation – often without a peer group on which to draw for learning and support – makes their role even more difficult to develop (CIPD, 2008) and solutions harder to identify. Solutions are likely to be highly tailored to the context and performance expectations of the role, and to the needs of the individual. A number of high-profile schemes exist that provide development pathways for leaders at the top of their organisational hierarchy (see **http://www. civilservice.gov.uk/about/leadership/developing-leaders**).

Developing professionals as managers

A number of authors and research projects have examined senior leadership training for those engaged in specific professions, e.g. education (Glatter, 2004; Bristow, 2007; Bennett, 2010) and the National Health Service (NHS) (Bristow, 2007), and considered the extent to which leadership and its development require special consideration or distinct models (Bush, 2008). In particular, changes in the nature of accountability and responsibility for management targets that accompany the move to management have been identified as key. Bittel (1998) argues that this is the main challenge for developers: the highly individualistic approach that professionals have towards their work, its intellectual challenge and their loyalty to their profession and its values, mean that when faced with the challenge of moving into management, professionals may display 'counterproductive characteristics':

- They over-apply their analytical skills and can become paralysed by analysis.
- They are insensitive to others and feel they are above organisational politics.
- They expect their technical expertise to solve organisational problems.
- They respect logic and intuition over emotion.
- They lack feeling and empathy.
- They lack awareness of common-sense solutions to problems.

Undoubtedly, some professionals make very good managers and are particularly good with people. Yet others face conflict between their role as professional and their role as manager. For example, research in secondary education amongst heads of department and deputy heads highlights the clash between the professional role as teacher and the role of middle manager (Adey, 2000), exposing the conflict between professional and managerial value systems. For example, in the NHS, a significant amount of research has been undertaken to explore the impact of development focused on core and leadership competencies. Earlier in this chapter we identified that competence-based approaches were likely to be generic, structured and prescriptive, which may cause tensions with professional values:

> Whilst recognising that every organisation is unique, the history and professional elaboration of groups in the public sector make a hospital particularly unique. The weakness of the competence approach and insensitivity of delivery to context reinforce the ideological gap between managerial and professional values.
>
> (Currie and Brown, 2003: 579)

Other research highlights the potential dangers of using what are perceived to be generic, simplistic, off-the-shelf training courses for developing professionals as managers. Research suggests that overall, professionals in education may prefer a more contingent, personalised approach to their development and the issues it raises, and, in particular, action learning in the development of leaders in the NHS has been well received (Bristow, 2007). The 'environmental complexity' inherent in many professional environments makes tailored provision particularly important (Glatter, 2004: 208; Bennett, 2010).

The spirit of this personalised approach is captured in the notion of continuous professional development (CPD): formal or informal development practices that continue beyond initial training or development (Collin *et al.*, 2012). Many professional associations – such as the CIPD – require or strongly recommend CPD as a condition of remaining part of the professional community (see **http://www.cipd.co.uk/cpd/guidance/**).

Graduate LMD

Graduates are covered in talent management activities by 51 per cent of respondents in the CIPD Annual Learning and Talent Development Survey (CIPD, 2012a); however, they are less likely to be developed as a specific group in non-profit or public-sector organisations. Graduates are recruited – usually directly from university or shortly after they graduate – for broadly two purposes. First, they provide essential specialist knowledge and skills, e.g. scientific, engineering, computing. Secondly, they 'create a pool of intelligent people with high potential as a means of providing for management of the future' (Mumford and Gold, 2006: 222; Connor and Shaw, 2008). What they lack are organisation-specific skills (Boyatzis *et al.*, 2002), which poses particular issues for LMD. Moreover, the schemes often represent significant expense for which demonstrating return on investment, particularly in the early stages, can be challenging (Bedingfield, 2005).

In respect of the way in which graduates are developed as managers, Mumford (1997: 223) argues:

> There is no mystery about what to do with graduates. There needs to be a formal development programme for them which will include appropriate courses; they need to have assignments in particular units or departments long enough to establish that they have done a definable piece of work.

Many large organisations (see Box 8.1) will have graduate LMD schemes designed to take graduates – with either professional or generalist degrees – with potential to senior management roles quickly and successfully.

Box 8.1 | **Graduate recruitment scheme for HR professionals in the civil service**

Continuing growth in the recruitment scheme for HR graduates aims to build a pipeline of candidates for top government jobs

The civil service has expanded its graduate recruitment scheme for HR professionals as it changes its delivery model and seeks the leaders of the future. Now in its fourth year, the scheme continues to grow and evolve, and is taking on 25 per cent more HR graduates in this autumn's intake. The programme is an important part of how the organisation is changing overall, explained Chris Last, HR director-general of the Department for Work and Pensions and head of government HR operations, responsible for 5,000 HR professionals.

➤

Box 8.1 continued

'We've upped the number of graduate recruits from between 40 and 50 to 60 for 2012–13 because we have changed the nature of the service. HR is changing from the classic Ulrich model to become more about added value,' said Last.

'A lot of senior level posts have been recruited externally, my own included, and actually we need to generate a pipeline of people that can become the future HR directors of the civil service.'

The three-year graduate programme is based on two 18-month assignments in which the trainees do 'real' jobs, rather than being seconded, Last said. Graduates master their HR skills and knowledge in three ways: learning on the job, studying for their CIPD accreditation and taking part in technical training.

'The value of these graduate schemes is all about the assignments and the stretches you give people during them,' said Last. 'The graduate training is constantly being reviewed and adjusted to ensure people get the maximum benefit from it', he added.

'The scheme is a more effective way of filling top posts than a previous strategy where HR people were selected from the line and administrative duties elsewhere in the service', he said. Last also recognises that the HR community overall has work to do to draw top graduates to choose a career in HR, especially in the public sector at a time of continuing service cuts.

'This scheme is partly about growing the professional badge of the HR function in the service, by changing the view that the function just does shared services-type work like payroll. HR can be lots of things: organisational design, talent management and business partnering,' he said. It is these expanded roles that the civil service is setting out to particularly highlight to undergraduates, as it takes the message to universities in its recruitment strategy.

The HR fast stream for graduates also continues to evolve in other ways: the service has just awarded the contract for delivering CIPD accreditation to Coventry University to ensure more consistency in delivery.

'The quality and outline of the CIPD training is standard but the quality of delivery depends on which academic institution is delivering the courses,' Last said. 'And the quality of our graduates' experience is important to us because at the end of this process we assess them and determine whether they can get promoted. So it's important that all the inputs are as common as they can be.'

'In the past we'd give the contract for delivering courses to the institution nearest to where the graduates had their assignment. This had given us a problem where people moved from one location to another as part of their assignment meaning their study would be out of kilter with their job.'

Another area of the graduate scheme that is constantly under scrutiny is technical training, which covers employment law, talent management, workforce training, and pay and reward. Last said they get feedback from graduates to determine whether or not the courses have the right content at the right speed 'and from this we try to make the courses more stretching,' he added.

'Some of the graduates we are hiring now are going to work for graduates we hired four years ago. These former graduate recruits have a better idea of the new recruits, their expectations and an understanding of what can be expected from them. So the quality of the training we can offer is better than four years ago as we get more practised at the scheme.'

This evolution appears to be working, as the retention rate for the scheme is above 80 per cent.

Source: Continuing growth in the recruitment scheme for HR graduates aims to build a pipeline of candidates for government jobs, *People Management* (Claire Churchard), 29 August 2012, with the permission of the publisher, the Chartered Institute of Personnel and Development, London (www.cipd.co.uk).

The competiveness in the job market has laid down significant challenges for graduates entering the workplace (Churchard, 2012). Internships have become a 'high-profile option' for graduates seeking employment on completion of their degree programmes. Internships are difficult to define and thus the legal protection for those engaged in them is unclear:

> An intern may expect to receive practical hands-on training and perhaps be given a project to complete over a short period of time. But an intern who is retained to perform a job, who receives no training, and who does not have a specific goal at the end of a pre-arranged period of time, may be an employee.
>
> (Scutt, 2012: 17)

While internships can offer benefits for graduates (developing technical or practical skills, experience in an industry) and employers (assessing potential employees, identifying the 'talent pipeline', bringing new ideas into the business) there are also significant challenges, not least about whether the internship is paid or not (CIPD, 2010). This latter theme has sparked considerable debate. In 2009, MP Alan Milburn (Cabinet Office, 2009) said:

> The cost of undertaking an internship can put many people off . . . . those with the least financial resources are less likely to be in a position to forgo the opportunity to earn more in order to undertake an internship. We have been shown research demonstrating that the less advantaged are most put off by the costs of undertaking [an unpaid] internship.

An unpaid Internships Bill, which sought to ban the advertisement of unpaid internships and regulate the conditions of employment (Scutt, 2012), failed to clear Parliament at its reading in March 2013 and the pressure put on workers in this position continues to attract high-profile press coverage (Malik and Quinn, 2013).

LMD in the small firm

The economic role of small and medium-sized firms (SMEs) in creating wealth and employment is widely acknowledged in the UK and beyond (BIS, 2011; van Wenroy *et al.*, 2011). The BIS Annual Small Business Survey in 2011 identified that despite economic challenges in the economy, employment levels were up in around a quarter of SMEs and over 66 per cent intended to upskill their workforce – including investment in increasing the leadership capability of managers – in the coming months. However, given the wide range of firms that fall under the 'SME' umbrella, knowledge is limited and generalisations difficult (Mayson and Barrett, 2005).

However, despite the relatively upbeat account of SMEs from some quarters, with managers being judged as good or very good and high levels of trust and participation (van Wenroy *et al.*, 2011), in the UK 65–75 per cent collapse or are sold during first-generation ownership tenure (Williams and Cowling, 2008). While there are many factors that may contribute to this high failure rate, the lack of management knowledge and expertise is viewed as a major factor (Fuller-Love, 2006; Coetzer *et al.*, 2011) and many small businesses fail to reach their potential because of the way their people are managed.

There appears to be sound evidence to suggest that few managers in small firms receive formal management training (Thompson, 2001) and, while there have been improvements in the development of managers in small firms in recent years, one in five managers receive no training at all (Fuller-Love, 2006).

Research has identified a number of challenges facing small businesses in investing in LMD:

- *Resources*. Significant challenges exist in terms of time, resources, previous formal education, concerns about realising returns on investment in management training, not knowing where or how to get advice and assistance, and a lack of appreciation of the complicated procedures and bureaucracy when applying for assistance (Fuller-Love, 2006).

- *Structure and organisation*. A more pervasive factor can explain the lack of formal LMD in SMEs: SMEs tend to be less formal generally in their operation and practice of HRM and HRD (Marlow *et al.*, 2010), posing challenges for formal planning, investment, control and measurement of LMD activities.

- *Size and accessibility.* Another significant barrier arises from the practicalities of having a smaller number of managers to develop, making the transfer and take-up of mainstream, large-organisation-focused methods problematic (Mayson and Barrett, 2005).

- *Availability of training and funding to support.* Over the years, easy access to full or match funding has almost entirely vanished. Funding for development is mostly linked to supporting the provision of apprenticeship or 'enterprise training', focusing on basic skills in operations, HRM marketing, finance, etc. Secondly, significant challenges are placed in the way of small firms seeking funding for more managerial interventions (see the complexity of UKCES's latest round of 'Employer Ownership of Skills' funding, 2013).

- *Owner characteristics and capabilities.* In small firms, success is often linked to strong owner (or family) identity and capability (Jones *et al.,* 2010) where family affiliation (Cater, 2009), individual action and entrepreneurship (Jones and Crompton, 2009; Mitchelmore, 2010) are valued over other capabilities.

Therefore, a strategy for developing managers in the small firm would include:

- identifying the knowledge and skills required by small firm owner/managers;
- delivering development in a way that acknowledges the sector's diversity and uniqueness;
- finding ways to overcome the bureaucracy and provide accessible and affordable approaches to development.

LMD in the public sector

Given the diversity of organisational forms that exist in the public sector in the UK (and across Europe), it is perhaps unwise to consider the sector as homogeneous. Nonetheless, public management may require particular sensitivity to the relationship between policy and operations, productivity and workplace ethos, quality and process, governance and public accountability, as well as the particular financial constraints that exist in a public-sector environment (Loffler and Bovaird, 2009). Some have argued that the context of public-sector management is 'staggeringly complex' (Alimo-Metcalfe and Alban-Metcalfe, 2010: 178) and so developing leadership skills has therefore been a key plank of the government's modernisation agenda (PIU, 2001) in, for example, the NHS, education, policing and the civil service (**http://www.civilservice.gov.uk/**).

Within the public sector, there is a huge range of contexts and work environments within which leaders face many challenges (Flynn, 2007). These can include:

- the management of limited resources that accompany the provision of a 'free' service;
- maintaining a public service ethos in a commercial society;
- managing complex environments with multiple goals and functions and different types of staff (e.g. professional and managerial);
- working within the constraints of unionised environments;
- managing professionals working in environments that may be substandard to that available in the private sector;
- performance standards and goals 'imposed' externally that cover issues not always within the control of the service.

These challenges and contradictions make for an interesting environment in which to develop the manager, often where there are limited funds available. That said, there are notable examples where considerable investment has been made in developing public sector managers, e.g.:

- the NHS Leadership Framework (**http://www.leadershipacademy.nhs.uk/discover/leadership-framework/**);
- the National College for School Leadership (**http://www.education.gov.uk/nationalcollege/**);

- the National Police Leadership Faculty – formerly the NPIA and, from early 2013, the College of Policing (**http://www.college.police.uk/**).

International LMD

Information and communication technologies have made working with suppliers, customers and connections across the globe part of everyday life for most managers (Melkman and Trotman, 2005). The globalisation of business has required the globalisation of management capability, with managers increasingly required to work sensitively and effectively across geographically and culturally diverse contexts (Dalton, 2010). A significant research base has developed to identify the competencies of international leaders and the LMD interventions best suited for their growth (Thorn, 2012).

Moreover, for some multinational organisations, the ability to manage across boundaries is a core competence and LMD has focused on the creation of elite cadres of international managers tasked with building efficient networks of organisations operating across national boundaries (McCall, 2010).

LMD for under-represented groups

Substantial recent attention has been paid to the differential treatment of women managers and their progression through organisations, drawing attention to enduring differences in perspectives on gendered LMD (Madsen, 2012; Kelan, 2013). For example, the Davies Report (Davies, 2011) identified the enduring impact of 'the old boys' network' as an explanation for the under-representation of women on boards in businesses in the UK. The report identified that development opportunities were high on the list of priority actions in order to improve women's representation. Although 15 per cent of board members are now women (Vinnicombe and Sealy, 2012), progress is slower than required to ensure equal representation in higher leadership roles (Clegg, 2012). The UK government has set a 'new aspiration that by the end of the current Parliament, 50% of all new appoints to public boards will be women (May, 2012).

Much less has been said about the position of the other diverse groups in society, and in microcosm in management. Much LMD is 'diversity-neutral' (Mabey and Finch-Lees, 2008) and fails to recognise how current approaches reinforce current prejudices and limitations. LMD is, after all, about conformity – building managers who reinforce corporate messages and approaches (Bailey *et al.*, 2010) – and difference is viewed as 'a liability' (Mabey and Finch-Lees, 2008). Taking a balanced view to LMD and recognising diversity require asking hard questions. Diversity issues are covered in detail elsewhere in the book (see Chapter 7) and ought to be explored before embarking on designing LMD.

Key Controversy

What is your view about the extent to which LMD should be tailored to different groups such as women or minority groups? Why do you hold this view? What are the organisational consequences of your view?

The future for LMD: the need for new thinking and new practices?

Explore

- List what you believe to be the way in which LMD might evolve over the next 10–15 years. Add a short sentence against each point to explain your reasoning.
- Discuss your ideas with a colleague(s). How do your ideas compare with theirs?

Leadership and management development – like so many aspects of organisational life – is in a state of considerable flux and transformation, giving rise to a number of issues and tensions that are continuing to influence the way LMD is interpreted, planned, organised and implemented across a wide range of contexts. As the economy contracts at record rate and a new financial order is emerging, any investment in employee development has to be worth the money invested. However, many employers report that a 'skills dearth' is restricting growth (Churchard, 2013), meaning perhaps that investment is more important than ever.

One of the challenges identified in this chapter was in evaluating LMD. If a clear case cannot be made for the link between LMD and organisational performance, and if this cannot be demonstrated within each organisation, then it will not be a priority in cash-strapped businesses. LMD will only be worth the money if clear links can be made with the business and its purposes (Tate, 2010). As such, LMD poses a 'strategic challenge':

- *Strategy must be put ahead of training.* Business leaders must take an informed view about what aspects of LMD support the business directly and jettison those that do not.

- *Development has to look outwards* at customers, markets, brands, products and competition – and inwards, at organisation, culture, structure, systems, relationships and rules.

- *LMD has to be targeted carefully.* Not all managers need the same level or quantity of development over the same timescales; identifying specific behaviours that have to change, and in which individuals, will allow a much more tailored offering.

- *Assumptions have to be challenged.* However 'self-evident' the value of LMD may be, it should not escape serious challenge.

- *The focus should be on leadership as it is practised, rather than as it is learned.* Solutions should then tailored to make this its business purpose.

In these ways, LMD can become a resource for the organisation, rather than a drain on its resources.

Concluding comments

A clear case has been made in this chapter that, for LMD to be effective, it must be linked to strategic goals and intentions. Chapter 2 introduced some of the realities of strategic flux and change in organisations – where intended strategies were not always realised and emerging strategies replaced those intended as the strategic environment changed over the process of planning cycles. If we are to achieve and maintain the required level of strategic fit, LMD has to be managed in a way that accepts and accommodates contextual diversity and organisational complexities. 'Managing' development therefore has to be seen as being just as important as 'doing' development.

So to what extent is LMD fulfilling its strategic role in this contextual and contingent manner? The answer has to be a qualified one. There has been evidence, over the years, of success (Mabey and Ramirez, 2005; Brown, 2007; Bailey *et al.,* 2010; Sheehan, 2012), but there is also evidence that in some situations LMD might be considered to be 'failing', in the sense that it is not fully delivering anticipated organisational and individual outcomes.

Explore

- To what extent do you feel that LMD is 'failing' to deliver anticipated outcomes in your organisation?
- Given what you have read in this chapter, what can be done to improve the situation?

In order to be strategic, organisations have to address several challenges (Clarke *et al.*, 2004; Bailey *et al.*, 2010):

- They must be clear about the nature of leadership and the qualities they value in the leaders in their business.
- They need clear evaluation strategies that demonstrate the multiple values of LMD.
- They must engage high-quality professionals to support LMD internally and to build networks externally.
- They must be 'in it for the long term' rather than following financial trends that drive piecemeal and partial investment.

Summary

- The terms 'leader' and 'manager' have become interchangeable in many organisations, but clarity is required around the nature of the role for which any development intervention is designed.
- LMD is a critical component to organisational success, where it is designed, delivered and evaluated in line with an organisation's strategy.
- Improving individual and organisational performance is at the heart of any LMD intervention.
- A number of choices have to be made when developing an LMD strategy:
  - Who to develop?
  - How to develop?
  - Who to involve?
  - How to evaluate?
- LMD comprises a range of interventions designed to enhance the skills of leaders and managers – a group of employees who have a significant impact on an organisation's performance.
- The context of LMD plays a significant part in the design of LMD interventions.

Questions

1 What do you understand by the term 'leadership and management development'?
2 To what extent can LMD support the business strategy?
3 Who are the stakeholders in LMD? Where can they support or block the process?
4 What are the important issues to consider in developing an LMD policy?
5 What are the challenges and issues that face LMD in the coming years?

Case study 1

Jersey Telecom's leadership development initiative

The experience of leadership development at Jersey Telecom proved to be more than an exercise in providing benefits for leaders. HR decision-makers identified the leadership development programme as an opportunity for culture change that focused on establishing commercial capabilities and an awareness of the global environment not currently embedded in their practice – their organisational history was as

Case study 1 continued

a state-owned telecommunications company, with a different set of cultural values and expectations. Moreover, leaders had the potential to be catalysts for greater change throughout the business – enabling them to lead by example was a goal of the programme so that others could be engaged in the process of growth and development.

The company learned from their experience of running development programmes previously and moved away from a traditional 'course' based on 'competencies'. At the outset, just five leadership competencies were identified, which were deliberately aspirational. Leadership capabilities of each of the 24 senior leaders were measured using bespoke assessments. Individual goals were set based on the assessments; the goals and competencies were intentionally challenging and stretching. Thereafter, leaders were invited to choose the learning interventions that they thought would best support them in achieving their goals. For example, for some, a coaching and support programme was put in place; for others, alternative forms of development were identified. The assessment process continued during and after the interventions when leaders' achievements were remeasured using the bespoke assessments. One-to-one sessions were provided to offer leaders feedback. The review process continued and leaders were reassessed after six months. The assessment and review process has been embedded in the company's appraisal process to ensure ongoing development.

On the whole, the process has been considered a success – with the board members rating the leaders more highly on the five competencies after the interventions than before: they are better at working with each other and at driving change. The leaders themselves were more pessimistic about their achievements: their expectations had been reset about the nature of 'good' performance and they appreciated that there were improvements to be made. The 'objective' feedback from the assessments had acted as a reality check.

The company plans to use a similar approach with the next level of leadership – those that are managed by the leaders in the pilot programme. For them, it is an opportunity for clearer succession planning and to enhance company growth more broadly.

Source: adapted from 'Jersey Telecom's leadership development initiative,' *People Management* (Nicola Reeves), 24 September 2012, with the permission of the publisher, the Chartered Institute of Personnel and Development, London (www.cipid.co.uk), and the author.

Questions

1 What challenges do organisations face in developing senior managers?

2 To what extent do senior managers present a special case in LMD?

3 As most organisations now prefer to develop internal managers through management succession than to recruit from outside, how can JT ensure they achieve this?

Case study 2

A thing worth doing is worth doing well: why are leaders losing faith in high-potential training?

Leadership and management development as an organisational intervention relies on the accepted wisdom that high-potential employees can be successfully and consistently indentified and developed usually in-company and usually through specially designed training interventions, and that doing so will ensure the health and success of the organization. However, reporting on a global survey by CEB of 6.6 million participants, Jo Faragher's article in *People Management* on the 15 November 2013 identified that 'half of HR professionals lack confidence in their programmes for high-potential workers and feel they are ineffective for developing future leaders'. Is

there, then, a pressing need to improve the quality and impact of such development interventions?

In detail, the research reported that:

- only about 17 per cent of employees who enter a programme for high-potential development do go on to succeed in a senior role;
- only 15 per cent of employees who perform well in their current role are effective after promotion;
- despite those statistics £1.2 million ($2m) is spent each year on learning and development for high-potential employees;

Case study 2 continued

- only half of those who replied to the survey had a systematic approach in place to enable them to identify staff with high potential;
- only around 33% of companies have valid evaluation and assessment methods to confirm their choices.

One of the authors of the survey, Eugene Burke, is quoted in the article as saying: 'Greater clarity is needed on how high-potential is defined' as very little information is available to programme designers to inform the development of effective criteria and content which has the appropriate impact.

Furthermore, there are risks associated with providing high-cost development for high-potential employees. Threats to managers' confidence in the programmes come at least in part from the potential for high-quality staff to use the development programme as a stepping stone to working with another company. CEB's research identified that as many as 50 per cent of candidates from high-potential programmes subsequently leave to work elsewhere.

A further part of the problem lies in the nature of the selection processes for high-potential development programmes. The process requires measurement and judgment of current performance as a determinant of future success. However, those that perform well now may not have the potential for future or higher leadership roles, or roles in a different context to the one in which they currently operate. The risk according to Eugene Burke is that 'companies risk giving too much responsibility to the wrong people, which could push them to leave the company, or increase performance issues as they struggle with elevated responsibility and expectation.'

So, what can companies do? There is a significant body of evidence to support investment in LMD generally and in high-potential programmes specifically. The findings suggest that at the very least companies should.

- adopt a clearer definition of what high potential is to ensure selection criteria are appropriate and clear;

- distinguish higher potential from high performance to ensure appropriate individuals are encouraged to participate in the programmes;
- identify an alignment in individuals between high potential and the desire to progress to senior roles in order to minimise the risk of individual failure and a decline in performance;
- identify engagement and commitment to the company to ensure that employees remain with the company on completion;
- consider alternatives to, or support mechanisms for, high-potential programmes such as assignment and seconded roles to ensure the individual has the opportunity to contextualise their learning to the company and its priorities.

The reasonable and balanced conclusion might be that, while too many companies may be directing resources and opportunities correctly, that in itself should not be a reason for non-investment, but rather should send a strong message to senior leaders that 'a thing worth doing is worth doing well'.

Questions

1 In the context of the evidence presented in this chapter, to what extent do you agree with the argument made by the authors of the CEB research?

2 The article interprets the results as disappointing: *only* 15 per cent of employees, and so on. In the context of your reading of this chapter, is this entirely fair? Is there an alternative interpretation?

3 How could greater clarity be achieved around the notion of 'high potential'?

4 What would need to be in place to convince you as a budget holder to invest in LMD for high-potential employees?

Source: Based on Faragher (2013) 'HR losing faith in high potential training, finds study', *People Management,* 15 November.

References and further reading

Adey, K. (2000) 'Professional development priorities: the views of middle managers in secondary schools', *Educational Management Administration and Leaders,* 28,4: 419–31.

Alimo-Metcalfe, B. and Alban-Metcalfe, J. (2010) 'Leadership in public and third sector organisations' in J. Storey (ed.) *Leadership in Organisations: Current Issues and Key Trends.* London: Routledge, pp. 225–48.

Allen, A. (2003) 'Out of the ordinary', *People Management,* 9, 24: 36–8.

Amagoh, F. (2009) 'Leadership development and leadership effectiveness', *Management Decision,* 47, 6: 989–99.

Antonacopoulou, E. and Bento, E. (2010) 'Learning leadership in practice' in J. Storey (ed.) *Leadership in Organisations: Current Issues and Key Trends.* London: Routledge, pp. 71–92.

Arkin, A. (2003) 'Shaken and stirred', *People Management*, 9, 24: 32–4.

Bailey, C., Clarke, M. and Butcher, D. (2010) *Strategically Aligned leadership Development, Leadership in Organisations: Critical Issues and Key Trends*. London: Routledge.

Bandura, A. (1997) *Self-efficacy: The Exercise of Control*. New York: W.H. Freeman.

Bedingfield, C. (2005) 'Transforming the ROI of your graduate scheme', *Industrial and Commercial Training*, 37, 4: 199–203.

Bennett, N. (2010) 'Leadership and leadership development in education' in J. Storey (ed.) *Leadership In Organisations: Current Issues and Key Trends*. London: Routledge, pp. 249–71.

BIS (2011) *BIS Small Business Survey*. London: Department for Business, Innovation and Skills.

Bittel, L. (1998) 'Management development for scientific and engineering personnel' in Prokopenko, J. (ed.) *Management Development: A Guide for the Profession*. Geneva: International Labour Office, pp. 426–45.

Boddy, D. (2010) *Management: An Introduction*. Harlow: FT/ Prentice Hall.

Bolton, G. (2010) *Reflective Practice: Writing and Professional Development*. London: Sage.

Boyatzis, R., Stubbs, E. and Taylor, S. (2002) 'Learning cognitive and emotional intelligence competencies through graduate management education', *Academy of Management Learning and Education*, 1, 2: 150–62.

Bristow, N. (2007) 'Clinical leadership in the NHS: evaluating change through action learning' in R. Hill and J. Stewart (eds) *Management Development: Perspectives from Theory and Practice*. Abingdon: Routledge, pp. 302–16.

Brown, P. (2005) 'The evolving role of strategic management development', *Journal of Management Development*, 24, 3: 209–22.

Brown, P. (2007) *Strategic Management Development. Management Development: Perspectives from Research and Practice*. Abingdon: Routledge.

Burgoyne, J. (1988) 'Management development for the individual and the organisation', *Personnel Management*, June: 40–44.

Burgoyne, J. and Jackson, B. (1997) 'The arena thesis: management development as a pluralistic meeting point' in J. Burgoyne and M. Reynolds (eds) *Management Learning: Integrating Perspectives in Theory and Practice*. London: Sage Publications Ltd, pp. 54–71.

Bush, T. (2008) *Leadership and Management Development in Education*. London: Sage.

Butler, L. and Leach, N. (2011) *Action Learning for Change: A Practical Guide for Managers*. Cirencester: Management Books 2000 Ltd.

Cabinet Office (2009) *Unleashing Aspiration: The Final Report of the Panel on Fair Access to the Professions*. London: Cabinet Office.

Cannon, J. and McGee, R. (2007) *Talent Management and Succession Planning*. London: CIPD.

Carter, L., Ulrich, D. and Goldsmith, M. (eds) (2005) *Best Practices in Leadership Development and Organisation Change: How the Best Companies Ensure Meaningful Change and Sustainable Leadership*. San Francisco, CA: Wiley.

Cater, J. (2009) 'The development of successors from followers to leaders in small family firms', *Family Business Review*, 22, 2: 109–24.

Churchard, C. (2012) 'University leavers apply for record number of jobs', *People Management*, 22 May. Online: **http://www.cipd.co.uk/pm/peoplemanagement/p/paymentgateway.**

aspx?returnURL=/pm/peoplemanagement/b/weblog/ archive/2012/05/22/university-leavers-apply-for-record-number-of-jobs-2012-05.aspx&blogid=2&postid=96183 (last accessed February 2014).

Churchard, C. (2013) 'Skills dearth restricts growth for fifth of employers, research finds', *People Management*, **14 February.** Online: **http://www.cipd.co.uk/pm/peoplemanagement/b/ weblog/archive/2013/02/14/skills-dearth-restricts-growth-for-fifth-of-employers-research-finds.aspx** (last accessed February 2014).

CIPD (2005) *Developing Managers for Business Performance (Toolkit)*. London: CIPD.

CIPD (2008) *Developing Senior Managers*, Factsheet. London: CIPD.

CIPD (2010) *Internships: To Pay or Not to Pay*. London: CIPD.

CIPD (2011) *UK Highlights: Global Leadership Forecast 2011*. London: CIPD.

CIPD (2012a) *Learning and Talent Development Survey*. London: CIPD.

CIPD (2012b) *Management Development*, Factsheet. London: CIPD. Online: **http://www.cipd.co.uk/hr-resources/factsheets/ management-development.aspx** (accessed February 2014).

Clarke, M., Butcher, D. and Bailey, C. (2004) 'Strategically aligned leadership development' in J. Storey (ed.) *Leadership in Organisations: Current Issues and Key Trends*. London: Routledge, pp. 271–92.

Clegg, A. (2012) 'Getting Women on boards: The new girl's network', *People Management*.

Coetzer, A., Battisti, M., Jurado, T. and Massey, C. (2011) 'The reality of management development in SMEs', *Journal of Management and Organisation* 17, 3: 290–306.

Collin, K., Van der Heijden, B. and Lewis, P. (2012) 'Continuing professional development', *International Journal of Training and Development*, 16, 3: 155–63.

Connor, H. and Shaw, S. (2008) 'Graduate training and development: current trends and issues', *Education and Training*, 50, 5: 357–65.

Crush, P. (2013) 'What you can learn from eBay: Top-rated feedback', *People Management*.

Cunliffe, A. and Eriksen, M. (2011) 'Relational leadership', *Human Relations*, 64: 1425–49.

Currie, G. and Brown, A.D. (2003) 'A narratological approach to understanding processes of organizing in a UK hospital', *Human Relations*, 56: 563–86.

Dalton, K. (2010) *Leadership and Management Development*. London: FT/Prentice Hall.

Davies (2011) *Women on Boards (The Davies Report)*. London: Department for Business. Online: **http://www.bis.gov.uk// assets/biscore/business-law/docs/w/11-745-women-on-boards.pdf** (accessed February 2014).

Duerden, D. (2006) *Management Development Activities*. London: CIPD.

Edwards, G. and Turnbull, S. (2013) 'Special issue on new paradigms in evaluating leadership development', *Advances in Developing Human Resources*, 15, 1: 3–9.

Flynn, N. (2007) *Public Sector Management*. London: Sage.

Fuller-Love, N. (2006) 'Management development in small firms', *International Journal of Management Reviews*, 8, 3: 175–90.

Geppert, M., Matten, D. and Williams, K. (2002) *Challenges for European Management in a Global Context: Experiences from Britain and Germany*. Basingstoke: Palgrave Macmillan.

Glatter, R. (2004) 'Leadership in education' in J. Storey (ed.) *Leadership in Organisations: Current Issues and Key Trends*. London: Routledge, pp. 203–22.

Gold, J., Thorpe, R. and Holt, R. (2007) 'Writing, reading and reason: the three Rs of manager learning' in R. Hill and J. Stewart (eds) *Management Development: Perspectives from Theory and Practice.* Abingdon: Routledge, pp. 271–84.

Gold, J., Thorpe, R. and Mumford, M. (2010) *Gower Handbook of Leadership and Management Development.* Aldershot: Gower.

Grandy, G. and Holton, J. (2013) 'Evaluating leadership development in a health care setting through a partnership approach', *Advances in Developing Human Resources,* 15, 1: 61–82.

Hamblin, B. (ed.) (2007) *Towards Evidence-based Management Development. Management Development: Perspectives from Research and Practice.* Abingdon: Routledge.

Hanson, B. (2013) 'The leadership development interface: aligning leaders and organisations towards more effective leadership learning', *Advances in Developing Human Resources,* 15, 1: 106–20.

Harrison, R. (2009) *Learning and Development,* 5th edn. London: CIPD.

Hatton, N. and Smith, D. (1995) 'Reflection in teacher education: towards definition and implementation', *Teacher and Teaching,* 11, 1: 33–49.

Hill, R. and Stewart, J. (eds) (2007) *Management Development: Perspectives from Research and Practice.* Abingdon: Routledge.

Honey, P. and Mumford, A. (1989) *Manual of Learning Opportunities.* Peter Honey.

House, R., Javidan, M., Hanges, P. and Dorman, P. (2002) 'Understanding cultures and implicit leadership theories across the globe: an introduction to project globe', *Personnel Review,* 24, 6: 19–28.

Hunt, C. (2005) 'Reflective practice' in J. Wilson (ed.) *Human Resource Development.* London: Kogan Page.

IDS (2012) *Competency Frameworks.* London: IDS.

Jarvis, C., Gulati, A., McCririck, V. and Simpson, P. (2013) 'Leadership matters: Tensions in evaluating leadership development', *Advances in Developing Human Resources,* 15, 1: 27–45.

Jones, O. and Crompton, H. (2009) 'Enterprise logic and small firms: a model of authentic entrepreneurial leadership', *Journal of Strategy and Management,* 2, 4: 329–51.

Jones, P. and Oswick, C. (2007) 'Inputs and outcomes of outdoor management development: of design, dogma and dissonance', *British Journal of Management,* 18, 4: 327–41.

Jones, O., Macpherson, A. and Thorpe, R. (2010) 'Learning in owner-managed small firms: mediating artefacts and strategic space', *Entrepreneurship and Regional Development,* 22(7–8): 649–73.

Kesby, D. (2008) 'Exploring the power of action learning', *Knowledge Management Review,* 11 (5) 26–9.

Kelan, E. (2013) 'The becoming of business bodies: gender, appearance and leadership development', *Management Learning,* 44, 1: 45–61.

Kolb, D. (1984) *Experiential Learning: Experience as the Source of Learning and Development.* Englewood Cliffs, NJ: Prentice-Hall.

Kyriakidou, O. (2012) 'Gender, management and leadership', *Equality, Diversity and Inclusion (Special Edition),* 31, 1: 4–9.

Lee, G. (2003). *Leadership Coaching.* London: CIPD.

Loffler, E. and Bovaird, T. (eds) (2009) *Public Management and Governance.* Abingdon: Routledge.

Mabey, C. (2002) 'Mapping management development practice', *Journal of Management Studies* 39, 8: 1139–56.

Mabey, C. (2013) 'Leadership development in organisations: multiple discourses and diverse practice', *International Journal of Management Reviews* 15, 4: 359–80.

Mabey, C. and Finch-Lees, T. (2008) *Management and Leadership Development.* London: Sage.

Mabey, C. and Ramirez, M. (2005) 'Does management development improve organisational productivity? a six-country analysis of European firms', *International Journal of Human Resource Management,* 16, 7: 1067–82.

Mabey, C. and Salaman, G. (1995) *Strategic Human Resource Management.* Oxford: Blackwell.

Madsen, S. (2012) 'Women and Leadership in Higher Education: Current Realities, Challenges, and Future Directions', *Advances in Developing Human Resources,* 14, 2: 131–9.

Malik, S. and Quinn, B. (2013) 'Bank of Amerca intern's death puts banks' working culture in the spotlight', *The Guardian,* 21 August, 2013.

Mankin, D. (2009) *Human Resource Development.* London: Oxford University Press.

Marlow, S., Taylor, S. and Thompson, A. (2010) 'Informality and formality in medium sized companies: contestation and synchronisation', *British Journal of Management,* 21, 4: 954–66.

Marsick, V. and Watkins, K. (1997) 'Lessons from informal and accidental learning' in J. Burgoyne and J. Reynolds (eds) *Management Learning: Integrating Perspectives in Theory and Practice.* London: Sage, pp. 295–311.

May, T. (2012) *Cranfield report Launch Speech by Home Secretary Theresa May,* 13 March 2012. Online: **http://www.home-office.gov.uk/media-centre/speeches/cranfield-speech-home-sec** (accessed February 2014).

Mayson, S. and Barrett, R. (2005) 'The science and practice of HRM in small firms', *Human Resource Management Review,* 16, 4: 447–55.

McCall, M. (2010) 'Recasting leadership development', *Industrial and Organisational Psychologist,* 3: 3–21.

McCauley-Smith, C., Williams, S., Gillon, A., Braganza, A. and Ward, C. (2013) 'Individual leader to interdependent leadershiop: a case study in leadership development and tripartite evaluation', *Advances in Developing Human Resources,* 15, 1: 83–105.

Melkman, A. and Trotman, K. (2005) *Training International Managers: Designing, Deploying and Delivering Effective training for Multi-cultural Groups.* Aldershot: Gower.

Mitchelmore, S. (2010) 'Entrepreneurial competences: a literature review and development agenda', *International Journal of Entrepreneurial Behaviour and Research,* 16, 2: 92–111.

Mole, G. (2010) 'Can leadership be taught?' in J. Storey (ed.) *Leadership in organizations: Current Issues and Key Trends,* 2nd edn. New York, NY: Routledge, pp. 114–26.

Moon, J. (2004) *A Handbook of Reflective and Experiential Learning.* London: Routledge.

Mumford, A. (1997) *Management Development: Strategies for Action.* London: CIPD.

Mumford, A. and Gold, J. (2006) *Management Development: Strategies for Action.* London: CIPD.

Mumford, M., Friedrich, T., Caughron, J. and Byrne, C. (2007) 'Leader cognition in real world settings: How do leaders think about the world?' *The Leadership Quarterly,* 18: 515–43.

Ng, K., Dyne, L. and Ang, S. (2009) 'From experience to experiential learning: Cultural intelligence as a learning capability for global leader development', *Academy of Management Learning,* 8, 4: 511–26.

Northhouse, P. (2013) *Leadership: Theory and Practice.* London: Sage.

Passmore, J. (ed.). (2010) *Leadership Coaching.* London: Association for Coaching.

Paton, R., Taylor, S., Storey, J. and Peters, G. (2010) 'Designing and delivering leadership education and development: the role of corporate universities', in J. Storey (ed.) *Leadership in Organisations: Current Issues and Key Trends*. London: Routledge, pp. 93–113.

Pedler, M. (2008) *Action Learning for Managers*. Aldershot: Gower.

Persaud, J. (2004) 'Higher Return', *People Management*, 8 April 2004.

Peters, L. and Baum, J. (2007) 'The importance of local context in leadership development and evaluation' in J. Martineau and C. Reinelt (eds) *The Handbook of Leadership Development Evaluation*. San Francisco, CA: Jossey Bass, pp. 261–83.

PIU (2001) *Strengthening Leadership in the Public Sector*. London: Cabinet Office Performance and Innovation Unit.

Rae, L. (2002) *Assessing the Value of Your Training: The Evaluation Process from Training Needs to the Report to the Board*. London: Gower.

Ramirez, M. (2004) 'Comparing European approaches to management education', *Advances in Developing Human Resources*, 6, 4: 428–50.

Revans, R. (1983) *The ABC of Action Learning*. Bromley: Chartwell Bratt.

Revans, R. (2011) *ABC of Action Learning*. Farnham: Gower.

Saks, A., Tamkin, P. and Lewis, P. (2011) 'Special issue: management training and development', *International Journal of Training and Development*, 15, 3: 179–83.

Salaman, G. (2004) 'Competences of managers, competences of leaders' in J. Storey (ed.) *Leadership in Organisations*. London: Routledge, pp. 58–78.

Salaman, G. (2010) 'Understanding the crises of leadership' in J. Storey (ed.) *Leadership in Organisations: Current Issues and Key Trends*. London: Routledge.

Schön, D. (1984) *The Reflective Practitioner: How Professionals Think in Action*. Massachusetts: Basic Books.

Scott, P. (2004) 'Innovative technologies and leadership development' in J. Storey (ed.) *Leadership in Organizations: Current Issues and Key Trends*. London: Routledge, pp. 138–51.

Scott-Ligon, G., Wallace, J. and Osburn, H. (2011) 'Experiential Development and Mentoring Processes for Leaders for Innovation', *Advances in Developing Human Resources*, 13, 3: 297–317.

Scutt, M. (2012) 'An end to interns?' *People Management*, 17 December 2012.

Sheehan, M. (2012) 'Investing in managment development in turbulent times and perceived organisational performance: a study of UK MNCs and their subsidiaries', *International Journal of Human Resource Management*, 23, 12: 2491–513.

Skipton-Leonard, H. (2009) 'Leadership development via action learning', *Advances in Developing Human Resources*, 12, 2: 225–40.

Stansfield, L. and Stewart, J. (2007) 'A stakeholder approach to the study of management development' in R. Hill and J. Stewart (eds) *Management Development: Perspectives from Theory and Practice*. Abindgon: Routledge, pp. 319–28.

Stevens, M. (2013) 'Staff performance hit as leaders fail to develop team working', *People Management*.

Storey, J. (2004) 'Changing theories of leadership and leadership development' in J. Story (ed.) *Leadership in Organisations*. London: Routledge, pp. 11–38.

Storey, J. (2010a) 'Changing theories of leadership and leadership development' in J. Story (ed.) *Leadership in Organisations: Current Issues and Key Trends*. London: Routledge, pp. 14–38.

Storey, J. (ed.) (2010b) *Leadership in Organisations: Current Issues and Key Trends*. London: Routledge.

Storey, J. (2010c) 'Signs of change: 'damned rascals' and beyond' in J. Story (ed.). *Leadership in Organisations: Current Issues and Key Trends*. London: Routledge, pp. 3–13.

Strack, R. and Krinks, P. (2008) 'The talent crunch', *People Management*, 26 June 2008.

Sturges, J. (2010) 'The individualization of the career and its implications for leadership' in J. Story (ed.) *Leadership in Organisations: Current Issues and Key Trends*. London: Routledge, pp. 150–64.

Tams, S. and Arthur, M. (2010) 'New directions for boundary-less careers: Agency and interdependence in a change world', *Journal of Organisational Behaviour*, 31, 5: 629–46.

Tansey, C., Turner, P., Foster, C., Harris, L., Sempik, A., Stewart, J. and Williams, H. (2007) *Talent: Strategy, Management and Measurement – Research into Practice*. London: CIPD.

Tarrant, D. (2005) 'Building a better team', *Management Today Australia*, May 14: 25–7.

Tate, W. (2010) 'Linking development with business' in J. Story (ed.) *Leadership in Organisations: Current Issues and Key Trends*. London: Routledge, pp. 185–206.

Thompson, A. (2001) 'Too much apple pie?' *People Management*, 03 May 2001.

Thompson, S. and Thompson, S. (2008) *The Critically Reflective Practitioner*. Basingstoke: Palgrave Macmillan.

Thompson, A., Mabey, C., Storey, J., Grey, C. and Iles, P. (2001) *Changing Patterns of Management Development*. Oxford, Blackwell.

Thorn, I. (2012) 'Leadership in international organisations: global leadership competencies', *The Psychologist-Manager Journal*, 15, 3: 158–63.

Trehan, K. and Rigg, C. (2008) 'Beware the unbottled genie: unspoken aspects of critical self reflection' in C. Elliot and S. Turnbull (eds) *Critical Thinking in Human Resource Development*. London: Routledge, pp. 11–25.

Trehan, K. and Shelton, R. (2007) 'Leadership development: A critical evaluation' in R. Hill and J. Stewart (eds) *Management Development: Perspectives from Theory and Practice*. Abingdon: Routledge, pp. 285–301.

Tyler, S. (2004) 'Making leadership and management development measure up' in J. Story (ed.) *Leadership in Organisations: Current Issues and Key Trends*. London: Routledge, pp. 152–70.

van Wenroy, B., Bewley, H., Bryson, A., Forth, J., Freeth, S., Stokes, L. and Woods, S. (2011) *The Workplace Employment Relations Study*. London: Department for Business Innovation and Skills.

Vinnicombe, S. and Sealy, R. (2012) *The Female FTSE Board Report 2012*. Cranfield: Cranfield University School of Management.

Warr, P., Bird, M.W. and Rackham, N. (1970) *Evaluation of Management Training*. Aldershot: Gower.

Whitmore, J. (2009) *Coaching for Performance*. London: Nicholas Brearley Publishing.

Williams, M. and Cowling, M. (2008) *Annual Small Business Survey 2007/8*. Institute for Employment Studies (**www.berr.gov.uk**).

Chapter 9

Organisational development

Mairi Watson

Objectives

- To define organisational development (OD).
- To outline the key stages in the history and discuss the contemporary view of OD.
- To explore the key theories which underpin the practice of OD.
- To investigate the techniques and practices of OD.
- To explore the nature of the change agent role and its impact on OD.
- To examine the links between OD and strategy, structure and culture.

Introductory case study

Taking first steps in making health clubs fit for purpose

Not long after he became chief executive of Fitness First last year, Andy Cosslett got his top team together and mooted the idea of putting up a price list in every club. 'There was a sharp intake of breath,' he recalled. Less than 12 months later, the former InterContinental Hotels Group chief executive has swept away the 'byzantine' terms and conditions that gave the fitness industry a bad name, put people off joining and attracted censure from the Office of Fair Trading.

'The business was driven by volume and getting people to sign up as members,' he said. 'It wasn't about retention. They used every deal, every promotion, to get people in. It was like buying a second-hand car. Now every Fitness First club has simple and transparent pricing and if somebody has to leave and we can't keep them, we'll make it as painless as possible.'

It is just one of the changes to entrenched business practices that he is making as he seeks to restore the battered fortunes of what was once the world's biggest fitness club operator. . . .

'The club environment has to be fit for purpose, the showers and air conditioning have to work, it

has to be sanitary, the ventilation has to be good. We've had great people who work very hard, but they couldn't overcome those basic factors. If you've got sticky floors, it doesn't matter how big your smile is.'

After last year's financial restructuring, which handed a controlling 55 per cent stake to Oaktree Capital Management and allowed the group to shed 68 of its 153 UK clubs, Fitness First has no external debt, giving Mr Cosslett at least £60 million to £70 million to invest in refurbishments over the next three years or so. He said that transforming the tired estate would not be a quick fix, but, on the evidence of the club in South Kensington, London, one of the first three new-look clubs, the changes are proving effective. 'We've doubled the rate yet doubled the number of members.'

As well as introducing modern showers and changing areas, complete with cool-down 'air showers' and hot yoga studios, he is revamping the foyers. 'Most of our clubs have football-style turnstiles. The first thing you see is a barrier that says please keep out.'

Not only is he changing the way the staff think – 'they have to have knowledge of people, not just fitness' –

but Mr Cosslett has also commissioned research into the psychology of different types of customer, from the fitness fanatics to more sociable exercise class junkies and the 'ladies who lunch'. He hopes that Fitness First can be 'built into a brand around some core groups'....In its results for the year to October 31, being released today, Fitness First, which the previous year had slumped to a £672 million loss after impairment and restructuring costs, reports a fall in revenues from £608.3 million to £587.9 million, with underlying profits down 1.6 per cent at £106 million. Any material improvement in the results would take time, Mr Cosslett admitted.

Questions

1 What factors in Fitness First's context have had, or will have, an impact on Andy Cosslett's change agenda?

2 As you read through the chapter, reflect on the extent to which Andy Cosslett is enacting the philosophy and practices of organisational development.

Source: extracted from Dominic Walsh, '', The *Times*, 29 April 2013 (http://www.thetimes.co.uk/tto/business/industries/leisure/article3751258.ece).

Introduction

This chapter grapples with the complex and demanding topic of organisational development (OD). It is so, because OD is, like HRM more generally, a field of enquiry (theory) as well as a field of practice (activity), offering the opportunity for students to engage with OD at both a critical and a strategic level (Garrow *et al.*, 2009; Francis *et al.*, 2012). It has been 'driven by the twin forces of academic rigour and practical relevance' with one or other in the ascendancy (Burnes and Cooke, 2012: 1396). The debate about the nature of OD and its place in contemporary organisations (and human resource management, HRM) has flourished recently as changes to the context of business operation have raised questions about the nature and function of organisational performance.

Organisational development today is typically enacted in organisations through formal, planned change efforts (which can be related, for example, to strategic planning, organisational redesign or leadership development) overseen by internal or external consultants (change agents) with behaviour change and/or performance improvement as the primary goals. OD relies on tried-and-tested models of change to communicate, structure, undertake and evaluate activities and efforts. As such, it is a profitable and extensive industry in its own right (Helms-Mills *et al.*, 2009).

In terms of theory, there has been a strong and well-known cadre of writers who had established OD in the mid-twentieth century as a field of applied behavioural science and a topic worthy of examination and implementation: as such, it predated – and perhaps acted as a precursor to – the development of HRM in the 1980s (CIPD, 2012; Francis *et al.*, 2012). Current debate shows a growing impetus for a critical re-examination of OD from the perspective of both researchers and academics and practitioners working in the field.

In terms of practice, a renewed interest in OD is demonstrably evident in the UK (Garrow *et al.*, 2009) not least in the explicit inclusion as one of the 10 areas of professional development on the HR Profession map and as one of the CIPD's advanced level 7 modules 'Organisational design and development', arguably because it has the potential to provide a language of organisational improvement. Organisationally, an interest in the strategic or performance impact of OD has led to the embedding of OD in the title and responsibilities of HR directors in many large organisations. In parallel, many of the practices associated with OD have been embraced and embedded by HR practitioners in their everyday activity. The language of OD is increasingly used as an umbrella term for the developmental practices associated with HR practice and can be said to be assuming greater strategic significance (CIPD, 2012).

The CIPD (2012) outlines the reasons why OD is so closely related to HR:

- OD work contributes to the sustained health and effectiveness of the organisation.
- OD work is based on thorough diagnosis that uses data from organisational, behavioural and psychological sources.
- OD work is planned and systemic in its focus, taking account of the whole organisation.
- OD practitioners create alignment between different activities, projects and initiatives.
- OD work involves groups of people in the organisation to maximise engagement, ownership and contribution.

In that way, OD can support the strategic goals of HR (see Box 9.1).

Box 9.1 Practical OD?

The CIPD's podcast on the link between OD and HR provides some insight into the two sets of challenges in the introduction. First, it offers a practical definition of how OD might have an impact on work:

Lee Sears (LS):
For me OD, I think it's a relatively simple definition. It's about the ability of a function to support an organisation to be successful now and in the future.

Ed Gryphon (EG):
People get so confused about those two letters 'OD', that for some people it means organisational design; some people are talking about organisational effectiveness; sometimes people are talking about training and development activities . . . Organisational development is about contributing to the sustained success of the organisation through the involvement of the people in that organisation at all levels. That is simply how I see it. In practical terms, I think that means you involve all levels of the organisation wherever you can in developing strategy and in implementing strategy.

Secondly, it identifies the extent to which OD and HR occupy a different space or whether they may share a joint future:

LS:
The debate about whether OD should be separate from HR or vice versa I think is a redundant one. They are very much occupying the same territory and from my point of view, for HR to be a meaningful and valuable function it has to have OD capabilities and skills and the ability to think and understand the organisation as an OD practitioner would. It has to be at the heart of HR. Similarly, though, for OD to be of any real value, it has to have touch points into all areas of the business and actually that is what HR does have; so they have to be an immediately supportive partnership rather than seen as separate entities to my mind.

EG:
The way I would see it is that actually HR offers practices, tools and approaches that OD practitioners can use. And I think very often it is about having an OD mindset. Sometimes it is referred to as systems thinking. I think it is about being curious and interested in the relationship between different parts of an organisation, the relationship between different activities. So it's not unusual in a big organisation today that you look at the list of changes and there are 125 different projects on the go and sometimes it feels like those are disconnected. I think the OD mindset is looking at how do you bring those together?

For more information, listen to the podcast or read the transcript at http://www.cipd.co.uk/podcasts/_articles/_organisationdevelopment.htm?link=title.

Source: HR and organisation development: separate past, joint future? Podcast 44, with the permission of the publisher, the Chartered Institute of Personnel and Development, London (www.cipd.co.uk).

Therefore, the chapter provides the background to the development of OD within the field of behavioural science and also offers an applied perspective.

While there are many ways of explaining the acronym OD (organisation, organisational, organisation or organisational development), this chapter refers throughout to 'organisational development'. Where a distinction in the use of the variety of terms is required, this will be made explicit.

Key Controversy

Ortenblad (2013), a contemporary philosopher, suggests that OD is one of a group of 'vague and attractive' management ideas – which also include the learning organisation, total quality management and business process re-engineering – which may be popular because of their very vagueness. Their ambiguity, he suggests, can provide symbolic legitimisation for a range of techniques and activities that otherwise may have no inherent value or impact.

As you read through this chapter, consider the proposition that OD may be popular for reasons other than its effectiveness.

Definitions and development of OD

Defining OD: 'extreme joined up thinking?'

OD has been, and arguably still is, the major approach to change across the western world, and increasingly globally.
Burnes and Cooke (2012: 1395)

A participant in the podcast described in Box 9.1 defined OD as 'extreme joined-up thinking', which sets the scene for the complexities inherent in an overarching definition of OD: 50 or 60 years of development have inevitably 'blurred the boundaries of the field and made it increasingly difficult to define' (Cummings, 2004: 25). Any definition has to take account of its complex history (considered later).

Beckhard's (1969:9) comprehensive and classic definition suggests it is:

an effort (1) planned, (2) organisation wide, (3) managed from the top, to (4) increase organisation effectiveness and health through (5) planned interventions in the organisation's 'processes' using behavioural-science knowledge.

In short, OD commences with an analysis of the problems and an initial appreciation of possible solutions and in the process pays significant attention to individual, team and organisational behaviour. An incremental process of change unfolds where the broadest selection of organisational members are involved – with the focus on team and interpersonal relationships. The process may be supported or facilitated by experts, but in all cases is driven by senior managers. A range of procedures and methods can be used depending on the nature and path of the change. On the whole, change can be achieved using OD methods if the problem or solution is clear (Boonstra, 2004). It treats change as a process that occurs over time (Cummings, 2004). It is a 'long-range effort to improve an organisation's problem solving processes' (French and Bell, 1984) and is a key factor in ensuring long-term sustained change in organisations. It 'applies behavioural science knowledge and practices to help organisations change to achieve greater effectiveness' (Cummings, 2004: 25).

The CIPD defines organisation development as a 'planned and systematic approach to enabling sustained organisation performance through the involvement of its people' (CIPD, 2012). That said, there have been multiple definitions offered over the years. However, there are similarities – CIPD (2012) identifies that all definitions of OD have the following features in common:

1. OD applies to changes in the strategy, structure, and/or processes of an entire system, such as an organisation, a single plant of a multi-plant firm, a department or work group, or individual role or job.

2. OD is based on the application and transfer of behavioural science knowledge and practice (such as leadership, group dynamics and work design), and is distinguished by its ability to transfer such knowledge and skill so that the system is capable of carrying out more planned change in the future.

3. OD is concerned with managing planned change, in a flexible manner that can be revised as new information is gathered.

4. OD involves both the creation and the subsequent reinforcement of change by institutionalising change.

5. OD is orientated to improving organisational effectiveness by:
   - helping members of the organisation to gain the skills and knowledge necessary to solve problems by involving them in the change process, and
   - promoting high performance including financial returns, high quality products and services, high productivity, continuous improvement and a high quality of working life.

However, to attempt to reach a single definition belies the eclecticism that exists in the field (Waclawski and Church, 2002; Garrow *et al.*, 2009). Helms-Mills *et al.* (2009: 50) describe it as 'cumbersome', including a 'myriad of theories and practices . . . however, it is safe to conclude that the field focuses on people, organisations and planned change'. Like most applied sciences, practice and research are founded on a variety of disciplines and concepts (Cummings, 2004). The theory within OD has been developed through interactions among psychology, sociology, anthropology and social psychology (Helms-Mills *et al.*, 2009). Practices rely on an understanding of individuals and their relationships and concepts, such as motivation, communication, conflict, participation, performance, group dynamics, leadership and organisational design (Cummings, 2004).

While OD recognises the centrality of 'people' in the process of change as both drivers and engines of change, and generally involves progression through a number of steps, facilitated by a change agent, the models have been criticised for their unitarist view of organisational goals and ambitions and positive assumptions about individual behaviour (Collins, 1998). For example, any political behaviour or resistance would be considered rational, and the possibility of malicious or self-interested behaviour could not be accommodated. Thus, OD pays scant attention to the complexity of the many competing perspectives of actors inherent in organisational change.

The development of a definition of OD therefore relies on a careful understanding of its past and the manner in which the field has developed since its establishment as a concept in the mid-twentieth century. While distinctions between different approaches may be less frequently or readily made in practice, it is important to understand the principles and beliefs that underlie the surface practices.

A brief history of OD

OD then . . .

A clear starting point for OD's history is in the late 1930s and early 1940s in behavioural research that took place in the USA during the Second World War. The work rejected previous theories of organisation, which emphasised efficiency and economy over human or social aspects of the workplace (e.g. scientific management – see Box 9.2; Garrow *et al.*, 2009). This body of work gained impetus from the need to rebuild the business environment and develop more effective ways of working in a new world order with dramatically changed political, social, financial and technical boundaries and expectations (Garrow *et al.,* 2009; Burnes and Cooke, 2012; Skipton-Leonard *et al.,* 2013).

From the 1940s to the 1960s, two parallel tracks of research and exploration into group and organisational activities were undertaken in the USA and the UK – originally work was carried out by Kurt Lewin at the Research Centre for Group Dynamics at the Massachusetts Institute of Technology in the USA. Eric Trist, influenced by Lewin's work, worked similarly at the Tavistock Institute of Human Relations – a charity – in the UK. The two tracks of work established organisational development as a field of enquiry and of practice (Stanford, 2012).

Box 9.2 Scientific management

Scientific management emerged from the work of a group of organisational theorists (e.g. Frederick Taylor) attempting to understand the nature of work at the turn of the twentieth century. The approach was epitomised by an increase in control over workers' activities and emphasised the need for rationality, clear objectives, the right of managers to manage and a 'man as machine' ethos. Work studies or time-and-motion studies were used to reduce tasks to their basic elements and group similar elements together to produce low-skilled, low-paid jobs: assembly line working was a common output. Workers were treated relatively impersonally and collectively (management and labour) and the nature of the psychological contract was calculative, with a focus on extrinsic rewards and incentives. Such a strategy encouraged a strong collective response from workers – hence the development of trade unions.

While this strategy epitomised the management approach of the first half of the twentieth century, it has left its legacy in many management practices, such as organisation and method study, job analysis and description, selection methods, an overriding concern for efficiency and the bottom line, appraisal and performance management.

The extremities of its impact led to the development of alternatives that paid closer attention to the human or social aspects of work in the form of the 'human relations movement' which provided the foundation for HRM as we know it today.

In the USA, Lewin's work arguably began the history of OD (Lewin, 1943–4; Andriopoulos and Dawson, 2009) as an intervention-based approach to planned change that directs attention to the importance of participation, collaboration and communication and a valuing of individual contributions (Bennis, 1969; French and Bell, 1984). Lewin's work began with the 'Harwood Studies' conducted between 1939 and 1947, which examined 'group behaviour in the real world' (Burnes, 2007) and laid the foundations for his 'three major contributions to OD' (Burnes and Cooke, 2012):

- A conceptualisation of planned change (including the three-step model of change discussed later, but also an emphasis on field theory – see Box 9.3 and the section on force-field analysis below – group dynamics and action research), which involved unfreezing the current situation, moving to the desired state and then freezing or sustaining the change.

- A demonstration of how psychological theories and techniques on group behaviour can be applied in organisations: one such intervention came in the form of 'T-Groups' (see Box 9.4), which were an important component of the processes of developing sensitivity to others in everyday interactions at work. Action research was also a central strand of work on group participation and collaboration (discussed later).

- A radical (at the time) approach to democracy and participation at work, initiated by Lewin's work on leadership behaviour in 1939 which identified that democratic leaders achieved better outcomes than autocratic leaders and that leaders had to change their own behaviour first before attempting to change others. This theme was sometimes referred to as 'group dynamics', reflecting the idea that workers should have a role in decision-making and that this increases cooperation and performance (Burnes and Cooke, 2012). During the 1960s, work on participative management mushroomed. This was, and remains, central to the ideas and ideals of OD.

Applying 'field theory' for organisational change and consulting requires an acceptance of its central premise. People and their surroundings and conditions depend closely on each other. In Lewin's words, 'to understand or to predict behaviour, the person and his environment have to be considered as one constellation of interdependent factors' (Lewin, 1946: 338). Thus, the notion of 'field' refers to: (a) all aspects of individuals in relationship with their surroundings and conditions; (b) that apparently influence the particular behaviours and developments of concern; (c) at a particular point in time. Field theory is closely related to systems theory – 'elements of any situation should be regarded as parts of a system'; that is, that the organisation should be considered a complex, interrelated system, where all parts relate to each other to form a whole. This approach requires us to understand the different levels of the organisation – individual, group, inter-group, organisational – and how they interact. In parallel to Lewin's work, the Tavistock Institute of Human Relations from the 1940s onwards (Trist and Bamforth, 1951; Trist and Murray, 1993; Benders *et al.*, 2000; Dawson, 2003b) was developing socio-technical systems theory; this work explored the joint relevance of social and technical components of work (e.g. Trist *et al.*, 1963; Willcocks and Mason, 1987; Dunphy and Griffiths, 1998). The socio-technical systems approach provided a more sensitive approach to the context of change through conceptualising organisations as complex open systems, where decisions in one area of operation had a profound impact across the business.

Box 9.3 Field theory

Lewin's field theory relies on the consideration of the individual and the environment together. His work has been much reviewed since its original development. For a more detailed description than is provided here, you may wish to explore The Tavistock Institute's series of articles by Dr Jean Neumann on the work of Lewin, especially that on Field Theory at http://www.tavinstitute.org/projects/field-theory-rule/

This collection of contributions represented a significant change in the way that workplaces were perceived and with this perception came a significant change in the nature of interventions in the process of improving organisational effectiveness. This chapter considers more of Lewin's work later.

Box 9.4 The T-Group approach

Training groups (T-Groups) are a form of intervention designed to increase people's sensitivity to their own behaviour and to increase participants' skills in working with others (Argyris, 1964; Burnes and Cooke, 2012). A significant proportion of the T-Group's time is spent discussing emotional reactions to the discussion that unfolds and thus their relationships with each other. The process encourages a greater understanding of how they and colleagues respond to the words and actions of others and what triggers particular emotional responses. Ordinarily, the T-Group has no structured agenda, but the facilitator encourages the expression of emotions – not judgments. Considerable skill is required on the part of the facilitator to avoid unintended damage to a working relationship or psychological health: some consider the practice to be unethical (Highhouse, 2002).

The effects of T-Groups were considered substantial in challenging authoritarian behaviour in managers and helping them develop behaviour that would ensure employee commitment (Argyris, 1964). However, the experience could be relatively unstructured and the effects

> **Box 9.4 continued**
>
> short-lived, as participants returned to the ongoing pressures and to their previous behaviours in the workplace (Porras and Bradford, 2004).
>
> Nowadays, the intended outcomes of T-Groups – improving interpersonal relationships and team behaviour – are more frequently and less controversially achieved through 'team-building' activities, the origins of which lie in the original principles of T-Groups (Rothwell and Sullivan, 2005).
>
> The label 'organisation development' came from the original T-Group experiments and was later blended with other practices such as action research and participative management to achieve organisational change (Burnes and Cooke, 2012).

Thus, a common interest in improving individual, group and organisational performance emerged (Stanford, 2012). For the founders of OD in the 1940s and 1950s, it was a credible, 'scientific' method of intervening in behaviour in organisations so as to improve performance – blending science with professionalism (Burnes and Cooke, 2012). The evidence base for intervention relied on a combination of in-depth understanding of behavioural sciences, such as psychology, sociology and anthropology, and the practice of management. Its power lay in an appeal to both scientific principles, which provide a strong evidence base, and strongly developed humanistic values, which provide the focus for the activity as being the organisation's people (Cummings, 2004).

From those early foundations, the next 30 years saw the establishment of empirical and practical fields of OD. In the 1960s, OD 'came to maturity' (Skipton-Leonard *et al.,* 2013) and 'took off' (Burnes and Cooke, 2012: 1400) as it 'matched the hippy, anti-authoritarian spirit of the age . . . attractive to adherents of flower power and new age religion [seeking] personal and social freedoms' at work and in life. OD could, it was believed, transform people and organisations (Porras and Bradford, 2004). In the late 1960s the OD Network (**www.ODnetwork.org**) was established to bring together practitioners, leaders and academics to lead advances in the practice and theory of OD.

In the 1970s and 1980s, with changing economic conditions, the softer, optimistic theories were overlaid with a more commercial focus on performance and results. More traditional work, such as Lewin's, was criticised as enabling only small-scale changes in stable conditions, which was not the situation in which organisations found themselves. The rise of guru-like OD practitioners – concerned with broader organisation-wide issues such as structure and strategy – and the fading from view of academics signalled a shift of power that was not entirely without consequence (Cummings, 2004; Burnes and Cooke, 2012; Skipton-Leonard *et al.,* 2013). Greiner's (1972: 19) 'red flags' were a response to this shift, as he raised questions about the way that the field of OD was developing: 'I wish to raise six red warning flags by questioning six trends that may be preventing the very changes being sought' (Figure 9.1). Greiner and Cummings (2004: 380) identified that, at the time, OD 'evolved and morphed into entirely new forms that seemed far afield from OD's traditional core'.

Beckhard's work continued to be influential. French and Bell (1984) provided seminal texts in the 1980s, as did Cummings and Worley (1991) in the early 1990s, so that OD became known as: 'a systematic process in which applied behaviour science principles and practices are introduced to achieve the goals of increasing individual and organisational effectiveness' (French and Bell, 1984).

French and Bell suggested eight characteristics that differentiated OD from other change interventions, with an emphasis on:

- group and organisational processes;
- the work team as the key unit for improving organisational effectiveness;
- management of work-team culture;
- management of the organisation's culture;

Figure 9.1 Greiner's red flags

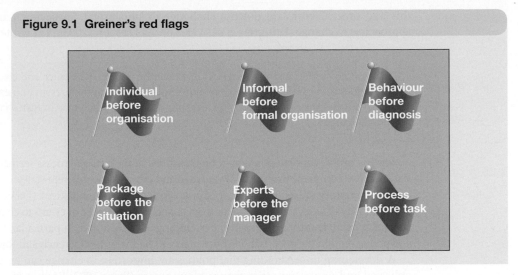

Source: Greiner and Cummings (2004), discussed in Burnes (2009: 345).

- understanding the whole organisational system and its consequences;
- an action research model;
- the use of change agents;
- change as an ongoing process.

The traditional approaches were joined by organisation-wide development practices, such as six sigma, total quality management and business process re-engineering, moving the focus away from the tried-and-tested group-based processes of the previous decades (Burnes and Cooke, 2012).

During the 1990s and early 2000s, OD's prominence was reduced (Skipton-Leonard *et al.*, 2013). In the field of practice, OD was conducted almost exclusively by external consultants zealously applying the principles of ethical OD practice (Robbins, 2001: 558):

- *Respect* – individuals considered to be responsible, conscientious and caring, to be treated with dignity and respect.
- *Trust* – the effective, health organisation is characterised by trust, openness and a supportive climate.
- *Power equalisation* – effective organisations de-emphasise hierarchical authority and control.
- *Confrontation* – problems shouldn't be swept under the rug, but should be openly confronted.
- *Participation* – the more that people who are affected by the change are involved in the decisions surrounding that change, the more they will be committed to implementation of those decisions.

In the field of theory, there was a growing emphasis on alternative conceptualisations of change which emphasised its complexities (Burnes and Cooke, 2012). For example, Pettigrew's (1985) influential case study of ICI challenged many of the dominant assumptions about how change happened (Pettigrew *et al.*, 1992). Pettigrew (1985) provided an extended critique of existing theories and practice of change and argued that the change process is 'a sequence of individual and collective events, actions and activities unfolding over time and in context' (Pettigrew, 1997: 344). The interplay between the content (the specific arena of change, e.g. technology, culture or what the change is in terms of its objectives, purpose and goals), the process (the 'actions, reactions and interactions' of human actors in producing and reproducing change; Pettigrew, 2003: 268) and the context of change (in terms of the internal and external environment) was identified as pivotal in conceptualising change as a process. Therefore, this and others' work laid down a challenge to 'ahistorical, aprocessual and acontextual' approaches to change (Pettigrew *et al.*, 1992: 6). As Dawson (2003a: 14) wrote:

> Change is a complex ongoing dynamic in which the politics, substance and context of change all interlock and overlay, and in which our understanding of the present and expectations for the future can influence our interpretation of past events, which may in turn shape our experience of change.

Lewin's simple conceptualisation of organisations in the change process seemed outmoded, not least because 'companies continuously move in and out of many different states, often concurrently, during the history of one or a number of organisational change initiatives' (Dawson, 2003a: 41). A growing body of work shifted the focus from change as a sequence of events to change as multivariate and cyclical, requiring a deeper understanding of context and, in particular, the role of power and politics within the organisation (Buchanan and Badham, 1999; French and Raven, 2001).

A developing understanding that politics are important in change can be attributed to the upheaval and uncertainty that change often causes (Staw, 1982; Ford *et al.*, 2008). The processes of organisational change were more frequently analysed as deeply political 'because the past can be interpreted in many different ways and future outcomes are contested, the system in the present is subject to the filtering of information brought about by relations of power and politics' (Pettigrew, 2003: 302) (see Box 9.5).

Box 9.5 Political behaviour and political skills

The term 'political' is typically used, loosely and pejoratively, to distinguish a category of interpersonal behaviour that includes a range of influence tactics, more or less covert, and more or less cunning.
Buchanan (1999: 74)

Political behaviour is a difficult subject to discuss in organisations, but here and later in the chapter, it is argued that understanding it is an important aspect of understanding, participating in or leading the process of change. Arguably, political behaviour has the potential to be more than self-interested (Ferris *et al.*, 2007) and can be employed to achieve organisational as well as individual purposes (Drory and Vigoda-Gadot, 2009).

What is political behaviour?

Dawson (1996) divides political behaviour into external and internal political activity, both of which involve decision-making and agenda-shaping in the process of change. External political activity includes the lobbying of politicians, strategic alliances, market positioning and stakeholder and competitor discussions. Internal political activity includes consultation, negotiation, conflicts and resistance within and between groups (such as trade unions and staff associations) and individuals, beyond 'mere' conflict and resistance. For example, Buchanan's (2008) candidate list of political behaviours, drawn from an extensive review of the literature, included the following as common political behaviours: building a network of useful contacts; using key players to support initiatives; making friends with power brokers; bending the rules to fit the situation; and self-promotion. Similarly, it was suggested that less common behaviours included: finding someone else to blame; claiming credit for the work of others; using social settings to discover opinions; using others to deliver bad news; deliberately withholding information; highlighting others' errors and flaws; using delaying tactics; breaking the rules; and compromising now to win later. Buchanan and Badham (2008) place political behaviour along a spectrum from conversational controls, impression management methods and influence tactics to dirty tricks and illegal acts, the former being routine, visible and unexceptional, and the latter being rare, exceptional and concealed. Moreover, the 'rich repertoire' (Buchanan and Badham 2008: 61) of political behaviours is triggered by contextual as well as individual factors, such as the need to achieve objectives and the complexity of organisational change.

Box 9.5 continued

What are the outcomes of political behaviour?

Buchanan's (1999) review of the literature identifies that political behaviours (individual and organisational) may have functional or dysfunctional outcomes. Functional outcomes of individual political behaviour include: the inspiration of confidence, trust and sincerity; increased self-confidence and reduced stress; power building; and career advancement. Dysfunctional outcomes of individual political behaviour include: frustration, anxiety and job dissatisfaction; individual harm through job loss; loss of strategic position and power; and damaged credibility. Likewise, organisational political behaviour can lead to the functional outcomes of support for desirable policies; opposition for undesirable policies; counter-action to legitimate tactics used to achieve illegitimate ends; support for implementation of legitimate decisions; resolution of conflict between competing views; and improved decision-making. On the other hand, dysfunctional outcomes include dysfunctional game playing; impeded efficiency; blocked goal achievement; misuse of resources; inflexibilities; barriers to communication; restricted information flows; and wasted time.

Question

1 What do you consider to be the acceptable boundaries of political behaviour in organisations?

This and other developments in our understanding of the change process (e.g. an interest in emergent change; Caldwell, 2006) meant that OD's influence had faded from immediate view – until recently.

OD today – the last 10 years

> The future of OD, its present relevance and continued viability, have been the subject of considerable debate in recent years.
> Marshak and Grant (2008:7)

Burnes and Cooke (2012) identify a turning point for OD in 2004 when as a field of theory there was a 'crisis of confidence' laid out in a special issue of the *Journal of Applied Behavioural Science* – the articles reflected on whether OD had any remaining currency in the modern world. However, alongside this there was a rekindling of interest by academics and practitioners in Lewin's work (Caldwell, 2006) and in developing new post-Lewinian theories (see the section on appreciative inquiry later in this chapter). As identified earlier, a closer alignment between OD and HR was also occurring.

Organisational development's revival in the late 2000s was based on its potential, it seemed, to address the 'perennial organisational dilemma' – how to meet individual needs while addressing organisational realities of improving performance. However, as a set of theories and practices, OD is arguably fundamentally different today from its original conceptions and activities (Francis et al., 2012).

Marshak and Grant (2008) provide a critical consideration of the history of OD. They argue that there is evident an 'old' and a 'new' approach in its theoretical and practical embodiment (see Table 9.1). 'Old' OD was firmly rooted in a positivist ideal. Its basis in classical behavioural sciences required a belief in the possibility of a discoverable reality and an objective truth. Change from this view is episodic, can be created, managed and planned. Resistance is problematic, should be diagnosed and treated, as any differences must be a consequence of misperceptions. The central emphasis of 'old' OD, then, was to change behaviour. By contrast, Marshak and Grant (2008) argue that modern OD is more culturally and socially aware and represents a more qualified and qualitative position. It draws on the two decades of research and theory development in organisational change, referred to earlier, and so it accepts the possibility of multiple viewpoints and perspectives. Change can be something, then, that is continuous and self-organising. Resistance to change is less problematic, and potentially positive, as it may reveal new information that may help to improve change processes and organisational relationships. The emphasis of 'new' OD then is in changing mindsets.

Aligned with this different approach then is a new set of practices. Marshak and Grant (2008: 7) argue that 'a new ensemble of OD practices have emerged' based on different foundations from the early writers which include practices such as appreciative enquiry, larger group interventions and new models of change. The chapter considers each of these 'new' areas of OD later on.

Moreover, there has been a growth in interest from academics that sees the emergence of new theories as well as new practices (Burnes and Cooke, 2012).

Key Controversy

What is ethically more acceptable? To attempt to change how someone behaves, or to attempt to change how someone thinks?

Table 9.1 Trends in organisational development

Classical OD (1950s onward)	New OD (1980s onward)
Based in classical science and modern thought and philosophy	Influenced by the new sciences and postmodern thought and philosophy
Truth is transcendent and discoverable; there is a single, objective reality	Truth is immanent and emerges from the situation; there are multiple, socially constructed realities
Reality can be discovered using rational and analytic processes	Reality is socially negotiated and may involve power and political processes
Collecting and applying valid data using objective problem-solving methods leads to change	Creating new mindsets or social agreements, sometimes through explicit or implicit negotiation, leads to change
Change is episodic and can be created, planned and managed	Change is continuous and can be self-organising
Emphasis on changing behaviour and what one does	Emphasis on changing mindsets and how one thinks

Source: from Marshak and Grant (2008: 8).

Explore

Read Marshak and Grant (2008).

Their article contends that the differences between OD then and now lie in differences in ontological and epistemological perspectives, and not necessarily differences in values or viability. That is to say, where OD then saw differences in perspective as aberrations to be repaired or removed in the process of OD, it now sees differences as competing realities, to be explored and embraced.

This is a complex argument, but one that helps to understand some of the criticisms of the older approaches to OD and to raise concerns about the impact of OD in its newer forms.

Francis et al. (2012), in their excellent account of OD's development and modern existence, identify a number of flaws still present in the contemporary view of OD. For example,

OD may still pay scant attention to power structures and political behaviour in organisations (Buchanan and Badham, 2008; Francis et al., 2012), identified earlier as one of the challenges to OD. This is a significant criticism as many, such as Dawson (2003b: 175) argue that:

> Change is a political process . . . political processes are central in shaping the speed, direction and outcomes of change . . . . Although the results of change may be presented in the form of some objective demonstrable outcome, the route and progression of change as well as evaluations of success and failure will be shaped by political processes.

Moreover, Helms-Mills et al. (2009) suggest that the easiest and most popular criticism of OD is that the plethora of publications, practitioners and processes have led to a dilution of the impact of OD, as practice has not kept pace with theory. While the extent to which the definition of OD can be contested will be discussed throughout the chapter, our working definition sees OD as a planned set of change activities to achieve organisational effectiveness through adjusting organisational processes – with people at the heart of the endeavour.

The theories of OD

> There is nothing so practical as a good theory. — Lewin (1943/4: 169)

As we saw earlier, the work of Kurt Lewin (1951), an influential psychologist in the early twentieth century, forms the basis of most OD interventions. Lewin's focus was group dynamics – he saw the group as the main level of study and intervention in the process of change (Helms-Mills et al., 2009). Lewin believed that organisations strive for balance or equilibrium in order to maintain stability. To disturb the equilibrium, dissatisfaction had to be created through either increasing the driving forces or reducing the restraining factors (Dawson, 2003b). Minimising the forces that restrain change and maximising those that support it are required to make change possible. Lewin used 'force-field analysis' as an analytical tool for understanding the restraining and driving forces for a particular change initiative (Figure 9.2).

Explore

You can use a force-field analysis to identify where conditions are supportive of a particular change or where there is resistance. If the driving forces outweigh the restraining forces, then the change can progress more easily. If the alternative is true, the change may have to be postponed or abandoned as there may be too many restraints or little enthusiasm for the change. If they are more or less in balance, then plans can be made to progress the change.

- List the stakeholders affected by the change or use a PESTLE analysis to identify the environmental factors that will affect the change.
- Split the list into drivers and restraints.
- Consider each factor in turn and identify its extent, relevance and scope. Draw an arrow on the diagram which represents its force (use breadth and length to represent the force) or give it a score or a rating.
- Identify actions that you will undertake to ensure the restraining forces are minimised and the driving forces maximised. Be careful, however, as increasing the driving forces can also increase resisting forces. It may be preferable to decrease the resisting forces first to reduce tension and challenge.

Figure 9.2 Example of a force-field analysis

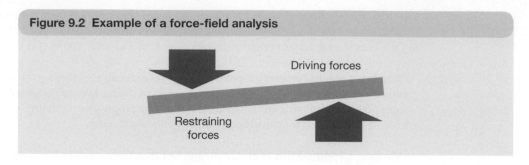

Driving forces

Restraining forces

Lewin also noticed, however, that group change was often short-lived, with a return to previous behaviour being highly likely. In order to achieve permanent change, Lewin proposed a solution in his three-step model. This model suggests that change consists of three stages: unfreezing, moving and freezing (often misquoted as re-freezing) (Figure 9.3). These three stages describe the process of moving from the current state, through a transitional state, to a final and established new state. This process takes the organisation through the stages in an orderly, controlled, planned and easily understood process.

The unfreezing stage is where dissatisfaction with the current situation is created through identifying the benefits of the change and the discomfort associated with the status quo. The group members must understand the reason for the change in order to engage in the process. The moving stage is where the activities and resources are aligned to achieve the desired change. New policies, procedures, values, behaviours and attitudes are established. Freezing is the stage where the changes are reinforced and established. Rewards and sanctions can be used to cement the new behaviours. The process requires considerable organisational commitment (Helms-Mills et al., 2009).

While revealing a basic appreciation of the need to see change as occurring in a context from which it has to be unfrozen and then frozen, Lewis's work has, however, been 'subject to reinterpretation or ridicule in almost equal measures' (Caldwell, 2006: 29). For example, inherent in Lewin's proposal on planned change is a particular set of beliefs about the change process: that change can be managed, that changes can be identified ahead of time, that the process of change is predictable, that the process is clear, and that if you follow the rules it will be successful (Stacey, 1996; Collins, 1998) and failure to succeed can simply be attributed to a failure to follow the rules. Thus, Lewin's approach can be argued to present a one-dimensional or unitary view of change and its context (Dawson, 2003a; Caldwell, 2006). That it is sometimes called a 'clinical' approach (Carnall, 2007) reflects intentions to diagnose or solve the 'problem' of change without considering or challenging the hegemonic qualities of talk and text (Abolafia, 2010). Moreover, the models take a largely unquestioning approach to the process of change, and do not consider the appropriateness of the change itself, but rather accept it as a 'given'.

Figure 9.3 Lewin's three-step model

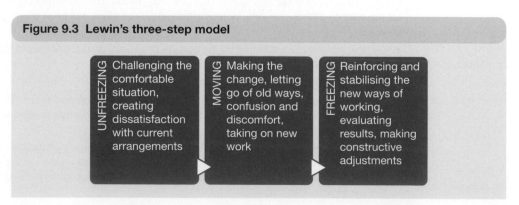

UNFREEZING Challenging the comfortable situation, creating dissatisfaction with current arrangements

MOVING Making the change, letting go of old ways, confusion and discomfort, taking on new work

FREEZING Reinforcing and stabilising the new ways of working, evaluating results, making constructive adjustments

Source: developed from Lewin (1951).

- What activities might each of the following undertake at each stage of Lewin's process to ensure that the process of change is achieved:
  - managers;
  - HR professionals.
- Who else would need to be involved to support the change process?
- How far can Lewin's model capture the processes of change in the dynamic world of modern organisations?

More recently, as we began to identify earlier, it has been argued that such approaches are no longer sustainable, given current understanding about the political nature of the processes of change (Caldwell, 2006). Moreover, the nature and speed of change in organisations today mean that there are likely to be multiple cycles of change in progress at any point in time. This presents several problems: cycles of change are almost certain to overlap and the stages of change as conceptualised by Lewin (1951) are likely to conflict with each other. Furthermore, the discomfort that comes with the process of moving is likely, in a constantly changing organisation, to be almost permanent and the freezing process will be difficult to achieve. Thus, the planned approaches appear weakened by organisational reality. Kanter et al.'s (1992: 10) view was that:

Lewin's model was a simple one with organisational change involving three stages . . . . Thus, the quaintly linear and static conception – the organisation as an ice-cube – is so wildly inappropriate that it is difficult to see why it has not only survived but prospered, except for one thing. It offers managers a very straightforward way of planning their actions, by simplifying an extraordinarily complex process . . . Suffice to say here, first, that organisations are never frozen, much less refrozen, but are fluid entities with many 'personalities'. Second, to the extent that there are stages, they overlap and interpenetrate one another in important ways.

Key Controversy

Organisational development relies on a structure for change that is top-down, controlled and controllable. Change is conceptualised as neat and tidy, linear, with boundaries, a defined beginning and a clear and definable end.

Reflecting this, OD relies on a mechanistic language (Fleetwood and Hesketh, 2010): 'managers are encouraged to find "levers" for change, and "drive" communications to effect change . . . consultants have a "toolkit" used to implement new ways of working . . .' (Francis et al., 2012: 7). Complexities are ignored or overlooked, politics marginalised and resistance considered dysfunctional.

Compare this with the reality of change, which is often emergent, messy, political, slow, iterative, repetitive, unsolved and unsolvable. What is your view?

Although strongly influenced by Lewin's model of organisational change, OD is often considered to be separate from mainstream change management because of the distinctive values and principles that underpin it.

Many other models have developed from Lewin's three-stage process. Collins (1998) refers to such models as 'n-step' and Buchanan and Huczynski (2010) to 'phase models' of change. All are based on the premise that there is a recipe to follow, and where change is unsuccessful it can be attributed to a failure to 'stick to the knitting'.

One of the most often-quoted models based on Lewin's work is Kotter (1995). In his examination of why change efforts normally fail, he identified eight steps to 'transforming your organisation'. Kotter acknowledges that his approach over-simplifies change and identifies that 'in reality, even successful change efforts are messy and full of surprises . . . but . . . a relatively simple vision is needed to guide people through a major change . . . and reduce the error rate' (p. 67):

1 Establish a sense of urgency, identify opportunities and threats.

2 Form a powerful guiding group to lead the change effort.

3 Create a vision to give direction and develop strategies to achieve it.

4 Communicate the new vision and strategies everywhere.

5 Give others the chance to act on the vision, remove obstacles.

6 Create the chance for short-term wins and visible improvements.

7 Consolidate the improvements and adjust.

8 Solidify the new approaches.

As well as a clear process for change, a key component of the model is strong leadership in the form of a 'guiding coalition' – a strong guiding group to lead the change effort. Some authors argue that this leadership must come from the top (Conger, 2000), whereas others argue for a more dispersed change agent role (Bennis, 2000; Dunphy, 2000). We discuss change agency later in the chapter.

Explore

The CIPD's toolkit 'Approaches to change: building capability and confidence' is an example of a phase model of change.

● Read the document and consider:
  – What benefits are suggested for you and your organisation in using the tool?
  – Examine the seven-part framework. What are its strengths and its weaknesses?
  – Given what we have covered so far in this chapter, is there anything missing from the guidance that is offered?

You may also want to read the CIPD report from 2005, called 'HR: Making change happen', which provides the background for the toolkit.

The techniques and practices of OD

Cheung-Judge and Holbeche (2011) suggest that the OD practitioner needs:

● an OD consultancy cycle which describes the phases of engagement;

● tools and techniques ('theories in action') which enable the 'shift';

● theoretical assumptions which are the primary principles that shape the practitioner's work (which include change theories such as Lewin's described earlier);

● values and ethics to give parameters and guidance.

In this section, having considered some of the theoretical assumptions earlier, we address the first two of the concerns in the list. A later section describes the role and skills of change agents.

The OD cycle

Organisational development is usually described as an 'intervention' during which skilled practitioners (change agents) apply established techniques in a process that addresses issues, problems and challenges associated with an organisational change or an improvement in performance. OD interventions take place within a cycle of process consultancy (Stanford, 2012): entry, diagnosis, planning, action and stabilisation/evaluation. Cheung-Judge and Holbeche (2011) identify an eight-stage cycle of:

- *Entry/contacting* – initial contract, define problem/need/client, explore readiness for change, agree contract outcomes (who, what, when, where).
- *Data collection* – prepare for data collection, collect data.
- *Data analysis* – analyse data, prepare a report and a summary.
- *Feedback* – plan feedback, produce feedback materials, deliver feedback, provide frameworks, diagnosis and planning.
- *Action planning* – assess problems/gaps/opportunities, prioritise opportunities, plan actions.
- *Action-taking* – carry out action plans, interventions: individual, interpersonal, group, intergroup, organisation, organisation/environment.
- *Evaluation* – review goals, assess progress, identify new learning, redirect where needed.
- *Termination* – assess need to continue, decide to end, phase out, stay open to be called.

The significant degree of planning that is required before intervention is notable.

Explore

- What are the skills that an OD practitioner needs to manage the consultancy process?
- Consider each of Cheung-Young and Holbeche's steps in turn:
  - Are they the same, or different, from those of other consultants?
  - How would the skills be different if the OD practitioner was an employee of the organisations, or an externally contracted consultant?

Tools and techniques

This section describes some of the established techniques that can be described as fitting with an 'OD mindset' (Francis et al., 2012).

> OD interventions are sets of structured activities in which selected organisational units engage in a sequence of tasks that will lead to organisational improvement. Interventions are actions taken to produce desired changes. French and Bell (1999: 118).

Deciding where to start

There are many models to assist practitioners in deciding where they should focus their attention and how they should intervene to achieve performance improvement using OD principles and practices. Authors provide comprehensive lists of activities that can be included under the umbrella of OD activity. McLean (2005), for example, offers a comprehensive list of interventions which combines both old and established approaches and new or emerging ideas, including a long list of activities that return us to our original proposition that many HR practices can sit under the OD umbrella:

- *Individual* – training groups, coaching, mentoring, self-awareness tools, training and development, leadership development, critical reflection, 360-degree feedback, job redesign, values clarification, conflict management, action learning.
- *Team* – cross-team development and awareness building, diversity, participation or collaboration projects.
- *Organisation* – organisational redesign, surveys, culture change projects, changes to reward systems and succession planning, strategic planning or scenario planning.

Stanford (2012) identifies an overlap between HR operation and OD activity and suggests the list starts with:

- business process redesign;
- change management;
- conflict management;
- culture analysis;
- executive coaching and leadership development;
- group problem-solving;
- large group interventions – e.g. Future Search, World Café and Openspace (see later);
- meeting design and facilitation;
- organisation assessments;
- organisation redesign;
- organisation dynamics;
- talent management;
- team-building.

A few authors provide guidance on the criteria for selection. For example, Pugh's (2009) 'OD matrix' provides a basis for understanding and diagnosing what change is necessary in an organisation, what methods to consider, and ways of initiating the change process (Table 9.2). His diagnostic tool provides guidance on the issues that can hinder change and the level at which they occur (Senior and Swailes, 2010). The matrix can be used to assist practitioners in the process of planning for intervention (recommended starting points for intervention are in italics). Selection is based on the level at which intervention should take place (organisational, inter-group, group or individual) and the scope of the change (behaviour, structure or context). The first column presents behaviours that can be tackled directly and most easily. The second suggests wider changes in the organisational structure and the last column presents the most challenging agenda or intervention which may involve significant disruption and cost and a high degree of commitment to the process from all involved.

Cheung-Judge and Holbeche (2011) summarise Schmuck and Miles' (1971) comprehensive decision tool – one of the first to be offered to enable selection of techniques by practitioners (the OD cube; see Figure 9.4). It encourages the practitioner to focus on the three interacting dimensions to be considered in the design process for interventions. Although quite old now, they argue that it still has a contribution to make. They suggest that using the cube requires both careful attention to the framework and also some imagination in tailoring the approach to the particular situation. The model encourages selection based on:

- *the diagnosed problems* – goals and plans, communication, culture and climate, leadership or authority, problem-solving, decision-making, conflict and cooperation and role definition;
- *the focus of attention* – the individual, the role, the dyad/triad, the team or group, intergroup or the total organisation;
- *the mode of intervention* – plan-making, confrontation, data-feedback, problem-solving, training, techno-structural activity, process consultation and coaching, and OD task force establishment.

Common to most lists or models is the need to identify the level of intervention – individual, team, inter-team or organisational. Others shy away from listing practices, and prefer to focus on the principles or defining characteristics of activity so as to ensure the outcome of organisational effectiveness. For example, Ramdhony (2012) presents a critical stance on OD and suggests the defining characteristics of activity include:

- a non-exclusive focus on performance;
- a commitment to critical reflection;

- a non-conformist posture;
- an emancipatory intent;
- a radical mindset;
- an ethical stance;
- a facilitator of participatory dialogue;
- an agent of workplace democracy.

Table 9.2 Organisational development matrix (Pugh, 2009)

	Behaviour (what is happening now?)	Structure (what is the required system?)	Context (what is the setting?)
Organisational level	General climate of poor morale, pressure, anxiety, suspicion, lack of awareness of, or response to, environmental changes *Survey Feedback Organisational Mirroring*	Systems goals – poorly defined or inappropriate and misunderstood; organisation structure inappropriate – centralisation, divisionalisation or standardisation; inadequacy of environmental monitoring *Change the structure*	Geographical setting, market pressures, labour market, physical condition, basic technology *Change strategy, location, physical condition, basic technology*
Inter-group level	Lack of effective cooperation between sub-units, conflict, excessive competition, limited war, failure to confront differences in priorities, unresolved feelings *Inter-group confrontation (with a third-party consultant), role negotiation*	Lack of integrated task perspective; sub-unit optimisation, required interaction difficult to achieve *Redefine responsibilities, change reporting relationships, improve coordination and liaison mechanism*	Different sub-unit values, lifestyle, physical distance *Reduce psychological and physical distance, exchange roles, attachments, cross-functional groups*
Group level	Inappropriate working relationships, atmosphere, participation, poor understanding and acceptance of goals, avoidance, inappropriate leadership style, leader not trusted, respected; leader in conflict with peers and superiors *Process consultation, team building*	Task requirements poorly defined; role relationships unclear or inappropriate; leaders' role overloaded, inappropriate reporting procedures *Redesign work relationships (socio-technical systems), self-directed working groups*	Insufficient resources, poor group composition for cohesion, inadequate physical setup, personality clashes *Change technology, layout and group composition*
Individual level	Failure to fulfil individual's needs; frustration responses; unwillingness to consider change, little chance for learning and development *Counselling, role analysis, career planning*	Poor job definition, task too easy or difficult *Job restructuring/ modification, redesign, enrichment, agree on key competencies*	Poor match of individual with job, poor selection or promotion, inadequate preparation or training, recognition and remuneration at variance with objectives *Personnel changes, improved selection and promotion procedures, improved training and education, bring recognition and remuneration in line with objectives*

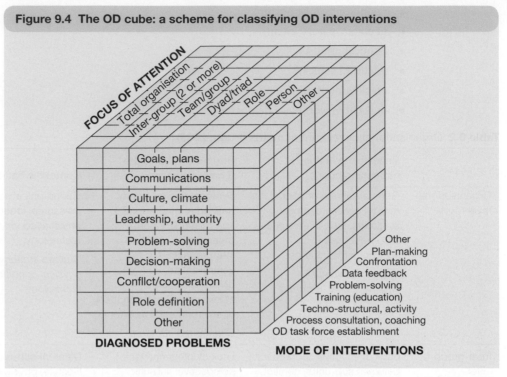

Figure 9.4 The OD cube: a scheme for classifying OD interventions

Source: Schmuck and Miles (1971: 5). Used with permission. For recent information about the OD cube, see Schmuck, R., Bell, S. and Bell, W. (2012) 'The Handbook of Organization Development in Schools and Colleges, 5th ed., Santa Cruz, CA: Exchange Pointe International.

Action research: the key philosophy of OD intervention

Lewin's pervasive influence in the development of OD is visible in the centrality of action research to its practice. OD involves deliberate intervention in an organisation and the observation of the results. Lewin developed the action research model to facilitate the examination by social scientists of practical problems without tight limits on the boundaries of the situation under examination (Dickens and Watkins, 1999; Hayes, 2010). According to Brydon-Miller et al. (2001: 15):

> ... action research goes beyond the notion that theory can inform practice, to a recognition that theory can and should be generated through practice, and ... that theory is really only useful insofar as it is put in the service of a practice focused on achieving social change.

Burnes and Cooke (2012) take the view that action research is based on the assumption that all situations and all organisations are unique and that the process of change has to be designed to accommodate this uniqueness, while, according to Anderson (2009) action research is based on the assumptions that:

● researchers are and should be involved in situations they are researching;

● researchers are and should be part of the cycle of improvement.

In that sense it is attractive to practitioners because of its tenets of direct involvement and opportunity for critical reflection.

The framework of action research facilitates a deep understanding of an organisational problem as it emerges: some argue that it is not, however, a method or a procedure for research, but 'a series of commitments to observe and problematize through practice a series of principles for conducting social enquiry' (McTaggart, 1996: 248). That is, unlike normal methods of research, which culminate in a point of revelation or solution, action research facilitates discovery and resolution as the process unfolds. Action research requires an open-ended process of planning, acting, observing and reflecting (Anderson, 2009). In the planning stage, information is gathered about the issue to be resolved and the context in which is it situated. Action is taken to implement the plan and the consequences carefully observed, recorded, and finally reflected on. The process continues cyclically until the desired improvement is achieved: Lewin (1946: 206) described this as a spiral of steps 'each of which is composed of a circle of planning, action and fact-finding about the result of the action'.

Burnes and Cooke (2012: 1402) identify that:

> though action research is often characterised as a diagnostic process . . . for Lewin it was much more about creating a dialogue amongst the particpants which would allow them to reach a common understanding of the context in which their behaviours took place.

Action learning sets

Action learning sets are considered in detail in the previous chapter (Chapter 8).

Appreciative inquiry (AI)

Appreciative inquiry is a conversation-based change process that does as its title suggests: an inquiry that is appreciative of the healthy, effective and positive aspects of the organisation. External as well as internal stakeholders may be included in the process. It is a 'glass half full' approach which offers an alternative to problem-based learning that focuses on what is wrong, or what needs to be improved. Its aim is to increase that which the organisation does well, rather than eliminate that which it does badly. There is significant potential for challenges during the process, as it may bring together stakeholders with very different views on the organisation. Moreover, AI requires a particular set of skills that enable high-quality conversational interactions in group settings.

Focusing on the positive is a central feature of AI. It allows stakeholders to express different views on key topics through a positive lens. David Cooperrider is generally considered to be the original architect of the process (Lewis et al., 2011).

Cooperrider and Whitney (2005) suggest a five-stage process:

- *Define* – where you identify the scope of the AI.
- *Discovery* – where you identify what is working, what is the best of the given situation.
- *Dream* – where you identify the vision for the future.
- *Design* – where you plan how to achieve the vision.
- *Destiny* – where you implement the design and sustain positive changes.

Large group interventions (LGIs)

World Café

World cafés provide an example of an LGI reliant on conversational activity. The focus of the activity is a set of questions or issues that are important to organisational life. The participants are seated in small groups in a café-style environment. Each table has a 'host', who is responsible for the activities of the group. The group is encouraged to write their ideas directly onto paper table covers. Participants engage in 'rounds' of conversations, moving table after each round to develop the work of the previous group. At the end, a whole group conversation takes place to reflect on insights and discoveries. The world café can be used for many purposes, such as strategy development, value elicitation, problem-solving, idea generation and organisational review. The environment is designed to encourage collaboration and dialogue both in the immediate task of problem-solving and in longer-term team relationships.

Future Search

Future Search enables action planning in larger groups over longer periods of time (three days) using storytelling and dialogue to elicit individuals' experiences of the past and present, and their vision for the future. It relies on a significant cross-section of all parties being present during the process and that the 'whole problem' is considered at once, before focusing on individual parts. The purpose is to identify common ground and to encourage individual responsibility for achieving the vision. Open Space Technology sets a similar agenda, but offers more flexibility in time and resources.

Explore

- Visit **www.theworldcafe.com**, **www.futuresearch.com** and **www.openspaceworld.org**, where you can find detailed explanations, free resources and case studies.
- Where could you use the World Café or Future Search approach in your organisation's development?

Swot analysis

A SWOT analysis (Box 9.6) usually appears somewhere in the process of OD. The tool was developed in the 1960s, originally by Albert Humphrey, as an analytical tool to evaluate strategic plans using the acronym SOFT – satisfactory, opportunities, faults and threats. In 1964, Urick and Orr, at a seminar in long-range planning in Zurich, Switzerland, where research on why corporate planning failed was being presented, adapted this to SWOT – strengths, weaknesses, opportunities and threats. The tool is usually presented as a grid to examine the issues around an organisational challenge or opportunity for improvement.

Box 9.6 ## A proper SWOT analysis

Complete this exercise either individually or in a group. Using sticky notes will allow you to move your responses around as you progress through the exercise.

Stage 1: Brainstorming

Brainstorm as many strengths, weaknesses, opportunities and threats relating to the situation as you can.

	Positive	Negative
Present Internal	Strengths	Weaknesses
Future External	Opportunities	Threats

Strengths and weaknesses describe the current/present and internal situation to whatever is being analysed.

Opportunities and threats describe the future and external situation to whatever is being analysed.

Strengths and opportunities are positive. Weaknesses and threats are negative.

Stage 2: Clustering

Cluster the reasons together to establish themes and linkages. Consider cause-and-effect relationships: is a weakness caused by another weakness?

Stage 3: Analyse weaknesses

At this stage, you should consider the extent to which the weakness is either easy or difficult to address and of high or low importance. This stage helps you to identify a way forward – you are able here to identify which weaknesses you can address first for fastest results.

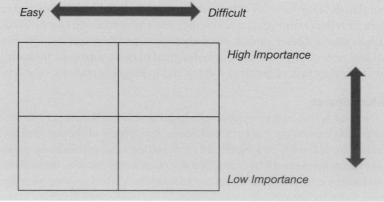

Box 9.6 continued

Stage 4: Creating objective statements

Look at each weakness in turn and reformulate as an objective statement. You can use SMART (specific, measurable, achievable, realistic, time-bounded) as an acronym to test your objective.

Stage 5: Risk analysis

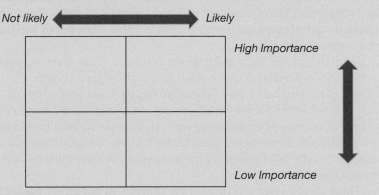

Consider the likelihood of the threat occurring and its relative importance. The risks you identify should lead to a contingency plan. The likely, and highly important, threats are the ones that require the most attention – accounting for these threats is essential to achieving the plan. Those in the bottom left quadrant are the least important and require little more than monitoring.

Stage 6: Focus on the positive

Return to strengths and opportunities and prepare practical plans for building on them.

Source: adapted from training materials provided by Frank Jordan, University of Northampton 2013.

The learning organisation

> The notion of the learning organisation is all about creating organisational results from individual learning.
>
> Senge (1990: 11)

The notion of the learning organisation has been, and continues to be, an influential one in conceptualisations of OD. Its roots can be traced in literature on organisational excellence (Peters and Waterman, 1972), total quality management (Deming, 1986), action learning (Revans, 1982, 1983, 2011), and organisational learning (Argyris and Schon, 1978; Argyris, 1992) – all influential in the parallel development of OD. Peter Senge (1990) is usually credited with bringing the concept to organisational life in the early 1990s in the US. In the UK, the work of Pedler *et al.* (1991) on 'The Learning Company Project' in the late 1980s and early 1990s provided organisationally useful tools for establishing a learning climate.

It has at its heart a 'whole company' perspective, like OD (not just an HR perspective), on learning and development. It links the development of the potential of everyone (not just managers, or 'talent' in the business) to the development of the company as a whole. It emphasises the importance of organisational flexibility, responsiveness, adaptability and conscious approach to change (Senge, 1990) and underlines the importance of breaking down outmoded ideas, attitudes and practices before building new skills, structures and values

(Pettigrew and Whipp, 1991). It is a 'systemic' rather than a 'systematic' approach, seeing everything as interconnected, rather than simple cause and effect, and because of this complexity, it is probably much less commonly adopted than the rhetoric would suggest (Gibb and Megginson, 2001: 153).

Pedler *et al.* (1991, 1997) explained that, at its heart, the learning company was about releasing the 'massive underdeveloped potential in our organisations' (Pedler *et al.*, 1997: 3) and seeking to differentiate the type of learning as one that happens 'at the whole organisation level'. For them, it is about being 'an organisation that facilitates the learning of all its members and consciously transforms itself and its context' (p. 3) and is about 'understanding and mastering the art of corporate learning . . . as learning is the key to survival and development for the companies of today' (p. 6).

Diagnostic tools are popular in the literature of the learning organisation. Pedler *et al.* (1991, 1997) developed an 11-point diagnostic jigsaw (Figure 9.5). Honey and Mumford (1989) generated an 11-point checklist and Bartram *et al.* (1993) a 70-item questionnaire that centred around seven broad categories (supportive management style, time pressures, degree of autonomy, encouraging team style, opportunities to develop, availability of written guidelines, atmosphere of satisfaction). These tools are intended as a structure for a gap analysis to establish the journey the business must make between where it is now and where it wants to be.

There are, however, criticisms of the concept. Its popularity peaked in the early 1990s, and since 2002 there has been considerably less discussion about the impact of the idea than in previous years. Even strong supporters point to the fact that it has not lived up to 'all our aspirations . . . or delivered its full potential' (Burgoyne, 1999). Garvin (1993: 78) identifies that important writers' work, Senge and Nonaka, in particular, is 'utopian . . . filled with near mystical terminology'.

Garvin (1993: 50) also highlights the aspirational nature of the ideas:

> . . . idyllic? Absolutely. Desirable? Without question. But does it provide a framework for action? Hardly. These recommendations are far too abstract, too many questions remain unanswered. How, for example, will managers know when their companies have become learning organisations? What concrete changes in behaviour are required? What policies and programmes must be in place? How do you get from here to there?

Sloman (1999: 31) agrees: 'the concept of the learning organisation should be redefined or declared redundant'. In its current manifestations, according to Stewart and Sambrook (2002: 183): 'The idea of learning organisations cannot be said to be capable of operationalisation in any meaningful sense.'

Overall, the models lack a convincing link between theory and practice (Lahteenmaki *et al.*, 1999), practice and outcomes. However, it must be noted that the original authors did not promise the learning organisation as a quick fix or simple solution (Pedler *et al.*, 1991), and the fact that organisations face challenges of culture, time, ownership and commitment is hardly surprising given the nature and size of the task. However, the debate is still live on how to promote individual learning for organisational advantage. Organisations still place 'enormous importance' on the creation of cultures that support learning and development for individuals, and for business benefit (CIPD, 2004c: 14), but the discussion has moved on, at least in part, to the development of a coaching culture.

The skills of OD practitioners

> All change processes are influence processes. All influence processes require awareness of, if not action in, the political processes of the organisations.
>
> Pettigrew (2000: 250)

Figure 9.5a The learning company profile

Company regularly takes stock and modifies direction and strategy as appropriate.	Policy and strategy formation structured as learning processes.	All members of the company take part in policy and strategy formation.	Policies are significantly influenced by the views of stakeholders.

1. The learning approach to strategy   **2. Participative policy making**

Managerial acts seen as conscious experiments.

Business plans are evolved and modified as we go along.

Commitment to airing differences and working through conflicts.

Company policies reflect the values of all members, not just those of top management.

Deliberate small scale experiments and feedback loops are built into the planning process to enable continuous improvement.

Appraisal and career planning discussions often generate visions that contribute to strategy and policy.

1.   2.

Information is used for understanding, not for reward or punishment.

Information technology is used to create databases and communication systems that help everyone understand what is going on.

Systems of accounting, budgeting and reporting are structured to assist learning.

Everyone feels part of a department or unit responsible for its own resources.

3. Informating   **4. Formative accounting and control**

You can get feedback on how your section or department is doing at any time by pressing a button.

We really understand the nature and significance of variation in a system, and interpret data accordingly.

Accountants and finance people act as consultants and advisers *as well as* score keepers and bean counters.

Control systems are designed and run to delight their customers.

Information technology is used to create databases, information and communication systems that help everyone to understand what is going on and to make sound decisions.

The financial system encourages departments and individuals to take risks with venture capital.

3.   4.

Departments see each other as customers and suppliers, discuss and come to agreements on quality, cost, delivery.

Each department strives to delight its internal customers *and* remains aware of the needs of the company as a whole.

The basic assumptions and values underpinning reward systems are explored and shared.

The nature of 'reward' is examined in depth.

5. Internal exchange   **6. Reward flexibility**

Departments speak freely and candidly with each other, both to challenge and to give help.

Managers facilitate communication, negotiation and contracting, rather than exerting top-down control.

Departments, sections and units are able to act on their own initiatives.

Alternative reward systems are examined, discussed, tried out.

Flexible working patterns allow people to make different contributions and draw different rewards.

We are all involved in determining the nature and share of reward systems.

5.   6.

Source: from *The Learning Company*, McGraw-Hill (Pedler, M., Burgoyne, J. and Boydell, T. 1991) pp. 26–7 © 1991.

(continued)

Figure 9.5b The learning company profile

Roles and careers are flexibly structured to allow for experimentation, growth and adaptation.

Appraisals are geared more to learning and development than to reward and punishment.

It is part of the work of all staff to collect, bring back, and report information about what's going on outside the company.

All meetings in the company regularly include a review of what's going on in our business environment.

7. Enabling structures

Departmental and other boundaries are seen as temporary structures that can flex in response to changes.

We have rules and procedures but they are frequently changed after review and discussion.

We experiment with new forms of structures.

7.

8. Boundary workers as environmental scanners

We meet regularly with representative groups of customers, suppliers, community members and so on to find out what's important to them.

We receive regular intelligence reports on the economy, markets, technological developments, socio-political events and world trends and examine how these may affect our business.

8.

There are systems and procedures for receiving, collating and sharing information from outside the company.

People from the company go on attachments to our business partners, including suppliers, customers and competitors.

We regularly meet with our competitors to share ideas and information.

If something goes wrong around here you can expect help, support and interest in learning lessons from it.

People make time to question their own practice, to analyse, discuss and learn from what happens.

9. Inter-company learning

10. Learning climate

We engage in joint ventures with our suppliers, customers and competitors, to develop new products and markets.

We participate in joint learning events with our suppliers, customers and other stakeholders.

There is a general attitude of continuous improvement – always trying to learn and do better.

When you don't know something, it's normal to ask around until you get the required help or information.

We use benchmarking in order to learn from the best practice in other industries.

3.

Differences of all sorts, between young and old, women and men, black and white, etc. are recognised and positively valued as essential to learning and creativity.

10.

People here have their own self-development budgets – they decide what training and development they want, and what to pay for it.

There are lots of opportunities, materials and resources available for learning on an 'open access' basis around the company.

11. Self-development opportunities for all

With appropriate guidance people are encouraged to take responsibility.

11.

Self-development resources are available to external stakeholders.

The exploration of an individual's learning needs is the central focus of appraisal and career planning.

Source: from *The Learning Company*, McGraw-Hill (Pedler, M., Burgoyne, J. and Boydell, T. 1991) pp. 26–7. © 1991.

Key Controversy

The expectations on OD practitioners – change agents – are high (see Figure 9.6). However, behind the debates about the skills that change agents require lies a serious critical discussion about the extent to which change can be managed as a rational or planned process in contemporary workplaces – whether there can be 'agency' in relation to change (Caldwell, 2006a). The assumptions that underlie the proposition that change can be managed have their roots in rationalist epistemologies which posit that human beings are rational actors and can act in an intentional and predictable manner towards goals or outcomes. A competing perspective is one that recognises that organisational change is simply too complex and high risk for one individual or group to lead and that human action is rarely rational or predictable. Therefore, agency in change is dispersed throughout the organisation and is dependent on an understanding of the cultural and historical context of the situation.

Caldwell's (2006) book provides an in-depth analysis of agency and change and provides a solid conceptual base for the discussion of the topic at an advanced level.

The idea of the OD consultant as change agent has its roots in Lewin's early work. Thereafter, most models of change agency focused on a process of planned change and the provision of technical or specialist assistance in the process (Caldwell, 2003). On this basis, OD practitioners require, first and foremost, process skills: 'to give the client insight into what is going on around him, within him and between him and other people' (Schein, 1988). We have already considered the extent to which process consultation is a vital part of OD models, as OD is applied to an organisation's business (Friedlander and Brown, 1974; Worren *et al.*, 1999) or social processes (Holbeche, 2009). Therefore, OD consultants are usually skilled in project management and/or process consulting (Baumgartner, 2009). Each stage of the process requires a different set of technical and practical skills to facilitate the client–consultant relationship, including facilitation, negotiation, coaching and relationship-building. However, Caldwell (2003) argues that this overplays the nature of change as strategic, top-down, planned and inevitable, and underplays the increasing dispersal of change roles among employees.

Many writers have subsequently attempted to provide more detail to the change agent's role. However, Caldwell (2003: 137) suggests that change agents' roles are 'exaggerated or misrepresented by one-dimensional models' and many have identified a significant skills gap (Withers *et al.*, 2009; Withers, 2012) despite the rise in popularity of OD as a job role and its position in the CIPD professional framework. This should, perhaps, be unsurprising, given the complexity and scope of change agents' roles (Caldwell, 2003).

From the broad base of work on change agency, Caldwell (2003: 140) provides evidence of four models of change agency (see Figure 9.7):

- *Leadership models* – which identify change agents as senior figures in the organisation, providing vision and charisma to transform the organisation.

- *Management models* – which identify change agents as middle managers who are experts at supporting strategic change initiated by others.

- *Consultancy models* – which identify change agents as external or internal consultants (e.g. OD consultants) who are adept at providing support for change at all levels of the organisation and can provide advice, support, expertise, process skills and programme coordination.

- *Team models* – which identify change agents as teams in the organisation who can operate at all levels.

In doing so, he argues that there is 'no universal model of change agency, or a single type of change agent with a fixed set of competencies'.

Figure 9.6 The change agent

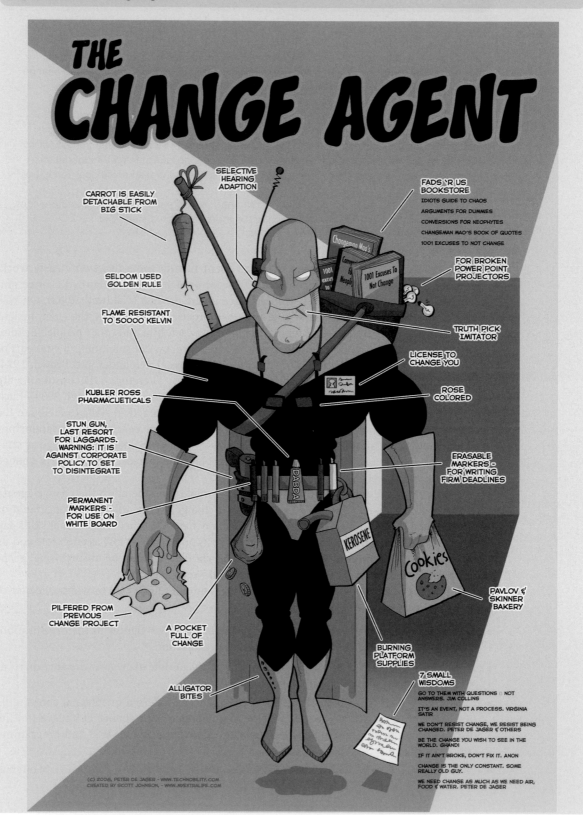

Figure 9.7 Four models of change agency

Leadership models	Management models	Consultancy models	Team models
Innovator (Kirton, 1980) Corporate entrepreneur (Karter, 1984) Transformational leader (Bass, 1990) Strategic architect (Prahalad and Hamal, 1990) Charismatic leader (Conger, 1993) Visionary (Bennis, 1993) Sponsor (Connor, 1998) Change leader (Kotter, 1996) Change champion (Unich, 1997)	Adaptor (Kirton, 1980) Empowerer (Lawler,1986) Developer (Pedler Burgoyna and Baydell, 1990) Changemaker (Storey, 1992) Pathfinder (Beatty and Lee, 1992) Change manager (Coldwell, 2001)	Action reseacher (Lewin, 1951) Facilitator (Tichy, 1974) Analyst (De Board, 1978) Process consultant (Schein, 1988) Catalyst (Blake and Mouton, 1983) Counsellor (Feltham, 1999) Expert (Cummings and Worley, 1997)	T-Group (Lewin, 1951) Composite group (Trist and Bamforth, 1951) Organic group (Meadows, 1951) Quality circle (Juran, 1985) TCI (West, 1990) Task group (Beer, Eisenstat and Spector, 1990) Guiding coalition (Kolter, 1996) Transition team (Karter, 1999) Pilot group (Senge, 1999)

Source: Caldwell (2003: 140).

In this section we consider the broader debate about the change-agency skills of OD practitioners and review a small selection of the literature on change agency, attempting to identify common themes.

In their detailed review of the individual differences literature, Nikolaou *et al.* (2007) identify a number of *personality traits* directly relevant to achieving organisational change:

- *Self-efficacy* – the belief that one can execute the behaviours required to achieve the outcomes.

- *Locus of control* – the belief that one can exercise control over the environment.

- *Core self-evaluations* – the belief that one is fundmentally worthy, effective and capable.

- *Openness to experience* – intelligence, perceptiveness, creativity, imagination, tolerance and inquisitiveness.

- *Personal resilience* – psychological resilience and the ability to 'bounce-back'.

They also identify the *skills and competencies* of a change agent as including facilitation skills: specifying goals, team-building, communication, negotiation and influencing. Bennis (1993), describing the skills associated with OD practitioners, identified four competencies:

- Broad knowledge of behavioural sciences and theories and methods of change.

- Operational and relational skills – the ability to listen, observe, identify and report and to form relationships based on trust.

- Sensitivity and maturity – including an understanding of self-motivation and that of others.

- Living in accordance with humanistic values – OD's behavioural science foundations sit in humanistic psychology, which is often criticised as too value-orientated to be a rigorous science (Cummings, 2004).

Cheung-Judge and Holbeche (2011) offer a comprehensive assessment of the skills of a change agent (Figure 9.8) and many before have summarised the skills required.

Throughout the work on change agency, political skill is argued to be part of the repertoire (McDermott *et al.,* 2010). For example, political skill is inherent in Ottoway's (1983) 10 change agency roles; Voss's (1992) 'political antennae'; Stjernberg and Philips' (1993) 'souls of fire'; Buchanan and Storey's (1997) range of roles, which involve role-taking and role-switching based on political skill and change management expertise; and Locock's (2001) 'opinion leaders'. The change agent relies on political competence ensuing from personal characteristics such as being

Figure 9.8 Profile of a competent organisational development practitioner

Conceptual competence	Ethics and values	Technical expertise	Strong individual and group processes and skills	Self-awareness	Self-confindence
Intellectual capability to see the big picture, understand the context in which organisations function and specialised knowledge on how organizations function.	Subscription in OD values, ability to role model those values in behaviour, and use the value to shape own consultancy practice.	Have in-depth knowledge of specific intervention methodologies.	Deep expertise in group dynamics and human dynamics. Able to understand how to facilitate both interpersonal work and group work, fluent in process consultation skills.	Committed to lifelong work in knowing oneself, interested to develop awareness as to how one impact others; able to make choices and not easily get hooked by others' issues.	Having a grounded sense of self, ability to centre oneself and not be dominated by the need for approval and the need to be needed in client's relationship.

Source: Cheung-Judge and Holbeche (2011).

articulate, sensitive, socially adept, competent, popular, and self-confident (Allen *et al.*, 1979; Kanter, 1989). Without political awareness and skills, they are likely to be out-manoeuvred or considered unprofessional (Buchanan, 2008). Within the literature on change agents, there is a recognition that individuals have different abilities, skills and willingness to exercise power, and 'skilful political activity may be required to overcome a lack of power sources, or in increasing the potency of a less valued set of power sources' (Pettigrew and McNulty, 1995: 852). Will and skill (Pettigrew and McNulty, 1995) are central aspects of political behaviour. Buchanan and Storey (1997) assert that the ability of individuals to both adopt and switch between a range of political roles – change initiators, sponsors, drivers and subversives – is a key skill in change agency. Where there are choices to be made or uncertainty concerning outcomes, political behaviour, exercised by those with the will and the skill to do so, shapes the progress of the change (Lipsky, 1980; Pettigrew and McNulty, 1995; Buchanan, 2008; Buchanan and Badham, 2008). Those who exercise political behaviour are demonstrating personal and organisational integrity, and political skill is central to performance, reputation and career (Buchanan, 2008).

OD: strategy, structure and culture

Organisational development can be considered a crossroads subject, which, in order to engage with it successfully, requires that other areas of organisational behaviour are understood. This section briefly introduces three of these areas, but there is insufficient space to give any full consideration. For more information and detail on the three areas – strategy, structure and culture – any good textbook on organisational behaviour will provide you with more detail on theory and practice.

OD and strategy

Many of the chapters in this textbook consider the link between the concept or field under discussion and an organisation's strategy. An underlying assumption of the book is that HR practitioners and the activities and interventions over which they preside have a role to play in the achievement of business objectives. However, where many organisations may espouse values that elevate the strategic role of people in the organisation (Gratton, 2000; Brockbank *et al.*, 2012), the reality may be somewhat different (Holbeche, 2008; Beatty, 2009). OD has 'expanded its focus beyond the social processes that occur mainly among individuals and within groups to include strategies . . . for the total organisation' (Francis *et al.*, 2012: 45). Cummings (2004: 26) identifies that, as OD involves planned change and the development of the organisation itself, it must inevitably engage with organisational strategies, design components and processes, as 'strategies have to do with how organisations use their resources to gain competitive advantage'.

Withers (2012: 71) argues that practitioners are more likely to identify with the notion of an 'OD agenda' than an 'OD strategy', because 'the way we think about how organisations work . . . has become . . . less distinguishable from approaches adopted by HR' generally. He quotes from Gallos (2006: 18), who suggests:

> many elements of OD have evolved into organisational routines that are nowadays taken for granted: better communications, team-building, management of intergroup relationships, change management, survey research, meeting designs, feedback and learning loops, organisational design, effective group processes, conflict resolution . . . to name but a few.

The taken-for-grantedness of OD activity means that the original justifications for these sets of activities have been lost. Nonetheless, he argues that OD has a role to play in:

- *Developing strategy content* – through organisation design, culture, developing change readiness and enhancing working practices across and between organisations.

- *Enabling strategy implementation* – through multi-level interventions which facilitate change leadership, employee engagement, restructuring, intra-group working, team-building, individual or organisational change.

- *Facilitating strategy process* – through using OD tools such as action research, process consultation, large group interventions, facilitation, change support, conflict resolution, focus groups and workshops.

Explore

- How is OD integrated into your organisation's strategic activities?
- Is there an individual or group of individuals with OD explicitly within their role and responsibilities? What are they responsible for, and how are they held to account? Or are the activities of OD 'taken-for-granted'?
- What are the consequences of your organisation's approach to OD?

OD and structure

Organisational development is frequently considered in parallel with organisation design or redesign. Stanford (2012: 58) argues that 'all organisation design work assumes a level of organisation development activity . . . the design elements . . . must mesh with the development aspects of how these are implemented'. OD can support organisation redesign so that there is better alignment between the design and its implementation.

The literature on organisational design reflects the significant changes in organisation design in practice, as organisations have grappled with the challenges of the complex and rapidly changing business environments of today. It is clear, then, that traditional, top-down bureaucratic structures have been replaced with lean and flexible alternatives, which enable organisations to respond quickly to changing environments (Cummings, 2004; Stanford, 2012).

While organisation design goes beyond 'mere' structure, this is usually where the consideration of design begins. However, changing the overall shape of the organisation – organisation redesign – requires consideration of both explicit and implicit aspects of the organisation's system. One way of considering both the implicit and explicit aspects of organisation design is to use a model such as the McKinsey 7-S model, still popular among OD practitioners (Figure 9.9; Stanford, 2012). This is a consulting tool, has no empirical basis and so should be used with care. Nonetheless it can help to frame thinking about the direction of the OD journey: it can be used to identify the current state and the desired state, so that activities can be planned to support the journey.

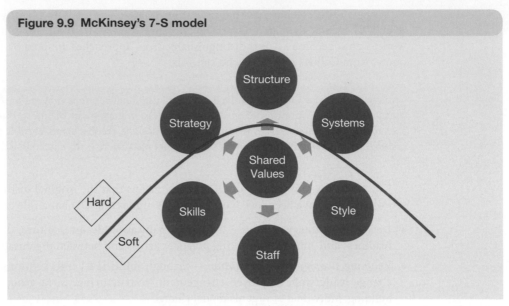

Figure 9.9 McKinsey's 7-S model

Source: adapted from Structure is not organization, Business Horizons, vol. 23 (3), p. 14 (Waterman Jr., R.H., Peters, T.J. and Phillips, J.R. 1980).

The diagram consists of 'hard' or explicit elements which can be easily defined and influenced, i.e. strategic elements such as strategy statements, plans, charts and formal processes:

- *Strategy* – the organisation's long-term plan for competitive advantage. What is the strategy? What are its timescales? What are the plans to support the strategy? What are the PESTLE factors related to the strategy?

- *Structure* – the structure of responsibility in the organisation. Who reports to whom? How is the company divided? Who manages whom? How are departments and teams linked? Where does decision-making responsibility lie? Where and how does communication flow?

- *Systems* – the activities undertaken to achieve the strategy. What are the influential systems in the organisation, e.g. HR, operations, finance, marketing? What are the rules that hold these together? How are the systems controlled?

The 'soft' or implicit elements are more difficult to describe and manage. These require the use of processes of influence and adaptation. Each of the elements is interdependent:

- *Shared values* – the company's culture or espoused values. What are the values? How are they conveyed? What is the climate or culture of the organisation?

- *Style* – the nature of leadership, sanctions and rewards. What is the leadership style like? How do employees respond to this? What controls are in place?

- *Staff* – the human resources in the organisation, their structure and roles. Where are the skills gaps, deficiencies or gluts? How easy are the competencies to find and retain?

- *Skills* – competences required to operate effectively in the company. What is the company known for doing well? How are skills developed?

OD and culture

Culture is an abstraction, yet the forces that are created in social and organisational situations that derive from culture are powerful. If we don't understand the operation of these forces, we become victim to them.
Schein (2004: 3)

Organisational development's humanist values highlight the importance of the less controlled, logical or rational aspects of organisations, and an organisation's culture – its values, beliefs, customs and traditions – fall within this scope. The notion of organisational culture is central to the OD because it captures 'organisational specialness'. Interest in it has been driven by the desire to identify and distil what makes one organisation 'better' than the next in terms of the performance of the organisation or the individuals within it. However, this interest is tempered by the challenges in capturing culture as it is an intangible or 'soft' part of the organisation, carried in people's minds, rather than written down or formally communicated. Thus, it is normally observed in patterns of action – 'the way we do things around here' (Deal and Kennedy, 1982). Moreover, it is used by individuals to interpret what happens around them, even where they are not aware of this, guiding their behaviour, and helping them to make judgments about what is right or wrong, appropriate or inappropriate in a particular organisational context.

Culture is a shifty, translucent concept. This is reflected in Morgan's (1986) description of culture as simply a 'metaphorical attempt' (Morgan, 1986: 3) that is frequently held responsible for the problems that organisations face. Culture is, as you will have grasped, an abstraction – you cannot see or touch 'culture'; you can only infer its existence from visible aspects of it (e.g. the layout of offices, decor, the furniture, the tone and language of literature, memos, notice boards, what people are wearing, what they are talking about, a sense of the history and the past, the type of technology that is in use, the rituals, language, symbols, ceremonies that are evident, the way people behave towards strangers and each other, and how they express what is important to them and what they value). The roots of an appreciation of culture lie in the HR approach to organisations, identified earlier as a reaction against scientific management and its consequences.

This poses particular challenges for managing or changing culture, not least because it plays a large part in how organisational success or failure is explained, even though it is intangible and invisible (see the Case study at the end of this chapter).

One of the most comprehensive attempts to analyse organisational cultures is that of the American academic and consultant Schein (1985). Schien's work tends towards the interpretive school of thought in that he argues that culture is difficult to discern and define, and that groups within organisations can work at cross-purposes to each other, bringing conflict and dissensus. Nonetheless, it works to cohere the organisation. Schein was concerned to describe and explain clearly what culture is and how it can be used to understand the characteristics of the organisation that bring stability and consistency. Schein (1992:9) explains that culture is 'a pattern of basic assumptions . . . that has worked well enough to be considered valuable and therefore to be taught to new members as the correct way to perceive, think and feel in relation to those problems'.

In describing culture, Schein (1985, 2004) identified three levels of culture, from the most to the least observable (Figure 9.10):

- *Artefacts* are the most visible aspect of an organisation's culture and include 'all the phenonema that one sees, hear and feels' (Schein, 2004: 25). These visible organisational processes and structures include architecture, myths, stories, rituals and ceremonies, as well as conversational rules and expectations. While this level is easy to observe, it may be difficult to understand what these mean to the group. Observers can be easily misled by these visible aspects, as they bring their own reactions and expectations to what they observe.

- *Espoused beliefs and values* are observable in action and are closely related to the 'way things are done around here'. These are the rules of behaviour that have been tested and proven to work in action and are what people 'say' are important to them in taking action in the organisation.

- *Underlying assumptions* are somewhat different – in contrast to the 'espoused' nature of beliefs and values, the basic assumptions are so 'deeply embedded' within the culture

Figure 9.10 Schein's three levels of culture

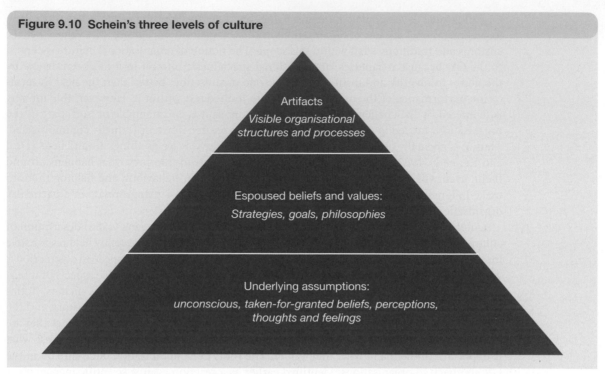

Source: adapted from Schein (2004: 26).

that they are taken for granted by organisational members and, over time, will cease to be questioned or challenged. Schein (2004: 32) describes them as 'nonconfrontable and nondebatable'. Using the example of McGregor's X and Y theories he identifies how these fundamental beliefs shape people's expectations, responses and behaviour in action.

The basic assumptions fall into six broad areas developed by Schein (1985) as a typology for cultural analysis, identifying the *content* of culture. Each dimension describes specific sets of assumptions that organisations have:

1 The organisation's relationship to its environment (beliefs that relate to the broader environment), e.g. their beliefs about their degree of dominance in the market which will affect their market behaviour.

2 The nature of human activity (beliefs about what the core activity of the business should be).

3 The nature of reality and truth (the methods used to establish 'facts' and what are perceived as relevant facts).

4 The nature of human nature (beliefs about what people are like): e.g. the beliefs embodied in McGregor's Theory X and Y.

5 The nature of human relationships (beliefs are about how people should relate to one another, both hierarchically and horizontally), e.g. the degree of formality or informality in the organisation.

6 Homogeneity versus diversity (beliefs about how similar or diverse the workforce should be), e.g. the degree to which compliance is enforced or maverick behaviour is accepted or encouraged.

Explore

Schein's typology raises our awareness of how visible aspects of culture can convey messages about the culture that, while helpful in interpretation, can be difficult to decipher. A common model that helps to access culture at this level is the 'cultural web' (Johnson and Scholes, 2006).

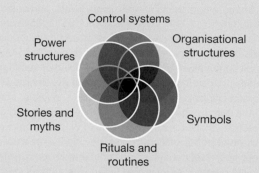

By interrogating each aspect of the web, evidence of the existence and nature of the culture can be gathered, e.g.:

Stories – What stories do people tell of success and failure in the organisation? What stories are told to new recruits or external stakeholders?

Rituals and routines – What is celebrated in the company? What happens when people exit the organisation? What happens if someone succeeds or fails?

Symbols – What is the company jargon? What is considered a status symbol? What are the perks of the job? What is the logo? What does it convey?

Organisational structures – Is the structure flat or hierarchical? What emphasis is there on formal or informal ways of getting things done?

Control systems – How tightly controlled is the company? How is success and failure reported? Who exercises the control in the company?

Power structures – Who has the real power in the organisation? Who are the role models? How is power used? Who has influence?

- Choose an organisation with which you are familiar – perhaps the university at which you are studying, or the business in which you work.

- Consider each category in turn. What does the overall picture tell you about the nature of the culture in that organisation?

  - Symbols
  - Stories
  - Power structures
  - Rituals and routines
  - Control systems
  - Organisational structures.

Schein's typology is one way among many of analysing an organisation's culture, but it has the advantages of being reasonably systematic, yet sufficiently comprehensive to enable its application to almost any organisation, whatever its size. Additionally, the typology is extremely useful for understanding the way, or how, an organisation behaves on both a macro-level (i.e. as a whole) and a micro-level (i.e. how individuals act). Understanding what makes someone 'tick' is not necessarily going to enable you to make that person do what you want them to, but it is likely to help you predict some of their behaviours in some circumstances (see Box 9.7).

Box 9.7 | **Dixon of Dock Green got shot!**

The nature of entrenched policing cultures has been the subject of much debate and discussion by academics and politicians alike. Academics have identified a distinct subculture that exists at grassroots levels, particularly among operational police officers (Waddington, 1999). Davies and Thomas (2008) explored how this strong culture acts to reinterpret policing priorities such as community policing so that they 'fit' the beliefs of this culture. They explore how difficult it is to embed new initiatives that challenge the beliefs, habits and values of police officers. Using an analogy that refers to a long-running TV series (21 years from the 1950s) about PC George Dixon, they use him as an example of community policing – high moral values, reliable, trustworthy and helpful to all members of the community – which, while once popular, and experiencing a renaissance in policing practice, challenges the beliefs held by police officers about the nature of policing. The culture of police officers is one they identify as valuing action, crime fighting, control and 'real policing' – fast cars, flashing lights and action. Community policing, however, is seen as a 'cushy number' or 'pink and fluffy'. The authors identify the process by which senior officers attempt to redefine community policing to be acceptable to the dominant culture ('Dixon of Dock Green: with attitude') so that it can be reinterpreted as 'real policing' ('[if officers can't show] that they can talk to the community . . . then they are not very good police officers').

However, Waddington's (1999) analysis of police culture resists this condemnatory position on canteen culture because he attempts to explain why this culture is as it is. He argues, very persuasively, that the culture serves a number of critical purposes. Put very simply, he suggests that it enables officers to make sense of and justify the importance of policing in societies where there is a high level of ambivalence about what the police can and should do. Moreover, he argues that the canteen culture exists more in talk than in action.

The strength of his analysis is in showing that the 'stocks of knowledge' that comprise culture are developed in specific social and historical contexts. Furthermore, culture not only enables organisation members to make sense of the world both inside and outside the organisation, but also provides them with a sense of identity.

Questions

1 In both analyses, the culture acts to adjust and change the intentions of senior managers and policy-makers. Can you think of any examples where the intentions of senior managers and policy-makers have changed the culture of an organisation?

2 Waddington's analysis suggests that there is a difference between culture as it is talked about and as it is practised. Can you think of an organisation where what people *say* is important is contradicted by what people in the organisation actually *do*?

Understanding organisational culture, then, should be a priority of OD practitioners, as it has the potential to have a significant impact on performance – or at least perceptions of performance – and effectiveness.

Key Controversy

Is OD a 'tool or a technique' or a 'theory' (Bunker *et al.*, 2004)?

Concluding comments

The use of the phrase 'people and organisational development' to recognise all – or a subset – of the practices, structure and function of HRM appears to have gathered some impetus in many organisations, particularly in the public and third sectors (e.g. **www.cfoa.org.uk**, **www.birming-ham.ac.uk**, **www.wateraid.org.uk** and many others). Holbeche (2012) argues that there are consequences of the increasing emphasis on the contribution of OD to organisational performance. She sees emerging roles for:

- Organisational prospectors who can scan and interpret the business environment so as to anticipate future business – and workforce – needs.

- Organisational architects who can design flexible, 'future-proof' structures that support agile shifts in behaviour within ethical and well-being expectations. This endeavour should support the creation of healthy working environments where individuals are enabled to increase their discretionary effort (Purcell *et al.*, 2003).

- Developers of individual and organisational capability who can grow skills and capture knowledge.

- Change agents who can initiate, manage and sustain the shifts needed, whilst managing competing political agendas.

Summary

The chapter has considered:

- Key similarities and differences in the definitions of OD.

- The historical development of OD as an academic and practical concept and the factors influencing renewed interest in the topic over the last 10 years.

- The key theories that underpin the practice of OD and the factors that differentiate it from mainstream change management.

- The techniques and practices of OD, including key stages in the OD cycle and the structured activities that are included in OD interventions.

- The nature of the change agent role and the skills, competencies and personality traits required by effective OD practitioners.

- The links between OD and strategy, structure and culture.

Questions

1 What do you understand by the term 'organisational development'?
2 To what extent can OD support the business strategy?
3 Who are the stakeholders in OD? Where can they support or block the process?
4 What are the important issues to consider in developing OD expertise in your organisation?
5 What are the challenges and issues that face OD in the coming years?
6 List the different methods and techniques used within OD? How would you evaluate their effectiveness?
7 Organisations are increasingly turning to OD as a technique to manage everyday change. Imagine you are the HR practitioner responsible for OD processes. What would you do to ensure you were appropriately skilled?

Case study

The world's biggest organisational development challenge?

Royles (2013) described the Public Inquiry into the events at Mid Staffordshire NHS Foundation Trust as 'what must rank as the world's largest organisational development (OD) challenge'. He identifies that:

'The report makes for harrowing reading, highlighting hundreds of unnecessary deaths and untold distress caused to some of our most vulnerable citizens. It raises concerns about the way NHS

➤

Case study continued

care has been regulated and the roles of different bodies that oversee the system. A system that is designed to ensure the NHS is safe for patients.'

The following article explains aspects of the report and its potential impact.

Stafford Hospital inquiry finds failures in leadership and culture

Hiding information about poor standards of NHS care should become a criminal offence, the public inquiry into failures at Stafford Hospital has concluded.

Health care staff who fail to adhere to basic standards that lead to death or serious harm should also face prosecution, according to the inquiry's chairman Robert Francis QC.

Releasing the findings of his year-long investigation into the Mid Staffordshire NHS Foundation Trust yesterday, Francis said that the health service needed a change of culture to 'make sure that patients come first'.

He added: 'As a result of poor leadership and staffing policies, a completely inadequate standard of nursing was offered on some wards in Stafford.'

Previous reviews had already uncovered 'appalling' levels of care at the hospital, and established that there were between 400 and 1,200 more deaths than would have been expected between 2005 and 2008.

Francis made 290 recommendations in his report, including a code of conduct for senior NHS managers – who could be disqualified for code breaches – plus a statutory obligation for a duty of candour among doctors and nurses, so that they were open with patients about mistakes.

Francis also advocated an increased focus on compassion in the recruitment, training and education of nurses, as well as regular competence checks for all clinical staff.

The report would require a major response from the NHS HR community, but was also an opportunity for the function to show its leadership mettle, said Dean Royles, director of NHS Employers.

'As a result of the inquiry all NHS organisations will be taking a hard look at their core HR approaches, and working on organisational development plans that will collectively affect the lives of the 1.3 million NHS employees and the millions of people who use our services each week,' explained Royles.

'This is going to be a major test of our HR community. But if we get it right we can turn what is undoubtedly a tragedy into an opportunity for exceptional staff engagement, driving improvement

in patient safety, patient experience and patient outcomes that would be a fitting tribute to those who suffered.'

The results of the independent inquiry came as the CIPD released new research that showed only 21 per cent of public sector employees trusted their senior leaders and just 29 per cent were actively engaged.

Furthermore, only a third of public sector workers were satisfied with their ability to voice concerns, found the *Employee Outlook* survey.

Ben Willmott, the CIPD's head of public policy, told PM that improving leadership at all levels within the NHS was something HR could take the lead on.

'Patient care will only improve if the quality of line management and other elements that support engagement – like communication, employee voice and trust in senior leadership – also fall into place,' he explained.

'I would hope there is a focus making sure that ward nurse managers have the necessary people management capability to do their jobs effectively. It is that key relationship with staff that will ultimately decide whether or not there is a "patient first" culture in organisations.'

The Francis report confirmed that some patients' complaints at Stafford Hospital had been ignored by senior managers, but did not apportion blame to individuals for the fatal lapses in care.

In response to the inquiry, prime minister David Cameron said that the government needed to 'purge' the culture of complacency in the health service and announced that a new post of chief inspector of hospitals would be created this autumn.

He also confirmed last night that there would be investigations into five other NHS trusts with high death rates. The hospitals in Colchester, Tameside, Blackpool, Basildon and Lancashire will all now face detailed inspections.

Source: NHS staff 'should face prosecution over mistake cover-ups', London: CIPD (Michelle Stevens) http://www.cipd.co.uk/pm/peoplemanagement/b/weblog/archive/2013/02/07/nhs-staff-should-face-prosecution-over-mistake-cover-ups.aspx, with the permission of the publisher, the Chartered Institute of Personnel and Development, London (www.cipd.co.uk)

Question

1 As an OD practitioner, where would you start in addressing the findings of the report?

References and further reading

Abolafia, M. (2010) 'Narrative construction as sensemaking', *Organisation Studies*, 31, 3: 349–67.

Allen, R.W., Madison, D.L., Porter, L.W., Renwick, P.A. and Mayes, B.T. (1979) 'Organizational politics: Tactics and characteristics of its actors', *California Management Review*, 22, 1: 77–83.

Anderson, V. (2009) *Research Methods in Human Resource Management*. London: CIPD.

Andriopoulos, C. and Dawson, P. (2009) *Managing Change, Creativity and Innovation*. London: Sage.

Argyris, C. (1992) *On Organisational Learning*. Oxford: Blackwell Business.

Argyris, C. (1964) 'T-Groups for organisational effectiveness', *Harvard Business Review*, 42, 2: 60–74.

Argyris, C. and Schon, D. A. (1978) *Organisational Learning: A Theory in Action Perspective*. Needham Heights, MA: Allyn & Bacon.

Bartram, D., Foster, J., Lindley, P.A., Brown, A.J. and Nixon, S. (1993) *The Learning Climate Questionnaire*. Employment Service and Newland Park Associates Ltd.

Baumgartner, S. (2009) 'How to develop your OD skills', *People Management, 12 February 2009*.

Beatty, R. (2009) 'HRM, the workforce, and the creation of economic value' in J. Storey, P. Wright and D. Ulrich (eds) *The Routledge Companion to Strategic Human Resource Management*. Abington: Routledge, pp. 479–87.

Beckhard, R. (1969) *Organisation Development: Strategies and Models*. London: Addison-Wesley.

Benders, J., Dooreward, H. and Poutsma, E. (2000) 'Modern sociotechnology' in M. Beyerlin (ed.) *Work Teams: Past, Present and Future*. New York: Kluwer Academic.

Bennis, W. (1969) *Organisation Development: Its Nature, Origins and Prospects*. Reading, MA: Addison-Wesley.

Bennis, W. (1993) *An Invented Life: Reflections on Leadership and Change*. Reading, MA: Addison-Wesley.

Bennis, W. (2000) 'Leadership of change' in M. Beer and Nohria, N. (eds) *Breaking the Code of Change*. Boston, MA: Harvard Business School Press, pp. 113-22.

Boonstra, J. (ed.) (2004) *Dynamics of Organisational Change and Learning*. London: John Wiley.

Brockbank, W., Ulrich, D., Younger, J. and Ulrich, J. (2012) 'Recent study shows impact of HR competences on business performance', *Employment Relations Today*, 39, 1: 1–7.

Brydon-Miller, M., Greenwood, D. and Macguire, P. (2001) 'Why action research?' *Action Research*, 1, 1: 9–14.

Buchanan, D. (1999) 'The logic of political action: An experiment with the epistemology of the particular', *British Journal of Management*, 10(special): S73-88.

Buchanan, D. (2008) You stab my back, I'l stab yours: Management experience and perceptions of organisational political behaviour', *British Journal of Management*, 19: 49–64.

Buchanan, D. and Badham, R. (1999) 'Politics and organisational change: the lived experience', *Human Relations*, 52, 5: 609–29.

Buchanan, D. and Badham, R. (2008) *Power, Politics and Organisational Change*. London: Sage.

Buchanan, D. and Huczynski, A. (2010) *Organisational Behaviour*. Harlow: FT/Prentice Hall.

Buchanan, D. and Storey J. (1997) 'Role taking and role switching in organizational change; The four pluralities' in I. McLoughlin and M. Harris (eds) *Innovation, Organizational Change and Technology*. London: International Thompson.

Bunker, B., Alban, B. and Lewicki, R. (2004) 'Ideas in currency and OD practice: has the well gone dry?', *Journal of Behavioural Science*, 40, 4: 403–21.

Burgoyne, J. (1999) 'Design of the times', *People Management*, 3 June: 39–44.

Burnes, B. (2007) 'Kurt Lewin and the Harwood Studies: the foundations of OD', *Journal of Applied Behavioural Science*, 43, 2: 213–31.

Burnes, B. (2009) *Managing Change*. Harlow: FT Prentice Hall.

Burnes, B. and Cooke, B. (2012) 'The past, present and future of organisation development: taking the long view', *Human Relations*, 65, 11: 1395–429.

Caldwell, R. (2003) 'Models of change agency: a fourfold classification', *British Journal of Management*, 14: 131–42.

Caldwell, R. (2006) *Agency and Change*. Abingdon, Routledge.

Carnall, C. (2007) *Managing Change in Organisations*. Harlow: FT/Prentice Hall.

Cheung-Judge, M.-Y. and Holbeche, L. (2011) *Organisation Development: A Practitioners Guide*. London: Kogan Page.

CIPD (2004) *Reflections: New Trends in Training and Development: Experts Views on the 2004 Training and Development Survey Findings*. London: CIPD.

CIPD (2012) *Organisation Development*, Fact sheet. London: CIPD. Online: **http://www.cipd.co.uk/hr-resources/factsheets/organisation-development.aspx** (accessed February 2014).

Collins, D. (1998) *Organisational Change: Sociological Perspectives*. London: Routledge.

Conger, J. (2000) 'Effective change begins at the top' in M. Beer and N. Nohria (eds) *Breaking the Code of Change*. Boston, MA: Harvard Business School Press, pp. 99–112.

Cooperrider, D. and Whitney, D. (2005) *Appreciative Inquiry: A Positive Revolution in Change*. California: Berrett-Koehler.

Cummings, T. (2004) 'Organisational development and change: foundations and applications' in J. Boonstra (ed.) *Dynamics of Organisational Change and Learning*. London: John Wiley, pp. 25–42.

Cummings, T. and Worley, C. (1991) *Organisational Development and Change*. Cincinatti, OH: Southwestern College Publishing.

Davies, A. and Thomas, R. (2008) 'Dixon of Dock Green got shot!: policing identity work and organisational change', *Public Administration*, 86, 3: 627–42.

Dawson, P. (1996) *Teaching and Quality: Change in the Workplace*. London: International Thompson Business Press.

Dawson, P. (2003a) *Reshaping Change: A Processual Perspective*. London: Routledge.

Dawson, P. (2003b) *Understanding Organisational Change: The Contemporary Experience of People at Work*. London: Sage.

Deal, T. and Kennedy, A. (1982) *Organisation Cultures: The Rights and Rituals of Organisation Life*. Reading, MA: Addison-Wesley.

Deming, W. E. (1986) *Out of Crisis*. Cambridge: Cambridge University Press.

Dickens, L. and Watkins, K. (1999) 'Action research: rethinking Lewin', *Management Learning*, 30, 2: 127–40.

Drory, A. and Vigoda-Gadot, E. (2009) 'Organisational politics and human resource management: a typology and the Israeli experience', *Human Resource Management Review*, 20, 1: 194–202.

Dunphy, D. (2000) 'Embracing paradox: top-down versus participative management of organisational change' in M. Beer and N. Nohnia (eds) *Breaking the Code of Change*. Boston, MA: Harvard Business School Press, pp. 125–35.

Dunphy, D. and Griffiths, A. (1998) *The Sustainable Corporation: Organisational Renewal in Australia*. St Leonards: Allen and Unwin.

Ferris, G., Treadway, D., P., Brouer, R., Douglas, C. and Lux, S. (2007) 'Political skill in organisations', *Journal of Management*, 33, 3: 290–320.

Fleetwood, S. and Hesketh, A. (2010) *Explaining the Performance or Human Resource Management*. Cambridge: Cambridge University Press.

Ford, J., Ford, L. W. and D'Amelio, A. (2008) 'Resistance to change: the rest of the story', *Academy of Management Review*, 33, 2: 362–77.

Francis, H., Holbeche, L. and Reddington, M. (eds) (2012) *People and Organisational Development: A New Agenda for Organisational Effectiveness*. London: CIPD.

French, W. and Bell, C. (1984) *Organisational Development*. Englewood Cliffs, NJ: Prentice Hall.

French, J. and Raven, B. (2001) 'The bases of social power' in I. Asherman, B. Pike and J. Randall (eds) *The Negotiation Source Book*. Amherst, MA: HRD Press.

Friedlander, F. and Brown, L. (1974) 'Organisation development', *Annual Review of Psychology*, 25: 313–41.

Gallos, J. (2006) *Organisational Development: A Reader*. San Fransisco, CA: John Wiley.

Garrow, V., Varney, S. and Lloyd, C. (2009) *Fish or Bird? Perspectives on Organisational Development (Report 463)*. London: IES.

Garvin, D. (1993) 'Building a learning organization', in P. Drucker and D. Garvin (eds) *The Harvard Business Review on Knowledge Management*. Boston, MA: Harvard Business School Press, pp. 47–80.

Gibb, S. and Megginson, D. (2001) 'Employee development' in T. Redman and A. Wilkinson (eds) *Contemporary Human Resource Management*. Harlow FT/Prentice Hall, pp. 128–67.

Gratton, L. (2000) *Living Strategy: Putting People at the Heart of Corporate Purpose*. Harlow: FT/Prentice Hall.

Greiner, L. (1972) 'Red flags in organisation development', *Business Horizons*, June: 17–24.

Greiner, L. and Cummings, T. (2004) 'Wanted: OD more alive than dead!', *Journal of Applied Behavioural Science*, 40, 4: 374–91.

Hayes, J. (2010) *The Theory and Practice of Change Management*. Basingstoke: Palgrave.

Helms-Mills, J., Dye, K. and Mills, A. (2009) *Understanding Organisational Change*. Abingdon: Routledge.

Highhouse, S. (2002) 'A history of the t-group and its early applications in management development', *Group Dynamics: Theory, Research and Practice*, 6, 4: 277–90.

Holbeche, L. (2008) *Aligning Human Resources and Business Strategy*. London: Butterworth-Heinemann.

Holbeche, L. (2009) *HR Leadership*. London: Butterworth-Heinemann.

Holbeche, L. (2012) 'The strategic context for the new OE' in H. Francis, L. Holbeche and M. Reddington (eds) *People and Organisational Development: A New Agenda for Organisational Effectiveness*. London: CIPD, pp. 22–41.

Honey, P. and Mumford A. (1989) *Manual of Learning Opportunities*. Peter Honey.

Johnson, G. and Scholes, K. (2006) *Exploring Corporate Strategy: Text and Cases*. Harlow: FT/Prentice Hall.

Kanter, R. (1989) *When Giants Learn to Dance: Mastering the Challenges of Strategy, Management and Careers in the 1990s*. London: Unwin.

Kanter, R., Stein, B. and Jick, T. (1992) *The Challenge of Organisational Change*. New York: Free Press.

Kotter, J. (1995) 'Leading change: why transformation efforts fail', *Harvard Business Review*, 73, 2: 59–67.

Lahteenmaki, S., Holden, L. and Roberts, I. (eds) (1999) *HRM and the Learning Organisation*. Turku, Finland: Turku School of Economics and Business Administration.

Lewin, K. (1943/4) 'Problems of research in social psychology', in D. Cartwright (ed.) *Field Theory is Social Science*. London: Social Science Paperbacks.

Lewin, K. (1946) 'Action research and minority problems', *Journal of Social Issues* 2, 4: 34–46.

Lewin, K. (1951) *Field Theory in Social Science*. New York: Harper & Row.

Lewis, S., Passmore, J. and Cantore, S. (2011) *Appreciative Inquiry for Change Management: Using AI to Facilitate Organisational Development*. London: Kogan Page.

Lipsky, M. (1980) *Street Level Bureaucrats: The Dilemmas of the Individual in Public Services*. New York, NY: Russell Sage Foundation.

Locock, L. (2001) *Maps and Journeys: Redesign in the NHS*. Birmingham: HMSC.

Marshak, R. and Grant, D. (2008) 'Organizational discourse and new organization development practices', *British Journal of Management*, 19: 7–19.

McDermott, A., Fitzgerald, L. and Watson, M. (2010) *Opportunity or imposition: local change agent responses to national policy initiatives*. Lisbon: European Group on Organization Studies.

McLean, G. (2005) *Organisation Development: Principles, Processes, Performance*. San Francisco, CA: in Berrett-Koehler.

McTaggart, R. (1996) 'Issues for participatory action researchers', in O. Zuber-Skerritt. (ed.) *New Directions in Action Research*. London: Falmer Press.

Morgan, G. (1997) *Images of Organization*. Thousand Oaks, CA: Sage.

Nikolaou, I., Gouras, A., Vakola, M. and Bourantas, D. (2007) 'Selecting change agents: exploring traits and skills in a simulated environment', *Journal of Change Management*, 7, 3–4: 291–313.

Ortenblad, A. (2013) 'Vague and attractive: five explanations of the use of ambiguous management ideas', *Philosophy of Management*, 5, 1: 45–54.

Ottoway, R. (1983) *Change Agents at Work*. London: Associated Business Press.

Pedler, M., Burgoyne, J. and Boydell, T. (1991) *The Learning Company*. Maidenhead: McGraw-Hill.

Pedler, M., Burgoyne, J. and Boydell, T. (1997) *The Learning Company*. Maidenhead: McGraw-Hill.

Peters, T. J. and Waterman, R.H. (1972) *In Search of Excellence: Lessons from America's Best Run Companies*. New York: Harper and Row.

Pettigrew, A. (1985) *The Awakening Giant*. Oxford: Blackwell.

Pettigrew, A. (1997) 'What is a processual analysis?' *Scandinavian Journal of Management*, 13, 4: 337–48.

Pettigrew, A. (2000) 'Linking change processes and outcomes: A commentary on Ghosal, Bartlett and Weick' in M. Beer and N. Nohria (eds) *Breaking the Code of Change*. Boston, MA: Harvard Business School Press, pp. 243–66.

Pettigrew, A. (2003) 'Strategy as process, power and change' in S. Cummings and D. Wilson (eds) *Images of Strategy*. Oxford: Blackwell, pp. 301–30.

Pettigrew, A. and McNulty, T. (1995) 'Power and influence in and around the boardroom', *Human Relations*, 48, 8: 845–73.

Pettigrew, A. and Whipp, R. (1991) *Managing Change for Competitive Success (ESRC Competitiveness Surveys)*. Oxford: Blackwell.

Pettigrew, A., Ferlie, E. and McKee, L. (1992) *Shaping Strategic Change. Making Change in Large Organisations: The Case of the National Health Service*. London: Sage.

Porras, J. and Bradford, D. (2004) 'A historical view of the future of OD: an interview with Jerry Porras', *Journal of Applied Behavioural Science*, 14, 2: 151–73.

Pugh, D. (2009) 'Planning and managing change' in D. Pugh and D. Mayle (eds) *Change Management Volume 2: Understanding and Managing Change Through Organisational Development*. Milton Keynes: Open University Business School.

Purcell, J., Kinnie, N., Hutchinson, S., Rayton, B. and Swart, J. (2003) *Understanding the People-Performance Link: Unlocking the Black Box*. London: CIPD.

Ramdhony, A. (2012) 'Critical HRD and organisational effectiveness' in H. Francis, L. Holbeche and M. Reddington (eds) *People and Organisational Development: A new Agenda for Organisational Effectiveness*. London: CIPD, pp. 161–79.

Revans, R. (ed.) (1982) *The enterprise as a learning system*. Action Learning in Practice. Aldershot: Gower.

Revans, R. (1983) *The ABC of Action Learning*. Bromley: Chartwell Bratt.

Revans, R. (2011) *ABC of Action Learning*. Farnham: Gower.

Robbins, S. (2001) *Organisational Behaviour*. Upper Saddle River, NJ: Prentice Hall.

Rothwell, W. and Sullivan, R. (eds) (2005) *Practicing Organisation Development*. San Francicso CA: John Wiley.

Royles, D. (2013) The world's biggest OD challenge? Online: **http://www.cipd.co.uk/pm/peoplemanagement/b/weblog/archive/2013/02/06/the-world-s-biggest-organisational-development-challenge.aspx** (accessed February 2014).

Schein, E. H. (1985) *Organisational Culture and Leadership*. London: Jossey-Bass.

Schein, E. (1988) *Process Consultation, Volume 1: Its role in organisational development*. Reading, MA: Addison-Wesley Publishing.

Schein, E. H. (2004) *Organisational Culture and Leadership*. London: Jossey-Bass.

Schmuck, R. and Miles, B. (1971) *Organizational Development in Schools*. Palo Alto, CA: National Press.

Senge, P. (1990) *The Fifth Discipline*. London: Random House Business Books.

Senior, B. and Swailes, S. (2010) *Organisational Change*. Harlow: FT/Prentice Hall.

Skipton-Leonard, H., Lewis, R., Freedman, A. and Passmore, J. (2013) *The Wiley Blackwell Handbook of The Psychology of Leadership, Change and Organisational Development*. Oxford: John Wiley.

Sloman, M. (1999) 'Learning centre: seize the day', *People Management*, 20 May: 31.

Stacey, R. (1996) *Complexity and Creativity in Organisations*. San Francisco, CA: Berrett-Koehler.

Stanford, N. (ed.). (2012) 'The historical and theoretical background to organisational development', *People and Organisational Development: A New Agenda for Organisational Effectiveness*. London: CIPD.

Staw, B. (1982) 'Counterforces to change' in P. S. Goodman. *Change in Organisations: New Perspectives on Theory, Research and Practice*. (ed.) San Francisco, CA: Jossey Bass.

Stewart, J. and Sambrook, S. (2002) 'Reflections and discussion' in J. Steward, S. Tjepkema, S. Sambrook, M. Mulder, H. Horst and J. Schreenrens (eds) *HRD and Learning Organisations in Europe*. London: Routledge pp. 178–87.

Stjernberg, T. and Philips, A. (1993) 'Organizational innovations in a long-term perspective: Legitimacy and souls-of-fire as critical factors of change and viability', *Human Relations* 46, 10: 1193–221.

Trist, E. and Bamforth, W. (1951) 'Some social and psychological consequences of the long wall method of coal-getting', *Human Relations*, 4: 3–38.

Trist, E. and Murray, H. (1993) 'Historical overview: the foundation and development of the Tavistock Institute' in E. Trist and H. Murray (eds) *The Social Engagement of Social Science Volume 2: The Socio-Technical Perspective*. Philadelphia, PA: University of Pennsylvania Press.

Trist, E., Higgin, G., Murray, H. and Pollock, A. B. (1963) *Organisational Choice*. London: Tavistock.

Voss, B. (1992) 'Office politics: A players guide', *Sales and Marketing Management*, 144, 12: 46–52.

Waclawski, J. and Church, A. (2002) 'Introduction and overview of organisation development as a data-driven approach for organisational change' in J. Waclawski and A. Church (eds) *Organisation Development: A Data-Driven Approach to Organisational Change*. San Francisco, CA: Jossey-Bass, pp. 3–26.

Waddington, P. (1999) 'Police (Canteen) sub-culture: an appreciation', *British Journal of Criminology*, 39, 2: 287–309.

Willcocks, L. and Mason, D. (1987) *Computerising Work: People, Systems Design and Workplace Relations*. London: Paradigm Publishing.

Withers, M. (2012) 'Developing an organisational development strategy from an HR perspective' in H. Francis, L. Holbeche and M. Reddington (eds) *People and Organisational Development: A New Agenda for Organisational Effectiveness*. London: CIPD, pp. 68–88.

Withers, M., Williamson, M. and Reddington, M. (2009) *Transforming HR: Creating Value through People*. Oxford: Butterworth-Heinemann.

Worren, N., Ruddle, K. and Moore, K. (1999) 'From organisational development to change management: The emergence of a new profession', *Journal of Applied Behavioural Science*, 35, 3: 273–86.

Part 4

THE EMPLOYMENT RELATIONSHIP

Introduction to Part 4

The employment relationship is key to understanding how employment is managed. It brings together the sources of power and legitimacy and rights and obligations that management and employees seek for themselves and apply to others. This part of the book is concerned with explaining the employment relationship and examining how it works out through a variety of applications, such as the law, collective bargaining, performance and reward, employee engagement and involvement.

Chapter 10 deals with the role and influence of the law in determining the nature of contract. The contract of employment is not simply a document that is presented to employees on appointment, but is a complex set of formal and informal rules that govern the whole basis of the employment relationship. Thus, the way employees and managers conform with, or break, those rules determines how that relationship works out in practice. Moreover, the nature of contract can have an important bearing on whether newer concepts such as human resource management (HRM) can fundamentally change a relationship that is so dependent upon the interaction of formal and informal legal regulation.

Chapter 11 follows on from the chapter on the employment relationship and employee rights at work to deal specifically with the pertinent issue of employee engagement. To support organisational agility and determine organisational success in an increasingly competitive marketplace, it is argued that employees need to be committed to the organisations they work for (organisational engagement) and to be engaged with the work they do within that organisation (job engagement). This chapter considers the antecedents and consequences of job and organisational engagement and suggests how levels of engagement might be enhanced. The chapter is also concerned with key supplementary issues, such as how organisations might measure and benchmark employee engagement.

Chapter 12 reviews approaches to performance management, in particular appraisal, and distinguishes between performance appraisal and the broader concept of performance management. It questions the ethics of performance appraisal as a means by which managers are able to engage in constant surveillance of their employees. The chapter argues that effective performance management will need to address changes in organisational structure and composition, in particular in relation to an increasingly global and competitive market, and a diverse and ageing workforce.

Chapter 13 examines developments in employee reward and the practical ways in which reward management can be used in conjunction with other HRM practices to promote employee engagement and drive individual and organisational performance. After tracing the historical development of reward systems, the chapter moves on to explore the contemporary meaning of reward, focusing on its role as a potential strategic lever to orient individuals and teams in the direction of business goals and values. The chapter also considers the economic and legal environment for reward and the challenges associated with designing a reward strategy that is affordable, equitable and relevant, paying particular attention to pragmatic reward choices and dilemmas experienced by contemporary organisations. These include decisions about the relative importance of internal equity and external pay comparability, the role of job evaluation, the factors which tend to be influential in shaping the reward 'mix', where to pitch pay and how to design pay structures and manage pay progression.

Chapter 14 is concerned with employee voice. The chapter identifies the three distinct but related concepts that comprise employee voice – employee involvement, employee participation and industrial democracy – and suggests that the difference between these constructs is best understood in terms of variations in employee power and influence. The chapter charts a trend towards employee involvement and a decline in representative participation and highlights that, as a result, large swathes of the British workforce are no longer covered by trade union representation. The chapter explores the growth in non-union forms of voice and questions the extent to which these are an effective substitute for independent trade union voice.

The employment relationship and employee rights at work

Alan J. Ryan

Objectives

- To introduce readers from a variety of backgrounds to the central significance of contract in the employment relationship.

- To examine the contractual and statutory regulation of employment contracts, with a central focus upon the manner in which employment rights need to be regulated and proceduralised in the workplace.

- To provide HR practitioners or other interested readers with the necessary basic information to enable them to make fair and reasonable decisions within the employment relationship.

- To add critical observations on the limitations of employee rights in the UK.

Introductory case study

Constructive unfair dismissal?

Ms Billingham answered a vocational call to become a Minister of Religion some 10 years ago. She was appointed as a 'superintendent minister' five years ago on the St Anywhere Circuit for a 10-year term. Ms Billingham was subject to annual appraisals and the possibility of disciplinary action, and received a stipend (salary), manse (accommodation furnished to a minimum standard) and a pension from the Church. She also received holiday pay and was entitled to claim sick pay. The Church issued a P60 to Ms Billingham at the end of each tax year, as well as payslips that included an 'employee reference number', and showed that it had deducted tax and National Insurance contributions. Recently Ms Billingham has resigned and is seeking to bring a claim for constructive unfair dismissal against the Church.

Introduction

This chapter opens with a brief discussion of the nature of employment law, suggesting ways in which the purpose of legal regulation of the employment relationship may be viewed. We then explore the manner in which, even in the twenty-first century, the relationship is dominated by the concepts of 'dependent' and 'non-dependent' labour and is wedded, in legal terms, to the central significance of contractual regulation in the employment relationship that allows for and legitimises managerial prerogative. In developing these arguments, we posit that the employment relationship should be seen as a process of socioeconomic exchange, which, unlike other contractual relationships, is incomplete. In this sense we will indicate that the act of hiring an employee does not complete the exchange; instead it simply initiates it as both parties intend the contract to continue until one of them decides to end it. We therefore focus on contractual processes in terms that highlight the legal (and human resource management, HRM) implications in the three key areas of formation, continuation and termination. The chapter concludes with a discussion of what are, at the time of writing, new or currently envisaged changes in the regulation of employment relationships.

In terms of the purpose of the regulation of employment relationships it has been argued (Arthurs, 2011; Hyde, 2011; Stone and Arthurs 2013) that, as in other social spheres, the law can be used to send signals to social actors in relation to the manner of their interactions, including indicating the boundaries of their rights and duties. So as Arthurs (2011) suggests, works by policy-makers, academics and the legal community make it possible to identify the ways in which, during different but overlapping eras, the law has been deployed to achieve a number of social policy aims. Arguments can be set out which indicate attempts to use regulation in an endeavour to encourage workers to meet the requirements of Christian morality, to develop a sense of one nation/national identity, to discourage the development of radical or revolutionary ideologies, to enable workers to earn a living and therefore to consume, to legitimate the 'web of rules' spun in individual workplaces, to support a system of countervailing power and, more recently, to integrate workers into business-level cultures designed to encourage engagement and manage their discontent. In pursuing these various aims, legislation, as interpreted and applied by the courts, is seen as a mechanism of social engineering rather than simply a matter of fairness or justice. From this position, it can be argued that the purpose of regulating the employment relationship, especially using the contractual paradigm, is centrally concerned with symbolism encased within the myth of equality within the relationship.

Hyde (1983) suggests that the public belief in the 'myth' of legal and judicial stability and infallibility encourages quiescence. This 'myth' supports the framework of legalism, especially within notions of a legitimate capitalism, by persuading people of the basic justice and equality of their world. This mechanism of myth generation asserts its own legitimacy to the extent that people regard themselves as obligated to the continuation of the regime (Hyde, 1983: 391). Such a regime overcomes any problems inherent in the creation of rational reasons for obedience, and consequently supports both the notion and the exercise of managerial prerogative. For Hyde the answer to the problem of 'why people obey laws' is related to this generation of ideological myths, located in the symbolic nature of the rituals of our legal institutions. Hyde (1990: 387–388). suggests that

> Battles over law are, enough of the time to matter, battles over cultural definition . . . the timing of labor [sic] legislation is shaped by the needs of the governing elites for symbolic definition of labor's place in society. . . . The content of labour legislation is shaped by the desire of legislators to have the legislation function effectively as such a symbolic statement.

The function of this symbolism, possibly even ideology, is to maintain a consensus amongst labour and management leaders. These 'battles over cultural definition' are therefore fought out on a battleground bounded by the confines of legal institutions and principles. Central to this battle are the principles of contract law that, however interpreted, set out the underlying rights and duties of the parties, including determining the nature of the relationship as dependent or non-dependent. From this foundation a number of propositions may be promulgated which suggest that labour legislation can be seen to be a response to social unrest/conflict, and in general illustrate the truth that when current relationships are unable to provide a basis for continued capital accumulation, legislative change is often the response. Further these laws, legal principles and the institutions that sustain them demonstrate an idealised view of society and labour relations. Thus, we see that these laws support both the contractual view of employment relationships and existing organisations representing workers, by the use of symbolic 'rights' and 'concessions'. Possibly more centrally, as symbolic actions, the impact of these 'laws' is never, and can never be, pre-determined, as results are negotiated on a case-by-case, law-by-law basis. We can then, and arguably should, as thinking HR managers challenge the simplistic view that the law states what 'is', considering really the law as symbolic of what 'ought to be' the reality. Employment law allows us to constitute ourselves and our organisations as 'a community' by excluding difference and 'untruths' (see Benhabib, 1994). The law silences and excludes many 'other voices' that are on the wrong side of the track. In this chapter we view the legal regulation of employment relationships as a 'discursive alchemy', within which the myth, the magic and the fantasy of received epistemological objectivity are engaged to sketch out employment law's promise of order, of security and of identity.

Explore

The key question for human resource managers revolves around the extent to which this symbolism, these laws, continue to provide support for the level of worker discipline that enables the continuation of capital accumulation at acceptable levels.

● Considering your organisation or one with which you are familiar, outline the manner in which the 'symbolism' of regulation affects the employment relationship.

Whilst we may argue that contract law in the twenty-first century continues to play a central role in supporting managerial prerogative, the extent to which it provides a stable relationship is declining. The speed of change, social and technological, has led to the development of new 'forms' of relationship which appear unsuited to the concept of relational contracts (see Wightman, 2013). As we move through our arguments, we will find a need to consider two specific features that result from these changes: the growth of non-standard employment and the decline in job tenure (Stone, 2013). Alongside other socioeconomic developments, the legal interference with HRM can be seen as a growing phenomenon that creates increasingly complex dilemmas in terms of managerial actions.

These dilemmas have their foundation in the reality that as a socioeconomic exchange the employment relationship not only contains an economic component – the exchange of work for payment – but also includes a sociological dimension centred on power and authority. These elements of the employment relationship are ordered through the principles embedded within notions of equality located at the centre of the contract of employment. Additionally, it is obvious that all employment relationships are subject to an assortment of other processes, including management competence, work group control, management motivation, worker engagement and the potential for workplace conflict. These factors combine to develop a relationship, which is apparently a rational process of economic exchange but is, in fact, much more complex. By this we suggest that contrary to the 'contractual paradigm', which indicates certainty at the outset, the terms of the relationship are vague in that the specific details are subject to ongoing negotiation and change. We will note that in these negotiations, employees – but in many instances not workers – have the protection of basic contractual and statutory employment rights which employers must respect. As indicated earlier, in order to provide readers with the necessary basic information on these matters the chapter is divided into four key themes or topics:

● formation of the contractual relationship, noting statutory employment rights;
● continuation of the relationship including variation;

- termination of the relationship;
- current issues.

The material in each part of the chapter, although necessarily legalistic in nature, is explained, as far as possible, in terms that are general and straightforward to assist the reader in their application. Some points are repeated as they affect areas of employment regulation detailed in successive parts of the chapter. Because the material is legalistic there are direct references to legal texts, cases and statutes – a list of law texts is provided at the end of the chapter for further reading – however, such references are set out in as reader-friendly a style as possible. The reader should view this chapter as a general introduction to the regulation of the employment relationship, and readers should be aware that more specialist information may be required in applying the general principles to specific situations.

Distinguishing contractual and statutory employment rights

In a chapter it is not possible to provide a complete and comprehensive analysis of the employment relationship and its legal regulation – employment contracts and employment statutes are subject to change as practices that were previously 'outwith the law' become subject to legal regulation; hence the law may be further updated after this edition is published. Equally, many areas of contractual and statutory regulation are extremely complicated, and disputes between an employer and an employee may require specialist analysis by employment lawyers. Examples of these areas include discrimination claims with respect to pension rights for part-time women employees, disability discrimination claims that relate to the status of an employee as HIV-positive, the interpretation of working time regulations for a particular group of employees and issues surrounding the transfer of undertakings. Thus, bearing in mind that contractual and statutory regulation of the employment relationship is a 'moving target', our examination of regulation within the employment relationship divides between a discussion of contractual and statutory employment rights.

Formation and contractual rights

All contracts can be seen to be based on a set of basic principles that begin with an 'invitation to treat', move through stages of 'offer' and 'acceptance' in which the terms of the deal are decided, before the parties undertake the performance of the duties accepted and the contract terminates. For the simple sale of a chocolate bar, this is uncontroversial –for the most part – having clear duties and obligations for each party at each stage. For employment contracts, the story is more complex because of the nature of the duties and obligations. The terms set following the offer and acceptance (that form the basis of the agreement) cannot stay fixed over the life of the agreement, nor can the agreement set out the performance level of either party. Further, the very nature of the relationship can be ambiguous in relation to dependent and non-dependent labour (see the discussion later in the chapter). That all employees have a contract of employment is a key concept in that it is the contract which governs the relationship between the employer and an individual employee. A key element in relation to these rights is the definition of the difference between an employee and a worker found in the Employment Rights Act 1996 (ERtsA) s. 230. It is this very issue that is at stake in the Introductory case study. As we discuss in the following, an employment contract has two types of terms within it: express terms that are usually written down and which govern the specific details of the employee's contract of employment; and implied terms, which fall into two groups and are unlikely to be written down but which nevertheless are considered to be part of an employee's contract of employment. For example, terms implied by statutory provision include the requirement that an employer is under a legally enforceable duty to provide a healthy and safe workplace. Further terms are implied under what is commonly referred to as the 'business efficacy' rule – in simple terms they are implied as a matter of fact and are needed in order for the contract to work. These are often derived from custom and practice arrangements in the workplace, even though many of them may be unwritten. The core principle in relation to 'business efficacy' is therefore the extent to which the parties would have agreed to the term had the issue involved been put to them at the outset of the contract (Collins *et al.,* 2012; see also *Devonald v. Rosser & Sons* [1906] 2 KB 728). In summary, contractual rights flow from the express and implied terms that create an individual contract of employment. It is important to point out that while employees receive protection via elements of these terms, they are also subject to regulation by them; hence the contract of employment is made up of a balance of rights and obligations between the employer and the employee.

Explore

Recent legislation has changed the employers' liability for health and safety issues.

- To what extent does this change the contractual relationship and weaken/strengthen the protection for employees in relation to the physical conditions under which work is undertaken?

Whilst the source of many of these rights is the agreement (contract) between the parties and the terms, which are 'nominally' agreed openly by the parties, some are underpinned by statutory enactments such as Acts of Parliament, Statutory Instruments and European Legislation that must be enacted into UK law – an example of the latter is the emergence in the UK of the statutory regulation of agency work. These statutory employment rights have been enacted in an attempt to provide a basic floor of rights for all workers, so the distinction between 'employees' and 'workers' becomes less relevant. In the drafting process, government and European Union civil servants seek to ensure that the legislation covers most eventualities. However, because such legislation is necessarily general in its coverage of a particular issue, the judiciary must interpret legislation. Interpretation of legislation is a complicated and controversial matter and often turns on the issue of what is 'reasonable'. For an employer's interpretation of a statute to be reasonable, the courts require the employer to demonstrate that another employer faced with the same or a similar situation would have acted in a similar way. If the issue is in dispute, an employee or worker needs to be able to demonstrate that another employer would not have acted in a particular manner. For example, it was common practice in setting the terms of the contract for many employers to exclude their part-time workforce from occupational pension schemes on the basis that the salary or wage level of part-timers was too low to generate a sufficient pension fund, particularly as this would reduce the take-home pay of such workers because of the necessary deduction of an employee's contribution to the pension scheme. After a long legal campaign, several trade unions, supported by the then Equal Opportunities Commission, established that this practice was unreasonable because many part-time workers were women and their exclusion from company pension schemes amounted to indirect sex discrimination. This was the case because, although the exclusion of part-time workers from pension schemes appears to be sex-neutral in its effects, such exclusion has a disproportionate effect on women, so the practice is discriminatory (see *R v. Secretary for Employment ex parte Seymour-Smith* [1999] IRLR 253). Common law precedent, i.e. judicial decisions of interpretation, guides decisions in disputes where there is no relevant Act of Parliament. It is clear therefore that a central principle of the English legal system operative is that of *reasonableness.* In employment contracts, the agreed terms and statutory interventions both have to be reasonable in their effects on the employer and employee. Thus, in many cases, judgments in disputes between employer and employee often turn on the question of reasonableness. The notions of reasonable and unreasonable behaviour or instructions are questions of interpretation in the circumstances of particular cases. As explained earlier, an express or implied term in a contract of employment is reasonable if, in a matter of dispute, it is held that a similar employer would have done the same thing (e.g. discipline or dismiss an employee) in similar circumstances. The discussion of this point is important for the following reasons. As statutory rights are subject to interpretation, challenge and eventual updating in the form either of statutory amendment or of a binding precedent created by a higher court, HR managers must keep abreast of developments in employment law to ensure that the procedures set in place by their employer reflect the spirit and the letter of the law.

The importance of the contract of employment

As indicated throughout this chapter, the regulation of the employment relation is fundamentally a matter of legal interpretation. It matters not whether we are focusing on wage, performance or termination; a key element on which the answer will turn is the status of the individual concerned. In simple terms, we are asking whether the individual concerned is a 'worker' or an 'employee', because the law attaches different levels of protection to each. As Freedland and Kountouris (2011) argue, the common law principles which establish a valid contract (see later) have both a different format and an alternative function in the framework relating to personal employment contracts. The existence of a contract of employment, and hence the classification of an individual as an employee, determines the availability of employment rights. As indicated in Figure 10.1, the legal categorisation of an individual as an 'employee' opens access to all employment rights, while other groups have restricted rights.

As can be seen, the division of rights between three different arrangements for offering and obtaining labour gives organisations options – some of which reduce the extent of their obligations to those undertaking the labour. Throughout the rest of this chapter, this division of rights will be highlighted where appropriate in order to draw out the importance of 'status' as defined within law by the existence of a contract of employment, and the extent to which there has been progression in the development of a more flexible relationship between those who carry out work and those for whom it is undertaken (von Prondzynski, 2000; Sciarra *et al.,* 2011; Stone and Arthurs, 2013). These more fluid relationships, such as those involving self-employed workers and sub-contract workers, are not well suited to regulation through the employment contract in its current form (Blanpain and Weiss, 2003; Conaghan and Rittich, 2005; Davidov and Langille, 2006; Njoya, 2007; Bercusson and Estlund, 2008; Collins *et al.,* 2012; Freedland and Kountouris, 2013).

Key Controversy

Whist this traditional – contractual – approach to the employment relationship may have provided a useful explanation in the past, can it be argued that a new approach is needed for the twenty-first century? See Freedland and Kountouris (2013) for guidance.

New approaches have been variously portrayed as the law relating to 'subordinate labour' (Davidov, 2005; Hyde, 2006), the law of 'the personal employment contract' (Freedland and

Figure 10.1 Employment rights

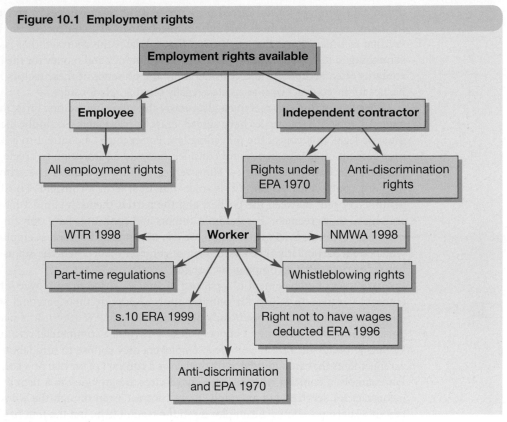

Kountouris, 2013) or the 'private/property law model' (Collins, 2000; Njoya, 2007). These various models are included in the following analysis at appropriate points.

Formation and the contract of employment

In order to explain the concept of contract, it is useful to develop our discussion in terms of the elements traditionally found within contract textbooks. Contracts are seen to contain five elements:

- invitation to treat;
- offer;
- acceptance;
- consideration;
- an intention to create legal relations.

To illustrate these elements, we can draw on the example of any purchase. An individual or organisation may decide to sell a particular item to any buyer and therefore display the item; this can be seen as an invitation to treat (or deal) with other parties. An individual may see this invitation and decide they would like to buy the item. As a result of this, they decide to make an *offer*. The current owner of the item may decide to *accept* this offer. If these requirements are fulfilled satisfactorily, a contract containing all the terms of the sale can be drawn up. In consideration for the agreed price, the existing owner agrees to give up their rights in the item and exchange them through the mechanism of a contract to the buyer. So we can say that *consideration* is the mechanism that validates the contract: that is, each party gives something to the contract, in this case an item for money and money for the item. If a contract contains offer, acceptance and consideration, the presence of these factors indicates that the parties to the contract wish to create a legally binding relationship.

A legally binding contract must also satisfy the following factors. First, the contents of the contract, to which the parties have agreed, must be reasonable. Secondly, the contract in itself must be legal, in terms of the prevailing law. For example, a contract to assassinate a person may contain offer, acceptance and consideration and an intention to create a legally binding relationship between the parties. However, conspiracy to murder is a criminal offence and thus any contractual relationship is void – the legal term for invalid. Thirdly, there must be genuine consent between the parties, and the parties themselves must have the capacity to consent to the agreement. For example, minors and bankrupts have only limited capacities in contract. From this brief introduction, we can now proceed to look at employment contracts, which are a particularly specialised form of contract that confers the status of employee and hence the rights that accompany such status.

A contract of employment is a *contract of service,* where an employee – the subject of the contract – agrees in return for remuneration to provide their personal service under the control of their employer (see *Ready Mix Concrete v. MPNI* 1968*)*. It is necessary to distinguish an employment contract of personal service from a commercial *contract for services*. As Collins *et al.* (2012: 187) makes clear, employers may choose to hire labour under different arrangements that are subdivided by the law as a contract of service or a contract for services. For example, a contract whereby catering services are provided to a firm by a second firm is a contract for services, not an employment contract, even though the work is performed by labour. Catering staff may be employees in the second firm, but the first has bought their services under a commercial contract for catering services.

A contract of employment differs from a contract for services in the sense that an employment contract of personal service to an employer is intended to be an open-ended relationship. It is a relationship that continues until either party decides to end it in a situation where they are allowed to do so with or without notice. Whilst some employment contracts are of a temporary or fixed-term nature, nonetheless an employment relationship is created, whereas in commercial contracts of a long-term duration (e.g. servicing agreements), an employment relationship is not created. Equally, such commercial contracts are likely to contain clear and precise contractual duties for each party. We can say therefore that commercial contracts are purely transactional contractual relationships and, unlike relational employment contracts, are not subject to the *common law duties* of an employer and employee which operate as implied terms and conditions within the contract of employment. By the common law we mean legal rules/principles that have been developed by the judiciary; that is, the common law is *judge-made law*. Now that we have defined contract and distinguished between contracts for services and contracts of service, it is possible to proceed with a discussion of the underlying assumptions behind contract theory.

Equality and freedom of entry: market individualism

The philosophical basis of a contract is derived from the principle of market individualism (see Atiyah, 1979; Deakin and Wilkinson, 2005). Market individualism suggests that individuals are the best judge of their own interests. From this suggestion the notion of *freedom of contract* is introduced, which assumes that individuals are self-determining agents who are primarily self-interested and are best able to fulfil their interests if they are free to enter into contracts with other parties in a free market.

Freedom of contract suggests that individuals act as free agents when they enter into contracts, as both parties to a contract have equal status before the law and, unless a standard form contract is used, they jointly determine the terms and conditions of the contract. It follows from such an assumption that the component elements of a contract – offer, acceptance and the consideration between the parties – are secured through a process of negotiation and then agreement to create legal relations. This may be the situation in the case of most purchases of goods, but in relation to the sale of labour inherent within employment the situation is somewhat different. As Fox (1985: 6) points out, contract theory alone, with all that it entails in terms of equality and references to adjudication by an outside body, cannot be an effective method of regulating terms and conditions of employment if the parties to the contract are in dispute. In the UK this is because the employment relationship remains one in which the status of the parties to the contract is unequal. The notion of status derives from paternalism in the master–servant relationship inherent in 'employment' prior to the rise of industrial economies (see Frank, 2010). Examples of paternal employment include domestic service and tied cottages for estate farmers and general agricultural labourers. In the nineteenth century, domestic servants and agricultural labourers were not employees in the modern sense of the word; rather they were subject to a crude form of commercial contract whereby they provided their labour services to a master in return for board and lodgings. However, once employment became contractually determined in a formal legal sense it did not constitute a clean break with the past. Consequently the contractual process incorporates characteristics from pre-industrial 'paternal' employment, e.g. the status bias of the master–servant relationship.

Fox (1985: 3–5) identifies paternalism as the basis of status within employment. Paternalism refers to a situation of subordination to legitimate authority. Prior to the development of the contract of employment, the process of subordination to legitimate authority was entirely within the master–servant relationship. Within contractually determined employment, the employee subordinates him or herself to the greater legal authority of the employer, the superiority of which is derived from the status-based relationship of master and servant. So, although employment contracts provide employees with a degree of independence from their employer (e.g. employees can terminate their employment through due notice), employees remain subordinate parties to the employment contract. They are subject to the reasonable and legitimate authority of their employer, to whom they provide personal service.

From this discussion it is clear that equality before the law in employment contracts is a fiction or myth because employers' authority is derived from their paternal status, which underpins the employment relationship. This is often referred to as the *managerial prerogative*. In most contracts, the agreeing parties are assumed to be the best judges of their own interests. However, in employment, the status bias of the employer gives them the privilege of determining their self-interest *and* having a partial say in the determination of employee interests. This privilege derives from the concept of *subordination,* which implies that the junior partner to the employment contract cannot perceive all their real interests. Kahn-Freund (1984: 15) described the individually based contract of employment as an act of submission on the part of the employee: 'In its operation it is a condition of subordination, however much the submission and the subordination may be concealed by that indispensable figment of the legal mind known as the contract of employment.'

An employer may determine the organisation of work, levels of payment and duration of working time. The employee is bound by such impositions if they are reasonable. Thus the notion of free employment contracts bears little resemblance to the real world (Hyman, 1975: 23). Relatedly, although all employees have an individual contract of employment, the terms and conditions of an individual's contract of employment are likely to be determined and regulated by means of a collective agreement, the details of which are normally incorporated in an individual's contract of employment. These agreements are often negotiated by a trade union through the process of collective bargaining. In the absence of a trade union and collective bargaining, 'collective agreements' are unilaterally determined by management on behalf of the employer; they are not the subject of negotiation. This point again illustrates that the notions of individual negotiation and freedom of contract exist at only a superficial level of relations between employer and employee.

Formation and the common law regulation of employment contracts

There are two features of the English legal system that highlight the contexts within which all aspects of the law operate. First, the English legal system, unlike most other legal systems (e.g. those of other European Union states), does not operate in conjunction with a written constitution or a Bill of Rights. In the specific area of employment, the absence of a written constitution or a Bill of Rights means that British subjects do not possess any specific inalienable rights as employees, e.g. the right to strike. Secondly, and relatedly, the system is very conservative – some would say obsessed with the past. This conservatism explains why 'precedent' has so prominent a role in the common law. Precedent operates based on decisions previously arrived at in a higher court. It is judge-made law that creates a rule for lower courts and subsequent future cases of a similar nature. Thus a precedent creates an example for subsequent cases or acts as a justification for subsequent decisions.

Advocates of Britain's unwritten constitution argue that its major benefit is adaptability over time, which contrasts with the rigid mechanism of a written constitution around which new developments have to be moulded. In matters of employment, many of the rights held by British subjects result from case law and precedent and from trade union activity in collective bargaining. Equally, trade unions have a consultative role in the formulation of statutory protections and provisions such as the national minimum wage or the statutory procedure for trade union recognition under the Employment Relations Act 1999 (ERA).

Common law duties of employer and employee

Earlier in the chapter, the concept of 'freedom of contract' was introduced. This concept assumes that individuals are self-determining agents who are primarily self-interested. It follows from this that individuals both freely enter into contractual arrangements and jointly determine the terms and conditions of an employment contract. In the case of employment, the notion of freedom of contract operates in conjunction with the common law duties of employer and employee. That is, although contracts of employment may be entered into freely, the contract of employment itself incorporates the common law duties of employee and employer.

Common law duties of the employer

These are (adapted from Cabrelli, 2008) as follows:

- To take reasonable care to ensure that all employees are safe at the workplace, and indemnify any employee for injury sustained during employment. Employers have both a common law duty and a statutory duty to provide a safe working environment for their employees. Aspects of this liability are codified in statute under the Health and Safety at Work Act 1974.

- To treat all employees in a manner that is in line with the duty of mutual trust and confidence – arguably therefore in a courteous and polite manner. That is, employers should not 'bully' or abuse their employees, or subject them to racist or sexist remarks. Aspects of this liability are codified in the Equality Act 2010 (EqA). The common law duties of the employer contrast with those of an employee.

- To provide a reasonable opportunity for the employee to work and pay the agreed wages as consideration for work performed. It is a matter of some debate as to whether the employer has a common law duty to actually provide work; the issue appears to turn on two distinct arguments. First, the notion of reasonableness, which will depend on the details of any particular case, and secondly, the operation of common law principles. The courts have held, for example, that the duty to provide work is a matter of fact rather than a matter of law. Thus in specific factual circumstances related to the nature of the work, such a duty may be implied into the contract of employment. The courts have indicated that where an employee needs to:
  - maintain or develop key skill levels;
  - keep up to date with developments in the industry, sector or trade within which they work; or

- there was an understanding between the parties that the employee would be given a reasonable amount of work in order that they could enjoy a specific level of earnings; or
- the failure to provide work may lead to a loss of reputation or publicity on the part of the employee,

they are willing to find the existence of an implied duty to provide work (for examples, see *Breach* [1976] IRLR 180, and *William Hill* [1998] IRLR 313).

Common law duties of the employee

These are broadly as follows:

- To be ready and willing to work for their employer.
- To offer personal service to the employer – that is not to send a substitute without agreement.
- To offer exclusive service to their employer – that is not hold a second job without agreement.
- To take reasonable care in the conduct and performance of their personal service.
- To work in the employer's time.
- To carry out all reasonable instructions during that time, except that the employee is not required to carry out instructions which are outwith his/her contract (for a discussion see *O'Brien v. Associated Fire Alarms Ltd* [1969] 1 All ER 93).
- To undertake not to disrupt the employer's business on purpose.
- To not disclose any trade secret to a third party (for a discussion, see *Faccenda Chicken Ltd v. Fowler* [1986] IRLR 69).

The common law duties of the employee and employer are not always detailed in the written particulars of a contract of employment; indeed, they are more often terms implied in the contract which are derived from custom and practice or statutes.

Explore

- To what extent is there equality of obligations within the principal 'implied terms' between the parties?
- Does this reflect contemporary views on issues such as the right to privacy, freedom of speech and a family life enshrined within the Human Rights Act 1998?
- How can employers use the duty of 'fidelity' in the age of social media?

In market economies, the law assumes that the contract of employment is entered into freely; however, the terms and conditions, whether they are express or implied, are not jointly determined, and in terms of employee and employer obligations, they are not equal in terms of their scope and coverage. In most cases, the employer is in the dominant bargaining position because they are offering employment. In such situations, the employer is able unilaterally to determine how the common law duties of the employee are to be fulfilled. The common law duties of the employee, as listed, appear to be clear and precise but are in reality open to considerable interpretation. In contrast to this, the common law obligations of the employer are imbued with the tenet of limited reasonableness: that is, the obligations imposed on the employer should not be unreasonable. Thus the general concept of reasonableness can only be tested in individual cases. As Hyman (1975: 24) argues, the status equality implied by the concept of self-determining individuals freely entering into contracts of employment is really status *inequality* because of the way the principles of equality before the law and freedom of entry operate in practice. Clearly, equality before the law belies the market power held by an employer. Individual equality before the law places firms that have access to necessarily expensive legal advice on the formulation of employment contracts and individuals bereft of such a capability on the same plane. As we pointed out earlier, within the contract of employment, freedom and equality are fused with the traditional status bias of employment, with the result that the reality of the employment relationship is that, rather than being one of exchange between equals, it is one of subordination of one party – the employee – to another – the employer (see *Bateman and Ors v. ASDA* [2010]).

Types of employment contract

Every employee has a contract of employment. However, as indicated earlier, not all *workers* have a contract of employment. Where an employer provides regular work, defines working hours, the place of work, determines holiday and sick pay arrangements, requires personal service, and deducts income tax and National Insurance through the PAYE system, the courts are predisposed to a finding that a contract of employment – and hence an employment relationship – exists and anyone engaged on these terms is likely to be an employee (however, see *Methodist Conference v. Preston* [2013]). By contrast, a worker who is not an employee will often pay their own income tax and National Insurance contributions, decide when, where and how they work, be allowed to arrange for a substitute to undertake their work, and make their own holiday and sick pay arrangements. However, in addition to self-employed contractors and freelance IT specialists, journalists, consultants, etc., some agency workers, casual workers and 'home workers' may be classified as having worker status rather than employee status. A contract of employment is not always written down in one document, and sometimes the contract may not be written down at all.

There are several types of employment contract, as detailed below.

Permanent, ongoing or open-ended contracts

This type of employment contract is assumed to continue until either side gives notice of an intention to terminate the contract.

Temporary contract

This type of contract has no specified duration; therefore it does not contain any restrictive fixed term or limiting event. It often does not contain waivers, e.g. the requirement that the employee waive their right to statutory protection in relation to redundancy. A temporary contract may be made permanent and the time served under the temporary contract will constitute continuity of service. Hence in the case of employment rights that are based on an employee's length of service (e.g. unfair dismissal, which is currently set at two years' length of service) it is unnecessary for the employee to serve another full two years to acquire this protection. However, although the general principle is clear, it is a complex area of law subject to the particular circumstances of individual cases. This complexity, in many cases, is the result of the triangular nature of such temporary contracts which involve the use of employment agencies. For example, in *Dacas v. Brook Street Bureau* [2004], despite the claimant having worked for the same client for an extended period, she did not enjoy the status of an employee and so, when her services were no longer required, could not claim unfair dismissal.

Fixed-term or limited event contract

This type of contract has a specified duration, i.e. a clear start date and a clear and unequivocal termination date or event which occasions termination. Examples of this might include situations where employment is subject to 'funding arrangements' that are not renewable, a specific one-off project or matters such as maternity and paternity leave. Both parties to such contracts should be aware that the contract is not renewable once the event or date occurs. More significant than this, many employees who are subject to such contracts are required to waive their statutory protections against unfair dismissal and redundancy. The ERA 1999 now prohibits employers from using waiver clauses against unfair dismissal; however, redundancy waivers continue. Since November 2001, employees under such contracts have equal rights to those of permanent employees in terms of pay rates and pension provision. Further, the Fixed-Term Employees (Prevention of Less Favourable Treatment) Regulations 2002 now provide that an individual who has worked on two or more such contracts over a period of four years has a right to a permanent contract.

'Casual', 'spot' or zero-hours contracts

Under this type of contract, the employee must be available for work, but the employer does not have to guarantee work; for example, a retired teacher may be on call to cover for sick colleagues. Equally, banks use on-call staff to cover busy periods such as lunchtime, whereas the Post Office employs many casual workers at Christmas. In most situations this type of contract is mutually beneficial and not open to abuse; however, if a worker is required to be at work but clock off during slack periods – a practice once common in many fast-food outlets – zero-hours contracts are open to abuse. For example, such a worker could remain at the workplace for long periods yet have a very low rate of hourly pay owing to continual clocking off. In an effort to overcome some of the abuses of zero-hours contracts, a person employed on such a contract is now entitled to the national minimum wage, whereas the Working Time Directive entitles the person to a paid holiday provided they worked during the preceding 13 weeks. The vast majority of individuals who are engaged under a zero-hours contract will be classified as an employee; however, some employers have attempted to argue that engagement under a zero-hours contract is compatible with worker status. The basis of this argument centres on the 'mutuality of obligation' between the employer and the worker or employee. If someone engaged under a zero-hours contract does not have regular hours of work and is able to decline offers of work and/or work elsewhere, there is unlikely to be a mutuality of obligation between the two parties. It is the presence of mutual obligation that creates the employment relationship establishing the employer and employee (see *Carmichael v. National Power* [1999]). This is a controversial area and the distinction between worker status and employee status is persistently criticised by the TUC and other employee groups. It has been the subject of much judicial comment and continues to cause concern amongst a wide range of organisations. Up to nine million workers in the UK may have worker status, many of whom are arguably *de facto* employees, e.g. long-term agency workers or temps engaged in one organisation. On the specific issue of agency and temporary workers, the UK's forthcoming adoption of European Union directives may provide the basis of some improvement in employment protection (see *Stringfellow Restaurants Ltd v. Quashie* [2012] for a recent judicial discussion of these debates). We have established that in the vast majority of cases the employer is the dominant party in the employment relationship. This dominance enables the employer to determine many terms and conditions contained within the employment contract. In modern practice, the employer offers employment on 'standard' terms in most cases and the idea of equality of bargaining power is one of the myths or symbols that generate obedience rather than a legally sustainable reality.

Terms within employment contracts

There are two types of terms and conditions within a contract of employment.

Express terms

These form an explicit part of an individual contract of employment. They are often referred to as the *written* terms and conditions of the contract that are included in the written *statement of the contract*. Any employee, irrespective of the number of hours they work, must be given a statement of the written terms and conditions of their contract within two months – eight weeks – of starting work (s.1(2) ERtsA 1996). The statement must include the following items:

- Name and address of employer.
- Name of the employee.
- Date employment began.
- Place or places of work.

- Rate of pay or salary point: for lower-paid employees the rate must adhere to the statutory national minimum wage, from 1 October 2013, £6.31 per hour for workers aged 22 or over, £5.03 per hour for those aged 18–21 and £3.72 for 16- and 17-year-olds. This rate is adjusted annually by amounts which are determined in consultation with the Low Pay Commission.

- Hours of work: as a result of the Human Rights Act 1998, it may be necessary for employers to specify the reasons for, frequency of and need to telephone employees at home. This legislation establishes that an employer does not have an automatic right to demand an employee's home phone number unless the express terms of an employment contract state that an employee has a duty to be available outside normal working hours.

- Holiday entitlements: as a result of the working time regulations (WTRs) all full-time employees are now entitled to 28 days' paid holiday, and part-time workers on a pro-rata basis. The situation with respect to temporary or agency workers is more complicated. All employees are entitled to a minimum of 28 days' paid holiday, but to qualify for this an employee must work for an employer for 13 weeks. Temps employed by an agency are entitled to paid holidays if they work for 13 weeks. This is the case even if they move between different workplaces, as long as the employment is continuous. The introduction of this right to paid holidays presented problems in relation to casual and part-time workers. One way employers – in some cases in agreement with recognised trade unions – sought to deal with this issue was the use of a system known as 'rolled-up holiday pay'. In simple terms this was a system whereby the hourly rate was supplemented by an agreed amount which was to represent holiday pay. In relation to casual, short-term assignments the worker is then deemed to take holiday at the end of the assignment, having already been paid for the time. The courts and the Employment Appeals Tribunal (EAT) in Scotland held such arrangements to be void as a form of contracting out of the legal requirements, In *Robinson-Steele v. R D Retail Services* [2006] IRLR 14 the English court finally referred the matter to the European Court of Justice (ECJ), having previously held such arrangements to comply with the WTRs. The difference in approach was a result of the Scottish courts arguing that the principle in 'rolled-up' schemes of 'receive as you earn' acted as a disincentive to take leave, whilst the English Tribunals argued that if the amount was genuine, sufficient and transparent the WTR permitted such arrangements. The ECJ reasoned that, as the purpose was to put the worker in the same position as regards payment, that the Directive prohibited the replacement of the period of leave by payment alone, and the 'rolled-up' scheme may lead to the replacement of leave with payment in lieu, such arrangements were excluded by the Directive. The ECJ went on to hold that the Directive does not outlaw 'the use of 'rolled-up' pay from being set off against any liability to pay in respect of any specific leave taken by the worker' (LexisNexis, 2013: A [922]). This in part offers legitimacy to the practice, at least in situations where the scheme currently exists. In relation to its continued use, Reg. 35 of the Directive, which makes void any provision excluding rights provided by the Directive, seals the demise of rolled-up holiday pay. Further confusion has arisen surrounding the right to holiday pay and/or accrued holiday time during periods of long-term illness or illness during a holiday period. Following recent cases there seems to be more clarity. The European Court held that untaken statutory holiday entitlement during periods of illness can be carried over but must be taken within 15 months, meaning that an individual cannot continually build up holiday leave by carrying over unused time each succeeding year (see *KHS AG v. Schulte* [2011]). In terms of individuals who have given notice of holiday leave or are indeed on holiday leave when they fall ill, the EAT has indicated that such holiday leave should be 'returned' to the individual and that it can be carried over (see *Fraser v. South West London St George's Mental Health Trust* [2011]).

- Sick pay arrangements.

- Notice entitlements.

- Pension rights, including auto-enrolment provisions.
- Details of the grievance procedure – including the identity of the person to whom the employee can apply for the purpose of seeking redress.
- Details of the discipline procedure.
- Job title.
- Period of employment if job not permanent.
- Details of any collective agreements which directly affect the terms and conditions.

Implied terms

These are terms and conditions that are not explicitly stated in an individual contract of employment but which are assumed to be included in the contract, e.g. workplace custom and practice arrangements and the common law duties of the employer and employee (see the earlier discussion).

Terms implied by statutory provision

These are terms and conditions that are incorporated into individual contracts of employment as either express or implied terms. Incorporated terms and conditions of employment include the statutory protections passed by the UK Parliament or the European Union. In English law, collective agreements negotiated between employers and trade unions through the process of collective bargaining are not legally binding. However, elements within collective agreements are legally binding if they are incorporated into individual contracts of employment, e.g. working hours and pay rates.

Key Controversy

The recent decline in the coverage and scope of collective bargaining has diminished the efficacy of 'incorporation' to such an extent it is no longer a pertinent concept in this area. This might affect the overall 'rights' of both parties and change the nature of the employment relationship. But do employers really benefit in a situation where individuals resort to employment tribunals to secure rights previously protected by collective agreements?

Continuation and changing the terms of employment

Employers are able to change terms and conditions of employment; however, employees have some rights if an employer seeks to change terms and conditions without consultation and agreement. A unilateral change in pay rates represents a serious breach of contract, as does the unilateral removal of a company car, reductions in holiday entitlements and suspension of an employer's pension contribution. Employees can accept unilateral changes and work normally under protest, i.e object to the changes and seek to minimise the effects of the unilateral change. However, a recent case, *Robinson v. Tescom* Corporation [2008] IRLR 408, made it clear that such objection, even if in writing and following the wording suggested by the Advisory, Conciliation and Arbitration Service (ACAS), is still acceptance of the change. Therefore, objecting to the new terms and conditions in writing and refusing to work to them when they are introduced later still amounts to gross disobedience, which may lead to summary dismissal. Such a dismissal could well be judged to be reasonable and fair under the 'some other substantial reason' provision (see the section on 'Termination of the employment contract'). This has the effect of allowing employees who object to the variation only one option: leave and claim 'constructive dismissal'.

Continuation and statutory rights relating to employment contracts

All employees have a contract of employment; equally, all employees receive some level of statutory protection against arbitrary and unreasonable treatment by an employer. Statutory protection can be framed in individual terms, e.g. protection against sexual and racial discrimination in the workplace; alternatively, rights may be collective, e.g. the statutory procedure for trade union recognition introduced by the Employment Relations Act 1999.

Since 1995 all workers, either full-time or part-time, have been subject to the same *day one statutory rights* irrespective of how many hours they work. Statutory day one rights provide a minimum level of protection to all workers. Some workers may have additional contractual rights negotiated by their employer and a recognised trade union. In addition to day one rights, other rights depend on an employee's length of service.

In 2010 the Government brought together all the previous anti-discrimination legislation into one Act (The Equality Act 2010). The following sections develop an analysis of the rights included within that legislation in relation to the nine protected characteristics and the prohibited actions associated with them.

Day one employment rights

Equal pay/equal value

Section 66(1) of the EqA 2010 inserts an *equality clause* into contracts of employment that can be enforced by an employment tribunal. Under the EqA terms within contracts of employment must be equal between the sexes. The equality clause enforces equal terms and conditions in the contracts of men and women in the same employment. The clause covers pay and all other contractual terms of employment. The EqA is applicable in three situations:

- *Like work*. Where men and women are employed to perform like work, i.e. the same work or work that is broadly similar, men and women must receive the same rate of pay or be paid on the same salary scale. This is the case even if part-time men and women work fewer hours than full-time men and women, i.e. a part-time worker may compare themselves to a full-time employee.

- *Work rated as equivalent under an analytical job evaluation scheme.* Job evaluation describes a set of methods that compare jobs with the view to assessing their relative and comparative worth (see Chapter 13). The process of job evaluation ranks jobs based on rational and objective assessment of key factors – such as skill, effort and decision-making – from a representative sample of jobs in a particular organisation. The purpose of job evaluation is to produce a reasonable and defensible ranking of jobs. By formalising and making explicit the basis of payment systems and associated differences in pay levels, employers can expose discriminatory practices and remove them (for more detail on job evaluation see Chapter 13 in this text).

- Where work is of *equal value,* even though it is not like work or work covered by a non-discriminatory job evaluation scheme in the same employment. Equal value is measured in terms of the demands upon the worker in terms of skill levels, effort and decision-making. If different work is held to be of equal value under these criteria then the two groups of workers must have the same pay levels. Pay is constituted in its widest sense and includes salary scales or pay rates, access to occupational pension schemes, redundancy protection, sick pay, travel concessions and other perks. In the 1980s, USDAW (the shop workers' trade union) and the Equal Opportunities Commission successfully fought equal value cases on behalf of supermarket checkout workers, who are predominantly women, against delivery dock and warehouse workers who were predominantly men. An employer may defend an equal value case on the grounds that differences in pay between men and women are justified on the grounds of a genuine material factor that is both relevant and significant in the particular case. The fact that a particular group of workers who are predominantly women includes a male worker does not constitute a genuine material factor: that is, men who receive lower pay than other men employed in the same organisation are able to claim that their work is of equal value. For example, the presence of a 'token' male checkout worker or school lunch assistant appears insufficient to defeat a claim for equal value. In summary, a claim to equal pay for work of equal value normally involves women in comparison to men; however, the presence of lower-paid men cannot undermine a claim, because men are also protected in respect of equal pay for work of equal value.

Discrimination/harassment – the protected characteristics and prohibited conduct

It is unlawful to discriminate against an employee, i.e. offer them less favourable treatment on grounds of any of the nine protected characteristics. In the following sections we note each and highlight specific HR issues that may arise. Whilst section 64 of the EqA 2010 covers discrimination in respect of terms and conditions including pay, sections 39–41 cover discrimination in respect of selection, training, promotion, termination (e.g. selection for redundancy) or any other detriment in employment. The EqA applies equally to men and women except with respect to pregnancy provisions, and defines discrimination in five ways:

- *Direct discrimination* (EqA s. 13). For example, denying a person employment on the grounds of any of the protected characteristics is likely to be direct discrimination. Such discrimination is often said to be covered by the 'but for' description. That is the treatment would not have been received 'but for' the fact of the characteristic.

- *Indirect discrimination* (EqA s. 19). This category refers to apparently neutral job requirements, provisions, criteria or practices that have a disproportional effect on individuals who possess the characteristic, e.g. height requirements, dress codes or age and length of service requirements for promotion that may preclude married women with children from having sufficient length of service to apply by an upper age limit. Some cases of indirect discrimination appear to be intentional, whereas other cases result from a failure to update HRM procedures in accordance with the law, e.g. dress codes that prevent women from wearing trousers (see *Schmidt v. Austicks Bookshops Ltd* [1977] IRLR 360). An employer may choose to defend a charge of indirect discrimination on the grounds that the apparently discriminatory provision is a proportionate means of achieving a legitimate objective, what can be classed as objective justification for the provision, criterion or practice. For example, in selection exercises for the fire service, candidates must be able to expand their lung capacity by a certain measurement. Many women applicants are unable to meet this requirement: hence it appears to have a disproportionate effect on women. However, many men are unable to meet the requirement. Lung expansion is a requirement of a firefighter's job because it plays a part in assessing whether or not a candidate would be able to escape from a variety of smoke-filled situations. Hence the requirement can be seen as a proportionate means of achieving a legitimate objective and therefore objectively justified. As Tolleys Employment Law Service (2009: B2001) notes '[a]s years go by, attitudes . . . alter and the courts have shown a willingness to take into consideration modern views and aspirations'.

- *Victimisation*. (EqA s. 27). In terms of legal definitions, this is a situation where a person discriminates against another because that other has brought proceedings, given evidence or indicated an intention to bring proceedings against the former under the various statutory provisions. The offence is committed by treating the individual less favourably than one treats other people on the broad range of issues covered with the Act (see *St Helen's Borough Council v. Derbyshire* [2007] IRLR 540).

- *Harassment* (EqA s. 26). This category covers verbal abuse, suggestive behaviour or conduct that has either the purpose or effects mentioned and is founded on the grounds of sex. Harassment and bullying occur when a person engages in such unwanted conduct which has the purpose or effect of violating another's dignity, creating an intimidating, hostile, degrading, humiliating or offensive environment for that individual. As an example, an employer who tolerates sexist jokes and/or pornographic images around the workplace might be said to have created an offensive environment, even if the employee is not able to claim the remark or image was aimed specifically at him or her. A key factor in determining whether such behaviour does have the effects indicated is the perception of the victim and reasonableness. This does not, however, give free rein to the oversensitive individual. Recently the EAT had to decide whether a Catholic could claim that the sub-editor at a newspaper twice shouting across the room 'What has happened to the f****** Pope?' amounted to harassment on the grounds of religious belief. The EAT held that adverse comments were not always discriminatory, that in this case the statement was not anti-Catholic and therefore no harassment had occurred, reinforcing the principle that reasonableness in the circumstances is a key element to be considered in cases brought under s. 26 of the EqA (*Heafield v. Times Newspapers* [2012]).

- *Discrimination on the basis of association or perception.* The courts have been faced with issues surrounding discrimination against an individual (often the person with caring responsibilities) who does not themselves possess the protected characteristic (see *Colemen v. Attridge Law* [2008]). This is further complicated in cases where an individual is singled out because of the perception that they possess the characteristic (see *English v. Thomas Sanderson Blinds Ltd* [2008]). It is clear from the decisions in both cases that the legislation does provide protection to the individual in both situations [see Collins *et al.* (2012) for further discussion].

Explore

- Is it reasonable that certain types of employment are exempt from the provisions of the EqA (2010)?
- Consider what these areas might be and justify their exclusion – as a start, consider areas of social work such as child protection and rape counselling.

Racial discrimination and harassment

Whilst previously this was covered under the Race Relations Act 1976 (as amended), it is now found within the EqA 2010 and the definitions of prohibited behaviour fall to be considered under the same provisions as indicated above. Examples of indirect racial discrimination in employment turn on the relevance of apparently race-neutral job requirements that have a disproportionate effect on ethnic minorities, e.g. requirements that preclude candidates on the basis that their grandparents were not British, or English language requirements. If these requirements are unrelated to the job they may well be indirectly discriminatory. Racial harassment in employment covers matters such as racial abuse, suggestive behaviour or the effects of tokenism. Certain types of employment are exempt from the provisions; for example, staff in specialised restaurants and community social workers who are required to speak particular ethnic languages may fall to be considered as legitimate aims for which the employers action is a proportionate response.

Maternity, adoption and paternity rights

The rules and regulations in respect of maternity rights are very complicated. It is important that both the employer and the employee follow them carefully. Some employees have better maternity arrangements than the statutory arrangements; this is usually the result of collective bargaining arrangements in the workplace.

All women are entitled to maternity leave, which under the provisions of the ERA 1996 was set at 26 weeks and was further extended by the maternity and paternity leave regulations to 52 weeks, of which up to 39 weeks are paid maternity leave. In April 2007 paid maternity leave was extended to nine months and the government has made a further commitment to increase paid leave to one year. The entitlement to paid maternity leave is unrelated to the number of hours worked or length of service. A pregnant employee must conform to the following requirements:

- provide written notice of pregnancy and due date;
- provide a medical certificate if requested;
- indicate the date the employee intends to begin leave – this cannot be before the 11th week;
- return to work within 39 weeks, which is the maternity pay period, or 52 weeks if the employee is taking a further 13 weeks unpaid maternity leave.

Maternity leave may be extended if the employee is sick or has an illness related to confinement. The day one employment rights establish that employees who are either pregnant or on maternity leave cannot be dismissed or made redundant because of pregnancy or a pregnancy-related illness contracted or diagnosed as commencing before or after the birth of the child.

An employee who fulfils the following criteria is entitled to *statutory maternity pay* when:

- their average weekly earnings are at least equal to the lower earnings limit;
- the employee provides the employer with a maternity certificate giving the due date;
- they were employed up to and including the 15th week before the baby was due;
- they have stopped working;
- they have given the employer 28 days' notice of their intention to stop working;
- at the end of the 15th week of confinement before the baby was due, the employee had worked for this employer for 26 weeks.

Statutory maternity pay is calculated on the basis of six weeks at 90 per cent of average earnings plus 33 weeks at 90 per cent of average earnings or the basic rate – currently £136.78 per week – whichever is the lower. After a period of maternity leave, an employee is entitled to return to the same job they held before going on leave. In April 2007, provisions were introduced that allow employers to 'keep in touch' and for employees to undertake a limited number of work days in order to keep up to date. In relation to the former, it is now considered good practice for the employer to inform the employee of any vacancies that arise during the maternity leave period. HR managers ought, therefore, to make it part of the maternity procedure to ensure they keep individuals on maternity leave informed. The same amendments to the regulations allow for a period of 10 working days during the maternity pay period when individuals could 'return to work' without losing the right to maternity pay.

After a great deal of pressure from family groups, trade unions and adoption agencies, the government enacted the Paternity and Adoption Leave Regulations (2002). These regulations provided, for the first time, rights to adoptive parents on the same footing as birth parents.

The same legislation introduced a period of two-week paternity leave which must be taken within 56 days of the date of birth. The leave can be taken either as two one-week blocks or a single two-week block. It is intended to make arrangements for parents to choose additional paternity leave of up to 26 weeks – in simple terms sharing the 52 weeks of family leave.

Disability discrimination

There are approximately nine million disabled working-age people in the UK, but only one-third of that figure are actually in employment, while many more would like to work but are unemployed or in receipt of incapacity benefit. The EqA 2010 (s. 6) makes it unlawful for an employer to discriminate against applicants for employment or against employees who have a disability in relation to job applications, promotion, training and contractual terms and benefits. The UK legislation has been influenced by both the Americans with Disabilities Act and, more recently, the European Framework Equal Treatment Directive (FETD) 2000/78/EC (see the 'Current issues' section for further discussion of the effects of the FETD).

There are two primary theories of disability, the most dominant of which has been the 'medical model'. Under this model an individual is disabled as a direct consequence of a physical or mental impairment. The UK legislation is firmly rooted in the medical model and we are presented with a number of legal and HR policy options – basically aimed at improving individual circumstances and caring for those unable to adapt to their social environment by facilitating changes to that environment. The ECJ has advocated a broader approach to disability more in line with the social model; the adoption of this definition would open the coverage of anti-disability discrimination legislation to a far wider group of individuals than a traditional medical model. In so doing, it places responsibilities on employers to eliminate structural barriers to participation, develop programmes of integration and create working conditions of individual empowerment. This covers a wider group to include the 'long-term sick' and hence adds to the operating costs imposed on organisations.

The provisions of the UK statute cover all employees, from permanent to casual. In addition, subcontract workers are also covered. The EqA is universal in application and the coverage of disability includes protection of employees with 'asymptomatic' conditions such as multiple sclerosis, HIV, attention deficit disorder and hyperactivity syndrome (ADDHS) and some forms of cancer from the time they are diagnosed by a doctor. This provision detailed in the legislation is intended to cover so-called 'hidden disabilities'.

The EqA (s. 6) defines *disability* as mental or physical impairment that has a long-term and substantial adverse effect on the ability of an individual to perform normal daily activities. The legislation goes on in Schedule 1 to amplify this definition under several headings. First, the nature of impairment is broadly interpreted in terms of its daily impact on an employee rather than being confined to those that are recognised medical conditions, e.g. HIV-positive status, schizophrenia, ADDHS and other forms of mental illness. Secondly, the requirement for a substantial effect rules out minor complaints such as hay fever or colour blindness. Thirdly, and related, a condition of impairment must last at least a year or the rest of a person's life to qualify as a long-term effect. Finally, the ability to undertake normal daily activity covers issues such as the ability to hear and learn, comprehend the perception and risk of physical danger, continence, eyesight, hearing, manual dexterity, memory, speech and physical coordination.

The Act and subsequent case law outline the tests for disability discrimination:

- *Less favourable treatment.* As with other anti-discrimination legislation, the law provides for a range of prohibited acts. Contravention of this regulation results in an individual being considered to have received less favourable treatment. This situation arises when a disabled employee is able to demonstrate less favourable treatment – in comparison with an able-bodied person – 'because of something arising in consequence' (EqA s. 15(1)) of their disability that cannot be shown to be a proportionate means of achieving a legitimate objective (i.e. cannot be objectively justified) by the employer. An employer can defend a claim for disability discrimination on the grounds of less favourable treatment if they can demonstrate a relevant or substantial justification for the treatment.

- *A duty to make reasonable adjustments.* This duty (EqA s. 20) comes into play when the employer could be reasonably judged to know that an individual with a disability would be placed at a substantial disadvantage by their work arrangements or premises. In such a situation, a failure to make reasonable adjustments in the workplace may result in disability discrimination. In addition to this, an employer can no longer justify disability discrimination with a substantial reason; they must rather demonstrate objective justification for their action or lack of action.

- *Harassment.* It is unlawful to harass a person for a reason that relates to the person's disability.

- *Victimisation.* As one of the protected characteristics in line with the others, the Act protects individuals who have asserted a statutory right or instigated proceedings under the legislation.

Under the provisions of the EU Framework Employment Directive (FED), the UK extended the coverage of anti-discrimination legislation to include groups previously excluded or poorly covered. A good example of this relates to the lesbian, gay, bi-sexual and transgender (LGBT) community. These specific issues are all now subsumed within the EqA (ss. 12, 10 and 5 respectively) along with gender reassignment (s. 7) marriage and civil partnership (s. 8) and pregnancy and maternity (s. 18).

Sexual orientation

The EqA 2010 puts in place provisions that attempt to prohibit discrimination on the basis of sexual orientation. The Act defines sexual orientation as an attraction to a person of the same sex, the opposite sex or both, as such covering the whole of the LGBT community. In principle, this means that all forms of discrimination can be based on the discriminator's perception, even where that perception is not accurate, or the perpetrators know the individual is not lesbian, gay, bisexual or transgender (*see English v. Thomas Sanderson Ltd* [2008] EWCA 1421). Further, individuals can be deemed to have discriminated against others where the action relates to someone with whom the victim of discrimination associates. Whilst direct discrimination can never be justified, the Act provides for objective justification of indirect discrimination in the same way as for other protected characteristics; similarly, harassment and victimisation are covered.

Religion and belief

The EqA 2010 includes the prohibition of discriminatory behaviour on the grounds of religion or belief. The Act does not contain any definition of 'religion or belief' and the UK government adopted a wide-ranging definition. By adopting a deliberately wide terminology ('any religion' and 'any religious or philosophical belief') the Act uses a concept in line with Article 9 of the European Convention on Human Rights. The effect of avoiding discrimination because of an individual's religion or belief should not be discrimination against the non-believer – thus it is unlawful for a Christian employer to refuse to employ an individual of no belief simply on that basis. The regulations do provide for an objective justification defence where belief is a central part of the role under the same interpretation as is found in relation to indirect discrimination – objective justification. Case law has highlighted that this enactment is designed to cover identifiable groups (see *Ewieda v. British Airways plc* [2009] IRLR 78) and that belief is separate from actions (see *Chondol v. Liverpool CC* [2009] EAT1298/08 and *Islington LBC v. Ladele* [2008] EAT1453/08). Both *Ewieda* and *Ladele* went to the European Court of Human Rights where the decision demonstrated that employers can objectively justify discriminatory behaviour (in the latter case based on the rights of others), but that the court will not simply agree with employer aims or 'brand' image.

Age discrimination

Until October 2006, age discrimination was regulated by a voluntary code of practice but is now regulated by s. 5 of the EqA 2010. This makes it unlawful for employers to specify age when recruiting staff, promoting staff or training staff. Similarly, terms such as 'youngish', 'recently qualified' 'under 40' become unlawful unless an employer is able to provide a clear business-related reason for the specification of the requirement. In addition, the cases suggest that advertisements that seek 'experienced' workers will require careful wording and person specifications to ensure that it is clear that recruitment decisions are not made on the basis of age and experience.

In addition to the above day one rights, all employees have the following day one rights where relevant:

- time off for trade union duties;
- protection against victimisation due to involvement in trade union duties, e.g. unfair selection for redundancy;

Table 10.1 Minimum notice periods

Length of service	Notice	Length of service	Notice
4 weeks to 2 years	1 week	7–8 years	7 weeks
2–3 years	2 weeks	8–9 years	8 weeks
3–4 years	3 weeks	9–10 years	9 weeks
4–5 years	4 weeks	10–11 years	10 weeks
5–6 years	5 weeks	11–12 years	11 weeks
6–7 years	6 weeks	Over 12 years	12 weeks

- protection against victimisation due to involvement in health and safety activity;
- the right to itemised payslips;
- protection against unlawful deductions from wages and/or claims that relate to entitlements under the provision of the national minimum wage or the provisions of the Working Time Directive, e.g. entitlements to paid holidays;
- written reasons for dismissal during pregnancy or maternity leave;
- time off for antenatal visits;
- Sunday working rights, where relevant;
- protection against victimisation for enforcing a day one or length of service statutory right;
- disclosure of wrongdoing under the provisions of the Public Interest Disclosure Act (1998), i.e. 'whistle-blowing'. Such cases can be expensive for an employer because the public interest disclosure legislation does not impose a cap on tribunal awards. Connex, the train operating company, was ordered to pay £55,000 to a train driver who successfully demonstrated his victimisation after he published concerns over safety risks; £18,000 of the award was for aggravated damages and injury to feelings. Connex declined to appeal the tribunal decision.

Rights that depend on length of service

Access to the following statutory rights is dependent upon an employee's length of service, but is unrelated to how many hours they work:

- Written statement of main terms and conditions of employment.
- Written reasons for dismissal: two years.
- Protection against unfair dismissal: two years.
- Dismissal due to redundancy: two years.
- Guaranteed lay-off pay: one month.
- Medical suspension pay – absence or suspension from work on medical grounds: 1 month.

Employers are required to provide employees with the periods of paid notice listed in Table 10.1. Employers must give employees full pay for the notice period even if the worker is off sick or on maternity leave.

Continuation – discrimination in employment

As we have seen, employees have statutory protection against discrimination on grounds of all the protected characteristics and unequal treatment in stipulation of terms and conditions (including pay). However, the presence of discrimination in employment is still evident [see Dickens (2005) for general discussion of the problem and elsewhere in this textbook for details of the relative positions of women and members of ethnic minorities in the labour market (Chapter 4)]. There are three possible explanations for the continued presence of discrimination in employment.

First, much discrimination goes unreported and is tolerated by employees, who feel that they have no voice mechanism to complain about such treatment; this is particularly the case in small firms and some non-union employers. That is, some employers know they are breaking the law but hope to get away with ignoring it. However, it is necessary to point out that even in workplaces that have collective bargaining and otherwise well-ordered HRM policies, discrimination may still occur.

A second explanation for the continued presence of discrimination relates to the rather limited nature of employment protection legislation during the 1980s. For much of its period of office the Conservative government operated differential employment protection legislation for full-time and part-time workers. However, many claims against this type of discrimination, unequal pay and indirect sex discrimination, lodged on the basis that more part-time workers were women than men, remain in the process of redress and resolution.

In an effort to reduce discrimination between full-time and part-time employees, the Part-time Workers' (Prevention of Less Favourable Treatment) Regulations came into force in July 2000. These regulations state that part-time workers should receive the same pay rates as full-time colleagues and receive the same hourly overtime rate once they exceed normal working hours. In addition to these equal rights, part-time workers must receive the same holiday, maternity and paternity leave entitlements as full-time colleagues on a pro-rata basis. Finally, part-time workers must be included in the provision of workplace training; that is, there must be a single framework for training in the workplace and not separate sets of arrangements for full-time and part-time workers. The regulations, although a marked improvement on the previous situation, remain limited.

A third explanation for the emergence of newly defined forms of discrimination in employment is the UK's further integration within the EU and the adoption by the Labour government of the EU's Social Charter of employment and social rights in 1997. This accession further exposed the limited protection provided for many British employees. The EU regulations also encourage the use of more permanent arrangements by requiring that individuals who have worked on two or more fixed-term contracts over a continuous period of four years (the 2 + 4 rule) become permanent employees.

The issue of workplace bullying further demonstrates the limited nature of the UK's discrimination and employment protection laws. It has been reported that every year 18.9 million working days are lost as a direct result of workplace bullying, costing the UK economy some £6 billion (see **www.bullyingatwork.com**). Equally disturbingly, it is clear that many organisations either do not have a policy on bullying or do not follow any policy when it is reported. Despite this feeling of an increase in bullying at work, it is still not specifically categorised in employment legislation, and while the practice may constitute discrimination or indirect discrimination, in other cases, employees may have to resign and possibly lodge a claim for constructive dismissal.

It is important for the HRM practitioner to note that an employer is liable to defend an allegation of discrimination in the workplace and act upon it even if the employer is not directly responsible for it but where another employee is responsible for the discriminatory behaviour. As some cases in City of London financial institutions demonstrate, it is not sufficient for an employer to argue that racist and sexist behaviour constitutes workplace 'banter' or that they were unaware that such behaviour occurred or that it is not discriminatory because all employees are subject to it.

The main themes that emerge from this part of the chapter centre around three issues, each of which is pertinent to the HRM practitioner. First, statutory protection is updated at parliamentary or EU level and it is essential that HR managers audit and monitor workplace practices and procedures that are likely to be affected by new legislation. Second, workplaces that have proceduralised systems for HRM must be vigilant and act quickly to prevent apparently one-off incidents developing into persistent behaviour consistent with emergent bullying or harassment. Finally, much remains to be done in order to remove discriminatory practices in the workplace, and it is clear that the discrimination agenda gets not only longer but also wider as new areas of activity have been drawn into the scope of existing measures, e.g. the extension of equal pay legislation to cover pension entitlements and before that, in the 1980s, the introduction of the equal value amendments for work of equal value to an employer in terms of skill, effort and decision-making.

Key Controversy

It is argued above that membership of the EU has driven UK anti-discrimination law. Some suggest (Confederation of British Industry, Institute of Directors, Federation of Small Businesses) that the UK 'gold plates' the legislation in a way that disadvantages UK businesses in terms of competition with organisations based within other EU member states. Will withdrawal from the EU improve the situation for employers whilst making it worse for employees?

Termination of the employment contract

Employment contracts can come to an end in a variety of ways, e.g. job redundancy, voluntary resignation, death in service, non-renewal of a fixed-term contract and termination (summary or otherwise) due to conduct – 'the sack'. This part of the chapter examines the issue of termination due to dismissal under the headings of fair dismissal, unfair dismissal, wrongful dismissal and constructive dismissal.

Fair dismissal

The days of 'at will' contracts of employment, when employers could sack people for any or no reason, arguably came to an end with the introduction of the concept of 'unfair dismissal' in the Industrial Relations Act 1971 (IRA). Since then, employers can be required to demonstrate that the termination was for one of the reasons listed in s. 98 of the ERtsA 1996. In general, it is correct to say that to be fair a dismissal must be contractually lawful, that is not in breach of any contractual provision and must also be lawful according to statute. In most situations when an employee is dismissed, the reasons for the dismissal are likely to be fair. An employer can fairly dismiss an employee on several grounds; dismissal is likely to be fair if it relates to the categories shown in Figure 10.2.

- *Employee conduct* (s. 98(2)(b)). Theft or fraud in the workplace, gross insubordination, fighting, etc.
- *Redundancy* (s. 98(2)(c)). Where a job is classed as redundant under s. 139 meaning that the employee is dismissed due to job redundancy through no fault of their own and has been correctly consulted about the situation and fairly selected for redundancy via an agreed process of selection. If an employee has two years of continuous service with the employer, they must be compensated for the redundancy.
- *Capability and qualifications* (s. 98(2)(a)). An employer can fairly dismiss an employee on these grounds but must demonstrate that dismissal relates to job capability, not the employee. For example, to obtain dismissal due to capability on the grounds of illness or disability an employer must demonstrate that they have already made changes to the work situation of an employee and cannot make further changes. Without this evidence the employee may have a claim under the EqA 2010 (s. 6) for disability discrimination. If an employee has falsified their qualifications or if they lose a practitioner qualification, for example, by being struck off the medical register if they are a doctor, dismissal is likely to be fair. If an employee is deemed to be incompetent, it will be necessary to demonstrate this – e.g. that they have been through an internal disciplinary procedure and been given a reasonable opportunity to improve their performance but failed to do so.

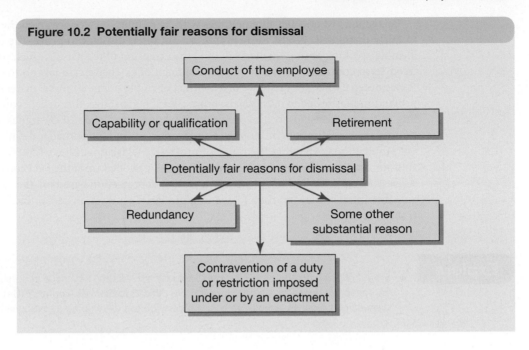

Figure 10.2 Potentially fair reasons for dismissal

- *Contravention of a duty or restriction imposed under or by an enactment* (s. 98(2)(d)). For example, if an employee is a driver or needs to be able to drive to perform their job, the loss of a driving licence is likely to be a fair reason for dismissal. Similarly, if there is another legal requirement that the employee can no longer meet, dismissal is likely to be fair; for example, for deep sea divers there are strict age and time limits due to health and safety considerations. Equally, lorry drivers may have to pass eyesight checks and pilots may have to meet strict health requirements. While dismissals may be fair in some situations, an employer may be expected to offer the employee another job. This is more likely if the firm has a collective bargaining agreement with a trade union.

- *Some other substantial reason* (s. 98(1)(b)). Here an employer must demonstrate, in a case where a dismissal is disputed, that the dismissal, while it does not relate to the categories listed above, is nonetheless fair and reasonable. Often this will be connected to reorganisation, and/or variation of contractual terms (for an example, see *Robinson v. Tescom Corporation* [2008], *Bateman v. ASDA* [2010] and *Lund v. St Edmund's School* [2013]).

Unfair dismissal

As distinct from 'wrongful dismissal', unfair dismissal is a statutory creation based originally in the IRA 1971, and now found within sections 94–132 of the ERtsA 1996. Where an employee believes that they have been dismissed unfairly, they have the right to lodge a claim at an employment tribunal (s. 111) and seek compensation, re-engagement or reinstatement. In order for us to understand the process of presenting a claim, it is possible to break it down into a number of issues and indicate on whom the burden to prove these issues falls:

	Issue	Burden of proof
1	Qualification (an employee with 12 months service)	Employee
2	Dismissal (under ERtsA s. 95)	Employee
3	Reason (under ERtsA s. 98)	Employer
4	Reasonableness (under ERtsA s. 98(4))	Neutral

Source: adapted from Jefferson (1997).

By sections 94 and 108 all employees with 24 months' service are given the right not to be unfairly dismissed. Whilst these points are not often difficult to prove, the development of 'flexible' working arrangements, including the extension of the use of casual, part-time and/or fixed-term contracts, has led to the development of extensive case law on the issue of status. As we noted earlier, the existence of a contract of employment is critical in deciding what legal protection is afforded to individuals. From a legal perspective, this debate concerns the labelling of the relationships for the provision of labour. Freedland (2003) argues that we need to remove the classifications of 'employee and worker' and adopt a broader definition of 'dependent labour', thus extending the range of protective legislation. Njoya (2007) suggests a legal solution based on the concept of property rights developed from the decision of Hawkins J in *Allen v. Flood* [1898], which postulates a regime of protection based on 'the full benefit of the valuable interest they (workers) have in a probable expectation of continuing employment' ([1898] at 16).

The courts have adopted, at various times, both a wide and a narrow interpretation of the concept of status. It was possibly seen at the broadest in *Dacas v. Brook Street Bureau* [2004], in which the Court of Appeal established that a temporary/agency worker could become an employee of the client company, despite a clause in the agreement to the contrary. These relationships can be visualised as 'triangular relationships' (see Figure 10.3).

Whilst these arrangements provide numerical, functional and financial flexibility for the client company (CC), they provide no security for the worker (W). In this model, while there are plenty of contracts floating around, the worker is not regarded as an employee of either of the other parties, because none of these contracts is a contract of employment. These 'temp' workers began to receive some form of protection in the late 1990s as the courts sought to identify an 'umbrella' contract of employment. Using this idea in *McMeechan v. Secretary of State for Employment* [1997] ICR 549 the Court of Appeal determined that, in specific circumstances, there could be two contracts between the worker and the employment business: an 'umbrella contract', referred to as 'being on the books'; and separate contracts for each assignment. They felt the latter was more likely, but that if sufficient assignments were undertaken over a long enough period of time, the 'umbrella contract' would make the worker an employee of the employment business (see also the decision in

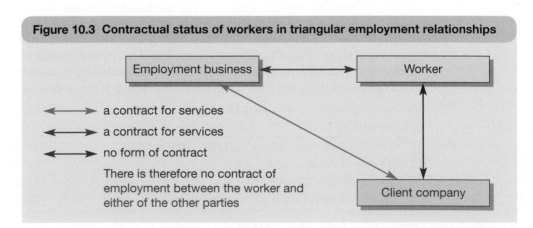

Figure 10.3 Contractual status of workers in triangular employment relationships

Consistent Group Ltd v. Kalwak [2008] IRLR 505). In *Dacas*, on similar facts, they reached the conclusion that the 'umbrella contract' would be with the client company, a decision that presents more acute problems for HR managers in terms of workforce planning and flexibility. The key issue, in both circumstances, appeared to be the length of time the worker had been engaged either as 'on the books' or within a specific client company. This length of service it, was held, creates obligations – notably based around issues of control and payment – for one or other of the organisations in relation to specific workers. The courts have now decided that such an 'umbrella contract' can only be implied where it is *necessary* to give the arrangement business sense (see *James v. London Borough of Greenwich* [2008] IRLR 302). HR managers can at present, therefore, develop flexibility plans which make extensive use of 'temps' without fear that these people will gain employment protection rights in relation to their organisation; that is, pending the next twist in this complex debate. This twist may come in relation to the development of the discussions about 'vulnerable workers' currently in progress and focusing on changes made by the Employment Act 2008 in relation to Employment Businesses and Employment Agencies. BERR (2008) noted that there are some 16,000 agencies making use of between 1.1 and 1.5 million temporary workers, that a larger proportion of the UK workforce (some 5 per cent) engages in temporary employment than in our major EU competitors (an average of 2.25 per cent), that some 225,000 of these workers are regularly on assignments of less than one week, while 55 per cent of engagements are less than 12 weeks. The report suggests that while a cornerstone of the recent achievements in the UK economy has been secured through the application of flexible workers, the vulnerable agency workforce is significantly slanted towards members of the minority ethnic groups. The results of this wide-ranging discussion can be seen in sections 8–18 of the Employment Act 2008, which address issues of minimum wages, enforcement of existing protections, and information-sharing between agencies. Despite these changes, the approach can still be described as 'light touch' in terms of regulation of this sector which reflects a policy towards vulnerable workers that conflicts with any move to provide substantive rights for agency workers or a change in the government's extended opposition to the implementation of the EU Temporary Agency Worker Directive (Wynn, 2009).

A similar story can be told in relation to homeworkers. While the current case law tends to involve textile workers (see *Nethermere of St Neots v. Gardiner* [1984] ICR 612) or assembly workers (see *Airfix Footwear Ltd v. Cope* [1978] ICR 1210), the arguments can be extended to cover casual workers (see *O'Kelly v. Trust House Forte* [1983] ICR 728). Indeed, it is possible to note that the two most litigated issues in the last decade, especially in relation to status, concern 'temps' and 'casual/homeworkers'. For twenty-first-century HR managers, these issues are likely to be more related to individuals using information technology at home as a means of managing work–life balance issues. Removing the work (and hence the worker) away from the normal place of work allows the individual to gain more self-control over pace, timing and organisation of work, and increases the likelihood that the courts will view the relationship as a contract of services rather than of service. The issue of status therefore continues to turn on the implied obligation of mutual trust and confidence (Brodie, 2008). Whether the HR manager is dealing with a casual worker, a homeworker or a temporary worker provided by an employment business, it is arguable that the application of this obligation is consistent with the protection of people's 'dignity, autonomy, respect, status or security' (Oliver, 1999: 86), values upon which the modern (ethical) HR manager would place importance and significance.

Job security in these terms can be defined as the right to have access to remedies for unfair dismissal, wrongful dismissal, discrimination and harassment, As Deakin and Morris (2012) suggest '[t]he key to the meaning of employment security is the existence of some form of regulatory intervention designed to protect workers against arbitrary managerial decisions' (p. 338). Despite pressure from various interest groups and trade unions, such protection within UK law is hard to identify, leaving much of the responsibility for ensuring this vulnerable section of the workforce enjoy the dignity, respect, and security afforded other workers in the hands of business leaders, a particular challenge for CIPD-qualified, ethical HR managers.

Having demonstrated that the individual is qualified to make a claim, the next issue is whether or not there was actually a dismissal. Section 95(1) (ERtsA 1996) lists three situations in which a dismissal will be deemed to have occurred:

- The contract under which he is employed is terminated by the employer (whether with or without notice).

- He is employed under a limited-term contract and that contract terminates by virtue of the limiting event without being renewed under the same contract.

- The employee terminates the contract under which he is employed (with or without notice) in circumstances in which he is entitled to terminate it without notice by reason of the employer's conduct.

Where the employer has followed a dismissal procedure, a redundancy procedure, or formally written to the employee stating the contract is terminated, proof that the situation meets the requirements of sub-section (1)(a) is not difficult. In many cases the same can be said of sub-section (1)(b). The final definition relates to what is commonly referred to as 'constructive dismissal' and poses many more difficulties. In these situations the employee has to show that the employer's behaviour was such as to amount to a 'repudiation' of the contract – put simply that the employer no longer intends to be bound by the terms of the contract. There is extensive case law on this issue, which is founded on the decision in *Western Excavating (ECC) Ltd v. Sharp* [1978] IRLR 27. In order for an employee to be able to mount a successful claim for constructive dismissal, four circumstances must be proved (these are adapted from *Harvey on Industrial Relations and the Law* Vol. 1 section D1@ [403]):

- There must be a breach of contract by the employer.

- That breach must be sufficiently important to justify the employee resigning, or else it must be the last in a series of incidents which justify his leaving.

- The employee must leave in response to the breach and not for some other, unconnected reason.

- The employee must not delay too long in terminating the contract in response to the employer's breach; otherwise he may be deemed to have waived the breach.

It is clear, therefore, that it is insufficient for the employee to terminate the contract because the employer has acted unreasonably; the conduct needs to be a breach of a fundamental term of the contract of employment. Unless the individual can demonstrate that there has been a breach of the fundamental terms of the contract, he or she is unlikely to succeed with a claim for unfair constructive dismissal.

Attention then turns to the stated reason for the dismissal, which, in order to be potentially fair, has to be one of the reasons detailed in the preceding section on 'fair dismissal'. In many cases, this is not at issue, as the employer will have stated in the letter of termination what the reason was, or the employee will have indicated the reason for his resignation on the claim form. The tribunal must then decide whether the employer acted reasonably or not in treating the reason as a sufficient cause for dismissal. However, as pointed out earlier in the chapter, many aspects of employment law turn on questions of interpretation and the reasonableness of a particular interpretation. So while an employer may deem a dismissal fair, an employee may disagree. If the details of a particular case do not meet the criteria for a potentially fair dismissal then the dismissal is unfair. In some circumstances, a reason for dismissal may be fair yet the dismissal may have been conducted in an unfair manner, i.e. a dismissal may be *procedurally unfair*. Hence, if there are internal procedures that should be followed that relate to grievance and discipline in the workplace, it is vital that an employer follows these procedures and is further able to demonstrate to the employee, their representatives and a tribunal that they have done so.

Unfair dismissals that relate to discriminatory behaviour, including those for unequal pay and those that relate to pregnancy, are automatically unfair and remedies are available to employees as day one rights. Other situations where no length of service is necessary to claim unfair dismissal include those that relate to trade union membership, participation in lawful industrial action that lasted less than eight weeks, participation as an employee representative for purposes of consultation (where there is no trade union presence), refusal to work on grounds of health and safety or where an employee seeks to assert a statutory right.

Wrongful dismissal

A wrongful dismissal is a dismissal that is in breach of contract, e.g. dismissal without notice or a failure to pay all due wages and remuneration during the notice period. It is settled law that the damages awarded for wrongful dismissal are the amount equivalent to that which would have been due in wages, together with the value of any fringe benefits, during the period between actual termination and when the contract could have been lawfully terminated (see *Silvey v. Pendragon plc* [2001] IRLR 685).

Constructive dismissal

As indicated earlier, claims for constructive dismissal are risky because an employee has to satisfy a tribunal that they had no alternative but to leave and in the majority of cases it is unlikely that the employee will get their job back.

Redundancy rights

Under current legislation – sections 105 and 162–170 ERtsA 1996 – employees require two years of continuous service in a particular employment to qualify for a lump sum compensation award. Such compensatory awards are detailed within the statutory provision in relation to age and years of service on the effective date of termination (EDT). For each complete year of service under the age of 22, they will receive half a week's pay. This increases to one week's pay for each completed year of service during which the employee was aged between 22 and 41 and rises to one and a half week's pay for each completed year of service during which the employee was over the age of 41. Redundancy payments and unfair dismissal compensation are unaffected by the number of hours an employee works, but the statutory limit for one week's pay currently is £450, only the best 20 years of service count, the basic award is capped at £13,500 and redundancy payments up to the value of £30,000 are tax-free. An employer must make the payment as soon as the employee is dismissed.

Employers are required to consult the workforce about redundancy and, where a trade union is recognised, it must be consulted in specific circumstances. In non-union workplaces, employers must establish a representative body of the workforce to consult over redundancy, e.g. multinational corporations may use existing European Works Councils for this purpose. The employer must consult with the consultative body or the trade union, giving information as to the reasons for redundancy, the numbers involved, mechanisms to minimise the numbers affected, the grades of job affected, the method of determining which jobs are redundant and how any payments that supplement the statutory requirements are to be worked out. If an employer has collective bargaining, it is likely that there will be an established redundancy procedure negotiated with the trade union. Whilst there is a statutory period for consultation that relates to the number of jobs being made redundant, the timing of these consultations is often a matter of dispute. The statute [Trade Union and Labour Relations (Consolidation) Act 1992 ss 188–196 – TULR(C)A] provides that if over 100 jobs are made redundant from an establishment within the period of 90 days, the employer must consult over a 45-day period, but only 30 days of consultation are necessary where the number of job redundancies is fewer than 100. Throughout the consultation period, an employer must seek alternatives to job redundancy and act in good faith. Both these issues are controversial. Many trade unions argue that it is easier to dismiss British employees than employees in other EU nations, because consultation occurs once the decision to make jobs redundant is taken rather than before the decision is made, as is required by law in most other EU nations.

Box 10.1	Unfair dismissal?

Zeena has worked for the organisation for many years and is seen as a good employee. Her line manager, Yvonne, received information that she was giving 'staff discount' to members of her family not covered by the agreement between the company and the staff association. When Yvonne spoke to Zeena about this, she admitted that she has done this on more than one occasion. Yvonne dismissed her with immediate effect. Yvonne has also recently dismissed Wallace who, following a road traffic accident, had been off sick. He is expected to make a complete recovery, but Yvonne decided they could wait no longer for his return.

Wallace is complaining bitterly and threatening legal action because he feels he should have been allowed to have a friend with him to plead his case in the meeting with Yvonne, in which he was told he was to be dismissed, and besides, Yvonne should not have acted without a medical report. Whilst Zeena claims she was unfairly dismissed.

Questions

1 Based on what you have read, do you think either claim would be successful?

2 Why have you arrived at this conclusion?

You should now attempt the problem above (Box 10.1) in order to test your understanding of the key principles discussed in the previous section.

The first section of the chapter has considered the detailed nature of the contract, including the use and effectiveness of both express and implied terms. This part of the chapter has illustrated how employers can fairly dismiss employees and how employees can respond by making a claim to an employment tribunal. The next section examines the issues that relate to the enforcement of employee rights in the employment relationship.

Enforcement of contractual and statutory employment rights

For the vast majority of employees, enforcement of employment rights is not an issue. Good employers, large and small, ensure that employment contracts reflect existing and new employment rights. In general, larger employers are likely to have a dedicated HRM function to do this and in some cases they are likely to recognise trade unions for the purposes of individual and collective representation. This union presence is likely to ensure that terms and conditions of employment and internal procedures reflect employee rights, be they contractual or statutory. However, some employers do seek to short-change employees by withholding certain rights, such as the minimum wage, or subjecting employees to arbitrary and unreasonable treatment.

If employees feel that a contractual or statutory employment right is absent, incorrectly proceduralised or not enforced, they have three main options. Discussion of the situation with a supervisor, line manager or the HRM advisor may result in corrective action. Alternatively, an employee can raise their grievance through their trade union representative or other employee representative. Lastly, and more often in cases of alleged unfair dismissal, an employee can instigate proceedings against their employer or former employer by making an application to an employment tribunal. In many cases, such an application may be sufficient to persuade the employer that they need to take corrective action. However, some cases will go to tribunal either because the dispute cannot be settled in any other way due to employer intransigence

Table 10.2 Data source: The Employment Tribunals and Employment Appeals Tribunals Fees Order 2013

Fee type	Issue fee	Hearing fee	Total
Type A	£160	£230	£390
Type B	£250	£950	£1,200

Source: http://www.legislation.gov.uk/ukdsi/2013/9780111538654.

or because an employer feels the case must be defended because of its future implications for themselves and other similar employers.

Employment tribunals are now long established and operate as specialist employment 'courts'. Tribunals are meant to be less formal than other courts, but over the years they have become increasingly legalistic and much more time-consuming, particularly in situations where a test case is being heard. Virtually all claims in relation to the employment relationship are heard in tribunals; however, some claims for wrongful, constructive and unfair dismissals that involve a breach of contract may be heard in civil courts.

The following discussion relates to the existing situation, and in the next section ('Current issues') we will highlight the plans to change the system from 2014. To begin an application to a tribunal, an employee or former employee must complete an application form ET1 within the time limit specified for the particular jurisdiction covering the event they intend to complain about (see Mansfield *et al.,* 2012 for a detailed list of time limits). The ET1 will contain details of the employee's claim and the remedy they are seeking – reinstatement, re-engagement or compensation. Along with the form the claimant is required to send an issue fee in line with Table 10.2.

Type A cases are those relating to 'small' sums of compensation or straightforward claims such as unlawful deduction from wages, holiday or notice pay disputes, etc. The more common jurisdictions – unfair dismissal, discrimination, equal pay and redundancy pay, etc. – will be classed as 'type B' claims and therefore attract the higher charging band. The Enterprise and Regulatory Reform Act (2013) introduces further changes with the removal of case manage ment decision meetings and pre-hearing reviews. These will be replaced by a single preliminary hearing, which will have more powers to strike out claims seen to have little prospect of success and impose deposit orders of up to the new limit of £1,000. More cases will be decided by an employment judge sitting alone (this does not apply to discrimination cases), and there will be a more stringent 'paper sift' in order to exclude 'weak' cases and a new regime of penalties that can be imposed on employers who defend cases with little prospect of success. The tribunal service will send the ET1 and an ET2 to the employer or former employer; the ET2 summonses the employer to appear before the tribunal. The employer must also complete an ET3, stating their side of the case, and return it to the tribunal service within 28 days of the date it was sent to them.

In 2012, the number of tribunal applications stood at 186,300 (Employment Tribunals Service, 2013). Whilst changes are spread across a number of jurisdictional areas, notable increases were seen in the areas of Transfer of Undertakings (Protection of Employment) Regulations (TUPE) and discrimination on the grounds of religion or belief. These changes seem difficult to stop because, as employers and government address one area, other areas increase. Employers continually claim that many of these applications are frivolous or vexatious. It is too early to say if the introduction of costs of up to £20,000 for making and losing will have a long-term effect; the median amount awarded as costs in 2012 was £5, the average was £1,292, and the highest was £36,466.

The statutory award for unfair dismissal is made up of two components. First, the basic award of up to £450 for each year of completed employment (making a maximum of $30 \times 450 = £13,500$) and, secondly, the compensatory award of up to a maximum of £74,200 (making a maximum combined award of £87,700). However, in cases that relate to discrimination, there is no upper limit on tribunal awards. For example, the average and highest awards in 2011/12 were as follows:

Jurisdiction	Highest	Average
Race discrimination	£4,445,023	£102,259
Sex discrimination	£89,700	£9,940
Disability discrimination	£390,871	£22,183
Religious discrimination	£59,522	£16,725
Sexual orientation	£27,473	£14,623
Age discrimination	£144,100	£19,327
Unfair dismissal	£173,408	£9,133

Source: Employment Tribunal Service Annual Report (20/09/2012).

While the maximum compensation awards may seem large, the table shows that the average award is much lower in the majority of cases. In 2011–12, only 60 unfair dismissal cases saw awards above £50,000, while 148 saw awards below £500, and over 1,500 were awarded less than £4,000; equally, in most cases former employees do not get their job back. The figures show that some 80 per cent of unfair dismissal claims never reach the tribunal – being either conciliated or withdrawn prior to the hearing – and of those that get to the tribunal only 10 per cent are successful. In those cases, compensation, as opposed to re-employment or re-engagement, is the preferred remedy of most tribunals. Tribunals are not, it would appear, the easy 'lottery win' for those who make a claim.

There is, in addition to these arguments, evidence that employers, and small employers in particular, lack confidence on the issue of employee rights. Arrowsmith *et al.* (2003), in a survey of small and medium-sized enterprises (SMEs), found that despite the growth of legislation, the impact on this sector appears relatively small. They wonder whether this is a result of lack of awareness rather than lack of impact. It is arguable that no better example of 'arbitrary managerial decisions' (Deakin and Morris, 2005) can be found than in the areas of grievance, discipline and dismissal. Despite extensive case law, this area remains one of the largest single areas of dispute and tribunal workload. Placing more emphasis on internal resolution enhances the role and duties of the HR function in handling disputes within the workplace.

What is missing is a realisation that discipline and grievance may represent a form of reactive conflict that stems primarily from the deteriorated state of the relationship between the parties (Lewin, 1999) and that workplace conflict resolution mechanisms need to address the imbalance of power within organisations. What appears to have been created by regulation is a 'new era in unfair dismissal law in which "economy prosperity" dominates "social justice" to a degree not seen before' (Sanders, 2009: 32).

Explore

For the CIPD-qualified, ethical HR manager, the challenge will be to implement and apply internal mechanisms that meet the organisation's business needs whilst retaining the dignity, respect and security required by employees.

- What policy options are available in this quest and what additional training will HR managers require to achieve the stated goal?

The evidence suggests that employers' claims of 'excessive red tape' and the burden of defending unnecessary tribunal applications are not proven. Many employees are denied the opportunity to go through internal grievance procedures, because of either fear of reprisals or the non-existence of clear procedures. Equally, the growth in employment rights caught some employers – good and bad – off guard, particularly in the area of unfair dismissal. Employer perception of red tape and the cost of defending at a tribunal must be measured against better regulation of the employment relationship and the need for improved best practice. While the majority of applications to tribunals to enforce employee rights are settled on a voluntary basis and withdrawn, the growth in the number of applications demonstrates the absence of best practice in many areas of employment. Lastly, the argument that a 'compensation culture' is emerging that is likely to damage the competitiveness of British industry is a very doubtful one, because if employees win a case at tribunal, it demonstrates that their rights were in some way infringed. Alternatively, if an employer settles a claim or takes corrective action in the workplace, this demonstrates that not all procedures were adequate. Furthermore, the actions of some employers in recent cases undermine claims of bureaucracy, red tape and time wasted in having to defend applications to employment tribunals. Applications to tribunals that are withdrawn or settled voluntarily may have been settled 'out of court' by employers.

While the growth of out-of-court settlements does undermine employers' claims of red tape and excessive costs in employment regulation, there are three specific problems with them in respect to the enforcement of employment rights. First, out-of-court settlements often prevent full disclosure of the facts and, while a former employee may be generously compensated, the provisions of a settlement usually remain confidential. Secondly, withdrawing a claim and settling out of court often enables employers to deny the charges made against them and, more importantly, prevents the creation of what might be a reference point – a precedent for future cases. Thirdly, an employer that settles a case out of court but denies the basis of the claim may fail to improve HRM procedures – a measure often enforced by tribunals or the Equalities and Human Rights Commission.

In summary, a well-resourced HRM function staffed by CIPD-qualified practitioners is one route to employer best practice in the area of employment rights; trade union recognition is another, and the latter is likely to lead to negotiation and partnership in the management of employee rights. Both routes are likely to become more fruitful for employers, bearing in mind the likelihood of further growth in employee rights and the medium- to longer-term impact of the membership of the EU.

Current issues

In September 2012 the Department for Business, Innovation and Skills issued a press release that set out plans to 'give firms more flexibility and confidence in managing their workforce and to reduce employment law red tape' (BIS, 2012). The plans included support for settlement agreements to end employment relationships in a consensual way, to limit compensation claims for unfair dismissal, to streamline employment tribunals, to change elements of the TUPE regulations and to improve the ACAS code of practice on discipline and grievance to consider small business more appropriately. As noted earlier, some of the streamlining of employment tribunals has been achieved and, as I write, many of the other areas are either timetabled to start in 2013 or scheduled for 2014. We have recently seen the publication of a wide range of legislation in the area of employment law and interesting developments in the application of principles surrounding 'contractual relationships' and 'some other substantial reason' (SOSR) dismissals. All this said, the general view is that the UK has one of the most lightly regulated, flexible labour markets in the OECD, behind only the USA and Canada (Scarpetta, 2013). In this section, we consider these developments and try to draw out the implications for human resource managers.

The Enterprise and Regulatory Reform Act 2013

A central plank of government plans to streamline employment tribunals is the proposal to introduce Early Conciliation in 2014. Facilitated by ACAS, the system is designed to give individuals and employers the opportunity to 'talk things through' before a tribunal claim is issued. The system will operate by requiring the individual to obtain a uniquely numbered certificate from ACAS before they can issue a claim that will be accepted by the tribunal office. Simply, the process will be as follows; the individual will contact ACAS using a simple electronic form that merely includes details of their name, address and contact details. ACAS will contact the individual within 24 hours, seeking further details, confirming they wish them to contact the employer and arranging for further contact. Interestingly, if they decline to have discussions with their employer, ACAS will simply issue the numbered certificate and things will progress as normal towards the tribunal. Where there is agreement, the ACAS conciliation officer will contact the employer and seek an agreement/settlement between the parties, meaning that no tribunal claim is issued, no fee is payable and both parties save the cost of solicitors. The regulations proposed envisage that once contact is made with ACAS, the 'time limitation' clock will stop, allowing time for the discussions to take place without the pressure of the limitation period being used. In conjunction with this, we should also note that there will be a process of remission of fees based on the traditional civil court system, which exempts individuals in receipt of specific benefits – one of which is Jobseekers' Allowance. The government is already looking at how this will apply to the regime of universal credits.

In terms of the role of HR managers, this will add a new dimension, or increase an existing role, especially for generalists in small/medium-sized organisations. ACAS will deal directly with the organisation rather than, as at present, with the legal representatives. It can therefore be seen to build on the preference to pursue enterprise-confined mediation and remove the need for solicitors to be contacted. In some ways, it can be seen to extend and supplement the idea of confidential negotiations before termination (discussed later in this chapter).

The Act inserts a new sub-section into s. 108 of the ERA 1996, making dismissal for political opinions or affiliation unfair as a day one right by removing the requirement for two years' service to dismissals where the principal reason for dismissal relates to political opinion or affiliation. This change simply brings us into line with other OECD and EU states making political freedom a day one protected right.

A further attempt to increase flexibility in the labour market is found with the introduction of new rules concerning the confidentiality of negotiations before termination – what have been termed 'settlement agreements'. Unlike compromise agreements, these agreements can be put in place where there is no existing dispute and may even come 'out of the blue' for the employee. The employer may write to the employee indicating that they wish to discuss an issue (e.g. performance, capability, attendance) and include within the letter terms upon which they are prepared to agree to the termination of the employment. Such letters cannot be submitted to tribunals as evidence in unfair dismissal claims, unless the employee can demonstrate that the decision to offer such an agreement was tainted by discrimination or covered by any other 'automatically unfair dismissal' regulation. The legislation also allows such attempts by the employer to be admissible 'to the extent that the tribunal considers just' [s. 111A(4)] if it was connected with improper behaviour or placing undue pressure on the individual. The ACAS draft code of practice indicates such behaviour will include: all forms of harassment, physical assault, victimisation, failure to allow at least seven working days to consider an offer (including changing the terms of the offer during that period) and telling an employee that, if the offer is rejected, they will be dismissed before any form of disciplinary action process has begun. These agreements differ also in that they do not need the protection of the 'without prejudice' rules, which will continue to apply to standard compromise agreements where there is already a dispute between the parties.

That these conversations have been variously described as 'grown up' or 'brutal' by commentators gives some indication of the division amongst practitioners and academic observers. For the HR manager it will mean a keener eye needs to be trained on line management and employee performance in order to make effective (fair) use of the new mechanisms.

Key Controversy

The description of these agreements as 'brutal' suggests that this new law will make employment more precarious for many employees, although it may make the efficient removal of older or less productive workers easier for businesses and so encourage them to recruit their first and subsequent employees, creating more jobs for workers.

On balance, considering existing legal provision and the current economic climate, do the advantages suggested outweigh the disadvantages for both parties?

The Growth and Infrastructure Bill 2013

An even more controversial development concerns the plans to introduce a new 'status' to the world of business. Section 27 of the Growth and Infrastructure Bill creates the possibility of employee shareholders. These are individuals who, in return for the issue or allotment of a minimum amount of shares (£2,000), would agree with the organisation to accept the status of employee shareholders. In so doing, they also agree to surrender rights to claim unfair dismissal (excepting in the case of discrimination), the right to claim a statutory redundancy payment, the right to request flexible working and, rather bizarrely, a change in maternity rights requiring 16 rather than eight weeks' notice if there is a wish to return early. Having twice been rejected by the House of Lords, the government eventually secured support by including a requirement that the individual must have taken 'professional advice' before entering such an agreement for it to be valid. There is, as I write, no clear guidance on what will/ should happen in a number of possible situations – e.g., in the case of transfers by the sale of shares, the resale value upon termination of employment, whether they are equity shares, voting shares, dividend-bearing shares, or all three. Guidance has been given that if the employee can trade the shares (either during employment or at the termination of employment), the first £50,000 profit will be free from capital gains tax, which could be useful if it was clear the individual would be able to sell the shares and we knew how the shares would be valued at both issue and resale.

For the HR manager, this simply adds another form for the purchase of labour and complicates discipline, grievance and performance issues, whilst apparently adding little to the ability to manage discontent. Further, whilst such employee shareholders may seem an easier group within which to develop engagement initiatives and indicate a greater willingness to accept change processes, we can also argue a greater cost to manage the process in terms of initial setup costs and ongoing communication to new group of stakeholders.

Contractual rights and wrongs?

In 1990, Denham (1990: 96) stated: 'The judicial deference to managerial prerogative is most apparent with respect to decisions in cases relating to dismissal for some other substantial reasons'. Nearly 25 years after Denham presented this argument the tribunals and courts show no indication of any softening in their position. In recent cases, including *Bateman and Ors v. ASDA Stores* [2010], the courts have continued to adopt an unquestioning approach to dismissals or unilateral variations in terms of employment where the business claims an economic, technical or organisational reason for the dismissal. These arguments are so wide as to catch all reasons for managerial decisions, and the courts decline the opportunity to examine the economic, technical or organisational imperatives claimed by management for their actions. As Denham goes on to assert, the courts provide ideological support by allowing fuzziness in the delineation of business needs. These principles are seen in action in two more recent cases, *Summers v. Handshake* [2013] and *Lund v. St Edmund's School* [2013]. While the EAT overturned the initial decision in each case, we can speculate how many individuals will be able to afford to pursue the matter to appeal in the new era of fees at both levels – the total cost to go to an EAT hearing will be £2,800. HR managers may be more confident, then, that in reorganisation, dismissal/demotions, where meagre business reasons need to be demonstrated, will be protected and managerial prerogative is likely to remain unchallenged.

Over recent years, the issue of employment status has been seen in tribunals to turn on the issue of mutuality of obligations. This trend continued in *Autoclenz Ltd v. Belcher* [2012], where the court looked at the obligations/terms of the contract and decided that the two were contradictory. They found that terms inserted making the individuals 'self-employed' contractors ran counter to the reality of the relationship, and that therefore there was a mutuality of obligation and the relevant terms were a 'sham'. Following that, in *StringfellowsRestaraunt v. Quashie* [2013], it was held that despite the lap-dancers being subject to a rota controlled by the organisation there was insufficient mutuality to create a contract of employment. In general, both cases merely add to an already developed body of law regarding employment status. More interesting is the rediscovery and application to employment relationships of the traditional common law contract principle of 'intention to create legal relationships'. In *Methodist Conference v. Preston* [2013], the courts were asked to decide whether a Methodist minister could, despite the spiritual nature of their calling, be an employee for the purposes of unfair dismissal. The answer, in the Supreme Court, was a resounding no, the reasoning given being that the parties did not have, when entering into the agreement, an intention to create a legally binding contract of employment. For HR managers, this opens another avenue for a defence against temporary, part-time or agency workers who wish to claim employee status, making it clear that there is not the requisite intention to create a legal relationship.

Finally in this section, we consider the thorny issue of the growth in the use of social media within and outside working time. It should go without qualification that all organisations ought to have a clear policy on the use and content of social media postings applicable to all employees. The courts have questioned whether Articles 8–10 of Schedule 1 of the Human Rights Act 1998 are engaged in relation to the use of social media and, having in general found it a difficult area, have fallen back on contract law principles. In this respect, a policy that is clear and has been communicated to all staff will be considered to fall under the heading of either a lawful instruction or part of the duty implied into all contracts of employment of fidelity. The lesson for HR managers is to make sure the organisation has a clear policy that is sufficiently robust, protects brand reputation and is unequivocal in setting out the punishments for failure to follow the rules.

Key Controversy

Should employers have the right to control what their employees' contributions to social media contain, even when these contributions are added outside working hours, using personal equipment from their own home? Consider your response to the preceding discussion relating to the Human Rights Act 1998. Should 'brand management' outweigh personal freedom of speech and expression?

Concluding comments

While many see the employment relationship as a private exchange between an employer and an employee, they are actually subject to significant contractual and statutory regulation. All employees have a contract of employment and some measure of statutory protection against unfair and unreasonable treatment by an employer. Whilst the period between 1997 and 2010 saw the contractual and statutory regulation of the employment relationship tightened, this is being eroded by recent legislation and the drive to develop the benefits of a flexible labour market. As a result of this, employees have less protection than was previously the case. This creates the need for improved vigilance from employees in terms of their performance, both within and outside the workplace, and for employers it reinforces the need in all areas of employment for an effective HRM function. In large and small employers, an HRM function staffed by CIPD-qualified, ethical, professionals is likely to increase employer confidence in the deregulation of employment and may help to avoid the infringement of employee rights. Equally, trade unions have a role to play in the enforcement of employee rights at work through collective bargaining. This is the case because, although there was a significant growth in statutory protection for individual employees between 1997 and 2010, a question remains about its effectiveness and durability. The growth in the number of applications to employment tribunals illustrates that the application of best-practice principles in the regulation of the employment relationship is far from universal. Similarly, the continued search for labour market flexibility, as demonstrated by the UK's idiosyncratic application of the Working Time Directive and the weakness in the framework for applications for flexible working, may infringe the employment rights of some workers but go unnoticed. Therefore, there is an issue of how to enforce recent changes to individual employment rights. Notwithstanding the drive for flexibility, specifically as identified by three features of a growth in non-standard employment, a decline in job tenure and a decline in union density (Stone, 2013: 366), the dignity and respect rightly desired by workers, alongside the need for employment security, mean that legislation must seek to establish enforceable rights and safeguards for both parties to the employment relationship. Indeed, as Standing (2011) notes, a key issue for employers is that 'Policies promoting labour flexibility erode processes of relational and peer-group interaction that are vital for reproducing skills and constructive attitudes to work' (p. 23) – both being key aims for HR managers and areas where they look for support from legal regulation.

If, as many employers assert, employees are the most valued assets within an organisation, fair and reasonable treatment consistent with contractual and statutory rights regulated on an individual basis is one measure of good employment practice. Moreover, the voluntary enforcement of employee rights by employers demonstrates the 'good employer' ethos – best practice in the regulation of the employment relationship. Employees who receive fair and reasonable treatment in the employment relationship are more likely to be retained by an employer, better motivated, more committed and deliver higher productivity than those employees who are not. As this chapter demonstrates, employee rights are extensive but not prohibitive in terms of coverage or the 'red tape' they create. Reasonable treatment requires regulation and enforcement. The evidence suggests that what some employers term 'red tape' actually results from problems created when unreasonable treatment occurs – i.e. when employers deviate from the good employer ethos and fail to follow best-practice procedures.

Summary

This chapter examined the employment relationship and its regulation through the contract of employment under four key themes. It then examined some of the 'hot topics/current issues' within the legal regulation of the employment relationship and sought to link them to contemporary HR practice.

Formation
Distinguishing contractual and statutory employment rights
- All employees have a contract of employment.
- All employees are protected by some statutory rights – these include day one rights and other rights that require some qualifying length of service.

The contract of employment

- Employment contracts are contracts of personal service between an employer and an employee.
- Employment contracts are based on the theory of market individualism, where individuals are seen as rational and self-interested.
- Employment contracts are subject to the common law.
- There are different types of employment contract.
- Employment contracts contain express, implied and statutory incorporated terms and conditions.

Continuation

Discrimination in employment

- Discrimination remains a persistent feature of the employment relationship.
- Some types of 'discrimination' remain lawful.

Termination

Termination of the employment contract

- Employees can be fairly, unfairly, wrongfully or constructively dismissed.
- Dismissals may be fair and potentially fair, otherwise they are unfair.

Enforcement of contractual and statutory employment rights

- Most employees are treated fairly.
- If employees are treated unreasonably or unfairly, they can complain to an employment tribunal.
- Tribunals, HRM departments, the Commission for Equality and Human Rights, and trade unions play a role in enforcing employment rights.

Current issues

- The development of a flexible workforce generated a long-standing debate between the rights of employers and the security of employment desired by employees.
- The changes in the legislation relating to settlement agreements, tribunal fees and employee shareholders.
- Further employment rights are constantly in the process of development and introduction, meaning that an understanding of the basic provisions becomes more important for a CIPD-qualified, ethical HR manager.

Questions

1 Look again at the introductory chapter case study. Is Ms Billingham an employee?
2 How can the ability of employers to make 'unilateral' changes to employment contracts be justified?
3 Should 'zero-hours' contracts be acceptable in the twenty-first century? Justify your response.
4 Do the unfair dismissal rules actually prevent unfair dismissal, or can they be seen more as part of the 'symbolism' of employment law?
5 Do the recent changes make life easier or more difficult for CIPD-qualified, ethically minded HR practitioners? Justify your response.

Case study

Age discrimination more widespread than sexism in the City

Age discrimination is now seen as a more widespread problem in the City than sex discrimination, a survey of more than 1,600 finance sector workers has found. While more than one-third of City employees said their employer was 'very committed' to gender diversity, less than a quarter felt the company was similarly committed to fighting age discrimination. The research also confirmed that problems over discrimination and lack of commitment to diversity were most likely to arise in areas such as trading and sales rather than within the middle or back office functions. 'The City is getting far better at supporting and developing female staff,' said Mark Cameron, chief operating officer at Astbury Marsden, a financial services recruiter, which carried out the survey. He added: 'The huge effort that London's financial services sector has made to broaden its workforce is clearly reflected in positive feedback we have had from employees.'

But while sex discrimination was on the decrease, negative attitudes towards co-workers on the basis of age and a lack of commitment to age diversity was seen as a wider problem. Mr Cameron said: 'We aren't saying that the negative consequences of age discrimination are bigger than other forms of discrimination, just that employees see it as more prevalent. They also see age diversity as something employers are not particularly focused on.'

The default retirement age, under which employers could force workers to retire at 65, was phased out in 2011. But Mr Cameron said that as with racial and gender diversity, it often took years for attitudes to change, and this seemed to be the case with age discrimination. 'With people likely to have longer working lives in the coming years, this is an issue that is going to become increasingly important,' he added.

Despite the findings, sex discrimination cases are still occurring. This year Latifa Bouabdillah, an investment banker, claimed sexual discrimination and unfair dismissal against Commerzbank at London Central employment tribunal. She had resigned from Deutsche Bank in 2011 and sued for £1m, claiming that men were promoted ahead of her and received bonuses up to three times larger. She moved to Commerzbank but alleged she was sacked when

her bosses found out about the Deutsche claim. Ms Bouabdillah told the tribunal she kept her Deutsche case secret because she feared Commerzbank would not offer her the £150,000-a-year role in its exotic vanilla funds team if it knew. Commerzbank said Ms Bouabdillah had made misleading statements on her application form and during interviews.

[The tribunal concluded: 'We find that the reason for the respondent's decision to dismiss the claimant was that she had brought tribunal proceedings. The respondent denies this and says that it was her failure to disclose the proceedings rather than the fact she had taken them which was the reason. We reject this. We do not accept that she misled the respondents at any stage. When asked direct questions she gave direct answers. They may not have been entirely full answers but that is not a matter of misleading or being dishonest. Had the respondent probed deeper, the claimant would have then had to decide whether to answer the more detailed questions or not, but failure to answer questions that were not asked does not in our view amount to a lack of honesty or trust' (Bouabdillah v. Commerzbank [2013]).]

Courts have faced many sex discrimination cases. Three years ago Oksana Denysenko won £1.5m damages from Credit Suisse after being made redundant when she returned from maternity leave. In 2010 Gill Switalski, a corporate lawyer, accepted a secret settlement worth millions after seeking a record £19m from F&C Asset Management over claims of sexist bullying.

Nearly half of employers would like the default retirement age reinstated, according to a survey of 300 employers by Eversheds, the law firm. It said fewer than 3 per cent of organisations now had a policy of mandatory retirement for their employees, down from 69 per cent two years ago. More than half said repeal of the DRA has led to an increase in the number of employees staying on beyond age 65 or normal pension age.

Prof Owen Warnock, Eversheds partner, said the end of the DRA had provided the impetus for change: 72 per cent of respondents said they would still be operating a mandatory retirement age if the law had

Case study continued

not been changed. A third felt the abolition had had a negative impact, but another third said the change had resulted in improvements in retaining important skills and knowledge.

'What's more, the much-feared increased in age-related retirement claims, has not, according to the survey respondents, in fact materialised,' he said.

 Source: Groom, B. (2013) Ageism more widespread than sexism, *Financial Times*, 31 March. Http://www.ft.com/cms/s/0/8a17e304-97d7-11e2-97e0-00144feabdc0.html?siteedition=uk#axzz30xwYk5hu
© The Financial Times Limited 2013. All Rights Reserved.

Questions

1 Compensation in age-discrimination cases is considerably lower than in other areas of discrimination. Why do you think this is so?

2 Considering your organisation (or one with which you are familiar), do you think age-discrimination is a major issue? What action is the organisation taking to address the issue?

3 Should the government permit organisations to reintroduce a default retirement age for their workers?

4 Mark Cameron comments, 'The City is getting far better at supporting and developing female staff.' To what extent do you think this is true for organisations in other sectors? Give examples.

5 Anti-sex discrimination legislation has been in place since the mid-1970s. Consider why sex discrimination cases such as Bouabdillah v. Commerzbank [2013] still arise. Can the law alone eradicate the problem of sexism in the workplace? Similarly, how optimistic are you that the law can successfully eliminate ageism at work?

References and further reading

Those texts marked with an asterisk are recommended for further reading.

*Anderman, S. (2000) *Labour Law, Management Decisions and Worker Rights*. London: Butterworths.

*Armstrong, P. and Baron, A. (1995) *The Job Evaluation Handbook*. London: CIPD.

Arrowsmith, J., Gilman, M., Edwards, P. and Ram, M. (2003) 'The impact of the national minimum wage on small firms', *British Journal of Industrial Relations*, 41, 3: 435–56.

Arthurs, H. (2011) 'Labour law after labour' in G. Davidov and B. Langille (eds) *The Idea of Labour Law*. Oxford: Oxford University Press, pp. 13–29.

Atiyah, P.S. (1979) *The Rise and Fall of Freedom of Contract*. Oxford: Oxford University Press.

*Barmes, L. (2007) 'Common law implied terms and behavioural standards at work', *Industrial Law Journal*, 36, 1: 35–47.

Benhabib, S. (1994) 'Democracy and difference: reflections on the metapolitics of Lyotard and Derrida', *Journal of Political Philosphy*, 2, 1: 1–23.

Bercusson, B. and Estlund, C. (2008) *Regulating Labour in the Wake of Globalisation: New Challenges, New Institutions*. Oxford: Hart Publishing.

BERR (2008) *Agency Working in the UK: A Review of the Evidence*. BERR.

BIS (2012) *New Proposals to Streamline Employment Law*, Press Release, September 14. Online: https://www.gov.uk/government/news/new-proposals-to-streamline-employment-law-will-boost-business (accessed January 2014).

*Blackburn, R. and Hart, M. (2002) *Small Firms' Awareness and Knowledge of Individual Employment Rights*. DTI Employment Relations Research Series No. 14.

Blanpain, R. and Weiss, M. (eds) (2003) *Changing Industrial Relations and Modernisation of Labour Law: Liber Amicorum in Honour of Professor Marco Biagi*. The Hague: Kluwer Law International.

*Braucher et al. (eds) (2013) *Revisiting the contractual scholarship of Stewart Macaulay*. Oxford: Hart Publishing.

Brodie, D. (2008) 'Mutual trust and confidence: catalysts, constraints and commonality', *Industrial Law Journal*, 37, 4: 329–75.

*Brown, E. (2008) 'Protecting agency workers: implied contract or legislation?', *Industrial Law Journal*, 37, 2: 178–96.

*Bryden, C. and Salter, M. (2009) 'Overstepping the Mark', *New Law Journal*, 159: 491.

*Burke, R. and Cooper, C. (eds) (2008) *The Long Work Hours Culture*. Bingley: Emerald.

Cabrelli, D. (2008) *Law Express: Employment Law*. London: Pearson Longman.

*Clark, I. (1996) 'The state and new industrial relations', in I. Beardwell (ed.) *Contemporary Industrial Relations: A Critical Analysis*. Oxford: Oxford University Press, pp. 37–64.

Collins, H. (2000) 'Justifications and techniques of legal regulation of the employment relation' in H. Collins, P. Davies and R. Rideout (eds) *Legal Regulation of the Employment Relation*. London: Kluwer Law International, pp. 2–30.

*Collins, H., Davies, P. and Rideout, R. (eds) (2000) *Legal Regulation of the Employment Relation*. London: Kluwer Law International.

Collins, H., Ewing K. and McColgan A. (2012) *Labour Law (Law in Context)*. Cambridge: Cambridge University Press.

Conaghan, J. and Rittich, K. (2005) *Labour Law, Work and Family*. Oxford: Oxford University Press.

*Craig, J. and Lynk, M. (2006) *Globalization and the Future of Labour Law*. Cambridge: Cambridge University Press.

*Daniels, G. and McIlroy, J. (eds) (2009) *Trade Unions in a Neoliberal World: British Trade Unions Under New Labour*. London: Routledge.

Davidov, G. (2005) 'Who is a worker', *Industrial Law Journal*, 34: 57–72.

Davidov, G. and Langille, B. (2006) *Boundaries and Frontiers of Labour Law*. Oxford: Hart Publishing.

*Davidov, G. and Langille, B. (eds) (2011) *The Idea of Labour Law*. Oxford: Oxford University Press.

*Davies, A. (2007) 'The contract for intermittent employment', *Industrial Law Journal*, 36, 1: 102–20.

*Davies, A. (2012) *EU Labour Law*. Cheltenham: Edward Elgar.

*Davis, P. and Freedland, M. (2007) *Towards a Flexible Labour Market: Labour Legislation and Regulation since the 1990s*. Oxford: Oxford University Press.

*Deakin, S. (2007) 'Does the 'Personal Employment Contract' provide a basis for the reunification of employment law?', *Industrial Law Journal*, 36, 1: 68–90.

*Deakin, S. (2008) 'Timing is everything: industrialization, legal origin and the evolution of the contract of employment in Britain and Continental Europe' in B. Bercusson and C. Estlund (eds) *Regulating Labour in the Wake of Globalisation: New Challenges, New Institutions*. Oxford: Hart Publishing, pp. 86–115.

Deakin, S. and Morris, G. (2012) *Labour Law*, 6th edn. Oxford: Hart Publishing.

Deakin, S. and Wilkinson, F. (2005) *The Law of the Labour Market: Industrialization, Employment and Legal Evolution*. Oxford: Oxford University Press.

Denham D.J. (1990) 'Unfair dismissal law and the legitimation of managerial control', *Capital and Class*, 14, 2: 83–101.

Dickens, L. (2005) 'Walking the talk? Equality and diversity in employment' in S. Bach (ed.) *The Management of Human Resources: Personnel Management in Britain*. Oxford: Blackwell, pp. 178–209.

Dickens, L. (ed.) (2012) *Making Employment Rights Effective*. Oxford: Hart Publishing.

Employment Tribunals Service (2013) *Employment Tribunal and EAT Statistics* (GB), 1 April 2011 to 31 March 2012. Online: **https://www.justice.gov.uk/downloads/statistics/tribs-stats/employment-trib-stats-april-march-2011-12.pdf** (accessed January 2014).

Fox, A. (1985) *History and Heritage*. London: Allen & Unwin.

Frank, C. (2010) *Master and Servant Law*. Farnham: Ashgate.

*Fredman, S. (2004) 'Women at work: the broken promise of flexicurity', *Industrial Law Journal*, 33: 299–310.

Freedland, M. (2003) *The Personal Employment Contract*. Oxford: Oxford University Press.

Freedland, M. and Kountouris, N. (2008) 'Towards a comparative theory of the contractual construction of personal work relations in Europe', *Industrial Law Journal*, 37: 49–60.

Freedland, M. and Kountouris, N. (2011) *The Legal Construction of Personal Work Relations*. Oxford: Oxford University Press.

*Fudge, J., McCrystal, S. and Sankaran, K. (2012) *Challenging the Legal Boundaries of Work Regulation*. Oxford: Hart Publishing.

*Gibbons, M. (2007) *Better Dispute Resolution: A Review of Employment Dispute Resolution in Great Britain*. London: Department of Trade and Industry.

*Gilmore, S. (2009) 'Introducing Human Resource Management' in S. Gilmore and S. Williams (eds) *Human Resource Management*. Oxford: Oxford University Press, pp. 3–20.

*Gilmore, S. and Williams, S. (2009) *Human Resource Management*. Oxford: Oxford University Press.

*Holland, J. and Burnett, S. (2009) *Employment Law: Legal Practice Course Guides*. Oxford: Oxford University Press.

*Horton, R. (2008) 'The end of disability-related discrimination in employment?', *Industrial Law Journal*, 37, 4: 376–400.

*Hosking, D. (2007) 'A high bar for EU disability rights', *Industrial Law Journal*, 36: 228–50.

Hyde, A. (1983) 'The concept of legitimation in the sociology of law', *Wisconsin Law Review* Mar/Apr, 379–426.

Hyde, A. (1990) 'A Theory of Labor Legislation', 38, *Buffalo Law Review*: 383–465.

Hyde, A. (2006) 'What is labour law?' in G. Davidov and B. Langille (eds) *Boundaries and Frontiers of Labour Law*. Oxford: Hart Publishing, pp. 37–62.

Hyde, A. (2011) 'The idea of labour law: a parable' in G. Davidov and B. Langille (eds) *The Idea of Labour Law*. Oxford: Oxford University Press, pp. 88–97.

Hyman, R. (1975) *Industrial Relations: A Marxist Introduction*. London: Macmillan.

*Jefferson, M. (1997) *Principles of Employment Law*, 3rd edn. London: Cavendish Publishing.

Kahn-Freund, O. (1984) *Labour and the Law*, 2nd edn. London: Stevens.

*Keen, S. (2008) 'Discrimination: blame it on the dog', *New Law Journal*, 158, September: 1216.

*Koukiadaki, A. (2009) 'Case law developments in the area of fixed-term work', *Industrial Law Journal*, 159, January: 89–103.

Lewin, D. (1999) 'Theoretical and empirical research on the grievance procedure and arbitration: a critical review' in A. Eaton and J. Keefe (eds) *Employment Dispute Resolution and Workers' Rights in the Changing Workplace*. Champaign IL: IRRA, pp. 137–86.

LexisNexis (2013) *Harvey on Industrial Relations and Employment Law* (5 vols) London: LexisNexis.

*Ley, C. (2009) 'Back to the future', *New Law Journal*, 159, April: 537.

*Luhmann, N. (2004) *Law as a Social System*. Oxford: Oxford University Press.

Mansfield, G., Bowers, J., Brown, D., Forshaw, S., Korn, A., Palca, J. and Reade, D. (2012) *Blackstone's Employment Law Practice*. Oxford: Oxford University Press, pp. 25–45.

*McCann, D. (2008) *Regulating Flexible Work*. Oxford: Oxford University Press.

*McKay, S. (2008) 'Employer motivations for using agency labour', *Industrial Law Journal*, 37: 296–9.

Njoya, W. (2007) *Property in Work: The Employment Relationship in the Anglo-American Firm*. Aldershot: Ashgate.

Oliver, B. (1999) Comparing corporate managers' personal values over three decades 1967–1995, *Journal of Business Ethics*, 20: 147–61.

*Peninsula (2003) *Survey on Flexible Hours*. London: Peninsula.

*Philips, K. and Eamets, R. (2007) *Approaches to Flexicurity: EU Models*. Dublin: European Foundation for the Improvement of Living and Working Conditions.

*Public Affairs (2001) *A Women's Place*.

*Reich, C. (1964) 'The new property', *Yale Law Journal*, 73, 5: 733–87.

*Reynold, QC. F. and Palmer, A. (2007) 'What place for hindsight in deciding whether a claimant was disabled?', *Industrial Law Journal*, 36, 4: 486–99.

*Rogowski, R. and Wilthagen, T. (1994) *Reflexive labour Law*. Deventer: Kluwer Law International.

*Ryan, A.J. and Pointon, J. (2007) 'Reward and performance management' in J. Beardwell and T. Claydon (eds) *Human Resource Management: A Contemporary Approach*, 5th edn. Harlow: FT/Prentice Hall, pp. 487–524.

Sanders A. (2009) 'Part One of the Employment Act 2008: "'better'" dispute resolution?', *Industrial Law Journal*, 159, January: 30–42.

Scarpetta, S. (2013) 'Unpublished paper from the Westminster Employment Forum session', 16 April 2013.

Sciarra, S., Davies, P. and Freedland M. (eds) (2011) *Employment Policy and the Regulation of Part-time Work in the European Union*. Cambridge: Cambridge University Press.

*Smith, I. (2009a) 'Hitting the buffers', *New Law Journal*, 159, February: 215.

*Smith, I. (2009b) 'Presidential protection', *New Law Journal*, 159, March: 369.

Standing G. (2011) *The Precariat; The New Dangerous Class*. London: Bloomsbury.

Stone K. (2013) 'The decline in the standard employment contract' in Stone, K. and Arthurs, H. (eds) *Rethinking Workplace Regulation; Beyond the standard contract of employment*. New York: Russell Sage Foundation, pp. 366–404.

Stone, K. and Arthurs, H. (eds) (2013) *Rethinking Workplace Regulation; Beyond the standard contract of employment*. New York: Russell Sage Foundation.

*TUC (2005) 'Government should investigate cause of tribunals drop', press release, 12 July.

*TUC (2008) *Hard Work, Hidden Lives, the Full Report of the TUC Commission on Vulnerable Employment*. London: TUC.

*Turner Hospital, J. (1992) *The Last Magician*. Virago: London.

*Various (2008) *New Developments in Employment Discrimination Law*. Tokyo: The Japan Institute for Labour Policy and Training.

Von Prondynski, F. (2000) 'Labour law as business facilitator' in H. Collins, P. Davies and R. Rideout (eds) *Legal Regulation of the Employment Relation*. London: Kluwer Law International, pp. 3–145.

*Von Wachter, V. (2009) 'Rearing its ugly head', *New Law Journal*, 159, February: 296.

*Wedderburn, W. (1986) *The Worker and the Law*. London: Penguin.

Wightman J. (2013) 'Contract in a pre-realist world' in Braucher *et al.* (eds) *Revisting the Contractual Scholarship of Stewart Macaulay*. Oxford: Hart Publishing, pp. 377–401.

*White, R. (2008) 'Notes: working under protest and variation of employment terms', *Industrial Law Journal*, 37: 365–80.

*Willey, B. (2012) *Employment Law in Context*, 4th edn. Harlow: Prentice Hall.

*Work Stress Management (2002) *Survey on Workplace Stress*. Online: **www.workstressmanagement.com**.

Wynn, M. (2009) 'Regulating rogues? Employment agency enforcement and sections 15–18 of the Employment Act 2008', *Industrial Law Journal*, 38, 2: 64–72.

Chapter 11

Employee engagement

Julia Pointon

Objectives

- To define employee engagement.
- To identify the similarities and differences between related concepts such as job satisfaction and organisational citizenship behaviour.
- To discuss the main drivers of employee engagement.
- To identify the organisational benefits of employee engagement.
- To outline strategies to enhance employee engagement.
- To consider employee engagement as a global concept.
- To reflect on the challenges associated with measuring employee engagement.

Introductory case study

A journey to award-winning employee engagement: Rainbow Trust

The Rainbow Trust provides emotional and practical support for families who have a child with a life-threatening or terminal illness. Family-support workers provide backing to around 1,200 families a year, from eight bases around the UK. In 2012, the Rainbow Trust was recognised as a *Sunday Times* Top 100 organisation. The charity was successful because employees felt something special towards the Trust they worked for. They felt passionate about what the Trust did, committed to ensuring its success, satisfied by the work they did and motivated by their own sense of personal and professional achievement. In other words, they were 'engaged'. The achievement of this relationship was not immediate or easy and required the Trust to undertake several initiatives explicitly designed to enhance levels of employee engagement.

The initiatives included the following:

- A monthly publication, which brought together business updates and stories from employees around the Trust, was launched to help everyone know and understand business priorities and each other's personal working styles and to plan effective teamworking.
- An employee engagement group was formed and met regularly throughout the year and consisted of employees from different functions, locations and levels. The group canvassed views and opinions across Rainbow and provided constructive feedback to the leadership team, providing a vehicle for two-way communication.
- The most ground-breaking initiative was the performance management process (PMP) launched

➤

in 2010. The goal was to introduce a performance management and performance-related pay (PRP) process that was fair, endorsed Rainbow values, encouraged exceptional performance and provided recognition to both individuals and teams for exceeding the agreed performance expectations. It also aimed to create a sense of joint responsibility among the geographically dispersed teams.

The process began with the chief executive presenting the business plan to the entire organisation and enabling employees to ask direct questions. The business plan was cascaded throughout Rainbow. Each staff member wrote their own specific, measurable, attainable, relevant and time-bound (SMART) objectives, and agreed them with line managers. Employees led their own performance reviews, providing supporting evidence, and rated their own performance on a scale of 1–5, where 2 represented solid performance. Line managers then proposed a rating for each of their direct reports to calibration which made the process fair. Based on the evidence provided and discussion, the calibration committee agreed a Rainbow Performance Review was one of the cornerstones in enhancing employee engagement.

Performance-related pay, rare for a third-sector organisation, was a natural progression. PMP rewarded employees for the part they played – the higher the performer, the higher the reward. When rating performance, Rainbow considered not only what was done but also how it was done. It was not just about hitting the numbers – it was about collaborating with colleagues and other stakeholders. Part of the PMP was the integration of feedback based on situation, behaviour and impact (SBI). In this approach, employees have to describe a situation they observed, the behaviour they witnessed and the impact of that

behaviour on themselves or a colleague. The Rainbow Trust expected all its employees to adopt this process, regardless of hierarchy. The rationale was to support the process of integration and transparency. The introduction of PMP was judged to be a key tool in enhancing employee engagement at the Rainbow Trust, because it involved people and the Trust believed that 'involved employees were motivated employees'.

The Trust leadership team decided to celebrate its 25th year with its first annual staff conference. It received 100 per cent feedback from the day and when staff were asked the question: 'Following the event do you have an increased sense of involvement and engagement with Rainbow Trust?' nine out of 10 respondents said yes!

In 2011 the employee survey response rate was 96 per cent, confirming that employees believed they were being listened to and they could effect change. It showed strong results in brand, purpose, credibility, pride and friendliness and improvement in almost every area. The Rainbow Trust was well placed to apply to the *Sunday Times* Top 100, receiving a one-star Best Companies rating, recognising it as a first-class organisation to work for. The head of marketing and communications stated: 'Rainbow Trust is a great place to work because employees are proud to work here and go the extra mile to get things done. There are high levels of trust in our service, in the organisation and in each other. Thanks to PMP and other measures, employees now feel that the organisation has a clear sense of direction and believe in its ambition. They understand the business priorities, where they fit within them, and can see the difference their contribution makes every day.'

Source: Anna Powis, (2012) 'A journey to award-winning employee engagement', *Human Resource Management International Digest*, Vol. 20 Iss: 5, pp.31-34, Copyright © 2012, Emerald Group Publishing Limited.

Introduction

Employee engagement has become an increasingly popular and well-used phrase in business vocabulary over recent years. Indeed, it is rare to find articles in the popular HR or management press without some mention of engagement and how to enable it. Yet there is still no one clear and agreed definition of engagement and, according to Soldati (2007), many researchers and practitioners continue to describe the term in very different ways. Nevertheless, there is an increasing awareness that employee engagement is pivotal to successful commercial and business performance, where engaged employees are the 'backbone of good working environments where people are industrious, ethical and accountable' (Cleland *et al.*, 2008). In his 2004 book entitled *The New Rules of Engagement*, Johnson wrote 'the ability to engage employees, to make them work with our business, is going to be one of the greatest organisational battles of the coming 10 years' (p. 1). Years on and employee engagement still remains a key challenge that is capturing the attention of executives and HR professionals alike and, increasingly, that of academics as well.

An 'engaged employee' can be thought of as one who is fully involved in, and enthusiastic about, their work, and so will act in a way that advances the interests of the organisation (Attridge, 2009). Employee engagement is therefore the degree of an employee's positive or negative emotional attachment to their job, colleagues and organisation, which profoundly influences their job satisfaction and their willingness to learn and perform at work.

Definitions from the practitioner literature

From the practitioner literature, the Chartered Institute of Personnel and Development (CIPD, 2010: 5) considers engagement to be: 'Positively present during the performance of work by willingly contributing intellectual effort, experiencing positive emotions and meaningful connections to others.'

CIPD (2012) defines it as:

> A combination of commitment to the organisation and its values plus a willingness to help out colleagues (organisational citizenship). It goes beyond job satisfaction and is not simply motivation. Engagement is something the employee has to offer: it cannot be 'required' as part of the employment contract.

A second practitioner-focused definition comes from The Institute of Employment Studies (IES) (Robinson *et al.*, 2004), which defines engagement as:

> A positive attitude held by the employee towards the organisation and its values. An engaged employee is aware of business context, and works with colleagues to improve performance within the job for the benefit of the organisation. The organisation must work to develop and nurture engagement, which requires a two-way relationship between employer and employee.

In 2006, the Conference Board, a non-profit consulting service, conducted an extensive review of the research literature on employee engagement and developed a blended definition of employee engagement, concluding it was 'a heightened emotional connection that an employee feels for his or her organisation, that influences him or her to exert greater discretionary effort to his or her work'.

Jack Welch, former General Electric CEO and also a business consultant, emphasises some of the same points as the IES, but concludes unequivocally that 'employee engagement is the number one measure of a company's health' (Welch and Welch, 2006).

Definitions from the academic literature

The first published mention of the term employee engagement occurred in 1990, when William Kahn of Boston University published his paper 'Psychological conditions of personal engagement and disengagement at work' in the *Academy of Management Journal*.

Kahn (1990: 694) completed some of the earliest academic work on engagement defining it as: 'The harnessing of organisation members' selves to their work roles; in engagement, people employ and express themselves physically, cognitively, and emotionally during role performances'. Thus, according to Kahn (1990, 1992), engagement means to be psychologically present when occupying and performing an organisational role. In the only study to empirically test Kahn's (1990) model, May *et al. (2004)* found that meaningfulness was found to have the strongest relation to different employee outcomes in terms of engagement. Although neither Kahn (1990) nor May *et al.* (2004) included outcomes in their studies, Kahn proposed that high levels of engagement can lead to positive outcomes for individuals, such as positive feelings associated with a job well done.

The work of Nelson and Simmons (2003) extends the focus of engagement as being primarily concerned with the relationship between the individual and the actual job, suggesting that engagement is identified when employees feel positive emotions towards their work, find their work to be personally meaningful, consider their workload to be manageable, and are hopeful about the future of their work.

May *et al. (2004)* refined the definition to include a three-dimensional concept of engagement. They proposed that engagement existed when the following criteria were perceived as being realised in the employee's work:

- a physical component ('I exert a lot of energy performing my job');
- an emotional component ('I really put my heart into my job');
- a cognitive component ('Performing my job is so absorbing that I forget about everything else').

Although employing slightly different terminology, Macy and Schneider (2008) also identified three core elements of employee engagement that once again focus explicitly on the job:

- intellectual engagement or thinking hard about the job and how to do it better;
- affective engagement, or feeling positively about doing a good job;
- social engagement or actively taking opportunities to discuss work-related improvements with others at work.

Rothwell (2010) defined engagement as a positive attitude towards the actual job. For Rothwell, engagement is a temporary and volatile phenomenon and is viewed as being present only when employees are intellectually and emotionally bound to their work role. Once again, this definition brings to the fore the relationship between individuals and their work as a central theme of employee engagement.

Explore

- Which of the different definitions resonates most with your own thoughts and why?
- Are there other aspects not covered in the definitions that you would like to have seen included?

The suggestion in the definitions outlined that engagement is concerned with individuals' psychological engagement with their actual job becomes a key differentiator in defining and understanding engagement as something separate and different from related concepts such as employee motivation, employee commitment, employee satisfaction and, more recently, concepts such as organisational citizenship behaviour (OCB). The commitment to viewing engagement as a relatively new and emerging construct that is similar to, but different from, other concepts is supported by the work of researchers, such as Meyer (1997), Buckingham (1999), Wright and Cropanzano (2000), Harter *et al.* (2003), Bakker (2009), Macey and Schneider (2008) and Avey *et al.* (2009). These researchers have taken time to investigate the broad range of work-related issues that affect, directly or indirectly, the links between, for example, organisational commitment and employee motivation, and have identified something new and slightly different, which they have called employee engagement.

Key Controversy

Is employee engagement something new, or simply old wine (long-standing management approaches) in new (fashionable management-speak) bottles? Is it just the latest management fad?

Characteristics of engaged employees

In 2010, Gallup commissioned research by the Kingston Employee Engagement Consortium Project. The research covered eight different organisations and resulted in over 180 interviews, generating 5,291 questionnaires. The conclusion confirmed the multi-faceted nature of engagement, highlighting that engagement is associated with a number of characteristics both at the level of the organisation and at the level of the individual (see Box 11.1).

Box 11.1 **Characteristics of engagement**

Employee engagement is associated with a range of positive outcomes at the individual and organisational levels:

- Engaged employees perform better.
- The majority of respondents were rated 'good' in their last appraisal.
- Engaged employees are more innovative than others.
- Engaged employees are more likely to want to stay with their employer. In the sample, 35 per cent indicate that they would like to continue working for their employer for five or more years, compared with 17 per cent who want to leave within the next two years.
- Engaged employees enjoy greater levels of personal well-being.
- Engaged employees perceive their workload to be more sustainable than others.
- One-third of employees are 'fit performers', enjoying high levels of personal well-being and performing well.
- Data indicated that excessively high levels of engagement might lead to ill-health and burnout.

Source: Gallup (2010).

The IES has undertaken valuable research in the area of employee engagement. One extensive study involving the NHS concluded that the characteristics of engagement and those of commitment were aligned and that engaged and committed employees perform better. Analysis of the NHS case study data (Robinson *et al.* 2004) indicated that the key characteristic of engaged employees is a sense of feeling valued and of being involved in the organisation's decision-making processes to the extent that they feel able to voice their ideas and know that managers listen to their views and value their contributions. The second key characteristic of an engaged employee in the NHS was a belief by the workers that they had the opportunity to develop their jobs by making suggestions as to how the work undertaken could be enhanced and improved. The third characteristic was the extent to which the organisation is concerned for their health and well-being. The key point here is that concern is demonstrated for both physical health and mental and emotional well-being. Clearly, in developing and sustaining the characteristics of an engaged employee, the role of the line manager is central in fostering employees' sense of involvement and value.

The CIPD (2010) found that employees who are engaged with the organisation tend to display particular recognisable primary behaviours. For example they tend to (p. 2):

- speak positively about the organisation to co-workers, potential employees and customers;
- have a strong desire to be a member of the organisation;
- give that extra effort to contribute to the organisation's success.

Gallup (Fleming and Asplund, 2007) identified 12 core elements that best predict and characterise employee engagement (see Box 11.2). If an individual employee affirms the following, their level of engagement is likely to be high.

Box 11.2 **Gallup: 12 factors of engagement**

- 'I know what is expected of me at work.'
- 'I have the materials and equipment I need to do my work right.'
- 'At work, I have the opportunity to do what I do best every day.'
- 'In the last seven days, I have received recognition or praise for doing good work.'
- 'My supervisor, or someone at work, seems to care about me as a person.'
- 'There is someone at work who encourages my development.'
- 'At work, my opinions seem to count.'
- 'The mission or purpose of my organisation makes me feel my job is important.'
- 'My associates or fellow employees are committed to doing quality work.'
- 'I have a best friend at work.'
- 'In the last six months, someone at work has talked to me about my progress.'
- 'This last year, I have had opportunities at work to learn and grow.'

Source: Fleming and Asplund (2007: 286–7).

In summary, engagement in practice is about creating alignment between the individual and with the organisation's goals. This alignment has both rational aspects, as evidenced by the statement 'I have the materials and equipment I need to do my work right', and emotional aspects, as evidenced by the statement 'In the last seven days, I have received recognition or praise for doing good work.' As a consequence of engagement, employees at all levels are prepared to give discretionary effort over and above the demands of the job.

Explore

The CIPD and Gallup both identify key characteristics of an 'engaged employee':
- Think about when you felt engaged? What was it that generated that feeling?
- Do you think you could repeat that same feeling with another organisation?

Employee disengagement

The emphasis thus far has been on understanding what employee engagement is, the organisational factors that contribute to enhancing levels of engagement among employees and the benefits that are derived from such actions. The other part of the equation, however, has to do with those employees who are not fully engaged. Kahn (1990: 694) defined disengagement as the uncoupling of selves from work roles. In disengagement, people withdraw and defend themselves physically, cognitively or emotionally during role performances. He identified three psychological conditions related to disengagement at work: meaningfulness, safety and availability. He argued that people asked themselves three fundamental questions in each role situation:

- How meaningful is it for me to bring myself into this performance?
- How safe is it to do so?
- How psychologically available am I to do so?

In 1999, Buckingham's book, *First, Break All the Rules*, he suggested that less than one in five workers was actively engaged in their work. This claim was later substantiated by Gallup in 2010, who found that 19 per cent of 1,000 people interviewed were actively disengaged at work. These workers complained that they did not have the tools they needed to do their jobs, did not know what was expected of them and their bosses did not listen to them.

In 2012 a special 'Engage for Success' task force was established in partnership with Bath University and Marks & Spencer. Data from a 2012 survey by Towers Watson and supplied to the task force evidenced that just 27 per cent of employees in the UK are 'highly engaged', with an equivalent proportion of employees being 'disengaged'. In terms of the extent and frequency of engagement, they found that fewer than one in five (18 per cent) people are engaged on a daily basis. Fifty-nine per cent reported being engaged 'once a week', 22 per cent 'a few times a year' or 'once a month', and just 1 per cent report 'never' being engaged. These findings suggest that a substantial majority of employees are not engaged with their work on a daily basis, but, equally, only a very small number are never engaged. These engagement levels compare unfavourably to a global average of 35 per cent who are 'highly engaged'.

This lack of engagement by UK employees has been demonstrated by research for over a decade and in some sectors shows no sign of abating. Of 2000 UK retail workers surveyed by engagement agency Maverick, 77 per cent are not engaged with their company brand values, with 63 per cent of workers in the sector indicating they had never been trained on the importance of these values and 60 per cent failed to understand how fundamental their employer's organisational values were to their own roles. CIPD (2010) research across eight UK organisations, resulting in a dataset of 5,291 questionnaires, considered levels of disengagement in respect of gender and found some interesting variations (see Box 11.3). For instance, they discovered that men were significantly more disengaged overall than women: while 74 per cent of women report being moderately engaged, only 68 per cent of men are moderately engaged, and 9 per cent of women are strongly engaged, while only 7 per cent of men are strongly engaged (Truss *et al.*, 2006).

Box 11.3   Disengaged employees

- Younger workers are less engaged than older workers.
- Non-managers are less engaged than managers.
- Public-sector employees are less frequently engaged than in the private sector.
- Public-sector employees show higher levels of social and intellectual engagement, whereas private-sector employees are more engaged affectively.

Key Controversy

How does an organisation 'limit' disengagement when the job is mundane and repetitive?
    Employee engagement figures (May 2013) highlight that the retail sector alone loses £628 million per year by failing to inspire its employees. The research also revealed that, by investing just 10 per cent more in staff engagement, UK businesses in all sectors could add £2,700 per employee per year in profits. This could result in a staggering £49 billion growth across UK plc, equivalent to 3 per cent of the country's current GDP.

The importance of effective management, clear and relevant communication, fairness and employee well-being are also identified in work undertaken for the CIPD. Case study research in two public-sector organisations and two private-sector firms (Gatenby *et al.*, 2009) identifies a number of barriers to employee engagement, including:

- Leadership style during organisational change and periods of low performance.
- Reactive decision-making that does not pick up problems until it is too late.
- Inconsistent management style leading to perceptions of unfairness.
- Low perceptions of senior management visibility and quality of downward communication.

- Incoherent communication channels – increasing the amount of communication does not necessarily contribute to employee perceptions of communication; clarity and timeliness are more important.
- Poor work–life balance due to a long-hours culture.
- Few opportunities for leadership development resulting in limited internal progression.

Explore

Consider a time when you were not engaged.

- Think about and reflect upon the reasons for your non-engagement – was there anything that could have prevented you feeling disengaged?

Employee engagement and related concepts

We have seen that engagement is concerned with the employee's connections with and feeling towards their job, but such sentiments do not occur in an organisational vacuum. There are other forces in play that directly or indirectly affect this relationship. In this section, we will explore the related themes of satisfaction and commitment.

Engagement is therefore closely linked to the idea of job satisfaction. Individuals benefit from having a job that they consider to be interesting and worthwhile, while at the same time organisations are seen to gain performance benefits from having employees who will give of their best and 'go the extra mile' (CIPD, 2009). Robinson (2004) and Penna (2007) both propose a model of engagement that incorporates job satisfaction. They suggest that feeling valued at work, alongside good two-way communication and opportunities for training and development, are important, as they act as key influences of positive job satisfaction. Robinson argues that satisfaction with the job of work alone will not produce an engaged workforce, but it is a significant contributory factor.

This phenomenon can be seen in positions where the actual job itself is intrinsically satisfying but the place of work is not, e.g. designers or engineers working in organisations where communication is poor, development opportunities are limited and career progression is restricted. In these situations, employees may take great pride in their work and derive an enormous amount of personal job satisfaction, but they may do so without feeling any emotional connection to the organisation.

Engagement is frequently associated with organisational commitment. However, a key distinction between the two concepts is that the attitudinal experience of commitment occurs apart from, or as a consequence of, day-to-day work activity, whereas engagement is developed and sustained through work and particularly the interaction with managers and co-workers (Jones and Harter, 2005). So, engaged employees are likely to display high levels of commitment, but not all committed employees are actively engaged. The extent to which engagement and commitment are aligned is dependent on the nature of commitment. Meyer and Allen (1991) identify three different types of commitment: normative, continuance and affective commitment. Normative or moral commitment occurs where an individual feels that they ought to be committed to the organisation, regardless of whether or not they actually believe in the organisation's values (Nickson *et al.*, 2008). Continuance commitment is where an individual chooses to remain with an organisation as long as they consider that the benefits of doing so outweigh the costs of leaving. With affective commitment, individuals feel an emotional attachment to the organisation. This type of commitment is most directly associated with engagement and is the form of commitment most likely to be measured by employers (Silverman, 2004). Individuals displaying affective commitment are more likely to go the extra mile for the organisation, so it is closely associated with the behavioural component of employee engagement, frequently expressed as organisational citizenship behaviour.

The term organisational citizenship behaviour (OCB) covers a range of different behaviours, but what they have in common is that they are discretionary and beyond the immediate demands of the job. As these types of behaviour are not usually part of the reward system, absence of such behaviours is not punishable by the organisation, but performance of them can contribute to enhanced organisational performance (Barkworth, 2004). Podsakoff *et al.* (2000: 516–25) groups OCBs into seven key themes:

- *Helping behaviour* – voluntarily helping others with, or preventing the occurrence of, work-related problems.
- *Sportsmanship* – maintaining a positive attitude even when things do not go your way, not being offended when others do not follow your suggestions, being willing to sacrifice personal interest for the good of the group.
- *Organisational loyalty* – promoting the organisation to outsiders, defending it against external threats, remaining committed to it even under adverse circumstances.
- *Organisational compliance* – scrupulous adherence to organisational regulations and procedures even when not being monitored or observed.
- *Individual initiative* – engaging in task-related behaviours at a level beyond generally expected levels, volunteering for extra responsibilities and encouraging others to do likewise.
- *Civic virtue* – showing willingness to participate in organisational governance, monitoring the environment for threats and opportunities, to look out for the organisation's best interests.
- *Self-development* – engaging in voluntary activities to improve knowledge, skills and abilities.

Commitment is conceptualised as a positive attachment and a willingness to exert energy for success of the organisation, a feeling of pride in being a member of the organisation and identifying with it at all levels. OCB is a behaviour observed within the work context that demonstrates itself through proactively taking innovative initiatives and actively seeking opportunities to contribute and 'go the extra mile' beyond the employment contract. Robinson *et al.* (2004) and Rafferty *et al.* (2005) make the point that while engagement has similarities with the two concepts, neither really sufficiently reflects the two-way nature of engagement, i.e. that it is a two-way mutual process between the employee and the organisation, or the extent to which engaged employees are expected to have an element of business awareness. Indeed, the precise definition offered by Robinson *et al.* (2004) clearly emphasises employee engagement as 'a positive attitude held by the employee towards the organisation and its value. An engaged employee is frequently aware of business context, and works with colleagues to improve performance within the job for the benefit of the organisation. The organisation must work to develop and nurture engagement, which requires a two-way relationship between employer and employee.' Saks (2006) draws a similar parallel between commitment and engagement, suggesting that organisational commitment differs from engagement in that it refers to a person's attitude and attachment towards their organisation. Engagement is not an attitude; it is the degree to which individuals are attentive and absorbed in the performance of their roles. And while OCB involves voluntary and informal behaviours that can help co-workers and the organisation, the focus of engagement is one's formal role performance rather than extra-role and voluntary behaviour (Saks, 2006: 602). May *et al.* (2004) offers a further refinement of the academic theory, holding that engagement is also distinct from job involvement. According to May *et al.* (2004), job involvement is the result of a cognitive judgment about the extent to which the job has the ability to satisfy an individual's 'needs' and is therefore closely aligned with one's self-image. Engagement has to do with how individuals employ themselves in the execution of their job. Furthermore, engagement involves the active use of emotions and behaviours in addition to cognitions. May *et al.* (2004: 12) conclude that 'engagement may be thought of as an antecedent to job involvement in that individuals who experience deep engagement in their roles should come to identify with their jobs'. In summary then, it is seen as a construct that consists of cognitive, emotional and behavioural components that are strongly associated with individual role performance.

From this stance, it can be see how employees who are totally absorbed in their job and understand how their specific function contributes to the overall business success would feel more passionate about the corporate goals and could and would exert their efforts beyond basic job requirements and responsibilities to meet customers' demands and so, by default, the aims of the organisation as a whole. This complex interplay of factors is described by others (Baumruk, 2004; Shaw, 2005; Richman, 2006) as an emotional and intellectual commitment or, as Franks and Taylor, (2004) described it, as the amount of discretionary effort exhibited by employees in their jobs.

Thus, engagement can be seen to include elements of commitment to the organisation and its values, plus a willingness to communicate and help out colleagues (organisational citizenship). It goes beyond job satisfaction and is not simply motivation. Engagement is something the employee has to feel an intrinsic motivation to offer, it cannot be 'required' as part of the employment contract and as such has strong links to the idea of the psychological contract, in that it is unwritten, is highly influenced by the relationship the employee has with their direct line manager, includes elements of trust and justice and is susceptible to being broken or violated.

In particular, engagement is two-way: organisations must work to engage the employee, who in turn has a choice about the level of engagement to offer the employer. Each reinforces the other. An engaged employee experiences a blend of job satisfaction, organisational commitment, job involvement and feelings of empowerment. It is a concept that is greater than the sum of its parts.

Despite there being some debate about the precise meaning of employee engagement, there are three things we know about it: it is measurable; it can be correlated with performance; and it varies from poor to great. Most importantly, employers can do a great deal to influence people's level of engagement. That is what makes it so important as a tool for business success.

Employee engagement as an exchange process

The idea of engagement being beneficial for all parties in the employment relationship suggests it is predicated on the principles of an 'exchange process'. The idea of explaining engagement as a mutually beneficial and reciprocal arrangement has strong theoretical links to 'social exchange theory'. Social exchange theory argues that obligations are generated through a series of interactions between two or more parties who are in a state of reciprocal interdependence; in the case of engagement, this is between the employee and the organisation. A basic principle of social exchange theory is that relationships evolve over time into trusting, loyal and mutual commitments, as long as the parties involved operate and follow certain expected patterns of behaviours or 'rules' of exchange (Cropanzano and Mitchell, 2005). The rules of exchange may be formalised in a contract of employment, or may, as is more likely, be shaped by the unwritten expectations of the organisational culture and be very similar in formation and operation to the psychological contract. The aspect of reciprocity or repayment is based on the actions of one party resulting in a response or actions by the other party. So, for example, when employees receive economic and socio-emotional resources from their organisation, they feel obliged to respond in kind and repay the organisation (Cropanzano and Mitchell, 2005). This is totally consistent with Robinson *et al*'s (2004) description of engagement as a two-way relationship between the employer and employee.

Explore

Think of a time when you have been highly committed to achieving a task or a particular assignment.
- Were you engaged with the organisation and committed to the task, or just committed to the task?

One obvious way for employees to repay their organisation is through their level of engagement. That is, employees can influence and control the extent to which they willingly engage with their job and the organisation, and the level of engagement they choose to offer will vary according to how obligated they feel and how much they consider the employer deserves. It stands to reason therefore, that if the employee feels the organisation is behaving in an open, transparent and respectful manner towards them, they will 'repay' in full. Conversely, if the employee considers the organisation has reneged on agreements, breached or violated promises or treated them disrespectfully or less favourably than others (the socio-emotional resources of the exchange), they will have little sense of needing to repay the organisation and will choose to withhold their engagement. It is often difficult for employees to limit or withhold or reduce the level of their actual performance, as job performance is often evaluated through a formal performance management appraisal process and may be associated with pay, career progression and job security (the economic resources part of the exchange). It would therefore not be in the interest of the employee to adversely affect their work rate, the quality of their work or the quality of their immediate relationships, e.g. with customers. Thus, the actual work behaviour of an employee may remain consistent and of a high quality, while their level of cognitive and emotional engagement may be consciously limited. Engagement and work behaviour can therefore be seen as two different constructs, although the antecedents of performance and organisational behaviour are consistent across the two aspects.

If the conditions of engagement are presented as the exchange of economic and socio-emotional resources, then in terms of social exchange theory, when employees receive these resources from their organisation they feel obliged to repay the organisation with greater levels of engagement. In terms of Kahn's (1990) definition of engagement that we considered at the start of the chapter, employees feel obliged to bring themselves more deeply into their role performances as repayment for the resources they receive from their organisation. When the organisation fails to provide these resources, employees are more likely to withdraw and disengage themselves from their roles. So the amount of cognitive, emotional and physical resources that an individual is prepared to devote in the performance of their work is contingent on the economic and socio-emotional resources they believe they receive from their organisation.

This scenario presents us with another poignant question. Namely, if employee engagement is part of an exchange relationship, is the exchange with the 'job' they are performing or the 'organisation' in which they are performing the job? In other words, can an employee be engaged with the job but not the organisation and vice-versa?

Key Controversy

Employers should really be concerned with paying employees to do their job – whether the employee is engaged or not is an irrelevance, providing they are doing their job correctly.

Saks (2006) was one of the first academics to take time to research this question in detail. The results demonstrated that while job and organisation engagement are indeed related they remain very distinct constructs. The study evidenced that employees can be significantly engaged with their particular job while simultaneously being less engaged with the organisation. In addition, the relationships between job and organisation engagement with the antecedents and consequences differed in a number of ways, suggesting that the psychological conditions that lead to job and organisation engagement, as well as the consequences, are not the same. Moreover, both job and organisation engagements explained significant and unique variance in job satisfaction, organisational commitment, intention to quit and OCB.

Given that we are dealing with human beings, it is not too much of a leap of faith to anticipate a situation in which one employee 'believes' the resource exchange is fair and is therefore fully engaged, while another employee, in the same situation, believes the exchange to be unfair and is therefore disengaged. The concept of justice provides a further antecedent to the concept of engagement.

The study by Saks (2006) was one of the first to suggest that a meaningful distinction between job and organisation engagement existed but that both could, to a certain extent, be predicted. Saks identified two particular sets of predicators: positive organisational support and justice. Let's examine each in turn. At the start of the chapter, we discussed some of the elements associated with engagement, e.g. Penna (2007) identified job satisfaction, feeling valued at work, communication and training and development as key influences of engagement, while the CIPD identified meaningfulness of work, voice, being able to feed your views upwards, senior management communication and vision, supportive work environment, person–job fit and line management style.

It can be discerned that some of the factors are related to wider organisational dimensions, e.g. a supportive work environment, while others are more job-specific, e.g. person–job fit. Saks (2006) found that employees who are provided with jobs that are high on positive job characteristics are more likely to reciprocate with greater job engagement and, further, that greater engagement at the level of the job resulted in higher levels of engagement with the organisation. Organisational engagement was positively related to employees' attitudes, intentions and behaviours, and, in particular, organisational commitment, intention to quit and OCB. The extent to which an employee was engaged with the organisation was influenced by the extent to which they considered they were being treated fairly, in other words, job characteristics predicted job engagement, and procedural justice predicted organisation engagement. The link with social exchange theory rests on the understanding that employees who perceive higher organisational support are more likely to reciprocate with greater levels of engagement in their job and in the organisation; employees who are provided with jobs that are high on the job characteristics are more likely to reciprocate with greater job engagement; and employees who have higher perceptions of procedural justice are more likely to reciprocate with greater organisation engagement. Engaged employees are also more likely to have a high-quality relationship with their employer, leading them also to have more positive attitudes, intentions and behaviours. Finally, the study by Saks (2006) found that out of the two aspects of job engagement and organisation engagement, organisation engagement was a much stronger predictor of all of the positive outcomes associated with employee engagement.

Employee engagement and psychological well-being

Employee engagement has a cognitive and emotional component, and therefore strong links with psychological well-being. This connection is explored in detail by Robertson and Cooper (2009, 2012). In the definitions discussed earlier, we noted how the research evidenced a link between engagement and positive organisational outcomes and how this approach contained the two well-established concepts of organisational citizenship and commitment. This perspective adopted by senior business practitioners (Meyer, 1997; Robinson *et al.*, 2004; Attridge, 2009) assumes that, broadly, positive employee attitudes, which organisations are keen to foster, are associated with better performance, and an employee with enhanced performance is likely to be happier and healthier (Wright and Cropanzano, 2000). However, Robertson and Cooper (2009) and Robertson and Cooper (2012: 226) state: 'such a narrow focus risks losing the gains associated with higher levels of psychological well being for both the organisation and the employees themselves'.

Their combined work was predicated on a belief that the construct of engagement needed to be wider and that 'full engagement' (Robertson and Cooper, 2009: 329) comprised commitment and citizenship and also the separate construct of psychological well-being. Their ongoing research therefore sought to disentangle the extent to which it may be distinguished from positive job and work attitudes (engagement) and the extent to which positive psychological well-being explains variance in productivity, over and above that which is explained by engagement (Robertson *et al.*, 2012: 227). The study in 2012 consisted of 9,930 individuals from 12 separate UK organisations across the public and private sector and assessed well-being using a standardised 11-point psychological health scale. They found support for the idea that although psychological well-being and positive job and work attitudes are related, they are in fact separate and distinctive constructs and evidence different relationships with productivity. Employees with higher levels of psychological well-being were found to be more optimistic, more resilient in the face of setbacks and have a stronger belief in their own ability to cope with things (Robertson, 2012: 320). This is important for HR practitioners, because if they focus only on employee work attitudes and ignore the psychological aspects, they will limit the benefits that can be obtained through initiatives designed to enhance engagement. A simple three-category system provides a way of organising the types of interventions that might be developed to improve psychological well-being:

- *Composition,* i.e. changing the composition of the people in the workforce through selection processes, redeployment and job placement.
- *Development,* i.e. developing people who are already part of the workforce through coaching, feedback, stress management training and the use of effective resilience building programmes.
- *Situational engineering,* i.e. re-engineering the situation that people work in through work and job redesign, changes in management and supervision and organisational change.

The findings from these two studies, in particular, place a strong emphasis on the individual psychological well-being of the employee being a major factor in determining the level of positive engagement. The work of Anderson and Keillher (2009) and Susi and Jawaharrani (2011) considered the factors contributing to a positive psychological state and found that employees who had a good work–life balance were more likely to feel psychologically healthy. Analysing this further, their work evidenced the importance of flexible working options as a significant contributory element. Defining flexible working as flexible work hours (e.g. flexitime, which permits workers to vary their start and finish times provided a certain number of hours are worked), a compressed work week (employees work a full week's worth of hours in four days and take the fifth off), working from home (remote working) and sharing a full-time job between two employees (job-sharing), they found that flexibility enhanced feelings of engagement:

- Flexible working builds commitment.
- Flexible workers feel more job satisfaction.
- Flexible workers go the extra mile.
- Flexible working attracts talent.

The conclusion was that organisations offering flexible working were demonstrating a higher level of trust in their employees and operating with a higher level of transparency. This enabled employees to have a greater degree of choice and control over their daily working patterns and it was this expression of trust, combined with the freedom of choice, that was the significant factor that positively influenced their feelings about their jobs, their individual psychological well-being and the organisations for which they worked (Anderson and Keillher, 2009: 14). Richman *et al.* (2008) reported similar findings that stressed the importance of choice and control as fundamental elements of well-being and engagement. They found the actual number of flexible time policies directly affected commitment to the employer and work-related stress, which mediated the costs of having flexible working to the organisation in terms of job performance, absenteeism and missed time.

The existence of supportive work–life practices, especially schedule flexibility and the presence of supportive supervisors, had direct positive effects on the employees' perceived control over work and family matters, as well as some direct effects on psychological, physiological and behavioural indicators of strain. Perceived control, in turn, was associated with lower levels of work–family conflict, and lower levels of job dissatisfaction, depression, somatic complaints and blood cholesterol. The availability of specific work–life programmes, work hours and distinct aspects of the work family culture (time demands, manager support and sensitivity, and negative career consequences of devoting time to family) were differentially related to outcomes of affective commitment, work–family conflict, and intention to leave the organisation.

Organisational drivers of engagement

Engagement does not occur by accident. It is the outcome of several highly integrated approaches to the management of human resources that shape and direct patterns of behaviour, thinking, action and culture. In this respect, it is possible to see how one policy, e.g. on absence management, may influence perceptions of equity and fairness and thereby affect morale among the workers. The task force of 2012, often referred to as the 'MacLeod Review', identified four key 'enablers' that are found in highly engaged organisations:

- Visible, empowering leadership providing a strong strategic narrative about the organisation, where it has come from and where it's going.
- Engaging managers who:
  - focus their people and give them scope;
  - treat their people as individuals;
  - coach and stretch their people.
- Employee voice throughout the organisation, for reinforcing and challenging views; between functions and externally; employees are seen as central to the solution.
- Organisational integrity – the values on the wall are reflected in day-to-day behaviours. There is no 'say–do' gap

So what can organisations do to improve levels of engagement? Research undertaken by the IES (Robinson *et al.*, 2004: 24) indicates that the following areas are of fundamental importance to engagement:

- *Good quality line management* – managers who care about their employees, treat them fairly, encourage them to perform well, take an interest in their career aspirations and provide opportunities for development.
- *Two-way, open communication* – allows employees to voice ideas and suggestions and keeps employees informed about the things that are relevant to them.
- *Effective co-operation* – between different departments and between management and trade unions.
- *Focus on employee development* – providing training that employees need for their current role and fair access to development opportunities.
- *Commitment to employee well-being* – taking health and safety seriously, working to minimise accidents, injuries, violence and harassment, and taking effective action should a problem occur.
- *Clear, accessible HR policies and practices* – senior management and line management commitment to appraisals, equal opportunities and family friendliness.
- *Fair pay and benefits* – in terms of comparison inside and outside the organisation.
- *Harmonious working environment* – encouraging employees to respect and help each other.

These drivers for engagement are represented in Figure 11.1 in a model adapted from the work of Robinson *et al.* (2004).

Employee engagement is more likely to occur when certain conditions exist. Employers can maximise employee engagement by improving these factors. Table 11.1 illustrates the 18 factors that most influence the level of employee engagement and their overall satisfaction with the listed condition of engagement.

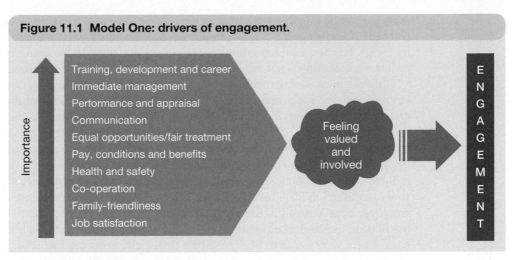

Figure 11.1 Model One: drivers of engagement.

Importance

Training, development and career
Immediate management
Performance and appraisal
Communication
Equal opportunities/fair treatment
Pay, conditions and benefits
Health and safety
Co-operation
Family-friendliness
Job satisfaction

Feeling valued and involved

ENGAGEMENT

Source: Robinson *et al.* (2004).

Table 11.1 Factors that most influence the level of employee engagement

18 conditions of engagement	Percentage overall satisfaction
The work itself	76%
Relationships with co-workers	76%
Opportunities to use skills and abilities	74%
Relationship with immediate supervisor	73%
Contribution of work to organisation's business goals	71%
Autonomy and independence	69%
Meaningfulness of job	69%
Variety of work	68%
Organisation's financial stability	63%
Overall corporate culture	60%
Management's recognition of employee job performance	57%
Job-specific training	55%
Communication between employees and senior management	54%
Organisation's commitment to professional development	54%
Networking	49%
Organisation's commitment to corporate social responsibility	49%
Career development opportunities	48%
Career advancement opportunities	42%

Source: Heathfield (2013).

Organisational benefits of employee engagement

Engaged employees may often feel 'better' about themselves and about their work, but are there any known organisational benefits to having an engaged workforce? Understanding the range of performance outcomes influenced by engagement is important because of the established connections between past engagement and future performance, and there is a wealth of evidence illustrating the value to business of leveraging this relationship. Buckingham is so convinced that he told the MacLeod Review team, that the relationship between engagement and performance was four times stronger than the reverse, leading him to conclude that it was engagement that drove performance (2009). The implication for business is that investing to secure engagement far outweighs and is far more effective than dealing with the outcomes of managing a non-engaged workforce. In a recent CBI Harvey Nash employment trends survey (July 2012), securing high levels of employee engagement was seen as the top workforce priority for UK businesses, ahead even of containing labour costs. In the same year, the head of the civil service identified increasing engagement among all public-sector employees as a priority.

Multiple meta-analytic studies have demonstrated robust cross-sectional links between employee engagement and increases in profits, productivity, innovation, beneficial discretionary effort, customer satisfaction and customer retention. Studies such as those by Podsakoff *et al.* (2002), Halsbesleben (2010) and Christian (2011) have demonstrated that employee engagement reduces absence, voluntary turnover, sabotage and a range of other negative behaviours. These studies have also demonstrated that employee engagement reduces absence, voluntary turnover, sabotage and a range of other negative behaviours. A study published in 2006 by ISR Global Research brought a greater sense of urgency to the employee engagement discussion. Simply stated, employee engagement was seen to affect the bottom line and so ultimately profitability. Organisations with high levels of employee engagement were found to perform better financially, reducing their cost base and increasing profits, compared with benchmarked organisations with lower levels of engagement. In 2010, Gallup, a world leading survey and consultancy organisation, suggested the world's top-performing organisations understood that employee engagement was a force that drove effective business outcomes. A Gallup (2006) study looking at data from over 23,000 business units demonstrated that those with the highest engagement scores (top 25 per cent) averaged 18 per cent higher productivity than those with the lowest engagement scores (bottom 25 per cent), leading them to conclude that engaged employees were more productive employees, more profitable, more customer-focused, safer and more likely to stay with the organisation.

Marks & Spencer's research shows that over a four-year period stores with improving engagement had, on average, delivered £62 million more sales to the business every year than stores with declining engagement. Sainsbury's have found a clear link between higher levels of engagement and sales performance, with the level of colleague engagement contributing up to 15 per cent of a store's year-on-year growth.

The Engagement Task Force of 2012 demonstrated how engagement spanned multiple aspects of organisational life. Employees themselves shared the view that engagement and customer satisfaction go hand in hand. In particular, 78 per cent of highly engaged employees in the UK public sector in 2007 said they could make an impact on public services delivery or customer service.

Management philosophies such as total quality management (TQM), quality circles, employee voice and feedback schemes are important for strategic leadership, communication and consultation, as well as systems and processes that encourage employee involvement in the generation and delivery of ideas that improve productivity. These ideas resonate strongly with the four enablers of employee engagement (visible, manager, voice and integrity). They also provide a convenient vehicle through which to enable employees to have a voice, to feel as though they are being consulted and that their opinions matter. By creating a business environment and a culture that suggests 'inclusion' and 'involvement', the likelihood that employees will feel more valued is greater, and it is known that employees who feel valued are more engaged, that engaged employees perform better and that enhanced performance leads to improved profitability. The employee engagement cycle is therefore virtuous, and thus the risk of employees being disengaged threatens the achievement of positive benefits.

Key Controversy

Organisations are clever at creating an environment in which employees are successfully duped into feeling their voice is being heard and their opinions matter.

Academics, alongside practitioners (e.g. Saks, 2006), also agree that the organisational and business benefits derived from having a fully engaged workforce can be tangible and extremely positive. Rentokil Initial (see Box 11.4) found a clear benefit from increased engagement in the form of improved staff retention. This positive correlation is further evidenced in Harter and Hayes, (2002) meta-analysis study in which they found significant correlations between high reported levels of engagement and the following business dimensions (Harter and Hayes, 2002: 272):

- Improved retention of talent.
- Enhanced levels of customer satisfaction.
- Improved individual performance.
- Higher team performance.
- Greater business unit productivity and profitability.
- Increased enterprise-level financial performance.

Box 11.4 Rentokil Initial

'Rentokil Initial plc has a 66,000 employee group, £2.5 billion turnover and services ranging from pest control to parcel delivery. . . . As a people-based service organisation, Rentokil Initial's service and business results depend heavily on how engaged their employees feel'. The determination and discretionary efforts of employees, particularly sales employees, are crucial to business success, and the cost of replacing employees is approximately 1.5–2 times annual salary plus opportunity costs. Rentokil employed a combination of correlation and gap analysis using 15 months of data and found that those teams that went on to produce the best gross margin began the period with higher engagement levels (+5 per cent) than the initial engagement levels of underperforming teams. The work revealed a key role for engagement in employee retention, especially for sales employees. Rentokil Initial found that 'a one percentage point improvement in engagement improved retention by 0.39 per cent. The teams that improved engagement the most saw retention increase by 6.7 percentage points, providing an estimated savings of £7 million'.

Source: Evidence Case Study: Rentokil Initial 1 April 2013 (**http://www.engageforsuccess.org/ideas-tools/evidence-case-study-rentokil-initial/**; accessed 17 June 2013).

The evidence provided indicates that employee engagement has a material effect on the bottom line in a wide variety of settings and that engaged employees can contribute in ways that affect business performance (profits, productivity, innovation and customer measures) as well as in ways that affect less tangible aspects of business performance, e.g. the people indicators (levels of innovation, morale, well-being, absence/turnover and health and safety). Engaged employees can provide things that are essential for organisations to navigate a turbulent business environment, and in the best-performing organisations employee engagement transcends HR initiatives and becomes a central feature of the prevailing culture. In summary, engagement is seen as a strategic approach to business which is supported by policies to drive improvement and organisational change.

Before we progress, we need to reflect on some of the less obvious implications of these comments. It is accepted by many commentators that employees are 'engaged' if they have a positive attitude towards work. Purcell *et al.* (2003) extends this thinking, suggesting that employee engagement is only really meaningful if there is a more genuine sharing of responsibility between management and employees on issues of substance. The CIPD survey conducted by Truss *et al.* (2006) suggested that strengthening the *employee voice* can make a real difference to organisational performance, in particular if they have the chance to feed their voice up the organisational chain of command. The CIPD survey concluded that currently many organisations are not that successful in doing this and as a result many employees felt they lacked opportunities to express their views and be involved in important decisions.

This finding provokes the following question: if organisations are capable of complex and integrated strategic thinking and the effective execution of complex business planning, how is it that they 'fail' in generating opportunities for employees to voice their views? Research by Robinson (2006) indicates that many employees are greatly under-utilised in the workplace through the lack of opportunities to become involved in work-based decisions and limited opportunities to have their voice heard. Could this be deliberate on the part of the organisations? Critics have argued that management is firmly in control and permits only very limited opportunities for employees to exert any real influence. Hyman and Mason (1995) argue that in reality, schemes to cultivate employee engagement 'extend little or no input into corporate or higher level decision making' (p. 387) and generally do not entail any significant sharing of power and authority. Similarly, Blyton and Turnbull (2004: 272) argued that employee involvement is 'soft on power', reinforcing a cycle of low-trust relationships. The suggestion is that while organisations recognise the potential value of having an engaged workforce, some are also fearful of letting go of their powerbase. In effect, they give scant recognition to the rhetoric of engagement, but actually do little in practice to really permit an equal involvement by the employees.

Key Controversy

Does the organisational rhetoric of employee engagement far exceed the opportunities for engagement that exist in reality?

Employee engagement and the older worker

Enhancing levels of engagement is important for all employees, and given that we know the average age of the working population is increasing, ensuring engagement among older workers is essential. Koc-Menard (2009) considers the role that older workers can play in the anticipated talent shortage. He points out that in both North America and Europe, the number of 55-year-old-plus (55+) workers who choose to extend their work life has increased steadily during the past decades and economists expect this trend to continue (Koc-Menard, 2009: 31). He continues, suggesting that older workers extend their work life either by delaying retirement or by working during retirement and that many companies find it attractive to employ 55+ workers because they bring in valuable assets, such as long experience, in-depth organisational and technical knowledge and rich networks of professional contacts. Attracting older workers has therefore become a key HR priority, but one with a potential problem because, although continued income can induce older workers to remain in employment, this may not be sufficient to ensure motivation and, specifically, engagement.

The engagement of older workers deserves particular attention, in part, because it has long been assumed that it was normative for workers to become disengaged from their work as they get older. To date, however, the academic literature has focused only limited attention on employers' efforts to adjust their strategies for engagement in response to differences in the ages of their employees. Keen to understand the relationship between the older worker and levels of engagement, Pitt-Catsouphes and Matz-Costa (2009) undertook a study involving 83,454 employees in 22 different companies. Four of these companies were in the pharmaceutical industry, five were in technology, five in manufacturing, four in finance and professional services and four were universities. Findings showed that, when compared, workers younger than 35 years old were engaged and, equally, workers aged 55 and older were also highly engaged. This could be explained by the removal of the retirement age, so those who remain in work do so because they want to rather than because they are required to by law. The findings have important implications for the older workers and employers.

Previous studies have found that increases in engagement can have ameliorative effects for employees; this effect suggests that flexibility can be one way to increase older workers' psychological well-being. The positive, moderating effect of flexibility, as described earlier, provides employers with one practical way to maintain the engagement of their talented older workers who want to extend their participation in the labour force. Providing employees with access to the flexibility they need provides managers with a tool to enhance the engagement of workers of all ages, but especially older workers. In summary, having access to much-needed flexibility can be beneficial for employees because older workers express a preference for having access to flexible work options; and, in turn, beneficial for employers because having access to needed flexibility augments engagement, which, as we have seen, is associated with positive outcomes for all parties in the employment relationship (see Box 11.5).

Box 11.5 Flexible working at BT

Since 2001, British Telecommunications (BT) has operated a flexible working portfolio. BT's flexible work portfolio, 'Achieving the balance', is open to all employees but is particularly aimed at 55+ workers. It includes compressed hours, part-time work opportunities and home working and is built on the following elements:

- Wind down: reducing the number of hours at work.
- Step down: moving to a position with fewer responsibilities.
- Time out: taking a career break or a sabbatical (for up to two years).
- Helping hands: taking up charity assignments (also for up to two years).
- Ease down: gradually reducing responsibilities.

Source: Foster (2005)

Foster (2005) suggested that this process enabled BT to develop an appropriate exchange relationship with older employees. The workers receive an opportunity to delay their retirement, while remaining high-value staff to the organisation. It enabled BT to address recruitment challenges related to technical positions and sustain an age-diverse workforce which is able to appreciate and respond to the needs of an ageing client base. As a consequence of being offered jobs that fit the needs of the person, the outcome enabled BT to gain the full engagement of these employees.

Measuring employee engagement

There is considerable interest in measuring levels of engagement, partly because of the numerous links that have been made between high levels of engagement and positive business and the natural tendency for organisations to interpret this connection as source of competitive advantage (Kular *et al.*, 2008). Most efforts to measure engagement have been at the level of the individual worker. Individual-level scores are most often aggregated to provide a level of engagement across all employees in a particular organisation or work cohort.

Many leading international business consulting companies have developed their own proprietary survey tools and processes for measuring work engagement, and while there is some variation among them, most address similar themes. One of the most popular approaches in this area comes from the Gallup Organisation (Harter *et al.*, 2003; Harter and Schmidt, 2008). Results of this work have yielded a 12-item Gallup Workplace Audit (Wagner and Harter, 2006; Rath, 2007; Rath and Conchie, 2009).

Explore

- Have you ever participated in an engagement or attitude survey at work?
- If so, did you feel it was really measuring valuable constructs and that it would enable the organisation to make effective changes to levels of employee engagement?
- Did you answer it with complete honesty or were you somewhat guarded in your responses? Why was this?

Casual observation suggests that much of the appeal to organisational management is driven by claims that employee engagement drives bottom-line results. Indeed, at least one HR consulting firm (Hewitt Associates LLC) indicates that they 'have established a conclusive, compelling relationship between engagement and profitability through higher productivity, sales, customer satisfaction, and employee retention' (Hewitt Associates LLC, 2005: 1). However, the extent to which these organisational benefits can be ascribed to engagement begs the question, as a minimum, as to whether engagement is a unique concept or merely a repackaging of other constructs, what Kelley (1927; cited in Lubinski, 2004: 98) called the 'Jangle Fallacy'. This is a matter of particular significance to those who develop and conduct employee surveys in organisations, because the end users of these products expect interpretations of the results to be in terms of actionable implications. Yet, if the organisation is not certain of precisely what it is measuring, the findings will be at best vague and, at worst, a leap of faith.

Subjective definitions and measurement without action can do more harm than good. Simply surveying for the current level of engagement and then doing nothing with that information may lead to employees feeling that they are being ignored, which may adversely affect morale and levels of trust. Identifying and analysing engagement levels and the drivers of success have to be the first step. However, many organisations continue to attempt to measure employee engagement through the use of surveys. Different names are used for this purpose, including an engagement survey, an attitude survey, a work climate improvement survey and an employee opinion survey.

In 2005, Shaw reviewed employee engagement research and the measurement proposals of many entities, but his study struggled to provide any real clarification. Shaw offered suggestions based on sifting through desk research and interviews and trying to subject the ideas to some reasoned analysis. Shaw broke engagement questions into three macro categories: climate, driver and outcome. In the end, however, Shaw (2005) concluded it is arguably unfeasible to directly measure in the survey all the actions behind engagement, due to the fact that there are potentially thousands of different individual actions, attitudes and processes that affect engagement.

Over and above the inherent problems of actually defining what is meant by the term 'employee engagement', other issues are associated with the use of engagement surveys. Ruck (2011) suggests that employee engagement surveys are so ubiquitous they are accepted as part of everyday working life, and while there are good reasons for surveys (e.g. they can identify, in general terms, what employees are thinking about managers and the organisation), they have a number of inherent problems, which he lists as:

- They measure the wrong factors.
- They are mainly quantitative.
- They are conducted too often.
- The expenditure would be better used for more communication with employees.
- They might be used as an excuse for not involving employees in day-to-day management.

Sullivan (2012) identified several other issues associated with the use of engagement surveys. Setting aside those we have already considered, such as problems associated with definition, some of the most significant issues include the following:

1 *Engagement is not productivity or an output.* A primary concern of organisations is often increasing productivity or output, and while employee engagement may contribute to

productivity, in and of itself, it is not productivity. An employee may be fully engaged and emotionally tied to the firm but without the proper training, leaders, resources or voice, no amount of engagement will improve productivity.

2 *Engagement is not a cause.* Many engagement studies attempt to demonstrate a statistical correlation between higher levels of engagement and enhanced levels of productivity, retention, customer satisfaction or being a top performer. But correlations alone can never prove cause and effect. Another alternative explanation for the apparent connection between engagement and productivity is that when employees are productive, well rewarded, recognised, well managed, and when they produce a great product, then it is those workplace factors that eventually increase their engagement. Equally, if an organisation is seeking to improve efficiency, they may limit overtime, implement pay and hiring freezes, and restrict training. These factors may precipitate a fall in expressed levels of engagement, but may in fact improve overall business performance and profitability.

3 *The ROI may be low.* The cost of employee surveys themselves is high, because in addition to the survey costs, each employee must spend paid time filling them out. The time spent analysing, interpreting and presenting the results can also be significant. This coupled with the fact that any 'action' to improve engagement must be implemented company-wide makes it a significant possibility that the costs outweigh the benefits.

4 *Outside factors may influence engagement.* It is accepted that morale and employee motivation are influenced by factors outside the organisation. It is possible that during periods of high unemployment, employees may feel closer emotional ties simply because they are in employment.

5 *High levels of engagement may not reduce employee turnover.* Much of the rhetoric around engagement suggests that high levels will contribute towards staff retention, but a study by Harris *et al.* (2010) showed a weak connection between engagement and turnover, finding that 43 per cent of the most highly engaged workers had a weak intention to stay. In addition, too strong a level of engagement may adversely affect judgment – there are organisations, including Kodak, Xerox and HP, who were extremely successful in building loyalty, but it was so strong that it resulted in group-think and discounting of external threats or the need for change. The study by Harris *et al.* was revealing, in that it found that in order to be successful, different approaches to engagement were required for different types of employees. For example, analysts are most engaged when they understand the business side of things as well as the analytics, when they know what is expected of them, and when they can keep their technical skills and expertise current. They are most likely to stay when they have a high degree of management support. But when they examined how well companies were arming analysts with critical information about the business, setting clear roles and expectations, feeding analysts' desire to keep up with the latest tools and techniques, and giving analysts the management support they needed, they suggested many organisations still had a long way to go in differentiating responses and actions to meet the needs of specific cohorts of employees (Harris *et al.*, 2010: 30).

Weaver (2013) expressed similar concerns over the unfettered use of engagement surveys and associated action, suggesting they:

- *reinforce* the limiting belief that employee engagement is a process or capability – something that the organisation and its leaders 'do' – rather than an outcome they need to strive to secure;

- *play* into the common preference for rational data driving pragmatic action and encourage a superficial, symptomatic view of what it takes to engage people (devaluing the concept of engagement along the way);

- *fragment focus* on what are perceived as specific engagement issues, driven by individual or clusters of questions, and draw attention away from the more fundamental issues that often undermine engagement;

- *legitimise waste* and, in extreme cases, destructive behaviours and initiatives that ironically often highlight, rather than resolve, the fundamental cultural and leadership issues they intend to address.

While it is clear from the preceding section that engagement is a current hot topic in HR and that many organisations are aware of the 'known' drivers of engagement, what is less clear is how organisations define the term and, as a consequence, exactly how valuable it is to really attempt to measure it or attempt statistical evaluations of levels of engagement. What also became apparent from the work of Harris *et al.* (2010) is the need to distinguish between the factors that promote engagement among different cohorts of workers and, finally, that even with the best intentions, measurements of engagement do not come with their own set of health warnings.

Key Controversy

How far do you agree with the claim that attempting to measure employee engagement via surveys is a waste of time and resources, as organisations are unclear about what it is they are measuring and employees are tired of being asked when nothing ever happens as a result of the comments?

Organisational strategies for enhancing employee engagement

Thus far the chapter has considered a range of issues related to the idea of employee engagement. We have come to understand the complex nature of the concept and to appreciate it as the cognitive, emotional and physical aspects of job performance, characterised by absorption, dedication and vigour, and dependent upon the psychological conditions of meaningfulness, safety and availability. In this final section, we will consider the strategies that organisations adopt in order to actively support and enhance the level of employee engagement.

It is known from studies that employees actively want to be engaged in their work. BlessingWhite (2006) confirms the desire of employees to be more engaged, finding that almost two-thirds (60 per cent) of the employees surveyed wanted more opportunities to grow and develop in their roles and as individuals. Wellins (2005: 11), in the Development Dimensions International report, which defines engagement as 'the extent to which people enjoy and believe in what they do and feel valued for doing it', stated that employees wanted (pp. 12–15):

- attachment to the job;
- agreeableness;
- emotional stability;
- openness to experience;
- achievement orientation;
- self-efficacy.

It was also stated that, in order to achieve this, managers must do five things to create a highly engaged workforce:

- Align efforts with strategy.
- Empower employees.
- Promote and encourage teamwork and collaboration.

- Help people grow and develop.
- Provide support and recognition where appropriate.

The challenge for organisations is to create and sustain an environment, culture, relationships and work roles that enable and facilitate employee engagement. Stated in this way, this sounds relatively straightforward; in reality, however, the approaches and strategies required are as multifaceted and complex as the concept itself and it almost goes without saying that, once again, 'one size will not fit all'.

For today's different generations, access to training and career opportunities, work/life balance and empowerment to make decisions are important factors in the working life. To foster a culture of employee engagement, changing expectations and patterns of behaviours need to be taken into consideration in the design of strategies to enhance levels of engagement. Vance (2006) details some of the changing workplace dynamics that have influenced the growing interest in employee engagement and the approaches that have been adopted:

- Employee–employer relationships are evolving into partnerships.
- There is an increased demand for work–life balance.
- HR has a more strategic role in promoting the links between employee performance and its impact on business goals.
- There is an increasing focus on selective retention for keeping mission-critical talent.
- There is greater work intensification as employers seek to increase productivity with fewer employees and resources.
- Acquiring and retaining key talent are re-emerging as top issues of concern.
- There is a decline in traditional communication methods and an increase in online communication.
- Needs, wants and behaviours of the talent pool are driving changes in attraction, selection and retention practices.

In acknowledging these factors, organisations have responded in ways designed to leverage levels of engagement.

Culture

Literature draws attention to the significance of creating and sustaining an appropriate culture. Research shows that organisations that provide a workplace culture with the psychological conditions of meaningfulness (job enrichment, work–role fit), safety (supportive manager and co-workers) and availability (sufficient and suitable resources) are more likely to have engaged employees (Kay and Jordan-Evans, 2003; May *et al.*, 2004; Lockwood, 2007).

Consequently, organisations considered as an 'employer of choice' are more likely to attract and retain the best talent and have higher levels of engagement. Beyond compensation and benefits, key retention factors include the mission and values of the company, treatment of people, learning and development opportunities, work–life balance policies and practices, and rewards to employees for their efforts.

In addition, employee loyalty must be earned through a culture of respect and integrity and learning and development. Therefore, an organisation that treats its employees with dignity and respect creates a workplace culture that fosters loyalty and engagement by weaving retention and engagement into the fabric of the workplace culture.

Communication

Clear, consistent and honest communication is an important management tool in leveraging employee engagement. HR therefore needs to ensure it promotes clear, concise information about the key business objectives and priorities. Most crucially, the organisation needs to ensure there are channels for employees to engage with the communication and that their voice is heard and responded to. Communication strategies that encourage employee engagement though open dialogue and where strategic and continuous communication lends credibility to the organisation's leadership are more likely to have an engaged workforce. On the other hand, a lack of communication or poorly communicated information can lead to distrust, dissatisfaction, scepticism, cynicism and unwanted turnover.

Effective managers

Research by BlessingWhite (2013) highlighted the manager–employee relationship as the number one factor that influences the level of employee engagement. The manager creates the connection between the employee and the organisation and, as a result, the manager–employee relationship is often the 'deal breaker' in relation to retention. Their study shows that employees who trust their managers appear to have more pride in the organisation and are more likely to feel they are applying their individual talents for their own success and that of the organisation. However, the findings also show that only 56 per cent of employees considered that their manager had a good understanding of their specific job function or fully utilised their unique talents.

BlessingWhite (2013) concluded that managers who demonstrate the following characteristics promote employee engagement:

- Showed a strong commitment to diversity.
- Took responsibility for successes and failures.
- Demonstrated honesty and integrity.
- Found solutions to problems.
- Respected and cared for employees as individuals.
- Set realistic performance expectations.
- Demonstrated passion for success.
- Defended their direct reports.

They also suggested that, by implication, organisations ought to rethink keeping managers who fostered disengaged employees and so lost valuable talent to competitors.

The working environment

Engagement levels are affected by the working environment. Where employees can see that they have support from others to help them do their job, there is a sense of teamwork and they can safely express themselves, then engagement will be higher. This is also linked to ensuring that employees are matched to their jobs. The extent to which there is synergy is a critical driver of engagement. This is one area where HR professionals can play an important role in helping line managers to design jobs effectively, and develop selection processes that match individual skills to jobs. There are clear links here with effective recruitment and selection and ongoing performance review, feedback and development opportunities. The absence of any of these essential actions will limit levels of engagement. There is a further consideration, which is the need for organisations to pay close attention to the selection, development and performance management of line managers to ensure they maximise their potential to be engaging leaders.

Governmental strategies for enhancing employee engagement

In 2009 the UK government commissioned a review of employee engagement. The group, chaired by David MacLeod and Nita Clarke, drew on studies of a wide range of organisations in both private and public sectors. It concluded that leadership, line management, employee voice and integrity are key enablers of engagement and that 'the correlation between engagement, well-being and performance is repeated too often for it to be a coincidence':

- The government should work to raise awareness of employee engagement benefits and techniques.
- A senior sponsor group bringing together business, the public sector, not-for-profit organisations and unions should be set up to boost understanding of this vital topic.
- The government and its agencies should work together to ensure that support is tailored to the needs of organisations in different sectors.

Following the report, in March 2011, the Prime Minister announced a new industry-led task force to build on the work of the earlier report. The government and the task force are committed to the idea that there is a better way to work. A practitioner group has been established which welcomes participation from UK-based private-, public- and third-sector organisations. The task force is charged with publishing evidence on the impact of employee engagement on performance, productivity and profitability; launching a major free-to-use interactive website with information, case studies, tools and techniques; holding engagement events in a wide range of companies and organisations; and rolling out a national practitioners' network. Employee engagement as a strategy to support economic growth has clearly secured the interest of the government.

Patterns of engagement across the world

So far this chapter has focused on engagement in the UK and the USA, but interest in the concept is worldwide, so it is important to consider whether the same engagement techniques work for employees in countries with different economies and cultures. In 2004, International Survey Research (ISR), the international research consultancy, completed a major survey into the nature and causes of employee engagement and how organisations can improve engagement to enhance business performance. The survey was conducted across 10 of the world's largest economies – Australia, Brazil, Canada, France, Germany, Hong Kong, the Netherlands, Singapore, the UK and the USA –involving nearly 160,000 employees from a range of sectors. The results show large variations among the 10 countries in terms of employees' overall commitment to, and involvement with, their employers (see Table 11.2). For example, in Brazil and in the USA, 75 per cent of employees were found to be engaged with their companies, whilst only 59 per cent

Table 11.2 Employee engagement worldwide

	Engagement	Satisfaction	Leadership	Willingness to change	Role clarity
Worldwide average	7.2	6.6	6.3	7.1	6.0
North america	7.2	6.7	6.6	7.1	6.2
South america	7.7	6.9	6.5	7.6	6.7
Europe	7.3	6.6	6.3	7.1	6.0
Africa	7.5	6.4	6.2	7.4	5.5
Asia	6.8	6.3	6.0	6.7	5.3
Australia	7.3	6.5	6.3	7.3	5.7

Source: Global Employee Engagement Index™, Effectory (2011) cited in Vilet, J. 2012 'Employee engagement: here's why it's a worldwide problem'.

of French employees were engaged. In Australia, Singapore and Hong Kong, the extent to which management is respected emerged as an influential determinant of engagement. In the UK and the USA, on the other hand, a more important factor was the degree to which organisations provide long-term employment and career opportunities. The research reveals that one size does not fit all when it comes to employee engagement with their organisation and/or work.

Ram and Prabhakar (2011) make reference to studies by the Gallup Organisation which show that 20 per cent of US employees are disengaged, 54 per cent are neutral about their work and only 26 per cent are actively engaged (Fleming *et al.*, 2005). The most comprehensive studies in this area have been undertaken by Towers Perrin, with the results compiled in a book by Gebauer and Lowman (2009). Data for the 2005 survey, entitled 'Winning strategies for a global workforce', were collected from more than 85,000 employees in 16 countries. The findings indicated that, worldwide, over 24 per cent of employees were disengaged, 62 per cent of employees were moderately engaged and only 14 per cent of employees were considered to be highly engaged (Towers Perrin, 2006). This study also showed a wide range between different countries in the percentage of their workforce who were highly engaged, with Mexico (40 per cent) and Brazil (31 per cent) being at the high end, the USA (21 per cent) and Canada (17 per cent) in the middle, and Europe (11 per cent) and Asia (7 per cent) at the low end.

Towers Perrin also conducted a Global Workplace survey in 2007–08 entitled 'Closing the engagement gap: a road map for driving superior business performance'. Data from 90,000 employees in 18 countries revealed that the business climate was, if anything, more complex, more volatile and more interconnected than it was in 2005. Based on a statistical analysis of their responses to the full set of questions, survey respondents were clustered into four groups (see Table 11.3):

● *Engaged* – those giving full discretionary effort, with high scores on all three dimensions.
● *Enrolled* – the partly engaged, with higher scores on the rational and motivational dimensions, but less connected emotionally.
● *Disenchanted* – the partly disengaged, with lower scores on all three components of engagement, especially the emotional connection.
● *Disengaged* – those who have disconnected rationally, emotionally and motivationally.

They concluded that the global workforce is not engaged, at least not to the extent that employers want or need their employees to be to drive results. They termed this the 'engagement gap' and defined it as the difference between the discretionary effort that organisations need for competitive advantage and the organisations' ability to elicit this effort from a significant portion of the workforce. Significantly, organisations were seen to have a pivotal role in forging the connections that define engagement and ensuring they keep their talent on the job and highly productive. Essentially, they suggested organisations can make a huge difference in creating a more engaged workforce if they focus on:

● effective and engaged leadership at the top;
● customising and shaping a work environment and culture to match their unique basis for competitive advantage, tangibly aligning workforce strategies with business priorities;

Table 11.3 Levels of engagement across 18 countries

Level of engagement	Percentage
Engaged	21%
Enrolled	41%
Disenchanted	30%
Disengaged	8%

- putting their workforce under the same microscope as they do their customers, in order to understand employees' needs, issues, values and 'buying' patterns to ensure they make the right choices about what tasks they will undertake with what level of focus and invest their time and energies most appropriately to drive the right business outcomes.

Towers Perrin found that almost four out of five workers were not achieving their full potential or doing what it takes to help their organisations succeed. More disturbing still, almost two out of five (the disenchanted and disengaged) have, what Towers and Perrin refer to as, already 'checked out'. This is significant because this and other studies consistently evidence a link between employee engagement and business performance. In two of their most recent surveys, Towers Perrin found that when they correlated engagement levels with financial results across 50 global companies over a one-year period, the companies with high employee engagement had a 19 per cent increase in operating income and almost a 28 per cent growth in earnings per share. Conversely, companies with low levels of engagement witnessed operating income drop more than 32 per cent and earnings per share decline over 11 per cent. In a similar study over a longer time horizon involving 40 global companies over three years, they found a spread of more than 5 per cent in operating margin and more than 3 per cent in net profit margin between the companies with high employee engagement and those with low engagement. The obvious question arising from these survey results is why, if organisations are aware of the link between engagement and business performance, are levels of engagement comparatively low. The answer, according to Towers Perrin is that it is 'chiefly because many, if not most, organisations and their leaders don't understand their role in the engagement equation and have, to a certain extent, lost sight of both their power and responsibility to drive engagement'. Based on this summary, the admissible conclusion is that most, if not all, employees want to be engaged and want to have the opportunity to deliver discretionary effort, but for some reason or other the organisations across the world are consistently failing to elicit this effort from a significant portion of the workforce.

Explore

- Based on your experience of working with employees from other countries, would you consider there are international differences in levels of engagement?
- How would you explain the differences?

In one of the most recent studies of this type, undertaken in 2012, Vilet, President of Vilet International, comments on the findings from research undertaken by Effectory using over 12,000 respondents in 47 countries. They paint a similar picture of differences between countries and of lower levels of engagement than might be possible. The scores were based on a 10-point scale, 10 being the most positive. The research found:

- Only two-thirds of employees worldwide are engaged.
- Company loyalty is at a five-year low.
- Over 40 per cent of the global workforce intends to leave their current employer within five years.

Employee engagement across the world has stagnated at 2008 levels.

Key Controversy

How far is a worldwide stagnation of levels of employee engagement a reflection of employee apathy or organisational mismanagement?

Summary

- This chapter has illustrated the complex nature of employee engagement. It has demonstrated the extent to which it is a managed workplace approach designed to ensure that employees are committed to their organisation's goals and values, motivated to contribute to organisational success, and are able at the same time to enhance their own sense of well-being. In broad terms, it can be understood as cognitive, emotional and physical role performance characterised by absorption, dedication and vigour, and dependent upon the psychological conditions of meaningfulness, safety and availability.

- The CIPD have defined the drivers of employee engagement as having opportunities to feed your views upwards, feeling well-informed about what is happening in the organisation and believing that your manager is committed to your organisation.

- The IES concluded that the main driver of engagement is a sense of feeling valued and involved. The main components of this are said to be:
  - involvement in decision-making; freedom to voice ideas (to which managers listen); feeling enabled to perform well; having opportunities to develop the job; and feeling the organisation is concerned for employees' health and well-being.

- Macy and Schneider (2008) suggested engagement has three dimensions: *intellectual engagement* – thinking hard about the job and how to do it better; *affective engagement* – feeling positively about doing a good job; and *social engagement* – actively taking opportunities to discuss work-related improvements with others at work.

- The concept of engagement has been compared with other similar constructs, such as employee motivation, employee commitment, employee satisfaction and, more recently, concepts such as OCB. However, supported by the work of researchers, such as Meyer (1997), Buckingham (1999), Wright and Cropanzano (2000), Harter *et al.* (2003), Bakker (2009), Macey and Schneider (2009) and Avey *et al.* (2009), the chapter concludes that engagement is something more, something new and slightly different which transcends related concepts.

- The link between high levels of engagement and organisational benefits has been cited by Harter *et al.* (2002) as improved retention of talent, enhanced levels of customer satisfaction, improved individual performance, higher team performance, greater business unit productivity and profitability and increased enterprise-level financial performance.

- The chapter considered the strategies organisations adopt in order to generate engagement. Four key aspects were mentioned in detail: the need to create an appropriate culture; the importance of open and transparent communication with the vital channel for upwards communication by the employees being open and robust; the need to ensure the integrity and competence of line managers and their skills in managing employees and ensuring their full potential was being realised; and the need to create an appropriate working environment in which employees had the resources they required in order to undertake their roles effectively.

- Engagement levels across the world vary, but the significant conclusion is that the global workforce is not engaged, at least not to the extent that employers want or need their employees to be in order to drive results. The findings indicated that, worldwide, over 24 per cent of employees were disengaged, 62 per cent of employees were moderately engaged and only 14 per cent of employees were considered to be highly engaged. This has been termed the 'engagement gap' and it is defined as the difference between the discretionary effort that organisations need for competitive advantage and the organisations' ability to elicit this effort from a significant portion of the workforce.

Questions

1 According to the 2006 Conference Board report 'Employee engagement, a review of current research and its implications', 12 major studies on employee engagement had been

published in the previous four-year period by top research firms such as Gallup, Towers Perrin, the Corporate Leadership Council and others. Each of the studies used different definitions and, collectively, came up with 26 key drivers of engagement. Given this context, what challenges may arise in attempting to measure employee engagement?

2 It is suggested that employee engagement is just the latest 'fad' and, by implication, has no antecedents. How far do you agree with this assertion? Use related academic material to support your argument.

3 What role can HR practitioners play in developing employee engagement as a means for improving organisational performance?

4 How far do you agree with the assumption that high levels of employee engagement will produce higher levels of profitability, which will benefit the viability of the business? What is your evidence base and what strategies could organisations employ to raise levels of engagement and profitability?

5 If employee engagement has become the Holy Grail, then employee disengagement has, by implication, become the organisational antithesis. What strategies and approaches would you advocate organisations to develop in an effort to discourage disengagement? How would you evaluate the relative success of these strategies and approaches?

Case study

A study of the link between performance management and employee engagement in Western multinational corporations operating across India and China

In the period between 2008 and 2011, four companies in four very different geographic areas participated in a research study to explore links between performance management and employee engagement. The four companies were:

- *GKN (UK, India, China)*. A 'leading global supplier to the world's automotive, off-highway and aerospace manufacturers. GKN provides technology-based, highly engineered products to virtually all of the world's major manufacturers of light vehicles, agricultural and construction equipment, aircraft and aero engines. Headquartered in the UK, some 40 000 people work in GKN companies and joint ventures in more than 30 countries'.

- *AkzoNobel (Netherlands, India, China)*. A 'major global paints and coatings company and a producer of speciality chemicals. The portfolio includes well-known brands such as Dulux, Sikkens, International and Eka. AkzoNobel is a Global Fortune 500 company and is consistently ranked one of the leaders on the Dow Jones Sustainability Indexes. Operations are based in more than 80 countries, involving 57 000 employees around the world. The corporate headquarters is based in Amsterdam, the Netherlands'.

- *Tesco HSC (India)*. 'Tesco HSC is the global services arm for Tesco, a major retailer operating in 14 countries, employing over 492 000 people in 2009, providing IT, business and finance services to its operations across Europe, Asia and America. Tesco HSC went live in May 2004, and at the time of the study had over 3000 employees. Tesco HSC has three functions: IT (1700 employees), Business Services (500 employees) and Financial services (600 employees). Tesco HSC designs, develops, tests and manages some of the retailer's mission-critical IT applications.'

- *InsureCo (Asia-Pacific)*. InsureCo Group (a pseudonym used for confidentiality reasons) is 'active in the fields of banking, investments, life insurance and retirement services in more than 40 countries. With its substantial worldwide experience and with nearly 125 000 employees, InsureCo Group provides a full range of integrated financial services to over 85 million customers globally, including individuals, families, small businesses, large corporations, institutions and governments'.

(*Source:* Farndale *et al.* 2011:5)

The study built on an understanding of the significance of effective employee engagement in leveraging business success, in particular in India and China, where staff turnover can run at almost epidemic proportions. Farndale *et al.*, suggest ' . . . learning how

Case study continued

to engage employees and build loyalty to the organization was identified as crucial for future success' (2011:4).

Cultural differences were recognised as a further significant dimension in understanding, developing and ultimately securing employee engagement. As the report indicates:

> In Western Countries (e.g. UK and the Netherlands) and Eastern (e.g. China and India) cultures have been shown to differ significantly, particularly with respect to the need for organisational hierarchies, and a focus on individuals versus groups (Hofstede, 1980). Such differences were thought likely to influence the manner in which employees respond to organisations, the systems in place to manage performance and the managers with whom they work. This in turn, was believed to have implications for their levels of engagement and the factors which influence this. The study therefore sought to develop a better understanding of the link between performance management and employee engagement in cross-cultural settings.

Source: Farndale *et al.* (2011: 4).

The case study respondents

InsureCo profiles the youngest respondents in the study, whilst the GKN sample included the oldest workers. AkzoNobel had a majority of people who designated themselves as middle managers, compared to a more even spread between professional, technical and middle management respondents in GKN and Tesco HSC. However, as a result of the criteria for the study, all samples were over-representative of higher levels of management and under-representative of employees with less than one year's service. GKN respondents had a relatively even spread across lengths of tenure, whereas in the remaining three companies many respondents had less than five years' service. As the report states:

> All the samples were dominated by male respondents with AkzoNobel having the largest relative proportion of female respondents. In all other respects, the samples were fairly representative of the employee populations. The average profile respondent was a male middle manager, aged 30–39, with up to five years' service with the company.

Source: Farndale *et al.* (2011: 7–8).

The case study design

'The research design involved constructing multiple case studies for each of the participating companies in the different country locations. There were two methods of data collection: qualitative semi-structured interviews or focus groups, and an online questionnaire' (Farndale *et al.*, 2011:6).

The dimensions

The study explored four dimensions of employee engagement based on two different foci of engagement, and whether employees' feelings (state) or behaviour were critical to engagement:

	Job-focused	**Organisation-focused**
State	Job state engagement	Organisation state engagement
Behaviour	Job behavioural engagement	Organisation behavioural engagement

Source: Farndale *et al.* (2011: 27).

Job state engagement was based on employees having great enthusiasm for their work which 'can lead to individuals talking passionately about their job, but not necessarily having loyalty to the company they work for (although the two can be highly correlated). Organisation state engagement' refers to employees who adore the company, often making effective ambassadors for the corporate brand. Behavioural engagement was defined as being less focused on the job or the organisation and being 'more about employees going the extra mile and putting in the extra effort to complete the work. Job behavioural engagement was about taking the initiative in daily work, and looking for development opportunities. Organisation behavioural engagement' was characterised as evidencing concern with 'employees being proactive in highlighting problems and suggesting improvements'.

Farndale *et al.* (2011) suggest that while 'behavioral engagement may be more beneficial to firms from a productivity perspective' p.27. Organisation state engagement was central in creating a pleasant environment for employees to work in. The key point emerging from the study was an acknowledgment that engagement is a multifaceted concept and that while all organisations may seek to enhance levels of engagement, it remains important for them to understand and be clear about what type is being sought and ultimately evaluated and to be aware of which of the four types identified in this case study are important for the operating context of the business.

Employee engagement has been acknowledged as important to the successful operation and development of organisations and as contributory factor to enhanced

Case study continued

competitive advantage and profitability. Engaging employees and building loyalty to the organisation is therefore crucial for future success. 'It is known through the work of Hofstede that cultures have been shown to differ significantly, particularly with respect to the need for organisational hierarchies, and a focus on individuals versus groups (Hofstede, 1980)'. Farndale *et al.* (2011) indicate: 'It has been argued that these differences are likely to influence the way employees respond to the organisations and managers they work for and the systems in place to manage their performance. This in turn is likely to have implications for their levels of engagement and the factors which influence this' p. 4.

Key findings

From the perspective of performance management, 'the study found employee involvement in target setting was linked positively to the two types of state engagement, but having' frequent appraisals was of least consequence, as it was only linked to organisation state engagement. A broad range of performance appraisal outcomes '(such as promotion, training, pay increase, etc.) were positively linked to all the desired engagement outcomes except for organisation behavioural engagement'.

'Work climate and job characteristics (available resources and demands), higher levels of job resources (with the occasional exception of autonomy and feedback) and the specific organisation resources of support and welfare were all positively related to the desired outcomes.'

In relation to 'demands on employees, high workload was linked to lower levels of organisation state engagement and organisation performance perceptions. Conversely, high emotional loads were linked to higher levels of job and organisational behavioural engagement, as was high pressure to produce at the organisation level. These organisation demands were also positively associated with job state engagement. The study suggested that rather than assuming pressures or demands in work always need to be minimised in order to maximise effectiveness and efficiency' a 'certain level of demand is positive for employee

engagement' although it stands to reason a 'balance' is required for optimal performance levels. From the data it can also be 'concluded that high levels of job and organisation resources in general are the key elements linked to all of the types of engagement studied'.

In summary, engagement can be viewed as a two-way process. Employees in the study appeared 'more willing to engage with the organisation when they considered they received something in return, such as extra pay in China or India, and work–life balance in the Netherlands. Engagement with the organisation as a whole, rather than just with a person's job, was generally seen as preferable and expected to lead ultimately to better productivity and profit'. However, the quality of the relationship with the line manager was seen as fundamentally critical to encouraging and supporting employee engagement. The better the individual relationship the more likely employee engagement would be realised.

Questions

1 The case study distinguishes between levels of engagement with the job and levels of engagement with the organisation and makes the point that behavioural engagement may be more beneficial to firms' productivity, whereas state engagement creates a pleasant environment for employees to work in. If this is the case, what HR strategies would you adopt to actively promote both behavioural engagement and state engagement?

2 The case study indicates that employee involvement in target setting was linked positively to the two types of state engagement, but having frequent appraisals was of least consequence, as it was only linked to organisation state engagement. As an HR professional, how would you achieve this level of participation in target setting?

Source: Farndale, E., Hope-Hailey, V., Kellier, C. and van Veldhoven, M. (2011) *A study of the link between Performance Management and Employee Engagement in Western multinational corporations operating across India and China.* Alexandria, VA: Society of Human Resource Management (SHRM). Excerpts in quotations within case study running text are from Farndale *et al.* (2011) unless stated otherwise.

References and further reading

Anderson, D. and Keillher, D. (2009) 'Flexible working and engagement; the importance of choice', *Strategic HR Review,* 8, 2: 13–18.

Attridge, M. (2009) 'Measuring and managing employee work engagement: a review of the research and business literature', *Journal of Workplace Behavioural Health,* 24, 4: 383–398.

Avey, J., Smith, R. and Palmer, N. (2010) 'Impact of positive psychological capital on employee well being over time', *Journal of Occupational Health Psychology,* 15, 1: 17–28.

Bakker, A., Leiter, M. and Trais, T. (2008) 'Work engagement an emerging concept in occupational psychology', *Work and Stress,* 22, 3: 187–200.

Barkworth, R. (2004) 'Organisational citizenship behaviour: A review of current research' in D. Robinson, S. Perryman and S. Hayday (eds) *The Drivers of Employee Engagement (Appendix)*. Institute of Employment Studies Report 408. Brighton: IES, pp. 41–50.

Baumruk, R. (2004) 'The missing link: the role of employee engagement in business success', *Workspan*, 47: 48–52.

BlessingWhite (2006) *Employee Engagement Report*. Princetown, NJ. Online: **http://www.blessingwhite.com/content/reports/engagement_report_2006.pdf** (accessed May 2013).

BlessingWhite (2013) *Employee Engagement Research Update Beyond the Numbers: A Practical Approach for Individuals, Managers, and Executives*. Online: http://www.blessingwhite. com/EEE__report.asp (accessed May 2013).

Blyton, P. and Turnball D. (2004) *The Dynamics of Employee Relations*. Basingstoke: Palgrave.

Buckingham, M. (1999) *First: Break All The Rules:What the World's Greatest Managers Do Differently*. New York, NY: Simon & Schuster.

Christian, M. (2011) 'Work engagement: a quantitative review and test of its relations with task and contextual performance', *Personnel Psychology*, 64, 1: 89–136.

CIPD (2009) *Promoting the Value of Learning in Adversity*. Guide. London: CIPD. Online: **http://www.cipd.co.uk/NR/rdonlyres/EEFFF289-1B3E-46BF-89FF-082A553B0ED6/0/4846ValueoflearningWEB.pdf** (accessed January 2014).

CIPD (2010) *Creating An Engaged Workforce: Findings from The Kingston Employee Engagement Consortium Project*. London: CIPD.

Cleland, A., Mitchinson, W. and Townend, A. (2008) *Engagement, Assertiveness and Business Performance – A New Perspective*. Charlbury: I. C. Ltd.

Conference Board (2006) *Employee Engagement A Review of Current Research and Its Implications*, Report by John Gibbons. Online: **http://www.conferenceboard.ca/e-library/abstract.aspx?did=1831** (accessed May 2013).

Cropanzano, M and Mitchell, N. (2005) 'Social exchange theory: an interdisciplinary review', *Journal of Management*, 31, 6: 874–900.

Effectory (2011) *Global Employee Engagement Index*. Online: **http://www.employee-engagement-index.com/?utm_source=Google&utm_medium=cpc&utm_campaign=1.08.11.058&gclid=CI6vwpu07rkCFXMQtAod11oA9w** (accessed May 2013).

Farndale, E., Hope-Hailey, V., Kellier, C. and van Veldhoven, M. (2011) *A Study of the Link between Performance Management and Employee Engagement in Western Multinational Corporations Operating across India and China*. Online: **http://www.shrm.org/about/foundation/research/documents/farndale%20final%20report%2010-11.pdf** (accessed May 2013).

Fleming, J.H. Ph.D. and Asplund, J. (2007) *Human Sigma: Managing the Employee–Customer Encounter*, Gallup Press.

Fleming, J., Coffman, C. and Harter, J. (2005) 'Manage your human Sigma', *Harvard Business Review*, 83, 7: 106–15.

Foster, C. (2005). 'BT – positive about age', *Equal Opportunities Review*, 138: 5–9.

Franks, D. and Taylor, R. (2004) 'The race for talent: retaining and engaging workers in the 21st century', *Human Resource Planning*, 27, 3: 12–25.

Gallup (2006) 'Gallup study: engaged employees inspire company innovation: national survey finds that passionate workers are most likely to drive organisations forward', *The Gallup Management Journal*, 12 October. Online: **http://**

gmj.gallup.com/content/24880/Gallup-Study-Engaged-Employees-Inspire-Company.aspx (accessed May 2013).

Gallup (2010) *Employee Engagement: What's Your Engagement Ratio?* Washington: Gallup.

Gatenby, C., Soane, E. and Truss, K. (2009) *Employee Engagement in Context*. London: CIPD.

Gebauer, J. and Lowman, D. (2009) *Closing the Engagement Gap: How Great Companies Unlock Employee Potential for Superior Results*. New York: Portfolio Penguin.

Harris, J., Craig. E. and Egan, H. (2010) *Counting on Analytical Talent*. Accenture.

Harter, J. and Hayes, T. (2002) 'Business unit level outcomes between employee satisfaction, employee engagement and business outcomes: a meta analysis', *Journal of Applied Psychology*, 87, 2: 268–279.

Harter, J. and Schmidt, F. (2008) 'Conceptual versus empirical distinctions among constructs: implications for discriminant validity', *Perspectives on Science and Practice*, 1, 1: 36–9.

Harter, J.K., Schmidt, F.L. and Keyes, C.L.M. (2003) 'Well-being in the workplace and its relationship to business outcomes: A review of the Gallup studies' in C. Keyes and J. Haidt (eds) *Flourishing: Positive Psychology and the Life Well Lived*. Washington, DC: American Psychological Association, pp. 205–224.

Heathfield, S. (2013) 18 *Critical Factors to Improve Employee Satisfaction and Engagement: Keys for Improving Employee Satisfaction and Engagement*. Online: http://humanresources. about.com/od/Employee-Engagement/a/keys-for-improving-employee-satisfaction-and-engagement.htm (accessed May 2013).

Hewitt Associates LLC. (2005) *Employee Engagement*. Online: **http://was4.hewitt.com/ hewitt/services/talent/subtalent/ee_engagement.htm** (accessed April 2013).

Hofstede, G. (1980) *Culture's Consequences: International Differences in Work-related Values*. Beverly Hills, CA: Sage Publications.

Hyman, J. and Mason, D. (1995) *Managing Employee Involvement and Participation*. London: Sage.

International Survey Research (2004) *Measuring Employee Engagement: A Three-part Model and its Link to Financial Performance*. Online: **http://www.isrsurveys.com/pdf/insight/casestudy_engagement04.pdf** (accessed May 2013).

Johnson, M. (2004) *The New Rules of Engagement*. London: CIPD.

Jones. J. and Harter, J. (2005) 'Race effects on the employee engagement-turnover intention relationship', *Journal of Leadership & Organizational Studies*, 11, 2: 78–88.

Kahn, W.A. (1990) 'Psychological conditions of personal engagement and disengagement at work', *Academy of Management Journal*, 33, 4: 692–724.

Kahn, W.A (1992) 'To Be Fully There: Psychological Presence at Work', *Human Relations*, 45, 4: 321–49.

Kaye, B. and Jordan-Evans, S. (2003) 'Engaging talent', *Executive Excellence*, 20, 8: 11.

Koc-Menard, S. (2009) 'Flexible work options for older workers', *Strategic HR Review*, 8, 2: 31–36.

Kular, S., Gatenby, M., Rees, C., Soane, E. and Truss, K. (2008) 'Employee engagement: a literature Review', *Working Paper 19*. K. B. S. Kingston: Kingston University.

Lockwood, N. (2007) 'Leveraging employee engagement for competitive advantage: hr's strategic role', *HR Magazine*, 52, 3: 1–11.

Lubinski, D. (2004) 'Introduction to the special section on cognitive abilities: 100 years after Spearman's (1904) 'general intelligence' objectively determined and measured', *Journal of Personality and Social Psychology*, 86, 1: 96–111.

Macey, W. and Schneider, B. (2008) 'The meaning of employee engagement', *Industrial and Organizational Psychology: Perspectives on Science and Practice*, 1, 1: 3–30.

MacLeod, D. (2009) *Engaging for Success: Enhancing Performance through Employee Engagement*. London: Department for Business.

May, R, Gilson, R. and Harter, M. (2004) 'The psychological conditions of meaningfulness, safety and availability and the engagement of the human spirit at work', *Occupational and Organisational Psychology*, 77, 3: 11–37.

Meyer, J. (ed.) (1997) *Organisational Commitment. International Review of Industrial and Organisational Psychology*. New York: John Wiley & Sons.

Meyer, J. and Allen, N. (1991) 'A three-component conceptualization of organizational Commitment', *Human Resource Management Review*, 1, 1: 61–89.

Nelson, D.L. and Simmons, B.L. (2003) 'Health psychology and work stress: a more positive approach' in J.C. Quick and L.E. Tetrick (eds) *Handbook of Occupational Health Psychology*. Washington, DC: American, pp. 97–119.

Penna (2007) *Meaning at Work Research Report*. Online: **http://www.e-penna.com/newsopinion/research.aspx** (accessed May 2013).

Pitt-Catsouphes, M. (2008) 'The multi-generational workforce: workplace flexibility and engagement', *Community, Work and Family*, 11, 2: 215–29.

Pitt-Catsouphes, M., Matz-Costa, C. and Besen, E. (2009) *Age & generations: Understanding experiences at the workplace*, Research Highlight No. 6. Chestnut Hill, MA: Sloan Center on Aging & Work at Boston College. Online: http://www.bc.edu/content/dam/files/research_sites/agingandwork/pdf/publications/RH06_Age_Generations.pdf (accessed May 2013).

Podsakoff, N. (2009) 'Individual and organisational-level consequences of organisational citizenship behaviours: a meta-analysis', *Journal of Applied Psychology*, 94, 1: 122–41.

Purcell, J., Kinnie, N., Hutchinson, S., Rayton, B. and Swart, J. (2003) *Understanding the People and Performance Link: Unlocking the Black Box*. London: CIPD.

Rafferty, A. (2005) *What makes a good employer?* Issue Paper 3. Geneva: International Council of Nurses.

Ram, T. and Prabhakar, R. (2011) 'The role of employee engagement in work-related outcomes', *Interdisciplinary Journal of Research in Business*, 1, 3: 47–61.

Rath, T. (2007) *The Strength Finder*. New York: Gallup Press.

Rath, T.and Conchie, T. (2009) *Strengths Based Leadership: Great Leaders, Teams, and Why People Follow*. New York: Gallup Press.

Richman, A. (2006) 'Everyone wants an engaged workforce how can you create it?' *Workspan*. 49: 36–9.

Robertson, I. and Cooper, C. (2009) 'Full engagement: the integration of employee engagement and psychological well being', *Leadership and Organisational Development Journal*, 31, 4: 324–336.

Robertson, I. and Cooper, C. (2012) 'Job and work attitudes, engagement and employee performance. Where does psychological well being fit in?', *Leadership and Organisational Development Journal*, 33, 2: 224–32.

Robinson, I. (2006) *Human Resource Management in Organisations*. London: CIPD.

Robinson, D., Perryman, S. and Hayday, S. (2004) *The Drivers of Employee Engagement Report 408*. Brighton: IES.

Rothwell, W. (2010) *Beyond Rules of Engagement: How Can Organizational Leaders Build a Culture that Supports High Engagement?*, A Dale Carnegie White Paper. University Park, PA: The Pennsylvania State University.

Ruck, K. (2011) *Five Problems with Employee Engagement Surveys*. E. I. Communication. Online: **http://www.exploring internalcommunication.com/five-problems-with-employee-engagement-surveys/#sthash.asmADqu6.dpuf** (accessed March 2013).

Saks, A. (2006) 'Antecedents and consequences of employee engagement', *Journal of Managerial Psychology*, 21, 7: 600–619.

Shaw, K. (2005) *Employee Engagement, How To Build A High-Performance Workforce*. London: Melcrum Publishing Limited.

Silverman, M. (2004) *Non-Financial Recognition: The Most Effective of Rewards?* Brighton: IES. Online: http://www.employment-studies.co.uk/pdflibrary/mp4.pdf accessed May 2013).

Soldati, P. (2007) *Employee Engagement: What Exactly Is It?* Online: **http://www.management-issues.com/opinion/4008/employee-engagement-what-exactly-is-it/** (accessed April 2013).

Sullivan, J. (2012) *What's Wrong with Employee Engagement? The Top Twenty Problems*. Online: **http://www.ere.net/2012/02/23/what%E2%80%99s-wrong-with-employee-engagement-the-top-20-potential-problems/** (accessed April 2013).

Susi, S. and Jawaharrani, K. (2011) 'Work life balance: the key driver of employee engagement', *Asian Journal of Management Research*, 2, 1: 474–83.

Towers Perrin-ISR (2006) *The ISR Employee Engagement Report*.

Towers Watson (2012) *Engagement at Risk: Driving Strong Performance in a Volatile Global Environment. Global Workforce Study*. Online: **http://towerswatson.com/assets/pdf/2012-Towers-Watson-Global-Workforce-Study.pdf** (accessed May 2013).

Truss, C., Soane, E., Edwards, C., Wisdom, K., Croll, A. and Burnett, J. (2006) *Working Life: Employee Attitudes and Engagement 2006*. London: CIPD.

Vance, R. (2006) *Effective Practice Guidelines: Employee Engagement and Commitment*. Alexandria, VA: SHRM Foundation. Online: **http://www.shrm.org/about/.../1006 employeeengagementonlinereport.doc** (accessed April 2013).

Wagner, R. and Harter, J. (2006) *12: The Great Elements of Managing*. Washington, DC: T.G. Organisation.

Weaver, M. (2013) 'Employee engagement surveys: please handle with care'. Online: **http://www.dpacoms.com/blog/employee-engagement-surveys-please-handle-with-care/** (accessed January 2014). DPA.

Welch, J. and Welch, S. (2006) 'Ideas the welch way: how healthy is your company?', *Business Week*, 8 May: 126.

Wellins, R. (2005) *Development Dimensions International Report*. Online: **http://www.ddiworld.com/home?lang=en-US** (accessed May 2013).

Wright, T. and Cropanzano, R. (2000) 'Psychological well being and job satisfaction as predictors of job performance', *Journal of Occupational Health Psychology*, 15, 1: 89–94.

Chapter 12

Performance management

Deborah Price

Objectives

- To demonstrate how management thinking has influenced current perceptions of performance management.
- To explore the motivations behind individual and organisational performance management.
- To consider the definition of performance management and to characterise this as a cycle.
- To critically review the means through which performance is managed.
- To explore the issues of performance appraisal.
- To discuss contemporary issues around surveillance and collaboration and their impact on managing individual and organisational performance.
- To look at the management of performance in relation to diverse and ageing workforces.

Introductory case study

Mouldaplas

Mouldaplas is a ceramics moulding firm making precision parts for aircraft engines. The company was established 40 years ago by Mr Thomas. Having worked at a major airline engine manufacturing company, he decided that there was scope in the market for a small firm to take over the smaller-scale precision ceramics work. Having started out with a few contracts from smaller airline engine manufacturers, he steadily grew the business. Today the firm employs 700 people in manufacturing, and produces the precision ceramics for the major airline company that Mr Thomas previously worked for. The business is largely non-unionised and the structure is functional, with different departments responsible for different product lines. Each department has been given a name, so that there is no evident hierarchy between those who deal with the prestige brand companies and those who deal with the smaller airlines. The departments are named after classic British war planes, and for the purpose of this case, we will focus on the Spitfire, Lancaster and Hurricane departments. Each of these departments is structured along traditional manufacturing sector lines, with work groups of about 10 people supervised by a shop floor supervisor. Each supervisor has three to four work groups and the supervisors are in turn managed by the departmental manager.

Performance management is a complicated issue in Mouldaplas, but needs to be at the heart of management control if the company is to meet the quality standards demanded by the organisation's customers. Requirements for International Organization for Standardization (ISO) accreditations are often augmented by specific quality specifications by product. The consequence of this is that the organisation not only has to have tight control on actual performance, but also needs additional people in quality assurance roles to make sure that the quality specifications are met. Failure to meet these could mean the loss of contracts worth in excess of £6 million per annum. External demands drive the quality standards, but there are also internal issues that make performance management critical. Wastage is a key cost to Mouldaplas. All products go through quality assurance inspection and those not meeting the specifications are discarded before there is any chance of them being delivered to the customer. The nature of the materials means that these cannot be reworked and they are scrapped. Wastage levels vary dramatically across the departments, with both Lancaster and Spitfire having relatively low wastage levels, whilst the Hurricane department has an unacceptably high level of wastage. The HR director has been asked to look into this issue and has found that the induction and the training and development of staff in all three departments have been exactly the same. The only thing that seems to differ is the nature of the managers. For Lancaster and Spitfire departments, supervisors and managers are seen as directive and controlling. They set standards within the department and will actively manage the performance of those who don't achieve the required standard. As such, performance appraisal is only ever used for those employees who are struggling. However, they have also introduced, at a local level, various initiatives to reward good performance. There is an employee of the month award for the person who has contributed most to ensuring that all the work gets done on time and to the appropriate standard – this is voted on by the other employees. There is a special award for innovations and new ideas that help to improve performance and there is a newly introduced 'this week's pint' award in which the managers 'buy a pint' for the person they think has worked best that week. All these awards are somewhat arbitrary and the workforce recognise that they are all somewhat subjective; however, everyone has a chance of being nominated and everyone has a chance of winning, so the teams buy in to these willingly.

There is also some element of external competition here, with Lancaster and Spitfire departments competing against each other for the lowest scrappage rates. The Hurricane department has admitted defeat in this competition, and their manager seems to spend most of his time explaining why his department has scrappage rates more than three times higher than the other departments. The blame has been put variously on the subcontractors who supply parts to the Hurricane department (they are the only department engaged in a collaborative relationship with an external supplier), the calibre of the workforce (some have been there for 30 years and are reluctant to take on change), the style of management (often described as laissez-faire) and the culture of the department. The difficulty for senior management here is in knowing whether the problems with performance are caused by just one of these, or all of them.

Introduction

The Introductory case study clearly illustrates the necessity for performance management. It shows how, even in a relatively small organisation, performance is driven by both external and internal demands and is ultimately a consequence of a wider range of influences. It also illustrates how crucial performance management is to the very survival of an organisation. Here, the loss of a single contract worth £6 million would have repercussions for the organisation's ability to employ its workforce – and that is without taking account of any collateral damage done by the impact the loss of such a contract would have on the organisation's reputation. The case also highlights the more complex aspects of performance management, emphasising the impact of nebulous issues such as culture, the difficulty of determining the causes of poor performance and showing how the subjective nature of performance measurement may or may not be an issue for performance management and performance monitoring.

This chapter explores many of these issues. It starts by taking a chronological view of the ways in which historical schools of thought have influenced contemporary practice. Building on a consideration of traditional methods of performance management, it then considers more recent sociological and psychological perspectives, before looking at performance management in practice. Having considered the methods available to us, and the strengths and limitations of these, the issues relating to performance management as surveillance and the complexities of managing performance in collaborative relationships are explored. Lastly, the chapter looks at managing performance in a range of diverse employment relationships, such as with an ageing workforce and voluntary workers.

The history of performance management

It is useful to look at the history of performance management over the last 100 years, because the systems that we develop today draw on key elements of these previous approaches. The roots of performance management can be traced back to the post-industrial revolution era, when advances in technology and the development of mechanisation irrevocably changed the nature of the work organisation. Business was no longer undertaken on a small, local scale but exploded into the creation of vast mills and factories where hundreds of people were employed. The need to control and direct the work of such a large number of people necessarily leads to the search for one best way to manage performance. Over the years, this search has taken a number of directions, and has seen the creation of numerous means and mechanisms through which management can ensure that the performance of people contributes meaningfully to the success of the organisation. In the early 1900s, Frederick Winslow Taylor's theory of scientific management proposed that the best way to manage performance was through the calculation of the optimally efficient way of working. Control of performance was determined by management, and worker discretion was removed so as to ensure operational consistency. Max Weber's suggestion of the ideal type bureaucracy set in place control by process and system. Performance here is determined by compliance with the rules and regulations of the organisation. The human relations school followed shortly after Taylor and Weber, and marked a shift away from a focus on process to a focus on people. Here, coming out the Hawthorne Experiments of Elton Mayo, we saw the development of theories which suggested that by meeting the individual needs of people, managers could direct individual performance to achieve organisational success. The human relations school was the backdrop to the creation of many of the traditional theories of motivation that we recognise today. Towards the 1970s, there was an increasing awareness across Western businesses that the management of performance needed to move away from such an individualist approach towards a more collectivist orientation. Two new approaches dominated. The management of corporate culture (Deal and Kennedy, 1982) was seen as a way of steering performance by appealing to people's shared sense of values, while total quality management (TQM; Oakland, 2003) was suggested as a way of allowing groups of people at different levels in the hierarchy to take responsibility for their own actions and therefore recognise their contributions to the wider organisational success. More recently, the end of the 1990s and the beginning of the 2000s have seen the development of both sociological and psychological models of performance management. From a sociological perspective, George Ritzer (1993), in his book on *The McDonaldization of Society*, notes how societal demands for efficiency, calculability, predictability and control have encouraged organisations to adopt a modern-day hybrid of scientific management and bureaucracy through the use of technological measurements of performance. Control of performance here is bound up in a combination of rules and regulations, and technological monitoring. What we see here is a pseudo-individualist perspective in which the focus is on measuring individual performance, but in a uniform and technical way across the organisation. The contemporary psychological perspectives return us again to the focus on the individual, and more recent work has looked at the impact that issues of person–organisation

(PO) fit, organisational citizenship behaviour, employee engagement and organisational identity have on performance. These newer psychological schools are premised on the assumption that where people have a positive psychological relationship with the organisation, be that through shared values, a sense of belonging or because they derive a better sense of themselves from that relationship, they will be inclined to perform in the best interest of that organisation.

What becomes apparent from our brief consideration of the history of performance management is that controlling and directing the actions of others, be that explicitly through the use of policy and procedure or implicitly through the use of motivational or engagement techniques, has been a key focus for HR practitioners and managers for some considerable time. There is, however, an argument that in the globalised world of 2014, the need for effective performance management is greater than ever.

The performance imperative: why manage performance?

In the late 1990s and early 2000s, performance management became more extensive and, arguably, more intensive, to the point where some authors (see Adair *et al.* 2003; Hyde *et al.*, 2006; Harris *et al.*, 2007; Bourgon, 2008) considered performance management to be one of the most striking features of the business agenda and, in particular, a central feature of the public sector reform agenda.

The fact that today's marketplace is more fiercely competitive than ever before is indeed widely acknowledged (Fawcett and Magnan 2002; Patterson *et al.* 2003). Globalisation, technological change and demanding stakeholders constantly push for better individual, collective and organisational performance. In response to this new global economic order, Bititci *et al.* (2004) suggest that over the past decade or so, businesses have been forced to become more responsive and adapt to a continuously changing business environment, to be more agile and frequently restructure themselves to find new ways of continuously improving processes, systems and performance. Longnecker and Fink (2001) and Longnecker *et al.* (1999) suggest that in response to both recognising the potential limitations of performance measurement and responding to the demands inherent in a new global business world, organisational processes and delivery systems are being re-engineered and streamlined so that cycle times are reduced and efficiencies are improved. Relationships with both customers and suppliers are being redefined so that 'strategic partnerships' may be forged and leveraged. Workforce effectiveness and productivity initiatives are being developed to improve employee performance. Total quality and customer service are no longer viewed as individual programmes, but rather are being integrated into corporate cultures and operating practices as 'simply a way of life'. In addition, technology is rapidly evolving, and must be properly integrated and implemented if it is to be leveraged to provide competitive advantage. Enlightened approaches to human resource management (HRM) are also being used as a vehicle to leverage human capital in the emerging global workplace.

Managing performance in the global workplace is complicated by the fact that companies operate on an international stage. Rather than national companies creating local business, organisations operate with subsidiaries, franchises and strategic partners across the globe, and while performance management systems are a fact of life in almost every organisation, 'cultural differences affect how such systems are designed and implemented, as well as their relative effectiveness' (Aguinis *et al.*, 2012, p. 385). For example, although India has seen a huge growth in foreign direct investment, the cultural values of the investors are often at odds with the paternalistic national culture values; likewise, performance management systems need to account for cultural practices such as 'Guanxi' in China and 'Wasta' in the Middle East.

For many organisations, dealing with global competitiveness is too big a challenge for them to take on alone, and as a way of both strengthening individual organisational performance and rationalising the competitiveness in the external environment, many have embarked on collaborative rather than competitive strategies. Indeed, Burgess *et al.* (1997) (cited in Busi and Bititci, 2006) suggest that in order 'to cope with today's increasing competitive marketplace, companies have, and should, become more collaborative' (p, 10) and form networks that boast, as a whole, all those resources and competencies needed to satisfy the end customer.

Such collaborative strategies, be they mergers, acquisitions or strategic alliances, have significant implications for performance management.

The implications arise because the collaborative model is based on breaking down traditional physical boundaries and getting the partners to behave as a single unit. Integrating different organisations implies forming teams of different people with different cultures, policies and routines (Holmberg, 2000). Managing a disparate range of newly formed teams poses a number of challenges related to communication, the psychological contract, trust and behaviour.

Explore

Virgin Atlantic and Singapore Airlines have a strategic business partnership which means that they share airspace, aircraft and crew. As such, if you book to fly to Singapore with Virgin Atlantic, you may find that the plane and the crew that take you there are from Singapore Airlines.

● What are the implications for performance management across such an embedded strategic partnership?

The imperatives for effective performance management are clear. International business, public sector efficiency and global economic austerity require managers to ensure that the performance of each individual, each group and each department within an organisation contributes in a meaningful way to the achievement of the strategic goals. Yet embedded within this objective is the assumption that we can in some way demonstrate the relationship between effective performance management and the wider performance of the organisation. A tension necessarily exists here for the contemporary organisation, one premised on how they assess the relative costs versus benefits of performance management. At the heart of the tension is the issue of proof. When the performance of an organisation is influenced by so many factors (technology, mechanisation, the style of management, the skills of the workforce, etc.), many of which are outside the control of the organisation itself (changing funding streams in the public sector, mergers, acquisitions and the growth of collaborative strategies in the private sector), how can HR practitioners demonstrate in any reliable way whether or not investment in performance management systems has had a direct impact on the performance of the organisation? As we continue to look at what performance management actually means, and the modes and mechanisms of performance management, we will draw on these tensions and the dilemmas faced by those trying to manage performance.

What is performance management?

Performance management can be seen as an overarching term that embraces all the ways in which an organisation and those who control the activities within it coordinate and direct actions in order to achieve the organisation's goals. Armstrong and Baron (1998) see performance management as a continuous process that focuses on the future rather than the past. They emphasise the strategic and integrated nature of performance management, which is aimed at 'increasing the effectiveness of organisations by improving the performance of the people who work in them and by developing the capabilities of teams and individual contributors' (Armstrong and Baron, 1998: 38–39). Performance management is about the coordinated control of potentially large groups of people across a range of units, departments and even organisations.

Performance measurement moves away from a singular focus on local level measurement to embrace more strategic, systematic, integrated and organisationally focused approaches to the holistic management of work activities, or the total performance system (TPS). Much early work on performance management dates back to the late 1980s, with commentators such as Johnson and Kaplan (1987), Lynch and Cross (1991), Eccles (1991), Kaplan and Norton (1992) and Thorpe (2004) setting the scene. Since then there have been a plethora of writers, each taking their own, slightly nuanced approach to the subject.

Armstrong and Baron (2005) define performance management as a process that operates in a continuous cycle and that 'contributes to the effective management of individuals and teams in order to achieve high levels of organisational performance' (p. 15) (see Figure 12.1).

Embedded within this is the understanding that formal 'performance management' is not the only thing that has an impact on the ways in which people and teams behave. Here performance management is not a single universally applicable process, but rather it needs to be contextually specific, what Armstrong and Baron (2004: 16) define as:

> a strategy which relates to every activity of the organisation set in the context of its human resource policies, culture, style and communications systems. The nature of the strategy depends on the organisational context and can vary from organisation to organisation.

What Armstrong and Baron's comments introduce here is a new element of complexity. Having noted the 'process' rather than 'event' orientation of performance management, they now suggest the need to tailor this process to the specific context. Their view suggests that performance management is a dynamic process which needs to be aligned to the developing

Figure 12.1 The performance cycle

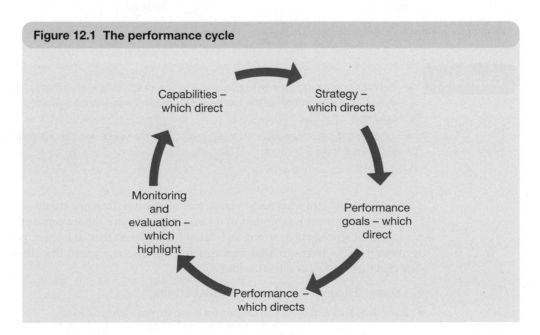

strategies of the organisation. Necessarily, then, they suggest that the principal activities of performance management are geared towards:

- communicating a shared vision of the purpose of the organisation;
- defining expectations of what must be delivered and how;
- ensuring that employees are aware of what high performance means and how they can achieve it;
- enhancing levels of motivation and enabling employees to monitor their own performance and understand what needs to be done to improve their overall level of performance.

London and Mone (2009) define performance management by the stages that this incorporates. For them, the performance management 'process' involves three stages, namely the setting of goals, the monitoring of performance to enable feedback and/or development as necessary and the use of appraisal as a means of evaluation and because this contributes to decisions about compensation.

The Chartered Institute of Personnel and Development (CIPD, 2009b) agrees and elaborates on these themes, suggesting that performance management should be:

- *Strategic* – it is about broader issues and longer-term goals.
- *Integrated* – it should link various aspects of the business, people management and individuals and teams.

It should incorporate elements of performance improvement to move the organisation forwards; aspects of people development to allow individuals to contribute meaningfully now and in the future; and control mechanisms that allow for the monitoring and management of performance. Performance management then can be seen as a range of things that it is, and that it is not, as in the following:

Performance management is . . .	Performance management is not . . .
Strategic	Purely operational
Context-specific	One size fits all
Dynamic	Static
A process	An event
Coherent	Fragmented
Integrated	Isolated

Explore

- Consider performance management systems with which you are familiar. To what extent do they conform to the issues raised in the 'Performance management is . . .' column?
- What might the consequences of any non-conformance be for the organisation and those who work there?

These insights into what performance management is draw our attention to the things that HR and management might need to do in order to ensure the success of their performance management strategy. Armstrong and Baron (2004) stress that, at its best, performance management is a tool to ensure that managers manage effectively, and that this involves making sure that their people and their teams:

- know and understand what is expected of them;
- have the skills and ability to deliver on these expectations;

- are supported by the organisation to develop the capacity to meet these expectations and are given feedback on their performance;
- have the opportunity to discuss and contribute to individual and team aims and objectives.

It is this set of criteria that necessarily underpins the practice of performance management.

Performance management in practice

In considering performance management in practice, it is useful to think about the aspects of HR practice through which performance is controlled and directed in order to achieve the organisational goals. If we consider performance management as a series of relationships, then the idea that these issues are interconnected and interdependent becomes more apparent (see Figure 12.2).

Recruitment and selection

Performance management at the time of recruitment and selection is crucial, and there are a number of reasons for this. The ways in which an organisation represents itself to the outside world are apparent through the recruitment and selection processes used, and this has a range of consequences. Adverts containing typographical errors, inaccurate or incorrect information communicate to potential applicants an image of carelessness and lack of monitoring systems in ensuring the quality of what leaves the organisation. Depending on the nature of the job, this may disincline strong candidates from applying. It also communicates the idea that substandard performance is acceptable. Selection processes are the mutual engagement of potential employers and potential employee and are the point at which each makes a value judgment as to whether or not they wish to formalise an employment relationship. The management of performance here has a number of manifestations. First there is the issue of process, and whether or not those people representing the organisation have both an

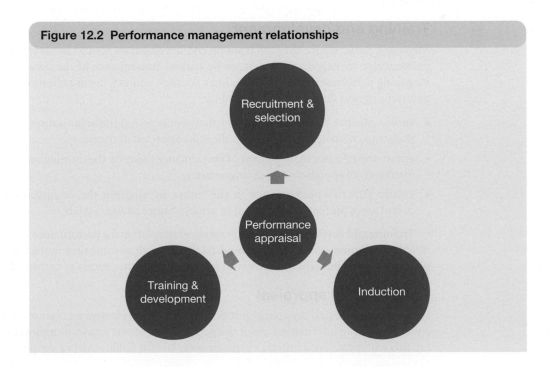

Figure 12.2 Performance management relationships

awareness of the processes and systems that they are to use, and the interpersonal skills to conduct the selection process appropriately. Secondly, there is the issue of communicating to the candidate, the levels, the types and the expectations of performance that they would need to deliver, but this is not always a positive thing. According to Sims and Brinkmann (2003) in their consideration of Enron, the selection system in use reflected the wider culture, in that 'It promoted greed, selfishness and jealousy within the organisation' (p. 252). Thirdly, there is the opportunity here to communicate the organisational values to applicants. These values, nebulous though they may seem, have a huge impact on performance, and can communicate not only the expected ways to behave within the organisation but also the ethical standards that underpin that behaviour. As Sims and Brinkmann (2003) point out in their consideration of the cultural values of Enron, 'Enron's leaders' primary message about their values was sent through their own actions' (p. 249). Where unethical behaviour is not only condoned, but rewarded, this is communicated as 'acceptable' to the wider organisation.

Induction

Performance management through a person's induction to the organisation contains a number of key elements. The first is the representation of the organisation by those inducting new people. By ensuring the appropriate skill levels of those involved in the processes and making sure that they communicate the correct messages about the required and expected levels of performance, the organisation is able to manage performance by example. Moreover, the most effective systems of performance management are a continuation of the induction process. The instigation of personal and career development plans as soon as people join the organisation, the effective communication of the ways in which the organisation monitors and manages performance, and clarity about the organisation's commitment to learning and development all ensure that the new person has a thorough understanding of performance management and their role in ensuring the strategic success of the organisation. Lastly, key to any induction programme is the issue of socialisation. This is often an informal consequence of the induction process but is, as with the issues relating to recruitment and selection, key to familiarising people with the social networks and the enacted norms and values of the organisation, as well as with the espoused values communicated through organisational visions and missions.

Training and development

Managing performance through training and development should be an integral part of the performance management process, and a natural consequence of the person's induction. In managing performance effectively within a strategic context, the organisation needs to ensure that training and development are used to:

- ensure effective performance today – that people within the organisation have the requisite skills and competences to perform the tasks expected of them;
- ensure the effective management of performance today by the training and development of managers, of appraisers and of interviewers;
- ensure effective performance in the future by aligning the organisational skills and competence profile to that needed to achieve future strategic goals.

Training and development, then, are means of translating the performance levels that we have into the performance levels that we need, be this today or at some time in the future. Key to this notion of reconciling what we have with what we need is the process of performance appraisal.

Performance appraisal

Performance appraisal represents just one tool in the performance measurement toolkit. It is a way of eliciting information about the performance of one or more employees and comparing this with predefined criteria or dimensions. DeNisi (2000) offers a simplistic definition of performance appraisal as 'the system whereby an organisation assigns some "score" to indicate the level of performance of a target person or group' (p. 121), whereas Fletcher (2001: 473) defines this more broadly as 'activities through which organisations seek to assess employees and develop their competence, enhance performance and distribute rewards'. What becomes apparent from this definition is the ways in which performance appraisal articulates with the wider issues of performance management. Rather than being a stand-alone process of measurement, the value of performance appraisal is seen in the ways in which this feeds reward structures, defines the direction for training and development, and contributes more widely to the success of the organisation.

Mondy *et al.* (2002) add another dimension to our characterisation of performance appraisal, that of the unit of appraisal, i.e. what we are actually appraising. Rather than working on the assumption of individual measurement, they comment on the ways in which appraisal may evaluate the performance of a collective unit, i.e. appraising a team.

The 2011 Workplace Employment Relations Study (WERS) (van Wanrooy *et al.*, 2013) has been mapping the growth in the use of performance appraisal and looking at the ways in which this is increasingly linked to reward and remuneration strategies. Of particular interest in their most recent survey was the growth in the use of performance appraisal for staff working in non-managerial positions. Figures here show a 26 per cent increase from 43 per cent in 2004 to 69 per cent in 2011. There is also embedded within these figures a very interesting divide between the use of appraisal in public and in private-sector organisations. While 67 per cent of private-sector organisations use performance appraisal for non-managerial staff, within the public sector, this figure rose to a massive 88 per cent (see Table 12.1).

Alongside this growth in the use of performance appraisal, an increase was found in the number of organisations who linked pay to the outcomes of appraisals. As such, the 2011 survey showed that 24 per cent of organisations surveyed use performance appraisal as a partial determinant of non-managerial pay, a rise from 15 per cent in 2004, but again, there were discrepancies between the results for the public and private sectors. Whilst the figures for linkage to pay are fairly equitable (24 per cent for the private sector and 25 per cent for the public sector), the more prevalent use of appraisal within the public sector means that they have a significantly higher rate of workplaces where appraisal is not linked to pay – 63 per cent as compared to 43 per cent in the private sector.

This link between performance appraisal and reward and remuneration is explored further in WERS to highlight the different types of reward that are becoming increasingly contingent on performance. It has been suggested that the growth in the use of performance appraisal has been linked to a rise in performance-related pay (PRP) schemes, but as Bach (2005) comments, this is not really the full picture, as there is in fact, 'little evidence to suggest that performance appraisal was introduced to support individual performance pay' (p. 297). Rather, Bach suggests, the increased use is more closely associated with the commitment of successive governments to introduce private-sector 'best practice' into the public sector in response to the need to increase efficiency and enhance managerial authority, as noted earlier. The most recent WERS report (van Wanrooy *et al.*, 2013) gives a further rationale for the introduction

Table 12.1 Appraisal of non-managerial employees as a percentage of all workplaces [the 2011 Workplace Employment Relations Study (WERS)]

	All private-sector workplaces	All public-sector workplaces*
Appraisal – link to pay	24%	25%
Appraisal – not linked to pay	43%	63%
No appraisal	33%	13%

*Rounding issues leading to totals of 101 per cent.

of pay for performance, that of allowing organisations 'to share risk with their employees in troubled times' (p. 24). By focusing reward on performance, and by using reward strategies such as share incentive plans and share options schemes, employers can not only gain increasing financial flexibility, they can also 'index link' the relative value of that reward to the value of the company. As such, should the value of the company fall, for whatever reason, then the values of the shares held by employees will also fall.

The organisational motivation for performance appraisal then, is clear. It is a means by which the performance of an individual or group is measured to enable remedial action to be taken where necessary, to enable appropriate rewards to be given and to identify areas where training and development are needed to ensure the skills needed for the future. Thus, framed performance appraisal serves two purposes in that it is both evaluative and developmental. At an operational level, there are a range of other reasons for undertaking performance appraisals, namely:

- informing promotion, separation and transfer decisions;
- giving feedback to the employee regarding how the organisation viewed the employee's performance;
- evaluating the relative contributions made by individuals, teams and/or departments in achieving higher-level organisation goals;
- evaluating the effectiveness of selection and placement decisions, including the relevance of the information used in the decisions within the organisation;
- informing reward decisions, including merit increases, promotions and other rewards;
- ascertaining and diagnosing training and development needs;
- evaluating the success of training and development decisions;
- gathering data to inform work scheduling plans, budgeting and human resources planning.

In many instances, the actual appraisal is undertaken via a face-to-face discussion, but it is important to note that this may be changing as the use of information technology and software packages such as 'Performance Pro' means that appraisals can easily be undertaken online.

Approaches to performance appraisal

The scope and method for reviewing performance vary between organisations, but typically, appraisal takes a 'free text' form, in which the appraiser and the appraisee review performance in general before focusing on specific objectives, targets or goals set in the previous appraisal. Although this qualitative form of appraisal allows for issues to emerge through the discussion process, this lack of rigid boundaries means that it is also open to accusations of partiality and bias. An alternative is to undertake a straight ranking of performance against predefined criteria or traits. On the basis of an assessment against the dimensions, employees are given the final rankings. Any approach using predetermined criteria has limitations, especially if the same criteria are employed across a wide range of job roles. It is also important to think about whether using such simple metrics really does solve the problem of subjectivity, as what people are ranking here is still only their perception of the levels of performance. Additionally, traits such as resourcefulness, loyalty or enthusiasm are not only subjective but may be open to different interpretations by different appraisers and the appraisee, leaving them open to bias and prejudice.

Because of the limitations of using either method in isolation, many appraisal systems have a dual process, which involves some form of ranking or rating and some scope for a more discursive consideration of performance between managers and employees.

Types of performance appraisal

Critical incident technique

Derived from the original 1954 work of John Flanagan, critical incident methods involve the identification of key events, be they positive or negative. In an appraisal setting, it is important to ensure that there is a balanced debate which draws on both positive and negative issues. It is also important to appreciate the impact that time can have on the recollection of events; for example, a really positive event that occurred 10 months ago may seem less important than a smaller negative incident that occurred more recently. The advantage of a critical incident approach is that it is individually oriented and therefore the issues raised are specific and relevant to the appraisee. The disadvantages include issues of subjectivity, the issue of timeliness mentioned previously and the fact that the individual focus can sometimes detract from the wider collective goals.

Key Controversy

To what extent are all performance management approaches simply a matter of subjective judgment? As HR practitioners, should our goal be to get rid of subjectivity or account for subjectivity?

Checklist approach

This is one in which the appraiser is given a list of statements or descriptions of the desired knowledge, skills and behaviours of the employees, drawn from key aspects of the role or from the job description. Often the appraisee and appraiser indicate which description most closely reflects the job performance of the employee. These tasks are often undertaken independently of each other at the start of the process, but later, during a formal discussion, the appraiser and appraisee seek to reach agreement as to which description is most appropriate. This approach is referred to as 'behaviourally anchored rating scales' (BARS) or 'behaviourally observed rating scales' (BORS). The advantage of this approach is that it focuses on role-relevant criteria and takes account of the views of both the appraiser and the appraisee. The limitations relate to the focus on a predefined range of criteria, when the priorities in the business may have changed since these criteria were set.

Goal-setting

This approach seeks to make the process even more transparent by establishing job objectives or goals, and reviewing (usually annually) the extent to which they have been met. In this style of appraisal, the CIPD (2009a) suggest the following points should be considered:

- What the appraisee has achieved during the review period, with examples and evidence.
- Any examples of objectives not achieved with explanations as to why.
- What the appraisee enjoys most about the job and how they might want to develop the role.
- Any aspect of the work in which improvement is required and how this might be achieved.
- Appraisee learning and development needs, with arguments to support their case for specific training.
- The level of support and guidance appraisees require from their manager.
- Appraisees' aspirations for the future, both in the current role and in possible future roles.
- Objectives for the next review period.

- Have you ever been appraised?
- How did you find the experience?
- How could it have been improved?

The extent to which the appraisee is involved in establishing performance goals varies between organisations, but motivational theory suggests goals are most effective in terms of motivating performance when the employee has been directly involved in setting them (see Box 12.1). A variation on this theme is to use a competency based framework against which performance is appraised. Many schemes use a combination of competency assessment, objectives and role accountabilities.

Performance may also be measured by gathering raw data (see Box 12.2). This is frequently used, for example, to monitor activity rates of computer operators, call handling speeds in call centres or throughput rates for staff in fast food restaurants. Performance measurement or employee monitoring can also be conducted using technology. For example, some cellular telephones have built-in global positioning systems that enable employers to track the physical location of employees at all times. Furthermore, employers can now conduct their own private investigations into employment applicants by accessing their presence on social media, or from driving records, vehicle registration records, bankruptcy proceedings, social security records, property ownership records, military records, sex offender lists, incarceration records, drug testing records, professional licensing records, workers' compensation records and credit reports. In performance measurement, electronic monitoring and surveillance of employees have grown, especially the monitoring of email and web browsing (Sipor and Ward, 1995; Stanton, 2000).

Explore

- What are the strengths, the limitations and ethical issues that might arise from checking an employee's presence on social media?

Box 12.1   **Goal-setting theory and performance management**

Goal-setting theory was established by Latham and Locke in 1984, when they argued that goals set for employees can play an important part in motivating them to improve their performance. Goals equate to targets and employees reflect on their performance and will modify their behaviour in order to hit the targets. Heslin *et al.* (2009) suggest a prime axiom of goal-setting theory is that specific, difficult goals lead to higher performance than when people strive to simply 'do their best' (Locke, 1966; Locke and Latham, 1990). The performance benefits of setting challenging and specific goals have been demonstrated in laboratory and field studies (Locke and Latham, 1990, 2002). However, setting specific and challenging goals is no guarantee of performance; the nature of the goals has to be such that achievement of these is appealing. Moreover, they need to be purposeful, achievable and offer the individual a chance to develop. For goals to be motivating they need:

- to be specific rather than vague;
- to be demanding but attainable and realistic;
- to generate feedback that is timely and meaningful;
- to be accepted by the employees as desirable.

SMART is an acronym often used to frame the desirable features of goals. The letters stand for Specific; Measurable; Appropriate; Relevant; and Time-limited.

Box 12.2

Wireless real-time production and employee performance measurement

One such system is referred to as the 20/20 Data Collection/Monitoring & Management System and it can be used in any production or manufacturing context, from assembling computers, to answering telephone calls in a call centre, to packing chocolate biscuits. It is a wireless real-time shop floor data collection and management system that is designed to enhance the production management to a higher level, thereby allowing productivity gains. It works by constantly monitoring the work rate of the operators to show if specific operators or assembly stations are constraining overall production throughput. Performance and line balancing reports rank the bottleneck operators and stations according to their constraint on system output. With real-time data access, managers are able to make well-informed decisions, such as reprioritising a job or reallocating staffing. Productivity analysis allows managers to measure individual employee performance and analyse labour costs by employee, department or work assembly station. In terms of performance management, real-time measurement data enables managers to:

- improve productivity by leveraging production monitoring and motivating the workers to meet the standards;
- access detailed analysis allowing managers to monitor performance and labour costs in terms of each employee;
- indicate and monitor individual operator efficiency and output;
- use the reported information to determine the precise cause of any defect and the action necessary to resolve the issue;
- identify poor operator performance before it causes a problem;
- use the data as part of a continuous total quality improvement programme.

Explore

- What, if any, are the ethical implications of wireless real-time production and employee performance measurement?

360-degree appraisal

An alternative approach to performance appraisal is the use of 360-degree feedback, or 'multi-rater feedback'. This approach was first developed and used by General Electric in the USA in 1992, and despite Newbold's (2008) suggestion that it went out of fashion for a while, it is now back in vogue, with many organisations using it. Aswathappa (2005: 234) lists GE (India) Reliance Industries, Godrej soaps, Wipro, Infosys, Thermex and Thomas Cook as examples of organisations currently using the 360-degree system of performance appraisal. It is an approach in which performance data are sought from peers, subordinates, superiors and nominated significant others who may be internal or external to the organisation.

Self-assessment is an indispensable part of 360-degree appraisals and they therefore have high employee involvement, For many, it is left to the appraisee to ask 'significant others' to take part in their appraisal. This level of personal investment in the process means that 360-degree systems usually have the strongest impact on behaviour and performance. Likewise, because the process involves numerous 'independent' views of the employee's performance, it is often considered to be one of the most credible performance appraisal methods. The 360-degree appraisal can be used as a powerful developmental tool because of the multiple views on the extent to which an individual is developing or refining their skills and competencies.

Explore

- What might be the advantages and limitations of 360-degree appraisal?

Performance appraisal can be operationalised using a number of different methods, or indeed any hybrid structure which combines elements of numerous approaches; however, in order to be successful, the CIPD suggest the use of five key elements:

- *Measurement* – assessing performance against agreed targets and objectives.
- *Feedback* – providing information to the individual on their performance and progress.
- *Positive reinforcement* – emphasising what has been done well and making only constructive criticism about what might be improved.
- *Exchange of views* – a frank exchange of views about what has happened, how appraisees can improve their performance, the support they need from their managers to achieve this, and their aspirations for their future career.
- *Agreement* – jointly coming to an understanding by all parties about what needs to be done to improve performance generally and overcome any issues raised in the course of the discussion (CIPD, 2009a).

Although the CIPD draw on these five key factors, from a practitioner perspective, Mr Satish Pradham of Tata introduces another key issue, that of continuity (see Box 12.3).

Explore

- How far do you agree with Mr Satish Pradhan, Executive Vice President – HR at Tata Sons (Box 12.3), that there should be 'no surprises' in a performance appraisal?
- Why do you think he is so keen to emphasise that non-financial rewards are also part of the system of performance recognition?

Box 12.3 **Performance appraisal at Tata Sons**

Mr Satish Pradhan, executive vice president – HR at Tata Sons, based in Mumbai, and with over 20 years of international and national experience in HRM, explained how performance appraisal at Tata Sons was built on two principles:

- no surprises;
- reward for performance.

Mr Pradhan took time to explain that effective performance appraisal was all about trust and development. He stated: 'If our employees trust that we have their best interests at heart and that we genuinely want them to succeed in their careers at Tata Sons, then their commitment to us and performance for us will excel.' He said that at no stage in the performance appraisal process should an employee be told anything they were not already aware of or had not had sufficient time to reflect upon. He was also keen to demonstrate that while financial incentives were part of the reward for performance, money was not the whole story. For Tata Sons, non-financial rewards, e.g. being chosen to represent the company on the platform of an international convention, are held in as much, if not more, esteem among the employees than a salary increase.

Limitations of performance measurement

Over recent years, there has been a growing discomfort with measuring performance through the use of appraisal indicators and targets. Callahan (2007) notes that all managers involved in measuring performance through such traditional indices need to think outside the performance box. He suggests that performance measurement is inadequate because it fails to recognise the key concepts of accountability and citizen participation and fails to emphasise the critical importance of their relationship. In other words, performance appraisals are compromised because they are used for a range of often conflicting purposes.

The problems of appraisal are compounded when the process of appraisal does not lead to any particular action. The ultimate test of the effectiveness of any performance management system is, according to Zients (2009; cited in Moynihan and Pandey, 2010), whether the information gathered through appraisal is used or not. The scenario of annual appraisals following which the paperwork sits filed away until the next appraisal 12 months later, is one that many people are familiar with, and this is problematic not only because it means that managers are not adequately using the systems available to them to both monitor and improve performance and develop their workforce, but also because this creates at best an apathy towards appraisal and at worse a resentment at the time wasted in a non-productive activity.

Appraisals are also in a 'catch 22' position. Problems can arise where the appraiser is to act as both manager and appraiser, a situation that occurs frequently. Managers are responsible for ensuring that the organisation has invested sufficiently in the development of the individual and has supported them effectively, yet in their role as appraiser they need to be able to point out realistically the consequences of any under-investment or the areas where the appraisee has not developed due to the lack of *their* support. On the other hand, it would be very difficult to have anyone but the manager undertake an appraisal, simply because they know the role, the job, the required competencies and the individual.

This tension develops further where the appraiser has a range of roles and responsibilities – which, again, may be conflicting (Wilson, 2002). To illustrate, the appraiser can be placed in the position, described by McGregor (1957) as being required to 'play God'. Appraisers invariably judge and rate the performance of their staff member. This role sits at odds with their responsibility to motivate and develop the same staff member, and may sit in opposition to their role as employee counsellor. Newton and Findlay (1996) make the point that employees are less likely to confide their limitations, development needs or anxieties about job competence to their appraiser, because it could adversely affect their rating at the next performance review and may affect reward levels if performance is linked to remuneration. Appraisers may equally be reluctant to give their staff a poor review because it might prove demotivating, could create conflict or may even suggest they lacked the necessary management skills to elicit high performance.

Lastly there are a range of rater biases that can also have a detrimental impact on the process of appraisal. The 'halo effect' is a perceptual bias on behalf of the appraiser, in which they focus almost entirely on the positive aspects of an employee, regardless of problem areas that require remedial action. The counter-side to this is the 'horns effect' in which an appraiser is predisposed to negative perceptions of the person and their performance. The 'comparing employees effect' is a system of judging relative performance, where the manager evaluates one employee against another without considering the different tasks they are required to perform. Lastly the 'recency effect' occurs when managers rate employees on the basis of their most recent encounter with them or on their most recent knowledge of their performance. This can mean that major successes that occurred some time back are underplayed and more recent minor errors come to the fore.

The type of appraisal system used may also facilitate difficulties. Where appraisers have to rank or rate staff, there may be an issue with the 'central tendency' effect. Here managers opt for the safe midway or central point, so as not to be overly lenient or overly harsh, or for fear of upsetting either the appraiser or their colleagues. This system necessarily reduces the effectiveness of appraisal by producing meaningless results. Research undertaken by Geddes and Konrad (2003) and Thornton and Rupp (2007) indicates that appraisal ratings are also influenced by gender, ethnic origins and physical attractiveness.

According to Bach (2005: 304), one of the most common responses to rater bias is to 'redouble training efforts to ensure managers are trained in conducting appraisals, and be aware of some of the potential limitations'. Another response has been to seek multiple sources of data from multiple stakeholders, e.g. 360-degree appraisal.

These points relate to limitations in the design and operation of performance appraisal. Another level of critical commentary has emerged which draws attention to the political and ethical considerations of performance appraisal and the fact that appraisal can be seen as a means of employee surveillance.

Performance management or surveillance?

From the earliest work of Frederick Winslow Taylor considered previously, the idea of performance management has always been premised on an assumption that managers are the principal agent of control. More critical schools of management thinking see performance management as being little more than a political structure premised on managerial objectives, their power to control, manipulate and direct employee behaviour and the extent to which they have a right to engage in the covert surveillance of employees. Indeed, drawing on the example of a call centre, Fernie and Metcalf (1997: 2) suggest that the 'tyranny of the assembly line is but a Sunday school picnic compared with the control that management can exercise in computer telephony'. Their empirical work demonstrated that in some respects the use of technological surveillance negates the need for direct management control, as immediate feedback to people allows them to self-monitor and remedy any performance shortfall before the 'wrath of management' is provoked. However, they also demonstrated the ways in which those being monitored created increasingly ingenious ways of circumventing the systems. Examples such as taking a call but remaining silent so the caller hangs up, or finishing the call abruptly but then not replacing the phone, meant that no further calls could be put through to them. As they can only be monitored for their ability to deal with the calls put through, they exert their own control on what will and will not be monitored.

Bach (2005) provides an excellent summary of this proposition, in which he suggests that those influenced by the work of French philosopher Michel Foucault view trends in appraisal as part of a more sinister management regime to control all aspects of employee behaviour and eliminate any scope for employee resistance or misbehaviour.

Understanding Foucault

Foucault's work involves reference to Jeremy Bentham's panopticon. Bentham was a utilitarian theorist, believing human beings are intrinsically bound to seek pleasure and avoid pain, wherever possible, and that 'good' and 'bad' are defined by what is pleasurable and painful. The object of legislation therefore, according to Bentham, should be to secure the greatest happiness for the greatest number of people; consequently, the pain of punishment should be proportional to the happiness that it secured. As a part of his vision of rational social control, Bentham devised an architectural device he called the 'panopticon', which is Greek for 'all seeing'. The panopticon was based on the design for a Russian factory that minimised the number of supervisors required, and it was proposed by Bentham for the design of prisons, workhouses, mental asylums and schools. The supervisors were able to view and monitor the inmates, but the inmates could not see the supervisors. The underlying principle is that the total and constant surveillance of inmates or workers would encourage them to conform to all the desired behaviours and beliefs and eventually each individual would themselves become an overseer of others. The strong illusion of a powerful, controlling and all-seeing eye would become an inner reality of self-policing. Bentham believed this approach could be successfully adopted in any environment, including work organisations, that involved any level of supervision – i.e. of employees (**http://www.mdx.ac.uk/www/study/ybenfou.htm**).

The same principles about power, control and observation were enshrined in much of Foucault's (1977) thinking about the role of managers controlling the behaviour and thoughts of their employees. In the example we saw earlier of the 20/20 data collection used as a wireless real-time production and employee performance measurement system (Box 12.2), it is easy to appreciate how this distant but all-embracing surveillance of the action, speed of work, quality and production can be regarded as an example of why Foucault exhibited concern over the extent to which employees were being manipulated, controlled and monitored by others and saw appraisal as epitomising a desire for observation in order to make every employee a knowable, calculable and administrative object (Miller and Rose, 1990: 5). Foucault, like Townley (1993b) and Grey (1994) in their work on appraisals and career management, questioned the ethics of such close and consistent intrusion into an employee's working life and saw such involvement as a negative feature of performance appraisal. However, to leave the story at that junction would be to tell only half of it, as others, in particular Findlay and Newton (1998), use their discussion of performance appraisal to highlight Foucault's apparent neglect of human agency (Newton, 1994) and to suggest that to see all aspects of intervention as a negative use of power is to ignore the mutuality of interests that characterises many aspects of the modern labour process.

Key Controversy

To what extent do you agree that performance appraisal is more about managerial control than it is about performance enhancement and individual development?

Collaborative performance management

Previously we have looked at the ways in which the economic climate has encouraged collaborative isomorphism, a process through which the competitive landscape is increasingly marked by organisations entering into similar types of collaborative strategies. These collaborative strategies have significant implications for the ways in which we can both measure and manage performance.

In this section, we consider some of what Waggoner *et al.* (1999: 52) call the 'various forces that shape organisational performance management systems'. In particular, we will consider the challenges of managing performance in an international context, managing performance of a diverse workforce, and managing the performance of an ageing workforce. Lastly we will consider whether managing the performance of a volunteer is in any respect different from managing the performance of salaried employees.

In determining the manner in which a collaborative/networked organisation should approach performance management, Longnecker and Fink (2001) suggest HR practitioners should ask the following critical questions, the answers to which will greatly influence the quality of performance management:

- Do all of our managers have a clear and unambiguous understanding of their role in our changing organisation?
- Do we provide all of our managers with ongoing and balanced performance feedback?
- Do we have a systematic approach to helping our managers 'learn by doing'?
- Is management development truly a management priority at our organisation?
- Do we take active steps to ensure that our management development efforts are designed to meet the actual needs of our managers?

Box 12.4   The aims of collaborative performance management

- Translate organisational vision into clear measurable outcomes that define success, and which are shared throughout the organisation and with customers and stakeholders.
- Provide a tool for assessing, managing and improving the overall health and success of performance management systems.
- Continue to shift from prescriptive, audit and compliance-based oversight to an ongoing, forward-looking strategic partnership.
- Include measures of quality, cost, speed, customer service and employee alignment, motivation and skills to provide an in-depth, predictive performance management system.
- Replace existing assessment models with a consistent approach to performance management.

Source: adapted from Procurement Executives' Association (1999).

Busi and Bititci (2006) build on this foundation and characterise a network-wide collaborative approach to performance management as focusing on:

- managing extended processes within and beyond the single company's boundaries;
- managing the collaborative enterprise performance, rather than only measuring it;
- creating and managing cross-organisational multidisciplinary teams;
- deploying integrated ICT across organisations;
- creating and sharing knowledge.

It is this issue of managing individual and organisational performance across what might be traditionally seen as the boundaries of the organisation that requires us to think in a more imaginative and nuanced way about how we measure and manage performance (see Box 12.4).

For many (Tung, 1993; Chiang and Birtch, 2010; Peretz and Fried, 2012) the difficulties in managing performance relate to the potential disparities between the cultures of the organisations wishing to collaborate. Indeed, such cultural incongruity is seen as a main cause of failures in mergers and acquisitions. Using a model adapted from Rieger and Wong-Rieger's work in 1991, Tung presents a useful taxonomy for thinking about the relationship between cultures (Figure 12.3).

Figure 12.3 Rieger and Wong-Rieger's Acculturation Taxonomy (Tung, 1993)

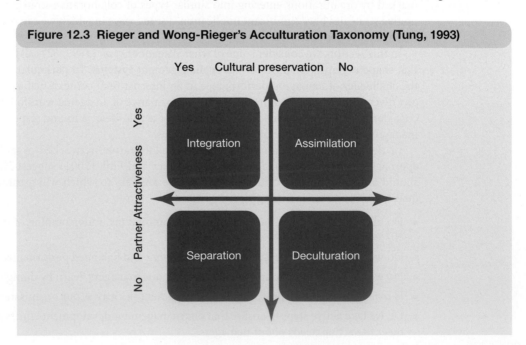

The taxonomy outlines four patterns of interaction between merging (or acquiring/ acquired) organisations, each of which is worth thinking about in relation to the management of performance:

- *Integration* – this occurs where there is a need to preserve the culture (i.e. there is no intention by management to create a 'new' culture) and both parties in the relationship perceive the other to be attractive (i.e. there is natural affinity between the two organisations). This is the most straightforward in terms of performance management which should be *synergistic,* as the similarities between the values of each organisation make it easier to extend the most effective performance management systems across the collaborative enterprise.

- *Assimilation* – this occurs when there is no need to preserve the culture of one or other of the organisations, but there is a high level of partner attractiveness. Here performance management can be in guise of a mutually agreed *synthesis* of the methods used in both organisations. The performance management tools and techniques used here need to be consistent with the desired culture of the new collaborative enterprise.

- *Deculturation* – this occurs where there is no need to preserve the culture of either organisation (perhaps a situation where two failing companies come together to try to marshal resources). Moreover, there is little partner attractiveness, i.e. the collaborative strategy is premised on purely business grounds and there is little in the way of shared values between the organisations. The management of performance here can be seen as *instrumental.* The newly created enterprise needs to use whichever tools and techniques are best to achieve the organisation's goals, regardless of cultural fit or fear of offending either partner.

- *Separation* – this is possibly the most difficult situation to deal with in terms of creating an effective performance management system. The organisations themselves 'disdain the culture or subculture of the other group' (Tung, 1993: 466), which results in 'an unhealthy tension and conflict'. Despite this, it is in the interest of the business to preserve the culture, which means that the creation of any performance management system may need to be *imposed* by management, cognisant of the reactions that this might create, so that performance can be managed explicitly whilst allowing time for new cultural norms to emerge.

As such, if we revisit the Rieger and Wong-Rieger (1991, cited in Tung, 1993) taxonomy, we can see more clearly the types of approaches that HR and management might need to consider in the design of performance management systems in a collaborative enterprise (Figure 12.4)

Busi and Bititci (2006) suggest that a collaborative performance management system would include the following key elements:

- a structured methodology to design the performance measurement system;

- a structured management process for using performance measurement information to help make decisions, set performance goals, allocate resources, inform management and report success (see also Amaratunga and Baldry, 2002);

- a set of specifications of the necessary electronic tools for data gathering, processing and analysis (see also Waggoner *et al.* 1999);

- theoretical guidelines on how to manage through measures [as Adair *et al.* (2003) point out, performance management systems are used to apply the information and knowledge arising from performance measurement systems];

- a review process to ensure that measures are constantly updated to reflect changes in strategy and/or market conditions (see also Waggoner *et al.,* 1999).

Many academics considering the impact of culture on performance management have grounded their empirical studies in the work of Geert Hofstede (1985). Although the idea of any one nation state having what might be deemed a uniform culture has been roundly criticised by many, Hofstede's work has stood the test of time in being seen as a way of appreciating national cultural difference. Looking at performance management through this lens,

Figure 12.4 Performance management implications of Rieger and Wong-Rieger's acculturation taxonomy (Tung, 1993)

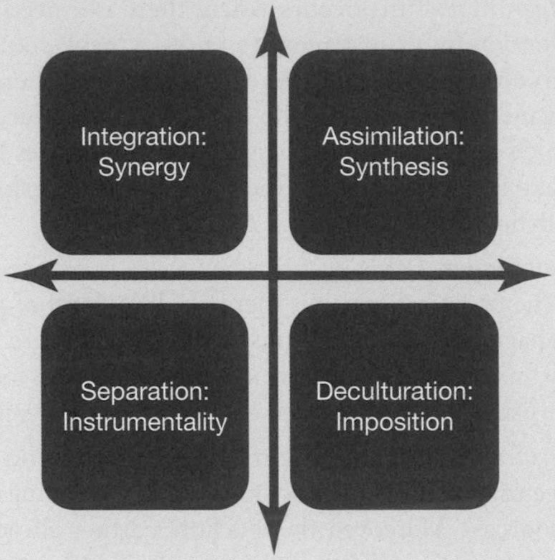

Peretz and Fried (2010) suggest that the choice of appraisal instruments should be guided by the culture in which they are to be used. Their empirical study across 21 countries revealed the importance of such selectivity; for example, despite the growing popularity of 360-degree appraisal systems, these systems really work best in countries where there is a low power distance, a high future orientation and an individualistic focus. Chiang and Birch (2010) take a more nuanced view of this by noting that even where there is an awareness of the national culture characteristics, there may still be different views on performance management:

> For variations between countries that exhibit similar cultural traits, HK attached by far the most importance to appraisal's evaluative role . . . this may be due to HK's highly assertive culture. Yet, Singapore, from a similar cultural heritage, utilized appraisal more for its communication development capabilities, and performance feedback was more frequent (p. 1384).

Consideration of the need for cross-cultural adaptations to the means by which we manage performance have been demonstrated through numerous empirical studies, but that then creates another issue for HR practitioners, one of equity. Where systems of performance management are altered, to what extent do one group of people feel that they are being treated differently? Where people are unhappy with the systems in situ, performance appraisal and performance management become counter-productive. Brown *et al.* (2010) suggest that people who are unhappy with the performance appraisal system are less committed to their work, have higher levels of job dissatisfaction and are more inclined to leave, whereas Thurston and McNall (2010: 225) suggest that 'employees' perceptions of fairness of performance appraisal practices are linked to organisationally relevant attitudes and behaviours; beyond the influence of the discrepancy between expected and actual performance'.

Explore

- What factors would you need to take into account when managing performance across national borders?

Managing performance in a diverse workforce

As the composition of the workforce continues to become more inclusive and diverse, understanding how this dimension affects performance has become an increasingly significant issue for HRM, and a number of organisations across different sectors have begun efforts to understand workforce diversity in relation to performance. Both scholars and practitioners have started to explore the consequences of increased diversity on work-related outcomes. Indeed, emphasis on diversity and its management has become a primary theme in the public management research literature, with inquiry devoted to diversity management programmes (Naff and Kellough, 2003; Kellough and Naff, 2004), the impact of diversity on performance outcomes (Wise and Tschirhart, 2000; Pitts and Wise, 2004; Pitts, 2005), the status of minority groups in public employment (Lewis and Smithey, 1998), and the role of diversity in public administration education (Tschirhart and Wise, 2002; Pitts and Wise, 2004).

In the USA, for example, Pitts (2009) suggested that almost 90 per cent of federal agencies reported they were actively managing diversity, but despite this high level of interest, there remained little empirical research to test the relationships between diversity management, job satisfaction and work group performance. To address this deficit, Pitts (2009) conducted a study among 140,000 federal government employees. His findings indicated that diversity management was positively and significantly related to job satisfaction. The most satisfied employees worked in units where they reported diversity management was strong. His work provides evidence for the argument that it is poor diversity management that is leading some segments of the workforce to be less satisfied with their jobs, rather than the jobs themselves.

The practical implications of his study are clear and direct: diversity management matters. At the organisational level, it means that resources should be devoted to diversity management programmes and training opportunities. Diversity should be viewed as a core competency for all employees, particularly managers. At the sub-organisational level, it means that managers who are concerned with the effective management of performance should put time and energy into understanding the different perspectives of employee groups. The managers who are likely to be most successful are those who effectively acknowledge and manage the diversity present in their groups. As a field, this means that HR practitioners must view diversity management as a core tool in the toolkit of performance management and should strive to include diversity-related competencies and raise levels of understanding and awareness across the entire organisation.

Explore

- What features distinguish a diverse workforce?
- How, if at all, might they affect an organisation's approach to managing performance?

Managing performance in an ageing workforce

As we have seen, effective performance management demands that organisations confront many of the demographic changes occurring in the workforce, such as increasing racial and ethnic diversity, along with greater numbers of women workers. Calo (2008) identifies a further aspect of performance management in the context of diversity, which involves recognising that in many developed economies, the workforce is steadily ageing, a reflection of declining birth rates. Most HR practitioners are vaguely aware that a major demographic shift is about to transform societies, and therefore companies. The statistics are compelling. For example, in the USA the percentage of the workforce between the ages of 55 and 64 is growing faster than any other age group. The situation is described by Strack *et al.* (2008), as being particularly acute in certain industries. In the US energy sector, more than a third of the workforce is already over 50 years old, and that age group is expected to grow by more than 25 per cent by 2020. In Japan, the number of workers over the age of 50 in the financial services sector is projected to rise by 61 per cent between now and then. Indeed, even in an emerging economy like China's, the number of manufacturing workers aged 50 or older will more than double by 2025.

An ageing workforce can also create a mismatch between labour supply and demand; for example, Germany currently faces an immediate shortage of qualified engineering graduates. Experienced engineers are retiring and, because engineering ceased to be an attractive career option in the late 1980s, there is a massive shortage of new recruits. In 2006 the country had a deficit of approximately 48,000 engineers and that figure is expected to grow significantly in coming years. At the same time, the country has too many unskilled workers: the unemployment rate of unskilled labour is more than six times higher than that of university graduates, and many industrialised countries face similar situations.

In terms of performance management, an ageing workforce has two important HR implications: first, organisations must ensure the transfer of the valuable knowledge that older workers possess before they retire; and secondly, organisations must address the issue of how to maintain efficient levels of performance among the older workers while they remain in the organisation.

As the workforce driving the knowledge economy ages, new challenges arise, particularly the risk of a significant loss of valuable knowledge as older workers retire from the workforce. Researchers and practitioners have discussed the importance of knowledge transfer to an organisation's success, and knowledge has become recognised as the most strategically significant resource of organisations. When Drucker (1993) originally alerted organisational leaders to the rise of the knowledge society, he described the radical change in the meaning of knowledge and how knowledge had assumed even greater importance than either capital or labour for nations. O'Dell and Grayson (1998: 6) referred to knowledge management as a broad concept, defining it as 'a conscious strategy of getting the right knowledge to the right people at the right time' and as a way of putting knowledge into action to improve organisational performance. How to transfer knowledge from one person to others or to the broader organisational knowledge base is a challenging aspect of the performance management process, because knowledge transfer does not occur spontaneously or naturally. While it is difficult to calculate accurately the financial consequences of losing critical knowledge, the risks certainly include lost productivity, increased errors and diminished creativity. The essential point, argues Calo (2008), is that organisational leaders need to recognise that once knowledge and expertise have left their organisation, they are difficult to recover, so difficult as to make their recovery unlikely. Knowledgeable older workers will be leaving organisations in record numbers over the coming decade, so before they leave it is imperative that organisations take steps to retain their knowledge. Calo (2008) suggests that conducting a knowledge risk assessment is one such strategy. It would involve all managers within the organisation being tasked with the responsibility of first identifying the at-risk positions, and then developing a plan to identify a successor, having an accelerated learning plan for the identified successor, and facilitating the transfer of knowledge from the incumbent workers to successors. This approach would serve to emphasise the overall institutional commitment to a knowledge transfer process.

Calo (2008) has drawn our attention to many of the concerns that have been expressed regarding the risk of the ageing workforce, including the loss of knowledge arising from the retirement of the baby boomers and the potential shortage of workers to fill the gaps left by exits from the workforce. A distinct, but related, concern is highlighted here and must be addressed: how to make the best use of older workers who remain in the workforce. Today, the workforce of most organisations has a higher overall age than at any time in history. While many older workers are members of the first wave of baby boomers, the 50–54 year age group is the fastest growing segment of the population, and the 45–49 year age group is the second fastest growing. The concerns, then, should not be only about the imminent retirement of the first wave of the baby boomers, but that organisations will need to confront many new performance issues as a result of having a greater number of older workers on their payrolls. As

Cappelli (2008) advised, managing an ageing workforce is going to be an ongoing and integral component part of an organisation's approach to performance management.

Strack *et al.* (2008) suggest that initiatives that focus on performance management of older workers can help to address the implications of an ageing workforce on productivity. They advise that conducting a systematic review of current HR policies and processes could alert the organisation to possible adjustments in a variety of areas to turn age-related challenges into competitive opportunities. The most obvious involves training programmes that help older workers update their skills and leverage their performance. However, in training older workers, it is important to remember that one-age-fits-all courses are not necessarily geared to the particular needs, knowledge and strengths of older workers. For example, older manufacturing employees' lack of familiarity with the internet may make typical web-based or blended training programmes unappealing to them.

Another obvious area for performance enhancement is healthcare management. On average, older employees do not become ill more often than younger employees; they just are ill for longer periods. Proactive measures, designed to prevent sickness and injury, can reduce the problem significantly. Such measures should be targeted at employees with a high risk of health problems and tailored to the jobs they do. Strack *et al.* (2008) reviewed RWE Power's strategy for managing older workers. RWE is a German electric power and natural gas public utility based in Essen and is the second largest electricity producer in Germany. Strack *et al.* report that in 2006, RWE Power found that an older workforce reduced performance in production-related job families. To counter this trend, it is managing the performance of older workers through personalised work schedules in which shift lengths are tailored to employees' abilities. It is also exploring the possibility of 'lifetime working programmes', in which employees accumulate credit for overtime hours that can be used to reduce work hours when they are older.

The performance of older workers can also be enhanced through the development of creative performance incentives. For example, Strack *et al.* (2008) suggest older workers might serve as mentors to new workers, which can increase motivation and performance. Employees with critical knowledge might be offered the chance to return to the company and work on special projects on a freelance basis after they have retired. This latter approach has demonstrated multiple benefits: reducing capacity shortfalls in a crucial job category and keeping valuable knowledge in the company, as well as motivating employees near retirement to perform well so that they will be considered for this post-retirement opportunity.

In summary, performance management of a diverse and ageing workforce is not a passing fad. It is a pressing and competitive priority for all organisations in this era of rapid demographic and social change.

Explore

- What features distinguish an ageing workforce?
- How, if at all, might these affect an organisation's approach to managing performance?

Managing performance in a volunteer workforce

Volunteers are the life blood of many non-profit organisations. Non-profit organisations have traditionally relied on volunteers to perform crucial agency functions. As staffing costs continue to rise, and as job seekers continue to look for valuable experience, non-profits will continue to rely more heavily on volunteers and other unpaid staff than do their for-profit counterparts. To put this into context, Cilenti *et al.* (2007) estimate that in the USA in 2000, adult volunteers devoted 15.5 billion hours of time to non-profit organisations throughout the nation, representing a total dollar value of $239 billion in volunteer time. Between September 2004 and September 2005, more than 65 million people did some kind of volunteer work, up from 59.8 million people in 2002.

The author of this article contends that well-managed non-profits have become expert at several crucial components of running a successful organisation, and can serve as examples to the for-profit sector. In short, non-profits often have well-defined, unwavering missions; they make wise use of their board of directors as a resource; and they seem to know a lot about managing paid employees and volunteers. Geber (1991) suggests that because volunteers often come from the ranks of the employees, it is vital to give them meaningful work that suits their level of expertise. This involves matching the volunteer's skills to an available position, preparing detailed job or project descriptions to facilitate a fast, thorough orientation, giving them high-quality but streamlined on-the-job training, and providing formal performance appraisals, while also offering less formal forms of feedback and recognition. Although these approaches may not sound much different from those that should be used with any paid employee, the importance of keeping volunteers satisfied and fulfilled with their assigned work, the necessity of expediency in their orientation and training, and the significance of giving recognition to their contribution accentuate the importance of these elements.

Performance managing volunteers at the CIPD

The CIPD, the professional lead body for all HRM practitioners, relies extensively on the use of volunteers to maintain the branch network and to operate as directors on the National Executive Board. In June 2008, under the Executive Leadership of Robin Jordan, the CIPD developed a series of competencies required at board level for all directors. In line with best performance management practice, the competencies are regularly reviewed and currently comprise:

- *Strategic direction* – the ability to contribute to setting the vision, values and purpose for CIPD, and ensure CIPD has the resources – people and financial – to achieve its goals. A person with the ability to think and plan ahead strategically.

- *Business judgment* – the ability to weigh evidence and analyse ideas before reaching an independent and objective conclusion, including an understanding of financial information at a complex business level; also the ability to assimilate information quickly and effectively.

- *Governance* – the ability to ensure that the CIPD is managed with integrity and probity, and to bring those qualities and independence of mind to the role.

- *Relationships* – the ability to work supportively and build team cohesiveness with fellow board members and executive management colleagues, while at the same time constructively probing, challenging and adding value to the strategic direction, decision-making and performance of CIPD.

The unique aspect of how the CIPD manages its volunteers at director level is that each volunteer board director has a 'conversation with purpose'. This is essentially a structured performance appraisal with the Chair. Whilst acknowledging the voluntary nature of board appointments, the principles associated with good governance suggest that this 'conversation with a purpose' involves:

- The opportunity for at least an annual meeting between the Chair and each director. (Opting out of the annual meeting is possible, except where the director indicates an intention to seek re-election.)

- The meeting is a two-way conversation, with an opportunity to discuss the contribution of the director and the Chair.

- Three areas should be covered:
  (i) Constructive feedback
    - considers examples to illustrate contributions made and behaviours apparent;
    - demonstrates appropriate preparation, attendance and commitment;
    - provides valuable input to board meetings;
    - asks demanding questions of the executive team;

- challenges others constructively within the board;
- contributes to strategy and policy discussion;
- involved in promoting the work of the CIPD outside board meetings;
- additional inputs in relation to feedback to the Chair may include management of board agendas;
- encouragement and participation of board members.

(ii) Aspirations for other roles
- What aspirations or potential have you considered for another role on the board or its subcommittees?
- Are you considering a second term (if applicable)? If so how do you meet the current requirements for non-executive directors?

(iii) Development needs
- What personal development would be appropriate and how might it be achieved?
- How might the board's development be addressed?

- A record of the meeting is held by both the director and the Chair, to be used in subsequent discussions and within the context of succession and development planning.

The 'conversations with a purpose' have aided effective performance management by clearly establishing the requirements of the role the volunteer is committing to. The conversations have the benefit of providing a formal opportunity for the volunteer board director to discuss with the Chair their performance and contribution, needs and aspirations and development plans. This serves to ensure the volunteer is aware of his or her role and is able to fulfil the requirements satisfactorily. In this respect, Robin Jordan, the retiring Chair, suggested that managing volunteers is no different from managing salaried staff: there is a role to be performed and there is an expectation about the way in which it will be undertaken. He said: 'There are roles and responsibilities and volunteers have a duty to undertake the performance of their work as effectively as possible.' In the approach to managing the performance of volunteers adopted by the CIPD, the level of support available from the host organisation is the same for volunteers and their needs and career aspirations are taken just as seriously as those of paid staff.

Many organisations are totally dependent on a volunteer workforce. For them, the innovative, creative and responsive approach adopted by the CIPD can be seen as a role model, and the adoption of the following is key to the successful management of volunteers:

- Understand individuals' motivations.
- Find the right fit.
- Manage the relationship with full-time staff.
- Match roles to talents.
- Implement best practices.
- Keep volunteers in the loop.

Explore

- To what extent do you agree with Robin Jordan, the retiring Chair of the National Executive of the CIPD, that managing volunteers is the same as managing paid staff?

Concluding comments

This chapter has focused on performance management. It has demonstrated how our understanding of contemporary performance management has evolved from earlier schools of thought, and how elements of previous practices can be seen in the ways in which we try to direct and control performance today. Traditional sociological modes of control, as characterised by Weber and Taylor, are reflected in Ritzer's notion of 'McDonaldisation'. The individualistic psychological focus of the motivational theorists are replicated today in our characterisations of employee engagement, identity and organisational citizenship behaviour. Insights into these schools of thought helps us to map the landscape of performance management and to see how this articulates with the wider issues affecting the world of work.

It is our consideration of the relationship between organisations and the environments in which they operate that has encouraged us to take a higher-level strategic view of the influences on performance management. Here we have looked specifically at the ways in which globalisation and the internationalisation of business have compelled HR practitioners and managers to think of newer and more nuanced ways of managing performance. In focusing on collaborative isomorphism, the discussions here draw attention to the problems of managing performance across networked organisations and across cultures, highlighting how the same processes of performance management and performance measurement may be perceived differently.

The distinction is made here between the management of performance and the measurement of performance and we have demonstrated that despite a growing understanding of the limitations of performance appraisal, it remains one of the most widely employed approaches in the contemporary measurement of employee performance. The critique related to operational limitations, such as rater bias and the trustworthiness of measurement, has given insights into the complexities of the process of performance measurement so that, in practice, we are cognisant of the types of conclusions we can realistically draw.

The chapter has explored the use of technology in the management of performance and has both discussed the ability of organisations to undertake covert surveillance of workers and encouraged thinking about the ethical implications of this. However, concerns over the ethical probity of monitoring the work of employees so closely, and possibly surreptitiously, has provoked many into thinking about the nature of management power and the ways in which this is wielded ostensibly for the corporate good. While for many the Orwellian prospects of covert surveillance present a daunting view of the future, it is important not to under-estimate the ways in which employees act in order to influence performance measurement, and it is probably dangerous to assume that managers are egotistical despots and villains!

Caution is needed here, because if we truly subscribe to the idea that effective HRM can lead to a genuine level of employee engagement and commitment, the desires, aims and objectives of the managers and the workers and their employment relationship cease to be characterised by antagonistic objectives, underpinned by adversarial and conflicting tensions, and become instead based on mutuality, trust and respect. In such circumstances, any power held by the manager would be used to further consolidate the effectiveness of the working relationship – rather than jeopardise it by trying to subvert workers or manipulate them through covert surveillance techniques. Performance appraisal does have the potential to be misused, but it also has the potential to help the development and career opportunities of many employees. In many respects, it appears that the jury is still out, with the culture of the organisation perhaps being the single biggest factor to influence the direction of the path followed.

This chapter has outlined a trend in the extension of performance measurement from that concerned solely with individual employees to an approach embracing the whole organisation. In this context, attention was drawn to the way in which organisational structures and operating boundaries are shifting, and bringing new demands and a need for new ways of approaching performance management. Working across cultures and between collaborating organisations requires the effective management of knowledge and the ability to translate organisational visions into clear measurable outcomes that define success, and are shared throughout the organisation with customers and stakeholders. This emerging perspective on performance management continues the shift from prescriptive, audit- and compliance-based oversight to an ongoing, forward-looking strategic partnership. Managing the performance of older workers and the performance of volunteers were also reviewed in the chapter and served to demonstrate the extent to which the management of performance will increasingly become an organisation-focused rather than an individual-focused activity. For further evidence of this trend, one only needs to review the press and observe the extent to which organisations are increasingly concerned with the effective management of their performance within society and within the community. The ability to demonstrate an active engagement with the corporate social responsibility agenda is growing rapidly. Perhaps, therefore, in the future, performance management will be less about quantifying the output of individual employees and more about the effective performance of the organisation in society.

Summary

- There are differences between performance measurement and performance appraisal.

- Approaches to performance measurement are typically represented in a performance appraisal process.

- Performance appraisal has limitations that result in part from the many competing aims it seeks to achieve.

- The ethics and probity of performance appraisal have been questioned, and some have represented it as a management tool that enables managers to monitor and engage in constant surveillance of their employees.

- Information and communication technology will change the nature and scope of performance management.

- Effective performance management will need to address changes in organisational structure and composition, in particular in relation to an increasingly global and competitive market, a diverse and ageing workforce and to manage a rising number of volunteer workers.

- In the future, performance management will be less about individual performance and more about the performance of the organisation as a world player and social partner with a conscience.

Questions

1 What are the organisational advantages and limitations of performance measurement?
2 Why has performance appraisal been so severely criticised?
3 What role do you envisage for ICT in the management of performance? Are there any associated risks?
4 What are the theoretical links between HRM and performance appraisal?
5 What new challenges will organisations face in managing performance in the years to come?
6 What factors would you take into account if you were designing an approach to performance management?

Case study

Performance improvement at TRW

TRW Inc. is a global automotive, aeronautics, electronics and information-systems company with 100,000 employees, based in 36 countries on five continents and with four core businesses. It was originally called 'Thompson Ramo Wooldridge Inc.', but was shortened to TRW Inc. in 1965.

In 2001, the company had a heavy debt load following a large acquisition in the automotive sector and, in the face of current adverse market conditions, TRW was challenged to become more competitive and performance-driven and to provide greater value to shareholders. To reach those goals, the senior

➤

449

Case study continued

management committee instituted dramatic change throughout the company. Business units were empowered to operate more autonomously than they had in the past, and the corporate headquarters itself was renamed the 'Business Support Centre.'

To guide the creation of a new and energised work culture, a new set of company-wide TRW 'behaviours' was developed and communicated throughout the company. The aim was to organise and operate a performance-appraisal, professional-development and succession-management system that not only attempted to create a more performance-driven, customer-oriented organisation, but also commanded respect and workers' acceptance. The solution was to select a team of IT experts and key HR people from each of the businesses. Each member was faced with the task of allowing their own particular business's way of doing things (some were used to working with two-page appraisal forms, others had 10) to be incorporated into a single system. The employee performance and development process they came up with, although common to the entire organisation, was allowed to flow within particular units as was felt best, both standardisation and flexibility being recognised as essentials.

To position TRW competitively for the twenty-first century, the company stands committed to excellence and quality, exploring new markets and satisfying its customers, shareholders and employees. To meet those commitments, TRW has created a set of six behaviours that distinguish it in the marketplace through performance and technology.

The six behaviours that guide performance management are:

1 Create trust:
   – create an open and constructive environment;
   – deal with reality;
   – communicate with candour and honesty;
   – honour commitments;
   – take personal accountability for results.

2 Energise people:
   – rigorously select, empower and grow people who demand the best of themselves and others;
   – reward performance and initiative.

3 Performance-driven:
   – deliver profitable growth;
   – develop and achieve demanding goals, both short- and long-term;
   – continuously improve productivity and quality;
   – execute with facts, urgency and decisiveness;
   – create energy that does not tolerate bureaucracy.

4 Embrace change:
   – passion for innovation;
   – a thirst for new ideas;
   – be adaptable and flexible;
   – know your markets; lead your competitors.

5 Customer-oriented:
   – understand your customers;
   – relentlessly focus on their needs;
   – develop lasting relationships.

6 Build teamwork:
   – share information and best practices;
   – speak up;
   – encourage diverse views;
   – get the facts, make decisions;
   – ACT!
   – support it.

Note: The TRW behaviours were instituted in 2001 to guide the culture of the company (Neary, 2002).

Questions

1 What are the strengths of TRW's approach to widespread organisational change aimed at performance improvements?

2 What are the limitations of this approach?

References and further reading

Those texts marked with an asterisk are recommended for further reading.

Adair, C., Simpson, L., Birdsell, J., Omelchuk, K., Casebeer, A., Gardiner, H., Newman, S., Beckjie, A. and Clelland, S. (2003) *Performance Measurement Systems in Health Care Services: Models, Practices and Effectiveness.* Alberta: The Alberta Heritage Foundation for Medical Research.

Aguinis, H., Joo, H. and Gottfredson, R. (2012) 'Performance management universals: think globally, act locally', *Business Horizons*, 55, 4: 385–92.

Amaratunga, D. and Baldry, D. (2002) 'Moving from performance measurement to performance management', *Facilities*, 20: 217–23.

Armstrong, M. and Baron, A. (1998) *Performance Management: The New Realistic.* London: IPD.

Armstrong, M. and Baron, A. (2004) *Managing Performance: Performance Management in Action.* London: CIPD.

Aswathappa, K. (2005) *Human Resource and Personal Management: Text and Cases,* 4th edn. Delhi: Tata McGraw-Hill.

Bach, S. (2005) *Managing Human Resources: Personnel Management in Transition,* 4th edn. Oxford: Blackwell.

Bentham, J. (1995) *The Panopticon Writings.* London: Verso.

Bititci, U., Martinez, V., Albores, P. and Parung, J. (2004) 'Creating and maintaining value in collaborative networks', *International Journal of Physical Distribution and Logistics Management,* 34: 251–68.

*Björkman, I. and Budhwar, P. (2007) 'When in Rome . . . ?', *Employee Relations,* 29: 595–610.

*Boselie, P., Dietz, G. and Boon, C. (2005) 'Commonalities and contradictions in HRM and performance research', *Human Resource Management Journal,* 15: 67–94.

*Boselie, P., Paauwe, J. and Jansen, P. (2001) 'Human resource management and performance: lessons from the Netherlands', *International Journal of Human Resource Management,* 12: 1107–25.

*Boxall, P. and Purcell, J. (2008) *Strategy and Human Resource Management.* Basingstoke: Palgrave Macmillan.

*Bourgon, J. (2008) 'Performance management: it's the results that count', *Asian Pacific Journal of Public Administration,* 30, 1: 41–58.

*Brown, M., Hyatt, D. and Benson, J. (2010) 'Consequences of the performance appraisal experience', *Personnel Review,* 39, 3: 375–96.

*Budhwar, P., Varma, A., Singh, V. and Dhar, R. (2006) 'HRM systems of Indian call centers in India: an exploratory study', *International Journal of Human Resource Management,* 17, 5: 881–97.

*Burgess, T., Gules, H. and Tekin, M. (1997) 'Supply chain collaboration and success in technology implementation', *Integrated Manufacturing Systems,* 8: 323–32.

Busi, M. and Bititci, U. (2006) 'Collaborative performance management: present gaps and future research', *International Journal of Productivity and Performance Management,* 55: 7–25.

Callahan, K. (2007) *Elements of Effective Governance: Measurement, Accountability and Participation.* New York: CRC Press: Taylor Francis.

Calo, T. (2008) 'Talent management in the era of the aging workforce: the critical role of knowledge transfer', *Public Personnel Management,* 37, 4: 403–41.

Cappelli, R. (2008) 'Talent management for the twenty-first century', *Harvard Business Review,* 86: 74–81.

Chiang, F. and Birtch, T. (2010) 'Appraising performance across borders: an empirical examination of the purposes and practices of performance appraisal in a multi-country context', *Journal of Management Studies,* 47, 7: 1365–93.

*Chand, M. and Katou, A. (2007) 'Human resource management: organisational performance; Hotel and Catering Industry, India', *Employee Relations,* 29: 576–94.

Cilenti, M., Guggenheimer, E. and Kramnick, R. (2007) *The Volunteer Workforce: Legal Issues and Best Practices for Nonprofits.* New York: Lawyers Alliance for New York.

CIPD (2009a) *Performance Appraisal,* Factsheet. London: CIPD.

CIPD (2009b) *Performance Management,* Factsheet. London: CIPD.

Deal, T. and Kennedy, A. (1982) *Corporate Cultures. The Rites and Rituals of Corporate Life.* New York: Penguin Books.

*Den-Hartog, D., Boselie, P. and Paauwe, J. (2004) 'Performance management: a model and research agenda', *Applied Psychology: An International Review,* 53: 556–69.

DeNisi, A. (ed.) (2000) *Performance Appraisal and Performance Management: A Multilevel Analysis.* San Francisco, CA: Jossey-Bass.

*Drucker, P. (1999) *The Practice of Management,* Oxford: Butterworth-Heinemann.

Drucker, R. (1993) 'The rise of the knowledge society', *Wilson Quarterly,* 17: 52–69.

Eccles, R. (1991) 'The performance measurement manifesto', *Harvard Business Review,* 69, 1: 131–7.

*Edwards, P. and Wright, M. (2001) 'High-involvement work systems and performance outcomes: the strength of variable, contingent and context-bound relationships', *International Journal of Human Resource Management,* 12, 4: 568–85.

Fawcett, S. and Magnan, G. (2002) 'The rhetoric and reality of supply chain integration', *International Journal of Physical Distribution and Logistics Management,* 32: 339–61.

Fernie, S. and Metcalf, D. (1997) *(Not) Hanging on the Telephone: Payment Systems in the New Sweat Shops.* Centre for Economic Performance, LSE.

*Ferris, G., Arthur, M., Berkson, H., Kaplan, D., Harell-Cook, G. and Frink, D. (1998) 'Toward a social context theory of the human resource management–organization effectiveness relationship', *Human Resource Management Review,* 8: 235–64.

Findlay, P. and Newton, T. (1998) 'Re-framing Foucault: the case of performance appraisal', in P. Findlay and T. Newton (eds) *Foucault, Management and Organization Theory.* London: Sage.

*Flanagan, J. (1954) 'The Critical Incident Technique'. *Psychological Bulletin,* 51, 4. Online: **http://www.apa.org/pubs/databases/psycinfo/cit-article.pdf** (accessed 28 January 2013).

Fletcher, C. (2001) 'Performance appraisal and management: the developing research agenda', *Journal of Occupational and Organisational Psychology,* 74: 473–88.

Foucault, M. (1977) *Discipline & Punish: The Birth of the Prison.* London: Penguin Books.

Geber, B. (1991) 'Managing volunteers', *Training,* 28: 21–6.

Geddes, D. and Konrad, A. (2003) 'Demographic differences and reactions to performance feedback', *Human Relations,* 56: 1485–514.

Grey, C. (1994) 'Career as a project of the self and labour process discipline', *Sociology,* 28: 479–97.

*Guest, D. (1997) 'Human resource management and performance: a review and research agenda', *Journal of Human Resource Management,* 8: 263–76.

*Guest, D. (2000) 'Human resource management, employee well-being and organizational performance', in D. Guest (ed.) *CIPD Professional Standards Conference 11th July.* Keele: Keele University.

*Hall, L. (2004) *HRM practices and employee and organizational performance: a critique of the research and guest's model,* Department of Business and Management Discussion Paper No. 5. Manchester: Manchester Metropolitan University.

Harris, C. Cortvriend, P. and Hyde, P. (2007) 'Human resource management and performance in healthcare organizations', *Journal of Health and Organization Management,* 21: 448–59.

Heslin, P. Carson, J. and VandeWalle, D. (2009) 'Practical applications of goal setting theory to performance management', in J.W. Smither (ed.) *Performance Management: Putting Research into Practice.* San Francisco, CA: Jossey Bass, pp. 89–114.

*Hofstede, G. (1985) 'The interaction between national and organizational value systems', *Journal of Management Studies,* 22, 347–57.

Holmberg, S. (2000) 'A system perspective on supply chain management', *International Journal of Physical Distribution and Logistics Management,* 30: 847–68.

*Huselid, M. (1995) 'The impact of human resource management practices on turnover, productivity and corporate financial performance', *Academy of Management Journal,* 38: 635–760.

Hyde, P., Boaden, R. Cortvriend, P. Harris, C., Marchington, M., Sparrow, P. and Sibbald, B. (2006) *Improving Health Through Human Resource Management.* London: CIPD.

*Industrial RS (2003a) 'Time to talk – how and why employers conduct appraisals', *Employment Trends,* 769: 8–14.

Johnson, H. and Kaplan, R. (1987) *Relevance Lost: The Rise and Fall of Management Accounting.* Boston, MA: Harvard Business School Press.

Kaplan, R. and Norton, D. (1992) 'The balanced scorecard – measures that drive performance', *Harvard Business Review,* 70, 1: 79–80.

*Kaplan, R. and Norton, D. (1996) 'Using the balanced scorecard as a strategic management system', *Harvard Business Review,* 74, 1: 75–85.

*Katou, A. and Budhwar, P. (2006) 'Human resource management systems and organisational performance: a test of a mediating model in the Greek manufacturing context', *The International Journal of Human Resource Management,* 17: 1223–53.

*Katou, A. and Budhwar, P. (2007) 'The effect of human resource management policies on organizational performance in Greek manufacturing firms', *Thunderbird International Business Review,* 49: 1–35.

Kellough, J. and Naff, K. (2004) 'Responding to a wake-up call: an examination of Federal Agency diversity management programs', *Administration& Society,* 36: 62–90.

*Kersley, B., Alpin, C., Bewley, H., Dix, G. and Oxenbridge, S. (2006) *Inside the Workplace: Findings from the 2004 Workplace Employment Relations Survey.* London: Routledge.

*Latham, G. and Locke, E. (1984) *Goal Setting: A Motivational Technique that Works.* Englewood Cliffs, NJ: Prentice-Hall.

*Legge, K. (1995) *Human Resource Management Rhetorics and Realities.* Basingstoke: Macmillan.

Lewis, G. and Smithey, P. (1998) 'Gender, race, and training in the Federal Civil Service', *Public Administration Quarterly,* 22: 204–8.

Locke, E. (1966) 'The relationship of intentions to level of performance', *Journal of Applied Psychology,* 50: 60–88.

Locke, E. and Latham, G. (1990) 'Work motivation and satisfaction: light at the end of the tunnel', *Psychological Science,* 1: 240–6.

Locke, E. and Latham, G. (2002) 'Building a practically useful theory of goal setting and task motivation: a 35-year odyssey', *American Psychologist,* 57: 705–17.

London, M. and Mone, E.M. (2009) 'Strategic Performance Management-Issues and Trends' in J. Storey, P.M. Wright and D. Ulrich (eds) *The Concise Companion to Strategic Human Resource Management.* Milton Keynes: Open University Press/Routledge, pp. 109–25.

*Longenecker, C. and Fink, L. (1997) 'Keys to designing and running an effective performance appraisal system: lessons learned', *Journal of Compensation and Benefits,* 13: 28–35.

Longnecker, C. and Fink, L. (2001) 'Improving management performance in rapidly changing organisations', *Journal of Management Development,* 20, 1: 7–18.

Longnecker, C. Simonetti, J. and Sharkey, T. (1999) 'Why organizations fail: the view from the front line', *Management Decision,* 15: 503–13.

Lynch, R. and Cross, K. (1991) *Measure Up! Yardstick for Continuous Improvement.* Cambridge, MA: Blackwell Business.

*MacDuffie, J. (1995) 'Human resource bundles and manufacturing performance: flexible production systems in the world auto industry', *Industrial Relations and Labour Review,* 48: 197–221.

McGregor, D. (1957) 'An uneasy look at performance appraisals', *Harvard Business Review,* 5: 89–95.

Miller, P. and Rose, N. (1990) 'Governing economic life', *Economy and Society,* 19: 1–31.

Mondy, R., Noe, R. and Premeaux, S. (2002) *Human Resource Management,* 8th edn. Upper Saddle River, NJ: Prentice-Hall.

Moynihan, D.P. and Pandey, S.K. (2010) 'The big question for performance management: why do managers use performance information?' *Journal of Public Administration Research and Theory,* 20, 4: 849–66.

Naff, K. and Kellough, E. (2003) 'Ensuring employment equity: are federal programs making a difference?', *International Journal of Public Administration,* 26: 1307–36.

Neary, D.B. (2002) 'Creating a company-wide, on-line, performance management system', *Human Resource Management,* 41: 491–8.

Newbold, C. (2008) '360-degree appraisals are now a classic', *Human Resource Management International Digest,* 16: 38–40.

Newton, T. (1994) 'Discourse and agency: the example of personnel psychology and assessment centers', *Organization Studies,* 15: 879–902.

Newton, T. and Findley, P. (1996) 'Playing God: the performance of appraisal', *Human Resource Management Journal,* 6: 42–58.

Oakland, J. (2003) *TQM: Text with Cases,* 3rd edn. Oxford. Butterworth-Heinemann.

O'Dell, C. and Grayson, C. (1998) *If Only We Knew What We Know.* New York: Free Press.

Patterson, K., Grimm, C. and Thomas, M. (2003) 'Adopting new technologies for supply chain management', *Transportation Research Part E,* 39: 95–121.

*Patterson, M., West, M., Lawthom, R. and Nickell, S. (1997) *The Impact of People Management on Business Performance.* London: IPD.

Peretz, H. and Fried, Y. (2012) 'National cultures, performance appraisal practices and organizational absenteeism and turnover: a study across 21 countries'. *Journal of Applied Psychology,* 97(2): 448–59.

Pitts, D. (2005) 'Diversity, representation, and performance: evidence about race and ethnicity in public organizations', *Journal of Public Administration Research and Theory,* 15: 615–31.

Pitts, D. (2009) 'Diversity management, job satisfaction, and performance: evidence from U.S. federal agencies', *Public Administration Review,* 69: 328–39.

Pitts, D. and Wise, L. (2004) 'Diversity in professional schools: a case study of public affairs and law', *Journal of Public Affairs Education,* 10: 142–60.

Procurement Executives Association (1999) *Guide to a Balanced Scorecard Performance Management Methodology.*

Procurement Executives' Association. Online: **http:// management. energy.gov/documents/BalancedScorecards PerfAndMeth.pdf.**

Purcell, J. 'Sustaining the HR and performance link in difficult times', University of Bath. Online: **http://www.bath.ac.uk/ werc/pdf/toughCIPD_8_02.pdf** (accessed 3 June 2009).

*Richardson, R. and Thompson, M. (1999) 'The impact of people management practices on business performance: a literature review', in *CIPD Issues in People Management*. London: CIPD.

Ritzer, G. (1993) *The McDonaldization of Society*. Thousand Oak, CA: Sage.

*Roberts, I. (2001) 'Reward and performance management', in I. Beardwell and L. Holden (eds) *Human Resource Management: A Contemporary Approach,* Harlow: FT/Prentice-Hall, pp. 506–58.

*Schuler, R. and Jackson, S. (1987) 'Linking competitive strategies with human resource management practices', *Academy of Management Executive,* 1: 207–19.

*Schuler, R. and Jackson, S. (1999) *Strategic Human Resource Management: A Reader*. London: Blackwell.

Sims, R.R. and Brinkmann, J. (2003) 'Enron ethics (or: culture matters more than codes)', *Journal of Business Ethics,* 45, 243–56.

Sipor, J. and Ward, B. (1995) 'The ethical and legal quandary of email privacy', *Communications of the Association for Computing Machinery,* 38: 8–54.

Stanton, J. (2000) 'Reactions to employee performance monitoring: framework, review and research directions', *Human Performance,* 13, 1: 85–113.

Strack, R., Baier, J. and Fahlander, A. (2008) 'Managing demographic risk', *Harvard Business Review,* 86: 119–28.

*Taylor, F. (1911) *The Principles of Scientific Management*. New York, NY: W.W. Norton. Published in Norton Library 1967 by arrangement with Harper & Row, Publishers, Inc.

Thornton III G. and Rupp, D. (2007) *Assessment Centers in Human Resource Management: Strategies for Prediction, Diagnosis and Development*. London: Taylor & Francis.

Thorpe, R. (2004) 'The characteristics of performance management research, implication and challenges', *International Journal of Productivity and Performance Management,* 53: 334–44.

Thurston, P and McNall, L. (2010) 'Justice perception of performance appraisal practices'. *Journal of Managerial Psychology*. 25(3): 201–28.

*Townley, B. (1993a) 'Foucault, power/knowledge and its relevance for HRM', *Academy of Management Review,* 18: 518–45.

Townley, B. (1993b) 'Performance appraisal and the emergence of management', *Journal of Management Studies,* 36: 287–306.

*Townley, B. (1994) *Reframing Human Resources Management: Power, Ethics and the Subject at Work*. London: Sage.

*Townley, B. (1997) 'The institutional logic of performance appraisal', *Organization Studies* 18: 261–85.

Tschirhart, M. and Wise, L. (2002) 'Responding to a diverse class: insights from seeing a course as an organization', *Journal of Public Affairs Education,* 8: 165–77.

Tung, R. (1993) 'Managing cross-national and intra-national diversity'. *Human Resource Management,* 32, 4: 461–77.

Waggoner, D., Neely, A. and Kennerley, M. (1999) 'The forces that shape organizational performance measurement systems: an interdisciplinary review', *International Journal of Production Economics,* 60: 53–60.

van Wanrooy, B., Bewley, H., Bryson, A., Forth, J., Freeth, S., Stokes, L. and Wood, S. (2013) *The 2011 Workplace Employment Relations Study; First Findings*. BIS, ESRC, ACAS, NIESR and UKCES.

Wilson, F. (2002) 'Dilemmas of appraisal', *European Management Journal,* 20: 620–29.

Wise, L. and Tschirhart, M. (2000) 'Examining empirical evidence on diversity effects: how useful is diversity research for public sector managers?', *Public Administration Review,* 60: 286–395.

Chapter 13

Employee reward

Amanda Thompson and Alan J. Ryan

Objectives

- To present the main historical and theoretical foundations underpinning contemporary employee reward practice.
- To define employee reward and identify the key components of reward.
- To explore the concept of reward management and the benefits and difficulties associated with introducing a strategic approach to reward.
- To consider key employee reward choices facing organisations in the contemporary era.
- To explore the economic and legal context for reward and the implications for employee reward practice.
- To identify the internal/organisational factors affecting organisational approaches to reward and the influence of sector.
- To consider key choices and emergent trends in terms of establishing pay levels, designing pay structures and determining criteria for pay progression.

Introductory case study

How do I get my pay up?

I've found out that one of my male colleagues who is in the rank below me has just negotiated a pay rise

29 January 2013

Dear Lucy

I work for a large firm that is getting much press on the importance of women's advancement in the workforce. I've recently found out by accident that one of my male colleagues who is in the rank below me has just negotiated a pay rise and is now paid slightly more than I am. I feel hard done by. What is the best strategy to get my pay up? Should I use my knowledge of his salary as a negotiating ploy? It feels wrong to me, but I'm sure others do it.

Middle manager, female, 45

Lucy's answer

The fact that this one man seems to be paid more than you doesn't prove a thing. It does not mean that you are underpaid. Even less does it mean your company is a great big hypocrite that doesn't actually care about women at all. It is a shame that you have let this unscientific snippet of data transform you from someone who was (I assume) fairly happy with her pay, into an aggrieved women, hinting darkly about discrimination.

The easiest thing for you to do is to try to erase this discovery from your mind, and go back to how you felt before. If you can't do that, then you should try to collect more information to see if you are, indeed, underpaid. I suspect you will find that your company is like most in that salaries are all over the place – that compared with some people you will look good, compared with others you'll look bad.

If you insist on obsessing about this one whippersnapper, at least do so logically. There are three reasons why he could be paid more than you: he might be perceived to be better at his work than you are; he might shout louder than you do; or he might recently have received an offer from another company and used that to get his salary up. If you want to play leapfrog, you'll find it hard to become demonstrably better at your work in a short space of time. It may also be tricky to rustle up a rival offer at a fat premium to your current salary in a hurry. That means all you have left is to try the shouting.

This is not an art, though it doesn't sound as if it comes easy to you. You need to marshal your arguments and make them loudly and unashamedly. Remember, people who make a nuisance tend to get paid more, as their bosses prefer quiet lives. However, do not even think of mentioning the pay of your colleague. I remember some years ago a woman journalist who made a discovery just like yours. When she complained to the boss that her pay was 20 per cent less than mine, she was told that was because she was 20 per cent less effective than I was. Result: she left the company shortly afterwards.

 Source: Kellaway, L. (2013), How do I get my pay up, *Financial Times*, 29 January. Http://www.ft.com/cms/s/0/534b36da-5b2a-11e2-8ccc-00144feab49a.html?siteedition=uk#axzz2tcGBag9f. © The Financial Times Limited 2013. All rights reserved.

Introduction

As the introductory case illustrates, reward can be a contentious and highly emotive matter for employees and one that is difficult to manage appropriately. Without the full facts, it is impossible to judge whether the manager in the scenario is being discriminated against because of her gender and/or if she is being paid fairly for the work she performs. The case, and in particular Lucy's 'no holds barred' response, does, however, raise some interesting issues concerning the way in which reward systems are designed and managed in organisations. We learn from this case that ad hoc decisions are not uncommon where reward is concerned, transparency does not always take centre stage and objective criteria are not, or cannot, be routinely applied to assess performance and determine pay rates/salaries. The case also reveals the 'dark art' of reward as practised at times by both employees, especially those with bargaining power, and employers, keen to ensure maximum return on investment while avoiding the financial and reputational risk associated with an equal pay challenge. It is suggested that pay can entice employees to stay, drive them to leave, encourage them to hold their employers to ransom or, worse, turn productive and content employees into embittered and disenchanted job incumbents.

This chapter identifies and discusses many of the issues raised by the introductory case study. It charts developments in employee reward and considers the practical ways in which reward management can be used, as part of a suite of human resource (HR) practices, to elicit employee engagement and drive individual and organisational performance. The chapter traces the historical path of reward, focusing initially on the nature of the wage–effort bargain and associated limited approaches to reward, revolving principally around the key construct of pay. The chapter then moves on to identify and explore the meaning of reward in the contemporary era, focusing upon reward as a potential strategic lever which can be used by organisations to encourage individuals and work teams to display behaviours that are consistent with organisational values and aligned with business goals. The overarching themes of the remainder of the chapter concern the economic and legal context for reward and the challenges associated with designing a reward strategy that is affordable, equitable and relevant, particularly in a testing economic environment. Embedded within these themes, emphasis is placed on pragmatic reward choices and dilemmas experienced by organisations in the twenty-first century, including decisions about the relative importance of internal equity and external pay comparability, the role of job evaluation, the factors which tend to be influential in shaping the reward 'mix', where to pitch pay, how to reward particular types of workers (e.g. top executives) and how to design pay structures and manage pay progression.

The historical and theoretical foundations of employee reward

We now outline and examine the extent to which human resource management (HRM) has developed current practical and theoretical issues surrounding the management of reward systems within modern organisations. A critical element of these discussions is the management of structures and strategies. This chapter introduces the notion of reward(s) as a central function in the development of a strategic role for HR functions and offers some explanation of the objectives of current reward management structures, strategies and systems.

'There's only one reason we come here – the money' has not been an unusual comment heard from employees in all organisations since the period of industrialisation. Such comments echo the nature of the employment relationship as a reward/effort bargain (Chapter 10). Whether openly, covertly, personally or collectively, we all become involved in the resolution of this bargain at some time during our working life. This chapter discusses how management have resolved and continue to resolve their problem of converting the labour potential, obtained by their transactions in the labour market, into the labour performance they desire, simply securing the required effort levels without rewarding at levels detrimental to the generation of sufficient profit. In this sense, we view reward as a core function for HR managers and rewards as composed of more than the mere 'notes' in the pay packet. Terms such as 'pay', 'compensation' and 'remuneration' are all recognisable expressions, but as we argue in the following sections, 'reward' is something qualitatively different in that the issues covered encompass both financial and non-financial benefits.

The development of reward systems

As a distinctive concern for managerial functions, the topic of reward is a recent addition; indeed it is fair to say that reward management has often been viewed as the 'poor relation'. Within the early labour management literature, it was discussed in terms of the management of figures and procedures (Yates, 1937; Urwick, 1958). Such discussions clearly view 'reward' as solely a matter of financial benefits (wage/effort) rather than including consideration of the non-financial benefits. We can argue from this initial analysis that during the development of a 'factory-based' system, in the late nineteenth/early twentieth centuries, it appears wage, rather than effort, was the central concern. Moreover, this period was accompanied by a system within which owners frequently found difficulty in securing consistent levels of control of the effort side of the bargain (Lovell, 1977; Zeitlin, 1983; Hinton, 1986). Employees, who were until that time self-controlled and in many respects driven by subsistence needs, had worked in small 'cottage' industries within which the product of labour was owned by the producers (workers themselves; notably in regard to the skilled artisans) and they worked only as hard as necessary in order to meet their subsistence needs. As Anthony (1977: 5) suggests, 'A great deal of the ideology of work is directed at getting men [*sic*] to take work seriously when they know that it is a joke'.

Explore

- How has a cataclysmic shift away from pure subsistence to extreme consumerism impacted workers' attitudes to financial recompense and issues of control within the workplace?

Owners found that getting workers to keep regular hours and to commit the effort owners considered to constitute 'a fair day's work' was problematic. In response to this dilemma they employed the 'butty' system of wage management. Under this system, owners committed a specific level of investment to a selected group of workers (normally skilled artisans) who then hired labour on 'spot contracts' by the day. The major problem for the owners with this system was that these 'subcontractors' had control over the effort/reward bargain and were able to enrich themselves at the expense of the owners. The owners enjoyed little or no control over the process of production, so the system was economically inefficient and failed to deliver the returns (rents/profits) required or, more importantly, the returns that were possible from the process of industrialisation.

From this group of 'favoured' workers, along with the introduction of some university graduates, there grew a new management cadre. This was a slow process: Gospel (1992: 17) notes that generally, in UK industry, this group (management, technical and clerical) amounted to only 8.6 per cent of the workforce in most manufacturing organisations by the start of the First World War. It can be further argued that even within these organisations, the development of a dedicated, specialised managerial function was uneven and patchy. These changes did little to address the problems associated with the wage/effort bargain, meaning productivity was below optimum levels. A key component in these problems was that they were underpinned by the actuality that 'the managers' brain was still under the workers' cap', or more precisely that these new managers rarely possessed the skills or knowledge of the production process held by the workers. This led to lower than optimum levels of production and reduced profits, a system F.W. Taylor described as 'systematic soldiering'. This activity was engaged in by workers, according to Taylor (1964: 74), 'with the deliberate object of keeping their employers ignorant of how fast work can be done'. From his observations Taylor took the view that workers acting in this manner were merely behaving as 'economically rational actors' desiring their own best interests. It was clear, therefore, that management needed to take the reins of the production process and reclaim their right to determine the outcome of the wage/effort bargain.

Explore

- Can you think of any contemporary work situations in which the brain is still 'under the worker's cap'?
- What impact does this have on reward decisions and outcomes?

Taylor, as the so-called 'father of scientific management', developed a system of measuring work, which assisted the process of reclaiming managerial rights. Jobs were broken down into specific elements which could then be timed and rated, while in the process, returning the determination of the speed of work to management and allowing for the development of pay systems which reflected, however crudely, performance. This scientific system devised by Taylor became the basis of countless pay systems operating effectively alongside the routinisation and deskilling of work, which is often associated with scientific management within the literature (see, for example, Braverman, 1974; Hill, 1981; Littler, 1982, 1985; Wood, 1982; Thompson, 1983; Burawoy, 1985). While this allowed management to reassert their control over the level of outputs, to relocate the managers' brain under their own hats and hence the determination of the wage/effort bargain, it did generate problems in relation to managerial attempts to convince workers to take work seriously. In straightforward terms, we can suggest that the 'measured work' techniques advocated by adherents of Taylorism further separated conception from execution and led to feelings of alienation. Alienation can be defined as 'various social or psychological evils which are characterised by a harmful separation, disruption or fragmentation which sunders things that properly belong together' (Wood, 2000: 24); in our terms that means the separation of workers from that which they produce. Blauner (1964) argued that such an objective state is created as an offshoot of the subjective feelings of separation which workers experience under modern production systems. These feelings and their outcomes can be briefly outlined in the following manner (adapted from Blauner, 1964):

- *Powerlessness* – the inability to exert control over work processes.
- *Meaninglessness* – the lack of a sense of purpose, as employees only concentrated on a narrowly defined and repetitive task and therefore could not relate their role to the overall production process and end product.
- *'Self-estrangement'* – the failure to become involved in work as a mode of self-expression.
- *Isolation* – the lack of sense of belonging.

Although scientific management originated at the beginning of the twentieth century, its legacy has lived on in many areas. Similar experiences have been reported in the design of work in service industries and call centres (Ritzer, 1997, 2000; Taylor and Bain, 1999, 2001; Callaghan and Thompson, 2001). The solution to this problem has been sought, following Taylor's notion of humans as economic actors, by the introduction of various reward systems and mechanisms, the core objectives of which were originally to operationalise effective control over the wage/effort bargain and later with current systems to alleviate the feelings of alienation and generate commitment to organisational goals.

In this regard, it is possible to argue that such reward systems are not designed in the 'perfect world' that some commentators have imagined. Rather they are controlled by various external and internal stimuli and operate within a complex landscape. These incentives or pressures can be broken down and identified in simple terms that highlight some of the more complex debates we address within this chapter. In no particular order, we can see that they include the ability of the organisation to pay, which in the current times of financial restraint and turbulence is greatly reduced. To this we can add the bargaining strength – both internally and more widely – of trade unions and of groups of workers in key organisational roles.

While the decline in trade union membership alongside the rise in non-union forms of representation (Dundon and Rollinson, 2004; Gollan, 2007), and the increased importance of small firms (Marlow *et al.*, 2005), especially within the private sector, may have weakened trade union power, there are still sectors within the economy where organisations have to make a judgment about the residual power available to trade unions. Such residual power is also a dynamic force behind moves to maintain differentials in line with existing custom and practice. A further element in this consideration is the wider increase in the 'cost of living', which places strains on employers and employees. This is exacerbated by rapid technological change which influences labour markets and available skills patterns. While organisational and technological change may have increased productivity, and hence arguably created increased profits, employers must decide what percentage of such increases can be used to develop wage systems that reflect current effort. These pressures have been crystallised into three main features that affect the amount of pay and/or level of increase awarded (Milkovitch and Newman, 1996):

- labour market pressures – supply and demand;
- product markets – competition and demand;
- organisational factors – sector, technology and size.

These considerations increase discussion of the extent to which employers can successfully develop, design and control reward systems in the current volatile economic climate.

Design and debates

While this chapter often discusses reward systems in a manner that appears to offer a chrono-logical explanation, we would note that the development of a 'new' system does not indicate the total removal of other older mechanisms. Evidence suggests that in many modern organi-sations we continue to find both 'old' and 'new' pay systems operating in tandem, deliver-ing control on different levels for various groups of workers (Armstrong and Stephens, 2005; Armstrong, 2012).

In terms of the types of reward mechanism applied, we can note the application of a number of different mechanisms based on 'time worked'. Time rates are mechanisms whereby reward is related to the number of hours worked and are often applied to manual workers in the form of hourly rates and non-manual workers by the application of monthly or annual salaries. In the past, these rates were set in a number of ways which relied on the power of employers to unilaterally lay down the appropriate amount, by statutory enactment or by collective bar-gaining. Employer discretion has been limited in a number of ways by the introduction of statutory rules and regulations, ranging from the Truck Acts, enacted in the mid-nineteenth century, which required payment in cash – an attempt to prevent the misuse by employers of 'factory shop vouchers' – to the 1891 Fair Wages Resolution, which obliged employers on local or national government projects to pay the standard/recognised rate for a job. Both of these measures, along with the Wage Councils, which were first established in 1909, were modified or repealed in the 1980s – with the Agricultural Wages Board, due in part to employer sup-port, being the only survivor. More recently the UK government put in place the National Minimum Wage Act (1999), which sets hourly rates across the whole economy for various groups of workers – primarily manual workers. These rates were set following meetings of the Low Pay Commission and gradated according to the age of the worker concerned. A new rate was established for apprentices (see page 475 for further details of the national minimum wage).

A criticism of time-based mechanisms is that they are often related to historic rather than current value, and can result in discrimination, demarcation disputes and a sense of injus-tice. Such time-related mechanisms are often based on the notion of a pay hierarchy in which groups of jobs/skills are banded. Although widely applied, basic versions of these instru-ments are poor in terms of relating wage to current effort, often rewarding effort that has been applied externally (gaining a recognised skill) and is inappropriate to current tasks. The advantages of these systems are that management can control wage costs by:

- limiting the access to various grades in the hierarchy;
- limiting the range of the grade (say 4 per cent top to bottom);
- demonstrating they are fair in relation to agreed procedures.

The problems created are not necessarily with the pay hierarchy system *per se,* but with the manner in which skills relating to specific grades are defined; solutions must then address the structure, strategy and rationale of the reward system rather than the application of such mechanisms.

Bowey and Lupton (1973) developed a scheme for highlighting the manner in which such hierarchies are built and sustained. They argued that five factors are in play when selecting and deciding the location of each job within the hierarchy:

- skill
- responsibility
- mental effort
- physical effort
- working conditions.

Using these factors it is possible to identify similarities between jobs rather than differences, as is the case with standard job evaluation schemes. Following the identification of these similarities, it is possible to locate various jobs within the pay hierarchy. What is more difficult is to translate this identification into a pay structure due to the various allocation or availability of the elements which make up an individual pay packet. Most conspicuous are the differences in the elements that are included in the individual pay packet at each level. So, for example, elements such as overtime, shift premium, individual bonus payments and other special allowances lead to increased earnings for some groups but not others. It is possible, in part, to explain the gender differences in earnings by reference to these elements. Hellerstein and Newmark (2006) argue that the difference in directly observable reward may be founded on either productivity differences or pure (taste-based) discrimination. In adopting this residual wage approach to wage discrimination, they suggest it is possible to estimate the true level of taste-based wage difference – whether looking at ethnicity, gender, age, disability or other forms of discrimination (see the discussion on equal pay later in this chapter).

Conboy (1976) noted that the key advantage of these time-based instruments is that both parties have a clear idea of the 'wage' element of the bargain. For management the problem is that these mechanisms do not give any clear indication of the 'effort' element of the bargain. This has led to time rate instruments being complicated by the addition of 'performance' elements, often in the form of 'piece-rates' or other complex 'bonus' calculations in an attempt to determine acceptable effort levels (e.g. predetermined motion time systems and measured daywork). The traditional form of such schemes can be demonstrated using the diagram shown in Figure 13.1.

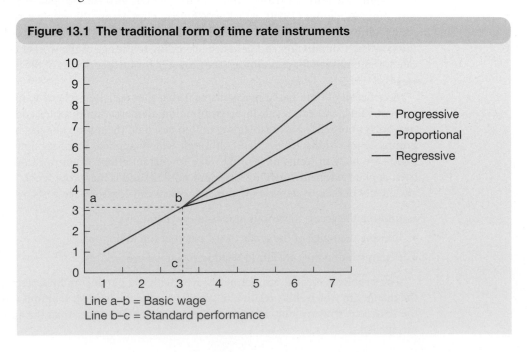

Figure 13.1 The traditional form of time rate instruments

Line a–b = Basic wage
Line b–c = Standard performance

Many schemes give guaranteed basic earnings which are then supplemented in ways which we can class as proportional (wages increase in direct relationship to output), progressive (wages increase more than output) or regressive (wages increase at a slower rate than output).

An important element in this discussion concerns the manner in which the 'base' element is decided. We have become familiar with the notion of a national minimum wage, which sets the minimum rate for specified groups; outside of this scheme, organisations need some mechanisms by which to assign values to various roles within the organisation. Traditional mechanisms (and in a slightly modified manner 'new pay' systems) have been related to hierarchy calculations or simplistic forms of job evaluation scheme. A job evaluation scheme operates by allocating values to each of a series of elements (e.g. skill or responsibility) and then measuring each 'job' in order to arrive at an agreed 'score'. The scores are then placed on the pay spine or grading structure in relation to accepted criteria. These criteria will be formed by the interaction of two sets of relativities. Scores will need to reflect 'external relativities', by which we mean the situation that appears to hold in relation to external markets and environmental conditions, and 'internal relativities', meaning an appearance of fairness in relation to other jobs/roles within the organisation. In the basic form, these schemes introduce us to the notion of reward packages under which different elements can be rewarded in various ways. However, these schemes fell out of favour in some respects because they were seen to 'pay the job' rather than 'pay the worker', and as such were difficult to relate to individual performance.

Time-based pay is clearly the simplest form of wage payment system, easily understood by both parties; it allows the development of 'overtime' payments for work completed in addition to the contracted hours in any given period and formed the basis of the creation of systems classed as payment by results (PBR). Early PBR schemes were time-based in that they used the time accumulated by the pace of work as a percentage of the time allowed to form a foundation for the calculation of performance payments. So, in a simple form, if a task is timed to take eight minutes but is completed in six then there is a saving of 25 per cent, but the increase in performance is 33.333 per cent in that if the job is completed in six minutes then the two minutes left is equal to a third of the new job time. From the employer's point of view, therefore, paying a 25 per cent bonus leaves a surplus per piece of 8.333 per cent. This adds to the perceived advantages of PBR when linked to hierarchical reward systems by providing increased worker effort. During the twentieth century, such structures/systems were widely used in British industry in an attempt to increase productivity. However, they are associated with a number of detrimental effects and disadvantages. Often the rates were negotiated following a work-measurement exercise which led to discontent and disillusionment. Too often operators can find easy ways around the rate in order to secure high earnings without the expected higher performance; these routes around the scheme often resulted in a reduced level of quality – in part because workers felt under pressure to produce and in part because quality and speed do not always combine. Further, by leaving the production levels in the hands of the workers, it undermines managerial attempts to secure control and, indeed, may even be said to have resulted in both a loss of managerial prerogative and the abrogation of managerial roles. As these rates were often set within tightly defined employer/trade union collective agreements, they encouraged the increase – notably during the 1950s–1970s – of local shop agreements, which resulted in considerable 'wage drift' during a period of economic restraint. Many of these problems are to some extent mirrored in the bonus schemes operating in the financial sector in the twenty-first century, which attract considerable disdain against the current backdrop of wage stagnation or decline in real wages for many others.

We can conclude then that such PBR systems, while originally crude, developed alongside the more extensive division of labour achieved by the increasing use and application of technology, ergonomics (pseudo-scientific work measurement) and mechanical production methods. These early techniques can easily be applied to such divided work because of four basic characteristics (adapted from Conboy, 1976):

- short job cycles;
- high manual content (which, using sophisticated ergonomic processes, can be measured);

- batch production (with repeated orders/processes);
- no marked fluctuations in required outputs.

The simplistic assumptions underlying these and other PBR systems are twofold. First, workers are motivated to increase performance (work harder) by money, and secondly, any increases in output will result in equivalent increases in wages. The schemes are intended to be self-financing and designed to reduce 'wasteful activity' in that they can be used to redesign the labour process. While such schemes now enjoy less popularity than they have in previous decades, there is still evidence that they are used in relation to specific groups of workers.

Hierarchial schemes in general continue to find favour, especially among salaried staff. A key element of such schemes is the practice of incremental progression. Such schemes operate on the simple premise that advancing years of service result in additional reward because of loyalty or greater experience. While they have recently been challenged – on the basis that they discriminate on the grounds of age – they continue to form a foundation for the solution to the labour problem for many organisations.

Explore

- To what extent do you think the solutions to the labour problem suggested so far reflect management's inability to clearly determine the 'effort' side of the bargain?

Having set out the basic framework within which the wage/effort bargain can be viewed, we now move on to consider more recent reward developments. In the discussion that follows we move from an analysis of solutions to the labour problem founded on 'cash' reward to a series of arguments that indicate more complex and considered solutions.

Employee reward in the contemporary era

The subject of reward, which has been described as a 'bundle of returns offered in exchange for a cluster of employee contributions' (Bloom and Milkovich, 1996: 25), is vast and continually evolving. This is a rather loose definition and sheds little light on what form 'returns' might take or what contribution employees might make to reap such returns. Usefully, the definition does, however, capture the multiplicity of returns and possible employee contributions, suggesting that reward comprises a blend of offerings and that employees' contributions can be numerous and eclectic.

The notion of a *range* of different forms of return in exchange for employee contributions of various types signals a departure from a narrow focus upon wages and effort. Wages or monetary return for the effort expended by employees, as discussed in the opening part of this chapter, remain important to the employment relationship; however, the advent of the concept of reward, and more pointedly reward management, prompts organisations to consider the differing ways in which employees positively impact the organisation via a range of contributions (not restricted to effort) and how best to signify organisational appreciation. The practice of reward veers away from a single dimensional focus on wages and instead emphasises a plethora of financial and non-financial returns employees might potentially receive in exchange for favourable contributions to the organisation. In terms of employee contributions to the organisation, effort becomes but one input among many potential offerings; indeed, its value to the organisation may well be considered less important and less attractive than other employee behaviours, e.g. measureable *outcome-related* contributions. It is thus clear that reward is a more inclusive term than wages or payment and that it is used to denote a diverse range of devices at the organisation's disposal to recognise the role played by individuals and teams in the operation, and ultimate success, of the business. Reward steps beyond the perimeters of compensation, remuneration and benefits terminology, where emphasis is placed on pay and other settlements which carry a monetary value, to a new plane in which almost anything could be construed as a return to employees for exhibiting desirable behaviour, from a cash bonus or health care benefit to employee involvement in decision-making, increased role responsibility, autonomy, access to more interesting work and other factors relating to the nature of the work itself and the environment in which it is carried out.

The aims of reward management, according to Armstrong (2012: 21), are to:

- support the achievement of business goals by developing a performance culture and stimulating high performance;
- define what is important in terms of behaviours and outcomes;
- align reward practices with employees' needs;
- reward people according to the value they create;
- motivate and win the engagement of employees;
- add value through the introduction of effective but affordable reward practices.

Components of reward

As indicated in the preceding section, reward comprises several elements, extending beyond base pay and thus presenting employers with a number of complex decisions. The first of these is which components to include in the reward package and the associated rationale for inclusion or rejection. Further decisions entail whether to permit employees a degree of choice in the reward 'mix' so that they can, for example, sacrifice salary in exchange for benefits or indeed choose from a menu of benefits to a defined value or cash limit. In addition, employers have fundamental decisions to make concerning whether the reward offering will be standardised and universal (applied to all employees), based upon performance or related to seniority (Marchington and Wilkinson, 2012). Such decisions will be influenced by the nature of the external operating environment, the behaviour of competitors and a range of internal organisational factors; these key determinants of the features of organisational reward systems will be explored later in the chapter.

For almost all workers, base pay forms the starting point in the reward package. The term is used to denote the hourly rate, wage or annual salary employees are paid for the work they do, based upon either some measure of job size or some aspect of the person, e.g. qualifications, skill set or demonstrable competencies. Base pay is a critical component, as it is used as the anchor rate for calculating redundancy payment entitlement, sick pay, pension level in a final salary scheme, overtime rates, as applicable, and other such employee rights. Base pay might be set deliberately low if, for example, commissions can be earned in excess and the organisation is keen to incentivise sales activity; base pay might also be suppressed where benefits are generous and so the overall worth of the reward bundle is considered to be commensurate with market rates. As is detailed later, however, the introduction of the national minimum wage in April 1999 imposed minimum limits on base pay in an attempt to curb the problem of low pay in the economy. As a result, employers are now obliged to adhere to minimum rates and review pay in accordance with periodic changes in the national minimum wage rates. The level of base pay awarded to employees and movement in base pay can be individually negotiated between managers and employees, unilaterally determined by owners/management, the subject of collective bargaining with relevant trade unions recognised within the industry and/or organisation, or, as occurs in some cases, set by National Pay Review Bodies.

Explore	
	• How fundamental is base pay within your own organisation?
	• How is the level of base pay determined?

Over and above base pay, further decisions may be made concerning supplementary payments attributable to skill or performance, for example, and other additions such as overtime, danger or dirt money, shift premium, bonuses or commissions. Dominant reward terminology refers to supplementary payments that are consolidated into base pay as forms of contingent pay and those that are non-consolidated as elements of variable pay (Armstrong, 2012). In practice, both forms of pay described are event- and/or behaviour-dependent and therefore not an assured, regular form of payment. Variable pay, in particular, is sometimes described as 'at risk' pay – by being non-consolidated, employees are compelled to repeat activities and behaviours to trigger variable pay in each subsequent business period and so secure a consistent level of reward. In addition, employees are disadvantaged in the sense that base pay, the driver of other entitlements (e.g. pension plans), remains unaffected by variable pay, regardless of how frequently variable pay is awarded or what portion of total salary comprises variable pay. The combination of base pay plus variable pay and/or contingent pay represents total earnings and is reflected in the employee's pay advice slip, yet entitlement to employee benefits enables the employee to accumulate additional remuneration. Employee benefits, sometimes called 'perks' (perquisites) or fringe benefits, carry a financial value or afford the recipient tax advantages that result in a net financial gain; however, in contrast to earnings, benefits are often presented in non-cash form. Where benefits are particularly generous and constitute a substantial component of the reward package, they tend to be identified in job advertisements to indicate the total financial value of the role to potential applicants (see Box 13.1).

Benefits can be classified as *immediate, deferred* or *contingent*. Employees derive value from immediate benefits instantaneously; such benefits might include the provision of a company car, a laptop computer, discounts, expensed mobile phone or subsidised meals. Where benefits are deferred, their value accrues and has a future rather than present value to the employee; a clear example of such a benefit is a pension plan or share scheme. Contingent benefits are those that are triggered in certain circumstances, e.g. sick pay schemes, paternity and maternity pay, and leave arrangements. Rather than deferring to the aforementioned classification, Wright (2004: 182) prefers to consider benefits in four distinct groupings:

- *Personal, security and health benefits* – e.g. pension, company sick pay scheme, life cover, medical insurance, loans.
- *Job, status or seniority-related benefits* – e.g. company car, holiday leave beyond statutory minimum, sabbaticals.
- *Family-friendly benefits* – e.g. childcare or eldercare facilities, nursery vouchers, enhanced maternity/paternity/parental leave arrangements.
- *Social or 'goodwill' or lifestyle benefits* – e.g. subsidised canteen, gym/sports facilities, cycle to work schemes, discounts, ironing collection/dry cleaning.

Benefits can be voluntary, affording employees the choice of whether to 'opt in' and use them according to their personal needs and financial position. Should employees elect to purchase benefits (eg. childcare vouchers, gym membership, healthcare plans), arrangements are usually set up for deductions to occur at source. This can attract tax advantages for the

---

Box 13.1 **HR Consultant (I.T. Sector), Hertfordshire**

Competitive Salary + Core and Voluntary Benefits Package
HR Manager (Distribution and Logistics), West Midlands
Salary £35,000 – £40,000 p.a. + Company Car + Pension
HR Manager (Chemicals, Oil and Gas), Finland
Salary £64,088 – £80,110 p.a. + Generous Bonus + Benefits

Source: www.jobs.personneltoday.com, 4 Feb, 2013.

employee and be an economical means of obtaining services applicable to an individual's lifestyle. In a recent CIPD survey, 24.7 per cent of respondents reported offering voluntary/ affinity benefits (CIPD, 2012) In other organisations, benefits are universal, in other words provided to all and regarded as 'perks' of the job. This is in direct contrast to status or seniority-related benefits, which employees only qualify for if they have accrued the requisite number of year's service or are employed at or beyond a prescribed grade or level; the benefits most commonly confined to senior employees at certain grades include private medical insurance, a company car and a car allowance (CIPD, 2012). Flexible benefit schemes or 'cafeteria benefits', so named because of the menu of choices presented to employees, continue to grow in popularity; in 2008, just 13 per cent of the organisations surveyed by the CIPD (2008) operated flexible benefits, while in 2012 approaching a quarter of all respondents (24.2 per cent) offered flexible benefits (CIPD, 2012). The latter survey demonstrates that systems of flexible benefits are more prevalent in large organisations employing 250–9,999 employees, possibly indicating that larger workplaces are more likely than small and medium-sized enterprises (SMEs) to be able to resource a system of flexible benefits, both financially and logistically. Flexible benefits are offered by divisions of internationally owned organisations (35.8 per cent) more so than by mainly UK-owned organisations (18.8 per cent), which perhaps reflects a response on the part of internationally owned organisations to create sufficient choice to appeal to both home and host country employees. The basic premise of a flexible or cafeteria benefits scheme is that employees can spend up to a points limit or cash total, purchasing benefits from a defined menu. Cafeteria schemes may comprise fixed (inflexible, core) benefits and flexible ones (a so-called 'core plus' scheme) or offer complete freedom of choice to the maximum cash value/points value. In other schemes, pre-packaged sets of benefits may be on offer to employees; these schemes are referred to as modularised benefits (Wright, 2004: 207).

It is difficult to generalise the provision of benefits as part of the overall reward package and predict the types of benefits any one organisation will deem appropriate to adopt. The impetus for providing benefits can be viewed from a number of perspectives (Wright, 2009):

- Do organisations see benefits as a way of compensating for lower pay or do higher pay and generous benefits tend to co-exist as part of a deliberate strategy aimed at attracting and retaining staff?

- Do employers select benefits in the belief that they will motivate employees and instil a greater sense of loyalty and commitment?

- Is benefit provision enhanced by employers where trade unions lobby successfully to expand the reward package on behalf of their members?

- Are benefits a mechanism for employer branding, the costs of which some organisations are prepared to bear?

The answers to these questions are intricate and beyond the scope of this chapter. We do know, however, that while employee benefits in themselves are a fairly steadfast feature of reward in the UK, recent years have witnessed some shifts in the types of benefits more commonly provided by employers. Wright (2009: 175) detects 'cutbacks in the most costly benefits and at the same time a growth in low-cost lifestyle and voluntary benefits'. She attributes such trends to the dual influences of the changing composition of the labour force (particularly the influx of mothers) and the need for employers to be economically prudent and focus on value for money as competition intensifies. These trends would seem to be reflected to some extent in the benefits top 10 (see Table 13.1), particularly in the list of benefits most commonly provided to all employees. While shifts in the type of benefits provided may be detectable, the 2012 CIPD reward survey shows that over half of respondents (55.2 per cent) predict spending as much on benefits in the year ahead as they had in the previous year, just over a third (34.7 per cent) anticipate spending more and only 10.2 per cent of respondents envisage a decrease in benefits spend (CIPD, 2012). Large organisations are most likely to be decreasing benefits spend, a finding inevitably influenced by changes taking place in some of

Table 13.1 Top 10 employer-provided benefits by provision

Provided to all employees		Provision dependent on grade/seniority		Part of a flexible benefit scheme only	
Benefit	% of respondents	Benefit	% of respondents	Benefit	% of respondents
Paid leave in excess of statutory entitlement	65.2%	Car allowance	61.8%	Dental insurance	45.5%
Training and career development	65.2%	Company car	53.8%	Cycle to work scheme loan	43.6%
Childcare vouchers	62.7%	Private medical insurance	40.2%	Childcare vouchers	41.8%
Free tea/coffee/ cold drinks	62.3%	Paid leave in excess of statutory entitlement	27.8%	Health screening	38.2%
Christmas party/ lunch	59.6%	Relocation assistance	24.9%	Critical illness insurance	30.9%
On-site parking	56.9%	Fuel allowance	20.7%	Private medical insurance	29.1%
Eye care vouchers	51.6%	Critical illness insurance	13.3%	Healthcare cash plans	23.6%
Employee assistance programme	48.9%	Permanent health insurance	12.7%	Gym on-site or membership	
Life assurance	48.4%	Health screening	10.7%	Permanent health insurance	16.4%
Enhanced maternity/ paternity leave	44%	Formal coaching/ mentoring schemes	10.7%	Life assurance	14.5%

Source: from *Reward Management,* Annual Survey Report 2012, London, CIPD, pp. 38–39, with the permission of the publisher, the Chartered Institute of Personnel and Development, London (**www.cipd.co.uk**).

the very large public-sector organisations in the sample, which are facing unprecedented cuts in funding. Setting aside multiple sector organisations, manufacturing and production firms are the most likely to be increasing spending, reflecting the expansion of this sector of the economy at present and the imperative to be able to compete for talent in a recovering market (CIPD, 2012).

Non-financial reward

While the components of reward identified and discussed so far have a financial basis, reward can also be non-financial or relational. In order to recognise the work that employees do, praise, thanks and publicly acknowledged awards such as 'employee of the month' can be appreciated by recipients while simultaneously communicating messages to the wider workforce of the employee behaviours that are valued by the organisation. There is arguably also greater awareness that for some workers extrinsic rewards alone, such as pay, do not motivate, and so a focus on the intrinsic rewards to be derived from the nature of the work itself (job content and context) is important (Marchington and Wilkinson, 2012). Consequently, non-financial rewards include the general quality of working life (QWL), e.g. the work environment, the degree of flexibility available, work–life balance, managerial style/attitude, line manager support, job-role autonomy and responsibility, plus opportunities for employee involvement and employee voice. 'Rewards' of this nature help to shape workers' experiences of work (either positively or negatively) and thus command the interest of scholars and practitioners seeking to better understand the key antecedents of job engagement and organisational engagement (see Chapter 11 on employee engagement). It might also be expected that in times of financial constraint the effective deployment and promotion of non-financial rewards becomes a paramount organisational concern.

The inclusion of non-financial reward to complement the other components of reward leads to the concept of total reward outlined in the next section. Put simply, total reward emphasises the potential benefits to be derived from considering reward in the broadest of senses, with a keen eye on the quality of the holistic employment experience.

Total reward

In recent years, there has been interest in the notion of managing rewards such that the various components are carefully crafted together to support one another and so maximise the satisfaction experienced by employees in the course of, and as a result of, their employment more broadly defined. The expression total reward is thus expansive terminology to denote everything that is rewarding about being an employee in a particular organisation and all the benefits the employee derives from that employment (Perkins and White, 2011: 304). WorldatWork (2000) concur, describing total reward as all of the tools an employer uses to attract, retain, motivate and satisfy employees, encompassing every single investment that an organisation makes in its people, and everything employees value in the employment relationship. The components of total rewards are succinctly presented in the model shown in Figure 13.2.

Thompson and Milsome (2001) insist that the concept of total rewards is necessarily holistic and integrative; it should also provide an approach to reward in the organisation that fits well with the business objectives and desired organisational culture and as such it is conflated with strategic approaches to reward. In addition, it is people centred, customised,

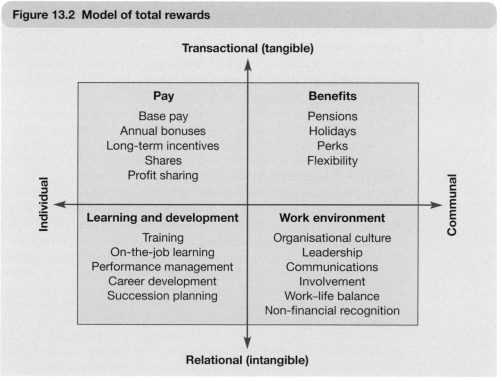

Figure 13.2 Model of total rewards

Source: Brown and Armstrong (1999: 81).

distinctive (offering support to a unique employer brand) and evolutionary, in the sense that it is developed incrementally as opposed to the product of drastic, sudden change. Armstrong (2012) argues that there is a compelling business case for creating a total reward approach; for example, he suggests it can provide a means of enhancing employee engagement, it can help the organisation to secure competitive advantage by offering choice and rewards tailored to the individual that are perhaps not provided by competitors and it can promote a performance culture. Adopting a total reward approach would certainly appear to tick a number of critical boxes for contemporary organisations as they grapple with issues of recruitment, retention and performance in fast-paced and highly competitive environments. In practice, however, the latest CIPD reward survey (CIPD, 2012) reports that only 17.8 per cent of respondents provide total reward statements to their employees, which would suggest that, despite the hype, the concept of total reward remains elusive to the majority of organisations.

Reward management and the emergence of strategic approaches to reward

The term 'reward management' was first used in 1988 by Armstrong and Murlis to denote the development of a new field or collective set of activities to emerge within the arena of HRM. The new term recognised that static techniques, principally concerned with salary administration, were fast giving way to a more dynamic approach emphasising the use of pay (and other rewards) in a strategic, flexible and innovative way with the aim of improving individual, team and organisational performance. The activity 'reward management' has been described as not only encompassing the development, maintenance, communication and evaluation of reward processes, but also being concerned with the development of appropriate organisational cultures, underpinning core values and increasing the commitment and motivation of employees (Armstrong and Murlis, 1998). Reward management in this sense is considered a strategic process and a key element of strategic HRM, as it has the power, if orchestrated appropriately, to leverage employee effort and performance aligned to organisational goals, it is integral to attempts to motivate and engage employees and it compels organisations to consider return on investment when making reward decisions, as opposed to viewing reward purely as a cost drain to the business (Fay, 2011; Perkins and White, 2011; Marchington and Wilkinson, 2012).

Armstrong (2012) proffers the notion of reward decisions corresponding to an underlying philosophy and set of guiding principles designed to convey the organisation's approach to managing reward. Logically, organisations should seek to ensure that the philosophy behind their approach to reward aligns with the organisation's values and beliefs and that reward strategy is consequently directed to support the achievement of wider corporate objectives. This is the essence of the 'total reward' approach referred to earlier, and such sentiments are strongly conveyed in the rhetoric of 'new pay' or 'strategic pay' first purported by American writers Lawler (1990, 1995, 2000) and Schuster and Zingheim (1992). The precise role played by reward in advancing organisational objectives is, however, unclear. Early models of strategic HRM, such as the Harvard model (Beer *et al.*, 1984), placed reward centrally as an integral HR activity, and Storey (1992) identified reward as a 'key strategic lever'. Resource-based models, too, suggest that pay acts as an important lever and can support a firm in achieving sustained competitive advantage. Kessler (2001), however, still needs to be convinced that there is sound evidence, based upon credible methodologies, that reward contributes to business performance and leads to sustained competitive advantage. There must also be a degree of reservation about the ease with which reward strategy can be matched seamlessly with business strategy and the extent to which employees will respond as intended to reward mechanisms designed to elicit certain desired behavioural patterns (Lewis, 2006).

Table 13.2 Examples of alignment: reward strategy and business strategy

Business strategy	Reward strategy
Achieve value added by improving employee motivation and commitment	Introduce or improve performance pay plans – individual, team, gain sharing
Achieve added value by improving performance/productivity	Introduce or improve performance pay plans and performance management processes
Achieve competitive advantage by developing and making the best use of distinctive core competencies	Introduce competence-related pay
Achieve competitive advantage by technological development	Introduce competence-related or skills-based pay
Achieve competitive advantage by delivering better value and quality to customers	Recognise and reward individuals and teams for meeting/exceeding customer service and quality standards/targets
Achieve competitive advantage by developing the capacity of the business to respond quickly and flexibly to new opportunities	Provide rewards for multi-skilling and job flexibility. Develop more flexible pay structures (e.g. broad-banding)
Achieve competitive advantage by attracting, developing and retaining high-quality employees	Ensure rates of pay are competitive. Reward people for developing their competencies and careers (e.g. using the scope made possible in a broad-banded grading structure)

Source: from *Reward Strategy: How to Develop a Reward Strategy. A CIPD Practical Tool,* CIPD (2005), with the permission of the publisher, the Chartered Institute of Personnel and Development, London (**www.cipd.co.uk**).

Despite these doubts, it appears to have become established orthodoxy that a strategic approach to reward can be used to leverage the kinds of employee behaviours that contribute to business goals (Perkins and White, 2011). Proponents of strategic reward suggest it is possible for reward strategies, intentionally or otherwise, to signal what the organisation considers important and what it clearly does not value. For example, reward strategies that rest on service-related salary increments are likely to convey messages that the organisation values loyalty and long tenure above all else, whereas the use of competence-related pay would suggest a need for employees to develop and demonstrate both core and job-specific competencies. Table 13.2 seeks to demonstrate a number of aligned relationships between the key thrust of business strategy and the direction of reward strategy.

Despite the rhetoric that strategic pay is the way forward to attract, retain and motivate employees to perform in particular ways, consistent with the goals and values of the organisation, we do not know a great deal about how organisations manage pay and other facets of reward strategically. We also know very little about whether strategic pay will leverage the desirable outcomes advocated.

Key Controversy

Can changes in reward structures and systems be facilitated to ensure that reward strategy is always aligned with organisational goals or is this operationally too difficult to achieve given the pace of change in most markets and organisations?

To what extent do you agree with the managerial assumption underpinning strategic approaches to reward that management can simply choose the most rational form of pay? Is it conceivable or naïve to think that reward alone can realise significant changes in employee behaviours with resultant bottom-line impact?

Reward strategy in practice

In the preceding section, we introduced the concept of strategic pay and began to tease out some of the difficulties associated with mounting strategic approaches to pay and other aspects of reward. There is no doubting that organisations are sold on the desirability of such approaches. In the CIPD (2011) reward survey, 58.5 per cent of respondents from all sectors placed alignment with business strategy as their top reward priority. The latest survey (CIPD, 2012) did not repeat this question and so direct comparison is not possible; however, the 2012 survey does indicate that organisations responding to the survey report were formulating *strategic choices* about reward by engaging in competitive pay positioning relative to comparator organisations (CIPD, 2012). In short there are data to support the idea that many organisations are seeking to offer competitive pay packages designed to attract, retain and engage employees as the economy makes tentative steps towards recovery, but is this adequate evidence of the presence of a strategic model of reward as advocated by the US 'new pay' writers in the 1990s, or a diluted version centred almost entirely on pay competitiveness? Druker and White (2009) suggest 'new pay' as heralded by the US scholars has failed to fully take hold in the UK; instead UK pay practices are dominated by concerns over internal and external equity. They argue that locating pay with the person rather than the job and relating reward to performance, the very concepts at the heart of 'strategic' or 'new pay' approaches, are both highly problematic and there are a number of pressures pushing internal and external equity to the forefront. Where internal equity is concerned, equal pay legislation is particularly influential in guiding practice in public services, which are now subject to equal pay reviews and equal pay reporting. Many, mainly private-sector employers, on the other hand, seek to align closely with the external market, particularly in tight and changing labour markets. Trevor (2009) would appear to concur by arguing that far from devising differentiated practices aligned closely to unique business goals and values, organisations are subject to coercive institutional pressures, such as laws, which promote conformity of practice. In addition, he argues, industry norms and trends are seductive and most organisations will conform accordingly, doing what others do in that sector to keep pace. Such a focus upon comparability may not be quite what the US writers had in mind when they extolled the benefits of 'new pay'/'strategic pay', but as Kessler (2007) argues, internal and external equity and business strategy need not be viewed as competing ideals in pay design; indeed, internal and external equity could quite legitimately be regarded as a key component of reward strategy.

Elsewhere in the CIPD (2012) reward survey, there is evidence of organisations using competitive pay positioning to set salaries for managerial and professional staff. Following Kessler's generous interpretation of reward strategy, the firms engaged in this type of activity can be considered to be making strategic decisions to invest greater resources in those individuals or tiers of the organisation perceived to bring greatest value to the organisation, so contributing to business strategy. In terms of sector-related trends, manufacturing and production firms appear to be positioning pay levels higher than other sectors as they compete for skills and expertise in a demanding market where pockets of skill shortage still prevail; again this form of pay posturing could be conceived as strategic pay in action rather than simply normative practice within industry grouping.

Is it possible to be strategic about reward?

Discussion concerning precisely what constitutes a strategic approach to reward is not new; there has also been long-standing doubt surrounding the ability of organisations to mount strategic approaches to reward. In research conducted by the Institute for Employment Studies, Bevan (2000: 2) commented that having a reward strategy sounded like a 'tall order'. To be successful, he argues, reward strategy is supposed to be downstream from business strategy and reinforce business goals, drive performance improvements within the business, deliver cultural and behavioural change, integrate horizontally with other HR practices and keep pay budgets under control, so 'little wonder that so many employers under-perform in the design and delivery of a truly strategic approach to reward – if such a thing exists'. In a similar vein, Druker and White (2009: 12) challenge the notion of 'new pay', which emphasises the importance of developing contingent approaches to reward, designed to align with business strategy. Specifically, Druker and White (2009: 12) question the view that 'new pay' supports the business case on the grounds that there are 'different interests at play within the business organisation and they cannot all be so easily in the pursuit of business goals'. They also argue that it is clear that 'strategic pay' may involve complex and sometimes contradictory objectives'. Trevor (2009) is similarly pessimistic. He argues that where centralised pay systems are in situ, standardised pay policies are seldom enacted as intended, and where systems are decentralised, line managers invariably elect to use pay in ways that are reminiscent of traditional pay management despite the hopes and desires of their superiors. Trevor (2009: 3) concludes that 'despite corporate rhetoric to the contrary, contemporary pay practice operationally is non-strategic'.

Explore

- Having read this section, are you convinced that your organisation delivers a strategic approach to reward?
- What evidence do you have to support your answer?

Key reward choices

Whether or not we accept that it is possible to be strategic about reward, to devise a reward system a number of key, value-laden choices must be made. Marchington and Wilkinson (2012: 376) suggest that there are seven essential reward decisions an organisation needs to draw consensus on:

- what to pay for, job size, time, performance, skills/qualifications or some other person-centred attribute or behaviour;
- whether to pay for seniority (time served) or for performance;
- what position to adopt in the market – at or close to the median pay levels in the market, within the upper quartile or the lower quartile;
- whether to place primary focus on internal equity when determining pay or be more concerned with external benchmarks;
- whether to operate a centralised or decentralised approach to reward or a hybrid with some central control and a degree of localised latitude;
- whether to build hierarchy into the reward system such that there are seniority or status related rewards or to devise a harmonised, single-status approach;
- the precise nature of the reward 'mix'.

Explore

Apply the preceding list of seven essential reward dilemmas to your own organisation or one with which you are familiar.

- What decisions has the organisation in question taken?
- Why do you think this particular stance has been adopted?

Getting these decisions right is deemed critical if reward is to begin to reinforce the strategic direction of the organisation. Similarly, the decisions made need to be ones most likely to motivate individuals to orientate their actions and behaviours in the interests of the organisation, not against it. This is demanding for any organisation given that motivation is individualised and complex. Thought needs to be invested in considering the extent to which different rewards are capable of motivating employees, the value of intrinsic and extrinsic motivation to employees, the role of pay in motivating people and the importance of equity in reward systems and reward management practices.

Motivation theory offers useful insight and can help to guide the design and management of reward processes. Notably, among the many theories of motivation, Herzberg's 'Two-Factor Theory' (Herzberg, 1966) suggests that pay is a *hygiene* factor rather than a motivator and so, in itself, is unlikely to motivate. Famously, Herzberg contends that pay needs to be adequate to prevent dissatisfaction but other factors induce a motivational state such as responsibility and autonomy. This is a salutary message indeed, particularly to those organisations that attempt to use pay or the prospect of financial rewards as an incentive for greater output, better quality or other outcomes they determine to be desirable. But could these organisations be treading the right path in presuming pay *does* motivate? Rynes *et al.* (2004) believe that there appears to be a continual (yet flawed) message to practitioners that pay is not a particularly effective motivator – a sentiment that, if believed, could very easily result in practitioners failing to recognise the motivational potential of a well-crafted reward system. The key thrust of the Rynes *et al.* argument is that, while employees may report that pay is not an important

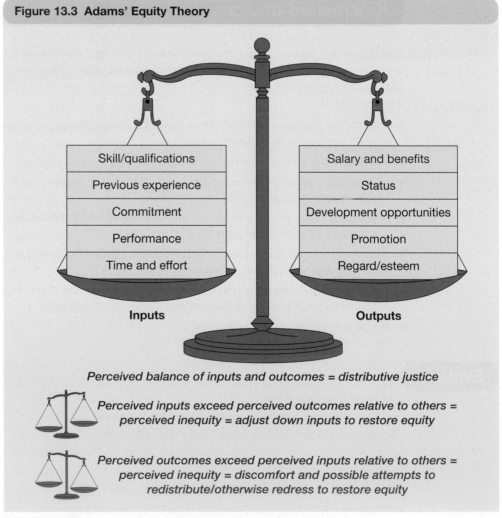

Figure 13.3 Adams' Equity Theory

Inputs	Outputs
Skill/qualifications	Salary and benefits
Previous experience	Status
Commitment	Development opportunities
Performance	Promotion
Time and effort	Regard/esteem

Perceived balance of inputs and outcomes = distributive justice

Perceived inputs exceed perceived outcomes relative to others = perceived inequity = adjust down inputs to restore equity

Perceived outcomes exceed perceived inputs relative to others = perceived inequity = discomfort and possible attempts to redistribute/otherwise redress to restore equity

Source: Adams (1965).

motivator, their actions indicate otherwise, suggesting that self-reports are subject to a degree of socially acceptable responding, as though employees feel it is somehow distasteful or morally reproachable to admit being motivated by money. Rynes *et al.* (2004) stress that despite their analysis, pay is probably not *the only* important motivator, nor always *the most important* motivator, nor indeed *equally important* in all situations; it is, however, overwhelmingly evident that it is an important motivator for most people.

In contrast to content theories of motivation, which focus on *what* motivates people, process theories of motivation such as 'expectancy theory' (Vroom, 1982) attempt to explain the internal thought processes that create a motivational state in individuals. Expectancy theory offers us the insight that employee motivation is the result of a complex set of decisions and assumptions made by the individual. For an employee to be motivated and therefore to expend effort, the rewards on offer have to be something that the individual values (hold 'valence') – hence the importance of the reward 'mix'. In addition, the individual must have belief that the rewards are achievable. An appreciation of expectancy theory encourages organisations to construct a clear 'line of sight', so that employees are in no doubt about what it is they need to do in order to gain the rewards offered. If there is ambiguity or partiality disturbing the line of sight, individuals are likely to be demotivated, even if the potential rewards hold personal valence.

Finally, Adams' 'Equity Theory' (Adams, 1965) prompts organisations to consider the perceived fairness of rewards and their application. Adams suggests that employees will compare the rewards they receive (outputs) in return for their effort, skill, qualifications, time and other contributions (inputs). Employees will be motivated where they perceive 'distributive justice' and demotivated where they perceive inequity. Employees may seek to adjust their inputs when they perceive inequity. Using the messages inherent in Adams' theory, organisations would be advised to take steps to ensure that their reward systems are fair, consistently applied and sufficiently transparent so that employees can see for themselves how reward decisions are determined (see Figure 13.3).

Factors influencing organisational approaches to reward practice and pay determination

An organisation's approach to reward generally, and to pay determination, will be shaped by both factors in the external environment within which it operates and an array of internal firm-specific characteristics, namely the nature of the business, the size of operation, organisational structure and culture, types of employees, jobs and technology, management and ownership and so forth. Each of the reward choices posited by Marchington and Wilkinson (2012) in the preceding section cascades a range of further ancillary choices, thus creating the potential for multiple models of reward practice. Because of this, it is difficult to generalise about approaches to reward and impossible to be prescriptive. More safely, an organisation's approach to developing a reward strategy ought to start from the standpoint, 'What makes sense for this organisation?' (Wright, 2004: 8), while subsuming relevant knowledge relating to the internal and external factors influencing choice. In this section of the chapter, we briefly discuss the key factors in the external and internal environment that shape and influence organisational approaches to reward.

The economic climate

In this chapter we have already alluded to some of the ways in which the economic environment might influence reward, notably the way in which employers may favour less costly benefits in tougher economic conditions (or pare back universal benefits) and the way in which employers can reduce risk and financial burden by making more extensive use of variable pay. The economic context is an important determinant of pay levels and a barometer for future trends. In setting pay levels, employers cannot help but be influenced by the market rates for jobs. As Kessler (2007: 167) remarks, 'organisations cannot survive if they fail to pay competitive labour market rates to attract employees with the skills needed to provide a service or manufacture a product'. Of course, there is no such thing as a single market rate for a job; rather, there are several rates or a zone of discretion, the spread of which is influenced by the supply of and demand for labour, the relative bargaining power of employees, geographical factors and the actions of employers competing for labour. In tight labour markets, where competition for resources is intensive and supply is low, market rates are driven higher, affecting the price employers have to pay to attract adequate resources. Economic activity rates and unemployment indicators are thus key factors influencing pay levels. In addition, for most organisations, the rate of growth in the economy is a critical benchmark for the salary review process and impacts upon organisations' ability to pay.

A key current concern in the public sector is the inability to raise pay levels due to budgetary constraints (CIPD, 2012) and the risk that stagnation of wage levels poses for employee engagement, productivity and attrition. Pay dispersion is also a sensitive issue for the public sector following the 2011 Hutton Review of Fair Pay, which debated but ultimately rejected a maximum ratio of 1:20 between the actual earnings of the lowest and the highest paid. Understandably amidst pay restraint for the many, the media is adept at drawing public attention to the pay rises and bonus payments awarded to executives in the very institutions widely considered to be responsible for the economic crisis, e.g. Barclays Bank and RBS. The jibes of rewards for mismanagement and misdemeanour that echo around the city are difficult to dissipate given that the UK's economic performance remains, at the time of writing, sluggish. The National Management Salary Survey 2013, published by the Chartered Institute of Management and XpertHR (XpertHR, 2013), claims that company bosses have experienced a 'bonus boom' that has raised their pay despite the state of the economy. According to the study, chief executives benefited from a 15.8 per cent increase in their salaries (largely attributable to big bonuses) in the year to 2013. The survey showed the average pay of a company chief executive to be more than £215,000, while middle managers earned, on average, £43,000.

Economic arguments are, of course, difficult to balance, and city institutions would defend salaries and bonuses awarded to senior executives on the grounds that reward packages need to be commensurate with those available to senior executive salaries on the global stage in order to retain talent in the UK. From an ethical perspective, increasing differentials between the highest paid and those on the lowest incomes are hard to countenance.

The legal context for reward

Since the rise of industrialisation, there have been numerous legal interventions into the realm of reward management. These have ranged from the Truck Acts of the nineteenth century, which were designed to ensure skilled workers were paid in cash, through to more recent interventions in terms of minimum wage regulation. These demonstrate the ways in which legal regulation can be seen to shape reward practices. Statutory regulation has been in place in the UK for some 30 years, which was intended to ensure pay equity in gender terms. More recently, legislation has been implemented to regulate pay at the lower extreme of the labour market, to impose minimum holiday entitlement and a restraint on working hours. Here we briefly discuss in turn the ways in which the equality of terms and conditions provisions of the Equality Act 2010, The National MinimumWage Regulations 1999 and the Working Time Directive 1998 constrain and influence employee reward practices.

The Equality Act 2010 (EqA), sections 64–80

Labour market discrimination occurs when groups of workers with equal average productivity are paid different average wages (Baldwin and Johnson 2006: 122). Equal pay regulations have a history founded in the Convention on Equal Pay approved by the International Labour Organisation in 1950–51, a regulation that had antecedents within the Treaty of Versailles in 1919, if not before (Jamieson, 1999). In the UK, the EqPA 1970 was enacted as part of the move towards membership of the European Economic Community (now the EU) in the early

1970s. Employers were allowed five years' 'grace' to voluntarily adjust and to permit them to get their reward structures in order before the legislation came into force in 1975. Broadly, the provisions within the legislation are restated in the EqA 2010 and can be seen as being designed to grant everyone the right to equal terms and conditions of employment in situations where they do the same work as a colleague of the opposite sex. The legislation reflects the pressures applied by the European Court of Justice (ECJ) to the extent that it includes colleagues of the opposite sex who do work that is 'like work', the same or has been rated as equivalent under a job evaluation scheme or where it can be proved by other mechanisms that the work is of equal value. The manner in which this is achieved is to insert into all contracts of employment an 'equality clause' (s. 66), which has the consequence of requiring the employer not to treat persons of different genders less favourably simply on the basis of gender. In spite of this legislation, there are still very significant inconsistencies between men's and women's pay. It does not matter whether wages are measured hourly or weekly; women currently receive approximately 86 per cent of the full-time male average, while in part-time work 'almost 50 per cent of women who work part-time earn nearer 60 per cent' of the average for their male counterparts (McColgan, 2008: 401). As McColgan (2008) notes, bringing equal pay claims is a sluggish, unwieldy and costly process, especially as the government refuses to go along with the development of class actions and shows even less willingness to implement legislation that places a positive obligation on employers to eliminate pay discrimination.

In spite of this lack of legislative backing to pursue equal pay, some employers seek to address such inequality within their reward structures. This can be achieved by the introduction of a number of reward policies and practices, such as those suggested by the Equality and Human Rights Commission (EHRC, **http://www.equalityhumanrights.com/**):

- ensuring employees reach the top of a given scale within a reasonable timescale;
- setting targets for all staff to reach pay points within a specific timescale;
- setting competency *and* experience criteria for each pay point;
- shortening the scales;
- reducing the number and range of performance measures.

As Fredman (2008) suggests, the fact that the current difference in gender-related pay was down to 12.6 per cent when measured using the median figure (rather than the usual mean, which rates it at 17.2 per cent) after 30 years of equal pay legislation gives no reason for satisfaction. Indeed, the change in the mechanisms for calculation merely masks the continuing inability of some groups to secure equality of treatment, especially where 'the median part-time gender pay gap was a scandalous 39.1% in 2007' (Fredman 2008: 193). The continuing gap indicates the need for a more complex response that addresses both government and employer unwillingness and the narrow coverage of the current legislation.

Explore

- While some inroads have been made, to what extent do you think the continued reliance upon the three requirements for equal pay claims (same or equivalent establishment, same employer and equal work) limits the progress towards equal pay?
- Consider an organisation of which you are aware and indicate mechanisms they could institute in order to address inequalities in terms and conditions of employment.

National Minimum Wage Regulations 1999

The regulation of wages is a central debate within the realm of 'worker protection, globalization, development and poverty reduction' (Evain, 2008: 20). These were put in place in order to develop the dual goals of fairness and efficiency. As the report of the Low Pay Commission suggested, it can be argued that low wages lead to a malevolent cluster comprising low morale, low performance and low productivity. The introduction of a national minimum wage is said to have benefited some 1.3 million workers (Low Pay Commission, 2001). Many of those affected worked in organisations where pay setting was inexact and did not recognise the need for formal systems; furthermore, the new wage levels benefited women more than men due to inequality and the extent of part-time work amongst women. The UK currently has rates covering those under 18 but over compulsory school age, 18–20 year-olds, those over 21, and apprentices under the age of 19, or over the age of 19 but in the first year of an apprenticeship scheme. The rates are changed in October each year and from October 2013 they were £3.72, £5.03, £6.31 and £2.68, respectively. As with the Wage Council rates before them, these rates are poorly policed and many small employers, especially those in the service sector, avoid enforcement (Arrowsmith and Gilman, 2005). Arrowsmith and Gilman (2005: 169) argue that in such small firms, 'pay levels reflect not only economic, product and labour market factors but also the informality of internal pay structures'. As we note below, such indeterminacy and informality support existing pay bias, as it is often based on predetermined skill patterns, time worked and length of service.

The level of the UK's statutory minimum wage is set at above the equivalent of US$1,000 per month (in the period 2006–07), which locates the UK in the top 18 per cent of countries where such a minimum is set (Evain, 2008) and within a group of industrialised countries where the rate is set other than by government alone. Evain (2008) notes that more than 100 countries that are members of the International Labour Organisation (ILO), which have ratified the Minimum Wage Fixing Convention 1970 (No 131), either enact minimum wage legislation or set such rates following the recommendation of a specialised body, or through collective bargaining. Worldwide, the average range of minimum rates varies from (in US$) $30 in Africa, $75 in many Asian countries, and $480 in Eastern Europe and Latin America to the US$1,000 or above in the majority of industrialised countries. These rates reflect national, regional, sectored and/or global imperatives and satisfy many competitive pressures. By removing wage calculation from competition, organisations can, in domestic and global settings, strive for alternative means of differentiation in terms of product or service. The issue then becomes the enforcement mechanism. Eyraud and Saget (2005) suggest that these regulations are often poorly enforced, leading to a continued decline in working conditions across the globe. The extent to which the legislation in the UK is enforced, and the individualised mechanisms for enforcement, tend to support the view that while the existence of such regulation is designed to ensure a high level of protection, the continued avoidance of such rules, as indicated by Arrowsmith and Gilman (2005), is widespread.

In 2001 a group of parents in East London, unhappy that the level of the minimum wage meant people with two jobs (which were needed to support a family) found they had little time for a family life, launched the 'Living Wage' campaign. The idea behind it was simply that an individual ought to be paid enough to live decently and take care of their family. The movement gained support from the trade unions, all political parties and many businesses – especially within the public sector. There are two 'levels' of living wage, one for London and one for the rest of the country. In 2013 these were hourly rates of £8.55 and £7.45, which were some £2.24 higher than the national minimum wage in London and £1.14 outside London. While businesses agree these higher rates on a voluntary basis, evidence from Unison (2013) suggests that 'paying the living wage is good for business, good for the individual and good for society' (**www.unison.org.uk**). The level is set by the Centre for Research in Social Policy and the Greater London Authority.

Key Controversy

Minimum wage legislation is said to advance a wide range of policy goals – what are these goals? To what extent does current UK regulation achieve these goals?

If the minimum wage rates are adequate, why did the Living Wage campaign receive so much support?

Working Time Regulations 1998

Placing limits on working hours is an essential activity in the quest for worker protection and ensuring the health and safety of those at work. In the current climate, it has also become a touchstone of the movement towards securing a sustainable work–life balance. In terms of the latter, there are two discourses, each of which has a separate focus: the *personal control of time* and the notion of *workplace flexibility* (see Humbert and Lewis, 2008). In terms of the reward agenda, we concentrate primarily on the latter, in that we are seeking solutions to the question of providing options for people with a workplace focus who also enjoy non-work (chiefly family) commitments. In that respect, the Working Time Regulations (1998) [WTR] offer some attempt to balance the demands of the employer with the needs of family life by placing limits on a range of working time issues. At a glance, the key provisions are:

- maximum 48-hour working week for many groups;
- an average eight-hour shift in each 24-hour period for night workers;
- a rest break after six consecutive hours' work;
- rest periods of 11 continuous hours daily and 35 continuous hours weekly;
- a minimum of 5.6 weeks' leave per annum.

The UK regulations have their basis in the EU Directive (93/104/EC), which is said to have introduced the new principle of 'humanisation' into EU social regulations, under which employers are required to take into account the general principle of adapting work and wage in order to alleviate monotonous work and work at a predetermined rate. That the UK has implemented the directive subject to a number of derogations does not alter the fact that reward managers need to consider the effects of the regulations. That the Employment Appeals Tribunal (EAT) could, in a recent case (*Corps of Commissionaires Management Ltd v Hughes* [2008] EAT`196`08), hold that the rest break is only triggered after six hours and not multiples thereof, is a simple indication of the minimalist approach of the UK government and the reluctance of management to extend the protection within the UK. During 2009, elements of the EU Directive relating to the definition of 'working time' – notably in relation to 'on-call' time and junior doctors – came into force and changed the options for UK reward managers. The development of 24/7 production and 'rolling shifts' has not been unduly limited by the daily or weekly rest periods, due to the availability of opt-outs; however, as these opt-outs are withdrawn, it will present fresh challenges for reward managers in the UK.

Worldwide, most members of the ILO have some form of regulation on working time. In a recent survey (Evain, 2008), attention was drawn to the fact that working time regulation was the subject of the very first ILO convention (Convention 1: 1919) and that the topic has been a major regulatory concern since that date. The general rule, where a normal hourly figure is placed on the working week, is that the figure of 40 or less is applied. In the UK we have no universal normal working limit because the WTR exclude 'professional workers' and/or workers who are not paid in relation to time. The latter group includes many clerical workers, most managers and almost all professional workers. This limitation is not unique to the UK and can be found in some 24 per cent of industrialised countries. A key result of such exceptions has been the development of 'extreme work' hours, most of which are unpaid. It is reported that managers in the UK work the longest hours in Europe, with 42 per cent working in excess of 60 hours a week; this phenomenon runs alongside evidence that work has also intensified (Burke and Cooper, 2008). Hewlett and Luce (2006) describe the amalgamation of these two factors, in the work of 'high earners', as the basis for the creation of 'extreme work'. Such work is portrayed as combining elements such as (adapted from Hewlett and Luce, 2006):

- unpredictable workflow;
- fast pace under tight deadlines;
- scope of responsibility that amounts to more than one job;
- work-related events outside regular working hours;

- availability to clients and/or more senior managers 24/7;
- large amounts of travel;
- a large (and increasing) number of direct reports;
- physical presence at the workplace on average at least 10 hours a day.

For reward managers, these elements present few problems because they tend to either describe the role chosen and adopted by the individual or take place within the terms of the existing contract of employment. As such, they are rewarded by existing reward structures, including PBR and other personalised reward agreements. In their survey of US business managers and professionals, Hewlett and Luce (2006: 54) found that 91 per cent cited unpredictability as a key pressure point, while 86 per cent also included increased pace within tight deadlines, 66 per cent included work-related events outside normal hours, and 61 per cent included 24/7 client demands. Perhaps the words of the eighteenth-century washer-woman Mary Collier are equally applicable to modern managers and professionals, both male and female (quoted in Thompson 1991: 81):

> Our toil and labour daily so extreme,
> that we have hardly ever the time to dream.

From this discussion we can begin to see that legislative activities, while a key source for elements that influence reward structures, are not the only, or perhaps the most important, influences.

Internal/organisational factors and the influence of sector

In addition to reflecting factors in the external environment, an organisation's chosen approach to reward will be shaped by the idiosyncratic nature of the firm and sector-specific factors. There are no hard and fast rules, so the full plethora of reward choices is theoretically at the disposal of the organisation. As far as its capabilities stretch, the organisation must seek to develop an approach to reward that is compliant, cost-effective and capable of attracting, retaining and motivating employees commensurate with the needs of the business. It is beyond the boundaries of this chapter to discuss in detail the complex configurations of reward and corresponding internal drivers that are likely to be significant in each case. Instead, a more general stance is adopted, which notes some of the discernible differences between reward practices according to workplace characteristics such as ownership/sector, unionisation and workplace size. We return to these themes in the final part of the chapter, where contemporary trends in pay and reward practices are discussed against the rhetoric of heightened strategic use of reward.

Large-scale surveys such as the Workplace Employment Relations Study (WERS) and the CIPD Annual Reward Survey allow changes and trends in employee reward practice to be tracked over time; they also provide a snapshot of employee reward practices at the time of the survey. CIPD research provides analysis by firm size (number of employees), firm sector (manufacturing and production, private-sector services, public services, voluntary, community and not-for-profit and multiple sectors, a new category since 2012), by employee category (management/professional, other employees) and by ownership (mainly UK-owned organisations, division of mainly UK-owned organisations, division of internationally-owned organisations). WERS provides further industry breakdown and, in addition, considers the variance between reward practices in unionised and non-unionised workplaces. A sample of observations is drawn from the 2011 WERS First Findings (van Wanrooy et al., 2013) and the latest CIPD (2012a) survey, and these are shown in Table 13.3.

Pay determination – internal or external focus?

As the final segment of Table 13.3 demonstrates, a key decision when setting levels of pay is whether to place emphasis on comparability with the external market or internal equity. As referred to earlier in the chapter, the lure of the external market would appear to be more

Table 13.3 Trends in reward practice

Pay structures	• According to the CIPD, almost half of all respondents said that their organisations use individual rates/ranges or spot salaries to manage base pay; this is the most common type of base pay management for all types of employee. • The management of base pay is an area where there is a marked difference of approach between sectors; in public services and voluntary, community and not-for-profit organisations, *pay spines* or some other forms of service-related structure form the dominant approach, while in manufacturing and production and private-sector services, *individual, flexible approaches* are commonplace.
Pay determination	• For manufacturing and production companies and private services organisations, the CIPD finds that generally ability to pay is the most important factor in pay determination; market rates are also a key factor. • More organisations (37.5 per cent) seek to maintain a level of internal pay equity through the use of a job evaluation scheme along with market rates than just paying attention to market rates without simultaneous use of job evaluation (31 per cent of all organisations). • In public services the most important factor in pay determination is collective bargaining. • WERS establishes that union influence over pay and conditions has continued to decline since the time of WERS 2004. • In the intervening period, 2004–2011, collective bargaining coverage in the public sector has significantly declined. Collective bargaining takes place in less than three-fifths (58 per cent) of public-sector workplaces, settling pay for 44 per cent of public-sector workplaces, down from over 66 per cent in 2004. • Strongly unionised workplaces where 100 per cent of employees have their pay set by collective bargaining have been a rarity in the private sector for some time and are increasingly uncommon in the public sector too.
Pay settlements	• WERS provides data on factors influencing the size of pay settlements; the survey finds that financial performance of the firm dominates in the private sector but is also a salient feature in the public sector. • The cost of living is mentioned by one-third of workplaces in both the public and private sectors as a factor guiding the size of pay settlements, but these figures were significantly lower than in 2004 when it was mentioned by 75 per cent of public-sector workplaces and 55 per cent of private-sector workplaces. • CIPD reveals that ability to pay, inflation and the movement in market rates were overall the three most important factors in determining pay reviews in 2011. Public services organisations, however, consider government funding or pay guidelines the most important factor in determining the outcome of pay reviews. • An increasing proportion of pay settlements result in a pay freeze, especially in the public sector. When periods of pay freeze end in the public sector, future increases are likely to be subject to a 1 per cent cap for two to three years. • As a whole, CIPD survey results show public services as being far more influenced by internal factors than by external market pressures when reviewing pay levels.
Pay progression	• The 2012 CIPD Reward Survey illustrates that length of service is by far the most common criterion for pay progression in public services. • For all other sectors, individual performance is the most used criterion, although market rates also feature highly. • Employers are considerably more likely to progress base pay for reasons relating to employee potential, value or retention for managerial or professional staff than for other employees. • Most in the private-service sector use three or more pay progression factors for managers and professionals and for other employees. The public sector is likely to use just one factor (performance or length of service) for both groups of workers.

(continued)

Table 13.3 Continued

Paying for performance/ incentives	• WERS shows that 20 per cent of employees received PBR in addition to their fixed wage and 3 per cent of employees were solely reliant on PBR, the remaining 77 per cent receiving a fixed wage only.
	• Only 7 per cent of public-sector employees received PBR compared with 27 per cent of private-sector employees.
	• Just over a half (54 per cent) of all workplaces use at least one incentive pay scheme, but private-sector workplaces are more than twice as likely as public-sector workplaces to do so.
	• While the percentage of workplaces using incentive schemes has remained broadly stable since WERS 2004, there have been notable changes in the types of schemes used, e.g. a move away from PBR towards merit pay and a halving of the use of share schemes in the private sector.
	• More non-managerial employees now have their performance formally appraised and the percentage of workplaces linking pay to the outcome of performance appraisal increased between the 2004 and 2011 WER surveys.
Pay dispersion (difference between the highest and lowest paid employees)	• According to WERS 2011, across all workplaces on average one-tenth of the workforce were paid an hourly rate at or below the adult rate of the national minimum wage. This proportion stood at 11 per cent in private-sector workplaces and 2 per cent in public-sector workplaces.
	• In 69 per cent of workplaces, no employees were being paid an hourly rate at or less than the adult national minimum wage rate. In 9 per cent of workplaces, at least half the workforce was receiving this rate.
	• Workplaces in the hotel and restaurant sector were most likely to have high proportions of low-paid workers.
	• Workplaces had an average of 13 per cent of their employees earning an hourly rate of £18.01 or more (the highest pay band specified); 16 per cent in public-sector workplaces and 12 per cent in private-sector workplaces.
	• In business services and public administration, more than one-third of all workplaces had at least a quarter of their workforce earning £18.01 or more an hour.
	• The CIPD Reward Survey tackles this issue too. It finds that there is greater pay dispersion for managerial and professional staff than there is for other employees. The highest median earnings for managerial and professional staff are more than three times higher than the lowest median earnings of workers in this group, whereas non-managerial staff have a differential between highest and lowest earnings of just over 100 per cent (highest median earnings are just over double the lowest median earnings).
	• The CIPD finds that for both employee categories, public-sector organisations have the highest levels of pay dispersion (gulf between the lowest and the highest paid).
Pay transparency	• The 2012 CIPD Reward Management Survey contained a new question concerning the extent to which organisations are prepared to reveal to employees information about pay scales, the provision of benefits and allowances, grading systems, job evaluation, performance-related pay schemes and how different individuals or groups of employees are treated in terms of pay decisions.
	• Overall findings demonstrate that organisations prefer pay confidentiality over transparency: 55.9 per cent of respondents agree or strongly agree that they are compliant with legislation but very much prefer to keep pay information as confidential as possible, while 38.6 per cent agree or strongly agree that they actively publicise pay information and intend to be as transparent as possible.
	• Most private-sector organisations' responses reflected the least transparent approach of the four choices presented, in contrast to most public services and third-sector organisations, which opted for the approach to disclosure that represents the most transparent and open of the four choices.

compelling for private-sector organisations, whereas the greater use of tools such as job evaluation and the equal pay review process in the public sector suggests that internal equity is more paramount here. Ultimately, however, any approach must try to reconcile the need to keep pace with external market rates with due concern for internal equity.

Suff and Reilly (2006) argue that, since it was first introduced in the 1920s, the popularity of job evaluation as a method for establishing the relative worth of jobs in the organisational hierarchy has ebbed and flowed according to patterns and fashions in reward management. The process has been criticised in the past for being excessively paperwork-driven and costly and too rigid to be of value to organisations trying to be adaptable and flexible in the face of intensive competitive pressures (Watson, 2005). It fell out of favour in the 1980s and 1990s as more flexible, flatter structures became characteristic of typical pay infrastructure, and market rates became the key method of setting pay levels (Suff and Reilly, 2006). Now there is evidence that job evaluation is reinventing itself as a credible tool to support structural pay decisions, to provide a defence against equal value claims, to support organisations following merger and acquisition and to complement broad-banding. Brown and Dive (2009: 29) would appear to agree:

> By evolving to meet the needs of organisations for more fluid structures, more market- and person-driven pay and more talented leaders – as well as performing its traditional function as a foundation for fair pay management – job evaluation seems to be securing its place in the HR professional's toolkit for the foreseeable future.

Job evaluation is described as 'a method of determining on a systematic basis the relative importance of a number of different jobs' (ACAS, 2010). As demonstrated by this definition and the information in Table 13.4, job evaluation is a systematic (yet not entirely scientific) process, as it is about making informed judgments, based upon an analytical process of gathering facts about jobs (based on job analysis techniques). It is also a structured process which occurs within a framework, allowing evaluators to arrive at consistent and rational decisions. Great care must be taken to focus on jobs and not on the qualities and performance standards of job incumbents; this distinction can sometimes be difficult to separate in practice.

It is clear, therefore, that job evaluation is not a 'perfect' determinant of job relativities. As we can see, it relies to some extent on subjective judgments and, as such, it may present some challenges in contemporary workplaces where there is likely to be greater fluidity in job roles. Nor does it pave the way for a perfect salary scale or grading structure or direct the organisation in terms of how much to pay employees for performing particular roles. It can, however, if designed, managed and maintained meticulously, provide the underpinning rationale for grading structures and help safeguard against unfair and discriminatory pay decisions.

Table 13.4 Job evaluation

Job evaluation is:	Job evaluation is not:
• Systematic	• Scientific
• Consistent	• An exact measurement of duties and tasks performed
• A good basis for a fair pay system	• A way of judging a job holder's performance
• A way of getting a hierarchy of jobs on which to base a grading structure	• A way of allocating pay rates

Source: ACAS (2010), *Job Evaluation; Considerations and Risks*, September 2010.

Devising pay structures

Whether or not organisations engage systematically with the process of job evaluation or take a stronger lead from benchmarking salaries in the external market without recourse to job evaluation techniques, most would agree with Armstrong (2012) that pay structures are necessary to supply a framework within which fair and consistent reward policies can be implemented. Indeed, Perkins and White (2011: 100) suggest that 'grading structures are the core building blocks of any organisation's human resource management system, not just for pay but often for conditions of service and career development as well'. The degree of sophistication characterising the design of pay structures in organisations can vary considerably according to firm size, sector and occupational group. For example, smaller firms are generally less likely to operate formal pay structures, especially during the formative stages of the business, relying perhaps instead on management discretion to set individual rates of pay for employees (Perkins and White, 2011). However, research in SMEs would indicate that as small firms grow, an informal approach to HRM becomes less tenable (Mazzarol, 2003; Barrett and Mayson, 2007; Barrett *et al.*, 2008); it is at this point that SMEs are likely to begin to inject greater levels of formalisation across a range of HR practices, including reward. Furthermore, the 2012 CIPD Reward Survey points to sectoral differences and occupational differences. Responses indicate that pay spines/service-related structures are prevalent in the public services and, to a slightly lesser extent, in the voluntary, community and not–for-profit sectors, while individual pay rates or spot salaries are more common in the manufacturing and production sector and in private-sector services. By occupation, management and professional staff are more likely to be subject to individual pay rates or spot salaries (43.8 per cent) than other employees (29.2 per cent).

According to the CIPD (2013a), a pay structure is a selection of pay levels, grades or bands which assimilates related jobs within a series or hierarchy. This in turn provides a framework within which reward strategies and policies can be applied. Pay structures are designed for several purposes:

- to bring order and clarity to an organisation in managing pay increases and pay progression;
- to assist with the process of aligning reward strategy with the business strategy;
- to help ensure pay decisions are fair and justified and protect the organisation against equal pay claims.

In essence, a pay structure defines the rate, or range of the payment rate, for jobs within the organisational structure. While this might sound a relatively simple task, there are a number of design choices to be made:

- Should the organisation establish spot rates for individual jobs or devise a more complex structure or series of pay structures?
- How many pay structures are necessary?
- What types of pay structures are suitable?
- If a grading structure is deemed appropriate, how many grades should there be; how wide should each grade or band be; and how close should grade differentials be?

Further decisions must subsequently be made about 'whether, or on what basis, employees will progress through the pay structure' (Perkins and White, 2011: 157).

General design features

As a rule, pay structures need to be flexible enough to accommodate change in the organisation or in the external market and sufficiently clear for individuals to understand where in the structure they are placed and how pay progression is achieved. Spot rates are set rates of base pay for individual jobs, independent of one another and not tied to a scale or range. Where there is a spot rate for a job, all employees incumbent in the role are paid the same base rate for the job; this may be supplemented by forms of variable pay, such as overtime and shift premium or attendance bonus. Spot rates tend to preside in manufacturing and warehouse/distribution centres and in other lower-skilled occupations, and they are also relatively common in small firms. On the other hand, they are also found at senior levels where the remuneration package may need to be designed to attract a particular individual (CIPD, 2013a). It is difficult to regard a series of spot rates as a pay structure *per se*; however, spot rates can be customised to personify typical features of a pay structure; for example, a mini-series of spot rates (generally referred to as an individual pay range) could be assigned to a role such that there is scope to pay a lesser training or learning rate to individuals new to the role, a target spot rate for a fully competent employee, and a further (higher) rate to recognise superior skill, experience or performance. In other circumstances, organisations may elect to manage spot rates in such a way as to incentivise consistently high levels of output. This might be attempted in a somewhat punitive fashion, by dropping lower-performing employees to a less favourable spot rate until such a time as higher productivity is resumed.

While, as illustrated, a degree of tailoring is possible, spot rates do not readily offer scope for pay progression; rather, they supply a series of detached job rates. Such an approach may be eminently suitable where jobs are fairly static in nature, and career development opportunities and expectations are limited. In contrast, grading, pay spines and job families more aptly fit the description of a framework for the enactment of pay policy. In addition, they offer options for pay progression, through the spine, grade or family of jobs, based upon length of service or other criteria best suited to the organisation's strategic business objectives.

A single structure or several structures?

An organisation may be able to design and implement a single pay structure to incorporate the entire range of jobs (or the vast majority of jobs) across it. Alternatively, two or more structures may be in place to assimilate different groups of roles represented within the organisation (e.g. a manual pay scale and an office and managerial salary structure). In recent times, both the National Health Service (NHS) and the higher education (HE) sector have untaken extensive pay reform, underpinned by job evaluation to develop single pay structures. The NHS scheme, 'Agenda for Change', succeeded in introducing a single national pay scale for NHS hospital employees (with the exception of doctors and consultants); similarly, the National Framework Agreement in Higher Education has created a single pay spine for support and academic staff in HE institutions.

Explore

- What benefits do you think hospitals and universities are likely to derive from the formulation of single pay structures in their respective organisations?

Pay spines

A pay spine is a series of fixed incremental salary points reflecting all jobs, from the highest paid through to the lowest paid, incorporated in the structure. Incremental points may increase at an evenly distributed rate throughout the spine; for example, each increment might be set at 2.5 per cent above the next, from the bottom to the top of the structure. Alternatively, increments might be wider at higher levels in the organisation. Pay spines are traditionally found in local government or voluntary organisations that mirror local government arrangements (CIPD, 2013a). In these work environments, pay grades are superimposed upon the pay spine to form a structure in which a series of increments apply within each grade. Employees' annual salaries are typically automatically raised to the next incremental point on the basis of length of service. This either occurs on an individual basis, triggered by the anniversary of the employee joining the organisation, or collectively at a fixed date in the calendar. Except in extreme cases of poor performance, where an increment might be withheld or where progression 'gateways' have to be crossed, employees continue to receive automatic annual increments (and possibly accelerated increments awarded according to performance criteria) until such time as they reach the top point in the grade. Pay progression thereafter, in the form of increments, is contingent on the employee gaining promotion to a higher grade. In some organisations, further additional discretionary points may be available beyond the upper limit of the grade boundary, reserved for those employees who have performed exceptionally throughout the year or those who have made a special contribution. In public services, where pay spines are prevalent, uplift to the pay spine is the subject of national pay bargaining between trade unions and employers; where a cost of living percentage increase in pay is agreed, the incremental scale is adjusted upwards accordingly. Pay spines offer employees a degree of pay progression certainty and give employers certainty in terms of total salary expenditure, but may be perceived as bureaucratic and excessively rigid.

Key Controversy

Do automatic increments based on length of service risk rewarding for incompetence and poor performance? On balance do you think incremental points are an equitable means of rewarding employees?

Graded pay structures

Aside from the use of a central pay spine, organisations opting for a formal pay structure are likely to use some form of grading. The general principles of a pay-grading structure are that jobs are grouped together into grades or bands, often according to some measure of job size. Graded structures require firms to determine how many grades or bands to build into the structure, the width of each grade ('bandwidth'), the degree of overlap to configure between grades and the size of grade differentials to apply throughout the structure. Jobs should be grouped together such that a distinction can be made between the characteristics of the jobs in different grades, and the grade hierarchy should broadly take account of the organisational hierarchy. Additionally, there should be a significant step in demands on job holders in the next highest grade, such that salary differentials can be suitably justified.

Narrow-graded pay structures

Narrow-graded pay structures, or 'traditional' graded structures as they are sometimes called, comprise a large number of grades, typically 10 or more, with jobs of broadly equivalent worth slotted into each of the grades (CIPD, 2013a). As the name would suggest, the width of each grade within the structure ('bandwidth') is narrow, perhaps amounting to a range where the upper salary limit of the grade is anywhere between 20 and 50 per cent higher than the lower salary limit. Salary differentials between pay ranges are invariably around 20 per cent (CIPD, 2013b), calculated with reference to the grade midpoint. There is usually an overlap between ranges, which can be as high as 50 per cent. The purpose of an overlap is to provide the employer with the scope to recognise and reward a highly experienced and/or qualified employee at the top of a grade more generously than someone who is still in the learning curve zone of the next higher grade (see Figure 13.4) Ultimately, however, individuals placed in the higher grade have greater scope for salary progression. They will be able to move closer towards, and eventually beyond, the target rate for a fully competent employee within the grade, contingent upon satisfying the criteria for pay progression used by the organisation.

For illustrative purposes, Figure 13.5 shows a single narrow grade with a bandwidth of 40 per cent, while Figure 13.6 shows an extract of a narrow-graded pay structure where the bandwidth is 40 per cent throughout the structure, a grade overlap of 20 per cent is applied and the differential between grades is set at 20 per cent.

It is common practice to identify a reference point or target rate in each grade which is the rate for a fully competent individual who is completely qualified and experienced to execute

Figure 13.4 Grade zones

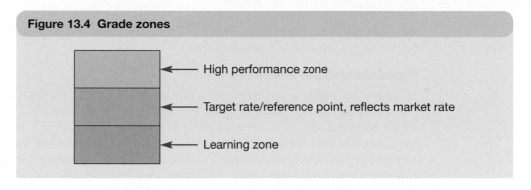

Figure 13.5 Narrow salary grade – 40% bandwidth

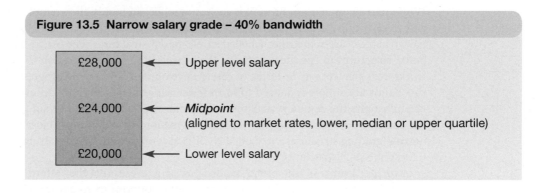

Figure 13.6 Extract of narrow-graded pay structure

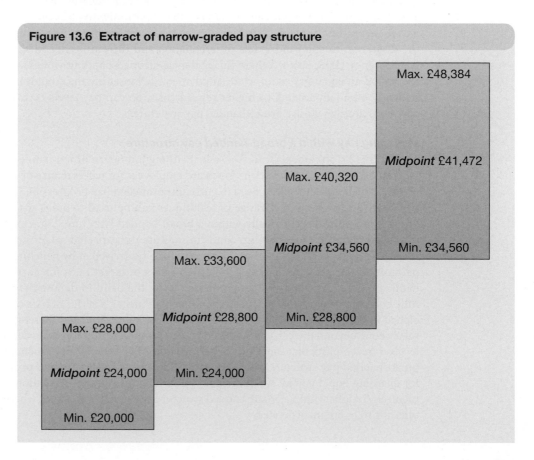

the job to the required standard. This target rate is frequently, but not always, the *midpoint* in the range, aligned to market rates for similar jobs and set in accordance with the organisation's pay stance (upper, median or lower quartile).

Broad-banded pay structures

In contrast to a narrow-graded pay structure, a broad-banded structure involves the use of a small number of pay bands, normally no more than five (Perkins and White, 2011), each with a bandwidth of up to 100 per cent or even more (CIPD, 2013b). The broader salary range attached to bands in the structure gives employers greater flexibility than is possible in a narrow-graded structure and is arguably more suitable for use in flatter organisations where employee development and career progression are not inextricably linked to vertical movement through the hierarchy. Flatter organisations tend to develop a more flexible outlook as far as careers are concerned, promoting lateral career development and 'zig-zag' careers. While narrow grades might inhibit such moves, broad bands allow employers to recognise and reward non-vertical career movement and role growth. For this reason, broad-banded pay structures are sometimes labelled career-based structures. For broad-banded or career-based structures to operate effectively, the organisation must reposition their own and their workforce's perceptions in terms of career development and salary progression. Where narrow bands are simply collapsed to form fewer wider bands, without an overarching change of philosophy the resultant structure might more aptly be termed broad-*graded* because of the continued attachment to the vertical progression mentality more closely associated with narrow-grading structures. In 2000, the CIPD also offered the less flattering term 'fat-graded' to describe such structures.

A further feature of true broad-banded pay structures is that they afford employers greater latitude in establishing starting salaries and so the opportunity to pay more to attract suitably qualified and experienced staff to 'hard to fill' positions. While this facility might be perceived as useful, especially in tight labour markets, the opportunity to place an employee on a salary anywhere within the wide range between the band minimum and maximum gives managers the discretion to apply individual differentiation and therein licence to cloud any notion of transparency (IDS, 2006). Where this is the case, broad-banding would appear to heighten the risk of an equal pay claim while simultaneously loosening the employer's rein on the pay budget, potentially leading to higher reward costs. So can pay levels be managed fairly and cost-consciously within a broad-banded pay structure?

Managing pay within a broad-banded pay structure

The CIPD (2013b) are quick to realise that although modern broad-banded structures allow greater flexibility and wider scope to reward employees for performance or some other measure of contribution, there is a need to curb untrammelled pay progression and maintain control over the pay budget. A range of techniques can be used to assist with controlling pay progression more systematically within a broad-banded structure. Some organisations have sought to mark out zones within bands to indicate the expected salary range for particular roles. The salary level reflected in the zone is likely be arrived at by benchmarking with comparators in the external market. Similarly, a series of target rates for particular jobs in the band could be identified and superimposed upon the band to denote the market rate for a fully competent individual performing in the job. Further, a series of bars or gateways can be etched into the band to serve as thresholds. To cross a threshold and thereby access the higher salary zone beyond the bar, job holders might be required to demonstrate defined competency levels or reach particular standards of performance. These methods of managing pay within a broad-banded pay structure would appear to improve transparency and provide a surer basis for ensuring equal pay for work of equal value. The role for job evaluation in establishing a hierarchy of jobs within a broad-banded structure is also more apparent where zones or target rates for roles are incorporated.

Explore

- Is there a grading structure within your organisation?
- How many grades/bands exist within your own organisation?
- Would you classify your own organisation's pay structure as *broad-graded, broad-banded* or *traditional* (*narrow-graded*)?
- What advantages and disadvantages are associated with the pay structure in place within your own organisation?

Number of bands	Senior executives	Managerial/professional	Staff/manual
3 or less	❑	❑	❑
4–5	❑	❑	❑
6–9	❑	❑	❑
10+	❑	❑	❑

Job families

Finally, pay structures can be characterised wholly or partially by the use of job family structures, or labour market structures as they are sometimes called. A job family structure consists of separate grade or pay structure for a series of jobs which are related by virtue of the activities carried out and the basic skills used. The jobs, though, will be differentiated by the level of responsibility, skill or competence required. Usually around six to eight levels are represented within a family structure (CIPD, 2013a), ranging from lower-ranking jobs through to higher-ranking posts. In essence, this approach to devising pay structures treats different occupations or functions separately and results in a series of pay ladders for different sets of jobs. Alternatively, a single job family structure could co-exist with a mainstream pay structure in an organisation where the family of jobs concerned cannot easily be assimilated in the mainstream structure without giving rise to anomalies. In practice, job family pay structures are beneficial where an organisation needs to recruit to job roles within a particular occupational group and there is fierce competition in the labour market forcing the price of wages up. A job family pay structure allows the organisation to align to the external market more closely and so improve its chances of attracting and retaining adequate resources.

Pay progression

As Wright (2004: 78) argues 'there is little point in organisations having elaborate pay structures unless they are offering employees some progression opportunities for their pay *within* the pay structure'. A number of means are at the organisation's disposal to manage employees' movement within the salary structure; indeed, the way in which this is done in different types of organisations tends to vary far more than actual levels of wages and salaries (Perkins and White, 2011). *How* organisations pay portrays their stance on reward and is in many ways a more strategic decision than *how much* to pay. Where a strategic approach to reward is manifest, methods of pay progression will be informed by a clear notion of the organisation's values and strategic imperatives, such that the 'right' individuals are recognised and rewarded for the 'right' behaviours. As was suggested earlier in this chapter, strategic approaches to reward are not universally applied, and even where they are, weaknesses and difficulties often mire best efforts. Where pay progression is concerned, sometimes pragmatic decisions, underscored by the lack of resources and expertise to design and manage more elaborate pay progression mechanisms, drive organisations to apply blanket solutions such as automatic annual increments linked to employee service and across-the-board percentage pay increases. Indeed, for some organisations, and the stakeholders involved in the particular employment relationship, annual service-related increments and unified pay awards may signify equity, parity and transparency and therefore be viewed more positively than other means of salary progression.

However, while service-related pay progression rewards the build-up of expertise in the job and may help employers with retention, it risks signalling to employees that longevity of service is more important than the quantity and/or quality of the work undertaken and the manner in which work is conducted. Similarly, universal pay increases, resulting in the same pay award to everyone regardless of their contribution, fail to take into account other factors that might justifiably be used to determine the speed and scale of individual salary progression. Service-related increments are a traditional method of pay progression in the public sector, but they are less frequently used by private-sector employers, who tend to prefer mechanisms that reward other factors such as performance, competence and skill (CIPD, 2012). The 2012 CIPD Reward Survey and the 2011 WERS survey (van Wanrooy *et al.*, 2013) also show that the use of collective bargaining, resulting in the same percentage pay increase for represented groups of employees, is more prevalent in the public sector than it is in private-sector and voluntary-sector organisations. The popularity of collective bargaining as a mechanism for settling pay and terms and conditions is, however, declining overall.

By contrast, a number of alternative means of managing salary progression are available and some of these are discussed in the following sections.

Individual performance-related pay (PRP)

Performance-related pay links individual pay progression with employee performance. The basic notion of individual PRP is that the promise of rewards contingent on performance will incentivise employees to perform optimally, thus raising individual performance and leading to improved levels of organisational performance. Within a PRP scheme, employee performance is typically assessed against pre-set targets or pre-agreed objectives, often at appraisal time, although a separate pay review meeting could be used to determine a PRP increase. PRP payments may be consolidated into base pay or paid as a bonus (variable pay). PRP schemes ebb and flow in popularity and have been the subject of much controversial debate in the reward literature. In particular, the supposed causal link between PRP and performance or productivity has been heavily questioned (Kessler and Purcell, 1992; Thompson, 1992; Marsden and Richardson, 1994). Indeed, rather than glowing accolades heralding the benefits of PRP, much attention has been drawn to the potential negative ramifications associated with using it. Reservations tend to revolve around the following issues:

- PRP schemes operate on the basis that employees will be motivated by money, whereas motivational theories suggest that money is not the only motivator, or even necessarily an effective motivator.
- The size of the 'pay pot' and how to divide this appropriately commensurate with individual performance achievements.
- Problems associated with measuring performance in a fair and objective manner.
- The ability of managers to manage the award of PRP; to make, communicate and justify difficult and potentially divisive reward decisions.
- Potential for pay discrimination/bias.
- Potential harm to efforts to engender teamwork as individual PRP encourages employees to focus on their own performance targets or objectives without concern for the greater good of the team, department or wider organisation.
- Focus on output/outcomes, but not the means used to accomplish performance outcomes.

Furthermore, Kessler and Purcell (1992) argue that linking assessments of performance to pay can induce tunnel vision, whereby employees concentrate on those aspects of their job that trigger pay increases and ignore other parts of their role. They also suggest that the limitations of the pay pot may mean that even employees with positive appraisal ratings only receive relatively small payouts that fail to measure up to the 'felt fair' principle. In view of the criticisms levelled against individual PRP, the CIPD (2013c) notes that the notion of linking pay to a wider definition of employees' contribution has gained ground. In this approach, individual performance is assessed taking into account processes and behaviour, not simply outcomes.

Pay for contribution

As indicated earlier, interest in paying for measures of contribution is partly prompted by concern that individual PRP takes too narrow an interpretation of performance by focusing on end results in isolation. Organisations expressing a preference for contribution-related pay signal an interest in how outcomes are achieved as well as the outcomes themselves. Indeed, the way in which employees conduct their work and the attitudes and behaviours they display may have been identified by such organisations as a critical factor in securing competitive advantage, so to try to match pay to softer measures of behaviours as well as harder results data would seem to indicate an attempt to design a pay progression mechanism that places due emphasis on strategic fit. Armstrong (2002: 309) defines contribution-related pay as 'a process for making pay decisions which are based on assessments of both the outcomes of the work carried out by individuals and the level of skill and competence which have influenced these outcomes'. It is thus an attempt at a mixed, blended or hybrid method incorporating the ethos of PRP and competence-based pay. It means paying for results (outcomes) and competence, for past performance and potential for future success (see Figure 13.7).

The mechanisms used to pay for contribution can vary considerably. Recognising that paying for contribution incorporates multi-dimensional measures, some organisations reward the acquisition and display of required competencies in base pay, and reward results achieved with an unconsolidated bonus (variable pay), while others arrive at a composite increase in base pay, taking into account both competence and results payouts. Rewards can also be given for combinations of organisational, team and individual performance, not just the latter (Brown and Armstrong, 1999). In essence, the model advocated by Brown and Armstrong entails a customised approach to reward.

Competence-related pay

Competence-related pay, used alone as means of pay progression, adopts a relatively narrow focus akin to the use of individual PRP; however, emphasis is placed on employees' input to the job, rather than performance or output. The aim of competence-related pay is to encourage and reward the development of particular competencies desired by the organisation; it amounts to a method of paying employees for *the ability* to perform as opposed to paying *for* performance (Armstrong, 2002). Perkins and White (2011: 182) comment that 'whereas individual performance-related pay can appear to be simply a punitive system to penalise workers,

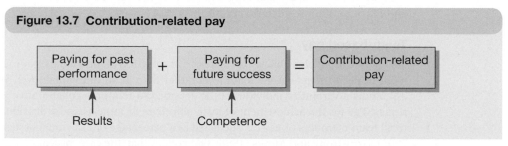

Figure 13.7 Contribution-related pay

Paying for past performance + Paying for future success = Contribution-related pay

Results   Competence

Source: adapted from Brown and Armstrong (1999: 137).

Table 13.5 The advantages and disadvantages of competence-related pay

Advantages	Disadvantages
• Encourages competence development	• Assessment of competence levels may be difficult
• Fits de-layered organisations by facilitating lateral career moves	• Might pay for irrelevant competencies
• Helps to integrate role and organisational core competencies	• Links to pay may be arbitrary
• Forms part of an integrated, competence-based approach to people management	• Costs may escalate if inappropriate or unused competencies are rewarded
• Delivers message that competence is important	
• Relies on appropriate, relevant and agreed competence profiles	

Source: from *Employee Reward*, 3rd edn, CIPD (Armstrong, M. 2002) p. 306, with the permission of the publisher, the Chartered Institute of Personnel and Development, London (**www.cipd.co.uk**).

competency-based systems can in contrast appear positive for employees' own career development'. The introduction of competence-based pay requires a competency framework to be in place and a means for measuring individual competence levels to be agreed and understood by managers and employees alike. Table 13.5 summarises the advantages and disadvantages of competence-related pay.

Skills-based pay

Skills-based pay is sometimes referred to as 'pay for knowledge' or 'knowledge-based pay' (Perkins and White, 2011: 187). The aim of skills-based pay is to encourage employees to acquire additional skills, units of skill or specific qualifications that are deemed important to meet business needs. Skills-based pay might be closely tied to National Vocational Qualifications (NVQs) and the units and levels of qualifications set out in modular qualification frameworks of this type; alternatively, the organisation may identify discernible skills or blocks of skills and arrange these in a hierarchy to indicate progressive skill levels. Marchington and Wilkinson (2012) identify both constraints and benefits in the use of skills-based pay. They argue that organisations must be able to anticipate and plan for future skills needs some years ahead to ensure they are rewarding for the acquisition of the *right* skills. They also warn that such a scheme may create frustration and demotivation amongst employees who exhaust the skills hierarchy and so lose access to pay progression. The costs of skills-based pay must also be carefully monitored both in terms of the investment in training to underpin the scheme and in terms of the identification and utilisation of the skills rewarded. While skills-based pay is likely to encourage a desire for upward mobility and thirst for skills acquisition amongst workers, thus enhancing organisational quality and capability, great care must be taken to ensure that only skills that are used are paid for, otherwise costs will escalate and the organisation will fail to profit.

Team-based pay

Team rewards involve linking pay increases or a portion of individuals' pay increase to an assessment of performance at the team level rather than at an individual level. Team-based pay is essentially a variant of individual PRP, designed to reinforce collaborative working and team results. Pay for the achievement of team objectives or targets can be distributed as a fixed sum to all team members or can be calculated as a percentage of individual base salary (Armstrong, 2002). Armstrong and Murlis (1998: 395) contest that 'the case for team pay looks good in theory but there are some formidable disadvantages', as follows:

- Its effectiveness relies on the existence of well-defined and mature teams.
- Distinguishing individual team members' contributions to the team could be problematic.
- It can be difficult to develop fair and objective methods for measuring team outcomes.
- Team rivalry may develop.
- Organisational flexibility may be hampered in the sense that employees in high-performing, well-rewarded teams might be unwilling to change roles.
- High performers in low-achieving teams may feel unduly penalised and dissatisfied.

Perkins and White (2011: 221) highlight the issue of the 'freeloader' as a particular problem. If individual performance within the team is not clearly discernible or is not closely monitored, those who fail to perform a fair share of the work may well remain eligible for the reward, resulting in resentment and disharmony within the team.

Pay progression based on measures of organisational performance

Finally, there are a three main ways in which individuals' pay can be linked to organisational performance, namely gain-sharing, profit-related pay and share-ownership schemes. The general premise of all three schemes is that by linking pay to organisational performance, employees will be encouraged to focus on value-added activities and will identify more closely with the goals of the organisation. Where the organisation is successful as a result of employees' efforts and contributions, due rewards are passed to employees in the form of a consolidated payment, a cash one-off payment (unconsolidated, variable pay) or the issue of company shares, and hence a financial stake in the organisation, where the preferred method of linking pay to organisational performance is a share-ownership scheme. Share schemes are considered to be long-term collective rewards and employees' fortunes are clearly dependent on the longer-term success of the organisation and the resultant rise and fall in share prices. Profit-sharing and gain-sharing, on the other hand, are collective rewards applied at organisational level which tend to deliver the reward within a period of 12 months or less (Perkins and White, 2011: 224). Briefly, gain-sharing schemes apply a formula to award individuals a share of the financial gains made by the organisation as a result of improvements in quality, productivity enhancements or cost-reduction strategies assisted by employees. Profit-related pay or profit-sharing, on the other hand, typically rewards employees with a slice of the company profits generated over and above a pre-specified profit target or level. The latest CIPD Reward Survey (2012) shows that gain sharing occurred in 21.6 per cent of organisations participating in the study and was more likely to be found within the manufacturing and production sector than in other sectors. Profit-sharing schemes were shown to be present in 38.1 per cent of all organisations and in 41.8 per cent of private-sector services firms. Around one in three respondents to the survey operate a share scheme or other long-term incentive plan such as executive deferred annual cash bonuses or an executive deferred/co-invest share plan.

Concluding comments

Trends in reward practice – towards a strategic approach or more traditionalism?

Since the early 1990s, 'new pay' enthusiasts (Lawler, 1990, 1995, 2000; Schuster and Zingheim, 1992) have consistently promoted the efficacy of transforming pay and reward such that it serves as a more effective driver of organisational performance. In essence, 'new pay' or 'dynamic pay' (Flannery *et al.*, 1996) advocate a far more managerialist view of the design and application of reward tools, resonating with the acclaimed superiority of strategic approaches to reward and the notion of 'total rewards'. Its key ingredients include a greater quotient of variable pay, a move away from rigid payment structures to fluid and flexible ones, pay centred on the person not on the job, pay progression dependent on performance, competence, skills, contribution or some other form of contingent pay and a shift away from collectivism to individualism in reward. Such practices are considered to offer the organisation greater agility to reward individual employees commensurate with the impact they make upon critical business objectives and greater control over the pay budget. In this final part of the chapter, we briefly discuss the extent to which organisations in the UK appear to echo the new pay rhetoric by marking out the support of business goals as the supreme priority governing reward objectives and throwing out traditional pay practices in favour of the new.

As we have learned throughout this chapter, there are a multitude of ways to do reward. At the same time, there is a strong tide running through business textbooks, the HR practitioner press and the professional body, persuading organisations that the right way to do reward is to align it with business strategy. Much of the evidence would suggest that despite the pressure to make the link to business strategy, few have grasped the nettle firmly. Indeed, the 2012 CIPD Reward Survey distils reward strategy down to measures of the proportion of organisations engaging in competitive remuneration positioning relative to comparative organisations, as if this captures the totality of reward strategy.

While there might be flimsy data to verify a swell of close adherence to the principles of a fully fledged reward strategy, there is evidence that elements of 'new pay' are permeating reward practices, particularly in the private sector. Here we see greater use of broad-banded pay structures, greater reference to market rates when determining salary levels and a higher propensity to use more varied and individualised methods of pay progression. Only in the public sector, voluntary sector and the not-for-profit sector is seniority-based pay (based on length of service) still the most common form of progression (CIPD, 2012). The decline of collective bargaining in the private sector and the rise in PRP would also seem to indicate that a managerial agenda of individualism and greater use of contingent pay in place of uniform rates for jobs is winning through (van Wanrooy *et al.*, 2013). By contrast, large sections of the public sector, at least in non-managerial roles, remain steeped in traditionalism.

Summary

This chapter began by outlining seven key objectives and these are revisited here:

- Historically, the area of HRM that we now recognise and understand as employee reward primarily concerned wages and payment systems and the ways in which these could be used to exert control over both sides of the wage/effort bargain, enlarge the area of managerial control and so maximise organisational profitability.

- Nowadays, employee reward is defined more broadly to include base pay, variable pay, benefits and non-financial rewards.

- Reward is now recognised by many employers as a key strategic lever that can be used to mould and direct employee behaviour such that it supports and reinforces business goals. Strategic approaches to reward emphasise the importance of matching reward systems and practices to corporate strategy, and integrating reward such that it complements other HR policies and practices. Debates persist, however, as to the precise contribution that reward can make to business performance, and doubts are cast on the ability of employers to design and implement reward strategy effectively. There would appear to remain a gap between rhetoric and practice in this respect.

- There are no right and wrong approaches to employee reward; rather, a myriad of choices are available to organisations. Key choices entail whether to pay for the person or pay for the job, whether to centralise or decentralise reward decision-making, whether to place primary focus on internal equity when determining pay or to be more concerned with external benchmarks, whether to build hierarchy into the reward system such that there are seniority or status-related rewards or to devise a harmonised, single-status approach and how to determine the precise nature of the reward 'mix'.

- Reward decisions are influenced by a range of factors in the external operating environment. In particular, the economic climate affects employers' ability to pay and it guides organisations in determining salary levels/size of the pay review. The legal framework surrounding reward is designed to protect the low-paid, set standards for hours of work and holiday entitlement and ensure equal pay for work of equal value.

- In practice, approaches to reward are influenced by the size and nature of the organisation, the presence of trade unions, ownership/sector and types of workers employed.

- Notable differences emerge between the public sector/voluntary sector and not-for-profit sectors and organisations in the private sector in terms of favoured methods for establishing pay levels, the design of pay structures and the criteria for pay progression.

- Despite the rhetoric of 'new pay' and the resounding case for strategic approaches to reward, traditionalism remains pervasive alongside experimentation with the new.

Questions

1 What do we mean by the term reward? How does it differ from 'wages', 'salary' or 'payment'?
2 Identify and briefly describe each of the components of reward.
3 In dominant reward terminology, contingent pay is distinguished from variable pay – explain what reward specialists mean when they use these terms.
4 Briefly suggest why strategic reward appears to be so difficult to achieve in practice.
5 Identify the key strands of the legislative framework affecting pay practices.
6 In a grading structure, what do the terms 'bandwidth' and 'salary differential' mean?
7 Why might an organisation use job family structures?
8 Explain the differences between individual performance-related pay, competence-based pay and pay related to contribution.

Case study

Shop Guru

Shop Guru is an independent consumer service operating on a not-for-profit basis. The service is funded primarily through membership subscription to its magazine and website. Shop Guru employs approximately 520 people across two sites: the Head Office in Cambridge and a call centre in Leicestershire. Its employees comprise researchers, editorial staff, PR experts, marketing officers and customer services representatives. Given the range of roles in the organisation, employee expectations and experiences vary considerably.

The diversity of the workforce posed the biggest challenge for the HR team as they set about the task of devising a reward strategy to align with organisational values. Historically, reward practices had developed in a piecemeal, ad hoc fashion, leading to an unmanageable number of salary bands (over 100 across the two sites) and considerable variation in the award of performance-related bonuses of managers. More fundamentally, however, there were divided views as to the role of reward and how it should be managed. For most managers and employees in the organisation, reward was considered in monetary terms only and in some factions of the organisation the firm belief was that service-related pay provided the only fair way to manage salary progression. Faced with an inordinate challenge,

Case study continued

the HR team constructed an evidence-based argument, using metrics, to persuade the senior management team that changes would reap dividends for the organisation. With senior management backing, the HR department embarked upon a lengthy consultation and communication process to explain the changes, collect employee views and elicit feedback.

The resultant reward process for Shop Guru rests on a strong set of total reward principles based upon pay, benefits, the values and culture of the organisation and learning and development. Pay is now linked to performance for all employees with expectations for each generic job level clearly identified in a transparent job family framework designed to reflect the discrete job groups within the organisation. The benefits package is generous and is benchmarked at the upper quartile level. Benefits are harmonised across the organisation and include a contributory pension scheme, personal private medical cover, flexible working practices and on-site Pilates classes and health screening. Career progression is facilitated via a range of learning and development interventions designed to provide opportunities for all members of the diverse workforce.

The most innovative feature of Shop Guru's new reward strategy is the way in which the organisation has linked the reward framework to its six core organisational values: aspiration, courage, flexibility, teamworking, personal responsibility and decisive action. Alongside performance measures for each job level within the framework, Shop Guru has translated how each of the values should be enacted; this brings the values to life for employees and ensures that positive behaviours are viewed alongside performance ouputs as critical to the reward proposition.

Source: Case based on *Case study – Which?*, CIPD Reward Management Annual Survey Report 2012, p. 24.

Questions

1 Suggest reasons why Shop Guru opted for a job family structure when re-configuring pre-existing pay structures.

2 What measures or mechanisms should Shop Guru put in place to help safeguard the organisation against equal pay claims?

3 Consider the factors you believe to be critical to the success of the new reward framework at Shop Guru.

4 What metrics / tools might Shop Guru use to assess the effectiveness of the new reward framework?

References and further reading

ACAS (2010) *Job Evaluation: Consideration and Risks.* London: ACAS, September 2010.

Adams, J. (1965) 'Inequity and social exchange' in L. Berkowitz (ed.) *Advances in Experimental Social Psychology 2.* New York: Academic Press, pp. 267–96.

Anthony, P.D. (1977) *The Ideology of Work.* London: Tavistock Publications.

Armstrong, M. (2002) *Employee Reward,* 3rd edn. London: CIPD.

Armstrong, M. (2012) *Armstrong's Handbook of Reward Management Practice: Improving Performance through Reward,* 4th edn. London: Kogan Page.

Armstrong, M. and Murlis, H. (1998) *Reward Management: A Handbook of Remuneration Strategy and Practice.* London: Kogan Page.

Armstrong, M. and and Stephens, T. (2005) *A Handbook of Employee Reward Management and Practice.* London: Kogan Page.

Arrowsmith, J. and Gilman, M. (2005) 'Small firms and the national minimum wage' in S. Marlow, D. Patton and M. Ram (eds) *Managing Labour in Small Firms.* London: Routledge, pp. 159–77.

Baldwin, M. and Johnson, W. (2006) 'A critical review of studies of discrimination against workers with disabilities' in W. Rodgers III (ed.) *Handbook on the Economics of Discrimination.* Gloucester: Edward Elgar, pp. 119–60.

Barrett, R. and Mayson, S. (2007) 'Human resource management in growing small firms', *Journal of Small Business and Enterprise Development,* 14, 2: 307–20.

Barrett, R., Mayson, S. and Warriner, M. (2008) 'The relationship between small firm growth and HRM practices' in R. Barrett and S. Mayson (eds) *International Handbook of Entrepreneurship and HRM.* Cheltenham: Edward Elgar, pp. 186–204.

Beer, M., Spector, B., Lawrence, P., Mills, D. and Walton, R. (1984) *Human Resource Management; A General Manager's Perspective.* New York: Free Press.

Bevan, S. (2000) *Reward Strategy: 10 Common Mistakes.* London: IES.

Blauner, R. (1964) *Alienation and Freedom: The Factory Worker and his Industry.* Chicago, IL: University of Chicago Press.

Bloom, M.C. and Milkovich, G. (1996) 'Issues in managerial compensation research' in C.L. Cooper and D.M. Rousseau (eds) *Trends in Organisational Behaviour,* vol. 3. Chichester: John Wiley, pp. 23–47.

Bowey, A. and Lupton, T. (1973) *Job and Pay Comparisions.* Aldershot: Gower.

Braverman, H. (1974) *Labour and Monopoly Capital: The Degradation of Work in the Twentieth Century.* London: Monthly Review Press.

Brown, D. and Armstrong, M. (1999) *Paying for Contribution; Real Performance-Related Pay Strategies.* London: Kogan Page.

Brown, D. and Dive, B. (2009) 'Level-pegging', *People Management,* 15 January: 26–29.

Burawoy, M. (1985) *The Politics of Production.* London: Verso.

Burke, R. and Cooper, C. (2008) *The Long Work Hours Culture: Causes, Consequences and Choices.* Bingley: Emerald.

Callaghan, G. and Thompson, P. (2001) 'Edwards revisited; technical control and call centres', *Economic and Industrial Democracy,* 22: 13–40.

CIPD (2008) *Reward Management*, CIPD Survey. London: CIPD.

CIPD (2011) *Reward Management*, Survey Report. London: CIPD.

CIPD (2012) *Reward Management*, Survey Report. London: CIPD.

CIPD (2013a) *Pay structures*, Factsheet. London: CIPD.

CIPD (2013b) *Pay progression*, Factsheet. London: CIPD.

CIPD (2013c) *Performance related pay*, Factsheet. London: CIPD.

Conboy, B. (1976) *Pay at Work.* London: Arrow Books.

Druker, J. and White, G. (2009) 'Introduction' in G. White and J. Druker (eds) *Reward Management: A Critical Text.* Abingdon: Routledge, pp. 1–22.

Dundon T. and Rollinson, D. (2004) *Employment Relations in Small Firms.* London: Routledge.

Evain, E. (2008) *Working Conditions Laws 2006–2007.* Geneva: ILO.

Eyraud, F. and Saget, C. (2005) *The Fundamentals of Minimum Wage Fixing.* Geneva: ILO.

Fay, C (2011) 'Compensation Strategies' in C. Rowley and K. Jackson (eds) *Human Resource Management; the Key Concepts.* London, Routledge.

Flannery, T.P., Hafrichter, D.A. and Platten, P.E. (1996) *People, Performance and Pay.* New York: The Free Press.

Fredman, S. (2008) 'Reforming equal pay laws', *Industrial Law Journal,* 37: 193–218.

Gollan, P. (2007) *Employee Representation in Non-Union Firms.* London: Sage.

Gospel, H. (1992) *Markets, Firms and the Management of Labour in Modern Britain.* Cambridge: Cambride University Press.

Hellerstein, J. and Newmark, D. (2006) 'Using matched employer-employee data to study labour market discrimination' in W. Rodgers III (ed.) *Handbook on the Economics of Discrimination.* Gloucester: Edward Elgar, pp. 29–60.

Herzberg, F. (1966) *Work and the Nature of Man.* Cleveland, OH: World Publishing.

Hewlett, S. and Luce, C. (2006) 'Extreme jobs: the dangerous allure of the 70-hour work week', *Harvard Business Review,* 84,12: 49–59.

Hill, S. (1981) *Competition and Control at Work.* London: Heinemann.

Hinton, J. (1986) *Labour and Socialism.* London: Wheatsheaf Books.

Humbert A.L. and Lewis, S. (2008) 'I have no life other than work – long working hours, blurred boundaries and family life' in R. Burke and C. Cooper (eds) *The Long Work Hours Culture: Causes, Consequences and Choices.* Bingley: Emerald, pp. 159–82.

IDS (2006) *Developments in Occupational Pay Differentiation. A Research Report of the Office for Manpower Economics, October 2006.* London: IDS.

Jamieson, S. (1999) 'Equal pay' in A. Morris and T. O'Donnell (eds) *Feminist Perspectives on Employment Law.* London: Cavendish, pp. 223–40.

Kessler, I. (2001) 'Reward system choices' in J. Storey (ed.) *Human Resource Management: A Critical Text,* 2nd edn. London: Thomson Learning, pp. 206–31.

Kessler, I. (2007) 'Reward choices: strategy and equity' in J. Storey (ed.) *Human Resource Management: A Critical Text,* 3rd edn. London: Thomson Learning, pp. 159–76.

Kessler, I. and Purcell, J. (1992) 'Performance related pay; objectives and application'. *Human Resource Management Journal,* 2, 3: 16–33.

Lawler, E. (1990) *Strategic Pay.* San Francisco, CA: Jossey-Bass.

Lawler, E. (1995) 'The new pay; a strategic approach', *Compensation and Benefits Review,* July/August: 46–54.

Lawler, E. (2000) 'Pay and strategy; new thinking for the new millennium', *Compensation and Benefits Review,* January/February: 7–12.

Lewis, P. (2006) 'Reward management' in T. Redman and A. Wilkinson (eds) *Contemporary Human Resource Management,* 2nd edn. London: FT/Pearson, pp. 126–52.

Little, C. (1982) *The Development of the Labour Process in Capitalist Societies.* London: Heinemann.

Littler, C. (ed.) (1985) *The Experience of Work.* Aldershot: Gower.

Lovell, J. (1977) *British Trade Unions 1875–1933.* London: MacMillan.

Low Pay Commision (2001) *1st Report of the Low Pay Commission.* London: HMSO.

Marchington, M. and Wilkinson, A. (2012) *Human Resource Management at Work,* 5th edn. London: CIPD.

Marlow, S., Patton, D. and Ram, M. (2005) *Managing Labour in Small Firms.* London: Routledge.

Marsden, D. and Richardson, R. (1994) 'Performing for pay? The effects of "merit pay" in a public service', *British Journal of Industrial Relations,* June: 243–61.

Mazzarol, T. (2003) 'A model of small business HR growth management', *International Journal of Entrepreneurial Behaviour and Research,* 9: 27–49.

McColgan, A. (2008) 'Equal pay' in P. Cane and J. Conaghan (eds) *The New Oxford Companion to Law.* Oxford: Oxford University Press, pp. 401–2.

Milkovitch, G. and Newman, J. (1996) *Compensation,* 5th edn. Burr Ridge, IL: Irwin.

Perkins, S.J. and White, G. (2011) *Employee Reward.* London: CIPD.

Ritzer, G. (1997) *The McDonaldization Theory.* London: Sage.

Ritzer, G. (2000) *The McDonaldization of Society.* London: Sage.

Rynes, S, Gerhart, B and Minette, K (2004) 'The importance of pay in employee motivation; discrepancies between what people say and what they do', *Human Resource Management Journal,* 43, 4: 381–94.

Schuster, J. and Zingheim, P. (1992) *The New Pay: Linking Employee and Organisational Performance.* New York: Lexington Books.

Storey, J. (1992) *Developments in the Management of Human Resources.* Oxford: Blackwell.

Suff, P and Reilly, P (2006) *The Appliance of an Inexact Science; Job Evaluation in the 21st Century.* Brighton: IES.

Taylor, F.W. (1964) *Scientific Management.* New York: Harper & Row.

Taylor, P. and Bain, P. (1999) 'An assembly line in the head', *Industrial Relations Journal,* 30: 101–17.

Taylor, P. and Bain, P. (2001) Trade unions, workers' rights and the frontier of control in UK call centres', *Economic and Industrial Democracy,* 22: 29–41

Thompson, P. (1983) *The Nature of Work*. London: Macmillian.

Thompson E.P. (1991) 'Time, work-discipline and Industrial Capitalism' in E.P. Thompson (ed.) *Customs in Common*. Harmondsworth: Penguin, pp. 68–92.

Thompson, M. (1992) *Pay and performance; the employer experience*, Report no. 218. London: Institute of Manpower Studies.

Thompson, P. and Milsome. S. (2001) *Reward Determination in the UK*, Research Report. London: CIPD.

Trevor, J (2009) *Exploring the strategic potential of pay; are we expecting too much?'*. Cambridge Judge Business School, Working Paper Series, 2/2009.

Urwick, L. (1958) *Personnel Management in Perspective*. Oxford: Oxford University Press.

Vroom, V. (1982) *Work and Motivation*. New York: John Wiley.

van Wanrooy, B, Bewley, H, Bryson, A, Forth, J, Freeth, S, Stokes, L and Wood, S (2013) *The 2011 Workplace Employment Relations Study; First Findings*. BIS, ESRC, ACAS, NIESR and UKCES, January 2013.

Watson, S. (2005) 'Is job evaluation making a comeback – or did it never go away?', *Benefits and Compensation International* 34, 10: 8–12, 14.

Wood, S. (ed.) (1982) *The Degradation of Work?* London: Hutchinson.

Wood, A.W. (2000) 'Alienation' in *Concise Routledge Encyclopedia of Philosophy*. London: Routledge, p. 24.

WorldatWork (2000) *Total Rewards: From Strategy To Implementations*. Scottsdale, AZ: WorldatWork.

Wright, A. (2004) *Employee Reward in Context*. London: CIPD.

Wright, A. (2009) 'Benefits' in G. White and J. Druker (eds) *Reward Management: A Critical Text*. Abingdon: Routledge, pp. 174–91.

XpertHR and The Chartered Institute of Management (2013) *The National Management Salary Survey*.

Yates, M.L. (1937) *Wages and Labour Conditions in British Engineering*. London: Macdonald and Evans.

Zeitlin, J. (1983) 'The labour strategies of British engineering employers 1890–1922' in H. Gospel and C. Littler (eds) *Managerial Strategies & Industrial Relations*. Aldershot: Gower, pp. 25–54.

Chapter 14

Employee voice

Peter Butler

Objectives

- To determine the meaning of employee voice and explore its constituent components.
- To clarify why trade union representation is no longer the dominant mode of voice in British workplaces.
- To explore the managerial motivation underpinning the use of 'direct' modes of voice and examine why certain forms of voice are closely allied to 'soft' HRM.
- To track shifting public policy *vis-à-vis* support for different modes of voice.
- To highlight the impact and limitations of European social policy on emergent voice regimes.

Introductory case study

Trade union warns of further strikes

By Brian Groom

The leader of the UK's biggest trade union has warned of a fresh wave of strikes and protests over the coming months as the labour movement seeks to press the government to soften its austerity programme.

Len McCluskey, general secretary of Unite, on Thursday said there was a 'real likelihood' of more industrial action over pay and other issues, following last November's walkout by 1.1m public sector workers over the coalition's pension changes.

The government is pressing ahead with the pension reforms, but Mr McCluskey said the issue was a 'festering sore' among workers in the health service, education and civil service and could erupt again.

Speaking ahead of the annual Trades Union Congress, which opens in Brighton on Sunday, Mr McCluskey also called for a change of direction to lift the economy out of recession.

Unite will press next week for a £1 an hour increase in the national minimum wage to boost low-paid workers' spending power and a cap on energy bills to protect consumers from higher prices this winter.

The TUC meets amid uncertainty about where the movement's campaign against public spending cuts goes next. Another mass demonstration is planned in London for October 20, but unions are divided on further strikes.

There are questions about whether members have the appetite for industrial action on the scale of last November, and whether there is an issue to rally around with the same potency as pensions.

But Mr McCluskey said: 'I see the issue of strikes and continuing protests actually increasing as we come closer and closer to a general election.'

He said 80 per cent of cuts had still to take effect and communities across the country would be 'shocked' when their full extent became known.

'I am not quite sure how that will manifest itself. The government seems deaf to calls to change its programme and I can foresee a breakdown in our communities. That is incredibly dangerous and anything can happen.'

Mr McCluskey said government policies were leading the country on a 'path to poverty'. A recent survey of 350,000 Unite members showed one in eight were turning to loan companies to make ends meet every month.

He said public sector workers had endured a three-year pay freeze and faced another two-year squeeze, leading to growing numbers having to rely on food banks. 'There is a real chance of co-ordinated industrial action, if not this winter, then early next year.'

 Source: Groom, B. (2012) Trade union warns of further strikes, *Financial Times*, 6 September. Http://www.ft.com/cms/s/0/7bb970f2-f836-11e1-b0e1-00144feabdc0.html#axzz2tcGBag9f.
© The Financial Times Limited 2012. All Rights Reserved.

Introduction

The topic of employee 'voice' continues to attract significant interest in both the academic and practitioner communities. Drawing on Lavelle *et al*. (2010: 396), 'voice' is defined here as 'any type of mechanism, structure or practice, which provides an employee with an opportunity to express an opinion or participate in decision-making within their organization'. In broad terms, the expanding empirical and theoretical focus is related to three dynamics. First, increased international competition, reaped by globalisation, and the desire for enhanced organisational performance, has encouraged organisations to seek new means of engaging workers. This links to discussions around behavioural change (e.g. motivation and commitment), soft HRM and the utilisation of high-performance work systems. Secondly, the desire for better systems of employee representation and corporate governance at European level has found expression through the regulation of workforce consultation. A mighty literature has emerged exploring the effect of 'mandated consultation' (e.g. the European Works Council Directive) on the democratic rights of employees, the operation of managerial prerogative and the broader macroeconomic implications of the 'juridification' of the employment relationship. Thirdly, the decline in the coverage of trade unions (indirect voice) and a growing 'representation gap' (Towers, 1997) has stimulated research into the efficacy of 'alternative' (direct) modes of voice. Efficiency in this sense is broadly understood and concerns both the democratic rights of workers and issues of productivity. The argument that employee representation may contribute to both finds voice via the concept of social partnership, a development we discuss in some detail.

Distilling the emergent data, it is clear that management is a far more sophisticated actor than was the case in the recent past when trade union representation was the dominant mode of voice. It is not uncommon to find a 'dualistic' direct and indirect approach in operation with trade unions, company councils, suggestion schemes, problem-solving groups and attitude surveys all utilised within a single organisation. There is evidence to suggest that this 'pick and mix' approach may yield benefits in the form of organisational performance. The precise configuration utilised will be driven by a range of factors, including ownership, sector, employment size and date of establishment (Lavelle *et al*., 2010). Highlighting the potential 'bundling' of interventions, Dundon *et al*. (2004: 1167) have argued that 'management is evidently thinking across the range of [voice] techniques'. This chapter seeks to explore the changing dynamics of workplace voice, shedding light on key developments and controversies. As we shall see, the precise meaning of 'voice' is ambiguous and the goals sought by the parties to the employment relationship 'can vary on economic, moral and pragmatic grounds' (Dundon *et al.*, 2004: 1153). Simply put, voice can ultimately serve different masters (see Muller and Hoffman, 2001: 76).

Given the potential for semantic confusion, this chapter will begin by looking at the voice construct in more depth. Here we draw a distinction between employee involvement and participation. Armed with some conceptual clarity, the subsequent section explores in greater depth the various means by which voice may be operationalised in the workplace, exploring both direct and indirect forms. In terms of the latter, trade union representation was once the dominant mode of voice within the British workplace. We hence pause to devote significant space to this theme, exploring the reasons for the demise of trade union representation and the strategies unions have utilised to recapture lost ground. The final section considers the important theme of 'mandated consultation', i.e. those modes of voice driven at supranational EU level (e.g. European Works Councils).

Definitions

As Dundon and Rollinson (2011: 276) note, the literature on voice can be confusing. Certainly the voice construct has 'multiple meanings' (Timming, 2012: 3253) and too often voice is treated as a loosely specified concept within which a myriad managerial interventions are collapsed. It is commonly accepted nonetheless that voice comprises two discrete components – employee involvement and employee participation (EPI) (see, e.g., Dundon and Rollinson, 2011: 276). Employee involvement and participation, while closely related, are conceptually and philosophically distinct and have similarly achieved prominence during differing historical periods. While writers in this field have long lamented the absence of universally accepted definitions (Pateman, 1970; Hespe and Little, 1971), we are today fortunate in that the terrain of voice is far less theoretically impoverished than it was a generation or so ago. Indeed, following the emergence of the topic as a discrete field of study, it is possible to construct a reasonably precise set of concepts, bringing some much-needed order to the subject matter. Lewis *et al.* (2003: 248) have argued that 'important differences . . . exist between the concepts in relation to the exercise of power, the locus of control, the nature of employee influence, and the driving force behind each approach in practice'. More empirically, Marchington (2005) suggests that it is possible to draw distinctions in terms of the degree of employee involvement; the form that the involvement takes; the level in the organisational hierarchy at which individuals are involved; and the scope of subject matter dealt with. In the final analysis, these models suggest that the essence of any distinction centres on issues of power and influence.

Employee involvement

Employee involvement is central to most models of HRM and, as such, the practice of this mode of voice is linked to aspects of employee engagement (Dundon and Rollinson, 2011: 299–303; see also Chapter 11). Employee involvement is of significant contemporary relevance in light of the economic downturn – according to Duncan Brown of the Institute of Employment Studies, mechanisms responsive to employees' concerns heightened by economically and politically turbulent contexts need to do more than manage and to *engage* people emotionally (cited in Gollan, 2010: 441). Hence employee involvement is characteristically seen as a central tenet of 'soft' HRM, where the focus is upon capturing the ideas of employees and securing their commitment and support for corporate goals. Storey (1992: 46) suggests

Box 14.1 Unitarism

Unitarism is a frame of reference that recognises the shared interests of all members in an organisation. It assumes there are compatible goals, a common purpose, and a single (unitary) interest which means that, if managed effectively the organisation will function harmoniously. This viewpoint assumes that conflict is abnormal and is caused by troublemakers, bad communication and poor management.

Source: Heery and Noon (2001: 388).

that 'soft' HRM 'connotes a style of approach whose touchstones are the careful nurturing of, and investment in, the human stock'. Legge (2005: 105–6) comments that the soft 'developmental humanism' model involves:

> treating employees as valued assets, a source of competitive advantage through their commitment, adaptability and high-quality (of skills, performance and so on) . . . the stress is therefore on generating commitment via 'communication, motivation and leadership'.

As with HRM, the concept of employee involvement is strongly grounded in unitary theory – put simply, it is assumed that managers and employees will 'march to the same tune' (See Box 14.1 and Box 14.2).

Characteristically, employee involvement initiatives are promoted by management with a view to mobilising the support and tacit knowledge of employees towards corporate goals. Marchington and Wilkinson (2005: 390) observe that employee involvement has 'focused on direct participation of small groups and individuals, it is concerned with information sharing at work-group level, and it has excluded the opportunity for workers to have any inputs into high-level decision-making'.

Critics have argued that employee involvement has management firmly in the driving seat and very limited real influence is relinquished or ceded to non-managerial actors. That is, employee involvement schemes 'extend little or no input into corporate or higher level decision making' and generally do not entail any significant sharing of power and authority (Hyman and Mason, 1995: 22). In contrast to employee participation (see the following section), employee involvement is regarded as a weak form of voice (Dundon and Rollinson, 2011: 276). Simply put, employee involvement is 'soft on power' (Blyton and Turnbull, 2004: 272), the hallmark being that management sets the agenda, and information disseminated by management is normally not subject to any decision-making input from employees (Rose, 2008: 341). To the extent that there is any granting of influence to employees, the locus is restricted to task or work-group level (Lewis *et al.*, 2003: 259; Rose, 2008: 341). Any employee 'involvement' in higher-order decisions is restricted to top-down information provision.

Box 14.2 Employee involvement

Practices and policies that emanate from management and sympathisers of free market commercial activity and that purport to provide employees with the opportunity to influence and, where appropriate, take part in the decision-making on matters that affect them.

Source: Hyman and Mason (1995: 21).

> ## Box 14.3 Pluralism
>
> Pluralism is a frame of reference that emphasises the different interests of the members of an organisation. It assumes there are diverse goals and objectives that reflect the many (plural) interests present in an organisation. These differences occur not only between employees and managers but also within these groups. . . . Therefore, the pluralist viewpoint assumes that conflict is a normal part of organsational life and can never be eliminated. Consequently a pluralist will seek ways to manage conflict and thereby limit the negative effects whilst developing some positive, creative aspects that emerge from differences of opinion and ideas.
>
> *Source*: Heery and Noon (2001: 272).

Participation

Employee participation is a very different mode of voice. It is grounded in pluralist thinking – a perspective that acknowledges the presence of divergent interests between different organisational stakeholders (Box 14.3). Henceforth, when using the term 'participation', we refer to *indirect* forms such as consultative committees. Operationally speaking, participation may be contrasted with employee involvement in that it invariably derives from employees, or their organisations (i.e. trade unions), as opposed to being employer-led (Harley *et al.*, 2005: 13). As Hyman and Mason (1995: 29) acknowledge, employee participation 'emerges from a collective employee interest to optimize the physical security and aspirational conditions under which employees are contracted to serve'. The motivation for participation therefore differs fundamentally from employee involvement in that it is born of a desire to increase the influence of employees *vis-à-vis* the employer rather than being concerned with technical issues of corporate efficiency (Box 14.4). Two outcomes follow. First, in contrast to the task-centred menu of practices that normally surround employee involvement, participative modes of voice are fundamentally power-orientated – they are concerned with 'distributive' (Rose, 2008: 340) joint decision-making or co-determination (Blyton and Turnbull, 2004: 59). While mechanisms of participation are concerned with the 'institutionalisation of conflict', industrial action may nevertheless occur in the absence of agreement. This could take the form of strikes, stoppages, working-to-rule or an employer lock-out. Recent examples of industrial discord include disputes within the public sector over pension reform. Secondly, participation is likely to give employees (usually via the agency of their representatives) access to a relatively higher-order 'range' of decisions (e.g. wage rates, introduction of new technology and training, etc.) than that provided by the machinery of employee involvement. In Abrahamsson's (1977: 189) terminology, participation can be viewed as a political process contributing to high-level decision-making as opposed to the 'socio-technical nature' of employee involvement, which restricts tangible employee influence to narrow production issues.

Because participatory schemes generally involve some dilution of managerial influence, there is a long history of employers seeking to resist their encroachment. Consequently, the more enduring examples, such as the works council format found in many European countries, tend to have a strong statutory underpinning and have often been initiated by social democratic governments sensitive to the needs of labour (Payne and Keep, 2005).

> ## Box 14.4 Workers' participation
>
> Workers' participation is about the distribution and exercise of power, in all its manifestations, between the owners and managers of organisations and those employed by them. It refers to the direct involvement of individuals in decisions relating to their immediate work organisation and to indirect involvement in decision-making, through representatives, in the wider socio-technical and political structures of the firm.
>
> *Source*: Brannen (1983: 16).

Table 14.1 Employee involvement and participation compared

Employee involvement	Employee participation
Management-inspired and controlled	Government or workforce-inspired; some control delegated to workforce
Geared to stimulating individual employee contributions	Aims to harness collective employee input through market regulation
Employees are often passive recipients	Employee representatives are actively involved
Tends to be task-based	Decision-making at higher organisational levels
Assumes common interests between employer and employees	Plurality of interests recognised and machinery for their resolution provided

Source: adapted from Hyman and Mason (1995).

In the UK, participation has traditionally found expression through the medium of collective bargaining, rather than via mandated works councils. Collective bargaining (see the section on 'Voice and the demise of collective bargaining') is the mechanism through which trade unions and employers jointly regulate certain aspects of the employment relationship (e.g. negotiating over pay and conditions such as leave entitlements, pensions and working hours). In terms of the level of influence exerted via this process, the traditional trade union preoccupation with wage issues or 'economism' (Hyman, 1989: 45) has ensured that strategic matters, e.g. decisions pertaining to capital investment, have rarely figured as substantive items on the bargaining agenda. Table 14.1 summarises some of the key differences between employee involvement and employee participation.

Key Controversy

If HRM genuinely seeks to empower workers, why is it associated with employee involvement rather than participation?

The practice of voice in the workplace

We will now examine the use of voice in contemporary organisations. As noted, voice comprises techniques of both employee involvement and participation. Drawing on Marchington *et al.* (1992) and Marchington and Wilkinson (2012), three categories of EPI initiatives are pertinent to the theme of voice:

- *Downward communications.* This refers to top-down communication from management to employees. Typical practices include company newspapers, team briefing, communication meetings, video briefing, employee reports and the use of the intranet.

- *Upward problem-solving forms and teamworking.* Upward problem-solving refers to bottom-up communication and involvement structures that are generally designed with the aim of capturing ideas and solving production/service problems (either individually or in small groups). Typical mechanisms include suggestion schemes and quality circles/problem-solving groups. This category could also include attitude surveys which management may implement (or commission) to try to understand more about the general climate within the company and as a mechanism to allow employees to raise concerns and/or ideas for future changes they would like to see. In addition to the typical forms of upward problem-solving already cited, Marchington and Wilkinson (2005) also identify task-based participation, e.g. teamworking and self-management.

- *Representative participation.* This refers to mechanisms for indirect participation, e.g. through trade unions, works councils and consultative committees. It means that employees are represented by elected representatives that have been drawn from their number.

Before we move on to discuss each of these categories in more detail, it is important to highlight a point raised by Marchington (2005) in respect of mechanisms for EPI. It is argued that these must be considered in respect of four dimensions:

1 the degree of involvement (the extent to which employees influence the final decision);

2 the level of involvement (whether at job, departmental or organisational level);

3 the forms of involvement (direct participation, indirect participation and financial);

4 the scope of decisions open to influence by workers, i.e. the type of subject matter dealt with, ranging from the trivial to the strategic.

By considering each of these four dimensions, one can appreciate the relative levels of power and influence that the respective mechanisms allow. As we have already highlighted, a criticism of those modes of voice founded on employee involvement (which are central to HRM) is that they afford very limited power and influence to employees. This is primarily because such mechanisms are essentially controlled by management, who have the final say as to what they will or will not accept. For example, in terms of *degree,* employees may have little influence over a final decision. In terms of *level* of involvement, employee involvement initiatives may essentially be dealing with locally-based production issues (e.g. problem-solving activities). The *form* this mode of voice takes will essentially be determined by management, and the *scope* of subject matter may, for example, revolve around work-based production problems rather than tackling higher-level issues of pay, conditions, redundancies and so on.

By contrast, representative participation (here we refer especially to trade union activities) is not primarily controlled by management, and in the case of trade unions, their organisation and structure are not circumscribed by management. We can contrast employee involvement to representative participation by considering once more the four levels identified by Marchington (2005). Take trade unions as an example – they are more likely to wield power and influence. They tend to have a higher *degree* of influence (if negotiations get tough, trade unions may coordinate industrial action); they may be negotiating at company or sector level (i.e. a high *level* of involvement); their *form* is not dictated by management, participation is indirect and they are likely to be involved in and negotiating on subjects wide in scope. Once the four dimensions are taken into account, one can understand why critics have argued that those voice initiatives associated with HRM represent 'pseudo-participation'.

We will now discuss each of the three categories in more detail.

Key Controversy

Why do critics argue that employee involvement as part of a wider HRM approach represents 'pseudo-participation'? Do employees in British workplaces have the ability to influence key decisions?

Downward communication

Downward communication means top-down communication from management to employees. As indicated, this includes team briefings, company newspapers, communication meetings and the use of the intranet.

A longstanding feature has been the popularity of meetings with the entire workforce or team briefings (see Table 14.2). Holden (2004) explains that team briefing systems are

Table 14.2 Mechanisms for employee involvement (per cent of workplaces)

	2004	2011
All staff workplace meetings	75	80
Team briefings	60	66
Provision of information on workplace finances	55	61
Staff surveys	36	37
Problem-solving groups	17	14

Source: abridged from van Wanrooy *et al.* (2013: 18).

normally used to cascade managerial messages down the organisation. Although team briefing arrangements may vary, they are normally given to relatively small groups and (in terms of content) often focus on issues affecting production or service, targets, etc. Team briefings are essentially a top-down form of communication, but there is often some opportunity for employees to exercise voice, e.g. by asking questions or perhaps even to lodge comments, queries or concerns. Evidence tends to show that team briefing systems work better when the briefers are properly trained. While evidence indicates that team briefing sessions are generally welcomed, problems can also emerge. For example, some studies have shown a tendency for team briefing sessions to be cancelled when production pressures are high (Glover, 2001). Also, critics have noted that team briefing sessions can be used to brief against existing trade unions or to try to dissuade employees from seeking union recognition in non-union firms. In 2011, 66 per cent of British workplaces utilised team briefings – up from 60 per cent in 2004 (van Wanrooy *et al.*, 2013: 18).

Newsletters remain popular, especially in the public sector. Holden (2004) notes that newsletters can often be welcomed, but a potential limitation is that management retain editorial control – as such, it is less likely that newsletters would be used as a direct form of voice to air employee grievances. It is likely that instances of usage of e-mail and intranet will increase in years to come as more companies make use of these facilities. The most widely used format for information dissemination is meetings involving all staff, used in 80 per cent of workplaces in 2011 – up from 75 per cent in 2004 (van Wanrooy *et al.*, 2013: 28).

Upward problem-solving and teamworking

Upward problem-solving mechanisms (such as suggestion schemes and problem-solving groups) are generally designed for the purpose of capturing ideas and solving production and service problems (see Table 14.2). Task-based participation and teamworking can also be considered here. They are more substantive in nature, as 'employees are encouraged or expected to extend the range and type of tasks undertaken' (Marchington and Wilkinson, 2012: 352). Surveys are another important source of upward communication, and are used in 37 per cent of British workplaces (Van Wanrooy *et al.*, 2013: 18).

Suggestion schemes work on the principle that employees submit suggestions. The suggestion is then reviewed by managers, and a decision will be made as to whether to accept the suggestion or reject it. If the suggestion is accepted, the employee will generally receive a direct financial reward. Such rewards may equate to a percentage of the overall saving that the suggestion will bring. Some companies may put a cap on the amount of cash that can be rewarded, but may 'top up' with other products or services.

Upward problem-solving also includes problem-solving groups (often referred to as quality circles in the 1990s). Problem-solving groups, utilised in 14 per cent of workplaces (Van Wanrooy *et al.*, 2013: 18), are generally small in nature (e.g. six to eight people) and normally meet on a voluntary basis. They are most common in education (27 per cent) and public administration (25 per cent) (van Wanrooy *et al.*, 2013: 18). The purpose of such 'offline' (Marchington and Wilkinson, 2012: 352) groups is to identify quality or work-related problems and to produce a solution to the problem. Some organisations will offer problem-solving groups administrative support, training and trained facilitators. Also, most groups will meet in work time. However, in contrast to suggestion schemes, there is not normally a direct financial reward for the solutions and ideas generated by such groups.

In addition to these more traditional forms of upward problem-solving, Marchington and Wilkinson (2012: 352) identify task-based participation and teamworking which, they argue, are 'integral to the work itself' rather than being additional or incidental to working arrangements. They explain that task-based participation can occur 'both horizontally and vertically' (Marchington and Wilkinson, 2005: 390). The former means that employees engage in a wider variety of tasks, but these are at a similar skill level. Vertical participation means that employees, 'may be trained to undertake tasks at a higher skill level or they may be given some managerial and supervisory responsibilities' (Marchington and Wilkinson, 2005: 392).

The concept of teamworking is closely linked to task-based participation and is now seen as a central feature of HRM (Mueller and Proctor, 2000). For example, the term 'multiskilling' is similar to horizontal task-based participation, essentially meaning that employees will move around tasks and will not be bound by strict job demarcation. While teamworking is widely reported in Britain, evidence still suggests that much of this is fairly low-level and that instances of semi-autonomous and self-managing teams are less common (Geary, 2003). Some would argue that self-managing teams are the ultimate in direct participation (and as such there is quite some way to go in the UK). Others, however, would argue that self-managing teams represent the ultimate form of management control in that they work on the basis of peer pressure and surveillance and are not genuinely liberating because they are always under the control of management (Garrahan and Stewart, 1992; Sewell and Wilkinson, 1992; Taylor et al., 2002). Yet others have argued that teamworking tends to offer mixed consequences – and it is too stark to argue that the outcomes of it are either 'all good' or 'all bad'.

Beyond these examples of 'formal' modes of voice, such practices may be 'informal' i.e. 'ad hoc or non-programmed interactions between managers and their staff' (Marchington and Wilkinson, 2012: 363). While limited attention has been paid to this mode of voice, Marchington and Wilkinson (2012: 363) observe that managers find such interactions useful – they may be used to inform workers about new developments in work organisation and to provide opportunities for discussion. Both sets of practices will often operate in tandem given their complementary nature, e.g. informal systems may be used to follow up on formal statements to allay worker fears and concerns.

Explore

- Do organisations make most use of formal or informal modes of voice?
- Might the balance be related to the size of the organisation?
- What are the advantages of each?

From teamworking to high-performance management

An important contemporary development closely allied to the theme of upward problem-solving and teamwork has been the emergence of the high-performance management (HPM) phenomenon– sometimes similarly referred as high-performance work practices (HPWP) or high-commitment management (see also Chapter 1). Following the work of Bélanger et al. (2002), HPM may be viewed as a combination of three elements. The first dimension, production management, is concerned with aspects of productive flexibility and process standardisation. A key facet here is *hard* quality management which characteristically involves the use of statistical tools to analyse variance from tolerance margins at each stage of the production process (Wilkinson et al., 1998), which is subsumed within a wider total quality management format. A quite distinct second dimension relates to work organisation. Here there has been a trend towards production activities based on knowledge, cognition and abstract labour. The centrepiece of the approach is teamworking. The practice of sharing skills across traditional demarcations 'is thus a fundamental feature of the emergent model' (Bélanger *et al.*, 2002: 39). The third sphere, 'employment relations', very much underpins the coherence of the former two components given the requirement for a committed, rather than a merely compliant workforce (Bélanger *et al.*, 2002: 42–48). Two significant features emerge. First, Bélanger *et al.* (2002) state there is a desire to align and support task flexibility via terms and conditions of employment. This is typically sought by making pay contingent on group performance (Appelbaum, 2002: 124). Secondly, HRM professionals are charged with the pursuit of social adhesion and commitment to the new production format and wider organisational goals. This involves 'efforts to fashion employment conditions and the modes of regulation of those conditions in such a way as to elicit the tacit skills of the workers and tie them more closely to the goals of the firm' (Bélanger *et al.*, 2002: 44). In other words, the central task becomes the inculcation of a unitary organisational culture, or, in Guest's (2002: 338) terms, the creation of a social system in support of the technical system.

There are clear linkages here to the soft HRM agenda. In considering how HPM or HPWP translate individual and group performance into financial performance, the resource-based view of the firm (see Chapter 2) has become the dominant theory (see Tregaskis *et al.*, 2013). In the resource-based view, an organisation gains competitive advantage if it possesses resources that enable it to act on the environment but are costly for competitors to imitate. HPM can achieve competitive advantage for an organisation by fostering valuable and unique contributions from workers with a system of HR practices that are difficult for competitors to imitate (see Tregaskis *et al.*, 2013 for a summary of the key literature).

The impact of HPM on organisational performance

The driving force behind the introduction of HPM is to enhance organisational performance. In recent years the underlying assumption that HPM necessarily gives rise to positive improvements in performance has been subject to detailed investigation. That HPM has the *potential* to enhance organisational performance appears to be well settled (see, e.g., Appelbaum *et al.*, 2000). However, as Tregaskis *et al.* (2013) argue, the research on HPM is open to criticism on several grounds. First, there is a heavy reliance on large-scale cross-sectional survey data, which are problematic with regard to claims of causality. Secondly, many studies rely on reports of managers, which might reflect organisational policy but not necessarily implementation of that policy. Thirdly, while some longitudinal research has been undertaken, the evidence is mixed, often because of a reliance on informant recall of past interventions or because objective performance indicators have only been collected following the event rather than before or during it.

Notwithstanding these caveats, research suggests a significant role for HPM *vis-à-vis* organisational competitiveness (e.g. Brewster *et al.*, 2008: Easterby Smith *et al.*, 2009; Bae *et al.*, 2011) and certainly, there is much anecdotal evidence to support such a proposition (see Stone *et al.*, 2012). These findings are reinforced by recent research by Tregaskis *et al.* (2013) into the implementation of HPM within a heavy engineering multinational company. Employing a longitudinal research design, the results indicate that the implementation of HPM in the form of training, performance management, communications (e.g. team briefings and newsletters) and work reorganisation was associated with sustained and beneficial changes in both productivity and safety. Tregaskis *et al.* (2013) move on to explore the important black box issue, i.e. they seek to explicate the rationale for the association. 'Tentatively' it is suggested that the introduction of HPM improvements in working conditions is followed by gains in motivation, which lead to enhanced skill use and productivity. However, an important issue remains as to whether the use of HPM has universal applicability – i.e. are such interventions only appropriate for certain types of industry or product market strategies (see Ashton and Sung, 2002: 165)? Schuler and Jackson (cited in Wood, 1999) have highlighted the need to link a Taylorist control approach with cost minimisation, and HPM to a quality-oriented strategy. In other words, HPM is only seen to be a suitable solution in certain circumstances; in others it may be economically rational to combine low involvement with low employee skill and commitment (see Boxall and Macky, 2009: 11). As such, an important policy issue concerns inadequate management skills, especially in small and medium-sized enterprises (SMEs), coupled with a lack of ambition for business improvements (Stone *et al.*, 2012: 82).

Explore

- Consider an organisation with which you are familiar – to what extent is there evidence of the use of HPM practices?

Representative participation

The final category of voice to be considered – representative participation – has been influential for over a century. This was traditionally the dominant mode of voice within the UK. As such, we devote significant space to this topic. This format is sometimes referred to as 'indirect participation' because it takes effect through the agency of elected representatives. Such mechanisms include non-union works councils (NERS), mandated modes of consultation (i.e. those invoked by recent European Directives) and trade unionism. The first two channels are afforded critical coverage later in this section. Here we focus on collective voice as provided by the major British trade unions, e.g. Unite, GMB and Unison.

Trade union representation

Trade union representation is of immense significance because it was the foremost mode of voice up until the 1980s. Trade union voice reached its zenith in the late 1970s when there were 13.3 million trade union members (Charlwood and Metcalfe, 2005), equating to 54 per cent of the working population (Dundon and Rollinson, 2011: 142). Members' demands and concerns were voiced by well over 300,000 workplace representatives or 'shop stewards' (Terry, 2010: 278). Expanding membership afforded the unions with immense industrial 'muscle' and political influence. Against the backdrop of an upsurge in industrial action, public policy became preoccupied with 'the challenge from below' (Flanders, 1965). The central concern was how the increasing power and influence of the unions might be harnessed constructively to tackle the principal political and economic issues of the day; namely, restrictive practices, strikes and inflation (cf. the Donovan Report, 1965–68). Much has changed, of course. Nowadays only around 26 per cent of the workforce is unionised (BIS, 2011: 7) and the number of workplace representatives is down, estimated at 125,000 (Charlwood and Forth, 2009). Academic commentators are predominantly preoccupied nowadays with the membership crisis and potential strategies for renewal (Terry, 2003).

Despite the evident atrophy of trade union power and influence, these institutions continue to warrant examination in any critical evaluation of voice for three principal reasons. First, levels of membership have held up well within certain parts of the economy, most notably the public sector where around 59 per cent of workers are unionised (Marchington *et al.*, 2011: 39). Secondly, it is commonly accepted that it is only through independent collective trade union representation that employees can overcome the asymmetry of power that resides at the heart of the employment relationship (see, e.g., Flanders, 1968). From this perspective, it is questionable whether the alternative (unitary and direct) modes of voice outlined earlier can ever be effective in articulating the demands of employees. They amount at best to 'pseudo' or 'phantom participation' (see Ramsay, 1980). Thirdly, trade unions have not been passive actors, and a range of tactics (e.g. partnership working) have been employed (see later) – with some degree of success to arrest membership decline. As such, we devote significant space to this once dominant mode of voice. Initially a brief overview is provided of the institution of 'collective bargaining', the classic means by which the voice of employees was traditionally mobilised to influence their terms and conditions of employment. We then pause to consider the reasons for membership decline, evaluating *inter alia* the impact of Thatcherism and structural change to the British economy. The shifting fortunes of trade unionism under New Labour (1997–2010) and the Conservative Liberal Democrat Coalition (2010–) are similarly considered.

Key Controversy

Trade union membership has declined significantly over the last 30 years or so. Does this indicate unions no longer have an important a role to play in the workplace?

Voice and the demise of collective bargaining

According to Brown (2010: 255), the term collective bargaining is used when trade unions are involved in negotiation about the employment relationship. The outcomes become, in effect, contractual terms of employment. Collective bargaining is hence concerned with *joint* regulation. As such, it represents a pluralist concept which recognises that the balance of bargaining power between the employer and single employee is uneven (Rose, 2008: 274). Through the institution of collective bargaining, workers are able to mobilise their collective power to influence certain – but by no means all – of the rules governing the employment relationship.

The outcome of negotiation and the collective bargaining process is a document called the 'collective agreement'. This contains both substantive and procedural rules. The former sets out the terms and conditions of employment, while the latter governs the behaviour and interaction of managers, workers and trade unions (Heery and Noon, 2001: 43). In line with the troubled fortunes of British trade unionism, there has been a significant contraction in the coverage of collective bargaining (see Tables 14.3 and 14.4). In 1970, such negotiations covered approximately 70 per cent of the workforce. It has since declined to around 23 per cent (van Wanrooy *et al.*, 2013: 22). In the private sector coverage has diminished to no more than one worker in five (Brown, 2010). As such, access to this form of voice is now a minority phenomenon in British workplaces. The influence of collective bargaining *where it is still found* has been similarly maginalised, i.e. the 'scope' of the issues covered by negotiation has narrowed. The percentage of all unionised workplaces normally negotiating over pay, hours and holidays fell from 33 per cent in 2004 to 25 per cent in 2011 (van Wanrooy *et al.*, 2013: 23). Similarly, as Terry (2010: 279–80) notes, a succession of Workplace Employment Relations Study (WERS) analyses point to a decline in joint regulation (negotiation) as the dominant mode of interaction between union representatives and management and its replacement by consultation or the provision of information. British trade unions have traditionally viewed consultation as a weak form of engagement (Terry, 2010: 285).

Table 14.3 Collective bargaining coverage – workplaces with any collective bargaining

	Public	Private	All
2004	70%	8%	16%
2011	58%	6%	13%

Table 14.4 Collective bargaining coverage – employees covered by collective bargaining

	Public	Private	All
2004	69%	17%	29%
2011	44%	16%	23%

Source: van Wanrooy *et al.* (2013: 22).

For some commentators (e.g. Brown, 2010: 272), these developments are disturbing because collective bargaining is deemed 'to lie at the heart of a pluralist approach to employment, one that expects management to make a case for changing workers' lives, and for those workers to have some opportunity [i.e. voice] to argue about it'. Ironically, beyond matters pertaining to pluralist ideals of organisational democracy, the collapse of collective bargaining and the resultant diminution of voice may have implications for organisational efficiency and HRM. It is well accepted that the provision of voice reduces the need for 'exit' (see Rogers and Streeck, 1994: 11–15), e.g. by affording a channel for employees to air grievances, thus cutting employers' hiring and training costs. This line of analysis is consistent with Chamberlain and Kuhn's (1965: 130) notion of collective bargaining as serving a 'decision making function' in giving employees the opportunity, if they wish, to participate in the determination of the policies which guide and rule their working lives.

Key Controversy

Does the collapse of collective bargaining in the private sector indicate workers have 'lost their voice'?

Trade union decline: rationale

The underlying reasons for the emasculation of trade union voice have attracted significant academic comment. The main lines of argument are well summarised elsewhere (see, e.g., Blyton and Turnbull, 2004; Rose, 2008: 161–63; Williams and Adam-Smith, 2010: 215–19). Here we restrict comment to a brief synopsis of the key arguments that have been advanced. First, it has been argued that the Conservative (1979–1997) legislative onslaught on the unions was critical in undermining union security and allowing managers to limit union influence. The Conservatives were influenced to a significant degree by the writings of the economist Friederich Hayek, who depicted unions as 'unjustifiably coercive institutions' (Smith, 2009: 338). It was thus argued by Hayek that the whole basis of a 'free society was threatened by the power arrogated by the unions' (cited in Smith, 2009: 338). Drawing inspiration from Hayek, the Conservatives proceeded to abolish most of the statutory and administrative supports for collective agreements (see Smith 2009: 340) and implemented much of Hayek's prescriptive agenda (e.g. restriction of picketing, abolition of the closed shop and liability in tort for the unions; see Smith, 2009: 339). The crucial mediating impact of the restrictive legal environment has been most fully developed by Freeman and Pelletier (1990). Secondly, the changing composition of employment has been influential. The essence of this argument is that employment has contracted in those areas where unions were once strong (e.g. coal mining and motor vehicle manufacturing). Most employment growth has been in the private service sector where work is often undertaken by, for example, women part-time workers (Williams and Adam-Smith, 2010: 218) who are difficult to mobilise. This thesis is sometimes referred to as the 'mountain gorilla hypothesis' (Blyton and Turnbull, 2004: 141) – the unions' natural habitat is seen to be dying out. A third related argument is that co-terminous with declining union power and influence, union membership no longer brings advantages in terms of a wage premium. The benefits of membership have plausibly been further eroded because of the floor of individual rights (e.g. the national minimum wage) enacted by the New Labour government and the emergence of a statutory system of employee representation (Terry, 2010: 282–9) under the Information and Consultation Directive (see later). Allied to this is the claim that workers are increasingly individualistic, consumer-orientated and less prone to the appeal of collective solidarity (Kelly, 1998), i.e. they have become 'turned off' by trade unionism. Finally, there is the potential impact of a more unitary managerial style to be considered. The decline in *collective* trade union voice coincided with the emergence of the HRM phenomenon which is premised on an *individualistic* approach to managing the employment relationship. 'Soft HRM' makes use of the direct managerially inspired modes of voice discussed earlier. The utilisation of these alternative voice arrangements may have contributed to a reduced enthusiasm for indirect voice.

Key Controversy

How might the collapse in trade union membership best be explained? Is the presence of strong and autonomous trade unionism compatible with organisational efficiency?

Opportunities for renaissance? Trade union voice under New Labour: 'Fairness not favours'

While the 1980s and 1990s represented an inhospitable backdrop for collective voice, the return of a (New) Labour government in 1997 signalled an apparent shift in public policy. As Dickens and Hall (2010: 303) observe, whereas the Conservatives had promoted flexibility at the expense of security, by contrast New Labour sought to create a flexible labour market underpinned by 'fair, minimum standards'. The ideological compass for this ambitious agenda was the so called 'third way'. The precise meaning of this somewhat nebulous construct has been subject to much debate. According to McIlroy (1998: 543), it was clearly neo-unitary as it represented, 'a modernised unitary perspective in which New Labour re-legitimised collectivism but on one central condition: that it imbricated with management objectives'. More optimistically perhaps, the third way could be conceived as an innovative brand of capitalism; a compromise between the harshness of liberal market economies (e.g. the USA and Thatcherite Britain) and the dirigisme of coordinated market economies of Western Europe (e.g. German and Scandinavia).

What is not in doubt is the fact that the practical outcome of the third way agenda was New Labour's 'adoption of much of the neo liberal inheritance' (Smith and Morton, 2006: 402) of their Conservative predecessors. Thus, by the close of the New Labour project in 2010, key elements of the Conservative's anti-union legislation (e.g. illegality of the closed shop and tight restrictions on industrial action) remained firmly in place with 'minor amendment' (Smith and Morton, 2006: 404). The principal point of departure was the legislation on trade union recognition contained within the Employment Relations Act 1999. The Act forces an employer to recognise a trade union and 'bargain in good faith' (Taylor and Emir, 2009: 539), where the majority of employees in a defined bargaining group or unit support union representation. According to Dickens and Hall (2010: 309), 'the recognition procedure *clearly* demarcated the New Labour government's approach to industrial relations from that of their Conservative predecessors' (emphasis added). Other commentators (e.g. Smith and Morton, 2006) are more critical in their appraisal (see the next section). The legislation (briefly summarised in Box 14.5) was significant because previously (in line with the 'voluntarist' tradition of British labour law) there was an absence of regulatory support for recognition – even in instances of high union membership.

Box 14.5 Statutory trade union recognition

1 Recognition can only be required by law if the parties fail to sign a voluntary agreement.
2 A trade union commences the process by requesting recognition from an employer. It must identify the 'bargaining unit' it wishes to represent. At this point the employer has three choices – accept the request; accept in principle but disagree with the bargaining unit; or refuse the request.
3 Where there is disagreement on the details, the employer and union are expected to negotiate an agreement – with the help of a government body – the Advisory Conciliation

Box 14.5 continued

and Arbitration Service (ACAS) if necessary. Where the employer refused the request the union can apply to the Central Arbitration Committee (CAC) for a decision.

4   Where the CAC is satisfied that 50 per cent of the members of the bargaining group are union members, a recognition is made unless:
    (a) It decides a ballot should be held in the interests of good industrial relations.
    (b) A significant number of union members write to inform the CAC that they do not wish the union to bargain on their behalf.
    (c) Other evidence is produced which leads to the same conclusion.
    In such circumstances, there must be a secret ballot.

5   Where the union does not have 50 per cent membership of the bargaining group, it can seek to persuade the CAC that the majority of the workforce would be likely to support recognition. In practice the union has to have the support of at least 10 per cent of the relevant workforce and to show that it would be more than likely to win a recognition ballot. Where the CAC is satisfied, it orders a recognition ballot to be held.

6   The union side wins the ballot if (a) the majority of those voting and (b) at least 40 per cent of the workers support the recognition proposal.

7   Where unions are successful under the statutory procedure, collective bargaining must cover pay, hours and holidays as a minimum.

Source: abridged from Taylor and Emir (2009: 539–41).

Statutory trade union recognition: a critique

While the statutory recognition procedure provided some support for collective trade union voice, collectivism was not reinstated as public policy (Smith, 2009: 340). Labour refused, for example, to rescind Conservative changes that removed the promotion of collective bargaining from the ACAS terms of reference (Smith, 2009: 340). The substantive content of the legislation has itself been robustly criticised at several levels. First, the statutory recognition procedure does not cover organisations with fewer than 20 employees. Employees in small organisations thus have no right to redress under the legislation, even where there is majority trade union support. Secondly, applications cannot be made to the CAC when an organisation already recognises either a union or another collective body (Taylor and Emir, 2009: 541), no matter how partially. As such, an employer can, for example, avoid recognising a *bona fide* trade union by 'negotiating' with a staff association that it has set up itself (Taylor and Emir, 2009: 541) in direct contravention of International Labour Organisation conventions (Smith and Morton, 2006: 407). Thirdly, in those instances where a union is successful in obtaining recognition, the designated 'scope' of any agreement is narrow, covering just pay, hours and holidays. Recognition agreements within the UK have traditionally been far more encompassing, covering, for example, working conditions, staffing levels and redeployment. Finally, the rules governing trade union access to workers during a recognition drive are complex (see Smith and Morton 2006: 407). Current procedures 'embody employers' wishes at almost every turn' (Smith and Morton, 2006: 407). One corollary has been an increase in anti-union consultants or American-style 'union busters' (Gall, 2003: 87) offering advice on how best to manipulate the various loopholes. Overall it has been argued that the complex statutory procedure has contributed to the unions' reduced effectiveness (Smith, 2009: 352). Certainly the decline in levels of union recognition has continued. The percentage of all workplaces with recognised unions fell from 24 to 21 per cent between 2004 and 2011 (van Wanrooy *et al.*, 2013: 14). Smith (2009: 348) argues that the key point of contrast between New Labour and their Conservative predecessors is that the former sought to 'domesticate rather than exclude workers' voice'. An important component of this 'domestication' was the promotion of workplace partnership – a theme we turn to in our consideration of the union response.

Key Controversy

Was New Labour's 'third way' (1997–2010) a genuine departure from Conservative policy (1979–1997)? Did New Labour adopt a unitary or pluralist approach as the basis for their dealings with the unions?

Trade union voice under the Coalition government

Coalition politics under the Conservatives and Liberal Democrats (2010–) has not significantly altered the dynamics of trade union voice. The favourable legislation on trade union recognition remains on the statute book, as does the restrictive Thatcherite legislation that sought to curb union militancy. As Dundon and Rollinson (2011: 183) observe, 'debate remains as to the substance of any similarity as well as any real or meaningful divergence in the respective ideological positions of all mainstream political parties in Britain'. Inevitably, the requirement to reduce the budget deficit and the imposition of a pay freeze for many workers have strained relations between the Coalition and public-sector unions (see the Introductory case study). While there has been some deregulation of the labour market (e.g. alterations to protection against unfair dismissal), the apparatus of collective labour law remains virtually intact. Guarded warnings have emanated from the Liberal Democrat business secretary Vince Cable that if strikes were to impose significant damage to the economy the pressure to further amend strike legislation 'would ratchet up' (BBC, 2011), but so far there has been an absence of legislation to match the rhetoric. Partly reflective of public-sector job losses, trade union membership has continued to decline under the coalition. Currently around 6.4 million people are trade union members, down by 143,000 in 2010. In the public sector, union membership levels fell by 186,000 to 3.9 million in 2011, after remaining broadly stable at around 4.1 million over the previous six years (BIS, 2011:7).

Trade union voice and membership loss: strategies for renewal

The overall environment in which British trade unions operate has become increasingly inhospitable in recent years. As noted, the reasons for this are manifold. Significantly, a shift to a more unitary managerial style, structural change to the economy (e.g. demise of manufacturing) and state policy severely impacted membership levels. The unions, however, have not been passive actors and a range of strategies have been implemented as the unions have sought to rejuvenate their fortunes and '[re]make their own histories' (Carter, 2000: 118). Implicit in the various responses is an acceptance that issues internal to the unions themselves, e.g. inadequate recruitment programmes and failure to deliver effective benefits to the membership, have, at least in part, contributed to their travails (Waddington and Kerr, 2009: 28).

Boosting trade union voice: servicing and organising

The use of the servicing and organising to stave off membership loss has attracted much controversy within the trade union movement. The servicing model, which was initially adopted in the late 1980s, is based on the notion that trade unions should embrace the increasing social tendencies towards instrumentality and consumerism and extend the range of individually orientated services on offer (e.g. credit cards, mortgages and legal advice). The utility of this approach has been robustly questioned by traditionalists; not least because data indicate that the provision of such services is not high on the list of reasons why working people join trade unions (see Waddington and Whitson, 1997). The inherent limitations of the above 'top-down' format premised on union members as 'passive recipients of service and support' (Waddington and Kerr, 2009: 28) resulted in increased interest in the so-called 'organising' model. This is a 'bottom up' approach, used successfully in the USA (e.g. 'justice for janitors') and Australia, which seeks to empower workers and stimulate activism (Heery, 2003: 27).

According to Waddington and Kerr (2009: 27–54), organising 'is an approach to union membership and renewal that encourages local union activity, greater self reliance and a collective identity'. Associated practices include person-to-person recruitment, based on the assumption that 'like recruits like', the mapping of workplaces to locate non-members and targeting of particular groups of potential members (Waddington and Kerr, 2009: 28). In terms of outcomes, organising unionism has delivered some success in recognition campaigns (Williams and Adam-Smith, 2010: 247), but overall it has failed to renew union fortunes on a national scale (Heery and Simms, 2008: 24).

Commentators suggest that a variety of constraints have impeded progress to date – the following list is by no means exhaustive. First, the overall proportion of resources devoted to organising is low and the most ambitious attempts to promote an 'organising culture' have been found in small to medium-sized unions (Heery, 2003:29). Secondly, it has been suggested there may be opposition to organising from within unions by those whose interests are threatened. These might include full-time officials whose skills (e.g. bargaining and representation) are ill-suited to an organising strategy (Heery and Simms, 2008: 25). Thirdly, unions have often encountered stiff opposition from employers and the use of US-style 'union busting tactics' (Gall, 2003). Given the latter problem, it is ironic that the third renewal strategy 'partnership', considered in the following section, is premised on cooperation and collaboration.

Key Controversy

Are trade unions in terminal decline? What opportunities exist for the rejuvenation of their fortunes?

Enter partnership

The limitations and partial gains attributable to 'servicing' and 'organising' afforded space for a third renewal strategy: partnership. This approach to industrial relations was strongly promoted by the New Labour government (1997–2010). During New Labour's first term, the administration sought to broker interest in partnership through a combination of legislative intervention, public-sector reform and 'micro level exhortation' (see Martinez Lucio and Stewart, 2002: 252). The creation of a dedicated Partnership Fund was particularly influential in showcasing a burgeoning number of partnership agreements, many of which were to be found in organisations undergoing substantial restructuring (Kelly, 2005: 191). These developments and their implications have attracted significant comment over the last decade or so (see Johnstone et al., 2009 for an overview).

Partnership is of interest within the HR field because there is evidence that its use is often associated with the take-up of employee involvement, which, as we have seen, is a central feature of mainstream HRM. Thus, Butler et al. (2013) refer to 'forward synergies' where partnership may be used to imbue organisational change programmes, which often utilise techniques of employee involvement, with a measure of legitimacy. This suggests that (pluralist) trade unionism and (unitary) HRM are not necessarily incompatible bedfellows. There is similarly evidence indicating that HR practitioners enjoy working under such systems (see Glover and Butler, 2012) because of the focus on collaborative industrial relations.

At a conceptual level, it is well accepted that partnership is an imprecise term (see Heery, 2003), comprising arrangements that can function at a variety of levels – state, sector and company (Heery, 2003:21). In the UK at least, partnership, where utilised, operates primarily at a workplace or company level. In this context, partnership refers to the negotiation of a distinctive partnership agreement between unions and management, which is intended to promote more cooperative relations within the firm (Heery, 2003: 21). Accordingly, for Guest and Peccei (cited in Johnstone et al., 2009), trust and mutuality are the key comments of a genuine partnership agreement. The precise nature of 'mutuality' or the *quid pro quo* will sometimes be formally defined within the partnership agreement (e.g. flexibility of labour in exchange for job security), although in so-called 'de facto' arrangements the precise 'trade-off' may be more implicit than explicit (see Butler *et al.*, 2011).

Partnership: impact on trade unions and their membership

Partnership, as a strategy for trade union renewal, has been the source of much contestation (see Box 14.6). There is some evidence that partnership working can strengthen the effectiveness of trade unions and, by inference, boost membership (Samuel, 2005). Critics, however, argue that the guarantees of security and union participation in the decision-making process are not realistic over the long term (see Heery, 2003 for a summary of the key arguments). From this perspective it is suggested that the credibility and legitimacy of unions will suffer if the partnership gamble 'fails to deliver'. A related argument is that under such arrangements union full-time officials are prone to incorporation or 'sell out'. That is, they become too close to their managerial counterparts – a development that is likely to undermine union autonomy and hence suppress, rather than boost, membership.

In terms of outcomes, the lion's share of the data points towards a 'constrained mutuality' (Guest and Peccei, 2001: 231). That is, the 'balance of advantage', in terms of the principles endorsed and practices in place, often leans heavily towards management. Hence, Martinez Lucio and Stuart (2002) have identified that concerns over employment security remain problematic and there is often a gap between the rhetoric of partnership and the experience of trade unionists on the ground. Suff and Williams (2004: 33) conclude that 'the reality of market relations and the balance of power in the employment relationship imply that genuine mutuality is likely to be unobtainable in practice'. More recently, Glover *et al.* (2013) have argued that approaches that are overly polarised may underplay the complexities of partnership – their research indicates the potential for a more variegated set of outcomes. In their study of partnership in the heavy engineering sector, it was found that, on the one hand, partnership resulted in heightened bonus payments and job security, while, on the other, there were examples of unfair managerial treatment and inconsistencies in managerial style. It is concluded that worker outcomes may be far from clear-cut and there is a need for researchers to differentiate between hard gains (e.g. bonuses and increased headcount) and soft gains (opportunities for personal growth and development) if the true implications for employees are to be accurately audited.

Box 14.6   Workplace partnership – polarised perspectives

Optimistic

- Union renewal, legitimacy, renaissance, organisation
- Organisational success, competitiveness, productivity
- Employee involvement, quality of working life
- Win–win
- Greater job security
- Better working conditions
- Higher productivity

Pessimistic

- Union incorporation, emasculation
- Work intensification
- Surveillance
- Co-option
- Employee disillusionment
- Zero sum

Source: Johnstone *et al.* (2009: 264).

Partnership: summary and prognosis

The weight of evidence suggests that partnership has failed to take root in the British context. The fragility of such pacts founded on voluntary consensus has been linked to the British variant of capitalism. It has long been accepted by institutional analysts that partnership and the 'shareholder primacy norm' (Deakin *et al.*, 2005: 68;) residing at the heart of neo-liberal systems of corporate governance are likely to make for uneasy bedfellows. The most tenacious exponent of this position is the German academic Wolfgang Streeck. Simply put, Streeck's thesis centres on the voluntaristic tradition of British industrial relations, which is viewed as incongruent with long-lasting union–management cooperation (see Butler *et al.*, 2011 for a summary). Streeck (1998: 200) has argued that within the British context 'short-term economic contingencies typically create temptations for employers to defect from long-term beneficial arrangements'. This contrasts with the German experience, where 'beneficial constraints' in the form of hard regulation, e.g. the laws on codetermination, 'impose sufficiently strong sanctions to make opportunistic withdrawal from reciprocal obligations highly unlikely' (Streeck, 1998: 202). In summary, successful partnership arrangements within the British context are unlikely to emerge unless there is a specific constellation of supportive factors in place that may substitute for 'hard regulation', e.g. strong trade unions, managerial skill and political sensitivity and trust. The dearth of such factors in the British context ultimately renders partnership a high-risk union strategy.

Distilling all this material, it is evident the once powerful mode of representative voice provided by trade unions has been severely weakened. It is unlikely that the level of trade union coverage will return to that experienced in the heady days of the 1970s – at least for the foreseeable future. This dynamic has stimulated interest in alternative modes of collective representation and it is to these that we now turn.

Non-union systems of employee voice: a unitary approach to collective representation?

It has become commonplace for commentators to posit the presence of a 'representation gap' (Towers, 1997). Given the scale of trade union decline outlined in the previous section, such accounts are often treated as beyond reproach. In one sense, however, this orthodoxy is problematic. As Millward *et al.* (2000: 124) acknowledge, the decline in trade union coverage has been matched by 'a major shift to non-union forms of voice'. While such non-union arrangements can take a variety of forms (including, of course, employee involvement), macro-level survey data (i.e. WERS) indicates that a significant number of non-union firms possess workplace-level joint consultative (i.e. non-union) modes of employee representation (NERs). Sometimes these may be used as part of a sophisticated HRM approach (Williams and Adam-Smith, 2010: 224). This might suggest that the absolute magnitude of the purported representation gap characteristically 'read off' from statistics relating to trade union coverage has been somewhat overplayed. At the very least, in view of the decline in both union recognition and the coverage of collective bargaining, questions concerning the effectiveness of non-union modes of voice become ever more pertinent. We consider the NER phenomenon in detail next.

NER defined

Non-union employee representation structures represent components of the wider phenomenon of employee participation (see Box 14.4). Being *representative* structures, NERs, like trade unions, embody indirect employee participation. Such institutions, therefore, perform an agency function and must consequently be distinguished from direct forms of employee voice (employee involvement), e.g. briefing and problem-solving groups discussed earlier. They may be viewed as a sub-species of the works council format, which Rogers and Streeck

(1995: 6) have defined as 'institutionalized bodies for representative communication between a single employer ("management") and the employees ("workforce") of a single plant or enterprise ("workplace")'. As Hespe and Little (1971: 329) observe, however, 'works councils can mean different things in different countries', and indeed within the UK the traditional lack of legal prescription renders the NER phenomenon particularly amorphous. Consequently, in terms of form, a diverse range of permutations are possible. Following Biagi's (1998: 484) modelling, workplace representative bodies may be analysed along two dimensions relating to their structural and functional properties. With regard to the former aspect, NERs may, for example, represent both managerial and non-managerial grades, or, as is common, solely the latter grouping. In respect of function, the terms of reference of the bodies might extend to issues distributional in character (e.g. wage bargaining) and/or items more integrational in nature, such as productivity matters. Additionally, and crucially, competence is similarly apt to vary from the right to information through to 'meaningful consultation'. Depending upon the context, such councils may consequently be more redolent of a mode of 'top-down' communication than a vehicle for the genuine expression of employee voice. Notwithstanding these ambiguities, Gollan (2001: 378) has usefully identified six common elements appertaining to NERs and this allows us to sketch a broad conceptualisation:

1 Only employees at the organisation can be members of the representative body.

2 There is no, or only limited, formal linkage to outside trade unions or external employee representative bodies.

3 A degree of resource is supplied by the organisation in which the employee representative body is based.

4 There is a representation of employees' interests or agency function, as opposed to more direct forms of individual participation and involvement.

5 Such structures predominantly deal with a range of issues at a workplace and/or organisational level.

6 There is no independent membership criterion based on individual employee contributions.

While this outline represents a useful point of entry, it nevertheless fails to emphasise the pre-eminent characteristic of these institutions – traditionally within the UK context, in contrast to the European variant, such structures have lacked legal institutionalisation. Prior to 2005 and the transposition of the Directive on Informational and Consultation (discussed later), they were exclusively managerial emanations, existing solely under the sufferance of employers. It is important, therefore, to stress that the institutions under review are typically not regarded as neutral structures; there is a need to emphasise in the vast majority of instances the primacy of management as architect, initiator and patron. Given their managerial genesis, there is consequently a strong *prima facie* presumption of a lack of independence. They would therefore appear, to various degrees, to be under the control or domination of the employer.

NER: exploring the effectiveness of the voice process

In line with the analysis in the previous section, the vast bulk of research in this area (e.g. Watling and Snook, 2003; Butler, 2005, 2009 a, b; Upchurch *et al.*, 2006) indicates that NER is a largely ineffectual mode of voice. Butler (2005) tracks the problems encountered by NER to deficiencies in four key areas: power, autonomy, competence and legitimacy (see Figure 14.1). The interplay of power and autonomy is deemed to be of particular significance. A major shortcoming in terms of the former is an absence of 'latent' power resources, i.e. the inability to engage in militant activity (e.g. strikes) to pursue demands (e.g. wage claims). With respect to autonomy, the terms of reference are typically managerially derived and the more contentious issues (e.g. pay and restructuring) are often deemed 'ultra vires', or beyond the scope of the remit of these forums. As eloquently argued by Donaghey *et al.* (2011: 59), management can, through the design of particular institutional arrangement, invoke a climate of 'silence' on certain issues. Outlining a similarly subtle approach to the emasculation of voice, Butler

Figure 14.1 NER and employee voice – key deficiencies

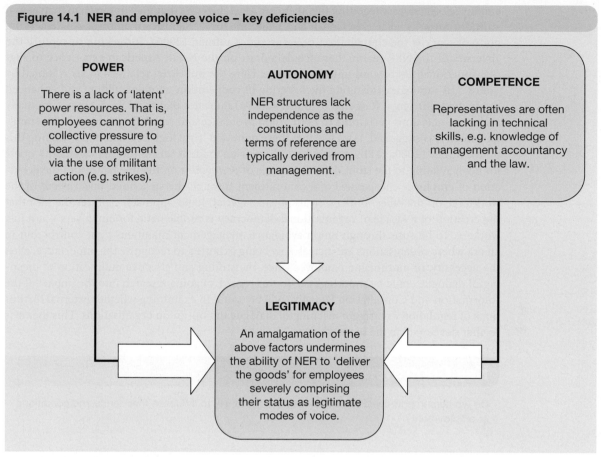

POWER

There is a lack of 'latent' power resources. That is, employees cannot bring collective pressure to bear on management via the use of militant action (e.g. strikes).

AUTONOMY

NER structures lack independence as the constitutions and terms of reference are typically derived from management.

COMPETENCE

Representatives are often lacking in technical skills, e.g. knowledge of management accountancy and the law.

LEGITIMACY

An amalgamation of the above factors undermines the ability of NER to 'deliver the goods' for employees severely comprising their status as legitimate modes of voice.

Source: Butler (2005).

(2005: 285), drawing on Poole's (1978) notion of 'mental resources', argues that in such contexts management will often seek to 'educate' delegates as to the cogency of managerial action and immerse them in corporate definitions of success. In the face of such unitary norms, the pressures for conformity are immense, damping the potential for independent action. As such, the bulk of the data indicates severe shortcomings in the effectiveness of this mode of voice – see, e.g., Gollan's (2003) study of Eurotunnel.

This is not to say NER cannot deliver benefits for employees in certain settings. Indeed, where NER is used as part of a strategic approach to HRM, management would be well advised to listen to such modes of voice, lest problems and issues become 'bottled up'. Furthermore, the Information and Consultation Directive (see the section on this later in the chapter) has the potential to transform NER. What data there are, however, indicate that NER is a far less effective form of representation than orthodox trade unionism.

NER: exploring the 'riddle' of managerial strategy

The shortcomings of this mode of voice beg an interesting question – why does management often commit significant resources to maintaining this form of representation? According to Butler (2009a: 200), until relatively recently it was customary to conceptualise NER as a more or less straightforward component of a broader strategy of trade union avoidance (see Gall, 2003: 88) or substitution. The argument here is that management erects a simulation of pluralist architecture in order to deactivate employee demands for independent external representation – often in response to the trade union recognition legislation discussed earlier. Latterly, however, scholars have started to question the idea of a single simple model of employee behaviour, suggesting that there are several factors that may impinge on managerial attitudes towards voice (see Gollan and Dundon, 2007). Significant amongst this emerging body of work is the contribution of Taras and Kaufman (2006). In seeking to capture the 'diversity of the NER realm', these scholars draw on the North American experience to suggest functionalities beyond union avoidance. Here the industrial relations focus is joined by 'softer' HR rationales, including the fostering of cooperation, morale building and enhanced production efficiency. Research by Butler (2009a) indicates that these goals are not mutually exclusive – i.e. aims pertaining to both union avoidance and soft HR may be pursued simultaneously. It is suggested, however, that these represent 'rival logics of action'. Developing this point, Butler (2009a: 211) stresses that 'there is an evident tension in management's quest for goals relating to the stout defence of goals of *prerogative* on the one hand, and the generation of employee engagement and commitment through the structured *involvement* of the workforce on the other'. Butler's 'rivals of (managerial) logic' approach captures the idea that the creation of a façade of organisational democracy is problematic for employers – not just workers. To be sure, through union avoidance, management maintains tight control, but in an era where organisations are increasingly being exhorted to recognise the importance, even the necessity, of maximising employee voice, the stifling and effective nullification of meaningful dialogue could be short-sighted. In this regard, ongoing research into the impact of the Information and Consultation Directive will be useful in examining whether external institutions of regulation can trigger meaningful dialogue in non-union organisations. This theme is further developed in the section below.

Key Controversy

Do workers in non-union organisations have the ability to influence their terms and conditions of employment?

Works councils and consultation in the European Union

At this point we will pause to consider some of the more recent developments in respect of collective or indirect employee voice. A recurrent theme within this chapter has been the ascendance of managerially inspired modes of voice, i.e. employee involvement. By and large, systems of indirect *participation,* i.e. mechanisms that seek to involve employees more fundamentally in the 'political structures of the firm' (Brannen, 1983: 16), fared less well throughout the 17-year period of Conservative government from 1979 to 1997. However, the decision of the Labour government to sign up to the European Agreement on Social Policy (the Social Chapter) in 1997 put employee participation firmly back on the agenda.

There is a long history of a European level of interest in employee participation. Plans for a 'fifth directive' that sought to provide workers with boardroom representation were suspended inconclusively in 1982. A new framework for a European Company Statute was again launched in 1989 (Hyman and Mason, 1995: 33). This also called for workers to have board-level input. However, pressure from employers and the British Conservative government ensured that the draft directive was never ratified (Hyman and Mason, 1995). As Leat (2003: 245) notes, ultimately such initiatives ran counter to the UK's voluntarist tradition and even more so to the *neo-laissez-faire* approach adopted by British governments after 1979. Consequently, the decision of the Blair government to bind Britain to the European Social Policy Protocol under the Treaty of Amsterdam (1999) marked a fundamental change in policy. Following this move, the directives agreed between 1994 and 1998 and all subsequent legislation under the Social Chapter became applicable to British companies. In terms of employee voice, the most far-reaching of these measures have been the directives on European Works Councils (1994) and Information and Consultation (2002).

The European Works Council Directive

Background

The European Works Council (EWC) directive, transposed into UK law in 1999, requires an EWC to be established in companies with at least 1000 employees within the EU and at least 150 employees in each of at least two member states. It is thus explicitly aimed at multinational companies (MNCs). It has been estimated that the directive covers around 1,850 MNCs (Kerckhofs, 2002). By 2003, 639 MNCs had negotiated agreements (Waddington and Kerckhofs, cited in Hall and Marginson, 2005: 208). The directive is a response to the concerns of the European Commission regarding the power of MNCs to take decisions in one member state that affect employees in others without their being involved in the decision-making process (Leat, 2003: 250). The legislation is thus intended to bridge the 'representation gap' between the growth of trans-national decision making and employees' hitherto strictly nationally defined information and consultation rights (Hall and Marginson, 2005). The EWC Directive is significant in that the requirement for mandated consultation (see Box 14.7) suggests some potential for the extension of employee influence.

Impact of the directive

Over a decade after the directive's inception, a reasonable amount of research has been conducted exploring the workings of these institutions. Reviewing the data, Blyton and Turnbull (2004: 373–74) argue that EWCs overwhelmingly tend to be management-led, with restrictions placed on the consultation procedure. These findings chime with an overview of the terrain by Hall and Marginson, who conclude that very few agreements depart from the formalised definition of consultation as set out in the directive, i.e. 'the exchange of views and establishment of dialogue' between employee representatives and management (Hall and Marginson, 2005: 207). Only sporadically are firmer consultation rights provided such as the right of employee representatives to be allowed to respond formally to managerial proposals and receive a considered response *before* management acts (Hall and Marginson, 2005). The balance of evidence is that limited headway has been made by EWCs in extending employee influence over strategic issues, with any impact restricted to the *implementation* of decisions rather than their actual substance (see, in particular, Stirling and Fitzgerald, 2000).

A plausible interpretation of the current situation is that companies operating EWCs have aligned them with their own organisational requirements, exploiting the directive for *corporate* purposes (see Waddington, 2011b: 225, emphasis added), rather than those of their employees. Hall and Marginson (2005) cite a study by Wills in which British managers generally had a positive view of the contribution of EWCs, seeing them as a way of reinforcing corporate communications and downplaying their consultative and representative role.

Box 14.7 | **The competence of EWCs**

European Works Councils have the right to meet with central management once a year. There must be information or consultation on:

- the structure, economic and financial situation of the business;
- developments in production and sales;
- the employment situation;
- investment trends;
- substantial changes concerning the introduction of new working methods or production processes, transfers of production, mergers, cutbacks or closures of undertakings.

Similarly, in Nakano's study of 14 Japanese MNCs (again cited in Hall and Marginson, 2005), managers perceived EWCs as providing benefits in terms of information provision, the fostering of cooperation between management and employee representatives and the development of a wider corporate identity among employee representatives (see also Timming, 2007 for a useful overview of the literature). Furthermore, as Waddington (2011a: 225) observes, citing a study by Vitols, managerial expectations that the establishment of EWCs would slow corporate decision-making have not been realised. Many studies hence suggest that the EWC machinery is prone to be hijacked by management, who then reconstruct these ostensibly pluralist structures along unitary lines to form part of the employee involvement apparatus. Arguably this stems from the original legislation that gave organisations considerable latitude in how to implement the directive. More alarmingly, Timming (2007: 251) points to the 'dark side' of the operation of EWCs, suggesting that management may use divide-and-rule tactics to 'encourage competition between geographically dispersed workforces'. Under such a scenario, managers are able to 'convert an ostensibly labour-friendly institution into a business friendly managerial tool'. So far the creation of EWCs appears to have done little to significantly improve the participation rights of British workers. Indeed, it is conceivable that, albeit unintentionally, mandated employee participation has significantly buttressed employee involvement arrangements. As Waddington (2011a: 232) observes, recent alterations to the directive (e.g. greater emphasis on the timely provision of information by management) may lead to improvement, but positive developments will be reliant on the efforts of EWC representatives and trade unionists.

Key Controversy

Are EWCs likely to result in European level collective bargaining? Does the evidence suggest that the directive has significantly increased the degree of employee influence? If not, why not?

EWCs and trade union voice

The potential implications for trade unions *vis-à-vis* the EWC regulations have been well explored at a theoretical level. The key issue preoccupying commentators has been the pan-European implications for organised labour. Banyuls *et al.* (2008: 532) have styled this the 'tensions of micro corporatism caught between international solidarity and regime competition'. Scholars have highlighted two potential dynamics within this 'tension'. First, at an optimistic level it has been suggested EWCs hold out the potential for cross-national collaboration of the labour movement. From within this perspective, EWCs are viewed as 'potential precursors towards European level collective bargaining and institutions providing an opportunity for trade union renewal' (Taylor and Mathers, 2002; cited in Banyuls, 2008: 534). This interpretation sees possibilities for 'horizontal integration', with EWCs acting as a bulwark against 'regime shopping' – the situation where organisations seek to move operations to deregulated low-cost economies. A more pessimistic strand of the early literature cautioned that EWCs might conversely become parochially orientated defenders of local interests (Schulten, 1996; cited in Weston and Martinez Lucio, 1998). Under this scenario, employee representation becomes fragmented into 'productivity coalitions' with local management, such pacts being sustained through competition with other units of production (see Weston and Martinez Lucio, 1998: 558–59 for a summary) via the invocation of 'coercive comparisons' (Ferner and Edwards, 1995). Representatives are tempted to 'free ride' using the information gathered from EWCs to consolidate and strengthen their own local position (see Weston and Martinez Lucio, 1998: 559) undermining international solidarity. Interestingly, this important theoretical dichotomy remains remarkably under-explored at an empirical level. Certainly it is well accepted that EWCs have not acted as engines for pan-European collective bargaining. There is some evidence of management using EWCs as a strategy of 'proactive fragmentation' (Timming, 2007: 251), encouraging divisiveness and competition between international plants with a view to securing local concessions (Timming, 2007: 251). There is similarly, however, some (albeit limited) evidence (e.g. Banyuls *et al.*, 2008) of EWCs being used to attenuate the consequences of regime competition, with international delegates acting in unison within a sense of international solidarity. However, the antecedent factors that might underpin the emergence of these very differing scenarios have not been significantly explored.

The Information and Consultation Directive

Background

These recent regulations (the Information and Consultation of Employees Regulations 2004, ICE) make provision for employees to be consulted and given information on major developments in their organisation. They differ from the EWC Directive, as here coverage extends to *all* companies in the EU with over 50 employees – not just MNCs. In the British context, the directive has been portrayed as a useful corrective to the failure of voluntarism (Sisson, 2002: 2) and the consequent 'representation gap' (Towers, 1997). The key significance of the legislation is that it is a vehicle for the extension of participation for employees without trade union representation. As such it has the potential 'to transform the UK industrial relations environment' (see Gollan and Wilkinson, 2007: 1145).

The original proposals were strongly backed by the French amid objections from Germany, Ireland, Denmark and the UK. Although the directive was initiated under the Social Chapter, and hence subject to qualified majority voting, these four dissenters comprised a sufficient blocking minority to initially keep the proposals off the statute book. The UK's objection was based on the notion of 'subsidiarity', the doctrine that the EU should only legislate where the objectives cannot be reached by legislation at national level (**www.eurofound.eu**). The proposals were, however, accepted by the European Parliament in February 2002. Under a compromise position, the UK (along with Ireland) had dispensation to phase in the legislation over a four-year period. Initially, only companies with 150 employees were covered.

Organisations with existing information and consultation arrangements that have the support of employees can continue operating them. In other circumstances, employees must 'trigger' negotiations with their employer to agree new information arrangements. If the negotiations do not produce an agreement, statutory information and consultation arrangements become applicable (see Box 14.8).

Impact of the directive

To date there has been limited research exploring the effectiveness of the directive. What evidence there is, however, mirrors much of the EWC's output. Thus, Hall *et al*'s (2007) 'provisional' study of Information and Consultation (I&C) arrangements in 13 case study organisations highlights how the forums 'were dominated by information provision by management' (p. 75). Developing this theme, it is noted that 'evidence of consultation as discussion *before* a decision and the even tougher criterion of influencing management plans were fairly

---

Box 14.8 | **The right to information and consultation**

The right to information and consultation covers the following:

- Information on the recent and probable development of the organisation's activities and economic situation.
- Information and consultation on the situation, structure and probable development of employment within the organisation.
- Information and consultation on decisions likely to lead to substantial changes in work organisation.

Source: www.eurofound.eu.

sparse' (p. 75, emphasis added). While induction training was provided in most instances, there was only 'limited evidence of subsequent training' (p. 72) and little indication that management went out of their way to build up representative effectiveness. Alarmingly, a significant proportion of workers across the study organisations were actually ignorant of the presence of the representative bodies. Bennett's (2010) public-sector study is similarly useful in highlighting the more limited awareness of union representatives of the regulations when compared with HR practitioners – a significant finding given the 'triggering' requirement. Hall *et al.*'s (2011; see also Hall and Purcell, 2012) broad conclusion based on a wider analysis of consultation in 25 organisations is that the directive has had only 'limited significance' (p. 22), sentiments echoed in other comparative case study research (Taylor *et al.*, 2009; Koukiadaki, 2010; Dobbins *et al.*, 2011).

Gollan and Wilkinson (2007: 1152) caution that there is a danger of viewing the legislation as a 'single shock to the system that will have a once and for all effect'. The argument here is that learning on all sides may develop the participation process. Consequently, 'managers may become more comfortable and employees more confident, changing an ineffectual consultation process into something with real meaning' (Gollan and Wilkinson, 2007). Hall *et al.*'s (2007) findings lend guarded support to this line of argument. Four of the ICE bodies under review had actually declined in effectiveness. Evidence of weakness and marginality was seen *inter alia* in a lack of weighty agenda issues, lack of consultation on major organisational change and a lack of training for new members. Nonetheless, in five cases there were signs of growing effectiveness being invoked through 'experiential learning' (Hall *et al.*'s (2007: 7). Taken as a whole – and in line with the emphasis on legislatively prompted voluntarism (Hall, 2005) – the emergent evidence suggests a variegated and complex set of outcomes rather than any sort of wholesale transformation to structures of participation and systems of corporate governance.

EWCs and ICE: a need for a more integrated research agenda?

As outlined in the preceding section, in recent years, parallel yet wholly discrete streams of EWC (e.g. Timming, 2006, 2007; Waddington, 2011a,b) and ICE (e.g. Taylor, 2009; Koukiadaki, 2010; Dobbins, *et al.* 2011) research have emerged. One important corollary is the absence of data dealing with the institutional interplay or interconnectedness of pan-European (EWC) and national (ICE) forums – more specifically, consideration of the cross-fertilisation of strategy, ideas and practice. This empirical dualism is untenable, not least because the twin instruments are viewed by the European Commission as *complementary* components of the European social dimension. The current emphasis on reductionism hence limits understanding of both the potential synergies and emergent tensions.

Scholars seeking to probe the EWC–ICE nexus might do well to look to elements of contemporary institutional theory for theoretical insight where knowledge of matters pertaining to spheres of interaction, networking and the cross-diffusion of practice are well developed. The theme of 'institutional complementarity', famously explored within the field of comparative political economy (e.g. Hall and Soskice, 2001), while potentially pertinent has been overlooked by EWC and ICE analysts. Researchers could usefully explore the degree of articulation and interest aggregation between the two institutional levels. Do ICE structures act as conduits through which EWC reps cascade matters downstream, as widely used in continental Europe (see Lecher *et al.*, 1999). Might ICE structures act as 'signaling mechanisms' (Marginson *et al.*, 2004: 211), alerting European works councillors to local decisions that may have a trans-national dimension? Do delegates at the two levels network and share intelligence and a common strategy *vis-à-vis* the pursuit of joint interests or is this stifled by jurisdictional claims, competition and tensions? These important issues warrant attention.

Key Controversy

Why might employers object to employees having legally mandated rights to consultation? Could the ICE directive form part of a strategic approach to HRM?

Concluding comments

It is evident that the expression of employee 'voice' remains central to the employment relationship. Recent years have witnessed a decline in the coverage of collective bargaining (e.g. van Wanrooy *et al.*, 2013), i.e. participation, towards managerially inspired forms of voice. The implications of this dynamic are open to differing interpretations. At one level there is concern that the increasing absence of independent representation renders workers vulnerable to exploitation by unscrupulous employers. Certainly, managers are using a variety of techniques to engage employees (van Wanrooy *et al.*, 2013: 18); however, 'while the majority of employees feel that managers are good at seeking their views, fewer employees feel that they influence decision making' (p. 18). Such data indicate grounds for concern – at least for those of a pluralist persuasion. These developments must nonetheless be set within the context of the enhanced 'juridification' or state regulation of the employment relationship. New Labour's 'floor of rights' approach (1997–2010) – which set out minimum acceptable standards of managerial behaviour in a variety of areas (e.g. the national minimum wage and family-friendly policy) – arguably reduced the potential for the widespread and systematic abuse of employees' rights. The issue of whether state regulation can fill the vacuum left by the decline of collective voice will remain contentious.

It is worth noting that employee participation – in the guise of the European regulation of consultation – has undergone something of a minor renaissance in recent years. The European Works Council and Information and Consultation directives both provide employees with significant rights to information and dialogue on economic, employment and strategic issues. What data there are, however, suggest these developments are unlikely to supply workers with effective voice (e.g. Hall and Marginson, 2005; Hall *et al.*, 2013). This juxtaposition of declining trade union coverage and lukewarm government support for 'mandated' consultation suggests that representative participation is likely to remain significantly eclipsed by employee involvement for many years to come.

Summary

- The topic of employee voice comprises three distinct but related concepts: employee involvement, employee participation and industrial democracy. The difference between these constructs is best understood in terms of variations in employee power and influence. Broadly speaking, there is a continuum ranging from narrow task-based employee input (employee involvement) through to elements of co-determination or joint decision-making (participation), extending to full-blown employee ownership (industrial democracy).

- The topic of voice has a long history. Interestingly, while employee involvement is nowadays ascendant, this is a relatively recent phenomenon. In the past, the field has been dominated by the themes of participation and industrial democracy. The current hegemony of employee involvement can be tracked to the 1980s and the emergence of neo-liberalism and various influential HRM models. While employee involvement is currently ascendant, developments at EU level have served to bolster the flagging fortunes of employee participation. The European Works Council and Information and Consultation directives provide employees with statutory rights to consultation hitherto denied to British workers. Academic commentators, however, have expressed reservations as to whether the legislation has the potential to seriously challenge managerial prerogative.

- Empirical research thus indicates a trend towards employee involvement and a decline in representative participation. An outcome of this trend is that large swathes of the British workforce are not covered by trade union representation. There is concern that a 'representation gap' has opened up and that such workers lack 'voice' and the ability to influence workplace decisions.

- There has been some experimentation with non-union forms of collective voice (NERs). Evidence suggests that such structures are managerial creations that lack power and autonomy. One corollary is that pluralist commentators argue these are a wholly ineffective substitute for *independent* trade union voice. Such structures may, however, be compatible with HRM given its unitary underpinnings.

Questions

1 Why is employee involvement described as unitarist?
2 What are the main trends in representative participation since 1980?
3 Why might management resist moves to greater industrial democracy?
4 Which approach to voice is more aligned with HRM – employee involvement or participation?
5 Why has trade union membership fallen over the last 30 years or so and do unions still serve a useful purpose?
6 What are the key differences between the EWC and ICE directives?

Case study

Union recognition and 'voice' issues in a retail organisation

This case study centres on issues of trade union recognition and union recognition avoidance. Although it is fictional, all of the issues are based around 'live' employee relations issues that have occurred over the last few years following the introduction of legislation on trade union recognition.

Company A, an American-based supermarket chain, with 300 units across the USA, has long sought a presence in the highly lucrative UK food retail sector. In August 2010, they were successful in purchasing a medium-sized British company, Company B. With 40 branches across the Midlands, Company B business strategy has been to concentrate on the lower, budget end of the market. The company has traditionally adopted a 'no frills', 'pile it high, sell it cheap' approach. In the face of the expansion of other budget retailers in the UK, Company B's profitability has shrunk considerably. As a consequence, the senior managerial team actively sought a suitor to inject some much-needed capital into the business.

At the time of the acquisition, Company B did not recognise any union for the purpose of collective bargaining. Collective representation was nonetheless provided by an in-house NER company forum – 'The Partners Council'. Introduced in 2000, employees from each of the stores elect two representatives. The body convenes on a monthly basis and provides employee representatives with an opportunity to raise issues of concern with management. Of late, however, the workforce has become increasingly disillusioned with the workings of the institution. One complaint centres on delegates not being sufficiently independent

of management – utilising the forum as a means of networking to further their own career interests. Another set of concerns focus on the nature of consultation. There is a feeling that the discussions are limited to a 'diet of trivia' – the body has no constitutional remit to discus key terms and conditions of employment, e.g. pay, hours, holidays and training. Subject to legally prescribed minima, these are areas of unfettered managerial prerogative. Common agenda items include matters pertaining to uniforms, canteen facilities and car parking. Representatives do not undertake any formal training and several delegates have resigned, feeling 'out of their depth' when dealing with their managerial counterparts, notwithstanding the fairly undemanding agenda. At the time of the takeover, several of the representative positions were unfilled; indeed there had been no formal meetings during the previous three months, the senior managerial team being preoccupied with the demands of the takeover. The structure and scope of the consultative apparatus have not been agreed with the workforce.

Beyond the Partners' Council there has been some experimentation with wider modes of communication (employee involvement). For over a decade a monthly newsletter has been sent directly to each worker's home address. There is also an intranet site where employees ('colleagues') can post comments and suggestions. The actual degree of readership and usage is not measured in any way. Team briefings have been used intermittently, as have attitude surveys.

While there is no trade union recognition, it is known that some employees are trade union members.

Case study continued

Each outlet operates an in-store bakery and a significant proportion of such workers are members of the Bakers and Associated Workers Union. This is an erstwhile craft union which now seeks to recruit more widely, given its shrinking membership base. The traditional stance of the union has been fairly militant. Protracted strike action, for example, ensued in two major food retailers in the mid-1990s following the introduction of Sunday trading. There was a more recent dispute over pay and flexibility that resulted in an unofficial 'wildcat' one day stoppage at a national bakery. Company A managers have had some dealings with full-time officials in disciplinary hearings – the tenor of such gatherings being routinely described as fractious and confrontational. More recently, Company A has been targeted by the National Union of Retail Workers. It is known that the lay activists have been moderately successful in recruiting members in four of the largest stores. It is no coincidence that these are the stores that were selected to undertake a 24-hour trading experiment. The pilot caused some disgruntlement amongst the shift workers – the £1.50-per-hour shift bonus being regarded as derisory. The NURW is a relatively large and well organised union that has secured several voluntary recognition agreements in recent years within the retail sector. Some of these have matured into formal partnership agreements, lauded as exemplars of best practice and management–union cooperation.

- *Pay rates*. The majority of shop floor staff (e.g. cashiers, shelf fillers, security, personnel and cleaners) are paid at a flat rate that tracks the national minimum wage. This is 60 pence below the industry norm. The other major work groups, warehouse staff and trades (i.e. butchers and bakers) are paid above the national minimum wage but below the industry norm With respect to employee benefits, the company operates a staff discount scheme. Sick pay and holiday entitlement are in line with statutory minima.
- *Profile of workforce*. There is a heavy reliance on female part-time workers (60 per cent), who work between 12 and 22 hours per week. In recent years the number of students recruited has also increased. These similarly work part-time (on average 12 hours per week), while a further cohort of students are employed seasonally (e.g. over the busy Christmas period) on fixed-term contracts. A central distribution unit employs around 300 workers. Approximately 25 per cent of these are eastern European migrants, while a further 25 per cent of total staff are supplied by a local recruitment agency.
- *Pension scheme*. The company offers a stakeholder scheme but does not provide any contributions.

- *Training*. All employees are provided with a two-day induction course. Trade staff, e.g. bakers and butchers, are given the opportunity to acquire related national vocational qualifications (NVQs), although there is no general provision for this.

Question

1 Respond to the following e-mail:

From: Head of HR, Company A
To: HR Consultancy
Subject: Union recognition and the 'Partners Council'

As you are aware from previous conversations, we have just acquired a majority shareholding in Company B. We are a predominantly US-based retailer and this is our first UK venture. As such we are unfamiliar with the traditions surrounding employee representation in the UK and the shifting legislative context. Our US operations are all non-unionised and this is our preferred approach to employee relations. It is evident that there is some dissatisfaction at Company B with the present in-house representative arrangements, especially amongst those workers with trade union sympathies. We are aware that matters relating to voice and representation in the UK are now quite complex in view of recent legislation on trade union recognition and information and consultation. Surveying the UK scene, our own HR team are somewhat confused – it is evident that some key sectoral players adopt an explicitly non-union approach while others are happy to work with organised labour. The US board has now asked for a briefing paper outlining and evaluating policy options.

As an HR consultant to Company A with expertise in this field, review the current situation at Company B and outline options that will resolve the growing managerial dilemma around employee representation. It is the responsibility of the senior managerial team to take final decisions so you do not need to recommend a particular course of action – they may all be hard to swallow for the evidently unitary US board – but you need to say what the likely consequences are for all options that you put forward. So, your task is not to find a 'best practice' solution to this problem but to outline possible options and critically evaluate the implications of these suggestions. Options might include, for instance, tactics of union substitution, e.g. 'beefing up' the current in-house NER forum or seeking to improve the current terms and conditions of employment on offer. All will have problems and consequences that you need to outline in your report.

Acknowledgement: The author would like to thank Dr Enda Hannon of Kingston University for use of the case study on which this exercise is based.

References and further reading

Abrahamsson, B. (1977) *Bureaucracy or Participation,* London: Sage.

Appelbaum, E. (2002) 'The impact of new forms of work organisations on workers', in G. Murray, J. Bélanger, G. Giles and P. Lapointe (eds) *Work and Employment Relations in the High Performance Workplace.* London: Continuum, pp. 120–49.

Appelbaum, E., Bailey, T., Berg, P. and Kellberg, A. (2000) *Manufacturing Advantage.* Ithaca, NY: Cornell University Press.

Ashton, D. and Sung, J. (2002) *Supporting Workplace Learning for High Performance Working.* Geneva: ILO.

Bae, K., Chuma., H., Kato, T., Kim, D. and Ohashi, I. (2011) 'High performance work practices and employee voice: a comparison of Japanese and Korean workers', *Industrial Relations,* 50, 1: 1–29.

Banyuls, J., Haipeter, T. and Neumann, L. (2008) 'European Works Council at General Motors Europe: Bargaining efficiency in regime competition', *Industrial Relations Journal,* 39, 6: 532–47.

BBC (2011) 'Vince Cable warns GMB against co-ordinated strikes', 6 June. Online: **http://www.bbc.co.uk/news/business-13661098** (accessed 30 September 2013).

Bélanger, P., Giles, A. and Murray, G. (2002) 'Workplace innovation and the role of institutions', in G. Murray, J. Bélanger, A. Giles and P. Lapointe (eds) *Work and Employment in the High Performance Workplace.* London: Continuum, pp. 150–80.

Bennett, T. (2010) 'Employee voice initiatives in the public sector: views from the workplace', *International Journal of Public Sector Management,* 23, 5: 444–55.

Biagi, M. (1998) 'Forms of employee representative participation' in R. Blainpan and C. Engels (eds) *Corporate Labour Law and Industrial Relations in Industrialized Economies.* The Netherlands: Kluwer Law International.

BIS (2011) *Department for Business Innovations and Skills: Trade Union Membership 2011.* London: National Statistics.

Blyton, P. and Turnbull, P. (2004) *The Dynamics of Employee Relations,* 3rd edn. Basingstoke: Palgrave.

Boxall, P. and Macky, K. (2009) 'Research and theory on high performance work systems: progressing the high involvement stream', *Human Resource Management Journal,* 19, 1: 3–23.

Brannen, P. (1983) *Authority and Participation in Industry.* London: Batsford.

Brewster, C. Wood, G. and Brookes, M. (2008) 'Similarity, isomorphism or duality? Recent survey evidence on the human resource management policies of multinational corporations', *British Journal of Management,* 19: 320–42.

Brown, W. (2010) 'Negotiation and Collective Bargaining' in T. Colling and M. Terry (eds) *Industrial Relations Theory and Practice.* Chichester: John Wiley.

Butler, P. (2005) 'Non union employee representation: Exploring the efficacy of the voice process', *Employee Relations,* 27, 3: 272–88.

Butler, P. (2009a) 'Non union employee representation: exploring the riddle of managerial strategy', *Industrial Relations Journal,* 40, 3: 198–214.

Butler, P. (2009b) 'Riding along on the crest of a wave: tracking the shifting rationale for non-union consultation at FinanceCo', *Human Resource Management Journal,* 19, 2: 176–93.

Butler, P., Glover, L. and Tregaskis, O. (2011) 'When the going gets tough . . . recession and the resilience of workplace partnership', *British Journal of Industrial Relations,* 49, 4: 666–87.

Butler, P., Tregaskis, O. and Glover, L. (2013) 'Workplace partnership and employee involvement – contradictions and synergies: Evidence from a heavy engineering case study', *Economic and Industrial Democracy,* 34, 1: 5–24.

Carter, B. (2000) 'Adoption of the organising model in British trade unions: Some evidence from the manufacturing science and finance', *Work, Employment and Society,* 14, 1: 117–36.

Chamberlain, N.W. and Kuhn, J.W. (1965) *Collective Bargaining.* New York: McGraw Hill.

Charlwood, A. and Forth, J. (2009) 'Employee representation' in W. Brown, A. Bryson, J. Forth and K. Whitfield (eds) *The Evolution of the Modern Workplace.* Cambridge: Cambridge University Press, pp. 74–96.

Charlwood, A. and Metcalfe, D. (2009) 'Appendix: union membership' in D. Metcalfe and S. Fernie (eds) *British Unions Resurgence or Perdition?* London: Routledge, pp. 231–9.

Deakin, S., Hobbs, R., Konzelmann, S. J. and Wilkinson, W. (2005) 'Working corporations: corporate governance and innovation in labour-management partnerships in Britain' in M. Stuart and M. Martinez Lucio (eds) *Partnership and Modernisation in Employment Relations.* Basingstoke: Palgrave, pp. 63–82.

Dickens, L. and Hall, M. (2010) 'Fairness – up to a point. Assessing the impact of New Labour's employment legislation', *Human Resource Management Journal,* 16, 4: 338–56.

Dobbins, T., Dundon, T., Cullinane, N., Donaghey, J. and Hickland, E. (2011) *The Information and Consultation of Employees (ICE) Directive: employer occupation of regulatory space for informing and consulting workers in liberal market regimes,* Bangor Business School Working Papers, 11/007. Bangor: Bangor University.

Donaghey, J., Cullinane, N., Dundon, T. and Wilkinson, A. (2011) 'Reconceptualising employee silence, problems and prognosis', *Work Employment and Society,* 25, 1: 51–67.

Dundon, T. and Rollinson, D. (2011) *Understanding Employment Relations.* Maidenhead: McGraw-Hill.

Dundon, T., Wilkinson, A., Marchington, M. and Ackers, P. (2004) 'The meaning and purpose of employee voice', *International Journal of Human Resource Management,* 15, 6: 1149–70.

Easterby-Smith, M., Lyles, M.A and Peteraf, M.A. (2009) 'Dynamic capabilities; current debates and future directions', *British Journal of Management,* 20: S1–S8.

Ferner, A. and Edwards, P.K. (1995) 'Power and Diffusion of Organizational Change within Multinational Enterprises', *European Journal of Industrial Relations,* 1, 2: 29–57.

Flanders, A. (1965) *Industrial Relations: What is wrong with the system.* London: Faber and Faber.

Flanders, A. (1968) *Trade Unions.* London: Hutchinson.

Freeman, R. and Pelletier, J. (1990) 'The impact of industrial relations legislation on British union density', *British Journal of Industrial Relations,* 28, 2: 141–64.

Gall, G. (2003) 'Employee opposition to union recognition' in G. Gall (ed.) *Union Organizing: Campaigning for Trade Union Recognition.* London: Routledge.

Garrahan, P. and Stewart, P. (1992) *The Nissan Enigma: Flexibility at Work in a Local Economy.* London: Mansell Publishing.

Geary, J.F. (2003) 'New forms of work organisation: still limited, still controlled, but still welcome?' in P.K. Edwards (ed.) *Industrial Relations: Theory and Practice in Britain.* Oxford: Blackwell, pp. 338–67.

Glover, L. (2001) 'Communication and consultation in a green field site company', *Personnel Review*, 30, 3: 297–316.

Glover, L. and Butler, P. (2012) 'High performance work systems, partnership and the working lives of HR professionals', *Human Resource Management Journal*, 22, 2: 199–215.

Glover, L., Tregaskis, O. and Butler, P. (2013) 'Mutual gains? The workers' verdict: a longitudinal study', *International Journal of Human Resource Management*.

Gollan, P. (2003) 'All talk but no voice: Employee voice at the Eurotunnel call centre', *Economic and Industrial Democracy*, 24, 4: 509–41.

Gollan, P. (2001) 'Tunnel vision: non union representation at Eurotunnel', *Employee Relations*, 3, 4: 376–400.

Gollan, P. (2010) 'Conference review; employee voice and value during a period of economic turbulence', *Human Resource Management Journal*, 20, 4: 440–43.

Gollan, P. and Dundon, T. (2007) 'Re-conceptualizing voice in the non-union workplace', *International Journal of Human Resource Management*, 18, 7: 1182–98.

Gollan, P. and Wilkinson, A. (2007) 'Implications of the EU Information and Consultation Directive and the Regulations in the UK – prospects for the future of employee representation. *International Journal of Human Resource Management*, 18, 7: 1145–58.

Guest, D. (2002) 'Human resource management, corporate performance and employee well-being: building the worker into HRM', *Journal of Industrial Relations*, 44, 4: 335–58.

Guest, D. and Peccei, R. (2001) 'Partnership at work: mutuality and the balance of advantage', *British Journal of Industrial Relations*, 39, 2: 207–63.

Hall, M. (2005) *How are employers and unions responding to the information and consultation of employee regulations*, Warwick Papers in Industrial Relations, No. 77.

Hall, M. and Marginson, P. (2005) 'Trojan horse or paper tiger? Assessing the significance of European Works Councils' in J. Hyman and P. Thompson (eds) *Participation at Work: Essays in Honour of Harvie Ramsay*. Basingstoke: Palgrave Macmillan, pp. 204–21.

Hall. M. and Purcell, J. (2012) *Consultation at Work: Regulation and Practice*. Oxford: Oxford University Press.

Hall, P. and Soskice, D. (2001) *Varieties of Capitalism: The Institutional Foundations of Comparative Advantage*. Oxford: Oxford University Press.

Hall, M., Hutchinson, S., Parker, J., Purcell, J. and Terry, M. (2007) *Implementing information and consultation: early experience under the ICE Regulations*, Employment Relations Research Series, No. 88. London: Department for Business Enterprise and Regulatory Reform.

Hall, M., Hutchinson, S., Purcell, J., Terry, M. and Parker, J. (2011) 'Promoting effective consultation? Assessing the impact of the ICE Regulations', *British Journal of Industrial Relations*, 51, 2: 355–81.

Harley, B., Hyman, J. and Thompson, P. (2005) 'The paradoxes of participation' in B. Harley, J. Hyman and P. Thompson (eds) *Participation and Democracy at Work: Essays in Honour of Harvie Ramsay*. Basingstoke: Palgrave Macmillan, pp. 1–19.

Heery, E. (2003) 'Partnership verses organising: alternative futures for British trade unionism', *Industrial Relations Journal*, 33, 1: 20–35.

Heery, E. and Noon, M. (2001) *A Dictionary of Human Resource Management*. Oxford, Oxford University Press.

Heery, E and Simms, M. (2008) 'Constraints on union organising in the United Kingdom', *Industrial Relations Journal*, 39, 1: 24–42.

Hespe, G. and Little, S. (1971) 'Some aspects of employee participation' in P. Warre (ed.) *Psychology at Work*. Harmondsworth: Penguin, pp. 325–47.

Holden, L. (2004) 'Employee involvement and empowerment' in I. Beardwell and L. Holden (eds) *Human Resource Management: A Contemporary Approach*, 4th edn. Harlow: Prentice Hall, pp. 539–78.

Hyman, R. (1989) *The Political Economy of Industrial Relations: Theory and Practice in a Cold Climate*. Basingstoke: Macmillan.

Hyman, J. and Mason, B. (1995) *Managing Employee Involvement and Participation*. London: Sage.

Johnstone, S., P. Ackers, and A. Wilkinson (2009). 'The British Partnership Phenomenon: A Ten Year Review'. *Human Resource Management Journal*, 19, 3: 260–79.

Kelly, J. (1998) *Rethinking Industrial Relations. Mobilization, Collectivism and Long Waves*. London: Routledge.

Kelly, J. (2005) 'Social partnership agreements in Britain' in M. Stuart and M. Martinez Lucio (eds) *Partnership and Modernisation in Employment Relations*. Basingstoke: Palgrave.

Kerckhofs, P. (2002) *European Works Councils; Facts and Figures*. Brussels: European Trade Union Institute.

Koukiadaki, A. (2010) 'The establishment and operation of information and consultation of employees arrangements in a capability based framework', *Economic and Industrial Democracy* 31, 3: 365–88.

Lavelle, J., Gunnigle, P. and McDonnell., A. (2010) 'Patterning employee voice in multinational companies', *Human Relations*, 63, 3: 395–418.

Leat, M. (2003) 'The European Union' in G. Hollinshead, P. Nicholls and S. Tailby (eds) *Employee Relations*. Harlow: Prentice Hall, pp. 202–61.

Lecher, W., Nagel, B. and Platzer, H.W. (1999) *The Establishment of European Works Councils – from Information Committee to Social Actor*. Aldershot: Ashgate.

Legge, K. (2005) *Human Resource Management: Rhetorics and Realities* (Anniversary ed.). Basingstoke: Palgrave Macmillan.

Lewis, P., Thornhill, A. and Saunders, M. (2003) *Employee Relations: Understanding the Employment Relationship*. Harlow: Prentice Hall.

Marchington, M. (2005) 'Employee involvement: patterns and explanations' in B. Harley, J. Hyman and P. Thompson (eds) *Participation and Democracy at Work: Essays in Honour of Harvie Ramsay*. Basingstoke: Palgrave Macmillan, pp. 20–37.

Marchington, M. and Wilkinson, A. (2005) 'Direct participation' in S. Bach (ed.) *Personnel Management: A Comprehensive Guide to Theory and Practice*. Oxford: Blackwell, pp. 382–404.

Marchington, M. and Wilkinson, A. (2012) *Human Resource Management at Work*. London: CIPD.

Marchington, M., Goodman, J., Wilkinson, A. and Ackers, P. (1992) *New Developments in Employee Involvement*, Department of Employment Research Series No. 2. London: HMSO.

Marchington, M., Waddington, J. and Timming, A. (2011) 'Employment relations in Britain', in G. Bamber, R. Lansbury and N. Wailes (eds) *International and Comparative Employment Relations*. London: Sage.

Marginson, P., Hall, M., Hoffmann, A. and Müller, T. (2004) 'The impact of European Works Councils on management decision in UK and US-based multinationals: A case study comparison', *British Journal of Industrial Relations*, 42, 2: 209–33.

Martinez Lucio, M. and Stuart, M. (2002) 'Assessing the principles of partnership: Workplace trade unions representatives' attitudes and experiences', *Employee Relations*, 24, 3: 305–20.

McIlroy, J. (1998) 'The enduring alliance? Trade unions and the making of New Labour, 1994–1997', *British Journal of Industrial Relations,* 36: 537–64.

Millward, N., Bryson, A. and Forth, J. (2000) *All Change at Work?* London: Routledge.

Mueller, F. and Proctor, S. (2000) *Teamworking.* Basingstoke: Macmillan.

Muller, T. and Hoffmann, A. (2001) *EWC Research: A Review of the Literature,* Warwick Papers in Industrial Relations, No. 65. Coventry: IRRU.

Pateman, C. (1970) *Participation and Democratic Theory.* Cambridge: Cambridge University Press.

Payne, J. and Keep, E. (2005) 'Promoting workplace development: Lessons for UK policy from Nordic approaches to job redesign and the quality of working life' in B. Harley, J. Hyman and P. Thompson (eds) *Participation and Democracy at Work: Essays in Honour of Harvie Ramsay.* Basingstoke: Palgrave Macmillan, pp. 145–65.

Ramsay, H. (1980) 'Phantom participation: patterns of power and conflict', *Industrial Relations Journal,* 11, 3: 46–59.

Rogers, J. and Streeck, W (1995) *Works Councils.* Chicago IL: University of Chicago Press.

Samuel, P. (2005) 'Partnership working and the cultivated activist', *Industrial Relations Journal,* 36, 1: 59–76.

Rose, E. (2008) *Employment Relations.* Harlow: Pearson.

Sewell, G. and Wilkinson, B. (1992) 'Empowerment or emasculation? Shopfloor surveillance in a total quality organisation' in P. Blyton and P. Turnbull (eds) *Reassessing Human Resource Management.* London: Sage, pp. 271–90.

Sisson, K. (2002) *The Information and Consultation Directive: unnecessary regulation or an opportunity to promote partnership,* Warwick Papers in Industrial Relations, No. 67.

Smith, P. (2009) 'New Labour and the commonsense of neo liberalism: trade unionism, collective bargaining and workers' rights', *Industrial Relations Journal,* 40, 4:337–55.

Smith. P. and Morton, D. (2006) 'Nine years of New Labour: Neo liberalism and workers' rights', *British Journal of Industrial Relations,* 44, 3: 410–20.

Stirling, J. and Fitzgerald, I. (2000) 'European works councils: representing workers on the periphery', *Employee Relations,* 23, 1: 13–25.

Stone, I., Braidford, P., Houston, M. and Bolger, F. (2012) *Promoting High Performance Working.* Durham: University of Durham Policy Research Group.

Storey, J. (1992) *Developments in the Management of Human Resources: An Analytical Review.* London: Blackwell.

Streeck, W. (1998) 'Beneficial constraints: On the economic limits of rational voluntarism' in J. Rogers Hollingsworth and R. Boyer (eds) *Contemporary Capitalism: The Embeddedness of Institutions.* Cambridge: Cambridge University Press.

Suff, R. and Williams, S. (2004) 'The myth of mutuality? Employee perceptions of partnership at Borg Warner', *Employee Relations,* 26, 1: 30–43.

Taras, D.G. and Kaufman, B.D. (2006) 'Non union employee representation in North America: Diversity, controversy and uncertain future', *Industrial Relations Journal,* 37, 5: 513–42.

Taylor, S. and Emir, A. (2009) *Employment Law: An Introduction.* Oxford: Oxford University Press.

Taylor, P., Mulvey, G., Hyman, J. and Bain, P. (2002) 'Work organization, control and the experience of work in call centres', *Work, Employment and Society,* 16, 1: 133–50.

Taylor, P., Baldry, C., Danford, A. and Stewart, P. (2009) '"An Umbrella Full of Holes?" Corporate restructuring, redundancy and the effectiveness of ICE Regulations', *Industrial Relations,* 64, 1.

Terry, M. (2003)'Partnership and the Future of Trade Unions in the UK', *Economic and Industrial Democracy,* 24, 4: 485–507.

Terry, M. (2010) 'Employee Representation', in T. Colling and M. Terry, (eds) *Industrial Relations Theory and Practice.* Chichester: John Wiley.

Timming, A. (2006) 'The problem of identity and trust in European Works Councils', *Employee Relations,* 28, 1: 9–25.

Timming, A. (2007) 'European Works Councils and the dark side of managing worker voice', *Human Resource Management Journal,* 17, 3: 248–64.

Timming, A. (2012) 'Tracing the effects of employee involvement and participation on trust in managers: an analysis of covariance structures', *The International Journal of Human Resource Management,* 23, 5: 3243–57.

Towers, B. (1997) *The Representation Gap: Change and Reform in the British and American Workplace.* Oxford: Oxford University Press.

Tregaskis, O., Daniels, K., Glover, L., Butler, P. and Meyer, M. (2013) 'High performance work practices and firm performance: a longitudinal case study', *British Journal of Management,* in press.

Upchurch, M., Richardson, M., Tailby, S., Danford, A. and Steward, P. (2006) 'Employee representation in the non union sector: A paradox of intention?', *Human Resource Management Journal,* 16, 4: 393–410.

Waddington, J. (2011a) 'European works Councils: The challenge for labour', *Industrial Relations Journal,* 42, 6: 508–29.

Waddington, J. (2011b) *European Works Councils.* London: Routledge.

Waddington, J. and Kerr, A. (2009) 'Transforming a trade union? An assessment of an Organizing Initiative', *British Journal of Industrial Relations,* 47, 1: 27–54.

Waddington, J. and Whitson, C. (1997) 'Why do people join trade unions during a period of membership decline?' *British Journal of Industrial Relations,* 35, 4: 515–46.

van Wanrooy, B., Bewley, H., Bryson, A., Forth, J., Freeth, S., Stokes, L. and Wood, S. (2013) *The 2011 Workplace Employment Relations Study: First Findings.* London: Department for Business, Innovation and Skills.

Watling, D. and Snook, J. (2003) 'Works Councils and trade unions complementary or competitive? The case of Sagco', Paper presented to the BUIRA Conference, 5–7 July, Manchester Metropolitan University.

Weston, S. and Martinez Lucio, M. (1998) 'In and beyond European Works. Councils: limits and possibilities for trade union influence', *Employee Relations,* 20, 6: 551–64.

Wilkinson, A., Redman, T., Snape, E. and Marchington, M. (1998) *Managing with Total Quality Management: Theory and Practice.* London: Macmillan.

Williams, S. and Adam-Smith, D. (2010) *Contemporary Employment Relations A Critical Introduction.* Oxford: Oxford University Press.

Wood, S. (1999) 'Human resource management and performance', *International Journal of Management Review,* 1, 4: 367–413.

Part 5

INTERNATIONAL HUMAN RESOURCE MANAGEMENT

Introduction to Part 5

The considerable growth of interest in international human resource management (HRM) stems from the rise of globalisation over the past half century, a phenomenon that has accelerated considerably since the millennium. This term describes the proliferation of international trading links, foreign direct investment, worldwide mergers and acquisitions and a burgeoning of telecommunications, faster and cheaper transport and rapid technological change. Globalisation has involved the integration of markets worldwide and on a regional level and is being stimulated further by emerging economies, particularly China and India.

The rise of the multinational company (MNC) has been one of the most visible manifestations of globalisation. As companies and organisations expand their cross-border activities, there has been a concomitant increase in business activity together with an increase in cross-border integration of their production processes. This, in turn, has created growing interest in the ways in which they achieve international management coordination and control, and what effect such coordination has on HRM in the countries in which their operations are based.

The possible role of MNCs as forces for change in national HRM systems is just one element in a wider debate that is developing concerning the effects of globalisation on national economic and business systems. Are there varieties of capitalism that are each efficient in their own national contexts, or is globalisation creating new conditions in which some of those varieties cease to be sustainable, causing convergence towards a dominant global model?

The chapters that comprise this part of the book cannot do justice to the complexity and scale of these issues. They merely serve to give you a flavour of some of the developments in the field and some of the debates that are now emerging. Chapter 15 gives a comparative perspective on HRM that explores the convergence and divergence of employment systems in Germany, Japan and the USA. In particular, the chapter focuses on the differing reactions to global financial crises in these employment systems.

Chapter 16 provides a detailed comparative examination of employment relations in two key emergent economies: China and India. It uses cultural and institutional perspectives to explore how historically rooted national characteristics interact with international, globalising influences to shape employment relations in these significant global players.

The final chapter, Chapter 17, combines a range of firm-level perspectives to examine how human resources are managed in MNCs. It starts by showing how international operations offer advantages in terms of enabling organisations to gain access to human resources and knowledge. It then explores the different ways in which MNCs might choose to structure the international HR function and discusses how HR networks and expatriate managers are used to generate and transfer HR knowledge internally. Finally, it explores how HRM practices are influenced by characteristics of country of origin and of the countries in which they operate.

Chapter 15

Comparative HRM and responses to global crises

Ian Clark and Tim Claydon

Objectives

- To demonstrate the distinctively national institutional character of employment systems in Germany, Japan and the USA.

- To demonstrate how institutional patterns of employment regulation are embedded within wider features of societies, specifically their business systems.

- To examine the nature and extent of change and diversity of reaction to global financial crises in the German, Japanese and American employment systems.

- To identify and explain recent pressures for change in employment systems, e.g. the adoption and diffusion of new business models.

- To examine the debate concerning whether change in national employment systems is leading convergence towards the American model of business and HRM.

Introductory case study

Good times, bad times – Kodak files for bankruptcy

Good times?

Prominent studies of human resources management (HRM) in the American business system refer to 'welfare capitalist' employers such as Kodak as the originators of HRM in the 1930s (Jacoby, 1997; Almond and Ferner, 2006). Welfare capitalism went on to constitute a pattern of employment practice that was markedly different to the New Deal employment model which became emblematic of the period from 1935 through to the late 1960s. Featuring as it did managerially inspired strategies to deter union membership, welfare capitalism came to represent a so-called transformation of American industrial relations (Kochan *et al.*, 1993). The transformation highlighted an ideological opposition to trade unions, often by 'founding father' employers, who had an ambition to see the firm, not the state, as the basis of employment security to employees. Similarly, innovations in personnel management, rather than 'job control unionism' formed the basis of commitment between employers and employees. Firms such as Kodak, which deployed welfare capitalism, diffused highly developed corporate cultures, mission statements, straplines, scripted speech, uniforms and dress codes and logos on uniforms. Commitment and performance were measured by employee rankings and appraisal systems, whereas performance was further measured by teamworking and team leaders. In return for tolerating these simple, technical and bureaucratic controls over work organisation and their autonomy, core or 'insider' workers and managers in internal labour markets received the following benefits: profit-sharing and share ownership, performance pay, in some cases unemployment insurance paid by employers, health care coverage including dental and rudimentary to sophisticated final salary pension schemes. The diffusion of these

➤

ideals, if not their empirical presence, in the American economy was captured during the 1980s and 1990s in the 'excellence' literature on American firms (Peters and Waterman, 1982). Kodak was emblematic of welfare capitalism – a household name which was identified as an 'excellent' employer offering workers a very good employment package.

Bad times?

By 2011 the firm was out of business filing for bankruptcy. Before the advent of digital cameras, in order to view pictures taken by an analogue camera it was necessary to put a roll of film in a camera, take the pictures, remove the film and then get the film developed and printed. Kodak controlled 90 per cent of the silver halide film market in the USA and a similar figure in the UK. Roll film had a 75 per cent mark-up and became Kodak's core business. Moreover, whilst Kodak researchers invented the digital camera and, with Apple, one of the first phone cameras, the firm never appreciated the potential threat of digital technology to their core business and, like record and film companies, book publishers and retailers, failed to innovate with digital technology. Kodak cited several factors to explain their 30-year slide into bankruptcy:

- What is now referred to as the firm's entitlement culture of guaranteed in-work benefits, health care coverage and final salary pensions for the firm's 19,000 former employees.
- Related to this, the burden of its past, i.e. the sophisticated package of HRM which became less sustainable as the firm's core market evaporated in the face of relentless change and innovation in the application of digital technology.
- Its botched strategy to reinvent itself in digital cameras then printers, the latter in the face of expert competition from Hewlett-Packard.
- The financial crisis delivered a double hit to Kodak in falling sales in the face of a weak economy and tighter margins reducing cash flow, which exposed a considerable pension scheme shortfall. The impact of the financial crisis combined with the weight of the previous three factors undermined the business, taking Kodak from a top 20 Fortune 500 firm in 1994 to bankruptcy in just 17 years.

Introduction

The Introductory case study informs the stated objectives of this chapter. First, the study demonstrates empirically how distinctively national characteristics in employment systems become embedded as part of established business strategies in particular firms. Further, it demonstrates the manner in which both particular business and HRM strategies can remain embedded, even in the face of threatening technological innovations. This is sometimes referred to as the 'old economy', featuring stable markets and established margins which sustain chosen approaches to employment regulation. It may prove instructive comparatively to look at how firms in the German and Japanese business systems have or have not been able to sustain established approaches to HRM and business in the face of similar developments. Secondly, it will be instructive to evaluate comparatively how firms in the three business systems have reacted to the various financial crises that have unfolded since 2007, in particular, how these crises have or have not challenged embedded patterns of employment regulation. Thirdly, it will be possible to examine the extent to which national employment systems demonstrate convergence towards aspects of the American model. Alternatively, it is possible to examine the extent to which the American, German and Japanese economies, associated business systems and related approaches to employment regulation and HRM have remained distinctively divergent in response to global crises.

Accordingly the chapter is divided into six sections. The first section outlines the field of scholarship in comparative HRM. The second examines the relationship between multinational firms and the strength or weakness of their country of origin in a particular national business system and the impact of this on the comparative diffusion of HRM in multinational firms of different nationalities. Thirdly, we look at varieties of HRM in the American business system. The fourth section looks at corporate paternalism in the Japanese business system and the penultimate section looks at so-called systematic social partnership in the German business system. There are two reasons for focusing on the employment systems of these particular countries: at different points in recent history each has been seen as an example of excellence based on the diffusion of multinational corporations (MNCs) and a model to be emulated by indigenous firms; and each of these models currently embodies a different paradigm of employment relations and HRM. The USA represents the liberal market model, Germany represents a model of social partnership and Japan is a model of enterprise-based partnership. The final section reveals a discussion of the financial crisis, 'financialisation', and the movement to financial capitalism, examining the impact of all three developments on comparative approaches to HRM which are embedded in particular business systems.

International and comparative HRM: the field of scholarship

What's the point of talking about international and comparative HRM? For critics there is not much point at all because HRM, let alone international or comparative HRM, is not a subject (see Thompson, 2011). However, for students of the sociology of work, work organisation and management strategy, there is a significant point in talking about international and comparative HRM. Take, for example, the British economy and the current state of employer strategies for the management of employees. Today, many standard HRM practices applied in both the public and private sectors originated beyond the UK; for example, appraisal and performance management, teamworking, team leadership strategies and associated approaches to the management of quality and logistics, non-unionism and union exclusion as a preferred management strategy all originated beyond the UK and were first substantively diffused into the British economy by subsidiaries of foreign multinational firms. So there is a point to talking about international HRM. This is the case because the term international HRM describes a set of distinct activities, functions and processes that are directed to attracting, developing and maintaining human resources in a multinational firm, i.e. a firm that operates in the global economy. However, at this stage, the talk is not complete. All firms, national and multinational, recruit, select, organise, motivate, promote, discipline, train and develop and terminate their employees, so is it enough to argue that all multinational firms undertake these activities in the same manner? No, it is necessary to go beyond international HRM and bring in a comparative dimension. Comparative HRM suggests that any appreciation of HRM is dependent on recognising the reasons for differences and similarities in HR practice across firms of different nationality. That is, how different national business systems create differences in approaches to the practice of HRM in different societies. Appreciation of these differences has led researchers to develop 'the country-of-origin effect' (see Dunning, 1999; Noorderhaven and Harzing, 2003). Whilst the country-of-origin effect remains contentious and ill-defined, the sources of its effect lie in the institutional framework and home country culture of a particular multinational firm. A significant mechanism through which the effect is manifest flows from the recruitment and selection of home country nationals by the multinational firm and the comparative embeddedness of administrative preferences of home country nationals in the organisational structures for business and HRM strategies, associated procedures and processes for aspects of HRM. The substantive characteristics of the home country and the extent to which these characteristics are institutionalised (in the home country), combined with the homogeneity of home country culture and the international diffusion of a particular multinational firm, all impact on the strength of the country-of-origin effect. Hence the comparative strength of country-of-origin effects in American, German and Japanese multinational firms is moderated by factors such as the cultural and institutional strength or weakness of 'Americanness', 'Germanness' and 'Japaneseness'. The strength or weakness of the country-of-origin effect is also moderated by the sector in which a multinational firm operates and the comparative strength or weakness of host country effects. This chapter further develops these points in part two whereas the remainder of this initial section summarises four phases in the development of comparative HRM.

Comparative HRM 1: Staffing decisions in multinational firms

Some of the earliest work on the development of multinational firms focused on the attitudes of executives in the home country to staffing decisions in overseas subsidiaries. Perlmutter (1969) developed the idea that executives in the company's headquarters could have one of three attitudes towards staffing in subsidiary operations: ethnocentric or home country-dominated; polycentric or host subsidiary country-dominated; or geocentric or world-orientated. In summary this early phase in the development of the subject focused on the management and use of expatriates in subsidiary operations to either reproduce home country-of-origin effects or set up and train host country nationals. In effect, international HRM had a practitioner focus that represented the international HR services of a multinational firm, i.e. recruitment, selection, pay and performance of expatriates plus housing, health, government relations, taxation, security and so forth.

Comparative HRM 2: International business strategy and the management of human resources

The 1980s witnessed a discernible change in the focus of debate away from ethnocentric, polycentric and geocentric studies towards two new themes. First, studies that focused on the transfer of policies across borders and the attempts of multinational firms to transfer international business and HRM strategies in the face of nationally distinctive styles of HRM and employment regulation in host countries (see, e.g. Bartlett and Ghosal, 1989). A central empirical theme that came out of this category of research was the persistence of differences, both culturally and institutionally, between national business systems, what it now termed divergence. The second theme focused on the presence of more common approaches to business and the management of human resources in multinational firms, which suggested that multinational firms were getting more similar. This argument is reminiscent of Kerr *et al.* (1960), who suggested that exposure to similar technologies would promote a similar diffusion of industrialisation across societies. In the contemporary period, this approach has re-emerged as globalisation and its attendant pressures towards convergence. As one of the chapter objectives identifies, the idea of convergence begs the question: convergence on what?

Comparative HRM 3: Organisational strategy, HRM in multinationals and divergence

Since the early 1990s, approaches to international and comparative HRM have attempted to cut through the cultural and technological prescription of convergence theory. More particularly, the study of HRM in multinational firms began to focus on the relationship between headquarters and subsidiaries and the moderating effects of embedded characteristics in national business systems which were identified by institutional theory, in particular the varieties of capitalism thesis associated with Hall and Soskice (2001). Here the literature began to entertain an explicit comparative dimension. This approach identified a convergence of practices, e.g. a growing focus on investor and shareholder value as a driver of management strategy. However, divergent responses, whereupon, say, German firms successfully accommodated these pressures, did not necessarily require German firms to become more like American or British firms in either business or HR strategies. That is, German multinational firms retained their Germanness, in that investor and shareholder value remains an important goal for private-sector firms, but were not required to give up well-established stakeholder approaches to business and employment relations management.

Comparative HRM 4: Potential drivers of change in comparative HRM in the contemporary period?

The contemporary period (i.e. the past 10 years to 2013) has witnessed considerable change in the global economy. Businesses are looking for new markets at lower costs, there has been rapid and extensive development in global communications and associated rapid development and transfer of new technology. These factors have, in turn, stimulated increased global travel and migration, which has improved and extended global education opportunities widening the global talent pool available to domestic and multinational firms. It is argued that there has been a further homogenisation of culture and consumer demand and a diffusion of new business models based on leverage and merger and acquisition. In addition to these factors, the period since 2008 has witnessed a sustained and deepening global financial crisis, an associated credit crunch, and a Eurozone crisis (see the section on 'financialisation' later in the chapter for more on this). All of these developments have an unfolding impact on established approaches to business and HRM as the Introductory case study establishes in relation to Kodak. These points are further developed in the next section. To summarise this section, one can say the following:

- International HRM is HRM in multinational firms.
- Comparative HRM centres on how HRM is affected by the characteristics of a business system and how MNCs are embedded within a national business system.
- That is, how a country of origin leads to points of difference and divergence in the manner in which MNCs address international business and international HRM.
- The relationship between these factors forms the basis of the next section of the chapter.

Key Controversy

Is comparative HRM a subject? How is comparative HRM substantively different from international HRM? Is comparative HRM a framework that academics use to describe differences? Are these differences of any relevance to HR practitioners and potential HR practitioners in MNCs or domestic firms?

HRM in a global, multinational and comparative context

This section examines the relationship between HRM, multinational firms and the country-of-origin business system within which a multinational firm is embedded. It also briefly outlines what we understand by the term multinational firm and then goes on to outline a conceptual framework to understand HRM in multinational firms.

This section establishes that national institutional frameworks of regulation create a comparative dimension of difference in terms of how multinational firms approach HRM. Key HR activities such as recruitment and selection, appraisal and performance management, learning and development, reward, remuneration, motivation and employment relations previously established in a national firm become exposed to an international dimension when the firm becomes a multinational. Therein a multinational firm may seek to export aspects of its domestic regulation to overseas subsidiaries. The extent of this preference brings into play the comparative strength or weakness of the country-of-origin effect associated with multinational firms of a particular nationality.

Multinationals

Traditionally multinational firms were based in one nation state, but today most firms trade internationally. At one stage this was manifest as exports of the goods produced by the firm, but in the contemporary period it is more likely to be manifest as direct foreign investment where a firm builds subsidiary operations in overseas territories. Therefore multinational firms operate in two or more nations; that is, they operate in and beyond their country of origin but are likely to remain embedded within and dominated by the institutional and cultural framework of their country of origin. Further, they may seek to transfer aspects of their home culture and institutional framework to host countries where foreign direct investment is located. In summary, multinational firms go through various stages of internationalisation, ranging from initially exporting the goods they produce to setting up local sales offices in different territories followed by licensing and franchising operations, which may see local host firms producing versions of their goods. These firms may then become more formal subcontractors, followed by the creation of wholly owned subsidiaries, together with the development of joint ventures or mergers and acquisitions, international consortia, alliances and partnerships.

So during the twentieth century most multinational firms grew from domestic firms, but in the twenty-first century the 'born global firm', e.g. Facebook, Google and other technology firms, represents a new phenomenon which the contemporary drivers of internationalisation identified in the preceding section make much more possible, particularly in digital services.

> **Explore**
>
> - Think of a multinational firm with which you are familiar – would you describe it as a 'traditional multinational' or a 'born global firm'?
> - What might be the implications of this distinction for the development of HR practices?

National business systems

The economic, political and social characteristics of individual nation states are shaped by and embedded within a social system which results in distinctively national characteristics. Within this variation, national employment systems reflect wider differences in national culture and institutions. They are the outcome of nationally distinctive histories of how national identity and statehood were forged, how industrialisation developed, and how the nature and outcomes of class conflicts shaped political institutions and relations between capital, labour and the state. It follows from this that national characteristics shape the strategies of actors such as capital, labour and the state. For firms, this is what makes US firms American and what emphasises the 'Germanness' and 'Japaneseness' of German and Japanese firms.

Since the late 1990s, academics have used a framework to evaluate differences and similarities between different business systems centred on comparative institutionalism. The 'varieties of capitalism' literature argues that capitalism comes in two broadly defined forms: liberal market economies, on the one hand, and liberal coordinated economies on the other (Hall and Soskice, 2001: 1–70). Market and coordinated economies are characterised by specific institutional complementarities, whereby the existence of two or more institutions stimulates improved performance of the economy; for example, the German business system, which is a coordinated, co-determination in employment relations, both promotes and sustains the system of vocational education and training that has helped sustain an innovative export-orientated manufacturing sector. By contrast, in the American business system, which is market-based, the ease with which businesses can be created and can hire and fire workers has promoted significant levels of innovation and the application of new business models based on venture capital and private equity, often summarised as the 'new economy'.

Both systems are sustainable and have specific comparative advantages, which suggest that neither system typology is inherently superior or preferable. Each system type has different patterns of control and coordination and these differences persist over time to embed different patterns of cooperation and conflict (Whitley, 1999). Based on market coordination, liberal market economies emphasise flexible labour markets, highly developed financial markets and highly competitive product markets. In contrast to this pattern, coordinated economies are based on non-market, more bureaucratic forms of coordination such as networks, regional alliances and cooperation. Moreover, traditionally finance is more long-term in orientation and the market for corporate control is less developed as family and long-term block shareholding by banks and other institutions is well established. Similarly, employment protection is stringent and often constitutionally guaranteed, which encourages firms to cooperate and form alliances in product markets. To summarise, a key theoretical theme in the literature is the persistence of differences between established business system types in the organisation and activities of the state, capital, labour and financial systems.

The country-of-origin effect

The country-of-origin effect suggests that multinational firms may seek to diffuse HR policies and strategies devised in the home country to their subsidiary operations in overseas territories (Ferner, 1997; Noorderhaven and Harzing, 2003). The sources of this effect can be found, both culturally and institutionally, in the home country of the multinational. The mechanisms by which this effect becomes manifest are in the recruitment of home country nationals of the multinational. This mechanism combines with the depth and strength of the embeddedness of the executive and administrative preferences of these home country nationals in home country organisational structures, procedures and operational processes. Hence, the country-of-origin effect can be strong where the substantive characteristics of the country of origin are deeply embedded to the extent that multinationals are highly ethnocentric in the manner in which they manage their overseas operations. For example, traditionally American multinationals are viewed as expressing, both culturally and where possible institutionally, a strong country-of-origin effect. However, the country-of-origin effect can be weaker; for example, German firms in Germany have a very strong country-of-origin effect, but the Germanness of overseas subsidiaries is less strong for a variety of reasons.

Explore

Consider a well-known multinational firm, such as McDonald's or Jaguar Land Rover.
- How strong is the country-of-origin effect?
- What factors lead you to draw this conclusion?

Host country effects

Host country effects refer to patterns of local regulation, custom and practice and statutory regulation, which may inhibit or encourage the transfer of country-of-origin effects of multinational firms. For example, it is well known that American multinational firms seek to manage through the managerial prerogative, which is often vulgarised in the term 'hire and fire'. The preference for a unitary managerial prerogative often manifests itself as non-unionism and sophisticated approaches to personnel management such as those associated with Kodak. Alternatively, the managerial prerogative may be manifest as anti-unionism or 'union busting'. Despite the embeddedness of these preferences, in some overseas territories where American multinationals decide to locate, union recognition may be a constitutional right. Because of this, American firms concede that they must recognise trade unions but may seek to do so in a manner which has only a minimal effect on the managerial prerogative. There is evidence that multinationals often associated with a strong country-of-origin effect are now seeking to get closer to the host country and may apply country-of-origin effects differentially to take into account the strength of particular host country effects. For example, Brewster *et al.* (2008) use a large international data set to demonstrate that the country-of-origin effect is weak. In addition, they find evidence of common global practices with sufficient diversity in practice to suggest that multinational firms face conflicting pressures towards and away from country-of-origin practices. These pressures may be further reinforced by regulatory factors and strategic choice options exercised by local managers as a form of subsidiary autonomy.

'Reverse diffusion' in multinational firms

Reverse diffusion involves practices that originate in overseas subsidiaries being repatriated to the multinational firm's country of origin, its headquarters in particular. These practices may then be adopted in domestic operations in the country of origin but, in addition, they are repackaged, reinvented and then diffused to other subsidiary operations beyond the one where the practice originated. The process of reverse diffusion is most likely to occur where the multinational firm has a weakness, but where particular subsidiaries have solutions to these weaknesses (see Edwards and Ferner, 2004 for detailed discussion of reverse diffusion).

'Sector effects' in multinational firms

Host country effects may mediate country-of-origin effects and reverse diffusion may redefine country-of-origin effects and host country effects. Sector effects may override country-of-origin effects and some aspects of host country effects. Put simply sector effects refer to the manner in which a particular sector operates. These effects may refer to the 'rules of the game' in a particular sector, where to operate effectively firms must assume a particular style and form which may override country-of-origin effects – even those associated with strongly ethnocentric business systems such as the American system. In the language introduced earlier in this chapter, firms in some sectors may converge on a particular form and style of operation. Colling and Clark (2002) found that sector effects in engineering contracting cut through country-of-origin effects, rendering nationality a poor predictor of internal style and operations. Similarly, Peston and Knight (2012) argue that operationally and managerially the vast majority of international banks conformed to a sector characteristic that diminished country-of-origin differences to the level of insignificance.

To summarise this section, it is possible to say:

- Multinational firms are embedded in the cultural and institutional framework of their parent country of origin.

- National business systems can be coordinated or market-orientated. The cultural and institutional embeddedness present within national business systems informs approaches to HRM and industrial relations.

- Multinational firms may seek to export or transfer domestic approaches to HRM to overseas subsidiaries. Host country factors may inhibit or reinforce the preference for transfer.

- Sector effects and reverse diffusion may further inhibit or inform country-of-origin effects.

- The country-of-origin effect remains conceptually influential, but in a period of globalisation is open to criticism as multinational firms evidently seek to get closer to host country territories in terms of HR strategies and policies.

Key Controversy

During a period of globalisation or contemporary convergence, is it possible to argue that country-of-origin effects remain significant indicators of MNC behaviour?
Why might MNCs seek to disguise or change their country of origin?

The American business system and HRM: varieties of HRM?

This section of the chapter outlines the characteristics of the American business system and then goes on to explain how these characteristics sustain varieties of Americanness in terms of patterns of HRM at the firm level. The characteristics and varieties of Americanness are best described as a pattern of managerial capitalism which exposes the visible hand of management and emphasises an unbridled managerial prerogative.

Hand in hand: the characteristics of the American business system

The managerial prerogative and freedom of action reflect the historical development of American capitalism, which exhibits a strong emphasis on individualism, private property rights and free market competition (Chandler, 1977, 1990; Lazonick, 1991). An ideology of egalitarian individualism is diffused throughout American society. Individual property rights are seen to be the foundation of democracy, creating a strong presumption against state regulation. In the field of employment relations, this is manifest in a strong bias against external interference with the rights of management whether by the state or trade unions. Therefore, compared with their counterparts in Germany and Japan, American managers are less constrained by legislation and social norms that restrict the employer's freedom to hire and fire and provide workers with rights to collective representation and participation in decision-making. This relative freedom flowed from and reinforces a comparatively poorly developed labour movement in the USA and allowed American employers to adopt a variety of managerially led approaches to workplace HRM and industrial relations. These included relatively sophisticated unitarist and pluralist approaches to employment regulation, as well as traditional approaches based on 'hire and fire'.

The American economy is characterised by market competition where, as firms grew in size, employers sought to innovate in production through the processes of simplification and standardisation. First encountered in the American armoury system of production (pistols and rifles) and then in meat packing, standardisation and simplification in production by the use of interchangeable parts grew to international prominence in automobile manufacturing, sometimes referred to as 'Fordism'. Employment in the American economy exhibits a pattern of highly contractual relations based on individualism and anti-trade unionism, both of which reinforce the managerial prerogative in employment. In the twentieth century, the pattern of market competition stimulated the creation of large, vertically integrated firms that controlled each stage of production. Extraction, manufacturing and retailing can be controlled either forward, as in the case of oil companies who drilled, refined and then sold petrol in their own petrol stations, or backwards as in the case of meat packing firms who owned ranches and cattle. The presence of large vertically integrated firms stimulated the growth of standardised mass intercontinental markets across the USA. These characteristics required strongly developed managerial bureaucracies and witnessed the development of centralised and professionalised managerial functions in accounting and finance, human resources, marketing and production and scientific management. Comparatively these functions developed well ahead of those found in other business systems. Marketing, in particular, saw the comparatively early development of nationally recognised branding and logos. Labour shortage dogged the development of the American economy and in response American governments encouraged successive waves of mass immigration in the late 19th century and inter-war period during the 20th century, often encouraging Europeans to get away from the war torn continent. Labour shortage not only encouraged immigration to stimulate economic development and growth, but in addition compelled the imperative of capital substitution in production. For American entrepreneurs and managers, this marked the beginning of work study, job analysis and work measurement as the scale of mass production necessitated managerial interventions to centralise, formalise and standardise production on what came to be known, not as production lines, but assembly lines (see Clark and Almond, 2006). It is in relation to production and the development of managerial controls that two iconic features of American managerial capitalism developed: de-skilling and managerial controls. The de-skilling thesis centred on wrest craft control of production away from labour and placing organisational capability for production in the hands of management. This development is often summarised in the phrase, 'the separation of the execution and control of production', and is characterised in the development of standardised assembly line production (see Braverman, 1974). As management wrested control over production from labour, this process of struggle and control witnessed the development of centralised managerial controls over labour. Edwards (1979) categorises these as simple, technical and bureaucratic controls. Simple controls are evident in the development of foreman, supervisors and, in more contemporary language, team leaders who retain a visual control over workers. Technical controls derive from the process of capital substitution already referred to, wherein workers become controlled by the pacing and technical characteristics of the machinery they work with, e.g. machine tools and presses in manufacturing processes, information technology systems, and scanners in food retailing and many other areas of work. The development of personnel and HR systems represents the best example of a bureaucratic control where HR innovations such as performance management and appraisals, time sheets, clocking or carding on and off of work, workplace discipline and reporting systems enable management not only to direct workers but also to monitor their performance. In more contemporary language, bureaucratic controls are often referred to as cultural controls in the workplace or in more post-structuralist approaches – workplace surveillance systems.

Business associations that play a significant role in regulating markets and relations among firms in other national systems are less prominent in the USA and firms prefer to 'go it alone'. This is because American business never had to define itself collectively in opposition to aristocratic or feudal interests (other than the conflict over slavery) in the way that European capitalists did. Consequently, the American business system is characterised by a relative absence of collective organisation among American businesses and therefore weak 'collective governance' in the private sector (Hollingsworth, 1997).

Employment models in the American business system: pluralism in the New Deal system

The late 1920s through to the early 1930s was a period of sustained economic collapse in the USA; often referred to as the 'Great Depression', this period witnessed the collapse of agriculture in the Midwest and California and the collapse of employment in many elements of manufacturing industry. Despite heavy unemployment and weak trade unions, however, there were pockets of sustained resistance to some of the worst excesses of management control and de-skilling within the American model of management. In 1933, recognising the threat of a total collapse of American capitalism, the newly elected President Roosevelt promised a 'New Deal' for Americans in a series of government interventions to create jobs, provide a measure of social security and address the historic imbalance of power in the employment relationship.

New Deal legislation, in the form of Section 7a of the 1933 National Industrial Recovery Act and the 1935 National Labour Relations Act, gave employees the legal right to organise and bargain collectively through representatives of their own choosing, free from employer coercion and interference (practices that were common during the 1920s). The New Deal approach to workplace trade unionism and collective bargaining introduced truly independent trade unions into American workplaces for the first time, but provided no authoritative enforcement procedures whilst theoretically compelling employers to bargain in good faith. The effect of this was both to stiffen employer resistance to collective bargaining and stimulate militant worker resistance to the development of more formalised, simple, technical and bureaucratic management controls. This led to a low-trust, adversarial system of industrial relations characterised by highly codified industrial relations practices, such as written contracts, detailed job descriptions, formalised grievance and disciplinary procedures, seniority rules to determine lay-offs and promotion between grades, provision for dispute arbitration and, in some cases, no-strike clauses (see Rupert, 1995; Towers, 1997; Clark and Almond, 2006).

In many respects, the New Deal system created a constitutional framework for workplace industrial relations, yet employer resistance to the system saw the development of employer-led, managerially controlled alternatives. A good number of large corporations refused to accept New Deal collective bargaining and kept unions out of their plants through a combination of paternalism and authoritarianism that came to be known as welfare capitalism (see the following section). Moreover, from the 1970s the New Deal system came under increasing strain due to increased international competition, the declining significance of domestic mass production and pressure for more flexible deployment of labour across work tasks as a way of improving competitiveness. In some cases, e.g. at General Motors and Delta Airlines, this led management and unions to seek a more cooperative relationship in which unions accepted new, more flexible working patterns and pay restraint in return for improved employment security, employee involvement and union participation in decision-making. More commonly, however, competitive pressures encouraged employers to turn towards non-union strategies that involved relocating operations away from the traditional industrial regions of the north-east to greenfield sites in tax- and employer-friendly states in the south where New Deal industrial relations were much less entrenched. At the same time, a shift in the labour force away from blue-collar towards white-collar and professional occupations encouraged employers to develop more individually focused HRM policies, reinforcing the non-union trend (Kochan *et al.,* 1993). In summary, New Deal employment protections and labour market regulations are weak compared with those found in most European states. At the individual level, American employment law is based on the doctrine of employment at will. At the collective level, the New Deal model has established only a decentralised industrial relations system in which employees can gain union recognition only if they win a majority of votes in workplace-level elections. It follows from this that unions must organise workers and negotiate contracts on a workplace by workplace firm-level basis. This limits union power by demanding high levels of union resource to administer contracts and organise new members. The 'pattern' of systematic job control contracts negotiated by American unions in the boom years of the 1950s–1960s across firms in a particular sector has, in the main, broken down as union power has eroded and membership density declined to less than 10 per cent of the American private-sector workforce.

Sophisticated unitarism: welfare capitalism

Welfare capitalism is a management approach to labour relations based on non-unionism and strong mutual commitment between employer and employees. Welfare capitalism is characterised by an ideological opposition to trade unions and collective bargaining in the workplace, much of which gained momentum because of what many 'founding father' employers saw as the politically centralising New Deal model. Further developed and extended during the 1930s, welfare capitalism co-existed with the New Deal model of labour relations. Welfare capitalist employers, in adopting sophisticated non-unionism, laid the origins for what is now termed HRM, developing an authoritarian yet paternalist approach to labour relations where the firm, rather than the state, trade unions or other third parties (such as the courts or arbitration panels), should provide for the security and welfare of employees.

Welfare capitalist employers devised strong corporate cultures and branding techniques, including the use and promotion of corporate mission statements, straplines, scripted speech and uniforms featuring company logos. Examples of welfare capitalist employers that you might be familiar with include Kodak, Procter & Gamble, Standard Oil, Heinz and IBM. To keep trade unions and collective bargaining out of their workplaces, welfare capitalist employers developed sophisticated union substitution strategies, including personnel management innovations such as provisions for employment security, severance pay, unemployment insurance, pensions and health care insurance (Foulkes, 1980). These strategies were supported by profits generated in strong, stable markets and often by being the dominant employer in a 'company town', which was an additional source of employee loyalty. More recently, welfare capitalist firms have been associated with the deployment of teamworking, profit-sharing and share ownership, workplace appraisals and employee rankings and performance-related pay schemes for both teams and individuals, in other words with the techniques associated with HRM (Jacoby, 1997).

Explore

- To what extent are sophisticated trade union substitution practices sufficient to sustain a union-free environment?

Welfare capitalist firms have not relied exclusively on sophisticated union substitution strategies; they have not hesitated to use more authoritarian methods to suppress attempts at unionisation when these have occurred. There is a thriving union avoidance industry made up of specialist consultants and law firms that advise companies on how to resist union recruitment drives and suppress union activity, and 'strike management' firms that provide workplace security in situations where an employer has replaced economic strikers. For more detail on union avoidance, see Logan (2006).

Traditional unitarism: 'lower road approaches'

American management has been influenced by the highly competitive nature of product markets and the attendant pressures for cost and price reduction. This, together with a scarcity of skilled labour, has encouraged the development of systems of management control over work organisation and product assembly that intensify and de-skill labour. In some sectors of employment, such as fast food, apparel and food retailing, meat packing, laundry services and delivery, cut-throat cost and price-based competition has encouraged employers to minimise labour costs by taking 'low road' non-union approaches to HRM and industrial relations (Katz and Darbishire, 2000). Here management focuses on standardisation, strict job controls and de-skilling, provides low wages and limited fringe benefits and only limited access to employee development and training. Initially lower road approaches, sometimes summarised as 'hire and fire', predominated in areas of employment not covered by New Deal and welfare capitalist employers. The retail giant Wal-Mart has often been portrayed as an example of this approach. More contemporary examples might include the retailer Amazon, where warehouse and packing work is highly de-skilled, and coffee retailers such as Starbucks that adopt an assembly line approach to coffee and snacks that incorporates the customer.

Explore

- What factors enable organisations that adopt 'low-road' practices to attract and retain staff?
- Why do you think these organisations are so successful?

Country-of-origin effects in subsidiaries of US MNCs

The dominant empirical finding in the literature on HRM in US MNCs is that American firms of any variety (i.e. New Deal, welfare capitalist or lower road) seek to transfer management styles to overseas subsidiaries (see Almond and Ferner, 2006). In terms of employment regulation and HRM, American firms are highly centralised, formalised and standardised, which historically reflects the highly ethnocentric approach to international business. In the contemporary period, there is some evidence to suggest that American firms do seek to get closer to host countries where they are located and may downplay formalised aspects of corporate cultures and standardisation in international business. So, in summary, the focus of contemporary debate on country-of-origin effects for US MNCs is on standardisation or local responsiveness in international business and associated approaches to HRM in subsidiary operations. Similarly, researchers have outlined the presence of subsidiary autonomy in the face of attempts by headquarters to secure centralisation and the impact of sector effects in defined areas of business such as engineering contracting or electricity (Colling and Clark, 2002, 2006; Ferner *et al.*, 2011). Both of these developments have the effect of blunting country-of-origin effects.

The nature of state regulation

American individualism is reflected in political commitment to the principles of the liberal market economy, i.e. free competition and as little state regulation of business as possible. Successive American governments have sustained minimal regulation of the labour market, supporting the 'hire at will' doctrine, which means that workers have few statutory protections against dismissal, other than on grounds of unfair discrimination. In addition to this, while the 1935 National Labour Relations Act provides workers with a legal right to vote for union representation, it leaves many avenues open to employers who wish to resist unionisation, so the law is of limited effectiveness (Kochan *et al.*, 1993). Weak statutory regulation of employment and weak statutory support for collective bargaining result in a very flexible labour market. The flexibility of the American labour market enables employers of whatever variety to make swift adjustments to the size of their labour force, a process that is often referred to as downsizing or 'right-sizing' a firm. Weak regulation also makes it easy for firms of any variety to adopt 'low road' employment strategies and deploy them against peripheral or core workers.

The financial system and corporate governance

Although some long-term inter-firm collaboration typical of more coordinated market economies is to be found in certain sectors, such as defence, health care, the digital economy, information technology and electronics (Locke, 1996; Hollingsworth, 1997), for the most part relations between American firms are arm's-length and contractual rather than long-term and relational (Chandler, 1977, 1990; Lazonick, 1991; Hall and Soskice, 2001). The arm's-length character of relations between firms in competitive demand-driven markets applies to the financial system too. In contrast to the close, long-term links between banks and firms typical of the post-war German and Japanese business systems, there is a much greater development of equity markets in the USA. Historically, share ownership has been much wider in the United States than elsewhere, and as enterprises grew in size and complexity, professional managers replaced owner-managers. This separation of ownership from control led to the development of sophisticated hierarchies of professional managers exercising considerable discretion in defining and achieving the goals of the firm. This development was captured in the term new 'managerial theories' of the firm (Baumol, 1959; Williamson, 1964). These theories developed what O'Sullivan (2000) later termed the 'retain and reinvest' pattern of corporate governance in the American business system. Although heavily focused on short-term results, managers nevertheless balanced the claims of shareholders against the need to retain profits to invest in product innovation. Professional managers also secured close control over labour through systematic mechanisation, labour de-skilling and bureaucratic forms of control (Braverman, 1974; Edwards, 1979; Littler, 1982).

The system of vocational education and training

The USA does not have a strongly developed system of vocational education and training. In particular, there is little organised training provision for high school leavers, who have to pick up skills through a mixture of informal and formal training once they enter employment (Cappelli *et al.*, 1997). In the absence of a training system that produces workers with formal occupational qualifications, employers design jobs to their own specifications and then fit the workers to the jobs (Marsden, 1999). Company-provided training has therefore aimed at providing workers with narrow skills related to their particular job rather than the broad occupational skills produced by German apprenticeships or the combinations of firm-specific skills generated by in-company training in Japan. This is in line with the tendency to substitute capital equipment for skilled labour and rely on systematic technical and bureaucratic control over workers rather than providing for their involvement in decision-making on the shop floor. This, in turn, has reinforced the 'arm's-length' relationship between management and labour.

Key Controversy

Are American firms inherently anti-trade union? Does the decline of welfare capitalism indicate a parallel decline in more sophisticated approaches to HRM?

Why do American firms fight to prioritise investor and shareholder value and the priorities of financial capitalism at the expense of stakeholder interests and those of employees in particular?

The Japanese employment system: firm-level welfare corporatism and corporate paternalism?

The Japanese employment system has been described as *welfare corporatism* or *corporate paternalism*. One way in which this has been expressed is in the nature of the relationship between the large Japanese company and its employees. This responsibility extends beyond the employee himself to include his family members. Thus Dore (1973) reported that at the Hitachi company during the 1950s and 1960s, all permanent employees were eligible for retirement bonuses, company pensions, social clubs and activities for retired workers, rented accommodation provided by the company, savings and loan schemes to aid house purchase, transport subsidies, sickness pay, educational loans for employees' children, gift payments made for weddings, births and marriages of children, and condolence gifts on an employee's death or the death of a family member.

Like many of the alleged economic miracles associated with the Japanese employment system, the details of the Hitachi case are economical with the truth. So to contextualise the modern Japan since 1945, the key characteristics of the Japanese employment system are briefly outlined. First, the focus of paternalism is the core permanent labour force in large Japanese firms, many of which are now well-known multinational firms. There is a dual system, comprising large employers supported by many more peripheral small to medium-sized firms within which many employees do not receive the benefits described in the previous paragraph. Originally, in the 1950s, employer paternalism was in fact an instrumental strategy to secure recruitment and retention of workers in the context of a severe labour shortage following the Second World War. Employer paternalism then and now focuses on the wage effort bargain and worker welfare.

The strength of welfare corporatism is largely due to the relative absence of a welfare state in post-Second World War Japan. In these circumstances, the provision of extensive welfare benefits by large Japanese companies was a way of attracting the best employees at a time of labour shortage. The range and level of welfare benefits also rapidly became an important issue for trade unions in negotiations with employers, as it did in the USA, where state welfare provision is also minimal. Welfare corporatism contributed to fostering what Sako (1997) describes as *community consciousness* among Japanese workers and managers. This is expressed in high levels of employee commitment and cooperation with management and low levels of industrial conflict. It is argued that Japanese workers see their relationship with their company as a 'partnership of fate', which involves a strong element of personal loyalty to the company and feelings of responsibility to colleagues and superiors in return for long-term material security provided by the firm (Matanle, 2003). By the 1980s these characteristics came to represent the embedded features of Japanese capitalism, which combined to secure continuous stable employment for core workers and created an internal dimension to management control strategies. The latter centred on employee commitment and the inclusion of employees in the process of management control in stark contrast to the American strategy of employee exclusion. There are three embedded features of Japanese capitalism that underpin welfare corporatism in Japan: lifetime employment, seniority-based pay and promotion, and enterprise unionism.

Lifetime employment

Traditionally large Japanese firms fill the vast majority of their permanent vacancies by recruiting school-leavers and university graduates as trainees. Once hired, these workers remain with the company until retirement. Essentially they enter an internal labour market (see Chapter 4) that provides long-term employment security and fills vacancies by internal promotion rather than external recruitment. Historically, Japanese employers have gone to great lengths to avoid dismissing workers during slack production periods. Depending on how long the slack period lasts, employers have used the time to provide workers with additional training, or they have transferred workers internally or to other companies either temporarily or permanently rather than simply dismiss them. Some firms have even set up new subsidiary companies to absorb redundant employees. This reluctance among large firms to dismiss workers on grounds of redundancy has been attributed to three factors: fear that dismissals would damage their reputation and make it harder for them to recruit high-quality university graduates in the future; legal restrictions that make dismissals difficult to defend in the courts; and a desire to avoid conflict with the union, which could lead to immediate disruption of production and weaken the basis for long-term cooperation (Rubery and Grimshaw, 2003).

Seniority-based pay and promotion

Historically, a distinctive feature of the Japanese approach to pay has been that, instead of pay being job-related, i.e. determined by the nature of the job being performed, it is person-related. A key person-related criterion for determining pay is seniority measured by age and length of service. Basic salaries are agreed for employees in different age bands, and annual salary increases are also related to seniority, with longer-serving workers receiving larger increases. In addition to basic salary, workers receive merit bonuses based on evaluation by their superiors. However, while merit bonuses mean that workers with the same length of service are paid different amounts, merit payments still incorporate a seniority element. This is because of agreements between employers and unions that specify that workers with longer service receive higher average merit ratings. Seniority-based promotion from one grade to another does not mean that the workers' function changes, it just means 'more status and a higher level of annual salary increases' (Dore, 1973: 99). More recently, employers have increased the weight attached to ability as opposed to age when determining pay, but how ability is determined is often vague (Matanle, 2003).

Enterprise unionism

While American trade unions are organised on an occupational or industrial basis and German trade unions on an industrial or sectoral basis, Japanese union organisation is based around individual enterprises. Thus firms such as Nissan or Toyota have their own enterprise unions and enterprise union federations. Unions do coordinate wage bargaining activity on a sectoral and national basis through the annual pay bargaining round – the 'spring wage offensive' (*shunto*); however, collective bargaining is essentially conducted at enterprise level. There is a debate over the effectiveness of enterprise unions as representatives of employees' interests. Critics have argued that enterprise unionism means that trade union power is fragmented and thus weakened. Critics also argue that enterprise-based unions identify too closely with the employing organisation and are too susceptible to interference from employers (Shirai, 1983). Supporters argue that enterprise-based unions make it easier for management and unions to work together to resolve problems. They also argue that Japanese enterprise unions exert considerable influence on management decision-making, to the benefit of workers (Nakamura, 1997). In summary, enterprise unions are employer-specific, focused on enterprise and production problem-solving and may or not be employer-controlled – i.e. in comparison to, say, British trade unions, the independence of Japanese trade unions is open to question. In addition to this enterprise, unions may not reflect the nature of Japanese labour. Before the Second World War, enterprise unions were not a key component in the Japanese economy. For some, American occupation and the Cold War saw more independent trade unions subject to suppression. Moreover, in the contemporary period of austerity and crisis, enterprise unions are subject to criticism that they are either ineffective or collude with management, only organise and represent full-time workers and have done little to oppose the growing use of temporary agency workers (Jeong and Aguilera, 2008; Royle and Urano, 2012). However, these three features of Japanese capitalism that underpin corporate paternalism in large Japanese firms focus on involvement and participation and the generation of employee commitment, i.e. the internal capability of a firm in terms of quality and consistency, a kind of paternal stakeholding approach to management control.

Explore

- How transferable are these characteristics – lifetime employment, seniority-based pay and promotion, and enterprise unionism – to non-Japanese organisations?

Dualism in Japan's employment system

The features discussed in the preceding sections have not applied equally to all enterprises and all workers in Japan. They are found in the large-firm corporate sector to a far greater extent than among small and medium-sized firms. Moreover, even within the corporate sector, not all employees enjoy lifetime employment and seniority-based pay and promotion. These conditions only apply to 'standard' employees, i.e. permanent, 'core' workers. A significant proportion of workers employed by large corporations in Japan are non-standard workers, i.e. seasonal, temporary and part-time workers. The exact proportion of Japanese workers who enjoy lifetime employment status has been a matter of debate. A common estimate during the 1980s was 35 per cent, but some estimates were as low as 10 per cent (Oliver and Wilkinson, 1992). Inagami (1988) however, reported that long-term, if not lifetime, employment was becoming increasingly common among smaller firms as well as large ones. This was the result of the development of close, long-term relationships between large corporations and their smaller suppliers, which gave the latter long-term commercial security and supported long-term employment contracts.

The employment system and the wider Japanese business system

Japan's employment system is embedded in a wider framework of institutionalised relationships, the most important of which are the role of the state, the principles of corporate governance and the system of vocational education and training.

State regulation

Japanese employment relations have sometimes been described as 'micro-corporatist'. This refers to the close links between unions and management and the degree of union involvement in business decision-making at the enterprise level. There are also close links between employers and government, and Japanese employers see their responsibilities as being not just to their shareholders but also to their employees and the nation as a whole. However, the absence of an authoritative central trade union confederation and the decentralised nature of collective bargaining have prevented Japanese trade unions from engaging in political exchange with employers and the government, so bargained corporatism has not developed in Japan. The absence of trade unions from policy-making has led to Japan being described as having 'corporatism without labour' (Shinoda, 1997). However, from the late 1980s, some observers argued that this situation was beginning to change and that Japanese trade unions were developing a more coherent political voice at national level following the formation of a unified peak organisation, Rengo (Shinoda, 1997).

In Japan, as in Germany, government legislation supports workers' right to organise and act collectively, although, unlike Germany, it has not laid out formal procedures for co-determination. Legislation also regulates labour market activity in Japan by establishing minimum standards with regard to wages, working time, dismissal and health and safety, although the operation of the law is nationally distinctive. For example, there is no statute that obliges employers to give valid reasons for dismissing workers. Nevertheless, despite the absence of a specific statute, the courts have developed strict standards governing employers' conduct regarding dismissals on the basis of case law, so the law has developed so as to reinforce the practice of lifetime employment (Sugeno and Suwa, 1997).

Corporate governance and finance

Japanese firms, like their German counterparts, operate on the stakeholder principle of governance. It can be argued that Japanese corporations operate a stronger version of the insider variant of this model than German firms, given their formal commitment to lifetime employment and to providing for the social welfare of their employees. This is supported by the system of corporate finance. As in Germany, Japanese corporations obtain most of their finance through bank loans and cross-investments (Oliver and Wilkinson, 1992). This reduces the pressure on Japanese managers to maximise short-run profits to satisfy investor and shareholder value, encourages them to take a long-term view of company performance and underpins Japanese employers' commitment to providing long-term employment security, training and career development for workers. In addition, the tendency to prioritise insider interests is reinforced by the fact that senior managers have themselves been part of the lifetime employment system, promoted from more junior positions within the company (Matanle, 2003).

The vocational education and training system

In contrast to German practice, new recruits in Japan are not selected on the basis of the occupational skills they possess, but on their ability to conform to company values, work cooperatively with others and benefit from training in company-specific skills. The Japanese training system and the system of lifetime employment are closely interlinked. Unlike Germany, Japan does not have a well-developed national system of vocational training. Instead, as in the American business system, training is enterprise-based. Employers take school leavers and college graduates and provide them with initial and continuing vocational training in sets of skills that are specific to the firm. Workers are trained using a mixture of formal training off the job and informal on-the-job training. A distinguishing feature of the enterprise-based system is its emphasis on continuing training over the employee's career in the firm. Permanent workers' careers typically involve gaining training and experience in a range of jobs within the company, updating and broadening their skills over time. Tasks are allocated on the basis of how workers are ranked in terms of their firm-specific skills and experience rather than their formal occupational qualifications (Marsden, 1999). Workers who are more highly ranked by their supervisors in terms of length of service and ability are allocated the more demanding tasks, which may include the design and control of production processes and the management of quality (Lincoln and Kalleberg, 1992; Nakamura, 1997). The Japanese approach to training supports the seniority-based pay and promotion system, as longer-serving workers are competent across a wider, more demanding range of tasks and therefore warrant higher pay.

HR departments in Japanese firms and overseas subsidiaries

In comparison to British and American firms, HR departments in large Japanese firms are more influential and have a clear organisational orientation, focusing on HR planning, learning and development, recruitment and employee welfare. HR departments are very centralised, particularly at the HQ level where policy is driven down to local units. HR departments are traditionally seen as 'king makers' in large Japanese firms as they have played a central role in planning out career pathways for graduate recruits. Turning to overseas subsidiary operations in the UK, the term 'Japanisation' during the 1980s described academic, policy and practitioner obsession with Japanese business and employment models recently diffused into the country. Many of the innovations associated with Japanese multinational firms, such as teamworking, logistics, quality circles and quality management, now represent standard HR and business practices in firms of any nationality and size. However, there are persistent questions over the extent to which 'Japanese' innovations are embedded in UK subsidiaries. HR functions in UK subsidiaries are not as large as those in Japan but remain comparatively distinctive. There is a strong country-of-origin effect on rhetoric and supply chain management, but other aspects of the three pillars system, e.g. enterprise unions, are less in evidence. In car manufacturing in the UK, Japanese employers chose to locate beyond traditional areas of motor manufacturing, but decided to recognise independent UK trade unions. Nonetheless, many Japanese firms are associated with what was once termed 'new industrial relations', where these firms pioneered single union recognition deals, often on a so-called beauty contest basis. These deals also included innovations such as no-strike deals and binding pendulum arbitration in cases of disagreement (Bassett, 1987; Wickens, 1987).

Change in Japan: the crumbling of the 'three pillars'?

Japan experienced a more marked slowing down in economic growth after 1990, with an annual average GDP growth rate of 1.6 per cent between 1991 and 1998. Unemployment in Japan also hit record levels of around 5 per cent, peaking at 5.3 per cent in 2003. It fell back to 3.9 per cent in 2007 but then rose again to 4.4 per cent in February 2009 (Inoue, 1999; OECD, 2008; *Wall Street Journal,* 2009). While this appears low by European standards, it has to be viewed in the context of the Japanese employment system and the extreme reluctance to dismiss workers. The unemployment figures mask a higher level of hidden unemployment and under-employment. The stagnation of Japan's economy, coupled with demographic and social changes, put considerable strain on the employment system. As in Germany, this led a growing number of observers, inside and outside of Japan, to argue that while the employment system may have underpinned Japan's economic success during the 1970s and 1980s, it was an obstacle to recovery in an increasingly globalised world economy. Thus, in 1998, the Japanese Congress on Economic Strategy, an advisory body to the government, argued that the Japanese system attached too much importance to equality and fairness and that Japan needed to restructure itself as a more 'competitive society' (Inoue, 1999:11). Critics also argued that the lifetime employment system had become socially and economically divisive. While older workers continued to enjoy the benefits of lifetime employment, such opportunities for young workers had become increasingly limited. The lifetime employment system was also criticised for being based on an outdated male model of employment that was increasingly at odds with Japanese women's changing aspirations.

The economy began to recover in 2002–03, with improved growth of GDP, and the unemployment rate fell to 3.8 per cent in 2007 (OECD, 2007). However, Japan has been hard hit by the global economic crisis caused by the 'credit crunch'. The value of exports fell by 49 per cent in the first quarter of 2009 and unemployment climbed again, hitting 4.4 per cent in February 2009. After the 'lost decade' of the 1990s, observers commented on how the economic crisis had initiated or accelerated currents of change in Japan's employment system and questioned its long-term viability (Hattori and Maeda, 2000; Hanami, 2004). The impact of the 'credit crunch' produced further challenges to the Japanese version of stakeholder capitalism and its associated employment system which are examined in the following and final sections of this chapter.

Explore

● Before reading on, outline the advantages and disadvantages of maintaining lifetime employment, seniority-based pay and promotion and enterprise unionism in the face of the economic downturn.

From stakeholder to shareholder capitalism?

As we have seen, the Japanese employment system is underpinned by a 'stakeholder capitalism' approach that is reflected in a system of corporate finance and governance that encourages a long-term management orientation and gives a relatively low priority to 'outsider' (i.e. shareholder) interests compared with those of 'insiders' (i.e. managers and managed employees). However, over the last 20 years, changes in patterns of ownership and changes in corporation law have raised the possibility that the stakeholder model is being eroded by growing shareholder influence. The most important developments, described by Araki (2005), are threefold:

● a decline in long-term and cross-shareholding in Japan, which, if it spreads, will destabilise the long-term relations between and within companies that have supported the Japanese employment system;

● a rising proportion of equity owned by foreign shareholders;

● legal reforms that have strengthened the power of shareholders over managers and made it possible for corporations to adopt new governance structures that include external, non-executive directors on boards of directors to represent shareholder interests.

Subsequently, Araki (2007: 281) concludes that these changes 'can best be viewed as the realignment of the priorities of different stakeholders within the framework of the stakeholder model', rather than indicating the collapse of the stakeholder approach. Many Japanese firms maintain cross-shareholding and remain committed to long-term, cooperative relations with other companies and these commitments operate as a form of countervailing power against the share of equity owned by foreign shareholders.

A decline in enterprise unionism?

The proportion of Japanese workers who are union members fell from 34.7 per cent in 1975 to 20.7 per cent in 2001. In more recent years, the figure has fallen further still, but remains significant and would be lower if employers cut their demand for labour to match the demand for goods and services. One reaction to the slowdown in Japanese economic performance is legislative support for the deployment of temporary agency workers, which has put further pressure on the number of new employees able to secure lifetime employment. These developments further reinforce the argument that enterprise unions and their confederations have been subject to a growing criticism that they serve only the interests of the elite group of workers in the leading corporations (Hanami, 2004). In the past, enterprise unions have played an important role as a channel for employee voice in Japanese companies, and as such have helped to create the basis for the high level of worker–management cooperation that has been a characteristic of Japanese employment relations for most of the post-war period. Therefore, the decline of enterprise unionism could threaten to weaken the system as a whole.

A decline in seniority-based pay and promotion?

An ageing workforce and slow economic growth since 1990 have undermined the seniority pay system. This is because seniority-based pay depends on the balance in the workforce between younger, junior employees and older, more senior employees. Younger workers are paid less than is warranted by their productivity, while older workers are paid more. As long as the proportions of younger and older workers are balanced, the overall wage bill is in line with the productivity of the workforce. However, it means that more young workers have to be hired each year to offset the effects of seniority-based wage increases for existing workers. But to be able to do this, the company has to keep expanding to create new vacancies at entry level. The economic stagnation of the Japanese economy has meant that corporations have cut back on their recruitment of young workers. Therefore the overall age profile of the workforce has increased, causing company wage bills increasingly to be out of line with workers' productivity, thus increasing production costs and reducing profitability and competitiveness (Hattori and Maeda, 2000). Reform of the wage and promotion system has also been encouraged by the increased pace of change in organisations. This means that skills and knowledge gained through seniority are at less of a premium. Therefore promotion is being linked more to individual performance. Finally, it is claimed that moves to base pay on individual performance are in tune with changing social attitudes, as younger generations of workers have developed more individualised sets of values and are less collectively orientated (Kusuda, 2000).

The outcome is that most Japanese corporations claim to be reducing the extent to which pay is determined by seniority and increasing the weight given to performance. A survey of large firms carried out by the Japan Productivity Centre for Socio-Economic Development in 1998 found that 76 per cent of respondents planned either to do away completely with seniority-based pay or to move to predominantly performance-based pay systems for their managerial employees (Hattori and Maeda, 2000). Regarding promotions, a survey carried out in 1999 for the Ministry of Labour found that over 80 per cent of companies said they used ability and performance as criteria for promotions to managerial grades, while 48 per cent used seniority. In addition to this, more companies claim to have introduced 'fast track' promotion routes and are promoting people at a younger age (Matanle, 2003; Conrad and Heindorf, 2006). At the same time, however, the extent of teamworking makes individual performance hard to measure, so some companies focus on team rather than individual performance. Lastly, skills and qualifications have become more rather than less important in determining basic pay. As employees need to have spent specified periods of time acquiring prescribed skills and abilities in order to gain promotion to the next grade, this blurs the distinction between seniority and ability/performance, and managers may continue to use age as a convenient proxy for performance. Moreover, the shift from seniority to performance-based pay has been concentrated on managerial staff (Inoue, 1999; Matanle, 2003; Conrad and Heindorf, 2006).

A retreat from lifetime employment?

The long period of economic stagnation throughout the 1990s has led companies to increase their use of fixed term contracts and temporary agency workers. Between 1990 and 2002, the proportion of 'atypical' workers, i.e. those on part-time and fixed-term contracts, rose from 20.2 per cent in 1990 to 29.8 per cent (Araki, 2005). This included a threefold increase in the number of registered temporary agency workers from 0.5 million in 1992 to 1.7 million in 2002 (Hanami, 2004; Macnaughtan, 2006). This has been encouraged by legislation that has relaxed restrictions on the use of fixed term contracts and made it easier to set up and run temporary employment agencies. At the same time, however, an amendment to the Labour Standards Law in 2003 tightened the restrictions on employers' right to dismiss workers (Hanami, 2004).

The late 1990s also saw household name companies being forced to make major cuts in their workforces. In 1999 Nissan Motor Corporation, which had just been taken over by Renault, announced the closure of five sites in Japan with the loss of over 10,000 jobs. This, together with other job cuts in Japanese corporations, was widely interpreted as signalling the end of the lifetime employment system in Japan. However, what was not so widely reported was that Nissan promised to achieve the reductions through natural wastage, early retirement, increasing part-time employment and selling non-core subsidiaries (Symonds, 1999). More generally, research has found that large Japanese companies remain reluctant to lay off workers, even when there is a need to cut jobs. As at Nissan, natural wastage, early retirement and temporary or permanent transfer of workers to subsidiaries are still the preferred methods of reducing headcount (Watanabe, 2000; Kato, 2001; Matanle, 2003). A Ministry of Labour survey of large firms in 1999 found that roughly a third of respondents planned to maintain their existing lifetime employment systems, while a little under half said that they planned to make

'Keidenran's Okuda lauds Japanese management for revival'

'Japan was able to overcome the protracted recession because companies focused on long-term growth and did their best to avoid massive lay-offs even while grappling with the need to restructure', Japan Business Federation Chairman Hiroshi Okuda said. . . . 'Japanese society has finally survived the long-standing economic slump because we, private firms, have stuck to the two bases of Japanese management: respect for people and long-term perspective.'

But Okuda's lecture was not an endorsement of the traditional management style. The corporate sector 'has been making necessary adjustments to accommodate the globalisation of the economy while giving consideration to job security,' he said. Companies have 'tackled various reforms, for example, reviewing their seniority systems and introducing merit-based compensation.'

Source: extracted from *The Nikkei Weekly,* 16 January 2006.

Question

1 Discuss why Japanese employers have been readier to reform the seniority wage system than retreat from lifetime employment.

partial revisions to their lifetime employment systems. Less than a fifth planned to make major changes (Hattori and Maeda, 2000; Matanle 2006). Signs of a revival of the Japanese economy during 2003–07 gave a further boost to confidence in the virtues of long-term employment.

The three key principles which define the Japanese employment system are subject to some erosion. The principle of seniority in determining pay and promotion is being downgraded, and companies have cut jobs and made more use of non-standard workers, i.e. temporary, fixed-term and part-time, when hiring. It may well be that these changes are having long-term effects on levels of trust and employee commitment, weakening the established basis for management–worker cooperation that has existed in Japan (Kwon, 2004). However, we can also see evidence of continuing commitment to the principle of long-term if not life-time employment, and we have noted the limits to the shift from seniority to performance in determining pay and promotion. Even where changes are being made, they continue to be constrained by features of the existing system (see Box 15.1).

Key Controversy

Are academics and practitioners too kind to Japanese employers? That is, are Japanese approaches to involvement and participation coercive and divisive?

Can Japanese firms maintain commitment to the Japanese model in the face of its successful adoption by lower cost producers such as South Korea and China?

Germany: employment regulation under systematic social partnership?

The German employment system

Germany's system of employment relations was established in the aftermath of the Second World War, but some of its features can be traced back to the Bismarck era of the late nineteenth century. The basic principle of the German system is one of collective self-regulation by employer and employee organisations within a systematic framework of law.

The German system has five key characteristics (Jacobi *et al.*, 1998). First, there is a framework of law that supports and regulates interest representation in employment relations. German employment relations law has established basic principles and institutional arrangements that allow employers and workers to regulate their own affairs with little direct interference from the state. Thus the 1949 Collective Agreement Act established collective bargaining rights for workers. The Works Constitution Act of 1952 and the Codetermination Acts of 1951 and 1976 gave workers the right to elect Works Councils in workplaces employing five or more workers. They also provided for workers to be represented on the supervisory boards of companies having more than 500 employees. In providing workers with legal rights to collective representation, the law made an important distinction between collective bargaining and co-determination, effectively creating the second key feature of the system, a dual structure of interest representation.

Secondly, there is a dual structure of interest representation. German employment relations law makes important distinctions between collective bargaining and co-determination in terms of their functions, institutions and the levels at which they operate. Collective bargaining establishes basic terms of employment such as wages and hours, what the Germans have called *issues of interest*. Co-determination deals with issues that arise from the application of industry-wide collective agreements at firm level in individual enterprises. These issues are known as *issues of rights*. Collective bargaining takes place at industry/regional level between trade unions and employers' associations. Co-determination is conducted between works councils and management at the firm level. Trade unions and works councils are therefore separate legal entities, with distinct functions and separate arenas of action. In practice, however, there has always been some overlap between the two. The majority of works councillors are trade union members, and works councils have for a long time engaged in informal workplace bargaining with management over pay (Jacobi *et al.*, 1998). Since the 1980s, the role of works councils in negotiating terms and conditions of employment has increased owing to decentralising tendencies in German industrial relations (see the section on 'Decentralisation of collective bargaining' later in this chapter).

The dual system of interest representation is reflected in the law on industrial action in Germany. Trade unions may call strikes in the event of disputes arising from a failure of collective bargaining negotiations to reach agreement on terms and conditions of employment (*disputes over issues of interest*). Works councils, on the other hand, have a legal obligation to work cooperatively with management for the good of the employees and the enterprise. Once a collective bargaining agreement has been concluded, there is a peace obligation on both sides for as long as the agreement lasts, and strikes during the currency of a collective agreement are unlawful. Disputes that may arise over the interpretation or application of the agreement (*disputes over issues of rights*) must be dealt with through co-determination procedure or by arbitration in the labour courts.

The third feature is the centralisation and co-ordination of collective bargaining at sectoral level, which is a key feature of the German model. In the private sector, collective bargaining has generally taken place in each region (*Lande*) between the trade union and the regional employers' association for the industry/sector concerned. In the public sector, collective bargaining is conducted at the national level. The centralisation of collective bargaining is a crucial aspect of the dual system of representation, as it means that collective bargaining operates at the industry/sector level, while co-determination operates at the enterprise or workplace level. If collective bargaining took place at the company or workplace level, as is the case in the USA or the UK, it would be much more difficult to differentiate between trade union activities and works committee activities. However, in recent years, there has been a move towards decentralisation of bargaining in much of German industry.

The fourth feature is the presence of encompassing organisations of workers and employers. Unions are legally required to represent all workers, not just their own members. Works councils represent all workers in a workplace. In addition, although not legally required to do so, employers' associations have historically represented all employers in their industries.

Collective agreements have therefore tended to cover all workers in each sector. This is recognised in law, so that workers effectively have a right to collective representation on basic terms and conditions of employment. Consequently, while the proportion of workers who are union members has always been relatively modest at around 35–37 per cent, 90 per cent have been covered by collective agreements (Jacobi *et al.,* 1998).

The fifth feature is summarised in the term social partnership. While the German system recognises that there are legitimate differences of interest between capital and labour, there is also a strong emphasis on labour–management cooperation supported by the state. At the level of the economy, the social partners, i.e. peak confederations of employers' associations and trade unions, participate in a three-way 'political exchange' with government on issues of national economic and social policy. At the sectoral level, trade unions have developed a role as mediators between employer and employee interests, rather than simply pursuing adversarial strategies against employers through collective bargaining (Jacobi *et al.,* 1998). At enterprise level, while works committees can constrain management actions on issues such as payments systems, work schedules, recruitment, transfer and dismissal, they are legally obliged to consider company aims and interests and not simply pursue immediate employee interests. This has supported the concept of the *professional enterprise community* (Lane, 1989). This term expresses a sense in which managers, employees and their representatives see themselves as the key stakeholders in the enterprise, acting as a coalition to guide its future.

These features of the German system of employment relations mean that employment issues are subject to a high degree of institutional regulation. In other words, the ability of management to exercise unilateral control over terms and conditions of employment is constrained by individual employment rights provided by state legislation and employees' rights to collective representation in decision-making through collective bargaining and co-determination. That is, collective bargaining and works councils constrain the managerial prerogative.

The employment system and 'Deutschland AG': the wider German business system

The German approach to employment regulation is an integral part of its broader approach to organising and regulating economic activity, i.e. its wider business system. This is often referred to as Deutschland AG, which describes an intricate web of cross-shareholdings between banks, founding families, insurance companies and leading industrial firms designed to protect many of Germany's leading firms from overseas corporate predators. In addition to the employment relations system, there are three key elements of the wider business system in Germany.

The nature of state regulation

Since the 1960s, *bargained corporatism* has been a guiding principle for state action in Germany (Strinati, 1982). Compared with the USA, where market individualism exerts a powerful influence on government policies for the labour market, there is much greater direct state intervention to regulate aspects of employment. Germany's employment protection laws are noticeably stricter in the way they constrain employers' freedom to dismiss workers than those of the USA or the UK, although they are not as strict as those in Italy, Spain or France. The second crucial element of bargained corporatism in Germany is active state support for the collective organisation and representation of workers and employers. This support takes the form of statutory rights to collective organisation, collective bargaining and other forms of collective worker participation in decision-making. Finally, as noted earlier, collective organisations of workers and employers have a role in negotiating with government over aspects of labour market regulation and wider issues of economic and social policy. Taken together, these three elements support a dense framework of institutional regulation of employment, and in this way bargained corporatism supports and is in many ways synonymous with the concept of social partnership in Germany.

Patterns of corporate governance and finance

German firms operate a 'stakeholder' model of governance. Therein management obligation is not only or even primarily to shareholders but to the various needs of a range of stakeholders in the company, including employees. The stakeholder principle is supported by the German system of company finance. German companies obtain finance through long-term bank loans and cross-investments by other companies rather than share flotation. This pattern of company finance has meant that enterprises have not been subject to strong pressure to maximise short-term profits. As long-term creditors, banks have focused more on long-term growth and performance than on immediate profits. This in turn has meant that firms have been able to make significant long-term investments in research and development and employee training, leading to high productivity and product innovation, which supports high wages and good working conditions. It has also meant that German employers have been willing to 'balance the pursuit of profit by a consideration of social justice' (Lane, 2000: 211). This is manifest in co-determination rights, employee involvement in decision-making on the shop floor, commitment to long-term employment security, and generous welfare benefits financed through company payroll taxes. This particular version of the stakeholder model has been termed 'insider capitalism', reflecting the priority given to the interests of those working inside the firm, both management and employees, in good working conditions, long-term security and career prospects, relative to those of 'outside' interests, such as the owners of the company. In this way, the system of corporate governance underpins the ideologies of the professional workplace community and social partnership at enterprise level.

The vocational education and training system (VET)

This is a system whereby many school leavers who do not go on to higher education spend three years as apprentices in the vocational education system. The system combines classroom-based training in vocational schools with practical training in companies. This provides apprentices with broadly based training for a defined occupation, e.g. engineer, baker. The costs of training are shared between employers, who are legally obliged to provide funding and resources for training, government and apprentices themselves. Firms finance the provision of practical, on-the-job training in the workplace, whereas the state funds the vocational schools and trainees accept relatively low wages. Trainees have to meet standards that are laid down by employers' organisations and trade unions and receive certificated qualifications that are universally recognised by employers.

The broad-based occupational nature of vocational training in Germany means that jobs are designed to match the range of occupational skills acquired by workers through formal training. Compared with the system of work organisation in the USA, where workers are fitted to jobs, under the German system jobs are designed to fit workers (Marsden, 1999). It also means that German workers are competent over a relatively wide range of tasks, some of which may include planning and coordination of production. The system also means that German workers are not tied to a single firm, as their skills are transferable across firms. Germany's system of VET has not only resulted in a large supply of highly skilled workers, but it has also helped to structure the high levels of worker–management cooperation that are characteristic of German industry. The apprenticeship system has historically enjoyed high regard in Germany and many German managers have been through apprenticeships, often in addition to taking higher education qualifications. Foremen, supervisors and many middle managers will have completed apprenticeships before obtaining further qualifications as a condition for promotion. This common grounding in technical education leads to workers, supervisors and managers sharing a common understanding of production issues and a common technical language. This in turn lays a basis for cooperation in the workplace that is founded on respect for superiors' technical expertise. In doing so, it contributes to the concept of the professional enterprise community, which is part of the ideological basis for the high level of worker–management cooperation at workplace level (Lane, 1989).

The HR function in the German business system and subsidiaries of German MNCs

Extensive institutional regulation in the German business system in large and small firms structures the system of co-determination, which constrains the managerial prerogative. Therefore, to a great extent, in large firms the HR function upholds and enforces the statutory system of employment regulation. This does not necessarily mean that trade unions run German firms, but rather that managers and workers often negotiate very hard to secure an agreement they can recommend to their constituencies. Once an agreement has been reached, more often than not both sides will abide by its details. Hence as the system is based on compliance and regulation there is a lesser need or less institutional room for more creative aspects of HRM associated with the American business system. In summary, because the German business system, and within that employment relations, is subject to a constitutional pattern of institutional regulation, employers and trade unions have less scope for strategic choice than in the American system. Strategic choice approaches to management strategy centre on the extent to which employers and management seek to shape the work environment to support the managerial prerogative. In the American and British business system, the comparative absence of extensive institutional regulation has allowed employers to pursue innovative business and management strategies. Initiatives such as HRM, non-unionism, downsizing, workforce offshoring and segmentation, and movement towards the priorities of shareholder and financial capitalism have been achieved with relatively little employee obstruction. By comparison, in the German business system management and trade unions, because they are subject to significant levels of institutional regulation, find themselves constrained by this and therefore operate on a more systematic basis. In turn, this is recognised as a strong country-of-origin effect inside Germany. In contrast to this, traditionally there is less evidence of a strong country-of-origin effect in overseas subsidiaries of German MNCs. There is, however, evidence that many erstwhile German firms employ reverse diffusion policies and some have even re-domiciled their country of origin to escape the rigours of the German business system; for example, Air Berlin, the engineering firm Linde and the broadcaster RTL are, at least in part, UK-listed businesses.

Explore

- In light of the above information, identify the key barriers to transferring features of the German business system to overseas subsidiaries.

It is evident that significant features of the German business system are less transferable to overseas subsidiaries precisely because of the embeddedness of aspects of the system in Germany. This was most evident in BMW's failure to revitalise Rover cars on the basis of German production methods such as diversified quality production. This method relies heavily on the system of vocational education and training which was not available in the UK, and BMW had no experience of managing its own training system, i.e. one that was not locked into local technical education providers. It is more likely that whilst German firms will seek to transfer aspects of their business and production models to overseas subsidiaries, they are less likely to transfer all aspects of the German employment relations systems. Rather there is evidence to suggest that notable German employers, such as EADS, the Airbus manufacturer, VW and BMW, use their overseas subsidiaries to learn about so-called Anglo-American business strategies. It follows from this that HR in subsidiaries of German MNCs is more focused on host country effects in terms of accepted patterns of regulation and compliance. Having argued this point, recent evidence suggests that the German model in the automobile sector may be going global as other manufacturers learn from BMW's experience. For example, Mercedes-Benz has exported its training system for apprentices to its American plants in the face of being unable to recruit locally trained and qualified apprentices capable of working within a system of diversified quality production.

Change in Germany: the erosion of social partnership

The 1980s and 1990s saw growing criticism of key features of the German employment system. Once seen as underpinning German economic success, it came to be viewed by many economic policy advisers and financial and business interests as a hindrance to renewed economic growth, competitiveness and job creation. There are several reasons for this disenchantment with the German model.

Economic stagnation and unemployment

Over the last 35 years, Germany has experienced relatively slow economic growth and high, persistent unemployment. Unemployment in West Germany rose from 2.6 per cent in 1980 to 7.2 per cent in 1985 and did not drop below 5 per cent until the early 1990s, when there was a short economic boom following German reunification in 1990 (OECD, 2006). Since 1995, the unemployment rate in Germany as a whole has not fallen below 7 per cent, and during 2005 it stood at 11.5 per cent before falling back to 7.4 per cent in 2008. However, the effects of the world economic crisis meant that it climbed rapidly to 8.6 per cent by March 2009 (Federal Statistical Office Germany, 2008; DW World, 2009).

The underlying reasons for Germany's unemployment problem are much debated. There is a strong case for arguing that it stems from the problems of economic adjustment in the former East Germany, where unemployment reached an official level of 18 per cent in 1999, with observers suggesting that the true level was nearer 25 per cent (Tuselman and Heise, 2000), and a monetary policy that has depressed levels of demand rather than being caused by features of the labour market (Teague and Grahl, 2004). However, economic advisers and financial and business interests became increasingly critical of aspects of the employment system in general, particularly the level of employment protection and social welfare benefits for workers and the centralised system of collective bargaining, and demanded reforms to increase labour market flexibility. However, the advent of the euro currency has seen many of these criticisms melt away, particularly in the period since 2008. Between 1999 and 2008, unit labour costs in Germany rose by 3 per cent, whereas in Spain they rose by 35 per cent and by over 20 per cent in France, Greece, Italy and Portugal. That is, even with Germany's extensive pattern of co-determination, comparatively it has become cheaper to manufacture goods in Germany, as German productivity growth has outstripped the rise in labour costs. In addition to this, the common currency has comparatively pushed the price of German goods down in many export markets.

The case against strong employment rights and social protection is that they raise the costs of employing labour and therefore discourage firms from creating more jobs. For example, because workers' strong employment rights make workforce reductions difficult and costly, employers prefer to achieve increases in output by raising the output of their existing workforce rather than hiring additional workers. Generous social welfare benefits are financed largely out of payroll taxes levied on employers. This means that non-wage costs of hiring workers are high, as well as wage costs. This reinforces employers' reluctance to add to the size of their workforces and also deters new business start-ups. They also contribute to high unemployment among low-skilled workers by setting a 'floor' to wages that prevents them from falling to a level that would lead to more unskilled jobs being offered.

The criticism of centralised collective bargaining is that it sets too high a minimum wage, which together with the social welfare system prevents wages for unskilled workers adjusting to a level that would lead to more jobs being created. It is also argued that it prevents enterprises from addressing the need to develop more flexible ways of using labour in order to raise productivity and reduce costs. The reforms that have been demanded are that restrictions on the use of flexible forms of employment such as temporary and fixed term employment should be eased, that the level of social benefits should be cut back to ease the tax burden on employers and enable wages to be more flexible at the lower end of the market, and that collective bargaining should be decentralised to allow for greater wage flexibility and permit negotiations on company-specific issues.

Weakening support for collective bargaining and co-determination?

The proportion of workers who are trade union members has fallen in Germany. At the same time, a growing number of small and medium-sized businesses do not have works councils, and by the end of the 1990s an estimated 60 per cent of German workers were outside co-determination (Teague and Grahl, 2004). Among employers, the coverage of employers' associations is declining. Many companies in the former East Germany either did not join or else withdrew from employers' associations after unification in order to avoid centralised wage bargaining. In the West, a number of small and medium-sized enterprises quit employers' associations in order to negotiate their own individual agreements with the trade unions, and many new companies are not joining employers' associations, often following the example of US MNCs. For example, General Motors infuriated the Opel works council by seeking to negotiate agreements on a plant-by-plant basis instead of centrally in an attempt to introduce an American-style New Deal model which often undermines nationally focused sector-wide bargaining. Nevertheless, trade unions retain considerable influence and the percentage of workers covered by collective agreements in the West is still very high – around 90 per cent – although the number is substantially lower in the East (Tuselman and Heise, 2000).

Decentralisation of collective bargaining

More significant than any overall decline in collective bargaining coverage has been the trend towards decentralisation of collective bargaining. This has reflected the growing relative importance of 'qualitative issues' concerning changes in working practices, new technology and flexibility, which are specific to companies or workplaces, compared with wage bargaining. At the same time, however, there have been examples of 'disorganised decentralisation' arising out of 'wildcat cooperation' between works councils and company management whereby they (illegally) agree to undercut or ignore the terms of collective agreements, usually on the grounds of preserving jobs. In an effort to eliminate wildcat cooperation and achieve a more coordinated and controlled decentralisation of bargaining, formal 'opening clauses' are being inserted into industry level agreements that allow enterprise managements and works committees to negotiate over more flexible working time arrangements or to undercut sectoral agreements on pay for limited time periods and in defined circumstances (Tuselman and Heise, 2000). This controlled decentralisation reflects the interests of the unions in maintaining an over-arching structure of centralised bargaining and owes much to the fact that employers continue to value the way that centralised bargaining moderates wage pressure and acts as a force for stability in industrial relations.

Changes in co-determination

The role of co-determination has been strengthened by legislation that has provided strong support for works council organisation and extended the influence of works councils over training and employment protection matters. Furthermore, decentralisation of collective bargaining has increased the role of works councils in establishing terms and conditions of employment. In particular, they became closely involved in company modernisation programmes during the 1980s, which focused on the introduction of new technologies, more flexible forms of working and new forms of employee involvement, such as quality circles and teamworking. In manufacturing firms, these programmes culminated in diversified quality production. For some the role of works councils in this evolution can be seen as an extension of the social partnership model in the workplace, whereas others view it as threatening to undermine the role of works councils as defenders of workers' employment rights. High unemployment and increasingly intense competition mean that works councils are under pressure to cooperate with management in 'building up an organisational consensus around corporate plans to succeed in global markets' that serve the interests of management, shareholders and the elite 'core' group of employees, but exposes other workers to increasing insecurity (Teague and Grahl, 2004: 566).

Germany's economic difficulties have strengthened the critics and weakened the defenders of its employment system, most notably the German trade unions. As some of the material in this chapter has sought to demonstrate, the high wages, comparatively low inequality in and between capital and labour, and high living standards that were once seen as strengths of 'Deutschland AG' are increasingly being represented as the source of persistent unemployment and comparatively weak growth. High unemployment has created fear of job loss and created a climate in which unions and works councils are on the defensive. At the same time, German firms are becoming more open to the disciplines of the stock market and influenced by the principle of shareholder value. However, while significant changes have taken place, reform of the German system has so far been gradual, hesitant and, at times, strongly resisted, particularly in the area of welfare reform, where there is strong continuing public support for Germany's extensive welfare state provision. Even so, pressure on the German system has been intensified recently by the effects of the credit crunch and world recession. Before the credit crunch and associated world recession, Germany's trade surplus sustained resistance to full-blown domestic reforms in business and employment regulation to meet the demands of globalisation, which were considered by many Germans to mean greater economic insecurity and stagnating wages.

In summary, irrespective of sustained criticism in the 1990s, the features of the German employment system and the wider business system described here have underpinned a distinctive strategy for competing in international markets. The high level of institutional regulation in Germany has made it difficult for employers to treat labour simply as a disposable commodity. Collective bargaining, co-determination and state legislation have resulted in high wages and restrictions on employers' freedom to dismiss workers. This means that employers have had to achieve competitiveness by ensuring that high wages are matched by high productivity and by competing on the basis of innovation and product quality rather than price. This has meant placing a relatively high emphasis on skill in the workforce and the production process. The consequences of the German system of VET are that German workers' broad skills mean that they are able to adapt to new technologies relatively easily and acquire additional skills within their occupational fields. They are also able to undertake aspects of production planning and problem-solving to a higher degree than in many other countries. This, together with the high level of cooperation that is partly due to the training system, means that workers need relatively little close supervision. Therefore, firms employ fewer staff not directly engaged in production, which contributes to high productivity levels and more autonomous working conditions. The centralisation of collective bargaining and its formal separation from co-determination, together with the influence of social partnership ideology, have resulted in low levels of industrial conflict and have also kept inflationary wage pressures low. In this way, the industrial relations system has contributed to quality of output in terms of reliability of supply and also to the control of wage costs. Often referred to as diversified quality production, the results have been high labour productivity and a competitive advantage in markets for sophisticated, innovative, high-value products based on high levels of research and development expenditure and sophisticated production techniques (Streeck, 1991). This has allowed German firms to pay high wages without becoming uncompetitive and also to fund, through taxation, a comprehensive and generous welfare state.

Explore

- Given this information, why haven't more multinationals of non-German origin attempted to emulate the German approach?

Financialisation, financial capitalism, the financial crisis and comparative HRM?

Financialisation and financial capitalism

Financialisation is most readily interpreted as the growing and systematic power of the finance sector broadly defined and with this the associated growth of financial engineering (Blackburn, 2006). Moreover, financialisation is reflected in the diffusion of new business models associated with financial capitalism, which give explicit priority to investor and shareholder value, promote short-term profit horizons and stimulate profitability and growth by downsizing, merger and acquisition rather than sector-driven longer-term development. Comparatively these pressures threaten the ability of employers in different national business systems to maintain commitment to established firm-level regimes whether they are lower road, focused on cultural change or higher commitment bargains (Thompson, 2003; Clark, 2009). Rather, a contemporary focus on the priorities of financial capitalism may witness business owners seeking to restructure firms they own through accounting and taxation arbitrage, application of business models that de-list plc firms, forced downsizing and re-domiciling a country of origin (Appelbaum *et al.*, 2013). The imperative of investor and shareholder value gives priority to the requirements of financial capitalism over and above culturally and institutionally embedded features of managerial capitalism in national business systems. So, in summary, in the period of benign economic conditions before the onset of financial crisis in 2008, the imperatives and priorities of globally focused financial capitalism emphasised the importance of investor and shareholder value. This imperative was reinforced by the diffusion of globally focused investors who often employed new business models. These models, particularly those associated with leveraged buyouts of established listed firms, began to challenge the institutional routine of embedded behaviour in national business systems often summarised as managerial capitalism. Both Appelbaum *et al.* (2013) and Heyes *et al.* (2012), in their respective critiques of employment relations research and the varieties of capitalism thesis, establish that within the managerial capitalism paradigm, researchers look at firms and workplaces comparatively – American firms, German firms or Japanese firms – but in the light of product market forces sometimes to the neglect of the capital market. These critiques are not just academic exercises – the limitations of the varieties of capitalism thesis, focused as it was on firms in apparently stable economic conditions, failed to predict the onset of the financial crisis or reactions to it.

Financial crisis

The seeds of the global crisis were sown in three separate but interrelated crises, each of which relates to excessive use of leverage. Low interest rates combined with low inflation and rising asset prices (bonds, shares, property – both commercial and residential) encouraged very high multiples of lending. Some banks in the UK provided 125 per cent mortgages, whereas in the USA mortgage providers innovated with so-called sub-prime or NINJAs – no-income-no-job-no-assets mortgages. These mortgages had very low start-up repayment rates and were given to purchasers who really were unable to maintain mortgage payments once they were exposed to real interest rates and rates of repayment. Sub-prime mortgage holders in the USA, buy-to-let mortgage holders in the UK and those who had remortgaged to fund consumption expenditure all faced significant problems when interest rates and inflation began to rise in 2008. More catastrophically, in the USA, sub-prime mortgages were rolled up by mortgage providers and sold in the market as 'secure and safe' mortgage-backed securities. As interest rates and inflation rates rose, they each had a dramatic effect on the ability of sub-prime mortgage holders to repay the loans. Owners of mortgage-backed securities saw they were becoming 'toxic', i.e. not worth the paper they were printed on, and began to sell out of the market very quickly. The trigger for this crisis was the failure of the Bear Sterns hedge fund in the USA in 2007, which led to the US Treasury buying up unsafe mortgage-backed securities. However, the damage was done: the bailout combined with mortgage defaults led to a collapse in property values. Worse, as all investors scrambled to get out of mortgage-backed securities, financial institutions in the USA and globally began to call in loans and stopped lending to one another. This led to a major slowdown in economic activity, of both consumption spending and investment spending.

The second crisis was most visible in the UK but also affected financial institutions in France and Germany. In blunt terms, financial institutions such as Royal Bank of Scotland, Halifax Bank of Scotland, Northern Rock and Bradford & Bingley ran out of money. More simply still, these financial institutions lent long and borrowed short on a revolving system to repay their own loans. Once the market for inter-bank lending dried up, they were in danger of not having enough cash to open their doors or stock their cash machines. There was a run on Northern Rock as investors queued to get their money out of the bank. Others were bailed out by the taxpayer and are now majority taxpayer-owned. So in the UK a banking crisis developed out of the risky use of leverage during benign economic conditions. This led to a credit crunch, even though interest rates are at record low levels, and a collapse of consumption and investment expenditure. It is likely that the UK will not recover to 2008 levels of economic activity until 2015 at the earliest. The third crisis centred on excessive leverage in the Eurozone. 'PIGS' (Portugal, Ireland, Greece and Spain), on entering the euro, suddenly to the delight of their respective financial ministries found their borrowing costs as low as those of Germany. To put it another way, the borrowing costs for PIGS was unrelated to the comparative efficiency of their economies. The fallacy of the euro was that in a common currency all members would have the same borrowing costs. In Greece the extent of leverage was far greater than officially recorded due to false accounting, which hid the depth of Greece's debt. In Spain and Ireland, government borrowing underpinned a property and construction boom. As global economic conditions went into reverse, demand for property collapsed as property developers and construction firms walked away from contracts. In Greece, once the false accounting was revealed by a change of government, the situation went beyond merely national debt to a sovereign debt crisis as the Greek government became unable to repay debt. As of 2013, this has become a now recurrent crisis which threatens political stability in Greece and Greece's continued membership of the Eurozone. With Europe in a euro and sovereign debt crisis, there are major implications for multinational firms sparking changes in how they operate in terms of output levels, manufacturing strategies, marketing and financial management. Each will have an unfolding effect on the management of human resources. The European Union represents more than 25 per cent of global gross domestic product – twice as large as China. Two effects of the crises are becoming evident in MNC behaviour. First, MNCs are looking to take costs out of European operations through downsizing and closure; for example, Pfizer the American pharmaceutical firm recently announced the closure of its research facility in Kent in the UK. Mitsubishi recently announced it would restructure forklift production in Europe due to the weakness of the European market. Secondly, to ride out the crisis, some MNCs – and American firms in particular – are seeking to get closer to their customers, taking into greater account host country effects in terms of consumer tastes. These developments have significant but contrary effects on the management of human resources. Downsizing and restructuring of subsidiary operations may represent the reassertion of country-of-origin effects, such as short-termism and a hire-and-fire reaction to tough economic conditions often found in US MNCs. However, at the same time some US MNCs are becoming less ethnocentric and less standardised in their approaches to embedded preferences in host countries to apply differentiated approaches to production. Downplaying centralised and standardised approaches requires such firms to generate more country-specific business and HR strategies.

Impacts on multinational firms and comparative HRM?

Reaction to financialisation and the emergence of financial capitalism, but more pertinently to financial crisis, are mediated by business system priorities, which are, in turn, informed by coordinated or liberal characteristics. First, crisis has witnessed a stalling in the movement to global firms. Whilst multinational firms are seeking to get closer to host countries, one effect of the crisis is that for many multinationals country-of-origin effects become more pronounced. Secondly, the financial crisis and reaction to it further reinforces debates about convergence and divergence and so-called 'convergent-divergence'. Therefore, while all business systems have experienced financial crisis, the extent to which financial crisis and the priorities of financial capitalism disrupt embedded national patterns of managerial capitalism varies. Business system and firm-level responses continue to exhibit divergence of response, but for business and HR strategy at firm level, divergence based on nationality is getting more difficult to sustain. In summary, reaction to financial crisis in national business systems begins from divergent positions. However, the impact of financial crisis and the priorities and imperatives of financial capitalism have pushed all business systems on a convergent pathway towards public spending cuts, tax increases and wage reductions, measures often summarised as 'austerity'. Austerity is evidently followed by bailouts of financial institutions and prominent firms, then fiscal difficulties (i.e. insufficient taxation revenue to sustain public spending and the public sector wage bill), then sustained political opposition to austerity and in some cases political unrest. Each of these developments has had a nationally specific impact on the management of labour and the employment relationship both at the level of the state and at the level of the firm.

Explore

Think about an MNC that you know well.

- To what extent has the country-of-origin effect become more pronounced as a result of the global economic crisis and how is this evident?

Concluding comments

National employment systems, national competitiveness and financial crisis

This subsection summarises and concludes on the depth of embeddedness of institutional routines in the American, German and Japanese economies in the light of local and global crises, where local crises interacted with global crises to challenge and renew established institutional practices.

The American employment system, national competitiveness and financial crisis

The wider impact of individualism on the American state, its financial institutions and patterns of industrial relations demonstrates that the central drivers of the American business system make it very dynamic. The institutional constraints on management are much weaker than in the German or Japanese business systems, resulting in distinctively *American* models of company organisation, patterns of finance and employment relations emerging alongside one another. The managerially led institutional features of the American employment system described earlier in the chapter underpin a distinctive strategy for domestic and international competition. The shallow depth of institutional regulation in the American employment system enables employers to treat labour as a disposable commodity and adjust wages and headcount in response to cyclical changes in labour and product market conditions or more pronounced crisis conditions. In the initial post-crisis period of 2008–09, American firms downsized significantly and rapidly. More significantly still, American workers are more accepting of plant closure, downsizing and unemployment than many European workers. This is demonstrated in comparatively high levels of labour mobility, whereby workers are willing to relocate long distances to find work. Take, for example, the city population of Detroit, which has declined by around 25 per cent since 2000 in response to the collapse of employment opportunities in the automobile sector, which has become more pronounced since 2007. In addition, workers work longer hours and have shorter holidays than in the UK and the EU (although not Japan), which contributes to high labour productivity in the USA.

The visible hand of management has moulded a business and employment system where management control and coordination of work organisation combines with substitution of capital for labour to create sustained international competitive advantage in terms of productivity and unit labour costs. However, in recent years, the growth of new technology, international competition and financial crisis has challenged American firms in a variety of ways. First, there is a marked distinction between so-called 'old economy' firms, such as in the car and retail sectors, and 'new economy' firms in social media and internet retailing. Essentially, some 'old economy' firms such as car manufacturers have relied on business models and products that have exhibited poor levels of production and management innovation. This reliance drove many of these firms into bankruptcy and then bailout and ownership by the American government. Hence, in some sectors American approaches to international business and labour management failed to respond effectively to new technology and international competition – Kodak is a good example of this tendency. Secondly, the past 20 years have witnessed an obsession with investor and shareholder value in corporate America where higher profit levels are not channelled into investment and innovation but returned to investors and shareholders. This obsession, combined with greater international competition, has put many welfare capitalist employers and their HR strategies under significant pressure, as investor and shareholder value has continued to be major corporate goals even in the face of financial crisis. This has further widened income differentials in the American economy as established stakeholder positions, in particular those of employees, within many firms are eroded to reduce bottom line costs with these savings re-distributed to investors and shareholders. This has had the effect of tightening the core workforce in many welfare capitalist firms and the few remaining New Deal-style employers, pushing many more employees towards peripheral low-road status. This development has the potential to widen further still income, skill and employment opportunity differentials in all varieties of American employer, a pressure that many American firms have attempted to diffuse in overseas subsidiaries. So, in summary, the American business system is able to maintain a variety of HR settlements which can co-exist not only between, but also within, individual firms. The New Deal model remains politically significant, e.g. in the manner in which the Obama administration bailed out Chrysler to the tune of $12.5 billion and General Motors to the tune of $50 billion of taxpayer dollars in association with the United Auto Workers Union. The union, a significant pension creditor, was given preferential treatment over other creditors, thereby securing the union pension fund to underwrite union agreement to the bailout and associated labour concessions. Given this political significance, New Deal empirical coverage at less than 10 per cent of the private-sector labour force is marginal. Welfare capitalism – the home of HRM – is also under challenge as a result of the combined pressures associated with investor and shareholder-focused financial capitalism, greater international competition, new technology and the erosion of established stable markets in the USA. Here foreign direct investment by American multinational firms plays some part in the explanation as assembly line and 'muscle' jobs have been exported to reduce costs. Hence, the core workforce in New Deal, welfare capitalist employers and lower road employers is being redefined and further tightened – yet all three varieties of HRM continue to co-exist in the American business system.

The Japanese employment system, national competitiveness and financial crisis

The embedded features of the Japanese employment system are widely seen as underpinning Japan's success in manufacturing, and while Japanese multinational firms have been significant innovators in aspects of HRM, the Japanese business system is now crisis-ridden and stagnant in terms of economic performance. Many Japanese firms beyond the automotive sector have found themselves outperformed by local lower-cost economies such as South Korea. For example, in 2008, JVC, which pioneered the development and manufacture of the flat-screen television, ceased production in Japan, ceding the regional market to South Korean manufacturers. However, significant Japanese multinational firms remain committed to production in Japan and continue to use lifetime employment for core employees. Hence, embedded features of the Japanese employment system remain so, even in the face of economic stagnation, financial crisis and disasters in the form of a tsunami, nuclear leaks and large-scale quality recalls of Toyota cars.

To summarise our discussion of the embeddedness of features of the Japanese business system and related approaches to HRM detailed earlier in the chapter, it is useful to divide the years since 1945 into four periods. Firstly, the period after the Second World War through to the 1980s laid and embedded the institutional features of the Japanese business model and related patterns of HRM. Highly competitive firms in motor manufacturing, electrical goods, consumer electronics, then personal computers, first domestically then internationally, secured well-paid employment for a sizeable core workforce at the plant level. The business model held management to account where block and cross shareholding rendered the capital market comparatively illiquid and the market for corporate control comparatively impotent. Stakeholders within the firm held significant power over any external shareholders, whereas Japanese institutional investors were comparatively passive in the face of bank-led monitoring of firm-level performance. Moreover, labour relations for core workers built a community firm based on lifetime employment, company unionism and internal promotion of management (Dore, 1973; Sheard, 1994). Firms had a growth dynamic generated via internal capabilities, which saw core employees integrated into decision-making and the values of a firm.

Second, the 1990s saw a significant slowdown in the Japanese business model and an emergent crisis in the system. As Peston and Knight (2012: 137–140, 298–306) observe, the post-Second World War period until the 1980s witnessed sustained export-led growth, which led to a stock market bubble where, in 1989, the value of the Tokyo stock market was greater than the value of the US stock market. However, a collapse in property and stock market prices began in 1990, ushering in what is often termed 'the lost decade', and in July 2012 the Nikkei index was 77 per cent below its 1989 peak. Poor economic performance continued throughout the decade as the yen rose in value, hitting the export price of many Japanese goods. In reaction to previous expansion, many Japanese firms chose to save and repay debt and not invest, whereas Japan's ageing population saw the wages share of national income increase due to the seniority-based system of recruitment and promotion. Third, the 1990s witnessed the emergence of pressures for change in the Japanese business system. A steady increase in foreign share ownership peaked at 28 per cent of the Japanese stock market in 2007. This growth increased pressures for investor and shareholder value and some reduction in the presence of cross shareholding, which had previously insulated Japanese firms and associated patterns of employment regulation from capital market pressures (Deakin and Whittaker, 2009). In turn, this reduced the growth of lifetime employment and stimulated a greater use of part-time and temporary agency workers (Sako, 2006). For many observers, Japan's 'lost decade' was most manifest as a 'balance sheet' recession, whereby the obsession with debt repayment by both firms and households meant that even zero interest rates could not encourage borrowing. This turned many businesses and banks into what are now termed 'zombie' businesses, but as many did not close, unemployment remained comparatively low at less than 6 per cent throughout the 1990s into the new century (see Peston and Knight, 2012: 299–301).

Lastly, by the end of the first decade of the twenty-first century, the Japanese economy and its business system, though remaining in recession, appeared very resilient. Hostile takeovers in the market for corporate control stalled and activist investors found only mixed success, whereas lifetime employment and a commitment to continue to produce goods in Japan remained present in firms such as Toyota (see Araki, 2009). However, as Jackson and Miyajima (2007) argue, while executive behaviour has changed and developed in response to more careful external monitoring by capital markets, Japanese approaches to efficiency remain committed to equity for core workers at least, and as Buchanan and Deakin (2009) suggest, unlike in the UK and the USA, the Japanese economy, its business system and associated approach to HRM remain wedded to producer capitalism and not the fledgling priorities of financial capitalism (see Appelbaum *et al.*, 2013).

The German business system, national competitiveness and financial crisis

The pressures for change and reform in the German business system are ever present. The period of financial crisis since 2008 initially saw these pressures further increase, but this time not necessarily because of inherent weaknesses in the Germany economy, but rather, because of the downturn in demand for German exports as a result of the impact of financial crisis in German export markets. Similarly, the strong pattern of institutional regulation in the German business system did not prevent some German financial institutions entertaining the same investment strategies that undermined the American and British financial systems. A few significant financial institutions had to be bailed out by the German government, but in contrast to the financial sector, the German manufacturing sector and other export-orientated sectors have been protected by the euro and the euro crisis. The crisis and the international weakness of the euro has effectively kept the price of German exports lower than they otherwise would be. In some ways, the period since 2010 has witnessed the resilience of the German business system and its established pattern of co-determination in employment relations. The German economy may be in transition, as evidenced in the passage of some labour reforms and the accommodation and incorporation of investor and shareholder capitalism, but the German business system has not collapsed or moved significantly closer to, say, the American business system.

In contrast to this strong country-of-origin effect in Germany, subsidiaries of German MNCs display less Germanness in subsidiary operations in HR strategies than might be expected. There is evidence from specific sectors to suggest that the growth of business education and the MBA culture is diffusing some Anglo-American traits into German business, particularly via younger graduates and managers, who appear less attached to embedded features of the German business system than more established managers (Carr, 2005). Further, while Germany still has many large firms where co-determination is a core feature of corporate governance, there is a growing recognition that smaller to medium-sized firms are becoming of greater significance. In 2004 there were 3.5 million small to medium-sized enterprises in Germany, which created 80 per cent of all apprenticeships and 70 per cent of all jobs (Guenterbeg and Kayser, 2004). This development may put further medium-term pressure on established features of co-determination.

Nonetheless, the success of the German business model and associated pattern of employment rights in the period since 1945 has resulted in the creation of what for many are a pattern of embedded institutional but beneficial constraints. These deter and prevent management from resorting to short-term contingencies, to satisfy investor and shareholder value at the expense of innovation and research and development, even in a period of sustained financial crisis (Streeck, 1998; Butler *et al.*, 2011). This is the case even where they have been sanctioned by the state, e.g. as in the Hartz reforms, which made downsizing and cost-cutting easier in small to medium-sized firms.

Summary

- There are noticeable differences in the way the employment relationship is regulated in different countries, such that we can identify different national employment systems.

- National employment systems can be compared on the basis of similarities and differences in the extent and patterns of institutionalised regulation of the employment relationship.

- Different countries' employment systems are embedded in and shaped by their wider business systems.

- Historically, Germany, Japan and the USA have adopted different employment paradigms based on, respectively, social partnership, welfare corporatism and a managerially led model.

- Each of the three paradigms has been embedded in distinctive business systems that have in turn produced and supported distinctive strategies for achieving competitiveness in domestic and international markets.

- Since the 1980s, each system has come under intense pressure to change in response to forces that many observers believe are encouraging the convergence of all employment systems towards the current US model, based as it is on shareholder capitalism. However, both the German and Japanese business systems have displayed resilience in the face of pressures towards convergence.

- Globalisation, if it means anything, means that international competitive pressures and reactions to them override the priorities of national business and employment systems, leading to the further marketisation of corporate governance and employment relations.

- In a global context, financial performance becomes much more important than previously, particularly as the stock market and the market for corporate control increasingly discipline management to ensure managerial efficiency on the basis that investors and shareholders are the dominant stakeholders.

- The diffusion of investor and shareholder approaches to corporate performance, combined with external shocks such as the recession caused by the credit crunch, encourages employers to see labour as a cost rather than a productive resource, leading to changes in HRM. At the same time, however, national systems of institutional regulation moderate this pressure.

The financial crisis is a global phenomenon which has contradictory results for HRM. As a reaction to crisis, many multinational firms have retreated to strong country of origin stereotypes but at the same time many multinationals have sought to accommodate the crisis by getting closer to host countries in terms of HRM. In summary, the financial crisis has reinforced ever present tensions within multinational firms between standardisation and localisation.

Questions

1 Has the country-of-origin effect which is so embedded in comparative HRM mediated the effect of global financial crisis in MNCs of different nationality?
2 In what ways, if at all, is the global crisis grounded for managers and workers in reforms in firm-level approaches to HRM?
3 Can the American, German and Japanese business models and related employment systems continue to main national distinctiveness in the face of global financial crisis?

Case study 1

'Toyota committed to Japan'

In summer 2012, Akio Toyoda, president of the Toyota Motor Corporation, committed the firm to maintaining itself as a Japanese car producer whereby the multinational will continue to produce three million cars, or 40 per cent of its global output, in Japan. This is only about one million cars fewer than before the onset of the global financial crisis. This commitment came in the face of the impact of a strong yen on Japanese exports and despite the fact that Toyota's domestic rivals, Honda and Nissan, produce about 75 per cent of their cars abroad to enable them to compete with local rivals such as South Korean firm Hyundai. Toyota has not closed any car plants in Japan or curtailed its pattern of lifetime employment for core workers – rather it has consolidated some of its subsidiary operations into the core of the firm and bought out minority shareholders who are more focused on global strategies and investor and shareholder value. Toyota's global operations secured its profitability worldwide, whereas its domestic operations lost nearly 400 billion yen.

Questions

1 What does Toyota's commitment tell us about the embeddedness of the Japanese business and HR model in some Japanese firms?

2 What is it that enables Toyota and other firms such as Honda and Nissan to retain a significant level of domestic production and more localised production in Europe and the USA?

Case study 2

Mercedes-Benz in Alabama

In Alabama, USA, Mercedes, in partnership with the state of Alabama, has formalised a $1.6 million contract to open a graduate training school to train and develop apprentices in mechtronics – the integration of mechanics, electronics and computer science in the manufacturing process, metallurgy, welding and electrical skills. Mechtronics students must complete seven terms of instruction, and after completing this and associated coursework will receive an associate degree. The top 75 per cent of students will secure jobs in full-time production. In addition, a percentage of these apprentices may go on to do further study that will qualify an apprentice for higher-grade maintenance positions in the plant. The Mercedes programme aims to secure, grow and develop the local workforce, and the local plant will be one of four global plants producing the Benz C-Class and its successor generation. Mercedes training programmes are identical across the world, in large measure because the firm does not produce different versions of cars for different territories. Mercedes has developed the programme recently diffused in Alabama throughout Asia, Europe and Canada.

Questions

1 Why is it necessary for Mercedes to do this in its global operations?

2 Does the global rollout of a German approach to VET represent a strong country-of-origin effect or Mercedes's aspiration to become a global firm?

References and further reading

Almond, P. and Ferner, A. (eds) (2006) *American Multinationals in Europe*. Oxford: Oxford University Press.

Appelbaum, E., Batt, R. and Clark, I. (2013) 'Implications for employment relations research: evidence from breach of trust and implicit contracts in private equity buy-outs' *British Journal of Industrial Relations*. Published online 1 March.

Araki, T. (2005) 'Corporate governance, labour and employment relations in Japan: the future of the shareholder model?'

in H. Gospel and A. Pendleton (eds) *Corporate Governance and Labour Management: An International Comparison*. Oxford: Oxford University Press, pp. 254–83.

Araki, T. (2009) 'Changes in Japan's practice-dependent stakeholder model and employee centred corporate governance' in Whittaker, D.H. and Deakin, S. (eds) *Corporate Governance and Managerial Reform in Japan*. Oxford: Oxford University Press, pp. 227–54.

Bartlett, C. and Ghoshal, S. (1989) *Managing Across Borders: The Transnational Solution.* Boston, MA: Harvard Business School Press.

Bassett, P. (1987) *Strike Free – New Industrial Relations in Britain.* London: Macmillan.

Baumol, W.J. (1959) *Business Behaviour, Value and Growth.* New York: Macmillan.

Blackburn, R. (2006) 'Finance and the fourth dimension', *New Left Review,* 39, May–June: 39–70.

Braverman, H. (1974) *Labour and Monopoly Capital.* New York: Monthly Review Press.

Brewster, C., Wood, J. and Brookes, M. (2008) 'Similarity, isomorphism or duality? Recent survey evidence on the human resource management policies of multinational corporations', *British Journal of Management,* 19: 320–42.

Buchanan, J. and Deakin, S. (2009) 'In the shadow of corporate governance reform: change and continuity in managerial practice at listed companies in Japan' in Whittaker, D. H. and Deakin, S. (eds) *Corporate Governance and Managerial Reform in Japan.* Oxford: Oxford University Press, pp. 28–70.

Butler, P., Glover, L. and Tregaskis, O. (2011) 'When the going gets tough. . . recession and the resilience of workplace partnership', *British Journal of Industrial Relations* 49, 4: 666–87.

Cappelli, P., Bassie, L., Katz, H., Knoke, D., Osterman, P. and Unseem, M. (1997) *Change at Work: How American Industry and Workers Are Coping with Corporate Restructuring and What Workers Must Do to Take Charge of Their Own Careers.* Oxford: Oxford University Press.

Carr, C. (2005) 'Are German, Japanese and Anglo-Saxon strategic decision styles still divergent in the context of globalisation?', *Journal of Management Studies,* 42, 6: 1155–88.

Chandler, A. (1977) *The Visible Hand: The Managerial Revolution in American Business.* Cambridge: Cambridge University Press.

Chandler, A. (1990) *Scale and Scope: The Dynamics of Industrial Capitalism.* Cambridge: Cambridge University Press.

Clark, I. (2009) 'Owners not Managers: disconnecting managerial capitalism? Understanding the take private equity business model.' *Work, Employment and Society* 23, 4: 359–78.

Clark, I. and Almond, P. (2006) 'An introduction to the American business system' in P. Almond and A. Ferner (eds) *American Multinationals in Europe: Human Resource Policies and Practices.* Oxford: Oxford University Press, pp. 37–56.

Colling, T. and Clark, I. (2002) '"Looking for Americanness": sector effects in engineering process plant contracting', *European Journal of Industrial Relations,* 8, 3: 301–25.

Colling, T. and Clark, I. (2006) 'What happened when the Americans took over Britain's electricity industry? Exploring trans-national sector effects on employment relations', *The International Journal of Human Resource Management,* 17, 9: 1625–44.

Conrad, H. and Heindorf, V. (2006) 'Recent changes in compensation practices in large Japanese companies: wages, bonuses and corporate pensions' in P. Matanle and W. Lunsing (eds) *Perspectives on Work, Employment and Society in Japan.* Basingstoke: Palgrave, pp. 79–97.

Deakin, S. and Whitakker, D. H. (2009) 'On a different path? The managerial reshaping of Japanese corporate governance' in Whittaker, D.H. and Deakin, S. (eds) *Corporate Governance and Managerial Reform in Japan.* Oxford: Oxford University Press, pp. 1–28.

Dore, R. (1973) *British Factory – Japanese Factory: The Origins of National Diversity in Industrial Relations.* London: Allen & Unwin.

Dunning, J. (1999) *American Investment in British Manufacturing Industry,* 2nd edn. London: Macmillan.

DW World (2009) *German Unemployment Rises Sharply,* 31 March. Online: **http://www.dw.de/german-unemployment-rises-sharply/a-4143056** (accessed January 2014).

Edwards, R. (1979) *Contested Terrain.* New York: Basic Books.

Edwards, T. and Ferner, A. (2004) 'Multinationals, reverse diffusion and national business systems', *Management International Review* 24, 1: 51–81.

Federal Statistical Office Germany (2008) Press release 136/1 April 2008, 'Upwards trend on labour market undiminished'.

Ferner, A. (1997) 'Country of origin effects and human resource management in multinational companies', *Human Resource Management Journal,* 7: 119–37.

Ferner, A., Tregaskis, O., Edwards, P., Edwards, T., Adam, D. and Meyer, M. (2011) 'HRM structures and subsidiaries in foreign multinational firms in the UK', *International Journal of Human Resource Management,* 22, 3: 483–509.

Foulkes, F. (1980) *Personnel Management in Large Non-union Companies.* Englewood Cliffs, NJ: Prentice Hall.

Guenterberg, B. and Kayser, G. (2004) *SMEs in Germany Facts and Figures 2004.* Bonn: Institut Fuer Mittelstandsforschinug.

Hall, P. and Soskice, D. (2001) 'An introduction to varieties of capitalism' in P. Hall and D. Soskice (eds) *Varieties of Capitalism: The Institutional Foundations of Comparative Advantage.* Oxford: Oxford University Press, pp. 1–72.

Hanami, T. (2004) 'The changing labour market, industrial relations and labour policy', *Japan Labour Review,* 1, 1: 4–16.

Hattori, R. and Maeda, E. (2000) 'The Japanese employment system (summary)', *Bank of Japan Monthly Bulletin* (January). Online: **www.boj.or.jp/en/type/ronbun/ron/research/ data/ ron0001a.pdf** (accessed December 2013).

Hollingsworth, J.R. (1997) 'The institutional embeddedness of American capitalism' in C. Crouch and W. Streeck (eds) *The Political Economy of Modern Capitalism.* London: Sage, pp. 133–48.

Heyes, J., Lewis, P. and Clark, I. (2012) 'Varieties of capitalism: the state, financialisation and the economic crisis of 2007–?' *Industrial Relations Journal,* 43, 3: 222–41.

Inagami, T. (1988) *Japanese Workplace Industrial Relations,* Japanese Industrial Relations Series 14. Tokyo: Japanese Institute of Labour.

Inoue, S. (1999) *Japanese trade unions and their future: opportunities and challenges in an era of globalisation,* International Institute for Labour Studies Discussion Paper No. 106. Geneva: ILO.

Jackson, K. and Miyajima, H. (2007) (eds) *Corporate Governance in Japan: Institutional Change and Organisational Diversity.* Oxford: Oxford University Press.

Jacobi, O., Keller, B. and Muller-Jentsch, W. (1998) 'Germany: facing new challenges' in A. Ferner and R. Hyman (eds) *Changing Industrial Relations in Europe.* Oxford: Blackwell, pp. 190–238.

Jacoby, S. (1997) *Modern Manors: Welfare Capitalism since the New Deal.* New York: Princeton University Press.

Jeong, D. and Aguilera, R. (2008) 'The evolution of enterprise unionism in Japan: a socio-political perspective', *The British Journal of Industrial Relations,* 46, 1: 98–132.

Kato, T. (2001) 'The end of lifetime employment in Japan? Evidence from national surveys and research', *Journal of the Japanese and International Economies,* 15: 489–514.

Katz, H. and Darbishire, O. (2000) *Converging Divergences: World Wide Changes in Employment Systems.* New York: Cornell University Press.

567

Kerr, C., Dunlop, J., Harbison, E. and Myers, C. (1960) *Industrialism and Industrial Man.* Cambridge, MA: Harvard University Press.

Kochan, T., Katz, H. and McKersie, R. (1993) *The Transformation of American Industrial Relations,* 2nd edn. New York: Cornell University Press.

Kusuda, K. (2000) 'Trends in wage systems in Japan', *Japanese Institute of Labour Bulletin,* April.

Kwon, Hyeong-ki (2004) 'Japanese employment relations in transition', *Economic and Industrial Democracy,* 25, 3: 325–45.

Lane, C. (1989) *Management and Labour in Europe.* Aldershot: Edward Elgar.

Lane, C. (2000) 'Globalisation and the German model of capitalism: erosion or survival?', *British Journal of Sociology,* 51, 2: 207–34.

Lazonick, W. (1991) *Business Organisation and the Myth of the Market Economy.* Cambridge: Cambridge University Press.

Lincoln, J. R. and Kalleberg, A.L. (1992) *Culture, Control and Commitment: A Study of Work Organisation and Attitudes in the United States and Japan.* Cambridge: Cambridge University Press.

Littler, C. (1982) *The Development of the Labour Process in Capitalist Economies.* London: Heinemann.

Locke, D. (1996) *The Collapse of American Management Mystique.* Oxford: Oxford University Press.

Logan, J. (2006) 'The union avoidance industry in the United States', *British Journal of Industrial Relations,* 44, 4: 651–75.

Macnaughtan, H. (2006) 'From 'post-war' to 'post-bubble': contemporary issues for Japanese working women', in P. Matanle and W. Lunsing (eds) *Perspectives on Work, Employment and Society in Japan.* Basingstoke: Palgrave, pp. 31–57.

Marsden, D. (1999) *A Theory of Employment Systems.* Oxford: Oxford University Press.

Matanle, P. (2003) *Japanese Capitalism and Modernity in a Global Era: Refabricating Lifetime Employment Relations.* London: Routledge Curzon.

Matanle, P. (2006) 'Beyond lifetime employment? Re-fabricating Japan's employment culture', in P. Matanle and W. Lunsing (eds) *Perspectives on Work, Employment and Society in Japan.* Basingstoke: Palgrave, pp. 58–78.

Nakamura, K. (1997) 'Worker participation: collective bargaining and joint consultation', in M. Sako and H. Sato (eds) *Japanese Labour and Management in Transition: Diversity, Flexibility and Participation.* London: Routledge, pp. 280–95.

Noorderhaven, N. and Harzing, A-W. (2003) 'The 'Country of origin effect' in multinational corporations: sources, mechanisms and moderating conditions', *Management International Review,* 43, 2: 47–66.

OECD (2006) *OECD Factbook 2006: Economic, Environmental and Social Statistics.* Paris: OECD Publishing.

OECD (2007) *OECD Economic Outlook 82.* Paris: OECD Publishing.

Oliver, N. and Wilkinson, B. (1992) *The Japanisation of British Industry: New Developments in the 1990s,* 2nd edn. Oxford: Blackwell.

O'Sullivan, M. (2000) *Contests for Corporate Control and Economic Performance in the United States and Germany.* Oxford: Oxford University Press.

Perlmutter, H. (1969) 'The tortuous evolution of the multinational corporation', *Columbia Journal of World Business,* 4, 1, 9–18.

Peston, R. and Knight, L. (2012) *How Do We Fix This Mess? The Economic Price of Having it All and the Route to Lasting Prosperity.* London: Hodder and Stoughton.

Peters, T. and Waterman R. (1982) *In Search of Excellence: Lessons from America's Best Run Companies.* London: Profile Books.

Royle, T. and Urano, E. (2012) 'A new form of union organising in Japan? Community unions and the case of McDonald's "McUnion"', *Work, Employment and Society,* 26, 4: 606–22.

Rubery, J. and Grimshaw, D. (2003) *The Organisation of Employment: An International Perspective.* Basingstoke: Palgrave.

Rupert, M. (1995) *Producing Hegemony: The Politics of Mass Production and American Global Power.* Cambridge: Cambridge University Press.

Sako, M. (1997) 'Introduction: forces for homogeneity and diversity in the Japanese industrial relations system', in M. Sako and H. Sato (eds) *Japanese Labour and Management in Transition: Diversity, Flexibility and Participation.* London: Routledge, pp. 1–26.

Shinoda, T. (1997) 'Rengo and policy participation: Japanese-style neocorporatism?' in M. Sako and H. Sato (eds) *Japanese Labour and Management in Transition: Diversity, Flexibility and Participation.* London: Routledge, pp. 24–87.

Shirai, T. (1983) *Contemporary Industrial Relations in Japan.* Madison, WI: Wisconsin University Press.

Streeck, W. (1991) 'On the institutional conditions for diversified quality production' in Matzner, E. and Streeck, W. (eds) *Beyond Keynsianism: the socio-economics of production and employment.* London: Edward Elgar, pp. 21–61.

Strinati, D. (1982) *Capitalism, the State and Industrial Relations.* London: Croom Helm.

Sugeno, K. and Suwa, Y. (1997) 'Labour law issues in a changing labour market: in search of a new support system' in M. Sako, and H. Sato (eds) *Japanese Labour and Management in Transition: Diversity, Flexibility and Participation.* London: Routledge, pp. 53–78.

Symonds, P. (1999) 'Nissan announces 21,000 jobs to go in Japan's first major downsizing' World Socialist Website, 2 October. Online: **http://www.wsws.org/en/articles/1999/10/niss-o20.html** (accessed January 2014).

Towers, B. (1997) *The Representation Gap.* Oxford: Oxford University Press.

Teague, P. and Grahl, J. (2004) 'The German model in danger', *Industrial Relations Journal,* 35, 6: 557–73.

Thompson, P. (2003) 'Disconnected capitalism: or why employers can't keep their side of the bargain', *Work, Employment and Society* 17, 2: 359–78.

Thompson, P. (2011) 'The Trouble with HRM', *Human Resource Management Journal,* 21, 4: 355–67.

Tuselman, H. and Heise, A. (2000) 'The German model at the crossroads: past, present and future', *Industrial Relations Journal,* 31, 3: 162–77.

Wall Street Journal (2009) 'OECD expects Japan 2009, GDP at –6.6% Vs –0.1% November forecast', 31 March. Online: **http://wsj.com/article/BT-CO-200090331-70342.html** (accessed April 2009).

Watanabe, S. (2000) 'The Japan model and the future of employment and wage systems', *International Labour Review,* 139, 3: 307–34.

Whitley, R. (1999) *Divergent Capitalisms: The Social Structuring and Change of Business Systems.* Oxford: Oxford University Press.

Wickens, P. (1987) *The Road to Nissan: Flexibility, Quality, Teamwork.* Basingstoke: Palgrave Macmillan.

Williamson, O. (1964) *The Economics of Discretionary Behaviour: Managerial Objectives in a Theory of the Firm.* Englewood Cliffs, NJ: Prentice Hall.

Chapter 16

Employment relations in emerging economies: China and India

Anita Hammer

Objectives

- To explore the advantages and challenges of the comparative capitalism framework for China and India.
- To examine the nature of employment relations in China and India in their institutional context.
- To assess the impact of globalisation and multinational firms on human resource management (HRM) in China and India.
- To undertake a comparative assessment of China and India.

Introductory case study

The miracle of Indian IT and software industry: can India retain the competitive advantage?

The Indian IT and software industry has grown phenomenally in recent decades, becoming the largest industry in India and employing six million people directly or indirectly. Some Indian multinational corporations (MNCs) in IT include TCS, Infosys and Wipro. The IT industry controls 20 per cent of the global customised software market, specialising in high-quality solutions and IT services, and is a key export revenue earner. The competitive advantage of India in this sector comes from a number of factors. There is a considerable population of highly trained Indian professionals who have returned to India after work experience in the USA and Europe. The knowledge of English, the low cost of labour and the time difference, which allows for a 24-hour software development project cycle, helps the industry. State support plays an important role through the development of software technology parks, the development of industrial clusters in Bangalore, Hyderabad and Madras, and by providing subsidies to the industry. Moreover,

US and European MNCs, such as Microsoft, Texas Instruments and Intel, have invested in R&D, technical and management training and even the local IT infrastructure.

Today, the industry increasingly faces competition from other countries. Since the mid-1990s, wages in India have increased around 25 per cent per year and they are much lower in China and Russia. Indian firms actively subcontract to lower-cost producers in China and elsewhere. Despite substantial investment – more than 100,000 engineering graduates and 70,000 software professionals join the industry, both indigenous private and multinational firms, every year – there is a skill shortage in the industry at the middle and lower levels. Also, India is one of the largest exporters of skilled migrants in areas of software engineering and financial services.

Aware of the challenge from other countries, the IT industry has moved up the value chain, focusing on quality and high-end R&D expertise. Indian IT firms

➤

are evolving from a competitive advantage based on cheap labour and low costs to one based on value-added expertise such as IT systems, design and development capabilities. The industry has diversified, Indian IT firms have entered into joint ventures with established players and strong industrial clusters are growing.

A number of firms, such as Prudential, British Airways, Reuters and Barclays, have outsourced jobs from the UK to Indian IT firms in the past decade. Time will tell if jobs will eventually move from India to other low-cost economies, or whether India will retain its expertise and competitive advantage in the field.

Source: based on NASSCOM (2011), *The IT-BPO sector in India: strategic review for 2011,* Executive Summary.

Introduction

This chapter presents and analyses the employment relations in two of the major emerging economies, China and India, assessed in their broader institutional context as well as in the nature of their integration into the global economy. They have gained significance in economic and political terms as two of the fastest growing economies in the world, encompassing two-fifths of the world's population. Both represent market-orientated, state-managed capitalist economies but are also characterised by high degrees of inequality. They attract the highest inward foreign investment and are increasingly important sources of foreign direct investment. China has been called the 'factory of the world' for its manufacturing and export-led growth, while India, the 'back office of the world', has become a popular base for IT-enabled services, such as call centre and business process outsourcing operations. As the Introductory case study shows, Indian IT firms enjoy a global competitive advantage that stems from the institutional context and are also taking advantage of global capitalism to move up the value chain. Chinese and Indian firms are becoming more established and some are buying well-known brands or forming strategic alliances in order to gain a global presence. Examples include Lenovo's acquisition of IBM's PC division, Nanjing Automotive's acquisition of part of the Rover group and the Tata group's acquisition of Tetley tea, Jaguar Land Rover and Corus Steel.

As the second and the fourth largest economies of the world, respectively, China and India present interesting case studies of comparative capitalisms. Both are continent-sized countries that exhibit considerable internal political and economic heterogeneity, resulting in national as well as sub-national patterns of economic and social development. Both are post-socialist economies transitioning towards a market-orientated approach, with a sizeable public sector/state-owned enterprises. Both are experiencing considerable changes in the nature of their labour markets (with a rising migrant, informal workforce) as well as employment relations (rolling back of comprehensive social security provided for formal workers). They face similar challenges of unemployment, regional disparities, enduring poverty of the peasantry and threat of social conflict. However, these commonalities need to be read alongside their differences. Neither economy has followed the same route as other industrialised economies or engaged with global capitalism in the same fashion. The Chinese model is one of political authoritarianism, while India has a democratic state, supposedly embedded enough to cope with social and political protest without its foundations being challenged (e.g. Bardhan, 1998). While China is the bigger economy and more advanced in terms of economic and human development, India is slower in economic growth and poor in redistributive terms. Not surprisingly, the academic debate centres on understanding the nature of their rapid development and to what extent existing theoretical frameworks, in particular the comparative capitalist framework, can explain the diversity of capitalism in the two countries (Bhattacharjee and Ackers, 2010; Fligstein and Zhang, 2011; Morgan, 2011; Peck and Zhang, 2013; Storz *et al.*, 2013; Witt and Redding, 2013).

This chapter presents and analyses the employment relations in China and India by situating the analysis in a comparative capitalist framework. This allows the identification of the similarities and differences of the economic patterns of development in the two economies with respect to each other as well as with industrialised economies. The main objective is, first, to show how the two countries have a number of distinctive institutional features ('institutions' include markets, firms, corporate governance, the role of the state, labour market, systems of vocational education and training and of industrial relations).These are underpinned by different social compromises between various interest groups that configure the specific employment relations in each economy. Secondly, such an understanding helps us to analyse the impact of globalisation and multinational firms on employment relations.

The structure of the chapter is as follows. The first section extends the comparative capitalism approach to China and India. The following section tracks the institutional change in Chinese employment relations from the 'iron rice bowl' to 'socialism with Chinese characteristics'. The third main section examines the institutional roots of India's economic development as it transitions from a 'socialist pattern' to a 'market-orientated' one and the changing employment system. The last section undertakes a comparative assessment of the two countries and explores possibilities for their future trajectory.

Comparative capitalism in Asia

One of the significant dimensions of research in social science today is to understand the nature of development and change in emerging economies, especially in Asia, in a comparative and historical perspective and its implications for the global economy. One of the frameworks for analysing the diverse economic systems of Asian economies is the comparative capitalist approach. It provides a conceptual frame for understanding diverse forms of capitalisms in their unique internal institutional arrangements, but also for comparing the diversity of these institutional arrangements, thereby dealing with the diversity and commonality of capitalism. Some of the main traditions in this approach include varieties of capitalism (Hall and Soskice, 2001), national business systems (Whitley, 1999) and regulation theory (Hollingsworth and Boyer, 1997; Amable, 2003). Each of these approaches identified key institutional dimensions of analysis that have been critically evaluated and augmented (summarised in Table 16.1).

Researchers in the comparative capitalist tradition argue that each societal context evolves its own unique culture and institutional pattern of economic development. The economic

Table 16.1 Institutional dimensions of leading models of comparative institutional analysis

Dimension	Whitley (1999)	Hall and Soskice (2001)	Amable (2003)	Redding (2005)	Hancké et al. (2007)
Civil society role				Yes	
Education and skills formation	Yes	Yes	Yes	Yes	Yes
Employment relations	Yes	Yes	Yes	Yes	Yes
Financial system	Yes	Yes	Yes	Yes	Yes
Interfirm networks	Yes	Yes		Yes	Yes
Internal dynamics of the firm	Yes	Yes		Yes	Yes
Ownership and corporate governance	Yes	Yes		Yes	Yes
Product markets			Yes		
Social capital (trust)	Yes			Yes	
Social protection			Yes		
State role	Yes			Yes	Yes

Source: Witt and Redding (2013: 268).

structures and relations evolve historically in a specific context and are politically enabled, institutionally mediated and socially embedded. Institutions refer to the state, law, the nature of family, education and training, interest groups or associations (especially trade unions and employer associations), labour markets and the financial system. They shape the structure and strategies of firms and how employment relations are configured, thus resulting in a variety of capitalist models. In its 'first wave', scholars compared the distinctive national forms of capitalisms in developed industrial economies, i.e. the USA, Europe and Japan, and focused on the relatively stable and well-organised institutions in those economies. The aim was to identify their comparative institutional advantage, i.e. how institutions interlock in specific ways to give a competitive advantage to the national economy and its firms (Deeg and Jackson, 2007). Based on this analysis, countries were identified as either liberal market economy (e.g. USA) or coordinated market economy (e.g. Germany) (Hall and Soskice, 2001) or were categorised according to five models of Amable (2003): market-based, social democratic, continental European, Mediterranean and Asian.

Research in the comparative capitalist tradition provided a powerful critique to the rhetoric that all economic systems would converge towards the apparently successful Anglo-Saxon form of neo-liberal capitalism, whereby firms would adopt universal management and employment practices. However, it has been critiqued for its inability to accommodate change, diversity and conflict in various national contexts as well as within a specific context. On one hand, the increasing internal diversity, change and conflict within the exemplars of comparative capitalism model, i.e. stable developed economies, has challenged many assumptions of the comparative capitalism analysis. On the other hand, it was criticised for its Western-centric focus as it was not extended to non-Western and non-industrialised parts of the world. Indeed, in view of the heterogeneity and change in China and India, some scholars argue that existing analytical frameworks are insufficient to explain changes in developing economies (Bhattacharjee and Ackers, 2010). According to Hamilton (2006: 70), China represents 'an independent vision of how a society can be put together and it must be understood in its own terms'. Chinese capitalism reveals the complexity of understanding the nature of institutions and change. The links between the state, the Chinese Communist Party (CCP), aspects of tradition (in the family system, social obligation, operation of *guanxi* – personal connections/networks) and aspects of foreign involvement provide the basis of a state-led, gradual institutional change and model of economic development (Fligstein and Zhang, 2011; Morgan, 2011). Similarly, India exhibits vast internal heterogeneity of modes of production, regulation and the nature of social compromise between different groups. This has resulted in very different routes to industrialisation and development between its different states (e.g. Gujarat and Kerala) and outcomes for various social groups (Sinha, 2005; Hammer, 2012). At the same time, many of its regions (as in China) are being articulated into the global economy in very specific ways, some as identified zones/clusters of knowledge, innovation or labour supply, where institutions and actors interact and struggle to mediate and modify global influences to suit regional/local ends (Bhattacharjee and Ackers, 2010; Hammer, 2010).

The critique of the comparative capitalist approach has become sharper in the last decade with the rise of China, India, Russia and Brazil as major economic players in the global economy. The 'second wave' of comparative capitalist research addresses many of the earlier gaps and has seen an increased focus of the comparative capitalist approach on Asia (Amable, 2003; Boyer *et al.*, 2011; Aoki, 2013; Storz *et al.*, 2013; Witt and Redding, 2013). The emergence and success of new economies with their complex institutional arrangements and internal diversity (China, India), rapid institutional change and, at times, the lack of institutional coherence (China) pose new analytical questions about institutional change, the role of the state and integration in the global economy (Morgan, 2011; Peck and Zhang, 2013; Storz *et al.*, 2013). As shown earlier in Table 16.1, Whitley (1999) and Redding (2005) have added further dimensions to the comparative institutional analysis for understanding Asia. More recently, Storz *et al.* (2013: 218) have argued for a differentiated understanding of the institutional patterns and variety within and across Asia. Apart from their increasing relevance economically, Asian economies provide an opportunity to extend and refine the existing comparative institutional analysis. The apparent lack of coherence and immense heterogeneity of capitalist production, regulation and related institution-building in China and the peculiar industrial specialisation in India based on textiles, IT or services require not only an application of the comparative capitalism approach to these economies, but also a renewed analysis of various modes of capitalist growth and institutional comparative advantage. While the key role of the state and institutional diversity of Asia support the existing analysis, the cases of countries like China where rapid institutional change co-exists with institutional stability and the role of exogenous shock in driving institutional change provide a better understanding of mechanisms and processes of change. One such work is that of Witt and Redding (2013), who identify five forms of Asian capitalism in a comparison of 13 Asian economies (including China and India): post-socialist economies, advanced city economies, emerging South-east Asian economies, advanced North-east Asian economies and Japan. These forms are all fundamentally distinct from Western types of capitalism. Not only do they extend the comparative institutional analysis to Asia but argue for further refinement of business system analysis to incorporate social capital (interpersonal and institutionalised trust), culture, the extent of informality and multiplexity (multiple business systems within the same economy).

In conclusion, with its focus on internal diversity and institutional change, the second wave of comparative capitalist analysis provides a welcome starting point for understanding and explaining the diversity of institutions and outcomes in Chinese and Indian capitalism in a comparative capitalist framework, as well as benefiting from what insights the two countries may bring to this framework. It informs the framework that is mobilised in the following sections to allow us to understand and analyse the institutional context of employment relations in China and India.

Key Controversy

Are China and India converging to a neo-liberal model of capitalism or do they reinforce the diversity of capitalism? What factors would prevent a convergence of employment practices in Asia?

China: state-led capitalist model

The People's Republic of China represents an interesting case of a Communist state that has achieved impressive economic growth since it started opening up in the 1970s. With a population of around 1.3 billion, which includes a workforce of about 780 million, China is the second largest economy in the world and is ranked second in absolute purchasing power. It has experienced average economic growth of 10 per cent and has attracted the highest flow of foreign direct investment in the world since 2001. China's growth was based on export-led manufacturing, and its external trade reached around $1.5 trillion in 2010 (World Development Indicators, 2013). Aware that over 50 per cent of the exports come from foreign-owned firms, recent state policy focuses on boosting domestic consumption and decreasing dependence on exports. In the context of a supportive state policy of 'going global', key firms and industries managed to move up the value chain into high-tech production (such as Haier and Lenovo).

The nature of Chinese capitalism is much debated because it is a Communist state ruled by one party, i.e. the CCP, that has embarked on a capitalist route: how socialist or capitalist is it? Others argue, instead, for a focus on its contradictions and paradoxes rather than trying to identify pure models (Fligstein and Zhang, 2011; Peck and Zhang, 2013). Thus, the socialist legacy is evident first in the ambiguous nature of private property rights and state ownership of land and natural resources. The state's presence in the economy also remains predominant through state-owned enterprises (SOEs) in strategic sectors, corporate governance and state-owned banks, while the CCP's control extends to shaping national, local and firm-level policies, as well as appointments to crucial positions in political and economic spheres. At the same time, capitalist elements are also clearly discernible in three areas: in the profit motive that drives the local growth in economic zones, in the private sector and increasingly even in SOEs; in the market coordination of prices, labour, wages and land, which is replacing price control of goods, *danwei* (work units), *hukou* (residency entitlement that provides citizenship rights) and socialist land tenure regimes; and in the rise of capitalist class interests (although in the shadow of the party-state) and increasing inequality and polarisation in society.

Four aspects stand out in the nature of industrialisation and development in China:

- the *high degree of direct state involvement* in the economy and its relationship with the CCP;
- the *gradual nature of economic and social change* from a command to a market economy with Chinese/socialist characteristics;
- the *combination of different traditions,* i.e. Confucian, Maoist and emerging values of materialism, which influence economic activity, firms and work practices in China;
- the *nature of foreign involvement* in China through investment and multinational firms.

All these aspects have an effect on the development of institutions and markets in China, which is discussed next.

Institutional context

This section outlines the historical pattern of institutional development in China through the dimensions of the state, firms, the financial system, the labour market, as well as the system of education and training. However, to explain the social foundations of Chinese capitalism, one needs to look beyond the set of institutions that the comparative capitalist framework mobilises for developed economies. Thus, aspects of tradition, i.e. the nature of the family system, social obligations and *guanxi* (personal connections/networks), or the social mechanisms that have traditionally supported Chinese economic activity and firms are also discussed (Hamilton, 2006; Morgan, 2011). Witt and Redding (2013) characterise similar social dimensions under social capital (trust), culture, informality and multiplexity of business systems within China.

State, regulation and reform

The role of the state remains predominant in the economic sphere, yet it is also changing in response to global economic pressures. The economy is state-controlled and planned. Economic activity and industrialisation was organised through SOEs and village and township enterprises (VTEs). Extensive regulations and a vast bureaucracy exist at the national and local level with political and economic interests fused together across all levels.

State and industrial governance in Maoist China

Child (1994: 36–38) identifies four main phases of industrial governance during the period from 1949 to 1976 and notes that social and political discipline was used as an effective force for controlling the Chinese people. In the first phase of central planning (1953–56), Mao Zedong who came to power in 1949 advocated that China move to an economy based upon socialist ownership. The Five Year Plan that was launched in 1953 emphasised centralised planning and control from the state. Trade unions existed, but their role was confined to welfare issues. In the second phase of Decentralisation and the Great Leap Forward (1957–61), the system of industrial governance that developed was influenced by the Soviet system and tended to be hierarchical, and not in sympathy with the collectivist orientation of the Chinese culture. The Great Leap Forward was a period when many of these collectivist values came to the fore. During 1957–61, control of much of industry passed from central to provincial government. However, great emphasis was placed upon allegiance to the Communist Party, and factory directors had to report to Party committees. The third phase refers to the period of readjustment, 1962–65.

The period 1959–61 saw a drop in agricultural output, followed by a famine. This was partly caused by an over-emphasis on expanding the manufacturing sector during the Great Leap Forward. The period of readjustment saw a move back towards more centralised planning; however, factory directors were given more control over day-to-day production issues.

The Cultural Revolution (1966–76) was a distinctive period, during which politics and ideology were the predominant concerns. There was a great emphasis upon allegiance to the Party. Factories moved away from hierarchical control towards using factory revolutionary committees as the management mechanism. In terms of rewards, 'competitive, individual and material incentive was rejected in favour of cooperative, collective and moral incentive' (Child, 1994: 37). Therefore, a context of collectivism and control developed. Child (1994: 39) comments that:

> the Cultural Revolution was seen to have dissipated incentive and responsibility for economic performance through egalitarianism, the weakening of management, the general devaluation of expertise and the claim that ideological fervour and inspired leadership could substitute for technical knowledge. . . The xenophobia of the period had denied the country opportunities for inward investment and technology transfer.

Economic reforms: post-1976

After the death of Mao Zedong in 1976, his successor Deng Xiaoping embarked on an economic reform programme. From the early 1980s, China allowed joint ventures to operate and from this point, foreign-invested enterprises became widespread. In 1982, Deng Xiaoping coined the phrase 'socialism with Chinese characteristics' to describe this approach to economic reform. Reforms are not conceived as a strategy to create a market or a capitalist economy, rather a socialist market economy. The formal legal institutions were therefore not conceived or designed as those to support a capitalist market economy, and legal independence of the judiciary has been poor. Gradual reform allowed an accommodation to reform, to reduce constraints to enterprise and to reinforce market processes without formally having to forego the political ideology of state control. The ongoing reform process has continually involved the state through its dominance in strategic and technological sectors, fostering indigenous innovation and forging national technological leadership through large-scale social science and engineering projects. The state, under Zhu Rongji, identified certain strategic industries, assets and technologies to become national industry champions (often SOEs) and pursue internationalisation strategies, taking China into the World Trade Organisation (WTO). This was upscaled by Wen Jiabao's policy of 'going global'. More recently, Hu Jintao focused on the high-technology sector through encouraging foreign direct investment (FDI), which more than doubled between 2001 and 2010, and providing state support to local start-up firms. More recent state strategy has focused on regional development and infrastructure development. Thus, the Chinese state has often been termed a socialist-developmental state, exhibiting links between the national state and industrial policies similar to the 'Asian' developmental state (Evans, 1995). However, what is significantly different in the Chinese model from other developmental states is the relationship between the central and local state, where political and economic interests are intertwined in very specific ways across different levels of the state, challenging the developmental orientations of the state.

Central–local state relations in economic development

Political centralisation and economic regionalisation drive Chinese reforms and economic development. Policy formulation and decision-making are a mix of top-down statism with strong bottom-up elements. Political centralisation is evident in the appointment and monitoring of sub-national state officials from above, while economic regionalisation is evident in the sub-national government's fairly comprehensive and autonomous management of local economic growth. This binds central and state governments where promotion and patronage flows from the top and loyalty is reciprocated from below, while encouraging competition between different regions. This has resulted in a variety of local state forms and models of economic development with successful institutional innovations within China, yet ones that have a historical legacy. Thus, more developed regions along the coast had better resources and leadership capacities and have tended towards developmental models, whereas resource-starved and agriculture-based regions have tended towards aggressive acquisition of land through dispossession of the peasantry for developing economic zones, high-tech parks and cities in order to attract mobile private and foreign investment. Also, the extent of government accountability and citizens' voice is very low. With the political power of capital embedded in the party-state and the CCP, there are elements of both a developmental and a predatory state (Peck and Zhang, 2013; Witt and Redding, 2013).

Corporate governance and financial systems

China's industrial production has been dominated by SOEs and Village and Township Enterprises (VTEs), although under the reform process they have become increasingly marketised. SOEs dominate in strategic technological sectors, often referred to as 'national champions'. The export-orientated sector is dominated by foreign firms and subject to open competition. Among the most dynamic sectors of the economy are the VTEs, which are not privately owned but are market-dependent. Private firms operate in the shadow of the state with a dominance of family and *guanxi* networks and patron–client ties.

Private ownership of property became legally permissible only in the 1990s. Ownership structures are relatively concentrated and there is not much protection for minority share-holders. Ownership rights in China are neither protected nor especially transparent. Thus, it is advantageous to disguise an enterprise's ownership as being state-owned or collectively owned, when in fact there is a private entrepreneur or family behind the scenes. The role of the state in organising such private enterprises around SOEs and the role of government policy in promoting them as substitutive institutions underlines the dominant role of the state in China. There exists considerable state ownership of privately listed companies, and the state or its agents carry out shareholder functions that would otherwise be performed by private owners in market economies. At the same time, although the formal institution of state own-ership has remained in place in many cases, the substantive role has changed dramatically (see Estrin and Prevezer, 2011 for details).

Not surprisingly, China's formal legal corporate governance structures are weak. There is a lack of legal infrastructure. Contract enforcement is weak. Intellectual property rights (IPRs) are shaky and IP theft is a serious concern for MNCs in China. According to Estrin and Prevezer (2011), it is informal institutions for corporate governance that substitute and compensate for ineffective formal corporate governance institutions in China. Informal insti-tutions create a favourable environment for firms in a variety of ways, such as cultivating relations with government officials; choosing geographical localities where it is known that private enterprise is more acceptable; taking over ailing state-owned enterprises; donating services to the local community; and concealing the private nature of ownership. The goals of informal mechanisms are supposedly not in conflict with those of the formal institutions, often promoting positive investment outcomes both domestically in terms of entrepreneur-ship and in relation to foreigners, leading to strong flows of FDI, e.g. by de facto recognition of ownership rights by the state. At the same time, such informal norms governing trust and authority relations based on personal and particularistic connections can also encourage cli-entelism and rent-seeking relations between the political elite and the capitalist class, e.g. in some SOEs. This has resulted in the perpetuation of vested interests and the concentration of political and economic power in the hands of a few (Peck and Zhang, 2013).

State influence on capital allocation is strong in China. Financial institutions are state-owned and China does not rely heavily on external financing. SOEs have preferential access to finance from state-owned banks compared with private firms. There are severe restric-tions on bank loans for certain types of businesses, especially for privately owned and riskier enterprises. Therefore, Chinese family-owned firms rely heavily on informal sources of finance, such as family networks, particularly small private firms with a lack of access to bank finance. Entrepreneurs go to unofficial and illegal credit institutions, not qualifying for credit from state-owned banks, which favour strategically important firms at the expense of small and medium-sized enterprises (SMEs). This informal banking sector is one-third of the size of the total financial system in China (Witt and Redding, 2013). There is increasingly large-scale foreign investment in technologically advanced sectors.

Aspects of tradition or social capital in inter-firm relations

Chinese economic activity and Chinese firms have traditionally relied on social and informal mechanisms for support that develop out of Chinese tradition, and the absence of institutionalised processes and formal procedures governing trust and authority. Child (1994: 28–32) states that there is a degree of agreement that Confucianism is the basis for many Chinese traditions. Confucianism emphasised a respect for elders and the family, order, hierarchy and a sense of duty. Individuals had a fixed position in society, and social harmony could be achieved when individuals behaved according to rank. Family is the fundamental institution that extends support and ensures the security of the individual. The family, and through it the individual, is rooted in a network of local, regional, national and international ties of social obligations, rights and responsibilities that are strictly defined and embedded in the practice of *guanxi*. *Guanxi* is intertwined with the preservation of 'face', which relates to a person's social standing, position and moral character. Whitley (1999) and Redding (2005) conceptualise these networks as social capital or interpersonal trust in Asian economies, expressed through relationships between individuals both inside and outside the firm. According to Morgan (2011), familial authority and extensive networks reign in a context where the state is a distant authoritarian presence and markets are controlled and restricted.

Chinese firms, locally as well as in the diaspora, have traditionally built on family and *guanxi* and continue to do so (Redding, 2005; Hamilton, 2006). The economic reform process was accompanied by links between the CCP and Chinese entrepreneurs in Hong Kong and Taiwan, who were and continue to be the main investors in China. The Chinese diaspora exploited the state-facilitated openings through pre-existing familiarity with local customs, language and kinship and community networks, as well as through donations to local institutions and preferential treatment from CCP officials. Likewise, local, small firms have been able to exploit dense networks of long-term, reciprocal ties and to participate in globalised supply chains (e.g. Wenzhou city model). According to some, such networks or informal institutions create a favourable environment for firms and construct supportive goals between owners and local states and government officials (Redding, 2005; Estrin and Prevezer, 2011). However, this form of network or *guanxi* capitalism can also result in clientelist exchanges between commercial/private entrepreneurs and bureaucratic/state power with weak accountability, termed as power-elite capitalism. This is evident in the 'insider' privatisation of SOEs where former party and government officials who moved into private business have amassed fortunes through their political, personal and family ties. Similarly, land development across China presents another opportunity for local officials and business interests to manipulate business opportunities for personal gains. This nexus between political power and economic wealth weaves formal hierarchies with *guanxi,* thereby creating exclusionary networks of vested interests based on patronage, co-option and corruption (Peck and Zhang, 2013).

Labour market and system of education and training

The labour market in China is deeply segmented along rural–urban lines, institutionalised through the *hukou* regime (household registration system) and creating a dualised form of economic citizenship. Of the total workforce, one-third are rural workers (rural-*hukou*) and one-third are urban workers (urban-*hukou*). The remaining rural-*hukou* are temporary migrants who work in cities, do not have access to the welfare benefits available to urban-*hukou,* and are also disenfranchised politically. Dispossessed of land acquired for industrial parks, economic zones and cities, these rural marginal workers provide the labour supply for urban projects and industry. Accommodated in dormitories provided by employers and/or the state, this migrant (often young and female) labour is available on tap, at low wages and without any social security coverage (Pun and Smith, 2007). The socialist *hukou*-cum-land regime makes this workforce vulnerable to workplace exploitation and social discrimination in the cities and by local officials and managers in their villages. Employment protection and welfare provision for the unemployed and marginal workers are minimal in China (Peck and Zhang, 2013). At the same time, there exists a shortage of educated staff, managerial employees and engineers.

The problem of labour market imbalance is rooted in Confucian ideology as well as the historical–economic development of modern China (Child, 1994). There is extensive basic education coverage, a Maoist legacy, but low enrolment in further and higher education. The traditional emphasis on general skills and weak vocational training was further exacerbated by severe disruption of education and training during the Cultural Revolution. Also, central planning meant that managers had little autonomy, mistakes were severely penalised and achievements were not rewarded. Important decisions were made by collective consensus, with managers seeing themselves as information conduits and individuals unwilling to take risky decisions that may lead them to 'lose face'. The acquisition of professional skill is left to private initiative and on-the-job training is limited (Witt and Redding, 2013). This is changing as the speed of economic development in China has led to a great demand for educated and skilled staff. More active state support for management development and training is accompanied by more emphasis on training in foreign firms (Gamble, 2003, 2006a). Not surprisingly, recent Chinese growth is based on superiority in labour-intensive sectors and limited technological innovation (Peck and Zhang, 2013).

To summarise, the Chinese institutional context comprises some institutions that are undergoing change (such as the Communist state) and others that are still being built (such as corporate governance structures, labour market and systems of skilling). The processes of institutional change and construction reveal a complex interplay of Communist legacies of state control, the continued role of traditional institutions of family and *guanxi* in economic activity, the coexistence of formal and informal institutions in economic and financial spheres, and a deeply segmented labour market. This has implications for employment relations in China, which are discussed next.

Explore

- Why is it important to consider aspects of tradition/social mechanisms to understand the Chinese institutional context?

Employment relations: from 'iron rice bowl' to a 'socialist market economy'

Chinese employment relations are transitioning from an egalitarian employment framework signified by lifelong employment, wage equality and comprehensive welfare provision for all its workers towards more market-driven relations. Three factors characterise the nature of change in employment relations:

- the endurance of some Maoist legacies at the workplace, e.g. low wage differentials, and of old traditions in economic activity, e.g. reliance on *guanxi*;
- the rise in unemployment, insecurity and social conflict in Chinese society;
- the continuing strong role of the state in employment relations.

The interaction between these aspects offers the possibility of institutional change in the Chinese capitalist model driven by the changes in social compromise (where the state/CCP is aware of the need to address inequality to ensure its survival).

'Iron rice bowl': work organisation, lifelong employment and comprehensive welfare

SOEs and VTEs have dominated industrial production and played both an economic and a social role. SOEs accounted for 80 per cent of industrial production in 1978 and still dominate in strategic sectors. Central to the enterprise were work units (*danwei*). These formed the core of the community. The enterprise provided lifetime employment and cradle-to-grave welfare structures through the system that became known as the 'iron rice bowl' (Ding *et al.*, 2000). This related to the provision of its employees with housing, medical support and education. There was no concept of a labour market, and individuals were not allowed to move within China to 'follow work'. Trade unions existed, but the All China Federation of Trade Unions (ACFTU) acted as a top-down transmission belt for mobilisation of workers for labour production on behalf of the State and the union role centred on production and welfare issues, and not negotiations on pay and conditions.

The 'iron rice bowl' has been criticised for encouraging a high degree of 'organisational dependency' (Ding *et al.*, 2000: 218). Under the full employment system that emerged, the dismissal of workers was allowed only if a worker had committed 'gross negligence', but the sanction was rarely used. In order to avoid the problems associated with unemployment, a system of 'featherbedding' was used, which resulted in enterprises that were overstaffed, with low levels of productivity (Child, 1994). Wages were based on seniority, and there was no real incentive for employees to strive for promotion. Managers were promoted according to Party allegiance rather than on the basis of merit. They are perceived to lack initiative, often avoid taking individual responsibility and are unwilling to delegate or to discipline staff. This resulted in problems of absenteeism, labour indiscipline and low motivation, and these have provided the basis for labour reforms.

Creating a socialist market economy: restructuring and labour reforms

Reforms have led to the commodification of land and labour, with significant changes in the labour market, in the provision of social security as well as in employment practices. Restructuring of SOEs and changes in labour laws have impacted upon workers socialised into the 'iron rice bowl' mentality with expectations of lifelong employment and comprehensive welfare. There is no longer a 'job for life': a 1988 bankruptcy law terminated the guarantee for lifelong employment. From 1998 the *danweis* were no longer allowed to allocate subsidised housing, and allowances for education and medical support were slowly being reduced. Labour reforms such as the *three systems reforms* of 1992 introduced labour contracts, performance-related rewards and social insurance reforms. Under the contract system, enterprises were able to downsize and reduce employees. Some of the labour market concerns were addressed by the 1994 Labour Law that provided some rights to workers, e.g. minimum wage levels, directives on working hours and provisions for dispute handling and resolution, but also partially decoupled welfare from the state. Likewise, the Labour Contract Law of the People's Republic of China 2008 provides employment protection, but in reality enforcement of labour law is weak and arbitrary, and protections for the unemployed and marginalised workers are minimal. Nichols *et al.* (2004) argue that the loss of lifelong employment and comprehensive welfare, along with a shift to performance-related pay and temporary employment contracts, has dismantled established labour and weakened workers' position *vis-à-vis* the employer. This often results in disharmony and conflict in workplaces which operate with tight control over labour and authoritarian discipline (Morris *et al.*, 2009; Nichols and Zhao, 2010; Danford and Zhao, 2012).

The labour market has become more decentralised and flexible with greater labour mobility, but largely to the detriment of workers, especially rural workers. The predatory state continues to acquire land for urban projects and economic zones developed to attract foreign investment by dispossessing peasantry, thereby creating a large unregulated labour market of internal migrant workers (rural-*hukou*) without proper registration, work permits and social protection. It was estimated that there were 42 million migrant workers in Guangdong – larger than the population of Poland (Harney, 2005) – and approximately 150 million rural-*hukou* who work in cities in China are subject to social discrimination and workplace exploitation (Peck and Zhang, 2013).

The social outcome of the reforms in China has been inequality and social unrest. Unemployment figures have risen sharply as a result of the global economic crisis. China's egalitarian social structure has become polarised in the past few decades into a rising economic elite interwoven with the part-state system at one end, with nearly two-thirds of the population located in the lowest socioeconomic stratum at the other (Peck and Zhang, 2013). Selective concentration of FDI in the coastal regions and large cities (accelerated by WTO accession) has contributed to growing income, opportunity and regional disparities. Worker unrest is evident in the increasing frequency of strikes and demonstrations, but also instances of violence and death (e.g. in the case of Foxconn, the large Chinese contract manufacturer that produces goods for MNCs such as Apple and HP, where, in 2010, there were a number of suicide attempts by employees, with a number of fatalities – some have argued these came about as a result of Foxconn's exploitative employment practices). Some have noted the potential for further unrest in the cities from migrant workers – particularly if such workers were laid off and unable to return home (Glover and Siu, 2000). This fear of social unrest may underlie the state's decision to institute a system of social security.

From comprehensive welfare to social security fund

Prior to the economic reforms, the enterprise provided comprehensive cover. Since the reforms, the state has continued to offload its welfare and social services, including pensions, healthcare, housing and education, to the private sector and households. A social insurance fund, contributed to by the state, the enterprise and individual employees, designed to act as a safety net has been created. The rising cost of social insurance has led to concerns that the social security fund will not be strong enough to support claims from it. The reasons for this include the following (Zhu and Warner, 2005: 363):

- the system is fairly new and, as a result, a mass of contributions has not built up;
- many retirees did not make contributions into the scheme but are now drawing from it;
- SOEs that have closed no longer make contributions for their employees.

It has been estimated that the cost of moving towards a fully funded pension system by 2030 could reach Rmb 3000 billion. Zhu and Warner (2005) comment that the problem is likely to be exacerbated in the future by an ageing population.

Explore

- What are the key characteristics and criticisms associated with the 'iron rice bowl'?
- How has it changed under the reform process?

Industrial relations

The legacy of Maoism is evident in industrial relations where the state and the CCP remain a powerful hegemonic force. Trade unions are party-controlled and unitary with limited worker involvement; for example, the ACFTU is the political instrument of the CCP used for top-down communication of state policies concerning work and employment. Membership of the ACFTU covers half of the workforce. Union density in 2007 was 16.1 per cent (Witt and Redding, 2013). Accession to the WTO saw the establishment of a 'tripartite negotiation system' at national level, and some legitimisation of the role of trade unions in protecting the economic interests of employees with some involvement in issues around lay-offs, re-employment and dispute settlement. In practice, the ACFTU functions in a bipartite rather than a tripartite fashion, and, as the political instrument of the CCP, aligns with management rather than workers (Witt, 2010).

Industrial relations are based on a regressive and piecemeal welfare system and the political deprivation of the workforce, especially the peasantry. Unions have concentrated on welfare and assisted in production issues, not on negotiating wages and working conditions. At the enterprise level, there is uncoordinated wage bargaining beyond state-stipulated minimum wage standards. In the private sector, management exercises extraordinary powers over employment relations issues (Witt, 2010). In a study of SOEs in the car industry, Nichols and Zhao (2010) demonstrate the dissatisfaction of workers with the tokenistic representation provided by the ACFTU and their own inability to form an independent trade union at the workplace. Overall, enforcement of labour is law is weak and arbitrary, while employment protection and provision for marginal workers (rural-*hukou* that form the large informal migrant worker group) and the unemployed are minimal (Peck and Zhang, 2013).

Employment practices: recruitment and reward

Employment practices such as recruitment and rewards exemplify the interplay of Maoist legacies, traditional mechanisms, nature of foreign involvement and the role of the state at the workplace. Recruitment practices show the influence of SOE practices, *guanxi* and proximity to the local state and bureaucracy, which carry over into MNC recruitment as well. Prior to the reforms, workers were assigned to firms from labour bureaux. This often meant that workers were assigned even when they did not hold the requisite skill and knowledge for the job. To some extent, processes of recruitment and selection are becoming less influenced by political bureaucracy and more by economic and market concerns. There is more emphasis on personal competency as a criterion, rather than on an individual's political background (Zhu and Dowling, 2002). Some powerful MNCs are also able to avoid such 'Chinese' influences in their recruitment practices, on account of their financial strength and position as 'outsiders', which allows them to sidestep societal expectation (Hutchings and Murray, 2003; Gamble, 2006a).

At the same time, Ahlstrom *et al.* (2005) reveal how personal networks and connections affect recruitment and selection practices in 16 foreign firms in China. They found that managers perceived potential benefits in strategic 'overstaffing' by taking on workers from SOEs that were downsizing in order to gain favour with local government officials. In effect, if companies took on additional staff, they could expect to 'negotiate some reciprocal benefits from the local government' (Ahlstrom *et al.*, 2005: 272). Managers also reported that recruiting members from retrenching SOEs could also bring useful industry contacts; for example, an SOE could be a customer of the foreign firm and deals could be helped by networks of personal contacts. The selection of well-connected individuals to management teams and boards of directors was seen as a paramount issue by some firms (not only to help deals but also to impart knowledge about local rules and regulations, so that the company could understand which rules had to be complied with). Finally, the study found that it was not unusual for companies to ask prospective employees for their list of connections with key officials and that, 'by hiring such connected individuals, firms ensure that they have a voice as officials at various levels and in different regions help to overcome difficulties' (Ahlstrom *et al.*, 2005: 277).

Similarly, reforms have increased flexibility within reward systems, but some aspects of the old system endure. The seniority-based flat rate system is being replaced by systems that often have some link to performance. Wages were determined by legislation and regional agencies until the mid-1980s, but factors such as responsibility and qualifications are being taken into account. Increased demand and shortage of skills have seen high labour turnover and a considerable increase in salaries and wages. However, SOEs are often unwilling to increase wage differentials. State enterprises have tended to pay equal bonuses to all employees regardless of the performance of individual employees. They have also retained a great degree of harmonisation of working conditions and tend not to penalise underperformance. The principle of equality has endured in the reward system post-Mao and also has an influence on MNCs, where wage differentials often remain much lower than in the parent country (Gamble, 2003).

In summary, employment relations are undergoing change in China, but these changes are gradual in nature and show elements of continuity from the past. Communist legacies of lifelong employment and comprehensive welfare in SOEs are gradually giving way to a more flexible labour market and a contributory social security fund. At the same time, wage equality from the Communist past and social mechanisms of *guanxi* in recruitment persist in the employment arena. Such legacies in employment practices are also evident in foreign firms operating in China, which are the focus of the next section.

Key Controversy

To what extent are employment relations in China undergoing a total transformation to market driven relations or do they display continuity from the past?

Globalisation and multinational firms in China

This section explores the interaction of the Chinese capitalist model with global capitalism. As a major global economic power, with the second largest and the fastest-growing economy of the world, China is building its model of capitalism while also re-entering the global capitalist order. The discussion so far has explored the change in institutions and employment relations in China as it transitions from a Communist to a market-orientated system, and also builds new institutions and markets. These processes are significantly influenced by global economic forces, in particular MNCs, through transfer of their employment and HR policies and practices, and the reorganisation of economic and social compromises that this engenders in the Chinese economy. After a brief overview of the nature and extent of foreign investment into China and Chinese foreign investment abroad, this section focuses on two areas of debate with regard to how MNCs are influencing employment relations in China: adoption of Western HRM by Chinese firms, and transfer of HRM to China by MNCs.

Inward foreign investment in China

China attracts the highest amount of FDI in the world, rising from $193 billion in 2000 to $473 billion in 2009. Most of the FDI is concentrated in China's eastern coastal regions, especially in Guangdong and Shanghai. Guangdong has seen the highest concentration of FDI, mainly due to its light regulation, relative remoteness from the capital Beijing (and therefore from central government control), its proximity to the region's largest port, Hong Kong, and the fact that it contained all but one of the country's special economic zones (SEZs). Shanghai has a strong industrial base and advantageous location as a major port at the mouth of the Yangtze. The third major development region is in the old industrial heartland of north-east coastal China. Attempts to boost FDI in China's less developed interior, namely Central and West China, are continuing. The nature of foreign investment has extended from cheap manufacturing and consumer market presence to research and development investment in information technology (Motorola, Microsoft), pharmaceuticals (GSK, Novartis) and automotive (GM, Ford, Toyota).

Outward foreign investment from China

Increasingly, Chinese firms are investing abroad and Chinese MNCs are becoming global players. China's outward FDI (OFDI) stock reached US$ 246 billion by the end of 2009, eight times the US$ 28 billion recorded in 2000. The bulk of China's OFDI goes to Asia in the tertiary sector, followed by the primary sector. China's overseas greenfield investments are concentrated mainly in the energy, raw materials, automotive and real estate sectors. The two largest Chinese MNCs are China International Trading and Investment Corporation (Citic), with foreign assets exceeding US$ 25 billion, and China Ocean Shipping (Group) Company (COSCO), with foreign assets of some US$ 21 billion. Other major MNCs include the China National Petroleum Corporation (CNPC), Sinochem Group, China National Offshore Oil Corporation (CNOOC) and Sinosteel Corporation. In the high-technology field, Haier (white goods) and Lenovo (PC) have a global presence.

The Chinese institutional context of strong state support and social networks has provided Chinese firms with a competitive advantage through opportunities to upgrade. The strong role of the state in the development of regions with clusters of knowledge and resources, control over the financial system and other resources, state support to SOEs and local start-up firms has allowed firms steady access to funds and organisational resources. Moreover, Chinese firms have enjoyed a 'latecomer advantage' in the adoption of new and specialist technology, e.g. the growth of Haier. The motive for internationalisation of Chinese firms has extended from resources and market-seeking to efficiency (e.g. Nanjing Automotives' acquisition of the Rover plant in the UK) and created-assets seeking (e.g. Lenovo's acquisition of IBM's computer division provided it with technology and expertise while developing a global brand) (World Investment Report, 2006). Therefore, international HRM in Chinese MNCs is an emerging area of research. For an account of this, see Zhang and Edwards (2007).

HRM in China

The nature and extent to which Western HRM is being adopted in China is a matter of debate. Child (1994: 157) questioned the extent to which one can utilise the term 'HRM' as a descriptor for the management of personnel in Chinese enterprises. Others, however, explicitly use mainstream HRM models to analyse employment issues in China (Ahlstrom et al., 2005; Zhu and Warner, 2005). More recent works emphasise the importance of traditional Chinese values of harmony and respect in shaping management, which has the potential of evolving a hybrid management model referred to as 'HRM with Chinese characteristics' or 'Confucian HRM' (Warner, 2008, 2010). However, this picture of harmonious workplace relations is challenged by other scholars who examine the employment relationship from worker perspectives (Nichols et al., 2004; Nichols and Zhao, 2010; Danford and Zhao, 2012). These scholars demonstrate the dissatisfaction of workers with the changes in employment contracts, work intensification, authoritarian control and weak and marginal ACFTU unions. Disharmony and conflict between workers and managers, rather than Confucian harmony, prevail at the workplace.

MNCs and transfer of HR practices

The debate about Western HRM and the role that traditional Chinese values play in it in China is also played out in international HRM in MNCs operating in China. Edwards et al. (2007) have formulated an integrated framework for analysing transfer of practices in MNCs that is responsive to market factors, cultural and institutional context, and political factors. They conceptualise the transfer process as complex and contested where not all MNCs transfer, not all practices are transferred, and the outcomes of transfer are varied. They identify four influences on the transfer process: home country (of MNC) context; global dominance (economic and/or political) of a national economy or firms; pressures for international integration on MNCs; and host country context. These influences can constrain or facilitate transfer, and can reinforce or contradict each other. Transfer of HR practices in MNCs operating in China is constrained by the specificity of the Chinese context. At the same time, it is facilitated by the fluid and dynamic nature of the Chinese capitalist model, as discussed in previous sections. MNCs, on their part, try to respond to the pressures for international integration, which includes standardisation of policies and practices, while remaining sensitive to local specificities, which means following local practices. Research on MNCs in China reveals this complexity (see Box 16.1).

Box 16.1

Confucian values and HRM: the case of the retail sector in China

China's social context and institutions play a major role in the way firms operate and manage their employees. Confucian values such as respect for authority, interpersonal harmony and role and importance of *guanxi* guide individual action and attitudes in modern Chinese society. This has led to some scholars claiming the emergence of 'Confucian HRM in China', a hybrid management model of Western HRM underpinned by the Chinese traditional value of harmony. A study of retail firms in China, SOEs and foreign MNCs, explored how these traditional norms might impact upon HRM. As the societal values interact with foreign ventures in the retail sector, some fundamental and far-reaching changes are noticeable in the HR practices of retail firms.

The respect for authority that stems from strong hierarchical and authoritarian traditions in China implies that a participative style of management is likely to be constrained. Chinese managers are likely to feel threatened and employees might not involve themselves in decision-making. This is often the case in SOEs where employee involvement and interpersonal communications are weak because of the traditional as well as Maoist legacy of hierarchical structures. By contrast, MNCs that have more developed HRM had significantly higher levels of employee participation practices. In a similar vein, the role and importance of *guanxi* prevail in aspects such as recruitment and career progression at the workplace, both in SOEs and in MNCs in China. However, many employees in MNCs prefer the management in MNCs to the complicated relationships and particularistic connections in Chinese firms. According to one employee, 'In state enterprises, relationships are more complicated. In foreign firms *guanxi* is much less relevant; instead there's good management. It's a real nuisance to be concerned with who is who's cousin.' Likewise, some MNCs have been able to transfer their flatter organisational structures to their Chinese workplace, which is in stark contrast to the rigid hierarchical structures in SOEs.

Thus, the MNCs in China are influenced by Chinese societal norms but can also successfully bypass such norms. One of the significant reasons is that they are not embedded in the traditional environment as are the SOEs. Their financial strength and prestige allow them to be more innovative. Also, being 'outsiders' MNCs can introduce novel practices without alienating traditional norms. Lastly, the retail sector employs a largely young Chinese workforce that is not influenced by norms or Maoist legacy to the same extent as the older SOE employees and is more open to new and innovative practices.

Source: based on Gamble (2006b, 2011).

Questions

1 How do traditional values impact on HRM? Assess with respect to either respect for authority or the role of *guanxi*.

2 Why do SOEs display many of the traditional norms in their employee management practices?

3 Why are MNCs able to bypass traditional norms in implementing HR practices?

4 To what extent are Confucian values likely to continue to exert an influence on HRM in a globalising China?

Early research on MNCs operating in China showed that the host country influence was stronger due to high cultural and institutional distance, and MNCs faced difficulty in implementing Western HR practices in China, e.g. performance appraisal systems (Child, 1994; Lu and Bjorkman, 1997; Gamble, 2003). *Guanxi* continued to operate in recruitment processes. Values such as respect for authority and seniority would make it difficult to encourage employee participation and avoidance of conflict, and saving 'face' implied difficulties in implementing performance management (Child, 1994). In addition, the Maoist legacy of low skill base and low emphasis on training alongside low wage differentials persists. In a study of a UK MNC operating in Shanghai, continued influence of local norms and expectations was evident in work pattern, employee representation and non-wage benefits (Gamble, 2003). However, large MNCs can overcome constraints posed by the institutional context. While *guanxi* continues to operate in many firms (Chinese and MNCs), some large MNCs do not rely on it (for Australian MNCs in China, see Hutchings and Murray, 2003; for UK MNCs, see Gamble, 2006a). Similarly, the tradition of respect for authority would imply that practices like flat hierarchy or employee participation will not work. Yet, flat hierarchy was appreciated in one firm (Gamble, 2003) and employee participation worked in another (Huang and Gamble, 2011). This is because these practices were novel and the predominantly younger workforce in foreign firms in China is more receptive towards new practices and market-based employment relations. Also, large MNCs can operate in innovative ways by virtue of their financial strength and of being 'outsiders' in the Chinese context.

A significant point to note is that outcomes of transfer may be different from the original practice. Thus, global and standardised HR policies or practices may be adopted by a subsidiary in principle, but they are interpreted and implemented in significantly different ways. In a study of 21 Western MNCs in China, Fu and Kamenou (2011) demonstrate a variation between global HR policies and practices of MNCs and their implementation at the local level. Chinese values and practices of *guanxi,* valuing seniority, and the importance of the 'human factor' influenced HR functions such as job rotation, performance and appraisal, training and development and reward management, and were adapted to suit local conditions by Chinese managers. Gamble and Huang (2009) echo a similar theme. Thus, the transfer and operation of Western HR practices to China is a complex and nuanced process.

This section has outlined the impact of global economic activity on the nature of foreign investment and employment practices of Chinese and foreign firms operating in China. It has explored how the Chinese institutional context influences the growth of Chinese MNCs and the transfer and adoption of HR practices, and how MNCs overcome the institutional constraints and/or modify and adapt their policies and practices to suit local conditions.

Key Controversy

Is the transfer of HR policies and practices a straightforward process? To what extent does the Chinese institutional context constrain or facilitate transfer?

Summary

The section on China has explored the historical pattern of development of the Chinese institutional context and employment relations and impact of globalisation on them. In summary:

- The Chinese institutional context is constituted of a strong state, weak corporate governance structures, economic role of social institutions of family and *guanxi,* and a segmented labour market with a surplus of low-skilled labour and a shortage of skilled staff. Some institutions are undergoing change (such as the Communist state) while others (such as corporate governance structures, labour market and systems of skilling) are still being built in very specific ways.

- Employment relations in China are also undergoing gradual change whilst showing continuity from the past. Communist legacies of lifelong employment and comprehensive welfare in SOEs are gradually giving way to a more flexible labour market and a contributory social security fund in the new model of a socialist market economy. At the same time, Maoist legacies of wage equality and traditions of *guanxi* in recruitment persist in the employment arena.

- Global capitalism is influencing the nature of investment into and out of China, and thereby employment relations. It is evident in the spread of HRM in Chinese firms and transfer of HR policies and practices in MNCs operating in China. What emerges is a complex picture of persistence of traditional and Maoist values and practices, but also the introduction of novel and innovative practices by MNCs in China. The outcomes of these processes show variation and modification in HR practices to suit the Chinese context.

India: state-guided capitalist model

India is an interesting case where, after five decades of following a 'socialist pattern of society' with a focus on a 'mixed economy' (according equal importance to the public and the private sector), the economy has been transitioning to a more market-orientated one since the 1990s. It is the fourth largest economy (according to purchasing power parities), exhibits the second fastest growing economy in the world, with an average annual growth rate of 8.8 per cent, and has a population of around 1.2 billion. The wide-ranging economic reforms initiated in the 1990s attracted FDI to India as a large consumer market and a source of surplus cheap labour. This attraction has since extended to its English-speaking population with a high level of skill in engineering, computing and software. Automobiles, telecommunications and software attract the greatest amount of FDI. As a player in the global economy, with major Indian MNCs in pharmaceuticals, steel, heavy engineering and IT (e.g. Ranbaxy, Tata, Reliance, Infosys, TCS and Wipro), India needs to move up the value chain and beyond the specialisation in certain sectors. Also, it is argued that India would be less adversely affected by the economic recession than other emerging markets because it relies less on exports than China (22 per cent of India's GDP vs 37 per cent of China's) and less on foreign capital than the overstretched economies of eastern Europe, but it has to address major challenges of poverty and inequality (*The Economist,* 2008).

As one of the largest democracies in the world and with a strategic location in South Asia, India is a counter to authoritarian China. It has a parliamentary form of government with a federal structure and a division of power between the centre and its 25 states and seven Union territories. India's vast internal economic and social heterogeneity of modes of production, regulation and social compromises between different groups has resulted in very different routes to industrialisation, development and outcomes for various social groups. The economic and social changes are filtered through electoral politics and result in complicated and regionally diverse socio-political compromises in this transitioning democracy. Therefore, India poses a challenge of understanding the sub-national variations in its institutional and employment context (Sinha, 2005).

Four aspects are prominent in terms of the nature of industrialisation and development in India:

- the *democratic nature of the Indian state* and its role in development, redistribution and avoidance of social conflict (Bardhan, 1984; Sen, 2001; Kohli, 2004);
- the *gradual nature of economic and social change* from a socialist mixed economy to a market economy;
- the *combination of different traditions,* i.e. social networks of family and caste, social hierarchy and materialism, which influence economic activity, firms and work practices in India;
- the *nature of foreign involvement* in India through investment and multinational firms.

All these aspects have an effect on the institutional context and change in India, as discussed in the following section.

Institutional context

This section traces the historical pattern of development of various institutions in India, i.e. the state, the financial system and corporate governance, as well as labour markets and systems of education and training. In addition, it incorporates a discussion of the social mechanisms of family and caste networks that play a role in the economic activity and firms.

State, regulation and reform

The state in India has changed its role from professed developmentalism to one that is more predatory in nature since the reforms of the 1990s (Witt and Redding, 2013). India adopted the model of a planned and mixed economy after independence from Britain in 1947, thereby emphasising the importance of both the public and private sector in economic development. The state played a strong role in the economy through a large public sector and the extension of licences/permits to private firms that often resulted in clientelist relations. The aim was to address the inequality and imbalances in regional development inherited from the colonial period through the public sector that would develop hitherto underdeveloped areas not attractive to private investment. The emphasis was on regulation to protect the domestic industry from foreign competition and to promote self-reliance through a policy of import substitution. Nevertheless, a small but strong private sector always existed.

Economic planning is carried out through five-year national plans (**www.ibef.org**). Currently, the 12th plan is running. The *first plan (1951–56)* focused on agriculture to ensure self-sufficiency in food grains and to address poverty, as a majority of the population relied on agriculture for subsistence. The *second plan (1956–61)* supported industrialisation and tried to shift from a predominantly agrarian economy to one that produced a wide variety of consumer and industrial goods. However, this plan failed, resulting in an under-utilisation of capacities and the emergence of a licence-quota regime based on political patronage. *Successive plans (1961–91)* witnessed a progressive decline in performance due to inflation, poverty and unemployment, although there were some achievements in defence and agriculture. According to Dreze and Sen (1995):

> Indian economic planning offered a good illustration of horrendous over activity in controlling industries, restraining gains from trade, and blighting competitiveness; and, soporific under activity in expanding school education, public health care, social security, gender equity and land reform.

Reforms: post-1991

The imposition of structural adjustment programmes by the World Bank and the International Monetary Fund in the 1980s started the trend towards liberalisation, privatisation and the economic reforms of 1991 in India (for an assessment of industrial development post-reform, see Kaplinsky, 1997). Successive plans have seen deregulation, liberalisation and the formulation of new industrial, fiscal and trade policies. Substantial reforms have been made in the financial, telecommunications and IT sectors. Liberalisation has encouraged foreign investment, and privatisation has permitted entry of the private sector in areas that were hitherto reserved for the public sector, e.g. transport, telecomms, banking and electricity, among others. For private firms, it implies a shift from protective regulation to market-driven competition that has created opportunities for expansion, diversification and internationalisation. Thus, the relatively strong role of the state in the economy has undergone a change since 1991: from a more interventionist role played through the public sector and the licence-quota regime pre-1991, the state now guides and facilitates the transition to a more market-orientated economy. On the one hand, this involves the withdrawal of the state from intervening on behalf of labour (replaced with targeted piecemeal social programmes for the poor), or the introduction of wide-ranging structural changes in the agricultural sector (60 per cent of the population, often in acute poverty, depend on agriculture). On the other hand, it actively assists capital through the acquisition of agricultural land for the development of industrial zones and parks or real estate development for the new Indian middle classes, while creating an underclass of rural migrant workers that supply labour to industry and private households.

Corporate governance and financial system

The public sector continues to be significant as the largest employer of organised labour in India and as a harbinger of social and economic change. In the private sector, there is extensive ownership and control of firms and business groups by families, and those firms and groups are again managed by family members. Considered a distinctive feature of private firms in India, this arrangement is referred to as a 'conglomerate business groups' model. Although firms are separate legal entities, listed separately with their own sets of shareholders, the family controls the strategic direction and regulates the firm. According to Khanna and Palepu (2000), business groups in the Indian private sector have filled institutional voids, such as imperfections in markets for capital, products and managerial talent. However, this has also encouraged clientelist relations between the state and certain business groups.

Since the 1991 liberalisation, India's formal corporate governance institutions have become more formal and, according to some, there is a gradual move from business groups to the Anglo-Saxon model (Reed, 2002). Capital markets have been liberalised. A takeover code was adopted in 1994, paving the way for a rudimentary market in corporate control. Steps have been taken to improve corporate governance norms and disclosure practices. Formal shareholder and creditor rights are relatively well formulated within a well-established legal framework. India's formal legal framework is more transparent, but less so in terms of where actual control resides, because of pervasive family or group control. The Indian legal system is characterised by extensive regulation but weak implementation. India fares poorly on the rule of law and corruption indices, although the efficiency of the judiciary is good. There are marked regional variations in the implementation of the legal system at the state level. In poorly performing states like Bihar, security of property, ownership rights and enforcement of the rule of law are poor, and formal legal codes are ineffective. The states that have high growth, such as Gujarat, display more effective legal procedures. Like China, informal institutions supposedly substitute and compensate for ineffective formal corporate governance institutions, and the goals of the two are not in conflict in India either. Indeed, according to some scholars, concentrated family ownership is beneficial for firm performance where there are weaker or less developed legal and regulatory institutions to protect shareholders (see Estrin and Prevezer, 2011 for details). Nevertheless, this can have a malign influence of exclusion, perpetuation of vested interests and clientelism. Recent coal and mobile phone corruption cases have laid bare the predatory nature of the Indian state and the intertwined political and private capital interests that appropriate resources for personal gain (Witt and Redding, 2013). Even the states feted for miraculous economic growth represent the interest of dominant socioeconomic groups that have extended into the political arena, where political parties reflect the close alliance among caste, class and business (Hammer, 2012).

The financial sector in India has been more open than in China and has improved since reforms in the financial sector post-1991. Access to finance has been more favourable for smaller firms, with over half of small businesses having active bank credit lines or overdraft facilities. There is a much lower reliance on retained earnings than in China. Aware of the competitive advantage of IT and computing firms, rules regarding equity and venture capital as well as other barriers of foreign involvement have been relaxed. Indeed, the state has extended active support to this sector (Witt and Redding, 2013).

Explore

- What is a 'corporate business group'?
- How is it distinctive to India?

Aspects of tradition in interfirm relations

A number of studies have examined the continued influence of traditional social mechanisms in economic activity, firms and employment relations in India (Hofstede 1991; Budhwar and Debrah, 2001; Budhwar and Khatri, 2001; Witt and Redding, 2013). India is a hierarchical society segmented by caste, religion and other group affiliations and a desire for proximity to sources of power. Interpersonal relations, age, seniority and status influence economic activity. Social institutions of family and extended family as well as religion-based networks influence firms' structures and their management (Khanna and Palepu, 2000; Estrin and Prevezer, 2011). This often translates into a paternalist management style and a preference for personalised social relationships where interpersonal trust is high, especially in the absence of institutionalised trust (Witt and Redding, 2013). Management practices draw on familial, cultural and moral registers at the workplace. Thus, employment practices like recruitment, rewards and career progression work through family and social networks and may be based on loyalty, status and political connections for both the employer and the employee.

Labour market and systems of education and training

The labour market is segmented and polarised in age composition, employment status as well as skill level. The working age population is fairly young, with half the working population under 25, and growing rapidly, as roughly 14 million is added to the labour market each year. Only 7 per cent of the total workforce is organised, i.e. having formal employment and being covered by legislative and social security provisions; 93 per cent is in unorganised/informal employment, with no legal or social protections. Women are predominantly in unorganised employment. Child labour, although illegal, continues to prevail in some sectors (Breman, 1996). Moreover, informal employment sees a concentration of migrant, rural inhabitants driven to seek temporary urban employment in agricultural off-peak seasons. The absence of meaningful land reforms and a lack of investment in agriculture forces this large segment of the population into multiple deprivations.

The inequality and discrimination that result from such informality is aggravated by labour being a concurrent subject (on which both the central and state government can legislate), which means that a plethora of labour laws exist but are poorly implemented (Harriss-White and Gooptu, 2001). From the 1920s to the 1940s, a number of legal provisions for workers and trade unions were instituted, followed by the appointment of the First National Commission on Labour in 1969. These provisions reflected the important role of labour and trade unions in the freedom struggle as well as the logic of industrial peace that influenced Indian industrial relations post-independence (Sengupta and Sett, 2000; Bhattacherjee and Ackers, 2010). Since liberalisation, the gradual shift to a strategy of economic competitiveness has instituted labour reforms that have increased managerial prerogative and weakened the power of workers and unions (Frenkel and Kuruvilla, 2002).

The education and training system has become more individualised as the state has shifted from a socialist to a market-orientated pattern. Literacy levels are around 60 per cent and provision of comprehensive education is incomplete. The acquisition of higher skills has always been left to private initiative (Witt and Redding, 2013). Pre-reform state legacy means that training infrastructure is extensive in the public sector, with apprenticeship systems instituted in all public sector firms. Industrial training institutes form the basis of organised industrial training in India. However, restructuring and downsizing mean the quality is steadily declining. Moreover, skill levels vary considerably. On the one hand, under-investment in education, inadequate provision for health and education, a bias against vocational skills and an occupational preference for non-production jobs have created an uneven skill base. Along with widespread low literacy, many are not obviously skilled at anything. Approximately 20 per cent of job seekers have had some sort of vocational training (*The Economist,* 2008). On the other hand, there is a growing number of educated and skilled personnel, especially in computing, software, medicine and engineering. India is one of the largest exporters of skilled migrants in software engineering and financial services. Every year, more than 100,000 engineering graduates and 70,000 software professionals join the industry, both indigenous private and multinational firms. According to Microsoft, India ranks second worldwide in the number of Microsoft-certified engineers produced. Still, skilled labour remains scarce in relation to the working population as a whole. Even in the information and communication technology industry where the highly skilled workforce exists, middle- and lower-level skilled personnel are in short supply (Venkata Ratnam, 2001).

To sum up, the Indian institutional context displays gradual institutional change. The state is shifting its role from a more direct involvement in the economy to that of guiding and managing its transition to a market-orientated one. Social institutions of family and networks define a distinctive structure of private firms in India, with a coexistence of formal and informal institutions in corporate governance mechanisms. The labour market reflects the nature of industrialisation: advanced specialisation and high skill levels in industries such as IT and computing alongside a vast pool of low-skilled surplus labour without any social security cover. This has implications for employment relations in India and these are discussed next.

Explore

- What are the distinctive features of the labour market in India?
- What is the main difference between formal/organised and informal/unorganised workers?

Employment relations: from a 'mixed' to an 'open' economy in India

Employment relations in India are shaped by two factors. First, economic liberalisation is recasting state–capital–labour relations where the earlier interventionist state (pro-labour) is withdrawing from capital–labour relations. There is a gradual transition from the logic of industrial peace and employment-income protection to the logic of competition guiding employment relations. The logic of industrial peace focused on limiting industrial conflict in order to promote economic development. This included strong protective legislation regarding union formation, collective bargaining, interventionist dispute resolution procedures and an avoidance of retrenchment and subcontracting. It exists alongside employment-income protection measures against lay-offs, long working hours, poor health and working conditions in a context of limited state social security provisions in India (Frenkel and Kuruvilla, 2002). This is giving way to labour flexibility and a weakening of union power. Secondly, employment relations exhibit the peculiarities of the labour market (a small percentage of a highly skilled workforce alongside surplus informal labour) and the nature of its industrialisation (basic and strategic industries in the public sector alongside globally competitive private firms in textiles, pharmaceuticals, IT, software and the services industry but in a predominantly agrarian society). This results in considerable variation in employment relations in a context where less than 10 per cent of those in formal employment have stable and secure employment (with an emphasis on training and a move towards sophisticated HRM policies and practices, e.g. IT, software and the services industry), while a majority (90 per cent) of the workforce are in informal employment and remain poor and insecure. This section outlines the labour reforms and the changes in the labour market, industrial relations and employment practices that have arisen from these factors.

Labour reforms and changes in the labour market

Since liberalisation, the logic of competition has increased the power of capital with demand for labour reforms by employers to rationalise labour law, increase labour flexibility, liberalise labour inspection and weaken unions. At the same time, the state is restrained from making radical changes in the formal framework of employment security or full-scale privatisation because of historic state–labour relations, especially political party–union links that are important in electoral mass politics. Therefore, while the central government has undertaken *soft* reforms such as an amendment to the trade union law, disinvestment rather than privatisation, the liberalisation of labour inspection, and special concessions to firms in special economic zones (SEZs), it is the state governments that have introduced wide-ranging and pro-employer labour reforms in order to retain and attract investment. Bardhan (2002, cited in Shyam Sundar, 2010: 590) refers to this as 'labour reforms by stealth'. Furthermore, judicial rulings by the Supreme Court have not supported the interests of workers and unions on issues such as privatisation, contract labour and the right to strike (Shyam Sundar, 2010).

Labour reforms at the state level have allowed more labour flexibility, control over work processes, union containment or avoidance, reduced regular workers (through voluntary retirement schemes), and led to an increase in contract labour and subcontracting at the workplace. A significant outcome of these labour market reforms has been an increase of temporary, casual and contract workers in the total workforce in the organised, manufacturing industry (Deshpande *et al.,* 2004). Overall, informal labour has grown in size supported by labour reforms that enable employers to replace formal with informal workers, to whom they are not required to extend social security or minimum wages. This weakens labour and its collective institutions. Informal employment almost forms a part of the state-capital strategy as 'the primary source of future work for all Indians' (NCL, 2002) and is particularly pronounced in the creation and development of new industrial areas or new industrial zones (NIZs) – often including export promotion zones (EPZs) and SEZs – built to attract investment. Units in EPZs and SEZs are often declared 'public utility services' in order to exempt them from labour laws, to relax labour inspections, or to make strikes difficult. This aids the increased use of informal workers and containment or avoidance of unions in the firms located here (Hammer, 2010).

With respect to skill upgrading in the labour market, one of the liberalisation arguments has been that the role played by the public sector in employment creation and training will be supplemented and/or replaced by MNCs. It is assumed that skill upgrading will occur in response to the requirements of new, technologically sophisticated industries. Individual workplace-based learning will, over time, enhance the social stock of knowledge and skills, thereby promoting growth (Okada, 2004).While this may be true in the new industries such as software and business process outsourcing (BPO) and for managers in some MNCs, it is more doubtful for junior management and workers, especially in manufacturing MNCs. On the one hand, Wipro, India's second largest software services exporter, recruits maths and science graduates and trains them for three years through on-the-job and classroom training at its Wipro Academy of Software Education. In BPO firms, there is increasing focus on talent recognition and prospects for career development through supported MBA courses and management diplomas (Kuruvilla and Ranganathan, 2010). On the other hand, in manufacturing MNCs in white goods and automobiles, deskilling and multi-tasking rather than multi-skilling, as well as the use of trainees for job completion rather than actual training, appear to be the norm, with the aim of minimising training requirements and facilitating the substitutability of labour (Trivedi, 2006; Hammer, 2010).

Industrial relations

Industrial relations systems are in a flux due to the changing role of the Indian state. The predominant political unionism model, in which unions and political parties maintain close relations, is increasingly challenged not only from labour reforms and the decentralisation of bargaining, but also from the rise of enterprise unions, anti-union workplaces and informal worker organisations. Also, the industrial relations system displays considerable variations within India. This is expressed in new strategies and forms of action for workers and unions.

Historically, the state has not only been the largest employer through the public sector but also a regulator, prosecutor and mediator in industrial relations. The key features that underpin Indian industrial relations include tripartite consultations at the national level, and works committees and joint management councils at the enterprise level. The dispute resolution machinery operates at four levels: bipartite negotiation, conciliation, arbitration and adjudication. Collective bargaining is conducted at different levels in different industries and is size-specific. Large firms that employ more than 300 people have collective bargaining, with the exception of those in electronics and a few in banking. At the managerial level, individual bargaining is more prevalent (Sengupta and Sett, 2000; Kuruvilla and Erickson, 2002; Bhattacharjee and Ackers, 2010).

The coverage and role of unions in India vary according to geography, sector and industry. While the state of West Bengal has a dominance of politically affiliated left-leaning trade unions, in Maharashtra enterprise-level unions, independent and unaffiliated, have a major presence. Gujarat has seen the rise of 'footpath unionism' (e.g. unions of hawkers) and social-movement unions of unorganised workers (e.g. the Self-Employed Women's Association, SEWA), whereas the industrially and socially backward states of Andhra Pradesh and Bihar have radical and militant trade unions. Unionism is stronger in manufacturing units and in the chemical, pharmaceutical and automobile industries than it is in electronics units. Both public- and private-sector Indian banks have entrenched unions but not foreign banks. Firms in IT, software and services are largely non-union (though UNITES Pro is a union in the BPO industry) and many MNCs have enterprise unionism or non-union plants. For example, in a NIZ near Delhi, some firms allow enterprise-based unions but resist and restrict cross-industry or wider political alliances, while others follow a clearly anti-union approach (Bhattacharjee and Ackers, 2010; Hammer, 2010). In another study, Hindustan Lever and Philips were hostile to any attempts to form federations of their company's unions (Venkata Ratnam, 1998).

Liberalisation and its assault on workers and unions have intensified the problems associated with the political unionism model that developed during the late colonial period, in conjunction with the freedom struggle, which created common ground between political leaders and unions. Political interests often overruled labour interests and generated splits and inter-union rivalry. Significantly, this also led trade unions to neglect the representation of informal labour, thereby furthering the latter's self-organisation and the emergence of new forms of informal workers' organisations. Increasingly, links between political parties and trade unions are becoming conflictual, as most political parties and their labour wings disagree on labour reforms. This is accompanied by new collective bargaining regulations such as the decentralisation of collective bargaining to the enterprise level in the private sector, the integration of long-term settlements and performance pay into public-sector bargaining, as well as increased managerialism – all trends that tend to weaken trade unions (Shyam Sundar, 2010). The increasing tension between party politics and trade union federations has implications for union strategies and action. It has led to cooperation between different unions in opposing neo-liberal policies of the state in many strikes and demonstrations since 1992. Moreover, trade unions have made efforts to become more inclusive and organise hitherto neglected informal workers in the face of their own declining membership. However, their interface with informal economy organisations has not always been cordial.

The organisation of informal workers into independent unions or cooperatives or civil society groups has been a significant development over the past two decades. Some examples include the National Federation of Construction Labour (an independent industry-level union formed in 1991 in Bangalore), SEWA (which organises Indian cigarette workers, waste pickers, construction workers) and the National Fishworkers' Forum. The National Centre for

Labour (NCL), formed in 1995, is an apex body of independent labour organisations working in the informal sector with a membership of about a million workers from 10 states (NCL website; Unni and Rani, 2003). Such organisations mobilise through social movements, in neighbourhoods and through discussion groups and reading circles. Some NGOs provide on-site child care and health services to workers (e.g. in construction), teach them about their welfare rights and get the workers registered with the welfare boards (e.g. NIRMAAN in Mumbai and SEWA in Gujarat and Delhi). The defining feature of such unions is the shift in their demand of workplace rights from employers to citizenship rights from the state. Instead of minimum wages, the demand is for reproductive and/or human/citizenship rights of education, health and welfare (basic needs). Moreover, workers ensure that production is not disrupted so that they do not lose their low incomes or jobs. Forms of action include demonstrations, petitions and hunger strikes all directed at politicians. Such organisations and their members argue that the welfare-orientated struggle is stronger and more appealing than the militant and violent movement of the past. Also, they have been successful in forming international networks, such as Women in Informal Employment: Globalizing and Organizing (WIEGO), and links with global union federations and the International Labour Organization (ILO) that can bring pressure on the state (Agarwala, 2006, 2008).

New mobilisation strategies are also employed by UNITES Pro, a union in the BPO industry with an estimated membership base of 7,000 across 150 different firms. Not only does the union defend workers' concerns within the workplace but it also responds to external issues such family and community issues. The union's innovative approaches include the role played by committed and energetic activists; a focus on the younger section of the workforce; and organising social events such as sporting events, spirituality classes, etc., which create the space for workers to raise their problems in a way that is more geographically appropriate to this industry (James and Vira, 2010).

Key Controversy

Do labour reforms benefit employers or labour? How is the labour market and trade union power affected by the reforms?

Employment practices: recruitment and rewards

Employment practices in firms display considerable variation across ownership forms (family/ state/foreign) and the nature of the labour market (surplus, largely informal labour alongside highly skilled workers in particular industries).

Public-sector firms have a formal system of recruitment based on a technical/rationalist approach, with standardised formal examinations and interviews. There are special provisions for quotas to recruit disadvantaged groups and communities as well as the local population. In family-owned private firms, forms of recruitment vary, although social networks have been predominant. For example, in the traditional trading *Marwari* community firms and concentrated in industries such as textiles and cement and in Kanpur and Nagpur, community and family networks play a major role. At the same time, the Tata corporate group, another family-based firm, was among the earliest to adopt a more corporate style of management and recruited a more diverse workforce through formal recruitment practices. Private firms are moving towards merit-based recruitment, particularly of junior managers. In high-tech industries like software and telecommunications, India has the comparative advantage of large numbers of highly skilled graduates who tend to be recruited on-campus. In the services sector, especially BPO, firms focus on recruiting from younger age groups, without paying much attention to working environments or career development options. Faced with a high rate of attrition (around 40 per cent), BPO firms have recently begun to recruit mature employees, i.e. people over 35 years of age, from provincial towns, and provided them with accommodation, travel and other facilities (for call centres, see Taylor and Bain, 2005; for BPO, see Kuruvilla and Ranganathan, 2010).

Multinational corporations display a similar variation in recruitment strategies and tiered systems of employment, depending on the sector. Manufacturing MNCs are often located in new industrial areas and set up greenfield plants. These regions have a concentration of workers, especially migrants, and are often free from union influence. Low-skilled workers are recruited from the local area and are often hired at the gate. Permanent skilled workers may be recruited from other regions of the country, often from industrial training institutes. Permanent workers are normally older than the young temporary workers. While production firms employ a predominantly male workforce, export units employ mainly women. At the management level, while some, e.g. Korean, firms rely more on expatriates as senior managers with local managers in middle management, most MNCs employ local managers as senior executives (Trivedi, 2006).

Reward systems reflect the inequalities of the labour market. While formal employees are well remunerated, informal workers often do not receive either minimum wages or any other statutory benefits. This is because there is no uniform wage policy for all sectors of the economy. Although the Minimum Wages Act 1948 is a centrally legislated act, minimum wages vary widely across states and implementation is weak. Moreover, liberalisation and relaxed labour laws have led firms to reduce regular workers and shift to temporary and contractual labour in order to avoid payment of minimum wages or benefits. The public sector is still largely characterised by standardised wages with other social benefits and security of employment. Increasingly, there is a move towards performance-related pay and promotion in private firms. In new industries such as information and communication technology, where the supply of technical skill is constrained and employee mobility very high, salary and benefits are also high. Schemes such as profit-sharing, share options and other perks, as well as a secure career and better communication, are often offered to retain employees in such sectors.

Multinational corporations tend to pay higher wages than local firms and the working conditions are usually better. This is true for employees at both ends of the spectrum: cheap labour for cost minimisation in manufacturing and call centres as well as the highly skilled workforce in computing and software. Korean firms are usually the highest paymasters, followed by Japanese and then indigenous firms. Segmentation of the workforce into permanent, company casual, trainee and contract workers means different packages for each group, thus reinforcing segmentation. Social security measures mandated by law, e.g. gratuity and provident funds, are provided to all workers, but pension funds are instituted only for senior executives. This is evident in both manufacturing and the services sector. Higher wages serve the twin purpose of employing better skilled personnel and, at times, acting as a means to curtail trade union developments. In manufacturing units, workers are often keen to secure higher wages and benefits even in the face of what they call an 'environment of fear and control' (Hammer, 2010). In the services sector, young graduates are willing to work in call centres for their comparatively higher remuneration packages despite the Taylorised work that denies the employees opportunities to channel grievances and improve their working conditions (Taylor and Bian, 2005; James and Vira, 2010).

We can see from this section that employment relations are being reshaped by the withdrawal of the state from capital–labour relations as well as the peculiarity of the labour market and industrialisation in India (a large, low-skilled informal labour force alongside high-skilled workers in new industries). Labour reforms have increased the flexibility of labour and weakened the bargaining power of workers and unions *vis-à-vis* employers, especially in new industrialised areas. This has resulted in new forms and strategies of unions. The state provision of skilling infrastructure is being replaced by individualised or firm-based training. Employment practices vary from one extreme (where informal workers barely receive minimum wages or benefits) to the other, in which public-sector firms and new industries follow sophisticated HRM with extensive reward packages and opportunities for training and learning.

Globalisation and multinational firms in India

This section explores the interaction of the Indian capitalism with global capitalism. As a major global economic power, with the second fastest growing economy in the world, India is engaging with the global capitalist order in its own way. The discussion so far has explored the changes in institutions and employment relations in India as the country transitions from a socialist to a market-orientated system. These processes are significantly influenced by global economic forces, in particular MNCs. This section focuses on some aspects of this development, i.e. the nature and extent of foreign investment into India and Indian foreign investment abroad, as well as patterns of HRM in the new economy in India.

Inward foreign investment in India

India attracts the second highest FDI in the world, after China. This is concentrated in industry clusters around cities like Delhi, Hyderabad, Bangalore and Madras, depending on the nature of investment. While many manufacturing MNCs are located in the Delhi region (Gurgaon and Noida/Greater Noida), Hyderabad and Bangalore have a concentration of IT and software industries. Initial inward investment into India was in production units for automobiles and the white goods industry, and call centres for sales/technical support and marketing research. This was accompanied by very fast growth of the IT and software industry from the late 1990s – this now commands 20 per cent of the world market and exports worth $47 billion in 2010 (NASSCOM, 2011). Services include BPO, providing back office operations such as billing, payroll and HRM (Kuruvilla and Ranganathan, 2010). This industry has benefited from English language skills as well as low-cost technical skills available in India. The nature of investment in the IT and services sectors has evolved from being based on cheap labour and low cost to being based on value-added expertise and design and development capabilities. Government support through the development of software technology parks and subsidies to ICT infrastructure has helped attract US and European MNCs, which are increasingly engaged in knowledge transfer and research and development.

Outward foreign investment from India

Dunning and Lundan's (2005) investment development path theory states that a country's level of development determines the nature of outward FDI, and the composition of FDI evolves from low-technology and resource-based to high-technology and efficiency-seeking. However, Indian firms have been internationalising before achieving the necessary level of economic development, and the nature of FDI is high-tech and efficiency-seeking. This has been explained both by special characteristics of MNCs from new economies (Lecraw, 1977) and the comparative advantage that arises not only from cheap labour. One of the strengths is expertise-based, e.g. Tata's in transportation equipment, Reliance in heavy industries, and IT firms such as Wipro, TCS and Infosys. IT and telecommunications have also benefited from a latecomer advantage in adoption of new technology. IT MNCs now subcontract to other lower-cost providers in China, while they have moved up the value chain and formed joint ventures with big MNCs, e.g. Infosys–Microsoft and Mahindra–British Telecom (NASSCOM, 2011). Some firms can produce high-quality goods at a low cost, e.g. Bharat Forgings, the second largest manufacturer in the world. The strong role of the state in the development of regions with clusters of knowledge and resources, such as IT hubs in Hyderabad and Bangalore, and other state subsidies have allowed firms steady access to funds and organisational resources. Networks of family, diaspora and cultural and institutional affinity play a role as well; for example, Indian MNCs are investing in Malaysia and South Africa, countries with which India has had a historical link. The motive for internationalisation of Indian firms has extended from resources (e.g. Oil and Natural Gas Corporation Ltd) to market-seeking (e.g. Tata and IT firms). Efficiency is a major motive for better integration, as Indian MNCs in electrical and electronics, automobiles, garments and IT services are suppliers or intermediate producers. Pharmaceutical firms such as Ranbaxy and Dr Reddy have expanded into Europe for created-assets seeking (World Investment Report, 2006).

HRM in the new economy

Research in the new economy has focused on the services sector, especially call centres and the BPO industry. Scholars have explored the nature of the labour process, work organisation and employment practices in call centres and the BPO industry (Taylor and Bain, 2005; Kuruvilla and Ranganathan, 2010; D'Cruz and Noronha, 2012). Nath (2013) provides evidence of stress, stigma and abuse associated with national identity and race in the emotional labour of call centre work. James and Vira (2010) examine the alternative forms of organising in the BPO industry, while Ravishankar *et al.* (2010) show complex processes of accommodation and resistance and subtle forms of cultural defiance of managerial actions in the industry.

In other industries, studies have compared HRM in the public and private sectors (Budhwar and Boyne, 2004; Haq, 2012) as well as researching specific HR practices, e.g. employee relations (Budhwar, 2003), industrial relations (Amba-Rao *et al.*, 2000; Frenkel and Kuruvilla, 2002; Hammer, 2010), innovative HRM (Jain *et al.,* 2012; Som, 2012) and diversity management (Cooke and Saini, 2010). Transfer, emulation and modification of HR practices in MNCs operating in India is also beginning to be explored (Amba-Rao *et al.*, 2000; Bjorkman and Budhwar, 2007; Hammer, 2010). More recently, there have been two special issues of academic journals on emerging patterns of HRM in the new economic environment in India: *Human Resource Management* (49/3, 2010) and *International Journal of Human Resource Management* (23/5, 2012).

The evolution of Indian MNCs is likely to have implications for HR both in India and in countries into which it is expanding. The Tata group is one example. It is a significant player in the Indian economy as one of the largest business groups, as well as being at the forefront of internationalisation by Indian firms. Almost 150 years old, the Tata group consists of 96 companies in seven major business lines: information system and communications, engineering, materials, services, energy, consumer products and chemicals. It has operations in 54 countries and its companies export products and services to 120 countries. The main drivers of its internationalisation include market access for exports, sourcing of raw materials and horizontal and vertical integration (for details on Tata, see Goldstein, 2008). Apart from being one of the earliest firms to adopt a corporate structure and management style, Tata also have rich experience of managing highly politicised industrial relations in the Indian context (Tata Steel at Jamshedpur) and place a strong emphasis on corporate social responsibility. These two factors may influence its HR policy and practices in Corus or Jaguar Land Rover in the UK.

This section has outlined the impact of global economic activity on the nature of foreign investment and employment practices of Indian and foreign firms operating in India. It explored how the India institutional context influences the growth of Indian MNCs and considered the possibilities for HR policies and practices that may evolve from the experience of Indian MNCs.

Explore

- What advantages has the Indian IT and software industry enjoyed?
- How has the nature of its growth changed over time?

Summary

The section on India has explored the historical pattern of development of the Indian institutional context and employment relations and considered the impact of globalisation on India. In summary:

- The Indian institutional context displays gradual change, where a formerly interventionist state is withdrawing from direct involvement in the economy as it transitions to a market-orientated one. Social institutions of family and networks define a distinctive structure of private firms in India with a coexistence of formal and informal institutions in corporate governance mechanisms. The labour market reflects the nature of industrialisation: advanced specialisation and therefore high skill level in industries such as IT and computing, alongside a vast pool of low-skilled surplus labour with no social security cover.

- Employment relations in India are being reshaped by liberal labour reforms, which have increased the flexibility of labour and weakened the bargaining power of workers and unions. This has resulted in new forms of unions and new union strategies. State provision of skilling infrastructure is being replaced by individualised or firm-based training. Employment practices show some variation, with informal workers barely getting minimum wages or benefits, whereas public-sector firms and new industries have adopted sophisticated HRM policies.

- Global capitalism is influencing the nature of investment into and out of India and thereby employment relations. It is evident in the spread of HRM in firms, the introduction of novel and innovative practices, and the transfer of HR policies and practices in MNCs.

China and India: a comparative assessment

Representing the two largest economies in Asia and the two fastest-growing economies in the world, comparisons between China and India are inevitable. They took divergent, yet similar, paths at the same time: China adopted a Communist model in 1949 while India opted for a socialist pattern of economy based on planned development in 1947. Both started altering their course, albeit gradually, from the 1970s, and have witnessed phenomenal growth in the last three decades as they have integrated into global capitalism. Understanding the particular factors behind these growth trajectories is important for a number of reasons: it allows the role of similar institutions to be investigated, demonstrates how different institutional configurations lead to high growth, and allows the specific role of work and employment to be examined. This section highlights the main dimensions from a comparative perspective (see Table 16.2), emphasising the comparative advantages enjoyed by the two countries as well as the particular challenges that each faces.

Significant dimensions of analysis: sub-national forms and informal labour

From an employment relations perspective, two dimensions need greater emphasis and elaboration in order to understand China and India. First, any analysis of the Chinese and Indian economies needs to incorporate *sub-national forms of governance and economic models*. Historically, both China and India have displayed regional variations in modes of production, regulation, institutions and the nature of social compromise between different groups. This has resulted in a variety of local state forms, very different routes to economic development, and different outcomes for various interest groups across regions (Sinha, 2005; Hammer, 2012; Peck and Zhang, 2013). Such sub-national variations often intensify, as many regions in China and India get articulated into the global economy in very specific ways (some as identified zones/clusters of knowledge, innovation or labour supply), and institutions and actors interact and struggle to mediate and modify global influences to suit regional/local ends (Bhattacharjee and Ackers, 2010; Hammer, 2010; Sinha, 2005). As mentioned earlier, recent works focusing on Asia have augmented the comparative institutional analysis by including further dimensions such as trust (Whitley, 1999; Redding, 2005), social capital (trust), culture, informality and multiplexity (Witt and Redding, 2013).

Secondly, one of the most significant implications of global capitalism for employment is the rise in informal work: 93 per cent of the workforce in India is informal and China has comparable numbers (Phillips, 2011). Therefore, employment relations in China and India cannot

Table 16.2 Comparative institutional analysis of China and India

Dimensions	China	India
Role of the state	Developmental and predatory Political authoritarianism State control of the economy: dominance through SOEs Variation in local state forms	Predatory and developmental Political democracy State guidance of economy Variation in local state forms
Corporate governance	Ownership: state (SOEs) and family SMEs Weak ownership and corporate governance Weak legal enforcement and intellectual property rights Informal institutions and processes: *guanxi* networks; patron–client relations between political power and capital	Ownership: state (public sector) and family/business groups Stronger ownership and corporate governance Variation between states in legal enforcement Informal institutions and processes: family and caste/religion-based networks, clientelist relations between state and business groups
Financial system	State-dominated banks Financing of SOEs, not private firms Private firms' recourse to informal sources of financing, e.g. *guanxi* networks	State-dominated banks Financing of state and private firms
Interfirm relations	State/party-dominated clientelist relations in SOEs Family and *guanxi* networks	State/business house clientelist relations Family/caste/religion-based networks Industrial clusters (e.g. IT)
Labour market and education and skill systems	Deeply segmented along urban–rural divide; dualised citizenship Large rural migrant workforce High literacy, low enrolment in further and higher education Emphasis on general skills, weak vocational training; skill acquisition left to private initiative Superiority in labour-intensive manufacturing	Segmented along formal–informal, with further segmentation within the informal Large rural migrant workforce Lower literacy, higher enrolment for further education Emphasis on general skills, declining vocational training structure, skill acquisition left to private initiative Superiority in services because of English and high technological skills in IT
Employment/industrial relations	Party-controlled unions with limited worker involvement High state intervention in wage bargaining Extraordinary power to managers in private firms Privatisation of social security Workers' protests in new industrial areas Minimal protection of the unemployed and marginalised rural workers	Variations in industrial relations models Medium and declining state intervention in wage bargaining Declining political unionism; rise of independent and enterprise unionism; informal worker organisations Minimal protection of informal workers

Source: based on Peck and Zhang (2013) and Witt and Redding (2013).

be understood without including *informal labour and labour agency* in the analytical framework. The National Commission for Enterprises in the Unorganised Sector in India defines informal workers as

> those working in the informal sector or households, excluding regular workers with social security benefits by the employers, and the workers in the formal sector without any employment and social security benefits provided by the employers.

Firms, both domestic and foreign, restructure work and employment via subcontracting, outsourcing and casualisation in order to shift from secure, permanent employment with social security benefits to insecure, temporary forms of employment. Nichols *et al.* (2004) and Danford and Zhao (2012) chart the dismantling of the factory regimes in China through changes in employment contracts, authoritarian control and work intensification. A large part of this informal workforce constitutes the most vulnerable segment: rural migrant workers. Around 200 million rural migrant workers in China provide the labour supply to industry and urban projects (Pun and Smith, 2007; Dong *et al.*, 2010; Peck and Zhang, 2013). Similarly, seasonal and circular migration of impoverished rural workers forms the underbelly of urban employment in India (Breman, 1996; Harriss-White, 2003). The enhanced exploitation in both societies has implications for labour agency. While some see this as leading to protests and limited resistance (Blecher, 2010; Dong *et al.*, 2010), for others it signifies 'higher levels of class awareness and identification in the workers' dormitories and social communities' (Chan *et al.*, 2010: 146) or new forms of resistance (Agarwala, 2008; Hammer, 2010).

Explore

- What additional dimensions can be added to the comparative analysis of employment relations in China and India?
- How does this help in our understanding of the two economies?

Comparative advantages of China and India

Much is made of the democratic character of the Indian state: knowledge of the English language, higher skills in computing, software and information technology, and the demographic premium. First, democracy certainly provides a sustainable framework to manage diversity with an equitable distribution of resources and opportunities, and to redress the imbalances created by differentiated globalisation. In reality, India has not delivered adequate material and human development benefits to the majority of its citizens. The processes and outcomes of the planned as well as current market-orientated development are disproportionately captured by the political and economic elite. Secondly, advantages arising from the English language are evident in the service sector growth, in call centres, the BPO and IT sectors, and the ever-increasing percentage of senior executives from India employed in multinational firms and international organisations. However, the premium enjoyed by India is being challenged by the Philippines, South Africa and increasingly China (i.e. placing a high emphasis on English in its educational system). Also, China is catching up on services while India still has to make up ground in manufacturing. Thirdly, to retain the comparative advantage in IT, the industry needs to upscale through diversification and research and innovation. At the same time, upgrading of middle level skills and wider vocational training are necessary. Finally, the demographic premium arising from a younger Indian workforce with a falling dependency ratio is in contrast to China's ageing population, and needs to be supported with increased health and education coverage, income and human development indicators (for a historically nuanced assessment, see Saith, 2008).

China's advantages arise from its manufacturing and export-led growth, state-led development of industry and innovation through SOEs ('national champions' and 'going global' strategies), and better human development indicators, translating into higher per-capita incomes and greater equality. However, the Chinese state is aware of the need to reduce dependence on manufacturing and exports. It has started to focus on increasing domestic consumption and development of the services sector in the 12th plan. Secondly, the dominance of SOEs, while likely to persist for political–economic reasons, needs to be supplemented with the growth of indigenous SMEs, especially in the high-technology sector. Moreover, the Communist legacy of comprehensive education and health that delivered 91 per cent adult literacy and better human development indicators overall is fast evaporating as these public goods are privatised. Low poverty levels and greater equality have given way to sharp acceleration of inequality since the economic reforms began. Human rights, workers' rights and intellectual property rights also remain areas of concern (Saith, 2008; Peck and Zhang, 2013).

Challenges faced by China and India

The major challenges faced by both economies can be attributed to their respective historical legacies, as well as the inability to address the social costs of reforms that have become more acute. These include governance issues, infrastructure, gender disadvantages, poverty and inequality. In India, the lack of a national consensus on reforms and of any real redistribution by the old and new elite is exacerbated by high levels of corruption. A study by Transparency International (2012) places India at the lower end of the table in terms of its institutions, the ease of doing business, and the average time taken to secure clearance for a start-up or to invoke bankruptcy. The Rights to Information Act 2005 and setting up of vigilance commissions are some attempts to address corruption through greater accountability and transparency. In China, political authoritarianism and intertwined political power–economic interests at all levels of government, coupled with a lack of accountability, have seen China catch up with India on the corruption index. The development of infrastructure is a priority in order to attract investment, especially in India. Poverty, exclusion, gender disadvantages and inequality interweave in both China and India, particularly so in the rural sector. The disadvantaged rural sector, with increased socioeconomic insecurity, migration and lack of access to education and health, has witnessed increasing poverty, patriarchal biases (evident in negative sex ratios, feminisation of agriculture, female and farmer suicides and crimes against women) and spiralling inequality (social, class and regional) in both societies. Most of the employment created is in the informal sector with low wages, poor working conditions, low job security and increased risk of safety and occupational health. The absence of adequate social security mechanisms has further increased and polarised inequalities.

In sum, prospects for the two economies remain uncertain. Politically, it depends on how far China can initiate political liberal reforms and the extent to which India can ensure redistributive measures. Economically, it could be that on account of their comparative advantages, both China and India continue to improve their position within the global division of labour while also growing their own MNCs and brands with global reach. However, economic growth over recent decades has given rise to new power dynamics. In both cases, economic progress is closely intertwined with the ability to develop new social compromises.

This section has undertaken a comparative assessment of China and India, summarising the analysis of the two economies from a comparative institutional perspective. Analytically, the section emphasised two significant dimensions that need to be included into any analysis of the two capitalisms: sub-national forms of governance and informal labour and labour agency. Thereafter, comparative advantages as well as challenges faced by the two economies were identified with some reflections on future prospects.

Key Controversy

Which economy is ahead: China or India? Critically assess the comparative advantages of, and challenges faced by, each economy.

Concluding comments

This chapter has analysed the employment relations in China and India, the two largest emerging economies in the world today. The analysis is situated within the comparative capitalist framework that facilitates the assessment of the two economies in their broader institutional context as well as in the nature of their integration into the global economy. This results in an understanding of how changes in employment relations are linked to other institutions.

The two economies are in a state of transition from a planned to market-oriented one, with distinctive role of the state, nature of firms and social institutions/relations. The picture that emerges is one of considerable variation in social and economic patterns, and employment relations, between the two economies but also within them. This has helped identify the comparative advantages as well as the challenges faced by each economy as they integrate into the global economy. Analytically, the chapter has emphasised two significant dimensions that need to be included within any analysis of the two capitalisms: subnational forms of governance and informal labour and labour agency. In doing so, it extends and augments the comparative institutional analysis.

Summary

- The chapter situated the analysis of employment relations in China and India in a comparative capitalist framework. It identified the similarities and differences in the economic patterns of development in the two economies with respect to each other as well as with other industrialised economies. It outlined the comparative capitalism approach before focusing on the challenges and advantages of applying it to China and India. Finally, it reviewed recent research on the 'second wave' of the comparative capitalist tradition and how this has evaluated and augmented the comparative institutional analysis with respect to China and India.

- The section on China explored the historical pattern of development of the Chinese institutional context in which the state–party dominates the economy through SOEs and state-owned banks. Weak corporate governance structures are supplemented by institutions of family and *guanxi* and patron–client relations between political power and capital. In the context of a deeply segmented labour market along rural–urban lines, which is institutionalised through dual citizenship, employment relations in China are undergoing a gradual change: from lifelong employment and comprehensive social security to a more flexible labour market, towards a contributory social security fund, and increased exploitation of rural migrant workers in the new model of the socialist market economy. As Chinese capitalism interacts with global capitalism, the influx of MNCs and the transfer of HR policies and practices reveal a complex picture where traditional and Maoist values and practices in employment relations persist and run in parallel to the introduction of novel and innovative practices by MNCs in China.

- The section on India outlined the Indian institutional context where a formerly interventionist state is withdrawing from direct involvement in the economy as it transitions to a market-orientated one. Institutions of family and social networks define the distinctive form of private firm in India, i.e. the business group, governed by both formal and informal institutions in corporate governance mechanisms. Formal–informal labour market segmentation reflects advanced specialisation and therefore high skill levels in industries such as IT and computing alongside a vast pool of low-skilled surplus informal labour without any social security cover. In this context, employment relations in India are being reshaped by liberal labour reforms, which have increased the flexibility of labour and weakened the bargaining power of workers and unions. This has resulted in new forms of unions and new union strategies, e.g. a decline in political unionism and a rise of enterprise unions and informal worker organisations. State provision of skilling infrastructure is being replaced by individualised or firm-based training. Regional variations of industrial relations models and local state–capital relations in India shape different employment dynamics. A peculiar feature of Indian capitalism as it interacts with global capitalism lies in the advanced industry and skills in certain sectors such as services and IT as well as prominent Indian MNCs.

- From a comparative institutional perspective, the chapter emphasised two significant dimensions that need to be included within any analysis of the two capitalisms: subnational forms of governance and informal labour and labour agency. Comparative advantages as well as challenges faced by the two economies were also discussed.

Questions

1 How are the changes in employment relations linked to other institutions?
2 Assess the changing role of the state in employment relations in China.
3 Examine HRM in India's new economy, i.e. IT, call centres and the BPO industry.
4 To what extent are the growth trajectories of China and India sustainable in the face of rising inequalities?

Case study

Unionism in an NIZ in India: a study of manufacturing MNCs

A considerable part of economic growth in India is driven by new industrial zones (NIZs). These have emerged since the 1990s, driven by the dynamics of high levels of FDI in manufacturing, neo-liberal state policies and a large pool of workers. An important aspect of NIZs is the deregulation of labour law by the state, which increases flexibility and control over labour and unions while reducing elements of employment protection. The strategy pursued is one that aims to increase productivity through increased managerialism and competition on lower labour cost rather than more cooperative labour–management relations. This 'facilitates' the flow of foreign investment to the region.

A result of this strategy is a shift away from established political unionism, i.e. one defined by common ground between political parties and trade unions, towards enterprise unionisms, i.e. workplace-based unions without wider or political affiliations. A study

of subsidiaries of manufacturing MNCs in an NIZ in India found the presence of different models of unionism. Of the eight firms studied, five had some form of union and four of these had enterprise unions. In the two Japanese firms, employer practices enforced strictly controlled work regimes and curbs on wider affiliation by unions. Attempts to forge alliances with central trade union federations by the union were disallowed in both firms. By contrast, in the Indian MNC, the union had broken its alliance with a central political federation because of the workers' dissatisfaction with it and switched from a politically affiliated union to an enterprise union. A third Japanese firm, the oldest in the region, had a politically affiliated union, while the only Korean firm was strictly 'non-union' or anti-union. Thus, workers and unions in the NIZ were responding to constraints at the workplace – increasing managerial control and NIZ-specific restrictive state policies – by focusing on the workplace either by

Case study continued

compulsion or by choice/pragmatism rather than as part of a political–industrial strategy.

However, the combination of state policy, managerialism and enterprise unionism in the NIZ has created interesting dynamics. Alternative strategies of workers and unions have emerged, characterised by the living space focus and community-based mobilisation. The expression denied to the workers at the workplace found an outlet in their living areas, where workers shared workplace experiences and where union leaders and officials actively mobilised. Three different types of effort were evident in three of the eight firms studied. This is a significant alternative in the longstanding debate on political versus enterprise unionism, but more so in the constrained context of an NIZ that restricts established forms of unionism. Yet the same constraints in the NIZ opened up alternative spaces in the living areas for workers' expression, resulting in new forms of labour organisation and strategies.

It is open to question whether the living space focus or community-based mobilisation evident in

the NIZ can be identified as a nascent form of social movement union or a 'modified' form of enterprise unionism. What is clear is a very vocal expression of workplace-specific grievances expressed in alternative spaces, with definite implications for unions in response to global capitalism exemplified in the NIZ.

Source: Hammer (2010).

Questions

1 What are the distinctive features of an NIZ? Do they have any implications for labour and unions?

2 What different models of unionism can you identify in the NIZ?

3 How can the trend towards enterprise unionism be explained?

4 What are the characteristics of alternative forms of unionism evident in the NIZ?

5 To what extent is the model of managerialist workplace and enterprise unionism sustainable within NIZs?

References and further reading

Agarwala, R. (2006), 'From work to welfare: a new class movement in India', *Critical Asian Studies,* 38, 4: 419–44.

Agarwala, R. (2008) Reshaping the social contract: emerging relations between the state and informal labour in India, *Theory and Society,* 37: 375–408.

Ahlstrom, D., Foley, S., Young, M.N. and Chan, E. (2005) 'Human resource strategies in post-WTO China', *Thunderbird International Business Review,* 47, 3: 263–385.

Amable, B. (2003) *The Diversity of Modern Capitalism.* Oxford: Oxford University Press.

Amba-Rao, S.C., Petrick, J.A., Gupta, J.N.D. and Von der Embse, T.J. (2000) 'Comparative performance appraisal practices and management values among foreign and domestic firms in India', *International Journal of Human Resource Management,* 11, 1: 60–89.

Aoki, M. (2013) 'Historical sources of institutional trajectories in economic development: China, Japan and Korea compared', *Socio-Economic Review,* 11/2: 233–64.

Bardhan, P. (1998) *The Political Economy of Development in India.* New Delhi: Oxford University Press.

Bhattacherjee, D. and Ackers, P. (2010) 'Introduction: employment relations in India – old narratives and new perspectives', *Industrial Relations Journal,* 41, 2: 104–21.

Bjorkman, I. and Budhwar, P. (2007) 'When in Rome. . .? Human resource management and the performance of foreign firms operating in India', *Employee Relations,* 29, 6: 595–610.

Blecher, M. (2010) 'Globalisation, structural reform, and labour politics in China', *Global Labour Journal* 1, 1: 92–111.

Boyer, R., Isogai, A. and Uemura, H. (2011) (eds) *Diversity and Transformations of Asian Capitalisms,* London: Routledge.

Breman, J. (1996) *Footloose Labour: Working in India's Informal Economy.* Cambridge: Cambridge University Press.

Budhwar, P. (2003) 'Employment relations in India', *Employee Relations,* 25, 2: 132–48.

Budhwar, P.S. and Boyne, G. (2004) 'Human resource management in the Indian public and private sector: an empirical comparison', *International Journal of Human Resource Management,* 15, 2: 346–70.

Budhwar, P.S. and Debrah Y.A. (eds) (2001) *Human Resource Management in Developing Countries.* London: Routledge.

Budhwar, P.S. and Khatri, N. (2001) 'A comparative study of HR practices in Britain and India', *International Journal of Human Resource management,* 12, 5: 800–826.

Chan, C., Ngai, P. and Chan, J. (2010) 'The role of the state, labour policy and workers' struggles in globalised China', *Global Labour Journal* 1, 1: 132–51.

Child, J. (1994) *Management in China in the Age of Reform.* Cambridge: Cambridge University Press.

Cooke, F. and Saini, D. (2010) '(How) Does the HR strategy support an innovation orientated business strategy? An investigation of institutional context and organisational practices in Indian firms', *Human Resource Management,* 49, 3: 377–400.

Danford, A. and Zhao, W. (2012) 'Confucian HRM or unitarism with Chinese characteristics? A study of worker attitudes to work reform and management in three state owned enterprises', *Work, Employment and Society,* 26, 5: 839–56.

D'Cruz, P. and Noronha, E. (2012) 'Cornered by conning: agents' experiences of closure of a call centre in India', *International Journal of Human Resource Management*, 23, 5: 1019–39.

Deeg, R., Jackson, G. (2007) 'Towards a more dynamic theory of capitalist variety', *Socio-Economic Review*, 5: 149–79.

Deshpande, I.K., Sharma, A.N., Karan, A.K. and Sarkar, S. (2004) *Liberalisation and Labour: Labour Flexibility in Indian Manufacturing*. New Delhi: Institute for Human Development.

Ding, Z., Goodall, K. and Warner, M. (2000) 'The end of the "iron rice-bowl": whither Chinese human resource management?', *International Journal of Human Resource Management*, 11, 2: 217–36.

Dong, X., Bowles, P. and Chang, H. (2010) 'Managing liberalisation and globalisation in rural China: trends in rural labour allocation, income and equality', *Global Labour Journal* 1, 1: 32–55.

Dreze, J. and Sen, A. (1995) *India – Economic Development and Social Opportunity*. Delhi: Oxford University Press.

Dunning, J. and Lundan, S. (2005) *Multinational Enterprises and the Global Economy*, 2nd edn. Aldershot: Edward Elgar.

Edwards, T., Colling, T. and Ferner, A. (2007) 'Conceptual approaches to the transfer of employment practices in multinational companies: an integrated approach', *Human Resource Management Journal*, 17: 201–17.

Estrin, S. and Prevezer, M. (2011) 'The role of informal institutions in corporate governance: Brazil, Russia, India, and China compared', *Asia Pacific Journal of Management*, 28: 41–67.

Evans, P. (1995) *Embedded Autonomy: States and Industrial Transformation*. Princeton, NJ: Princeton University Press.

Fligstein, N. and Zhang, J. (2011) 'A new agenda for research on the trajectory of Chinese capitalism', *Management and Organisation Review*, 7: 39–62.

Frenkel, S. and Kuruvilla, S. (2002) 'Logics of action, globalisation and changing employment relations in China, India, Malaysia and the Philippines', *Industrial and Labour Relations Review*, 55, 3: 387–412.

Fu, Y. and Kamenou, N. (2011) 'The impact of Chinese cultural values on human resource policies and practices within transnational corporations in China', *International Journal of Human Resource Management*, 22, 16: 3270–89.

Gamble, J. (2003) 'Transferring HR practices from the UK to China: the limits and potential for convergence', *International Journal of Human Resource Management*, 14, 3: 369–87.

Gamble, J. (2006a) 'Introducing western style HRM practices to China: shopfloor perceptions in British Multinationals', *Journal of World Business*, 41: 328–43.

Gamble, J. (2006b) 'Multinational retailers in China: proliferating "McJobs" or developing skills?' *Journal of Management Studies*, 43, 7: 1463–90.

Gamble, J. (2011) *Multinational Retailers and Consumers in China: Transferring Organizational Practices from the United Kingdom and Japan*, Palgrave.

Gamble, J. and Huang, Q. (2009) 'The transfer of organisational practices: a diachronic perspective from China', *International Journal of Human Resource Management*, 20, 8, 1683–703.

Glover, L. and Siu, N. (2000) 'The human resource barriers to the management of quality in China', *International Journal of Human Resource Management*, 11, 4: 867–82.

Goldstein, A. (2008) 'Emerging economies' transnational corporations: the case of Tata', *Transnational Corporations*, 17, 3: 85–108 (UNCTAD).

Hall, P. A. and Soskice, D. (eds) (2001) *Varieties of Capitalism: The Institutional Foundations of Comparative Advantage*. Oxford: Oxford University Press.

Hamilton, G. (2006) *Commerce and Capitalism in Chinese Societies*. London: Routledge.

Hammer, A. (2010) 'Trade unions in a constrained environment: workers' voices from a New Industrial Zone in India', *Industrial Relations Journal*, 41, 2: 168–84.

Hammer, A. (2012) 'Institutional analysis and collective mobilisation in a comparative assessment of two cooperatives in India' in Atzeni, M. (ed.) *Alternative Work Organisation*. London: Palgrave, pp. 157–78.

Hancké, B., Rhodes, M. and Thatcher, M. (eds) (2008) *Beyond Varieties of Capitalism: Conflict. Contradictions, and Complementarities in the European Economy*. Oxford: Oxford University Press.

Haq, R. (2012) 'The managing diversity mindset in public versus private organisations in India', *International Journal of Human Resource Management*, 23, 5: 892–914.

Harney, A. (2005) 'Guangdong: paying the price of rapid development', *Financial Times*, 7 November.

Harriss-White, B. (2003) 'Inequality at work in the informal economy: key issues and illustrations, *International Labour Review*, 142, 4: 459–69.

Harriss-White, B. and Gooptu, N. (2001) 'Mapping India's world of unorganised labour' in L. Panitch and C. Leys (eds) *Socialist Register 2001: Working Classes. Global Realities*, 89–118. London: Merlin Press.

Hofstede, G. (1991) *Cultures and Organisations: Software of the Mind*. London: McGraw-Hill.

Hollingsworth, J. R. and Boyer, R. (eds) (1997) *Contemporary Capitalism: The Embeddedness of Institutions*. New York: Cambridge University Press.

Huang, Q. and Gamble, J. (2011) 'Informal institutional constraints and their impact on HRM and employee satisfaction: evidence from China's retail sector', *International Journal of Human Resource Management*, 22, 15: 3168–86.

Hutchings, K. and Murray, G. (2003) 'Family, face and favours: do Australians adjust to accepted business conventions in China?', *Singapore Management Review*, 25, 2: 25–49.

Jain, H., Mathew, M. and Bedi, A. (2012) 'HRM innovations by Indian and foreign MNCs operating in India: a survey of HR professionals', *International Journal of Human Resource Management*, 23, 5: 1006–18.

James, A. and Vira, B. (2010) 'Unionising the new spaces of the economy? Alternative labour organising in India's IT enabled services- BPO industry', *Geoforum*, 41: 364–76.

Kaplinsky, R. (1997) 'India's industrial development: an interpretive survey', *World Development*, 25, 5: 681–94.

Khanna, T. and Palepu, K. (2000) 'Is group affiliation profitable in emerging markets? An analysis of diversified Indian business groups', *Journal of Finance*, 55, 2: 867–91.

Kohli, A. (2004) *State-directed Development: Political Power and Industrialisation in the Global Periphery*. Cambridge: Cambridge University Press.

Kuruvilla, S. and Erickson, C.L. (2002) 'Change and transformation in Asian industrial relations', *Industrial Relations*, 41, 2: 171–227.

Kuruvilla, S. and Ranganathan, A. (2010) 'Globalisation and outsourcing: confronting new HR challenges in India's BPO industry', *Industrial Relations Journal*, 41, 2: 136–53.

Lecraw, D. (1977) 'Direct investment by firms from less developed countries', *Oxford Economic Papers*, 29, 3: 442–57.

Lu, Y. and Björkman, I. (1997) MNC standardisation versus localisation: MNC practices in China-Western joint ventures, *International Journal of Human Resource Management*, 8: 614–28.

Morgan, G. (2011) 'Comparative capitalisms: a framework for the analysis of emerging and developing economies', *International Studies of Management and Organisation*, 41, 1: 12–34.

Morris, J., Wilkinson, B. and Gamble, J. (2009) 'Strategic IHRM or the bottom line? The cases of electronics and garments commodity chains in China', *International Journal of Human Resource Management*, 20, 2: 348–71.

NASSCOM (2011) The IT-BPO sector in India: strategic review for 2011. Foundation Report: Executive summary.

Nath, V. (2013) 'Aesthetic and emotional labour through stigma: national identity management and racial abuse in offshored Indian call centres', *Work, Employment and Society*, 25, 4: 709–25.

Nichols, T. and Zhao, W. (2010) 'Disaffection with trade unions in China: some evidence from the SOEs in the auto industry', *Industrial Relations Journal*, 41, 1: 19–33.

Nichols, T., Cam, S., Chou, W.C.G., Chun, S. *et al.* (2004) 'Factory regimes and the dismantling of established labour in Asia: a review of cases from large manufacturing plants in China, S Korea and Taiwan', *Work, Employment and Society*, 18, 4: 663–85.

Okada, A. (2004) 'Skills development and interfirm learning linkages under globalisation: lessons from the Indian automobile industry', *World Development*, 32, 7: 1265–88.

Peck, J. and Zhang, J. (2013) 'A variety of capitalism . . . with Chinese characteristics?', *Journal of Economic Geography*, 13, 3: 357–96.

Phillips, N. (2011) 'Informality, global production networks and the dynamics of "adverse incorporation"', *Global Networks*, 11, 3: 380–97.

Pun, N. and Smith, C. (2007) 'Putting the transnational labour process in its place: the dormitory labour regime in post-socialist China', *Work, Employment and Society*, 21, 1: 27–45.

Redding, G. (2005) 'The thick description and comparison of societal systems of capitalism', *Journal of International Business Studies*, 36: 123–55.

Reed, A. (2002) 'Corporate governance reforms in India', *Journal of Business Ethics*, 37: 249–68.

Report of the Second National Commission on Labour (NCL) (2002). Ministry of Labour, Government of India, Delhi.

Ravishankar, M.N., Cohen, L. and El-Sawad, A. (2010) 'Examining resistance, accommodation and the pursuit of aspiration in the Indian IT-BPO space: reflections on two case studies', *Industrial Relations Journal*, 41, 2: 154–67.

Saith, A. (2008) 'China and India: the institutional roots of differential performance', *Development and Change*, 39, 5: 723–57.

Sen, A. (2001) *Development as Freedom*. Oxford: Oxford University Press.

Sengupta, A.K. and Sett, P.K. (2000) 'Industrial relations law, employment security and collective bargaining in India: myths, realities and hopes', *Industrial Relations Journal*, 31, 2: 144–53.

Shyam Sundar, K.R. (2010) 'Emerging trends in employment relations in India', *Indian Journal of Industrial Relations*, 45, 4: 585–95.

Sinha, A. (2005) *The Regional Roots of Developmental Politics in India: A Divided Leviathan*. Bloomington, IN: Indiana University Press.

Som, A. (2012) 'Organisational response through innovative HRM and re-design: a comparative study from France and India', *International Journal of Human Resource Management*, 23, 5: 952–76.

Storz, C., Amable, B., Casper, S. and Lechevalier, S. (2013) 'Bringing Asia into the comparative capitalism perspective', *Socio-Economic Review*, 11, 2: 217–32.

Taylor, P. and Bain, P. (2005) 'India calling to the far away towns': the call centre labour process and globalisation', *Work, Employment and Society*, 19, 2: 261–82.

The Economist (2008) Special edition on China and India: Asia's wounded giants, 11 December.

Transparency International (2012) See Global Corruption Barometer: Corruption Perceptions Index; and Regional and national surveys and indices on **www.transparency.org**.

Trivedi, A. (2006) 'Global factory, Indian worker', unpublished PhD thesis, University of London.

Unni, J. and Rani, U. (2003) 'Social protection for informal workers in India: Insecurities, instruments and institutional mechanisms', *Development and Change*, 34, 1: 127–61.

Venkata Ratnam, C.S. (1998) 'Multinational companies in India' *International Journal of Human Resource Management*, 9, 4: 567–89.

Venkata Ratnam, C.S. (2001) *Globalisation and Labour-management Relations: Dynamics of Change*. New Delhi: Response Books.

Warner, M. (2008) 'Reassessing HRM "with Chinese characteristics": an overview', *International Journal of Human Resource Management*, 19, 5: 771–801.

Warner, M. (2010) 'In search of Confucian HRM: theory and practice in greater China and beyond', *International Journal of Human Resource Management*, 21, 12: 2053–78.

Whitley, R. (1999) *Divergent Capitalisms: The Social Structuring and Change of Business Systems*. Oxford: Oxford University Press.

Witt, M. A. (2010) *China: What Variety of Capitalism?* INSEAD Faculty & Research Working Paper 2010/88/EPS. Online: **http://www.insead.edu**.

Witt, M. A. and Redding, G. (2013) 'Asian business systems: institutional comparison, clusters and implications for varieties of capitalism and business systems theory', *Socio-Economic Review*, 11, 2: 265–300.

World Development Indicators (2013) Online: **http://data.worldbank.org/country/china** (accessed September 2013).

World Investment Report (2006) UNCTAD. Online: **http://unctad.org/en/docs/wir2006_en.pdf** (accessed January 2014).

Zhang, M. and Edwards, C. (2007) 'Diffusing 'best practice' in Chinese multinationals: the motivation, facilitation and limitations', *International Journal of Human Resource Management*, 18, 12: 2147–65.

Zhu, C. and Dowling, P.J. (2002) 'Staffing practices in translation: some empirical evidence from China', *International Journal of Human Resource Management*, 13, 4: 569–97.

Zhu, Y. and Warner, M. (2005) 'Changing Chinese employment relations since WTO accession', *Personnel Review*, 34, 3: 354–69.

Chapter 17

International HRM

Phil Almond and Olga Tregaskis

Objectives

- To examine factors that help to explain the strategy and structure of multinational corporations (MNCs).

- To examine the structure, role and activities of international human resource management (HRM) functions in MNCs and the factors influencing these configurations.

- To consider the role of international HR networks and expatriates in generating and transferring HR knowledge in MNCs.

- To examine the influence of MNC country of origin and location on HRM practice.

Introductory case study

Labour unrest at Maruti Suzuki

Maruti Suzuki, the Indian subsidiary of Japan's Suzuki, has been India's biggest carmaker for two-and-a-half decades. But this year, its position as India's market leader – and as a major driver of Suzuki's profits – has been undermined by labour unrest that has severely disrupted production and led to long waiting periods for Maruti's most popular models.

Since June, workers at the company's five-year-old Manesar plant, in the northern state of Haryana, have gone on strike three times, initially to press for a new, independent union, and later against management's punitive moves against strike leaders. Tensions culminated this month, when 1,500 workers occupied the factory compound for eight days, halting production completely, until they were evicted by police.

Maruti said on Friday that it had finally resolved its differences with the workers after days of intensive talks brokered by the state government, and that normal production would resume. But labour activists say it is likely to be a fragile peace. 'How long this truce will last is going to depend on management,' says Gautam Mody, secretary of the New Trade Union Initiative, which has closely followed the agitation. 'They need to change their style in being able to accept a union of the workers' choice and not trying to dictate terms of how industrial relations will work.'

The unrest at Maruti reflects the increasingly combative mood among Indian industrial workers, who toil in highly-automated, ultra-modern factories – often owned by, or supplying to, foreign companies – but feel they are not getting an adequate share of India's rising prosperity.

Prabhu Mohapatra, a Delhi University labour historian, says the agitation at Maruti had similar causes as the labour unrest that has rocked many foreign-owned factories in China in the past few years. 'Auto component companies have made enormous profits, and workers have gotten peanuts,' he said. 'How many months would it take a worker at the Manesar plant to buy a Maruti, compared to a German worker? The difference is 20 times. You have to increase the purchasing power of workers to create a mass market, but here, you think "We will squeeze these workers so we can export",' he added.

 Source: Kazmin, A. (2011) Indian workers demand greater rewards, Financial Times, 24 October. http://www.ft.com/cms/s/0/8c5d92f2-fbdo-11e0-9283-00144feab49a.html#axzz2tcGBag9f.
© The Financial Times Limited 2011. All rights reserved.

Introduction

This chapter deals with issues relating to the management of human resources within multinational corporations (MNCs), i.e. firms that directly employ people in more than one country. As the Introductory case study illustrates, this is a matter of considerable economic and social importance in an increasingly globalised economy.

In the UK, more than 25 per cent of manufacturing employment is in the subsidiaries of foreign multinationals, as well as 12 per cent of total employment in services (OECD, 2006). In addition, of course, many UK-owned firms have international operations, and therefore also have to engage in international HRM. Finally, it has long been argued that the management practices of foreign MNCs have a wider influence on HRM in domestic firms (cf. Dunning, 1958; Oliver and Wilkinson, 1992). This is particularly the case when firms are part of the supply chain to, or operate in competition with, foreign MNCs (Rutherford and Holmes, 2008; Brandl *et al.,* 2013). Overall, then, a large proportion of UK managers and workers are, directly or indirectly, affected by the HR decisions of MNCs.

But are the HR issues facing managers in MNCs different from those in purely domestic firms? In other words, do MNCs, which form a diverse group, have something in common that is distinctive from other firms, which means we should analyse them together? This chapter will argue that MNCs should be considered as a distinct group of organisations, similar to the way in which academics have long recognised that public-sector organisations, for example, need to be treated as a distinct group of employers.

The chapter will therefore explain what makes the process of HRM distinctive in an MNC. It will, for instance, reflect the fact that managing the human resources of a firm becomes more complex when those human resources work in different national societies, for reasons that can be related back to the cross-national differences in employment relations systems introduced in previous chapters in this part of the book. Differences in employment law and industrial relations systems between countries mean that some HR policies and practices may be legally and socially acceptable in a firm's operations in one country, but not in another country. Equally, differences in national training and education systems may mean that the skill and competence profile of the workers available on the labour market will differ from one country to another. Finally, differences in national management cultures may mean that some management styles are more appropriate in some national settings than in others.

These national differences, though, are not just a 'problem' for the managers of MNCs to deal with; they can also be exploited to the advantage of the firm. Indeed, much of the literature on international HRM seeks to identify and understand how MNCs manage their geographically dispersed workforces for both local and global competitive advantage. Questions typically asked in this literature concern the circumstances in which MNCs broadly attempt to pursue uniformity of HR policies across their international operations, and those in which there are advantages to having different policies in different countries. Such differentiation may in some cases be useful in order to meet the demands of local product markets, where national differences in customer demands mean that firms have to adapt their management of labour. In other cases, differentiation may take place in order to exploit the local labour market most efficiently. MNCs that originate in high-cost, highly regulated economies may well choose not to transfer high-cost elements of their HR systems to lower-wage or lightly regulated economies, although as our Introductory case study showed, this decision has heavy social consequences, as well as potentially provoking labour unrest.

Despite the demands for and benefits that MNCs can accrue from differentiation, there are strong competitive reasons for these organisations to want to coordinate and integrate their activities across geographical boundaries. To maximise economies of scale, MNCs attempt to coordinate activities involving scarce and/or costly resources. Equally, it is argued that the more management processes and activities that can be integrated across geographical boundaries, the easier it is to share resources and knowledge. The HRM function in MNCs plays a critical role in developing systems and processes that promote internal consistency in how employees are treated. HR professionals also need to consider how they can identify and best use the skill and management talent that exists across the distributed MNC network. At the same time, the desire for standardisation and integration in HRM needs to take account of the country differences that give rise to different employee expectations, perceptions and skill levels.

This raises questions about how the international HR function can organise itself to address both the demands for integration and localisation. Which HRM activities should be coordinated or controlled by the central corporate HR function and which activities should be localised? How can the HR function structure itself to best address these competing demands for integration and localisation? Finally, more recently, the literature in the field has been concerned with how HR knowledge can be transferred across the MNC and whether global HR practices can be created from knowledge drawn from the subsidiaries as much as from that generated by the centre or corporate HR function.

These varying reports in the literature and various debates are considered in this chapter. We begin with the organisational-focused literature by introducing the international strategic context within which MNCs operate. We then look at the alternative models that have been proposed to explain how the international HR function is organised and its role. Next, we consider how HR knowledge is transferred, focusing specifically on the role of international HR networks and expatriates. The chapter then analyses national context and considers the extent to which international HRM is affected by the national ownership of firms and by the countries in which they operate. The role of managers in dealing with different national systems of employment relations (see Chapter 15) is also highlighted here.

The international strategic context

As discussed in the introduction, additional insights are necessary in order to understand HR management in MNCs, for the simple reason that one thing that all MNCs share is the challenge of coordinating managers and workers in more than one country. At the most basic level, this creates dilemmas for managers about the extent to which the firm should pursue consistent HR policies across its different national operations, or allow foreign subsidiaries to pursue the policies that are seen as appropriate for the specific national employment systems involved.

Clearly, however, all MNCs are not the same; they vary enormously along dimensions such as size, the number of foreign countries in which they have workforces, and their degree of internationalisation, i.e. the proportion of the firm's workforce, and of its sales, that are outside the original home country. These differences impact greatly on the nature of management within such firms.

Differences in MNC structure

It is sometimes argued that some of the differences between international firms mean that, when discussing international management, we should distinguish between MNCs with different structural forms, and discuss the nature of management processes within each, rather than simply referring to 'multinational corporations' as if this group of firms were homogenous.

International business strategists have attempted to generate theory that makes it easier to interpret the complex world of international business. One of the best known is Prahalad and Doz's (1987) integration–responsiveness (I–R) grid. They argue that MNCs are faced with pressures, on the one hand, to integrate and coordinate their activities and, on the other, to respond to local (national) variations. The pressures driving integration and responsiveness faced by MNCs are summarised in Table 17.1.

MNCs adopt different strategies and structures depending on where they sit within this grid (see Harzing, 1999 for an in-depth review). So, for example, in a multi-domestic industry, such as utilities (e.g. water services), consumer demands and service provision are highly context-specific. Thus, the competitive strategy of a multinational's French subsidiary, for example, is in this case largely independent of that of its UK counterpart. This is necessary

Table 17.1 Summary of the pressures making up the integration–responsiveness (I–R) grid

I–R grid	Pressures
Strategic coordination is where:	• Multinational customers are a large proportion of the customer base, need is high. For example, it is important to coordinate pricing, service and product support worldwide as the multinational customer has the ability to compare prices on this basis. • Global competition is likely. If companies operate in multiple markets, global competition is highly likely. As such, it is important to monitor and collect information on competitors' activities in the different countries in readiness for an appropriate and timely strategic response. • Investment in one or more parts of the business is high. For example, high-tech manufacturing and R&D are common high fixed costs. To maximise the benefits and yield the best return on capital investments, global coordination is necessary.
Operational integration is high where:	• Technological intensity is high. Technology-intensive businesses often require a small number of manufacturing sites that enable quality and costs to be centrally controlled while serving wide geographically dispersed markets. • Cost reduction is a priority. This can be achieved through locating in low-cost economies or building plants designed to maximise economies of scale. • The product is universal and requires minimal adaptation to local markets. This is typical in consumer electronics. • Manufacturing needs to be located close to essential raw materials or energy, such as in the petrochemicals business.
Local responsiveness is high where:	• Customer demands vary across nations or regions. • Distribution channels need to be tailored to the characteristics of the country or region. For example, marketing of products may need to be nationally specific. • There are other similar products where the product needs to be adapted to local needs. • Local competitors rather than multinational competitors define the market competition. • The host country places restrictions on the operating subsidiary.

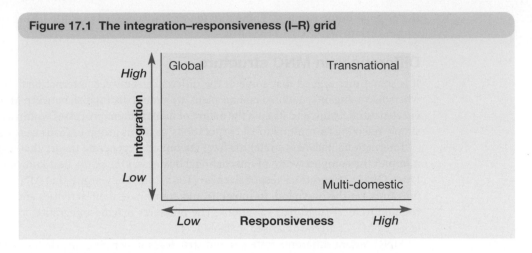

Figure 17.1 The integration–responsiveness (I–R) grid

because regulatory requirements, customer norms or government policy require a strategy that is responsive to local conditions. As such, these subsidiaries compete in domestic markets and frequently with domestic companies. Equally, a decentralised organisational structure where subsidiaries are given a high degree of strategic and operational autonomy from its parent is the most efficient. However, often the parent retains some degree of control through setting performance targets. This type of organisation would be located in the bottom right-hand side of the grid (Figure 17.1). By contrast, in a global industry, such as consumer electronics, standardised product/service demands by customers mean economies of scale dominate. The organisation's strategy prioritises efficiencies by producing standardised products, locating in the most cost-effective economies and coordinating expensive resources such as equipment or R&D. These organisations tend to centralise resources and responsibilities to the parent company, while the role of the subsidiaries tends to be in sales and services. The strategic responsibility and operational freedom of subsidiaries is usually fairly tightly controlled by the parent. This type of organisation would be located in the top left-hand side of the grid.

There is a considerable degree of empirical evidence supporting the existence of multi-domestic and global organisational forms (Bartlett and Ghoshal, 1989, 1990; Roth and Morrison, 1990; Leong and Tan, 1993; Moenaert *et al.*, 1994; Harzing, 2000). And the I–R grid is a simple and effective tool for explaining the key priorities shaping these organisations' strategies and structures. However, it is less effective at capturing the significance of the transfer of learning and innovation, which is an important strategic priority for the third type of international organisation, namely the transnational.

Another prominent model in the international management literature is that developed by Bartlett and Ghoshal (1989, 1990). Their work elaborates on issues around innovation and knowledge transfer in MNCs. Like Prahalad and Doz (1987), they identify the different pressures facing firms, which push them towards different structural forms. Two of the pressures they identify share much in common with Prahalad and Doz's concepts of integration and responsiveness. However, they also identify a third pressure, namely, worldwide innovation. Each of these is discussed in more detail in the following:

- *Local differentiation*. This refers to pressures emanating from 'local' (which usually in this context means national) markets to offer distinctive products, or to offer services in a distinctive way. This can be caused by consumer tastes; for example, a supermarket chain seeking to operate in both the UK and Spain would have to take account of the fact that there is a much higher demand for fresh produce, and regional products, in Spain, and a higher demand for packaged meals in the UK. This might affect the necessary skills profile of the workforce in the two countries, and would also be likely to affect the way in which the national operations think about distribution and marketing. In other cases, pressures for local differentiation are brought about by national regulations; this is often the case in the utilities sector, for example.

- *Global integration.* Bartlett and Ghoshal (1989) argue that the technological developments of the last half-century mean that economies of scale became increasingly crucial to competitive success. In order to achieve the scale necessary to gain competitive advantage, firms may seek to create integrated production processes in different parts of the world. For example, in automobile production, it is common for different parts of vehicles to be manufactured in different national subsidiaries of the major companies.

- *Worldwide innovation.* Here, the argument is that firms have come under increasing pressure to increase the pace of innovation, as markets and technologies evolve rapidly. In this context, Bartlett and Ghoshal (1989) argue that a logical response for many international firms is to encourage and support innovation in a coordinated way across their different international operations, rather than simply to rely on the innovative capacities of the original home country operations of the firm.

Explore

Select a multinational firm you see on your local high street.

- Use the internet to find out as much as you can about its products and business in your country and worldwide.
- Drawing on the three demands outlined in the I–R grid (strategic coordination, operational integration and local responsiveness), can you describe the extent to which this firm's activities in your local high street are driven by these demands?

Suggested reading: Ghoshal and Bartlett (1998).

Ghoshal and Bartlett (1998) further argue that these different pressures exist to differing extents. This will partly depend on which sector(s) the MNC is operating in; national differences in markets, for example, may be important in food retail, but far less so (if at all) in the market for computer chips, while economies of scale and the extent of radical innovation will also be greater in some sectors than in others. They also argue that the nature and extent of these pressures have altered over time, with greater pressures for global integration and particularly for worldwide innovation, meaning that the predominant structural forms of MNCs should change to fit these.

They identify four main structural forms of international firms:

- *The multinational ('multi-domestic') form.* Ghoshal and Bartlett (1998), in common with a number of other writers on international management, use the term 'multinational' to refer to a specific type of structure, rather than to international firms in general. As we have chosen in this chapter to use MNC as a generic term for all international firms, to minimise terminological confusion we will refer to the type of firm Bartlett and Ghoshal mean here as 'multi-domestic'. A multi-domestic structure means that the headquarters of the MNC does not attempt to control strictly what happens in overseas subsidiaries, so these operate on a largely autonomous basis. Such firms are highly decentralised in HR, with little or no attempt to transfer practices across borders. Equally, few attempts are made at knowledge transfer. To a large extent, the relations between the HQ and foreign subsidiaries are confined to flows of finance. This structure is associated with circumstances in which customer tastes vary greatly from one nation to another, or where there are strong regulatory differences between countries, creating markets that are strongly national in nature. Bartlett and Ghoshal associate this form with the first half of the twentieth century, but it should be noted that the multi-domestic form of MNC continues to exist in markets such as utility sectors, where national regulation makes extensive attempts at international coordination by HQ largely counterproductive.

- *The global form.* This is essentially a model in which HQ management takes home country management approaches, and tries to replicate them abroad in order to achieve economies of scale. In this model, there is a clear hierarchy, with the HQ instructing foreign managers how to manage their operations, or using a high number of expatriate managers for the same reason. Strategic decisions will be taken exclusively at HQ level, with research and development also concentrated in the home country. This model of international management is most likely in markets where economies of scale are critical to competitive advantage. Bartlett and Ghoshal associate this model with the period between 1950 and 1980, although cases where HQ strongly directs policy abroad and concentrates knowledge in the home base continue to exist.

- *The international form.* In the global form, MNCs replicate a production technology worldwide, in order to produce an identical product in different national operations. The international firm goes one step beyond this, in that HQs become increasingly cognisant of cross-national differences in consumer demands. They export knowledge and expertise to foreign subsidiaries, but allow local management the ability to alter the nature of products and services to suit the nature of the local market. In these firms, control is somewhat less tight than in global firms, but the general tone of policy is still likely to flow from the HQ to subsidiaries.

- *The transnational firm.* In this final type of MNC, the firm moves away from being a hierarchy, with the HQ at the top and the various national subsidiaries below, and towards what is sometimes referred to as a 'heterarchy' (Nohria and Ghoshal, 1997), or network form of organisation. In such 'transnational' firms, then, management control is dispersed across the corporation, rather than being concentrated at HQ. Unlike in the previous three forms of international organisation, the various international units of the enterprise are highly interdependent. Because of this, there are extensive flows of people, knowledge and resources, not just from HQ to foreign subsidiaries (as is frequent in the global and international forms), but also from foreign subsidiaries to HQ, and between different foreign subsidiaries. Such firms achieve coordination through shared decision-making, aided by attempts to create a common managerial culture across the firm (sometimes referred to as 'normative integration'; see Birkinshaw and Morrison, 1995: 737), rather than through rule-making from HQ. According to Bartlett and Ghoshal (1990), this network form of organisation allows international firms systematically to transfer learning and knowledge across their various international operations, while offering a more flexible, responsive form of coordination than the three previous models of organisation.

Key Controversy

The models of organisational structures – multi-domestic, global form, international form and the transnational – represent ideal types. As such there is considerable debate around the extent to which the transnational firm exists. However, there is greater agreement around the existence of the characteristics of each model. What structural indicators would you associate with transnational structures?

Suggested reading: Tregaskis, O., Edwards, T., Edwards, P., Ferner, A. and Marginson, P. (2010) 'Transnational learning structures in multinational firms: organisational context and national embeddedness', *Human Relations*, 63, 4: 471–499.

As mentioned earlier, Bartlett and Ghoshal (1995) argue that the most appropriate structure for MNCs has altered over time, with a broad movement from the multi-domestic through to the transnational form. In the current context of internationalised markets, rapid transformations in production technology and product markets, and the need to combine global economies of scale with local or regional adaptability, they clearly argue that large MNCs, at least, should follow the transnational model.

In reality, though, even many of the larger MNCs do not follow the transnational model. There are several reasons for this. First, as Bartlett and Ghoshal (1989) would acknowledge, there remain product markets that are so nationally specific as to make the transnational structure an inappropriate organisational structure. Secondly, their models play down the importance of organisational politics (Edwards and Rees, 2006: 77–81); the transnational structure is difficult to coordinate as, in reality, managers in different countries are liable to pursue their own objectives, with the result that the strategy of an international organisation that is not strongly hierarchical is more likely to be the result of continual negotiation rather than of rational planning. In other words, it is difficult for the senior executives of an organisation to create a rational network structure – how the network operates in reality will be affected by the range of managerial actors within the international organisation. Finally, Bartlett and Ghoshal largely ignore the extent to which MNC structures and strategies are affected by both the countries they originate from and the countries they operate in. Such effects will be examined in a later section of this chapter.

In summary, Prahalad and Doz provided an effective and simple model for appreciating the two competing pressures – integration and responsiveness – and their impact on MNC structures. However, their work under-emphasised the importance of global innovation and knowledge transfer. This is addressed to a greater extent by Bartlett and Ghoshal (1989), who offer a fourfold typology of MNC structures; some of the effects of positioning along these dimensions on HRM and the international transfer of knowledge and learning will be explored in the following sections. They argue that pressures on such organisations to combine local differentiation, global integration and worldwide innovation mean that the transnational model is increasingly the most appropriate model to follow. However, the evidence also suggests that international business models, such as those of Bartlett and Ghoshal, under-estimate the role of organisational politics and institutional context in determining how MNCs operate (Edwards and Rees, 2006; Tregaskis *et al.,* 2010; Ferner *et al.,* 2011). For this reason, many MNCs, even if they are seeking to achieve local differentiation, global integration and worldwide innovation, may not in reality operate according to the transnational model.

Configuration of the international HRM function

International HRM is defined as (Taylor *et al.,* 1996: 960):

> The set of distinct activities, functions and processes that are directed at attracting, developing and maintaining an MNC's human resources. It is thus the aggregate of the various HRM systems used to manage people in the MNC, both at home and overseas.

Here we consider the models of international HRM that have been put forward to explain how the HR function is configured, the activities and roles undertaken and the factors affecting these. It is interesting to consider how external and institutional factors are treated within these models, an issue that will be explored in more detail in the latter part of this chapter. Since the early 1990s, the international HRM literature has been dominated by models and typologies aimed at identifying the role and structure of international HRM functions aligned with organisational strategy. As a result of the attempt to 'explicitly link IHRM with the strategy of the MNC' (Taylor *et al.,* 1996: 960), this body of work is tightly tied to developments in multinational strategy–structure and is 'built on antecedents that are decades old' (p. 961). The HRM systems at the international and national levels are seen as the mechanisms through which competitive demands are potentially realised. The key theoretical work in the field of international HRM thus draws heavily on the strategy–structure work of the international management researchers, most notably Bartlett and Ghoshal (1989), Hedlund (1986) and Prahalad and Doz (1987). The questions that dominate this field include: how can such organisations most efficiently structure their geographically dispersed operations to meet both global and local competitive demands, and what is the nature of the control relationship between the parent and its subsidiaries? These questions in turn raise issues for international HRM in terms of what types of HRM activity should be centralised to maximise integration and meet globalisation strategic imperatives, and what should be decentralised to allow localisation of policy and practice, and to maximise local competitive advantage.

Explore

- Why might the parent company want to control its subsidiaries' activities?
- Do you think it is reasonable for the parent to control the subsidiaries' activities? Consider the case for support from the parent's perspective and from the subsidiary's perspective.

The five approaches reviewed here have each had a profound effect on the debates and theoretical development in this field. However, they each differ in the nature of the contribution they make. First, we will consider the Schuler *et al.* (1993) model, which was developed as an analytical framework pulling together various conceptual and empirical work in the field, providing researchers with a potential roadmap of the internal and external organisational factors influencing the issues, function, practices and impacts of international HRM. The importance of national context is recognised but not specified. Second, Taylor *et al.* (1996) focused on the conditions under which the parent was more likely to exercise control over its subsidiaries' activities. In particular, the model emphasised the resource dependencies that existed between the parent and its subsidiaries. This says little about national contextual issues, but is important as, unlike much previous writing in the field, it recognises that subsidiaries of multinationals have considerable ability to control their own action and influence the degree of parent control over them by using resources that the parent needs as a means of trading or negotiating. The third model shifts its focus from the international HR function to the influence of management perceptions on multinational strategy. Perlmutter (1969) identifies variation in the mindsets or ways of thinking about the international environment, which he argues can affect the international nature of the organisation's management processes. This model has had a profound effect on international HRM debates, as it underpins much of the theorising on the role of corporate HR functions in multinationals (e.g. Schuler *et al.*, 1993). The fourth and fifth models, by Adler and Ghadar (1990) and Milliman and Von Glinow (1990), respectively, are models of organisational change. They focus more on the relative influence of host and home country factors in shaping the role of the international HR function and, in particular, the role of expatriate managers in enabling international strategy. Both models adopt a similar perspective in terms of seeing the multinational progress through various stages of internationalisation, with each stage bringing into focus the importance of home and host country priorities. Here we see the potential for overlap between much of the comparative work and international HR theory; however, as will be illustrated, the discussion of home and host contextual issues is scant.

Schuler, Dowling and De Cieri (1993): integrative framework of international HRM

The Schuler *et al.* (1993) integrative framework of international HRM was, in essence, a conceptual framework that attempted to map HRM activity to the varying strategic requirements for integration and local responsiveness which define MNC strategy (Figure 17.2). Because of this, it is extremely comprehensive in terms of the breadth of issues addressed, although this is at the expense of depth in the explanation of these issues. This framework was built upon the work of strategic HRM theorists researching HRM in domestic companies (Lengnick-Hall and Lengnick-Hall, 1988; Boam and Sparrow, 1992; Schuler, 1992; Wright and McMahan, 1992). As such, Schuler *et al.* (1993: 422) define strategic international HRM (SIHRM) as:

Figure 17.2 Integrative framework of strategic international HRM (SIHRM) in multinational enterprises

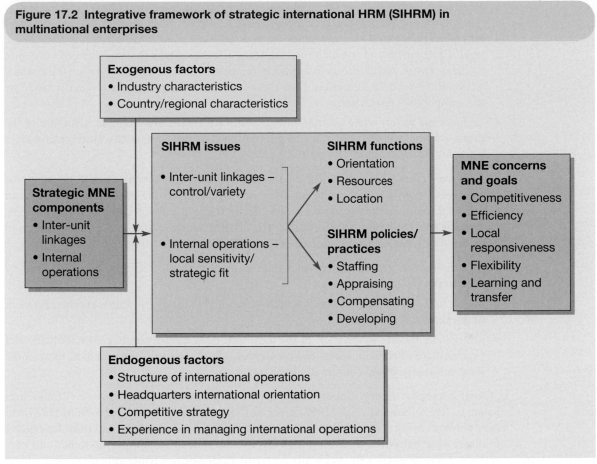

Source: Schuler *et al.* (1993: 423).

Human resource management issues, functions, policies and practices that result from the strategic activities of multinational enterprises and that impact the international concerns and goals of those enterprises.

The overlap between the study of domestic and international HRM is discussed explicitly by Taylor *et al.* (1996: 960):

Strategic Human Resource Management (SHRM) . . . is used to explicitly link with the strategic management processes of the organisation and to emphasise coordination or congruence among various human resource management practices. Thus, SIHRM is used to explicitly link IHRM with the strategy of the MNC.

This integrative framework of SIHRM identifies a series of strategic multinational enterprise (MNE) components, endogenous factors and exogenous factors that shape the issues, policy, practices and functions of HRM in international organisations. These determinants are explained briefly here:

● *Strategic MNE components* include inter-unit linkages and internal operations. Inter-unit linkage is concerned with the need to differentiate or integrate several operations which are geographically dispersed (Prahalad and Doz, 1987; Ghoshal and Bartlett, 1998). Internal operations refer to how each unit operates within its local environment. The restrictions of national institutional or legislative frameworks are recognised, along with the cultural diversity in attitudes towards work, management, authority and so forth (Hofstede, 1980; Laurent, 1983; Schein, 1984).

- *Exogenous factors* relate to issues external to the organisation, e.g. industry characteristics (such as type of business and technology available, nature of competitors, degree of change) and country/regional characteristics (such as political conditions, economic conditions, legal requirements and socio-cultural context). They also argue that an extended version of this framework would include issues such as industry maturity, history, national industrial policy and level of unionisation. Here there is a clear overlap with the issues discussed by the comparative researchers.

- *Endogenous factors* relate to internal organisational issues. For example, structure of the organisation, experience or stage of internationalisation, competitive strategy and HQ's international orientation.

Essentially, these three aspects of the framework bring together the work of international management theorists and argue for their impingement on the management of human resources throughout the organisation. Specifically, they argue that the strategic components, exogenous and endogenous factors affect the SIHRM function and associated policies and practices. The function can be affected in terms of:

- *its orientation,* i.e. the extent to which control of local activities is centralised or decentralised;

- *the amount of financial and time resources* committed to the development and management of international managers;

- *where activities are located,* i.e. in the local unit or at the corporate centre. Policies and practices are affected in terms of how they are developed and implemented to promote local autonomy, global coordination and integration.

Using agency theory (Jones, 1984) and resource dependency theory (Pfeffer and Salancik, 1978), Schuler *et al.* (1993) propose that an organisation's approach to HRM will vary between using a high level of parent country nationals and normative control measures to direct local behaviour and using high levels of local or third-country nationals and normative control measures to enable the centre to guide policies while still allowing for local adaptation. HR philosophy will play a key role in providing local sites with general statements to guide their practices so they are in tune with the corporate approach but locally sensitive. There is also a need for local HR policy to fit with corporate policy if personnel are to be able to be selected, transferred and developed as an organisational resource as opposed to a subsidiary resource. As such, they argue that in order for MNCs to be flexible and adaptable to local circumstances, to transfer learning and to retain strategic integration, HR practices need to match strategic and cultural demands at the local level. A *modus operandi* needs to be developed to enable HR practices to fit changing circumstances, while global HR policies need to be developed to be flexible enough to be applied to local HR practice. This perspective, therefore, focuses not only on HR policies and practices for the management of international managers but also on HR policies and practices for the management of local employees.

As indicated earlier, the role of national institutional factors is incorporated within the framework. Specifically, they argue that uncertain political environments and high economic risk demand greater monitoring and control from the parent, while high levels of heterogeneity, and complexity in legislative conditions affecting labour relations are likely to lead to the greater utilisation of local employees, rather than expatriates, in senior management positions at the subsidiary level. They also recognise that cultural diversity will demand greater attention by HR professionals in contexts where there is a business demand for integration and coordination. Thus, the effects of the national institutional context are recognised in terms of the degree of control or autonomy given to the subsidiary by the parent and in terms of the centrality of expatriates.

The relationship between organisational structures and SIHRM policy and practice is discussed in relation to four organisational strategy–structure configurations, namely, the international divisional structure, the multinational structure, the global and the transnational. Schuler *et al.* (1993: 446) state that:

> Different structures of international operations create different requirements for autonomy, localisation and co-ordination, thus affecting the nature of and extent of SIHRM policies and practices; and the structures of the international operations of the MNE will impact the need for the units to develop mechanisms to respond to local conditions and to develop a flexible capability.

Given this, Schuler *et al.* propose that international divisional structures result in a SIHRM orientation that focuses on a single issue, namely the selection of senior managers to head up local operations. The multinational structure focuses on selecting managers from anywhere in the company that can run local operations autonomously and with sensitivity to local conditions. The global structure requires a SIHRM orientation that selects managers who can operate under centralised control conditions. The transnational structure requires selecting and developing managers that can balance both local and global perspectives. Here again we see that the focus of the model is on explaining and matching the internal HR resources, via recruitment, selection or development, to meet the strategic needs of the organisations.

Schuler *et al.* (1993: 451) conclude that SIHRM is concerned with 'developing a fit between exogenous and endogenous factors and balancing the competing demands of global versus local requirements as well as the needs of coordination, control and autonomy'.

While the model is comprehensive, it has been criticised for failing to explain the micro-political processes that underpin parent–subsidiary relations (Quintanilla, 1999) and for being overly descriptive (Holden, 2001). In addition, while the model alludes to the impact of international HRM on both the international and local workforces, in reality the discussion tends to focus on management employees only (Ferner, 1994).

Explore

- Using Schuler *et al.*'s framework of SIHRM, consider the role of the HRM function at the headquarter and the subsidiary level.
- In what ways might they differ in terms of the scope of their activities, the types of employees they support and the competencies of the HR professionals.
- Would you expect the subsidiary level HRM function to be a replica of the HQ HRM function?

Suggested reading: Schuler *et al.* (1993).

Taylor, Beechler and Napier (1996): exportive, integrative and adaptive model

Taylor *et al.* (1996) apply the resource-based theory of the firm to explain and predict why international organisations adopt different forms of SIHRM. Resource-based theory of the firm (Barney, 1991) applied to HR issues (Lado and Wilson, 1994) argues that HR can facilitate strategic goals by developing competencies within the organisation that are valuable, rare, hard to imitate and non-substitutable. Competencies are:

- *valuable* – if they are differentiated and provide the company with something that they lack;
- *rare* – if they are scarce or in short supply;
- *hard to imitate* – where, for example, they are embedded within the firm's culture or history and are thus based on collective values;
- *non-substitutable* – where they cannot easily be replaced through recruitment, e.g. in the case of tacit knowledge.

Applying this perspective, Taylor *et al.* suggested that the multinational could leverage resources at the national, firm and subsidiary levels, which could contribute to competitive advantage. Some of these resources would be context-specific while others were context-generalisable. This is illustrated by the exportative, integrative and adoptive SIHRM orientations towards corporate, subsidiary and employee group level HR issues, policies and practices. The concepts of these three SIHRM forms are based on previous work in international management and SIHRM (Perlmutter, 1969; Hedlund, 1986; Rosenzweig and Singh, 1991; Rosenzweig and Nohria, 1994). Each of these three orientations is explained here:

- *Adaptive*. HRM reflects subsidiary HRM systems designed to match the local environment. Differentiation is emphasised and HRM is concerned with the appointment of local senior managers but with little transfer of HRM philosophies, policies or practices from the parent to subsidiary or between subsidiaries. This approach focuses on attending to local differentiation needs and is polycentric in nature.

- *Exportive*. HRM focuses on replication of parent HR systems in subsidiaries. Integration is a key priority and all HRM functions are affected, not just the international 'cadre' (managers). This approach focuses on maximising global integration and is ethnocentric in nature.

- *Integrative*. HRM is based on the notion of taking the best HRM systems from anywhere in the company and allowing for both global integration and local differentiation and is geocentric in nature.

At the level of the subsidiary, the SIHRM orientation determines the level of transfer of parent HRM systems, which is based on the resource–dependency relationship between the parent and subsidiary. For example, exportive HRM leads to high control by the parent which promotes a high level of transfer of its HRM systems to achieve global integration. Under these conditions, the subsidiary is highly dependent on the parent for HR systems and processes to enable integration. By contrast, the adaptive HRM orientation demands little control and transfer of practices by the parent, as differentiation is the priority. Under these conditions, resource dependency by both the parent and subsidiary is low. In the middle we have the integrative orientation which demands a balance between the transfer of some systems while maintaining the flexibility in the system to allow the subsidiary to adapt to the local context. Under these conditions, there is a parent–subsidiary interdependency. Finally, from the resource-dependence perspective they argue that parent control and standardisation of parent and subsidiary practice will be greater in those areas affecting employees 'most critical to the MNC's performance' (Taylor *et al.*, 1996: 978).

Taylor *et al.* also recognise that there are a number of factors that are likely to constrain the degree of parent control over subsidiary behaviour, namely method of subsidiary establishment, cultural and legal distance of host country from the parent or home country of the multinational. With respect to the first of these points, the evidence suggests that subsidiaries that have been acquired have less in common with their parent HR systems than those that are greenfield sites, although this pattern may change over time. Equally, the greater the dissimilarity between the parent company's national culture and legal context, the less commonality there is between the parent' and the subsidiary's HR systems. This would follow from many of the institutional arguments outlined earlier in the book (see Chapter 15).

Their work raises a number of implications. First, unlike much of the previous work, Taylor *et al.* (1996) are more explicit about the impact of SIHRM on different occupational groups. They recognise that not all employees provide the same level of value to the company or the same level of critical resources. Traditionally, broad distinctions have been made between white-collar and blue-collar workers. However, there is a need to refine this further by looking at other occupational groups that may be critical to competitive advantage, such as research staff or product designers. Secondly, their work raises a key question about the generalisability of HR practice beyond the context in which it was developed. What aspects of HRM practice are generalisable? Why? Finally, their model lacks specificity with regard to what is transferred and how.

Explore

Many multinationals now operate not only in many countries, but also across very distinct regions of the world. This often exposes the parent firm to very different or institutionally distant socio-legal and cultural contexts. In addition, much international expansion occurs through mergers and acquisitions, which can often involve very distinct organisational cultures being brought together.

● Given the diversity in the operating context, to what extent are the three approaches outlined by Taylor *et al.* (1996) – adaptive, exportive and integrative – likely to be viable strategies?

Suggested reading: Taylor *et al.* (1996).

Perlmutter (1969): mindsets

Perlmutter (1969) is widely recognised as one of the first theorists to propose a network-based model of how international companies organise globally. Perlmutter's classification has been applied primarily in the international HRM literature rather than the international business field, from where it originated. Kobrin (1994) explains that Perlmutter's adoption by the international HRM theorists is largely because the classification is defined in terms of HRM issues (e.g. training, recruiting, selecting people and resources). Perlmutter initially defined three organisational types based on senior management's cognitions or mindsets: the ethnocentric, polycentric and geocentric organisation. Later he defined a fourth mindset, namely the regiocentric. He argues that senior management mindsets reflect the extent to which home, host, global or regional values are perceived as important and in turn influence the international nature of management processes used in the company. These mindsets have been adopted by many in the international HRM field as a way of classifying different HRM approaches, for example:

● *The ethnocentric mindset* reflects a focus on home country values and ways of operating. As a consequence, key positions in subsidiaries are filled by parent country nationals (i.e. expatriates). This gives the parent a high degree of direct control over the subsidiary's operations.

● *The polycentric mindset* focuses on host country values and ways of operating. As a result, key positions in the subsidiary are more likely to be filled by local employees and the parent company is less interested in controlling and homogenising the organisational culture.

● *The geocentric mindset* focuses on global values and ways of operating. These global values are not nationally specific but instead transcend national boundaries and become almost acultural. This approach looks to use the best people for the job, selecting from all over the global organisation.

● *The regiocentric mindset* focuses on regional values and ways of operating. As a result, the organisation is usually structured along regional geographical lines (e.g. Europe, America and the Asia/Pacific Rim) and employees move around within these regions. This approach allows some degree of integration, but recognises regional diversity.

Schuler *et al.* (1993) incorporate Perlmutter's ideas into their framework, arguing that these attitudes underpin a multinational's SIHRM orientation in terms of autonomy and standardisation of local HR practice (e.g. staffing, appraisal, compensation and training). The ethnocentric mindset promotes control and centralisation of HR activity, the polycentric mindset is aligned with local decentralisation, and the geocentric mindset does not develop HR activity on the basis of nationality. We also saw how these mindsets were associated with Taylor *et al.*'s (1996) integrative, adaptive and exportive orientations. While these relationships are somewhat scant in their detail, they allude to the widening scope of the role of a corporate SIHRM function, as organisational structures become more complex and network-like rather than hierarchical in nature. One of the primary problems with Perlmutter's approach is that it provides little explanation of how or why the organisation may move from one type of mindset orientation to another.

Explore

Perlmutter's global mindsets have been linked to international organisational forms.

- Taking each mindset in turn – ethnocentric, polycentric, geocentric and regiocentric – identify the type of international organisational form with which it is most likely to be associated.
- Can you think of any examples of firms you are familiar with that are likely to adopt any of the mindsets identified by Perlmutter?

Adler and Ghadar (1990) and Milliman and Von Glinow (1990): organisational change models

Two models have been put forward that are based on organisational change models: the product life cycle model of Adler and Ghadar (1990) and the organisational life cycle model of Milliman and Von Glinow (1990). These models have been designed to explain how and why the international HRM orientation of a multinational change over time in line with changes in its corporate strategy. Both approaches also recognise the variable importance of the parent or home country context and the host country context throughout each stage. In doing so, they take a largely cultural approach.

The Adler and Ghadar (1990) model is based on the product life cycle during internationalisation, first observed and described by Vernon (1966), and is a stage model of organisational change. In Adler and Ghadar's model, they describe how the role of culture changes in salience and how HRM activities are modified at each stage in response to product strategic requirements and cultural requirements. These phases are described briefly here (see also Table 17.2):

- *Phase I – Domestic.* Here the focus is on the home market. The products/services are unique, they have not been available before, and therefore the price is high relative to cost and competition is minimal. As the products are unique, there is no need for cultural sensitivity and, if they are exported, they are in a significantly strong position not to need adaptation. Indeed exportation of the product/service is based on the premise that 'foreigners' want the product/service unadapted. The HR needs are therefore not that demanding in international terms, i.e. expatriate assignments, internal business trips and cross-cultural training are not warranted for the export market. The international work is restricted to product- or project-specific technical competence (Mendenhall *et al.*, 1989). As domestic sales tend to dominate profits, international aspects of management are not given to the best people or seen as a valuable career move. International organisational development is not seen as relevant.

- *Phase II – International.* Here competition increases and international markets become more important for profit. There is a shift in focus from product development (R&D) to manufacturing and plants are set up locally and divisional structures emerge. Cultural sensitivity becomes critical to effective corporate strategies. However, decision-making and control tend to remain with the parent. HR performs a vital role in attaining control of local operations. Home country personnel are used to transfer technology and management systems overseas where replication, rather than innovation, is the prime objective. Training in cultural sensitivity and adaptability is key at this stage.

- *Phase III –Multinational.* Here the product/service reaches maturity, competition is intense and the price has fallen. Coordination of resources becomes a vital tool in the reduction of costs. The role of culture becomes less important as the issue of reducing costs takes central

Table 17.2 Globalisation and HRM

	Phase I – Domestic	Phase II – International	Phase III – Multinational	Phase IV – Global
Primary orientation	Product or service	Market	Price	Strategy
Strategy	Domestic	Multi-domestic	Multinational	Global
Worldwide strategy	Allow foreign clients to buy product/service	Increase market internationally, transfer technology abroad	Source, produce and market internationally	Gain global strategic competitive advantage
Staffing expatriates	None (few)	Many	Some	Many
Why sent	Junket	To sell control or transfer technology	Control	Coordination and integration
Whom sent		'OK' performers, salespeople	Very good performers	High-potential managers and top executives
Purpose	Reward	Project 'to get job done'	Project and career development	Career and organisational development
Career impact	Negative	Bad for domestic career	Important for global career	Essential for executive suite
Professional re-entry	Somewhat difficult	Extremely difficult	Less difficult	Professionally easy
Training and development	None	Limited	Longer	Continuous throughout career
For whom	No one	Expatriates	Expatriates	Managers
Performance appraisal	Corporate bottom line	Subsidiary bottom line	Corporate bottom line	Strategic positioning
Motivation assumption	Money motivates	Money and adventure	Challenge and opportunity	Challenge, opportunity, advancement
Rewarding	Extra money to compensate for foreign hardship		Less generous, global packages	
Career 'fast track'	Domestic	Domestic	Token international	Global
Executive passport	Home country	Home country	Home country, token foreigners	Multinational
Necessary skills	Technical and managerial	Plus cultural adaption	Plus recognising cultural differences	Plus cross-cultural interaction, influence and synergy

Source: Adler and Ghadar (1990).

position. As such, the best people are usually chosen for international posts to increase profits and control costs. The management assumption at this phase is that organisational culture is more important than national culture, and therefore sensitivity to local cultures is seen to be less important and recruitment of international managers tends to be from those familiar with the parent culture.

- *Phase IV – Global.* The three prior phases were based on hierarchical structures. This phase is based on the assumption that the organisation will need to operate in all three phases simultaneously and therefore build 'complex networks of joint ventures, wholly owned subsidiaries and organisational and project defined alliances' (Adler and Ghadar, 1990: 240). Under such conditions, the role of culture comes again to the fore. These organisations operate at a strategic level to combine responsive design and delivery quickly and cheaply. This negates the development of global R&D, production and marketing and therefore requires the management of culture and relationships external to the organisation. Success is based on international managers being able to communicate effectively in a culturally diverse environment. The delineation between expatriate and local managers disappears and the organisation needs to manage the dual demands of integration and local responsiveness (Doz and Prahalad, 1986).

Explore

Expatriates are identified as having a key role to play in each of the phases of internationalisation.

- How might the role and the skills/competencies of the expatriate change depending on the phase of internationalisation of the firm?
- How might the global mindset of the expatriate change at each phase? Is it likely to influence their performance in any way?

	Phase I	Phase II	Phase III	Phase IV
Expatriates	• Expatriates are from the parent company			
	• Focus on the transfer of technical competence to overseas operations; otherwise input is limited			

Suggested reading: Adler and Ghadar (1990).

However, the Adler and Ghadar (1990) model is criticised for its emphasis on the role of the expatriate manager and management expertise, with little reference to other employee groups. Milliman and Von Glinow (1990) also argue that as it focuses on a product life cycle it is too narrow. International organisations often have multiple products and the stage of the cycle may vary across the strategic business units (SBUs), changing the parent–SBU relationship. Therefore, in response, Milliman and Von Glinow (1990) apply the organisational life cycle (OLC) approach to provide a more general framework to understanding SIHRM at the parent and subsidiary level. This model was further refined in the paper by Milliman *et al.* (1991). The OLC approach is based on the premise that HRM responses will predictably vary in line with stages of organisational development. Milliman and Von Glinow's (1990) work highlights the importance of recognising the interrelationships between the parent and subsidiary level in defining the nature of international HRM. They note that 'the degree to which the corporate business and human resource strategies affect the SBU's strategic choices and practices depends on a number of fundamental characteristics of the MNC, such as its organisational culture, management style and control systems' (p. 28).

The Milliman and Von Glinow (1990) model identifies four international HRM objectives:

- *Timing* – refers to whether the organisation takes a short-term or long-term perspective in its business and international HRM strategy. The former requires quick responses, while the latter allows a longer period for implementation, which can mean longer international assignments and commitment to overseas operations.

- *Cost* – refers to whether the organisation needs to focus on lowering costs or can focus on longer-term development issues in its overseas operations and the career paths of its expatriate managers.
- *Integration* – relates to the use of expatriate managers in implementing informal control systems.
- *Differentiation* – refers to the development of a network of home and host country managers to facilitate communication and control between the parent and subsidiary.

These four objectives change over four OLC stages, leading to a different pattern of international HRM, as follows:

- *Stage 1.* As the firm starts out, most of the international HRM is conducted on an *ad hoc* basis and international assignments focus on technical work skills, with little emphasis on cultural training. The need for integration or differentiation is minimal.
- *Stage 2.* The number and extent of commitment in overseas operation increase. Short-term savings remain a priority and the need of integration is minimal. However, for successive growth of the overseas markets, greater knowledge of the local environment is needed. Thus expatriate training in cultural sensitivity and languages becomes more important.
- *Stage 3.* As the business becomes well established, the organisation can take a longer-term perspective and integration becomes key, particularly for controlling costs. Home country expatriates provide control along with the transfer of home HRM systems and organisational culture. But as cultural sensitivity is less important, training in this area for expatriates diminishes and career development for this group is not so long-term. Sophisticated control systems, such as socialisation, mentoring and succession planning, are vital for promoting a unified organisational culture and integration.
- *Stage 4.* The demands for both integration and differentiation are evident. In response, organisations need to invest in training and development to enhance the flexibility of the organisation to meet these demands. They also need to evolve a 'multicentric cultural perspective' (Milliman and Von Glinow, 1990: 32), which ensures awareness of the national cultures and subcultures at the subsidiary level.

The Milliman and Von Glinow (1990) model parallels closely the stages models proposed by Adler and Ghadar (1990). Both models provide prescriptions of international HRM types. While stages 1–3 are themselves supported by empirical work, the associated international HRM forms are theoretically extrapolated. Stage 4, like the work of the international management theorists, is largely a theoretical concept. Mayrhofer and Brewster (1996) argue that, in practice, MNCs, irrespective of their need for integration or diversity, adopt an ethnocentric approach to international HRM, with many relying heavily on the use of expatriate managers to control overseas operations. Another problem with the stages model is that it has become less relevant as MNCs adopt both domestic and international markets simultaneously (Taylor and Beechler, 1993), and with acquisitions, mergers and demergers there is less evidence that multinationals have to pass through each of these phases in order to internationalise.

In this part we have looked at the organisational processes, policies and practices adopted by MNCs to address their international strategic goals. This has considered the question of the role of the international HR function, how it is organised and the activities undertaken. Furthermore, complex relationships between the internal configuration of organisational strategies and structures have been considered in terms of how these meet variable external influences. The resource-dependent nature of parent–subsidiary relations as a mechanism of influence highlighted the multiple levels at which international HRM operates, and its differential impact on home and host country employees.

Knowledge and the transfer of HR policy and practice in international organisations

The models outlined in the preceding section emphasise the importance of integrating HRM and creating global HRM practices that transcend national boundaries. This presupposes that HR knowledge can be easily packaged and transferred across multinational units and across national borders. A survey conducted by Brewster *et al.* (2002) for the CIPD found that 45 per cent of organisations in their study identified knowledge management as a central plank of their international HRM strategy. In this section, we consider some of the difficulties associated with knowledge transfer and the role of international HR networks and expatriates in facilitating the transfer of HR policy and practice.

The nature of knowledge

Knowledge is most frequently defined in terms of its explicit and tacit qualities (Nonaka and Takeuchi, 1995). This classification is based on Polanyi's (1962) expression of knowledge as having two complementary elements: the tacit, which cannot be articulated, and the explicit, which can be articulated. Most of our knowledge is tacit in nature, particularly when we think of operational skills or know-how (Lam, 2000). This point is illustrated by Athanssiou and Nigh (2000: 474), who suggest that while an individual may know how to ride a bike, they may not be able to explain how this is possible in relation to the laws of physics; thus, often, 'one knows more than one can tell'. By contrast, explicit knowledge, because it can be articulated, can be codified, which makes it easier to transfer (Lam, 2000).

In terms of the transfer of knowledge, it is argued that the transfer of tacit and explicit knowledge requires different mechanisms. While the latter can be accumulated or stored at a central location or 'repositories' (Argote and Ingram, 2000), the former is dependent on close interaction. Tacit knowledge is personal and not subject-independent. As such, it is scattered throughout an organisation. Its transfer is highly dependent on the transferor's 'deeper awareness of the communicable details' (Athanassiou and Nigh, 2000: 474) and the transferee's ability to understand what is being communicated. Developing a shared understanding, or what Polanyi (1966: 61) refers to as the 'same kind of indwelling', is fundamental to the effective transfer of tacit knowledge. Such shared understandings can best be generated through close interaction. There is a significant body of evidence that suggests that developing a common understanding of the tacit dimension of knowledge is best achieved via face-to-face personal communications or strong social interaction (Nohria and Eccles, 1992).

Both modes of knowledge also demand differing methods for acquisition and accumulation purposes (Lam, 2000). It is argued that explicit knowledge can be generated through reasoning and deduction, and can be acquired from formal learning mechanisms such as reading, training and educational programmes. In contrast, tacit knowledge is dependent on practical context-specific experience. Thus, in organisations, tacit knowledge is acquired through personal experiences of different environments and face-to-face communications, and close interactions are critical for the diffusion of this knowledge.

In sum, the tacit or explicit nature of knowledge requires alternative mechanisms for its effective transfer, accumulation and generation. Because explicit knowledge can be codified, it becomes a public as opposed to an individual or private possession. In so doing, this makes it easier to copy or replicate. As a result, organisations are particularly interested in harnessing tacit knowledge for competitive purposes, which is by its nature much more difficult for competitors to replicate. However, the context-specific nature of tacit knowledge and its non-articulation places emphasis on personal interaction as a means of transferring and generating tacit knowledge. It is argued that the HR function is a source of a considerable degree of tacit HR knowledge (Lado and Wilson, 1994; Huselid, 1995).

The role of the social context in generating and transferring HR knowledge

Many of the models of international HRM discussed previously imply that explicit HR knowledge is contained within the policies and practices of the company, but clearly overlook *how* this knowledge is transferred. Building on the earlier debates, this section considers the importance of the social context for the generation and transfer of HR knowledge.

Taylor (2006) argues that HR functions play an important role in building social capital as a means of developing and transferring HR policies to achieve strategic integration. Social capital is defined as 'an asset embedded in relationships, communities, networks or societies' (Leana and van Buren, 1999: 539). It potentially provides a means through which tacit knowledge can be transferred because it creates a conducive social or relational context (Tregaskis *et al.*, 2005). Nahapiet and Ghoshal (1998) identified three dimensions of social capital, underpinning knowledge creation and diffusion in organisations: structural, cognitive and social dimensions (Box 17.1). This work emphasises the importance of personal interaction in networks for harnessing tacit knowledge.

Box 17.1 Dimensions of social capital

Structural dimension of social capital

This refers to the structure of the network, the nature of the ties in terms of being weak or strong, and how they are combined to transfer knowledge and to combine knowledge. Evidence suggests that weak ties facilitate the search for information; however, they can hinder the transfer of knowledge, particularly tacit knowledge. When the network is dealing with tacit knowledge, strong ties have been found to be more effective (Hansen, 1999). The intensity of ties, their density, connectivity and hierarchy all influence the level of contact among network members and the ease with which information can be exchanged. The structural elements are also important in terms of the opportunity they offer to exchange knowledge more quickly than would be the case in the absence of such a network, and in facilitating flows of knowledge, providing network members with opportunities to combine and exchange knowledge that would not arise if the network did not exist.

Cognitive dimension of social capital

This refers to the resources that foster the shared meanings and understanding among network members, such as common codes and language or shared narratives that represent the way things are done. This cognitive dimension provides a shared context between group members that facilitates more effectively and efficiently the sharing of tacit knowledge and the potential to combine this knowledge in new and novel ways (Gulati *et al.*, 2000).

A number of studies have found that network members that have worked together longer tend to work better together because they have developed shared routines and understandings that enable them to leverage the distinctiveness of group members for organisational purposes (Bantel and Jackson, 1989; Fisher and Pollock, 2004).

Relational dimension of social capital

This refers to the nature of the personal relationships that exist between network members in terms of, for example, the degree of trust, identification with others, a sense of obligation to others, and the norms or expectations within the group regarding cooperation. These elements can affect access to knowledge and the motivation to engage in knowledge exchange and combination activities.

Source: Tregaskis *et al.* (2005: 10).

Implications for the generation and transfer of HR knowledge

The knowledge and social capital literature suggests that the generation and transfer of knowledge is socially embedded. As such, one of the key mechanisms for the generation and diffusion of HR knowledge is the network. There has been an increasing body of work examining the role of transnational teams or networks in multinationals in knowledge creation and diffusion (Athanassiou and Nigh, 2000). However, fewer studies have looked at networks involved in developing HR-related knowledge in international organisations. One of the few studies to explore this issue in detail was conducted by Tregaskis *et al.* (2005), who examined the role of international HR networks in 13 multinational organisations. This research identified companies that had explicitly adopted formal international HR networks comprising HQ-level (e.g. parent or regional) HR directors and senior subsidiary-level HR managers. The case study evidence revealed that these forums had seven primary functions:

- global policy development;
- global HR policy implementation;
- best practice creation and sharing;
- exploitation of the distributed HR expertise;
- creating buy-in to policy initiatives;
- information exchange;
- socialisation of the HR community.

These functions reflected the organisation's desire to achieve integration in certain areas of HR activity, such as performance management, succession planning, talent spotting and expatriate careers. They also reflected the ambition by some of the companies to generate new global HR knowledge by drawing together expertise and tacit knowledge of how HR issues operated in divergent national contexts. There was also evidence of two alternative decision-making processes (i.e. top-down vs collaborative) at play in the performance of these functions. The collaborative decision-making process embraced national variation as part of the process towards integration. In contrast, the top-down decision-making process tended to ignore or sideline national variation. The implication for the generation of new HR knowledge was stark. In the collaborative networks, there was more opportunity for tacit knowledge to be exchanged among network members that had spent considerable time building the structural, relational and cognitive dimensions of the network. This tacit knowledge was used to create new global policies based, to a greater extent, on the joint experiences of the network members. The top-down model relied more heavily on HR knowledge that was generated at the centre, then codified and transferred through extensive implementation measures.

The value of networks for the rapid transfer of knowledge has also been explored by Brown and Duguid (1991) through what they refer to as 'communities of practice' (COP). Unlike the formal networks examined in the research by Tregaskis *et al.*, a COP may be informal in nature. Desouza (2003: 29) defines a COP as 'a group of people who have common tasks, interact and share knowledge with each other, either formally or informally'. These communities have a tacit and shared understanding of the group's identity and generate knowledge that is unique because the membership and the tacit knowledge of its membership are unique. Sparrow *et al.* (2004: 97) argue that the types of structures needed to support such communities include 'team processes for learning, reflection and appreciative enquiry, and co-enquiry, as opposed to simple expert–student relationships (headquarter-country operation)'. This suggests the generation of global HR practices within international HR communities of practice would require collaborative relations across subsidiary HR functions and between headquarters and subsidiary-level HR functions. It also challenges the nature of the parent–subsidiary control relationship that underpins many of the models explaining the configuration of the international HRM function.

Social capital is increasingly being recognised by organisations and individuals as having an important impact on the quality of performance outcomes at multiple levels, e.g. individual, team, department, organisational. However, creating and fostering social capital in practice are fraught with difficulty.

- Consider some of the factors that are likely to facilitate or hinder the development of social capital in the workplace.

Another significant mechanism for the generation and transfer of international HR knowledge is the expatriate manager. The role of the expatriate manager in knowledge diffusion in transnational organisations was recognised by Bartlett and Ghoshal (1995). However, work in this area is generally limited (but see Bonache and Brewster, 2001; Cerdin, 2003). Kostova and Roth (2003) suggest that social capital is accumulated by international managers because of their boundary-spanning roles. These roles refer to management roles that cross networks, functional or geographical boundaries (Thomas, 1994; Aldrich and Herker, 1977). These individuals often act as the lynchpin between horizontal or vertical structures within the multinational network (Thomas, 1994; Au and Fukuda, 2002; Beechler *et al.*, 2004; Brannen and Thomas, 2010). As such, international managers can act to help diffuse HR practices across these boundaries. But equally, there is a need for the HR function to consider utilising international HR professionals in boundary-spanning roles to facilitate the diffusion and generation of tacit HR knowledge (Tregaskis *et al.*, 2005).

This section has considered how HR knowledge is generated and transferred across the international organisation. It is suggested that the tacit nature of knowledge and its context-specificity demands organisational structures and processes that enable a social context for the generation and transfer of knowledge. In terms of the international HR function, this raises possibilities for the role of formal networks, communities of practice and boundary-spanning international HR roles. These are all issues relevant to the future direction of international HR research.

Country effects

This section considers influences on the international HRM policies and practices of MNCs that are related to the country from which they originate, and the foreign countries in which they operate. As we will see, there is evidence that countries of ownership, and of subsidiary operation, have effects both on processes of international learning within MNCs and on specific HRM practices, such as the management of pay or collective industrial relations.

It should be noted that some writers on international management play down the importance of such influences, or even, in some cases, virtually deny their existence. In particular, writers on globalisation have sometimes made the claim that globalising trends in the world economy militate against cross-national differences in management in general, driving a convergence of capitalisms generally towards a single model, heavily influenced by the American model. At the extreme, the work of authors such as Kenneth Ohmae (1991) suggested a 'borderless world', or 'interlinked economy' in which the globalisation of production chains, product markets, corporate structures and financial flows makes national boundaries and the nation-state largely irrelevant. Following a similar logic, Reich (1991: 3) speculated about a future with 'no national products or technologies, no national corporations, no national industries'.

Against this, however, arguments are frequently made that the vast majority of MNCs retain a national identity. For example, the capital on which MNCs depend for investment remains predominantly based in the country of origin (Doremus *et al.*, 1998). Equally, in general, managerial control tends to be exerted by nationals of the original home country; for example,

Ruigrok and van Tulder (1995) found that 25 of the 30 largest American-owned MNCs had no foreign nationals on their boards of directors. Additionally, it has been argued that MNCs are often less 'transnational' than they may appear to be at first glance. Frequently, operations, particularly strategic functions such as research and development centres, remain disproportionately concentrated in the country of origin (Pauly and Reich, 1997; Hirst and Thompson, 1999).

Additionally, there are both economic and social reasons to expect that MNCs with their origins in different national systems of business and employment may operate in somewhat distinctive ways, with effects on the nature of HR policies in their subsidiary operations across the world. From an economic perspective, it is commonly argued that the ways in which firms choose to internationalise, as well as their use of specific management practices, is a result of their embeddedness in specifically national institutional contexts which coincide with the firms' country of origin (cf. Porter, 1990; Whitley, 1999; Lane, 2001; Morgan, 2001; Kristensen and Morgan, 2007). The basic argument here is that firms' competitive advantage is rooted in their home country business systems and that they will seek to replicate such advantages abroad. A good example of this can be found in the early development of the automobile industry. Faced with a lack of craft workers, but a plentiful supply of semi-skilled workers, and a large domestic market with relatively homogenous tastes due to (at the time) relatively small class distinctions compared with European countries, American firms such as Ford developed a mass production system which they later sought to internationalise. More recently, Japanese firms developed a competitive advantage in some areas of manufacturing, which can be related to elements of the Japanese business and employment systems such as the close links between companies within supply chains, enterprise unionism and employment security for core workers in large firms. This permitted the development of the employee involvement and quality management programmes necessary to achieve more flexible forms of mass production (see Chapter 15). Again, in many cases, Japanese companies abroad have sought to replicate (or provide equivalents for) some of these policies.

In the international HRM literature, then, the term 'country-of-origin effects' (Ferner, 1997), sometimes referred to as 'home country effects', means those elements of the behaviour of MNCs that can be traced back to the characteristics of the national business system from which the MNC originates. Country-of-origin business systems can influence HRM in many areas. For example, the preferred nature of industrial relations management may well be affected by senior executives' domestic experiences, affecting both how MNCs deal with trade unions in foreign subsidiaries, and policies in areas such as employee involvement and participation. Equally, the nature of training and education in the home country may affect managers' understanding of the appropriate competencies of workers and managers, and of work organisation. Employment-related policy may also be affected by business system effects outside the direct area of employment. For example, the nature of corporate finance in the country of origin may affect the extent to which senior executives adopt a short-termist 'shareholder value' mentality, which in turn may affect the extent to which they adopt a short-term or long-term approach to employment issues, with American or British firms perhaps, all other things being equal, being less willing to offer secure employment in subsidiaries than their Japanese counterparts, as managers in the latter group of firms have generally had less need to worry about short-term fluctuations in profitability (Whitley, 1999; Hall and Soskice, 2001).

Key Controversy

Ruidrok and Van Tulder argued in 1995 that the corporate boards of MNCs remained largely made up of personnel from the home country. But does this remain true today? Visit the websites of any five large MNCs and examine the details provided of members of their corporate boards. Would you say their senior executive personnel is 'globalised' or largely home country-based? What effects, if any, might this have on the way these firms think about management?

Evidence on country-of-origin effects

Research into the HR and industrial relations practices and policies of foreign firms in the UK has revealed a number of ways in which subsidiary policy is often influenced by firms' embeddedness in their country-of-origin business system. Here, we review evidence on the influence of such 'country-of-origin effects' in foreign-owned firms in the UK. We particularly use evidence from two research projects. The first, Almond and Ferner (2006), examined employment relations and HRM in the European subsidiaries of US MNCs, while the second, Edwards *et al.* (2007), was a representative survey of MNCs operating in the UK.

Almond and Ferner (2006) argued that the 'Americanness' of US MNCs affected the nature of their management of human resources in a number of ways. First, the management of the majority of the US MNCs is quite highly centralised (Ferner *et al.*, 2006a). In contradiction to predictions that MNCs are evolving into devolved networks (cf. Nohria and Ghoshal, 1997), centralised rule-setting from the US headquarters of firms remained commonplace. Most of the firms involved in the research pursued uniformity of HR policies across countries, and subsidiary managers had to give strong arguments to global HQ when they wished to deviate from 'global' policy, which, as we argue in the following, was often fairly 'American' in nature. Control was achieved by measuring outcomes (such as the achievement of diversity targets, number of employees in each grade) at the HQ, rather than by high numbers of expatriate managers. This pattern of centralisation across international operations is an extension of the way American firms developed formalised, bureaucratic control systems in order to coordinate their varied activities across the USA, as analysed by Chandler (1976) and confirmed for the UK operations of US MNCs by Edwards *et al.* (2007). Recently, the increased need for business units within US MNCs to be financially accountable in the short term, due to pressures for 'shareholder value' (O'Sullivan, 2000), has probably led to a tightening of central control in some US MNCs.

Given this pattern of centralisation, it is perhaps unsurprising that, for nearly all of the organisations studied, there was a considerable amount of 'forward' policy transfer of HR policy (i.e transfer of US policy to foreign subsidiary operations), but relatively little evidence of 'reverse' transfer from subsidiaries to the USA (Edwards *et al.*, 2006). In this respect, most of the firms resembled Bartlett and Ghoshal's (1989) global, or international, forms more than the transnational form. Edwards *et al.* argue that this pattern of organisational learning in the area of HR is influenced by the fact that US management theories and policies emanate from a liberal business and employment system, where there are relatively few 'constraints' on management decision-making in the area of HR. This means that US managerial techniques are seen as relatively independent of the context in which they operate, when compared with HR policies developed in societies that are more actively regulated. For example, many German firms, and German subsidiaries of foreign MNCs, develop policies which allow them to develop high levels of functional flexibility, in response to their relative lack of freedom to compete on labour cost due to the nature of German collective bargaining, the need to consult with their workers through co-determination institutions, and the skills available to firms because of the nature of the co-determination system. However, such policies are difficult to export to countries such as the USA and the UK, which do not share these institutions, as the appropriate skills might not be so readily available, and the forms of cooperation between local workers and managers that are said to characterise large German firms might not be replicable in countries with substantially different industrial relations systems. Evidence from German MNCs suggests, for example, that they make relatively little attempt to 'export' elements of the German system of employment to their UK operations (Ferner and Varul, 2000; Edwards *et al.*, 2007).

With regard to specific HR practices, the first area of policy on which US MNCs often exhibit country-of-origin effects is that of collective industrial relations. It is well known that employers in the USA are, on average, more resistant to trade union organisation than their counterparts in other developed industrial democracies (Colling *et al.*, 2006) and that the legal supports for trade union organisation and collective bargaining in the USA are weak in comparison to those in other countries. Both these facts reflect a variety of historical factors in the pattern of industrialisation in the USA (for more details, see Colling, 2000), which are distinct to those in Europe.

There have long been large subsidiaries of US MNCs in the UK that have operated non-union, human relations-style policies (what would now be termed 'soft HRM'), even before the 1980s, when changes to the UK industrial relations climate made large non-union workplaces somewhat less unusual. The prototypical example here would be a firm such as IBM, which would historically offer relatively high pay and employment security to its workers, but would strongly resist efforts at trade union organisation. These firms were generally monopolistic firms in which the founding family retained substantial influence, under an ideology, often known as 'welfare capitalism' (Jacoby, 1997), that the firm, rather than trade unions or the state, should be responsible for the welfare of workers. Although changes to the American business system, and increased global competition, meant that firms from this group no longer offered 'jobs for life' well before the current economic crisis, there continue to be a substantial number of US MNCs that make the avoidance of trade unions abroad a central part of their HR strategy (see Ferner *et al.*, 2005; Colling *et al.*, 2006). In some cases, the American HQ of such firms makes explicit written guidelines, sometimes even published on corporate websites, that subsidiary managers should discourage trade union organisation. Additionally, as the above authors reflect, a number of firms that have not been able to avoid unionisation in the USA are anxious to do so abroad, perhaps due to their experience of highly conflictual industrial relations in their home country. Finally, of course, there are a number of 'low road' MNCs, such as McDonald's, which are strongly anti-union (cf. Royle, 2000). This is not to say, however, that all foreign subsidiaries of US firms operate non-union or anti-union policies. Some US MNCs, although seeking to avoid trade unions in the USA, make little effort to intervene in foreign industrial relations systems, providing that such systems do not impinge too heavily on their ability to pursue their desired HR policies (Ferner *et al.*, 2005). However, on the whole, survey evidence (Edwards *et al.*, 2007) shows US MNCs as being the least likely, and German firms the most likely, to recognise trade unions in their UK operations.

Further effects can be seen in the management of pay and performance (Almond *et al.*, 2006). In particular, US MNCs were innovators in the area of formalised systems of performance-related pay in Europe (Muller, 1998), which can be seen as a reflection of the particularly market-orientated American employment system. Although this practice is now also diffused widely among large non-American firms (Faulkner *et al.*, 2004), they remain more prevalent in US MNCs than those of other nationalities, and least common in German and Japanese MNCs (Edwards *et al.*, 2007). It can still be argued, however, that the form the practice often takes in US MNCs – with forced distributions pushing given percentages of employees into high- and low-performing categories, and in some cases the threat of dismissal or reduced job security for lower performing groups – reflects specifically American managerial beliefs about employment. In particular, this type of practice can be related to the American notion of 'employment at will', meaning there is, for most US employees, little protection from unfair dismissal (cf. Almond *et al.*, 2006). Systems of performance management tend to be tightly controlled by US HQ, with relatively little freedom for national subsidiaries to adopt distinctive policies.

A number of US MNCs also export workforce 'diversity' policies from the USA. These are clearly linked to the social and legislative context of equal opportunity law, and to US firms' attempts to interpret equal opportunity law to their own advantage (Ferner *et al.*, 2006b). In many cases, US firms, having devised diversity policies for the USA, chose to export these abroad, thus imposing targets for the proportion of women, and sometimes other disadvantaged labour market groups, in management positions. This reflects how the nature of country-of-origin effects can change over time, as the home country institutional context changes. Political sensitivities to equality issues in the USA, prompted by the civil rights movement and reactions to it, have led to the development of a range of diversity policies, which have in many cases been internationalised through the formal management systems of US firms.

It has also frequently been argued that Japanese MNCs betray specifically 'Japanese' characteristics when operating abroad. Japanese economic success in the 1970s and 1980s sparked considerable academic interest in Japanese management methods, with a wave of interest both in the HR policies of Japanese subsidiaries themselves [see, e.g., Kenney and Florida (1993) and Milkman (1991) for US subsidiaries of Japanese MNCs, and Morris *et al.,* (2000) and Elger and Smith (1994) for their UK subsidiaries] and, in Britain, in 'Japanese' practices that were being imitated by UK firms (see, e.g., Oliver and Wilkinson, 1992).

It is difficult to compare the HR policies of the UK subsidiaries of Japanese MNCs directly with those of US MNCs. The main reason for this is that the overwhelming majority of Japanese foreign direct investment in the UK has taken place in the last 25 years, into a UK industrial relations environment which had already been affected by Thatcherism and the economic crisis of the late 1970s/early 1980s. Much US investment is much older, going back in some cases to the Victorian era, meaning that many UK subsidiaries of US MNCs, such as Ford or General Motors, have a much more substantial 'British' heritage than Toyota or Nissan. Equally, much Japanese investment has involved so-called 'greenfield' sites, meaning that the Japanese MNCs involved had the opportunity to 'start from scratch' in terms of their management systems, and to recruit and select an entire new workforce.

Indeed, one of the notable features of many Japanese subsidiaries investigated in this period was their very selective recruitment procedures, in many cases focusing on the recruitment of a young workforce with the ability to learn, rather than looking for experienced workers with substantial experience of other UK firms (Oliver and Wilkinson, 1992). This reflects practice among core workers in the largest Japanese firms, where workers are selected directly from school or university and are expected to remain with the same employer for the majority of their career.

At least some of the larger Japanese inward investors also sought to replicate Japanese-type structures in their industrial relations policies. Rather than taking advantage of the 1980s industrial relations climate by seeking to exclude trade unions, some Japanese MNCs sought to reach single union agreements, whereby one trade union, usually the very moderate Amalgamated Engineering and Electrical Union (AEEU), represented all the different workforce groups within the firm. This differs from the more typical UK pattern in manufacturing, in which different occupational groups are represented by different trade unions, and replicates, to the extent that this is possible in a UK context, the company unionism present in the core Japanese firms at home. One 1990s survey of Japanese subsidiaries in South Wales found that 75 per cent had a single union deal (Innes and Morris, 1995). The Japanese firms in the same survey tended to have fewer job grades, reflecting a lesser degree of job demarcation than in US firms, and were less likely to have performance-related pay (see earlier), but slightly more likely to have elements of single-status practices such as equal holiday leave, and the wearing of company uniforms by all employees. Perhaps surprisingly, however, in view of the 'Japanisation' literature, flexible work organisation arrangements such as teamworking were only slightly more prevalent than in US-owned firms. This is in spite of the fact that considerable case study evidence from the larger Japanese subsidiaries in the UK does suggest that these policies are used.

Part of the explanation for this could lie with the extent to which Japanese practices, then seen as a model to be emulated (Womack *et al.*, 1990), were being copied by rival firms. If this is the case, it remains possible that the nature of policies such as teamworking is qualitatively different in Japanese-owned and American-owned firms. Just as important, however, as argued by Elger and Smith (2006) in an important work based on a long-term study of Japanese firms in Telford, the portrait of Japanese management generally found in the English-language management literature is somewhat stereotypical. Specifically, the commonly understood Japanese HRM model only really applies to core workers in a small number of well-known firms. Elements of the model, such as employment security and internal career structures, do not extend to peripheral firms in supply chains or to peripheral groups of the workforce, and very often Japanese MNCs use foreign workforces as part of this periphery.

The picture painted by Elger and Smith (2006) of Japanese management in Telford, of union avoidance and intensified assembly line work and modest wages, is much more reminiscent of the less glorified peripheral work systems of Japan than of the more paternalist HRM policies experienced by the core workers of core firms.

Finally, country-of-origin effects are likely to be stronger where the home country retains a substantial proportion of the MNC's operations. This is usually the case with US and Japanese firms, but for obvious reasons is less common with large MNCs based in smaller countries. In these cases, internationalisation of the firm may mean a much greater degree of internationalisation of its management cadre, and often of its capital base (i.e. the larger continental European MNCs will tend to raise finance from the US stock market as well as from domestic sources), meaning that country-of-origin effects may tend, over time, to diminish. The work of Hayden and Edwards (2001) examines this process in the Swedish case.

Overall, one can say that the various effects of firms and their managers originating from one particularly national business system may lead them to be more likely to choose some policies than others. This is not an automatic process, however. One cannot simply say that firms will adopt a certain style of HRM just because they are from a given country, but they may predispose managers to certain choices over others in given contexts. A major survey of HR practices shows the extent of some of these tendencies (Edwards *et al.*, 2007).

Key Controversy

Examine Edwards *et al.* (2007)'s survey findings on employee representation and consultation (available at **http://www2.warwick.ac.uk/fac/soc/wbs/projects/mncemployment/ conference_papers/full_report_july.pdf**). Can you think of some reasons why German firms are the most likely to recognise unions in the UK, and US firms the least likely? Why might Japanese MNCs favour the forms of indirect participation mentioned?

Host country effects

'Host country effects' is the term used to describe elements of MNC HR policy that are shaped by the context of the foreign countries in which subsidiaries are located. In other words, this concerns the way in which subsidiary HR policies and practices are shaped by a foreign MNC's interaction with employees and host country managers, working under different national rules and different national cultural and social systems. These rules and systems, along with levels of economic development and ease of access to markets, also provide countries with different competitive advantages. MNCs may sometimes choose to (or need to) deviate from their original, home country, policies, in order to exploit these advantages fully, while dealing with societal and cultural differences.

The broad term of 'host country effects' can perhaps be usefully split into a number of groups. First, there are effects that are imposed on the foreign MNC by host country constraints. These may arise directly from labour market regulation; as illustrated earlier in the book (see Chapter 15), host countries, even within EU countries, still differ considerably in their regulation of core elements of the employment relationship, such as wage protection, working time, employment security, worker participation and the trade union and collective bargaining rights of employees. In most western European countries, for example, it is very difficult for MNCs simply to choose to refuse to offer union recognition to employees. Equally, it is much harder, and more expensive, to dismiss permanent employees in some countries than in others. In other words, certain policies are either obligatory or prohibited in some societies, which has the effect of reducing the (legitimate) scope for strategic choice for foreign MNCs.

To this group of effects, one can also add elements of national cultural/societal understandings of the employment relationship that may not be written down in law, but which will affect the ways in which given HR practices will be interpreted by workers. For example, due to the nature of gender relations in Britain (see Chapter 4), employers in the UK, including foreign MNCs, benefit from a large workforce that is eager to take part-time employment with flexible working hours (i.e. working-class women and, increasingly, students) (Almond and Rubery, 2000). In France, while it is possible to recruit flexible part-timers due to the current high levels of unemployment in that country, most women in employment have historically tended to work full-time hours, meaning that part-time workers may be less content with their situation. While this does not, of course, stop a foreign MNC from employing a part-time workforce in France, managers should not be surprised if, as a result, their French employees display less 'commitment' than their British counterparts.

Secondly, host country effects are not only constraints on foreign MNCs. Indeed, if they were, there would be much less foreign direct investment. In fact, MNCs are constantly taking advantage of differences between different host countries (and other potential host countries) (Kristensen and Morgan, 2007). Much production, and indeed increasing proportions of service provision, takes place in global supply chains that seek to exploit national socioeconomic differences. If the employment system of one country offers expensive, but skilled, workers with a high capacity for learning, while that of another offers largely untrained, but cheap labour, MNCs may locate the higher skilled work in the first and the less skilled in the second. Similarly, the policies required to be seen as a 'good' or 'fair' employer in contemporary China are clearly not as resource-intensive as those in Germany, meaning that many firms will not choose to employ the same types of HR policies in these two very different environments. It should also be noted that MNCs' coordination of work extends beyond workplaces they directly own, through various forms of contractual and alliance relationships in global value chains (Coe *et al.*, 2008; Herrigel and Zeitlin, 2011). While issues concerning subcontracted work are not generally well integrated within the international HRM literature, it is necessary to recognise their importance in a fuller analysis of how MNCs manage human resources.

Finally, where an MNC locates a subsidiary in a country partly or mainly in order to exploit the national or regional product market, differences in consumer demand between nations may necessitate different ways of managing human resources. This was discussed briefly earlier in relation to the 'multi-domestic' form of MNC organisation, but will also apply to many firms that do not share that type of structure. While market differences may equally well be present in manufacturing as in the service sector, they are perhaps more likely to impact on HRM where there is direct contact between the employee and the customer.

The extent to which host country effects will cause differentiation in HR policies obviously depends on the nature of host country patterns of employment relations, and how different these are from those in the country of origin. This is sometimes referred to as 'institutional distance' (Kostova, 1999). For example, a US firm attempting to export a non-union system of HRM with a high performance-related element to pay would probably face far more difficulties in Germany than it would in the UK (for an example, see Almond *et al.*, 2005). By the same token, if the training system of one host country supplies the firm with a plentiful quantity of workers who have an otherwise scarce skill, it might well not choose to export all the elements of its corporate training programme to that country.

However, it should be noted that the strength of host country effects cannot simply be read off from a broad understanding of the nature of its institutions. In particular, the degree to which national economies depend on foreign MNCs for their success varies quite considerably from country to country. In countries such as Hungary or Ireland, where nearly half the manufacturing workforce works directly for foreign MNCs, one would expect this group of firms to have considerable lobbying power, and thus potentially a substantial collective impact on the nature of the overall business and employment systems (cf. Gunnigle *et al.*, 2003 for the Irish case).

Equally, as nations and localities compete for foreign direct investment, MNCs may have substantial negotiating power over political and other 'governance actors' in their host economies (Almond, 2011).The impact of 'constraining' host country effects may, in practice, be reduced if the MNC has a substantial choice about which countries it is located in. If the firm can produce credible threats that it may move part or all of its operations to more lightly regulated and/or lower cost countries, it is possible that some host country constraints can be 'negotiated' (particularly with local unions and local/regional governments), lessening their real impact. Less dramatically, the practice of 'coercive comparisons' (Marginson and Sisson, 2002), by which MNCs threaten (explicitly or implicitly) to withdraw investment in one subsidiary unless it matches the performance of another, is commonplace.

Another way of dealing with undesirable host country regulations, of course, is simply to disobey them. This is commonplace in the multinational fast food industry (Royle, 2000), but it also happens in firms that do not follow 'hard', cost-minimisation strategies quite so obviously (Almond *et al.*, 2005; Colling *et al.*, 2006). The subsidiaries of MNCs, whose home country practices may challenge the assumptions behind host country employment relations systems, will frequently attempt to find ways of exploiting the 'malleability' of those systems (Muller-Camen *et al.*, 2001). When foreign MNCs succeed in avoiding the constraints of host country systems, they may begin to alter the nature of those systems, in that their practices may well be imitated by domestic firms. For instance, while some medium-large British non-union firms did exist in the post-war era, one might argue that US MNCs became a template for later attempts to create non-union 'soft HRM' workplaces in the UK. More recently, German employers have followed closely the attempts of German subsidiaries of US multinationals to create more flexible pay structures.

The negotiation of home and host country effects

Neither home nor host country effects are automatic in their operation. It is important to take into account the fact that different organisational members, such as national and local managers, down to groups of shopfloor employees, have interests and goals of their own, which cannot simply be reduced to those of the 'corporation'. In particular, it is important to take account of the ways in which host country socialisation affects the rationality of host country managers (Broad, 1994). In other words, host country managers may, because of their 'embeddedness' in their own society, have different ideas about what is 'good management' and what is 'fair' and 'just' from those of their foreign superiors. For example, in the recent study of US MNCs in Europe discussed earlier, German and British subsidiary managers, both coming from countries with much more pluralist industrial relations traditions than their American counterparts, often applied HQ industrial relations policy in a fairly pragmatic and accommodating way, allowing a greater role for collective labour than a strict reading of corporate policy might suggest (Colling *et al.*, 2006). Similar processes can be seen to operate in the UK subsidiaries of Japanese firms (Elger and Smith, 2006)

In other words, HR outcomes at a subsidiary level result from different actors, at different levels of the organisation, with different power resources negotiating on the extent to which it is desirable to follow a 'global' policy or to make allowances for local contingencies. In particular, local managers should have specific knowledge about the local situation and will have their own interpretations of the realities of what is likely to work in the local context. It may be difficult for an HQ manager to predict exactly how a foreign subsidiary workforce is likely to respond to a given HR initiative or how strictly an element of employment law is enforced. Local managers therefore have a role in interpreting and negotiating precisely what the nature of 'host country effects' are in a given context. In other words, any analysis of policy transfer within MNCs needs to take account of organisational politics and the power resources of various actors (Edwards, 2004).

Concluding comments

In this chapter, we have considered how multinational firms manage their geographically dispersed workforces. We have explored the effects of firms' internal organisational structures and processes, on the one hand, and the external national contextual factors they encounter on the other.

Globalisation of the market place means that multinational firms are often required to find ways of accommodating dual demands for integration and co-ordination alongside differentiation to leverage competitive resources. The creation of transnational learning capabilities for the diffusion of global standards and innovation has become ever more critical. At the same time these firms operate within institutional environments consisting of regulatory and normative influences that shape the human capital resources available to firms, the expectations of workers, and the nature of employment contracts.

The research evidence has demonstrated that the response by firms is anything but simple, universal or consistent. Instead we have seen firms adapt to often conflicting demands for global consistency and local differences through the development of new structural and knowledge capabilities. For example, complex sets of inter- and intra-organisational links fostered through social relations are used to access tacit knowledge resources, interpret cognitive frames of reference and leverage resources from power groups and stakeholders that may otherwise remain inaccessible.

Multinationals have also become adept at building multi-level organisational structures that enable competing goals for global and local embeddedness to be addressed to different degrees at the subnational, national and transnational levels. Care must be taken not to interpret such multi-level structures as always effective or strategically intentional; we have noted how the nature of, for example, country of origin and host country effects are often negotiated within the company, including by managers at different levels of the multinational. However, the presence of these firms in transnational policy forums, national and subnational policy areas demonstrates their potential to influence the legislative, human capital and R&D capabilities of the environments on which they rely.

Summary

- This chapter has analysed international HRM by combining a range of academic perspectives in the area, from strategic approaches to those focusing more on MNCs' relations with their institutional environment. It highlights the fact that internationalised operations offer firms advantages in terms of access to human resources and knowledge, while also dealing with the increasingly complicated nature of HRM when firms internationalise.

- The chapter highlights how HRM decisions in MNCs may be related to business strategy and structure, but with the added complication that global as well as national strategic factors would need to be taken into account by senior managers. It then examines the ways in which MNCs might choose to structure their international HR function in order to cope with the complexities of international management and the role of networks and expatriates in the generation and transfer of HR knowledge. The final section examines the potential effects on HRM strategies and structures of the country of ownership of MNCs, as well as of the countries in which they operate.

- As the chapter reflects, the coordination of human resources in MNCs is a socially complex affair. It should be emphasised that none of the models, or explanations, presented to explain MNCs' behaviour in HRM fully succeeds in unwrapping this complexity. In examining the process of HRM in the international firm, it is necessary to take account of strategies, internal structures and institutions together.

Questions

1 Explain how, with the rise of the transnational firm and network structures, the concepts of integration and local responsiveness are relevant to understanding the contemporary structures of international firms.

2 How significant is the expatriate/international manager in delivering the strategic goals of multinational firms? Use the relevant literature to support your argument.

3 Resource-dependency and configurational models of multinational strategies dominate our understanding of how these complex firms operate. Explain the merits and limitations of each approach.

4 Identify the ways in which a firm can capture and diffuse learning across its geographically dispersed subsidiaries. What incentives might you have to put in place to encourage diffusion of learning and explain why these incentives may be necessary.

5 How might host country effects both constrain and benefit the operations of foreign-owned MNCs? Use examples from the literature to support your argument.

6 Would you expect a German firm operating in the UK to make different HR policy choices from those of a US-owned firm? Use relevant data to justify your position.

7 In what ways do host country institutions and culture potentially give host country managers power within the firm? What might HQ managers do to try to control this.

8 What are the risks, or lost opportunities, involved for a firm that seeks to have uniform HR policies throughout the world?

Case study

HRM at ITco

ITco is a world leader in the field of IT manufacture and services. Although it is US-owned, more than half of the global workforce is located outside the USA, and the bulk of annual revenues is derived from overseas operations. The firm has operations in virtually all countries of any size.

European operations are headquartered in Germany, with a number of expatriate American managers working in European management positions. At the same time, spending time working in both the European headquarters and the US operations is normal for European managers of 'high potential' who wish to gain senior management positions in the firm.

ITco was long known as a 'welfare capitalist' company (see Jacoby, 1997; Almond and Ferner, 2006): employees had a high degree of employment security and were relatively well paid, while the company was strongly non-union. These policies, including where possible the non-union approach, tended to be exported overseas to foreign subsidiaries. In recent years, partly due to business crises and the changing nature of the product market, long-term guarantees of employment security have all but disappeared. The company continues to resist union influence, however, both in the USA and, where possible, overseas.

The company follows a matrix structure of geographical regions and business divisions. In recent years, the organisational importance of national subsidiaries has declined, with multi-national 'regions' (such as Europe, the Middle-East and Africa, or the Asia–Pacific) acting alongside business divisions as centres of decision-making. The structure of the HR function has also changed. The firm has moved away from a national geography-based structure, with national HR managers responsible for affairs in their subsidiary, to a regional European structure, with responsibilities divided into functions (compensation, recruitment, etc.) reporting to a European head. For example, all job applications anywhere in the European operations are processed at one central location. The employee relations function, however, has been kept at a national level.

Questions

1 From this summary, which characteristics of ITco's policies or structures might be related to its American origins?

2 Why do you think all the functions within HR, except for employee relations, were centralised at the European level?

3 For what reasons do you think ITco tends to send managers on international assignments?

In recent years, many large MNCs have moved towards supplying HR service functions via a central phone and intranet-based service centre. This, it is normally argued, allows firms to cut costs by reducing the number of HR managers and officers at the individual sites. Many also believe that moving to a service centre model has allowed senior HR managers to concentrate on strategy, rather than having to deal with day-to-day administrative issues.

Until now, ITco has preferred to retain HR managers and officers at each location, rather than moving

Case study continued

to a service centre model. With the current economic crisis, however, the corporate director of human resources believes that the costs of the HR function in the European region are unacceptably high. She says the obvious solution is to set up a service centre dealing with the enquiries of employees on a regional basis.

As she discusses this proposal with some of the national HR managers from the different European subsidiaries, she finds that a number of them have objections to the idea. They argue that it will be impossible for the employees of a European-level service centre to understand the differences between employment law, and more general differences in employee attitudes, between the different European countries. They say that setting up a European-level centre would be too complicated, given the difficulties of finding people with the necessary linguistic capabilities and country knowledge. Single-country service centres might work, they say, but to unite the HR administration of European, Middle East and African workforces under one roof is a step too far.

After this discussion, however, managers of the British and Romanian subsidiaries approach the European director of HR and say they might be interested in hosting a cross-national service centre, should one be set up. The British manager points out that there is spare space available at the UK headquarters, that UK labour law is very flexible and that it will be easy to attract employees with the required competencies to a site within a couple of hours of London. The Romanian manager argues that the site should be in the centre of Europe and points out that Romanian labour costs are much lower than the European average. Some time later, the managing director of the German operations phones his contacts on the corporate board just to check that any service centre would be located at the European headquarters in Berlin; it would be dangerous, he argues, to effectively have two European centres.

Exercise

As an HR consultant advising ITco, what advice would you give them? You have the following choices:

1 To set up a European HR service centre.

2 To stick with the existing model and establish national HR service centres in the larger countries.

3 To come up with your own model of HR service delivery, different from models 1 and 2.

If you choose option 1, you need to consider how you would deal with the practical issues involved in setting up a multilingual service centre, and to answer the charge that workers might feel alienated if their HQ queries are being dealt with by people in another country. You also need to consider where might be a good location for such a centre.

If you choose option 2, you must defend it against the charge that the costs of replicating facilities across a number of different countries is inevitably higher than one large service centre. What are the advantages of this model that offset this cost? Also, what is to be done in countries where there is an insufficient number of employees to justify setting up a service centre? You will also need to think of alternative ways of cutting the costs of the HR function.

Is there an alternative model (option 3) that succeeds both in cutting costs and in avoiding worker alienation across the many different national operations of ITco?

References and further reading

Adler, N. and Ghadar, F. (1990) 'Strategic human resource management: a global perspective' in R. Pieper, *Human Resource Management: An International Comparison.* Berlin: Walter de Gruyter, pp. 235–60.

Aldrich, H. E. and Herker. D. (1977) 'Boundary spanning roles and organisation structure', *Academy of Management Review,* 2, 2: 217–30.

Almond, P. (2011) 'The sub-national embeddedness of international HRM', *Human Relations,* 64, 4: 531–51.

Almond, P. and Ferner, A. (eds) (2006) *American Multinationals in Europe: Managing Employment Relations Across Borders.* Oxford: Oxford University Press.

Almond, P. and Rubery, J. (2000) 'Deregulation and societal systems' in M. Maurice and A. Sorge (eds) *Embedding Organisations.* Amsterdam: John Benjamin, pp. 277–94.

Almond, P., Muller-Camen, M., Collings, T. and Quintanilla, J. (2006) 'Pay and performance' in P. Almond and A. Ferner (eds) *American Multinationals in Europe: Managing*

Employment Relations Across Borders. Oxford: Oxford University Press, pp. 119–45.

Almond, P., Edwards, T., Colling, T., Ferner, A., Gunnigle, P., Muller-Camen, M., Quintanilla, J. and Wachter, H. (2005) 'Unravelling home and host country effects: an investigation of the HR policies of an American multinational in four european countries', *Industrial Relations (Berkeley)*, 44, 2: 276–306.

Argote, L. and Ingram, P. (2000) 'Knowledge transfer: a basis for competitive advantage in firms', *Organisational Behaviour and Human Decision Processes*, 82: 152–69.

Athanassiou, N. and Nigh, D. (2000) 'Internationalisation, tacit knowledge and the top management teams of MNCs', *Journal of International Business Studies*, 31, 3: 471–88.

Au, K. Y. and Fukuda, J. (2002) 'Boundary spanning behaviours of expatriates', *Journal of World Business*, 37: 285–96.

Bantel, K.A. and Jackson, S.E. (1989) 'Top management and innovations in banking: does the composition of the top team make a difference?', *Strategic Management Journal*, 13: 338–55.

Barney, J. (1991) 'Firm resources and sustained competitive advantage', *Journal of Management*, 17: 99–120.

Bartlett, C.A. and Ghoshal, S. (1989) *Managing Across Borders: The Transnational Solution.* Boston. MA: Harvard Business School Press.

Bartlett, C.A. and Ghoshal, S. (1990) 'The multinational corporation as an interorganisational network', *Academy of Management Review*, 15, 4: 603–25.

Bartlett, C.A. and Ghoshal, S. (1995) *Transnational Management*, 2nd edn. Boston, MA: Irwin.

Beechler, S., Sondergaard, M., Miller, E.L. and Bird, A. (2004) 'Boundary spanning' in H. Lane, M. Maznevksi, M.E. Mendenhall and J. McNett (eds) *The Handbook of Global Management: A Guide to Managing Complexity.* Oxford: Blackwell, pp. 121–33.

Birkinshaw, J. and Morrison, A. (1995) 'Configurations of strategy and structure in subsidiaries of multinational companies', *Journal of International Business Studies*, 26, 4: 729–54.

Boam, R. and Sparrow, P. (1992) *Designing and Achieving Competency.* London: McGraw-Hill.

Bonache, J. and Brewster, C. (2001) 'Knowledge transfer and the management of expatriation', *Thunderbird International Business Review*, 43, 1: 145–68.

Brandl, B., Strohmer, S. and Traxler, F. (2013) 'Foreign direct investment, labour relations and sector effects: US investment outflows to Europe', *The International Journal of Human Resource Management* (ahead-of-print), 1–24.

Brannen, M. K. and Thomas, D. (2010) 'Bicultural individuals in organisations', *International Journal of Cross Cultural Management*, 10, 1: 5–16.

Brewster, C., Harris, H. and Sparrow, P.R. (2002) *Globalising HR Executive Brief.* London: CIPD.

Broad, G. (1994) 'The managerial limits to Japanisation: a manufacturing case study', *Human Resource Management Journal*, 4, 3: 52–69.

Brown, J.S. and Duguid, P. (1991) 'Organisational learning and communities-of-practice: towards a unified view of working, learning and innovation', *Organisation Science*, 2, 1: 40–57.

Cerdin, J-L. (2003) 'International diffusion of HRM practices: the role of expatriates', *Beta: Scandinavian Journal of Business Research*, 17, 1: 48–58.

Chandler, A. (1976) *The Visible Hand: The Managerial Revolution in America.* Cambridge, MA: Belknap.

Coe, N. M., Dicken, P. and Hess, M. (2008) 'Global production networks: realising the potential', *Journal of Economic Geography*, 8, 3: 271–95.

Colling. T. (2000) 'In a state of bliss there is no need for a ministry of bliss. Power, consent and the limits of innovation in American non-union companies'. Occasional paper, Leicester Business School, De Montfort University.

Colling, T., Gunnigle, P., Quintanilla, J. and Tempel, A. (2006) 'Collective representation and participation', in P. Almond and A. Ferner (eds) *American Multinationals in Europe: Managing Employment Relations Across Borders.* Oxford: Oxford University Press, pp. 95–118.

Desouza, K.C. (2003) 'Knowledge management barriers: why the technology imperative seldom works', *Business Horizons*, January–February: 25–9.

Doremus, P., Keller, W., Pauly, L. and Reich, S. (1998) *The Myth of the Global Corporation.* Princeton, NJ: Princeton University Press.

Doz, Y.L. and Prahalad, C.K. (1986) 'Controlled variety: a challenge for human resource management in the MNC', *Human Resource Management*, 25, 1: 55–72.

Dunning, J. (1958) *American Investment in British Manufacturing.* London: Allen & Unwin.

Edwards, T. (2004) 'The transfer of employment practices across borders in multinational companies', in A.-W. Harzing and J. van Ruysseveldt (eds) *International Human Resource Management*, 2nd edn. London: Sage pp. 389–410.

Edwards, T. and Rees, C. (eds) (2006) *International Human Resource Management: Globalisation, National Systems and Multinational Companies.* London: FT/Prentice Hall.

Edwards, T., Collings, D., Quintanilla, J. and Tempel, A. (2006) 'Innovation and the transfer of organisational learning', in P. Almond and A. Ferner (eds) *American Multinationals in Europe: Managing Employment Relations Across Borders.* Oxford: Oxford University Press, pp. 223–47.

Edwards, P., Edwards, T., Ferner, A., Marginson, P. and Tregaskis, O. (2007) *Employment practices of MNCs in organisational context: a large-scale survey. Report of Main Survey.* Online: **http://www2.warwick.ac.uk/fac/soc/wbs/projects/ mncemployment/conference_papers/full_report_july.pdf** (accessed February 2014).

Elger, T. and Smith, C. (eds) (1994) *Global Japanization? The Transnational Transformation of the Labour Process.* Oxford: Oxford University Press.

Elger, T. and Smith, C. (2006) *Assembling Work. Remaking Factory Regimes in Japanese Multinationals in Britain.* Oxford: Oxford University Press.

Faulkner, D., PitKethley, R. and Child, J. (2004) 'International mergers and acquisitions in the UK 1985–1994: A comparison of national HRM practices', *International Journal of Human Resource Management*, 13, 1: 94–111.

Ferner, A. (1994) 'Multinational companies and human resource management: an overview of research issues', *Human Resource Management Journal*, 4, 2: 79–102.

Ferner, A. (1997) 'Country of origin effects and HRM in multinational enterprises', *Human Resource Management Journal*, 7, 1: 19–37.

Ferner, A. and Varul, M. (2000) 'Vanguard' subsidiaries and the diffusion of new practices: a case study of German multinationals', *British Journal of Industrial Relations*, 38, 1: 115–40.

Ferner, A., Almond, P., Colling, T. and Edwards, T. (2005) 'Policies on union representation in US multinationals in the UK: between micro-politics and macro-institutions', *British Journal of Industrial Relations*, 43, 4: 703–28.

Ferner, A., Gunnigle, P., Wachter, H. and Edwards, T. (2006a) 'Centralisation' in P. Almond and A. Ferner (eds) *American Multinationals in Europe: Managing Employment Relations Across Borders*. Oxford: Oxford University Press, pp. 197–222.

Ferner, A., Muller-Camen, M., Morley, M. and Susaeta, L. (2006b) 'Workforce diversity policies', in P. Almond and A. Ferner (eds) *American Multinationals in Europe: Managing Employment Relations Across Borders*. Oxford: Oxford University Press, pp. 146–71.

Ferner A., Tregaskis O., Edwards P., Edwards T. and Marginson P. (2011) 'The determinants of central control and subsidiary discretion in multinationals,' *International Journal of Human Resource Management,* 22, 3: 483–509.

Fisher, H.M. and Pollock, T.G. (2004) 'Effects of social capital and power on surviving transformational change: the case of initial public offerings', *Academy of Management Journal,* 47, 4: 463–82.

Ghoshal, S. and Bartlett, C.A. (1998) *Managing Across Borders*. London: Random House, pp. 1–81.

Gulati, T., Nohria, N. and Zaheer, A. (2000) 'Strategic networks', *Strategic Management Journal,* 21: 203–15.

Gunnigle, P., Collings, D., Morley, M. and McAvinue, A.O. (2003) 'US multinationals and human resource management in Ireland: towards a qualitative research agenda', *Irish Journal of Management,* January: 7–25.

Hall, P. and Soskice D. (2001) *Varieties of Capitalism: The Institutional Foundations of Comparative Advantage*. Oxford: Oxford University Press.

Hansen, M.T. (1999) 'The search-transfer problem: the role of weak ties in sharing knowledge across organisation subunits', *Administrative Science Quarterly,* 44, 1: 82–111.

Harzing, A.-W. (1999) *Managing the Multinationals: an International Study of Control Mechanisms*. Cheltenham: Edward Elgar.

Harzing, A.-W. (2000) 'An empirical analysis and extension of the Bartlett and Ghoshal Typology of Multinational Companies', *Journal of International Business Studies,* 31, 1: 101–19.

Hayden, A. and Edwards, T. (2001) 'The erosion of the country of origin effect: a case study of a Swedish multinational company', *Relations Industrielles,* 56, 1: 116–40.

Hedlund, G. (1986) 'The hypermodern MNC – a heterarchy?' *Human Resource Management,* 25, 1: 9–35.

Herrigel, G. and Zeitlin, J. (2011) 'Inter-firm relations in global manufacturing: disintegrated production and its globalisation' in G. Morgan, J. Campbell, C. Crouch, P.H. Kristensen, O. Pedersen and R. Whitley (eds) *The Oxford Handbook of Comparative Institutional Analysis,* Oxford: Oxford University Press, pp. 527–63.

Hirst, P. and Thompson, G. (1999) *Globalisation in Question,* 2nd edn. Cambridge: Polity Press.

Hofstede, G. (1980) *Culture's Consequences: International Differences in Work-Related Values*. Beverly Hills, CA: Sage.

Holden L. (2001) 'International human resource management', in I. Beardwell and L. Holden (eds) *Human Resource Management*. London: Prentice Hall, pp. 633–76.

Huselid, M. (1995) 'The impact of human resource management practices on turnover, productivity and corporate financial performance', *Academy of Management Journal,* 38, 3: 635–72.

Innes, E. and Morris, J. (1995) 'Multinational corporations and employee relations: continuity and change in a mature industrial region', *Employee Relations,* 17, 6: 25–42.

Jacoby, S. (1997) *Modern Manors: Welfare Capitalism since the New Deal*. Princeton, NJ: Princeton University Press.

Jones, G. (1984) 'Task visibility, free riding, and shirking: explaining the effect of structure and technology on employee behaviour', *Journal of Financial Economics,* 3: 305–60.

Kenney, M. and Florida, R. (1993) *Beyond Mass Production*. New York: Oxford University Press.

Kobrin, S.J. (1994) 'Is there a relationship between a geocentric mind-set and multinational strategy?' *Journal of International Business Studies,* third quarter: 493–511.

Kostova, T. (1999) 'Transnational transfer of strategic organisational practices: a contextual perspective', *Academy of Management Review,* 24, 2: 308–24.

Kostova, T. and Roth, K. (2003) 'Social capital in multinational corporations and a micro-macro model of its formation', *Academy of Management Review,* 28, 2: 297–317.

Kristensen, P. and Morgan, G. (2007) 'Multinationals and institutional competitiveness', *Regulation and Governance,* 1: 197–212.

Lado, A. and Wilson, M. (1994) 'Human resource systems and sustained competitive advantage: a competency based perspective', *Academy of Management Review,* 19: 699–727.

Lam, A. (2000) 'Tacit knowledge, organisational learning and societal institutions: an integrated framework', *Organisation Studies,* 21, 3: 487–513.

Lane, C. (2001) 'Understanding the globalisation strategies of German and British multinational companies: is a 'societal effects' approach still useful' in M. Maurice and A. Sorge (eds), *Embedding Organisations*. Amsterdam: John Benjamins, pp. 189–208.

Laurent, A. (1983) 'The cultural diversity of Western conceptions of management', *International Studies of Management and Organisation,* 13, 1–2: 75–96.

Leana, C. and van Buren, H. (1999) 'Organisational social capital and employment practices', *Academy of Management Review,* 24, 3: 538–55.

Lengnick-Hall, C. and Lengnick-Hall, M. (1988) 'Strategic human resource management: A review of the literature and proposed typology', *Academy of Management Review,* 13: 454–70.

Leong, S.M. and Tan, C.T. (1993) 'Managing across borders: an empirical test of the Bartlett and Ghoshal [1989] organisational typology', *Journal of International Business Studies,* 24, 3: 449–64.

Marginson, P. and Sisson, K. (2002) 'Coordinated bargaining – a process for our times?', *British Journal of Industrial Relations,* 40, 2: 197–220.

Mayrhofer, W. and Brewster, C. (1996) 'In praise of ethnocentricity: expatriate policies in European multinationals', *International Executive,* 36, 6: 749–78.

Mendenhall, M., Dunbar, E. and Oddou, G. (1989) 'Expatriate selection, training and career pathing: a review and critique', *Human Resource Management,* 26: 331–45.

Milkman. R. (1991) *Japan's California factories: Labour relations and economic globalisation*. Berkeley, CA: Institute Industrial Relations, UCLA.

Milliman, J.F. and Von Glinow, M.A. (1990) 'A life cycle approach to strategic international human resource management in MNCs', *Research in Personnel and Human Resources Management,* Supp. 2: 21–35.

Milliman, J.M., Von Glinow, A. and Nathan, M. (1991) 'Organizational life cycles and strategic international human resource management in multinational companies: Implications for congruence theory', *Academy of Management Review,* 16, 2: 318–39.

Moenaert, R.K., Souder, W.E., De Meyer, A. and Deschoolmeester, D. (1994) 'R&D-marketing, integration mechanisms, communication flows and innovation success', *Journal of Product Innovation Management,* 11, 1: 31–45.

Morgan, G. (2001) *The Multinational Firm*. Oxford: Oxford University Press.

Morris, J., Wilkinson, B. and Munday, M. (2000) 'Farewell to HRM? Personnel practices in Japanese manufacturing plants in the UK', *International Journal of Human Resource Management*, 11, 6: 1047–60.

Muller, M. (1998) 'Human resource and industrial relations practices of UK and US multinationals in Germany', *International Journal of Human Resource Management*, 9, 4: 732–49.

Muller-Camen, M., Almons, P., Gunnigle, P., Quintanilla, J. and Tempel, A. (2001) 'Between home and host country: multinationals and employment relations in Europe', *Industrial Relations Journal*, 32, 5: 435–48.

Nahapiet, J. and Ghoshal, S. (1998) 'Social capital, intellectual capital, and the organisation advantage', *Academy of Management Review*, 23: 243–66.

Nohria, N. and Eccles, R.G. (1992) 'Face-to-face: making network organisations work' in N. Nohria and R.G. Eccles (eds) *Networks and Organisations: Structure, Form and Action*. Boston, MA: Harvard Business School Press, pp. 288–323.

Nohria, N. and Ghoshal, S. (1997) *The Differentiated Network: Organising Multinational Companies For Value Creation*. London: Routledge.

Nonaka, I. and Takeuchi, H. (1995) *The Knowledge Creating Company*. New York: Oxford University Press.

OECD (2006) OECD Factbook (2006) *Economic, Environmental and Social Statistics*. Paris: OECD.

Ohmae, K. (1991) *The Borderless World*. London: Macmillan.

Oliver, N. and Wilkinson, B. (1992) *The Japanization of British Industry*. Oxford: Blackwell.

O'Sullivan, M. (2000) *Contests for Corporate Control: Corporate Governance and Economic Performance in the United States and Germany*. Oxford: Oxford University Press.

Pauly, L. and Reich, S. (1997) 'National structures and multinational corporate behaviour: enduring differences in the age of globalisation', *International Organisation*, 51, 1: 1–30.

Perlmutter, H.V. (1969) 'The tortuous evolution of the multinational corporation', *Columbia Journal of World Business*, 4, 1: 9–18.

Pfeffer, J. and Salancik, G.R. (1978) *The External Control of Organisations*. New York: Harper and Row.

Polanyi, M. (1962) *Personal Knowledge*. Chicago, IL: University of Chicago Press.

Polanyi, M. (1966) *The Tacit Dimension*. Garden City, NY: Doubleday.

Porter, M. (1990) *The Competitive Advantage of Nations* (with a new introduction). Basingstoke: Macmillan.

Prahalad, C.K. and Doz, Y. (1987) *The Multinational Mission: Balancing Local Demands and Global Vision*. New York: The Free Press.

Quintanilla, J. (1999) 'The configuration of human resource management policies and practices in multinational subsidiaries: the case of European retail banks in Spain'. *Unpublished PhD thesis*, University of Warwick.

Reich, R. (1991) *The Work of Nations: Preparing Ourselves for 21st Century Capitalism*. New York: Alfred A. Knopf.

Rosenzweig, P.M. and Nohria, N. (1994) 'Influences on human resource management practices in multinational corpo-rations', *Journal of International Business Studies*, second quarter: 229–51.

Rosenzweig, P.M. and Singh, J.V. (1991) 'Organisational environments and the multinational enterprise', *Academy of Management Review*, 16, 2: 304–16.

Roth, K. and Morrison, A.J. (1990) 'An empirical analysis of the integration-responsiveness framework in global industries', *Journal of International Business Studies*, 22, 4: 541–61.

Royle, T. (2000) *Working for McDonald's in Europe*. London: Routledge.

Ruigrok, W. and van Tulder, R. (1995) *The Logic of International Restructuring*. London: Routledge.

Rutherford, T. and Holmes, J. (2008) 'The flea on the tail of the dog': power in global production networks and the restructuring of Canadian automotive clusters', *Journal of Economic Geography*, 8, 4: 519–44.

Schein, E. (1984) 'The role of the founder in creating organizational culture', *Organisational Dynamics*, Summer: 13–28.

Schuler, R. (1992) 'Strategic human resources management: linking the people with the strategic needs of the business', *Organisational Dynamics*, summer: 18–32.

Schuler, R., Dowling P. and De Cieri, H. (1993) 'An integrative framework of strategic international human resource management', *Journal of Management*, 19, 2: 419–59.

Sparrow, P., Brewster, C. and Harris, H. (2004) *Globalising Human Resource Management*. London: Routledge.

Taylor, S. (2006) 'Emerging motivations for global HRM integration' in A. Ferner, J. Quintanilla and C. Sanchez-Runde (eds) *Multinational, Institutions and the Construction of Transnational Practices*. London: Palgrave, pp. 109–30.

Taylor, S. and Beechler, S. (1993) 'Human resource management integration and adaption in multinational firms' in S. Prasad and R. Peterson (eds) *Advances in International Comparative Management*, 8. Greenwich, CT: JAI Press, pp. 155–74.

Taylor, S., Beechler, S. and Napier, N. (1996) 'Towards an integrative model of strategic international human resource management', *Academy of Management Review*, 21, 4: 959–85.

Thomas, D. C. (1994) 'The boundary spanning role of expatriates in the multinational corporation'. *Advances in International and Comparative Management*, 9: 145–70.

Tregaskis, O., Glover, L. and Ferner, A. (2005) *International HR Networks*. London: CIPD.

Tregaskis, O., Edwards, T., Edwards, P., Ferner, A. and Marginson, P. (2010) 'Transnational learning structures in multinational firms: organisational context and national embeddedness', *Human Relations*, 63, 4: 471–99.

Vernon, R. (1966) 'International investment and international trade in the product cycle', *Quarterly Journal of Economics*, May: 190–207.

Whitley, R. (1999) *Divergent Capitalisms*. Oxford: Oxford University Press.

Womack, J., Jones, D. and Roos, G. (1990) *The Machine that Changed the World*. New York: Rawson.

Wright, P. and McMahan, G. (1992) 'Theoretical perspectives for strategic human resource management', *Journal of Management*, 18, 3: 295–320.

Glossary of terms and abbreviations

Academy Schools State-maintained independent schools set up with the help of external sponsors – usually business, religious or voluntary organisations.

Advisory, Conciliation and Arbitration Service (ACAS) Founded in 1975, aims to improve employment relations. It provides information, advice and training and will work with employers and employees to solve problems.

ACFTU The All China Federation of Trade Unions.

Added value Technically the difference between the value of a firm's inputs and its outputs; the additional value is added through the deployment and efforts of the firm's resources. Can be defined as FVA (financial value added), CVA (customer value added) and PVA (people value added).

AEL Accreditation of Experiential Learning.

Alienation Marx suggests it is a condition in which a worker loses power to control the performance, processes and product of his/her labour. Thus the very worker becomes a thing rather than a human being, in which state they experience powerlessness, meaninglessness, isolation and self-estrangement.

Androgogy 'The art and science of helping adults learn' (Knowles *et al.*, 1984: 60).

Annualised hours contract Relatively novel form of employment contract that offers management, and sometimes workers, a considerable degree of flexibility. The hours that an employee works can be altered within a very short time frame within a day, a week, or even a month. So long as the total hours worked do not exceed the contractually fixed annual amount an employee can be asked and expected to work from zero up to anything in excess of 80 hours in any one week.

APL Accreditation of Prior Learning.

Appraisal The process through which an assessment is made of an employee by another person using quantitative and/or qualitative assessments.

Appraisal (360 degree) A system of appraisal which seeks feedback from 'all directions' – superiors, subordinates, peers and customers.

Attitude survey Survey, usually conducted by questionnaire, to elicit employees' opinions about issues to do with their work and the organisation.

Balanced scorecard An integrated framework for balancing shareholder and strategic goals, and extending these balanced performance measures down the organisation.

BERR Department for Business, Enterprise and Regulatory Reform, now part of the Department for Business, Innovation and Skills – *see* **BIS**.

Best fit Models of HRM that focus on alignment between HRM and business strategy and the external context of the firm. Tend to link or 'fit' generic type business strategies to generic HRM strategies.

Best practice A 'set' or number of human resource practices that have the potential to enhance organisational performance when implemented. Usually categorised as 'high commitment', 'high involvement' or 'high performance'.

BIS Department for Business, Innovation and Skills.

Broadbanding Pay systems which have a wide range of possible pay levels within them. Unlike traditional narrow systems, there is normally a high degree of overlap across the grades.

BS 5750 British standard of quality, originally applied to the manufacture of products but now also being used to 'measure' quality of service. Often used in employee involvement (EI) as a way of getting employees to self-check their quality of work against a standardised norm.

Bundles A coherent combination of human resource practices that are horizontally integrated.

Business process re-engineering (BPR) System that aims to improve performance by redesigning the processes through which an organisation operates, maximising their value-added content and minimising everything else (Peppard and Rowland, 1995: 20).

Cabinet Office A senior government department alongside the Treasury, the Cabinet Office supports the Prime Minister, the Cabinet and the Civil Service in managing government policy.

Career 'The evolving sequence of a person's work experiences over time' (Arthur *et al.*, 1989: 8); 'the individual's development in learning and work throughout life' (Collin and Watts, 1996: 393).

Causal ambiguity The cause or source of an organisation's competitive advantage is ambiguous or unclear, particularly to the organisation's competitors.

CBI Confederation of British Industry. Powerful institution set up in 1965 to promote and represent the interests of British industry. Financed by subscription and made up of employers' associations, national business associations and over 10,000 affiliated companies. Works to advise and negotiate with the government and the Trades Union Congress.

CCT   Compulsory competitive tendering.

Chaos and complexity theories   In contrast to traditional science, these more recent theories draw attention to the uncertainty, non-linearity and unpredictability that result from the interrelatedness and interdependence of the elements of the universe.

CIPD   Chartered Institute of Personnel and Development – the professional organisation for human resource and personnel managers and those in related fields such as training and development. Website: www.cipd.co.uk.

Closed system   System that does not interact with other subsystems or its environment.

Collective bargaining   Process utilised by trade unions, as the representatives of employees, and management, as the representatives of employers, to establish the terms and conditions under which labour will be employed.

Competence   'The ability to perform the activities within an occupational area to the levels of performance expected in employment' (Training Commission, 1988).

Competences   Behavioural repertoires that people input to a job, role or organisation context, and which employees need to bring to a role to perform to the required level (*see also* **Core competences**).

Competency-based pay   An approach to reward based on the attainment of skills or talents by individuals in relation to a specific task at a certain standard.

Competitive advantage   The ability of an organisation to add more value for its customers than its rivals, and therefore gain a position of advantage in the marketplace.

Configurational approach   An approach that identified the benefits of identifying a set of horizontally integrated HR practices that were aligned to the business strategy, thus fitting the internal and external context of the business.

Constructivism   Concerned with individual experience and emphasises the individual's cognitive processes.

Contingent pay   Elements of the reward package which are contingent on other events (performance, merit, attendance) and are awarded at the discretion of the management.

Cooperatives   Organisations and companies that are collectively owned either by their customers or by their employees.

Core competences   Distinctive skills and knowledge, related to product, service or technology, that can be used to gain competitive advantage.

Corporate governance   The set of systems, principles and processes by which a company is governed.

Cost minimisation   This refers to a managerial approach that perceives human resources as costs to be controlled as tightly as possible. HR practices are likely to include low wages, minimal training, close supervision and no employee voice mechanisms.

CPSA   Civil and Public Servants Association.

Culture   The prevailing pattern of values, attitudes, beliefs, assumptions, norms and sentiments.

Danwei   Work units around which social and economic organisation was structured and were central to the state owned enterprises in Communist China.

DCSF   Department for Children, Schools and Families.

DfES   Department for Education and Skills now subsumed into the Department for Business, Innovation and Skills – *see* **BIS**.

Deskilling   The attempt by management to appropriate and monopolise workers' knowledge of production in an effort to control the labour process. To classify, tabulate and reduce this knowledge to rules, laws and formulae, which are then allocated to workers on a daily basis.

DETR   Department of the Environment, Transport and the Regions.

Development   The process of becoming increasingly complex, more elaborate and differentiated, by virtue of learning and maturation, resulting in new ways of acting and responding to the environment.

Development centres   Normally used for the selection of managers. They utilise a range of intensive psychological tests and simulations to assess management potential.

Discourse   The shared language, metaphors, stories that give members of a group their particular way of interpreting reality.

Disengagement   the converse of **engagement**. Employees feel psychologically remote from the organisational values and isolated from other employees.

DIUS   Department for Innovation, Universities and Skills. Now part of the Department for Business, Innovation and Skills – *see* **BIS**.

Downsizing   Possibly the simplest explanation is given by Heery and Noon (2001: 90) as 'getting rid of employees'. A modern 'buzzword' used to indicate the reduction of employment within organisations.

Double-loop learning   See **Single-loop learning**.

DTI   Department for Trade and Industry, now subsumed into the Department for Business, Innovation and Skills – *see* **BIS**.

Dual system   German system of vocational training for apprentices, which combines off-the-job training at vocational colleges with on-the-job training under the tutelage of *meister* (skilled craft) workers.

Efficiency   The sound management of resources within a business in order to *maximise* the return on investment.

Efficiency wages   Wages paid above the market rate to attract better workers, induce more effort and reduce turnover and training costs.

Effectiveness   The ability of an organisation to meet the demands and expectations of its various stakeholders, albeit some more than others.

EHRC Equality and Human Rights Commission, UK statutory body with a remit to promote and monitor human rights; and to protect, enforce and promote equality across the nine 'protected' grounds – age, disability, gender, race, religion and belief, pregnancy and maternity, marriage and civil partnership, sexual orientation and gender reassignment.

EI Employee involvement; a term to describe the wide variety of schemes in which employees can be involved in their work situation.

EIRO European Industrial Relations Observatory – produces regular reports on employment relations in EU Member States.

e-Learning Use of new technology such as e-mail, the internet, intranets and computer software packages to facilitate learning for employees.

Emergent Strategies which emerge over time, sometimes with an element of trial and error. Some emergent strategies are incremental changes with embedded learning, others may be adaptive in response to external environmental changes.

Employability The acquisition and updating of skills, experience, reputation – the investment in human capital – to ensure that the individual remains employable, and not dependent upon a particular organisation.

Empowerment Recent term that encompasses **EI** (employee involvement) initiatives to encourage the workforce to have direct individual and collective control over their work processes, taking responsibility for improved customer service to both internal and external customers. Generally confined to workplace-level issues and concerns.

Engagement Generally seen as an internal state of being – physical, mental and emotional – that brings together earlier concepts of work effort, organisational commitment, job satisfaction and 'flow' (or optimal experience).

Enterprise unions Japanese concept of employee unions associated with only one enterprise and the only one recognised by the company. One of the 'three pillars' of the Japanese employment system.

Epistemology The assumptions made about the world which form the basis for knowledge.

ESOPS Employee share option scheme, whereby employees are allowed to purchase company shares or are given them as part of a bonus.

ET Employment training.

Ethnic penalties The economic and non-economic disadvantages black and minority ethnic groups experience in the labour market compared to non-ethnic minority groups of the same human and social capital.

EU European Union, so named in 1992 (formerly EC).

Exit policy Policy/procedures that facilitate prompt and orderly recovery or removal of failing institutions through timely and corrective action. There were restrictions placed on closure and retrenchment in view of the social costs and their political ramifications that are now being eased.

Factor of production An input into the production process. Factors of production were traditionally classified as *land* (raw materials), *capital* (buildings, equipment, machinery) and *labour*. Labour is usually seen as a variable factor of production because labour inputs can be varied quite easily at short notice, unlike capital, the amount of which cannot be varied easily in the short run. Internalising the employment relationship transforms labour into a *quasi-fixed factor of production* because it restricts the employer's freedom to cut jobs at short notice.

FIEs Foreign invested enterprises.

Firm-specific skills Skills that can be used in only one or a few particular organisations.

Fit The level of integration between an organisation's business strategy and its human resource policies and practices. 'Fit' tends to imply a top-down relationship between the strategy makers and the strategy implementers.

Forked lightning, the Mae West Language and concepts used by city financiers working on the international currency and commodity markets. Used to describe the patterns formed by fluctuating price movements as they get represented on dealers' screens.

Foundation schools State-financed schools that own school land and other physical assets of the school, are the employers of school staff and which have authority over admissions.

FSB Federation of Small Businesses.

FTSE The FTSE Group provides a series of indices (measures) relating to share prices and other aspects of economic activity. The **FTSE100 index** is an index of the share prices of the top 100 firms by share value.

Functional flexibility The ability of management to redeploy workers across tasks. Functional flexibility can be horizontal – redeployment across tasks at the same level of skill, and/or vertical – the ability to perform tasks at different (higher) levels of skill.

GDP Gross domestic product – a measure of the total value of goods and services produced within a country, excluding income from investments abroad.

Glass ceiling Metaphor used to describe the barrier facing women who seek to gain access to senior management positions, often women can see the jobs at the very top but find there is an impenetrable barrier which prevents them securing the positions.

Globalisation A controversial term that has generated considerable debate as to its meaning. Generally seen to involve increased internationalisation of investment and production, the growing importance of multinational companies and the emergence of transnational regulation of economic activity.

GNVQs   General National Vocational Qualifications.

Guanxi   Chinese term that refers to the concept of drawing on connections or networks to secure favours in personal or business relations.

Hard HRM   A view of HRM that identifies employees as a cost to be minimised, and tends to focus on 'flexibility techniques' and limited investment in learning and development (*see also* **Soft HRM**).

Hegemony   The imposition upon others of a powerful group's interpretation of reality.

High-commitment management   Used to describe a set of HR practices aimed at enhancing the commitment, quality and flexibility of employees.

High-performance work practices   A term that gained currency in the 1990s that sought to link bundles of HR practices with outcomes in terms of increased employee commitment and performance which in turn enhances the firm's sustained competitive advantage, efficiency and profitability.

HMSO   Her Majesty's Stationery Office. Publishers of parliamentary proceedings, official government documents and reports. Privatised in 1996 and now known as The Stationery Office (TSO).

Holistic   Treatment of organisations, situations, problems as totalities or wholes as opposed to a specific, reductionist approach.

Horizontal integration   Level of alignment across and within functions, such that all functional policies and practices are integrated and congruent with one another.

HRD   Human resource development.

Hukou   The household registration system required by law in China that provides residency entitlement and citizenship rights to its citizens.

Human capital   The knowledge, skill and attitudes, the intangible contributions to high performance, that make employees assets to the organisation.

Human relations   Associated with the pioneering work of Roethlisberger and Dickson, Elton Mayo and others, who studied the importance of community and collective values in work organisations. These studies first identified that management needed to attend to the 'social needs' of employees.

ICT   Information and communication technology.

Ideology   The set of ideas and beliefs that underpins interpretations of reality.

IIP   Investors in People.

ILO   International Labour Organization. International body set up in 1919 to promote employment rights and decent employment standards. Now an agency of the United Nations.

IMS   The Institute of Manpower Studies. Located at the University of Sussex.

Independent Pay Review Bodies   These are in place to offer expert advice to the government on the pay of certain groups of public-sector employees: armed forces, doctors and dentists, school teachers, certain groups of NHS nursing and healthcare staff, police officers and highly paid public officials such as judges and senior civil servants.

Indexation   Procedure linking pay, pensions or other financial benefits to changes in the retail price index to protect against inflation or in some cases to the growth of average earnings to protect the relative as well as the absolute value of pay, etc.

Informal labour   Workers without any legal, employment or social security benefits provided by the employers. They are often the most vulnerable, poor and exploited segment of workers.

Institutions   Social structures and processes of a society and structure, its social patterns and norms. They are historically embedded and constitute the social organisation and economy of a country.

Institutional vacuum/representation gap   Situation in which collective bargaining is no longer the dominant form of establishing terms and conditions of employment, but no recognisable or regulated channel of employee representation or employee voice has emerged to replace it.

Intellectual capital   The hidden value, and capital, tied up in an organisation's people (knowledge, skills and competencies), which can be a key source of competitive advantage and differentiate it from its competitors.

Iron rice bowl   The system of lifelong employment, wage equality and comprehensive welfare provision for workers in China.

IRDAC   Industrial Research and Development Advisory Committee of the Commission of the European Communities.

IRS   Industrial Relations Services. A data gathering and publications bureau that collects and analyses movement in key variables of importance to the study and practice of industrial relations.

ITBs   Industrial Training Boards. Set up in 1964 to monitor training in various sectors of the economy. Most were abolished in 1981, but a few still survive.

JCC   Joint consultative committee; body made up of employee representatives and management, which meets regularly to discuss issues of common interest.

Job enlargement   Related to job rotation, whereby a job is made bigger by the introduction of new tasks. This gives greater variety in job content and thereby helps to relieve monotony in repetitive jobs such as assembly line working.

Job enrichment   Adds to a cycle of work not only a variety of tasks but also increased responsibility to workers. Most associated with autonomous work groups introduced into Volvo's Kalmar plant in Sweden in the 1970s.

Job rotation   Originally introduced in the 1970s for members of a team to exchange jobs to enliven work interest, but also used recently to promote wider skills experience and flexibility among employees.

JV Joint venture.

Keiretsu A form of inter-company organisation in Japan that consists of a set of companies that hold shares in each other and have shared business relationships.

Knowledge-based age Reflects the move to a global environment, where tacit and explicit knowledge becomes a key source of competitive advantage for organisations.

Knowledge-based organisation One that manages the generation of new knowledge through learning, capturing knowledge and experience, sharing, collaborating and communicating, organising information and using and building on what is known.

Labour process The application of human labour to raw materials in the production of goods and services that are later sold on the free market. Labour is paid a wage for its contribution, but capital must ensure that it secures value added over and above what it is paying for. Some call this efficiency. Others prefer the term 'exploitation'.

Learning Complex cognitive, physical and affective process that results in the capacity for changed performance.

Learning cycle Learning seen as a process having different identifiable phases. Effective learning may be facilitated if methods appropriate to the various phases are used.

Learning style Individuals differ in their approaches to learning, and prefer one mode of learning, or phase of the learning cycle, to others.

Learning organisation (LO) 'A Learning Company is an organisation that facilitates the learning of all its members and consciously transforms itself and its context' (Pedler *et al.*, 1997: 3).

LECs Local Enterprise Companies. Locally based agencies in Scotland whose function is to promote training and business and wider economic development. There are 22 in existence. For the UK *see* **LSC**.

Leverage The exploitation by an organisation of its resources to their full extent. Often linked to the notion of stretching resources.

Licence-quota regime The practice in a state-regulated economy where a business has to obtain permission to manufacture (licence) as well as the quantity to produce (quota) from the licensing authority (state) before commencing production.

Lifetime employment Japanese concept whereby in large corporations employees are guaranteed a job for life in exchange for loyalty to the organisation. One of the 'three pillars' of the Japanese employment system.

Living wage Promoted by the Living Wage Foundation, the living wage is based on the amount an individual needs to earn to cover the basic costs of living. The living wage differs from the minimum wage in that the latter is set by law (see **National Minimum Wage**) yet can fail to be sufficient to meet requirements for a basic quality of life.

Loose labour market Sometimes called a 'surplus' labour market, where unemployment is running high and labour supply exceeds demand.

LMS Local management of schools.

LSC Learning and Skills Council. Set up in 2001 to replace the Training and Enterprise Council the LSC is responsible for funding and planning post-16 education and training in England. The equivalent body in Wales is Education and Learning Wales (ELWa). The LSC has 47 local offices known as Local Learning and Skills Councils (LLSCs) and ELWa has four regional offices.

Maastricht Protocol Part of the Maastricht Treaty dealing with the Social Chapter (Social Charter), allowing Britain to sign the treaty without signing the Maastricht Protocol or Social Chapter.

Maastricht Treaty The content was agreed at a meeting at Maastricht in the Netherlands and signed in a watered-down form in Edinburgh in 1992. It was rejected and then accepted by the voters of Denmark in two referendums. It concerns extending aspects of European political union (EPU) and European and Monetary Union (EMU).

Management gurus Phenomenon of the 1980s, when academics, consultants and business practitioners began to enjoy celebrity status as specialists on the diagnosis of management problems and the development of 'business solutions'. Includes people such as Tom Peters, Rosabeth Moss Kanter, John Harvey Jones and M.C. Robert Beeston.

McDonaldisation The reduction of organisation to simple, repetitive and predictable work processes that make the labour process more amenable to standardised calculation and control.

MCI (Management Charter Initiative) Employer-led initiative with the aim of developing recognised standards in management practice.

Measured day work (MDW) A system within which pay is fixed against specific levels of performance during the 'day' rather than by the hourly performance or piece-rates.

Mentor More experienced person who guides, encourages and supports a younger or less experienced person.

MSC (Manpower Services Commission) Previously had responsibility for training but was abolished in 1988.

Mission statement A statement setting out the main purpose of the business.

NACETT National Advisory Council for Education and Training Targets, now incorporated into the Learning and Skills Councils.

NALGO   National and Local Government Officers Association. *See* **Unison**.

NASUWT   National Association of School Masters/ Union of Women Teachers.

National curriculum   Obligatory subjects of the UK school system, introduced via the Education Reform Act 1989.

National Minimum Wage   Introduced by the National Minimum Wage Act 1998, this sets the minimum rate of reward any worker can receive on an hourly basis. The scale is age-related and linked to inflation through an annual upgrade.

NATO   North Atlantic Treaty Organization. Western defensive alliance set up originally in 1949 to promote economic and military cooperation among its members. The original members were Belgium, Britain, Canada, France, Italy, Norway, Portugal and the Netherlands. Greece and Turkey joined in 1952, and the former West Germany in 1955.

NCU   National Communications Union.

NCVQ (National Council for Vocational Qualifications)   Government-backed initiative to establish a national system for the recognition of vocational qualifications.

Nenko   Japanese term meaning seniority and ability. One of the 'three pillars' of the Japanese employment system.

Networking   Interacting for mutual benefit, usually on an informal basis, with individuals and groups internal and external to the organisation.

New Deal   Government initiative that provides training for 18–24 year-olds who have been out of work for more than six months, and 25-year-olds and over who have been unemployed for longer than two years.

New Deal in America   Programme of economic and social reconstruction initiated by President F.D. Roosevelt in 1933 that aimed to lift the USA out of the Great Depression that hit the country in 1929.

NHS   National Health Service.

NHS Trusts   Local NHS organisations responsible for distributing NHS funds and managing services. Primary Care Trusts (PCTs) are responsible for managing 80 per cent of NHS funds and they cover GP services, dentists, opticians and pharmacists. Other trusts are ambulance trusts, hospital trusts and mental health and social care trusts.

NIZ (New Industrial Zone)   These are new industrial zones in India, which have emerged since the 1990s, driven by the dynamics of high levels of foreign direct investment in manufacturing, neoliberal state policies and a large pool of workers.

Non-union firms   Organisations which do not recognise trade unions for collective bargaining purposes; this may be throughout the organisation or at plant or business unit level. So, for example, IBM, frequently quoted as an example of a soft-HRM non-union firm, does in fact recognise unions in Germany, as does McDonald's, another organisation strongly associated with an anti-union stance.

NSTF   National Skills Task Force.

Numerical flexibility   The ability of management to vary headcount in response to changes in demand.

NVQs   National Vocational Qualifications. An attempt to harmonise all **VET** qualifications within the UK by attributing five levels to all qualifications, from level 1, the lowest, to level 5, the highest.

ONS   Office of National Statistics.

Open system   System that is connected to and interacts with other subsystems and its environment.

OSC   Occupational Standards Council.

Over-education or over-qualification   A situation whereby people hold qualifications over and above those required for their job.

Paired comparisons   A system of appraisal that seeks to assess the performance of pairs of individuals, until each employee has been judged in relation to each other.

Paradigm   A well-developed, and often widely held, set of associated assumptions that frames the interpretation of reality. When these assumptions are undermined by new knowledge or events, a 'paradigm shift' occurs as the old gives way (often gradually and painfully) to a new paradigm.

Payment by results   Reward systems under which worker output or performance determines elements of the package.

PCT   Primary Care Trust – *see* **NHS Trusts**.

Performance-related pay   Payment systems which in some way relate reward to either organisational or individual performance. Often used as a way to motivate white-collar workers, usually based on a developed appraisal system.

Phenomenology   Concerned with understanding the individual's conscious experience. It takes a holistic approach and acknowledges the significance of subjectivity.

Pluralism   Theoretical analysis of the employment relationship that recognises inequality between capital and labour where each of the interest groups has some conflicting and some common aims. To address these issues, pluralists argue that employees should be facilitated to act collectively, usually as a trade union, to redress such imbalances. Management, as the representatives of employers, should engage in collective bargaining with trade unions to establish consensual agreements on issues of conflict and commonality.

Positivism   The orthodox approach to the understanding of reality, and the basis for scientific method.

Post-Fordism   A claimed epochal shift in manufacturing that sees a move away from mass production assembly lines and the development of flexible systems that empower and reskill line workers. Associated with the move towards niche products and volatile consumer demand.

Postmodernism A term used (often loosely) to denote various disjunctions from, fragmentations in, or challenges to previously common understandings of knowledge and social life.

PRB Pay review body.

Predetermined motion time (PDMT) systems A member of the time-rate pay systems family under which rewards are calculated based on time and piece. As a standard form of incentive bonus scheme, PDMT schemes rewards are set using the pseudo-scientific measurement of activity.

Profit sharing Scheme whereby employees are given a bonus or payment based on a company's profits.

Private Finance Initiative (PFI) Where the government contracts out projects such as prison management, hospital building, road construction, etc. to the private sector, then leases back the service over an extended period of time.

Privatisation The transfer of productive activities from public to private ownership and control. Privatisation was a key element of economic policy under the Conservative governments of the 1980s and 1990s when the coal and steel industries, the telephone service, water, gas and electricity supply and railways among others were transferred from public to private ownership.

Psychological contract The notion that an individual has a range of expectations about their employing organisation and the organisation has expectations of them.

Psychological (psychometric) testing Specialised tests used for selection or assessing potential. Usually in the form of questionnaires. They construct a personality profile of the candidate.

Public–Private Partnerships (PPP) Collaboration between public bodies, e.g. government or local authorities, and private businesses to provide goods and services. *See* **Private Finance Initiative**.

Quality circle (QC) Group made up of six to 10 employees, with regular meetings held weekly or fortnightly during working time. The principal aim is to identify problems from their own area.

Ranking A method of assessing and ordering individual performance using a predetermined scale.

Rating A determined measure or scale against which an individual's performance is measured.

Reification The conceptualisation and treatment of a person or abstraction as though they were things.

Resource-based view Strategy creation built around the further exploitation of core competencies and strategic capabilities.

RCN Royal College of Nursing.

Rhetoric The often subtle and unacknowledged use of language to 'persuade, influence or manipulate'.

Rightsizing *–see* **Downsizing**.

Scientific management *– see* **Taylorism**.

Single-loop learning Detection and correction of deviances in performance from established (organisational or other) norms. Double-loop learning is the questioning of those very norms that define effective performance (compare efficiency and effectiveness).

Single-table bargaining Arrangement under which unions on a multi-union site develop a mutually agreed bargaining agenda, which is then negotiated jointly with management.

Single-union deal Arrangement under which one trade union operates to represent all employees within an organisation; this is usually a preferred union sponsored by management.

Social Chapter Another name for the Social Charter, which emerged from the Maastricht meeting in 1989.

Social Charter A programme to implement the 'social dimension' of the single market, affording rights and protection to employees.

Social complexity The complex interpersonal relationships that exist within organisations, within and between teams and individuals.

Social constructionism Holds that an objective reality is not directly knowable. The reality we do know is socially constructed through language, discourse and social interaction.

Social partnership Process whereby employers and employees establish a framework of rights based upon minimum standards in employment, flexibility, security, information sharing and cooperation between management and employees' representatives.

Social relations of production The patterns and dynamics produced and reproduced in action by individuals and collectives employed in the labour process.

Sociotechnical The structuring or integration of human activities and subsystems with technological subsystems.

SOE State-owned enterprise.

Soft HRM A view of HRM that recognises employees as a resource worth investing in, and tends to focus on high-commitment/high-involvement human resource practices; *see also* **Hard HRM**.

Stakeholders Any individual or group capable of affecting or being affected by the performance and actions of the organisation.

Stakeholder society One in which individuals recognise that only by making a positive contribution to contemporary society can they expect a positive outcome from society.

Stakeholders in social partnership Those groups with an interest in promoting strong social partnerships at work, i.e. the state, employers and their organisations, employees and their organisations.

Strategic management The process by which an organisation establishes its objectives, formulates strategies to meet these objectives, implements actions and measures and monitors performance.

Suggestion scheme Arrangement whereby employees are encouraged to put forward their ideas for improving efficiency, safety or working conditions. Payment or reward is often given related to the value of the suggestion.

Supervisory boards Part of the dual management board structure required by law in all German enterprises listed on the German stock exchange. Day-to-day management is the responsibility of the management board, which is accountable to the supervisory board. The supervisory board appoints, oversees and advises the management board. It also participates directly in key strategic decisions. Supervisory boards are elected by shareholders and where firms employ more than 500 employees in Germany, membership of the board must also include employee representatives. Employee representatives make up one-third of the supervisory board membership in companies having 500–2000 employees and half of the membership in companies having over 2000 employees.

Sustainable competitive advantage The ability of an organisation to add more value than its rivals in order to gain advantage and maintain that advantage over time.

SVQs Scottish Vocational Qualifications.

Synergy Added value or additional benefit that accrues from cooperation between team members, or departments, such that the results are greater than the sum of all the individual parts.

System Assembly of parts, objects or attributes inter-relating and interacting in an organised way.

Systemic Thinking about and perceiving situations, problems and difficulties as systems.

Tacit knowledge Knowledge that is never explicitly taught, often not verbalised, but is acquired through doing and expressed in know-how.

Taylorism, Taylorist a systematic approach to work organisation named after Frederick Winslow Taylor. Involves time and motion study, specialised sub-division of labour and close management control. Also referred to as 'scientific management'.

Team briefing Regular meeting of groups of between four and 15 people based round a common production or service area. Meetings are usually led by a manager or supervisor and last for no more than 30 minutes, during which information is imparted, often with time left for questions from employees.

TECs Training and Enterprise Councils. These operated in England and Wales and were made up of local employers and elected local people, to create local training initiatives in response to local skill needs. Their function was taken over in 2002 by Learning and Skills Councils – *see* **LSC**.

Theory 'X' and 'Y' Based on McGregor's thesis on managerial change. Two contrasting views of people and work. Theory X sees people as inherently lazy, unambitious and avoiding responsibility. Theory Y sees work as natural as rest or play and being capable of providing self-fulfilment and a sense of achievement for those involved.

Thinking performer A set of competencies that should guide CIPD members (Chartered Institute of Personnel and Development) through their careers.

Tight labour market Sometimes called a 'shortage' labour market, where there a high levels of employment and demand exceeds supply or the supply for certain types of workers with specific skills sets is insufficient to meet demand.

TQM Total quality management, an all-pervasive system of management-controlled employee involvement based on the concept of quality throughout the organisation in terms of product and service, whereby groups of workers are each encouraged to perceive each other (and other departments) as internal customers. This ensures the provision of quality products and services to external customers.

Transferable skills Skills that can be used anywhere in the economy.

Tripartism Systems of industrial relations whereby the state, employers' associations and trade unions oversee and govern labour market initiatives and related policies, e.g. wage levels and increases.

Trust Schools State-funded schools supported by a charitable trust that has enhanced freedom to manage its own operations; *see also* **Foundation schools**.

TUC Trades Union Congress.

TUPE Transfer of Undertakings (Protection of Employment) Regulations.

UNICE Union of Industrial and Employers' Confederations of Europe.

Underemployment An employment situation that is insufficient in some important way for the worker, relative to a standard. The term is most widely used to explain the predicament individuals find themselves in when they occupy a part-time job despite desiring full-time work.

Unison Public service union formed following merger of COHSE, NALGO and NUPE.

Unitarism Theoretical analysis of the employment relationship based on managerial prerogative, valuing labour individually according to market assessments, and which views organised resistance to management authority as pathological.

Value chain A framework for identifying where value is added and where costs are incurred.

VET Vocational education and training.

Vertical integration   In terms of SHRM, the level of alignment between an organisation's business strategy and its HR strategy, policies and practices.

Vision (statement)   A desired future state, or an attempt by an organisation to articulate that desired future state.

VQs   Vocational qualifications.

Wa   Japanese term for harmony.

Wage drift   A gradual and uneven increase in wages in certain sectors of the economy resulting from variable, informal bargaining activities reflecting areas of localised union strength. Such increases are supplementary to any formally agreed wages formula. If allowed to grow unchecked, this practice can lead to inflationary measures.

Weberian bureaucracy   Associated with the research and writing of the sociologist Max Weber (1864–1920), who observed and studied the growth of vast organisational bureaucracies. Notable for the extreme degree of functional specialisation, formal rules and procedures, and long lines of command and authority. Staffed by professional, full-time, salaried employees who do not own the resources and facilities with which they work.

WERS   Workplace Employment Relations Study. The Workplace Employment Relations Study (WERS) series commenced in 1980 and has mapped employment relations extensively over three decades. It provides insights into employment relations in Britain by collecting data from a representative sample of British workplaces. The sixth survey was carried out in 2011.

Works councils   Committees made up either solely of workers or of joint representatives of workers, management and shareholders, which meet, usually at company level, to discuss a variety of issues relating to workforce matters and sometimes general, wider-ranging organisational issues. Usually supported by legislation, which compels organisations to set them up.

YT   Youth Training (formerly Youth Training Service, YTS).

Zaibatsu   Large, diversified Japanese business groups, which rose to prominence in the early twentieth century, such as Mitsubishi, Mitsui and Sumitomo.

Zero-hours contract   A contract of employment containing provisions which create an 'on call' arrangement between employer and employee. It does not oblige the employer to provide work for the employee, nor does it oblige the employee to accept the work offered. The employee receives compensation only for hours worked.

References

Arthur, M.B., Hall, D.T. and Lawrence, B.S. (eds) (1989) *Handbook of Career Theory*. Cambridge: Cambridge University Press.

Collin, A. and Watts, A.G. (1996) 'The death and transfiguration of career: and of career guidance?', *British Journal of Guidance and Counselling*, 24, 3: 385–98.

Heery, A. and Noon, M. (2001) *Dictionary of Human Resource Management*. Oxford: Oxford University Press.

Knowles, M.S. and Associates (1984) *Androgogy in Action*. San Francisco, CA: Jossey-Bass.

Pedler, M., Burgoyne, J. and Boydell, T. (1997) *The Learning Company: A Strategy for Sustainable Development*. London: McGraw-Hill.

Peppard, J. and Rowland, P. (1995) *The Essence of Business Process Re-engineering*. Hemel Hempstead: Prentice Hall.

Training Commission (1988) *Classifying the Components of Managing Competencies*. Sheffield: Training Commission.

Index